Critical acclaim for *PROGRAM*

D1091415

"Just take it as a given—if you're going to program for Windows, buy this book. It will pay for itself in a matter of hours."

Computer Language

"The classic book on Windows programming, of course, is Charles Petzold's PROGRAMMING WINDOWS. If you don't already have a copy, you need one."

Windows Tech Journal

"Windows programmers are in great demand these days, and this is the best book for programmers who want to cash in on the craze. It is a thorough introduction for anyone who wants to look behind the curtain."

The New York Times

"As you are building your library of the best Windows books, you want to make sure you include the classic—Petzold's best-selling PROGRAMMING WINDOWS. . . . The best part is that Petzold's technical discussions are crystal clear."

PC Techniques

"This remains the classic Windows programming guide."

Programmer's Journal

"Charles Petzold has done it again. . . . Whether you're new to Windows development or write Windows code every day, this book belongs on your bookshelf—within easy reach."

Computer Shopper

"The serious programmer's guide . . . has been and continues to be Charles Petzold's PROGRAMMING WINDOWS. If you want to program Windows applications and haven't read this book, you need to do so."

IEEE Micro

"There are just three books that I regard as crucial texts for serious Windows programming: First, of course, is the classic PROGRAMMING WINDOWS by Charles Petzold."

INFOWORLD

"Broad in scope and omitting little, this book is a must for anyone serious about Windows."

Byte Magazine

"The definitive book on Windows programming is, of course, Charles Petzold's."

Dr. Dobb's Journal

Programming
Windows®
95

Charles
Petzold

PUBLISHED BY
Microsoft Press
A Division of Microsoft Corporation
One Microsoft Way
Redmond, Washington 98052-6399

Copyright © 1996 by Charles Petzold

All rights reserved. No part of the contents of this book may be reproduced or transmitted
in any form or by any means without the written permission of the publisher.

Library of Congress Cataloging-in-Publication Data
Petzold, Charles, 1953–
    Programming Windows 95 / Charles Petzold. -- 4th ed.
        p.   cm.
    Includes index.
    ISBN 1-55615-676-6
    1. Microsoft Windows (Computer file)   2. Operating systems
(Computers) I. Title.
QA76.76.O63P533 1996
005.265--dc20   95-49555
                                                 CIP

Printed and bound in the United States of America.

3 4 5 6 7 8 9 QMQM 1 0 9 8 7 6

Distributed to the book trade in Canada by Macmillan of Canada, a division of Canada Publishing
Corporation.

A CIP catalogue record for this book is available from the British Library.

Microsoft Press books are available through booksellers and distributors worldwide. For further information about international editions, contact your local Microsoft Corporation office. Or contact Microsoft
Press International directly at fax (206) 936-7329.

PageMaker is a trademark of Adobe Systems, Inc. Apple, LaserWriter, Lisa, Macintosh, and TrueType
are registered trademarks of Apple Computer, Inc. ToolBook is a registered trademark of Asymetrix
Corporation. Borland, Delphi, SideKick, and Turbo C are registered trademarks of Borland International,
Inc. Corel and Design is a registered trademark of Corel Systems Corporation. DEC is a trademark of Digi-
tal Equipment Corporation. Digital Research and GEM are registered trademarks of Digital Research, Inc.
ColorPro, Hewlett-Packard, and HP are registered trademarks of Hewlett-Packard Company. IBM, OS/2, and
TopView are registered trademarks and Current and Graphics Assistant are trademarks of International
Business Machines Corporation. Lotus and VisiCalc are registered trademarks of Lotus Development Corporation. Micrografx Designer is a trademark of Micrografx, Inc. Microsoft, Microsoft Press, Microsoft Press
and Design, MS-DOS, MultiPlan, QuickC, Visual Basic, Windows, and the Windows operating system logo
are registered trademarks of Microsoft Corporation. NEC is a registered trademark of NEC Corporation.
PowerBuilder is a trademark of Powersoft Corporation. DESQview is a registered trademark of Quarterdeck Office Systems. Visio is a registered trademark of Visio Corporation. UNIX is a registered trademark
in the United States and other countries, licensed exclusively through X/Open Company, Ltd. Xerox is
a registered trademark of Xerox Corp. All other trademarks and service marks are the property of their
respective owners.

Acquisitions Editor: Eric Stroo
Project Editor: Jack Litewka
Technical Editor: Marc Young

Contents

Section III
Using Resources

Acknowledgments

This book would have been impossible without the help and encouragement of very many special people, starting with the past and current editors and writers at *PC Magazine* and *Microsoft Systems Journal*, two magazines for which I've always enjoyed writing.

Over the past almost-decade, all the folks at Microsoft Press have been wonderful in their Job-like patience and tolerance of my procrastination and crankiness (traits often unfortunately common to writers) during the production of the four editions of this book. Many other people at Microsoft also helped out in the earlier editions, including the unsung heroic developers of Microsoft Windows and the staff of MS Online System Support.

For this fourth edition, I particularly want to thank Beck Zaratian of Witzend Software (Seattle), who reviewed a number of chapters from the last edition and helpfully identified many changes that had to be made for Windows 95. Paul Yao definitely deserves a very-long standing ovation for helping get the book into production by taking on the work of two new chapters, Chapters 12 and 20. Thanks also to Kraig Brockschmidt, Nancy Cluts, and Evangelos Petroutsos for reviewing chapters.

I also thank the most important people in my life: my friends (especially Lynn, who incessantly prodded me to finish the book, I think mostly so I wouldn't complain about it so much); and my Mom; and the rest of my family, growing by leaps and bounds, most recently by Linda and Mike's contribution-in-progress (good luck, guys!).

Charles Petzold
January 5, 1996

Getting Started

Chapter 1

README.TXT

This is a book for people skilled in the C programming language who wish to learn how to write applications for the Microsoft Windows 95 operating system. Your familiarity with C is one of three prerequisites for using this book. The second is that you've installed Microsoft Visual C++ version 4.0 for 32-bit development. The third is that you have actually used Windows 95 and understand the fundamentals of its user interface design.

As you probably know, Windows 95 is the most recent incarnation of a graphical operating system first introduced in November 1985 to run on IBM PCs and compatibles. In terms of market penetration, Windows has almost entirely blown away any competition it may have once had over the past decade, and it has become the de facto standard for personal computer environments. These days, if you're writing a program for PC compatibles, you're writing for Windows.

Think of this chapter as your first day in class. Despite the tendency of some sadistic teachers to launch immediately into the brutal guts of the course material, most of us prefer a more relaxed introduction. So, in this chapter I'll discuss some historical background of Windows, the ground rules of this book, and even (if you'll indulge me) a bit about myself and how this book came to be written.

I can't, however, guarantee that this chapter will be entirely stress-free. You are a programmer, you are an engineer of software, and like any other engineer, your role is to take on the difficult (and challenging—and fortunately often satisfying) job of making the world an easier place to use. You are building roads and bridges that bring people closer to their destinations and goals, and those structures must be sturdy and solid and fast.

THE PROGRAMMER'S CHALLENGE

In the movie *Grand Canyon,* a father is helping his 15-year-old son learn to drive and makes the observation that "Making a left turn in L.A. is one of the harder things you're going to learn in life." He could also have said that about Windows-based programming.

I'm not speaking specifically of the mechanics of Windows-based programming. I'll begin with that nasty subject in the next chapter. I'm thinking more of the program-design philosophy of bending over backwards to make things easy for the user. This is a relatively new concept.

Back in the early days of computers, the only users were also programmers. Old-time computer programs would suck up some data, muck around with it for a while, and then spit out some paper output. Naive users simply weren't a factor. Even when computer software became somewhat interactive and presented a command-line prompt on a teletype or video display, users were expected to remember often cryptic commands and options.

Perhaps the real revolution in program design came about with early interactive word processors (WordStar, for example) and spreadsheets (VisiCalc) that incorporated primitive forms of the most fundamental element of modern user interface design. This is, of course, the menu. The menus in these early interactive applications were not well implemented, but the idea was present and it slowly developed in sophistication. In retrospect, the menu seems obvious: It presents all the program options available to the user. Of course, in the early days, the lack of memory constrained the programmer in designing a good user interface. User-unfriendly programs are shorter and easier to write; friendly programs are bigger and more difficult to write.

The principle of TANSTAAFL ("There Ain't No Such Thing As A Free Lunch") is clearly at work here. Somebody has to do the hard work. As a programmer, you have elected to be that person.

Fortunately, a good part of this hard work has already been done for you by the designers and programmers of the Microsoft Windows 95 operating system. These unsung heroes have implemented much of the code required to create modern user interface objects and to display program output using richly formatted text and graphics. In doing so, however, they have also necessarily created an extensive application programming interface (API) that can be quite intimidating to programmers coming to Windows for the first time. This is not atypical with Windows—it is true of every modern graphical user interface.

Originally it was commonly estimated that a programmer needed about 6 months to get up to speed with Windows programming. (I often joked that by using my book, this could be cut down to 26 weeks, or perhaps even 180 days.) Windows has become more extensive in recent years, but there are also tools available that will help you out with the hard parts, so the 6-month rule probably still applies.

I'm telling you this because I don't want you to feel professionally inadequate or mentally deficient if you don't "get it" right away. If you're new to programming for graphical environments, Windows can be very strange. You'll get it eventually.

THE GROUND RULES

What I'm going to teach you in this book is what I think of as "classical" Windows programming. I use the plain old C programming language (not C++), and I use the raw application programming interface (API) directly rather than any "wrappers" that hide the API under easier interfaces. Despite the advances in Windows 95 over earlier versions of Windows, most of the programs in this book don't look a lot different from programs that would have been (and were) written for Microsoft Windows version 1.0 about 10 years ago.

In one sense, this book shows the hard way to do Windows programming—but it is also the most basic, fundamental, versatile, and powerful way. You really can't do anything more with Windows using other approaches. Moreover, by learning classical Windows programming using C and the raw APIs, you can more clearly understand how Windows and your application interact, and this can often be very useful knowledge. This approach establishes a firm foundation that you will never regret. Believe me.

Although I teach classical Windows programming, I don't necessarily recommend that you limit yourself to it. These days you have a variety of options that may make Windows programming easier. One popular option is C++, generally used in conjunction with class libraries such as the Microsoft Foundation Classes (MFC) or Borland's Object Windows Library (OWL). Other options are Microsoft's Visual Basic and Borland's Delphi. Code-generation products are also available that take some of the grunt work out of Windows programming. You can even create Windows applications using simple scripting languages such as Asymetrix's ToolBook.

I can't tell you which of these options is best; it really depends on the application you're writing and how much you're willing to sacrifice by insulating yourself from the environment.

Another subject I don't approach in this book is the use of interactive development environments (IDEs) such as Microsoft Visual C++ version 4.0. These environments often assist you by helping out with the creation of resources (such as menus and dialog boxes), by generating make files, and by giving you a common environment in which to write, compile, run, and debug your code. I have nothing against IDEs. I think they're great. However, their workings often hinder rather than aid the learning of classical Windows programming. In short, I don't want to teach you how to learn how to fill in IDE dialog boxes; rather, I want to teach you how to design your own dialog boxes and handle the processing of input to them.

For this reason, the code in this book is shown as though it were created in an ordinary text editor, and the program compiled from an old-fashioned command line. This will be most obvious when we get to the subject of resource scripts, which contain text descriptions of your program's menus, dialog boxes, and other resources. The resource scripts in this book are written to be readable, which is not usually the case when resource scripts are generated by an IDE. I do this because I want you to understand what the statements in a resource script mean. Make files—those files that contain statements that compile and link your program to create an executable—are notoriously long and complex when generated by an IDE. Mine are short and simple, and I won't apologize for that! The only nontext resources in this book are icons, mouse cursors, and bitmapped pictures, which by their very nature usually require tools to create them.

The advantage of this approach is that you can simply copy the source files to your hard disk, call up an MS-DOS command-line window, run the make file to create an executable, and run the executable right off the command line.

Most of the programs in this book are very short, designed to demonstrate one or two salient concepts. Otherwise, they are stripped down to bare essentials. The programs are teaching tools and not models for complete Windows-based programs. For example, every real Windows program should have a unique icon; very few of mine do because it would simply be clutter. Also, it is recommended that text strings used in a program should be put in a resource script to facilitate translation into different languages. Again, doing this would add clutter and obscure the point I'm trying to make. It is my experience that the shorter the program, the more likely a reader is to study it carefully.

This book cannot possibly cover every aspect of programming for Windows 95. It is also no substitute for the official documentation. After assimilating the contents of this book, you will still be spending many hours reading documentation of Windows 95 features and function calls.

This is not the only Windows programming book published by Microsoft Press. For an alternative to programming for Windows in C using the native APIs, you may want to pick up *Programming Windows 95 with MFC* by Jeff Prosise (to be published in summer of 1996). To get a better insight into the inner workings of Windows 95, look at *Inside Windows 95* by Adrian King. The discussion of advanced user interface options in Chapter 12 is more extensively explored in *Programming the Windows 95 User Interface* by Nancy Winnick Cluts. The cursory discussion of OLE in Chapter 20 should be supplemented by *Inside OLE* by Kraig Brockschmidt. Miscellaneous Windows 95 programming topics can be found in the *Programmer's Guide to Microsoft Windows 95*. Also of interest are *Inside Visual C++* by David J. Kruglinski, *OLE Controls Inside Out* by Adam Denning, and *Hardcore Visual Basic* by Bruce McKinney.

The final ground rule for my writing (and your reading) this book is that I'm not going to delve into "undocumented" or "unauthorized" aspects of programming for Windows 95. While this information may often be interesting, I don't think it is of much significance for all but the oddest of Windows applications. As I've matured as a programmer, I've tried more and more not to rely upon implementation details because these may change in future versions of the operating system. Instead, I try to treat the API as if it were fully described by the technical documentation. This is not always the case, of course, and there are often some "gotchas" that the documentation fails to address. Bugs may exist as well. I won't ignore these problems.

A BRIEF HISTORY OF WINDOWS

Soon after the introduction of the IBM PC in the fall of 1981, it became evident that the predominant operating system for the PC (and compatibles) would be MS-DOS, which stands for Microsoft Disk Operating System. The early versions of MS-DOS provided a command-line interface to the user, featuring such commands as DIR and TYPE, which was capable of loading application programs into memory for execution and offered services to these programs for accessing files, reading the keyboard, and writing to the video display (in character mode only) and the printer port.

Due to memory and hardware constraints, sophisticated graphical environments were slower in coming. Apple Computers demonstrated a possible alternative when it released its ill-fated Lisa in January 1983, and then set a standard for graphical environments with the Macintosh in January 1984, which (despite its declining market share) is still considered the standard against which all other graphical environments are measured.

Windows was announced by Microsoft Corporation in November 1983 (post-Lisa but pre-Macintosh) and was released two years later in November 1985. Over the next two years, Microsoft Windows version 1.0 was followed by several updates to support the international market and to provide drivers for additional video displays and printers.

Windows version 2.0 was released in November 1987. This version incorporated several changes to the user interface. The most significant of these changes involved the use of overlapping windows rather than the "tiled" windows found in Windows 1.*x*. Windows 2.0 also included enhancements to the keyboard and mouse interface, particularly for menus and dialog boxes.

Up until this time, Windows required only an Intel 8086 or 8088 microprocessor running in "real-mode" to access 1 megabyte (MB) of memory. Windows/386 (released shortly after Windows 2.0) used the "virtual 86" mode of the Intel 80386 microprocessor to window and multitask many MS-DOS programs that directly access hardware. For symmetry, Windows version 2.1 was renamed Windows/286.

Windows version 3.0 was introduced on May 22, 1990. The earlier Windows/286 and Windows/386 versions were merged into one product with this release. The big change in Windows 3.0 was the support of the protected mode operation of Intel's 80286, 80386, and 80486 microprocessors. This gave Windows and Windows applications access to up to 16 MB of memory. The Windows "shell" programs for running programs and maintaining files were completely revamped. Windows 3.0 was the first version to become common on many users' machines, both in the home and office.

Windows version 3.1 was released in April 1992. Several significant features included the TrueType font technology (which brought scalable outline fonts to Windows), multimedia (sound and music), OLE, and common dialog boxes. Also, Windows 3.1 ran *only* in protected mode and required an 80286 or 80386 processor with at least 1 MB of memory.

Any history of Windows must also include a mention of OS/2, an alternative to DOS and Windows that was originally developed by Microsoft in collaboration with IBM. OS/2 version 1.0 (character-mode only) ran on the Intel 80286 (or later) microprocessors and was released in late 1987. The graphical Presentation Manager (PM) came about with OS/2 version 1.1 in October 1988. PM was originally supposed to be a protected mode version of Windows, but the graphical API was changed to such a degree that it proved very difficult for software manufacturers to support both platforms.

By September 1990, conflicts between IBM and Microsoft reached a peak and required that the two companies go their separate ways. IBM took over OS/2 and Microsoft made it clear that Windows was the center of their strategy for operating systems. While OS/2 still has some fervent admirers, it has not nearly approached the popularity of Windows.

Windows NT, introduced in July 1993, was the first version of Windows to support the 32-bit programming model of the Intel 80386, 80486, and Pentium microprocessors. Windows NT has a 32-bit flat address space and 32-bit integers. Windows NT is also portable and runs on several RISC-based workstations.

Windows 95 (previously code-named Chicago and sometimes referred to as Windows version 4.0) was introduced in August 1995. Like Windows NT, Windows 95 also supports a 32-bit programming model (thus requiring an 80386 or better microprocessor). Although it lacks some of the features of Windows NT such as high security and portability to RISC machines, Windows 95 has the advantage of running on machines with as little as 4 MB of memory.

Obviously, programs written for the 16-bit versions of Windows prior to Windows NT and Windows 95 are usually not transparently portable to the newer 32-bit versions of Windows; I'll discuss some of the changes necessary for porting in the chapters ahead.

Microsoft has attempted to differentiate their various platforms by defining sets of APIs. The Win16 API is that supported by Windows 3.1. The Win32 API is supported by Windows NT and Windows 95. But wait—there's more. Microsoft made it possible for programmers to write 32-bit applications for Windows 3.1; the 32-bit function calls were translated to 16-bit calls by a dynamic link library (DLL). The API was named Win32s ("s" for "subset" because the API only supported functions in Win16). Also, at one time the Windows 95 API was named Win32c ("c" for "compatible"), but this term has been abandoned.

At this time, Windows NT and Windows 95 are both considered to support the Win32 API. However, each operating system supports some features not supported by the other. The overlap is considerable, so it is possible to write programs that run under both systems. Also, it is widely assumed that the two products will be merged at some time in the future.

A BRIEF HISTORY OF THIS BOOK

In early 1988, the first edition of *Programming Windows* was one of the first books on Windows programming to hit the bookstore shelves. As I prepared to revise *Programming Windows* for Windows 95, I was startled to realize that 1995 is the 10-year anniversary of Windows, and consequently the 10-year anniversary of the origins of this very book. That fact is both exhilarating and just a little bit scary.

As I look back over the history of this book, I realize that it came about largely due to chance occurrences and my association with many wonderful people in the computer industry. Here's how it began.

In the spring of 1985, I was doing some freelance writing for *PC Magazine* and spending a lot of time hanging around their offices at One Park Avenue in New York City. On an irregular basis, the magazine would be visited by Microsoft's Steve Ballmer (now executive vice president of sales and support), who would drop off the latest beta version of the long-awaited product known as Windows. Those of us interested in Windows would gather in senior editor John Dickinson's office to check it out. John was one of the few people at *PC Magazine* who had an EGA on his machine and who could hence run Windows in color. We'd play with these early versions of Windows for a while (usually until we got tired of it crashing) and then wait for the next time Ballmer would come by with a more stable version.

One day in that spring of 1985, I asked John Dickinson how one actually writes a program that runs under Windows. John quickly pulled open a desk drawer and unloaded on me several inches of photocopied papers and about 10 diskettes that Ballmer had left with him a couple weeks earlier. John's only request was that I not bring the stuff back to his office.

The pile of paper and diskettes turned out to be the preliminary version of the first Windows Software Development Kit (SDK), complete with a C compiler. I took the bundle home, installed the SDK on a Bernoulli box (at that time I was working with a two-floppy IBM PC), and instantly became a Windows programmer after about six months of total confusion. Throughout this learning experience and struggling with the documentation, one sentence ran through my mind: "I could explain this stuff a whole lot better than Microsoft has."

Windows version 1.0 was finally introduced in November 1985, but at that time no one could have foreseen that Windows would one day rule the market. Indeed, it had competitors, including IBM's TopView, Digital Research's GEM, and Quarterdeck's DESQview. The February 25, 1985, cover of *PC Magazine* proclaimed "Window Wars!" This was the first cover story I wrote for the magazine, although I was relegated to reviewing TopView rather than Windows.

It took almost another year before I was confident enough to actually discuss Windows programming in print, which happened in the December 1986 issue of *Microsoft Systems Journal*. I believe that this piece—which presented an early version of my WHATSIZE program that you'll find in Chapter 4—is the first article about Windows programming to appear in a magazine. I happened to know the first editor of *MSJ* (Jonathan Lazarus) because he was earlier a vice president at Ziff-Davis, which published *PC Magazine*. Jon later went on to work at Microsoft, where he currently holds the position of vice president of strategic relations.

Writing about Windows for *MSJ* brought me to the attention of Microsoft Press, but also in a roundabout way. I met Tandy Trower (currently director of user interface design at Microsoft) at a Microsoft language conference in Redmond, Washington, in October 1986, and I told him how excited I was to write about Windows programming for *MSJ*. He gave my name to Susan Lammers, who was then editor-in-chief of Microsoft Press. People at Microsoft Press already knew my name because I was the first potential magazine reviewer of the infamous first edition of the *MS-DOS Encyclopedia* to inform them that it contained numerous flaws and errors, which led to its being withdrawn from the market and totally redone under the more skillful oversight of Ray Duncan.

During the November 1986 Fall Comdex in Las Vegas, I met with Microsoft Press acquisitions editor Claudette Moore (now a computer-book literary agent based in Massachusetts), and we hammered out an outline. Originally, *Programming Windows* was supposed to be a much smaller book, and targeted to both programmers and advanced users. As I worked on the book over the next year (during which I had to change the focus from Windows 1.0 to Windows 2.0), it grew in size and narrowed in scope.

What you're holding in your hands is the fourth edition of *Programming Windows*. I revised it for Windows 3.0 and then again for Windows 3.1. Since the book was first published, I've had many Windows programmers tell me that *Programming Windows* gave them their start with this often strange environment. Nothing could please me more—not necessarily for the ego rush, but because I've helped somehow in making Windows the success that it is.

LET'S GET STARTED

OK, the first day of class is nearly over. In the next chapter, we'll begin banging out some Windows code. To do this, you'll need to have installed Microsoft Visual C++ version 4.0. In your AUTOEXEC.BAT file you need to include the statement:

```
CALL \MSDEV\BIN\VCVARS32.BAT
```

This is a file included with VC++ that sets up DOS environment variables for compiling programs from the MS-DOS command line. It simply indicates paths to the header files, library files, and binary files. You'll also need to use a second CALL statement in your AUTO-EXEC.BAT file to run the MSC.BAT file, shown in Figure 1-1. This also defines environment variables which are used in the make files in the chapters to come.

MSC.BAT

```
REM ------------------------------------------------------------
REM  MSC.BAT -- Set up environment for Microsoft C/C++ 7.0 NMAKE
REM ------------------------------------------------------------
SET CC=cl
SET CFLAGS=-c -DSTRICT -G3 -Ow -W3 -Zp -Tp
SET CFLAGSMT=-c -DSTRICT -G3 -MT -Ow -W3 -Zp -Tp
SET LINKER=link
SET GUIFLAGS=-SUBSYSTEM:windows
SET DLLFLAGS=-SUBSYSTEM:windows -DLL
SET GUILIBS=-DEFAULTLIB:user32.lib gdi32.lib winmm.lib comdlg32.lib comctl32.lib
SET RC=rc
SET RCVARS=-r -DWIN32
```

Figure 1-1. *Run this file to compile the programs in this book.*

The MSC.BAT file can be found in the CHAP01 directory of the companion CD-ROM included with this book.

I'll describe what these statements do in the chapters ahead.

Chapter 2

Hello, Windows 95

If you are new to programming for a graphical environment such as Microsoft Windows 95, you will probably find it very different from anything else in your experience. Windows has the reputation of being easy for users but difficult for programmers. It is quite common for newcomers to be baffled by the architecture of Windows and the structure of the applications that run under the system. If this happens to you, please do not fear that you are missing some vital part of your brain that is required to become a successful Windows programmer. This initial confusion is normal, and don't let anyone tell you differently.

Windows-based programming is strange. It's weird, it's warped, it's awkward, it's convoluted, it's mind-boggling. It's definitely not immediately obvious, and it may take some time before you experience the thrill of shouting "Eureka!" (otherwise known as the student's "Oh, *now* I get it!" revelation of which teachers are so fond). One common estimation is that programmers must endure a 6-month learning curve before becoming adept at writing Windows programs, and even after that, the learning never ends. My only hope is that this book may cut some weeks (or maybe a month or two) from that typical learning curve.

You may therefore be asking, "If Windows programming is so difficult, why bother?"

Well, the easy answer is, "You probably don't have much of a choice." After all, Windows has achieved such a widespread penetration in the PC-compatible market that programming for bare MS-DOS (using either character mode or graphics) is no longer feasible. If you write off-the-shelf commercial applications, software reviewers for computer magazines will virtually ignore your product if it is not written for Windows. If you do specialized corporate programming, your users (and your employers!) won't like the fact that your program does not fluidly integrate with the existing Windows applications they use.

But there are better reasons for choosing Windows as your platform.

THE WINDOWS DIFFERENCE

Windows provides significant advantages to both users and programmers over the conventional MS-DOS environment. The benefits to users and the benefits to program developers are really quite similar because the job of a program developer is to give users what they need and want. Windows 95 makes this possible.

The Graphical User Interface (GUI)

Windows is a graphical user interface (GUI), sometimes also called a "visual interface" or "graphical windowing environment." The concepts behind this type of user interface date from the mid-1970s, with the pioneering work done at the Xerox Palo Alto Research Center (PARC) for machines such as the Alto and the Star and for environments such as Smalltalk. This work was later brought into the mainstream and popularized by Apple Computer, Inc., first in the ill-fated Lisa and then a year later in the much more successful Macintosh, introduced in January 1984.

Since the introduction of the Macintosh, graphical user interfaces have bloomed like wildflowers throughout the personal-computer industry and the not-so-personal computer industry as well. It is now quite obvious that the graphical user interface is (in the words of Microsoft's Charles Simonyi) the single most important "grand consensus" of the personal-computer industry.

GUI Concepts and Rationale

All graphical user interfaces make use of graphics on a bitmapped video display. Graphics provides better utilization of screen real estate, a visually rich environment for conveying information, and the possibility of a WYSIWYG (what you see is what you get) video display of graphics and formatted text prepared for a printed document.

In earlier days, the video display was used solely to echo text that the user typed on a keyboard. In a graphical user interface, the video display itself becomes a source of user input. The video display shows various graphical objects in the form of icons and input devices such as buttons and scroll bars. Using the keyboard (or, more directly, a pointing device such as a mouse), the user can directly manipulate these objects on the screen. Graphics objects can be dragged, buttons can be pushed, and scroll bars can be scrolled.

The interaction between the user and a program thus becomes more intimate. Rather than the one-way cycle of information from the keyboard to the program to the video display, the user directly interacts with the objects on the display.

The Consistent User Interface

Users no longer expect to spend long periods of time learning how to use the computer or mastering a new program. Windows helps because all Windows-based programs have the same fundamental look and feel. The program occupies a window—a rectangular area on the screen. It is identified by a title bar. Most program functions are initiated through the program's menu. The display of information too large to fit on a single screen can be viewed using scroll bars. Some menu items invoke dialog boxes, into which the user enters additional information. One dialog box found in almost every large Windows program opens a file. This dialog box looks the same (or very similar) in many different Windows programs, and it is almost always invoked from the same menu option.

Once you know how to use one Windows program, you're in a good position to easily learn another. The menus and dialog boxes allow a user to experiment with a new program and explore its features. Most Windows programs have both a keyboard interface and a mouse interface. Although most functions of Windows programs can be controlled through the keyboard, using the mouse is often easier for many chores.

From the programmer's perspective, the consistent user interface results from using the routines built into Windows for constructing menus and dialog boxes. All menus have the same keyboard and mouse interfaces because Windows—rather than the application program—handles this job.

The Multitasking Advantage

Although some people continue to question whether multitasking is really necessary on a single-user computer, users definitely are ready for multitasking and can benefit from it. The popularity of MS-DOS RAM-resident programs such as Sidekick proved that many years ago. Although popups are not, strictly speaking, multitasking programs, they do allow fast context switching. This context switching involves many of the same concepts as multitasking.

Under Windows, every program in effect becomes a RAM-resident popup. Several Windows programs can be displayed and running at the same time. Each program occupies a rectangular window on the screen. The user can move the windows around on the screen, change their size, switch among different programs, and transfer data from one program to another. Because this looks something like a desktop (in the days before the desk became dominated by the computer itself, of course), Windows is sometimes said to use a "desktop metaphor" for the display of multiple programs.

Earlier versions of Windows used a system of multitasking called "nonpreemptive." This meant that Windows did not use the system timer to allocate processing time among the various programs running under the system. The programs themselves had to voluntarily give up control so that other programs could run. Under Windows 95, multitasking is preemptive, and programs themselves can split into multiple threads of execution that seem to run concurrently.

Memory Management

An operating system cannot implement multitasking without doing something about memory management. As new programs are started up and old ones terminate, memory can become fragmented. The system must be able to consolidate free memory space. This requires the system to move blocks of code and data in memory.

Even Windows 1, running on an 8088 microprocessor, was able to perform this type of memory management. Under real mode, this can only be regarded as an astonishing feat of software engineering. Programs running under Windows can overcommit memory; a program can contain more code than can fit into memory at any one time. Windows can discard code from memory and later reload the code from the program's .EXE file. A user can run several copies, called "instances," of a program; all these instances share the same code in memory. Programs running in Windows can share routines located in other files called "dynamic link libraries." Windows includes a mechanism to link the program with the routines in the dynamic link libraries at run time. Windows itself is basically a set of dynamic link libraries.

Thus, even in Windows 1, the 640-kilobyte (KB) memory limit of the PC's architecture was effectively stretched without requiring any additional memory. But Microsoft didn't stop there: Windows 2 gave the Windows applications access to expanded memory (EMS), and Windows 3 ran in protected mode to give Windows applications access to up to 16 MB of extended memory. And now Windows 95 blows these old restrictions away by being a full-fledged 32-bit operating system with a flat memory space.

The Device-Independent Graphics Interface

Windows is a graphical interface, and Windows programs can make full use of graphics and formatted text on both the video display and the printer. A graphical interface is not only more attractive in appearance, but it can also impart a high level of information to the user.

Programs written for Windows do not directly access the hardware of graphics display devices such as the screen and printer. Instead, Windows includes a graphics programming language (called the Graphics Device Interface, or GDI) that makes it easy to display graphics and formatted text. Windows virtualizes display hardware. A program written for Windows will run with any video board or any printer for which a Windows device driver is available. The program does not need to determine what type of device is attached to the system.

Putting a device-independent graphics interface on the IBM PC was not an easy job for the developers of Windows. The PC design was based on the principle of open architecture. Third-party hardware manufacturers were encouraged to develop peripherals for the PC and have done so in great number. Although several standards have emerged, conventional MS-DOS programs for the PC must individually support many different hardware configurations. For example, it is fairly common for an MS-DOS word-processing program to be sold with one or two disks of small files, each one supporting a particular printer. Windows 95 programs do not require these drivers because their support is part of Windows.

The Windows Commitment

Programming for Windows 95 is an all-or-nothing proposition. For example, you cannot write an MS-DOS application and use Windows only for some graphics. If you want to use any part of Windows, you must make the commitment to write a full-fledged Windows program.

The reason for this will become more obvious as you learn about the structure of a Windows program. Everything in Windows is interconnected. If you want to draw some graphics on the video display, you need something called a "handle to a device context." To get that, you need a "handle to a window." To get that, you must create a window and be prepared to receive "messages" to the window. To receive and process messages, you need a "window procedure." And at that point you're writing a Windows program. You can't fly unless you leave the ground.

The Function Calls

Windows 95 supports well over a thousand function calls that applications can use. It is highly unlikely that you will ever memorize the syntax to all these calls. Most Windows programmers spend a good chunk of their time looking up the various function calls, either in printed sources or in online references.

Each Windows function has a descriptive name written in mixed uppercase and lowercase letters, such as *CreateWindow*. This function (as you might guess) creates a window for your program. Another example: The function *IsClipboardFormatAvailable* determines whether the clipboard is holding data of a particular format.

All the main Windows functions are declared in header files. The main header file is named WINDOWS.H, and this header file includes many other header files. These header files are supplied in any C-based programming environment that supports Windows 95. The header files are an important part of the Windows technical documentation. You may want to print out copies of the header files or use a file browser for quick reference.

In your Windows program, you use the Windows function calls in generally the same way you use C library functions such as *strlen*. The primary difference is that the code for C library functions is linked into your program code, whereas the code for Windows functions is located outside of your program in dynamic link libraries (DLLs).

When you run a Windows program, it interfaces to Windows through a process called "dynamic linking." A Windows .EXE file contains references to the various dynamic link libraries it uses and the functions therein. Most of these DLLs are located in the SYSTEM subdirectory of your Windows directory. When a Windows program is loaded into memory, the calls in the program are resolved to point to the entries of the functions in the dynamic link libraries, which are also loaded into memory if not already there.

When you link a Windows program to produce an executable, you must link with special "import libraries" provided with your programming environment. These import libraries contain the dynamic link library names of, and reference information for, all the Windows functions. The linker uses this information to construct the table in the .EXE file that Windows uses to resolve calls to Windows functions when loading the program.

Object-Oriented Programming

When programming for Windows, you're really engaged in a type of object-oriented programming (OOP). This is most evident in the object you'll be working with most in Windows—the object that gives Windows its name, the object that will soon seem to take on anthropomorphic characteristics, the object that may even show up in your dreams, the object known as the "window."

As I mentioned earlier, windows are rectangular areas on the screen. A window receives user input from the keyboard or the mouse and displays graphical output on its surface.

An application window usually contains the program's title bar, menu, sizing border, and perhaps some scroll bars. Dialog boxes are additional windows. Moreover, the surface of a dialog box always contains several additional windows called "child windows." These child windows take the form of push buttons, radio buttons, check boxes, text entry fields, list boxes, and scroll bars.

The user sees these windows as objects on the screen and interacts directly with these objects by pushing a button or scrolling a scroll bar. Interestingly enough, the programmer's perspective is analogous to the user's perspective. The window receives this user input in the form of "messages" to the window. A window also uses messages to communicate with other windows.

Understanding these messages is one of the hurdles you'll have to jump in becoming a Windows programmer.

Message-Driven Architecture

The first time I saw a graphical user interface in action, I was puzzled. The demonstration included a rudimentary word processor running in a window. The word processor would reformat its text when the program's window was resized.

It was obvious to me that the operating system itself was handling the details of the window-resizing logic and that the program was capable of responding to this system function. How did the program *know* when its window was resized? What was the mechanism the operating system used to convey this information to the window? My previous programming experience was useless in understanding how this worked.

It turns out that the answer to these questions is central to understanding the architecture used in graphical user interfaces. In Windows, when a user resizes a window, Windows sends a message to the program indicating the new window size. The program can then adjust the contents of its window to reflect the new size.

"Windows sends a message to the program." I hope you didn't read that statement without blinking. What on earth could it mean? We're talking about program code here, not an electronic mail system. How can an operating system send a message to a program?

When I say that "Windows sends a message to the program," I mean that Windows calls a function within the program. The parameters to this function describe the particular message. This function located in your Windows program is known as the "window procedure."

The Window Procedure

You are undoubtedly accustomed to the idea of a program making calls to the operating system. This is how a program opens a disk file, for example. What you may not be accustomed to is the idea of an operating system making calls to a program. Yet this is fundamental to Windows 95's object-oriented architecture.

Every window that a program creates has an associated window procedure. This window procedure is a function that could be either in the program itself or in a dynamic link library. Windows sends a message to a window by calling the window procedure. The window procedure does some processing based on the message and then returns control to Windows.

More precisely, a window is always created based on a "window class." The window class identifies the window procedure that processes messages to the window. The use of a window class allows multiple windows to be based on the same window class and hence use the same window procedure. For example, all buttons in all Windows programs are based on the same window class. This window class is associated with a window procedure (located in a Windows dynamic link library) that processes messages to all the button windows.

In object-oriented programming, an "object" is a combination of code and data. A window is an object. The code is the window procedure. The data is information retained by the window procedure and information retained by Windows for each window and window class that exists in the system.

A window procedure processes messages to the window. Very often these messages inform a window of user input from the keyboard or the mouse. This is how a push-button window knows that it's being "pressed," for example. Other messages tell a window when it is being resized or when the surface of the window needs to be redrawn.

When a Windows program begins execution, Windows creates a "message queue" for the program. This message queue stores messages to all the various windows a program might create. The program includes a short chunk of code called the "message loop" to retrieve these messages from the queue and dispatch them to the appropriate window procedure. Other messages are sent directly to the window procedure without being placed in the message queue.

If your eyes are beginning to glaze over with this excessively abstract description of Windows architecture, maybe it will help to see how the window, the window class, the window procedure, the message queue, the message loop, and the window messages all fit together in the context of a real program.

Let's go.

YOUR FIRST WINDOWS PROGRAM

In their classic book *The C Programming Language* (2d ed., Prentice Hall, 1988), Brian Kernighan and Dennis Ritchie begin discussing C with the now-famous "Hello, world" program:

```
#include <stdio.h>

main ()
    {
    printf ("Hello, world\n") ;
    }
```

In this chapter, I will show you the analogous program written for Microsoft Windows 95. The program is called HELLOWIN, and it creates a window that displays the text string "Hello, Windows 95!" and also plays a sound file with my voice reciting those same words.

Lest you collapse from shock when you first look at the HELLOWIN code, I'll warn you now that the HELLOWIN.C source code file is over 80 lines long. Most of these 80 lines are overhead. You'll have similar overhead in almost every Windows program you write.

Rather than ask why the "Hello, Windows 95!" program is so long and complex, let's ask why the traditional "Hello, world" program is so short and simple.

What's Wrong with This Program?

The output model for the "Hello, world" program and other traditional C programs is an antique piece of hardware known as the teletype. The teletype resembles a typewriter with a continuous roll of paper. In the not-too-distant past, programmers would sit at a teletype and type in commands that were echoed to the paper. The computer responded by printing its output on the paper.

In the early days of mainframe terminals and personal computers, the teletype metaphor was extended to the video display. The video display became a "glass teletype" that simply scrolled when text reached the bottom of the screen.

How can the traditional "Hello, world" program display text without telling the operating system the particular output device on which the text is to appear? Because there is only one output device—the video display, used as if it were a teletype. If the user wishes the output to go elsewhere, it must be redirected from the command line.

How can the program display text without telling the system where on the output device the text is to appear? Because the text always appears where the cursor happens to be, probably on the next line after you execute the program. If you wanted to display "Hello, world" in the center of the screen, you'd have to use some device-dependent control codes to first position the cursor at the desired location.

Let's say you want to run several "Hello, world" programs at one time and see their output on the screen. What a mess! The copies of the program would interfere with each other. There is nothing in the teletype metaphor to separate output from several programs running concurrently.

It's also interesting that you see the "Hello, world" output even after the program terminates. Rather than properly cleaning up after itself, the program leaves remnants of its existence on the video display.

The "Hello, world" program is so simple because it's designed for a simpler age and simpler computers and simpler output devices. It's not in the same ballpark as what we think of today as modern software, and it's not even playing the same game.

The HELLOWIN Files

Two of the three files necessary to create the "HELLOWIN" program are shown in Figure 2-1. These are the HELLOWIN.MAK "make" file and the HELLOWIN.C source code file. The third file is stored on the companion CD-ROM as HELLOWIN.WAV. This is an audio waveform file containing the spoken text.

HELLOWIN.MAK

```
#------------------------
# HELLOWIN.MAK make file
#------------------------

hellowin.exe : hellowin.obj
    $(LINKER) $(GUIFLAGS) -OUT:hellowin.exe hellowin.obj $(GUILIBS)

hellowin.obj : hellowin.c
    $(CC) $(CFLAGS) hellowin.c
```

Figure 2-1. *The HELLOWIN program.*

(continued)

HELLOWIN.C

```
/*-------------------------------------------------------------
   HELLOWIN.C -- Displays "Hello, Windows 95!" in client area
                 (c) Charles Petzold, 1996
   -------------------------------------------------------------*/

#include <windows.h>

LRESULT CALLBACK WndProc (HWND, UINT, WPARAM, LPARAM) ;

int WINAPI WinMain (HINSTANCE hInstance, HINSTANCE hPrevInstance,
                    PSTR szCmdLine, int iCmdShow)
     {
     static char szAppName[] = "HelloWin" ;
     HWND         hwnd ;
     MSG          msg ;
     WNDCLASSEX   wndclass ;

     wndclass.cbSize        = sizeof (wndclass) ;
     wndclass.style         = CS_HREDRAW | CS_VREDRAW ;
     wndclass.lpfnWndProc   = WndProc ;
     wndclass.cbClsExtra    = 0 ;
     wndclass.cbWndExtra    = 0 ;
     wndclass.hInstance     = hInstance ;
     wndclass.hIcon         = LoadIcon (NULL, IDI_APPLICATION) ;
     wndclass.hCursor       = LoadCursor (NULL, IDC_ARROW) ;
     wndclass.hbrBackground = (HBRUSH) GetStockObject (WHITE_BRUSH) ;
     wndclass.lpszMenuName  = NULL ;
     wndclass.lpszClassName = szAppName ;
     wndclass.hIconSm       = LoadIcon (NULL, IDI_APPLICATION) ;

     RegisterClassEx (&wndclass) ;

     hwnd = CreateWindow (szAppName,        // window class name
                 "The Hello Program",       // window caption
                 WS_OVERLAPPEDWINDOW,       // window style
                 CW_USEDEFAULT,             // initial x position
                 CW_USEDEFAULT,             // initial y position
                 CW_USEDEFAULT,             // initial x size
                 CW_USEDEFAULT,             // initial y size
                 NULL,                      // parent window handle
                 NULL,                      // window menu handle
                 hInstance,                 // program instance handle
                 NULL) ;                    // creation parameters

     ShowWindow (hwnd, iCmdShow) ;
     UpdateWindow (hwnd) ;
```

(continued)

```
        while (GetMessage (&msg, NULL, 0, 0))
              {
              TranslateMessage (&msg) ;
              DispatchMessage (&msg) ;
              }
        return msg.wParam ;
        }

LRESULT CALLBACK WndProc (HWND hwnd, UINT iMsg, WPARAM wParam, LPARAM lParam)
        {
        HDC         hdc ;
        PAINTSTRUCT ps ;
        RECT        rect ;

        switch (iMsg)
              {
              case WM_CREATE :
                    PlaySound ("hellowin.wav", NULL, SND_FILENAME | SND_ASYNC) ;
                    return 0 ;

              case WM_PAINT :
                    hdc = BeginPaint (hwnd, &ps) ;

                    GetClientRect (hwnd, &rect) ;

                    DrawText (hdc, "Hello, Windows 95!", -1, &rect,
                              DT_SINGLELINE | DT_CENTER | DT_VCENTER) ;

                    EndPaint (hwnd, &ps) ;
                    return 0 ;

              case WM_DESTROY :
                    PostQuitMessage (0) ;
                    return 0 ;
              }

        return DefWindowProc (hwnd, iMsg, wParam, lParam) ;
        }
```

In Chapter 9, you'll encounter another type of file common in Windows programming called the "resource script" with a filename extension of .RC. But until then, most of the sample programs will use simply a make file and a C source code file and perhaps a header file.

As I mentioned earlier, most of HELLOWIN.C is overhead found in virtually every Windows program. Nobody really memorizes all the syntax to write this overhead; generally, Windows programmers begin a new program by copying an existing program and making appropriate changes to it. You're free to use the programs on the companion CD-ROM in this manner.

If you have Windows 95 and Microsoft Visual C++ 4.0 installed, and have executed the VCVARS32.BAT batch file included with Visual C++ and the MSC.BAT batch file shown in Chapter 1, you should be able to create HELLOWIN.EXE by running:

```
NMAKE HELLOWIN.MAK
```

on the MS-DOS command line.

If all goes well, you can simply run the program from the MS-DOS command line by entering:

```
HELLOWIN
```

The program creates a normal application window as shown in Figure 2-2 on the facing page. The window displays "Hello, Windows 95!" in the center of its client area. If you have a sound board installed, you will also hear the spoken message. (And if you don't have a sound board, what are you waiting for?)

When you think about it, this window has an amazing amount of functionality in its mere 80-odd lines of code. You can grab the title bar with the mouse pointer and move the window around the screen. You can grab the sizing borders and resize the window. When the window changes size, the program will automatically reposition the "Hello, Windows 95!" text string in the new center of the client area. You can click the maximize button and zoom HELLOWIN to fill the screen. You can click the minimize button and clear it from the screen. You can invoke all these options from the system menu. You can also close the window to terminate the program either by selecting that option from the system menu, clicking the close button at the far right of the title bar, or double-clicking the icon at the far left of the title bar.

While you may be pleased to see that HELLOWIN has all the functionality of a normal Windows program, you may not be so happy when you examine the source code required to create this program. But let's be brave while I proceed to dissect this program piece by piece and analyze it to death.

The Make File

To ease compilation of Windows-based programs, you can use the NMAKE utility included with Microsoft Visual C++ version 4.0. Whenever you want to change something in the HELLOWIN.C source code file, all you need do is run NMAKE as shown above to create the updated HELLOWIN.EXE executable.

A make file consists of one or more sections, each of which begins with a left-justified line that lists a target file, followed by a colon, followed by one or more dependent

Figure 2-2. *HELLOWIN running under Windows 95.*

files. This line is followed by one or more indented command lines. These commands create the target file from the dependent files. If the last modification date and time of any of the dependent files is later than the last modification date and time of the target file, NMAKE executes the indented command lines.

Normally, NMAKE will update only the target file in the first section of the make file. However, if one of the dependent files is itself a target file in another section of the make file, NMAKE will update that target first.

The HELLOWIN.MAK make file contains two sections. The first section runs the linker if HELLOWIN.OBJ has been altered more recently than HELLOWIN.EXE. The second section runs the C compiler if HELLOWIN.C has been changed more recently than HELLOWIN.OBJ. Because HELLOWIN.OBJ is a dependent file in the first section of the make file and a target file in the second section, NMAKE will check whether HELLOWIN.OBJ needs updating before re-creating HELLOWIN.EXE. Thus, the make file is actually executed from the bottom up. Running the C compiler creates the HELLOWIN.OBJ object module from the HELLOWIN.C source code file. Running the linker creates the HELLOWIN.EXE executable from HELLOWIN.OBJ.

In Chapter 1, I discussed how the macro identifiers in the make file are provided by environment variables set by the batch files I showed in that chapter. These mostly involve setting various compiler flags and linker library names, so refer back to that section of Chapter 1 if you're interested in these details.

The C Source Code File

The second file in Figure 2-1 is HELLOWIN.C (see pages 22–23), the C source code file. It may take a while before you recognize that this program is indeed written in C!

Let's first take a global look at HELLOWIN.C before getting into details. The file contains only two functions: *WinMain* and *WndProc. WinMain* is the entry point to the program. It is the equivalent of the standard C *main* function. Every Windows program has a *WinMain* function.

WndProc is the "window procedure" for HELLOWIN's window. Every window— be it something as large as a program's main application window or as small as a little push button—has an associated window procedure. The window procedure is a way of encapsulating code that responds to input (generally from the keyboard or mouse) and displays graphics output to the screen. As we'll discover, the window procedure does this by processing "messages" to the window. Don't worry about how this works just yet. You'll have plenty of time later to wrestle with this concept.

No code in HELLOWIN.C calls *WndProc* directly: *WndProc* is called only from Windows. However, there is a reference to *WndProc* in *WinMain*, which is why the function is declared near the top of the program before *WinMain*.

The Windows Function Calls

HELLOWIN makes calls to no less than 17 Windows functions. In the order they occur in HELLOWIN, these functions (with a brief description) are:

■ *LoadIcon*—loads an icon for use by a program.

■ *LoadCursor*—loads a mouse cursor for use by a program.

■ *GetStockObject*—obtains a graphics object (in this case a brush used for painting the window's background).

■ *RegisterClassEx*—registers a window class for the program's window.

■ *CreateWindow*—creates a window based on a window class.

■ *ShowWindow*—displays the window on the screen.

■ *UpdateWindow*—directs the window to paint itself.

■ *GetMessage*—obtains a message from the message queue.

■ *TranslateMessage*—translates some keyboard messages.

■ *DispatchMessage*—sends a message to a window procedure.

■ *PlaySound*—plays a sound file.

- *BeginPaint*—initiates the beginning of window painting.

- *GetClientRect*—obtains the dimensions of the window's client area.

- *DrawText*—displays a text string.

- *EndPaint*—ends window painting.

- *PostQuitMessage*—inserts a "quit" message into the message queue.

- *DefWindowProc*—performs default processing of messages.

These functions are documented in books or online references included with your compiler, and they are declared in various header files from WINDOWS.H.

Uppercase Identifiers

You'll notice the use of quite a few uppercase identifiers in HELLOWIN.C. These identifiers are defined in the Windows header files. Several of these identifiers contain a two-letter or three-letter prefix followed by an underscore:

CS_HREDRAW	DT_VCENTER	WM_CREATE
CS_VREDRAW	IDC_ARROW	WM_DESTROY
CW_USEDEFAULT	IDI_APPLICATION	WM_PAINT
DT_CENTER	SND_ASYNC	WS_OVERLAPPEDWINDOW
DT_SINGLELINE	SND_FILENAME	

These are simply numeric constants. The prefix indicates a general category to which the constant belongs, as indicated in this table:

Prefix	*Category*
CS	Class style option
IDI	ID number for an icon
IDC	ID number for a cursor
WS	Window style
CW	Create window option
WM	Window message
SND	Sound option
DT	Draw text option

You almost never need to remember numeric constants when programming for Windows. Virtually every numeric constant used in Windows has an identifier defined in the header files.

New Data Types

Some other identifiers used in HELLOWIN.C are new data types, also defined in the header files using either *typedef* statements or *#define* statements. This was originally done to ease the transition of Windows programs from the original 16-bit system to future operating systems that would be based on 32-bit (or other) technology. This didn't quite work as smoothly and transparently as everyone thought at the time, but the concept was fundamentally sound.

Sometimes these new data types are just convenient abbreviations. For example, the UINT data type used for the second parameter to *WndProc* is simply an *unsigned int*, which in Windows 95 is a 32-bit value. The PSTR data type used for the third parameter to *WinMain* is a pointer to a character string, that is, a *char* *.

Others are less obvious. For example, the third and fourth parameters to *WndProc* are defined as WPARAM and LPARAM, respectively. The origin of these names requires a bit of historical perspective: When Windows was a 16-bit system, the third parameter to *WndProc* was defined as a WORD, which was a 16-bit *unsigned short* integer, and the fourth parameter was defined as a LONG, which was a 32-bit signed *long* integer, and that's the reason for the "W" and "L" prefixes on the word "PARAM." In Windows 95, WPARAM is defined as a UINT and LPARAM is defined as a LONG (which is simply the C *long* integer type), so both parameters to the window procedure are 32-bit values. This may be a little confusing because the WORD data type is still defined as a 16-bit *unsigned short* integer in Windows 95, so the "W" prefix to "PARAM" creates somewhat of a misnomer.

The *WndProc* function returns a value of type LRESULT. That's simply defined as a LONG. The *WinMain* function is given a type of WINAPI (as is every Windows function defined in the header files), and the *WndProc* function is given a type of CALLBACK. Both these identifers are defined as _ _*stdcall*, which refers to a special calling sequence for function calls that occur between Windows itself and your application.

HELLOWIN also uses four data structures (which I'll discuss later in this chapter) defined in the Windows header files. These data structures are:

Structure	Meaning
MSG	Message structure
WNDCLASSEX	Window class structure
PAINTSTRUCT	Paint structure
RECT	Rectangle structure

The first two data structures are used in *WinMain* to define two structures named *msg* and *wndclass*. The second two are used in *WndProc* to define two structures named *ps* and *rect*.

Getting a Handle on Handles

Finally, there are three uppercase identifiers for various types of "handles":

Identifier	*Meaning*
HINSTANCE	Handle to an "instance"—the program itself
HWND	Handle to a window
HDC	Handle to a device context

Handles are used quite frequently in Windows. Before the chapter is over, you will also encounter HICON (a handle to an icon), HCURSOR (a handle to a mouse cursor), and HBRUSH (a handle to a graphics brush).

A handle is simply a number (usually 32 bits in size) that refers to an object. The handles in Windows are similar to file handles used in conventional C or MS-DOS programming. A program almost always obtains a handle by calling a Windows function. The program uses the handle in other Windows functions to refer to the object. The actual value of the handle is unimportant to your program, but the Windows module that gives your program the handle knows how to use it to reference the object.

Hungarian Notation

You might also notice that some of the variables in HELLOWIN.C have peculiar-looking names. One example is *szCmdLine*, passed as a parameter to *WinMain*.

Many Windows programmers use a variable-naming convention known as Hungarian notation, in honor of the legendary Microsoft programmer Charles Simonyi. Very simply, the variable name begins with a lowercase letter or letters that denote the data type of the variable. For example, the *sz* prefix in *szCmdLine* stands for "string terminated by zero." The *h* prefix in *hInstance* and *hPrevInstance* stands for "handle"; the *i* prefix in *iCmdShow* stands for "integer." The last two parameters to *WndProc* also use Hungarian notation, although, as I explained before, *wParam* should more properly be named *uiParam* (for "unsigned integer"). But because these two parameters are defined using the data types WPARAM and LPARAM, I've chosen to retain their traditional names.

When naming structure variables, you can use the structure name (or an abbreviation of the structure name) in lowercase either as a prefix to the variable name or as the entire variable name. For example, in the *WinMain* function in HELLOWIN.C, the *msg* variable is a structure of the MSG type; *wndclass* is a structure of the WNDCLASSEX type. In the *WndProc* function, *ps* is a PAINTSTRUCT structure and *rect* is a RECT structure.

Hungarian notation helps you avoid errors in your code before they turn into bugs. Because the name of a variable describes both the use of a variable and its data type, you are much less likely to make coding errors involving mismatched data types.

The variable name prefixes I'll generally be using in this book are shown in the following table:

Prefix	Data Type
c	char
by	BYTE (unsigned char)
n	short
i	int
x, y	int (used as x-coordinate or y-coordinate)
cx, cy	int (used as x or y length; c stands for "count")
b or f	BOOL (int); f stands for "flag"
w	WORD (unsigned short)
l	LONG (long)
dw	DWORD (unsigned long)
fn	function
s	string
sz	string terminated by 0 byte
h	handle
p	pointer

The Program Entry Point

With this global look at HELLOWIN.C out of the way, we can now begin the line-by-line dissection of the program. The code begins with an *#include* statement to include the WINDOWS.H header file:

```
#include <windows.h>
```

WINDOWS.H includes many other header files containing declarations of the Windows functions, the Windows structures, the new data types, and numeric constants.

The *#include* statement is followed by a forward declaration of *WndProc*:

```
LRESULT CALLBACK WndProc (HWND, UINT, WPARAM, LPARAM) ;
```

The forward declaration is required because *WndProc* is referenced by some code in the *WinMain* function.

In a C program written for a conventional environment, the entry point is a function called *main*. This is where the program begins execution. (Actually, the *main* function is the entry point to the part of the program written by the programmer. Usually the C compiler will insert some start-up code in the executable file. The start-up code then calls *main.*) The entry point of a Windows program is a function called *WinMain*. *WinMain* is always defined like this:

```
int WINAPI WinMain (HINSTANCE hInstance, HINSTANCE hPrevInstance,
                    PSTR szCmdLine, int iCmdShow)
```

This function uses the WINAPI calling sequence and returns an integer back to Windows when it terminates. The function must be named *WinMain*. It has four parameters:

The *hInstance* parameter is called the "instance handle." This is a number that uniquely identifies the program when it is running under Windows. It could be that the user is running multiple copies of the same program under Windows. Each copy is called an "instance," and each has a different *hInstance* value. The instance handle is comparable to a "task ID" or "process ID" number common in multitasking operating systems.

The *hPrevInstance* ("previous instance") parameter is now obsolete. In previous versions of Windows, it referred to the instance handle of the most recent previous instance of the same program that is still active. If no other copies of the program were currently loaded, then *hPrevInstance* was 0 or NULL. Under Windows 95, this parameter is always NULL.

The *szCmdLine* parameter is a pointer to a 0-terminated string that contains any command-line parameters passed to the program. You can run a Windows program with a command-line parameter by including the parameter after the program name on the MS-DOS command line, or by typing the program name and the parameter into the Run dialog box invoked from the Start menu.

The *iCmdShow* parameter is a number indicating how the window is to be initially displayed in Windows. This number is assigned by whatever other program executes the program to run. Programs do not often need to examine this number, but they can if they want to. In most cases the number is either a 1 or a 7. But it's best not to think of the value as a 1 or as a 7. Rather, think of the value as SW_SHOWNORMAL (defined in the Windows header files as 1) or SW_SHOWMINNOACTIVE (defined as 7). The SW prefix in these identifiers stands for "show window." This indicates whether the user launched the program to be displayed as a normal window or to be initially minimized.

Registering the Window Class

A window is always created based on a window class. The window class identifies the window procedure that processes messages to the window. This is important, so I'll repeat it: A window is always created based on a window class. The window class identifies the window procedure that processes messages to the window.

More than one window can be created based on a single window class. For example, all button windows in Windows are created based on the same window class. The window class defines the window procedure and some other characteristics of the windows that are created based on that class. When you create a window, you define additional characteristics of the window that are unique to that window.

Before you create a window for your program, you must register a window class by calling *RegisterClassEx*. This is an extended (hence the "*Ex*") version of the *RegisterClass* function found in previous versions of Windows. *RegisterClass* still works under Windows 95, however.

The *RegisterClassEx* function requires a single parameter: a pointer to a structure of type WNDCLASSEX. The WNDCLASSEX structure is defined in the Windows header files like this:

```
typedef struct tagWNDCLASSEX
    {
    UINT        cbSize ;
    UINT        style ;
    WNDPROC     lpfnWndProc ;
    int         cbClsExtra ;
    int         cbWndExtra ;
    HINSTANCE   hInstance ;
    HICON       hIcon ;
    HCURSOR     hCursor ;
    HBRUSH      hbrBackground ;
    LPCSTR      lpszMenuName ;
    LPCSTR      lpszClassName ;
    HICON       hIconSm ;
    }
    WNDCLASSEX ;
```

A few notes on some of the data types and Hungarian notation here: Those *LP* and *lp* prefixes stand for "long pointer," which is a remnant of 16-bit Windows, where programmers had to distinguish between short (or near) 16-bit pointers and long (or far) 32-bit pointers. In Windows 95, all pointers are 32 bits in size. I've attempted to remove all *l* prefixes on pointer types in the sample programs in this book, but you'll undoubtedly see them elsewhere.

You'll also notice some other uses of Hungarian notation: The *lpfn* prefix stands for "long pointer to a function." The *cb* prefix stands for "count of bytes." The *hbr* prefix is "handle to a brush."

In *WinMain*, you must define a structure of type WNDCLASSEX, generally like this:

```
WNDCLASSEX wndclass ;
```

You then define the 12 fields of the structure and call *RegisterClassEx*:

```
RegisterClassEx (&wndclass) ;
```

The two most important fields are the second to last and the third. The second to last field is the name of the window class (which in programs that create only one window is generally set to the name of the program). The third field (*lpfnWndProc*) is the address of the window procedure used for all windows created based on this class (which is the function *WndProc* in HELLOWIN.C). The other fields describe characteristics of all windows based on this window class.

The *cbSize* field is the size of the structure. The statement:

```
wndclass.style = CS_HREDRAW ¦ CS_VREDRAW ;
```

combines two "class style" identifiers with a C bitwise OR operator. In the Windows header files, the various identifiers beginning with the CS prefix are defined as 32-bit constants with 1 bit set. For example, CS_VREDRAW is defined as 0x0001, and CS_HREDRAW is defined as 0x0002. Identifiers defined in this way are sometimes called "bit flags." You combine the bit-flag identifiers with the C bitwise OR operator.

These two class-style identifiers indicate that all windows created based on this class are to be completely repainted whenever the horizontal window size (CS_HREDRAW) or the vertical window size (CS_VREDRAW) of the window changes. If you resize HELLOWIN's window, you'll see that the text string is redrawn to be in the new center of the window. These two identifiers ensure that this happens. We'll see shortly how the window procedure is notified of this change in window size.

The third field of the WNDCLASSEX structure is initialized by the statement:

```
wndclass.lpfnWndProc = WndProc ;
```

This sets the window procedure for this window class to *WndProc*, which is the second function in HELLOWIN.C. This window procedure will process all messages to all windows created based on this window class. As I mentioned, the *lpfn* prefix in the field name is Hungarian notation for "long pointer to a function."

The next two statements:

```
wndclass.cbClsExtra = 0 ;
wndclass.cbWndExtra = 0 ;
```

reserve some extra space in the class structure and the window structure that Windows maintains internally. A program can use this extra space for its own purpose. HELLOWIN does not use this feature, so 0 is specified. Otherwise, as the Hungarian notation indicates, the field would be set to a "count of bytes."

The next field is simply the instance handle of the program (which is one of the parameters to *WinMain*):

```
wndclass.hInstance = hInstance ;
```

The statement:

```
wndclass.hIcon = LoadIcon (NULL, IDI_APPLICATION) ;
```

and the statement:

```
wndclass.hIconSm = LoadIcon (NULL, IDI_APPLICATION) ;
```

set an icon for all windows created based on this window class. The icon is a small bitmap picture that appears in the Windows taskbar and at the left side of the window's title bar. Later in this book you'll learn how to create customized icons for your Windows programs. Right now, we'll take an easy approach and use a predefined icon.

To obtain a handle to a predefined icon, you call *LoadIcon* with a first parameter set to NULL. (When loading your own customized icon, this parameter would be set to the instance handle of the program.) The second parameter is an identifier beginning with IDI ("ID for an icon") defined in the Windows header files. The IDI_APPLICATION icon is simply a little picture of a window. The *LoadIcon* function returns a handle to this icon. We don't really care about the value of this handle. It's simply used to set the value of the *hIcon* and *hIconSm* fields. These fields are defined in the WNDCLASSEX structure to be of type HICON, which stands for "handle to an icon."

The statement:

```
wndclass.hCursor = LoadCursor (NULL, IDC_ARROW) ;
```

is very similar to the two previous statements. The *LoadCursor* function loads a predefined mouse cursor known as IDC_ARROW and returns a handle to the cursor. This handle is assigned to the *hCursor* field of the WNDCLASSEX structure. When the mouse cursor appears over the client area of a window that is created based on this class, the cursor becomes a small arrow.

The next field specifies the background color of the client area of windows created based on this class. The *hbr* prefix of the *hbrBackground* field name stands for "handle to a brush." A brush is a graphics term that refers to a colored pattern of pixels used to fill an area. Windows has several standard, or "stock," brushes. The *GetStockObject* call shown here returns a handle to a white brush:

```
wndclass.hbrBackground = GetStockObject (WHITE_BRUSH) ;
```

This means the background of the client area of the window will be solid white, which is a common choice.

The next field specifies the window class menu. HELLOWIN has no application menu, so the field is set to NULL:

```
wndclass.lpszMenuName = NULL ;
```

Finally the class must be given a name. For a small program, this can be simply the name of the program, which is the "HelloWin" string stored in the *szAppName* variable:

```
wndclass.lpszClassName = szAppName ;
```

When all 12 fields of the structure have been initialized, HELLOWIN registers the window class by calling *RegisterClassEx*. The only parameter to the function is a pointer to the WNDCLASSEX structure:

```
RegisterClassEx (&wndclass) ;
```

Creating the Window

The window class defines general characteristics of a window, thus allowing the same window class to be used for creating many different windows. When you actually create a window by calling *CreateWindow*, you specify more detailed information about the window.

Programmers new to Windows are sometimes confused about the distinction between the window class and the window, and why all the characteristics of a window can't be specified in one shot. Actually, dividing information in this way is quite convenient. For example, all push-button windows are created based on the same window class. The window procedure associated with this window class is located inside Windows itself. The window class is responsible for processing keyboard and mouse input to the push button and defining the button's visual appearance on the screen. All push buttons work the same way in this respect. But not all push buttons are the same. They may have different sizes, different locations on the screen, and different text strings. These latter characteristics are part of the window definition.

Rather than using a data structure as *RegisterClassEx* does, the *CreateWindow* call requires all the information to be passed as parameters to the function. Here's the *Create-Window* call in HELLOWIN.C:

```
hwnd = CreateWindow (szAppName,        // window class name
               "The Hello Program", // window caption
               WS_OVERLAPPEDWINDOW, // window style
               CW_USEDEFAULT,       // initial x position
               CW_USEDEFAULT,       // initial y position
               CW_USEDEFAULT,       // initial x size
               CW_USEDEFAULT,       // initial y size
               NULL,                // parent window handle
               NULL,                // window menu handle
               hInstance,           // program instance handle
               NULL) ;              // creation parameters
```

For your reading convenience, I've used the // symbol for single-line comments to describe the parameters to the *CreateWindow* function.

The parameter marked "window class name" is *szAppName*, which contains the string "HelloWin"—the name of the window class we just registered. This is how the window is associated with the window class.

The window created by this program is a normal overlapped window with a title bar; a system menu box to the left of the title bar; minimize, maximize, and close icons to the right of the title bar; and a thick window-sizing border. That's a standard style for windows, and it has the name WS_OVERLAPPEDWINDOW, which appears as the "window style" parameter. The "window caption" is the text that will appear in the title bar.

The parameters marked "initial x position" and "initial y position" specify the initial position of the upper left corner of the window relative to the upper left corner of the screen. By using the identifier CW_USEDEFAULT for these parameters, we are indicating we want Windows to use the default position for an overlapped window. (CW_USEDEFAULT is defined as 0x80000000.) By default, Windows positions successive overlapped windows at stepped horizontal and vertical offsets from the upper left corner of the display. Similarly, the "initial x size" and "initial y size" parameters specify the width and height of the window. The CW_USEDEFAULT identifier again indicates that we want Windows to use a default size for the window.

The parameter marked "parent window handle" is set to NULL because this window has no parent window. (When a parent-child relationship exists between two windows, the child window always appears on the surface of its parent.) The "window menu handle" is also set to NULL because the window has no menu. The "program instance handle" is set to the instance handle passed to the program as a parameter of *WinMain*. Finally, a "creation parameters" pointer is set to NULL. You could use this parameter to point to some data that you might later want to reference in the program.

The *CreateWindow* call returns a handle to the created window. This handle is saved in the variable *hwnd*, which is defined to be of type HWND (handle to a window). Every window in Windows has a handle. Your program uses the handle to refer to the window. Many Windows functions require *hwnd* as a parameter so that Windows knows to which window the function applies. If a program creates many windows, each has a different handle. The handle to a window is one of the most important handles that a Windows program (pardon the expression) handles.

Displaying the Window

After the *CreateWindow* call returns, the window has been created internally in Windows. However, the window does not yet appear on the video display. Two more calls are needed. The first is:

```
ShowWindow (hwnd, iCmdShow) ;
```

The first parameter is the handle to the window just created by *CreateWindow*. The second parameter is the *iCmdShow* value passed as a parameter to *WinMain*. This determines how the window is to be initially displayed on the screen. If *iCmdShow* is SW_SHOWNORMAL (equal to 1), the window is displayed normally. If *iCmdShow* is SW_SHOWMINNOACTIVE (equal to 7), then the window is not displayed but its name and icon appear on the taskbar.

The *ShowWindow* function puts the window on the display. If the second parameter to *ShowWindow* is SW_SHOWNORMAL, the client area of the window is erased with the background brush specified in the window class. The function call:

```
UpdateWindow (hwnd) ;
```

then causes the client area to be painted. It accomplishes this by sending the window procedure (the *WndProc* function in HELLOWIN.C) a WM_PAINT message. We'll soon examine how *WndProc* deals with this message.

The Message Loop

After the *UpdateWindow* call, the window is fully visible on the video display. The program must now make itself ready to read keyboard and mouse input from the user. Windows maintains a "message queue" for each Windows program currently running under Windows. When an input event occurs, Windows translates the event into a "message" that it places in the program's message queue.

A program retrieves these messages from the message queue by executing a block of code known as the "message loop":

```
while (GetMessage (&msg, NULL, 0, 0))
     {
     TranslateMessage (&msg) ;
     DispatchMessage (&msg) ;
     }
return msg.wParam ;
```

The *msg* variable is a structure of type MSG, which is defined in the Windows header files as follows:

```
typedef struct tagMSG
     {
     HWND     hwnd ;
     UINT     message ;
     WPARAM   wParam ;
     LPARAM   lParam ;
     DWORD    time ;
     POINT    pt ;
     }
     MSG ;
```

The POINT data type is yet another structure, defined like this:

```
typedef struct tagPOINT
     {
     LONG x ;
     LONG y ;
     }
     POINT ;
```

The *GetMessage* call that begins the message loop retrieves a message from the message queue:

```
GetMessage (&msg, NULL, 0, 0)
```

This call passes to Windows a pointer to the MSG structure called *msg*. The second, third, and fourth parameters are set to NULL or 0 to indicate that the program wants all messages for all windows created by the program. Windows fills in the fields of the message structure with the next message from the message queue. The fields of this structure are:

■ *hwnd*—the handle to the window to which the message is directed. In the HELLOWIN program, this is the same as the *hwnd* value returned from *CreateWindow*, because that's the only window this program has.

■ *message*—the message identifier. This is a number that identifies the message. For each message, there is a corresponding identifier defined in the Windows header files that begins with the prefix WM ("window message"). For example, if you position the mouse pointer over HELLOWIN's client area and press the left mouse button, Windows will put a message in the message queue with a *message* field equal to WM_LBUTTONDOWN, which is the value 0x0201.

■ *wParam*—a 32-bit "message parameter," the meaning and value of which depend on the particular message.

■ *lParam*—another 32-bit message parameter dependent on the message.

■ *time*—the time the message was placed in the message queue.

■ *pt*—the mouse coordinates at the time the message was placed in the message queue.

If the *message* field of the message retrieved from the message queue is anything except WM_QUIT (which equals 0x0012), then *GetMessage* returns a nonzero value. A WM_QUIT message causes the program to fall out of the message loop. The program then terminates, returning the *wParam* member of the *msg* structure.

The statement:

```
TranslateMessage (&msg) ;
```

passes the *msg* structure back to Windows for some keyboard translation. (I'll discuss this more in Chapter 5.) The statement:

```
DispatchMessage (&msg) ;
```

again passes the *msg* structure back to Windows. Windows then sends the message to the appropriate window procedure for processing—that is, Windows calls the window procedure. That window procedure is the *WndProc* function in HELLOWIN. After *WndProc* processes the message, it returns to Windows, which is still servicing the *DispatchMessage* call. When Windows returns to HELLOWIN following the *DispatchMessage* call, the message loop continues with the next *GetMessage* call.

The Window Procedure

All that I've described so far is really just overhead: The window class has been registered, the window has been created, the window has been displayed on the screen, and the program has entered a message loop to retrieve messages from the message queue.

The real action occurs in the window procedure, which Windows programmers commonly call a "window proc" (pronounced "prock"). The window procedure determines what the window displays in its client area and how the window responds to user input.

In HELLOWIN, the window procedure is the function called *WndProc*. A window procedure can have any name (as long as it doesn't conflict with some other name, of course). A Windows program can contain more than one window procedure. A window procedure is always associated with a particular window class that you register by calling *RegisterClassEx*. The *CreateWindow* function creates a window based on a particular window class. More than one window can be created based on the same window class.

A window procedure is always defined like this:

```
LRESULT CALLBACK WndProc (HWND hwnd, UINT iMsg, WPARAM wParam, LPARAM lParam)
```

Notice that the four parameters to the window procedure are identical to the first four fields of the MSG structure.

The first parameter is *hwnd*, the handle to the window receiving the message. This is the same handle returned from the *CreateWindow* function. For a program like HELLOWIN, which creates only one window, this is the only window handle the program knows about. If a program creates multiple windows based on the same window class (and hence the same window procedure), then *hwnd* identifies the particular window receiving the message.

The second parameter is a number (specifically, a 32-bit unsigned integer or UINT) that identifies the message. The last two parameters (a WPARAM called *wParam* and an LPARAM called *lParam*) provide more information about the message. These are called "message parameters." What these parameters contain is specific to each type of message.

Processing the Messages

Each message that a window procedure receives is identified by a number, which is the *iMsg* parameter to the window procedure. The Windows header files define identifiers beginning with the prefix WM ("window message") for each message parameter.

Generally, Windows programmers use a *switch* and *case* construction to determine what message the window procedure is receiving and how to process it accordingly. When a window procedure processes a message, it should return 0 from the window procedure. All messages that a window procedure chooses not to process must be passed to a Windows function named *DefWindowProc*. The value returned from *DefWindowProc* must be returned from the window procedure.

In HELLOWIN, *WndProc* chooses to process only three messages: WM_CREATE, WM_PAINT, and WM_DESTROY. The window procedure is structured like this:

```
switch (iMsg)
    {
    case WM_CREATE :
        [process WM_CREATE message]
        return 0 ;

    case WM_PAINT :
        [process WM_PAINT message]
        return 0 ;

    case WM_DESTROY :
        [process WM_DESTROY message]
        return 0 ;
    }

return DefWindowProc (hwnd, iMsg, wParam, lParam) ;
```

It is essential to call *DefWindowProc* for default processing of all messages that your window procedure does not process.

Playing a Sound File

The very first message that a window procedure receives—and the first that *WndProc* chooses to process—is WM_CREATE. *WndProc* receives this message while Windows is processing the *CreateWindow* function in *WinMain*. That is, when HELLOWIN calls *CreateWindow*, Windows does what it has to do and, in the process, Windows calls *WndProc* with the first parameter set to the window handle and the second parameter set to WM_CREATE. *WndProc* processes the WM_CREATE message and returns control back to Windows. Windows can then return from the *CreateWindow* call back to HELLOWIN to continue further progress in *WinMain*.

Often a window procedure performs one-time window initialization during WM_CREATE processing. HELLOWIN chooses to process this message by playing a wave-form sound file named HELLOWIN.WAV. It does this using the simple *PlaySound* function. The first parameter is the name of the file. It could also be a sound alias name defined in the Sounds section of the Control Panel, or a program resource. The second parameter is used only if the sound file is a resource. The third parameter specifies a couple of options. In this case I've indicated that the first parameter is a filename, and that the sound is to be played asynchronously, that is, the *PlaySound* function call is to return as soon as the sound file starts playing without waiting for it to complete.

WndProc concludes the WM_CREATE processing by returning 0 from the window procedure.

The WM_PAINT Message

The second message that *WndProc* processes is WM_PAINT. This message is extremely important in Windows programming. It informs a program when part or all of the window's client area is "invalid" and must be repainted.

How does a client area become invalid? When the window is first created, the entire client area is invalid because the program has not yet drawn anything on the window. The first WM_PAINT message (which normally occurs when the program calls *UpdateWindow* in *WinMain*) directs the window procedure to draw something on the client area.

When you resize HELLOWIN's window, the client area also becomes invalid. You'll recall that the *style* parameter of HELLOWIN's *wndclass* structure was set to the flags CS_HREDRAW and CS_VREDRAW. This directs Windows to invalidate the whole window when the size changes. The window procedure then receives a WM_PAINT message.

When you minimize HELLOWIN and then restore the window again to its previous size, Windows does not save the contents of the client area. Under a graphical environment, this would be too much data to retain. Instead, Windows invalidates the window. The window procedure receives a WM_PAINT message and itself restores the contents of its window.

When you move windows around so that they overlap, Windows does not save the area of a window covered by another window. When that area of the window is later uncovered, it is flagged as invalid. The window procedure receives a WM_PAINT message to repaint the contents of the window.

WM_PAINT processing almost always begins with a call to *BeginPaint*:

```
hdc = BeginPaint (hwnd, &ps) ;
```

and ends with a call to *EndPaint*:

```
EndPaint (hwnd, &ps) ;
```

In both cases, the first parameter is a handle to the program's window and the second parameter is a pointer to a structure of type PAINTSTRUCT. The PAINTSTRUCT structure contains some information that a window procedure can use for painting the client area. (I'll discuss the fields of this structure in the next chapter.)

During the *BeginPaint* call, Windows erases the background of the client area if it hasn't been erased already. It erases the background using the brush specified in the *hbrBackground* field of the WNDCLASSEX structure used to register the window class. In the case of HELLOWIN, this is a stock white brush, which means that Windows erases the background of the window by coloring it white. The *BeginPaint* call validates the entire client area and returns a "handle to a device context." A device context refers to a physical output device (such as a video display) and its device driver. You need the device context handle to display text and graphics in the client area of a window. Using the device context handle returned from *BeginPaint*, you cannot draw outside the client area, even if you try. *EndPaint* releases the device context handle so that it is no longer valid.

If a window procedure does not process WM_PAINT messages (which is very rare), they must be passed on to *DefWindowProc*. *DefWindowProc* simply calls *BeginPaint* and *EndPaint* in succession so that the client area is validated.

After *WndProc* calls *BeginPaint*, it calls *GetClientRect*:

```
GetClientRect (hwnd, &rect) ;
```

The first parameter is the handle to the program's window. The second parameter is a pointer to a variable named *rect*, defined as type RECT in *WndProc*.

RECT is a "rectangle" structure defined in the Windows header files. It has four LONG fields named *left*, *top*, *right*, and *bottom*. *GetClientRect* sets these four fields to the dimensions of the client area of the window. The *left* and *top* fields are always set to 0. The *right* and *bottom* fields are set to the width and height of the client area in pixels.

WndProc doesn't do anything with this RECT structure except pass a pointer to it as the fourth parameter of *DrawText*:

```
DrawText (hdc, "Hello, Windows 95!", -1, &rect,
        DT_SINGLELINE | DT_CENTER | DT_VCENTER) ;
```

DrawText (as the name implies) draws text. Because this function draws something, the first parameter is a handle to the device context returned from *BeginPaint*. The second parameter is the text to draw, and the third parameter is set to −1 to indicate that the text string is terminated with a 0 byte.

The last parameter is a series of bit flags defined in the Windows header files. The flags indicate that the text should be displayed as a single line centered horizontally and vertically within the rectangle specified by the fourth parameter. This function call thus causes the string "Hello, Windows 95!" to be displayed centered in the client area.

Whenever the client area becomes invalid (as it does when you change the size of the window), *WndProc* receives a new WM_PAINT message. *WndProc* obtains the updated window size by calling *GetClientRect* and again displays the text in the new center of the window.

The WM_DESTROY Message

The WM_DESTROY message is another important message. This message indicates that Windows is in the process of destroying a window based on a command from the user. The message is a result of the user clicking on the Close button or selecting Close from the program's system menu or pressing Alt-F4.

HELLOWIN responds to this message in a standard way by calling:

```
PostQuitMessage (0) ;
```

This function inserts a WM_QUIT message in the program's message queue. I mentioned earlier that *GetMessage* returns nonzero for any message other than WM_QUIT that it retrieves from the message queue. When *GetMessage* retrieves a WM_QUIT message, *GetMessage* returns 0. This causes *WinMain* to drop out of the message loop and exit, terminating the program.

THE WINDOWS PROGRAMMING HURDLES

Even with my explanation of HELLOWIN, the structure and workings of the program are probably still somewhat mysterious. In a short C program written for a conventional environment, the entire program may be contained in the *main* function. In HELLOWIN, *WinMain* contains only program overhead necessary to register the window class, create the window, and retrieve and dispatch messages from the message queue.

All the real action of the program occurs in the window procedure. In HELLOWIN, this action is not much—it simply plays a sound file and displays a text string in its window. But in later chapters you'll find that almost everything a Windows program does is in response to a message to a window procedure. This is one of the major conceptual hurdles that you must leap to begin writing Windows programs.

Don't Call Me, I'll Call You

As I mentioned earlier, programmers are familiar with the idea of calling on the operating system to do something. For instance, C programmers use the *fopen* function to open a file. The library functions provided with the compiler have code that eventually calls the operating system to open the file. No problem.

But Windows is different. Although Windows has well over a thousand functions that your program can call, Windows also makes calls to *your* program, specifically to the window procedure we have called *WndProc*. The window procedure is associated with a window class that the program registers by calling *RegisterClassEx*. A window that is created based on this class uses this window procedure for processing all messages to the window. Windows sends a message to the window by calling the window procedure.

Windows calls *WndProc* when a window is first being created. Windows calls *WndProc* when the window is later destroyed. Windows calls *WndProc* when the window has been resized or moved or minimized. Windows calls *WndProc* when an item has been selected from a menu. Windows calls *WndProc* when a scroll bar is manipulated or clicked with the mouse. Windows calls *WndProc* to tell it when it must repaint its client area.

All these calls are in the form of messages. In most Windows programs, the bulk of the program is dedicated to handling these messages. The over 200 different messages that Windows can send to a window procedure are all identified with names that begin with the letters "WM" and are defined in the Windows header files.

Actually, the idea of a routine within a program that is called from outside the program is not unheard of in normal programming. The *signal* function in C can trap a Ctrl-Break. You may have experience with intercepting hardware interrupts in assembly language or with using one of the ON constructions in Microsoft BASIC. The Microsoft Mouse driver has a method that nonWindows programs can use to be notified of mouse activity.

In Windows, this concept is extended to cover everything. Everything that happens to a window is relayed to the window procedure in the form of a message. The window procedure then responds to this message in some way or passes the message to *DefWindowProc* for default processing.

The *wParam* and *lParam* parameters to the window procedure are not used in HELLOWIN except as parameters to *DefWindowProc*. These parameters give the window procedure additional information about the message. The meaning of the parameters is message-dependent.

Let's look at an example. Whenever the client area of a window changes in size, Windows calls that window's window procedure. The *hwnd* parameter to the window procedure is the handle of the window changing in size. The *iMsg* parameter is WM_SIZE. The *wParam* parameter for a WM_SIZE message is the value SIZENORMAL, SIZEICONIC, SIZEFULLSCREEN, SIZEZOOMSHOW, or SIZEZOOMHIDE (defined in the Windows header files as the numbers 0 through 4). The *wParam* parameter indicates whether the window is being minimized, maximized, or hidden (as a result of another window being maximized). The *lParam* parameter contains the new size of the window. The new width (a 16-bit value) and the new height (a 16-bit value) have been stuck together in the 32-byte *lParam*. The Windows header files include macros to help you extract these two values from *lParam*. We'll do this in the next chapter.

Sometimes messages generate other messages as a result of *DefWindowProc* processing. For example, suppose you run HELLOWIN and select Close from the system menu using either the keyboard or the mouse. *DefWindowProc* processes this keyboard or mouse input. When it detects that you have selected the Close option, it sends a WM_SYSCOMMAND message to the window procedure. *WndProc* passes this message to *DefWindowProc*. *DefWindowProc* responds by sending a WM_CLOSE message to the window procedure. *WndProc* again passes this message to *DefWindowProc*. *DefWindowProc* responds to the WM_CLOSE message by calling *DestroyWindow*. *DestroyWindow* causes Windows to send a WM_DESTROY message to the window procedure. *WndProc* finally responds to this message by calling *PostQuitMessage* to put a WM_QUIT message in the message queue. This message causes the message loop in *WinMain* to terminate and the program to end.

Queued and Nonqueued Messages

I've talked about Windows sending messages to a window, which means that Windows calls the window procedure. But a Windows program also has a message loop that retrieves messages from a message queue by calling *GetMessage* and dispatches them to the window procedure by calling *DispatchMessage*.

So, does a Windows program poll for messages (exactly as a normal program polls for keyboard data) and then route these messages to some location? Or does it receive messages directly from outside the program? Well, both.

Messages can be either "queued" or "nonqueued." The queued messages are those that are placed in a program's message queue by Windows and retrieved and dispatched in the message loop. The nonqueued messages are sent to the window directly when Windows calls the window procedure. The result is that the window procedure gets all the messages—both queued and nonqueued—for the window. Structurally, Windows programs are very clean because they have one central point of message processing. It is said that queued messages are *posted* to a message queue and that nonqueued messages are *sent* to the window procedure.

The queued messages are primarily those that result from user input in the form of keystrokes (such as WM_KEYDOWN and WM_KEYUP), characters that result from keystrokes (WM_CHAR), mouse movement (WM_MOUSEMOVE), and mouse button clicks (WM_LBUTTONDOWN). Queued messages also include the timer message (WM_TIMER), the repaint message (WM_PAINT), and the quit message (WM_QUIT). The nonqueued messages are everything else. In many cases the nonqueued messages result from queued messages. When you pass a nonqueued message to *DefWindowProc* within the window procedure, Windows often processes the message by sending the window procedure other messages.

This process is obviously complex, but fortunately most of the complexity is Windows' problem rather than our program's. From the perspective of the window procedure, these messages come through in an orderly, synchronized manner. The window procedure can do something with these messages or ignore them. For this reason, the window procedure has been called the "ultimate hook." Messages notify the window procedure of almost everything that affects the window.

The nonqueued messages often result from calling certain Windows functions or from explicitly sending a message by calling *SendMessage*. (Messages can also be placed in a message queue by calling *PostMessage*.)

For example, when *WinMain* calls *CreateWindow*, Windows creates the window and in the process sends the window procedure a WM_CREATE message. When *WinMain* calls *ShowWindow*, Windows sends the window procedure WM_SIZE and WM_SHOWWINDOW messages. When *WinMain* calls *UpdateWindow*, Windows sends the window procedure a WM_PAINT message.

Messages are not like hardware interrupts. While processing one message in a window procedure, the program will not be interrupted by another message. Only when the window procedure calls a function that generates a new message will the window procedure process the message before the function returns.

The message loop and the window procedure do not run concurrently. When the window procedure is processing a queued message, it is the result of a call to *DispatchMessage* in *WinMain*. *DispatchMessage* does not return until the window procedure has processed the message.

But notice that the window procedure must be reentrant. That is, Windows often calls *WndProc* with a new message as a result of *WndProc* calling *DefWindowProc* with a previous message. In most cases the reentrancy of the window procedure presents no problem, but you should be aware of it.

For example, suppose you set a variable while processing a message in the window procedure, and then you call a Windows function. Upon return from that function, can you be assured that the variable is still the same? Not necessarily—not if the particular Windows function you called generated another message, and the window procedure changed the variable while processing that second message. This is one of the reasons why certain forms of compiler optimization must be turned off when compiling Windows programs.

In many cases, the window procedure must retain information it obtains in one message and use it while processing another message. This information must be saved in variables defined as *static* in the window procedure, or saved in global variables.

Of course, you'll get a much better feel for all this in later chapters as the window procedures are expanded to process more messages.

Don't Be a Pig

Windows 95 is a preemptive multitasking environment. This means that as one program is doing a lengthy job, Windows can allow the user to switch control to another program. This is a good thing, and it is one advantage of Windows 95 over previous DOS-based versions of Windows.

However, because of the way that Windows is structured, this preemptive multitasking does not always work the way you might like. For example, suppose your program spends a minute or so processing a particular message. Yes, the user can switch to another program. But the user cannot do anything with *your* program. The user cannot move your program's window, resize it, minimize it, close it, nothing. That's because your window procedure must perform these functions and your window procedure is busy doing a lengthy job. Oh, it may not seem like the window procedure performs its own moving and sizing operations, but it does. That's part of the job of *DefWindowProc*, which must be considered as part of your window procedure.

If your program needs to perform lengthy jobs while processing particular messages, there are ways to do so politely that I'll describe in Chapter 14. Even with preemptive multitasking, it's not a good idea to leave your window sitting inert on the screen. It annoys users, and they'll begin to think of your program as a pig.

The Learning Curve

Yes, as you've undoubtedly determined from this chapter, Windows programming is certainly different from programming for a conventional environment like MS-DOS. Nobody will claim that Windows programming is easy.

When I first started learning Windows programming, I decided to do what I had always done when learning a new operating system or a new language—write a simple "hex dump" program to display the contents of a file. In the conventional MS-DOS environment, such a program involves command-line processing, rudimentary file I/O, and screen output formatting. My Windows hex-dump program, however, turned into a monster. It required that I learn about menus, dialog boxes, scroll bars, and the like. As a first Windows program, it was definitely a mistake, demanding that I absorb too much all at once.

Yet when this program was finished, it was quite unlike any hex-dump program I had ever written. Rather than obtain the filename from a command line, WINDUMP (as I called it) presented a list box showing all the files in the current directory. Rather than write its output to the screen in a simple teletype fashion, WINDUMP had scroll bars, so I could move to any part of the file. As an extra bonus, I could even run two copies of WINDUMP to compare two files side by side. In short, WINDUMP was the first hex-dump program I wrote that I was actually proud of.

What you have to ask yourself is this: Do I want my programs to use a modern and productive user interface, one that includes menus, dialog boxes, scroll bars, and graphics? If you answer yes, then the question becomes: Do I want to write all this menu, dialog box, scroll bar, and graphics code myself? Or would I rather take advantage of all the code already inside Windows for this? In other words, is it easier to learn how to use over 1000 function calls or to write them yourself? Is it easier to orient your programming mind to the message-driven architecture of Windows or struggle with using several different sources of user input in a traditional model?

If you're going to write your own user interface logic, you had better close this book and get to work right away. Meanwhile, the rest of us are going to learn how to display and scroll text in a window.

Chapter 3

Painting with Text

In the previous chapter, you saw a simple Windows 95 program that displayed a single line of text in the center of its window, or rather—to be more precise—in the center of its client area. The distinction between the application window and its client area is quite important: The client area is that part of the total application window that is not taken up by the title bar, the window-sizing border, the menu bar (if any), and scroll bars (if any). In short, the client area is the part of the window on which a program is free to draw and deliver visual information to the user.

You can do almost anything you want with your program's client area—anything, that is, except assume that it will be a particular size or that the size will remain constant while your program is running. If you are accustomed to writing programs for MS-DOS, these stipulations may come as a bit of a shock. You can no longer think in terms of 25 (or 43 or 50) lines of text with 80 characters across the screen. Your program must share the video display with other Windows programs. The Windows user controls how the programs' windows are arranged on the screen. Although it's possible to create a window of a fixed size (which is appropriate for calculators and similar utilities), in most cases windows are sizeable. Your program must accept the size it's given and do something reasonable with it.

This works both ways. Just as your program may find itself with a client area barely large enough in which to say "Hello," it may also someday be run on a big-screen, high-resolution video system and discover a client area large enough for two entire pages of text and plenty of closet space besides. Dealing intelligently with both eventualities is an important part of Windows programming.

Although Windows has extensive Graphics Device Interface (GDI) functions for displaying graphics, in this chapter I'll stick to displaying simple lines of text. I'll also ignore the various fonts (typefaces) and font sizes that Windows makes available and use only Windows' default "system font." This may seem limiting, but it really isn't. The problems we encounter—and solve—in this chapter apply to all Windows programming. When you display a combination of text and graphics (as, for instance, the Windows Calculator program does), the character dimensions of Windows' default system font often determine the dimensions of the graphics.

This chapter is ostensibly about learning how to paint, but it's really about learning the basics of device-independent programming. Windows programs can assume little about the size of their client areas or even the size of text characters. Instead, they must use the facilities that Windows provides to obtain information about the environment in which the program runs.

PAINTING AND REPAINTING

Under MS-DOS, a program using the display in a full-screen mode can write to any part of the display. What the program puts on the display will stay there and will not mysteriously disappear. The program can then discard information needed to re-create the screen display. If another program (such as a RAM-resident popup) overlays part of the display, then the popup is responsible for restoring the display when it leaves.

In Windows, you can display only in the client area of your window, and you cannot be assured that what you display in the client area will remain there until your program specifically writes over it. For instance, a dialog box from another application may overlay part of your client area. Although Windows will attempt to save and restore the area of the display underneath the dialog box, it sometimes cannot do so. When the dialog box is removed from the screen, Windows will request that your program repaint this portion of your client area.

Windows is a message-driven system. Windows informs applications of various events by posting messages in the application's message queue or sending messages to the appropriate window procedure. Windows informs a window procedure that part of the window's client area needs updating by posting a WM_PAINT message.

The WM_PAINT Message

Most Windows programs call the function *UpdateWindow* during initialization in *WinMain* shortly before entering the message loop. Windows takes this opportunity to send the window procedure its first WM_PAINT message. That message informs your window procedure that the client area is ready to be painted. Thereafter, that window procedure should be ready at any time to process additional WM_PAINT messages and even to repaint the entire client area of the window if necessary. A window procedure receives a WM_PAINT message whenever one of the following occurs:

■   A previously hidden area of the window is brought into view when a user moves a window or uncovers a window.

- The user resizes the window (if the window class style has the CS_HREDRAW and CS_VREDRAW bits set).

- The program uses the *ScrollWindow* or *ScrollDC* function to scroll part of its client area.

- The program uses the *InvalidateRect* or *InvalidateRgn* function to explicitly generate a WM_PAINT message.

In some cases in which part of the client area is temporarily written over, Windows attempts to save an area of the display and restore it later. This is not always successful. Windows may sometimes post a WM_PAINT message when:

- Windows removes a dialog box or message box that was overlaying part of the window.

- A menu is pulled down and then released.

In a few cases, Windows always saves the area of the display it overwrites and then restores it. This is the case whenever:

- The mouse cursor is moved across the client area.
- An icon is dragged across the client area.

Dealing with WM_PAINT messages requires that you alter your thinking about how you write to the display. Your program should be structured so that it accumulates all the information necessary to paint the client area but paints only "on demand"—when Windows sends the window procedure a WM_PAINT message. If your program needs to update its client area, it can force Windows to generate this WM_PAINT message. This may seem a roundabout method of displaying something on the screen, but the structure of your program will benefit from it.

Valid and Invalid Rectangles

Although a window procedure should be prepared to update the entire client area whenever it receives a WM_PAINT message, it often needs to update only a smaller area (most often a rectangular area within the client area). This is most obvious when part of the client area is overlaid by a dialog box. Repainting is required only for the rectangular area uncovered when the dialog box is removed.

That area is known as an "invalid region" or "update region." The presence of an invalid region in a client area is what prompts Windows to place a WM_PAINT message in the application's message queue. Your window procedure receives a WM_PAINT message only if part of your client area is invalid.

Windows internally maintains a "paint information structure" for each window. This structure contains (among other information) the coordinates of the smallest rectangle that encompasses the invalid region. This is known as the "invalid rectangle"; sometimes it is also called the "invalid region." If another region of the client area becomes invalid before the window procedure processes the WM_PAINT message, Windows calculates a new invalid region that encompasses both areas and stores this updated information in the paint information structure. Windows does not place multiple WM_PAINT messages in the message queue.

A window procedure can invalidate a rectangle in its own client area by calling *InvalidateRect*. If the message queue already contains a WM_PAINT message, Windows calculates a new invalid rectangle. Otherwise, it places a new WM_PAINT message in the message queue. A window procedure can obtain the coordinates of the invalid rectangle when it receives a WM_PAINT message (as we'll see later in this chapter). It can also obtain these coordinates at any other time by calling *GetUpdateRect*.

After the window procedure calls *BeginPaint* during the WM_PAINT message, the entire client area is validated. A program can also validate any rectangular region in the client area by calling the *ValidateRect* function. If this call has the effect of validating the entire invalid area, then any WM_PAINT message currently in the queue is deleted.

AN INTRODUCTION TO GDI

To paint the client area of your window, you use Windows' Graphics Device Interface (GDI) functions. (An overview of GDI awaits us in the next chapter.) Windows provides several GDI functions for writing text strings to the client area of the window. We've already encountered the *DrawText* function in Chapter 2, but the most popular text output function by far is *TextOut*. This function has the following format:

```
TextOut (hdc, x, y, psString, iLength) ;
```

TextOut writes a character string to the display. The *psString* parameter is a pointer to the character string, and *iLength* is the length of the string in characters. The *x* and *y* parameters define the starting position of the character string in the client area. (More details soon.) The *hdc* parameter is a "handle to a device context," and it is an important part of GDI. Virtually every GDI function requires this handle as the first parameter to the function.

The Device Context

A handle, you'll recall, is simply a number that Windows uses for internal reference to an object. You obtain the handle from Windows and then use the handle in other functions. The device context handle is your window's passport to the GDI functions. With that device context handle you are free to paint your client area and make it as beautiful or as ugly as you like.

The device context (also called the "DC") is really just a data structure maintained internally by GDI. A device context is associated with a particular display device, such as a printer, plotter, or video display. For a video display, a device context is usually associated with a particular window on the display.

Some of the values in the device context are graphics "attributes." These attributes define some particulars of how GDI drawing functions work. With *TextOut*, for instance, the attributes of the device context determine the color of the text, the color of the text background, how the *x*-coordinate and *y*-coordinate in the *TextOut* function are mapped to the client area of the window, and what font Windows uses when displaying the text.

When a program needs to paint, it must first obtain a handle to a device context. After it has finished painting, the program should release the handle. When a program releases the handle, the handle is no longer valid and must not be used. The program should obtain the handle and release the handle during the processing of a single message. Except for a device context created with a call to *CreateDC* (a function I won't discuss in this chapter), you should not keep a device context handle around from one message to another.

Windows applications generally use two methods for getting a device context handle in preparation for painting the screen.

Getting a Device Context Handle: Method One

You use this method when you process WM_PAINT messages. Two functions are involved: *BeginPaint* and *EndPaint*. These two functions require the handle to the window (passed to the window procedure as a parameter) and the address of a structure variable of type PAINTSTRUCT. Windows programmers usually name this structure variable *ps* and define it within the window procedure, like so:

```
PAINTSTRUCT ps ;
```

While processing a WM_PAINT message, the window procedure first calls *BeginPaint* to fill in the fields of the *ps* structure. The value returned from *BeginPaint* is the device context handle. This is commonly saved in a variable named *hdc*. You define this variable in your window procedure like this:

```
HDC hdc ;
```

The HDC data type is defined as a 32-bit unsigned integer. The program may then use GDI functions such as *TextOut*. A call to *EndPaint* releases the device context handle.

Typically, processing of the WM_PAINT message looks like this:

```
case WM_PAINT :
     hdc = BeginPaint (hwnd, &ps) ;
     [use GDI functions]
     EndPaint (hwnd, &ps) ;
     return 0 ;
```

The window procedure must call *BeginPaint* and *EndPaint* as a pair while processing the WM_PAINT message. If a window procedure does not process WM_PAINT messages, then it must pass the WM_PAINT message to *DefWindowProc* (the default window procedure) located in Windows.

DefWindowProc processes WM_PAINT messages with the following code:

```
case WM_PAINT :
     BeginPaint (hwnd, &ps) ;
     EndPaint (hwnd, &ps) ;
     return 0 ;
```

This sequence of *BeginPaint* and *EndPaint* with nothing in between simply validates the previously invalid region. But don't do this:

```
case WM_PAINT :
     return 0 ;    // WRONG !!!
```

Windows places a WM_PAINT message in the message queue because part of the client area is invalid. Unless you call *BeginPaint* and *EndPaint* (or *ValidateRect*), Windows will not validate that area. Instead, Windows will send you another WM_PAINT message. And another, and another, and another...

The Paint Information Structure

Earlier I mentioned a "paint information structure" that Windows maintains for each window. That's what PAINTSTRUCT is. The structure is defined as follows:

```
typedef struct tagPAINTSTRUCT
     {
     HDC        hdc ;
     BOOL       fErase ;
     RECT       rcPaint ;
     BOOL       fRestore ;
     BOOL       fIncUpdate ;
     BYTE       rgbReserved[32] ;
     }
     PAINTSTRUCT ;
```

Windows fills in the fields of this structure when your program calls *BeginPaint*. Your program may use only the first three fields. The others are used internally by Windows.

The *hdc* field is the handle to the device context. In a redundancy typical of Windows, the value returned from *BeginPaint* is also this device context handle.

In most cases, *fErase* will be flagged TRUE (nonzero), meaning that Windows has erased the background of the invalid rectangle. Windows erases the background using the brush specified in the *hbrBackground* field of the WNDCLASSEX structure that you use when registering the window class during *WinMain* initialization. Many Windows programs use a white brush:

```
wndclass.hbrBackground = (HBRUSH) GetStockObject (WHITE_BRUSH) ;
```

However, if your program invalidates a rectangle of the client area by calling the Windows function *InvalidateRect*, the last parameter of the function specifies whether you want the background erased. If this parameter is FALSE (or 0), then Windows will not erase the background and the *fErase* field will also be FALSE.

The *rcPaint* field of the PAINTSTRUCT structure is a structure of type RECT. As you learned in Chapter 2, the RECT structure defines a rectangle. The four fields are *left, top, right,* and *bottom.* The *rcPaint* field in the PAINTSTRUCT structure defines the boundaries of the invalid rectangle, as shown in Figure 3-1. The values are in units of pixels relative to the upper left corner of the client area. The invalid rectangle is the area that you should repaint. Although a Windows program can simply repaint the entire client area of the window whenever it receives a WM_PAINT message, repainting only the area of the window defined by that rectangle saves time.

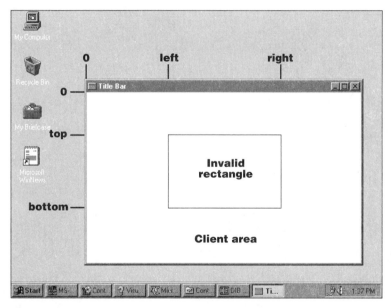

Figure 3-1. *The boundaries of the invalid rectangle.*

The *rcPaint* rectangle in PAINTSTRUCT is not only the invalid rectangle; it is also a "clipping" rectangle. This means that Windows restricts painting to within the clipping rectangle. (More precisely, if the invalid region is not rectangular, Windows restricts painting to within that region.) When you use the device context handle from the PAINTSTRUCT structure, Windows will not paint outside the *rcPaint* rectangle.

To paint outside this *rcPaint* rectangle while processing WM_PAINT messages, you can make this call:

```
InvalidateRect (hWnd, NULL, TRUE) ;
```

before calling *BeginPaint*. This invalidates the entire client area and erases the background. A FALSE value in the last parameter will not erase the background, however. Whatever was there will stay.

In the HELLOWIN program in Chapter 2, we didn't care about invalid rectangles or clipping rectangles when processing the WM_PAINT message. If the area where the text was displayed happened to be within the invalid rectangle, *DrawText* restored it. If not, then at some point during processing of the *DrawText* call, Windows determined it didn't have to write anything to the display. But this determination takes time. A programmer concerned about performance and speed will want to use the invalid-rectangle dimensions during processing of WM_PAINT to avoid unnecessary GDI calls.

Getting a Device Context Handle: Method Two

You can also obtain a handle to a device context if you want to paint the client area when processing messages other than WM_PAINT or if you need the device context handle for other purposes, such as obtaining information about the device context. Call *GetDC* to obtain the handle to the device context, and call *ReleaseDC* after you're done with it:

```
hdc = GetDC (hwnd) ;
[use GDI functions]
ReleaseDC (hwnd, hdc) ;
```

Like *BeginPaint* and *EndPaint*, the *GetDC* and *ReleaseDC* functions should be called in pairs. When you call *GetDC* while processing a message, you should call *ReleaseDC* before you exit the window procedure. Do not call *GetDC* in response to one message and *ReleaseDC* in response to another.

Unlike the device context handle obtained from the PAINTSTRUCT structure, the device context handle returned from *GetDC* has a clipping rectangle equal to the entire client area. You can paint on any part of the client area, not merely on the invalid rectangle (if indeed there is an invalid rectangle). Unlike *BeginPaint*, *GetDC* does not validate any invalid regions.

Generally, you'll use the *GetDC* and *ReleaseDC* calls in response to keyboard messages (such as in a word processing program) or mouse messages (such as in a drawing program). This allows the program to update the client area in prompt reaction to the user's keyboard or mouse input without deliberately invalidating part of the window to generate WM_PAINT messages. Still, your program must accumulate enough information to be able to update the display whenever you *do* receive a WM_PAINT message.

TextOut: The Details

When you obtain the handle to the device context, Windows fills the internal device context structure with default values. As you'll see in later chapters, you can change these defaults with GDI functions. The GDI function we're interested in right now is *TextOut*:

```
TextOut (hdc, x, y, psString, iLength) ;
```

Let's examine this function in more detail.

The first parameter is the handle to the device context—either the *hdc* value returned from *GetDC* or the *hdc* value returned from *BeginPaint* during processing of a WM_PAINT message.

The attributes of the device context control the characteristics of this displayed text. For instance, one attribute of the device context specifies the text color. The default color is conveniently black. The default device context also defines a background color of white. When a program writes text to the display, Windows uses this background color to fill in the rectangular space surrounding each character, called the "character box."

This text background color is not the same background you set when defining the window class. The background in the window class is a brush—which is a pattern that may or may not be a pure color—that Windows uses to erase the client area. It is not part of the device context structure. When defining the window class structure, most Windows applications use WHITE_BRUSH so that the background color in the default device context is the same color as the brush Windows uses to erase the background of the client area.

The *psString* parameter is a pointer to a character string, and *iLength* is the length of the string, that is, the number of characters in the string. The string should not contain any ASCII control characters such as carriage returns, linefeeds, tabs, or backspaces. Windows displays these control characters as boxes or solid blocks. *TextOut* does not recognize a 0 as denoting the end of a string and requires the *iLength* parameter for the string's length.

The *x* and *y* values in *TextOut* define the starting point of the character string within the client area. The *x* value is the horizontal position; the *y* value is the vertical position. The upper left corner of the first character in the string is positioned at the coordinate point (x, y). In the default device context, the origin (the point where *x* and *y* both equal 0) is the upper left corner of the client area. If you use 0 values for *x* and *y* in *TextOut*, the character string starts flush against the upper left corner of the client area.

GDI coordinates are documented as "logical coordinates." What this means exactly we'll examine in more detail in the next chapter. For now, be aware that Windows has a variety of "mapping modes" that govern how the logical coordinates specified in GDI functions are translated to the physical pixel coordinates of the display. The mapping mode is defined in the device context. The default mapping mode is called MM_TEXT (using the identifier defined in the Windows header files). Under the MM_TEXT mapping mode, logical units are the same as physical units, which are pixels, relative to the upper left corner of the client area. Values of *x* increase as you move to the right in the client area, and values of *y* increase as you move down in the client area. (See Figure 3-2 on the following page.) The MM_TEXT coordinate system is identical to the coordinate system that Windows uses to define the invalid rectangle in the PAINTSTRUCT structure. Very convenient. (This is not the case with other mapping modes, however.)

The device context also defines a clipping region. As you've seen, the default clipping region is the entire client area for a device context handle obtained from *GetDC* and the invalid region for the device context handle obtained from *BeginPaint*. Windows will not display any part of the character string that lies outside the clipping region. If a character is partly within the clipping region, Windows displays only the portion of the character inside the region. Writing outside the client area of your window isn't easy to do, so don't worry about doing it inadvertently.

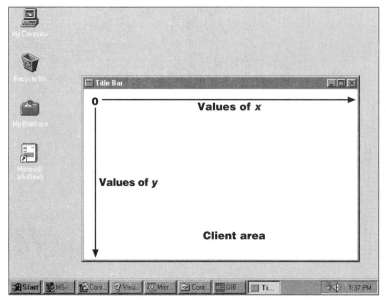

Figure 3-2. *The x-coordinate and y-coordinate in the MM_TEXT mapping mode.*

The System Font

The device context also defines the font that Windows uses when writing text to the client area. The default is a font called the "system font" or (using the identifier in the Windows header files) SYSTEM_FONT. The system font is the font that Windows uses for text in title bars, menus, and dialog boxes.

In the early days of Windows, the system font was a fixed-pitch font, which means that all the characters had the same width, much like a typewriter. However, beginning with Windows 3.0 (and continuing through Windows 95), the system font became a variable-pitch font, which means that different characters have different widths. A "W" is wider than an "i," for example. It has been well established that text printed with variable-pitch fonts is more readable than fixed-pitch fonts. But as you might imagine, this change from a default fixed-pitch font to a default variable-pitch font broke a lot of early Windows code and required that programmers learn some new techniques for working with text.

The system font is a "raster font," which means that the characters are defined as blocks of pixels. The retail version of Windows includes several system fonts in various sizes for use with different video display adapters. When manufacturers of a new video board develop a new Windows display driver, they are also responsible for developing a new system font appropriate for the resolution of the display. Alternatively, the manufacturer might specify that one of the system font files supplied with the retail version of Windows be used. The system font must be designed so that at least 25 lines of 80-character text can fit on the display. That is the only guarantee you have about the relationship between screen size and font size in Windows.

The Size of a Character

To display multiple lines of text using the *TextOut* function, you need to determine the dimensions of font characters. You can space successive lines of text based on the height of a character, and you can space columns of text across the client area based on the average width of the characters in the font.

You can obtain character dimensions with the *GetTextMetrics* call. *GetTextMetrics* requires a handle to the device context because it returns information about the font currently selected in the device context. Windows copies the various values of text metrics into a structure of type TEXTMETRIC. The values are in units that depend on the mapping mode selected in the device context. In the default device context, this mapping mode is MM_TEXT, so the dimensions are in units of pixels.

To use the *GetTextMetrics* function, you first need to define a structure variable (commonly called *tm*):

```
TEXTMETRIC tm ;
```

Next, get a handle to the device context and call *GetTextMetrics*:

```
hdc = GetDC (hwnd) ;
GetTextMetrics (hdc, &tm) ;
ReleaseDC (hwnd, hdc) ;
```

You can then examine the values in the text metric structure and probably save a few of them for future use.

Text Metrics: The Details

The TEXTMETRIC structure provides a wealth of information about the current font selected in the device context. However, the vertical size of a font is defined by only five values, as shown in Figure 3-3 on the following page.

These are fairly self-explanatory. The *tmInternalLeading* value is the amount of space allowed for an accent mark above a character. If the value is set to 0, accented capital letters are made a little shorter so that the accent fits within the ascent of the character. The *tmExternalLeading* value is the amount of space that the designer of the font suggests be added between character rows. You can accept or reject the font designer's suggestion for including external leading when spacing lines of text.

The TEXTMETRIC structure contains two fields that describe character width: *tmAveCharWidth* (a weighted average width of lowercase characters) and *tmMaxCharWidth* (the width of the widest character in the font). For a fixed-pitch font, these two values are the same.

The sample programs in this chapter will require another character width—the average width of uppercase letters. This can be calculated fairly accurately as 150% of *tmAve-CharWidth*.

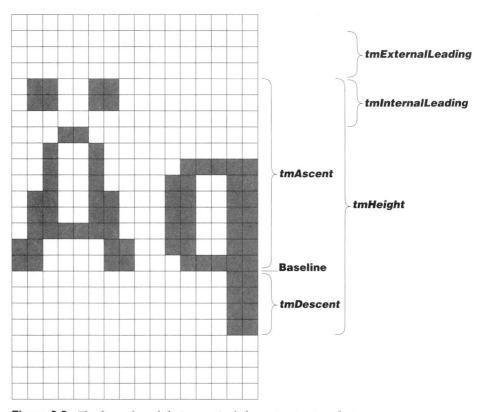

Figure 3-3. *The five values defining vertical character size in a font.*

It's important to realize that the dimensions of the system font are dependent on the resolution of the video display on which Windows runs. Windows provides a device-independent graphics interface, but you have to help. Don't write your Windows program so that it guesses at character dimensions. Don't hard code any values. Use the *GetTextMetrics* function to obtain this information.

Formatting Text

Because the dimensions of the system font do not change during a Windows session, you need to call *GetTextMetrics* only once when your program executes. A good place to make this call is while processing the WM_CREATE message in the window procedure. The WM_CREATE message is the first message the window procedure receives. Windows calls your window procedure with a WM_CREATE message when you call *CreateWindow* in *WinMain*.

Suppose you're writing a Windows program that displays several lines of text running down the client area. You'll want to obtain values for the character width and height. Within the window procedure you can define two variables to save the average character width (*cxChar*) and the total character height (*cyChar*):

```
static int cxChar, cyChar ;
```

The prefix *c* added to the variable names stands for "count," and in combination with *x* or *y* refers to a width or a height. These variables are defined as *static* because they must be valid when the window procedure processes other messages (such as WM_PAINT). If the variables are defined globally outside any functions, they need not be defined as *static*.

Here's the WM_CREATE code:

```
case WM_CREATE :
     hdc = GetDC (hwnd) ;

     GetTextMetrics (hdc, &tm) ;
     cxChar = tm.tmAveCharWidth ;
     cyChar = tm.tmHeight + tm.tmExternalLeading ;

     ReleaseDC (hwnd, hdc) ;
     return 0 ;
```

If you do not want to include external leading to space lines of text, you can use:

```
cyChar = tm.tmHeight ;
```

How you use this character size to calculate display coordinates is up to you. A simple method is to leave a *cyChar* margin at the top of the client area and a *cxChar* margin at the left. To display several lines of left-justified text, use the following *x*-coordinate value when calling the *TextOut* function:

```
cxChar
```

The *y*-coordinate value in *TextOut* is:

```
cyChar * (1 + i)
```

where *i* is the line number starting at 0.

You'll often find it necessary to display formatted numbers as well as simple character strings. If you were programming in MS-DOS using standard C library functions, you would probably use *printf* for this formatting. You cannot use *printf* in Windows because *printf* writes to the standard output device, and that concept makes no sense under Windows.

Instead, you can use *sprintf*. The *sprintf* function works just like *printf* except that it puts the formatted string into a character array. You can then use *TextOut* to write the string to the display. Very conveniently, the value returned from *sprintf* is the length of the string—you can pass this value to *TextOut* as the *iLength* parameter. This code shows a typical *sprintf* and *TextOut* combination:

```
int  iLength ;
char szBuffer [40] ;
[other program lines]
iLength = sprintf (szBuffer, "The sum of %d and %d is %d",
                   nA, nB, nA + nB) ;
TextOut (hdc, x, y, szBuffer, iLength) ;
```

For something as simple as this you could dispense with the *iLength* definition and combine the two statements into one:

```
TextOut (hdc, x, y, szBuffer,
    sprintf (szBuffer, "The sum of %d and %d is %d",
             nA, nB, nA + nB)) ;
```

It's not pretty, but it works.

If you don't need to display floating-point numbers, you can use *wsprintf* rather than *sprintf*. The *wsprintf* function has the same syntax as *sprintf*, but it's included in Windows, so using it won't increase the size of your .EXE file.

Putting It All Together

Now we seem to have everything we need to write a simple program that displays multiple lines of text on the screen. We know how to get a handle to a device context, how to use the *TextOut* function, and how to space text based on the size of a single character. The only thing left to do is to display something interesting.

The information available in the Windows *GetSystemMetrics* call looks interesting enough. This function returns information about the size of various graphical items in Windows, such as icons, cursors, title bars, and scroll bars. These sizes vary with the display adapter and driver. *GetSystemMetrics* requires a single parameter called an "index." This index is one of 73 integer identifiers defined in the Windows header files. *GetSystemMetrics* returns an integer, usually the size of the item specified in the parameter.

Let's write a program that displays some of the information available from the *GetSystemMetrics* call in a simple one-line-per-item format. Working with this information is easier if we create a header file that defines an array of structures containing both the Windows header-file identifiers for the *GetSystemMetrics* index and the text we want to display for each value returned from the call. This header file is called SYSMETS.H and is shown in Figure 3-4.

SYSMETS.H

```
/*-------------------------------------------------
   SYSMETS.H -- System metrics display structure
  -------------------------------------------------*/

#define NUMLINES ((int) (sizeof sysmetrics / sizeof sysmetrics [0]))

struct
{
int   iIndex ;
char *szLabel ;
char *szDesc ;
}
sysmetrics [] =
{
SM_CXSCREEN,          "SM_CXSCREEN",          "Screen width in pixels",
SM_CYSCREEN,          "SM_CYSCREEN",          "Screen height in pixels",
SM_CXVSCROLL,         "SM_CXVSCROLL",         "Vertical scroll arrow width",
SM_CYHSCROLL,         "SM_CYHSCROLL",         "Horizontal scroll arrow height",
SM_CYCAPTION,         "SM_CYCAPTION",         "Caption bar height",
SM_CXBORDER,          "SM_CXBORDER",          "Window border width",
SM_CYBORDER,          "SM_CYBORDER",          "Window border height",
SM_CXDLGFRAME,        "SM_CXDLGFRAME",        "Dialog window frame width",
SM_CYDLGFRAME,        "SM_CYDLGFRAME",        "Dialog window frame height",
SM_CYVTHUMB,          "SM_CYVTHUMB",          "Vertical scroll thumb height",
SM_CXHTHUMB,          "SM_CXHTHUMB",          "Horizontal scroll thumb width",
SM_CXICON,            "SM_CXICON",            "Icon width",
SM_CYICON,            "SM_CYICON",            "Icon height",
SM_CXCURSOR,          "SM_CXCURSOR",          "Cursor width",
SM_CYCURSOR,          "SM_CYCURSOR",          "Cursor height",
SM_CYMENU,            "SM_CYMENU",            "Menu bar height",
SM_CXFULLSCREEN,      "SM_CXFULLSCREEN",      "Full screen client area width",
SM_CYFULLSCREEN,      "SM_CYFULLSCREEN",      "Full screen client area height",
SM_CYKANJIWINDOW,     "SM_CYKANJIWINDOW",     "Kanji window height",
SM_MOUSEPRESENT,      "SM_MOUSEPRESENT",      "Mouse present flag",
```

Figure 3-4. *SYSMETS.H.*

(continued)

```
SM_CYVSCROLL,        "SM_CYVSCROLL",          "Vertical scroll arrow height",
SM_CXHSCROLL,        "SM_CXHSCROLL",          "Horizontal scroll arrow width",
SM_DEBUG,            "SM_DEBUG",              "Debug version flag",
SM_SWAPBUTTON,       "SM_SWAPBUTTON",         "Mouse buttons swapped flag",
SM_RESERVED1,        "SM_RESERVED1",          "Reserved",
SM_RESERVED2,        "SM_RESERVED2",          "Reserved",
SM_RESERVED3,        "SM_RESERVED3",          "Reserved",
SM_RESERVED4,        "SM_RESERVED4",          "Reserved",
SM_CXMIN,            "SM_CXMIN",              "Minimum window width",
SM_CYMIN,            "SM_CYMIN",              "Minimum window height",
SM_CXSIZE,           "SM_CXSIZE",             "Minimize/Maximize icon width",
SM_CYSIZE,           "SM_CYSIZE",             "Minimize/Maximize icon height",
SM_CXFRAME,          "SM_CXFRAME",            "Window frame width",
SM_CYFRAME,          "SM_CYFRAME",            "Window frame height",
SM_CXMINTRACK,       "SM_CXMINTRACK",         "Minimum window tracking width",
SM_CYMINTRACK,       "SM_CYMINTRACK",         "Minimum window tracking height",
SM_CXDOUBLECLK,      "SM_CXDOUBLECLK",        "Double click x tolerance",
SM_CYDOUBLECLK,      "SM_CYDOUBLECLK",        "Double click y tolerance",
SM_CXICONSPACING,    "SM_CXICONSPACING",      "Horizontal icon spacing",
SM_CYICONSPACING,    "SM_CYICONSPACING",      "Vertical icon spacing",
SM_MENUDROPALIGNMENT,"SM_MENUDROPALIGNMENT",  "Left or right menu drop",
SM_PENWINDOWS,       "SM_PENWINDOWS",         "Pen extensions installed",
SM_DBCSENABLED,      "SM_DBCSENABLED",        "Double-Byte Char Set enabled",
SM_CMOUSEBUTTONS,    "SM_CMOUSEBUTTONS",      "Number of mouse buttons",
SM_SHOWSOUNDS,       "SM_SHOWSOUNDS",         "Present sounds visually"
} ;
```

The program that displays this information is called SYSMETS1. The files required to create SYSMETS1.EXE (make file and C source code file) are shown in Figure 3-5. Most of the code should look familiar by now. With the exception of the program name, the make file is identical to that for HELLOWIN. In SYSMETS1.C, *WinMain* is virtually identical to HELLOWIN.

SYSMETS1.MAK

```
#----------------------
# SYSMETS1.MAK make file
#----------------------

sysmets1.exe : sysmets1.obj
     $(LINKER) $(GUIFLAGS) -OUT:sysmets1.exe sysmets1.obj $(GUILIBS)

sysmets1.obj : sysmets1.c sysmets.h
     $(CC) $(CFLAGS) sysmets1.c
```

Figure 3-5. *The SYSMETS1 program.*   *(continued)*

SYSMETS1.C

```
/*------------------------------------------------------
   SYSMETS1.C -- System Metrics Display Program No. 1
                 (c) Charles Petzold, 1996
   ------------------------------------------------------*/

#include <windows.h>
#include <string.h>
#include "sysmets.h"

LRESULT CALLBACK WndProc (HWND, UINT, WPARAM, LPARAM) ;

int WINAPI WinMain (HINSTANCE hInstance, HINSTANCE hPrevInstance,
                    PSTR szCmdLine, int iCmdShow)
     {
     static char szAppName[] = "SysMets1" ;
     HWND         hwnd ;
     MSG          msg ;
     WNDCLASSEX   wndclass ;

     wndclass.cbSize        = sizeof (wndclass) ;
     wndclass.style         = CS_HREDRAW | CS_VREDRAW ;
     wndclass.lpfnWndProc   = WndProc ;
     wndclass.cbClsExtra    = 0 ;
     wndclass.cbWndExtra    = 0 ;
     wndclass.hInstance     = hInstance ;
     wndclass.hIcon         = LoadIcon (NULL, IDI_APPLICATION) ;
     wndclass.hCursor       = LoadCursor (NULL, IDC_ARROW) ;
     wndclass.hbrBackground = (HBRUSH) GetStockObject (WHITE_BRUSH) ;
     wndclass.lpszMenuName  = NULL ;
     wndclass.lpszClassName = szAppName ;
     wndclass.hIconSm       = LoadIcon (NULL, IDI_APPLICATION) ;

     RegisterClassEx (&wndclass) ;

     hwnd = CreateWindow (szAppName, "Get System Metrics No. 1",
                          WS_OVERLAPPEDWINDOW,
                          CW_USEDEFAULT, CW_USEDEFAULT,
                          CW_USEDEFAULT, CW_USEDEFAULT,
                          NULL, NULL, hInstance, NULL) ;

     ShowWindow (hwnd, iCmdShow) ;
     UpdateWindow (hwnd) ;

     while (GetMessage (&msg, NULL, 0, 0))
          {
          TranslateMessage (&msg) ;
```

(continued)

```
            DispatchMessage (&msg) ;
            }
     return msg.wParam ;
     }

LRESULT CALLBACK WndProc (HWND hwnd, UINT iMsg, WPARAM wParam, LPARAM lParam)
     {
     static int   cxChar, cxCaps, cyChar ;
     char         szBuffer[10] ;
     HDC          hdc ;
     int          i ;
     PAINTSTRUCT  ps ;
     TEXTMETRIC   tm ;

     switch (iMsg)
          {
          case WM_CREATE :
               hdc = GetDC (hwnd) ;

               GetTextMetrics (hdc, &tm) ;
               cxChar = tm.tmAveCharWidth ;
               cxCaps = (tm.tmPitchAndFamily & 1 ? 3 : 2) * cxChar / 2 ;
               cyChar = tm.tmHeight + tm.tmExternalLeading ;

               ReleaseDC (hwnd, hdc) ;
               return 0 ;

          case WM_PAINT :
               hdc = BeginPaint (hwnd, &ps) ;

               for (i = 0 ; i < NUMLINES ; i++)
                    {
                    TextOut (hdc, cxChar, cyChar * (1 + i),
                             sysmetrics[i].szLabel,
                             strlen (sysmetrics[i].szLabel)) ;

                    TextOut (hdc, cxChar + 22 * cxCaps, cyChar * (1 + i),
                             sysmetrics[i].szDesc,
                             strlen (sysmetrics[i].szDesc)) ;

                    SetTextAlign (hdc, TA_RIGHT | TA_TOP) ;

                    TextOut (hdc, cxChar + 22 * cxCaps + 40 * cxChar,
                             cyChar * (1 + i), szBuffer,
                             wsprintf (szBuffer, "%5d",
                             GetSystemMetrics (sysmetrics[i].iIndex))) ;
```

(continued)

```
                SetTextAlign (hdc, TA_LEFT | TA_TOP) ;
                }
            EndPaint (hwnd, &ps) ;
            return 0 ;

        case WM_DESTROY :
            PostQuitMessage (0) ;
            return 0 ;
        }

    return DefWindowProc (hwnd, iMsg, wParam, lParam) ;
    }
```

Figure 3-6 shows SYSMETS1 running on a VGA. As you can see from the program's window, the screen width is 640 pixels and the screen height is 480 pixels. These two values, as well as many of the other values shown by the program, may be different for different types of video displays.

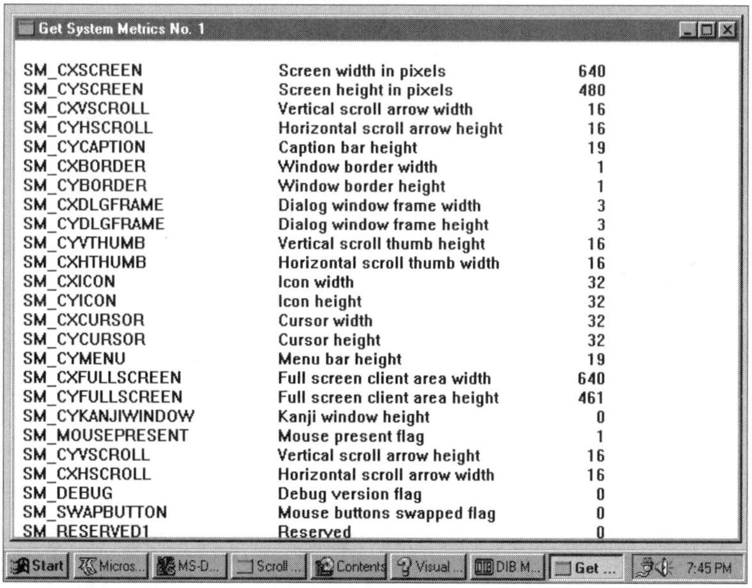

SM_CXSCREEN	Screen width in pixels	640
SM_CYSCREEN	Screen height in pixels	480
SM_CXVSCROLL	Vertical scroll arrow width	16
SM_CYHSCROLL	Horizontal scroll arrow height	16
SM_CYCAPTION	Caption bar height	19
SM_CXBORDER	Window border width	1
SM_CYBORDER	Window border height	1
SM_CXDLGFRAME	Dialog window frame width	3
SM_CYDLGFRAME	Dialog window frame height	3
SM_CYVTHUMB	Vertical scroll thumb height	16
SM_CXHTHUMB	Horizontal scroll thumb width	16
SM_CXICON	Icon width	32
SM_CYICON	Icon height	32
SM_CXCURSOR	Cursor width	32
SM_CYCURSOR	Cursor height	32
SM_CYMENU	Menu bar height	19
SM_CXFULLSCREEN	Full screen client area width	640
SM_CYFULLSCREEN	Full screen client area height	461
SM_CYKANJIWINDOW	Kanji window height	0
SM_MOUSEPRESENT	Mouse present flag	1
SM_CYVSCROLL	Vertical scroll arrow height	16
SM_CXHSCROLL	Horizontal scroll arrow width	16
SM_DEBUG	Debug version flag	0
SM_SWAPBUTTON	Mouse buttons swapped flag	0
SM_RESERVED1	Reserved	0

Figure 3-6. *The SYSMETS1 display.*

The SYSMETS1.C Window Procedure

The *WndProc* window procedure in the SYSMETS1.C program processes three messages: WM_CREATE, WM_PAINT, and WM_DESTROY. The WM_DESTROY message is processed in the same way as the HELLOWIN program in Chapter 2.

The WM_CREATE message is the first message the window procedure receives. It is generated by Windows when the *CreateWindow* function creates the window. During the

WM_CREATE message, SYSMETS1 obtains a device context for the window by calling *GetDC* and gets the text metrics for the default system font by calling *GetTextMetrics*. SYSMETS1 saves the average character width in *cxChar* and the total height of the characters (including external leading) in *cyChar*.

SYSMETS1 also saves an average width of uppercase letters in the static variable *cxCaps*. For a fixed-pitch font, *cxCaps* would equal *cxChar*. For a variable-width font, *cxCaps* is set to 150% of *cxChar*. The low bit of the *tmPitchAndFamily* field of the TEXTMETRIC structure is 1 for a variable-width font and 0 for a fixed-pitch font. SYSMETS1 uses this bit value to calculate *cxCaps* from *cxChar*:

```
cxCaps = (tm.tmPitchAndFamily & 1 ? 3 : 2) * cxChar / 2 ;
```

SYSMETS1 does all window painting during the WM_PAINT message. As normal, the window procedure first obtains a handle to the device context by calling *BeginPaint*. A *for* statement loops through all the lines of the *sysmetrics* structure defined in SYSMETS.H. The three columns of text are displayed with three *TextOut* functions. In each case, the third parameter to *TextOut* is set to:

```
cyChar * (1 + i)
```

This parameter indicates the pixel position of the top of the character string relative to the top of the client area. Thus, the program leaves a margin at the top equal to *cyChar*. The first line of text (when *i* equals 0) begins *cyChar* pixels below the top of the client area.

The first *TextOut* statement displays the uppercase identifiers in the first of the three columns. The second parameter to *TextOut* is *cxChar*. This leaves a one-character margin between the left edge of the client area and the text string. The text is obtained from the *szLabel* field of the *sysmetrics* structure. I use the C runtime function *strlen* to obtain the length of the string, which is required as the last parameter to *TextOut*.

The second *TextOut* statement displays the description of the system metrics value. These descriptions are stored in the *szDesc* field of the *sysmetrics* structure. In this case, the second parameter to *TextOut* is set to:

```
cxChar + 22 * cxCaps
```

The longest uppercase identifier displayed in the first column is 20 characters, so the second column must begin at least *20 × cxCaps* to the right of the beginning of the first column of text.

The third *TextOut* statement displays the numeric values obtained from the *GetSystemMetrics* function. The variable-width font makes formatting a column of right-justified numbers a little tricky. All the digits from 0 through 9 have the same width, but this width is greater than the width of a space. Numbers can be one or more digits wide, so different numbers can begin at different horizontal positions.

Wouldn't it be easier if we could display a column of right-justified numbers by specifying the pixel position where the number *ends* rather than where it *begins?* This is what the *SetTextAlign* function lets us do. After SYSMETS1 calls:

```
SetTextAlign (hdc, TA_RIGHT | TA_TOP) ;
```

the coordinates passed to subsequent *TextOut* functions will specify the top-right corner of the text string rather than the top-left corner.

The *TextOut* function to display the column of numbers has a second parameter set to:

```
cxChar + 22 * cxCaps + 40 * cxChar
```

The *40 × cxChar* value accommodates the width of the second column and the width of the third column. Following the *TextOut* function, another call to *SetTextAlign* sets things back to normal for the next time through the loop.

Not Enough Room!

One little nasty problem exists with the SYSMETS1 program: Unless you have a gigantic big-screen, high-resolution video adapter, you can't see the last chunk of lines of the system metrics list. If you make the window narrower, you can't even see the values.

SYSMETS1 doesn't know how large its client area is. It begins the text at the top of the window and relies on Windows to clip everything that drifts beyond the edges of the client area. This is not desirable. Our first job in solving this problem is to determine how much of the program's output can actually fit within the client area.

The Size of the Client Area

If you experiment with existing Windows applications, you'll find that window sizes can vary widely. At the most (assuming the window does not have a menu or scroll bars), the window can be maximized, and the client area will occupy the entire screen except for the program's title bar. The total dimension of this maximized client is available from the *GetSystemMetrics* function using the SM_CXFULLSCREEN and SM_CYFULLSCREEN parameters. For a VGA the values returned are 640 and 461 pixels. The minimum size of the window can be quite small, sometimes almost nonexistent, virtually eliminating the client area.

One common method for determining the size of a window's client area is to process the WM_SIZE message within your window procedure. Windows sends a WM_SIZE message to a window procedure whenever the size of the window changes. The *lParam* variable passed to the window procedure contains the width of the client area in the low word and the height in the high word. The code to process this message often looks like this:

```
static int cxClient, cyClient ;
[other program lines]
case WM_SIZE :
```

```
cxClient = LOWORD (lParam) ;
cyClient = HIWORD (lParam) ;
return 0 ;
```

The LOWORD and HIWORD macros are defined in the Windows header files. Like *cxChar* and *cyChar*, the *cxClient* and *cyClient* variables are defined as static inside the window procedure because they are used later when processing other messages.

The WM_SIZE message will eventually be followed by a WM_PAINT message. Why? Because when we define the window class, we specify that the class style is:

```
CS_HREDRAW | CS_VREDRAW
```

This class style tells Windows to force a repaint if either the horizontal or vertical size changes.

You can calculate the number of full lines of text displayable within the client area with the formula:

```
cyClient / cyChar
```

This may be 0 if the height of the client area is too small to display a full character. Similarly, the approximate number of lowercase characters you can display horizontally within the client area is equal to:

```
cxClient / cxChar
```

If you determine *cxChar* and *cyChar* during a WM_CREATE message, don't worry about dividing by 0 in these calculations. Your window procedure receives a WM_CREATE message when *WinMain* calls *CreateWindow*. The first WM_SIZE message comes a little later when *WinMain* calls *ShowWindow*, at which point *cxChar* and *cyChar* have already been assigned positive non-zero values.

Knowing the size of the window's client area is the first step in providing a way for the user to move the text within the client area if the client area is not large enough to hold everything. If you're familiar with other Windows-based applications that have similar requirements, you probably know what we need: This is a job for those wonderful inventions known as scroll bars.

SCROLL BARS

Scroll bars are one of the best features of a graphics and mouse interface. They are easy to use and provide good visual feedback. You can use scroll bars whenever you need to display anything—text, graphics, a spreadsheet, database records, pictures—that requires more space than is available in the client area of the window.

Scroll bars are positioned either vertically (for up and down movement) or horizontally (for left and right movement). You can click with the mouse on the arrows at each end of a scroll bar or on the area between the arrows. A "scroll box," or "thumb," travels the length of the scroll bar to indicate the approximate location of the material shown on the display in relation to the entire document. You can alsc drag the thumb with the mouse to move to a particular location. Figure 3-7 shows the recommended use of a vertical scroll bar for text.

Programmers sometimes have problems with scrolling terminology because their perspective is different from the user's: A user who scrolls down wants to bring a lower part of the document into view; however, the program actually moves the document up in relation to the display window. The Windows documentation and the header file identifiers are based on the user's perspective: Scrolling up means moving toward the beginning of the document; scrolling down means moving toward the end.

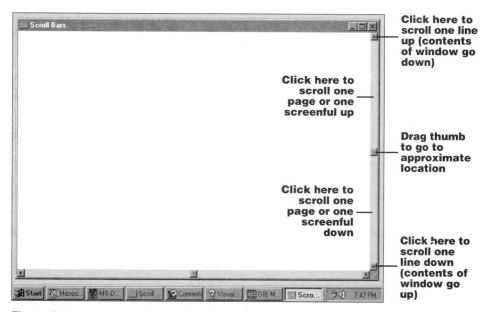

Figure 3-7. *The vertical scroll bar.*

It is very easy to include a horizontal or vertical scroll bar in your application window. All you need to do is include the identifier WS_VSCROLL (vertical scroll) or WS_HSCROLL (horizontal scroll) or both in the window style in the *CreateWindow* statement. These scroll bars are always placed against the right side or bottom of the window and extend the full length or width of the client area. The client area does not include the space occupied by the scroll bar. The width of a vertical window scroll bar and the height of a horizontal window scroll bar are constant for a particular display driver. If you need these values, you can obtain them (as you may have observed) from the *GetSystemMetrics* call.

Windows takes care of all mouse logic for the scroll bars. However, window scroll bars do not have an automatic keyboard interface. If you want the cursor keys to duplicate some of the window scroll bars' functions, you must explicitly provide logic for that (as we'll do when we return to this program in Chapter 5, which covers the keyboard).

Scroll Bar Range and Position

Every scroll bar has an associated "range" (which is a pair of integers representing a minimum and maximum value) and a "position" (which is the location of the thumb within the range). When the thumb is at the top (or left) of the scroll bar, the position of the thumb is the minimum value of the range. At the bottom (or right) of the scroll bar, the thumb position is the maximum value of the range.

By default, the range of a scroll bar is 0 (top or left) through 100 (bottom or right), but it's easy to change the range to something that is more convenient for the program:

```
SetScrollRange (hwnd, iBar, iMin, iMax, bRedraw) ;
```

The *iBar* parameter is either SB_VERT or SB_HORZ, *iMin* and *iMax* are the minimum and maximum positions of the range, and *bRedraw* is set to TRUE if you want Windows to redraw the scroll bar based on the new range.

The thumb position is always a discrete integral value. For instance, a scroll bar with a range of 0 through 4 has five thumb positions, as shown in Figure 3-8. You can use *SetScrollPos* to set a new thumb position within the scroll bar range:

```
SetScrollPos (hwnd, iBar, iPos, bRedraw) ;
```

The *iPos* parameter is the new position and must be within the range of *iMin* through *iMax*. Windows provides similar functions (*GetScrollRange* and *GetScrollPos*) to obtain the current range and position of a scroll bar.

When you use scroll bars within your program, you share responsibility with Windows for maintaining the scroll bars and updating the position of the scroll bar thumb. These are Windows' responsibilities for scroll bars:

- Handles all scroll bar mouse logic.

- Provides a "reverse video" flash when the user clicks on the scroll bar.

- Moves the thumb as the user drags the thumb within the scroll bar.

- Sends scroll bar messages to the window procedure for the window containing the scroll bar.

These are your program's responsibilities:

- Initialize the range of the scroll bar.

- Process the scroll bar messages.

- Update the position of the scroll bar thumb.

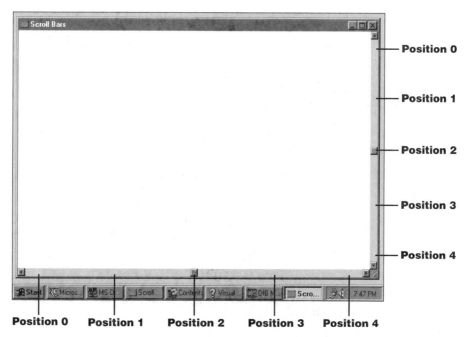

Figure 3-8. *Scroll bars with five thumb positions.*

Scroll Bar Messages

Windows sends the window procedure WM_VSCROLL and WM_HSCROLL messages when the scroll bar is clicked with the mouse or the thumb is dragged. Each mouse action on the scroll bar generates at least two messages, one when the mouse button is pressed and another when it is released.

The low word of the *wParam* parameter that accompanies the WM_VSCROLL and WM_HSCROLL messages is a number that indicates what the mouse is doing to the scroll bar. These values correspond to defined identifiers that begin with SB_, which stands for "scroll bar." Although some of these identifiers use the words "UP" and "DOWN," they apply to horizontal as well as vertical scroll bars, as shown in Figure 3-9 on the following page. Your window procedure can receive multiple SB_LINEUP, SB_PAGEUP, SB_LINEDOWN, or SB_PAGEDOWN messages if the mouse button is held down while positioned on the scroll bar. The SB_ENDSCROLL message signals that the mouse button has been released. You can generally ignore SB_ENDSCROLL messages.

When the low word of *wParam* is SB_THUMBTRACK or SB_THUMBPOSITION, the high word of *wParam* is the current position of the dragged scroll bar. This position is within the minimum and maximum values of the scroll bar range. For other scroll bar actions, the high word of *wParam* should be ignored. You can also ignore *lParam*; that's used for scroll bars usually created within dialog boxes.

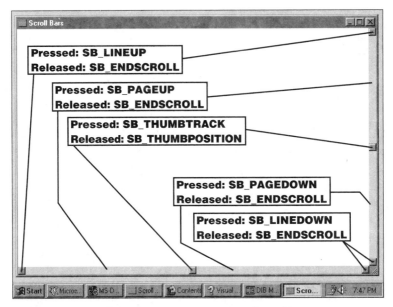

Figure 3-9. *Identifiers for the* wParam *values of scroll bar messages.*

The Windows documentation indicates that the low word of *wParam* can also be SB_TOP or SB_BOTTOM, indicating that the scroll bar has been moved to its minimum or maximum position. However, you will never receive these values for a scroll bar created as part of your application window.

Handling the SB_THUMBTRACK and SB_THUMBPOSITION messages is problematic. If you set a large scroll bar range and the user quickly drags the thumb inside the scroll bar, Windows sends your window function a barrage of SB_THUMBTRACK messages. Your program may have problems keeping up with these messages. For this reason, most Windows applications ignore these messages and take action only on receipt of SB_THUMB-POSITION, which means that the thumb is again at rest.

However, if you can update your display quickly, you may want to include SB-_THUMBTRACK processing in your program. But be aware that users who discover that your program scrolls immediately as they move the scroll bar thumb will undoubtedly try to move it as quickly as possible to see if your program can keep up—and they will get an inordinate amount of satisfaction if it cannot.

Scrolling SYSMETS

Enough explanation. It's time to put this stuff into practice. Let's start simply. We'll begin with vertical scrolling because that's what we desperately need. The horizontal scrolling can wait. SYSMETS2 is shown in Figure 3-10.

The new *CreateWindow* call adds a vertical scroll bar to the window by including the WS_VSCROLL window style in the *CreateWindow* call:

```
WS_OVERLAPPEDWINDOW ¦ WS_VSCROLL
```

SYSMETS2.MAK

```
#-----------------------
# SYSMETS2.MAK make file
#-----------------------

sysmets2.exe : sysmets2.obj
     $(LINKER) $(GUIFLAGS) -OUT:sysmets2.exe sysmets2.obj $(GUILIBS)

sysmets2.obj : sysmets2.c sysmets.h
     $(CC) $(CFLAGS) sysmets2.c
```

SYSMETS2.C

```
/*-------------------------------------------------------
   SYSMETS2.C -- System Metrics Display Program No. 2
                 (c) Charles Petzold, 1996
   -------------------------------------------------------*/

#include <windows.h>
#include <string.h>
#include "sysmets.h"

LRESULT CALLBACK WndProc (HWND, UINT, WPARAM, LPARAM) ;

int WINAPI WinMain (HINSTANCE hInstance, HINSTANCE hPrevInstance,
                    PSTR szCmdLine, int iCmdShow)
     {
     static char szAppName[] = "SysMets2" ;
     HWND        hwnd ;
     MSG         msg ;
     WNDCLASSEX  wndclass ;

     wndclass.cbSize        = sizeof (wndclass) ;
     wndclass.style         = CS_HREDRAW ¦ CS_VREDRAW ;
     wndclass.lpfnWndProc   = WndProc ;
     wndclass.cbClsExtra    = 0 ;
     wndclass.cbWndExtra    = 0 ;
     wndclass.hInstance     = hInstance ;
     wndclass.hIcon         = LoadIcon (NULL, IDI_APPLICATION) ;
     wndclass.hCursor       = LoadCursor (NULL, IDC_ARROW) ;
```

Figure 3-10. *The SYSMETS2 program.*

(continued)

```
        wndclass.hbrBackground = (HBRUSH) GetStockObject (WHITE_BRUSH) ;
        wndclass.lpszMenuName  = NULL ;
        wndclass.lpszClassName = szAppName ;
        wndclass.hIconSm       = LoadIcon (NULL, IDI_APPLICATION) ;

        RegisterClassEx (&wndclass) ;

        hwnd = CreateWindow (szAppName, "Get System Metrics No. 2",
                        WS_OVERLAPPEDWINDOW | WS_VSCROLL,
                        CW_USEDEFAULT, CW_USEDEFAULT,
                        CW_USEDEFAULT, CW_USEDEFAULT,
                        NULL, NULL, hInstance, NULL) ;

        ShowWindow (hwnd, iCmdShow) ;
        UpdateWindow (hwnd) ;

        while (GetMessage (&msg, NULL, 0, 0))
            {
            TranslateMessage (&msg) ;
            DispatchMessage (&msg) ;
            }
        return msg.wParam ;
        }

LRESULT CALLBACK WndProc (HWND hwnd, UINT iMsg, WPARAM wParam, LPARAM lParam)
        {
        static int  cxChar, cxCaps, cyChar, cyClient, iVscrollPos ;
        char        szBuffer[10] ;
        HDC         hdc ;
        int         i, y ;
        PAINTSTRUCT ps ;
        TEXTMETRIC  tm ;

        switch (iMsg)
            {
            case WM_CREATE :
                hdc = GetDC (hwnd) ;

                GetTextMetrics (hdc, &tm) ;
                cxChar = tm.tmAveCharWidth ;
                cxCaps = (tm.tmPitchAndFamily & 1 ? 3 : 2) * cxChar / 2 ;
                cyChar = tm.tmHeight + tm.tmExternalLeading ;

                ReleaseDC (hwnd, hdc) ;

                SetScrollRange (hwnd, SB_VERT, 0, NUMLINES, FALSE) ;
                SetScrollPos   (hwnd, SB_VERT, iVscrollPos, TRUE) ;
                return 0 ;
```

(continued)

```
     case WM_SIZE :
          cyClient = HIWORD (lParam) ;
          return 0 ;

     case WM_VSCROLL :
          switch (LOWORD (wParam))
               {
               case SB_LINEUP :
                    iVscrollPos -= 1 ;
                    break ;

               case SB_LINEDOWN :
                    iVscrollPos += 1 ;
                    break ;

               case SB_PAGEUP :
                    iVscrollPos -= cyClient / cyChar ;
                    break ;

               case SB_PAGEDOWN :
                    iVscrollPos += cyClient / cyChar ;
                    break ;

               case SB_THUMBPOSITION :
                    iVscrollPos = HIWORD (wParam) ;
                    break ;

               default :
                    break ;
               }
          iVscrollPos = max (0, min (iVscrollPos, NUMLINES)) ;

          if (iVscrollPos != GetScrollPos (hwnd, SB_VERT))
               {
               SetScrollPos (hwnd, SB_VERT, iVscrollPos, TRUE) ;
               InvalidateRect (hwnd, NULL, TRUE) ;
               }
          return 0 ;

     case WM_PAINT :
          hdc = BeginPaint (hwnd, &ps) ;

          for (i = 0 ; i < NUMLINES ; i++)
               {
               y = cyChar * (1 - iVscrollPos + i) ;

               TextOut (hdc, cxChar, y,
```

(continued)

```
                        sysmetrics[i].szLabel,
                        strlen (sysmetrics[i].szLabel)) ;

            TextOut (hdc, cxChar + 22 * cxCaps, y,
                        sysmetrics[i].szDesc,
                        strlen (sysmetrics[i].szDesc)) ;

            SetTextAlign (hdc, TA_RIGHT | TA_TOP) ;

            TextOut (hdc, cxChar + 22 * cxCaps + 40 * cxChar, y,
                        szBuffer,
                        wsprintf (szBuffer, "%5d",
                        GetSystemMetrics (sysmetrics[i].iIndex))) ;

            SetTextAlign (hdc, TA_LEFT | TA_TOP) ;
            }

        EndPaint (hwnd, &ps) ;
        return 0 ;

    case WM_DESTROY :
        PostQuitMessage (0) ;
        return 0 ;
    }

return DefWindowProc (hwnd, iMsg, wParam, lParam) ;
}
```

The *WndProc* window procedure has two additional lines to set the range and position of the vertical scroll bar during processing of the WM_CREATE message:

```
SetScrollRange (hwnd, SB_VERT, 0, NUMLINES, FALSE) ;
SetScrollPos   (hwnd, SB_VERT, iVscrollPos, TRUE) ;
```

The *sysmetrics* structure has NUMLINES lines of text, so the scroll bar range is set from 0 through NUMLINES. Each position of the scroll bar corresponds to a line of text displayed at the top of the client area. If the scroll bar thumb is at position 0, a blank line is left at the top of the screen for a margin. As you increase the position of the scroll bar by scrolling down, the text should move up. When the scroll bar position is at the bottom, the last line of the structure is at the top.

To help with processing of the WM_VSCROLL messages, a static variable named *iVscrollPos* is defined within the *WndProc* window procedure. This variable is the current position of the scroll bar thumb. For SB_LINEUP and SB_LINEDOWN, all we need to do is adjust the scroll position by 1. For SB_PAGEUP and SB_PAGEDOWN, we want to move the text by the contents of one screen, or *cyClient* divided by *cyChar*. For SB_THUMBPOSITION, the new thumb position is the high word of *wParam*. SB_ENDSCROLL and SB_THUMB-TRACK messages are ignored.

The *iVscrollPos* is then adjusted using the *min* and *max* macros to ensure that it is between the minimum and maximum range values. If the scroll position has changed, it is updated using *SetScrollPos*, and the entire window is invalidated by an *InvalidateRect* call.

The *InvalidateRect* call generates a WM_PAINT message. When the original SYSMETS1 processed WM_PAINT messages, the *y*-coordinate of each line was calculated as:

```
cyChar * (1 + i)
```

In SYSMETS2, the formula is:

```
cyChar * (1 - iVscrollPos + i)
```

The loop still displays NUMLINES lines of text, but for values of *iVscrollPos* of 2 and above, the loop begins displaying lines above the client area. This is outside the client area, so Windows doesn't display those lines.

I told you we'd start simply. This is rather wasteful and inefficient code. We'll fix it shortly, but first consider how we update the client area after a WM_VSCROLL message.

Structuring Your Program for Painting

The window procedure in SYSMETS2 does not repaint the client area after processing a scroll bar message. Instead, it calls *InvalidateRect* to invalidate the client area. This causes Windows to place a WM_PAINT message in the message queue.

It is best to structure your Windows programs so that you do all client-area painting in response to a WM_PAINT message. Because your program should be able to repaint the entire client area of the window at any time on receipt of a WM_PAINT message, you will probably duplicate code if you also paint in other parts of the program.

At first, you may rebel at this dictum because it is so different from normal PC programming. I won't deny that, on occasion, painting in response to messages other than WM_PAINT is much more convenient. (The KEYLOOK program in Chapter 5 is an example of such a program.) But in many cases it's simply unnecessary, and after you master the discipline of accumulating all the information you need to paint in response to a WM_PAINT message, you'll be pleased with the results. However, your program will often determine that it must repaint a particular area of the display when processing a message other than WM_PAINT. This is where *InvalidateRect* comes in handy. You can use it to invalidate specific rectangles of the client area or the entire client area.

Simply marking areas of the window as invalid to generate WM_PAINT messages may not be entirely satisfactory in some applications. After you make an *InvalidateRect* call, Windows places a WM_PAINT message in the message queue, and the window procedure eventually processes it. However, Windows treats WM_PAINT messages as low priority, so if a lot of other activity is occurring in the system, it may be a while before you get it. Everyone has seen blank white "holes" in programs when dialog boxes disappear.

If you prefer to update the invalid area immediately, you can call *UpdateWindow* after you call *InvalidateRect*:

```
UpdateWindow (hwnd) ;
```

UpdateWindow causes the window procedure to be called immediately with a WM_PAINT message if any part of the client area is invalid. (It will not call the window procedure if the entire client area is valid.) This WM_PAINT message bypasses the message queue. The window procedure is called directly from Windows. When the window procedure has finished repainting, it exits, and Windows returns control to the program at the statement following the *UpdateWindow* call.

You'll note that *UpdateWindow* is the same function used in *WinMain* to generate the first WM_PAINT message. When a window is first created, the entire client area is invalid. *UpdateWindow* directs the window procedure to paint it.

Building a Better Scroll

Because SYSMETS2 is too inefficient a model to be imitated in other programs, let's clean it up. SYSMETS3—our final version of the SYSMETS program in this chapter—is shown in Figure 3-11. This version adds a horizontal scroll bar for left and right scrolling and repaints the client area more efficiently.

SYSMETS3.MAK

```
#-----------------------
# SYSMETS3.MAK make file
#-----------------------

sysmets3.exe : sysmets3.obj
    $(LINKER) $(GUIFLAGS) -OUT:sysmets3.exe sysmets3.obj $(GUILIBS)

sysmets3.obj : sysmets3.c sysmets.h
    $(CC) $(CFLAGS) sysmets3.c
```

SYSMETS3.C

```
/*-------------------------------------------------------------
   SYSMETS3.C -- System Metrics Display Program No. 3
                 (c) Charles Petzold, 1996
   -----------------------------------------------------------*/

#include <windows.h>
#include "sysmets.h"

LRESULT CALLBACK WndProc (HWND, UINT, WPARAM, LPARAM) ;
```

Figure 3-11. *The SYSMETS3 program.*   *(continued)*

```
int WINAPI WinMain (HINSTANCE hInstance, HINSTANCE hPrevInstance,
                    PSTR szCmdLine, int iCmdShow)
     {
     static char szAppName[] = "SysMets3" ;
     HWND        hwnd ;
     MSG         msg ;
     WNDCLASSEX  wndclass ;

     wndclass.cbSize        = sizeof (wndclass) ;
     wndclass.style         = CS_HREDRAW | CS_VREDRAW ;
     wndclass.lpfnWndProc   = WndProc ;
     wndclass.cbClsExtra    = 0 ;
     wndclass.cbWndExtra    = 0 ;
     wndclass.hInstance     = hInstance ;
     wndclass.hIcon         = LoadIcon (NULL, IDI_APPLICATION) ;
     wndclass.hCursor       = LoadCursor (NULL, IDC_ARROW) ;
     wndclass.hbrBackground = (HBRUSH) GetStockObject (WHITE_BRUSH) ;
     wndclass.lpszMenuName  = NULL ;
     wndclass.lpszClassName = szAppName ;
     wndclass.hIconSm       = LoadIcon (NULL, IDI_APPLICATION) ;

     RegisterClassEx (&wndclass) ;

     hwnd = CreateWindow (szAppName, "Get System Metrics No. 3",
                          WS_OVERLAPPEDWINDOW | WS_VSCROLL | WS_HSCROLL,
                          CW_USEDEFAULT, CW_USEDEFAULT,
                          CW_USEDEFAULT, CW_USEDEFAULT,
                          NULL, NULL, hInstance, NULL) ;

     ShowWindow (hwnd, iCmdShow) ;
     UpdateWindow (hwnd) ;

     while (GetMessage (&msg, NULL, 0, 0))
          {
          TranslateMessage (&msg) ;
          DispatchMessage (&msg) ;
          }
     return msg.wParam ;
     }

LRESULT CALLBACK WndProc (HWND hwnd, UINT iMsg, WPARAM wParam, LPARAM lParam)
     {
     static int  cxChar, cxCaps, cyChar, cxClient, cyClient, iMaxWidth,
                 iVscrollPos, iVscrollMax, iHscrollPos, iHscrollMax ;
     char        szBuffer[10] ;
     HDC         hdc ;
```

(continued)

```
int        i, x, y, iPaintBeg, iPaintEnd, iVscrollInc, iHscrollInc ;
PAINTSTRUCT ps ;
TEXTMETRIC  tm ;

switch (iMsg)
    {
    case WM_CREATE :
        hdc = GetDC (hwnd) ;

        GetTextMetrics (hdc, &tm) ;
        cxChar = tm.tmAveCharWidth ;
        cxCaps = (tm.tmPitchAndFamily & 1 ? 3 : 2) * cxChar / 2 ;
        cyChar = tm.tmHeight + tm.tmExternalLeading ;

        ReleaseDC (hwnd, hdc) ;

        iMaxWidth = 40 * cxChar + 22 * cxCaps ;
        return 0 ;

    case WM_SIZE :
        cxClient = LOWORD (lParam) ;
        cyClient = HIWORD (lParam) ;

        iVscrollMax = max (0, NUMLINES + 2 - cyClient / cyChar) ;
        iVscrollPos = min (iVscrollPos, iVscrollMax) ;

        SetScrollRange (hwnd, SB_VERT, 0, iVscrollMax, FALSE) ;
        SetScrollPos   (hwnd, SB_VERT, iVscrollPos, TRUE) ;

        iHscrollMax = max (0, 2 + (iMaxWidth - cxClient) / cxChar) ;
        iHscrollPos = min (iHscrollPos, iHscrollMax) ;

        SetScrollRange (hwnd, SB_HORZ, 0, iHscrollMax, FALSE) ;
        SetScrollPos   (hwnd, SB_HORZ, iHscrollPos, TRUE) ;
        return 0 ;

    case WM_VSCROLL :
        switch (LOWORD (wParam))
            {
            case SB_TOP :
                iVscrollInc = -iVscrollPos ;
                break ;

            case SB_BOTTOM :
                iVscrollInc = iVscrollMax - iVscrollPos ;
                break ;
```

(continued)

82

```
                    case SB_LINEUP :
                         iVscrollInc = -1 ;
                         break ;

                    case SB_LINEDOWN :
                         iVscrollInc = 1 ;
                         break ;

                    case SB_PAGEUP :
                         iVscrollInc = min (-1, -cyClient / cyChar) ;
                         break ;

                    case SB_PAGEDOWN :
                         iVscrollInc = max (1, cyClient / cyChar) ;
                         break ;

                    case SB_THUMBTRACK :
                         iVscrollInc = HIWORD (wParam) - iVscrollPos ;
                         break ;

                    default :
                         iVscrollInc = 0 ;
                    }
               iVscrollInc = max (-iVscrollPos,
                         min (iVscrollInc, iVscrollMax - iVscrollPos)) ;

               if (iVscrollInc != 0)
                    {
                    iVscrollPos += iVscrollInc ;
                    ScrollWindow (hwnd, 0, -cyChar * iVscrollInc, NULL, NULL) ;
                    SetScrollPos (hwnd, SB_VERT, iVscrollPos, TRUE) ;
                    UpdateWindow (hwnd) ;
                    }
               return 0 ;

          case WM_HSCROLL :
               switch (LOWORD (wParam))
                    {
                    case SB_LINEUP :
                         iHscrollInc = -1 ;
                         break ;

                    case SB_LINEDOWN :
                         iHscrollInc = 1 ;
                         break ;
```

(continued)

```
          case SB_PAGEUP :
               iHscrollInc = -8 ;
               break ;

          case SB_PAGEDOWN :
               iHscrollInc = 8 ;
               break ;

          case SB_THUMBPOSITION :
               iHscrollInc = HIWORD (wParam) - iHscrollPos ;
               break ;

          default :
               iHscrollInc = 0 ;
          }
     iHscrollInc = max (-iHscrollPos,
                     min (iHscrollInc, iHscrollMax - iHscrollPos)) ;

     if (iHscrollInc != 0)
          {
          iHscrollPos += iHscrollInc ;
          ScrollWindow (hwnd, -cxChar * iHscrollInc, 0, NULL, NULL) ;
          SetScrollPos (hwnd, SB_HORZ, iHscrollPos, TRUE) ;
          }
     return 0 ;

case WM_PAINT :
     hdc = BeginPaint (hwnd, &ps) ;

     iPaintBeg = max (0, iVscrollPos + ps.rcPaint.top / cyChar - 1) ;
     iPaintEnd = min (NUMLINES,
                     iVscrollPos + ps.rcPaint.bottom / cyChar) ;

     for (i = iPaintBeg ; i < iPaintEnd ; i++)
          {
          x = cxChar * (1 - iHscrollPos) ;
          y = cyChar * (1 - iVscrollPos + i) ;

          TextOut (hdc, x, y,
                    sysmetrics[i].szLabel,
                    strlen (sysmetrics[i].szLabel)) ;

          TextOut (hdc, x + 22 * cxCaps, y,
                    sysmetrics[i].szDesc,
                    strlen (sysmetrics[i].szDesc)) ;

          SetTextAlign (hdc, TA_RIGHT | TA_TOP) ;
```

(continued)

```
                    TextOut (hdc, x + 22 * cxCaps + 40 * cxChar, y,
                            szBuffer,
                            wsprintf (szBuffer, "%5d",
                                GetSystemMetrics (sysmetrics[i].iIndex))) ;

               SetTextAlign (hdc, TA_LEFT | TA_TOP) ;
               }

          EndPaint (hwnd, &ps) ;
          return 0 ;

     case WM_DESTROY :
          PostQuitMessage (0) ;
          return 0 ;
     }

     return DefWindowProc (hwnd, iMsg, wParam, lParam) ;
     }
```

These are the improvements in SYSMETS3 and how they are implemented in the program:

■   You can no longer scroll the display so that the last line appears at the top of the client area. You can scroll only far enough to see the last line at the bottom of the client area. This requires that the program calculate a new scroll bar range (and possibly a new thumb position) when it processes a WM_SIZE message. The WM_SIZE logic calculates the scroll bar range based on the number of lines of text, the width of the text, and the size of the client area. This approach results in a smaller range—only that necessary to bring into view the text that falls outside the client area.

   This offers an interesting dividend. Suppose that the client area of the window is large enough to display the entire text with top and bottom margins. In this case, both the minimum position and maximum position of the scroll bar range will equal 0. What will Windows do with this information? It will remove the scroll bar from the window! It's no longer needed. Similarly, if the client area is wide enough to show the full 60-column width of the text, no horizontal scroll bar is displayed in the window.

■   The WM_VSCROLL and WM_HSCROLL messages are processed by first calculating an increment of the scroll bar position for each scroll bar action. This value is then used to scroll the existing contents of the window using the Windows *ScrollWindow* call. This function has the following format:

```
ScrollWindow (hwnd, xInc, yInc, pRect, pClipRect) ;
```

The *xInc* and *yInc* values specify an amount to scroll in pixels. In SYSMETS3, the *pRect* and *pClipRect* values are set to NULL to specify that the entire client area should be scrolled. Windows invalidates the rectangle in the client area "uncovered" by the scrolling operation. This generates a WM_PAINT message. *InvalidateRect* is no longer needed. (Note that *ScrollWindow* is *not* a GDI procedure because it does not require a handle to a device context. It is one of the few non-GDI Windows functions that changes the appearance of the client area of a window.)

■ The WM_PAINT processing now determines which lines are within the invalid rectangle and rewrites only those lines. It does this by analyzing the top and bottom coordinates of the invalid rectangle stored in the PAINTSTRUCT structure. The program paints only those text lines within the invalid rectangle. The code is more complex, but it is much faster.

■ Because WM_PAINT was speeded up, I decided to let SYSMETS3 process SB_THUMBTRACK operations for WM_VSCROLL messages. Previously, the program would ignore SB_THUMBTRACK messages (which occur as the user drags the scroll bar thumb) and would act only on SB_THUMBPOSITION messages, which occur when the user stops dragging the thumb. The WM_VSCROLL code also calls *UpdateWindow* to update the client area immediately. When you move the thumb on the vertical scroll bar, SYSMETS3 will continually scroll and update the client area. I'll let you decide whether SYSMETS3 (and Windows) is fast enough to justify this change.

But I Don't Like to Use the Mouse

In the early days of Windows, a significant number of users didn't care for using the mouse, and indeed, Windows itself (and many Windows programs) did not require a mouse. Although mouseless PCs have now generally gone the way of monochrome displays and dot matrix printers, it is still recommended that you write programs that duplicate mouse operations with the keyboard. This is particularly true for something as fundamental as scroll bars, because our keyboards have a whole array of cursor movement keys that should perform the same operations.

In Chapter 5, you'll learn how to use the keyboard and how to add a keyboard interface to this program. You'll notice that SYSMETS3 seems to process WM_VSCROLL messages when the low word of *wParam* equals SB_TOP and SB_BOTTOM. I mentioned earlier that a window procedure doesn't receive these messages for scroll bars, so right now this is superfluous code. When we come back to this program in Chapter 5, you'll see the reason for including these operations.

Chapter 4

Essential Graphics

The Graphics Device Interface (GDI) is the subsystem of Windows 95 responsible for displaying graphics (including text) on video displays and printers. As you might imagine, GDI is a very important part of Windows. Not only do the applications that you write for Windows 95 use GDI exclusively for the display of visual information, but Windows itself uses GDI extensively for the visual display of user interface items such as menus, scroll bars, icons, and mouse cursors.

Perhaps due to the "anything goes" tradition of MS-DOS programming, often newer (and sometimes even veteran) Windows programmers are tempted to "sneak around" GDI and write directly to the video display. Please—don't even think about it. It will only cause you many headaches, including interference with other Windows 95 programs and incompatibilities with future versions of the operating system.

Unlike some newer features of Windows 95, GDI has been around from the very beginning. Internally, Windows 1.0 consisted basically of three dynamic link libraries, KERNEL (handling tasking, memory management, and file I/O), USER (the user interface), and GDI. Successive versions of Windows have added some functionality to GDI while (for the most part) maintaining backward compatibility with existing programs, but the core of GDI—for better or for worse—has remained about the same.

Unfortunately, a comprehensive coverage of GDI would require an entire book, and this is not that book. In this chapter, I want to provide you with enough knowledge of GDI to understand the drawing routines demonstrated in the remainder of this book, plus some other information that you may find useful.

THE GDI PHILOSOPHY

Graphics in 32-bit Windows are handled primarily by functions exported from the GDI32.DLL dynamic link library, which in turn uses the 16-bit GDI.EXE dynamic link library. (Dynamic link libraries in earlier versions of Windows had a .EXE extension rather than .DLL.) These modules call routines in the various display driver files—a .DRV file for the video display screen and possibly one or more other .DRV driver files that control printers or plotters. The video driver accesses the hardware of the video display, or converts GDI commands into codes or commands that various printers understand. Different video display adapters and printers require different driver files.

Because very many different display devices can be attached to PC compatibles, one of the primary goals of GDI is to support device-independent graphics. Windows programs should be able to run without problems on any graphics output device that Windows supports. GDI accomplishes this goal by providing facilities to insulate your programs from the particular characteristics of different output devices.

The world of graphics output devices is divided into two broad groups: raster devices and vector devices. Most PC output devices are raster devices, which means that they represent images as a pattern of dots. This category includes video display adapters, dot-matrix printers, and laser printers. Vector devices, which draw images using lines, are generally limited to plotters.

Much of traditional computer graphics programming is based solely on vectors. This means that a program using one of these graphics languages is a level of abstraction away from the hardware. The output device is using pixels for a graphics representation, but the program is not talking to the interface in terms of pixels. While you can certainly use Windows GDI as a high-level vector drawing system, you can also use it for relatively low-level pixel manipulation.

In this respect, Windows GDI is to traditional graphics interface languages what C is to other programming languages. C is well known for its high degree of portability among different operating systems and environments. Yet C is also well known for allowing a programmer to perform low-level system functions that are often impossible in other high-level languages. Just as C is sometimes thought of as a "high-level assembly language," you can think of GDI as a high-level interface to the hardware of the graphics device.

As you've seen, by default Windows uses a coordinate system based on pixels. Most traditional graphics languages use a "virtual" coordinate system with horizontal and vertical axes that range (for instance) from 0 to 32,767. Although some graphics languages don't let you use pixel coordinates, Windows GDI lets you use either system (as well as additional coordinate systems based on physical measurements). You can use a virtual coordinate system and keep your program distanced from the hardware, or you can use the device coordinate system and snuggle right up to the hardware.

Some programmers think that after you start working in terms of pixels, you've abandoned device independence. We've already seen in Chapter 3 that this is not necessarily true. The trick is to use the pixels in a device-independent fashion. This requires that the graphics interface language provide facilities for a program to determine the hardware characteristics of the device and make appropriate adjustments. For example, in the SYSMETS programs we used the pixel size of a standard system font character to space text on the screen. This approach allowed the programs to adjust to different display adapters with different resolutions, text sizes, and aspect ratios. You'll see other methods in this chapter for determining display sizes.

In the early days, many users ran Windows with a monochrome display. Even in more recent years laptop users were restricted to gray shades. For this reason, GDI was constructed so that you can write a program without worrying very much about color—that is, Windows can convert colors to gray shades. Even today, video displays used with Windows 95 have different color capabilities (16 colors, 256 colors, or "full-color"), and most users are still stuck with noncolor printers. It is possible to use these devices blindly, but your program can also determine how many colors are available on the particular display device and take best advantage of the hardware.

Of course, just as you can write C programs that have subtle portability problems when they run on other computers, you can also inadvertently let device dependencies creep into your Windows programs. That's part of the price of not being fully insulated from the hardware. We'll examine some of these device-dependent traps in this chapter.

You should also be aware of the limitations of Windows GDI. GDI is not (at this time) capable of doing everything you may want a graphics interface to do. Although you can move graphics objects around the display, GDI is generally a static display system with only limited animation support. As implemented in Windows 95, GDI provides no direct support for three-dimensional representations or for rotations of objects. For instance, when you draw an ellipse, the ellipse axes must be parallel to the horizontal and vertical coordinates. Although some graphics languages use floating-point numbers for virtual coordinates, Windows 95—for performance reasons—always uses 16-bit signed integers. This, unfortunately, is one deficiency of Windows 95. Windows NT supports 32-bit coordinates.

THE STRUCTURE OF GDI

From the programmer's perspective, GDI consists of several hundred function calls and some associated data types, macros, and structures. But before we begin looking at some of these functions in detail, let's step back and get a feel for the overall structure of GDI.

The Types of Function Calls

Generally, the function calls associated with GDI can be classified in several broad groups. These are not cut-and-dried, and there are some overlaps, but here they are nonetheless:

■ *Functions that get (or create) and release (or destroy) a device context*—As we saw in Chapter 3, you need a handle to a device context in order to draw. The

GetDC and *ReleaseDC* functions let you do this during messages other than WM_PAINT, and the *BeginPaint* and *EndPaint* functions (although technically a part of the USER subsystem in Windows) are used during the WM_PAINT message for drawing. We'll examine some other functions regarding device contexts shortly.

■ *Functions that obtain information about the device context*—Again, in the SYSMETS programs in Chapter 3, we used the *GetTextMetrics* function to obtain information about the dimensions of the font currently selected in the device context. Later on in this chapter, we'll look at the DEVCAPS1 program to obtain very general device context information.

■ *Functions that draw something*—Obviously, once all the preliminaries are out of the way, this is the really important stuff. In Chapter 3, we used the *TextOut* function to display some text in the client area of the window. As we'll see, other GDI functions let us draw lines, filled areas, and bit-mapped images.

■ *Functions that set and get attributes of the device context*—An "attribute" of the device context determines various details regarding how the drawing functions work. For example, you use *SetTextColor* to specify the color of any text you draw using *TextOut* (or other text output functions). In the SYSMETS programs in Chapter 3, we used *SetTextAlign* to tell GDI that the starting position of the text string in the *TextOut* function should be the right side of the string rather than the left, which is the default. All attributes of the device context have default values that are set when the device context is obtained. For all *Set* functions there are *Get* functions that let you obtain the current device context attributes.

■ *Functions that work with GDI objects*—Now here's where GDI gets a little messy. First, an example: By default, any lines you draw using GDI are solid and of a standard width. You may wish to draw thicker lines, or use lines composed of a series of dots or dashes. This line width and this line style are *not* attributes of the device context. Instead, they are characteristics of a "logical pen." You can create a logical pen by specifying these characteristics in the *CreatePen*, *CreatePenIndirect*, or *ExtCreatePen* function. The functions return a handle to a logical pen. (Although these functions are considered to be part of GDI, unlike most GDI function calls they do *not* require a handle to a device context.) To use this pen, you "select" the handle into the device context. From then on, whatever lines you draw use this pen. Later on, you deselect the pen object from the device context and destroy the object. Besides pens, you also use GDI objects for creating brushes that fill enclosed areas, for fonts, for bitmaps, and for other aspects of GDI that I'll be covering in this chapter.

The GDI Primitives

The types of graphics you display on the screen or the printer can themselves be divided into several categories, often called "primitives." These are:

- *Lines and curves*—Lines are the foundation of any vector graphics drawing system. GDI supports straight lines, rectangles, ellipses (including that subset of ellipses known as circles), "arcs" that are partial curves on the circumference of an ellipse, and Bezier splines, all of which I'll discuss in this chapter. Any more complex curves can be drawn as a polyline, which is generally a collection of very short lines that define a curve. Lines are drawn using the current pen selected in the device context.

- *Filled areas*—Whenever a series of lines or curves encloses an area, that area can be filled with the current GDI brush object. This brush can be a solid color, a pattern (which can be a series of horizontal, vertical, or diagonal hash marks), or a bitmapped image that repeats vertically or horizontally within the area.

- *Bitmaps*—Bitmaps are a rectangular array of bits that correspond to the pixels of a display device. They are the fundamental tool of raster graphics. Bitmaps are generally used for displaying complex (often real-world) images on the video display or printer. Bitmaps are also used for displaying small images (such as icons and mouse cursors and buttons that appear in application toolbars) that must be drawn very quickly. GDI supports two types of bitmaps—the old (although still quite useful) "device-dependent" bitmap, which is a GDI object, and the newer (as of Windows 3.0) "device-independent" bitmap (or DIB), which can be stored in disk files.

- *Text*—Text is not quite as mathematical as the other aspects of computer graphics. Text as we know it is bound to hundreds of years of traditional typography, which many typographers consider an art. For this reason, text is often the most complex part of any computer graphics system, but also (assuming literacy remains the norm) the most important. Data structures used for defining GDI font objects and for obtaining font information are among the largest in Windows. Beginning with Windows 3.1, GDI began supporting TrueType fonts, which are based on filled outlines that can be manipulated with other GDI functions. Windows 95 continues to support the older bitmap-based fonts (such as the default system font) for compatibility and memory size.

Other Stuff

Other aspects of GDI are not so easily classifiable. These are:

- *Mapping modes and transforms*—Although by default you draw in units of pixels, you are not limited to that. The GDI mapping modes allow you to draw in units of inches (or rather, fractions of inches), or millimeters, or anything you want. (Windows NT also supports a traditional "world transform" expressed as a 3-by-3 matrix. This allows for skewing and rotation of graphics objects. Unfortunately, the world transform is not supported under Windows 95.)

- *Metafiles*—A metafile is a collection of GDI commands stored in a binary form. Metafiles are primarily used to transfer representations of vector graphics drawings through the clipboard.

- *Regions*—A region is a complex area of any shape, and is generally defined as a Boolean combination of simpler regions. Regions are generally stored internal to GDI as a series of scan lines apart from any combination of lines that may have been used to define the region originally. You can use regions for outlining, filling, and clipping.

- *Paths*—A path is a collection of straight lines and curves stored internally to GDI. Paths can be used for drawing, filling, and clipping. Paths can also be converted to regions.

- *Clipping*—Drawing can be restricted to a particular section of the client area. This is known as clipping, and the clipping area can be either rectangular or any non-rectangular area that you can mathematically define as a series of short lines. Clipping is generally defined by a region or a path.

- *Palettes*—The use of a customized palette is generally restricted to displays that show 256 colors. Windows reserves only 20 of these colors for use by the system. You can alter the other 236 colors to accurately display the colors of real-world images stored as bitmaps.

- *Printing*—Although this chapter is restricted to the video display, everything you learn in this chapter can also be applied to printing. (See Chapter 15 for a discussion of printing.)

THE DEVICE CONTEXT

Before we begin drawing, let's examine the device context with more rigor than we did in Chapter 3.

When you want to draw on a graphics output device (such as the screen or a printer), you must first obtain a handle to a device context (or DC). In giving your program this handle, Windows is giving you permission to use the device. You then include the handle as a parameter in the GDI functions to identify to Windows the device you want to draw on.

The device context contains many current "attributes" that determine how the GDI functions work on the device. These attributes allow the parameters to the GDI functions to include only starting coordinates or sizes and not everything else that Windows needs to display the object on the device. For example, when you call *TextOut*, you need specify in the function only the device context handle, the starting coordinates, the text, and the length of the text. You don't need to specify the font, the color of the text, the color of the background behind the text, and the intercharacter spacing, because these attributes are part of the device context. When you want to change one of these attributes, you call a function that changes the attribute in the device context. Subsequent *TextOut* calls to that device context use the changed attribute.

Getting the Handle to the Device Context

Windows provides several methods for obtaining a device context handle. If you obtain a device context handle while processing a message, you should release it (or delete it) before exiting the window procedure. After you release the handle, it is no longer valid.

The most common method for obtaining a device context handle and then releasing it involves using the *BeginPaint* and *EndPaint* calls when processing the WM_PAINT message:

```
hdc = BeginPaint (hwnd, &ps) ;
[other program lines]
EndPaint (hwnd, &ps) ;
```

The variable *ps* is a structure of type PAINTSTRUCT. The *hdc* field of this structure is the handle to the device context that *BeginPaint* returns. The PAINTSTRUCT structure also contains a RECT (rectangle) structure named *rcPaint* that defines a rectangle encompassing the invalid region of the window's client area. With the device context handle obtained from *BeginPaint*, you can draw only within this region. The *BeginPaint* call validates this region.

Windows programs can also obtain a handle to a device context during processing of messages other than WM_PAINT:

```
hdc = GetDC (hwnd) ;
[other program lines]
ReleaseDC (hwnd, hdc) ;
```

This device context applies to the client area of the window whose handle is *hwnd*. The primary difference between the use of these calls and the use of the *BeginPaint* and *EndPaint* combination is that you can draw on your entire client area with the handle returned from *GetDC*. However, *GetDC* and *ReleaseDC* don't validate any possibly invalid regions of the client area.

A Windows program can also obtain a handle to a device context that applies to the entire window and not only to the window's client area:

```
hdc = GetWindowDC (hwnd) ;
```

```
[other program lines]
ReleaseDC (hwnd, hdc) ;
```

This device context includes the window title bar, menu, scroll bars, and frame in addition to the client area. The *GetWindowDC* function is rarely used by application programs. If you want to experiment with it, you should trap WM_NCPAINT ("nonclient paint") messages, which prevents Windows from drawing on the nonclient area of the window.

The *BeginPaint*, *GetDC*, and *GetWindowDC* calls obtain a device context associated with a particular window on the video display. A much more general function for obtaining a handle to a device context is *CreateDC*:

```
hdc = CreateDC (pszDriver, pszDevice, pszOutput, pData) ;
[other program lines]
DeleteDC (hdc) ;
```

For example, you can obtain a device context handle for the entire display by calling:

```
hdc = CreateDC ("DISPLAY", NULL, NULL, NULL) ;
```

Writing outside your windows is generally impolite, but it's convenient for some unusual applications. (Although this fact is undocumented, you can also retrieve a device context for the entire screen by calling *GetDC* with a NULL parameter.) In Chapter 15 we'll use the *CreateDC* function to obtain a handle to a printer device context.

Sometimes you only need to obtain some information about a device context and not to do any drawing. In these cases, you can obtain a handle to an "information context" using *CreateIC*. The parameters are the same as for the *CreateDC* function, for example:

```
hdcInfo = CreateIC ("DISPLAY", NULL, NULL, NULL) ;
[other program lines]
DeleteDC (hdcInfo) ;
```

You can't write to the device using this information context handle.

When working with bitmaps, it can sometimes be useful to obtain a "memory device context":

```
hdcMem = CreateCompatibleDC (hdc) ;
[other program lines]
DeleteDC (hdcMem) ;
```

This is a rather abstract concept. But basically what you do is select a bitmap into the memory device context and then use GDI function calls to draw on the bitmap. I'll discuss this later in this chapter and use the technique in the GRAFMENU program in Chapter 10.

As I mentioned earlier, a metafile is a collection of GDI calls encoded in binary form. You can create a metafile by obtaining a metafile device context:

```
hdcMeta = CreateMetaFile (pszFilename) ;
[other program lines]
hmf = CloseMetaFile (hdcMeta) ;
```

During the time that the metafile device context is valid, any GDI calls you make using *hdcMeta* are not displayed but become part of the metafile. When you call *CloseMetaFile*, the device context handle becomes invalid. The function returns a handle to the metafile (*hmf*).

Getting Device Context Information

A device context usually refers to a physical display device such as a video display or a printer. Often, you need to obtain information about this device, including the size of the display (in terms of both pixels and physical dimensions) and its color capabilities. You can get this information by calling the *GetDeviceCaps* ("get device capabilities") function:

```
iValue = GetDeviceCaps (hdc, iIndex) ;
```

The *iIndex* parameter is one of 28 identifiers defined in the Windows header files. For instance, the *iIndex* value of HORZRES causes *GetDeviceCaps* to return the width of the device in pixels; a VERTRES parameter returns the height of the device in pixels. If *hdc* is a handle to a screen device context, that's the same information you can get from *GetSystemMetrics*. If *hdc* is a handle to a printer device context, then *GetDeviceCaps* returns the height and width of the printer display area in pixels.

You can also use *GetDeviceCaps* to determine the device's capabilities of processing various types of graphics. This is unimportant for the video display, but it becomes more important when working with printers. For instance, most plotters can't draw bitmapped images—and *GetDeviceCaps* can tell you that.

The DEVCAPS1 Program

The DEVCAPS1 program, shown in Figure 4-1, displays some (but not all) the information available from the *GetDeviceCaps* function using a device context for the video display. (A second expanded version of this program, called DEVCAPS2, will be presented in Chapter 15 to get information for the printer.)

DEVCAPS1.MAK

```
#-----------------------
# DEVCAPS1.MAK make file
#-----------------------


devcaps1.exe : devcaps1.obj
     $(LINKER) $(GUIFLAGS) -OUT:devcaps1.exe devcaps1.obj $(GUILIBS)

devcaps1.obj : devcaps1.c
     $(CC) $(CFLAGS) devcaps1.c
```

Figure 4-1. *The DEVCAPS1 program.*   *(continued)*

DEVCAPS1.C

```
/*------------------------------------------------------------
   DEVCAPS1.C -- Device Capabilities Display Program No. 1
                 (c) Charles Petzold, 1996
   ------------------------------------------------------------*/

#include <windows.h>
#include <string.h>

#define NUMLINES ((int) (sizeof devcaps / sizeof devcaps [0]))

struct
     {
     int  iIndex ;
     char *szLabel ;
     char *szDesc ;
     }
     devcaps [] =
          {
          HORZSIZE,      "HORZSIZE",      "Width in millimeters:",
          VERTSIZE,      "VERTSIZE",      "Height in millimeters:",
          HORZRES,       "HORZRES",       "Width in pixels:",
          VERTRES,       "VERTRES",       "Height in raster lines:",
          BITSPIXEL,     "BITSPIXEL",     "Color bits per pixel:",
          PLANES,        "PLANES",        "Number of color planes:",
          NUMBRUSHES,    "NUMBRUSHES",    "Number of device brushes:",
          NUMPENS,       "NUMPENS",       "Number of device pens:",
          NUMMARKERS,    "NUMMARKERS",    "Number of device markers:",
          NUMFONTS,      "NUMFONTS",      "Number of device fonts:",
          NUMCOLORS,     "NUMCOLORS",     "Number of device colors:",
          PDEVICESIZE,   "PDEVICESIZE",   "Size of device structure:",
          ASPECTX,       "ASPECTX",       "Relative width of pixel:",
          ASPECTY,       "ASPECTY",       "Relative height of pixel:",
          ASPECTXY,      "ASPECTXY",      "Relative diagonal of pixel:",
          LOGPIXELSX,    "LOGPIXELSX",    "Horizontal dots per inch:",
          LOGPIXELSY,    "LOGPIXELSY",    "Vertical dots per inch:",
          SIZEPALETTE,   "SIZEPALETTE",   "Number of palette entries:",
          NUMRESERVED,   "NUMRESERVED",   "Reserved palette entries:",
          COLORRES,      "COLORRES",      "Actual color resolution:"
          } ;

LRESULT CALLBACK WndProc (HWND, UINT, WPARAM, LPARAM) ;

int WINAPI WinMain (HINSTANCE hInstance, HINSTANCE hPrevInstance,
                    PSTR szCmdLine, int iCmdShow)
     {
     static char szAppName[] = "DevCaps1" ;
```

(continued)

```
    HWND        hwnd ;
    MSG         msg ;
    WNDCLASSEX  wndclass ;

    wndclass.cbSize        = sizeof (wndclass) ;
    wndclass.style         = CS_HREDRAW | CS_VREDRAW ;
    wndclass.lpfnWndProc   = WndProc ;
    wndclass.cbClsExtra    = 0 ;
    wndclass.cbWndExtra    = 0 ;
    wndclass.hInstance     = hInstance ;
    wndclass.hIcon         = LoadIcon (NULL, IDI_APPLICATION) ;
    wndclass.hCursor       = LoadCursor (NULL, IDC_ARROW) ;
    wndclass.hbrBackground = (HBRUSH) GetStockObject (WHITE_BRUSH) ;
    wndclass.lpszMenuName  = NULL ;
    wndclass.lpszClassName = szAppName ;
    wndclass.hIconSm       = LoadIcon (NULL, IDI_APPLICATION) ;

    RegisterClassEx (&wndclass) ;

    hwnd = CreateWindow (szAppName, "Device Capabilities",
                         WS_OVERLAPPEDWINDOW,
                         CW_USEDEFAULT, CW_USEDEFAULT,
                         CW_USEDEFAULT, CW_USEDEFAULT,
                         NULL, NULL, hInstance, NULL) ;

    ShowWindow (hwnd, iCmdShow) ;
    UpdateWindow (hwnd) ;

    while (GetMessage (&msg, NULL, 0, 0))
         {
         TranslateMessage (&msg) ;
         DispatchMessage (&msg) ;
         }
    return msg.wParam ;
    }

LRESULT CALLBACK WndProc (HWND hwnd, UINT iMsg, WPARAM wParam,
                                               LPARAM lParam)
    {
    static int  cxChar, cxCaps, cyChar ;
    char        szBuffer[10] ;
    HDC         hdc ;
    int         i ;
    PAINTSTRUCT ps ;
    TEXTMETRIC  tm ;
```

(continued)

```
switch (iMsg)
    {
    case WM_CREATE :
        hdc = GetDC (hwnd) ;

        GetTextMetrics (hdc, &tm) ;
        cxChar = tm.tmAveCharWidth ;

        cxCaps = (tm.tmPitchAndFamily & 1 ? 3 : 2) * cxChar / 2 ;
        cyChar = tm.tmHeight + tm.tmExternalLeading ;

        ReleaseDC (hwnd, hdc) ;
        return 0 ;

    case WM_PAINT :
        hdc = BeginPaint (hwnd, &ps) ;

        for (i = 0 ; i < NUMLINES ; i++)
            {
            TextOut (hdc, cxChar, cyChar * (1 + i),
                        devcaps[i].szLabel,
                        strlen (devcaps[i].szLabel)) ;

            TextOut (hdc, cxChar + 22 * cxCaps, cyChar * (1 + i),
                        devcaps[i].szDesc,
                        strlen (devcaps[i].szDesc)) ;

            SetTextAlign (hdc, TA_RIGHT | TA_TOP) ;

            TextOut (hdc, cxChar + 22 * cxCaps + 40 * cxChar,
                        cyChar * (1 + i), szBuffer,
                        wsprintf (szBuffer, "%5d",
                            GetDeviceCaps (hdc, devcaps[i].iIndex))) ;

            SetTextAlign (hdc, TA_LEFT | TA_TOP) ;
            }

        EndPaint (hwnd, &ps) ;
        return 0 ;

    case WM_DESTROY :
        PostQuitMessage (0) ;
        return 0 ;
    }

return DefWindowProc (hwnd, iMsg, wParam, lParam) ;
}
```

As you can see, this program is quite similar to the SYSMETS1 program shown in Chapter 3. To keep the code short, I didn't include scrollbars because I knew the information would fit on one screen. The results for my 256-color VGA are shown in Figure 4-2.

HORZSIZE	Width in millimeters:	169
VERTSIZE	Height in millimeters:	127
HORZRES	Width in pixels:	640
VERTRES	Height in raster lines:	480
BITSPIXEL	Color bits per pixel:	8
PLANES	Number of color planes:	1
NUMBRUSHES	Number of device brushes:	-1
NUMPENS	Number of device pens:	16
NUMMARKERS	Number of device markers:	0
NUMFONTS	Number of device fonts:	0
NUMCOLORS	Number of device colors:	20
PDEVICESIZE	Size of device structure:	1112
ASPECTX	Relative width of pixel:	36
ASPECTY	Relative height of pixel:	36
ASPECTXY	Relative diagonal of pixel:	51
LOGPIXELSX	Horizontal dots per inch:	96
LOGPIXELSY	Vertical dots per inch:	96
SIZEPALETTE	Number of palette entries:	256
NUMRESERVED	Reserved palette entries:	20
COLORRES	Actual color resolution:	18

Figure 4-2. *The DEVCAPS1 display for a 256-color VGA.*

The Size of the Device

The most important information that your Windows program can obtain about the video device from *GetDeviceCaps* is the size of the display (measured in both millimeters and pixels) and the display's pixel aspect ratio. These dimensions can help in scaling images to be displayed.

The HORZSIZE and VERTSIZE values are the width and height of the display area in millimeters. Of course, the Windows driver doesn't really know the exact size of the display you have attached to your video adapter. These dimensions are based on standard display sizes for the adapters.

The HORZRES and VERTRES values are the width and height of the display area in pixels. For a device context for a video display, these are the same values as those returned from *GetSystemMetrics*. Using these values along with HORZSIZE and VERTSIZE you can obtain the device resolution in pixels per millimeter. If you know that there are 25.4 millimeters (mm) to the inch, you can also obtain the resolution in dots per inch.

The ASPECTX, ASPECTY, and ASPECTXY values are the relative width, height, and diagonal size of each pixel, rounded to the nearest integer. ASPECTXY equals the square root of the sum of squares of ASPECTX and ASPECTY, as you'll recall from Pythagoras.

The LOGPIXELSX and LOGPIXELSY values are the number of pixels per a horizontal and a vertical "logical inch." For a video display, a logical inch is not a real inch (25.4 mm), as you can easily determine by performing a few calculations using the HORZSIZE, VERTSIZE, HORZRES, and VERTRES values. These LOGPIXELSX and LOGPIXELSY values require a little explanation. You may have noticed that most word processing programs for Windows display a ruler that isn't quite right: If you measure the ruler as displayed on a VGA monitor, you'll find that what it declares as 1 inch is really more like 1½ inches. These programs are using the LOGPIXELSX and LOGPIXELSY values for the ruler. If the programs used actual physical dimensions, normal 10-point or 12-point text would be so small as to be nearly illegible. These logical dimensions in effect blow up the display to allow an adequate size for displaying text. When we start working with text, we'll wrestle again with this problem. It affects only video displays; for printers, all the dimensions returned from *GetDeviceCaps* are consistent.

Finding Out About Color

Color displays require more than one bit per pixel. The more bits, the more colors, or more specifically, the number of unique simultaneous colors is equal to 2 to the number of bits. Sixteen-color video adapters require 4 bits per pixels. These bits are generally organized in color planes—a red plane, a green plane, a blue plane, and an intensity plane. Adapters with 8, 16, or 24 bits per pixel have a single color plane in which a number of adjacent bits represent the color of each pixel.

GetDeviceCaps lets you determine the organization of memory in the video adapter and the number of colors it can represent. This call returns the number of color planes:

```
iPlanes = GetDeviceCaps (hdc, PLANES) ;
```

This call returns the number of color bits per pixel:

```
iBitsPixel = GetDeviceCaps (hdc, BITSPIXEL) ;
```

Most graphics display devices that are capable of color use either multiple color planes or multiple color bits per pixel, but not both; in other words, one of these calls will return a value of 1. The number of colors that can be rendered on the video adapter can be calculated by the formula:

```
iColors = 1 << (iPlanes * iBitsPixel) ;
```

This value may or may not be the same as the number of colors obtainable with the NUMCOLORS parameter:

```
iColors = GetDeviceCaps (hdc, NUMCOLORS) ;
```

For example, these two numbers will be different for most plotters. For a plotter, both the PLANES and BITSPIXEL values will equal 1, but the NUMCOLORS value will reflect the number of colored pens that the plotter has. For monochrome devices, *GetDeviceCaps* returns a 2 for the NUMCOLORS parameter.

More importantly, these two values can also be different for 256-color video adapters that support loadable color palettes. *GetDeviceCaps* with the NUMCOLORS parameter returns the number of colors reserved by Windows, which will be 20. The remaining 236 colors can be set by a Windows program using the palette manager.

Windows uses an unsigned long (32-bit) integer value to represent a color. The data type for a color is called COLORREF. The lowest three bytes specify red, green, and blue values that range from 0 through 255, as illustrated by Figure 4-3. This results in a potential palette of 2^{24} (or about 16 million) colors.

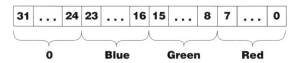

Figure 4-3. *The 32-bit color value.*

This unsigned long is often referred to as an "RGB color." The Windows header files provide several macros for working with RGB color values. The *RGB* macro takes three arguments representing red, green, and blue values and combines them into an unsigned long:

```
#define RGB(r,g,b) ((COLORREF)(((BYTE)(r) | \
                    ((WORD)(g) << 8)) | \
                    (((DWORD)(BYTE)(b)) << 16)))
```

Thus, the value:

```
RGB (255, 0, 255)
```

is really 0x00FF00FF, an RGB color value for magenta. When all three arguments are set to 0, the color is black; when the arguments are set to 255, the color is white. The *GetRValue*, *GetGValue*, and *GetBValue* macros extract the unsigned character primary-color values from an unsigned long RGB color value. These macros are sometimes handy when you're using Windows functions that return RGB color values to your program.

The number of colors returned from *GetDeviceCaps* is the number of pure colors that the device can display. Windows can use dithering (which involves a pixel pattern that combines pixels of different colors) to represent colors in addition to the pure colors. Not all unique combinations of red, green, and blue bytes produce different dithering patterns. For instance, on a 16-color VGA, a red, green, or blue value must generally be incremented by 4 to produce a different dithering pattern. So for these adapters, you have 2^{18} (or 262,144) dithered colors.

You can determine the closest pure color of a particular color value by calling *Get-NearestColor*.

```
rgbPureColor = GetNearestColor (hdc, rgbColor) ;
```

The Device Context Attributes

As I noted above, Windows uses the device context to store "attributes" that govern how the GDI functions operate on the display. For instance, when you display some text using the *TextOut* function, you don't have to specify the color of the text or the font. Windows uses the device context to obtain this information.

When a program obtains a handle to a device context, Windows creates a device context with default values for all the attributes. The device context attributes are shown in the following table. A program can change or obtain any of the attributes.

Device Context Attribute	Default	Function(s) to Change	Function to Get
Mapping mode	MM_TEXT	SetMapMode	GetMapMode
Window origin	(0, 0)	SetWindowOrgEx OffsetWindowOrgEx	GetWindowOrgEx
Viewport origin	(0, 0)	SetViewportOrgEx OffsetViewportOrgEx	GetViewportOrgEx
Window extents	(1, 1)	SetWindowExtEx SetMapMode ScaleWindowExtEx	GetWindowExtEx
Viewport extents	(1, 1)	SetViewportExtEx SetMapMode ScaleViewportExtEx	GetViewportExExt
Pen	BLACK_PEN	SelectObject	SelectObject
Brush	WHITE_BRUSH	SelectObject	SelectObject
Font	SYSTEM_FONT	SelectObject	SelectObject
Bitmap	None	SelectObject	SelectObject
Current pen position	(0, 0)	MoveToEx LineTo PolylineTo PolyBezierTo	GetCurrentPositionEx
Background mode	OPAQUE	SetBkMode	GetBkMode
Background color	White	SetBkColor	GetBkColor
Text color	Black	SetTextColor	GetTextColor
Drawing mode	R2_COPYPEN	SetROP2	GetROP2
Stretching mode	BLACKONWHITE	SetStretchBltMode	GetStretchBltMode
Polygon filling mode	ALTERNATE	SetPolyFillMode	GetPolyFillMode

Device Context Attribute	Default	Function(s) to Change	Function to Get
Intercharacter spacing	0	*SetTextCharacterExtra*	*GetTextCharacterExtra*
Brush origin	(0, 0) in screen coordinates	*SetBrushOrgEx*	*GetBrushOrgEx*
Clipping region	None	*SelectObject* *SelectClipRgn* *IntersectClipRect* *OffsetClipRgn* *ExcludeClipRect* *SelectClipPath*	*GetClipBox*

Saving Device Contexts

Throughout this chapter, you'll encounter various functions to change the device context attributes. Normally, Windows gets a new device context with default values when you call *GetDC* or *BeginPaint*. All changes you make to the attributes are lost when the device context is released with the *ReleaseDC* or the *EndPaint* call. If your program needs to use nondefault device context attributes, you'll have to initialize the device context every time you obtain a device context handle:

```
case WM_PAINT :
    hdc = BeginPaint (hwnd, &ps) ;
    [initialize device context attributes]
    [paint client area of window]
    EndPaint (hwnd, &ps) ;
    return 0 ;
```

Although this approach is generally satisfactory, you might prefer that changes you make to the device context attributes be saved when you release the device context so that they will be in effect the next time you call *GetDC* or *BeginPaint*. You can accomplish this by including the CS_OWNDC flag as part of the window class when you register the window class:

```
wndclass.style = CS_HREDRAW | CS_VREDRAW | CS_OWNDC ;
```

Now each window that you create based on this window class will have its own private device context that exists until the window is destroyed. When you use the CS_OWNDC style, you need to initialize the device context attributes only once, perhaps during processing of the WM_CREATE message:

```
case WM_CREATE :
    hdc = GetDC (hwnd) ;
    [initialize device context attributes]
    ReleaseDC (hwnd, hdc) ;
```

The attributes continue to be valid until you change them.

The CS_OWNDC style affects only the device contexts retrieved from *GetDC* and *BeginPaint* and not device contexts obtained from the other functions (such as *GetWindowDC*). The CS_OWNDC style is not without its cost: Windows requires about 800 bytes to store the device context for each window created with this style. Even if you use CS_OWNDC, you must still release the device context before exiting the window procedure.

You can also use the CS_CLASSDC style:

```
wndclass.style = CS_HREDRAW | CS_VREDRAW | CS_CLASSDC ;
```

This causes each window class to have its own device context that is shared by all windows created based on that class. In general, the CS_CLASSDC type of device context is more difficult to use than the CS_OWNDC type, because any changes you make to the device context attributes affect all windows based on the same window class. This could have some strange effects.

In some cases you might want to change certain device context attributes, do some painting using the changed attributes, and then revert to the original device context. To simplify this process, you save the state of a device context by calling:

```
iSavedID = SaveDC (hdc) ;
```

Now you change some attributes. When you want to return to the device context as it existed before the *SaveDC* call, you use:

```
RestoreDC (hdc, iSavedID) ;
```

You can call *SaveDC* any number of times before calling *RestoreDC*. If you want to revert to the device context as it existed before the last *SaveDC* call, you call:

```
RestoreDC (hdc, -1) ;
```

DRAWING LINES

In theory, all that a display device driver needs for drawing is a *SetPixel* (and in some cases, a *GetPixel*) function. Everything else could be handled with higher-level functions, perhaps implemented in the GDI module itself or even in your application program code. Drawing a line, for instance, simply requires that you call the "write pixel" routine numerous times, adjusting the *x*- and *y*-coordinates appropriately.

In reality, you can indeed do almost any drawing you need with only "write pixel" and "read pixel" routines—that is, if you don't mind waiting for the results. It is much more efficient for a graphics system to do line drawing and other complex graphics operations at the level of the device driver, which can have its own optimized code to perform the operations. Moreover, as video display technology becomes more sophisticated, the adapter boards will contain graphics coprocessors that allow the video hardware itself to draw the figures.

The Windows GDI does indeed include *SetPixel* and *GetPixel* functions. Although I'll use the *SetPixel* function in the CONNECT program in Chapter 7, in real-life graphics programming these functions are rarely used. For most purposes, the lowest-level vector graphics primitive must be considered to be the line.

Windows can draw straight lines, elliptical lines (a curved line on the circumference of an ellipse), and Bezier splines. The seven functions supported under Windows 95 that draw lines are *LineTo* (straight lines), *Polyline* and *PolylineTo* (a series of connected straight lines), *PolyPolyline* (multiple polylines), *Arc* (elliptical lines), *PolyBezier*, and *PolyBezierTo*. (The Windows NT GDI supports three more line-drawing functions—*ArcTo*, *AngleArc*, and *PolyDraw*. These are not supported under Windows 95.) Five attributes of the device context affect the appearance of lines that you draw using these functions: current pen position (for *LineTo, PolylineTo,* and *PolyBezierTo* only), pen, background mode (for nonsolid pens), background color (for the OPAQUE background mode), and drawing mode.

For reasons I'll discuss shortly, I'll also cover the *Rectangle, Ellipse, RoundRect, Chord* and *Pie* functions in this section, even though these functions fill enclosed areas as well as drawing lines.

The *LineTo* function is one of a few GDI functions that does not include the full dimensions of the object to be drawn. Instead, *LineTo* draws a line from the "current position" defined in the device context up to (but not including) the point specified in the *LineTo* function. The current position is simply a starting point for several other GDI functions. In the default device context, the current position is initially set at the point (0, 0). If you call *LineTo* without first setting the current position, it draws a line starting at the upper left corner of the client area.

To draw a line from the point (*xStart, yStart*) to the point (*xEnd, yEnd*), you first must use *MoveToEx* to set the current position to the point (*xStart, yStart*):

```
MoveToEx (hdc, xStart, yStart, &pt) ;
```

where pt is a structure of type POINT, defined like this in the Windows header files:

```
typedef struct tag POINT
    {
    LONG x ;
    LONG y ;
    }
    POINT ;
```

MoveToEx doesn't draw anything. It simply changes the current position. The previous current position is stored in the POINT structure. You can then use *LineTo* to draw the line:

```
LineTo (hdc, xEnd, yEnd) ;
```

This draws the line up to (but not including) the point (*xEnd, yEnd*). Following the *LineTo* call, the current position is set to (*xEnd, yEnd*).

A brief historical note: In the 16-bit versions of Windows, the function to change the current position was *MoveTo*, which had just three parameters—the device context handle, and *x*- and *y*-coordinates. The function returned the previous current position packed as two 16-bit values in a 32-bit unsigned long. However, in the 32-bit versions of Windows (including Windows NT and Windows 95), coordinates are 32-bit values. Because the 32-bit versions of C do not define a 64-bit integral data type, this change required that *MoveTo* be replaced with *MoveToEx*. This change was necessary even though the return value from *MoveTo* was almost never used in real-life programming!

Here's the good news: If you don't need the previous current position—which is almost always the case—you can simply set the last parameter of *MoveToEx* to NULL. In fact, to convert some of your existing 16-bit code to Windows 95, you may want to define a macro like this:

```
#define MoveTo(hdc, x, y) MoveToEx (hdc, x, y, NULL)
```

I use this macro in several programs shown in subsequent chapters.

Now the bad news: Even though coordinate values in Windows 95 appear to be 32-bit values, only the lower 16-bits are used. Coordinate values are effectively restricted to −32,768 through 32,767.

You can obtain the current pen position by calling:

```
GetCurrentPositionEx (hdc, &pt) ;
```

The following code draws a grid in the client area of a window, spacing the lines 100 pixels apart starting from the upper left corner. The variable *hwnd* is assumed to be a handle to the window, *hdc* is a handle to the device context, and *x* and *y* are integers:

```
GetClientRect (hwnd, &rect) ;
for (x = 0 ; x < rect.right ; x += 100)
     {
     MoveToEx (hdc, x, 0, NULL) ;
     LineTo   (hdc, x, rect.bottom) ;
     }

for (y = 0 ; y < rect.bottom ; y += 100)
     {
     MoveToEx (hdc, 0, y, NULL) ;
     LineTo   (hdc, rect.right, y) ;
     }
```

Although it may seem like a nuisance to be forced to use two functions to draw a single line, the current position attribute comes in handy when you want to draw a series of connected lines. For instance, you might want to define an array of 5 points (10 values) that draw the outline of a rectangle:

```
POINT pt [5] = { 100, 100, 200, 100, 200, 200,
                 100, 200, 100, 100 } ;
```

Notice that the last point is the same as the first. Now you need only use *MoveToEx* for the first point and *LineTo* for the successive points:

```
MoveToEx (hdc, pt[0].x, pt[0].y, NULL) ;

for (i = 1 ; i < 5 ; i++)
    LineTo (hdc, pt[i].x, pt[i].y) ;
```

Because *LineTo* draws from the current point up to (but not including) the point in the *LineTo* function, no coordinate gets written twice by this code. While overwriting points is not a problem with a display, it might not look good on a plotter or with some drawing modes (to be covered shortly).

When you have an array of points that you want connected with lines, you can draw the lines more easily using the *Polyline* function. This statement draws the same rectangle as in the code shown above:

```
Polyline (hdc, pt, 5) ;
```

The last parameter is the number of points. We could also have represented this value by (*sizeof (pt)* / *sizeof* (POINT)). *Polyline* has the same effect on drawing as an initial *MoveToEx* function followed by multiple *LineTo* functions. However, *Polyline* doesn't use or change the current position. *PolylineTo* is a little different. This function uses the current position for the starting point and sets the current position to the end of the last line drawn. The code below draws the same rectangle as that shown above:

```
MoveToEx (hdc, pt[0].x, pt[0].y, NULL) ;
PolylineTo (hdc, pt + 1, 4) ;
```

Although you can use *Polyline* and *PolylineTo* with just a few lines, the functions are most useful when drawing a complex curve composed of hundreds or even thousands of lines. For example, suppose you want to draw a sine wave. The SINEWAVE program in Figure 4-4 shows how to do it.

SINEWAVE.MAK

```
#-----------------------
# SINEWAVE.MAK make file
#-----------------------

sinewave.exe : sinewave.obj
    $(LINKER) $(GUIFLAGS) -OUT:sinewave.exe sinewave.obj $(GUILIBS)

sinewave.obj : sinewave.c
    $(CC) $(CFLAGS) sinewave.c
```

Figure 4-4. *The SINEWAVE program.*   *(continued)*

SINEWAVE.C

```c
/*-------------------------------------------
   SINEWAVE.C -- Sine Wave Using Polyline
                 (c) Charles Petzold, 1996
   -----------------------------------------*/

#include <windows.h>
#include <math.h>

#define NUM    1000
#define TWOPI  (2 * 3.14159)

LRESULT CALLBACK WndProc (HWND, UINT, WPARAM, LPARAM) ;

int WINAPI WinMain (HINSTANCE hInstance, HINSTANCE hPrevInstance,
                    PSTR szCmdLine, int iCmdShow)
     {
     static char szAppName[] = "SineWave" ;
     HWND         hwnd ;
     MSG          msg ;
     WNDCLASSEX   wndclass ;

     wndclass.cbSize        = sizeof (wndclass) ;
     wndclass.style         = CS_HREDRAW | CS_VREDRAW ;
     wndclass.lpfnWndProc   = WndProc ;
     wndclass.cbClsExtra    = 0 ;
     wndclass.cbWndExtra    = 0 ;
     wndclass.hInstance     = hInstance ;
     wndclass.hIcon         = LoadIcon (NULL, IDI_APPLICATION) ;
     wndclass.hCursor       = LoadCursor (NULL, IDC_ARROW) ;
     wndclass.hbrBackground = (HBRUSH) GetStockObject (WHITE_BRUSH) ;
     wndclass.lpszMenuName  = NULL ;
     wndclass.lpszClassName = szAppName ;
     wndclass.hIconSm       = LoadIcon (NULL, IDI_APPLICATION) ;

     RegisterClassEx (&wndclass) ;

     hwnd = CreateWindow (szAppName, "Sine Wave Using Polyline",
                         WS_OVERLAPPEDWINDOW,
                         CW_USEDEFAULT, CW_USEDEFAULT,
                         CW_USEDEFAULT, CW_USEDEFAULT,
                         NULL, NULL, hInstance, NULL) ;

     ShowWindow (hwnd, iCmdShow) ;
     UpdateWindow (hwnd) ;
```

(continued)

```
    while (GetMessage (&msg, NULL, 0, 0))
         {
         TranslateMessage (&msg) ;
         DispatchMessage (&msg) ;
         }
    return msg.wParam ;
    }

LRESULT CALLBACK WndProc (HWND hwnd, UINT iMsg, WPARAM wParam,
                                           LPARAM lParam)
    {
    static int  cxClient, cyClient ;
    HDC         hdc ;
    int         i ;
    PAINTSTRUCT ps ;
    POINT       pt [NUM] ;

    switch (iMsg)
         {
         case WM_SIZE :
              cxClient = LOWORD (lParam) ;
              cyClient = HIWORD (lParam) ;
              return 0 ;

         case WM_PAINT :
              hdc = BeginPaint (hwnd, &ps) ;

              MoveToEx (hdc, 0,        cyClient / 2, NULL) ;
              LineTo   (hdc, cxClient, cyClient / 2) ;

              for (i = 0 ; i < NUM ; i++)
                   {
                   pt[i].x = i * cxClient / NUM ;
                   pt[i].y = (int) (cyClient / 2 *
                             (1 - sin (TWOPI * i / NUM))) ;
                   }

              Polyline (hdc, pt, NUM) ;

              return 0 ;

         case WM_DESTROY :
              PostQuitMessage (0) ;
              return 0 ;
         }

    return DefWindowProc (hwnd, iMsg, wParam, lParam) ;
    }
```

This program has an array of 1000 POINT structures. As the *for* loop is incremented from 0 through 999, the *x* members of the structure are set to incrementally increasing values from 0 to *cxClient*. The *y* members of the structure are set to sine curve values for one cycle and enlarged to fill the client area. The whole curve is drawn using a single *Polyline* call. Because the *Polyline* function is implemented at the device driver level, it is much faster than calling *LineTo* 1000 times. The results are shown in Figure 4-5.

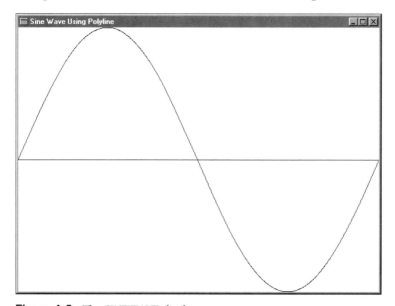

Figure 4-5. *The SINEWAVE display.*

The Bounding Box

I next want to discuss the *Arc* function, which draws an elliptical curve. However, the *Arc* function does not make much sense without first discussing the *Ellipse* function, and the *Ellipse* function doesn't make much sense with first discussing the *Rectangle* function, and if I discuss *Ellipse* and *Rectangle*, I might as well discuss *RoundRect*, *Chord*, and *Pie*.

The problem is, the *Rectangle, Ellipse, RoundRect, Chord,* and *Pie* functions are not strictly line-drawing functions. Yes, the functions draw lines, but they also fill an enclosed area with the current area-filling brush. This brush is solid white by default, so it may not be that obvious that these functions do more than draw lines when you first begin experimenting with them. Strictly speaking, these functions belong in the later section on "Drawing Filled Areas" but I'll discuss them here regardless.

The functions I've indicated above are all similar in that they are built up from a rectangular "bounding box." You define the coordinates of a box that encloses the object— a bounding box—and Windows draws the object within this box.

The simplest of these functions draws a rectangle:

```
Rectangle (hdc, xLeft, yTop, xRight, yBottom) ;
```

The point (*xLeft, yTop*) is the upper left corner of the rectangle, and (*xRight, yBottom*) is the lower right corner. A figure drawn using the *Rectangle* function is shown in Figure 4-6. The sides of the rectangle are always parallel to the horizontal and vertical sides of the display.

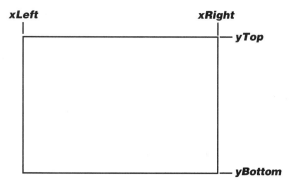

Figure 4-6. *A figure drawn using the* Rectangle *function.*

Programmers who have worked with graphics before are accustomed to the problem of being off by one pixel. Some graphics systems draw a figure to encompass the right and bottom coordinates, and some draw figures up to (but not including) the right and bottom coordinates. Windows uses the latter approach, but there's an easier way to think about it. Consider the function call:

```
Rectangle (hdc, 1, 1, 5, 4) ;
```

I mentioned above that Windows draws the figure within a "bounding box." You can think of the display as a grid where each pixel is within a grid cell. The imaginary bounding box is drawn on the grid, and the rectangle is then drawn within this bounding box. Here's how the figure would be drawn:

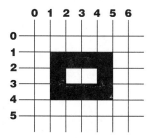

The area separating the rectangle from the top and left of the client area is 1 pixel wide. Windows uses the current brush to color the 2 pixels inside the rectangle.

Once you know how to draw a rectangle, you also know how to draw an ellipse, because it uses the same parameters:

```
Ellipse (hdc, xLeft, yTop, xRight, yBottom) ;
```

A figure drawn using the *Ellipse* function is shown (with the imaginary bounding box) in Figure 4-7.

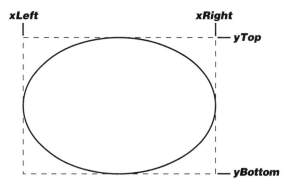

Figure 4-7. *A figure drawn using the* Ellipse *function.*

The function to draw rectangles with rounded corners uses the same bounding box as the *Rectangle* and *Ellipse* functions but includes two more parameters:

```
RoundRect (hdc, xLeft, yTop, xRight, yBottom,
                xCornerEllipse, yCornerEllipse) ;
```

A figure drawn using this function is shown in Figure 4-8.

Windows uses a small ellipse to draw the rounded corners. The width of this ellipse is *xCornerEllipse*, and the height is *yCornerEllipse*. Imagine Windows splitting this small ellipse into four quadrants and using one quadrant for each of the four corners. The rounding of the corners is more pronounced for larger values of *xCornerEllipse* and *yCornerEllipse*. If *xCornerEllipse* is equal to the difference between *xLeft* and *xRight* and *yCornerEllipse* is equal to the difference between *yTop* and *yBottom*, then the *RoundRect* function will draw an ellipse.

The rounded rectangle shown in Figure 4-8 was drawn using corner ellipse dimensions calculated with these formulas:

```
xCornerEllipse = (xRight - xLeft) / 4 ;
yCornerEllipse = (yBottom - yTop) / 4 ;
```

This is an easy approach, but the results admittedly don't look quite right, because the rounding of the corners is more pronounced along the larger rectangle dimension. To correct this problem, you'll probably want to make *xCornerEllipse* equal to *yCornerEllipse* in real dimensions.

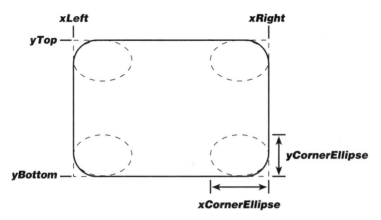

Figure 4-8. *A figure drawn using the* RoundRect *function.*

The *Arc, Chord,* and *Pie* functions all take identical parameters:

```
Arc (hdc, xLeft, yTop, xRight, yBottom,
        xStart, yStart, xEnd, yEnd) ;

Chord (hdc, xLeft, yTop, xRight, yBottom,
        xStart, yStart, xEnd, yEnd) ;

Pie (hdc, xLeft, yTop, xRight, yBottom,
        xStart, yStart, xEnd, yEnd) ;
```

A line drawn using the *Arc* function is shown in Figure 4-9; figures drawn using the *Chord* and *Pie* functions are shown in Figures 4-10 and 4-11. Windows uses an imaginary line to connect (*xStart, yStart*) with the center of the ellipse. At the point at which that line intersects the bounding box, Windows begins drawing an arc in a counterclockwise direction around the circumference of the ellipse. Windows also uses an imaginary line to connect (*xEnd, yEnd*) with the center of the ellipse. At the point at which that line intersects the bounding box, Windows stops drawing the arc.

For the *Arc* function, Windows is now finished, because the arc is an elliptical line rather than a filled area. For the *Chord* function, Windows connects the endpoints of the arc. For the *Pie* function, Windows connects each endpoint of the arc with the center of the ellipse. The interiors of the chord and pie-wedge figures are filled with the current brush.

You may wonder about this use of starting and ending positions in the *Arc, Chord,* and *Pie* functions. Why not simply specify starting and ending points on the circumference of the ellipse? Well, you can, but you would have to figure out what those points are. Windows' method gets the job done without requiring such precision.

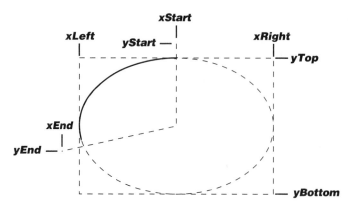

Figure 4-9. *A line drawn using the* Arc *function.*

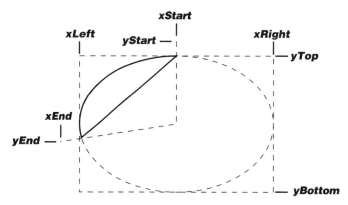

Figure 4-10. *A figure drawn using the* Chord *function.*

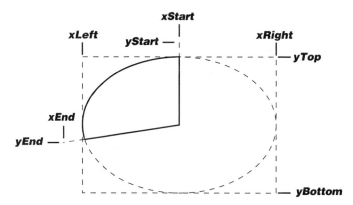

Figure 4-11. *A figure drawn using the* Pie *function.*

The LINEDEMO program shown in Figure 4-12 draws a rectangle, an ellipse, a rectangle with rounded corners, and two lines, but not in that order. The program demonstrates that these functions that define closed areas actually do fill them, because the lines are hidden behind the ellipse. The results are shown in Figure 4-13.

LINEDEMO.MAK

```
#------------------------
# LINEDEMO.MAK make file
#------------------------

linedemo.exe : linedemo.obj
     $(LINKER) $(GUIFLAGS) -OUT:linedemo.exe linedemo.obj $(GUILIBS)

linedemo.obj : linedemo.c
     $(CC) $(CFLAGS) linedemo.c
```

LINEDEMO.C

```
/*----------------------------------------------------
     LINEDEMO.C -- Line-Drawing Demonstration Program
                    (c) Charles Petzold, 1996
     ----------------------------------------------------*/

#include <windows.h>

LRESULT CALLBACK WndProc (HWND, UINT, WPARAM, LPARAM) ;

int WINAPI WinMain (HINSTANCE hInstance, HINSTANCE hPrevInstance,
                    PSTR szCmdLine, int iCmdShow)
     {
     static char szAppName[] = "LineDemo" ;
     HWND        hwnd ;
     MSG         msg ;
     WNDCLASSEX  wndclass ;

     wndclass.cbSize        = sizeof (wndclass) ;
     wndclass.style         = CS_HREDRAW | CS_VREDRAW ;
     wndclass.lpfnWndProc   = WndProc ;
     wndclass.cbClsExtra    = 0 ;
     wndclass.cbWndExtra    = 0 ;
     wndclass.hInstance     = hInstance ;
```

Figure 4-12. *The LINEDEMO program.*

(continued)

```
        wndclass.hIcon       = LoadIcon (NULL, IDI_APPLICATION) ;
        wndclass.hCursor     = LoadCursor (NULL, IDC_ARROW) ;
        wndclass.hbrBackground = (HBRUSH) GetStockObject (WHITE_BRUSH) ;
        wndclass.lpszMenuName = NULL ;
        wndclass.lpszClassName = szAppName ;
        wndclass.hIconSm      = LoadIcon (NULL, IDI_APPLICATION) ;

        RegisterClassEx (&wndclass) ;

        hwnd = CreateWindow (szAppName, "Line Demonstration",
                             WS_OVERLAPPEDWINDOW,
                             CW_USEDEFAULT, CW_USEDEFAULT,
                             CW_USEDEFAULT, CW_USEDEFAULT,
                             NULL, NULL, hInstance, NULL) ;

        ShowWindow (hwnd, iCmdShow) ;
        UpdateWindow (hwnd) ;

        while (GetMessage (&msg, NULL, 0, 0))
             {
             TranslateMessage (&msg) ;
             DispatchMessage (&msg) ;
             }
        return msg.wParam ;
        }

LRESULT CALLBACK WndProc (HWND hwnd, UINT iMsg, WPARAM wParam,
                                              LPARAM lParam)
        {
        static int  cxClient, cyClient ;
        HDC         hdc ;
        PAINTSTRUCT ps ;

        switch (iMsg)
             {
             case WM_SIZE :
                  cxClient = LOWORD (lParam) ;
                  cyClient = HIWORD (lParam) ;
                  return 0 ;

             case WM_PAINT :
                  hdc = BeginPaint (hwnd, &ps) ;

                  Rectangle (hdc,      cxClient / 8,      cyClient / 8,
                                  7 * cxClient / 8, 7 * cyClient / 8) ;
```

(continued)

```
            MoveToEx  (hdc,          0,         0, NULL) ;
            LineTo    (hdc, cxClient, cyClient) ;

            MoveToEx  (hdc,          0, cyClient, NULL) ;
            LineTo    (hdc, cxClient,          0) ;

            Ellipse   (hdc,      cxClient / 8,      cyClient / 8,
                             7 * cxClient / 8, 7 * cyClient / 8) ;

            RoundRect (hdc,      cxClient / 4,      cyClient / 4,
                             3 * cxClient / 4, 3 * cyClient / 4,
                                 cxClient / 4,      cyClient / 4) ;

            EndPaint (hwnd, &ps) ;
            return 0 ;

      case WM_DESTROY :
            PostQuitMessage (0) ;
            return 0 ;
      }

   return DefWindowProc (hwnd, iMsg, wParam, lParam) ;
   }
```

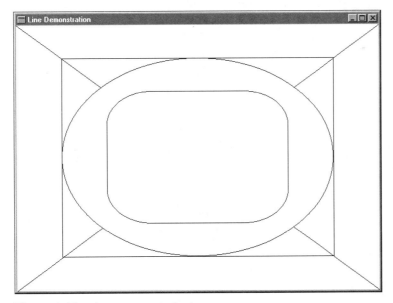

Figure 4-13. *The LINEDEMO display.*

Bezier Splines

The word "spline" once referred to a piece of flexible wood, rubber, or metal used to draw curves on a piece of paper. For example, if you had some disparate graph points, and you wanted to draw a curve between them (either for interpolation or extrapolation), you'd first mark the points on a piece of graph paper. You'd then anchor a spline to the points and use a pencil to draw the curve along the spline as it bent around the points. (Please don't laugh. This may sound like 19th century technology, but I know from personal experience that mechanical splines as well as slide rules were used by insurance actuaries as recently as 15 years ago.)

Nowadays, of course, splines are mathematical formulas. They come in many different flavors. The Bezier spline is one of the most popular for computer graphics programming. It is a fairly recent addition to the arsenal of graphics tools available on the operating system level, and it comes from an unlikely source. In the 1960s, the Renault automobile company was switching over from a manual design of car bodies (which involved clay) to a computer-based design. Mathematical tools were required, and Pierre Bezier came up with a set of formulas that proved to be very useful for this job.

Since then, the two-dimensional form of the Bezier spline has shown itself to be the most useful curve (after the straight line and ellipse) for computer graphics. For example, in PostScript, the Bezier spline is used for *all* curves—elliptical lines are approximated from Beziers. Bezier curves are also used to define the character outlines of PostScript fonts. (TrueType uses a simpler and faster form of spline.)

A single two-dimensional Bezier spline is defined by four points—two end points and two control points. The ends of the curve are anchored at the two end points. The control points act as "magnets" to pull the curve away from the straight line between the two end points. This is best illustrated by an interactive program, called BEZIER, shown in Figure 4-14.

BEZIER.MAK

```
#---------------------
# BEZIER.MAK make file
#---------------------

bezier.exe : bezier.obj
    $(LINKER) $(GUIFLAGS) -OUT:bezier.exe bezier.obj $(GUILIBS)

bezier.obj : bezier.c
    $(CC) $(CFLAGS) bezier.c
```

Figure 4-14. *The BEZIER program.*

(continued)

BEZIER.C

```c
/*-----------------------------------------
   BEZIER.C -- Bezier Splines Demo
               (c) Charles Petzold, 1996
   -----------------------------------------*/

#include <windows.h>

LRESULT CALLBACK WndProc (HWND, UINT, WPARAM, LPARAM) ;

int WINAPI WinMain (HINSTANCE hInstance, HINSTANCE hPrevInstance,
                    PSTR szCmdLine, int iCmdShow)
     {
     static char szAppName[] = "Bezier" ;
     HWND        hwnd ;
     MSG         msg ;
     WNDCLASSEX  wndclass ;

     wndclass.cbSize        = sizeof (wndclass) ;
     wndclass.style         = CS_HREDRAW | CS_VREDRAW ;
     wndclass.lpfnWndProc   = WndProc ;
     wndclass.cbClsExtra    = 0 ;
     wndclass.cbWndExtra    = 0 ;
     wndclass.hInstance     = hInstance ;
     wndclass.hIcon         = LoadIcon (NULL, IDI_APPLICATION) ;
     wndclass.hCursor       = LoadCursor (NULL, IDC_ARROW) ;
     wndclass.hbrBackground = (HBRUSH) GetStockObject (WHITE_BRUSH) ;
     wndclass.lpszMenuName  = NULL ;
     wndclass.lpszClassName = szAppName ;
     wndclass.hIconSm       = LoadIcon (NULL, IDI_APPLICATION) ;

     RegisterClassEx (&wndclass) ;

     hwnd = CreateWindow (szAppName, "Bezier Splines",
                          WS_OVERLAPPEDWINDOW,
                          CW_USEDEFAULT, CW_USEDEFAULT,
                          CW_USEDEFAULT, CW_USEDEFAULT,
                          NULL, NULL, hInstance, NULL) ;

     ShowWindow (hwnd, iCmdShow) ;
     UpdateWindow (hwnd) ;

     while (GetMessage (&msg, NULL, 0, 0))
```

(continued)

```
            {
            TranslateMessage (&msg) ;
            DispatchMessage (&msg) ;
            }
       return msg.wParam ;
       }

void DrawBezier (HDC hdc, POINT apt [])
       {
       PolyBezier (hdc, apt, 4) ;

       MoveToEx (hdc, apt[0].x, apt[0].y, NULL) ;
       LineTo   (hdc, apt[1].x, apt[1].y) ;

       MoveToEx (hdc, apt[2].x, apt[2].y, NULL) ;
       LineTo   (hdc, apt[3].x, apt[3].y) ;
       }

LRESULT CALLBACK WndProc (HWND hwnd, UINT iMsg, WPARAM wParam,
                                               LPARAM lParam)
       {
       static POINT apt [4] ;
       HDC          hdc ;
       int          cxClient, cyClient ;
       PAINTSTRUCT  ps ;

       switch (iMsg)
           {
           case WM_SIZE :
                cxClient = LOWORD (lParam) ;
                cyClient = HIWORD (lParam) ;

                apt[0].x = cxClient / 4 ;
                apt[0].y = cyClient / 2 ;

                apt[1].x = cxClient / 2 ;
                apt[1].y = cyClient / 4 ;

                apt[2].x =     cxClient / 2 ;
                apt[2].y = 3 * cyClient / 4 ;

                apt[3].x = 3 * cxClient / 4 ;
                apt[3].y =     cyClient / 2 ;

                return 0 ;
```

(continued)

120

```
          case WM_MOUSEMOVE :
               if (wParam & MK_LBUTTON || wParam & MK_RBUTTON)
                    {
                    hdc = GetDC (hwnd) ;

                    SelectObject (hdc, GetStockObject (WHITE_PEN)) ;
                    DrawBezier (hdc, apt) ;

                    if (wParam & MK_LBUTTON)
                         {
                         apt[1].x = LOWORD (lParam) ;
                         apt[1].y = HIWORD (lParam) ;
                         }

                    if (wParam & MK_RBUTTON)
                         {
                         apt[2].x = LOWORD (lParam) ;
                         apt[2].y = HIWORD (lParam) ;
                         }

                    SelectObject (hdc, GetStockObject (BLACK_PEN)) ;
                    DrawBezier (hdc, apt) ;
                    ReleaseDC (hwnd, hdc) ;
                    }

               return 0 ;

          case WM_PAINT :
               InvalidateRect (hwnd, NULL, TRUE) ;

               hdc = BeginPaint (hwnd, &ps) ;

               DrawBezier (hdc, apt) ;

               EndPaint (hwnd, &ps) ;
               return 0 ;

          case WM_DESTROY :
               PostQuitMessage (0) ;
               return 0 ;
          }

     return DefWindowProc (hwnd, iMsg, wParam, lParam) ;
     }
```

Because this program uses some mouse processing logic that we won't learn about until Chapter 6, I won't discuss its inner workings (which might be obvious nonetheless). Instead, use the program to experiment with manipulating Bezier splines. In this program, the two end points are set to be halfway down the client area, and ¼ and ¾ of the way across the client area. The two control points are manipulable, the first by pressing the left mouse button and moving the mouse, the second by pressing the right mouse button and moving the mouse. Figure 4-15 shows a typical display.

Aside from the Bezier spline itself, the program also draws a straight line from the first control point to the first end point (also called the begin point) at the left, and from the second control point to the end point at the right.

Bezier splines are considered to be useful for computer-assisted design work because of several characteristics:

First, with a little practice, you can usually manipulate the curve into something close to a desired shape.

Second, the Bezier spline is very well controlled. In some forms of splines, the curve does not pass through any of the points that define the curve. The Bezier spline is always anchored at the two end points. (This is one of the assumptions that is used to derive the Bezier formulas.) Also, some forms of splines have singularities where the curve veers off into infinity. In computer-based design work, this is rarely desired. Indeed, the Bezier curve is always bounded by a four-sided polygon (called a "convex hull") that is formed by connecting the end points and control points.

Third, another characteristic of the Bezier spline involves the relationship between the end points and the control points. The curve is always tangent to and in the same direction as a straight line drawn from the begin point to the first control point. (This is visually illustrated by the BEZIER program.) Also, the curve is always tangent to and in the same direction as a straight line drawn from the second control point to the end point. These are two other assumptions used to derive the Bezier formulas.

Fourth, the Bezier spline is often aesthetically pleasing. I know this is a subjective criteria, but I'm not the only person who thinks so.

Prior to Windows 95, you'd have to create your own Bezier splines using the *Polyline* function. You would also need knowledge of the following parametric equations for the Bezier spline. The beginning point is (x_0, y_0), and the end point is (x_3, y_3). The two control points are (x_1, y_1) and (x_2, y_2). The curve is drawn for values of *t* ranging from 0 to 1:

$$x(t) = (1–t)3x0 + 3t(1–t)2x1 + 3t2(1–t)x2 + t3x3$$
$$y(t) = (1–t)3y0 + 3t(1–t)2y1 + 3t2(1–t)y2 + t3y3$$

You don't need to know these formulas in Windows 95. To draw one or more connected Bezier splines, you use:

```
PolyBezier (hdc, pt, iCount) ;
```

or

```
PolyBezierTo (hdc, pt, iCount) ;
```

In both cases, *pt* is an array of POINT structures. With *PolyBezier*, the first four points indicate (in this order) the begin point, first control point, second control point, and end point of the first Bezier curve. Each subsequent Bezier requires three more points because the begin point of the second Bezier curve is the same as the end point of the first Bezier curve, and so on. The *iCount* parameter is always one plus three times the number of connected curves you're drawing.

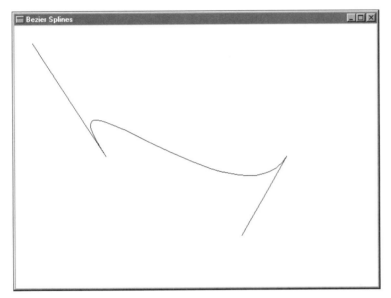

Figure 4-15. *The BEZIER display.*

The *PolyBezierTo* function uses the current position for the first begin point. The first and each subsequent Bezier spline requires only three points. When the function returns, the current position is set to the last end point.

One note of caution: When you draw a series of connected Bezier splines, the point of connection will be smooth only if the second control point of the first Bezier, the end point of the first Bezier (which is also the begin point of the second Bezier), and the first control point of the second Bezier are colinear, that is, they lie on the same straight line.

Using Stock Pens

When you call any of the line-drawing functions that I've discussed in this section, Windows uses the "pen" currently selected in the device context to draw the line. The pen determines the line's color, its width, and its style, which can be solid, dotted, or dashed. The pen in the default device context is called BLACK_PEN. This pen draws a solid black line with a width of one pixel regardless of the mapping mode. BLACK_PEN is one of three "stock pens" that Windows provides. The other two are WHITE_PEN and NULL_PEN. NULL_PEN is a pen that doesn't draw. You can also create your own customized pens.

In your Windows programs, you refer to pens with a handle. The Windows header files include a type definition named HPEN, a handle to a pen. You can define a variable (for instance, *hPen*) using this type definition:

```
HPEN hPen ;
```

You obtain the handle to one of the stock pens by a call to *GetStockObject*. For instance, suppose you want to use the stock pen called WHITE_PEN. You get the pen handle like this:

```
hPen = GetStockObject (WHITE_PEN) ;
```

Now you must make that pen the currently selected pen in the device context, which requires a call to *SelectObject*:

```
SelectObject (hdc, hPen) ;
```

After this call, the lines you draw will use WHITE_PEN until you select another pen into the device context or release the device context.

Rather than explicitly defining an *hPen* variable, you can instead combine the *GetStockObject* and *SelectObject* calls in one statement:

```
SelectObject (hdc, GetStockObject (WHITE_PEN)) ;
```

If you then want to return to using BLACK_PEN, you can get the handle to that stock object and select it into the device context in one statement:

```
SelectObject (hdc, GetStockObject (BLACK_PEN)) ;
```

SelectObject returns the handle to the pen that had been previously selected into the device context. If you start off with a fresh device context and call:

```
hPen = SelectObject (hdc, GetStockObject (WHITE_PEN)) ;
```

then the current pen in the device context will be WHITE_PEN, and the variable *hPen* will be the handle to BLACK_PEN. You can then select BLACK_PEN into the device context by calling:

```
SelectObject (hdc, hPen) ;
```

Creating, Selecting, and Deleting Pens

Although the pens defined as stock objects are certainly convenient, you are limited to only a solid black pen, a solid white pen, or no pen at all. If you want to get fancier than that, you must create your own pens. Here's the general procedure: You create a "logical pen," which is merely the description of a pen, using the function *CreatePen* or *CreatePenIndirect*.

(You can also use *ExtCreatePen*, which I'll describe later in this chapter while discussing GDI paths.) These functions return a handle to the logical pen. You select the pen into the device context by calling *SelectObject*. You can then draw lines with this new pen. Only one pen can be selected into the device context at any one time. After you release the device context (or after you select another pen into the device context), you can delete the logical pen you've created by calling *DeleteObject*. When you do so, the handle to the pen is no longer valid.

A logical pen is a "GDI object." You create and use the pen, but the pen doesn't belong to your program. The pen really belongs to the GDI module. A pen is one of six GDI objects that you can create. The other five are brushes, bitmaps, regions, fonts, and palettes. Aside from palettes, all of these objects are selected into the device context using *SelectObject*.

Three rules govern the use of GDI objects such as pens:

- Eventually delete all GDI objects that you create.

- Don't delete GDI objects while they are selected into a valid device context.

- Don't delete stock objects.

These are not unreasonable rules, but they can be a little tricky sometimes. We'll run through some examples to get the hang of how the rules work.

The general syntax for the *CreatePen* function looks like this:

```
hPen = CreatePen (iPenStyle, iWidth, rgbColor) ;
```

The *iPenStyle* parameter determines whether the pen draws a solid line or a line made up of dots or dashes. The parameter can be one of the following identifiers defined in Windows header files. Figure 4-16 shows the kind of line that each style produces.

PS_SOLID	——————
PS_DASH	— — — —
PS_DOT	· · · · · · · · · · ·
PS_DASHDOT	—·—·—
PS_DASHDOTDOT	—··—···
PS_NULL	
PS_INSIDEFRAME	——————

Figure 4-16. *The seven pen styles.*

For the PS_SOLID, PS_NULL, and PS_INSIDEFRAME styles, the *iWidth* parameter is the width of the pen. An *iWidth* value of 0 directs Windows to use one pixel for the pen width. The stock pens are 1 pixel wide. If you specify a dotted or dashed pen style with a physical width greater than 1, Windows will use a solid pen instead.

The *rgbColor* parameter to *CreatePen* is an unsigned long integer specifying the color of the pen. For all the pen styles except PS_INSIDEFRAME, when you select the pen into the device context, Windows converts this parameter to the nearest pure color that the device can represent. The PS_INSIDEFRAME style is the only pen style that can use a dithered color, and then only when the width is greater than 1.

The PS_INSIDEFRAME style has another peculiarity when used with functions that define a filled area: For all pen styles except PS_INSIDEFRAME, if the pen used to draw the outline is greater than 1 pixel wide, then the pen is centered on the border so that part of the line may be outside the bounding box. For the PS_INSIDEFRAME pen style, the entire line is drawn inside the bounding box.

You can also create a pen by setting up a structure of type LOGPEN ("logical pen") and calling *CreatePenIndirect*. If your program uses a lot of different pens that you initialize in your source code, this method is more efficient. First you define a structure variable of type LOGPEN—for instance, *logpen*:

```
LOGPEN logpen ;
```

This structure has three members: *lopnStyle* (UINT) is the pen style, *lopnWidth* (POINT) is the pen width in logical units, and *lopnColor* (COLORREF) is the pen color. The *lopnWidth* member is a structure of type POINT, but Windows uses only the *lopnWidth.x* value for the pen width and ignores *lopnWidth.y*. Then you create the pen by passing the address of the structure to *CreatePenIndirect*:

```
hPen = CreatePenIndirect (&logpen) ;
```

You can also obtain the logical pen information for an existing pen. If you already have a handle to a pen, you can copy the data that defines the logical pen into a structure of type LOGPEN by using the *GetObject* call:

```
GetObject (hPen, sizeof (LOGPEN), (LPVOID) &logpen) ;
```

Note that the *CreatePen* and *CreatePenIndirect* functions do not require a handle to a device context. These functions create logical pens that have no connection with a device context until you call *SelectObject*. For instance, you can use the same logical pen for several different devices, such as the screen and a printer.

Here's one method for creating, selecting, and deleting pens. Suppose your program uses three pens—a black pen of width 1, a red pen of width 3, and a black dotted pen. You can first define variables for storing the handles to these pens:

```
static HPEN hPen1, hPen2, hPen3 ;
```

During processing of WM_CREATE, you can create the three pens:

```
hPen1 = CreatePen (PS_SOLID, 1, 0) ;
hPen2 = CreatePen (PS_SOLID, 3, RGB (255, 0, 0)) ;
hPen3 = CreatePen (PS_DOT,   0, 0) ;
```

During processing of WM_PAINT (or any other time you have a valid handle to a device context), you can select one of these pens into the device context and draw with it:

```
SelectObject (hdc, hPen2) ;
[line-drawing functions]
SelectObject (hdc, hPen1) ;
[other line-drawing functions]
```

During processing of WM_DESTROY, you can delete the three pens you created:

```
DeleteObject (hPen1) ;
DeleteObject (hPen2) ;
DeleteObject (hPen3) ;
```

This is the most straightforward method for creating, selecting, and deleting pens, but it requires that the logical pens take up memory space during the entire time your program is running. You might instead want to create the pens during each WM_PAINT message and delete them after you call *EndPaint*. (You can delete them before calling *EndPaint*, but you have to be careful not to delete the pen currently selected in the device context.)

You might also want to create pens on the fly and combine the *CreatePen* and the *Select Object* calls in the same statement:

```
SelectObject (hdc, CreatePen (PS_DASH, 0, RGB (255, 0, 0))) ;
```

Now when you draw lines, you'll be using a red dashed pen. When you're finished drawing the red dashed lines, you can delete the pen. Whoops! How can you delete this pen when you haven't saved the pen handle? Recall that *SelectObject* returns the handle to the pen previously selected in the device context. So you can delete the pen by selecting the stock BLACK_PEN into the device context and deleting the value returned from *SelectObject*:

```
DeleteObject (SelectObject (hdc, GetStockObject (BLACK_PEN))) ;
```

Here's another method. When you select a newly created pen into the device context, save the handle to the pen that *SelectObject* returns:

```
hPen = SelectObject (hdc, CreatePen (PS_DASH, 0, RGB (255, 0, 0))) ;
```

What is *hPen*? If this is the first *SelectObject* call you've made since obtaining the device context, *hPen* is a handle to the BLACK_PEN stock object. You can now select that pen into the device context and delete the pen you created (the handle returned from this second *SelectObject* call) in one statement:

```
DeleteObject (SelectObject (hdc, hPen)) ;
```

Filling In the Gaps

The use of dotted pens and dashed pens raises an interesting question: What happens to the gaps between the dots and the dashes? The coloring of the gaps depends on both the background mode and the background color attributes defined in the device context. The default background mode is OPAQUE, which means that Windows fills in the gaps with the background color, which by default is white. This is consistent with the WHITE_BRUSH that many programs use in the window class for erasing the background of the window.

You can change the background color that Windows uses to fill in the gaps by calling:

```
SetBkColor (hdc, rgbColor) ;
```

As with the *rgbColor* value used for the pen color, Windows converts this background color to a pure color. You can obtain the current background color defined in the device context by calling *GetBkColor*.

You can also prevent Windows from filling in the gaps by changing the background mode to TRANSPARENT:

```
SetBkMode (hdc, TRANSPARENT) ;
```

Windows will ignore the background color and will not fill in the gaps. You can obtain the current background mode (either TRANSPARENT or OPAQUE) by calling *GetBkMode*.

Drawing Modes

The appearance of lines drawn on the display is also affected by the drawing mode defined in the device context. Imagine drawing a line that has a color based not only on the color of the pen but also on the original color of the display area where the line is drawn. Imagine a way in which you could use the same pen to draw a black line on a white surface and a white line on a black surface without knowing what color the surface is. Could such a facility be useful to you? It's made possible by the drawing mode.

When Windows uses a pen to draw a line, it actually performs a bitwise Boolean operation between the pixels of the pen and the pixels of the destination display surface. Performing a bitwise Boolean operation with pixels is called a "raster operation," or "ROP." Because drawing a line involves only two pixel patterns (the pen and the destination), the Boolean operation is called a "binary raster operation," or "ROP2." Windows defines 16 ROP2 codes that indicate how Windows combines the pen pixels and the destination pixels. In the default device context, the drawing mode is defined as R2_COPYPEN, meaning that Windows simply copies the pixels of the pen to the destination, which is how we normally think about pens. There are 15 other ROP2 codes.

Where do these 16 different ROP2 codes come from? For illustration purposes, let's assume a monochrome system. The destination color (the color of the window's client area) can be either black (which we'll represent by a 0) or white (1). The pen also can be either black or white. There are four combinations of using a black or white pen to draw on a black or white destination: a white pen on a white destination, a white pen on a black destination, a black pen on a white destination, and a black pen on a black destination.

What happens to the destination after you draw with the pen? One possibility is that the line is always drawn as black regardless of the pen or destination color: This drawing

128

mode is indicated by the ROP2 code R2_BLACK. Another possibility is that the line is drawn as black except when both the pen and destination are black, in which case the line is drawn as white. Although this might be a little strange, Windows has a name for it: The drawing mode is called R2_NOTMERGEPEN. Windows performs a bitwise OR operation on the destination pixels and the pen pixels and then inverts that result.

The table below shows all 16 ROP2 drawing modes. The table indicates how the original pen (P) and destination (D) colors are combined for the resultant destination color. The column labeled "Boolean Operation" uses C notation to show how the destination pixels and pen pixels are combined.

| *Pen (P):* | *1* | *1* | *0* | *0* | *Boolean* | |
Destination (D):	*1*	*0*	*1*	*0*	*Operation*	*Drawing Mode*
Results:	0	0	0	0	0	R2_BLACK
	0	0	0	1	~(P ¦ D)	R2_NOTMERGEPEN
	0	0	1	0	~P & D	R2_MASKNOTPEN
	0	0	1	1	~P	R2_NOTCOPYPEN
	0	1	0	0	P & ~D	R2_MASKPENNOT
	0	1	0	1	~D	R2_NOT
	0	1	1	0	P ∧ D	R2_XORPEN
	0	1	1	1	~(P & D)	R2_NOTMASKPEN
	1	0	0	0	P & D	R2_MASKPEN
	1	0	0	1	~(P ∧ D)	R2_NOTXORPEN
	1	0	1	0	D	R2_NOP
	1	0	1	1	~P ¦ D	R2_MERGENOTPEN
	1	1	0	0	P	R2_COPYPEN (default)
	1	1	0	1	P ¦ ~D	R2_MERGEPENNOT
	1	1	1	0	P ¦ D	R2_MERGEPEN
	1	1	1	1	1	R2_WHITE

You can set a new drawing mode in the device context by:

```
SetROP2 (hdc, iDrawMode) ;
```

The *iDrawMode* parameter is one of the values listed in the "Drawing Mode" column of the table. You can obtain the current drawing mode by using the function:

```
iDrawMode = GetROP2 (hdc) ;
```

The device context default is R2_COPYPEN, which simply transfers the pen color to the destination. The R2_NOTCOPYPEN mode draws white if the pen color is black and black if the pen color is white. The R2_BLACK mode always draws black, regardless of the color of the pen or the background. Likewise, the R2_WHITE mode always draws white. The R2_NOP mode is a "no operation": It leaves the destination unchanged.

We started out using an example of a pure monochrome system. In reality, on a monochrome display Windows can simulate various shades of gray by dithering black and white pixels. When drawing a pen on a dithered background, Windows simply performs the bitwise operation on a pixel-by-pixel basis. The R2_NOT mode always inverts the destination, again regardless of the color of the pen. This mode is useful when you don't know the color of the background, because it guarantees that the pen will be visible. (Well, *almost* guarantees—if the background is a 50 percent gray, the pen will be virtually invisible.) I'll demonstrate the use of R2_NOT in the BLOKOUT programs in Chapter 6.

DRAWING FILLED AREAS

Now let's take the next step up, from drawing lines to drawing figures. Windows' seven functions for drawing filled figures with borders are listed in the table below:

Function	Figure
Rectangle	Rectangle with square corners
Ellipse	Ellipse
RoundRect	Rectangle with rounded corners
Chord	Arc on the circumference of an ellipse with endpoints connected by a chord
Pie	Pie wedge on the circumference of an ellipse
Polygon	Multisided figure
PolyPolygon	Multiple multisided figures

Windows draws the outline of the figure with the current pen selected in the device context. The current background mode, background color, and drawing mode are all used for this outline, just as if Windows were drawing a line. Everything we learned about lines also applies to the borders around these figures.

The figure is filled with the current brush selected into the device context. By default, this is the stock object called WHITE_BRUSH, which means that the interior will be drawn as white. Windows defines six stock brushes: WHITE_BRUSH, LTGRAY_BRUSH, GRAY_BRUSH, DKGRAY_BRUSH, BLACK_BRUSH, and NULL_BRUSH (or HOLLOW_BRUSH).

You can select one of the stock brushes into your device context the same way you select a stock pen. Windows defines HBRUSH to be a handle to a brush, so you can first define a variable for the brush handle:

```
HBRUSH hBrush ;
```

You can get the handle to GRAY_BRUSH by calling *GetStockObject*:

```
hBrush = GetStockObject (GRAY_BRUSH) ;
```

You can select it into the device context by calling *SelectObject*:

```
SelectObject (hdc, hBrush) ;
```

Now when you draw one of these figures, the interior will be gray.

If you want to draw a figure without a border, select the NULL_PEN into the device context:

```
SelectObject (hdc, GetStockObject (NULL_PEN)) ;
```

If you want to draw the outline of the figure without filling in the interior, select the NULL_BRUSH into the device context:

```
SelectObject (hdc, GetStockObject (NULL_BRUSH)) ;
```

You can also create customized brushes just as you can create customized pens. We'll cover that topic shortly.

The *Polygon* Function and the Polygon Filling Mode

I've already discussed the first five area-filling functions. *Polygon* is the sixth function for drawing a bordered and filled figure. The function call is similar to the *Polyline* function:

```
Polygon (hdc, pt, iCount) ;
```

The *pt* parameter is an array of POINT structures, and *iCount* is the number of points. If the last point in this array is different from the first point, Windows adds another line that connects the last point with the first point. (This does not happen with the *Polyline* function.)

Windows fills this bounded area with the current brush in one of two ways, depending on the current polygon filling mode defined in the device context. By default, the polygon filling mode is ALTERNATE, which means that Windows fills in only those interiors accessible from the outside of the polygon by crossing an odd number of lines (1, 3, 5, and so forth). The other interiors are not filled. You can also set the polygon filling mode to WINDING, in which case Windows generally fills in all the interior areas. You set the filling mode using:

```
SetPolyFillMode (hdc, iMode) ;
```

The two polygon filling modes are most simply demonstrated with a five-pointed star. In Figure 4-17, the star on the left was drawn with the ALTERNATE mode, and the star on the right was drawn with the WINDING mode.

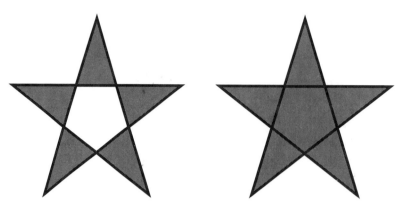

Figure 4-17. *Figures drawn with the two polygon filling modes: ALTERNATE (left) and WINDING (right).*

Brushing the Interior

The interiors of the *Rectangle, RoundRect, Ellipse, Chord, Pie, Polygon*, and *PolyPolygon* figures are filled in with the current brush (also sometimes called a "pattern") selected in the device context. A brush is an 8-by-8 bitmap that is repeated horizontally and vertically to fill the area.

When Windows uses dithering to display more colors than are normally available on a display, it actually uses a brush for the color. On a monochrome system, Windows can use dithering of black and white pixels to create 64 different shades of gray. More precisely, Windows can create 64 different monochrome brushes. For pure black, all bits in the 8-by-8 bitmap are 0. One bit out of the 64 is made 1 (that is, white) for the first gray shade, two bits are white for the second gray shade, and so on, until all bits in the 8-by-8 bitmap are 1 for pure white. On a color video system, dithered colors are also bitmaps, and a much wider range of color is available.

Windows has four functions that let you create logical brushes. You select the brush into the device context with *SelectObject*. Like logical pens, logical brushes are GDI objects. Any brush that you create must be deleted, but it must not be deleted while it is selected into the device context.

Here's the first function to create a logical brush:

```
hBrush = CreateSolidBrush (rgbColor) ;
```

The word *Solid* in this function doesn't really mean that the brush is a pure color. When you select the brush into the device context, Windows creates an 8-by-8 bitmap for a dithered color and uses that bitmap for the brush.

You can also create a brush with "hatch marks" made up of horizontal, vertical, or diagonal lines. Brushes of this style are most commonly used for coloring the interiors of bar graphs and when drawing to plotters. The function for creating a hatch brush is:

```
hBrush = CreateHatchBrush (iHatchStyle, rgbColor) ;
```

The *iHatchStyle* parameter describes the appearance of the hatch marks. The parameter can be one of the following styles: HS_HORIZONTAL, HS_VERTICAL, HS_FDIAGONAL, HS__BDIAGONAL, HS_CROSS, and HS_DIAGCROSS. Figure 4-18 shows the kind of hatch marks that each of these styles produces.

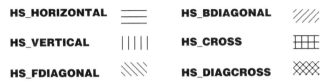

Figure 4-18. *The six hatch brush styles.*

The *rgbColor* parameter of *CreateHatchBrush* is the color of the hatch lines. When you select the brush into a device context, Windows converts this color to the nearest pure color. The area between the hatch lines is colored based on the background mode and background color defined in the device context. If the background mode is OPAQUE, the background color (which is also converted to a pure color) is used to fill in the spaces between the lines. In this case, neither the hatch lines nor the fill color can be a dithered color. If the background mode is TRANSPARENT, Windows draws the hatch lines without filling in the area between them.

Because brushes are always 8-by-8 bitmaps, the appearance of hatch brushes will also vary according to the resolution of the device on which they are displayed. Each of the hatch marks shown in Figure 4-18 was drawn in a 32-by-16-pixel rectangle, which means that the 8-by-8 bitmap was repeated four times horizontally and two times vertically. On a 300-dots-per-inch laser printer, the same 32-by-16-pixel rectangle would occupy an area about $1/9$ inch wide and $1/19$ inch high.

You can also create your own brushes based on bitmaps using *CreatePatternBrush*:

```
hBrush = CreatePatternBrush (hBitmap) ;
```

I'll discuss this function when I discuss bitmaps later in this chapter.

Windows also includes a function that encompasses the three other functions for creating brushes (*CreateSolidBrush*, *CreateHatchBrush*, and *CreatePatternBrush*):

```
hBrush = CreateBrushIndirect (&logbrush) ;
```

The variable *logbrush* is a structure of type LOGBRUSH ("logical brush"). The three fields of this structure are shown below. The value of the *lbStyle* field determines how Windows interprets the other two fields:

lbStyle (UINT)	lbColor (C OLORREF)	lbHatch (LONG)
BS_SOLID	Color of brush	Ignored
BS_HOLLOW	Ignored	Ignored
BS_HATCHED	Color of hatches	Hatch brush style
BS_PATTERN	Ignored	Handle to bitmap

Earlier we used *SelectObject* to select a logical pen into a device context, *DeleteObject* to delete a logical pen, and *GetObject* to get information about a logical pen. You can use these same three functions with brushes. Once you have a handle to a brush, you can select the brush into a device context using *SelectObject*:

```
SelectObject (hdc, hBrush) ;
```

You can later delete a created brush with the *DeleteObject* function:

```
DeleteObject (hBrush) ;
```

Do not delete a brush that is currently selected into a device context, however. If you need to obtain information about a brush, you can call *GetObject*:

```
GetObject (hBrush, sizeof (LOGBRUSH), (LPVOID) &logbrush) ;
```

where *logbrush* is a structure of type LOGBRUSH.

THE MAPPING MODE

Up until now, I've been assuming that we've been drawing in units of pixels relative to the upper left corner of the client area. Yes, this is the default, but it's not your only choice.

One device context attribute that affects virtually all the drawing you do on the client area is the "mapping mode." Four other device context attributes—the window origin, the viewport origin, the window extents, and the viewport extents—are closely related to the mapping mode attribute.

Most of the GDI drawing functions require coordinate values or sizes. For instance, this is the *TextOut* function:

```
TextOut (hdc, x, y, szBuffer, iLength) ;
```

The x and y parameters indicate the starting position of the text. The x parameter is the position on the horizontal axis, and the y parameter is the position on the vertical axis. Often the notation (x, y) is used to indicate this point.

In *TextOut*, as in virtually all GDI functions, these coordinate values are in terms of "logical units." Windows must translate the logical units into "device units," or pixels. This translation is governed by the mapping mode, the window and viewport origins, and the window and viewport extents. The mapping mode also implies an orientation of the x-axis and the *y*-axis; that is, it determines whether values of *x* increase as you move toward the left or right side of the display and whether values of *y* increase as you move up or down the display.

Windows defines eight mapping modes. These are listed in the following table using the identifiers defined in the Windows header files:

		Increasing Values	
Mapping Mode	*Logical Unit*	*x-axis*	*y-axis*
MM_TEXT	Pixel	Right	Down
MM_LOMETRIC	0.1 mm	Right	Up
MM_HIMETRIC	0.01 mm	Right	Up
MM_LOENGLISH	0.01 in.	Right	Up
MM_HIENGLISH	0.001 in.	Right	Up
MM_TWIPS*	$^1/_{1440}$ in.	Right	Up
MM_ISOTROPIC	Arbitrary ($x = y$)	Selectable	Selectable
MM_ANISOTROPIC	Arbitrary ($x != y$)	Selectable	Selectable

* *Twip* is a fabricated word meaning "twentieth of a point." A point, which is a unit of measurement for type, is approximately $^1/_{72}$ inch but often assumed in graphics systems such as GDI to be exactly $^1/_{72}$ inch. A twip is $^1/_{20}$ point and hence $^1/_{1440}$ inch.

You can set the mapping mode by using:

```
SetMapMode (hdc, iMapMode) ;
```

where *iMapMode* is one of the eight mapping mode identifiers. You can obtain the current mapping mode by calling:

```
iMapMode = GetMapMode (hdc) ;
```

The default mapping mode is MM_TEXT. In this mapping mode, logical units are the same as physical units, which allows us (or, depending on your perspective, forces us) to work directly in terms of pixels. In a *TextOut* call that looks like this:

```
TextOut (hdc, 8, 16, szBuffer, iLength) ;
```

the text begins 8 pixels from the left of the client area and 16 pixels from the top.

If the mapping mode is set to MM_LOENGLISH, then logical units are in terms of hundredths of an inch:

```
SetMapMode (hdc, MM_LOENGLISH) ;
```

Now the *TextOut* function call might look like this:

```
TextOut (hdc, 50, -100, szBuffer, iLength) ;
```

The text begins 0.5 inch from the left and 1 inch from the top of the client area. (The reason for the negative sign in front of the *y*-coordinate will become clear later, when I discuss the mapping modes in more detail.) Other mapping modes allow programs to specify coordinates in terms of millimeters, a printer's point size, or an arbitrarily scaled axis.

If you feel comfortable working in terms of pixels, you don't need to use any mapping modes except the default MM_TEXT mode. If you need to display an image in actual inch or millimeter dimensions, you can obtain the information you need from *GetDeviceCaps* and do your own scaling. The other mapping modes are simply a convenient way to avoid doing your own scaling.

Regardless of the mapping mode, all coordinates you specify in Windows functions must be signed short integers in the range −32,768 through 32,767. Some Windows functions that use coordinates for the starting point and ending point of a rectangle also require that the width and height of the rectangle be 32,767 or less.

Device Coordinates and Logical Coordinates

You may ask: If I use the MM_LOENGLISH mapping mode, will I start getting WM_SIZE messages in terms of hundredths of an inch? Absolutely not. Windows continues to use device coordinates for all messages (such as WM_MOVE, WM_SIZE, and WM_MOUSE-MOVE), for all non-GDI functions, and even for some GDI functions. Think of it this way: The mapping mode is an attribute of the device context, so the only time the mapping mode comes into play is when you use GDI functions that require a handle to the device context as one of the parameters. *GetSystemMetrics* is not a GDI function, so it will continue to return sizes in terms of device units, which are pixels. And although *GetDeviceCaps* is a GDI function that requires a handle to a device context, Windows continues to return device units for the HORZRES and VERTRES indexes, because one of the purposes of this function is to provide a program with the size of the device in pixels.

However, the values in the TEXTMETRIC structure that you obtain from the *GetTextMetrics* call are in terms of logical units. If the mapping mode is MM_LOENGLISH at the time the call is made, *GetTextMetrics* provides character widths and heights in terms of hundredths of an inch. When you call *GetTextMetrics* for information about the height and width of characters, the mapping mode should be set to the same mapping mode that you'll be using when you draw text based on these sizes. As I cover the various GDI functions in this chapter, I'll note whether they use device coordinates or logical coordinates. All functions discussed so far use logical coordinates, except for the spacing between the dots and dashes in styled lines, and the spacing between hash marks in patterns. These are independent of the mapping mode.

The Device Coordinate Systems

Windows maps logical coordinates specified in GDI functions to device coordinates. Before we discuss the logical coordinate systems used with the various mapping modes, let's examine the different device coordinate systems that Windows defines for the video display area. Although we have been working mostly within the client area of our window, Windows uses two other device coordinate areas at various times. In all device coordinate systems, units are in terms of pixels. Values on the horizontal, or *x*, axis increase from left to right, and values on the vertical, or *y*, axis increase from top to bottom.

When we use the entire screen, we are working in terms of "screen coordinates." The upper left corner of the screen is the point (0, 0). Screen coordinates are used in the WM_MOVE message (for nonchild windows) and in the following Windows functions: *CreateWindow* and *MoveWindow* (both for nonchild windows), *GetMessagePos*, *GetCursorPos*, *SetCursorPos*, *GetWindowRect*, *WindowFromPoint*, and *SetBrushOrgEx*. These are generally either functions that don't have a window associated with them (such as the two cursor functions) or functions that must move (or find) a window based on a screen point. If you use *CreateDC* with a DISPLAY parameter to obtain a device context for the entire screen, then logical coordinates specified in GDI calls will be mapped to screen coordinates.

"Whole-window coordinates" refer to a program's entire window, including the title bar, menu, scroll bars, and window frame. For a normal window, the point (0, 0) is the upper left corner of the sizing border. Whole-window coordinates are rare in Windows, but if you obtain a device context from *GetWindowDC*, logical coordinates in GDI functions will be mapped to whole-window coordinates.

The third device coordinate system—the one we've been working with the most—uses "client-area coordinates." The point (0, 0) is the upper left corner of the client area. When you obtain a device context using *GetDC* or *BeginPaint*, logical coordinates in GDI functions are translated to client-area coordinates.

You can convert client-area coordinates to screen coordinates and vice versa using the functions *ClientToScreen* and *ScreenToClient*. You can also obtain the position and size of the whole window in terms of screen coordinates using the *GetWindowRect* function. These three functions provide enough information to translate from any one device coordinate system to any other.

The Viewport and the Window

The mapping mode defines how Windows maps logical coordinates that are specified in GDI functions to device coordinates, where the particular device coordinate system depends on the function you use to obtain the device context. To continue our discussion of the mapping mode, we need some additional terminology: The mapping mode is said to define the mapping of the "window" (logical coordinates) to the "viewport" (device coordinates).

The use of the words *window* and *viewport* is unfortunate. In other graphics interface languages, *viewport* often implies a clipping region. We've been using the word *window* to talk about the area that a program occupies on the screen. We'll have to put aside our preconceptions about these words during this discussion.

The "viewport" is in terms of device coordinates (pixels). Most often, the viewport is the same as the client area, but it can also refer to whole-window coordinates or screen coordinates if you've obtained a device context from *GetWindowDC* or *CreateDC.* The point (0, 0) is the upper left corner of the client area (or the whole window or the screen). Values of x increase to the right, and values of y increase going down.

The "window" is in terms of logical coordinates, which may be pixels, millimeters, inches, or any other unit you want. You specify logical window coordinates in the GDI functions.

For all mapping modes, Windows translates window (logical) coordinates to view port (device) coordinates by the use of two formulas:

$$xViewport = (xWindow - xWinOrg) * \frac{xViewExt}{xWinExt} + xViewOrg$$

$$yViewport = (yWindow - yWinOrg) * \frac{yViewExt}{yWinExt} + yViewOrg$$

where (*xWindow, yWindow*) is a logical point to be translated, and (*xViewport, yViewport*) is the translated point in device coordinates. If the device coordinates are client-area coordinates or whole-window coordinates, then Windows must also translate these device coordinates to screen coordinates before drawing an object.

These formulas use two points that specify an "origin" of the window and the viewport: (*xWinOrg, yWinOrg*) is the window origin in logical coordinates; (*xViewOrg, yViewOrg*) is the viewport origin in device coordinates. In the default device context, these two points are set to (0, 0), but they can be changed. The formulas imply that the logical point (*xWinOrg, yWinOrg*) is always mapped to the device point (*xViewOrg, yViewOrg*).

The formulas also use two points that specify "extents": (*xWinExt, yWinExt*) is the window extent in logical coordinates; (*xViewExt, yViewExt*) is the viewport extent in device coordinates. In most mapping modes, the extents are implied by the mapping mode and cannot be changed. Each extent means nothing by itself, but the ratio of the viewport extent to the window extent is a scaling factor for converting logical units to device units. The extents can be negative: This implies that values on the logical *x*-axis don't necessarily have to increase to the right and that values on the logical *y*-axis don't necessarily have to increase going down.

Windows can also translate from viewport (device) coordinates to window (logical) coordinates:

$$xWindow = (xViewport - xViewOrg) * \frac{xWinExt}{xViewExt} + xWinOrg$$

$$yWindow = (yViewport - yViewOrg) * \frac{yWinExt}{yViewExt} + yWinOrg$$

Windows provides two functions that let you convert device points to logical points and vice versa within a program. The following function converts device points to logical points:

```
DPtoLP (hdc, pPoints, iNumber) ;
```

The variable *pPoints* is a pointer to an array of POINT structures, and *iNumber* is the number of points to be converted. You'll find this function useful for converting the size of the client area obtained from *GetClientRect* (which is always in terms of device units) to logical coordinates:

```
GetClientRect (hwnd, &rect) ;
DPtoLP (hdc, (PPOINT) &rect, 2) ;
```

This function converts logical points to device points:

```
LPtoDP (hdc, pPoints, iNumber) ;
```

Working with MM_TEXT

For the MM_TEXT mapping mode, the default origins and extents are shown below:

Window origin:	(0, 0)	Can be changed
Viewport origin:	(0, 0)	Can be changed
Window extent:	(1, 1)	Cannot be changed
Viewport extent:	(1, 1)	Cannot be changed

The ratio of the viewport extent to the window extent is 1, so no scaling is performed between logical coordinates and device coordinates. The formulas shown on the preceding page reduce to these:

```
xViewport = xWindow - xWinOrg + xViewOrg
yViewport = yWindow - yWinOrg + yViewOrg
```

This mapping mode is called a "text" mapping mode not because it's most suitable for text but because of the orientation of the axes. We read text from left to right and top to bottom, and MM_TEXT defines values on the axes to increase the same way:

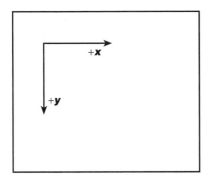

Windows provides the functions *SetViewportOrgEx* and *SetWindowOrgEx* for changing the viewport and window origins. These functions have the effect of shifting the axes so that the logical point (0, 0) no longer refers to the upper left corner. Generally, you'll use either *SetViewportOrgEx* or *SetWindowOrgEx* but not both.

Here's how these functions work: If you change the viewport origin to (*xViewOrg*, *yViewOrg*), then the logical point (0, 0) will be mapped to the device point (*xViewOrg*, *yViewOrg*). If you change the window origin to (*xWinOrg*, *yWinOrg*), then the logical point (*xWinOrg*, *yWinOrg*) will be mapped to the device point (0, 0), which is the upper left corner. Regardless of any changes you make to the window and viewport origins, the device point (0, 0) is always the upper left corner of the client area.

For instance, suppose your client area is *cxClient* pixels wide and *cyClient* pixels high. If you want to define the logical point (0, 0) to be the center of the client area, you can do so by calling:

```
SetViewportOrgEx (hdc, cxClient / 2, cyClient / 2, NULL) ;
```

The arguments to *SetViewportOrgEx* are always in terms of device units. The logical point (0, 0) will now be mapped to the device point (*cxClient / 2, cyClient / 2*). Now you use your client area as if it had the following coordinate system:

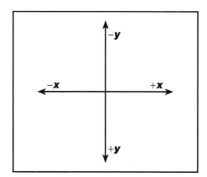

The logical *x*-axis ranges from −*cxClient / 2* to +*cxClient / 2*, and the logical *y*-axis ranges from −*cyClient / 2* to +*cyClient / 2*. The lower right corner of the client area is the logical point (*cxClient / 2, cyClient / 2*). If you want to display text starting at the upper left corner of the client area, which is the device point (0, 0), you need to use negative coordinates:

```
TextOut (hdc, -cxClient / 2, -cyClient / 2, "Hello", 5) ;
```

You can achieve the same result with *SetWindowOrgEx* as you did with *SetViewportOrgEx*:

```
SetWindowOrgEx (hdc, -cxClient / 2, -cyClient / 2, NULL) ;
```

The arguments to *SetWindowOrgEx* are always in terms of logical units. After this call, the logical point (−*cxClient / 2*, −*cyClient / 2*) is mapped to the device point (0, 0), the upper left corner of the client area.

What you probably don't want to do (unless you know what's going to happen) is to use both functions together:

```
SetViewportOrgEx (hdc, cxClient / 2, cyClient / 2, NULL) ;
SetWindowOrgEx (hdc, -cxClient / 2, -cyClient / 2, NULL) ;
```

This means that the logical point ($-cxClient/2, -cyClient/2$) is mapped to the device point ($cxClient/2, cyClient/2$), giving you a coordinate system that looks like this:

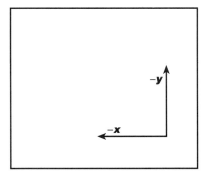

You can obtain the current viewport and window origins from these functions:

```
GetViewportOrgEx (hdc, &pt) ;
```

```
GetWindowOrgEx (hdc, &pt) ;
```

where *pt* is a POINT structure.

The values returned from *GetViewportOrgEx* are in device coordinates; the values returned from *GetWindowOrgEx* are in logical coordinates.

You might want to change the viewport or window origin to shift display output within the client area of your window—for instance, in response to scroll bar input from the user. Changing the viewport or window origin doesn't shift the display output immediately, of course. You change the origin and then repaint the display. For instance, in the SYSMETS2 program in Chapter 2, we used the *iVscrollPos* value (the current position of the vertical scroll bar) to adjust the *y*-coordinates of the display output:

```
case WM_PAINT :
    BeginPaint (hwnd, &ps) ;

    for (i = 0 ; i < NUMLINES ; i++)
        {
        y = cyChar * (1 - iVscrollPos + i) ;
        [display text]
        }

    EndPaint (hwnd, &ps) ;
    return 0 ;
```

We can achieve the same result using *SetWindowOrgEx*:

```
case WM_PAINT :
     BeginPaint (hwnd, &ps) ;

     SetWindowOrgEx (ps.hdc, 0, cyChar * iVscrollPos) ;

     for (i = 0 ; i < NUMLINES ; i++)
         {
         y = cyChar * (1 + i) ;
         [display text]
         }

     EndPaint (hwnd, &ps) ;
     return 0 ;
```

Now the calculation of the *y*-coordinate for the *TextOut* functions doesn't require the *iVscrollPos* value. This means you can put the text output functions in a subroutine and not have to pass the *iVscrollPos* value to the subroutine, because we adjust the display of the text by changing the window origin.

If you have some experience working with rectangular (or Cartesian) coordinate systems, moving the logical point (0, 0) to the center of the client area as we did earlier may have seemed a reasonable action. However, there's a slight problem with the MM_TEXT mapping mode: Usually a Cartesian coordinate system defines values on the *y*-axis to increase as you move up the axis, whereas MM_TEXT defines the values to increase as you move down. In this sense, MM_TEXT is an oddity, and these next five mapping modes do it correctly.

The "Metric" Mapping Modes

Windows includes five mapping modes that express logical coordinates in physical measurements. Because logical coordinates on the *x*-axis and *y*-axis are mapped to identical physical units, these mapping modes help you to draw round circles and square squares.

The five "metric" mapping modes are arranged below in order of lowest precision to highest precision. The two columns at the right show the size of the logical units in terms of inches (in.) and millimeters (mm) for comparison:

Mapping Mode	Logical Unit	Inch	Millimeter
MM_LOENGLISH	0.01 in.	0.01	0.254
MM_LOMETRIC	0.1 mm	0.00394	0.1
MM_HIENGLISH	0.001 in.	0.001	0.0254
MM_TWIPS*	$^1/_{1440}$ in.	0.000694	0.0176
MM_HIMETRIC	0.01 mm	0.000394	0.01

* A *twip* equals $^1/_{20}$ point (which itself equals $^1/_{72}$ inch) and hence $^1/_{1440}$ inch.

To give you an idea of how the MM_TEXT mode fits in with these resolutions, on a standard VGA display each pixel is 0.325 mm wide and high, so VGA device coordinates are coarser than the logical coordinates for any of the metric mapping modes.

On a 300-dots-per-inch laser printer, each pixel is 0.0033 inch—a higher resolution than MM_LOENGLISH and MM_LOMETRIC but not as high as MM_HIENGLISH, MM_TWIPS, or MM_HIMETRIC.

The default origins and extents are shown below:

Window origin:	(0, 0)	Can be changed
Viewport origin:	(0, 0)	Can be changed
Window extent:	(?, ?)	Cannot be changed
Viewport extent:	(?, ?)	Cannot be changed

The window and viewport extents depend on the mapping mode and the aspect ratio of the device. As I mentioned earlier, the extents aren't important by themselves but take on meaning only when expressed as ratios. Here are the translation formulas again:

$$xViewport = (xWindow - xWinOrg) * \frac{xViewExt}{xWinExt} + xViewOrg$$

$$yViewport = (yWindow - yWinOrg) * \frac{yViewExt}{yWinExt} + yViewOrg$$

For MM_LOENGLISH, for instance, Windows calculates the extents to be the following:

$$\frac{xViewExt}{xWinExt} = number\ of\ horizontal\ pixels\ in\ 0.01\ in.$$

$$\frac{-yViewExt}{yWinExt} = negative\ number\ of\ vertical\ pixels\ in\ 0.01\ in.$$

For many display devices (such as the VGA), this ratio will be less than 1. Because Windows works entirely with integers, the use of a ratio rather than an absolute scaling factor is necessary to reduce loss of precision when converting logical and device coordinates.

Notice the negative sign in front of the ratio of extents for the vertical axis. This negative sign changes the orientation of the *y*-axis. For these five mapping modes, *y* values increase as you move up the device. The default window and viewport origins are (0, 0). This fact has an interesting implication. When you first change to one of these five mapping modes, the coordinate system looks like this:

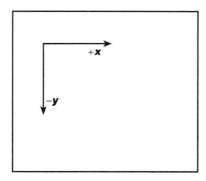

The only way you can display anything in the client area is to use negative values of *y*. For instance, this code:

```
SetMapMode (hdc, MM_LOENGLISH) ;
TextOut (hdc, 100, -100, "Hello", 5) ;
```

displays *Hello* 1 inch from the top and left edges of the client area.

To preserve your sanity, you'll probably want to avoid this. One solution is to set the logical (0, 0) point to be the lower left corner of the client area. Assuming that *cyClient* is the height of the client area in pixels, you can do this by calling *SetViewportOrgEx*:

```
SetViewportOrgEx (hdc, 0, cyClient, NULL) ;
```

Now the coordinate system looks like this:

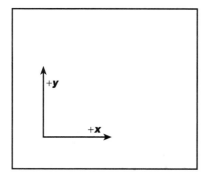

Alternatively, you can set the logical (0, 0) point to the center of the client area:

```
SetViewportOrgEx (hdc, cxClient / 2, cyClient / 2, NULL) ;
```

The coordinate system looks like this:

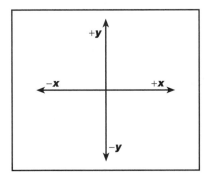

Now we have a real four-quadrant Cartesian coordinate system with equal logical units on the *x*-axis and *y*-axis in terms of inches, millimeters, or twips.

You can also use the *SetWindowOrgEx* function to change the logical (0, 0) point, but the task is a little more difficult because the parameters to *SetWindowOrgEx* have to be in logical coordinates. You would first need to convert (*cxClient*, *cyClient*) to a logical coordinate using the *DPtoLP* function. Assuming that the variable *pt* is a structure of type POINT, this code changes the logical (0, 0) point to the center of the client area:

```
pt.x = cxClient ;
pt.y = cyClient ;
DPtoLP (hdc, &pt, 1) ;
SetWindowOrgEx (hdc, -pt.x / 2, -pt.y / 2, NULL) ;
```

The "Roll Your Own" Mapping Modes

The two remaining mapping modes are called MM_ISOTROPIC and MM_ANISOTROPIC. These are the only two mapping modes for which Windows lets you change the viewport and window extents, which means that you can change the scaling factor that Windows uses to translate logical and device coordinates. The word *isotropic* means "equal in all directions"; *anisotropic* is the opposite—"not equal." Like the metric mapping modes shown earlier, MM_ISOTROPIC uses equally scaled axes. Logical units on the *x*-axis have the same physical dimensions as logical units on the *y*-axis. This helps when you need to create images that retain the correct aspect ratio regardless of the aspect ratio of the display device.

The difference between MM_ISOTROPIC and the metric mapping modes is that with MM_ISOTROPIC you can control the physical size of the logical unit. If you want, you can adjust the physical size of the logical unit based on the size of the client area so that the images you draw are always contained within the client area, shrinking and expanding appropriately. For instance, the ANACLOCK ("analog clock") program in Chapter 7 is an example of an isotropic image. The clock is always round. As you size the window, the image is resized appropriately. A Windows program can handle the resizing of an image entirely through adjusting the window and viewport extents. The program can then use the same logical units in the drawing functions regardless of the size of the window.

Sometimes the MM_TEXT and the "metric" mapping modes are called "fully constrained" mapping modes. This means that you cannot change the window and viewport extents and the way Windows scales logical coordinates to device coordinates. MM_ISOTROPIC is a "partly constrained" mapping mode. Windows allows you to change the window and viewport extents, but it adjusts them so that x and y logical units represent the same physical dimensions. The MM_ANISOTROPIC mapping mode is "unconstrained." You can change the window and viewport extents, and Windows doesn't adjust the values.

The MM_ISOTROPIC mapping mode

The MM_ISOTROPIC mapping mode is ideal for using arbitrary axes while preserving equal logical units on the two axes. Rectangles with equal logical widths and heights are displayed as squares. Ellipses with equal logical widths and heights are displayed as circles.

When you first set the mapping mode to MM_ISOTROPIC, Windows uses the same window and viewport extents that it uses with MM_LOMETRIC. (Don't rely on this fact, however.) The difference is that you can now change the extents to suit your preferences by calling *SetWindowExtEx* and *SetViewportExtEx*. Windows will then adjust the extents so that the logical units on both axes represent equal physical distances.

Generally, you'll use parameters to *SetWindowExtEx* with the desired logical size of the logical window, and parameters to *SetViewportExtEx* with the actual height and width of the client area. When Windows adjusts these extents, it has to fit the logical window within the physical viewport, which can result in a section of the client area falling outside the logical window. You should call *SetWindowExtEx* before you call *SetViewportExtEx* to make the most efficient use of space in the client area.

For instance, suppose you want a "traditional" one-quadrant virtual coordinate system where (0, 0) is at the lower left corner of the client area and the width ranges from 0 to 32,767 and the height from 0 to 32,767. You want the x and y units to have the same physical dimensions. Here's what you need to do:

```
SetMapMode (hdc, MM_ISOTROPIC) ;
SetWindowExtEx (hdc, 32767, 32767, NULL) ;
SetViewportExtEx (hdc, cxClient, -cyClient, NULL) ;
SetViewportOrgEx (hdc, 0, cyClient, NULL) ;
```

If you then obtain the window and viewport extents using *GetWindowExtEx* and *GetViewportExtEx*, you'll find that they are not the values you specified. Windows adjusts the extents based on the aspect ratio of the display device so that logical units on the two axes represent the same physical dimensions.

If the client area is wider than it is high (in physical dimensions), Windows adjusts the x extents so that the logical window is narrower than the client-area viewport. The logical window will be positioned at the left of the client area:

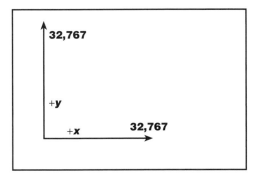

You can't display anything starting on the right side of the client area beyond the range of the *x*-axis, because that requires a logical *x*-coordinate greater than 32,767.

If the client area is higher than it is wide (in physical dimensions), Windows adjusts the *y* extents. The logical window will be positioned at the bottom of the client area:

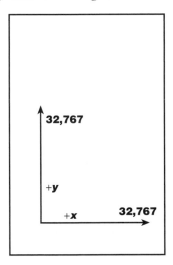

Now you can't display anything at the top of the client area, because you need a logical *y*-coordinate greater than 32,767.

If you prefer that the logical window always be positioned at the left and top of the client area, you can change the code on the preceding page to the following:

```
SetMapMode (hdc, MM_ISOTROPIC) ;
SetWindowExtEx (hdc, 32767, 32767, NULL) ;
SetViewportExtEx (hdc, cxClient, -cyClient, NULL) ;
SetWindowOrgEx (hdc, 0, 32767, NULL) ;
```

In the *SetWindowOrgEx* call we're saying that we want the logical point (0, 32767) to be mapped to the device point (0, 0). Now if the client area is higher than it is wide, the coordinates are arranged like this:

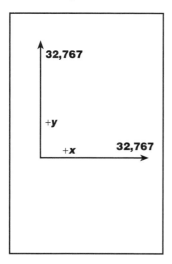

For an ANACLOCK-like image, you might want to use a four-quadrant Cartesian coordinate system with arbitrarily scaled axes in four directions where the logical point (0, 0) is in the center of the client area. If you want each axis to range from 0 to 1000 (for instance), you use this code:

```
SetMapMode (hdc, MM_ISOTROPIC) ;
SetWindowExtEx (hdc, 1000, 1000, NULL) ;
SetViewportExtEx (hdc, cxClient / 2, -cyClient / 2, NULL) ;
SetViewportOrgEx (hdc, cxClient / 2, cyClient / 2, NULL) ;
```

The logical coordinates look like this if the client area is wider than it is high:

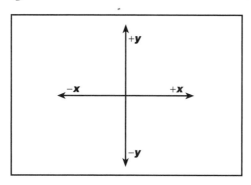

The logical coordinates are also centered if the client area is higher than it is wide:

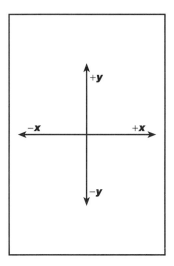

Keep in mind that no clipping is implied in window or viewport extents. When calling GDI functions, you are still free to use logical x and y values less than −1000 and greater than +1000. Depending on the shape of the client area, these points may or may not be visible.

With the MM_ISOTROPIC mapping mode, you can make logical units larger than pixels. For instance, suppose you want a mapping mode with the point (0, 0) at the upper left corner of the display and values of y increasing as you move down (like MM_TEXT) but with logical coordinates in sixteenths of an inch. This mapping mode would let you draw a ruler starting at the top and left side of the client area with divisions of sixteenths of an inch:

```
SetMapMode (hdc, MM_ISOTROPIC) ;

SetWindowExtEx (hdc, 160 * GetDeviceCaps (hdc, HORZSIZE) / 254,
                     160 * GetDeviceCaps (hdc, VERTSIZE) / 254, NULL) ;

SetViewportExtEx (hdc, GetDeviceCaps (hdc, HORZRES),
                       GetDeviceCaps (hdc, VERTRES), NULL) ;
```

In this code, the viewport extents are set to the pixel dimensions of the entire screen. The window extents must be set to the dimensions of the entire screen in units of sixteenths of an inch. The HORZSIZE and VERTSIZE indexes to *GetDeviceCaps* return the dimensions of the device in millimeters. If we were working with floating-point numbers, we would convert the millimeters to inches by dividing by 25.4 and then convert inches to sixteenths of an inch by multiplying by 16. However, because we're working with integers, we must multiply by 160 and divide by 254.

For most output devices, this code makes the logical unit much larger than the physical unit. Everything you draw on the device will have coordinate values that map to an increment of $1/16$ inch. You cannot draw two horizontal lines that are $1/32$ inch apart, however, because that would require a fractional logical coordinate.

MM_ANISOTROPIC: Stretching the image to fit

When you set the viewport and window extents in the MM_ISOTROPIC mapping mode, Windows adjusts the values so that logical units on the two axes have the same physical dimensions. In the MM_ANISOTROPIC mapping mode, Windows makes no adjustments to the values you set. This means that MM_ANISOTROPIC does not necessarily maintain the correct aspect ratio.

One way you can use MM_ANISOTROPIC is to have arbitrary coordinates for the client area, as we did with MM_ISOTROPIC. This code sets the point (0, 0) at the lower left corner of the client area with both the *x*- and *y*-axes ranging from 0 to 32,767:

```
SetMapMode (hdc, MM_ANISOTROPIC) ;
SetWindowExtEx (hdc, 32767, 32767, NULL) ;
SetViewportExtEx (hdc, cxClient, -cyClient, NULL) ;
SetViewportOrgEx (hdc, 0, cyClient, NULL) ;
```

With MM_ISOTROPIC, similar code caused part of the client area to be beyond the range of the axes. With MM_ANISOTROPIC, the upper right corner of the client area is always the point (32767, 32767) regardless of its dimensions. If the client area is not square, then logical *x* and *y* units will be different physical dimensions.

In the previous section on the MM_ISOTROPIC mapping mode, I discussed drawing an ANACLOCK-like image in the client area where both the *x*- and *y*-axes ranged from −1000 to 1000. You can do something similar with MM_ANISOTROPIC:

```
SetMapMode (hdc, MM_ANISOTROPIC) ;
SetWindowExtEx (hdc, 1000, 1000, NULL) ;
SetViewportExtEx (hdc, cxClient / 2, -cyClient / 2, NULL) ;
SetViewportOrgEx (hdc, cxClient / 2,  cyClient / 2, NULL) ;
```

The difference with MM_ANISOTROPIC is that in general the clock would be drawn as an ellipse rather than a circle.

Another way to use MM_ANISOTROPIC is to set *x* and *y* units to fixed but unequal values. For instance, if you have a program that displays only text, you may want to set coarse coordinates based on the height and width of a single character:

```
SetMapMode (hdc, MM_ANISOTROPIC) ;
SetWindowExtEx (hdc, 1, 1, NULL) ;
SetViewportExtEx (hdc, cxChar, cyChar, NULL) ;
```

(This assumes that *cxChar* and *cyChar* are the width and height of a character in pixels, for a fixed-pitch font.) Now you can specify character row and column coordinates in the *TextOut* call rather than pixel coordinates. For instance, the following statement displays the text *Hello* three character spaces from the left and two character rows from the top:

```
TextOut (hdc, 3, 2, "Hello", 5) ;
```

This is almost like working in text mode in the non-Windows MS-DOS environment!

When you first set the MM_ANISOTROPIC mapping mode, it always inherits the extents of the previously set mapping mode. This can be very convenient. One way of thinking about MM_ANISOTROPIC is that it "unlocks" the extents; that is, it allows you to change the extents of an otherwise fully constrained mapping mode. For instance, suppose you want to use the MM_LOENGLISH mapping mode because you want logical units to be 0.01 inch. But you don't want the values along the *y*-axis to increase as you move up the screen—you prefer the MM_TEXT orientation, where *y* values increase moving down. Here's the code:

```
SIZE size ;
[other program lines]
SetMapMode (hdc, MM_LOENGLISH) ;
SetMapMode (hdc, MM_ANISOTROPIC) ;

GetViewportExtEx (hdc, &size) ;

SetViewportExtEx (hdc, size.cx, -size.cy, NULL) ;
```

We first set the mapping mode to MM_LOENGLISH. Then we liberate the extents by setting the mapping mode to MM_ANISOTROPIC. The *GetViewportExtEx* obtains the viewport extents in a SIZE structure. Then we call *SetViewportExtEx* with the extents except that we make the *y* extent negative.

The WHATSIZE Program

We'll use various mapping modes as we explore the GDI functions in the next four chapters. Right now, let's simply look at the size of a client area in terms of inches and millimeters. The WHATSIZE program, shown in Figure 4-19, displays the size of the client area in terms of units associated with the six fully constrained mapping modes: MM_TEXT, MM_LOMETRIC, MM_HIMETRIC, MM_LOENGLISH, MM_HIENGLISH, and MM_TWIPS.

WHATSIZE.MAK

```
#------------------------
# WHATSIZE.MAK make file
#------------------------

whatsize.exe : whatsize.obj
    $(LINKER) $(GUIFLAGS) -OUT:whatsize.exe whatsize.obj $(GUILIBS)

whatsize.obj : whatsize.c
    $(CC) $(CFLAGS) whatsize.c
```

Figure 4-19. *The WHATSIZE program.*

WHATSIZE.C

```c
/*----------------------------------------------
   WHATSIZE.C -- What Size is the Window?
                 (c) Charles Petzold, 1996
   ----------------------------------------------*/

#include <windows.h>
#include <stdio.h>

LRESULT CALLBACK WndProc (HWND, UINT, WPARAM, LPARAM) ;

int WINAPI WinMain (HINSTANCE hInstance, HINSTANCE hPrevInstance,
                    PSTR szCmdLine, int iCmdShow)
     {
     static char szAppName[] = "WhatSize" ;
     HWND        hwnd ;
     MSG         msg ;
     WNDCLASSEX  wndclass ;

     wndclass.cbSize        = sizeof (wndclass) ;
     wndclass.style         = CS_HREDRAW | CS_VREDRAW ;
     wndclass.lpfnWndProc   = WndProc ;
     wndclass.cbClsExtra    = 0 ;
     wndclass.cbWndExtra    = 0 ;
     wndclass.hInstance     = hInstance ;
     wndclass.hIcon         = LoadIcon (NULL, IDI_APPLICATION) ;
     wndclass.hCursor       = LoadCursor (NULL, IDC_ARROW) ;
     wndclass.hbrBackground = (HBRUSH) GetStockObject (WHITE_BRUSH) ;
     wndclass.lpszMenuName  = NULL ;
     wndclass.lpszClassName = szAppName ;
     wndclass.hIconSm       = LoadIcon (NULL, IDI_APPLICATION) ;

     RegisterClassEx (&wndclass) ;

     hwnd = CreateWindow (szAppName, "What Size is the Window?",
                          WS_OVERLAPPEDWINDOW,
                          CW_USEDEFAULT, CW_USEDEFAULT,
                          CW_USEDEFAULT, CW_USEDEFAULT,
                          NULL, NULL, hInstance, NULL) ;

     ShowWindow (hwnd, iCmdShow) ;
     UpdateWindow (hwnd) ;

     while (GetMessage (&msg, NULL, 0, 0))
          {
          TranslateMessage (&msg) ;
```

(continued)

```
            DispatchMessage (&msg) ;
            }
     return msg.wParam ;
     }

void Show (HWND hwnd, HDC hdc, int xText, int yText, int iMapMode,
          char *szMapMode)
     {
     char szBuffer [60] ;
     RECT rect ;

     SaveDC (hdc) ;

     SetMapMode (hdc, iMapMode) ;
     GetClientRect (hwnd, &rect) ;
     DPtoLP (hdc, (PPOINT) &rect, 2) ;

     RestoreDC (hdc, -1) ;

     TextOut (hdc, xText, yText, szBuffer,
              sprintf (szBuffer, "%-20s %7d %7d %7d %7d", szMapMode,
                  rect.left, rect.right, rect.top, rect.bottom)) ;
     }

LRESULT CALLBACK WndProc (HWND hwnd, UINT iMsg, WPARAM wParam,
                                            LPARAM lParam)
     {
     static char  szHeading [] =
                  "Mapping Mode          Left    Right    Top Bottom" ;
     static char  szUndLine [] =
                  "------------          ----    -----    --- ------" ;
     static int   cxChar, cyChar ;
     HDC          hdc ;
     PAINTSTRUCT  ps ;
     TEXTMETRIC   tm ;

     switch (iMsg)
         {
         case WM_CREATE :
             hdc = GetDC (hwnd) ;
             SelectObject (hdc, GetStockObject (SYSTEM_FIXED_FONT)) ;

             GetTextMetrics (hdc, &tm) ;
             cxChar = tm.tmAveCharWidth ;
             cyChar = tm.tmHeight + tm.tmExternalLeading ;
```

(continued)

```
                    ReleaseDC (hwnd, hdc) ;
                    return 0 ;

          case WM_PAINT :
                    hdc = BeginPaint (hwnd, &ps) ;
                    SelectObject (hdc, GetStockObject (SYSTEM_FIXED_FONT)) ;

                    SetMapMode (hdc, MM_ANISOTROPIC) ;
                    SetWindowExtEx (hdc, 1, 1, NULL) ;
                    SetViewportExtEx (hdc, cxChar, cyChar, NULL) ;

                    TextOut (hdc, 1, 1, szHeading, sizeof szHeading - 1) ;
                    TextOut (hdc, 1, 2, szUndLine, sizeof szUndLine - 1) ;

                    Show (hwnd, hdc, 1, 3, MM_TEXT,      "TEXT (pixels)") ;
                    Show (hwnd, hdc, 1, 4, MM_LOMETRIC,  "LOMETRIC (.1 mm)") ;
                    Show (hwnd, hdc, 1, 5, MM_HIMETRIC,  "HIMETRIC (.01 mm)") ;
                    Show (hwnd, hdc, 1, 6, MM_LOENGLISH, "LOENGLISH (.01 in)") ;
                    Show (hwnd, hdc, 1, 7, MM_HIENGLISH, "HIENGLISH (.001 in)") ;
                    Show (hwnd, hdc, 1, 8, MM_TWIPS,     "TWIPS (1/1440 in)") ;

                    EndPaint (hwnd, &ps) ;
                    return 0 ;

          case WM_DESTROY :
                    PostQuitMessage (0) ;
                    return 0 ;
          }
     return DefWindowProc (hwnd, iMsg, wParam, lParam) ;
     }
```

For ease in displaying the information using the *TextOut* function, WHATSIZE uses the MM_ANISOTROPIC mapping mode with logical units set to character dimensions:

```
SetMapMode (hdc, MM_ANISOTROPIC) ;
SetWindowExtEx (hdc, 1, 1, NULL) ;
SetViewportExtEx (hdc, cxChar, cyChar, NULL) ;
```

The program can then specify logical coordinates to *TextOut* in character row and character column coordinates for a fixed-pitch font.

When WHATSIZE needs to obtain the size of the client area for one of the six mapping modes, it saves the current device context, sets a new mapping mode, obtains the client-area coordinates, converts them to logical coordinates, and then restores the original mapping mode before displaying the information. This code is in WHATSIZE's *Show* function:

```
SaveDC (hdc) ;

SetMapMode (hdc, iMapMode) ;
GetClientRect (hwnd, &rect) ;
DPtoLP (hdc, (PPOINT) &rect, 2) ;

RestoreDC (hdc, -1) ;
```

Figure 4-20 shows a typical display from WHATSIZE.

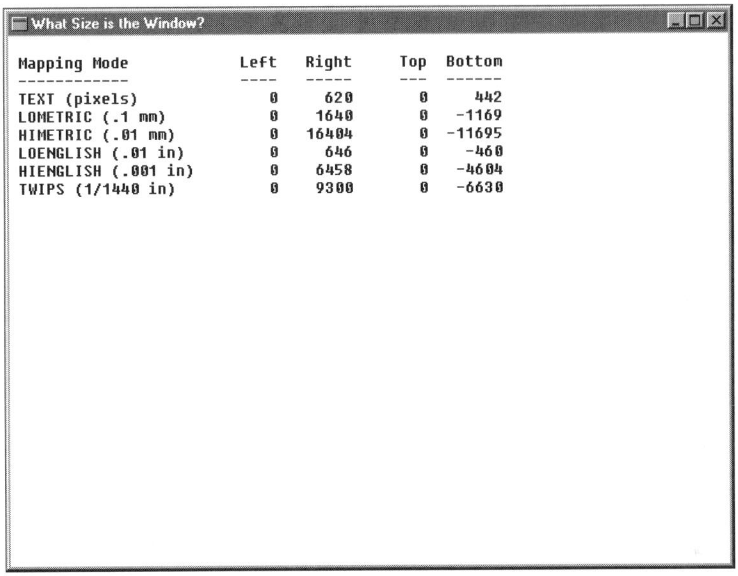

```
 What Size is the Window?                                      _ □ ×

 Mapping Mode            Left    Right     Top   Bottom
 -----------             ----    -----     ---   ------
 TEXT (pixels)              0      620       0      442
 LOMETRIC (.1 mm)           0     1640       0    -1169
 HIMETRIC (.01 mm)          0    16404       0   -11695
 LOENGLISH (.01 in)         0      646       0     -460
 HIENGLISH (.001 in)        0     6458       0    -4604
 TWIPS (1/1440 in)          0     9300       0    -6630
```

Figure 4-20. *A typical WHATSIZE display.*

You'll notice that I've used something called SYSTEM_FIXED_FONT for selecting a fixed-pitch font. I'll discuss this soon.

RECTANGLES, REGIONS, AND CLIPPING

Microsoft Windows 95 includes several drawing functions that work with RECT (rectangle) structures and "regions." A region is an area of the screen that is a combination of rectangles, polygons, and ellipses.

Working with Rectangles

These three drawing functions require a pointer to a rectangle structure:

```
FillRect (hdc, &rect, hBrush) ;
FrameRect (hdc, &rect, hBrush) ;
InvertRect (hdc, &rect) ;
```

In these functions, the *rect* parameter is a structure of type RECT with four fields: *left, top, right,* and *bottom.* The coordinates in this structure are treated as logical coordinates.

FillRect fills the rectangle (up to but not including the right and bottom coordinates) with the specified brush. This function doesn't require that you first select the brush into the device context.

FrameRect uses the brush to draw a rectangular frame, but it does not fill in the rectangle. Using a brush to draw a frame may seem a little strange, because with the functions that you've seen so far (such as *Rectangle*), the border is drawn with the current pen. *FrameRect* allows you to draw a rectangular frame that isn't necessarily a pure color. This frame is one logical unit wide. If logical units are larger than device units, then the frame will be 2 or more pixels wide.

InvertRect inverts all the pixels in the rectangle, turning ones to zeros and zeros to ones. This function turns a white area to black, a black area to white, and a green area to magenta.

Windows also includes nine functions that allow you to manipulate RECT structures easily and cleanly. For instance, to set the four fields of a RECT structure to particular values, you would conventionally use code that looks like this:

```
rect.left   = xLeft ;
rect.top    = yTop ;
rect.right  = xRight ;
rect.bottom = yBottom ;
```

By calling *SetRect*, however, you can achieve the same result with a single line:

```
SetRect (&rect, xLeft, yTop, xRight, yBottom) ;
```

The other eight functions can also come in handy when you want to do one of the following:

■ Move a rectangle a number of units along the *x* and *y* axes:

```
OffsetRect (&rect, x, y) ;
```

■ Increase or decrease the size of a rectangle:

```
InflateRect (&rect, x, y) ;
```

■ Set the fields of a rectangle equal to 0:

```
SetRectEmpty (&rect) ;
```

■ Copy one rectangle to another:

```
CopyRect (&DestRect, &SrcRect) ;
```

■ Obtain the intersection of two rectangles:

```
IntersectRect (&DestRect, &SrcRect1, &SrcRect2) ;
```

■   Obtain the union of two rectangles:

```
UnionRect (&DestRect, &SrcRect1, &SrcRect2) ;
```

■   Determine if a rectangle is empty:

```
bEmpty = IsRectEmpty (&rect) ;
```

■   Determine if a point is in a rectangle:

```
bInRect = PtInRect (&rect, point) ;
```

In most cases, the equivalent code for these functions is simple. For example, you can duplicate the *CopyRect* function call with:

```
DestRect = SrcRect ;
```

Random Rectangles

A fun program in any graphics system is one that runs "forever," simply drawing a hypnotic series of images with random sizes and colors—for example, rectangles of a random size and color. You can create such a program in Windows, but it's not quite as easy as it first seems. I hope you realize that you can't simply put a *while (TRUE)* loop in the WM_PAINT message. Sure, it will work, but the program will effectively prevent itself from processing other messages. The program cannot be exited or minimized.

One acceptable alternative is setting a Windows timer to send WM_TIMER messages to your window function. (I'll discuss the timer in Chapter 7.) For each WM_TIMER message, you obtain a device context with *GetDC*, draw a random rectangle, and then release the device context with *ReleaseDC*. But that takes some of the fun out of the program, because the program can't draw the random rectangles as quickly as possible. It must wait for each WM_TIMER message, and that's based on the resolution of the system clock.

There must be plenty of "dead time" in Windows—time during which all the message queues are empty and Windows is just sitting around waiting for keyboard or mouse input. Couldn't we somehow get control during that dead time and draw the rectangles, relinquishing control only when a message is added to a program's message queue? That's one of the purposes of the *PeekMessage* function. Here's one example of a *PeekMessage* call:

```
PeekMessage (&msg, NULL, 0, 0, PM_REMOVE) ;
```

The first four parameters (a pointer to a MSG structure, a window handle, and two values indicating a message range) are identical to those of *GetMessage*. Setting the second, third, and fourth parameters to NULL or 0 indicates that we want *PeekMessage* to return all messages for all windows in the program. The last parameter to *PeekMessage* is set to PM_REMOVE if the message is to be removed from the message queue. You can set it to PM_NOREMOVE if the message isn't to be removed. This is why *PeekMessage* is a "peek" rather than a "get"—it allows a program to check the next message in the program's queue without actually removing it.

GetMessage doesn't return control to a program unless it retrieves a message from the program's message queue. But *PeekMessage* always returns right away regardless of whether a message is present or not. When there's a message in the program's message queue, the return value of *PeekMessage* is TRUE (nonzero) and the message can be processed as normal. When there is no message in the queue, *PeekMessage* returns FALSE (0).

This allows us to replace the normal message loop, which looks like this:

```
while (GetMessage (&msg, NULL, 0, 0))
     {
     TranslateMessage (&msg) ;
     DispatchMessage (&msg) ;
     }
return msg.wParam ;
```

with an alternative message loop like this:

```
while (TRUE)
     {
     if (PeekMessage (&msg, NULL, 0, 0, PM_REMOVE))
          {
          if (msg.message == WM_QUIT)
               break ;

          TranslateMessage (&msg) ;
          DispatchMessage (&msg) ;
          }
     else
          {
          [other program lines to do some work]
          }
     }
return msg.wParam ;
```

Notice that the WM_QUIT message is explicitly checked. You don't have to do this in a normal message loop, because the return value of *GetMessage* is FALSE (0) when it retrieves a WM_QUIT message. But *PeekMessage* uses its return value to indicate whether a message was retrieved, so the check of WM_QUIT is required.

If the return value of *PeekMessage* is TRUE, the message is processed normally. If the value is FALSE, the program can do some work (such as displaying yet another random rectangle) before returning control to Windows.

(Although the Windows documentation notes that you can't use *PeekMessage* to remove WM_PAINT messages from the message queue, this isn't really a problem. After all, *GetMessage* doesn't remove WM_PAINT messages from the queue either. The only way to remove a WM_PAINT message from the queue is to validate the invalid regions of the window's client area, which you can do with *ValidateRect*, *ValidateRgn*, or a *BeginPaint* and *EndPaint* pair. If you process a WM_PAINT message normally after retrieving it from the queue with *PeekMessage*, you'll have no problems. What you can't do is use code like this to empty your message queue of all messages:

```
while (PeekMessage (&msg, NULL, 0, 0, PM_REMOVE)) ;
```

This statement removes and discards all messages from your message queue except WM_PAINT. If a WM_PAINT message is in the queue, you'll be stuck inside the *while* loop forever.)

PeekMessage was much more important in earlier versions of Windows than in Windows 95. This is because the 16-bit versions of Windows employed non-preemptive multitasking (which I'll discuss in Chapter 14). The Windows Terminal program used a *PeekMessage* loop to check for incoming data from a communications port. The Print Manager program used this technique for printing, and Windows applications that printed also generally used a *PeekMessage* loop. With the preemptive multitasking of Windows 95, programs can create multiple threads of execution, as we'll see in that later chapter.

Armed only with the *PeekMessage* function, however, we can write a program that relentlessly displays random rectangles. The program, RANDRECT, is shown in Figure 4-21.

RANDRECT.MAK

```
#------------------------
# RANDRECT.MAK make file
#------------------------

randrect.exe : randrect.obj
     $(LINKER) $(GUIFLAGS) -OUT:randrect.exe randrect.obj $(GUILIBS)

randrect.obj : randrect.c
     $(CC) $(CFLAGS) randrect.c
```

RANDRECT.C

```
/*------------------------------------------
   RANDRECT.C -- Displays Random Rectangles
                (c) Charles Petzold, 1996
   ------------------------------------------*/

#include <windows.h>
#include <stdlib.h>

LRESULT CALLBACK WndProc (HWND, UINT, WPARAM, LPARAM) ;
void DrawRectangle (HWND) ;
```

Figure 4-21. *The RANDRECT program.*   *(continued)*

```
int cxClient, cyClient ;

int WINAPI WinMain (HINSTANCE hInstance, HINSTANCE hPrevInstance,
                    PSTR szCmdLine, int iCmdShow)
    {
    static char szAppName[] = "RandRect" ;
    HWND        hwnd ;
    MSG         msg ;
    WNDCLASSEX  wndclass ;

    wndclass.cbSize        = sizeof (wndclass) ;
    wndclass.style         = CS_HREDRAW | CS_VREDRAW ;
    wndclass.lpfnWndProc   = WndProc ;
    wndclass.cbClsExtra    = 0 ;
    wndclass.cbWndExtra    = 0 ;
    wndclass.hInstance     = hInstance ;
    wndclass.hIcon         = LoadIcon (NULL, IDI_APPLICATION) ;
    wndclass.hCursor       = LoadCursor (NULL, IDC_ARROW) ;
    wndclass.hbrBackground = (HBRUSH) GetStockObject (WHITE_BRUSH) ;
    wndclass.lpszMenuName  = NULL ;
    wndclass.lpszClassName = szAppName ;
    wndclass.hIconSm       = LoadIcon (NULL, IDI_APPLICATION) ;

    RegisterClassEx (&wndclass) ;

    hwnd = CreateWindow (szAppName, "Random Rectangles",
                         WS_OVERLAPPEDWINDOW,
                         CW_USEDEFAULT, CW_USEDEFAULT,
                         CW_USEDEFAULT, CW_USEDEFAULT,
                         NULL, NULL, hInstance, NULL) ;

    ShowWindow (hwnd, iCmdShow) ;
    UpdateWindow (hwnd) ;

    while (TRUE)
        {
        if (PeekMessage (&msg, NULL, 0, 0, PM_REMOVE))
            {
            if (msg.message == WM_QUIT)
                break ;

            TranslateMessage (&msg) ;
            DispatchMessage (&msg) ;
            }
```

(continued)

160

```
        else
            DrawRectangle (hwnd) ;
        }

     return msg.wParam ;
     }

LRESULT CALLBACK WndProc (HWND hwnd, UINT iMsg, WPARAM wParam,
                                        LPARAM lParam)
     {
     switch (iMsg)
         {
         case WM_SIZE :
             cxClient = LOWORD (lParam) ;
             cyClient = HIWORD (lParam) ;
             return 0 ;

         case WM_DESTROY :
             PostQuitMessage (0) ;
             return 0 ;
         }
     return DefWindowProc (hwnd, iMsg, wParam, lParam) ;
     }

void DrawRectangle (HWND hwnd)
     {
     HBRUSH hBrush ;
     HDC    hdc ;
     RECT   rect ;

     if (cxClient == 0 || cyClient == 0)
         return ;

     SetRect (&rect, rand () % cxClient, rand () % cyClient,
                     rand () % cxClient, rand () % cyClient) ;


     hBrush = CreateSolidBrush (RGB (rand () % 256, rand () % 256,
                                            rand () % 256)) ;
     hdc = GetDC (hwnd) ;

     FillRect (hdc, &rect, hBrush) ;

     ReleaseDC (hwnd, hdc) ;

     DeleteObject (hBrush) ;
     }
```

The program uses the *SetRect* and *FillRect* functions I discussed above, basing rectangle coordinates and solid brush colors on random values obtained from the C *rand* function. I'll show another version of this program using multiple threads of execution in Chapter 14.

Creating and Painting Regions

A region is a description of an area of the display that is a combination of rectangles, polygons, and ellipses. You can use regions for drawing or for clipping. You use a region for clipping (that is, restricting drawing to a specific part of your client area) by selecting the region into the device context. Like pens, brushes, and bitmaps, regions are GDI objects. You should delete any regions that you create by calling *DeleteObject*.

When you create a region, Windows returns a handle to the region of type HRGN. The simplest type of region describes a rectangle. You can create a rectangular region in one of two ways:

```
hRgn = CreateRectRgn (xLeft, yTop, xRight, yBottom) ;
```

or:

```
hRgn = CreateRectRgnIndirect (&rect) ;
```

You can also create elliptical regions using:

```
hRgn = CreateEllipticRgn (xLeft, yTop, xRight, yBottom) ;
```

or:

```
hRgn = CreateEllipticRgnIndirect (&rect) ;
```

The *CreateRoundRectRgn* creates a rectangular region with rounded corners.

Creating a polygonal region is similar to using the *Polygon* function:

```
hRgn = CreatePolygonRgn (&point, iCount, iPolyFillMode) ;
```

The *point* parameter is an array of structures of type POINT, *iCount* is the number of points, and *iPolyFillMode* is either ALTERNATE or WINDING. You can also create multiple polygonal regions using *CreatePolyPolygonRgn.*

So what, you say? What makes these regions so special? Here's the function that unleashes the power of regions:

```
iRgnType = CombineRgn (hDestRgn, hSrcRgn1, hSrcRgn2, iCombine) ;
```

This combines two source regions (*hSrcRgn1* and *hSrcRgn2*) and causes the destination region handle (*hDestRgn*) to refer to that combined region. All three region handles must be valid, but the region previously described by *hDestRgn* is destroyed. (When you use this function, you might want to make *hDestRgn* refer initially to a small rectangular region.)

The *iCombine* parameter describes how the *hSrcRgn1* and *hSrcRgn2* regions are to be combined:

iCombine Value	New Region
RGN_AND	Overlapping area of the two source regions
RGN_OR	All the two source regions
RGN_XOR	All the two source regions excluding the overlapping area
RGN_DIFF	All of *hSrcRgn1* not in *hSrcRgn2*
RGN_COPY	All of *hSrcRgn1*

The *iRgnType* value returned from *CombineRgn* is one of the following: NULLREGION, indicating an empty region; SIMPLEREGION, indicating a simple rectangle, ellipse, or polygon; COMPLEXREGION, indicating a combination of rectangles, ellipses, or polygons; and ERROR, meaning that an error has occurred.

Once you have a handle to a region, you can use it with four drawing functions:

```
FillRgn (hdc, hRgn, hBrush) ;
FrameRgn (hdc, hRgn, hBrush, xFrame, yFrame) ;
InvertRgn (hdc, hRgn) ;
PaintRgn (hdc, hRgn) ;
```

The *FillRgn*, *FrameRgn*, and *InvertRgn* functions are similar to the *FillRect*, *FrameRect*, and *InvertRect* functions. The *xFrame* and *yFrame* parameters to *FrameRgn* are the logical width and height of the frame to be painted around the region. The *PaintRgn* function fills in the region with the brush currently selected in the device context. All these functions assume the region is defined in logical coordinates.

When you're finished with a region, you can delete it using the same function that deletes other GDI objects:

```
DeleteObject (hRgn) ;
```

Clipping with Rectangles and Regions

Regions can also play a role in clipping. The *InvalidateRect* function invalidates a rectangular area of the display and generates a WM_PAINT message. For example, you can use the *InvalidateRect* function to erase the client area and generate a WM_PAINT message:

```
InvalidateRect (hwnd, NULL, TRUE) ;
```

You can obtain the coordinates of the invalid rectangle by calling *GetUpdateRect*, and you can validate a rectangle of the client area using the *ValidateRect* function. When you receive a WM_PAINT message, the coordinates of the invalid rectangle are available from the PAINTSTRUCT structure that is filled in by the *BeginPaint* function. This invalid rectangle also defines a "clipping region." You cannot paint outside the clipping region.

Windows has two functions similar to *InvalidateRect* and *ValidateRect* that work with regions rather than rectangles:

```
InvalidateRgn (hwnd, hRgn, bErase) ;
```

and:

```
ValidateRgn (hwnd, hRgn) ;
```

When you receive a WM_PAINT message as a result of an invalid region, the clipping region will be a region that is not necessarily rectangular.

You can create a clipping region of your own by selecting a region into the device context using either:

```
SelectObject (hdc, hRgn) ;
```

or:

```
SelectClipRgn (hdc, hRgn) ;
```

A clipping region is assumed to be in device coordinates.

GDI makes a copy of the clipping region, so you can delete the region object after you select it in the device context. Windows also includes several functions to manipulate this clipping region, such as *ExcludeClipRect* to exclude a rectangle from the clipping region, *IntersectClipRect* to create a new clipping region that is the intersection of the previous clipping region and a rectangle, and *OffsetClipRgn* to move a clipping region to another part of the client area.

The CLOVER Program

The CLOVER program forms a region out of four ellipses, selects this region into the device context, and then draws a series of lines emanating from the center of the window's client area. The lines appear only in the area defined by the region. The resulting display is shown in Figure 4-22.

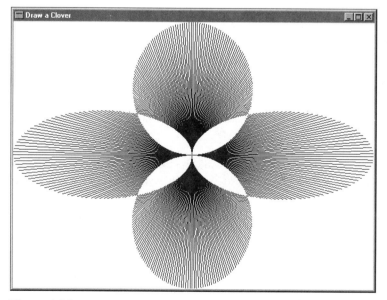

Figure 4-22. *The CLOVER display, drawn using a complex clipping region.*

To draw this graphic by conventional methods, you would have to calculate the end point of each line based on formulas involving the circumference of an ellipse. By using a complex clipping region, you can draw the lines and let Windows determine the end points. The CLOVER program is shown in Figure 4-23.

CLOVER.MAK

```
#----------------------
# CLOVER.MAK make file
#----------------------

clover.exe : clover.obj
     $(LINKER) $(GUIFLAGS) -OUT:clover.exe clover.obj $(GUILIBS)

clover.obj : clover.c
     $(CC) $(CFLAGS) clover.c
```

CLOVER.C

```
/*-------------------------------------------------
   CLOVER.C -- Clover Drawing Program using Regions
               (c) Charles Petzold, 1996
  -------------------------------------------------*/

#include <windows.h>
#include <math.h>

#define TWO_PI (2.0 * 3.14159)

LRESULT CALLBACK WndProc (HWND, UINT, WPARAM, LPARAM) ;

int WINAPI WinMain (HINSTANCE hInstance, HINSTANCE hPrevInstance,
                    PSTR szCmdLine, int iCmdShow)
     {
     static char szAppName[] = "Clover" ;
     HWND        hwnd ;
     MSG         msg ;
     WNDCLASSEX  wndclass ;

     wndclass.cbSize       = sizeof (wndclass) ;
     wndclass.style        = CS_HREDRAW | CS_VREDRAW ;
     wndclass.lpfnWndProc  = WndProc ;
     wndclass.cbClsExtra   = 0 ;
     wndclass.cbWndExtra   = 0 ;
     wndclass.hInstance    = hInstance ;
```

Figure 4-23. *The CLOVER program.* (continued)

```
wndclass.hIcon          = LoadIcon (NULL, IDI_APPLICATION) ;
wndclass.hCursor        = LoadCursor (NULL, IDC_ARROW) ;
wndclass.hbrBackground  = (HBRUSH) GetStockObject (WHITE_BRUSH) ;
wndclass.lpszMenuName   = NULL ;
wndclass.lpszClassName  = szAppName ;
wndclass.hIconSm        = LoadIcon (NULL, IDI_APPLICATION) ;

RegisterClassEx (&wndclass) ;

hwnd = CreateWindow (szAppName, "Draw a Clover",
                     WS_OVERLAPPEDWINDOW,
                     CW_USEDEFAULT, CW_USEDEFAULT,
                     CW_USEDEFAULT, CW_USEDEFAULT,
                     NULL, NULL, hInstance, NULL) ;

ShowWindow (hwnd, iCmdShow) ;
UpdateWindow (hwnd) ;

while (GetMessage (&msg, NULL, 0, 0))
     {
     TranslateMessage (&msg) ;
     DispatchMessage (&msg) ;
     }
return msg.wParam ;
}

LRESULT CALLBACK WndProc (HWND hwnd, UINT iMsg, WPARAM wParam,
                                               LPARAM lParam)
     {
     static HRGN hRgnClip ;
     static int  cxClient, cyClient ;
     double      fAngle, fRadius ;
     HCURSOR     hCursor ;
     HDC         hdc ;
     HRGN        hRgnTemp [6] ;
     int         i ;
     PAINTSTRUCT ps ;

     switch (iMsg)
          {
          case WM_SIZE :
               cxClient = LOWORD (lParam) ;
               cyClient = HIWORD (lParam) ;

               hCursor = SetCursor (LoadCursor (NULL, IDC_WAIT)) ;
               ShowCursor (TRUE) ;

               if (hRgnClip)
                    DeleteObject (hRgnClip) ;
```

(continued)

```
            hRgnTemp [0] = CreateEllipticRgn (0, cyClient / 3,
                              cxClient / 2, 2 * cyClient / 3) ;
            hRgnTemp [1] = CreateEllipticRgn (cxClient / 2, cyClient / 3,
                              cxClient, 2 * cyClient / 3) ;
            hRgnTemp [2] = CreateEllipticRgn (cxClient / 3, 0,
                              2 * cxClient / 3, cyClient / 2) ;
            hRgnTemp [3] = CreateEllipticRgn (cxClient / 3, cyClient / 2,
                              2 * cxClient / 3, cyClient) ;
            hRgnTemp [4] = CreateRectRgn (0, 0, 1, 1) ;
            hRgnTemp [5] = CreateRectRgn (0, 0, 1, 1) ;
            hRgnClip     = CreateRectRgn (0, 0, 1, 1) ;

            CombineRgn (hRgnTemp [4], hRgnTemp [0], hRgnTemp [1], RGN_OR) ;
            CombineRgn (hRgnTemp [5], hRgnTemp [2], hRgnTemp [3], RGN_OR) ;
            CombineRgn (hRgnClip,     hRgnTemp [4], hRgnTemp [5], RGN_XOR) ;

            for (i = 0 ; i < 6 ; i++)
                DeleteObject (hRgnTemp [i]) ;

            SetCursor (hCursor) ;
            ShowCursor (FALSE) ;
            return 0 ;

       case WM_PAINT :
            hdc = BeginPaint (hwnd, &ps) ;

            SetViewportOrgEx (hdc, cxClient / 2, cyClient / 2, NULL) ;
            SelectClipRgn (hdc, hRgnClip) ;

            fRadius = _hypot (cxClient / 2.0, cyClient / 2.0) ;

            for (fAngle = 0.0 ; fAngle < TWO_PI ; fAngle += TWO_PI / 360)
                 {
                 MoveToEx (hdc, 0, 0, NULL) ;
                 LineTo (hdc, (int) ( fRadius * cos (fAngle) + 0.5),
                              (int) (-fRadius * sin (fAngle) + 0.5)) ;
                 }
            EndPaint (hwnd, &ps) ;
            return 0 ;

       case WM_DESTROY :
            DeleteObject (hRgnClip) ;
            PostQuitMessage (0) ;
            return 0 ;
       }
  return DefWindowProc (hwnd, iMsg, wParam, lParam) ;
  }
```

Because regions always use device coordinates, the CLOVER program has to re-create the region every time it receives a WM_SIZE message. This may require several seconds. CLOVER begins by creating four elliptical regions that are stored as the first four elements of the *hRgnTemp* array. Then the program creates three "dummy" regions:

```
hRgnTemp [4] = CreateRectRgn (0, 0, 1, 1) ;
hRgnTemp [5] = CreateRectRgn (0, 0, 1, 1) ;
hRgnClip     = CreateRectRgn (0, 0, 1, 1) ;
```

The two elliptical regions at the left and right of the client area are combined:

```
CombineRgn (hRgnTemp [4], hRgnTemp [0], hRgnTemp [1], RGN_OR) ;
```

Similarly, the two elliptical regions at the top and bottom of the client area are combined:

```
CombineRgn (hRgnTemp [5], hRgnTemp [2], hRgnTemp [3], RGN_OR) ;
```

Finally, these two combined regions are in turn combined into *hRgnClip*:

```
CombineRgn (hRgnClip, hRgnTemp [4], hRgnTemp [5], RGN_XOR) ;
```

The RGN_XOR identifier is used to exclude overlapping areas from the resultant region. Finally, the six temporary regions are deleted:

```
for (i = 0 ; i < 6 ; i++)
    DeleteObject (hRgnTemp [i]) ;
```

The WM_PAINT processing is simple, considering the results. The viewport origin is set to the center of the client area (to make the line drawing easier), and the region created during the WM_SIZE message is selected as the device context's clipping region:

```
SetViewportOrg (hdc, xClient / 2, yClient / 2) ;
SelectClipRgn (hdc, hRgnClip) ;
```

Now all that's left is drawing the lines—360 of them, spaced 1 degree apart. The length of each line is the variable *fRadius*, which is the distance from the center to the corner of the client area:

```
fRadius = _hypot (xClient / 2.0, yClient / 2.0) ;

for (fAngle = 0.0 ; fAngle < TWO_PI ; fAngle += TWO_PI / 360)
    {
    MoveToEx (hdc, 0, 0, NULL) ;
    LineTo (hdc, (int) ( fRadius * cos (fAngle) + 0.5),
                 (int) (-fRadius * sin (fAngle) + 0.5)) ;
    }
```

During processing of WM_DESTROY, the region is deleted:

```
DeleteObject (hRgnClip) ;
```

PATHS

A path is a collection of straight lines and curves stored internally to GDI. Paths were introduced to Windows in Windows NT and are also supported under Windows 95. Paths and regions may seem very similar at first, and, indeed, you can convert a path to a region and use a path for clipping. However, we'll see shortly how they differ.

Creating and Rendering Paths

To begin a path definition, you simply call:

```
BeginPath (hdc) ;
```

After this call, any line you draw (straight lines, arcs, and Bezier splines) will be stored internally to GDI as a path and not rendered on the device context. Often a path consists of *connected* lines. To make connected lines, you use the *LineTo, PolylineTo,* and *BezierTo* functions, all of which draw lines beginning at the current position. If you change the current position using *MoveToEx,* or if you call any of the other line-drawing functions, or if you call one of the window/viewport functions that cause a change in the current position, you create a new subpath within the entire path. Thus, a path contains one or more subpaths, where each subpath is a series of connected lines.

Each subpath within the path can be open or closed. A closed subpath is one in which the first point of the first connected line is the same as the last point of the last connected line, and, moreover, the subpath is concluded by a call to *CloseFigure. CloseFigure* will close the subpath with a straight line if necessary. Any subsequent line-drawing function begins a new subpath. Finally, you end the path definition by calling:

```
EndPath (hdc) ;
```

At this point you then call one of the following five functions:

```
StrokePath (hdc) ;
FillPath (hdc) ;
StrokeAndFillPath (hdc) ;
hRgn = PathToRegion (hdc) ;
SelectClipPath (hdc, iCombine) ;
```

Each of these functions destroys the path definition after completion.

StrokePath draws the path using the current pen. You may wonder: What's the point? Why can't I just skip all this path stuff and draw the lines normally? I'll tell you why shortly.

The other four functions close any open paths with straight lines. *FillPath* fills the path using the current brush according to the current polygon filling mode. *StrokeAndFillPath* does both jobs in one shot. You can also convert the path to a region or use the path for a clipping area. The *iCombine* parameter is one of the RGN_ constants used with the *CombineRgn* function, and indicates how the path is combined with the current clipping region.

Paths are more flexible than regions for filling and clipping because regions can be defined only by combinations of rectangles, ellipses, and polygons. Paths can be composed of Bezier splines and (at least in Windows NT) arcs. In GDI, paths and regions are stored quite differently. A path is a collection of line and curve definitions, and a region (in the general sense) is a collection of scan lines.

Extended Pens

When you call *StrokePath*, the path is rendered using the current pen. Earlier in this chapter I discussed the *CreatePen* function that you use to create a pen object. With the introduction of paths, Windows NT and Windows 95 also support an extended pen function call *ExtCreatePen*. This function reveals why it's sometimes useful to create a path and stroke it rather than to draw lines without using a path. The *ExtCreatePen* function looks like this:

```
hPen = ExtCreatePen (iStyle, iWidth, &lBrush, 0, NULL) ;
```

You can use this function for normal line drawing, but in that case some of the features aren't supported by Windows 95. Even when used for rendering paths, some features are still not supported by Windows 95, which I've indicated above by setting the last two parameters to 0 and NULL.

For the first parameter to *ExtCreatePen* you can use any of the styles described earlier for *CreatePen*. You can additionally combine these styles with PS_GEOMETRIC (where the *iWidth* parameter denoting the width of the line is in logical units and is subject to transforms) or PS_COSMETIC (where the *iWidth* parameter must be 1). In Windows 95, pens with a dashed or dotted style must be PS_COSMETIC. (This restriction is lifted for Windows NT.)

One of the parameters to *CreatePen* is a color; rather than a color, *ExtCreatePen* uses a brush to color the interiors of PS_GEOMETRIC pens. That brush can even be defined by a bitmap.

When you're drawing wide lines, you might also be concerned about the appearance of the ends of the lines. When lines or curves are connected, you might also be concerned about the appearance of the joins between the lines. With pens created by *CreatePen*, these ends and joins are always rounded. With *ExtCreatePen*, you have a choice. (Actually, in Windows 95, you only have a choice when you use the pen to stroke a path; Windows NT is more flexible.) The ends of wide lines can be defined using one of the following pen styles in *ExtCreatePen*:

```
PS_ENDCAP_ROUND
PS_ENDCAP_SQUARE
PS_ENDCAP_FLAT
```

The "square" style is different from the "flat" style in that it extends the line for one-half the width. Similarly, joins between lines in a path can be specified by:

```
PS_JOIN_ROUND
PS_JOIN_BEVEL
PS_JOIN_MITER
```

The "bevel" style cuts off the end of the join, and the "miter" style turns it into a spike. This can be better illustrated with a program called ENDJOIN and shown in Figure 4-24.

ENDJOIN.MAK

```
#----------------------
# ENDJOIN.MAK make file
#----------------------

endjoin.exe : endjoin.obj
     $(LINKER) $(GUIFLAGS) -OUT:endjoin.exe endjoin.obj $(GUILIBS)

endjoin.obj : endjoin.c
     $(CC) $(CFLAGS) endjoin.c
```

ENDJOIN.C

```
/*-----------------------------------------
   ENDJOIN.C -- Ends and Joins Demo
               (c) Charles Petzold, 1996
   -----------------------------------------*/

#include <windows.h>

LRESULT CALLBACK WndProc (HWND, UINT, WPARAM, LPARAM) ;

int WINAPI WinMain (HINSTANCE hInstance, HINSTANCE hPrevInstance,
                    PSTR szCmdLine, int iCmdShow)
     {
     static char szAppName[] = "EndJoin" ;
     HWND        hwnd ;
     MSG         msg ;
     WNDCLASSEX  wndclass ;

     wndclass.cbSize        = sizeof (WNDCLASSEX) ;
     wndclass.style         = CS_HREDRAW | CS_VREDRAW ;
     wndclass.lpfnWndProc   = WndProc ;
     wndclass.cbClsExtra    = 0 ;
     wndclass.cbWndExtra    = 0 ;
     wndclass.hInstance     = hInstance ;
     wndclass.hIcon         = LoadIcon (NULL, IDI_APPLICATION) ;
     wndclass.hCursor       = LoadCursor (NULL, IDC_ARROW) ;
```

Figure 4-24. *The ENDJOIN program.* *(continued)*

```
    wndclass.hbrBackground = (HBRUSH) GetStockObject (WHITE_BRUSH) ;
    wndclass.lpszMenuName  = NULL ;
    wndclass.lpszClassName = szAppName ;
    wndclass.hIconSm       = LoadIcon (NULL, IDI_APPLICATION) ;

    RegisterClassEx (&wndclass) ;

    hwnd = CreateWindow (szAppName, "Ends and Joins Demo",
                         WS_OVERLAPPEDWINDOW,
                         CW_USEDEFAULT, CW_USEDEFAULT,
                         CW_USEDEFAULT, CW_USEDEFAULT,
                         NULL, NULL, hInstance, NULL) ;

    ShowWindow (hwnd, iCmdShow) ;
    UpdateWindow (hwnd) ;

    while (GetMessage (&msg, NULL, 0, 0))
        {
        TranslateMessage (&msg) ;
        DispatchMessage (&msg) ;
        }
    return msg.wParam ;
    }

LRESULT CALLBACK WndProc (HWND hwnd, UINT iMsg, WPARAM wParam,
                                               LPARAM lParam)
    {
    static int  iEnd  [] = { PS_ENDCAP_ROUND, PS_ENDCAP_SQUARE,
                             PS_ENDCAP_FLAT } ;
    static int  iJoin [] = { PS_JOIN_ROUND,   PS_JOIN_BEVEL,
                             PS_JOIN_MITER } ;
    static int  cxClient, cyClient ;
    HDC         hdc ;
    int         i ;
    LOGBRUSH    lb ;
    PAINTSTRUCT ps ;

    switch (iMsg)
        {
        case WM_SIZE :
             cxClient = LOWORD (lParam) ;
             cyClient = HIWORD (lParam) ;
             return 0 ;

        case WM_PAINT :
             hdc = BeginPaint (hwnd, &ps) ;
```

(continued)

```
                SetMapMode (hdc, MM_ANISOTROPIC) ;
                SetWindowExtEx (hdc, 100, 100, NULL) ;
                SetViewportExtEx (hdc, cxClient, cyClient, NULL) ;

                lb.lbStyle = BS_SOLID ;
                lb.lbColor = RGB (128, 128, 128) ;
                lb.lbHatch = 0 ;


                for (i = 0 ; i < 3 ; i++)
                     {
                     SelectObject (hdc,
                         ExtCreatePen (PS_SOLID | PS_GEOMETRIC |
                                      iEnd [i] | iJoin [i], 10,
                                      &lb, 0, NULL)) ;

                     BeginPath (hdc) ;

                     MoveToEx (hdc, 10 + 30 * i, 25, NULL) ;
                     LineTo   (hdc, 20 + 30 * i, 75) ;
                     LineTo   (hdc, 30 + 30 * i, 25) ;


                     EndPath (hdc) ;

                     StrokePath (hdc) ;

                     DeleteObject (
                         SelectObject (hdc,
                             GetStockObject (BLACK_PEN))) ;

                     MoveToEx (hdc, 10 + 30 * i, 25, NULL) ;
                     LineTo   (hdc, 20 + 30 * i, 75) ;
                     LineTo   (hdc, 30 + 30 * i, 25) ;
                     }


                EndPaint (hwnd, &ps) ;
                return 0 ;

                case WM_DESTROY :
                PostQuitMessage (0) ;
                return 0 ;
          }

     return DefWindowProc (hwnd, iMsg, wParam, lParam) ;
     }
```

The program draws three V-shaped wide lines using the end and join styles in the order listed above. The program also draws three identical lines using the stock black pen. This shows how the wide line compares with the normal thin line. The results are shown in Figure 4-25.

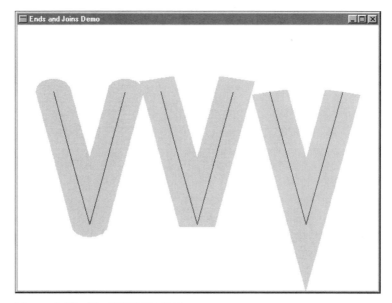

Figure 4-25. *The ENDJOIN display.*

I hope it's now apparent why Windows 95 supports a *StrokePath* function: If you were to draw the two lines individually, GDI would be forced to use the line ends on each of them. Only if they're in a path definition does GDI know that the lines are connected and then use a line join.

BITS AND BLTS

Bitmaps represent one of two methods for storing pictorial information in a Windows 95 program. A bitmap is a digital representation of an image. Each pixel in the image corresponds to one or more bits in the bitmap. Monochrome bitmaps require only 1 bit per pixel; color bitmaps require additional bits to indicate the color of each pixel. The other form of storing pictorial information is the metafile, which I'll cover later in this chapter. A metafile is a description of a picture rather than a digital representation of it.

Both bitmaps and metafiles have their place in computer graphics. Bitmaps are very often used for very complex images originating from the real world, such as digitized photographs or video captures. Metafiles are more suitable for human- or machine-generated images, such as architectural drawings. Both bitmaps and metafiles can exist in memory or be stored on a disk as files, and both can be transferred among Windows applications using the clipboard.

You can construct a bitmap "manually" using the Paint program included with Windows 95. You can then include the bitmap as a resource in a resource script file and load it into a program using the *LoadBitmap* function, as we'll see in Chapter 9. In Chapter 10, we'll see how bitmaps can substitute for text in a menu. Bitmaps can also be used to construct customized brushes.

Bitmaps have two major drawbacks. First, they are susceptible to problems involving device dependence. The most obvious device dependency is color. Displaying a color bitmap on a monochrome device is often unsatisfactory. Another problem is that a bitmap often implies a particular resolution and aspect ratio of an image. Although bitmaps can be stretched or compressed, this process generally involves duplicating or dropping rows or columns of pixels, and this can lead to distortion in the scaled image. A metafile can be scaled to almost any size without distortion.

The second major drawback of bitmaps is that they require a large amount of storage space. For instance, a bitmap representation of an entire 640-by-480-pixel, 16-color VGA screen requires over 150 KB. Metafiles usually require much less storage space than bitmaps. The storage space for a bitmap is governed by the size of the image and number of colors it contains, whereas the storage space for a metafile is governed by the complexity of the image and the number of individual GDI instructions it contains.

One advantage of bitmaps over metafiles, however, is speed. Copying a bitmap to a video display is usually much faster than rendering a metafile.

Color and Bitmaps

Each pixel in an image corresponds to one or more bits in a bitmap. A monochrome image requires 1 bit per pixel. A color image requires more than 1 bit per pixel. The number of different colors that can be represented by a bitmap is equal to 2 to the power of the number of bits per pixel. For example, a 16-color bitmap requires 4 bits per pixel, and a 256-color bitmap requires 8 bits per pixel. "Full-color" bitmaps require 24 bits per pixel, 8 each for red, green, and blue.

Prior to Windows 3.0, the only bitmaps supported under Windows were GDI objects, which were referenced using a bitmap handle. These bitmaps were either monochrome or had the same color organization as a real graphics output device, such as a video display. For example, a bitmap compatible with a 16-color VGA had four color planes. The problem was that these color bitmaps could not be saved and used on a graphics output device with a different color organization, for example, one having 8 bits per pixel and capable of rendering 256 colors.

Beginning in Windows 3.0, a new bitmap format was defined, called the device-independent bitmap, or DIB. The DIB included its own color table that showed how the pixel bits correspond to RGB colors. DIBs can be displayed on any raster output device. The only problem is that the colors of the DIB must be converted to the nearest colors that the device can actually render.

The Device-Independent Bitmap (DIB)

The DIB format is called "device independent" because it contains a color table. The color table describes how the pixel values correspond to RGB color values. This color table may not necessarily be compatible with a particular graphics output device. The DIB format is an extension of the bitmap format supported in the OS/2 1.1 Presentation Manager. The Windows header files contain some structures for working with OS/2 bitmaps.

With the introduction of the DIB, the GDI bitmap objects are sometimes called "device-dependent bitmaps" (DDBs). They are device dependent because they must be compatible with a specific graphics output device. The DIB is not a GDI object. GDI cannot store DIBs. Maintaining a DIB in a memory block is the responsibility of your program. Once GDI gets hold of a DIB, it turns it into a device-dependent bitmap, compatible with some real output device. DIBs are primarily for interchange among programs. They can be passed among programs either by storing them in files or copying them to the clipboard.

A DIB can be converted to a device-dependent GDI bitmap object; in such a case, the device-independent color information in the DIB is lost. A GDI bitmap object can also be used to construct a DIB, in which case the DIB will contain a color table compatible with the graphics output device with which the GDI bitmap object is compatible.

If you need to store bitmap information in a file or to read bitmap files or to pass bitmap information into and out of the clipboard in a device-independent format, you should use DIBs. However, if you only need to create or use monochrome bitmaps, or if you only need bitmaps within your own program that are compatible with the video display, then using device-dependent GDI bitmap objects is usually easier.

The DIB File

You can create a device-independent bitmap and save it on a disk file in the Microsoft Developer Studio or the Paint program included in the retail Windows 95 product. The files generally have the extension .BMP, although some DIBs can be found with the extension .DIB.

The DIB file begins with a file header section defined by the BITMAPFILEHEADER structure. This structure has five fields:

Field	Size	Description
bfType	WORD	The bytes "BM" (for bitmap)
bfSize	DWORD	Total size of the file
bfReserved1	WORD	Set to 0
bfReserved2	WORD	Set to 0
bfOffBits	DWORD	Offset to the bitmap bits from the beginning of the file

This is followed by another header defined by the BITMAPINFOHEADER structure. This structure has 11 fields:

Field	Size	Description
biSize	DWORD	Size of this structure in bytes
biWidth	LONG	Width of the bitmap in pixels
biHeight	LONG	Height of the bitmap in pixels
biPlanes	WORD	Set to 1
biBitCount	WORD	Color bits per pixel (1, 4, 8, or 24)
biCompression	DWORD	Compression scheme (0 for none)
biSizeImage	DWORD	Size of bitmap bits in bytes (only required if compression is used)
biXPelsPerMeter	LONG	Horizontal resolution in pixels per meter
biYPelsPerMeter	LONG	Vertical resolution in pixels per meter
biClrUsed	DWORD	Number of colors used in image
biClrImportant	DWORD	Number of important colors in image

All fields following the *biBitCount* field may be set to 0 for default values (or may not even appear in the file). Thus, the structure can be as small as 16 bytes in length. It can also contain additional fields beyond those shown here.

If *biClrUsed* is set to 0 and the number of color bits per pixel is 1, 4, or 8, the BITMAP-INFOHEADER structure is followed by a color table, which consists of two or more RGBQUAD structures. The RGBQUAD structure defines an RGB color value:

Field	Size	Description
rgbBlue	BYTE	Blue intensity
rgbGreen	BYTE	Green intensity
rgbRed	BYTE	Red intensity
rgbReserved	BYTE	Set to 0

The number of RGBQUAD structures is usually determined by the *biBitCount* field: 2 RGBQUAD structures are required for 1 color bit, 16 for 4 color bits, and 256 for 8 color bits. However, if the *biClrUsed* field is nonzero, then the *biClrUsed* field contains the number of RGBQUAD structures in the color table.

The color table is followed by the array of bits that define the bitmap image. This array begins with the bottom row of pixels. Each row begins with the leftmost pixels. Each pixel corresponds to 1, 4, 8, or 24 bits. For a monochrome bitmap with 1 color bit per pixel, the first pixel in each row is represented by the most significant bit of the first byte in each row. If this bit is 0, the color of the pixel can be obtained from the first RGBQUAD structure in the color table. If the bit is 1, the color is given by the second RGBQUAD structure in the color table.

For a 16-color bitmap with 4 color bits per pixel, the first pixel in each row is represented by the most significant four bits of the first byte in each row. The color of each pixel is obtained by using the 4-bit value as an index into the 16 entries in the color table.

For a 256-color bitmap, each byte corresponds to one pixel. The color of the pixel is obtained by using the 8-bit value as an index into the 256 entries in the color table.

If the bitmap image contains 24 color bits per pixel, each set of three bytes is an RGB value of the pixel. There is no color table unless the *biClrUsed* field in the BITMAPINFO-HEADER structure is nonzero.

In each case, each row of the bitmap data contains a multiple of 4 bytes. The row is padded to the right to ensure this.

The bitmap format supported in OS/2 1.1 and later is very similar. It begins with a BITMAPFILEHEADER structure but is followed by a 12-byte BITMAPCOREHEADER structure. (You can determine whether a bitmap file uses this format or the Windows format by examining the first field of this structure.) The color table consists of RGBTRIPLE structures rather than RGBQUAD structures.

Beginning with Windows 95, a third information header is defined, called BITMAP-V4HEADER. (Windows 95 is sometimes also known as Windows 4.0, hence the V4 or "version 4" indication.) This contains some additional information for correctly rendering colors on different devices.

The Packed-DIB Memory Format

If you encounter a DIB file that you'd like to read into a Windows program, you can read it directly into a block of allocated memory. This is known as the "packed-DIB memory format." It consists of everything in the DIB file except the BITMAPFILEHEADER structure. Thus the memory block begins with an information header structure, followed by a color table (if one is present), followed by the bitmap bits themselves. The packed-DIB memory format is used for copying DIBs to and from the clipboard.

You can also use the packed-DIB memory format to display the bitmap on the screen using the *SetDIBitsToDevice* or *StretchDIBits* function, to create a brush based on a DIB (*CreateDIBPatternBrush*) or to create a device-dependent GDI bitmap object from a DIB (*CreateDIBitmap*).

In any case, you must calculate the address within the global memory block where the bitmaps bits begin. You can do this by examining the information header structure and determining the size of the color table.

Displaying a DIB

Windows has two functions to display a DIB from a packed-DIB memory block. The most general is *StretchDIBits*, which allows the bitmap to be stretched or compressed and which can use various raster operations discussed later in this chapter. The *SetDIBitsToDevice* function is somewhat simpler; it displays the bitmap without stretching or compressing, and it cannot use any raster operations.

Both functions require a pointer to a BITMAPINFOHEADER structure—the beginning of the DIB memory block—and a pointer to the bitmap bits. The *StretchDIBits* function is particularly versatile—allowing you to display any rectangle within the bitmap at a specified logical width and height on the display.

Converting DIBs to Bitmap Objects

If you have a 16-color or 256-color video display and display a full-color bitmap with 24 bits per pixel, you'll notice that the bitmap requires some time to be displayed. This is because the device driver must perform a nearest-color search for each of the pixels in the bitmap.

You can speed up the display process by converting the DIB to a device-dependent GDI bitmap object using the *CreateDIBitmap* function. The nearest-color search would have to be performed only once, and then the bitmap object would be in the same format as the video display.

Contrary to the name of this function, *CreateDIBitmap* does not create a DIB. It creates a device-dependent GDI bitmap object from a DIB specification, and it returns a handle to the object. This GDI bitmap object is compatible with the graphics output device whose handle is passed as the first parameter. As when displaying a DIB, GDI must convert the device-independent colors to the colors of the device.

Following this call, you can display the bitmap by selecting the bitmap handle into a memory device context and using *BitBlt*, as shown later in this chapter.

You can also use the *CreateDIBitmap* to create an uninitialized GDI bitmap object:

```
hBitmap = CreateDIBitmap (hdc, &bmih, 0, NULL, NULL, 0) ;
```

Two functions are available to set and obtain the bits of the bitmap. The first function sets the bits:

```
SetDIBits (hdc, hBitmap, iStart, iNum, pBits, &bmi, iUsage) ;
```

The last three parameters are the same as those in the *CreateDIBitmap* function. The *iStart* parameter indicates the beginning scan line addressed by *pBits*. This can range from 0 (for the bottom scan line) to the height of the bitmap in pixels minus 1 (for the top scan line). The *iNum* parameter indicates the number of scan lines to set into the bitmap.

The *GetDIBits* function has identical parameters:

```
GetDIBits (hdc, hBitmap, iStart, iNum, pBits, &bmi, iUsage) ;
```

But in this case, *pBits* points to a buffer to receive the bitmap bits. The function sets the fields of the BITMAPINFO structure to indicate the dimensions of the bitmap and the color table.

THE GDI BITMAP OBJECT

The old bitmap format that originated in Windows 1 is very limited and highly dependent on the output device for which the bitmap is created. You should use the DIB format rather than the old bitmap format for storing bitmap files on disk. However, when you need a bitmap solely for use within a program, working with device-dependent bitmaps is much easier and gives better performance.

Creating Bitmaps in a Program

Windows includes five functions that let you create a device-dependent GDI bitmap object in your program. The first is the *CreateDIBitmap* function discussed above. The others are:

```
hBitmap = CreateBitmap (cxWidth, cyHeight, iPlanes, iBitsPixel, pBits) ;
hBitmap = CreateBitmapIndirect (&bitmap) ;
hBitmap = CreateCompatibleBitmap (hdc, cxWidth, cyHeight) ;
hBitmap = CreateDiscardableBitmap (hdc, cxWidth, cyHeight) ;
```

In all cases, the *cxWidth* and *cyHeight* parameters are the width and the height of the bitmap in pixels. In *CreateBitmap*, the *iPlanes* and *iBitsPixel* parameters are the number of color planes and the number of color bits per pixel in the bitmap. At least one of these parameters should be set to 1. If both parameters are 1, the function creates a monochrome bitmap. (I'll discuss how the color planes and color bits represent color shortly.)

In the *CreateBitmap* function, *pBits* can be set to NULL if you are creating an uninitialized bitmap. The resultant bitmap contains random data. In the *CreateCompatibleBitmap* and *CreateDiscardableBitmap* functions, Windows uses the device context referenced by *hdc* to obtain the number of color planes and the number of color bits per pixel. The bitmap created by these functions is uninitialized.

CreateBitmapIndirect is similar to *CreateBitmap* except that it uses the bitmap structure of type BITMAP to define the bitmap. The following table shows the fields of this structure:

Field	Type	Description
bmType	LONG	Set to 0
bmWidth	LONG	Width of bitmap in pixels
bmHeight	LONG	Height of bitmap in scan lines
bmWidthBytes	LONG	Width of bitmap in bytes (must be even)
bmPlanes	WORD	Number of color planes
bmBitsPixel	WORD	Number of color bits per pixel
bmBits	LPVOID	Pointer to array of bits

The *bmWidthBytes* field must be an even number—the lowest even number of bytes required to store one scan line. The array of the bits referenced by *bmBits* must be organized based on the *bmWidthBytes* field. If *bm* is a structure variable of type BITMAP, you can calculate the *bmWidthBytes* field by using the following statement:

```
bm.bmWidthBytes = (bm.bmWidth * bm.bmBitsPixel + 15) / 16 * 2 ;
```

If Windows cannot create the bitmap (generally because not enough memory is available), it will return a NULL. You should check the return values from the bitmap creation functions, particularly if you're creating large bitmaps.

Once you create a bitmap, you cannot change the size, the number of color planes, or the number of color bits per pixel. You would have to create a new bitmap and transfer the bits from the original bitmap to this new bitmap. If you have a handle to a bitmap, you can get the size and color organization using:

```
GetObject (hBitmap, sizeof (BITMAP), (LPVOID) &bitmap) ;
```

This copies the information about the bitmap into a structure (called *bitmap* here) of type BITMAP. This function doesn't fill in the *bmBits* field. To get access to the actual bits of the bitmap, you must call:

```
GetBitmapBits (hBitmap, dwCount, pBits) ;
```

This copies *dwCount* bits into a character array referenced by the pointer *pBits*. To ensure that all the bits of the bitmap are copied into this array, you can calculate the *dwCount* parameter based on the fields of the bitmap structure:

```
dwCount = (DWORD) bitmap.bmWidthBytes * bitmap.bmHeight * bitmap.bmPlanes ;
```

You can also direct Windows to copy a character array containing the bitmap bits back into an existing bitmap using the function:

```
SetBitmapBits (hBitmap, dwCount, pBits) ;
```

Because bitmaps are GDI objects, you should delete any bitmap you create:

```
DeleteObject (hBitmap) ;
```

The Monochrome Bitmap Format

For a monochrome bitmap, the format of the bits is relatively simple and can almost be derived directly from the image you want to create. For instance, suppose you want to create a bitmap that looks like this:

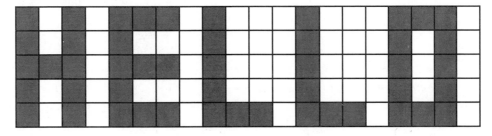

You can write down a series of bits (0 for black and 1 for white) that directly corresponds to this grid. Reading these bits from left to right, you can then assign each group of 8 bits a hexadecimal byte. If the width of the bitmap is not a multiple of 16, pad the bytes to the right with zeros to get an even number of bytes:

```
0 1 0 1 0 0 0 1 0 1 1 1 0 1 1 1 0 0 0 1 = 51 77 10 00
0 1 0 1 0 1 1 1 0 1 1 1 0 1 1 1 0 1 0 1 = 57 77 50 00
0 0 0 1 0 0 1 1 0 1 1 1 0 1 1 1 0 1 0 1 = 13 77 50 00
0 1 0 1 0 1 1 1 0 1 1 1 0 1 1 1 0 1 0 1 = 57 77 50 00
0 1 0 1 0 0 0 1 0 0 0 1 0 0 0 1 0 0 0 1 = 51 11 10 00
```

The width in pixels is 20, the height in scan lines is 5, and the width in bytes is 4. You can set up a BITMAP structure for this bitmap with the following statement:

```
static BITMAP bitmap    = { 0, 20, 5, 4, 1, 1 } ;
```

and you can store the bits in a BYTE array:

```
static BYTE   byBits [] = { 0x51, 0x77, 0x10, 0x00,
                            0x57, 0x77, 0x50, 0x00,
                            0x13, 0x77, 0x50, 0x00,
                            0x57, 0x77, 0x50, 0x00,
                            0x51, 0x11, 0x10, 0x00 } ;
```

Creating the bitmap with *CreateBitmapIndirect* requires two statements:

```
bitmap.bmBits = (LPVOID) byBits ;
hBitmap = CreateBitmapIndirect (&bitmap) ;
```

Another approach is:

```
hBitmap = CreateBitmapIndirect (&bitmap) ;
SetBitmapBits (hBitmap, sizeof (byBits), byBits) ;
```

You can also create the bitmap in one statement:

```
hBitmap = CreateBitmap (20, 5, 1, 1, byBits) ;
```

The Color Bitmap Format

An old-style color bitmap is a little more complex and extremely device dependent. A color bitmap is organized to facilitate the transfer of the bits to a particular output device. Whether the bitmap is organized as a series of color planes or as multiple color bits per pixel depends on the device for which the bitmap is suitable.

Let's look first at a bitmap that has a *bmBitsPixel* value of 1 (which means that it has 1 color bit per pixel) but a *bmPlanes* value greater than 1. A color bitmap for a 16-color VGA is a good example. Windows uses the four color planes of the VGA to display 16 colors, so *bmPlanes* is 4. The array of bits begins with the top scan line. The color planes for each scan line are stored sequentially—the red plane first, the green plane, the blue plane, and the intensity plane. The bitmap then continues with the second scan line.

A bitmap can also represent color as a multiple number of bits per pixel. Suppose the video device can represent 256 colors using 8 color bits (1 byte) per pixel. For each scan line, the first byte represents the color for the leftmost pixel, the second byte represents the color for the next pixel, and so forth. The *bmWidthBytes* value in the BITMAP structure reflects the increased byte width of each scan line, but the *bmWidth* value is still the number of pixels per scan line.

Here's the catch: Nothing in the bitmap specifies how these multiple color planes or multiple color bits correspond to actual display colors. A particular color bitmap is suitable only for an output device with display memory organized like the bitmap. Thus, creating an initialized color bitmap using *CreateBitmap* or *CreateBitmapIndirect* is not recommended. You should use these functions only for creating initialized or uninitialized monochrome bitmaps.

To create a color bitmap, use *CreateCompatibleBitmap*, which ensures that the format is compatible with a real graphics output device. You get an image into a color bitmap by selecting it into a memory device context (described shortly) and then drawing on this device context or by using the *BitBlt* function.

To create a color bitmap that is not necessarily compatible with a real graphics output device, use DIBs.

The Memory Device Context

Two functions—*SetDIBitsToDevice* and *StretchDIBits*—allow you to render an array of bits on an output device. However, if you have a handle to a bitmap, there is no function to draw the bitmap on the display surface of a device context. You'll search in vain for a function that looks like this:

```
DrawBitmap (hdc, hBitmap, xStart, yStart) ; // No such function!!!
```

This function would copy a bitmap to the device context represented by *hdc* beginning at the logical point (*xStart, yStart*). We'll write our own *DrawBitmap* function later in this chapter. First, however, you need to become familiar with several concepts, starting with the memory device context.

A memory device context is a device context that has a "display surface" that exists only in memory. You can create a memory device context using the function:

```
hdcMem = CreateCompatibleDC (hdc) ;
```

The *hdc* handle is a handle to an existing valid device context. The function returns a handle to the memory device context. Upon creation of the memory device context, all the attributes are set to the normal default values. You can do almost anything you want with this memory device context. You can set the attributes to nondefault values, obtain the current settings of the attributes, and select pens, brushes, and regions into it. And yes, you can even draw on it. But it doesn't make much sense to do so just yet. Here's why.

When you first create a memory device context, it has a "display surface" that contains exactly 1 monochrome pixel. That is a very small display surface. (Don't rely on *GetDeviceCaps* to tell you this. The HORZSIZE, VERTSIZE, HORZRES, VERTRES, BITSPIXEL, and PLANES values for *hdcMem* will all be set to the values associated with the original *hdc*. If *GetDeviceCaps* really returned the correct values associated with the memory device context when it is first created, then the HORZRES, VERTRES, BITSPIXEL, and PLANES indexes would all return 1.) What you need to do is make the display surface of the memory device context larger. You do this by selecting a bitmap into the device context:

```
SelectObject (hdcMem, hBitmap) ;
```

Now the display surface of *hdcMem* has the same width, height, and color organization as the bitmap referenced by *hBitmap*. With the default window and viewport origins, the logical point (0, 0) of the memory device context corresponds to the upper left corner of the bitmap.

If the bitmap had some kind of picture on it, then that picture is now part of the memory device context's display surface. Any changes you make to that bitmap (for instance, by using *SetBitmapBits* to set a different array of bits to the bitmap) are reflected in this display surface. Anything you draw on the memory device context is actually drawn on the bitmap. In short, the bitmap is the display surface of the memory device context.

Earlier I discussed the various functions to create bitmaps. One of them is:

```
hBitmap = CreateCompatibleBitmap (hdc, xWidth, yHeight) ;
```

If *hdc* is the handle to the normal device context for a screen or a printer, then the number of color planes and number of bits per pixel of this bitmap are the same as for the device. However, if *hdc* is the handle to a memory device context (and no bitmap has yet been selected into the memory device context), then *CreateCompatibleBitmap* returns a monochrome bitmap that is *xWidth* pixels wide and *yHeight* pixels high.

A bitmap is a GDI object. Earlier in this chapter we saw how to use *SelectObject* to select a pen, brush, or region into a device context, and later on we'll see how to use this function to select a font into a device context. You can use *SelectObject* to select these four GDI objects into a memory device context also. However, you cannot select a bitmap into a normal device context, only into a memory device context.

When you've finished with the memory device context, you must delete it:

```
DeleteDC (hdcMem) ;
```

Well, you may say, this is all very nice, but we haven't yet solved the problem of getting the bitmap on the display. All we've done is select it into a memory device context. Now what? Now we have to learn how to "blt" (pronounced "blit") the bits from one device context to another.

The Mighty Blt

Computer graphics involves writing pixels to a display device. Earlier we looked at the more refined ways of doing this, but for power pixel manipulation, nothing in Windows comes close to *BitBlt* and its two cousins, *PatBlt* and *StretchBlt*. *BitBlt* (pronounced "bit blit") stands for "bit-block transfer." *BitBlt* is a pixel-mover, or (more vividly) a raster-blaster. The simple word "transfer" doesn't really do justice to *BitBlt*. It does more than a transfer—it actually does a logical combination of three sets of pixels using 1 of 256 different types of raster operations.

The *PatBlt* function

PatBlt ("pattern block transfer") is the simplest of the three "blt" functions. It's really quite different from *BitBlt* and *StretchBlt* in that it uses only one device context. But *PatBlt* is nonetheless a reasonable place to begin.

Earlier you encountered the device context attribute called the drawing mode. This attribute can be set to 1 of 16 binary raster operation (ROP2) codes. When you draw a line, the drawing mode determines the type of logical operation that Windows performs on the pixels of the pen and the pixels of the device context destination. *PatBlt* is similar to the drawing mode except that it alters a rectangular area of the device context destination rather than merely a line. It performs a logical operation involving the pixels in this rectangle and a "pattern." This "pattern" is nothing new—*pattern* is simply another name for a brush. For this pattern, *PatBlt* uses the brush currently selected in the device context.

The syntax of *PatBlt* is:

```
PatBlt (hdc, xDest, yDest, xWidth, yHeight, dwROP) ;
```

The *xDest*, *yDest*, *xWidth*, and *yHeight* parameters are in logical units. The logical point (*xDest*, *yDest*) specifies the upper left corner of a rectangle. The rectangle is *xWidth* units wide and *yHeight* units high. (See the following section, entitled "Blt Coordinates," for a more precise definition of these values.) This is the rectangular area that *PatBlt* alters. The logical operation that *PatBlt* performs on the brush and the destination device context is determined by the *dwROP* parameter, which is a doubleword (32-bit integer) ROP code—not one of the ROP2 codes used for the drawing mode.

Windows has 256 ROP codes. These define all possible logical combinations of a source display area, a destination display area, and a pattern (or brush). The device driver for the video display supports all 256 raster operations through the use of a "compiler" of sorts. This compiler uses the 32-bit ROP code to create a set of machine-language instructions that can carry out this logical operation on the pixels of the display; it then executes these instructions. The high word of the 32-bit ROP code is a number between 0 and 255. The low word is a number that assists the device driver "compiler" in constructing the machine code for the logical operation. Fifteen of the 256 ROP codes have names.

Because the *PatBlt* function uses only a destination device context and a pattern (and not a source device context), it can accept only a subset of these 256 ROP codes—that is, the 16 ROP codes that use only the destination device context and a pattern. The 16 raster operations supported by *PatBlt* are shown in the table below. You'll notice that this is similar to the table showing ROP2 codes on page 129.

Pattern (P):	1	1	0	0	Boolean	ROP	
Destination (D):	1	0	1	0	Operation	Code	Name
Result:	0	0	0	0	0	0x000042	BLACKNESS
	0	0	0	1	~(P¦D)	0x0500A9	
	0	0	1	0	~P & D	0x0A0329	
	0	0	1	1	~P	0x0F0001	
	0	1	0	0	P & ~D	0x500325	
	0	1	0	1	~D	0x550009	DSTINVERT
	0	1	1	0	P ∧ D	0x5A0049	PATINVERT
	0	1	1	1	~(P & D)	0x5F00E9	
	1	0	0	0	P & D	0xA000C9	
	1	0	0	1	~(P ∧ D)	0xA50065	
	1	0	1	0	D	0xAA0029	
	1	0	1	1	~P¦D	0xAF0229	
	1	1	0	0	P	0xF00021	PATCOPY
	1	1	0	1	P¦~D	0xF50225	
	1	1	1	0	P¦D	0xFA0089	
	1	1	1	1	1	0xFF0062	WHITENESS

For a monochrome device context, a 1 bit corresponds to a white pixel and a 0 bit to a black pixel. Destinations and patterns that are either pure black or pure white are the easiest to consider when you start thinking about *PatBlt*. For instance, if you call:

```
PatBlt (hdc, xDest, yDest, xWidth, yHeight, 0x5F00E9L) ;
```

then the rectangular area that begins at the logical point (*xDest, yDest*) and that is *xWidth* pixels wide and *yHeight* pixels high will be colored black only if the destination was originally white and you had WHITE_BRUSH selected in the device context. Otherwise, the destination will be colored white. Of course, even in a monochrome device context, destinations and brushes can be dithered combinations of black and white pixels. In this case, Windows performs the logical combination on a pixel-by-pixel basis, which can lead to some odd results. For instance, if your destination has been colored with GRAY_BRUSH, and GRAY_BRUSH is also the current brush selected into the device context, then:

```
PatBlt (hdc, xDest, yDest, xWidth, yHeight, PATINVERT) ;
```

will set the destination to either pure white or pure black, depending on how the dithered pixels of the destination coincide with the dithered pixels of the brush.

Color introduces more complexities. Windows performs the logical operation for each color plane separately or each set of color bits separately, depending on how the memory of the device is organized.

Some of the more common uses of *PatBlt* are shown below. If you want to draw a black rectangle, you call:

```
PatBlt (hdc, xDest, yDest, xWidth, yHeight, BLACKNESS) ;
```

To draw a white rectangle, use:

```
PatBlt (hdc, xDest, yDest, xWidth, yHeight, WHITENESS) ;
```

The function:

```
PatBlt (hdc, xDest, yDest, xWidth, yHeight, DSTINVERT) ;
```

always inverts the colors of the rectangle. If WHITE_BRUSH is currently selected in the device context, then the function:

```
PatBlt (hdc, xDest, yDest, xWidth, yHeight, PATINVERT) ;
```

also inverts the rectangle.

You'll recall that the *FillRect* function fills in a rectangular area with a brush:

```
FillRect (hdc, &rect, hBrush) ;
```

The *FillRect* function is equivalent to the following code:

```
hBrush = SelectObject (hdc, hBrush) ;
PatBlt (hdc, rect.left, rect.top,
              rect.right - rect.left,
              rect.bottom - rect.top, PATCOPY) ;
SelectObject (hdc, hBrush) ;
```

In fact, this code is what Windows uses to execute the *FillRect* function. When you call:

```
InvertRect (hdc, &rect) ;
```

Windows translates it into the function:

```
PatBlt (hdc, rect.left, rect.top,
              rect.right - rect.left,
              rect.bottom - rect.top, DSTINVERT) ;
```

Blt coordinates

When I introduced the syntax of the *PatBlt* function, I said that the point (*xDest, yDest*) specifies the upper left corner of a rectangle and that this rectangle is *xWidth* units wide and *yHeight* units high. The statement is not entirely accurate. *BitBlt*, *PatBlt*, and *StretchBlt* are the only GDI drawing functions that specify logical rectangular coordinates in terms of a logical width and height measured from a single corner. All the other GDI drawing functions that use rectangular bounding boxes require that coordinates be specified in terms of an upper left corner and a lower right corner. For the MM_TEXT mapping mode, the above description of the *PatBlt* parameters is accurate. For the metric mapping modes, however, it's not. If you use positive values of *xWidth* and *yHeight*, then the point (*xDest*, *yDest*) will be the lower left corner of the rectangle. If you want (*xDest*, *yDest*) to be the upper left corner of the rectangle, the *yHeight* parameter must be set to the negative height of the rectangle.

To be more precise, the rectangle that *PatBlt* colors has a logical width given by the absolute value of *xWidth* and a logical height given by the absolute value of *yHeight*. These two parameters can be negative. The rectangle is defined by two corners given by the logical points (*xDest*, *yDest*) and (*xDest* + *xWidth*, *yDest* + *yHeight*). The upper left corner of the rectangle is always included in the area that *PatBlt* modifies. The lower right corner is outside the rectangle. Depending on the mapping mode and the signs of the *xWidth* and *yHeight* parameters, the upper left corner of this rectangle could be the point:

```
(xDest, yDest)
```

or:

```
(xDest, yDest + yHeight)
```

or:

```
(xDest + xWidth, yDest)
```

or:

```
(xDest + xWidth, yDest + yHeight)
```

If you've set the mapping mode to MM_LOENGLISH and you want to use *PatBlt* on the square inch at the upper left corner of the client area, you can use:

```
PatBlt (hdc, 0, 0, 100, -100, dwROP) ;
```

or:

```
PatBlt (hdc, 0, -100, 100, 100, dwROP) ;
```

or:

```
PatBlt (hdc, 100, 0, -100, -100, dwROP) ;
```

or:

```
PatBlt (hdc, 100, -100, -100, 100, dwROP) ;
```

The easiest way to set the correct parameters to *PatBlt* is to set *xDest* and *yDest* to the upper left corner of the rectangle. If your mapping mode defines *y*-coordinates as increasing as you move up the display, use a negative value for the *yHeight* parameter. If your mapping mode defines *x*-coordinates as increasing to the left (which is almost unheard of), use a negative value for the *xWidth* parameter.

Transferring Bits with *BitBlt*

In one sense, *BitBlt* is a superset of *PatBlt*. It does everything *PatBlt* does but also introduces a second device context into the logical operation. Here's the general syntax:

```
BitBlt (hdcDest, xDest, yDest, xWidth, yHeight,
        hdcSrc,  xSrc,  ySrc,  dwROP) ;
```

The *BitBlt* call modifies the destination device context (whose handle is *hdcDest*) within the rectangle defined by the logical point (*xDest, yDest*) and the *xWidth* and *yHeight* parameters, both of which are in logical units. These parameters define a rectangle as described in the previous section. *BitBlt* also uses a rectangle in a source device context (whose handle is *SrcDC*). This rectangle begins at the logical point (*xSrc, ySrc*) and is also *xWidth* logical units wide and *yHeight* logical units high.

BitBlt performs a logical combination of three elements: the brush selected into the destination device context, the pixels in the source device context rectangle, and the pixels in the destination device context rectangle. The result is written to the destination device context rectangle. You can use any of the 256 ROP codes for the *dwROP* parameter to *BitBlt*. The 15 ROP codes that have names are shown in the following table.

Pattern (P):	1	1	1	1	0	0	0	0	Boolean	ROP	
Source (S):	1	1	0	0	1	1	0	0	Operation	Code	Name
Destination (D):	1	0	1	0	1	0	1	0			
Result:	0	0	0	0	0	0	0	0	0	0x000042	BLACKNESS
	0	0	0	1	0	0	0	1	~ (S¦D)	0x1100A6	NOTSRCERASE
	0	0	1	1	0	0	1	1	~ S	0x330008	NOTSRCCOPY
	0	1	0	0	0	1	0	0	S & ~D	0x440328	SRCERASE
	0	1	0	1	0	1	0	1	~D	0x550009	DSTINVERT
	0	1	0	1	1	0	1	0	P ∧ D	0x5A0049	PATINVERT
	0	1	1	0	0	1	1	0	S ∧ D	0x660046	SRCINVERT
	1	0	0	0	1	0	0	0	S & D	0x8800C6	SRCAND
	1	0	1	1	1	0	1	1	~S¦D	0xBB0226	MERGEPAINT
	1	1	0	0	0	0	0	0	P & S	0xC000CA	MERGECOPY
	1	1	0	0	1	1	0	0	S	0xCC0020	SRCCOPY
	1	1	1	0	1	1	1	0	S¦D	0xEE0086	SRCPAINT
	1	1	1	1	0	0	0	0	P	0xF00021	PATCOPY
	1	1	1	1	1	0	1	1	P¦~S¦D	0xFB0A09	PATPAINT
	1	1	1	1	1	1	1	1	1	0xFF0062	WHITENESS

Look at the eight 0's and 1's that show the result of the logical combination. The two-digit hexadecimal number that corresponds to these bits is the high word of the ROP code. If we can create a table of the result we want from the pattern, source, and destination, we can easily determine the ROP code from the table of ROP codes in the Reference section of the Microsoft Developer Studio. We'll be doing this a little later. If you use 1 of the 16 ROP codes shown in the earlier table, then you can use *PatBlt* instead of *BitBlt*, because you're not referencing a source device context.

You can set *hdcSrc* and *hdcDest* to the same device context handle, in which case *BitBlt* will perform a logical combination of the destination rectangle, the source rectangle, and the current brush selected into the device context. However, it's a little risky to do this in your client-area device context. If part of the source rectangle is covered by another window, then Windows will use the pixels of this other window as the source. Windows doesn't know what's underneath that other window in your client area.

However, examples of the *BitBlt* function using the same device context for the source and destination are the easiest to grasp. The function:

```
BitBlt (hdc, 100, 0, 50, 100, hdc, 0, 0, SRCCOPY) ;
```

copies the rectangle beginning at logical point (0, 0) that is 50 logical units wide and 100 logical units high to the rectangular area beginning at the logical point (100, 0).

The *DrawBitmap* Function

BitBlt becomes most valuable in working with bitmaps that have been selected into a memory device context. When you perform a "bit-block transfer" from the memory device context to a device context for your client area, the bitmap selected in the memory device context is transferred to your client area.

Earlier I mentioned a hypothetical *DrawBitmap* function that would draw a bitmap on a display surface. Such a function would have the syntax:

```
DrawBitmap (hdc, hBitmap, xStart, yStart) ;
```

I promised we'd write a *DrawBitmap* function; here it is:

```
void DrawBitmap (HDC hdc, HBITMAP hBitmap, int xStart, int yStart)
     {
     BITMAP     bm ;
     HDC        hdcMem ;
     DWORD      dwSize ;
     POINT      ptSize, ptOrg ;

     hdcMem = CreateCompatibleDC (hdc) ;
     SelectObject (hdcMem, hBitmap) ;
     SetMapMode (hdcMem, GetMapMode (hdc)) ;

     GetObject (hBitmap, sizeof (BITMAP), (LPVOID) &bm) ;
```

```
        ptSize.x = bm.bmWidth ;
        ptSize.y = bm.bmHeight ;
        DPtoLP (hdc, &ptSize, 1) ;

        ptOrg.x = 0 ;
        ptOrg.y = 0 ;
        DPtoLP (hdcMem, &ptOrg, 1) ;

        BitBlt (hdc, xStart, yStart, ptSize.x, ptSize.y,
                hdcMem, ptOrg.x, ptOrg.y, SRCCOPY) ;

        DeleteDC (hdcMem) ;
        }
```

I'm assuming here that you don't want the height or width of the bitmap stretched or compressed in any way. That is, if your bitmap is 100 pixels wide, you want it to cover a 100-pixel-wide rectangle of your client area regardless of the mapping mode.

DrawBitmap first creates a memory device context using *CreateCompatibleDC* and then selects the bitmap into it with *SelectObject*. The mapping mode of the memory device context is set to the same mapping mode as the video device context. Because *BitBlt* works with logical coordinates and logical sizes and you don't want the bitmap stretched or compressed, the *xWidth* and *yHeight* parameters to *BitBlt* must be logical units that correspond to the physical pixel size of the bitmap. For this reason, *DrawBitmap* gets the dimensions of the bitmap using *GetObject* and makes a POINT structure out of the width and height. It then converts this point to logical coordinates. This is done similarly for the origin of the bitmap—the point (0, 0) in device coordinates.

Notice that it doesn't matter which brush is currently selected into the destination device context (*hdc*), because SRCCOPY doesn't use the brush.

Using Different ROP Codes

SRCCOPY is definitely the most popular *dwROP* parameter to *BitBlt*, and you may be hard-pressed to find uses for the other 255 ROP codes. So I'll give you a couple of examples in which other ROP codes show their stuff.

In the first example, you have a monochrome bitmap that you want to transfer to the screen. However, you want to display the bitmap so that the black (0) bits don't affect anything currently on the client area. Moreover, you want all the white (1) bits to color the client area with a brush, perhaps a colored brush created from *CreateSolidBrush*. How do you do it?

I'll assume that you're working in the MM_TEXT mapping mode and that you want to write the bitmap starting at the point (*xStart, yStart*) in your client area. You already have a handle to the monochrome bitmap (*hBitmap*) and a handle to the colored brush (*hBrush*). You know the width and height of the bitmap and have them stored in a BITMAP structure named *bm*. Here's the code:

```
hdcMem = CreateCompatibleDC (hdc) ;
SelectObject (hdcMem, hBitmap) ;
hBrush = SelectObject (hdc, hBrush) ;

BitBlt (hdc, xStart, yStart, bm.bmWidth, bm.bmHeight,
        hdcMem, 0, 0, 0xE20746L) ;

SelectObject (hdc, hBrush) ;
DeleteDC (hdcMem) ;
```

BitBlt performs a logical combination of a destination device context (*hdc*), a source device context (*hdcMem*), and the brush currently selected in the destination device context. So you create a memory device context, select the bitmap into it, select the colored brush into your client-area display context, and call *BitBlt*. Then you select the original brush into your display device context and delete the memory device context.

The only puzzling part of this code is the ROP code 0xE20746. This ROP code causes Windows to perform the logical operation:

```
((Destination ^ Pattern) & Source) ^ Destination
```

Still not obvious? Try this approach:

Pattern:	1	1	1	1	0	0	0	0
Source:	1	1	0	0	1	1	0	0
Destination:	1	0	1	0	1	0	1	0
Result:	?	?	?	?	?	?	?	?

For every black bit in the bitmap (which will be selected into the source memory device context), you want the destination device context to be unchanged. This means that everywhere the Source is 0, you want the Result to be the same bit as the Destination:

Pattern:	1	1	1	1	0	0	0	0
Source:	1	1	0	0	1	1	0	0
Destination:	1	0	1	0	1	0	1	0
Result:	?	?	1	0	?	?	1	0

We're halfway there. For every white bit in the bitmap, you want the destination device context to be colored with the pattern. The brush you select into the destination device context is this pattern. So everywhere the Source is 1, you want the Result to be the Pattern:

Pattern:	1	1	1	1	0	0	0	0
Source:	1	1	0	0	1	1	0	0
Destination:	1	0	1	0	1	0	1	0
Result:	1	1	1	0	0	0	1	0

This means that the high word of the ROP code is 0xE2. You can look that up in the ROP table in the Microsoft Developer Studio and find that the full ROP code is 0xE20746.

Perhaps at this point you discover that you mixed up the white and black bits when first you created the bitmap. That's easy to fix. It's merely a different logical operation:

Pattern:	1	1	1	1	0	0	0	0
Source:	1	1	0	0	1	1	0	0
Destination:	1	0	1	0	1	0	1	0
Result:	1	0	1	1	1	0	0	0

Now the high word of the ROP code is 0xB8, and the entire ROP code is 0xB8074A, which performs the logical operation:

```
((Destination ^ Pattern) & Source) ^ Pattern
```

Here's the second example: When we get to the subject of icons and cursors, you'll find that they are made up of two bitmaps. The use of two bitmaps allows these figures to be "transparent" in spots or to invert the display surface underneath. For a monochrome icon or cursor, the two bitmaps are coded as follows:

Bitmap 1:	0	0	1	1
Bitmap 2:	0	1	0	1
Result:	Black	White	Screen	Inverse Screen

Windows selects Bitmap 1 into a memory device context and uses *BitBlt* with a ROP code called SRCAND to transfer the bitmap to the display. This ROP code performs the logical operation:

```
Destination & Source
```

In Bitmap 1, the destination is left unchanged for 1 bits and set to 0 for 0 bits. Windows then selects Bitmap 2 into the device context and uses *BitBlt* with SRCINVERT. The logical operation is:

```
Destination ^ Source
```

In Bitmap 2, this leaves the destination unchanged for all 0 bits and inverts the destination for all 1 bits.

Look at the first and second columns of the table: Bitmap 1 with SRCAND blacks out the bits, and Bitmap 2 with SRCINVERT turns selected bits to white by inverting the black bits. These operations set the black and white bits that make up the icon or cursor. Now look at the third and fourth columns of the table: Bitmap 1 with SRCAND leaves the display unchanged, and Bitmap 2 with SRCINVERT inverts the colors of selected bits. These operations let the icon or cursor be transparent or invert the underlying colors.

Another example of the creative use of ROP codes accompanies the description of the *GrayString* function later in this chapter.

More Fun with Memory Device Contexts

We've been using memory device contexts to transfer an existing bitmap to the display. You can also use memory device contexts to draw on the surface of a bitmap. We'll do this in the GRAFMENU program in Chapter 10. First, you create a memory device context:

```
hdcMem = CreateCompatibleDC (hdc) ;
```

Next, you create a bitmap of the desired size. If you want to create a monochrome bitmap, you can make it compatible with *hdcMem*:

```
hBitmap = CreateCompatibleBitmap (hdcMem, xWidth, yHeight) ;
```

Or to make the bitmap have the same color organization as the video display, you can make the bitmap compatible with *hdc*:

```
hBitmap = CreateCompatibleBitmap (hdc, xWidth, yHeight) ;
```

You can now select the bitmap into the memory device context:

```
SelectObject (hdcMem, hBitmap) ;
```

Now you can draw on this memory device context (and by extension, the bitmap) using all the GDI functions discussed in this chapter. When you first create the bitmap, it contains random bits, so you may want to begin by using the *PatBlt* function with a ROP code of WHITENESS or BLACKNESS to erase the background of the memory device context.

When you've finished drawing on the memory device context, simply delete it:

```
DeleteDC (hdcMem) ;
```

Now you're left with a bitmap containing everything you drew on it while it was selected in the memory device context.

The SCRAMBLE program, shown in Figure 4-26, is very rude, and I probably shouldn't even be showing it to you. But it uses a memory device context as a temporary holding space for *BitBlt* operations that swap the contents of two rectangles of the display.

SCRAMBLE.MAK

```
#-----------------------
# SCRAMBLE.MAK make file
#-----------------------

scramble.exe : scramble.obj
     $(LINKER) $(GUIFLAGS) -OUT:scramble.EXE scramble.obj $(GUILIBS)

scramble.obj : scramble.c
     $(CC) $(CFLAGS) scramble.c
```

Figure 4-26. *The SCRAMBLE program.*

(continued)

SCRAMBLE.C

```
/*-------------------------------------------------
   SCRAMBLE.C -- Scramble (and Unscramble) Screen
                 (c) Charles Petzold, 1996
   -------------------------------------------------*/

#include <windows.h>
#include <stdlib.h>

#define NUM 200

LRESULT CALLBACK WndProc (HWND, UINT, WPARAM, LPARAM) ;

int WINAPI WinMain (HINSTANCE hInstance, HINSTANCE hPrevInstance,
                    PSTR szCmdLine, int iCmdShow)
     {
     static int iKeep [NUM][4] ;
     HDC        hdc, hdcMem ;
     int        cx, cy ;
     HBITMAP    hBitmap ;
     int        i, j, x1, y1, x2, y2 ;

     if (LockWindowUpdate (GetDesktopWindow ()))
         {
         hdc     = CreateDC ("DISPLAY", NULL, NULL, NULL) ;
         hdcMem  = CreateCompatibleDC (hdc) ;
         cx  = GetSystemMetrics (SM_CXSCREEN) / 10 ;
         cy  = GetSystemMetrics (SM_CYSCREEN) / 10 ;
         hBitmap = CreateCompatibleBitmap (hdc, cx, cy) ;

         SelectObject (hdcMem, hBitmap) ;

         srand ((int) GetCurrentTime ()) ;

         for (i = 0 ; i < 2 ; i++)
             for (j = 0 ; j < NUM ; j++)
                 {
                 if (i == 0)
                     {
                     iKeep [j] [0] = x1 = cx * (rand () % 10) ;
                     iKeep [j] [1] = y1 = cy * (rand () % 10) ;
                     iKeep [j] [2] = x2 = cx * (rand () % 10) ;
                     iKeep [j] [3] = y2 = cy * (rand () % 10) ;
                     }
```

(continued)

```
                     else
                         {
                         x1 = iKeep [NUM - 1 - j] [0] ;
                         y1 = iKeep [NUM - 1 - j] [1] ;
                         x2 = iKeep [NUM - 1 - j] [2] ;
                         y2 = iKeep [NUM - 1 - j] [3] ;
                         }
                     BitBlt (hdcMem, 0, 0, cx, cy, hdc,  x1, y1, SRCCOPY) ;
                     BitBlt (hdc,   x1, y1, cx, cy, hdc,  x2, y2, SRCCOPY) ;
                     BitBlt (hdc,   x2, y2, cx, cy, hdcMem, 0, 0, SRCCOPY) ;

                     Sleep (10) ;
                     }

            DeleteDC (hdcMem) ;
            DeleteDC (hdc) ;
            DeleteObject (hBitmap) ;

            LockWindowUpdate (NULL) ;
            }

     return FALSE ;
     }
```

SCRAMBLE doesn't have a window procedure. In *WinMain*, it obtains a device context for the entire screen:

```
hdc = CreateDC ("DISPLAY", NULL, NULL, NULL) ;
```

and also a memory device context:

```
hdcMem = CreateCompatibleDC (hdc) ;
```

Then it determines the dimensions of the full screen and divides them by 10:

```
xSize = GetSystemMetrics (SM_CXSCREEN) / 10 ;
ySize = GetSystemMetrics (SM_CYSCREEN) / 10 ;
```

The program uses these dimensions to create a bitmap:

```
hBitmap = CreateCompatibleBitmap (hdc, xSize, ySize) ;
```

and selects it into the memory device context:

```
SelectObject (hdcMem, hBitmap) ;
```

Using the C *rand* function, SCRAMBLE finds four random values that are multiples of the *xSize* and *ySize* values:

```
x1 = xSize * (rand () % 10) ;
y1 = ySize * (rand () % 10) ;
x2 = xSize * (rand () % 10) ;
y2 = ySize * (rand () % 10) ;
```

The program swaps two rectangular blocks of the display through the use of three *BitBlt* functions. The first copies the rectangle beginning at point (*x1, y1*) to the memory device context:

```
BitBlt (hdcMem, 0, 0, xSize, ySize, hdc, x1, y1, SRCCOPY) ;
```

The second copies the rectangle beginning at point (*x2, y2*) to the location beginning at point (*x1, y1*):

```
BitBlt (hdc, x1, y1, xSize, ySize, hdc, x2, y2, SRCCOPY) ;
```

The third copies the rectangle in the memory device context to the area beginning at point (*x2, y2*):

```
BitBlt (hdc, x2, y2, xSize, ySize, hdcMem, 0, 0, SRCCOPY) ;
```

This process effectively swaps the contents of the two rectangles on the display. SCRAMBLE does this 200 times, after which the screen should be thoroughly scrambled. But do not fear, because SCRAMBLE keeps track of this mess and then unscrambles the screen, returning it to normal before exiting.

You can also use memory device contexts to copy the contents of one bitmap to another. For instance, suppose you want to create a bitmap that contains only the upper left quadrant of another bitmap. If the original bitmap has the handle *hBitmap*, you can copy the dimensions into a structure of type BITMAP:

```
GetObject (hBitmap, sizeof (BITMAP), (LPVOID) &bm) ;
```

and create a new uninitialized bitmap of one-quarter the size:

```
hBitmap2 = CreateBitmap (bm.bmWidth / 2, bm.bmHeight / 2,
                         bm.bmPlanes, bm.bmBitsPixel, NULL) ;
```

Now create two memory device contexts and select the original bitmap and the new bitmap into them:

```
hdcMem1 = CreateCompatibleDC (hdc) ;
hdcMem2 = CreateCompatibleDC (hdc) ;

SelectObject (hdcMem1, hBitmap) ;
SelectObject (hdcMem2, hBitmap2) ;
```

Finally, copy the upper left quadrant of the first bitmap to the second:

```
BitBlt (hdcMem2, 0, 0, bm.bmWidth / 2, bm.bmHeight / 2,
        hdcMem1, 0, 0, SRCCOPY) ;
```

You're done, except for cleaning up:

```
DeleteDC (hdcMem1) ;
DeleteDC (hdcMem2) ;
DeleteObject (hBitmap) ;
```

Color Conversions

If the destination and source device contexts in the *BitBlt* call have different color characteristics, Windows must convert the bitmap from one color format to another. The best color
conversion occurs when the source bitmap is monochrome. Windows uses the text color
and background color attributes in the destination device context for this conversion:

Monochrome DC *(Source)*	*Color DC* *(Destination)*
0 (Black)	Text color (default is black)
1 (White)	Background color (default is white)

The background color attribute is also the color Windows uses to fill in the gaps in
dotted and dashed lines and between the hatches in hatched brushes. You can change the
background color with *SetBkColor*. The text color, which we'll encounter later in this chapter, determines the color of text. You can change this with *SetTextColor*. With default settings, the monochrome bitmap simply turns into a black-and-white bitmap on the color
device context.

Translating a bitmap in a color source device context to a monochrome destination
device context is less satisfactory:

Color DC *(Source)*	*Monochrome DC* *(Destination)*
Pixel != Background color	0 (Black)
Pixel == Background color	1 (White)

In this case, Windows uses the background color of the source device context to determine what color is translated to white. Every other color is translated to black.

Here's another color-related problem: Windows needs to equate a particular combination of color bits in the bitmap (either in different planes or in the same plane) to the
24-bit color value of the background color. This means that the color device context must
refer to a real device or be a memory device context based on a real device. For instance,
suppose you have a monochrome device driver. You create a memory device context based
on the screen device context and select a color bitmap into that memory device context.
You now try to transfer that bitmap to a monochrome device context. It won't work, because Windows doesn't know how the multiple planes or multiple bits per pixel in the
memory device context bitmap relate to real colors.

Mapping Mode Conversions

The *BitBlt* call requires different starting coordinates for the source and destination device contexts, but it needs only one width and one height:

```
BitBlt (hdcDest, xDest, yDest, xWidth, yHeight,
        hdcSrc, xSrc, ySrc, dwROP) ;
```

The *xWidth* and *yHeight* values are in logical units, and they apply to both the rectangle in the source device context and the rectangle in the destination device context. *BitBlt* must convert all coordinates and sizes to device coordinates before calling on the driver file to perform the actual operation. Because the *xWidth* and *yHeight* values are used for both the source and destination device contexts, the values must be converted to device units (pixels) separately for each device context.

When the source and destination device contexts are the same, or when both device contexts use the MM_TEXT mapping mode, then the size of this rectangle in device units will be the same in both device contexts. Windows can then do a simple pixel-to-pixel transfer. However, when the size of the rectangle in device units is different in the two device contexts, Windows turns the job over to the more versatile *StretchBlt* function.

Stretching Bitmaps with *StretchBlt*

StretchBlt adds two parameters to the *BitBlt* call:

```
StretchBlt (hdcDest, xDest, yDest, xDestWidth, yDestHeight,
            hdcSrc, xSrc, ySrc, xSrcWidth, ySrcHeight, dwROP) ;
```

Because *StretchBlt* accepts different width and height parameters for the source and destination rectangles, it allows you to stretch or compress a bitmap in the source device context to fit a larger or smaller area in the destination device context.

Just as *BitBlt* provides a superset of *PatBlt*'s functionality, *StretchBlt* expands on *BitBlt* by allowing you to specify the sizes of the source and destination rectangles separately. As with *PatBlt* and *BitBlt*, all coordinates and values in *StretchBlt* are in logical units. *StretchBlt* also allows you to flip an image vertically or horizontally. If the signs of *xSrcWidth* and *xDestWidth* (when converted to device units) are different, then *StretchBlt* creates a mirror image: Left becomes right, and right becomes left. If *ySrcHeight* and *yDestHeight* are different, then *StretchBlt* turns the image upside down.

StretchBlt can be slow, particularly when it works with a large bitmap. *StretchBlt* also has some problems related to the inherent difficulties of scaling bitmaps. When expanding a bitmap, *StretchBlt* must duplicate rows or columns of pixels. If the expansion is not an integral multiple, then the process can result in some distortion of the image.

When shrinking a bitmap, *StretchBlt* must combine two or more rows or columns of pixels into a single row or column. It does this in one of three ways, depending on the stretching mode attribute in the device context. You can use the *SetStretchBltMode* function to change this attribute:

```
SetStretchBltMode (hdc, iMode) ;
```

The value of *iMode* can be one of the following:

- BLACKONWHITE (default)—If two or more pixels have to be combined into one pixel, *StretchBlt* performs a logical AND operation on the pixels. The resulting pixel is white only if all the original pixels are white, which in practice means that black pixels predominate over white pixels.

- WHITEONBLACK—If two or more pixels have to be combined into one pixel, *StretchBlt* performs a logical OR operation. The resulting pixel is black only if all the original pixels are black, which means that white pixels predominate.

- COLORONCOLOR—*StretchBlt* simply eliminates rows or columns of pixels without doing any logical combination. This is often the best approach for color bitmaps, because the other two modes can cause color distortions.

Brushes and Bitmaps

When you use the *CreatePatternBrush* or *CreateBrushIndirect* function with the *lbStyle* field set to BS_PATTERN, you first need a handle to a bitmap. The bitmap must be at least 8 pixels wide and 8 pixels high. If it's larger, Windows uses only the upper left corner of the bitmap for the brush.

Because brushes and bitmaps are GDI objects, you must delete any that you create in your program before the program terminates. When you create a brush based on a bitmap, Windows makes a copy of the bitmap bits for use when drawing with the brush. You can delete the bitmap immediately after calling *CreatePatternBrush* (or *CreateBrushIndirect*) without affecting the brush. Similarly, you can delete the brush without affecting the bitmap.

Let's say that you want to draw a rectangle filled in with a brush that looks like little bricks, as shown in Figure 4-27.

Figure 4-27. *A figure filled in with a customized brush.*

200

The bitmap you need has a pixel pattern that looks like this:

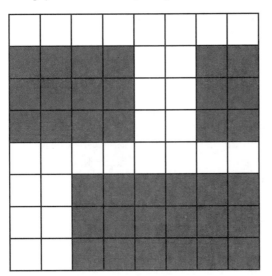

This is a monochrome bitmap with a height and width of 8.

As I'll demonstrate in Chapter 9, you can create this bitmap as a small file in the Microsoft Developer Studio and define it in your program as a resource. Loading it returns a handle to the bitmap:

```
hBitmap = LoadBitmap (hInstance, "Brick") ;
hBrush  = CreatePatternBrush (hBitmap) ;
```

When you have a valid device context, select the brush into the device context and display the rectangle:

```
SelectObject (hdc, hBrush) ;
Rectangle (hdc, xLeft, yTop, xRight, yBottom) ;
```

When you release the device context, delete the brush and bitmap:

```
DeleteObject (hBrush) ;
DeleteObject (hBitmap) ;
```

You don't have to wait until you release the device context to delete the bitmap—you can do so anytime after you create the brush based on the bitmap.

You could also define the bitmap pixels within your program as an array of eight unsigned integers. Each integer corresponds to a scan line in the bitmap pattern. A 1 bit is used for white and a 0 bit for black:

```
HBITMAP hBitmap ;
HBRUSH  hBrush ;
static  WORD wBrickBits [] =
     { 0xFF, 0x0C, 0x0C, 0x0C, 0xFF, 0xC0, 0xC0, 0xC0 } ;
```

The bitmap is created using *CreateBitmap* by referencing this array of integers:

```
hBitmap = CreateBitmap (8, 8, 1, 1, (LPVOID) wBrickBits) ;
hBrush = CreatePatternBrush (hBitmap) ;
```

You then continue as above.

METAFILES

Metafiles are to vector graphics as bitmaps are to raster graphics. Metafiles are constructed by humans or computer programs. The metafile consists of a series of records that correspond to graphics function calls, for example, to draw straight lines and curves, filled areas, and text. In essence, a metafile is a collection of graphics function calls encoded in binary form.

Paint programs create bitmaps; drawing programs create metafiles. In a drawing program, you can easily "grab" a particular graphical object (such as a line) and move it somewhere else. That's because all the individual components of the picture are stored as separate records. In a paint program, such feats are not possible—you're generally restricted to removing or inserting rectangular chunks of the bitmap.

Because the metafile describes an image in terms of graphical drawing commands, the image can be scaled without loss of resolution. Bitmaps don't work that way. If you display a bitmap at twice the size, you don't get twice the resolution. The bits in the bitmap are just replicated horizontally and vertically.

A metafile can be converted to a bitmap, but with the loss of information. The graphical objects that make up the metafile are no longer separate and become blended together in one big image. Converting bitmaps to metafiles is a much more difficult job, usually restricted to very simple images and requiring a lot of processing power to analyze edges and outlines.

Metafiles are used most often for sharing pictures between programs through the clipboard, although they can also exist on disk as clip art. Because metafiles describe a picture as a collection of GDI calls, they take up much less space and are more device independent than bitmaps.

I'll first discuss the metafile functions supported since Windows 1.0 (and still supported under Windows 95), and then discuss the "enhanced metafile" developed for Windows NT and also supported under Windows 95. The enhanced metafiles have several improvements over the old metafile format and are much better suited for disk storage.

Simple Use of Memory Metafiles

You create a metafile by first creating a metafile device context by calling *CreateMetaFile*. You can then use most of the GDI drawing functions to draw on this metafile device context. These GDI calls don't really draw on anything, however. Instead, they are stored within the metafile. When you close the metafile device context, you get back a handle to the metafile. You can then "play" this metafile on a real device context and execute the GDI functions in the metafile.

CreateMetaFile takes a single parameter. This can be either NULL or a filename. If NULL, the metafile is stored in memory. If it's a filename (the extension .WMF—"Windows Metafile"—is customary), then the metafile is stored in a disk file.

The program METAFILE shown in Figure 4-28 shows how to create a memory metafile during the WM_CREATE message and display the image 100 times during the WM_PAINT message.

METAFILE.MAK

```
#------------------------
# METAFILE.MAK make file
#------------------------

metafile.exe : metafile.obj
     $(LINKER) $(GUIFLAGS) -OUT:metafile.exe metafile.obj $(GUILIBS)

metafile.obj : metafile.c
     $(CC) $(CFLAGS) metafile.c
```

METAFILE.C

```
/*-----------------------------------------------
   METAFILE.C -- Metafile Demonstration Program
                (c) Charles Petzold, 1996
   -----------------------------------------------*/

#include <windows.h>

LRESULT CALLBACK WndProc (HWND, UINT, WPARAM, LPARAM) ;

int WINAPI WinMain (HINSTANCE hInstance, HINSTANCE hPrevInstance,
                   PSTR szCmdLine, int iCmdShow)
     {
     static char szAppName [] = "Metafile" ;
     HWND        hwnd ;
     MSG         msg ;
     WNDCLASSEX  wndclass ;

     wndclass.cbSize         = sizeof (wndclass) ;
     wndclass.style          = CS_HREDRAW | CS_VREDRAW ;
```

Figure 4-28. *The METAFILE program.*

(continued)

```
        wndclass.lpfnWndProc   = WndProc ;
        wndclass.cbClsExtra    = 0 ;
        wndclass.cbWndExtra    = 0 ;
        wndclass.hInstance     = hInstance ;
        wndclass.hIcon         = LoadIcon (NULL, IDI_APPLICATION) ;
        wndclass.hCursor       = LoadCursor (NULL, IDC_ARROW) ;
        wndclass.hbrBackground = (HBRUSH) GetStockObject (WHITE_BRUSH) ;
        wndclass.lpszMenuName  = NULL ;
        wndclass.lpszClassName = szAppName ;
        wndclass.hIconSm       = LoadIcon (NULL, IDI_APPLICATION) ;

        RegisterClassEx (&wndclass) ;

        hwnd = CreateWindow (szAppName, "Metafile Demonstration",
                            WS_OVERLAPPEDWINDOW,
                            CW_USEDEFAULT, CW_USEDEFAULT,
                            CW_USEDEFAULT, CW_USEDEFAULT,
                            NULL, NULL, hInstance, NULL) ;

        ShowWindow (hwnd, iCmdShow) ;
        UpdateWindow (hwnd) ;

        while (GetMessage (&msg, NULL, 0, 0))
            {
            TranslateMessage (&msg) ;
            DispatchMessage (&msg) ;
            }
        return msg.wParam ;
        }

LRESULT CALLBACK WndProc (HWND hwnd, UINT iMsg, WPARAM wParam,
                                                LPARAM lParam)
    {
    static HMETAFILE hmf ;
    static int       cxClient, cyClient ;
    HBRUSH           hBrush ;
    HDC              hdc, hdcMeta ;
    int              x, y ;
    PAINTSTRUCT      ps ;

    switch (iMsg)
        {
        case WM_CREATE :
            hdcMeta = CreateMetaFile (NULL) ;
            hBrush  = CreateSolidBrush (RGB (0, 0, 255)) ;

            Rectangle (hdcMeta, 0, 0, 100, 100) ;
```

(continued)

```
            MoveToEx (hdcMeta,   0,   0, NULL) ;
            LineTo   (hdcMeta, 100, 100) ;
            MoveToEx (hdcMeta,   0, 100, NULL) ;
            LineTo   (hdcMeta, 100,   0) ;

            SelectObject (hdcMeta, hBrush) ;
            Ellipse (hdcMeta, 20, 20, 80, 80) ;

            hmf = CloseMetaFile (hdcMeta) ;

            DeleteObject (hBrush) ;
            return 0 ;

       case WM_SIZE :
            cxClient = LOWORD (lParam) ;
            cyClient = HIWORD (lParam) ;
            return 0 ;

       case WM_PAINT :
            hdc = BeginPaint (hwnd, &ps) ;

            SetMapMode (hdc, MM_ANISOTROPIC) ;
            SetWindowExtEx (hdc, 1000, 1000, NULL) ;
            SetViewportExtEx (hdc, cxClient, cyClient, NULL) ;

            for (x = 0 ; x < 10 ; x++)
                 for (y = 0 ; y < 10 ; y++)
                      {
                      SetWindowOrgEx (hdc, -100 * x, -100 * y, NULL) ;
                      PlayMetaFile (hdc, hmf) ;
                      }

            EndPaint (hwnd, &ps) ;
            return 0 ;

       case WM_DESTROY :
            DeleteMetaFile (hmf) ;
            PostQuitMessage (0) ;
            return 0 ;
       }
  return DefWindowProc (hwnd, iMsg, wParam, lParam) ;
  }
```

This program demonstrates the use of four metafile functions involved in using a memory metafile. The first is *CreateMetaFile*, which is called with a NULL parameter during processing of the WM_CREATE message. The function returns a handle to a metafile device context. METAFILE then draws a rectangle, two lines, and one blue ellipse using this metafile DC. These function calls are stored in a binary form in the metafile. The *CloseMetaFile* function returns a handle to the metafile. Notice that the metafile handle is stored in a static variable because it will be used later.

The metafile contains a binary representation of the GDI function calls—which are a *Rectangle* call, two *MoveToEx* calls, two *LineTo* calls, a *SelectObject* call (indicating the blue brush), and an *Ellipse* call. No mapping mode or transform is implied by the coordinates. They are simply stored as numbers in the metafile.

During the WM_PAINT message, METAFILE sets up a mapping mode and calls *PlayMetaFile* to draw the object 100 times in the window. The coordinates of the function calls in the metafile are interpreted in the context of the current transform set up for the destination device context. In calling *PlayMetaFile*, in effect you're repeating all the calls that you made between *CreateMetaFile* and *CloseMetaFile* when you originally created the metafile during the WM_CREATE message.

As with any GDI object, metafile objects should be deleted before a program terminates. This occurs during the WM_DESTROY message with the *DeleteMetaFile* function.

The results of the METAFILE program are shown in Figure 4-29.

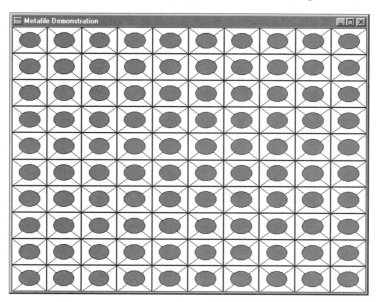

Figure 4-29. *The METAFILE display.*

Storing Metafiles on Disk

In the above example, the NULL parameter to *CreateMetaFile* meant that we wanted to create a metafile stored in memory. We can also create a metafile stored on a disk as a normal file. This method is preferred for large metafiles because it uses less memory space. Windows

206

has to maintain a relatively small area in memory to store the name of the file containing the metafile. On the down side, a metafile stored on disk requires a disk access every time you play it.

To convert METAFILE to using a disk-based metafile, you need to replace the NULL parameter to *CreateMetaFile* with a filename. At the conclusion of the WM_CREATE processing, you can call *DeleteMetaFile* with the metafile handle. The handle has been deleted but the disk file remains behind.

During processing of the WM_PAINT message, you can get a metafile handle to this disk file by calling *GetMetaFile*:

```
hmf = GetMetaFile (szFileName) ;
```

Now you can play this metafile just as before. When processing of the WM_PAINT message is over, you can delete the metafile handle:

```
DeleteMetaFile (hmf) ;
```

When it comes time to process the WM_DESTROY message, you don't have to delete the metafile, because it was deleted at the end of the WM_CREATE message and at the end of each WM_PAINT message. But you should still delete the disk file:

```
remove (szFileName) ;
```

unless, of course, you want to keep the file around. In Chapter 9, I'll discuss user-defined resources. Resources are usually binary data stored in the .EXE file of a program but apart from the normal code and data areas. A metafile can be such a resource. If you have a block of data with the contents of a metafile, you can create a metafile using:

```
hmf = SetMetaFileBitsEx (iSize, pData) ;
```

SetMetaFileBitsEx has a companion function, *GetMetaFileBitsEx*, that copies the contents of a metafile to a block of memory.

ENHANCED METAFILES

The old (but still supported) metafiles I've described above have certain problems. In particular, a program that uses a metafile created by another program cannot easily determine the size of the visual image represented in the metafile. It would have to go into the internals of the metafile and examine all the drawing commands. This is a big problem.

Early on, Microsoft recommended that metafiles do not contain calls to *SetMapMode* or other functions that change the window/viewport transform. Doing so could make the metafile device-dependent or prevent an application from altering the size of the displayed image. Thus, all the coordinates in the metafile are just numbers and are not associated with any particular coordinate system.

As we'll see in Chapter 16, the old-style metafiles are not passed through the clipboard directly. Instead, the clipboard deals with something called a "metafile picture." This is a structure of type METAFILEPICT. The metafile handle is a field of this structure, as are a mapping mode identifier (indicating the units of all the coordinates of the GDI function calls encoded within the metafile) and the dimensions of the image. This information assists the program importing the metafile with setting up the proper GDI environment for displaying the image.

The metafile picture structure is a classical kludge. It was obviously added to GDI to correct deficiencies in the metafile format. Moreover, a similar facility was not developed for disk-based metafiles, and that's why you do not see a whole lot of them used for interchanging pictures. They're simply too difficult to use.

Doing It Better

Like Windows NT, Windows 95 supports a new "enhanced metafile" format, and it involves a bunch of new function calls, a couple of new data structures, a new clipboard format, and a new filename extension—EMF.

The most important enhancement is that the new metafile format includes more extensive header information accessible through a function call. This information aids in helping an application display the metafile image.

Some of the enhanced metafile functions allow you to translate back and forth between the enhanced metafile (EMF) format and what's now called the Windows metafile (WMF) format. Of course, this conversion may not proceed without hitches. The old metafile format does not support some of the new graphics features (such as paths).

The Basic Procedure

Figure 4-30 shows the EMF1 program, which creates and displays an enhanced metafile with a fairly minimal amount of distraction.

EMF1.MAK

```
#--------------------
# EMF1.MAK make file
#--------------------

emf1.exe : emf1.obj
    $(LINKER) $(GUIFLAGS) -OUT:emf1.exe emf1.obj $(GUILIBS)

emf1.obj : emf1.c
    $(CC) $(CFLAGS) emf1.c
```

Figure 4-30. *The EMF1 Program.*   *(continued)*

EMF1.C

```c
/*-------------------------------------
   EMF1.C -- Enhanced Metafile Demo #1
            (c) Charles Petzold, 1996
   -------------------------------------*/

#include <windows.h>

LRESULT CALLBACK WndProc (HWND, UINT, WPARAM, LPARAM) ;

int WINAPI WinMain (HINSTANCE hInstance, HINSTANCE hPrevInstance,
                    PSTR szCmdLine, int iCmdShow)
     {
     static char szAppName[] = "EMF1" ;
     HWND         hwnd ;
     MSG          msg ;
     WNDCLASSEX   wndclass ;

     wndclass.cbSize        = sizeof (wndclass) ;
     wndclass.style         = CS_HREDRAW | CS_VREDRAW ;
     wndclass.lpfnWndProc   = WndProc ;
     wndclass.cbClsExtra    = 0 ;
     wndclass.cbWndExtra    = 0 ;
     wndclass.hInstance     = hInstance ;
     wndclass.hIcon         = LoadIcon (NULL, IDI_APPLICATION) ;
     wndclass.hCursor       = LoadCursor (NULL, IDC_ARROW) ;
     wndclass.hbrBackground = (HBRUSH) GetStockObject (WHITE_BRUSH) ;
     wndclass.lpszMenuName  = NULL ;
     wndclass.lpszClassName = szAppName ;
     wndclass.hIconSm       = LoadIcon (NULL, IDI_APPLICATION) ;

     RegisterClassEx (&wndclass) ;

     hwnd = CreateWindow (szAppName, "Enhanced Metafile Demo #1",
                          WS_OVERLAPPEDWINDOW,
                          CW_USEDEFAULT, CW_USEDEFAULT,
                          CW_USEDEFAULT, CW_USEDEFAULT,
                          NULL, NULL, hInstance, NULL) ;

     ShowWindow (hwnd, iCmdShow) ;
     UpdateWindow (hwnd) ;

     while (GetMessage (&msg, NULL, 0, 0))
          {
          TranslateMessage (&msg) ;
```

(continued)

```
                DispatchMessage (&msg) ;
                }
        return msg.wParam ;
        }


LRESULT CALLBACK WndProc (HWND hwnd, UINT iMsg, WPARAM wParam,
                                            LPARAM lParam)
        {
        static HENHMETAFILE hemf ;
        HDC                 hdc, hdcEMF ;
        PAINTSTRUCT         ps ;
        RECT                rect ;

        switch (iMsg)
            {
            case WM_CREATE :
                hdcEMF = CreateEnhMetaFile (NULL, NULL, NULL, NULL) ;

                Rectangle (hdcEMF, 100, 100, 200, 200) ;

                MoveToEx  (hdcEMF, 100, 100, NULL) ;
                LineTo    (hdcEMF, 200, 200) ;

                MoveToEx  (hdcEMF, 200, 100, NULL) ;
                LineTo    (hdcEMF, 100, 200) ;

                hemf = CloseEnhMetaFile (hdcEMF) ;

                return 0 ;

            case WM_PAINT :
                hdc = BeginPaint (hwnd, &ps) ;

                GetClientRect (hwnd, &rect) ;

                rect.left   =     rect.right  / 4 ;
                rect.right  = 3 * rect.right  / 4 ;
                rect.top    =     rect.bottom / 4 ;
                rect.bottom = 3 * rect.bottom / 4 ;

                PlayEnhMetaFile (hdc, hemf, &rect) ;

                EndPaint (hwnd, &ps) ;
                return 0 ;

            case WM_DESTROY :
                DeleteEnhMetaFile (hemf) ;
```

(continued)

210

```
            PostQuitMessage (0) ;
            return 0 ;
      }
   return DefWindowProc (hwnd, iMsg, wParam, lParam) ;
   }
```

During WM_CREATE message processing in EMF1's window procedure, the program creates the enhanced metafile, beginning with a call to *CreateEnhMetaFile*. This function requires four parameters, but you can set all of them to NULL. (How convenient!) I'll be discussing how to use this function with non-NULL parameters shortly.

Like *CreateMetaFile*, the *CreateEnhMetaFile* function returns a special device context handle. The program uses this handle to draw a rectangle and two lines connecting the opposite corners of the rectangle. These function calls and their parameters are converted to a binary form and stored in the metafile.

Finally, a call to *CloseEnhMetaFile* wraps up the creation of the enhanced metafile and returns a handle to it. This is stored in a static variable of type HENHMETAFILE.

During the WM_PAINT message, EMF1 obtains the dimensions of the program's client window in a RECT structure. The four fields of the structure are adjusted so that the rectangle is half the width and height of the client window, and centered within it. EMF1 then calls *PlayEnhMetaFile*. The first parameter is a handle to the window's device context, the second parameter is the handle to the enhanced metafile, and the third parameter is a pointer to the RECT structure.

What happens here is that during creation of the metafile GDI figures out the entire dimensions of the metafile image. In this case, the image is 100 units high and wide. When displaying the metafile, GDI stretches the image to fit the rectangle specified in the *PlayEnhMetaFile* function. Three instances of EMF1 running under Windows 95 are shown in Figure 4-31.

Finally, during the WM_DESTROY message, EMF1 deletes the metafile by calling *DeleteEnhMetaFile*.

Let's take note of a few things we can learn from the EMF1 program.

First, in this particular program, the coordinates used in the rectangle and line-drawing functions when creating the enhanced metafile don't really mean all that much. You can double them all or subtract a constant from them all, and the results will be the same. All that matters is that the coordinates have a relationship among themselves in defining an image.

Second, the image is stretched to fit the rectangle passed to the *PlayEnhMetaFile* function. Thus, as Figure 4-31 clearly shows, the image can be distorted. The metafile coordinates imply that the image is square, but that's not what we get in the general case.

Sometimes that's exactly what you want. For imbedding images in a word processing text, you may want the user to specify a rectangle for the image and be assured that the entire image fits exactly within the rectangle without any wasted space. Let the user worry about the correct aspect ratio by adjusting the rectangle appropriately.

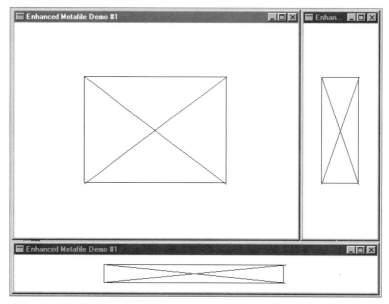

Figure 4-31. *The EMF1 Display.*

However, there are times when something else is appropriate. You may want to maintain the aspect ratio of the original image because it may be vitally important to rendering the visual information. For example, a police sketch of a crime suspect shouldn't be fatter or squatter than it was originally drawn. Or, you may want to preserve the metrical size of the original image. It may be important that the image is two inches high, and shouldn't normally be reproduced otherwise.

Looking Inside

The EMF2 program shown in Figure 4-32 creates a disk-based metafile.

EMF2.MAK

```
#--------------------
# EMF2.MAK make file
#--------------------

emf2.exe : emf2.obj
    $(LINKER) $(GUIFLAGS) -OUT:emf2.exe emf2.obj $(GUILIBS)

emf2.obj : emf2.c
    $(CC) $(CFLAGS) emf2.c
```

Figure 4-32. *The EMF2 Program.*   *(continued)*

EMF2.C

```
/*-------------------------------------
   EMF2.C -- Enhanced Metafile Demo #2
             (c) Charles Petzold, 1996
   -------------------------------------*/

#include <windows.h>

LRESULT CALLBACK WndProc (HWND, UINT, WPARAM, LPARAM) ;

int WINAPI WinMain (HINSTANCE hInstance, HINSTANCE hPrevInstance,
                    PSTR szCmdLine, int iCmdShow)
     {
     static char szAppName[] = "EMF2" ;
     HWND         hwnd ;
     MSG          msg ;
     WNDCLASSEX   wndclass ;

     wndclass.cbSize        = sizeof (wndclass) ;
     wndclass.style         = CS_HREDRAW : CS_VREDRAW ;
     wndclass.lpfnWndProc   = WndProc ;
     wndclass.cbClsExtra    = 0 ;
     wndclass.cbWndExtra    = 0 ;
     wndclass.hInstance     = hInstance ;
     wndclass.hIcon         = LoadIcon (NULL, IDI_APPLICATION) ;
     wndclass.hCursor       = LoadCursor (NULL, IDC_ARROW) ;
     wndclass.hbrBackground = (HBRUSH) GetStockObject (WHITE_BRUSH) ;
     wndclass.lpszMenuName  = NULL ;
     wndclass.lpszClassName = szAppName ;
     wndclass.hIconSm       = LoadIcon (NULL, IDI_APPLICATION) ;

     RegisterClassEx (&wndclass) ;

     hwnd = CreateWindow (szAppName, "Enhanced Metafile Demo #2",
                          WS_OVERLAPPEDWINDOW,
                          CW_USEDEFAULT, CW_USEDEFAULT,
                          CW_USEDEFAULT, CW_USEDEFAULT,
                          NULL, NULL, hInstance, NULL) ;

     ShowWindow (hwnd, iCmdShow) ;
     UpdateWindow (hwnd) ;

     while (GetMessage (&msg, NULL, 0, 0))
          {
          TranslateMessage (&msg) ;
```

(continued)

```
            DispatchMessage (&msg) ;
            }
        return msg.wParam ;
        }

LRESULT CALLBACK WndProc (HWND hwnd, UINT iMsg, WPARAM wParam,
                                              LPARAM lParam)
        {
        HDC          hdc, hdcEMF ;
        HENHMETAFILE hemf ;
        PAINTSTRUCT  ps ;
        RECT         rect ;

        switch (iMsg)
            {
            case WM_CREATE :
                hdcEMF = CreateEnhMetaFile (NULL, "emf2.emf", NULL,
                                            "EMF2\0EMF Demo #2\0") ;

                Rectangle (hdcEMF, 100, 100, 200, 200) ;

                MoveToEx  (hdcEMF, 100, 100, NULL) ;
                LineTo    (hdcEMF, 200, 200) ;

                MoveToEx  (hdcEMF, 200, 100, NULL) ;
                LineTo    (hdcEMF, 100, 200) ;

                hemf = CloseEnhMetaFile (hdcEMF) ;

                DeleteEnhMetaFile (hemf) ;
                return 0 ;

            case WM_PAINT :
                hdc = BeginPaint (hwnd, &ps) ;

                GetClientRect (hwnd, &rect) ;

                rect.left   =     rect.right  / 4 ;
                rect.right  = 3 * rect.right  / 4 ;
                rect.top    =     rect.bottom / 4 ;
                rect.bottom = 3 * rect.bottom / 4 ;

                hemf = GetEnhMetaFile ("emf2.emf") ;

                PlayEnhMetaFile (hdc, hemf, &rect) ;

                DeleteEnhMetaFile (hemf) ;
```

(continued)

```
            EndPaint (hwnd, &ps) ;
            return 0 ;

      case WM_DESTROY :
            PostQuitMessage (0) ;
            return 0 ;
      }
   return DefWindowProc (hwnd, iMsg, wParam, lParam) ;
   }
```

Notice that here the first parameter to *CreateEnhMetaFile* is a device context handle. GDI uses this parameter to insert metrical information in the metafile header, as we'll see shortly. If the parameter is set to NULL, GDI assumes that this metrical information is based on the video device context.

The second parameter to *CreateEnhMetaFile* is a filename. If you set this parameter to NULL (as EMF1 does but EMF2 does not), then the function creates a memory metafile. EMF2 creates a disk-based metafile with the name EMF2.EMF.

The third parameter to the function is an address of a RECT structure that indicates the total dimensions of the metafile. This piece of vital information (one of the deficiencies of the earlier Windows metafile format) goes into the metafile header, as we'll see shortly. If you set this parameter to NULL, GDI will figure out the dimensions for you. I like the idea of operating systems doing things for me, so I've set the parameter to NULL. If performance is critical in your application, you might want to use this parameter to avoid some extraneous work on GDI's part.

Finally, the last parameter is a text string describing the metafile. This text string is specified in two pieces: The first piece is the name of the application (not necessarily the program filename) followed by a NULL character, and the second piece describes the visual image, followed by two NULL characters. For example, using the C notation of '\0' for a NULL character, the description string could be "HemiDemiSemiCad V6.4\0Flying Frogs\0\0". Because C normally puts a NULL character at the end of quoted strings, you need only one '\0' at the very end, as EMF2 demonstrates.

After creating the metafile, EMF2 proceeds like EMF1, by calling a few GDI function calls using the device context handle returned from the *CreateEnhMetaFile* function. These draw a rectangle and two lines connecting the opposite corners of the rectangle. The program then calls *CloseEnhMetaFile* to destroy the device context handle and obtain a handle to the completed metafile.

Then, still during WM_CREATE processing, EMF2 does something EMF1 does not: Right after obtaining the metafile handle, the program calls *DeleteEnhMetaFile*. That gets rid of all memory resources required to maintain the metafile. However, the disk-based metafile stays behind. (If you ever want to get rid of that file, use a normal file-deletion function.) Notice that the metafile handle is not stored as a static variable as in EMF1, which implies that it is not required to be saved between messages.

Now, in order to use that metafile, EMF2 needs to access the disk file. It does this during the WM_PAINT message by calling *GetEnhMetaFile*. The single parameter to the function is the metafile filename, and the function returns a handle to the metafile. EMF2 passes this handle to the *PlayEnhMetaFile* function, just as in EMF1. The metafile image is displayed in the rectangle described by the last parameter to the function. But unlike EMF1, EMF2 deletes the metafile before concluding WM_PAINT processing. During any following WM_PAINT messages, EMF2 gets the metafile again, plays it, and deletes it.

Keep in mind that deleting the metafile involves deleting only the memory resources required for maintaining the metafile. The disk-based metafile stays behind, even after the program has concluded execution.

Because EMF2 leaves behind a disk-based metafile, you can take a look at it. It is composed of variable length records described by the ENHMETARECORD structure defined in the Windows header files. The enhanced metafile always begins with a header record. This corresponds to a structure of type ENHMETAHEADER.

You do not need to access the actual disk-based metafile to obtain the header information. If you have a handle to the metafile, you can use the *GetEnhMetaFileHeader* function:

```
GetEnhMetaFileHeader (hemf, cbSize, &emh) ;
```

The first parameter is the metafile handle, the last is a pointer to an ENHMETAHEADER structure, and the second is the size of this structure. You can use the similar *GetEnhMetaFileDescription* function to obtain the description string. The *rclBounds* field of the ENHMETAHEADER is a rectangle structure that indicates the size of the image in pixels. The *rclFrame* field is another rectangle structure that provides the same information but in units of 0.01 millimeters.

The header record concludes with two SIZE structures, which contain two 32-bit fields, *szlDevice* and *szlMillimeters*. The *szlDevice* field indicates the size of the output device in pixels, and the *szlMillimeters* is the size of the output device in millimeters. This is based on the device context indicated by the handle passed as the first parameter to the *CreateEnhMetaFile* call. If the parameter is set to NULL, GDI uses the video display. GDI obtains the metric sizing information from *GetDeviceCaps*.

Displaying Accurate Images

The great thing about metafile images is that they can be stretched to any size and still maintain reasonable fidelity. Enlarging or compressing the image simply involves scaling all the coordinate points that define these primitives. Bitmaps, on the other hand, can lose vital information when compression results in dropping entire rows and columns of pixels.

Sometimes, however, arbitrarily scaling a metafile is not such a hot idea. While it may be fun to stretch a metafile image of a person's face into a fat face or a thin face, it's also helpful to know the correct aspect ratio of the image. Also, some metafile images may make sense only at a specific metrical size. (Counterfeiters will appreciate this concept.)

As we've seen, the last parameter to *PlayEnhMetaFile* is a RECT structure that indicates to GDI where you want the image displayed within the destination device context. GDI stretches the image to fit snugly within that rectangle. Accurately displaying a metafile image—either in specific metrical sizes or with a proper aspect ratio—requires using the size information in the metafile header and setting the rectangle structure accordingly.

This can be tricky, but it's more fun when the image is also displayed on a printer, so I'll save that job for Chapter 15.

TEXT AND FONTS

The first Windows programming job we tackled in this book was displaying a simple one-line text string in the center of a window. In the last chapter we moved on to displaying multiple (and scrollable) lines of text. Now it's time to examine the mechanics of text display in a more rigorous manner. The discussion of text will not end here. In Chapter 11 we'll see how the Common Dialog Box library (introduced in Windows 3.1) greatly simplifies programs that must allow users to choose fonts. In Chapter 15 we'll explore the problems with displaying text on the screen that will accurately show how it will eventually look on the printer page.

Simple Text Output

Let's begin by looking at the different functions Windows provides for text output, the device context attributes that affect text, and the use of "stock" fonts.

The most common text output function is the one I used in the SYSMETS programs in Chapter 3:

```
TextOut (hdc, xStart, yStart, pString, iCount) ;
```

The *xStart* and *yStart* parameters are the starting position of the string in logical coordinates. Normally, this is the point at which Windows begins drawing the upper left corner of the first character. *TextOut* requires a far pointer to the character string and the length of the string. The function does not recognize NULL-terminated character strings.

The meaning of the *xStart* and *yStart* parameters to *TextOut* can be altered by the *SetTextAlign* function. The TA_LEFT, TA_RIGHT, and TA_CENTER flags affect how *xStart* is used to position the string horizontally. The default is TA_LEFT. If you specify TA_RIGHT in the *SetTextAlign* function, subsequent *TextOut* calls position the right side of the last character in the string at *xStart*. For TA_CENTER, the center of the string is positioned at *xStart*.

Similarly, the TA_TOP, TA_BOTTOM, and TA_BASELINE flags affect the vertical positioning. TA_TOP is the default, which means that the string is positioned so that *yStart* specifies the top of the characters in the string. Using TA_BOTTOM means that the string is positioned above *yStart*. You can use TA_BASELINE to position a string so that the baseline is at *yStart*. The baseline is the line below which descenders (such as those on the lower-case p, q, and y) hang.

If you call *SetTextAlign* with the TA_UPDATECP flag, Windows ignores the *xStart* and *yStart* parameters to *TextOut* and instead uses the current position previously set by *MoveToEx* or *LineTo,* or any other function that changes the current position. The TA_UPDATECP flag also causes the *TextOut* function to update the current position to the end of the string (for TA_LEFT) or the beginning of the string (for TA_RIGHT). This is useful for displaying a line of text with multiple *TextOut* calls. When the horizontal positioning is TA_CENTER, the current position remains the same after a *TextOut* call.

You'll recall that displaying columnar text in the series of SYSMETS programs in Chapter 3 required that one *TextOut* call be used for each column. An alternative is the *TabbedTextOut* function:

```
TabbedTextOut (hdc, xStart, yStart, pString, iCount,
                iNumTabs, piTabStops, xTabOrigin) ;
```

If the text string contains embedded tab characters ('\t' or 0x09), *TabbedTextOut* will expand the tabs into spaces based on an array of integers you pass to the function.

The first five parameters to *TabbedTextOut* are the same as those to *TextOut*. The sixth parameter is the number of tab stops, and the seventh parameter is an array of tab stops in units of pixels. For example, if the average character width is 8 pixels and you want a tab stop every 5 characters, then this array would contain the numbers 40, 80, 120, and so forth, in ascending order.

If the sixth and seventh parameters are 0 or NULL, tab stops are set at every eight average character widths. If the sixth parameter is 1, the seventh parameter points to a single integer, which is repeated incrementally for multiple tab stops. (For example, if the sixth parameter is 1 and the seventh parameter points to a variable containing the number 30, tab stops are set at 30, 60, 90, ... pixels.) The last parameter gives the logical *x*-coordinate of the starting position from which tab stops are measured. This may or may not be the same as the starting position of the string.

Another advanced text output function is *ExtTextOut* (the *Ext* prefix stands for *extended*):

```
ExtTextOut (hdc, xStart, yStart, iOptions, &rect,
             pString, iCount, pxDistance) ;
```

The fifth parameter is a pointer to a rectangle structure. This is either a clipping rectangle (if *iOptions* is set to ETO_CLIPPED) or a background rectangle to be filled with the current background color (if *iOptions* is set to ETO_OPAQUE). You can specify both options or neither.

The last parameter is an array of integers that specify the spacing between consecutive characters in the string. This allows a program to tighten or loosen intercharacter spacing, which is sometimes required for justifying a single word of text in a narrow column. The parameter can be set to NULL for default character spacing.

A higher-level function for writing text is *DrawText*, which we first encountered in the HELLOWIN program in Chapter 2. Rather than specifying a coordinate starting position, you provide a structure of type RECT that defines a rectangle in which you want the text to appear:

```
DrawText (hdc, pString, iCount, &rect, iFormat) ;
```

As with the other text output functions, *DrawText* requires a far pointer to the character string and the length of the string. However, if you use *DrawText* with NULL-terminated strings, you can set *iCount* to −1, and Windows will calculate the length of the string.

When *iFormat* is set to 0, Windows interprets the text as a series of lines that are separated by carriage-return characters ('\r' or 0x0D) or linefeed characters ('\n' or 0x0A). The text begins at the upper left corner of the rectangle. A carriage return or linefeed is interpreted as a "newline" character, so Windows breaks the current line and starts a new one. The new line begins at the left side of the rectangle, spaced one character height (without external leading) below the previous line. Any text, including parts of letters, that would be displayed to the right or below the bottom of the rectangle is clipped.

You can change the default operation of *DrawText* by including an *iFormat* parameter, which consists of one or more flags. The DT_LEFT flag (the default) specifies a left-justified line, DT_RIGHT specifies a right-justified line, and DT_CENTER specifies a line centered between the left and right sides of the rectangle. Because the value of DT_LEFT is 0, you needn't include the identifier if you want text to be left-justified only.

If you don't want carriage returns or linefeeds to be interpreted as newline characters, you can include the identifier DT_SINGLELINE. Windows then interprets carriage returns and linefeeds as displayable characters rather than control characters. When using DT_SINGLELINE, you can also specify whether the line is to be placed at the top of the rectangle (DT_TOP, the default), at the bottom of the rectangle (DT_BOTTOM), or halfway between the top and bottom (DT_VCENTER).

When displaying multiple lines of text, Windows normally breaks the lines only at carriage returns or linefeeds. If the lines are too long to fit in the rectangle, however, you can use the DT_WORDBREAK flag, which causes Windows to create breaks at the ends of words within lines. For both single-line and multiple-line displays, Windows truncates any part of the text that falls outside the rectangle. You can override this by including the flag DT_NOCLIP, which also speeds up the operation of the function. When Windows spaces multiple lines of text, it normally uses the character height without external leading. If you prefer that external leading be included in the line spacing, then you can use the flag DT_EXTERNALLEADING.

If your text contains tab characters ('\t' or 0x09), you need to include the flag DT_EXPANDTABS. By default, the tab stops are set at every eighth character position. You can specify a different tab setting by using the flag DT_TABSTOP, in which case the upper byte of *wFormat* contains the character-position number of each new tab stop. I recommend that you avoid using DT_TABSTOP, however, because the upper byte of *iFormat* is also used for some other flags.

Device Context Attributes for Text

Several device context attributes affect text. In the default device context, the text color is black, but you can change that with:

```
SetTextColor (hdc, rgbColor) ;
```

As with pen colors and hatch brush colors, Windows converts the value of *rgbColor* to a pure color. You can obtain the current text color by calling *GetTextColor.*

The spaces between the character strokes are colored in, based on the setting of the background mode and the background color. You can change the background mode using:

```
SetBkMode (hdc, iMode) ;
```

where *iMode* is either OPAQUE or TRANSPARENT. The default background mode is OPAQUE, which means that Windows uses the background color to fill in the area between the character strokes. You can change the background color by using:

```
SetBkColor (hdc, rgbColor) ;
```

The value of *rgbColor* is converted to that of a pure color. The default background color is white. If the background mode is set to TRANSPARENT, Windows ignores the background color and doesn't color the area between the character strokes. Windows also uses the background mode and background color to color the spaces between dotted and dashed lines and the area between the hatches of hatched brushes, as I discussed earlier.

Many Windows programs specify WHITE_BRUSH as the brush that Windows uses to erase the background of a window. The brush is specified in the window class structure. However, you may want to make the background of your program's window consistent with the system colors that a user can set in the Control Panel. In that case, you would specify the background color this way in the WNDCLASS structure:

```
wndclass.hbrBackground = (HBRUSH) (COLOR_WINDOW + 1) ;
```

When you want to write text to the client area, you can then set the text color and background color using the current system colors:

```
SetTextColor (hdc, GetSysColor (COLOR_WINDOWTEXT)) ;
SetBkColor (hdc, GetSysColor (COLOR_WINDOW)) ;
```

If you do this, you'll want your program to be alerted if the system colors change:

```
case WM_SYSCOLORCHANGE :
    InvalidateRect (hwnd, NULL, TRUE) ;
    break ;
```

Another device context attribute that affects text is the intercharacter spacing. By default it's set to 0, which means that Windows doesn't add any space between characters. You can insert space by using the function:

```
SetTextCharacterExtra (hdc, iExtra) ;
```

The *iExtra* parameter is in logical units. Windows converts it to the nearest pixel, which can be 0. If you use a negative value for *iExtra* (perhaps in an attempt to squeeze characters closer together), Windows takes the absolute value of the number: You can't make the value less than 0. You can obtain the current intercharacter spacing by calling *GetText-CharacterExtra*. Windows converts the pixel spacing to logical units before returning the value.

Using Stock Fonts

When you call *TextOut*, *TabbedTextOut*, *ExtTextOut*, or *DrawText* to write text, Windows uses the font currently selected in the device context. The font defines a particular typeface and a size. The easiest way to display text with various fonts is to use the stock fonts that Windows provides. However, the range of these is quite limited.

You can obtain a handle to a stock font by calling:

```
hFont = GetStockObject (iFont) ;
```

where *iFont* is one of several identifiers, only two of which are commonly used. You can then select that font into the device context:

```
SelectObject (hdc, hFont) ;
```

Or you can accomplish this in one step:

```
SelectObject (hdc, GetStockObject (iFont)) ;
```

GetStockObject is the same function we used earlier to obtain stock pens and brushes; *SelectObject* we used to select pens, brushes, bitmaps, and regions into the device context.

The font selected in the default device context is called the system font and is identified by the *GetStockObject* parameter SYSTEM_FONT. This is the proportional ANSI character set font that Windows uses for text in menus, dialog boxes, message boxes, and window caption bars. Specifying SYSTEM_FIXED_FONT in *GetStockObject* (which I did in the WHATSIZE program earlier in this chapter) gives you a handle to a fixed-pitch font compatible with the system font used in versions of Windows prior to version 3. This is very convenient when all font characters have the same width.

When you select a new font into a device context, you must calculate the font's character height and average character width using *GetTextMetrics*. If you've selected a proportional font, be aware that the average character width is really an average and that some characters have a lesser or greater width. Later in this chapter you'll learn how to determine the full width of a string made up of variable-width characters.

Although *GetStockObject* certainly offers the easiest access to different fonts, you don't have much control over which font Windows gives you. You'll see shortly how you can be very specific about the typeface and size that you want.

The Types of Fonts

Windows supports two broad categories of fonts, "GDI fonts" and "device fonts." The GDI fonts are stored in files on your hard disk. Device fonts are native to the output device. For example, it is very common for printers to have a collection of built-in device fonts.

GDI fonts come in three flavors—raster fonts, stroke fonts, and TrueType fonts.

A raster font is sometimes called a bitmap font, because in a raster font file each character is stored as a bitmap pixel pattern. Each raster font is designed for a specific aspect ratio and character size. Windows can create larger character sizes from GDI raster fonts by simply duplicating rows or columns of pixels. However, this can be done only in integral multiples and within certain limits. For this reason, GDI raster fonts are termed "nonscalable" fonts. They cannot be expanded or compressed to an arbitrary size. The primary advantages of raster fonts are performance (because they are very fast to display) and readability (because they have been hand-designed to be as legible as possible).

Prior to Windows 3.1, the only other GDI fonts supplied with Windows were the GDI stroke fonts. The stroke fonts are defined as a series of line segments in a "connect-the-dots" format. Stroke fonts are continuously scalable, which means that the same font can be used for graphics output devices of any resolution, and the fonts can be increased or decreased to any size. However, performance is poor, legibility suffers greatly at small sizes, and at large sizes the characters look decidedly weak because their strokes are single lines. Stroke fonts are now sometimes called "plotter fonts" because they are particularly suitable for plotters but not for anything else.

For both GDI raster fonts and GDI stroke fonts, Windows can "synthesize" boldface, italics, underlining, and strikethroughs without storing separate fonts for each attribute. For italics, for instance, Windows simply shifts the upper part of the character to the right.

Then there is TrueType, to which the remainder of this chapter will be devoted.

TrueType Fonts

The introduction of TrueType in Windows 3.1 greatly enhances the ability to work with text in a flexible manner. TrueType is an outline font technology that was developed by Apple Computer, Inc., and Microsoft Corporation; it is supported by many font manufacturers. The individual characters of TrueType fonts are defined by an outline of straight lines and curves. Thus, Windows can scale these fonts by altering the coordinates that define the outlines. TrueType fonts can be used on both video displays and printers, enabling true WYSIWYG ("what-you-see-is-what-you-get").

When your program wants to use a TrueType font of a particular size, Windows "rasterizes" the font. This means that Windows scales the coordinates connecting the lines and curves of each character using "hints" that are included in the TrueType font file. These hints compensate for rounding errors that would otherwise cause a resultant character to be unsightly. (For example, in some fonts the two legs of a capital H should be the same width. A blind scaling of the font could result in one leg being a pixel wider than the other. The hints prevent this from happening.) The resultant outline of each character is then used to create a bitmap of the character. These bitmaps are cached in memory for future use.

Windows 95 comes equipped with 13 TrueType fonts. They have "typeface names," which are:

> Courier New
>
> Courier New Bold
>
> Courier New Italic
>
> Courier New Bold Italic
>
> Times New Roman
>
> Times New Roman Bold
>
> Times New Roman Italic
>
> Times New Roman Bold Italic
>
> Arial
>
> Arial Bold
>
> Arial Italic
>
> Arial Bold Italic
>
> Symbol

Courier New is a fixed-pitch font (that is, every character has the same width) designed to look like the output from an antique piece of hardware known as a typewriter. Times New Roman is a clone of the Times font originally designed for the *Times of London* and used in many printed materials. It is considered to be highly readable. Arial is a clone of Helvetica, a sans serif font. This means that the characters do not have the small turns at the ends of the strokes. The Symbol font contains a collection of handy symbols.

In traditional typography, you specify a font by its typeface name and its size. The type size is expressed in units called points. A point is very close to $^1/_{72}$ inch, so close that it is often defined as $^1/_{72}$ inch in computer typography. The text of this book is printed in 12-point type. The type size is sometimes described as the height of the characters from the top of the ascenders to the bottom of the descenders. That's a convenient way to think of the type size, but it's not accurate for all fonts. Sometimes a font designer will do something different.

The EZFONT System

The introduction of TrueType—and its basis in traditional typography—has provided Windows with a solid foundation for displaying text in its many varieties. However, some of the Windows font-selection functions are based on older technology, in which raster fonts on the screen had to approximate printer device fonts.

In previous editions of this book, I extensively discussed the *EnumFonts* function, which provides a program with LOGFONT ("logical font") and TEXTMETRIC structures for every GDI font installed for use by Windows and all the device fonts. The *ChooseFont* dialog box (to be discussed in Chapter 11) largely eliminates the use of this function and all that it entails. Similarly, I extensively discussed the *CreateFontIndirect* function, which allows a program to describe a desired font without directly naming it. This is how printer fonts were approximated on the video display.

Instead, in this chapter I'll propose something quite different. I want to show you how to use the various standard TrueType fonts in your programs with a minimum of overhead and in a manner consistent with traditional typography. This involves specifying the name of the font (one of the 13 names listed above) and its size (which I'll discuss shortly). I call it EZFONT ("easy font"), and the two files you need are shown in Figure 4-33.

EZFONT.H

```
/*---------------------
    EZFONT.H header file
   ------------------*/

HFONT EzCreateFont (HDC hdc, char * szFaceName, int iDeciPtHeight,
                    int iDeciPtWidth, int iAttributes, BOOL fLogRes) ;

#define EZ_ATTR_BOLD            1
#define EZ_ATTR_ITALIC          2
#define EZ_ATTR_UNDERLINE       4
#define EZ_ATTR_STRIKEOUT       8
```

EZFONT.C

```
/*------------------------------------------
    EZFONT.C -- Easy Font Creation
              (c) Charles Petzold, 1996
   ------------------------------------*/

#include <windows.h>
#include <string.h>
```

Figure 4-33. *The EZFONT files.*

(continued)

```
#include <math.h>
#include "ezfont.h"

HFONT EzCreateFont (HDC hdc, char * szFaceName, int iDeciPtHeight,
                    int iDeciPtWidth, int iAttributes, BOOL fLogRes)
     {
     FLOAT      cxDpi, cyDpi ;
     HFONT      hFont ;
     LOGFONT    lf ;
     POINT      pt ;
     TEXTMETRIC tm ;

     SaveDC (hdc) ;

     SetGraphicsMode (hdc, GM_ADVANCED) ;
     ModifyWorldTransform (hdc, NULL, MWT_IDENTITY) ;
     SetViewportOrgEx (hdc, 0, 0, NULL) ;
     SetWindowOrgEx   (hdc, 0, 0, NULL) ;

     if (fLogRes)
         {
         cxDpi = (FLOAT) GetDeviceCaps (hdc, LOGPIXELSX) ;
         cyDpi = (FLOAT) GetDeviceCaps (hdc, LOGPIXELSY) ;
         }
     else
         {
         cxDpi = (FLOAT) (25.4 * GetDeviceCaps (hdc, HORZRES) /
                              GetDeviceCaps (hdc, HORZSIZE)) ;

         cyDpi = (FLOAT) (25.4 * GetDeviceCaps (hdc, VERTRES) /
                              GetDeviceCaps (hdc, VERTSIZE)) ;
         }
     pt.x = (int) (iDeciPtWidth  * cxDpi / 72) ;
     pt.y = (int) (iDeciPtHeight * cyDpi / 72) ;

     DPtoLP (hdc, &pt, 1) ;

     lf.lfHeight       = - (int) (fabs (pt.y) / 10.0 + 0.5) ;
     lf.lfWidth        = 0 ;
     lf.lfEscapement   = 0 ;
     lf.lfOrientation  = 0 ;
     lf.lfWeight       = iAttributes & EZ_ATTR_BOLD      ? 700 : 0 ;
     lf.lfItalic       = iAttributes & EZ_ATTR_ITALIC    ?   1 : 0 ;
     lf.lfUnderline    = iAttributes & EZ_ATTR_UNDERLINE ?   1 : 0 ;
     lf.lfStrikeOut    = iAttributes & EZ_ATTR_STRIKEOUT ?   1 : 0 ;
     lf.lfCharSet      = 0 ;
```

(continued)

```
lf.lfOutPrecision   = 0 ;
lf.lfClipPrecision  = 0 ;
lf.lfQuality        = 0 ;
lf.lfPitchAndFamily = 0 ;

strcpy (lf.lfFaceName, szFaceName) ;

hFont = CreateFontIndirect (&lf) ;

if (iDeciPtWidth != 0)
    {
    hFont = (HFONT) SelectObject (hdc, hFont) ;

    GetTextMetrics (hdc, &tm) ;

    DeleteObject (SelectObject (hdc, hFont)) ;

    lf.lfWidth = (int) (tm.tmAveCharWidth *
                        fabs (pt.x) / fabs (pt.y) + 0.5) ;

    hFont = CreateFontIndirect (&lf) ;
    }

RestoreDC (hdc, -1) ;

return hFont ;
}
```

EZFONT.C has only one function, called *EzCreateFont*, which you can use like so:

```
hFont = EzCreateFont (hdc, szFaceName, iDeciPtHeight,
                      iDeciPtWidth, iAttributes, fLogRes) ;
```

The function returns a handle to a font. The font can be selected in the device context by calling *SelectObject*. You should then call *GetTextMetrics* or *GetOutlineTextMetrics* to determine the actual size of the font dimensions in logical coordinates. Before your program terminates, you should delete any created fonts by calling *DeleteObject*.

The *szFaceName* parameter is one of the 13 TrueType typeface names listed earlier. If you have other TrueType fonts installed in your system, you can use those names also, but the 13 faces listed earlier are guaranteed for all Windows 95 systems.

The third parameter indicates the desired point size, but it's specified in "decipoints," which are $1/10$ of a point. Thus, if you want a point size of $12\,1/2$, use a value of 125.

Normally, the fourth parameter should be set to zero or identical to the third parameter. However, you can create a TrueType font with a wider or narrower size by setting this parameter to something different. (This is sometimes called the "em-width" of the font and describes the width of the font in points. Don't confuse this with the average width of the font characters or anything like that. Back in the early days of typography, a capital 'M' was as wide as it was high. So, the concept of an "em-square" came into being, and that's the origin of the em-width measurement. When the em-width equals the em-height (the point size of the font), the character widths are as the font designer intended. A smaller or wider em-width lets you create slimmer or wider characters.)

The *iAttributes* parameter can be set to one or more of the following values defined in EZFONT.H:

EZ_ATTR_BOLD
EZ_ATTR_ITALIC
EZ_ATTR_UNDERLINE
EZ_ATTR_STRIKEOUT

Normally, you probably wouldn't use EZ_ATTR_BOLD or EZ_ATTR_ITALIC because these attributes are part of the complete TrueType typeface name. If you use them, Windows will synthesize these effects.

Finally, you set the last parameter to TRUE to base the visible font size on the "logical resolution" returned by the *GetDeviceCaps* function. Otherwise, it's based on the actual resolution.

The Inner Workings

The *EzCreateFont* function is designed for use with either Windows 95 or Windows NT. The NT compatibility is indicated by the use of the *SetGraphicsMode* and *ModifyWorldTransform* functions, which have no effect in Windows 95. (In short, the Windows NT world transform should have the effect of modifying the visible size of the font, so the world transform is set to the default—no transform—before the font size is calculated.)

EzCreateFont basically sets the fields of a LOGFONT structure and calls *CreateFontIndirect*, which returns a handle to the font. For selecting TrueType fonts, most of the fields can be set to zero. The fields you need set are:

- *lfHeight*—This is the desired height of the characters (including internal leading but not external leading) in logical units. Because the point size of the font itself is the height of the font less internal leading, you're really specifying line spacing here. You can set *lfHeight* to 0 for a default size. If you set *lfHeight* to a negative number, Windows treats the absolute value of that number as a desired font height size rather than a line spacing. If you want a font of a particular point size, the point size must be converted to logical units, and the *lfHeight* field set to the negative of that value.

- *lfWidth*—This is the desired width of the characters in logical units. In most cases, you set this to 0 and let Windows choose a font based solely on the height.

- *lfWeight*—This field allows you to specify boldface by setting it to 700.

- *lfItalic*—When nonzero, this specifies italics.

- *lfUnderline*—When nonzero, this specifies underlining.

- *lfStrikeOut*—When nonzero, this specifies that the font should have a line drawn through the characters.

- *lfFaceName* (BYTE array)—This is the name of a typeface (such as Courier New, Arial, or Times New Roman).

One chore of the *EzCreateFont* function is to convert a point size to logical units to set up the LOGFONT structure. It turns out that the point size must be converted to device units (pixels) first, and then to logical units. To perform the first step, we use information available from the *GetDeviceCaps* function.

Calling *GetDeviceCaps* with the HORZRES and VERTRES parameters gives us the width and height of the video display (or printable area of the printer page) in pixels. Calling *GetDeviceCaps* with the HORZSIZE and VERTSIZE parameter gives us the physical width and height of the video display (or printable area of the printer page) in units of millimeters. If the last parameter is set to FALSE, the *EzCreateFont* function uses these values to obtain a resolution of the devices in dots-per-inch.

There's an alternative approach. You can obtain the device resolution in dots-per-inch directly, using the LOGPIXELSX and LOGPIXELSY parameters to the *GetDeviceCaps* function. This is called the "logical resolution" of the device. For printers, the normal resolution and the logical resolution are identical (ignoring rounding errors). For video displays, however, the logical resolution is finer than the normal resolution. For example, for a VGA the above formulas for the normal resolution yield about 68 dots per inch. The logical resolution is 96 dots per inch.

The difference is dramatic: Let's assume we're working with a 12-point font, which is $\frac{1}{6}$ inch high. Assuming a normal resolution of 68 dots per inch, the full point-height of the characters comes out to about 11 pixels. With a logical resolution of 96 dots per inch, it's 16 pixels. That's about a 45 percent increase.

Why the difference? Well, if you think about it, there is no true resolution of a VGA. A standard VGA displays 640 pixels by 480 pixels, but the size of the actual screen may range from a tiny notebook computer to a big VGA projector. Windows itself has no way to determine the actual screen size. The HORZSIZE and VERTSIZE values are based on a "standard" desktop VGA screen size, probably one of the early IBM models that some anonymous Microsoft programmer measured with a ruler way back in 1987.

If you think about it some more, you really don't *want* fonts displayed on the screen in their true size. Suppose you're using a VGA projector in a presentation before hundreds of people, and you display 12-point fonts that actually measure ⅙ inch on the projection screen. There's no doubt your audience will be confused and possibly hostile.

People who use text in applications are often working with word processing programs and desktop publishing programs. Quite often that work is destined for 8½-by-11-inch paper output (8 inches by 10 inches, considering margins). Many VGA displays are wider than 8 inches. Displaying larger characters based on the logical resolution takes better advantage of the screen real estate.

However, if you use the logical font resolution, you may have a problem mixing text with other graphics. If you use the *SetMapMode* function to draw graphics in units of inches or millimeters, and you use the logical device resolution for sizing fonts, you'll run into inconsistencies—not on printer output (because normal resolution and logical resolution are identical there) but on the video display, where there's a 45 percent difference. A solution will be demonstrated later in this chapter in the JUSTIFY1 program.

The LOGFONT structure you pass to *CreateFontIndirect* requires a font height in logical units. Once you have the value in pixels, getting logical units would seem to involve a fairly simple call to the *DPtoLP* ("device point to logical point") function. But in order for the *DPtoLP* conversion to work correctly, the same mapping mode must be in effect when you later display text using the created font. This means that you should set your mapping mode before calling the *EzCreateFont* function. In most cases, you use only one mapping mode for drawing on a particular area of the window, so this requirement should not be a problem.

Simple Text Formatting

Equipped with the EZFONT files, it's time to try our hand at text formatting. The process involves placing each line of text within margins in one of four ways: aligned on the left margin, aligned on the right margin, centered between the margins, or justified—that is, running from one margin to the other, with equal spaces between the words. For the first three jobs, you can use the *DrawText* function with the DT_WORDBREAK parameter, but this approach has limitations. For instance, you can't determine what part of the text *DrawText* was able to fit within the rectangle. *DrawText* is convenient for some simple jobs, but for more complex formatting tasks, you'll probably want to employ *TextOut*.

One of the most useful functions for working with text is *GetTextExtentPoint32*. (This is a function whose name reveals some changes since the early versions of Windows.) The function tells you the width and height of a character string based on the current font selected in the device context:

```
GetTextExtentPoint32 (hdc, pString, iCount, &size) ;
```

The width and height of the text in logical units are returned in the *cx* and *cy* fields of the SIZE structure. I'll begin with an example using one line of text. Let's say that you have selected a font into your device context and now want to write the text:

```
char *szText [] = "Hello, how are you?" ;
```

You want the text to start at the vertical coordinate *yStart*, within margins set by the coordinates *xLeft* and *xRight*. Your job is to calculate the *xStart* value for the horizontal coordinate where the text begins. This job would be considerably easier if the text were displayed using a fixed-pitch font, but that's not the general case. First, you get the text extents of the string:

```
GetTextExtentPoint32 (hdc, szText, strlen (szText), &size) ;
```

If *size.cx* is larger than (*xRight* – *xLeft*), then the line is too long to fit within the margins. Let's assume it can fit.

To align the text on the left margin, you simply set *xStart* equal to *xLeft* and then write the text:

```
TextOut (hdc, xStart, yStart, szText, strlen (szText)) ;
```

This is easy. You can now add the *size.cy* to *yStart*, and you're ready to write the next line of text.

To align the text on the right margin, you use this formula for *xStart*:

```
xStart = xRight - size.cx ;
```

To center the text between the left and right margins, use this formula:

```
xStart = (xLeft + xRight - size.cx) / 2 ;
```

Now here's the tough job—to justify the text within the left and right margins. The distance between the margins is (*xRight* – *xLeft*). Without justification, the text is *size.cx* wide. The difference between these two values, which is:

```
xRight - xLeft - size.cx
```

must be equally distributed among the three space characters in the character string. It sounds like a terrible job, but it's not too bad. To do it, you call:

```
SetTextJustification (hdc, xRight - xLeft - size.cx, 3)
```

The second parameter is the amount of space that must be distributed among the space characters in the character string. The third parameter is the number of space characters—in this case, 3.

Now set *xStart* equal to *xLeft* and write the text with *TextOut*:

```
TextOut (hdc, xStart, yStart, szText, strlen (szText)) ;
```

The text will be justified between the *xLeft* and *xRight* margins.

Whenever you call *SetTextJustification*, it accumulates an error term if the amount of space doesn't distribute evenly among the space characters. This error term will affect subsequent *GetTextExtent* calls. Each time you start a new line, you should clear out the error term by calling:

```
SetTextJustification (hdc, 0, 0) ;
```

Working with Paragraphs

If you're working with a whole paragraph, you have to start at the beginning and scan through the string looking for blanks. Every time you encounter a blank, you call *GetTextExtentPoint32* to determine if the text still fits between the left and right margins. When the text exceeds the space allowed for it, you backtrack to the previous blank. Now you have determined the character string for the line. If you want to justify the line, call *SetTextJustification* and *TextOut*, clear out the error term, and proceed to the next line.

The JUSTIFY1 program, shown in Figure 4-34, does this job for the first paragraph of Herman Melville's *Moby Dick*. It's hard-coded for a 15-point Times New Roman font, but you can change that in the *MyCreateFont* function defined near the top of the program and recompile. You can also change the alignment using the identifiers at the top of the program. Figure 4-35 shows the JUSTIFY1 display.

JUSTIFY1.MAK

```
#-----------------------
# JUSTIFY1.MAK make file
#-----------------------

justify1.exe : justify1.obj ezfont.obj
     $(LINKER) $(GUIFLAGS) -OUT:justify1.exe justify1.obj ezfont.obj $(GUILIBS)

justify1.obj : justify1.c
     $(CC) $(CFLAGS) justify1.c

ezfont.obj : ezfont.c
     $(CC) $(CFLAGS) ezfont.c
```

JUSTIFY1.C

```
/*-------------------------------------------
   JUSTIFY1.C -- Justified Type Program
                (c) Charles Petzold, 1996
   -------------------------------------------*/
```

Figure 4-34. *The JUSTIFY1 program.*   *(continued)*

```
#include <windows.h>
#include "ezfont.h"

#define LEFT            0
#define RIGHT           1
#define CENTER          2
#define JUSTIFIED       3


#define ALIGN           JUSTIFIED


#define MyCreateFont EzCreateFont (hdc, "Times New Roman", 150, 0, 0, TRUE)


LRESULT CALLBACK WndProc (HWND, UINT, WPARAM, LPARAM) ;

int WINAPI WinMain (HINSTANCE hInstance, HINSTANCE hPrevInstance,
                    PSTR szCmdLine, int iCmdShow)
     {
     static    char szAppName[] = "Justify1" ;
     HWND       hwnd ;
     MSG        msg ;
     WNDCLASSEX wndclass ;

     wndclass.cbSize        = sizeof (wndclass) ;
     wndclass.style         = CS_HREDRAW | CS_VREDRAW ;
     wndclass.lpfnWndProc   = WndProc ;
     wndclass.cbClsExtra    = 0 ;
     wndclass.cbWndExtra    = 0 ;
     wndclass.hInstance     = hInstance ;
     wndclass.hIcon         = LoadIcon (NULL, IDI_APPLICATION) ;
     wndclass.hCursor       = LoadCursor (NULL, IDC_ARROW) ;
     wndclass.hbrBackground = (HBRUSH) GetStockObject (WHITE_BRUSH) ;
     wndclass.lpszMenuName  = szAppName ;
     wndclass.lpszClassName = szAppName ;
     wndclass.hIconSm       = LoadIcon (NULL, IDI_APPLICATION) ;

     RegisterClassEx (&wndclass) ;

     hwnd = CreateWindow (szAppName, "Justified Type",
                          WS_OVERLAPPEDWINDOW,
                          CW_USEDEFAULT, CW_USEDEFAULT,
                          CW_USEDEFAULT, CW_USEDEFAULT,
                          NULL, NULL, hInstance, NULL) ;

     ShowWindow (hwnd, iCmdShow) ;
     UpdateWindow (hwnd) ;
```

(continued)

```
    while (GetMessage (&msg, NULL, 0, 0))
        {
        TranslateMessage (&msg) ;
        DispatchMessage (&msg) ;
        }
    return msg.wParam ;
    }

void DrawRuler (HDC hdc, RECT *prc)
    {
    static int iRuleSize [16] = { 360, 72, 144, 72, 216, 72, 144, 72,
                                  288, 72, 144, 72, 216, 72, 144, 72 } ;

    int        i, j ;
    POINT      ptClient ;

    SaveDC (hdc) ;
                    // Set Logical Twips mapping mode

    SetMapMode (hdc, MM_ANISOTROPIC) ;
    SetWindowExtEx (hdc, 1440, 1440, NULL) ;
    SetViewportExtEx (hdc, GetDeviceCaps (hdc, LOGPIXELSX),
                        GetDeviceCaps (hdc, LOGPIXELSY), NULL) ;

                    // Move the origin to a half inch from upper left

    SetWindowOrgEx (hdc, -720, -720, NULL) ;

                    // Find the right margin (quarter inch from right)

    ptClient.x = prc->right ;
    ptClient.y = prc->bottom ;
    DPtoLP (hdc, &ptClient, 1) ;
    ptClient.x -= 360 ;

                    // Draw the rulers

    MoveToEx (hdc, 0,            -360, NULL) ;
    LineTo   (hdc, ptClient.x, -360) ;
    MoveToEx (hdc, -360,           0, NULL) ;
    LineTo   (hdc, -360, ptClient.y) ;

    for (i = 0, j = 0 ; i <= ptClient.x ; i += 1440 / 16, j++)
        {
        MoveToEx (hdc, i, -360, NULL) ;
        LineTo   (hdc, i, -360 - iRuleSize [j % 16]) ;
        }
```

(continued)

```
        for (i = 0, j = 0 ; i <= ptClient.y ; i += 1440 / 16, j++)
            {
            MoveToEx (hdc, -360, i, NULL) ;
            LineTo   (hdc, -360 - iRuleSize [j % 16], i) ;
            }

    RestoreDC (hdc, -1) ;
    }

void Justify (HDC hdc, PSTR pText, RECT *prc, int iAlign)
    {
    int  xStart, yStart, iBreakCount ;
    PSTR pBegin, pEnd ;
    SIZE size ;

    yStart = prc->top ;
    do                              // for each text line
        {
        iBreakCount = 0 ;
        while (*pText == ' ')
                                    // skip over leading blanks
            pText++ ;
        pBegin = pText ;

        do                          // until the line is known
            {
            pEnd = pText ;

            while (*pText != '\0' && *pText++ != ' ') ;
            if (*pText == '\0')
                break ;
                                    // for each space, calculate extents
            iBreakCount++ ;
            SetTextJustification (hdc, 0, 0) ;
            GetTextExtentPoint32 (hdc, pBegin, pText - pBegin - 1, &size) ;
            }
        while ((int) size.cx < (prc->right - prc->left)) ;

        iBreakCount-- ;
        while (*(pEnd - 1) == ' ')   // eliminate trailing blanks
            {
            pEnd-- ;
            iBreakCount-- ;
            }
```

(continued)

```
            if (*pText == '\0' || iBreakCount <= 0)
                pEnd = pText ;

        SetTextJustification (hdc, 0, 0) ;
        GetTextExtentPoint32 (hdc, pBegin, pEnd - pBegin, &size) ;

        switch (iAlign)                    // use alignment for xStart
            {
            case LEFT :
                xStart = prc->left ;
                break ;

            case RIGHT :
                xStart = prc->right - size.cx ;
                break ;

            case CENTER :
                xStart = (prc->right + prc->left - size.cx) / 2 ;
                break ;

            case JUSTIFIED :
                if (*pText != '\0' && iBreakCount > 0)
                    SetTextJustification (hdc,
                        prc->right - prc->left - size.cx,
                        iBreakCount) ;
                xStart = prc->left ;
                break ;
            }

        TextOut (hdc, xStart, yStart, pBegin, pEnd - pBegin) ;
        yStart += size.cy ;
        pText = pEnd ;
        }
    while (*pText && yStart < prc->bottom) ;

    }


LRESULT CALLBACK WndProc (HWND hwnd, UINT iMsg, WPARAM wParam,
                                               LPARAM lParam)
    {
    static char szText[] = "Call me Ishmael. Some years ago -- never mind "
                        "how long precisely -- having little or no money "
                        "in my purse, and nothing particular to interest "
```

(continued)

```
                         "me on shore, I thought I would sail about a "
                         "little and see the watery part of the world. It "
                         "is a way I have of driving off the spleen, and "
                         "regulating the circulation.  Whenever I find "
                         "myself growing grim about the mouth; whenever "
                         "it is a damp, drizzly November in my soul; "
                         "whenever I find myself involuntarily pausing "
                         "before coffin warehouses, and bringing up the "
                         "rear of every funeral I meet; and especially "
                         "whenever my hypos get such an upper hand of me, "
                         "that it requires a strong moral principle to "
                         "prevent me from deliberately stepping into the "
                         "street, and methodically knocking people's hats "
                         "off -- then, I account it high time to get to sea "
                         "as soon as I can. This is my substitute for "
                         "pistol and ball.  With a philosophical flourish "
                         "Cato throws himself upon his sword; I quietly "
                         "take to the ship. There is nothing surprising "
                         "in this. If they but knew it, almost all men in "
                         "their degree, some time or other, cherish very "
                         "nearly the same feelings towards the ocean with "
                         "me." ;

HDC           hdc ;
PAINTSTRUCT ps ;
RECT          rcClient ;

switch (iMsg)
     {
     case WM_PAINT :
          hdc = BeginPaint (hwnd, &ps) ;

          GetClientRect (hwnd, &rcClient) ;
          DrawRuler (hdc, &rcClient) ;

          rcClient.left  += GetDeviceCaps (hdc, LOGPIXELSX) / 2 ;
          rcClient.top   += GetDeviceCaps (hdc, LOGPIXELSY) / 2 ;
          rcClient.right -= GetDeviceCaps (hdc, LOGPIXELSX) / 4 ;

          SelectObject (hdc, MyCreateFont) ;

          Justify (hdc, szText, &rcClient, ALIGN) ;

          DeleteObject (SelectObject (hdc, GetStockObject (SYSTEM_FONT)));
          EndPaint (hwnd, &ps) ;
          return 0 ;
```

(continued)

```
        case WM_DESTROY :
                PostQuitMessage (0) ;
                return 0 ;
        }
    return DefWindowProc (hwnd, iMsg, wParam, lParam) ;
    }
```

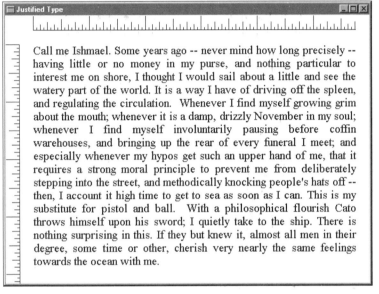

Figure 4-35. *The JUSTIFY1 display.*

JUSTIFY1 displays a ruler (in logical inches, of course) across the top and down the left side of the client area. The *DrawRuler* function draws the ruler. A rectangle structure defines the area in which the text must be justified.

The bulk of the work involved with formatting this text is in the *Justify* function. JUSTIFY1 starts searching for blanks at the beginning of the text and uses *GetTextExtentPoint32* to measure each line. When the length of the line exceeds the width of the display area, JUSTIFY1 returns to the previous space and uses the line up to that point. Depending on the value of the ALIGN constant, the line is left aligned, right aligned, centered, or justified.

JUSTIFY isn't perfect. In particular, the justification logic falls apart when there are fewer than two words in each line. Even if we solve this problem (which isn't a particularly difficult one), the program still won't work properly when a single word is too long to fit within the left and right margins. Of course, matters can become even more complex when you start working with programs that can use multiple fonts on the same line (as Windows word processors do with apparent ease). But nobody ever claimed this stuff was easy. It's just easier than if you were doing all the work yourself.

Means of Input

Chapter 5

The Keyboard

Like most interactive programs that run on personal computers, Windows 95 applications rely heavily on the keyboard for user input. Although Windows also supports a mouse as an input device, the keyboard still rules supreme. Indeed, because some older PC users prefer using the keyboard rather than a mouse, it is recommended that program developers attempt to implement complete program functionality from the keyboard. (Of course, in some cases, such as drawing programs or desktop publishing programs, this is simply not practical and a mouse will be required.)

The keyboard cannot be treated solely as an input device in isolation from other program functions. For example, programs often echo keyboard input by displaying typed characters in the client area of a window. Thus, handling keyboard input and displaying text must be treated together. If adapting your program to foreign languages and markets is important to you, you'll also need to know something about the Windows 95 support of the extended ASCII character set (codes of 128 and above), double-byte character sets (DBCS), and the Windows NT support of the 16-bit keyboard encoding known as Unicode.

KEYBOARD BASICS

As you might guess, the message-based architecture of Windows is ideal for working with the keyboard. Your program learns about keystrokes through messages that are delivered to your window procedure.

Actually, it's a bit more complicated than that: As the user presses and releases keys, the keyboard driver passes the keystrokes to Windows. Windows saves the keystrokes (in the form of messages) in the *system* message queue. It then transfers the keyboard messages one at a time to the message queue of the program that contains the window with the current "input focus" (which I'll discuss shortly). The program then dispatches the messages to the proper window procedure.

The reason for this two-step process—storing messages first in the system message queue and then passing them to the application message queue—involves synchronization. When a user types on the keyboard faster than a program can process the keys, Windows stores the extra keystrokes in the system message queue because one of these extra keystrokes may have the effect of switching input focus to another program. The successive keys should then go to the other program. Windows correctly synchronizes such keyboard messages.

Windows sends eight different messages to programs to indicate various keyboard events. That may seem like a lot, but your program can safely ignore many of them. Also, in most cases, the keyboard information encoded in these messages is probably more than your program needs. Part of the job of handling the keyboard is knowing which messages are important and which are not.

Ignoring the Keyboard

Although the keyboard is the primary source of user input to Windows programs, your program does not need to act on every keyboard message it receives. Windows handles many keyboard functions itself. For instance, you can ignore keystrokes that pertain to system functions. These keystrokes generally involve the Alt key.

A program need not monitor these keystrokes because Windows notifies a program of the *effect* of the keystrokes. (A program can monitor the keystrokes if it wants to, however.) For instance, if the Windows user selects a menu item with the keyboard, Windows sends the program a message that the menu item has been selected, regardless of whether it was selected by using the mouse or by using the keyboard. (Menus are covered in Chapter 10.)

Some Windows programs use "keyboard accelerators" to invoke common menu items. The accelerators generally involve the function keys or a letter in combination with the Ctrl key. These keyboard accelerators are defined in a program's resource script. (Chapter 10 shows how Windows translates the accelerators into menu command messages. You don't have to do the translation yourself.)

Dialog boxes (covered in Chapter 11) also have a keyboard interface, but programs usually do not need to monitor the keyboard when a dialog box is active. The keyboard interface is handled by Windows, and Windows sends messages to your program about the effects of the keystrokes. Dialog boxes can contain "edit" controls for text input. These are generally small boxes in which the user types a character string. Windows handles all the edit control logic and gives your program the final contents of the edit control when the user is done.

Even within your main window you can define child windows that function as edit controls. An extreme example of this is the POPPAD program shown in Chapter 8. This program is little more than a large multiline edit control and relies on Windows to handle all the dirty work.

Focus, Focus, Who's Got the Focus?

The keyboard must be shared by all applications running under Windows. Some applications may have more than one window, and the keyboard must be shared by these windows within the same application. When a key on the keyboard is pressed, only one window procedure can receive a message that the key has been pressed. The window that receives this keyboard message is the window with the "input focus."

The concept of input focus is closely related to the concept of "active window." The window with the input focus is either the active window or a child window of the active window. The active window is usually easy to identify. If the active window has a title bar, Windows highlights the title bar. If the active window has a dialog frame (a form most commonly seen in dialog boxes) instead of a title bar, Windows highlights the frame. If the active window has been minimized, then Windows highlights the title bar text.

The most common child windows are controls such as push buttons, radio buttons, check boxes, scroll bars, edit boxes, and list boxes that usually appear in a dialog box. Child windows are never themselves active windows. If a child window has the input focus, then the active window is its parent. Child window controls indicate that they have the input focus generally by using a flashing cursor or caret.

If the active window has been minimized, then no window has the input focus. Windows continues to send keyboard messages to the program, but these messages are in a different form from keyboard messages sent to active windows that are not minimized.

A window procedure can determine when it has the input focus by trapping WM_SETFOCUS and WM_KILLFOCUS messages. WM_SETFOCUS indicates that the window is receiving the input focus, and WM_KILLFOCUS signals that the window is losing the input focus.

Keystrokes and Characters

The messages that an application receives from Windows about keyboard events distinguish between "keystrokes" and "characters." This is in accordance with the two ways you can view the keyboard. First, you can think of the keyboard as a collection of keys. The keyboard has only one A key. Pressing that key is a keystroke. Releasing that key is a keystroke. But the keyboard is also an input device that generates displayable characters. The A key can generate several characters depending on the status of the Ctrl, Shift, and Caps Lock keys. Normally, the character is a lowercase a. If the Shift key is down or Caps Lock is toggled on, the character is an uppercase A. If Ctrl is down, the character is a Ctrl-A. On a foreign-language keyboard, the A keystroke may be preceded by a "dead-character key" or by Shift, Ctrl, or Alt in various combinations. The combinations could generate a lowercase a or an uppercase A with an accent mark.

For keystroke combinations that result in displayable characters, Windows sends a program both keystroke messages and character messages. Some keys do not generate characters. These include the shift keys, the function keys, the cursor movement keys, and special keys such as Insert and Delete. For these keys, Windows generates only keystroke messages.

KEYSTROKE MESSAGES

When you press a key, Windows places either a WM_KEYDOWN or WM_SYSKEYDOWN message in the message queue of the window with the input focus. When you release a key, Windows places either a WM_KEYUP or WM_SYSKEYUP message in the message queue.

	Key Pressed	*Key Released*
Nonsystem Keystroke:	WM_KEYDOWN	WM_KEYUP
System Keystroke:	WM_SYSKEYDOWN	WM_SYSKEYUP

Usually the "down" and "up" messages occur in pairs. However, if you hold down a key so that the typematic (autorepeat) action takes over, Windows sends the window procedure a series of WM_KEYDOWN (or WM_SYSKEYDOWN) messages and a single WM_KEYUP (or WM_SYSKEYUP) message when the key is finally released. Like all queued messages, keystroke messages are time-stamped. You can obtain the relative time a key was pressed or released by calling *GetMessageTime*.

System and Nonsystem Keystrokes

The "SYS" in WM_SYSKEYDOWN and WM_SYSKEYUP stands for "system" and refers to keystrokes that are more important to Windows than to the Windows application. The WM_SYSKEYDOWN and WM_SYSKEYUP messages are usually generated for keys typed in combination with the Alt key. These keystrokes invoke options on the program's menu or system menu, or they are used for system functions such as switching the active window (Alt-Tab or Alt-Esc) or for system menu accelerators (Alt in combination with a function key). Programs usually ignore the WM_SYSKEYUP and WM_SYSKEYDOWN messages and pass them to *DefWindowProc*. Because Windows takes care of all the Alt-key logic, you really have no need to trap these messages. Your window procedure will eventually receive other messages concerning the result of these keystrokes (such as a menu selection). If you want to include code in your window procedure to trap the system keystroke messages (as we will do in the KEYLOOK program later in this chapter), pass the messages to *DefWindowProc* after you process them so that Windows can still use them for their normal purposes.

But think about this for a moment. Almost everything that affects your program's window passes through your window procedure first. Windows does something with the message only if you pass the message to *DefWindowProc.* For instance, if you add the lines:

```
case WM_SYSKEYDOWN :
case WM_SYSKEYUP :
case WM_SYSCHAR :
      return 0 ;
```

to a window procedure, then you effectively disable all Alt-key operations (menu commands, Alt-Tab, Alt-Esc, and so on) when your program has the input focus. Although I doubt you would want to do this, I trust you're beginning to sense the power in your window procedure.

The WM_KEYDOWN and WM_KEYUP messages are usually generated for keys that are pressed and released without the Alt key. Your program may use or discard these keystroke messages. Windows itself doesn't care about them.

The *lParam* Variable

For all four keystroke messages, the 32-bit *lParam* variable passed to the window procedure is divided into six fields: Repeat Count, OEM Scan Code, Extended Key Flag, Context Code, Previous Key State, and Transition State. (See Figure 5-1.)

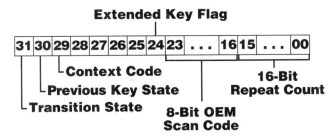

Figure 5-1. *The six keystroke-message fields of the* lParam *variable.*

Repeat Count

The Repeat Count is the number of keystrokes represented by the message. In most cases the Repeat Count is set to 1. However, if a key is held down and your window procedure is not fast enough to process key-down messages at the typematic rate (approximately a 10-character-per-second default), Windows combines several WM_KEYDOWN or WM-_SYSKEYDOWN messages into a single message and increases Repeat Count accordingly. The Repeat Count is always 1 for a WM_KEYUP or WM_SYSKEYUP message.

Because a Repeat Count greater than 1 indicates that typematic keystrokes are occurring faster than your program can process them, you may want to ignore the Repeat Count when processing the keyboard messages. Almost everyone has had the experience of "overscrolling" a word-processing document or spreadsheet because extra keystrokes have stacked up in the keyboard buffer. Ignoring the Repeat Count in your program will significantly reduce the possibilities for overscrolling. However, in other cases you will want to use the Repeat Count. You should probably try your programs both ways and see which approach feels the most natural.

OEM Scan Code

The OEM Scan Code is the keyboard scan code generated by the hardware of the computer. (If you're familiar with assembly language programming, this scan code is the same as the value passed back to a program in register AH during a BIOS Interrupt 16H call.) Windows applications generally ignore the OEM Scan Code because there are better ways to decode keyboard information.

Extended Key Flag

The Extended Key Flag is 1 if the keystroke results from one of the additional keys on the IBM Enhanced Keyboard. (The IBM Enhanced Keyboard has function keys across the top and a separate [combined] keypad for cursor keys and number keys.) This flag is set to 1 for the Alt and Ctrl keys at the right of the keyboard, the cursor movement keys (including Insert and Delete) that are not part of the numeric keypad, the Slash (/) and Enter keys on the numeric keypad, and the Num Lock key. Windows programs generally ignore the Extended Key Flag.

Context Code

The Context Code is 1 if the Alt key is pressed. This bit will always be 1 for the WM_SYS-KEYUP and WM_SYSKEYDOWN messages and 0 for the WM_KEYUP and WM_KEYDOWN messages, with two exceptions:

- If the active window is minimized, it does not have the input focus. All keystrokes generate WM_SYSKEYUP and WM_SYSKEYDOWN messages. If the Alt key is not pressed, the Context Code field is set to 0. (Windows uses SYS keyboard messages so that the active window that is minimized doesn't process these keystrokes.)

- On some foreign-language keyboards, certain characters are generated by combining Shift, Ctrl, or Alt with another key. In these cases the *lParam* variable that accompanies WM_KEYUP and WM_KEYDOWN messages has a 1 in the Context Code field, but the messages are not system keystroke messages.

Previous Key State

The Previous Key State is 0 if the key was previously up and 1 if the key was previously down. It is always set to 1 for a WM_KEYUP or WM_SYSKEYUP message, but it can be 0 or 1 for a WM_KEYDOWN or WM_SYSKEYDOWN message. A 1 indicates second and subsequent messages for keys that are the result of typematic action.

Transition State

The Transition State is 0 if the key is being pressed and 1 if the key is being released. The field is set to 0 for a WM_KEYDOWN or WM_SYSKEYDOWN message and to 1 for a WM_KEYUP or WM_SYSKEYUP message.

Virtual Key Codes

Although some information in *lParam* might be useful for processing WM_KEYUP, WM_KEYDOWN, WM_SYSKEYUP, and WM_SYSKEYDOWN messages, the *wParam* parameter is much more important. This parameter contains the "virtual key code" that identifies the key that was pressed or released. The developers of Windows have attempted to define virtual keys in a device-independent manner. For this reason, some virtual key codes cannot be generated on the IBM PC and strict compatibles but may be found on other manufacturer's keyboards.

The virtual key codes you use most often have names defined in the Windows header files. The table below shows these names along with the numeric key codes and the IBM PC key that corresponds to the virtual key. Although all keys cause keystroke messages, the table does not include any symbol keys (such as the key with the / and ? symbols). These keys have virtual key codes of 128 and above, and they are often defined differently for international keyboards. You can determine the values of these virtual key codes using the KEYLOOK program that is shown later in this chapter, but normally you should not process keystroke messages for these keys.

VIRTUAL KEY CODES

Decimal	Hex	WINDOWS.H Identifier	Required	IBM Keyboard
1	01	VK_LBUTTON		
2	02	VK_RBUTTON		
3	03	VK_CANCEL	✓	Ctrl-Break
4	04	VK_MBUTTON		
8	08	VK_BACK	✓	Backspace
9	09	VK_TAB	✓	Tab

(continued)

VIRTUAL KEY CODES *continued*

Decimal	Hex	WINDOWS.H Identifier	Required	IBM Keyboard
12	0C	VK_CLEAR		Numeric keypad 5 with Num Lock OFF
13	0D	VK_RETURN	✓	Enter
16	10	VK_SHIFT	✓	Shift
17	11	VK_CONTROL	✓	Ctrl
18	12	VK_MENU	✓	Alt
19	13	VK_PAUSE		Pause
20	14	VK_CAPITAL	✓	Caps Lock
27	1B	VK_ESCAPE	✓	Esc
32	20	VK_SPACE	✓	Spacebar
33	21	VK_PRIOR	✓	Page Up
34	22	VK_NEXT	✓	Page Down
35	23	VK_END		End
36	24	VK_HOME	✓	Home
37	25	VK_LEFT	✓	Left Arrow
38	26	VK_UP	✓	Up Arrow
39	27	VK_RIGHT	✓	Right Arrow
40	28	VK_DOWN	✓	Down Arrow
41	29	VK_SELECT		
42	2A	VK_PRINT		
43	2B	VK_EXECUTE		
44	2C	VK_SNAPSHOT		Print Screen
45	2D	VK_INSERT	✓	Insert
46	2E	VK_DELETE	✓	Delete
47	2F	VK_HELP		
48–57	30–39		✓	0 through 9 on main keyboard
65–90	41–5A		✓	A through Z
96	60	VK_NUMPAD0		Numeric keypad 0 with Num Lock ON
97	61	VK_NUMPAD1		Numeric keypad 1 with Num Lock ON
98	62	VK_NUMPAD2		Numeric keypad 2 with Num Lock ON
99	63	VK_NUMPAD3		Numeric keypad 3 with Num Lock ON
100	64	VK_NUMPAD4		Numeric keypad 4 with Num Lock ON
101	65	VK_NUMPAD5		Numeric keypad 5 with Num Lock ON
102	66	VK_NUMPAD6		Numeric keypad 6 with Num Lock ON
103	67	VK_NUMPAD7		Numeric keypad 7 with Num Lock ON

VIRTUAL KEY CODES *continued*

Decimal	Hex	*WINDOWS.H* Identifier	Required	IBM Keyboard
104	68	VK_NUMPAD8		Numeric keypad 8 with Num Lock ON
105	69	VK_NUMPAD9		Numeric keypad 9 with Num Lock ON
106	6A	VK_MULTIPLY		Numeric keypad *
107	6B	VK_ADD		Numeric keypad +
108	6C	VK_SEPARATOR		
109	6D	VK_SUBTRACT		Numeric keypad -
110	6E	VK_DECIMAL		Numeric keypad .
111	6F	VK_DIVIDE		Numeric keypad /
112	70	VK_F1	✔	Function key F1
113	71	VK_F2	✔	Function key F2
114	72	VK_F3	✔	Function key F3
115	73	VK_F4	✔	Function key F4
116	74	VK_F5	✔	Function key F5
117	75	VK_F6	✔	Function key F6
118	76	VK_F7	✔	Function key F7
119	77	VK_F8	✔	Function key F8
120	78	VK_F9	✔	Function key F9
121	79	VK_F10	✔	Function key F10
122	7A	VK_F11		Function key F11 (enhanced keyboard)
123	7B	VK_F12		Function key F12 (enhanced keyboard)
124	7C	VK_F13		
125	7D	VK_F14		
126	7E	VK_F15		
127	7F	VK_F16		
144	90	VK_NUMLOCK		Num Lock
145	91	VK_SCROLL		Scroll Lock

A checkmark (✔) in the column labeled "Required" indicates that the key is mandatory for any Windows implementation. Windows also requires that a keyboard and keyboard driver allow the Shift, Ctrl, and Shift and Ctrl keys together to be combined with all letter keys, all required cursor keys, and all required function keys. The VK_LBUTTON, VK_MBUTTON, and VK_RBUTTON virtual key codes refer to the left, middle, and right buttons of a mouse. However, you will never receive keystroke messages with *wParam* set to these values. The mouse generates its own messages, as we'll see in the next chapter.

Shift States

The *wParam* and *lParam* parameters that accompany WM_KEYDOWN, WM_KEYUP, WM_SYSKEYDOWN, and WM_SYSKEYUP messages do not tell your program about the state of the shift keys. You can obtain the current state of any virtual key using the *GetKeyState* function. This function generally is used to obtain the state of shift keys (Shift, Ctrl, and Alt) and toggle keys (Caps Lock, Num Lock, and Scroll Lock). For instance:

```
GetKeyState (VK_SHIFT) ;
```

returns a negative value (that is, the high bit is set) if the Shift key is down. The value returned from:

```
GetKeyState (VK_CAPITAL) ;
```

has the low bit set if the Caps Lock key is toggled on. You can also obtain the state of the mouse buttons using the virtual key codes VK_LBUTTON, VK_RBUTTON, and VK_MBUTTON. However, most Windows programs that need to monitor a combination of mouse buttons and keystrokes usually do it the other way around—by checking keystrokes when they receive a mouse message. In fact, shift-state information is included in the mouse messages (as you'll see in the next chapter).

Be careful with *GetKeyState*. It is not a real-time keyboard status check. Rather, it is a check of the keyboard status up to and including the current message being processed. *GetKeyState* does not let you retrieve keyboard information independent of normal keyboard messages. For instance, you may want to hold up processing in your window procedure until the user presses the F1 function key:

```
while (GetKeyState (VK_F1) >= 0) ;  // WRONG !!!
```

Don't do it! Your program must retrieve the keyboard message from the queue before *GetKeyState* can retrieve the state of the key. This synchronization actually works to your advantage because if you need to know the shift state for a particular keystroke message, *GetKeyState* is guaranteed to be accurate, even if you are processing the message after the shift key has been released. If you really need the current state of the key, you can use *GetAsyncKeyState*.

Using Keystroke Messages

The idea of a program getting information about every keystroke is certainly nice; however, most Windows programs ignore all but a few keystroke messages. The WM_SYSKEYDOWN and WM_SYSKEYUP messages are for Windows system functions, and you don't need to look at them. If you process WM_KEYDOWN messages, you can usually also ignore WM_KEYUP messages.

Windows programs generally use WM_KEYDOWN messages for keystrokes that do not generate characters. Although you may think that it's possible to use keystroke messages in combination with shift-state information to translate keystroke messages into character messages, don't do it. You'll have problems with international keyboard differences. For instance, if you get a WM_KEYDOWN message with *wParam* equal to 33H, you know the user pressed the 3 key. So far, so good. If you use *GetKeyState* and find out that the Shift key is down, you might assume that the user is typing a pound sign (#). Not necessarily so. A British user is typing a £. So the WM_KEYDOWN messages are most useful for the cursor movement keys, the function keys, and special keys such as Insert and Delete. However, sometimes Insert, Delete, and the function keys appear as menu accelerators. Because Windows translates menu accelerators into menu command messages, you don't have to process the keystrokes themselves. Some non-Windows programs for the PC use function keys extensively in combination with the Shift, Ctrl, and Alt keys. You can do something similar in your Windows programs, but it's not recommended. If you want to use the function keys, they should duplicate menu commands. One objective in Windows is to provide a user interface that doesn't require memorization or using complex command charts.

We've managed to eliminate everything except one final case: Most of the time, you will process WM_KEYDOWN messages only for cursor movement keys. When you use the cursor keys, you can check the Shift-key and Ctrl-key states through *GetKeyState*. Windows functions often use the Shift key in combination with the cursor keys to extend a selection in (for instance) a word-processing document. The Ctrl key is often used to alter the meaning of the cursor key. (For example, Ctrl in combination with the Right Arrow key might mean to move the cursor one word to the right.)

One of the best ways to determine how to use the keyboard is to examine how the keyboard is used in existing popular Windows programs. If you don't like those definitions, you are free to do something different. But keep in mind that doing so may be detrimental to a user's ability to quickly learn your program.

ENHANCING SYSMETS: ADDING A KEYBOARD INTERFACE

When we wrote the three versions of the SYSMETS program in Chapter 3, we didn't know anything about the keyboard. We were able to scroll the text only by using the mouse on the scroll bars. Now that we know how to process keystroke messages, let's add a keyboard interface to SYSMETS. This is obviously a job for cursor movement keys. We'll use most of the cursor movement keys (Home, End, Page Up, Page Down, Up Arrow, and Down Arrow) for vertical scrolling. The Left Arrow key and the Right Arrow key can take care of the less-important horizontal scrolling.

Adding WM_KEYDOWN Logic

One obvious way to create a keyboard interface is to add some WM_KEYDOWN logic to the window procedure that parallels the WM_VSCROLL and WM_HSCROLL logic:

```
case WM_KEYDOWN :
     iVscrollInc = iHscrollInc = 0 ;

     switch (wParam)
         {
         case VK_HOME :          // same as WM_VSCROLL, SB_TOP
              iVscrollInc = -iVscrollPos ;
              break ;

         case VK_END :           // same as WM_VSCROLL, SB_BOTTOM
              iVscrollInc = iVscrollMax - iVscrollPos ;
              break ;

         case VK_UP :            // same as WM_VSCROLL, SB_LINEUP
              iVscrollInc = -1 ;
              break ;

         case VK_DOWN :          // same as WM_VSCROLL, SB_LINEDOWN
              iVscrollInc = 1 ;
              break ;

         case VK_PRIOR :         // same as WM_VSCROLL, SB_PAGEUP
              iVscrollInc = min (-1, -cyClient / cyChar) ;
              break ;

         case VK_NEXT :          // same as WM_VSCROLL, SB_PAGEDOWN
              iVscrollInc = max (1, cyClient / cyChar) ;
              break ;

         case VK_LEFT :          // same as WM_HSCROLL, SB_PAGEUP
              iHscrollInc = -8 ;
              break ;

         case VK_RIGHT :         // same as WM_HSCROLL, SB_PAGEDOWN
              iHscrollInc = 8 ;
              break ;

         default :
              break ;
         }

     if (iVscrollInc = max (-iVscrollPos,
             min (iVscrollInc, iVscrollMax - iVscrollPos)))
```

```
            {
            iVscrollPos += iVscrollInc ;
            ScrollWindow (hwnd, 0, -cyChar * iVscrollInc, NULL, NULL) ;
            SetScrollPos (hwnd, SB_VERT, iVscrollPos, TRUE) ;
            UpdateWindow (hwnd) ;
            }

     if (iHscrollInc = max (-iHscrollPos,
               min (iHscrollInc, iHscrollMax - iHscrollPos)))
            {
            iHscrollPos += iHscrollInc ;
            ScrollWindow (hwnd, -cxChar * iHscrollInc, 0, NULL, NULL) ;
            SetScrollPos (hwnd, SB_HORZ, iHscrollPos, TRUE) ;
            }

     return 0 ;
```

Do you dislike this code as much as I do? Simply duplicating all the scroll bar code is unwise, because if we ever wanted to change the scroll bar logic, we'd have to make parallel changes in WM_KEYDOWN. There has to be a better way. And there is.

Sending Messages

Wouldn't it be better to simply translate each of these WM_KEYDOWN messages into an equivalent WM_VSCROLL and WM_HSCROLL message and then perhaps fool *WndProc* into thinking that it's getting a WM_VSCROLL or WM_HSCROLL message, perhaps by sending a phony scroll bar message to the window procedure? Windows lets you do this. The function is called *SendMessage*, and it takes the same parameters as those passed to the window procedure:

```
SendMessage (hwnd, message, wParam, lParam) ;
```

When you call *SendMessage*, Windows calls the window procedure whose window handle is *hwnd*, passing to it these four parameters. When the window procedure has completed processing the message, Windows returns control to the next statement following the *SendMessage* call. The window procedure to which you send the message could be the same window procedure, another window procedure in the same program, or even a window procedure in another application.

Here's how we might use *SendMessage* for processing WM_KEYDOWN codes in the SYSMETS program:

```
case WM_KEYDOWN :
     switch (wParam)
          {
          case VK_HOME :
               SendMessage (hwnd, WM_VSCROLL, SB_TOP, 0L) ;
               break ;
```

```
        case VK_END :
                SendMessage (hwnd, WM_VSCROLL, SB_BOTTOM, 0L) ;
                break ;

        case VK_PRIOR :
                SendMessage (hwnd, WM_VSCROLL, SB_PAGEUP, 0L) ;
                break ;
```

[other program lines]

OK, you get the general idea. Our goal was to add a keyboard interface to the scroll bars, and that's exactly what we've done. We've made the cursor movement keys duplicate scroll bar logic by actually sending the window procedure a scroll bar message. Now you see why I included SB_TOP and SB_BOTTOM processing for WM_VSCROLL messages in the SYSMETS3 program. It wasn't used then, but it's used now for processing the Home and End keys. The final SYSMETS program, shown in Figure 5-2, incorporates these changes. You'll also need the SYSMETS.H file from Chapter 3 (Figure 3-4) to compile this program.

SYSMETS.MAK

```
#----------------------
# SYSMETS.MAK make file
#----------------------

sysmets.exe : sysmets.obj
     $(LINKER) $(GUIFLAGS) -OUT:sysmets.exe sysmets.obj $(GUILIBS)

sysmets.obj : sysmets.c sysmets.h
     $(CC) $(CFLAGS) sysmets.c
```

SYSMETS.C

```
/*---------------------------------------------------------
   SYSMETS.C -- System Metrics Display Program (Final)
                (c) Charles Petzold, 1996
   ---------------------------------------------------------*/

#include <windows.h>
#include <string.h>
#include "sysmets.h"

LRESULT CALLBACK WndProc (HWND, UINT, WPARAM, LPARAM) ;
```

Figure 5-2. *The SYSMETS program.*   *(continued)*

```
int WINAPI WinMain (HINSTANCE hInstance, HINSTANCE hPrevInstance,
                    PSTR szCmdLine, int iCmdShow)
     {
     static char szAppName[] = "SysMets" ;
     HWND        hwnd ;
     MSG         msg ;
     WNDCLASSEX  wndclass ;

     wndclass.cbSize        = sizeof (wndclass) ;
     wndclass.style         = CS_HREDRAW | CS_VREDRAW ;
     wndclass.lpfnWndProc   = WndProc ;
     wndclass.cbClsExtra    = 0 ;
     wndclass.cbWndExtra    = 0 ;
     wndclass.hInstance     = hInstance ;
     wndclass.hIcon         = LoadIcon (NULL, IDI_APPLICATION) ;
     wndclass.hCursor       = LoadCursor (NULL, IDC_ARROW) ;
     wndclass.hbrBackground = (HBRUSH) GetStockObject (WHITE_BRUSH) ;
     wndclass.lpszMenuName  = NULL ;
     wndclass.lpszClassName = szAppName ;
     wndclass.hIconSm       = LoadIcon (NULL, IDI_APPLICATION) ;

     RegisterClassEx (&wndclass) ;

     hwnd = CreateWindow (szAppName, "System Metrics",
                          WS_OVERLAPPEDWINDOW | WS_VSCROLL | WS_HSCROLL,
                          CW_USEDEFAULT, CW_USEDEFAULT,
                          CW_USEDEFAULT, CW_USEDEFAULT,
                          NULL, NULL, hInstance, NULL) ;

     ShowWindow (hwnd, iCmdShow) ;
     UpdateWindow (hwnd) ;

     while (GetMessage (&msg, NULL, 0, 0))
          {
          TranslateMessage (&msg) ;
          DispatchMessage (&msg) ;
          }
     return msg.wParam ;
     }

LRESULT CALLBACK WndProc (HWND hwnd, UINT iMsg, WPARAM wParam, LPARAM lParam)
     {
     static int  cxChar, cxCaps, cyChar, cxClient, cyClient, iMaxWidth,
                 iVscrollPos, iVscrollMax, iHscrollPos, iHscrollMax ;
```

(continued)

```
char        szBuffer[10] ;
HDC         hdc ;
int         i, x, y, iPaintBeg, iPaintEnd, iVscrollInc,
            iHscrollInc ;
PAINTSTRUCT ps ;
TEXTMETRIC  tm ;

switch (iMsg)
    {
    case WM_CREATE :
        hdc = GetDC (hwnd) ;

        GetTextMetrics (hdc, &tm) ;
        cxChar = tm.tmAveCharWidth ;
        cxCaps = (tm.tmPitchAndFamily & 1 ? 3 : 2) * cxChar / 2 ;
        cyChar = tm.tmHeight + tm.tmExternalLeading ;

        ReleaseDC (hwnd, hdc) ;

        iMaxWidth = 40 * cxChar + 22 * cxCaps ;
        return 0 ;

    case WM_SIZE :
        cxClient = LOWORD (lParam) ;
        cyClient = HIWORD (lParam) ;

        iVscrollMax = max (0, NUMLINES + 2 - cyClient / cyChar) ;
        iVscrollPos = min (iVscrollPos, iVscrollMax) ;

        SetScrollRange (hwnd, SB_VERT, 0, iVscrollMax, FALSE) ;
        SetScrollPos   (hwnd, SB_VERT, iVscrollPos, TRUE) ;

        iHscrollMax = max (0, 2 + (iMaxWidth - cxClient) / cxChar) ;
        iHscrollPos = min (iHscrollPos, iHscrollMax) ;

        SetScrollRange (hwnd, SB_HORZ, 0, iHscrollMax, FALSE) ;
        SetScrollPos   (hwnd, SB_HORZ, iHscrollPos, TRUE) ;
        return 0 ;

    case WM_VSCROLL :
        switch (LOWORD (wParam))
            {
            case SB_TOP :
                iVscrollInc = -iVscrollPos ;
                break ;
```

(continued)

```
          case SB_BOTTOM :
               iVscrollInc = iVscrollMax - iVscrollPos ;
               break ;

          case SB_LINEUP :
               iVscrollInc = -1 ;
               break ;

          case SB_LINEDOWN :
               iVscrollInc = 1 ;
               break ;

          case SB_PAGEUP :
               iVscrollInc = min (-1, -cyClient / cyChar) ;
               break ;

          case SB_PAGEDOWN :
               iVscrollInc = max (1, cyClient / cyChar) ;
               break ;

          case SB_THUMBTRACK :
               iVscrollInc = HIWORD (wParam) - iVscrollPos ;
               break ;

          default :
               iVscrollInc = 0 ;
          }
     iVscrollInc = max (-iVscrollPos,
                    min (iVscrollInc, iVscrollMax - iVscrollPos)) ;

     if (iVscrollInc != 0)
          {
          iVscrollPos += iVscrollInc ;
          ScrollWindow (hwnd, 0, -cyChar * iVscrollInc, NULL, NULL) ;
          SetScrollPos (hwnd, SB_VERT, iVscrollPos, TRUE) ;
          UpdateWindow (hwnd) ;
          }
     return 0 ;

case WM_HSCROLL :
     switch (LOWORD (wParam))
          {
          case SB_LINEUP :
               iHscrollInc = -1 ;
               break ;
```

(continued)

```
                        case SB_LINEDOWN :
                             iHscrollInc = 1 ;
                             break ;

                        case SB_PAGEUP :
                             iHscrollInc = -8 ;
                             break ;

                        case SB_PAGEDOWN :
                             iHscrollInc = 8 ;
                             break ;

                        case SB_THUMBPOSITION :
                             iHscrollInc = HIWORD (wParam) - iHscrollPos ;
                             break ;

                        default :
                             iHscrollInc = 0 ;
                        }
                   iHscrollInc = max (-iHscrollPos,
                                 min (iHscrollInc, iHscrollMax - iHscrollPos)) ;

                   if (iHscrollInc != 0)
                        {
                        iHscrollPos += iHscrollInc ;
                        ScrollWindow (hwnd, -cxChar * iHscrollInc, 0, NULL, NULL) ;
                        SetScrollPos (hwnd, SB_HORZ, iHscrollPos, TRUE) ;
                        }
                   return 0 ;

              case WM_KEYDOWN :
                   switch (wParam)
                        {
                        case VK_HOME :
                             SendMessage (hwnd, WM_VSCROLL, SB_TOP, 0L) ;
                             break ;

                        case VK_END :
                             SendMessage (hwnd, WM_VSCROLL, SB_BOTTOM, 0L) ;
                             break ;

                        case VK_PRIOR :
                             SendMessage (hwnd, WM_VSCROLL, SB_PAGEUP, 0L) ;
                             break ;
```

(continued)

```
            case VK_NEXT :
                 SendMessage (hwnd, WM_VSCROLL, SB_PAGEDOWN, 0L) ;
                 break ;

            case VK_UP :
                 SendMessage (hwnd, WM_VSCROLL, SB_LINEUP, 0L) ;
                 break ;

            case VK_DOWN :
                 SendMessage (hwnd, WM_VSCROLL, SB_LINEDOWN, 0L) ;
                 break ;

            case VK_LEFT :
                 SendMessage (hwnd, WM_HSCROLL, SB_PAGEUP, 0L) ;
                 break ;

            case VK_RIGHT :
                 SendMessage (hwnd, WM_HSCROLL, SB_PAGEDOWN, 0L) ;
                 break ;
            }
       return 0 ;

case WM_PAINT :
       hdc = BeginPaint (hwnd, &ps) ;

       iPaintBeg = max (0, iVscrollPos + ps.rcPaint.top / cyChar - 1) ;
       iPaintEnd = min (NUMLINES,
                       iVscrollPos + ps.rcPaint.bottom / cyChar) ;

       for (i = iPaintBeg ; i < iPaintEnd ; i++)
            {
            x = cxChar * (1 - iHscrollPos) ;
            y = cyChar * (1 - iVscrollPos + i) ;

            TextOut (hdc, x, y,
                     sysmetrics[i].szLabel,
                     strlen (sysmetrics[i].szLabel)) ;

            TextOut (hdc, x + 22 * cxCaps, y,
                     sysmetrics[i].szDesc,
                     strlen (sysmetrics[i].szDesc)) ;

            SetTextAlign (hdc, TA_RIGHT | TA_TOP) ;
```

(continued)

```
                            TextOut (hdc, x + 22 * cxCaps + 40 * cxChar, y,
                                    szBuffer,
                                    wsprintf (szBuffer, "%5d",
                                            GetSystemMetrics (sysmetrics[i].iIndex))) ;

                            SetTextAlign (hdc, TA_LEFT | TA_TOP) ;
                            }

                    EndPaint (hwnd, &ps) ;
                    return 0 ;

            case WM_DESTROY :
                    PostQuitMessage (0) ;
                    return 0 ;
            }

    return DefWindowProc (hwnd, iMsg, wParam, lParam) ;
    }
```

CHARACTER MESSAGES

Earlier I discussed the idea of translating keystroke messages into character messages by taking into account shift-state information, and I warned that shift-state information is not enough: You also need to know about country-dependent keyboard configurations. For this reason, you should not attempt to translate keystroke messages into character codes yourself.

Windows does it for you. You've seen this code before:

```
while (GetMessage (&msg, NULL, 0, 0))
    {
    TranslateMessage (&msg) ;
    DispatchMessage (&msg) ;
    }
```

This is a typical message loop that appears in *WinMain*. The *GetMessage* function fills in the *msg* structure fields with the next message from the queue. *DispatchMessage* calls the appropriate window procedure with this message.

Between these two functions is *TranslateMessage*, which translates keystroke messages into character messages. If the message is WM_KEYDOWN or WM_SYSKEYDOWN, and if the keystroke in combination with the shift state produces a character, then *TranslateMessage* places a character message in the message queue. This character message will be the next message that *GetMessage* retrieves from the queue after the keystroke message.

There are four character messages:

	Characters	*Dead Characters*
Nonsystem Characters:	WM_CHAR	WM_DEADCHAR
System Characters:	WM_SYSCHAR	WM_SYSDEADCHAR

The WM_CHAR and WM_DEADCHAR messages are derived from WM_KEYDOWN messages. The WM_SYSCHAR and WM_SYSDEADCHAR messages are derived from WM_SYS-KEYDOWN messages. In most cases, your Windows program can ignore everything except WM_CHAR messages. The *lParam* parameter passed to the window procedure with the character code message is the same as the *lParam* parameter for the keystroke message that generated the character code message. The *wParam* parameter is the ASCII code for the character (yes, good old familiar ASCII).

The character messages are delivered to your window procedure sandwiched between keystroke messages. For instance, if Caps Lock is not toggled on and you press and release the A key, the window procedure receives the following three messages:

Message	*Key or Code*
WM_KEYDOWN	Virtual key A
WM_CHAR	ASCII code a
WM_KEYUP	Virtual key A

If you type an uppercase A by pressing the Shift key, pressing the A key, releasing the A key, and then releasing the Shift key, the window procedure receives five messages:

Message	*Key or Code*
WM_KEYDOWN	Virtual key VK_SHIFT
WM_KEYDOWN	Virtual key A
WM_CHAR	ASCII code A
WM_KEYUP	Virtual key A
WM_KEYUP	Virtual key VK_SHIFT

The Shift key by itself does not generate a character message.

If you hold down the A key so that the typematic action generates keystrokes, you'll get a character message for each WM_KEYDOWN message:

Message	Key or Code
WM_KEYDOWN	Virtual key A
WM_CHAR	ASCII code a
WM_KEYDOWN	Virtual key A
WM_CHAR	ASCII code a
WM_KEYDOWN	Virtual key A
WM_CHAR	ASCII code a
WM_KEYDOWN	Virtual key A
WM_CHAR	ASCII code a
WM_KEYUP	Virtual key A

If some of the WM_KEYDOWN messages have a Repeat Count greater than 1, the corresponding WM_CHAR messages will have the same Repeat Count.

The Ctrl key in combination with a letter key generates ASCII control codes from 01H (Ctrl-A) through 1AH (Ctrl-Z). You can also use other keys to generate these control codes. The following table shows the value of *wParam* in a WM_CHAR message for keys that generate control codes:

Key	ASCII Code	Duplicated by
Backspace	08H	Ctrl-H
Tab	09H	Ctrl-I
Ctrl-Enter	0AH	Ctrl-J
Enter	0DH	Ctrl-M
Esc	1BH	Ctrl-[

Windows programs sometimes use the Ctrl key in combination with letter keys for menu accelerators, in which case the letter keys are not translated into character messages.

WM_CHAR Messages

When your Windows program needs to process characters from the keyboard (for instance, in a word-processing or communications program), it will process WM_CHAR messages. You'll probably want some special processing for the Backspace, Tab, and Enter keys (and perhaps the Linefeed key), but you'll treat all other characters the same:

```
case WM_CHAR :

     switch (wParam)
         {
         case '\b' :    // backspace
```

```
             [other program lines]
             break ;

    case '\t' :     // tab
             [other program lines]
             break ;

    case '\n' :     // linefeed
             [other program lines]
             break ;

    case '\r' :     // carriage return
             [other program lines]
             break ;

    default :       // character code
             [other program lines]
             break ;
    }
return 0 ;
```

This program fragment is virtually identical to keyboard character processing in regular MS-DOS programs.

Dead-Character Messages

Windows programs can usually ignore WM_DEADCHAR and WM_SYSDEADCHAR messages. On some non-U.S. keyboards, certain keys are defined to add a diacritic to a letter. These are called "dead keys" because they don't create characters by themselves. For instance, when the German keyboard is installed, the key that is in the same position as the +/= key on a U.S. keyboard is a dead key for the acute accent (´) when unshifted and the grave accent (`) when shifted.

When a user presses this dead key, your window procedure receives a WM_DEAD-CHAR message with *wParam* equal to the ASCII code for the diacritic by itself. When the user then presses a letter key (for instance, the A key), the window procedure receives a WM_CHAR message where *wParam* is the ASCII code for the letter a with the diacritic. Thus, your program does not have to process the WM_DEADCHAR message, because the WM_CHAR message gives the program all the information it needs. The Windows logic even has built-in error handling: If the dead key is followed by a letter that can't take a diacritic (such as the letter s), then the window procedure receives two WM_CHAR messages in a row—the first with *wParam* equal to the ASCII code for the diacritic by itself (the same *wParam* value delivered with the WM_DEADCHAR message) and the second with *wParam* equal to the ASCII code for the letter s.

Looking at Keyboard Messages

If you'd like to see how Windows sends keyboard messages to a program, KEYLOOK (shown in Figure 5-3) will help. This program displays in its client area all the information that Windows sends the window procedure for the eight different keyboard messages.

KEYLOOK.MAK

```
#----------------------
# KEYLOOK.MAK make file
#----------------------

keylook.exe : keylook.obj
     $(LINKER) $(GUIFLAGS) -OUT:keylook.exe keylook.obj $(GUILIBS)

keylook.obj : keylook.c
     $(CC) $(CFLAGS) keylook.c
```

KEYLOOK.C

```c
/*------------------------------------------------------
   KEYLOOK.C -- Displays Keyboard and Character Messages
                (c) Charles Petzold, 1996
   ------------------------------------------------------*/

#include <windows.h>
#include <stdio.h>

LRESULT CALLBACK WndProc (HWND, UINT, WPARAM, LPARAM) ;

RECT rect ;
int  cxChar, cyChar ;

int WINAPI WinMain (HINSTANCE hInstance, HINSTANCE hPrevInstance,
                    PSTR szCmdLine, int iCmdShow)
     {
     static char szAppName[] = "KeyLook" ;
     HWND        hwnd ;
     MSG         msg ;
     WNDCLASSEX  wndclass ;

     wndclass.cbSize       = sizeof (wndclass) ;
     wndclass.style        = CS_HREDRAW | CS_VREDRAW ;
     wndclass.lpfnWndProc  = WndProc ;
     wndclass.cbClsExtra   = 0 ;
```

Figure 5-3. *The KEYLOOK program.*

(continued)

```
        wndclass.cbWndExtra    = 0 ;
        wndclass.hInstance     = hInstance ;
        wndclass.hIcon         = LoadIcon (NULL, IDI_APPLICATION) ;
        wndclass.hCursor       = LoadCursor (NULL, IDC_ARROW) ;
        wndclass.hbrBackground = (HBRUSH) GetStockObject (WHITE_BRUSH) ;
        wndclass.lpszMenuName  = NULL ;
        wndclass.lpszClassName = szAppName ;
        wndclass.hIconSm       = LoadIcon (NULL, IDI_APPLICATION) ;

        RegisterClassEx (&wndclass) ;

        hwnd = CreateWindow (szAppName, "Keyboard Message Looker",
                             WS_OVERLAPPEDWINDOW,
                             CW_USEDEFAULT, CW_USEDEFAULT,
                             CW_USEDEFAULT, CW_USEDEFAULT,
                             NULL, NULL, hInstance, NULL) ;

        ShowWindow (hwnd, iCmdShow) ;
        UpdateWindow (hwnd) ;

        while (GetMessage (&msg, NULL, 0, 0))
             {
             TranslateMessage (&msg) ;
             DispatchMessage (&msg) ;
             }
        return msg.wParam ;
        }

void ShowKey (HWND hwnd, int iType, char *szMessage,
              WPARAM wParam, LPARAM lParam)
        {
        static char *szFormat[2] = {
                       "%-14s %3d    %c %6u %4d %3s %3s %4s %4s",
                       "%-14s    %3d %c %6u %4d %3s %3s %4s %4s" } ;
        char       szBuffer[80] ;
        HDC        hdc ;

        ScrollWindow (hwnd, 0, -cyChar, &rect, &rect) ;
        hdc = GetDC (hwnd) ;

        SelectObject (hdc, GetStockObject (SYSTEM_FIXED_FONT)) ;

        TextOut (hdc, cxChar, rect.bottom - cyChar, szBuffer,
                 wsprintf (szBuffer, szFormat [iType],
                     szMessage, wParam,
                     (BYTE) (iType ? wParam : ' '),
```

(continued)

```
                        LOWORD (lParam),
                        HIWORD (lParam) & 0xFF,
                        (PSTR) (0x01000000 & lParam ? "Yes"  : "No"),
                        (PSTR) (0x20000000 & lParam ? "Yes"  : "No"),
                        (PSTR) (0x40000000 & lParam ? "Down" : "Up"),
                        (PSTR) (0x80000000 & lParam ? "Up"   : "Down"))) ;

          ReleaseDC (hwnd, hdc) ;
          ValidateRect (hwnd, NULL) ;
          }

LRESULT CALLBACK WndProc (HWND hwnd, UINT iMsg, WPARAM wParam, LPARAM lParam)
     {
     static char szTop[] =
               "Message         Key Char Repeat Scan Ext ALT Prev Tran" ;
     static char szUnd[] =
               "_____         ___ ____ _____ ____ ___ ___ ____ ____" ;
     HDC          hdc ;
     PAINTSTRUCT ps ;
     TEXTMETRIC  tm ;

     switch (iMsg)
          {
          case WM_CREATE :
               hdc = GetDC (hwnd) ;

               SelectObject (hdc, GetStockObject (SYSTEM_FIXED_FONT)) ;

               GetTextMetrics (hdc, &tm) ;
               cxChar = tm.tmAveCharWidth ;
               cyChar = tm.tmHeight ;

               ReleaseDC (hwnd, hdc) ;

               rect.top = 3 * cyChar / 2 ;
               return 0 ;

          case WM_SIZE :
               rect.right  = LOWORD (lParam) ;
               rect.bottom = HIWORD (lParam) ;
               UpdateWindow (hwnd) ;
               return 0 ;

          case WM_PAINT :
               InvalidateRect (hwnd, NULL, TRUE) ;
               hdc = BeginPaint (hwnd, &ps) ;
```

(continued)

266

```
          SelectObject (hdc, GetStockObject (SYSTEM_FIXED_FONT)) ;
          SetBkMode (hdc, TRANSPARENT) ;
          TextOut (hdc, cxChar, cyChar / 2, szTop, (sizeof szTop) - 1) ;
          TextOut (hdc, cxChar, cyChar / 2, szUnd, (sizeof szUnd) - 1) ;
          EndPaint (hwnd, &ps) ;
          return 0 ;

     case WM_KEYDOWN :
          ShowKey (hwnd, 0, "WM_KEYDOWN", wParam, lParam) ;
          return 0 ;

     case WM_KEYUP :
          ShowKey (hwnd, 0, "WM_KEYUP", wParam, lParam) ;
          return 0 ;

     case WM_CHAR :
          ShowKey (hwnd, 1, "WM_CHAR", wParam, lParam) ;
          return 0 ;

     case WM_DEADCHAR :
          ShowKey (hwnd, 1, "WM_DEADCHAR", wParam, lParam) ;
          return 0 ;

     case WM_SYSKEYDOWN :
          ShowKey (hwnd, 0, "WM_SYSKEYDOWN", wParam, lParam) ;
          break ;          // ie, call DefWindowProc

     case WM_SYSKEYUP :
          ShowKey (hwnd, 0, "WM_SYSKEYUP", wParam, lParam) ;
          break ;          // ie, call DefWindowProc

     case WM_SYSCHAR :
          ShowKey (hwnd, 1, "WM_SYSCHAR", wParam, lParam) ;
          break ;          // ie, call DefWindowProc

     case WM_SYSDEADCHAR :
          ShowKey (hwnd, 1, "WM_SYSDEADCHAR", wParam, lParam) ;
          break ;          // ie, call DefWindowProc

     case WM_DESTROY :
          PostQuitMessage (0) ;
          return 0 ;
     }
return DefWindowProc (hwnd, iMsg, wParam, lParam) ;
}
```

KEYLOOK uses the display like an old-fashioned teletype output device. When KEYLOOK receives a keystroke message, it calls *ScrollWindow* to scroll the contents of the entire client area of the window so that the contents move up the height of one character. *TextOut* is used to display the line of new information beginning one character height from the bottom. This is about as simple as a teletype output can get. Figure 5-4 shows what the KEYLOOK display looks like when you type the word "Windows." The first column shows the keyboard message, the second shows the virtual key code for keystroke messages, the third shows the character code (and the character itself) for character messages, and the other six columns show the states of the six fields in the *lParam* message parameter.

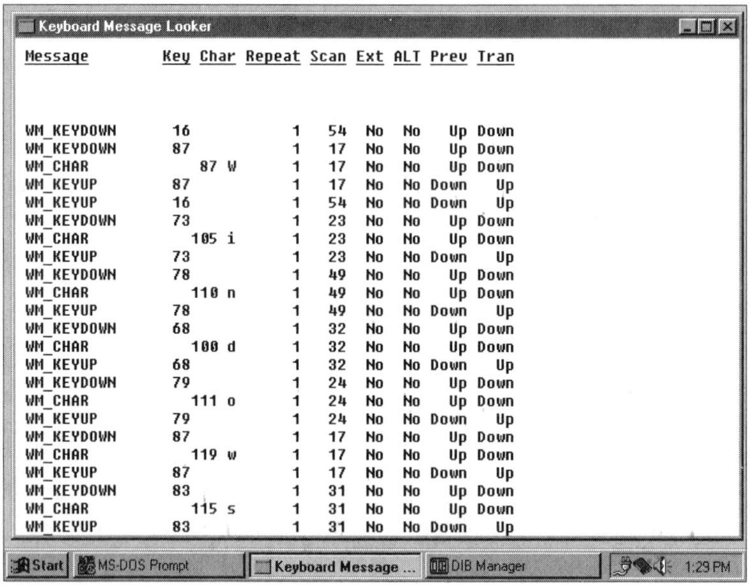

Message	Key	Char	Repeat	Scan	Ext	ALT	Prev	Tran
WM_KEYDOWN	16		1	54	No	No	Up	Down
WM_KEYDOWN	87		1	17	No	No	Up	Down
WM_CHAR		87 W	1	17	No	No	Up	Down
WM_KEYUP	87		1	17	No	No	Down	Up
WM_KEYUP	16		1	54	No	No	Down	Up
WM_KEYDOWN	73		1	23	No	No	Up	Down
WM_CHAR		105 i	1	23	No	No	Up	Down
WM_KEYUP	73		1	23	No	No	Down	Up
WM_KEYDOWN	78		1	49	No	No	Up	Down
WM_CHAR		110 n	1	49	No	No	Up	Down
WM_KEYUP	78		1	49	No	No	Down	Up
WM_KEYDOWN	68		1	32	No	No	Up	Down
WM_CHAR		100 d	1	32	No	No	Up	Down
WM_KEYUP	68		1	32	No	No	Down	Up
WM_KEYDOWN	79		1	24	No	No	Up	Down
WM_CHAR		111 o	1	24	No	No	Up	Down
WM_KEYUP	79		1	24	No	No	Down	Up
WM_KEYDOWN	87		1	17	No	No	Up	Down
WM_CHAR		119 w	1	17	No	No	Up	Down
WM_KEYUP	87		1	17	No	No	Down	Up
WM_KEYDOWN	83		1	31	No	No	Up	Down
WM_CHAR		115 s	1	31	No	No	Up	Down
WM_KEYUP	83		1	31	No	No	Down	Up

Figure 5-4. *The KEYLOOK display.*

Most of KEYLOOK.C uses features of Windows that have already been covered in the various SYSMETS programs, but a few new functions are used here. Note, however, that the column formatting of KEYLOOK would be difficult with the default proportional font. The code to display each line would need to be broken into nine sections to get everything lined up. For something like this, a much easier approach is to simply switch to a fixed-pitch font. As I discussed in the last chapter, this requires two functions that I've combined in a single statement:

```
SelectObject (hdc, GetStockObject (SYSTEM_FIXED_FONT)) ;
```

KEYLOOK calls these two functions whenever it obtains a device context. This occurs in three places: the *ShowKey* function, while processing the WM_CREATE message in *WndProc*, and while processing the WM_PAINT message. The *GetStockObject* function obtains a handle to the stock graphics object that is the fixed-pitch font that was used in versions of Windows prior to Windows 3.0. The *SelectObject* call selects that object into the device context. Following this call, all text that is displayed will use the fixed-pitch font. It is possible to switch back to the default proportional font by calling:

```
SelectObject (hdc, GetStockObject (SYSTEM_FONT)) ;
```

The *ShowKey* function calls *ScrollWindow* to scroll the previous lines of keystrokes up before displaying a new line. Normally this would cause part of the window to become invalid and hence generate a WM_PAINT message. The *ShowKey* function concludes with a call to *ValidateRect* to prevent this.

KEYLOOK does not save the keystrokes it receives, so on receipt of a WM_PAINT message it cannot re-create the window. For this reason, KEYLOOK simply displays the header at the top of the client area during the WM_PAINT message. Before calling *BeginPaint* during the WM_PAINT message, KEYLOOK invalidates the entire window. This allows the whole window to be erased rather than just the invalid rectangle.

(That KEYLOOK does not save the keystrokes and hence cannot redraw the window during a WM_PAINT message is certainly a flaw. The TYPER program shown later in this chapter corrects this flaw.)

KEYLOOK draws a header at the top of the client area identifying the nine columns. Although it's possible to create an underlined font, I took a slightly different approach here. I defined two character string variables named *szTop* (which has the text) and *szUnd* (which has the underlining) and displayed both of them at the same position at the top of the window during the WM_PAINT message. Normally, Windows displays text in an "opaque" mode, meaning that Windows erases the character background area while displaying a character. This would cause the second character string (*szUnd*) to erase the first (*szTop*). To prevent this, switch the device context into the "transparent" mode:

```
SetBkMode (hdc, TRANSPARENT) ;
```

THE CARET (NOT THE CURSOR)

When you type text into a program, generally a little underline or box shows you where the next character you type will appear on the screen. You may know this as a "cursor," but you'll have to get out of that habit when programming for Windows. In Windows, it's called the "caret." The word "cursor" is used for the bitmap image that represents the mouse position.

The Caret Functions

There are five essential caret functions:

- *CreateCaret*—creates a caret associated with a window.

- *SetCaretPos*—sets the position of the caret on the window.

- *ShowCaret*—shows the caret.

- *HideCaret*—hides the caret.

- *DestroyCaret*—destroys the caret.

There are also functions to get the caret position (*GetCaretPos*) and to get and set the caret blink time (*GetCaretBlinkTime* and *SetCaretBlinkTime*).

The caret is customarily a horizontal line or a box that is the size of a character or a vertical line. The vertical line is recommended when you use a proportional font such as the Windows default system font. Because the characters in a proportional font are not a fixed size, the horizontal line and box can't be set to the size of a character.

You cannot simply create a caret during the WM_CREATE message and destroy it during the WM_DESTROY message. The caret is what is known as a "systemwide resource." What this means is that there is only one caret in the system. In effect, a program "borrows" the caret from the system when it needs to display a caret in its window.

Does this sound bizarrely restrictive? It's really not. Think about it: The display of a caret in a window makes sense only when the window has the input focus. This indicates to the user that he or she may enter text in the program. Only one window has the input focus at any time, so only one caret is needed in the whole system.

A program can determine if it has the input focus by processing the WM_SETFOCUS and WM_KILLFOCUS messages. A window procedure receives a WM_SETFOCUS message when it receives the input focus, and a WM_KILLFOCUS message when it loses the input focus. These messages occur in pairs: A window procedure will always receive a WM_SETFOCUS message before it receives a WM_KILLFOCUS message, and it always receives an equal number of WM_SETFOCUS and WM_KILLFOCUS messages over the course of the window's lifetime.

The main rule for using the caret is simple: A window procedure calls *CreateCaret* during the WM_SETFOCUS message and *DestroyCaret* during the WM_KILLFOCUS message.

There are a few other rules: The caret is created hidden. After calling *CreateCaret*, the window procedure must call *ShowCaret* for the caret to be visible. In addition, the window procedure must hide the caret by calling *HideCaret* whenever it draws something on its window during a message other than WM_PAINT. After it finishes drawing on the window, it calls *ShowCaret* to display the caret again. The effect of *HideCaret* is additive: If you call *HideCaret* several times without calling *ShowCaret*, you must call *ShowCaret* the same number of times before the caret becomes visible again.

The TYPER Program

The TYPER program shown in Figure 5-5 brings together much of what we've learned in this chapter. You can think of TYPER as an extremely rudimentary text editor. You can type in the window, move the cursor (I mean caret) around with the cursor movement (or are they caret movement?) keys, and erase the contents of the window by pressing Escape. The contents of the window are also erased when you resize the window. There's no scrolling, no search and replace, no way to save files, and no spell checker, but it's a start.

To make things easy for me, TYPER uses a fixed-pitch font. Writing a text editor for a proportional font is, as you might imagine, much more difficult. The program obtains a device context in several places: during the WM_CREATE message, the WM_KEYDOWN message, the WM_CHAR message, and the WM_PAINT message. Each time, calls to *GetStockObject* and *SelectObject* select the fixed-pitch font.

During the WM_SIZE message, TYPER calculates the character width and height of the window and saves these values in the variables *cxBuffer* and *cyBuffer*. It then uses *malloc* to allocate a buffer to hold all the characters that can be typed in the window. The *xCaret* and *yCaret* variables store the character position of the caret.

During the WM_SETFOCUS message, TYPER calls *CreateCaret* to create a caret that is the width and height of a character, *SetCaretPos* to set the caret position, and *ShowCaret* to make the caret visible. During the WM_KILLFOCUS message, TYPER calls *HideCaret* and *DestroyCaret*.

TYPER.MAK

```
#--------------------
# TYPER.MAK make file
#--------------------

typer.exe : typer.obj
    $(LINKER) $(GUIFLAGS) -OUT:typer.exe typer.obj $(GUILIBS)

typer.obj : typer.c
    $(CC) $(CFLAGS) typer.c
```

TYPER.C

```
/*-----------------------------------------
   TYPER.C -- Typing Program
           (c) Charles Petzold, 1996
   -----------------------------------------*/
```

Figure 5-5. *The TYPER program.*   *(continued)*

```
#include <windows.h>
#include <stdlib.h>

#define BUFFER(x,y) *(pBuffer + y * cxBuffer + x)

LRESULT CALLBACK WndProc (HWND, UINT, WPARAM, LPARAM) ;

int WINAPI WinMain (HINSTANCE hInstance, HINSTANCE hPrevInstance,
                    PSTR szCmdLine, int iCmdShow)
     {
     static char szAppName[] = "Typer" ;
     HWND         hwnd ;
     MSG          msg ;
     WNDCLASSEX   wndclass ;

     wndclass.cbSize        = sizeof (wndclass) ;
     wndclass.style         = CS_HREDRAW | CS_VREDRAW ;
     wndclass.lpfnWndProc   = WndProc ;
     wndclass.cbClsExtra    = 0 ;
     wndclass.cbWndExtra    = 0 ;
     wndclass.hInstance     = hInstance ;
     wndclass.hIcon         = LoadIcon (NULL, IDI_APPLICATION) ;
     wndclass.hCursor       = LoadCursor (NULL, IDC_ARROW) ;
     wndclass.hbrBackground = (HBRUSH) GetStockObject (WHITE_BRUSH) ;
     wndclass.lpszMenuName  = NULL ;
     wndclass.lpszClassName = szAppName ;
     wndclass.hIconSm       = LoadIcon (NULL, IDI_APPLICATION) ;

     RegisterClassEx (&wndclass) ;

     hwnd = CreateWindow (szAppName, "Typing Program",
                         WS_OVERLAPPEDWINDOW,
                         CW_USEDEFAULT, CW_USEDEFAULT,
                         CW_USEDEFAULT, CW_USEDEFAULT,
                         NULL, NULL, hInstance, NULL) ;

     ShowWindow (hwnd, iCmdShow) ;
     UpdateWindow (hwnd) ;

     while (GetMessage (&msg, NULL, 0, 0))
          {
          TranslateMessage (&msg) ;
          DispatchMessage (&msg) ;
          }
     return msg.wParam ;
     }
```

(continued)

```
LRESULT CALLBACK WndProc (HWND hwnd, UINT iMsg, WPARAM wParam, LPARAM lParam)
    {
    static char *pBuffer = NULL ;
    static int  cxChar, cyChar, cxClient, cyClient, cxBuffer,
                cyBuffer, xCaret, yCaret ;
    HDC         hdc ;
    int         x, y, i ;
    PAINTSTRUCT ps ;
    TEXTMETRIC  tm ;

    switch (iMsg)
        {
        case WM_CREATE :
            hdc = GetDC (hwnd) ;

            SelectObject (hdc, GetStockObject (SYSTEM_FIXED_FONT)) ;
            GetTextMetrics (hdc, &tm) ;
            cxChar = tm.tmAveCharWidth ;
            cyChar = tm.tmHeight ;

            ReleaseDC (hwnd, hdc) ;
            return 0 ;

        case WM_SIZE :
                            // obtain window size in pixels

            cxClient = LOWORD (lParam) ;
            cyClient = HIWORD (lParam) ;

                            // calculate window size in characters

            cxBuffer = max (1, cxClient / cxChar) ;
            cyBuffer = max (1, cyClient / cyChar) ;

                            // allocate memory for buffer and clear it

            if (pBuffer != NULL)
                free (pBuffer) ;

            if ((pBuffer = (char *) malloc (cxBuffer * cyBuffer))
                == NULL)
                MessageBox (hwnd, "Window too large.  Cannot "
                                  "allocate enough memory.",
                                  "Typer",
                                  MB_ICONEXCLAMATION | MB_OK) ;
```

(continued)

273

```
        else
            for (y = 0 ; y < cyBuffer ; y++)
                for (x = 0 ; x < cxBuffer ; x++)
                    BUFFER(x,y) = ' ' ;

                            // set caret to upper left corner
        xCaret = 0 ;
        yCaret = 0 ;

        if (hwnd == GetFocus ())
            SetCaretPos (xCaret * cxChar, yCaret * cyChar) ;

        return 0 ;

case WM_SETFOCUS :
                        // create and show the caret

        CreateCaret (hwnd, NULL, cxChar, cyChar) ;
        SetCaretPos (xCaret * cxChar, yCaret * cyChar) ;
        ShowCaret (hwnd) ;
        return 0 ;

case WM_KILLFOCUS :
                        // hide and destroy the caret
        HideCaret (hwnd) ;
        DestroyCaret () ;
        return 0 ;

case WM_KEYDOWN :
        switch (wParam)
            {
            case VK_HOME :
                xCaret = 0 ;
                break ;

            case VK_END :
                xCaret = cxBuffer - 1 ;
                break ;

            case VK_PRIOR :
                yCaret = 0 ;
                break ;

            case VK_NEXT :
                yCaret = cyBuffer - 1 ;
                break ;
```

(continued)

```
            case VK_LEFT :
                 xCaret = max (xCaret - 1, 0) ;
                 break ;

            case VK_RIGHT :
                 xCaret = min (xCaret + 1, cxBuffer - 1) ;
                 break ;

            case VK_UP :
                 yCaret = max (yCaret - 1, 0) ;
                 break ;

            case VK_DOWN :
                 yCaret = min (yCaret + 1, cyBuffer - 1) ;
                 break ;

            case VK_DELETE :
                 for (x = xCaret ; x < cxBuffer - 1 ; x++)
                      BUFFER (x, yCaret) = BUFFER (x + 1, yCaret) ;

                 BUFFER (cxBuffer - 1, yCaret) = ' ' ;

                 HideCaret (hwnd) ;
                 hdc = GetDC (hwnd) ;

                 SelectObject (hdc,
                      GetStockObject (SYSTEM_FIXED_FONT)) ;

                 TextOut (hdc, xCaret * cxChar, yCaret * cyChar,
                         & BUFFER (xCaret, yCaret),
                         cxBuffer - xCaret) ;

                 ShowCaret (hwnd) ;
                 ReleaseDC (hwnd, hdc) ;
                 break ;
            }

       SetCaretPos (xCaret * cxChar, yCaret * cyChar) ;
       return 0 ;

case WM_CHAR :
     for (i = 0 ; i < (int) LOWORD (lParam) ; i++)
          {
          switch (wParam)
               {
               case '\b' :                      // backspace
```

(continued)

```
          if (xCaret > 0)
               {
               xCaret-- ;
               SendMessage (hwnd, WM_KEYDOWN,
                            VK_DELETE, 1L) ;
               }
          break ;

case '\t' :                  // tab
     do
          {
          SendMessage (hwnd, WM_CHAR, ' ', 1L) ;
          }
     while (xCaret % 8 != 0) ;
     break ;

case '\n' :                  // line feed
     if (++yCaret == cyBuffer)
          yCaret = 0 ;
     break ;

case '\r' :                  // carriage return
     xCaret = 0 ;

     if (++yCaret == cyBuffer)
          yCaret = 0 ;
     break ;

case '\x1B' :                // escape
     for (y = 0 ; y < cyBuffer ; y++)
          for (x = 0 ; x < cxBuffer ; x++)
               BUFFER (x, y) = ' ' ;

     xCaret = 0 ;
     yCaret = 0 ;

     InvalidateRect (hwnd, NULL, FALSE) ;
     break ;

default :                    // character codes
     BUFFER (xCaret, yCaret) = (char) wParam ;

     HideCaret (hwnd) ;
     hdc = GetDC (hwnd) ;
```

(continued)

```
                              SelectObject (hdc,
                                   GetStockObject (SYSTEM_FIXED_FONT)) ;

                              TextOut (hdc, xCaret * cxChar,
                                        yCaret * cyChar,
                                        & BUFFER (xCaret, yCaret), 1) ;

                              ShowCaret (hwnd) ;
                              ReleaseDC (hwnd, hdc) ;

                              if (++xCaret == cxBuffer)
                                   {
                                   xCaret = 0 ;

                                   if (++yCaret == cyBuffer)
                                        yCaret = 0 ;
                                   }
                              break ;
                         }
                    }

          SetCaretPos (xCaret * cxChar, yCaret * cyChar) ;
          return 0 ;

     case WM_PAINT :
          hdc = BeginPaint (hwnd, &ps) ;
          SelectObject (hdc, GetStockObject (SYSTEM_FIXED_FONT)) ;

          for (y = 0 ; y < cyBuffer ; y++)
               TextOut (hdc, 0, y * cyChar, & BUFFER(0,y), cxBuffer) ;

          EndPaint (hwnd, &ps) ;
          return 0 ;

     case WM_DESTROY :
          PostQuitMessage (0) ;
          return 0 ;
     }
return DefWindowProc (hwnd, iMsg, wParam, lParam) ;
}
```

The processing of the WM_KEYDOWN and WM_CHAR messages is more extensive. The WM_KEYDOWN processing mostly involves the cursor movement keys. Home and End send the caret to the beginning and end of a line, and Page Up and Page Down send the caret to the top and bottom of the window. The arrow keys work as you would expect. For the Delete key, TYPER must move everything remaining in the buffer from the next caret position to the end of the line and then display a blank at the end of the line.

The WM_CHAR processing handles the Backspace, Tab, Linefeed (Ctrl-Enter), Enter, Escape, and character keys. Notice I've used Repeat Count in *lParam* when processing the WM_CHAR message (under the assumption that every character the user types is important) but not during the WM_KEYDOWN message (to prevent inadvertent overscrolling). The Backspace and Tab processing is simplified somewhat by the use of the *SendMessage* function. Backspace is emulated by the Delete logic, and Tab is emulated by a series of spaces.

As I mentioned earlier, you should hide the caret when drawing on the window during messages other than WM_PAINT. The program does this when processing the WM_KEYDOWN message for the Delete key and the WM_CHAR message for character keys. In both these cases, TYPER alters the contents of the buffer and then draws the new character or characters on the window.

I use TYPER when working on speeches, as shown in Figure 5-6.

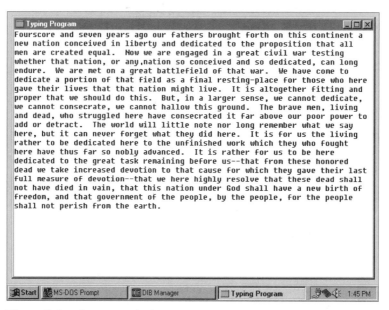

Figure 5-6. *The TYPER display.*

THE WINDOWS CHARACTER SETS

I mentioned earlier that letter keys preceded by dead-character keys generate WM_CHAR messages where *wParam* is the ASCII code for a character with a diacritic. This may be a little puzzling because the ASCII character set doesn't include any codes for characters with diacritics. What exactly is the value of *wParam* in this case? The answer to this question requires that we tackle the subject of character sets, a topic that may at first seem more appropriate for a discussion about character fonts. However, it is also of vital importance in keyboard handling.

The standard 7-bit ASCII character set defines codes from 0 through 31 (0x1F) and 127 (0x7F) as control characters, and it defines codes from 32 (0x20) through 126 (0x7E) as displayable characters. None of these characters have diacritics. Because personal computers use 8-bit bytes, computer manufacturers often define character sets that use 256 codes rather than the 128 ASCII codes. The additional codes may be assigned characters with diacritics. The resultant "extended character set" then includes the ASCII character set and up to 128 other characters.

If Windows supported such an extended character set, displaying characters with diacritics would be easy. But Windows doesn't support a simple extended character set. Windows supports two extended character sets. Unfortunately, the presence of these two character sets doesn't make things twice as easy.

The OEM Character Set

First, let's go back to the hardware that Windows runs on—the IBM PC and compatibles. In the early 1980s, the developers of the IBM PC decided to extend the ASCII character set as shown in Figure 5-7 on the following page. The codes from 0x20 through 0x7E are displayable characters from the ASCII character set. The rest are nonstandard—or at least were at the time.

This character set cannot be ignored. It is encoded in millions of ROM chips in IBM video adapters, printers, and system board BIOS's. It has been duplicated in the hardware of numerous manufacturers of IBM-compatible computers and peripherals. This character set is part of what is meant by the phrase "the IBM standard." Many non-Windows text-mode programs written for the IBM PC require this extended character set because they use the block-drawing and line-drawing characters (codes B0H through DFH) in their screen output.

The only problem is this: The IBM extended character set is inappropriate for Windows. First, the block-drawing and line-drawing characters commonly used by PC programs in text-mode applications are not needed in Windows because Windows does real graphics. If you want to draw a horizontal line in Windows, it's easier to draw a line than to display a string of 0xC4 characters. Second, the Greek alphabet and mathematical symbols are less important in Windows than are the accented letters used in most European languages. A program that needs to display mathematical symbols can best draw them using graphics functions.

In short, Windows supports the IBM character set, but it is relegated to secondary importance—mostly for old applications that run in a window. Windows applications do not normally use the IBM character set. In Windows documentation, the IBM character set is referred to as the "OEM character set." The OEM character set is more precisely defined as the character set that is native to the machine currently running Windows.

	0	1	2	3	4	5	6	7	8	9	A	B	C	D	E	F
00:	☺	☻	♥	♦	♣	♠	•	◘	○	◙	♂	♀	♪	♫	☼
10:	►	◄	↕	‼	¶	§	▬	↨	↑	↓	→	←	∟	↔	▲	▼
20:		!	"	#	$	%	&	'	(	)	*	+	,	-	.	/
30:	0	1	2	3	4	5	6	7	8	9	:	;	<	=	>	?
40:	@	A	B	C	D	E	F	G	H	I	J	K	L	M	N	O
50:	P	Q	R	S	T	U	V	W	X	Y	Z	[	\	]	^	_
60:	`	a	b	c	d	e	f	g	h	i	j	k	l	m	n	o
70:	p	q	r	s	t	u	v	w	x	y	z	{	¦	}	~	⌂
80:	Ç	ü	é	â	ä	à	å	ç	ê	ë	è	ï	î	ì	Ä	Å
90:	É	æ	Æ	ô	ö	ò	û	ù	ÿ	Ö	Ü	¢	£	¥	₧	ƒ
A0:	á	í	ó	ú	ñ	Ñ	ª	º	¿	⌐	¬	½	¼	¡	«	»
B0:	░	▒	▓	│	┤	╡	╢	╖	╕	╣	║	╗	╝	╜	╛	┐
C0:	└	┴	┬	├	─	┼	╞	╟	╚	╔	╩	╦	╠	═	╬	╧
D0:	╨	╤	╥	╙	╘	╒	╓	╫	╪	┘	┌	█	▄	▌	▐	▀
E0:	α	β	Γ	π	Σ	σ	µ	τ	Φ	Θ	Ω	δ	∞	φ	ε	∩
F0:	≡	±	≥	≤	⌠	⌡	÷	≈	°	∙	·	√	ⁿ	²	■	

Figure 5-7. *The IBM extended character set arranged by character code.*

International support under DOS

There are a number of variants on the IBM PC character set, called "code pages." The variant used in the United States and in most European countries is called Code Page 437. Systems sold in Norway, Denmark, Portugal, and a few other European countries use different, special, code pages, which contain more of the special characters required by the languages of those countries. Recently, a number of these countries began to use Code Page 850, which contains fewer graphics symbols and more accented letters and other special characters.

Windows supports code pages by installing OEM fonts (used for running DOS applications in windows and in the clipboard viewer), which correspond to the system's code page, and by installing appropriate translation tables for the *CharToOem* and *OemToChar* functions (discussed later).

The Windows Setup program will select the appropriate code pages based on the regional settings of the current system configuration.

The ANSI Character Set

The extended character set that Windows and Windows programs use for most purposes is called the "ANSI character set," but which is actually an ISO standard. When your program receives a WM_CHAR message, the *wParam* parameter is the ANSI character code. The ANSI character set is shown in Figure 5-8. As you can see, the codes from 0x20 through 0x7E represent the same characters that appear in the OEM character set and the ASCII character set. The characters displayed as solid blocks are undefined characters. They may appear differently on other output devices (such as a printer). TrueType fonts define some additional characters for ANSI codes 0x80 through 0x9F.

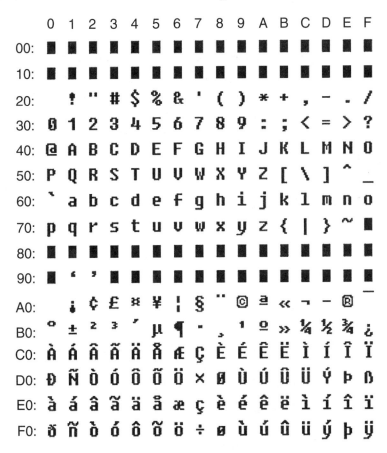

Figure 5-8. *The ANSI character set arranged by character code.*

OEM, ANSI, and Fonts

Windows has different fonts for displaying the ANSI and OEM character sets. When you first obtain a handle to a device context, one of the attributes in the device context is a font. By default this is the SYSTEM_FONT or "system font," which uses the ANSI character set. If you want to display characters from the OEM character set, you can select the OEM_FIXED_FONT (also called the "terminal font") in the device context by using the following code:

```
SelectObject (hdc, GetStockObject (OEM_FIXED_FONT)) ;
```

INTERNATIONALIZATION CONCERNS

Here's why we have to talk about fonts in the middle of the keyboard chapter. We've established that when a Windows user on a non-U.S. keyboard types a character with a diacritic, the *wParam* parameter of the WM_CHAR message is the code for that character in the ANSI character set.

So, if you need to echo that character to the display, you had better be using a font with the ANSI character set (such as the SYSTEM_FONT or SYSTEM_FIXED_FONT). If you instead use the OEM_FIXED_FONT, the character you write to the display will be incorrect and will surprise the user. A few other simple rules will allow the keyboard logic in your Windows programs to survive intact when you convert your programs for a European market.

Working with the Character Set

When you get a WM_CHAR message, keep in mind that *wParam* may legitimately have values above 128. Don't assume that anything above 127 is an invalid character.

You may want to convert a character to uppercase. Don't use your own algorithm:

```
if (ch >= 'a' && ch <= 'z')
     ch -= 32 ;              // WRONG !!!
```

That's a poor practice even when writing non-Windows C. But don't use the standard C function either:

```
ch = toupper (ch) ;         // WRONG !!!
```

Both these functions work only for the lower half of the ANSI character set. They will not convert a 0xE0 to a 0xC0.

Instead, you should use the Windows functions *CharUpper* and *CharLower*. If *pString* is a zero-terminated character string, you can convert it to uppercase using *CharUpper*:

```
CharUpper (pString) ;
```

or using the *CharUpperBuff* function for character strings that are not 0-terminated:

```
CharUpperBuff (pString, nLength) ;
```

You can also use *CharUpper* to convert a single character, but some casting is required because the high-order word of the parameter must be 0:

```
ch = CharUpper ((PSTR) (LONG) (BYTE) ch) ;
```

If *ch* is defined as an unsigned character, the initial BYTE cast is not required. Windows also includes *CharLower* and *CharLowerBuff* functions for converting to lowercase.

If you are really serious about writing Windows programs that can be easily converted to foreign languages, you should also investigate the *CharNext* and *CharPrev* functions. These functions facilitate handling of multibyte character sets, often used in far-eastern countries. These character sets require more than 256 characters, some of which use 2 bytes. If you use normal C pointer arithmetic to scan a string (perhaps searching for a backslash character in a directory path string), you may think you've found the character when you've really found the second byte of a 2-byte character code. *CharNext* and *CharPrev* take a far pointer to a character string and return a far pointer that has been correctly incremented or decremented past 2-byte character codes.

Talking with MS-DOS

If Windows were the only operating environment running on a machine, you could forget about the OEM character set and use only the ANSI character set. However, users can create files in the MS-DOS environment and use them in Windows; they can also create files in Windows and use them when back in MS-DOS. Unfortunately, MS-DOS uses the OEM character set.

Here's an example of the communications problems that can occur. Suppose that a German-speaking PC user creates a file named ÜBUNGEN.TXT ("practice exercises") in an MS-DOS program such as EDLIN. On the IBM PC, the Ü is part of the IBM (that is, OEM) character set and has a code of 154 or 0x9A. (When using MS-DOS with a U.S. keyboard on an IBM PC, you can also create this letter by typing Alt-154 using the numeric keypad.) MS-DOS uses that character code in the directory entry of the file.

If a Windows program uses MS-DOS function calls to obtain a directory of files and then writes them directly to the display using an ANSI character set font, the first letter of ÜBUNGEN.TXT will show up as a solid block, because code 154 is one of the undefined characters in the ANSI character set. The Windows program needs to convert the IBM extended character set code of 154 (0x9A) to an ANSI character set code of 220 (or 0xDC), which is the letter Ü in the ANSI character set. That's what the Windows function *OemToChar* does for you. It requires two far pointers to strings. The OEM characters in the first string are converted to ANSI characters and stored in the second string:

```
OemToChar (lpszOemStr, lpszAnsiStr) ;
```

Now let's take the opposite example. The German-speaking user wants your Windows program to create a file named ÜBUNGEN.TXT. The filename entered by the user has a 220 (0xDC) as the first character. If you use an MS-DOS function call to open the file, MS-DOS uses that character in the filename. When the user later looks at the file under MS-DOS, the first character shows up as a block. Before you use the MS-DOS function calls, you must convert the filename to the OEM character set:

```
CharToOem (lpszAnsiStr, lpszOemStr) ;
```

This converts a 220 (0xDC) to a 154 (0x9A). Windows also includes two functions named *CharToOemBuff* and *OemToCharBuff* that do not require a 0-terminated string.

Windows has an *OpenFile* call that will convert this for you. If you use *OpenFile*, don't do your own *CharToOem* conversion. If you use MS-DOS function calls to obtain lists of filenames (as the Windows File Manager program does), then these filenames should be passed through *OemToChar* before being displayed.

Converting the contents of files is another problem that arises when files are used in both Windows and MS-DOS. If your Windows program uses files that you are certain have been created in an MS-DOS program, then you may need to pass the text contents of the file through the *OemToChar* function. Similarly, if your Windows program is preparing a file for use in an MS-DOS program, you may want to use *CharToOem* to convert the text.

The *OemToChar* and *CharToOem* functions are located in the keyboard driver. They incorporate very simple lookup tables. The *OemToChar* routine converts an OEM code from 0x80 through 0xFF to a character code in the ANSI set that most closely resembles the OEM character. In some cases, this conversion is only grossly approximate. For instance, most of the line-drawing characters in the IBM character set are translated as plus signs, dashes, and vertical lines. Most of the OEM codes from 0x00 through 0x1F are not translated to ANSI codes.

The *CharToOem* routine converts ANSI codes from 0xA0 through 0xFF into codes in the OEM set. The accented characters in the ANSI character set that do not appear in the OEM character set are translated into regular ASCII codes for the characters, without the diacritics.

Using the Numeric Keypad

As you probably know, the IBM PC keyboard and BIOS let you enter codes for the IBM extended character set by pressing and holding down the Alt key, typing on the numeric keypad the three-digit decimal code representing the OEM character, and releasing the Alt key. This facility is duplicated in Windows in two ways.

First, when you type Alt-[*OEM code*] on the numeric keypad, Windows gives you the ANSI character code (in the *wParam* parameter of the WM_CHAR message) that most closely approximates the OEM character represented by the OEM code. That is, Windows passes the code through the *OemToChar* function before generating the WM_CHAR message. This facility is for the user's convenience: If you do not have a foreign-language keyboard and you are accustomed to typing a Ü by typing Alt-154, you can do the same thing in a Windows program. You don't need to relearn the ANSI character codes.

Second, if you want to generate ANSI extended character codes from the U.S. keyboard, type Alt-0[*OEM code*] on the numeric keypad. The *wParam* parameter of the WM_CHAR message is that OEM code. Thus, Alt-0220 is also a Ü. You can try this out in the KEYLOOK or TYPER programs.

The Unicode Solution for Windows NT

Program developers involved with creating applications for an international market have had to deal with inadequate solutions for the deficiencies of pure 7-bit ASCII, such as code pages and double-byte character sets. A better solution is sorely needed, and that solution may well be Unicode.

Unicode is a character encoding that uses a uniform 16-bit code for each character. This allows the representation of every character in every written language of the world that is likely to be used in computer communication, including the logographic symbols of Chinese, Japanese, and Korean. Unicode was developed by a consortium of computer industry companies (including all the big ones) and is documented in the book *The Unicode Standard* published by Addison-Wesley.

Unfortunately, Windows 95 has only rudimentary support of Unicode, and it cannot deliver Unicode characters through the keyboard driver. This is quite in contrast to Windows NT, which has Unicode support from the ground up.

Obviously, adapting programs (and the minds of programmers) to the idea of 16-bit characters is a significant job, but one that is well worth doing if we are to be allowed to display all the world's languages on the screens and printers of personal computers. If you're interested in the concepts and mechanics of Unicode as implemented under Windows NT, you may want to check out my "Environments" column in *PC Magazine* for the 1993 issues dated October 26, November 9, November 23, and December 7 (where it was inadvertently omitted from the table of contents but appears starting on page 426).

Chapter 6

The Mouse

The mouse is a pointing device with one or more buttons. Despite much experimentation with input devices such as touch screens and light pens, the mouse (and variations such as trackballs common on laptop computers) is the only device to achieve a massive penetration in the PC market.

This was not always the case. Indeed, the early developers of Windows felt that they shouldn't require users to buy a mouse in order to run the product. So, they made the mouse an optional accessory and provided a keyboard interface to all operations in Windows and the "applets" distributed with Windows. Third-party developers were also encouraged to duplicate mouse functions with a keyboard interface, and earlier editions of this book did likewise.

Although the mouse has become nearly universal on Windows machines, I still believe in this philosophy. Touch typists in particular prefer keeping their hands on the keyboard, and I suppose everyone has had the experience of "losing" their mouse on a cluttered desk. For this reason, I still recommend that—whenever possible—you add a keyboard interface to duplicate mouse functions.

MOUSE BASICS

Windows 95 can support a one-button, two-button, or three-button mouse or use a joystick or light pen to mimic a one-button mouse. Because a one-button mouse is the lowest common denominator, many Windows programmers have traditionally avoided the use of the second and third buttons. However, the two-button mouse has become the de facto standard, so the traditional reticence to use the second button is no longer justified. Indeed, the second mouse button is being promoted for invoking a "context menu," which is a menu that appears in a window outside of the normal menu bar, or for special dragging operations. (Dragging will be explained shortly.)

You can determine if a mouse is present by using the *GetSystemMetrics* function:

```
fMouse = GetSystemMetrics (SM_MOUSEPRESENT) ;
```

The value of *fMouse* will be TRUE (nonzero) if a mouse is installed. To determine the number of buttons on the installed mouse, use:

```
cButtons = GetSystemMetrics (SM_CMOUSEBUTTONS) ;
```

This function will return 0 if a mouse is not installed.

Left-handed users can switch the mouse buttons using the Windows Control Panel. Although an application can determine whether this is the case by passing the SM_SWAP-BUTTON parameter to *GetSystemMetrics*, this is not usually necessary. The button triggered by the index finger is considered to be the left button, even if it's physically on the right side of the mouse. However, in a training program, you may want to draw a mouse on the screen, and in that case, you may want to know if the mouse buttons have been swapped.

Some Quick Definitions

When the Windows user moves the mouse, Windows moves a small bitmapped picture called the "mouse cursor" on the display. The mouse cursor has a single-pixel "hot spot" that points to a precise location on the display.

The display driver contains several predefined mouse cursors that programs may use. The most common is the slanted arrow called IDC_ARROW defined in the Windows header files. The hot spot is the tip of the arrow. The IDC_CROSS cursor (used in the BLOKOUT programs shown in this chapter) has a hot spot in the center of a crosshair pattern. The IDC_WAIT cursor is an hourglass generally used by programs to indicate they are busy. Programmers can also design their own cursors (as we'll do in Chapter 9). The default cursor for a particular window is specified when defining the window class structure. For instance:

```
wndclass.hCursor = LoadCursor (NULL, IDC_ARROW) ;
```

The following terms describe the actions you take with mouse buttons:

■ Clicking—pressing and releasing a mouse button

■ Double-clicking—pressing and releasing a mouse button twice in quick succession

■ Dragging—moving the mouse while holding down a button

On a three-button mouse, the buttons are called the left button, the middle button, and the right button. Mouse-related identifiers defined in the Windows header files use the abbreviations LBUTTON, MBUTTON, and RBUTTON. A two-button mouse has only a left button and a right button. The single button on a one-button mouse is a left button.

CLIENT-AREA MOUSE MESSAGES

In the previous chapter you saw how Windows sends keyboard messages only to the window with the input focus. Mouse messages are different: A window procedure receives mouse messages whenever the mouse passes over the window or is clicked within the window, even if the window is not active or does not have the input focus. Windows defines 21 messages for the mouse. However, 11 of these messages do not relate to the client area (hereinafter, "nonclient-area" messages), and Windows programs usually ignore them.

When the mouse is moved over the client area of a window, the window procedure receives the message WM_MOUSEMOVE. When a mouse button is pressed or released within the client area of a window, the window procedure receives these messages:

Button	*Pressed*	*Released*	*Pressed (Second Click)*
Left	WM_LBUTTONDOWN	WM_LBUTTONUP	WM_LBUTTONDBLCLK
Middle	WM_MBUTTONDOWN	WM_MBUTTONUP	WM_MBUTTONDBLCLK
Right	WM_RBUTTONDOWN	WM_RBUTTONUP	WM_RBUTTONDBLCLK

Your window procedure receives "MBUTTON" messages only for a three-button mouse and "RBUTTON" messages only for a two-button or three-button mouse. The window procedure receives "DBLCLK" (double-click) messages only if the window class has been defined to receive them (as described below).

For all these messages, the value of *lParam* contains the position of the mouse. The low word is the *x*-coordinate, and the high word is the *y*-coordinate relative to the upper left corner of the client area of the window. You can extract the *x*-coordinate and *y*-coordinate from *lParam* using the LOWORD and HIWORD macros defined in the Windows header files. The value of *wParam* indicates the state of the mouse buttons and the Shift and Ctrl keys. You can test *wParam* using the bit masks defined in the header files. The MK prefix stands for "mouse key."

MK_LBUTTON	Left button is down
MK_MBUTTON	Middle button is down
MK_RBUTTON	Right button is down
MK_SHIFT	Shift key is down
MK_CONTROL	Ctrl key is down

As you move the mouse over the client area of a window, Windows does *not* generate a WM_MOUSEMOVE message for every possible pixel position of the mouse. The number of WM_MOUSEMOVE messages your program receives depends on the mouse hardware and on the speed at which your window procedure can process the mouse movement messages. You'll get a good idea of the rate of WM_MOUSEMOVE messages when you experiment with the CONNECT program described below.

If you click the left mouse button in the client area of an inactive window, Windows changes the active window to the window that is being clicked and then passes the WM_LBUTTONDOWN message to the window procedure. When your window procedure gets a WM_LBUTTONDOWN message, your program can safely assume the window is active. However, your window procedure can receive a WM_LBUTTONUP message without first receiving a WM_LBUTTONDOWN message. This can happen if the mouse button is pressed in one window, moved to your window, and released. Similarly, the window procedure can receive a WM_LBUTTONDOWN without a corresponding WM_LBUTTONUP message if the mouse button is released while positioned over another window.

There are two exceptions to these rules:

■ A window procedure can "capture the mouse" and continue to receive mouse messages even when the mouse is outside the window's client area. You'll learn how to capture the mouse later in this chapter.

■ If a system modal message box or a system modal dialog box is on the display, no other program can receive mouse messages. System modal message boxes and dialog boxes prohibit switching to another window program while the box is active. (An example of a system modal message box is the one that appears when you shut down your Windows session.)

Simple Mouse Processing: An Example

The CONNECT program, shown in Figure 6-1, does some simple mouse processing to let you get a good feel for how Windows sends mouse messages to your program.

CONNECT.MAK

```
#------------------------
# CONNECT.MAK make file
#------------------------

connect.exe : connect.obj
    $(LINKER) $(GUIFLAGS) -OUT:connect.exe connect.obj $(GUILIBS)

connect.obj : connect.c
    $(CC) $(CFLAGS) connect.c
```

Figure 6-1. *The CONNECT program.*

(continued)

CONNECT.C

```
/*-----------------------------------------------------
   CONNECT.C -- Connect-the-Dots Mouse Demo Program
                (c) Charles Petzold, 1996
   -----------------------------------------------------*/

#include <windows.h>

#define MAXPOINTS 1000
#define MoveTo(hdc, x, y) MoveToEx (hdc, x, y, NULL)

LRESULT CALLBACK WndProc (HWND, UINT, WPARAM, LPARAM) ;

int WINAPI WinMain (HINSTANCE hInstance, HINSTANCE hPrevInstance,
                    PSTR szCmdLine, int iCmdShow)
     {
     static char szAppName[] = "Connect" ;
     HWND        hwnd ;
     MSG         msg ;
     WNDCLASSEX  wndclass ;

     wndclass.cbSize        = sizeof (wndclass) ;
     wndclass.style         = CS_HREDRAW | CS_VREDRAW ;
     wndclass.lpfnWndProc   = WndProc ;
     wndclass.cbClsExtra    = 0 ;
     wndclass.cbWndExtra    = 0 ;
     wndclass.hInstance     = hInstance ;
     wndclass.hIcon         = LoadIcon (NULL, IDI_APPLICATION) ;
     wndclass.hCursor       = LoadCursor (NULL, IDC_ARROW) ;
     wndclass.hbrBackground = (HBRUSH) GetStockObject (WHITE_BRUSH) ;
     wndclass.lpszMenuName  = NULL ;
     wndclass.lpszClassName = szAppName ;
     wndclass.hIconSm       = LoadIcon (NULL, IDI_APPLICATION) ;

     RegisterClassEx (&wndclass) ;

     hwnd = CreateWindow (szAppName, "Connect-the-Points Mouse Demo",
                          WS_OVERLAPPEDWINDOW,
                          CW_USEDEFAULT, CW_USEDEFAULT,
                          CW_USEDEFAULT, CW_USEDEFAULT,
                          NULL, NULL, hInstance, NULL) ;

     ShowWindow (hwnd, iCmdShow) ;
     UpdateWindow (hwnd) ;

     while (GetMessage (&msg, NULL, 0, 0))
```

(continued)

```
         {
         TranslateMessage (&msg) ;
         DispatchMessage (&msg) ;
         }
     return msg.wParam ;
     }

LRESULT CALLBACK WndProc (HWND hwnd, UINT iMsg, WPARAM wParam, LPARAM lParam)
     {
     static POINT points[MAXPOINTS] ;
     static int    iCount ;
     HDC           hdc ;
     PAINTSTRUCT   ps ;
     int           i, j ;

     switch (iMsg)
         {
         case WM_LBUTTONDOWN :
              iCount = 0 ;
              InvalidateRect (hwnd, NULL, TRUE) ;
              return 0 ;

         case WM_MOUSEMOVE :
              if (wParam & MK_LBUTTON && iCount < 1000)
                   {
                   points[iCount  ].x = LOWORD (lParam) ;
                   points[iCount++].y = HIWORD (lParam) ;

                   hdc = GetDC (hwnd) ;
                   SetPixel (hdc, LOWORD (lParam), HIWORD (lParam), 0L) ;
                   ReleaseDC (hwnd, hdc) ;
                   }
              return 0 ;

         case WM_LBUTTONUP :
              InvalidateRect (hwnd, NULL, FALSE) ;
              return 0 ;

         case WM_PAINT :
              hdc = BeginPaint (hwnd, &ps) ;

              SetCursor (LoadCursor (NULL, IDC_WAIT)) ;
              ShowCursor (TRUE) ;

              for (i = 0 ; i < iCount - 1 ; i++)
                   for (j = i + 1 ; j < iCount ; j++)
```

(continued)

```
                               {
                               MoveTo (hdc, points[i].x, points[i].y) ;
                               LineTo (hdc, points[j].x, points[j].y) ;
                               }

                    ShowCursor (FALSE) ;
                    SetCursor (LoadCursor (NULL, IDC_ARROW)) ;

                    EndPaint (hwnd, &ps) ;
                    return 0 ;

               case WM_DESTROY :
                    PostQuitMessage (0) ;
                    return 0 ;
               }
          return DefWindowProc (hwnd, iMsg, wParam, lParam) ;
          }
```

CONNECT processes three mouse messages:

■ WM_LBUTTONDOWN—CONNECT clears the client area.

■ WM_MOUSEMOVE—If the left button is down, CONNECT draws a black dot on the client area at the mouse position.

■ WM_LBUTTONUP—CONNECT connects every dot drawn in the client area to every other dot. Sometimes this results in a pretty design, sometimes in a dense blob. (See Figure 6-2 on the following page.)

To use CONNECT, bring the mouse cursor into the client area, press the left button, move the mouse around a little, and release the left button. CONNECT works best for a curved pattern of a few dots, which you can draw by moving the mouse quickly while the left button is depressed. CONNECT uses several simple Graphics Device Interface (GDI) functions. *SetPixel* draws a one-pixel dot of a particular color—in this case black. (On high-resolution displays, the pixel may be nearly invisible.) Drawing the lines requires two functions: *MoveTo* marks the *x*-coordinate and *y*-coordinate of the beginning of the line, and *LineTo* draws the line. (Notice I've defined *MoveTo* as a macro using *MoveToEx*.)

If you move the mouse cursor out of the client area before releasing the button, CONNECT does not connect the dots because it doesn't receive the WM_LBUTTONUP message. If you move the mouse back into the client area and press the left button again, CONNECT clears the client area. (If you want to continue a design after releasing the button outside the client area, press the left button again while the mouse is outside the client area and then move the mouse back inside.)

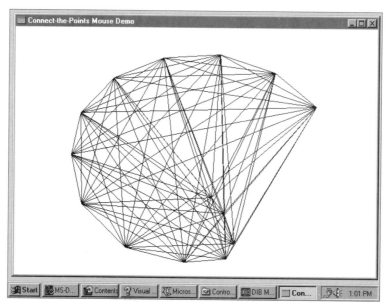

Figure 6-2. *The CONNECT display.*

CONNECT stores a maximum of 1000 points. The number of lines it draws is equal to:

$$\frac{(P) \times (P - 1)}{2}$$

where *P* is the number of points. With 1000 points, this involves almost 500,000 lines, which can take several minutes to draw. Because Windows 95 is a preemptive multitasking environment, you can switch to other programs at this time. However, you can't do anything else with the CONNECT program (such as move it or change the size) while the program is busy. In Chapter 14, we'll examine methods for dealing with this problem.

Because CONNECT may take some time to draw the lines, it switches to an hourglass cursor and then back again while processing the WM_PAINT message. This requires two calls to the *SetCursor* function using two stock cursors. CONNECT also calls *ShowCursor* twice, once with a TRUE parameter and the second time with a FALSE parameter. I'll discuss these calls in more detail later in this chapter, in the section "Emulating the Mouse with the Keyboard."

If CONNECT is busy drawing lines, you can press the mouse button, move the mouse around, and release the mouse button, but nothing will happen. CONNECT does not receive these messages because it is busy and not making any *GetMessage* calls. After CONNECT finishes drawing the lines, it does not receive these messages because the mouse button has been released already. In this respect, the mouse is not like the keyboard. Windows treats every keystroke as if it were important. However, if a mouse button is pressed and released in the client area while a program is busy, the mouse clicks are discarded.

Now try this: While CONNECT is engaged in a lengthy drawing routine, hold down the mouse button and move the mouse around. After CONNECT is finished drawing, it will retrieve the WM_LBUTTONDOWN message from the queue (and clear the client area) because the button is currently down. However, it receives only the WM_MOUSEMOVE messages that occur after it receives the WM_LBUTTONDOWN message.

Sometimes the word "tracking" is used to refer to the way that programs process mouse movement. Tracking does not mean, however, that your program sits in a loop in its window procedure attempting to follow the mouse's movements on the display. The window procedure instead processes each mouse message as it comes and then quickly exits.

Processing Shift Keys

When CONNECT receives a WM_MOUSEMOVE message, it performs a bitwise AND operation on the value of *wParam* and MK_LBUTTON to determine if the left button is depressed. You can also use *wParam* to determine the state of the Shift keys. For instance, if processing must be dependent on the status of the Shift and Ctrl keys, you might use logic that looks like this:

```
if (MK_SHIFT & wParam)
     if (MK_CONTROL & wParam)
          {
          [Shift and Ctrl keys are down]
          }
     else
          {
          [Shift key is down]
          }
else if (MK_CONTROL & wParam)
          {
          [Ctrl key is down]
          }
     else
          {
          [neither Shift nor Ctrl key is down]
          }
```

If you want to use both the left and right mouse buttons in your programs, and if you also want to accommodate those users with a one-button mouse, you can write your code so that Shift in combination with the left button is equivalent to the right button. In that case, your mouse button-click processing might look something like this:

```
case WM_LBUTTONDOWN :
     if (!MK_SHIFT & wParam)
```

```
               {
               [left button logic]

               return 0 ;
               }
                              // fall through
     case WM_RBUTTONDOWN :
          [right button logic]

          return 0 ;
```

The Windows function *GetKeyState* (described in Chapter 4) can also return the status of the mouse buttons or shift keys using the virtual key codes VK_LBUTTON, VK_RBUTTON, VK_MBUTTON, VK_SHIFT, and VK_CONTROL. The button or key is down if the value returned from *GetKeyState* is negative. Because *GetKeyState* returns mouse or key states as of the message currently being processed, the status information is properly synchronized with the messages. But just as you cannot use *GetKeyState* for a key that has yet to be pressed, so you cannot use it for a mouse button that has yet to be pressed. Don't do this:

```
     while (GetKeyState (VK_LBUTTON) >= 0) ;  // WRONG !!!
```

The *GetKeyState* function will report that the left button is depressed only if the button is already depressed when you process the message during which you call *GetKeyState*.

Mouse Double-Clicks

A mouse double-click is two clicks in quick succession. To qualify as a double-click, the two clicks must occur in close proximity within a specific interval called the "double-click time." If you want your window procedure to receive double-click mouse messages, you must include the identifier CS_DBLCLKS when initializing the window style in the window class structure before calling *RegisterClassEx*:

```
     wndclass.style = CS_HREDRAW | CS_VREDRAW | CS_DBLCLKS ;
```

If you do *not* include CS_DBLCLKS in the window style and the user clicks the left mouse button twice in quick succession, your window procedure receives these messages: WM_LBUTTONDOWN, WM_LBUTTONUP, WM_LBUTTONDOWN, and WM_LBUTTONUP. (The window procedure might also receive other messages between these button messages.) If you want to implement your own double-click logic, you can use the Windows function *GetMessageTime* to obtain the relative times of the WM_LBUTTONDOWN messages. This function is discussed in more detail in Chapter 7.

If you include CS_DBLCLKS in your window class, the window procedure receives these messages for a double-click: WM_LBUTTONDOWN, WM_LBUTTONUP, WM_LBUTTONDBLCLK, and WM_LBUTTONUP. The WM_LBUTTONDBLCLK message simply replaces the second WM_LBUTTONDOWN message.

Double-click messages are much easier to process if the first click of a double-click performs the same action as a single click. The second click (the WM_LBUTTONDBLCLK message) then does something in addition to the first click. For example, look at how the mouse works with the file list in Windows Explorer. A single click selects the file. Windows Explorer highlights the file with a reverse-video bar. A double-click performs two actions: The first click selects the file, just as a single click does; the second click directs Windows Explorer to run the file. That's fairly easy logic. Mouse-handling logic could get more complex if the first click of a double-click does not perform the same action as a single click.

NONCLIENT-AREA MOUSE MESSAGES

The 10 mouse messages discussed so far occur when the mouse is moved or clicked within the client area of a window. If the mouse is outside a window's client area but still within the window, Windows sends the window procedure a "nonclient-area" mouse message. The nonclient area includes the title bar, the menu, and window scroll bars.

You do not usually need to process nonclient-area mouse messages. Instead, you simply pass them on to *DefWindowProc* so Windows can perform system functions. In this respect, the nonclient-area mouse messages are similar to the system keyboard messages WM_SYSKEYDOWN, WM_SYSKEYUP, and WM_SYSCHAR.

The nonclient-area mouse messages parallel almost exactly the client-area mouse messages. The messages include the letters "NC" to indicate "nonclient." If the mouse is moved within a nonclient area of a window, then the window procedure receives the message WM_NCMOUSEMOVE. The mouse buttons generate these messages:

Button	*Pressed*	*Released*	*Pressed (Second Click)*
Left	WM_NCLBUTTONDOWN	WM_NCLBUTTONUP	WM_NCLBUTTONDBLCLK
Middle	WM_NCMBUTTONDOWN	WM_NCMBUTTONUP	WM_NCMBUTTONDBLCLK
Right	WM_NCRBUTTONDOWN	WM_NCRBUTTONUP	WM_NCRBUTTONDBLCLK

The *wParam* and *lParam* parameters for nonclient-area mouse messages, however, are different from those for client-area mouse messages. The *wParam* parameter indicates the nonclient area where the mouse was moved or clicked. It is set to one of the identifiers beginning with HT (standing for "hit-test") that are defined in the Windows header files.

The *lParam* variable contains an *x*-coordinate in the low word and a *y*-coordinate in the high word. However, these are screen coordinates, not client-area coordinates as they are for client-area mouse messages. For screen coordinates, the upper left corner of the display area has *x* and *y* values of 0. Values of *x* increase as you move to the right, and values of *y* increase as you move down. (See Figure 6-3.)

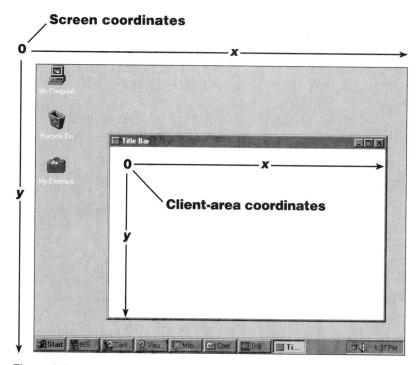

Figure 6-3. *Screen coordinates and client-area coordinates.*

You can convert screen coordinates to client-area coordinates and vice versa with two Windows functions:

```
ScreenToClient (hwnd, pPoint) ;
ClientToScreen (hwnd, pPoint) ;
```

The *pPoint* parameter is a pointer to a structure of type POINT. These two functions convert the values stored in the structure without preserving the old values. Note that if a screen-coordinate point is above the window's client area, then the converted client-area *y*-coordinate will be negative. Similarly, a screen coordinate to the left of a client area is a negative *x* value when expressed as a client-area coordinate.

The Hit-Test Message

If you've been keeping count, you know that we've covered 20 of the 21 mouse messages. The last message is WM_NCHITTEST, which stands for "nonclient hit test." This message precedes all other client-area and nonclient-area mouse messages. The *lParam* parameter contains the *x* and *y* screen coordinates of the mouse position. The *wParam* parameter is not used.

Windows applications usually pass this message to *DefWindowProc*. Windows then uses the WM_NCHITTEST message to generate all other mouse messages, based on the position of the mouse. For nonclient-area mouse messages, the value returned from *Def-WindowProc* when processing WM_NCHITTEST becomes the *wParam* parameter in the mouse message. This value can be any of the *wParam* values that accompany the nonclient-area mouse messages plus the following:

HTCLIENT	Client area
HTNOWHERE	Not on any window
HTTRANSPARENT	A window covered by another window
HTERROR	Causes *DefWindowProc* to produce a beep

If *DefWindowProc* returns HTCLIENT after it processes a WM_NCHITTEST message, then Windows converts the screen coordinates to client-area coordinates and generates a client-area mouse message.

If you remember how we disabled all system keyboard functions by trapping the WM_SYSKEYDOWN message, you may wonder if you can do something similar by trapping mouse messages. Sure. If you include the lines:

```
case WM_NCHITTEST :
     return (LRESULT) HTNOWHERE ;
```

in your window procedure, you will effectively disable all client-area and nonclient-area mouse messages to your window. The mouse buttons will simply not work while the mouse is anywhere within your window, including the system menu icon, the sizing buttons, and the close button.

Messages Beget Messages

Windows uses the WM_NCHITTEST message to generate all other mouse messages. The idea of messages giving birth to other messages is common in Windows. Let's take an example. As you know, if you double-click the system menu icon of a Windows program, the program will be terminated. The double-click generates a series of WM_NCHITTEST messages. Because the mouse is positioned over the system menu icon, *DefWindowProc* returns a value of HTSYSMENU and Windows puts a WM_NCLBUTTONDBLCLK message in the message queue with *wParam* equal to HTSYSMENU.

The window procedure usually passes that mouse message to *DefWindowProc*. When *DefWindowProc* receives the WM_NCLBUTTONDBLCLK message with *wParam* equal to HTSYSMENU, it puts a WM_SYSCOMMAND message with *wParam* equal to SC_CLOSE in the message queue. (This WM_SYSCOMMAND message is also generated when a user selects Close from the system menu.) Again, the window procedure usually passes that message to *DefWindowProc*. *DefWindowProc* processes the message by sending a WM_CLOSE message to the window procedure.

If a program wants to require confirmation from a user before terminating, the window procedure can trap WM_CLOSE. Otherwise, *DefWindowProc* processes WM_CLOSE by calling the *DestroyWindow* function. Among other actions, *DestroyWindow* sends a WM-_DESTROY message to the window procedure. Normally, a window procedure processes WM_DESTROY with the code:

```
case WM_DESTROY :
     PostQuitMessage (0) ;
     return 0 ;
```

The *PostQuitMessage* causes Windows to place a WM_QUIT message in the message queue. This message never reaches the window procedure because it causes *GetMessage* to return 0, which terminates the message loop and the program.

HIT-TESTING IN YOUR PROGRAMS

Earlier I discussed how Windows Explorer responds to mouse clicks and double-clicks. Obviously, the program must determine at which file the user is pointing with the mouse. This is called "hit-testing." Just as *DefWindowProc* must do some hit-testing when processing WM_NCHITTEST messages, very often a window procedure must do some hit-testing within the client area. In general, hit-testing involves calculations using the x- and y-coordinates passed to your window procedure in the *lParam* parameter of the mouse message.

A Hypothetical Example

Here's an example. Your program displays several columns of alphabetically sorted files. The file list starts at the top of the client area, which is *cxClient* pixels wide and *cyClient* pixels high; each character is *cyChar* pixels high. The filenames are stored in a sorted array of pointers to character strings called *szFileNames*.

Let's assume that the columns are *cxColWidth* pixels wide. The number of files you can fit in each column is:

```
iNumInCol = cyClient / cyChar ;
```

You receive a mouse click message with the coordinates *cxMouse* and *cyMouse* derived from *lParam*. You can determine which column of filenames the user is pointing to by using the formula:

```
iColumn = cxMouse / cxColWidth ;
```

The position of the filename in relation to the top of the column is:

```
iFromTop = cyMouse / cyChar ;
```

Now you can calculate an index to the *szFileNames* array:

```
iIndex = iColumn * iNumInCol + iFromTop ;
```

Obviously, if *iIndex* exceeds the number of files in the array, the user is clicking on a blank area of the display.

In many cases, hit-testing is more complex than this example suggests. For instance, it can become very messy in a word-processing program (such as WORDPAD) that uses variable font sizes. When you display something in the client area, you must determine the coordinates for each item you display. In hit-testing calculations, you must go backward from the coordinates to the object. However, if the object you display is a string, then going backward involves finding the character position within the string.

A Sample Program

The CHECKER1 program, shown in Figure 6-4, demonstrates some simple hit-testing. The program divides the client area into a 5-by-5 array of 25 rectangles. If you click the mouse on one of the rectangles, the rectangle is filled with an X. If you click there again, the X is removed.

CHECKER1.MAK

```
#------------------------
# CHECKER1.MAK make file
#------------------------

checker1.exe : checker1.obj
     $(LINKER) $(GUIFLAGS) -OUT:checker1.exe checker1.obj $(GUILIBS)

checker1.obj : checker1.c
     $(CC) $(CFLAGS) checker1.c
```

CHECKER1.C

```
/*-------------------------------------------------
   CHECKER1.C -- Mouse Hit-Test Demo Program No. 1
                 (c) Charles Petzold, 1996
   -------------------------------------------------*/

#include <windows.h>

#define DIVISIONS 5
#define MoveTo(hdc, x, y) MoveToEx (hdc, x, y, NULL)

LRESULT CALLBACK WndProc (HWND, UINT, WPARAM, LPARAM) ;

int WINAPI WinMain (HINSTANCE hInstance, HINSTANCE hPrevInstance,
                    PSTR  szCmdLine, int iCmdShow)
     {
     static char szAppName[] = "Checker1" ;
```

Figure 6-4. *The CHECKER1 program.*   *(continued)*

```
      HWND        hwnd ;
      MSG         msg ;
      WNDCLASSEX  wndclass ;

      wndclass.cbSize        = sizeof (wndclass) ;
      wndclass.style         = CS_HREDRAW | CS_VREDRAW ;
      wndclass.lpfnWndProc   = WndProc ;
      wndclass.cbClsExtra    = 0 ;
      wndclass.cbWndExtra    = 0 ;
      wndclass.hInstance     = hInstance ;
      wndclass.hIcon         = LoadIcon (NULL), IDI_APPLICATION ;
      wndclass.hCursor       = LoadCursor (NULL, IDC_ARROW) ;
      wndclass.hbrBackground = (HBRUSH) GetStockObject (WHITE_BRUSH) ;
      wndclass.lpszMenuName  = NULL ;
      wndclass.lpszClassName = szAppName ;
      wndclass.hIconSm       = LoadIcon (NULL, IDI_APPLICATION) ;

      RegisterClassEx (&wndclass) ;

      hwnd = CreateWindow (szAppName, "Checker1 Mouse Hit-Test Demo",
                           WS_OVERLAPPEDWINDOW,
                           CW_USEDEFAULT, CW_USEDEFAULT,
                           CW_USEDEFAULT, CW_USEDEFAULT,
                           NULL, NULL, hInstance, NULL) ;

      ShowWindow (hwnd, iCmdShow) ;
      UpdateWindow (hwnd) ;

      while (GetMessage (&msg, NULL, 0, 0))
           {
           TranslateMessage (&msg) ;
           DispatchMessage (&msg) ;
           }
      return msg.wParam ;
      }

LRESULT CALLBACK WndProc (HWND hwnd, UINT iMsg, WPARAM wParam, LPARAM lParam)
      {
      static BOOL fState[DIVISIONS][DIVISIONS] ;
      static int  cxBlock, cyBlock ;
      HDC         hdc ;
      PAINTSTRUCT ps ;
      RECT        rect ;
      int         x, y ;

      switch (iMsg)
           {
           case WM_SIZE :
```

(continued)

```
                cxBlock = LOWORD (lParam) / DIVISIONS ;
                cyBlock = HIWORD (lParam) / DIVISIONS ;
                return 0 ;

        case WM_LBUTTONDOWN :
                x = LOWORD (lParam) / cxBlock ;
                y = HIWORD (lParam) / cyBlock ;

                if (x < DIVISIONS && y < DIVISIONS)
                     {
                     fState [x][y] ^= 1 ;

                     rect.left   = x * cxBlock ;
                     rect.top    = y * cyBlock ;
                     rect.right  = (x + 1) * cxBlock ;
                     rect.bottom = (y + 1) * cyBlock ;

                     InvalidateRect (hwnd, &rect, FALSE) ;
                     }
                else
                     MessageBeep (0) ;
                return 0 ;

        case WM_PAINT :
                hdc = BeginPaint (hwnd, &ps) ;

                for (x = 0 ; x < DIVISIONS ; x++)
                     for (y = 0 ; y < DIVISIONS ; y++)
                          {
                          Rectangle (hdc, x * cxBlock, y * cyBlock,
                                    (x + 1) * cxBlock, (y + 1) * cyBlock) ;

                          if (fState [x][y])
                               {
                               MoveTo (hdc,  x    * cxBlock,
                                             y    * cyBlock) ;
                               LineTo (hdc, (x+1) * cxBlock,
                                            (y+1) * cyBlock) ;
                               MoveTo (hdc,  x    * cxBlock,
                                            (y+1) * cyBlock) ;
                               LineTo (hdc, (x+1) * cxBlock,
                                             y    * cyBlock) ;
                               }
                          }
                EndPaint (hwnd, &ps) ;
                return 0 ;
```

(continued)

```
        case WM_DESTROY :
              PostQuitMessage (0) ;
              return 0 ;
        }
    return DefWindowProc (hwnd, iMsg, wParam, lParam) ;
    }
```

Figure 6-5 shows the CHECKER1 display. All 25 rectangles have the same width and height. These width and height values are stored in *cxBlock* and *cyBlock* and are recalculated when the size of the client area changes. The WM_LBUTTONDOWN logic uses the mouse coordinates to determine which rectangle has been clicked. It flags the current state of the rectangle in the array *fState* and invalidates the rectangle to generate a WM_PAINT message. If the width or height of the client area is not evenly divisible by five, a small strip of client area at the left or bottom will not be covered by a rectangle. For error processing, CHECKER1 responds to a mouse click in this area by calling *MessageBeep*.

When CHECKER1 receives a WM_PAINT message, it repaints the entire client area by drawing rectangles using the GDI *Rectangle* function. If the *fState* value is set, CHECKER1 draws two lines using the *MoveTo* and *LineTo* functions. During WM_PAINT processing, CHECKER1 does not check the validity of each rectangular section before repainting it, but it could. One method for checking validity involves building a RECT structure for each rectangular block within the loop (using the same formulas as in the WM_LBUTTONDOWN logic) and checking whether it intersects the invalid rectangle (*ps.rcPaint*) by using the function *IntersectRect*. Another method is to use *PtInRect* to determine if any of the four corners of the rectangular block are within the invalid rectangle.

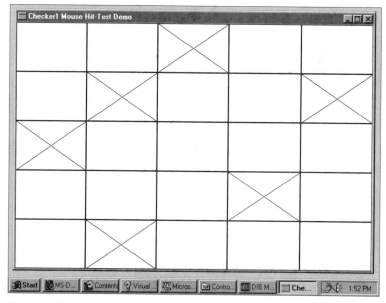

Figure 6-5. *The CHECKER1 display.*

Emulating the Mouse with the Keyboard

CHECKER1 works only if you have a mouse. We'll be adding a keyboard interface to the program shortly, as we did for the SYSMETS program in Chapter 5. However, adding a keyboard interface to a program that uses the mouse cursor for pointing purposes requires that we also must worry about displaying and moving the mouse cursor.

Even if a mouse device is not installed, Windows can still display a mouse cursor. Windows maintains a "display count" for this cursor. If a mouse is installed, the display count is initially 0; if not, the display count is initially −1. The mouse cursor is displayed only if the display count is 0 or positive. You can increment the display count by calling:

```
ShowCursor (TRUE) ;
```

and decrement it by calling:

```
ShowCursor (FALSE) ;
```

You do not need to determine if a mouse is installed before using *ShowCursor*. If you want to display the mouse cursor regardless of the presence of the mouse, simply increment the display count. After you increment the display count once, decrementing it will hide the cursor if no mouse is installed but leave it displayed if a mouse is present. The display count applies to all of Windows, so you should ensure that you increment and decrement the display count an equal number of times.

You may want to use the following simple logic in your window procedure:

```
case WM_SETFOCUS :
     ShowCursor (TRUE) ;
     return 0 ;

case WM_KILLFOCUS :
     ShowCursor (FALSE) ;
     return 0 ;
```

A window procedure receives the WM_SETFOCUS message when the window obtains the keyboard input focus and WM_KILLFOCUS when it loses the input focus. These are ideal times to display and hide the mouse cursor. First, the WM_SETFOCUS and WM_KILLFOCUS calls are balanced—that is, the window procedure will increment and decrement the mouse cursor display count an equal number of times. Second, for versions of Windows installed without a mouse, using the WM_SETFOCUS and WM_KILLFOCUS messages causes the cursor to be visible only when the window has the input focus. That is also the only time the user can move the cursor using the keyboard interface that you'll design.

Windows maintains a current mouse cursor position even if a mouse is not installed. If a mouse is not installed, and you display the mouse cursor, it may appear in any part of the display and will remain in that position until you explicitly move it. You can obtain the cursor position by using:

```
GetCursorPos (pPoint) ;
```

where *pPoint* is a pointer to a POINT structure. The function fills in the POINT fields with the *x*- and *y*-coordinates of the mouse. You can set the cursor position by using:

```
SetCursorPos (x, y) ;
```

In both cases, the *x* and *y* values are screen coordinates, not client-area coordinates. (This should be evident because the functions do not require a *hwnd* parameter.) As noted earlier, you can convert screen coordinates to client-area coordinates and vice versa by using *Screen-ToClient* and *ClientToScreen*.

If you call *GetCursorPos* while processing a mouse message and convert to client-area coordinates, the coordinates may still be slightly different from those in *lParam* of the mouse message. The coordinates returned from *GetCursorPos* indicate the current position of the mouse. The coordinates in *lParam* of a mouse message are the coordinates of the mouse when the message was generated.

You'll probably want to write keyboard logic to move the mouse cursor with the keyboard arrow keys and simulate the mouse button with the Spacebar or Enter key. What you *don't* want to do is move the mouse cursor one pixel per keystroke. That forces a user to hold down an arrow key for more than a minute to move the mouse cursor from one side of the display to the other.

If you need to implement a keyboard interface to the mouse cursor but still maintain the ability to position the cursor at precise pixel locations, then process keystroke messages in such a way that, when you hold down an arrow key, the mouse cursor starts moving slowly but then speeds up. You'll recall that the *lParam* parameter in WM_KEYDOWN messages indicates if the keystroke messages are the result of typematic action. This is an excellent application of that information.

Adding a Keyboard Interface to CHECKER

The CHECKER2 program, shown in Figure 6-6, is the same as CHECKER1 except that it includes a keyboard interface. You can use the Left, Right, Up, and Down arrow keys to move the cursor among the 25 rectangles. The Home key sends the cursor to the upper left rectangle; the End key drops it down to the lower right rectangle. Both the Spacebar and Enter keys toggle the X mark.

CHECKER2.MAK

```
#-----------------------
# CHECKER2.MAK make file
#-----------------------

checker2.exe : checker2.obj
     $(LINKER) $(GUIFLAGS) -OUT:checker2.exe checker2.obj $(GUILIBS)
```

Figure 6-6. *The CHECKER2 program.*

(continued)

```
checker2.obj : checker2.c
     $(CC) $(CFLAGS) checker2.c
```

CHECKER2.C

```
/*----------------------------------------------------
   CHECKER2.C -- Mouse Hit-Test Demo Program No. 2
                 (c) Charles Petzold, 1996
   --------------------------------------------------*/

#include <windows.h>

#define DIVISIONS 5
#define MoveTo(hdc, x, y) MoveToEx (hdc, x, y, NULL)

LRESULT CALLBACK WndProc (HWND, UINT, WPARAM, LPARAM) ;

int WINAPI WinMain (HINSTANCE hInstance, HINSTANCE hPrevInstance,
                    PSTR szCmdLine, int iCmdShow)
     {
     static char szAppName[] = "Checker2" ;
     HWND        hwnd ;
     MSG         msg ;
     WNDCLASSEX  wndclass ;

     wndclass.cbSize        = sizeof (wndclass) ;
     wndclass.style         = CS_HREDRAW | CS_VREDRAW ;
     wndclass.lpfnWndProc   = WndProc ;
     wndclass.cbClsExtra    = 0 ;
     wndclass.cbWndExtra    = 0 ;
     wndclass.hInstance     = hInstance ;
     wndclass.hIcon         = LoadIcon (NULL, IDI_APPLICATION) ;
     wndclass.hCursor       = LoadCursor (NULL, IDC_ARROW) ;
     wndclass.hbrBackground = (HBRUSH) GetStockObject (WHITE_BRUSH) ;
     wndclass.lpszMenuName  = NULL ;
     wndclass.lpszClassName = szAppName ;
     wndclass.hIconSm       = LoadIcon (NULL, IDI_APPLICATION) ;

     RegisterClassEx (&wndclass) ;

     hwnd = CreateWindow (szAppName, "Checker2 Mouse Hit-Test Demo",
                     WS_OVERLAPPEDWINDOW,
                     CW_USEDEFAULT, CW_USEDEFAULT,
```

(continued)

```
                              CW_USEDEFAULT, CW_USEDEFAULT,
                              NULL, NULL, hInstance, NULL) ;

     ShowWindow (hwnd, iCmdShow) ;
     UpdateWindow (hwnd) ;

     while (GetMessage (&msg, NULL, 0, 0))
          {
          TranslateMessage (&msg) ;
          DispatchMessage (&msg) ;
          }
     return msg.wParam ;
     }

LRESULT CALLBACK WndProc (HWND hwnd, UINT iMsg, WPARAM wParam, LPARAM lParam)
     {
     static BOOL fState[DIVISIONS][DIVISIONS] ;
     static int  cxBlock, cyBlock ;
     HDC         hdc ;
     PAINTSTRUCT ps ;
     POINT       point ;
     RECT        rect ;
     int         x, y ;

     switch (iMsg)
          {
          case WM_SIZE :
               cxBlock = LOWORD (lParam) / DIVISIONS ;
               cyBlock = HIWORD (lParam) / DIVISIONS ;
               return 0 ;

          case WM_SETFOCUS :
               ShowCursor (TRUE) ;
               return 0 ;

          case WM_KILLFOCUS :
               ShowCursor (FALSE) ;
               return 0 ;

          case WM_KEYDOWN :
               GetCursorPos (&point) ;
               ScreenToClient (hwnd, &point) ;

               x = max (0, min (DIVISIONS - 1, point.x / cxBlock)) ;
               y = max (0, min (DIVISIONS - 1, point.y / cyBlock)) ;
```

(continued)

```
        switch (wParam)
            {
            case VK_UP :
                y-- ;
                break ;

            case VK_DOWN :
                y++ ;
                break ;

            case VK_LEFT :
                x-- ;
                break ;

            case VK_RIGHT :
                x++ ;
                break ;

            case VK_HOME :
                x = y = 0 ;
                break ;

            case VK_END :
                x = y = DIVISIONS - 1 ;
                break ;

            case VK_RETURN :
            case VK_SPACE :
                SendMessage (hwnd, WM_LBUTTONDOWN, MK_LBUTTON,
                            MAKELONG (x * cxBlock, y * cyBlock)) ;
                break ;
            }
        x = (x + DIVISIONS) % DIVISIONS ;
        y = (y + DIVISIONS) % DIVISIONS ;

        point.x = x * cxBlock + cxBlock / 2 ;
        point.y = y * cyBlock + cyBlock / 2 ;

        ClientToScreen (hwnd, &point) ;
        SetCursorPos (point.x, point.y) ;
        return 0 ;

case WM_LBUTTONDOWN :
    x = LOWORD (lParam) / cxBlock ;
    y = HIWORD (lParam) / cyBlock ;

    if (x < DIVISIONS && y < DIVISIONS)
```

(continued)

```
                        {
                        fState[x][y] ^= 1 ;

                        rect.left   = x * cxBlock ;
                        rect.top    = y * cyBlock ;
                        rect.right  = (x + 1) * cxBlock ;
                        rect.bottom = (y + 1) * cyBlock ;

                        InvalidateRect (hwnd, &rect, FALSE) ;
                        }
                else
                        MessageBeep (0) ;
                return 0 ;

        case WM_PAINT :
                hdc = BeginPaint (hwnd, &ps) ;

                for (x = 0 ; x < DIVISIONS ; x++)
                        for (y = 0 ; y < DIVISIONS ; y++)
                                {
                                Rectangle (hdc, x * cxBlock, y * cyBlock,
                                        (x + 1) * cxBlock, (y + 1) * cyBlock) ;

                                if (fState [x][y])
                                        {
                                        MoveTo (hdc,  x    * cxBlock,
                                                      y    * cyBlock) ;
                                        LineTo (hdc, (x+1) * cxBlock,
                                                     (y+1) * cyBlock) ;
                                        MoveTo (hdc,  x    * cxBlock,
                                                     (y+1) * cyBlock) ;
                                        LineTo (hdc, (x+1) * cxBlock,
                                                      y    * cyBlock) ;
                                        }
                                }
                EndPaint (hwnd, &ps) ;
                return 0 ;

        case WM_DESTROY :
                PostQuitMessage (0) ;
                return 0 ;
        }
    return DefWindowProc (hwnd, iMsg, wParam, lParam) ;
    }
```

The WM_KEYDOWN logic in CHECKER2 determines the position of the cursor (*GetCursorPos*), converts the screen coordinates to client-area coordinates (*ScreenToClient*), and divides the coordinates by the width and height of the rectangular block. This produces *x* and *y* values that indicate the position of the rectangle in the 5-by-5 array. The mouse cursor may or may not be in the client area when a key is pressed, so *x* and *y* must be passed through the *min* and *max* macros to ensure that they range from 0 through 4.

For arrow keys, CHECKER2 increments or decrements *x* and *y* appropriately. If the key is the Enter key (VK_RETURN) or Spacebar (VK_SPACE), CHECKER2 uses *SendMessage* to send a WM_LBUTTONDOWN message to itself. This technique is similar to the method used in the SYSMETS program in Chapter 5 to add a keyboard interface to the window scroll bar. The WM_KEYDOWN logic finishes by calculating client-area coordinates that point to the center of the rectangle, converting to screen coordinates (*ClientToScreen*), and setting the cursor position (*SetCursorPos*).

Using Child Windows for Hit-Testing

Some programs, like the Windows PAINT program, divide the client area into several smaller logical areas. The PAINT program, shown in Figure 6-7, has an area at the left for its icon-based menu and an area at the bottom for the color menu. PAINT, when hit-testing on these two menus, must take into account the location of the menu within the client area before determining the menu item being selected by the user.

Figure 6-7. *The Windows PAINT program.*

Or maybe not. In reality, PAINT simplifies the menu drawing and hit-testing through the use of "child windows." The child windows divide the entire client area into several smaller rectangular regions. Each child window has its own window handle, window procedure, and client area. Each window procedure receives mouse messages that apply only to its child window. The *lParam* parameter in the mouse message contains coordinates relative to the upper left corner of the client area of the child window, not of the parent window.

Child windows used in this way can help you structure and modularize your programs. If the child windows use different window classes, each child window can have its own window procedure. The different window classes can also define different background colors and different default cursors. In Chapter 8, we'll look at "child window controls"—predefined child windows that take the form of scroll bars, buttons, and edit boxes. Right now, let's see how we can use child windows in the CHECKER program.

Child Windows in CHECKER

Figure 6-8 shows CHECKER3. This version of the program creates 25 child windows to process mouse clicks. It does not have a keyboard interface, but one could easily be added.

CHECKER3 has two window procedures called *WndProc* and *ChildWndProc*. *Wnd-Proc* is still the window procedure for the main (or parent) window. *ChildWndProc* is the window procedure for the 25 child windows. Both window procedures must be defined as CALLBACK functions.

Because the window procedure is defined by the window class structure that you register with Windows by using the *RegisterClassEx* call, the two window procedures in CHECKER3.C require two window classes. The first window class is for the main window and has the name "Checker3". The second window class is given the name "Checker3_Child".

Most of the fields of the *wndclass* structure variable are simply reused when "Checker3_Child" is registered in *WinMain*. The *lpszClassName* field is set to "Checker3-_Child" (the name of the class). The *lpfnWndProc* field is set to *ChildWndProc*, the window procedure for this window class, and the *hIcon* and *hIconSm* fields are set to NULL because icons are not used with child windows. For the "Checker3_Child" window class, the *cbWndExtra* field in the *wndclass* structure variable is set to 2 bytes, or more precisely, *sizeof (WORD)*. This field tells Windows to reserve 2 bytes of extra space in a structure that Windows maintains for each window based on this window class. You can use this space to store information that may be different for each window.

CHECKER3.MAK

```
#------------------------
# CHECKER3.MAK make file
#------------------------

checker3.exe : checker3.obj
    $(LINKER) $(GUIFLAGS) -OUT:checker3.exe checker3.obj $(GUILIBS)

checker3.obj : checker3.c
    $(CC) $(CFLAGS) checker3.c
```

Figure 6-8. *The CHECKER3 program.*   *(continued)*

CHECKER3.C

```
/*-------------------------------------------------
   CHECKER3.C -- Mouse Hit-Test Demo Program No. 3
                 (c) Charles Petzold, 1996
   -------------------------------------------------*/

#include <windows.h>

#define DIVISIONS 5
#define MoveTo(hdc, x, y) MoveToEx (hdc, x, y, NULL)

LRESULT CALLBACK WndProc     (HWND, UINT, WPARAM, LPARAM) ;
LRESULT CALLBACK ChildWndProc (HWND, UINT, WPARAM, LPARAM) ;

char       szChildClass[] = "Checker3_Child" ;

int WINAPI WinMain (HINSTANCE hInstance, HINSTANCE hPrevInstance,
                    PSTR szCmdLine, int iCmdShow)
     {
     static char szAppName[] = "Checker3" ;
     HWND        hwnd ;
     MSG         msg ;
     WNDCLASSEX  wndclass ;

     wndclass.cbSize        = sizeof (wndclass) ;
     wndclass.style         = CS_HREDRAW | CS_VREDRAW ;
     wndclass.lpfnWndProc   = WndProc ;
     wndclass.cbClsExtra    = 0 ;
     wndclass.cbWndExtra    = 0 ;
     wndclass.hInstance     = hInstance ;
     wndclass.hIcon         = LoadIcon (NULL, IDI_APPLICATION) ;
     wndclass.hCursor       = LoadCursor (NULL, IDC_ARROW) ;
     wndclass.hbrBackground = (HBRUSH) GetStockObject (WHITE_BRUSH) ;
     wndclass.lpszMenuName  = NULL ;
     wndclass.lpszClassName = szAppName ;
     wndclass.hIconSm       = LoadIcon (NULL, IDI_APPLICATION) ;

     RegisterClassEx (&wndclass) ;

     wndclass.lpfnWndProc   = ChildWndProc ;
     wndclass.cbWndExtra    = sizeof (WORD) ;
     wndclass.hIcon         = NULL ;
     wndclass.lpszClassName = szChildClass ;
     wndclass.hIconSm       = NULL ;

     RegisterClassEx (&wndclass) ;

     hwnd = CreateWindow (szAppName, "Checker3 Mouse Hit-Test Demo",
```

(continued)

```
                              WS_OVERLAPPEDWINDOW,
                              CW_USEDEFAULT, CW_USEDEFAULT,
                              CW_USEDEFAULT, CW_USEDEFAULT,
                              NULL, NULL, hInstance, NULL) ;

     ShowWindow (hwnd, iCmdShow) ;
     UpdateWindow (hwnd) ;

     while (GetMessage (&msg, NULL, 0, 0))
          {
          TranslateMessage (&msg) ;
          DispatchMessage (&msg) ;
          }
     return msg.wParam ;
     }

LRESULT CALLBACK WndProc (HWND hwnd, UINT iMsg, WPARAM wParam, LPARAM lParam)
     {
     static HWND hwndChild[DIVISIONS][DIVISIONS] ;
     int         cxBlock, cyBlock, x, y ;

     switch (iMsg)
          {
          case WM_CREATE :
               for (x = 0 ; x < DIVISIONS ; x++)
                    for (y = 0 ; y < DIVISIONS ; y++)
                         {
                         hwndChild[x][y] = CreateWindow (szChildClass, NULL,
                              WS_CHILDWINDOW | WS_VISIBLE,
                              0, 0, 0, 0,
                              hwnd, (HMENU) (y << 8 | x),
                              (HINSTANCE) GetWindowLong (hwnd, GWL_HINSTANCE),
                              NULL) ;
                         }
               return 0 ;

          case WM_SIZE :
               cxBlock = LOWORD (lParam) / DIVISIONS ;
               cyBlock = HIWORD (lParam) / DIVISIONS ;

               for (x = 0 ; x < DIVISIONS ; x++)
                    for (y = 0 ; y < DIVISIONS ; y++)
                         MoveWindow (hwndChild[x][y],
                              x * cxBlock, y * cyBlock,
                              cxBlock, cyBlock, TRUE) ;
               return 0 ;
```

(continued)

```
          case WM_LBUTTONDOWN :
               MessageBeep (0) ;
               return 0 ;

          case WM_DESTROY :
               PostQuitMessage (0) ;
               return 0 ;
          }
     return DefWindowProc (hwnd, iMsg, wParam, lParam) ;
     }

LRESULT CALLBACK ChildWndProc (HWND hwnd, UINT iMsg, WPARAM wParam, LPARAM lParam)
     {
     HDC        hdc ;
     PAINTSTRUCT ps ;
     RECT       rect ;

     switch (iMsg)
          {
          case WM_CREATE :
               SetWindowWord (hwnd, 0, 0) ;        // on/off flag
               return 0 ;

          case WM_LBUTTONDOWN :
               SetWindowWord (hwnd, 0, 1 ^ GetWindowWord (hwnd, 0)) ;
               InvalidateRect (hwnd, NULL, FALSE) ;
               return 0 ;

          case WM_PAINT :
               hdc = BeginPaint (hwnd, &ps) ;

               GetClientRect (hwnd, &rect) ;
               Rectangle (hdc, 0, 0, rect.right, rect.bottom) ;

               if (GetWindowWord (hwnd, 0))
                    {
                    MoveTo (hdc, 0,           0) ;
                    LineTo (hdc, rect.right, rect.bottom) ;
                    MoveTo (hdc, 0,          rect.bottom) ;
                    LineTo (hdc, rect.right, 0) ;
                    }

               EndPaint (hwnd, &ps) ;
               return 0 ;
          }
     return DefWindowProc (hwnd, iMsg, wParam, lParam) ;
     }
```

The *CreateWindow* call in *WinMain* creates the main window based on the "Checker3" class. This is normal. However, when *WndProc* receives a WM_CREATE message, it calls *CreateWindow* 25 times to create 25 child windows based on the "Checker3_Child" window class. The following table provides a comparison of the parameters to the *CreateWindow* call in *WinMain* that creates the main window and the *CreateWindow* call in *WndProc* that creates the 25 child windows:

Parameter	*Main Window*	*Child Window*
window class	"Checker3"	"Checker3_Child"
window caption	"Checker3..."	NULL
window style	WS_OVERLAPPEDWINDOW	WS_CHILDWINDOW ¦ WS_VISIBLE
horizontal position	CW_USEDEFAULT	0
vertical position	CW_USEDEFAULT	0
width	CW_USEDEFAULT	0
height	CW_USEDEFAULT	0
parent window handle	NULL	*hwnd*
menu handle/child ID	NULL	(HMENU) $(y << 8$ ¦ $x)$
instance handle	*hInstance*	(HINSTANCE) *GetWindowLong* (*hwnd*, GWL_HINSTANCE)
extra parameters	NULL	NULL

Normally the position, width, and height parameters are required for child windows, but in CHECKER3 the child windows are positioned and resized later in *WndProc*. The parent window handle is NULL for the main window because it is the parent. The parent window handle is required when using the *CreateWindow* call to create a child window.

The main window doesn't have a menu, so that parameter is NULL. For child windows, the same parameter position is called a "child ID." This is a number that uniquely identifies the child window. The child ID becomes much more important when working with child window controls because messages to the parent window are identified by this child ID, as we'll see in Chapter 8. For CHECKER3, I've set the child ID to the position that each child window occupies in the 5-by-5 array within the main window.

The instance handle is *hInstance* in both cases. When the child window is created, the *hInstance* value is extracted using the function *GetWindowLong* from the structure that Windows maintains for the window. (Rather than use *GetWindowLong*, I could have saved the value of *hInstance* in a global variable and used it directly.)

Each child window has a different window handle that is stored in the *hwndChild* array. When *WndProc* receives a WM_SIZE message, it calls *MoveWindow* for each of the 25 child windows. The parameters indicate the upper left corner of the child window relative to the parent window client-area coordinates, the width and height of the child window, and whether the child window needs repainting.

Now let's take a look at *ChildWndProc*. This window procedure processes messages for all 25 child windows. The *hwnd* parameter to *ChildWndProc* is the handle to the child window receiving the message. When *ChildWndProc* processes a WM_CREATE message (which will happen 25 times because there are 25 child windows), it uses *SetWindowWord* to store a 0 in the extra area reserved within the window structure. (Recall that we reserved this space by using the *cbWndExtra* field when defining the window class structure.) *ChildWndProc* uses this value to store the current state (X or no X) of the rectangle. When the child window is clicked, the WM_LBUTTONDOWN logic simply flips the value of this word (from 0 to 1 or from 1 to 0) and invalidates the entire child window client area. This area is the single rectangle being clicked. The WM_PAINT processing is trivial because the size of the rectangle it draws is the same size as the client window.

Because the C source code file and the .EXE file of CHECKER3 are larger than those for CHECKER1 (to say nothing of my explanation of the programs), I will not try to convince you that CHECKER3 is "simpler" than CHECKER1. But note that we no longer have to do any mouse hit-testing! If a child window in CHECKER3 gets a WM_LBUTTONDOWN message, the window has been hit, and that's all it needs to know.

If you want to add a keyboard interface to CHECKER3, keep in mind that the main window still gets keyboard messages because it has the input focus. We'll explore child windows more in Chapter 8.

CAPTURING THE MOUSE

A window procedure normally receives mouse messages only when the mouse cursor is positioned over the client or nonclient area of the window. A program may need to receive mouse messages when the mouse is outside the window. If so, the program can "capture" the mouse.

Blocking Out a Rectangle

To examine why capturing the mouse may be necessary, let's look at the BLOKOUT1 program shown in Figure 6-9.

BLOKOUT1.MAK

```
#-----------------------
# BLOKOUT1.MAK make file
#-----------------------

blokout1.exe : blokout1.obj
     $(LINKER) $(GUIFLAGS) -OUT:blokout1.exe blokout1.obj $(GUILIBS)
```

Figure 6-9. *The BLOKOUT1 program.*

(continued)

```
blokout1.obj : blokout1.c
    $(CC) $(CFLAGS) blokout1.c
```

BLOKOUT1.C

```c
/*------------------------------------------
   BLOKOUT1.C -- Mouse Button Demo Program
                 (c) Charles Petzold, 1996
   ------------------------------------------*/

#include <windows.h>

LRESULT CALLBACK WndProc (HWND, UINT, WPARAM, LPARAM) ;

int WINAPI WinMain (HINSTANCE hInstance, HINSTANCE hPrevInstance,
                    PSTR szCmdLine, int iCmdShow)
     {
     static char szAppName[] = "BlokOut1" ;
     HWND         hwnd ;
     MSG          msg ;
     WNDCLASSEX   wndclass ;

     wndclass.cbSize        = sizeof (wndclass) ;
     wndclass.style         = CS_HREDRAW | CS_VREDRAW ;
     wndclass.lpfnWndProc   = WndProc ;
     wndclass.cbClsExtra    = 0 ;
     wndclass.cbWndExtra    = 0 ;
     wndclass.hInstance     = hInstance ;
     wndclass.hIcon         = LoadIcon (NULL, IDI_APPLICATION) ;
     wndclass.hCursor       = LoadCursor (NULL, IDC_ARROW) ;
     wndclass.hbrBackground = (HBRUSH) GetStockObject (WHITE_BRUSH) ;
     wndclass.lpszMenuName  = NULL ;
     wndclass.lpszClassName = szAppName ;
     wndclass.hIconSm       = LoadIcon (NULL, IDI_APPLICATION) ;

     RegisterClassEx (&wndclass) ;

     hwnd = CreateWindow (szAppName, "Mouse Button Demo",
                          WS_OVERLAPPEDWINDOW,
                          CW_USEDEFAULT, CW_USEDEFAULT,
                          CW_USEDEFAULT, CW_USEDEFAULT,
                          NULL, NULL, hInstance, NULL) ;

     ShowWindow (hwnd, iCmdShow) ;
     UpdateWindow (hwnd) ;
```

(continued)

```
        while (GetMessage (&msg, NULL, 0, 0))
            {
            TranslateMessage (&msg) ;
            DispatchMessage (&msg) ;
            }
        return msg.wParam ;
        }


void DrawBoxOutline (HWND hwnd, POINT ptBeg, POINT ptEnd)
        {
        HDC hdc ;

        hdc = GetDC (hwnd) ;

        SetROP2 (hdc, R2_NOT) ;
        SelectObject (hdc, GetStockObject (NULL_BRUSH)) ;
        Rectangle (hdc, ptBeg.x, ptBeg.y, ptEnd.x, ptEnd.y) ;

        ReleaseDC (hwnd, hdc) ;
        }


LRESULT CALLBACK WndProc (HWND hwnd, UINT iMsg, WPARAM wParam, LPARAM lParam)
        {
        static BOOL  fBlocking, fValidBox ;
        static POINT ptBeg, ptEnd, ptBoxBeg, ptBoxEnd ;
        HDC          hdc ;
        PAINTSTRUCT  ps ;

        switch (iMsg)
            {
            case WM_LBUTTONDOWN :
                    ptBeg.x = ptEnd.x = LOWORD (lParam) ;
                    ptBeg.y = ptEnd.y = HIWORD (lParam) ;

                    DrawBoxOutline (hwnd, ptBeg, ptEnd) ;

                    SetCursor (LoadCursor (NULL, IDC_CROSS)) ;

                    fBlocking = TRUE ;
                    return 0 ;

            case WM_MOUSEMOVE :
                    if (fBlocking)
                        {
                        SetCursor (LoadCursor (NULL, IDC_CROSS)) ;
```

(continued)

```
                        DrawBoxOutline (hwnd, ptBeg, ptEnd) ;

                        ptEnd.x = LOWORD (lParam) ;
                        ptEnd.y = HIWORD (lParam) ;

                        DrawBoxOutline (hwnd, ptBeg, ptEnd) ;
                        }
               return 0 ;

     case WM_LBUTTONUP :
          if (fBlocking)
               {
               DrawBoxOutline (hwnd, ptBeg, ptEnd) ;

               ptBoxBeg   = ptBeg ;
               ptBoxEnd.x = LOWORD (lParam) ;
               ptBoxEnd.y = HIWORD (lParam) ;

               SetCursor (LoadCursor (NULL, IDC_ARROW)) ;

               fBlocking = FALSE ;
               fValidBox = TRUE ;

               InvalidateRect (hwnd, NULL, TRUE) ;
               }
          return 0 ;

     case WM_CHAR :
          if (fBlocking & wParam == '\x1B')        // ie, Escape
               {
               DrawBoxOutline (hwnd, ptBeg, ptEnd) ;

               SetCursor (LoadCursor (NULL, IDC_ARROW)) ;

               fBlocking = FALSE ;
               }
          return 0 ;

     case WM_PAINT :
          hdc = BeginPaint (hwnd, &ps) ;

          if (fValidBox)
               {
               SelectObject (hdc, GetStockObject (BLACK_BRUSH)) ;
               Rectangle (hdc, ptBoxBeg.x, ptBoxBeg.y,
                               ptBoxEnd.x, ptBoxEnd.y) ;
               }
```

(continued)

```
                    if (fBlocking)
                         {
                         SetROP2 (hdc, R2_NOT) ;
                         SelectObject (hdc, GetStockObject (NULL_BRUSH)) ;
                         Rectangle (hdc, ptBeg.x, ptBeg.y, ptEnd.x, ptEnd.y) ;
                         }

               EndPaint (hwnd, &ps) ;
               return 0 ;

          case WM_DESTROY :
               PostQuitMessage (0) ;
               return 0 ;
          }
     return DefWindowProc (hwnd, iMsg, wParam, lParam) ;
     }
```

This program demonstrates a little something that might be implemented in a Windows drawing program. You begin by depressing the left mouse button to indicate one corner of a rectangle. You then drag the mouse. The program draws an outlined rectangle with the opposite corner at the current mouse position. When you release the mouse, the program fills the rectangle. Figure 6-10 shows one rectangle already drawn and another one in progress.

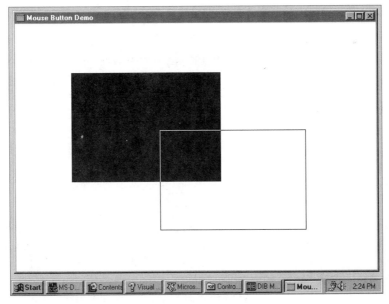

Figure 6-10. *The BLOKOUT1 display.*

When the left mouse button is depressed, BLOKOUT1 saves the mouse coordinates and calls the function *DrawBoxOutline* for the first time. The function draws a rectangle with the raster operations R2_NOT. This inverts the color of the client area. During subsequent WM_MOUSEMOVE messages, the program draws the same rectangle again, effectively erasing the previous version. It then uses the new mouse coordinates to draw a new rectangle. Finally, when BLOKOUT1 receives a WM_LBUTTONUP message, the mouse coordinates are saved and the window is invalidated, generating a WM_PAINT message to display the fixed rectangle.

So, what's the problem?

Try this: Press the left mouse button within BLOKOUT1's client area and then move the cursor outside the window. The program stops receiving WM_MOUSEMOVE messages. Now release the button. BLOKOUT1 doesn't get that WM_LBUTTONUP message because the cursor is outside the client area. Move the cursor back within BLOKOUT1's client area. The window procedure still thinks the button is pressed.

This is not good. The program doesn't know what's going on.

The Capture Solution

BLOKOUT1 shows some common program functionality, but the code is obviously flawed. This is the type of problem for which mouse capturing was invented. If the user is dragging the mouse, it should be no big deal if the cursor drifts out of the window for a moment. The program should still be in control of the mouse.

Capturing the mouse is easier than baiting a mousetrap. You need only call:

```
SetCapture (hwnd) ;
```

After this function call, Windows sends all mouse messages to the window procedure for the window whose handle is *hwnd*. The mouse messages are always client-area messages, even when the mouse is in a nonclient area of the window. The *lParam* parameter still indicates the position of the mouse in client-area coordinates. These x- and y-coordinates, however, can be negative if the mouse is to the left of or above the client area.

While the mouse is captured, system keyboard functions are also disabled. When you want to release the mouse, call:

```
ReleaseCapture () ;
```

This returns processing to normal.

Under Windows 95, mouse capturing is a little more restrictive than it was in previous versions of Windows. Specifically, if the mouse has been captured, and a mouse button is not currently down, and the mouse cursor passes over another window, the window underneath the cursor will receive the mouse messages rather than the window that captured the mouse. This is necessary to prevent one program from messing up the whole system by capturing the mouse and not releasing it.

In other words, capture the mouse only when the button is depressed in your client area. Release the capture when the button is released.

The BLOKOUT2 Program

The BLOKOUT2 program that demonstrates mouse capturing is shown in Figure 6-11.

BLOKOUT2.MAK

```
#-----------------------
# BLOKOUT2.MAK make file
#-----------------------

blokout2.exe : blokout2.obj
     $(LINKER) $(GUIFLAGS) -OUT:blokout2.exe blokout2.obj $(GUILIBS)

blokout2.obj : blokout2.c
     $(CC) $(CFLAGS) blokout2.c
```

BLOKOUT2.C

```c
/*----------------------------------------------------
   BLOKOUT2.C -- Mouse Button & Capture Demo Program
                 (c) Charles Petzold, 1996
   ----------------------------------------------------*/

#include <windows.h>

LRESULT CALLBACK WndProc (HWND, UINT, WPARAM, LPARAM) ;

int WINAPI WinMain (HINSTANCE hInstance, HINSTANCE hPrevInstance,
                    PSTR szCmdLine, int iCmdShow)
     {
     static char szAppName[] = "BlokOut2" ;
     HWND        hwnd ;
     MSG         msg ;
     WNDCLASSEX  wndclass ;

     wndclass.cbSize        = sizeof (wndclass) ;
     wndclass.style         = CS_HREDRAW | CS_VREDRAW ;
     wndclass.lpfnWndProc   = WndProc ;
     wndclass.cbClsExtra    = 0 ;
     wndclass.cbWndExtra    = 0 ;
     wndclass.hInstance     = hInstance ;
     wndclass.hIcon         = LoadIcon (NULL, IDI_APPLICATION) ;
     wndclass.hCursor       = LoadCursor (NULL, IDC_ARROW) ;
     wndclass.hbrBackground = (HBRUSH) GetStockObject (WHITE_BRUSH) ;
     wndclass.lpszMenuName  = NULL ;
```

Figure 6-11. *The BLOKOUT2 program.*   *(continued)*

```
        wndclass.lpszClassName = szAppName ;
        wndclass.hIconSm        = LoadIcon (NULL, IDI_APPLICATION) ;

        RegisterClassEx (&wndclass) ;

        hwnd = CreateWindow (szAppName, "Mouse Button & Capture Demo",
                             WS_OVERLAPPEDWINDOW,
                             CW_USEDEFAULT, CW_USEDEFAULT,
                             CW_USEDEFAULT, CW_USEDEFAULT,
                             NULL, NULL, hInstance, NULL) ;

        ShowWindow (hwnd, iCmdShow) ;
        UpdateWindow (hwnd) ;

        while (GetMessage (&msg, NULL, 0, 0))
            {
            TranslateMessage (&msg) ;
            DispatchMessage (&msg) ;
            }
        return msg.wParam ;
        }

void DrawBoxOutline (HWND hwnd, POINT ptBeg, POINT ptEnd)
        {
        HDC hdc ;

        hdc = GetDC (hwnd) ;

        SetROP2 (hdc, R2_NOT) ;
        SelectObject (hdc, GetStockObject (NULL_BRUSH)) ;
        Rectangle (hdc, ptBeg.x, ptBeg.y, ptEnd.x, ptEnd.y) ;

        ReleaseDC (hwnd, hdc) ;
        }

LRESULT CALLBACK WndProc (HWND hwnd, UINT iMsg, WPARAM wParam, LPARAM lParam)
        {
        static BOOL  fBlocking, fValidBox ;
        static POINT ptBeg, ptEnd, ptBoxBeg, ptBoxEnd ;
        HDC          hdc ;
        PAINTSTRUCT  ps ;

        switch (iMsg)
            {
            case WM_LBUTTONDOWN :
                 ptBeg.x = ptEnd.x = LOWORD (lParam) ;
                 ptBeg.y = ptEnd.y = HIWORD (lParam) ;
```

(continued)

```
            DrawBoxOutline (hwnd, ptBeg, ptEnd) ;

            SetCapture (hwnd) ;
            SetCursor (LoadCursor (NULL, IDC_CROSS)) ;

            fBlocking = TRUE ;
            return 0 ;

       case WM_MOUSEMOVE :
            if (fBlocking)
                 {
                 SetCursor (LoadCursor (NULL, IDC_CROSS)) ;

                 DrawBoxOutline (hwnd, ptBeg, ptEnd) ;

                 ptEnd.x = LOWORD (lParam) ;
                 ptEnd.y = HIWORD (lParam) ;

                 DrawBoxOutline (hwnd, ptBeg, ptEnd) ;
                 }
            return 0 ;

       case WM_LBUTTONUP :
            if (fBlockin g)
                 {
                 DrawBoxOutline (hwnd, ptBeg, ptEnd) ;

                 ptBoxBeg   = ptBeg ;
                 ptBoxEnd.x = LOWORD (lParam) ;
                 ptBoxEnd.y = HIWORD (lParam) ;

                 ReleaseCapture () ;
                 SetCursor (LoadCursor (NULL, IDC_ARROW)) ;

                 fBlocking = FALSE ;
                 fValidBox = TRUE ;

                 InvalidateRect (hwnd, NULL, TRUE) ;
                 }
            return 0 ;

       case WM_CHAR :
            if (fBlocking & wParam == '\x1B')          // i.e., Escape
                 {
                 DrawBoxOutline (hwnd, ptBeg, ptEnd) ;
                 ReleaseCapture () ;
```

(continued)

```
                    SetCursor (LoadCursor (NULL, IDC_ARROW)) ;

                    fBlocking = FALSE ;
                    }
               return 0 ;

          case WM_PAINT :
               hdc = BeginPaint (hwnd, &ps) ;

               if (fValidBox)
                    {
                    SelectObject (hdc, GetStockObject (BLACK_BRUSH)) ;
                    Rectangle (hdc, ptBoxBeg.x, ptBoxBeg.y,
                                    ptBoxEnd.x, ptBoxEnd.y) ;
                    }

               if (fBlocking)
                    {
                    SetROP2 (hdc, R2_NOT) ;
                    SelectObject (hdc, GetStockObject (NULL_BRUSH)) ;
                    Rectangle (hdc, ptBeg.x, ptBeg.y, ptEnd.x, ptEnd.y) ;
                    }

               EndPaint (hwnd, &ps) ;
               return 0 ;

          case WM_DESTROY :
               PostQuitMessage (0) ;
               return 0 ;
          }
     return DefWindowProc (hwnd, iMsg, wParam, lParam) ;
     }
```

BLOKOUT2 is the same as BLOKOUT1 except with three new lines of code: a call to *SetCapture* during the WM_LBUTTONDOWN message and calls to *ReleaseCapture* during the WM_LBUTTONUP and WM_CHAR messages. (Processing the WM_CHAR message allows the mouse capture to be released when the user presses the Escape key.)

And check this out: Make the window smaller than the screen size, begin blocking out a rectangle within the client area, and then move the mouse cursor outside the client area to the right or bottom, and finally release the mouse button. The program will have the coordinates of the entire rectangle. Just enlarge the window to see it.

Capturing the mouse isn't something suited only for oddball applications. You should do it anytime you need to track WM_MOUSEMOVE messages after a mouse button has been depressed in your client area until the mouse button is released. Your program will be simpler, and the user's expectations will have been met.

Chapter 7

The Timer

The Windows timer is an input device that periodically notifies an application when a specified interval of time has elapsed. Your program tells Windows the interval, in effect saying, for example, "Give me a nudge every 10 seconds." Windows then sends your program recurrent WM_TIMER messages to signal the intervals.

At first, the Windows timer may seem a less important input device than the keyboard or mouse, and certainly it is for many applications. But the timer is more useful than you may think, and not only for programs that display time, such as the Windows clock that appears in the taskbar. (This chapter includes two clock programs—one analog and one digital.) Here are other uses for the Windows timer, some perhaps not so obvious:

■ Multitasking—Although Windows 95 is a preemptive multitasking environment, sometimes it is more efficient for programs to return control to Windows as quickly as possible. If a program must do a large amount of processing, it can divide the job into smaller pieces and process each piece on receipt of a WM_TIMER message. (I'll have more to say on this subject in Chapter 14.)

■ Maintaining an updated status report—A program can use the timer to display "real-time" updates of continuously changing information, regarding either system resources or the progress of a certain task.

■ Implementing an "autosave" feature—The timer can prompt a Windows program to save a user's work on disk whenever a specified amount of time has elapsed.

■ Terminating demonstration versions of programs—Some demonstration versions of programs are designed to terminate, say, 30 minutes after they begin. The timer can signal such applications when the time is up.

■   Pacing movement—Graphical objects in a game or successive displays in a computer-assisted instruction program may need to proceed at a set rate. Using the timer eliminates the inconsistencies that might result from variations in microprocessor speed.

■   Multimedia—Programs that play CD audio, sound, or music often let the audio data play in the background. A program can use the timer to periodically determine how much of the audio has played and to coordinate on-screen visual information.

This chapter also explores topics that extend beyond the timer to other areas of Windows programming. We've already encountered the concept of the call-back function in our work with window procedures, but call-back functions also show up in timer programming. This chapter also discusses what to do when a program cannot gain access to a timer. This is no longer nearly as likely as under previous versions of Windows, but the method presented here can also be applied to error handling in other programs. Finally, the sample programs shown here deal with such decidedly nontimer issues as using a type of window known as a "popup," accessing the WIN.INI file to obtain information about international time and date formats, and using trigonometry to effectively rotate graphics objects on the screen.

TIMER BASICS

You can allocate a timer for your Windows program by calling the *SetTimer* function. *SetTimer* includes an integer parameter specifying an interval that can range (in theory) from 1 msec (millisecond) to 4,294,967,295 msec, which is nearly 50 days. The value indicates the rate at which Windows sends your program WM_TIMER messages. For instance, an interval of 1000 msec causes Windows to send your program a WM_TIMER message every second.

When your program is done using the timer, it calls the *KillTimer* function to stop the timer messages. You can program a "one-shot" timer by calling *KillTimer* during the processing of the WM_TIMER message. The *KillTimer* call purges the message queue of any pending WM_TIMER messages. Your program will never receive a stray WM_TIMER message following a *KillTimer* call.

The System and the Timer

The Windows timer is a relatively simple extension of the timer logic built into the PC's hardware and ROM BIOS. The PC's ROM BIOS initializes a timer chip to generate a hardware interrupt. This interrupt is sometimes called the "clock tick" or "timer tick" interrupt. These interrupts occur every 54.925 msec, or about 18.2 times per second. Some programs written for MS-DOS trapped this hardware interrupt themselves to implement clocks and timers.

Windows-based programs don't do this. Windows itself handles the hardware interrupt so that applications don't have to. For every program that currently has a timer set, Windows handles the timer interrupt by decrementing the counter value originally passed through the *SetTimer* call. When this counter value reaches 0, Windows places a WM_TIMER message in the appropriate application's message queue and resets the counter to its original value.

Because a Windows application retrieves WM_TIMER messages from the normal message queue, you never have to worry about your program being "interrupted" by a sudden WM_TIMER message while doing other processing. In this way, the timer is similar to the keyboard and mouse: the driver handles the asynchronous hardware interrupt events, and Windows translates these events into orderly, structured, serialized messages.

The Windows timer has the same 54.925-msec resolution as the underlying PC timer. This fact has two important implications:

■ A Windows application cannot receive WM_TIMER messages at a rate faster than about 18.2 times per second when using a single timer.

■ The time interval you specify in the *SetTimer* call is always rounded down to an integral multiple of clock ticks. For instance, a 1000-msec interval divided by 54.925 msec is 18.207 clock ticks, which is rounded down to 18 clock ticks, which is really a 989-msec interval. For intervals shorter than 55 msec, each clock tick generates a single WM_TIMER message.

Timer Messages Are Not Asynchronous

As I mentioned, non-Windows programs written for the IBM PC and compatibles can use the hardware timer tick interrupt by intercepting the hardware interrupt. When the hardware interrupt occurs, the program currently running is suspended, and control passes to the interrupt handler. When the interrupt handler is done, it passes control back to the interrupted program.

Like the hardware keyboard and mouse interrupts, the hardware timer tick interrupt is sometimes called an asynchronous interrupt because it occurs randomly with respect to the program that it interrupts. (Actually, the term "isochronous" is more accurate than "asynchronous" for a timer interrupt because the interrupts occur at equal intervals. But the interrupts are still asynchronous with respect to other processing.)

Although Windows also handles asynchronous timer interrupts, the WM_TIMER messages that Windows sends to applications are not asynchronous. The WM_TIMER messages are placed in the normal message queue and ordered with all the other messages. Therefore, if you specify 1000 msec in the *SetTimer* call, your program is not guaranteed to receive a WM_TIMER message every second or even (as I mentioned above) every 989 msec. If your application is busy for more than a second, it will not get any WM_TIMER messages during that time. You can demonstrate this to yourself using the programs shown in this chapter. In fact, Windows handles WM_TIMER messages much like WM_PAINT messages. Both these messages are low priority, and the program will only receive them if the message queue has no other messages.

The WM_TIMER messages are similar to WM_PAINT messages in another respect: Windows does not keep loading up the message queue with multiple WM_TIMER messages. Instead, Windows combines several WM_TIMER messages in the message queue into a single message. Therefore, the application won't get a bunch of them all at once, although it may get two WM_TIMER messages in quick succession. An application cannot determine the number of "missing" WM_TIMER messages that result from this process.

If you use the title bar of a clock program to move the window around the screen, the clock will stop receiving WM_TIMER messages. When the clock regains control and jumps ahead to the correct time, it isn't because it gets several WM_TIMER messages in a row. The program must determine the actual time and then set itself. The WM_TIMER messages only inform the program when it should be updated. A program can't keep time itself solely by counting WM_TIMER messages. (Later in this chapter, we'll write two clock applications that update every second, and we'll see precisely how this is accomplished.)

For convenience, I'll be talking about the timer in terms such as "getting a WM_TIMER message every second." But keep in mind that these messages are not precise clock tick interrupts.

USING THE TIMER: THREE METHODS

If you need a timer for the entire duration of your program, you'll probably call *SetTimer* from the *WinMain* function or while processing the WM_CREATE message, and *KillTimer* in response to a WM_DESTROY message. Setting the timer in *WinMain* provides the easiest error handling if a timer is unavailable. You can use a timer in one of three ways, depending on the parameters to the *SetTimer* call.

Method One

This method, the easiest, causes Windows to send WM_TIMER messages to the normal window procedure of the application. The *SetTimer* call looks like this:

```
SetTimer (hwnd, 1, iMsecInterval, NULL) ;
```

The first parameter is a handle to the window whose window procedure will receive the WM_TIMER messages. The second parameter is the timer ID, which should be a non-zero number. I have arbitrarily set it to 1 in this example. The third parameter is a 32-bit unsigned integer that specifies an interval in milliseconds. A value of 60000 will deliver a WM_TIMER message once a minute.

You can stop the WM_TIMER messages at any time (even while processing a WM_TIMER message) by calling:

```
KillTimer (hwnd, 1) ;
```

The second parameter is the same timer ID used in the *SetTimer* call. You should kill any active timers in response to a WM_DESTROY message before your program terminates.

When your window procedure receives a WM_TIMER message, *wParam* is equal to the timer ID (which in the above case is simply 1), and *lParam* is 0. If you need to set more than one timer, use a different timer ID for each timer. The value of *wParam* will differentiate the WM_TIMER messages passed to your window procedure. To make your program more readable, you may want to use *#define* statements for the different timer IDs:

```
#define TIMER_SEC   1
#define TIMER_MIN   2
```

You can then set the two timers with two *SetTimer* calls:

```
SetTimer (hwnd, TIMER_SEC, 1000, NULL) ;
SetTimer (hwnd, TIMER_MIN, 60000, NULL) ;
```

The WM_TIMER logic might look something like this:

```
case WM_TIMER :
     switch (wParam)
          {
          case TIMER_SEC :
               [once-per-second processing]
               break ;
          case TIMER_MIN :
               [once-per-minute processing]
               break ;
          }
     return 0 ;
```

If you want to set an existing timer to a different elapsed time, kill the timer and call *SetTimer* again. This code assumes that the timer ID is 1:

```
KillTimer (hwnd, 1) ;
SetTimer (hwnd, 1, iMsecInterval, NULL) ;
```

The *iMsecInterval* parameter is the new elapsed time in milliseconds. You may want to use this technique in a clock program if there's an option to show seconds or not. You'd simply change the timer interval between 1000 msec and 60,000 msec.

What to do if no timer is available

In the early days of Windows, only 16 timers could be active at any time throughout the entire system. Windows users discovered this fact early on by attempting to run as many Clock programs as possible. The 17th would come up with an error message saying "No more clocks or timers!" While Windows 3.0 doubled the number of timers to 32, and Windows 95 has done away with any practical limitation, it's still a good idea to code a lot of error processing in your Windows program. For purposes of clarity, I have not done this in my earlier sample code, but here is as good a place as ever to discuss handling some rudimentary problems.

If no timer is available, *SetTimer* returns NULL. Your program might be able to function reasonably well without the timer, but if you need the timer (as a clock program certainly does), the application has no choice but to terminate if it can't get one. If you call *SetTimer* in *WinMain*, you can terminate the program simply by returning FALSE from *WinMain*.

Let's assume you want a 1000-msec timer. Following the *CreateWindow* call but before the message loop, you might have a statement such as this:

```
if (!SetTimer (hwnd, 1, 1000, NULL))
    return FALSE ;
```

This is the unfriendly way to terminate. The user is left wondering why the application will not load. It's much friendlier—and fairly easy—to use a Windows message box for displaying a message. (A complete discussion of message boxes awaits you in Chapter 12, but this will get you started.)

A message box is a popup window that always appears in the center of the display. Message boxes have a title bar but no sizing border. The title bar usually contains the name of the application. The message box encloses a message and one, two, or three buttons (some combination of OK, Retry, Cancel, Yes, No, and others). The message box can also contain a predefined icon: a lowercase "i" (which stands for "information"), an exclamation point, a question mark, or a forbidding white X on a red background (formerly a stop sign). You have probably seen plenty of message boxes when working with Windows.

This code creates a message box that you can use when *SetTimer* fails to allocate a timer:

```
if (!SetTimer (hwnd, 1, 1000, NULL))
    {
    MessageBox (hwnd,
        "Too many clocks or timers!",
        "Program Name",
        MB_ICONEXCLAMATION | MB_OK) ;
    return FALSE ;
    }
```

This message box is shown in Figure 7-1. When the user presses Enter or clicks the OK button, *WinMain* terminates by returning FALSE.

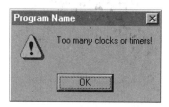

Figure 7-1. *A message box for "friendly termination."*

By default, message boxes are "application modal" windows. This means that a user must respond to the message box before the application will continue. The user can, however switch to other applications. So, why not give the user the opportunity to close one of the other applications using the timer and successfully load your application? That's what this code does:

```
while (!SetTimer (hwnd, 1, 1000, NULL))
    if (IDCANCEL == MessageBox (hwnd,
            "Too many clocks or timers!",
            "Program Name",
            MB_ICONEXCLAMATION | MB_RETRYCANCEL))
        return FALSE ;
```

This message box, shown in Figure 7-2, has two buttons, labeled Retry and Cancel. If the user clicks the Cancel button, the *MessageBox* function returns a value equal to IDCANCEL, and the program terminates. If the user clicks the Retry button, *SetTimer* is called again.

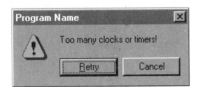

Figure 7-2. *A message box that offers a choice.*

A sample program

Figure 7-3 shows a sample program that uses the timer. This program, called BEEPER1, sets a timer for 1-second intervals. When it receives a WM_TIMER message, it alternates coloring the client area blue and red, and it beeps by calling the function *MessageBeep*. Although *MessageBeep* is documented as a companion to *MessageBox*, it's really an all-purpose beep function. In PCs equipped with sound boards, you can use the various MB_ICON parameters in *MessageBeep* to make different sounds selected by the user.

BEEPER1 sets the timer in the *WinMain* function and processes the WM_TIMER messages in the *WndProc* window procedure. During the WM_TIMER message, BEEPER1 calls *MessageBeep*, inverts the value of *bFlipFlop*, and invalidates the window to generate a WM_PAINT message. During the WM_PAINT message, BEEPER1 obtains a RECT structure for the size of the window by calling *GetClientRect* and colors the window by calling *FillRect*.

BEEPER1.MAK

```
#-----------------------
# BEEPER1.MAK make file
#-----------------------

beeper1.exe : beeper1.obj
    $(LINKER) $(GUIFLAGS) -OUT:beeper1.exe beeper1.obj $(GUILIBS)

beeper1.obj : beeper1.c
    $(CC) $(CFLAGS) beeper1.c
```

Figure 7-3. *The BEEPER1 program.*

(continued)

BEEPER1.C

```
/*-------------------------------------------
   BEEPER1.C  -- Timer Demo Program No. 1
                 (c) Charles Petzold, 1996
   -------------------------------------------*/

#include <windows.h>

#define ID_TIMER    1

LRESULT CALLBACK WndProc (HWND, UINT, WPARAM, LPARAM) ;

int WINAPI WinMain (HINSTANCE hInstance, HINSTANCE hPrevInstance,
                    PSTR szCmdLine, int iCmdShow)
     {
     static char szAppName[] = "Beeper1" ;
     HWND        hwnd ;
     MSG         msg ;
     WNDCLASSEX  wndclass ;

     wndclass.cbSize        = sizeof (wndclass) ;
     wndclass.style         = CS_HREDRAW | CS_VREDRAW ;
     wndclass.lpfnWndProc   = WndProc ;
     wndclass.cbClsExtra    = 0 ;
     wndclass.cbWndExtra    = 0 ;
     wndclass.hInstance     = hInstance ;
     wndclass.hIcon         = LoadIcon (NULL, IDI_APPLICATION) ;
     wndclass.hCursor       = LoadCursor (NULL, IDC_ARROW) ;
     wndclass.hbrBackground = (HBRUSH) GetStockObject (WHITE_BRUSH) ;
     wndclass.lpszMenuName  = NULL ;
     wndclass.lpszClassName = szAppName ;
     wndclass.hIconSm       = LoadIcon (NULL, IDI_APPLICATION) ;

     RegisterClassEx (&wndclass) ;

     hwnd = CreateWindow (szAppName, "Beeper1 Timer Demo",
                     WS_OVERLAPPEDWINDOW,
                     CW_USEDEFAULT, CW_USEDEFAULT,
                     CW_USEDEFAULT, CW_USEDEFAULT,
                     NULL, NULL, hInstance, NULL) ;

     while (!SetTimer (hwnd, ID_TIMER, 1000, NULL))
          if (IDCANCEL == MessageBox (hwnd,
                          "Too many clocks or timers!", szAppName,
                          MB_ICONEXCLAMATION | MB_RETRYCANCEL))
             return FALSE ;
```

(continued)

```
      ShowWindow (hwnd, iCmdShow) ;
      UpdateWindow (hwnd) ;

      while (GetMessage (&msg, NULL, 0, 0))
           {
           TranslateMessage (&msg) ;
           DispatchMessage (&msg) ;
           }
      return msg.wParam ;
      }

LRESULT CALLBACK WndProc (HWND hwnd, UINT iMsg, WPARAM wParam, LPARAM lParam)
      {
      static BOOL fFlipFlop = FALSE ;
      HBRUSH      hBrush ;
      HDC         hdc ;
      PAINTSTRUCT ps ;
      RECT        rc ;

      switch (iMsg)
           {
           case WM_TIMER :
                MessageBeep (0) ;

                fFlipFlop = !fFlipFlop ;
                InvalidateRect (hwnd, NULL, FALSE) ;

                return 0 ;

           case WM_PAINT :
                hdc = BeginPaint (hwnd, &ps) ;

                GetClientRect (hwnd, &rc) ;

                hBrush = CreateSolidBrush (fFlipFlop ? RGB(255,0,0) :
                                                       RGB(0,0,255)) ;
                FillRect (hdc, &rc, hBrush) ;
                EndPaint (hwnd, &ps) ;
                DeleteObject (hBrush) ;
                return 0 ;

           case WM_DESTROY :
                KillTimer (hwnd, ID_TIMER) ;
                PostQuitMessage (0) ;
                return 0 ;
           }
      return DefWindowProc (hwnd, iMsg, wParam, lParam) ;
      }
```

Because BEEPER1 audibly indicates every WM_TIMER message it receives, you can get a good idea of the erratic nature of WM_TIMER messages by loading BEEPER1 and performing some other actions within Windows. For instance, try moving or resizing the BEEPER1 window. This causes the program to enter a "modal message loop." Windows prevents anything from interfering with the move or resize operation by trapping all messages through a message loop inside Windows rather than the message loop in your program. Most messages to a program's window that come through this loop are simply discarded, which is why BEEPER1 stops beeping. When you complete the move or resize, you'll note that BEEPER1 doesn't get all the WM_TIMER messages it has missed, although the first two messages may be less than a second apart.

Method Two

The first method for setting the timer causes WM_TIMER messages to be sent to the normal window procedure. With this second method, you can direct Windows to send the timer messages to another function within your program.

The function that will receive these timer messages is termed a "call-back" function. This is a function within your program that is called by Windows. You tell Windows the address of this function, and Windows later calls the function. This should sound familiar because a program's window procedure is really a type of call-back function. You tell Windows the address of the window procedure when registering the window class, and then Windows calls the function when sending messages to the program.

SetTimer is not the only Windows function that uses a call-back function. The *CreateDialog* and *DialogBox* functions (discussed in Chapter 14) use call-back functions to process messages in a dialog box; several Windows functions (*EnumChildWindows*, *EnumFonts*, *EnumObjects*, *EnumProps*, and *EnumWindows*) pass enumerated information to call-back functions; and several less-commonly used functions (*GrayString*, *LineDDA*, and *SetWindowsHookEx*) also require call-back functions.

Like a window procedure, a call-back function must be defined as CALLBACK because it is called by Windows from outside the code space of the program. The parameters to the call-back function and the value returned from the call-back function depend on the purpose of the call-back function. In the case of the call-back function associated with the timer, the input parameters are the same as the input parameters to a window procedure. The timer call-back function does not return a value to Windows.

Let's name the call-back function *TimerProc*. (You can name it anything you like.) It will process only WM_TIMER messages.

```
VOID CALLBACK TimerProc (HWND hwnd, UINT iMsg, UINT iTimerID,
                                              DWORD dwTime)
    {
    [process WM_TIMER messages]
    }
```

The *hwnd* input parameter is the handle to the window specified when you call *SetTimer*. Windows will send only WM_TIMER messages to *TimerProc*, so the *iMsg* parameter will always equal WM_TIMER. The *iTimerID* value is the timer ID, and the *dwTime* value is the system time.

As I noted earlier, the first method for setting a timer requires a *SetTimer* call that looks like this:

```
SetTimer (hwnd, iTimerID, iMsecInterval, NULL) ;
```

When you use a call-back function to process WM_TIMER messages, the fourth parameter to *SetTimer* is instead the address of the call-back function, like so:

```
SetTimer (hwnd, iTimerID, iMsecInterval, (TIMERPROC) TimerProc) ;
```

A sample program

Let's look at some sample code so you can see how this stuff fits together. The BEEPER2 program, shown in Figure 7-4, is functionally the same as BEEPER1 except that Windows sends the timer messages to *TimerProc* rather than *WndProc*. Notice that *TimerProc* is declared at the top of the program along with *WndProc*.

BEEPER2.MAK

```
#---------------------
# BEEPER2.MAK make file
#---------------------

beeper2.exe : beeper2.obj
     $(LINKER) $(GUIFLAGS) -OUT:beeper2.exe beeper2.obj $(GUILIBS)

beeper2.obj : beeper2.c
     $(CC) $(CFLAGS) beeper2.c
```

BEEPER2.C

```
/*------------------------------------------
   BEEPER2.C -- Timer Demo Program No. 2
              (c) Charles Petzold, 1996
   ------------------------------------------*/

#include <windows.h>

#define ID_TIMER    1

LRESULT CALLBACK WndProc    (HWND, UINT, WPARAM, LPARAM) ;
```

Figure 7-4. *The BEEPER2 program.* (continued)

```
VOID    CALLBACK TimerProc (HWND, UINT, UINT,   DWORD ) ;

int WINAPI WinMain (HINSTANCE hInstance, HINSTANCE hPrevInstance,
                    PSTR szCmdLine, int iCmdShow)
    {
    static char szAppName[] = "Beeper2" ;
    HWND        hwnd ;
    MSG         msg ;
    WNDCLASSEX  wndclass ;

    wndclass.cbSize        = sizeof (wndclass) ;
    wndclass.style         = CS_HREDRAW | CS_VREDRAW ;
    wndclass.lpfnWndProc   = WndProc ;
    wndclass.cbClsExtra    = 0 ;
    wndclass.cbWndExtra    = 0 ;
    wndclass.hInstance     = hInstance ;
    wndclass.hIcon         = LoadIcon (NULL, IDI_APPLICATION) ;
    wndclass.hCursor       = LoadCursor (NULL, IDC_ARROW) ;
    wndclass.hbrBackground = (HBRUSH) GetStockObject (WHITE_BRUSH) ;
    wndclass.lpszMenuName  = NULL ;
    wndclass.lpszClassName = szAppName ;
    wndclass.hIconSm       = LoadIcon (NULL, IDI_APPLICATION) ;

    RegisterClassEx (&wndclass) ;

    hwnd = CreateWindow (szAppName, "Beeper2 Timer Demo",
                        WS_OVERLAPPEDWINDOW,
                        CW_USEDEFAULT, CW_USEDEFAULT,
                        CW_USEDEFAULT, CW_USEDEFAULT,
                        NULL, NULL, hInstance, NULL) ;

    while (!SetTimer (hwnd, ID_TIMER, 1000, (TIMERPROC) TimerProc))
        if (IDCANCEL == MessageBox (hwnd,
                        "Too many clocks or timers!", szAppName,
                        MB_ICONEXCLAMATION | MB_RETRYCANCEL))
            return FALSE ;

    ShowWindow (hwnd, iCmdShow) ;
    UpdateWindow (hwnd) ;

    while (GetMessage (&msg, NULL, 0, 0))
        {
        TranslateMessage (&msg) ;
        DispatchMessage (&msg) ;
        }
    return msg.wParam ;
    }
```

(continued)

338

```
LRESULT CALLBACK WndProc (HWND hwnd, UINT iMsg, WPARAM wParam, LPARAM lParam)
    {
    switch (iMsg)
        {
        case WM_DESTROY :
            KillTimer (hwnd, ID_TIMER) ;
            PostQuitMessage (0) ;
            return 0 ;
        }
    return DefWindowProc (hwnd, iMsg, wParam, lParam) ;
    }

VOID CALLBACK TimerProc (HWND hwnd, UINT iMsg, UINT iTimerID, DWORD dwTime)
    {
    static BOOL fFlipFlop = FALSE ;
    HBRUSH      hBrush ;
    HDC         hdc ;
    RECT        rc ;

    MessageBeep (0) ;
    fFlipFlop = !fFlipFlop ;

    GetClientRect (hwnd, &rc) ;

    hdc = GetDC (hwnd) ;
    hBrush = CreateSolidBrush (fFlipFlop ? RGB (255,0,0) : RGB (0,0,255)) ;

    FillRect (hdc, &rc, hBrush) ;
    ReleaseDC (hwnd, hdc) ;
    DeleteObject (hBrush) ;
    }
```

Method Three

The third method of setting the timer is similar to the second method, except that the *hwnd* parameter to *SetTimer* is set to NULL, and the second parameter (normally the timer ID) is ignored. Instead, the function returns a timer ID:

```
iTimerID = SetTimer (NULL, 0, wMsecInterval, (TIMERPROC) TimerProc) ;
```

The *iTimerID* returned from *SetTimer* will be NULL if no timer is available.

The first parameter to *KillTimer* (usually the window handle) must also be NULL. The timer ID must be the value returned from *SetTimer*.

```
KillTimer (NULL, iTimerID) ;
```

The *hwnd* parameter passed to the *TimerProc* timer function will also be NULL.

This method for setting a timer is rarely used. It might come in handy if you do a lot of *SetTimer* calls at different times in your program and don't want to keep track of which timer IDs you've already used.

Now that you know how to use the Windows timer, you're ready for a couple of useful timer programs.

USING THE TIMER FOR A CLOCK

A clock is the most obvious application for the timer, so let's look at two of them, one digital and one analog. The DIGCLOCK program, shown in Figure 7-5, creates a popup window that positions itself in the upper right corner of the display. The program displays the day of the week, the date, and the time, as shown in Figure 7-6 on page 344.

DIGCLOCK.MAK

```
#-----------------------
# DIGCLOCK.MAK make file
#-----------------------

digclock.exe : digclock.obj
     $(LINKER) $(GUIFLAGS) -OUT:digclock.exe digclock.obj $(GUILIBS)

digclock.obj : digclock.c
     $(CC) $(CFLAGS) digclock.c
```

DIGCLOCK.C

```
/*------------------------------------------
     DIGCLOCK.C -- Digital Clock Program
               (c) Charles Petzold, 1996
     ------------------------------------*/

#include <windows.h>
#include <time.h>

#define ID_TIMER    1

#define YEAR  (datetime->tm_year % 100)
#define MONTH (datetime->tm_mon  + 1)
#define MDAY  (datetime->tm_mday)
#define WDAY  (datetime->tm_wday)
#define HOUR  (datetime->tm_hour)
```

Figure 7-5. *The DIGCLOCK program.*

(continued)

```
#define MIN   (datetime->tm_min)
#define SEC   (datetime->tm_sec)

LRESULT CALLBACK WndProc (HWND, UINT, WPARAM, LPARAM) ;
void SizeTheWindow (int *, int *, int *, int *) ;

char  sDate[2], sTime[2], sAMPM[2][5] ;
int   iDate, iTime ;

int WINAPI WinMain (HINSTANCE hInstance, HINSTANCE hPrevInstance,
                    PSTR szCmdLine, int iCmdShow)
    {
    static char szAppName[] = "DigClock" ;
    HWND        hwnd ;
    MSG         msg ;
    int         xStart, yStart, xClient, yClient ;
    WNDCLASSEX  wndclass ;

    wndclass.cbSize        = sizeof (wndclass) ;
    wndclass.style         = CS_HREDRAW | CS_VREDRAW ;
    wndclass.lpfnWndProc   = WndProc ;
    wndclass.cbClsExtra    = 0 ;
    wndclass.cbWndExtra    = 0 ;
    wndclass.hInstance     = hInstance ;
    wndclass.hIcon         = NULL ;
    wndclass.hCursor       = LoadCursor (NULL, IDC_ARROW) ;
    wndclass.hbrBackground = (HBRUSH) GetStockObject (WHITE_BRUSH) ;
    wndclass.lpszMenuName  = NULL ;
    wndclass.lpszClassName = szAppName ;
    wndclass.hIconSm       = NULL ;

    RegisterClassEx (&wndclass) ;

    SizeTheWindow (&xStart, &yStart, &xClient, &yClient) ;

    hwnd = CreateWindow (szAppName, szAppName,
                         WS_POPUP | WS_DLGFRAME | WS_SYSMENU,
                         xStart,  yStart,
                         xClient, yClient,
                         NULL, NULL, hInstance, NULL) ;

    if (!SetTimer (hwnd, ID_TIMER, 1000, NULL))
        {
        MessageBox (hwnd, "Too many clocks or timers!", szAppName,
                    MB_ICONEXCLAMATION | MB_OK) ;
        return FALSE ;
        }
```

(continued)

```
    ShowWindow (hwnd, SW_SHOWNOACTIVATE) ;
    UpdateWindow (hwnd) ;

    while (GetMessage (&msg, NULL, 0, 0))
         {
         TranslateMessage (&msg) ;
         DispatchMessage (&msg) ;
         }
    return msg.wParam ;
    }

void SizeTheWindow (int *pxStart,  int *pyStart,
                    int *pxClient, int *pyClient)
    {
    HDC        hdc ;
    TEXTMETRIC tm ;

    hdc = CreateIC ("DISPLAY", NULL, NULL, NULL) ;
    GetTextMetrics (hdc, &tm) ;
    DeleteDC (hdc) ;

    *pxClient = 2 * GetSystemMetrics (SM_CXDLGFRAME) + 16*tm.tmAveCharWidth ;
    *pxStart =      GetSystemMetrics (SM_CXSCREEN)   - *pxClient ;
    *pyClient = 2 * GetSystemMetrics (SM_CYDLGFRAME) + 2*tm.tmHeight ;
    *pyStart =      0 ;
    }

void SetInternational (void)
    {
    static char cName[] = "intl" ;

    iDate = GetProfileInt (cName, "iDate", 0) ;
    iTime = GetProfileInt (cName, "iTime", 0) ;

    GetProfileString (cName, "sDate",  "/",  sDate,    2) ;
    GetProfileString (cName, "sTime",  ":",  sTime,    2) ;
    GetProfileString (cName, "s1159", "AM", sAMPM[0], 5) ;
    GetProfileString (cName, "s2359", "PM", sAMPM[1], 5) ;
    }

void WndPaint (HWND hwnd, HDC hdc)
    {
    static char szWday[] = "Sun\0Mon\0Tue\0Wed\0Thu\0Fri\0Sat" ;
    char       cBuffer[40] ;
    int        iLength ;
```

(continued)

342

```
        RECT        rect ;
        struct tm  *datetime ;
        time_t      lTime ;

        time (&lTime) ;
        datetime = localtime (&lTime) ;

        iLength = wsprintf (cBuffer, "  %s  %d%s%02d%s%02d  \r\n",
                   (PSTR) szWday + 4 * WDAY,
                   iDate == 1 ? MDAY  : iDate == 2 ? YEAR  : MONTH, (PSTR) sDate,
                   iDate == 1 ? MONTH : iDate == 2 ? MONTH : MDAY,  (PSTR) sDate,
                   iDate == 1 ? YEAR  : iDate == 2 ? MDAY  : YEAR) ;

        if (iTime == 1)
            iLength += wsprintf (cBuffer + iLength, "  %02d%s%02d%s%02d  ",
                                 HOUR, (PSTR) sTime, MIN, (PSTR) sTime, SEC) ;
        else
            iLength += wsprintf (cBuffer + iLength, "  %d%s%02d%s%02d %s  ",
                                 (HOUR % 12) ? (HOUR % 12) : 12,
                                 (PSTR) sTime, MIN, (PSTR) sTime, SEC,
                                 (PSTR) sAMPM [HOUR / 12]) ;

        GetClientRect (hwnd, &rect) ;
        DrawText (hdc, cBuffer, -1, &rect, DT_CENTER | DT_NOCLIP) ;
        }

LRESULT CALLBACK WndProc (HWND hwnd, UINT iMsg, WPARAM wParam, LPARAM lParam)
        {
        HDC         hdc ;
        PAINTSTRUCT ps ;

        switch (iMsg)
            {
            case WM_CREATE :
                 SetInternational () ;
                 return 0 ;

            case WM_TIMER :
                 InvalidateRect (hwnd, NULL, FALSE) ;
                 return 0 ;

            case WM_PAINT :
                 hdc = BeginPaint (hwnd, &ps) ;
                 WndPaint (hwnd, hdc) ;
                 EndPaint (hwnd, &ps) ;
```

(continued)

```
                return 0 ;

        case WM_WININICHANGE :
                SetInternational () ;
                InvalidateRect (hwnd, NULL, TRUE) ;
                return 0 ;

        case WM_DESTROY :
                KillTimer (hwnd, ID_TIMER) ;
                PostQuitMessage (0) ;
                return 0 ;
        }
    return DefWindowProc (hwnd, iMsg, wParam, lParam) ;
    }
```

```
Tue 5/02/95
12:45:12 PM
```

Figure 7-6. *The DIGCLOCK window.*

All the programs shown so far have used the window style WS_OVERLAPPEDWIN-
DOW as the third parameter to the *CreateWindow* function. DIGCLOCK uses the window style:

```
WS_POPUP ¦ WS_DLGFRAME ¦ WS_SYSMENU
```

This creates a style of window known as "popup," with a dialog box frame and a system menu. The popup style is most commonly used for dialog boxes and message boxes,
and only rarely for applications. DIGCLOCK also uses yet another variation of the *Show-
Window* call:

```
ShowWindow (hwnd, SW_SHOWNOACTIVATE) ;
```

Normally, a program becomes the active window when you run it. SW_SHOWNOACTI-
VATE tells Windows that the program that loaded DIGCLOCK should remain the active
window. You can make DIGCLOCK active, however, by clicking on its window with the
mouse or by pressing Alt-Tab or Alt-Esc. Although DIGCLOCK has no system menu box,
you can still access the system menu when DIGCLOCK is active by pressing Alt-Spacebar.
If you select Move, you can move the window with the keyboard.

Positioning and Sizing the Popup

The DIGCLOCK popup window is positioned at the upper right corner of the display. The
window must be large enough to accommodate two lines of text of 16 characters each. The
SizeTheWindow procedure in DIGCLOCK.C determines the correct parameters to use in

the *CreateWindow* call. Normally, a program cannot obtain a text size without first creating a window because it needs the window handle to obtain a device context handle. DIGCLOCK gets around this problem by obtaining an information device context handle for the screen using *CreateIC*. This function is similar to *CreateDC* normally used for creating a device context for a printer (as I'll demonstrate in Chapter 15) but is used to obtain information from the device context. The text size in combination with information available from *GetSystemMetrics* is enough to derive an initial starting position and window size.

Getting the Date and Time

In its *WndPaint* function, DIGCLOCK uses the *time* and *localtime* C functions to determine the current date and time. The *localtime* function puts all the information we need into a structure; several macro definitions near the top of the program help make the *wsprintf* calls more readable. (You should avoid making MS-DOS or ROM BIOS function calls in your Windows programs; use Windows functions or the C run-time library instead.)

Going International

Windows includes international support. The WIN.INI file created during installation of Windows contains a section headed *[intl]*. This lists information concerning formats of dates, time, currency, and numbers. You can display dates in one of three different formats: month-day-year, year-month-day, or day-month-year. The separator between these three numbers can be a slash, a dash, a period, or, in fact, any character you like. You can display the time in either 12-hour or 24-hour format; a colon or a period is commonly used to separate hours, minutes, and seconds.

The *SetInternational* function in DIGCLOCK retrieves this formatting information from the WIN.INI file by using the Windows *GetProfileInt* (for integers) and *GetProfileString* (for strings). These calls must include default values if Windows cannot find the values in WIN.INI. *SetInternational* stores the values in global variables that have the same names as the text strings that identify them in WIN.INI. The *WndPaint* function uses the values obtained from WIN.INI to format the date and time displays and then calls *DrawText* to center the two lines of text within the window.

As you would expect, whenever DIGCLOCK's window procedure receives a WM_TIMER message, it invalidates the window to generate a WM_PAINT message. But *WndProc* also invalidates the window when it receives a WM_WININICHANGE message. Any application that changes WIN.INI sends the WM_WININICHANGE message to all active Windows applications. If the *[intl]* section of WIN.INI is changed, DIGCLOCK will know and will obtain the new international information. To see how this works, load DIGCLOCK, double-click the Regional Settings icon in the Control Panel, and change either the date format, the date separator, the time format, or the time separator. Now press Enter. The WIN.INI file gets updated, and DIGCLOCK's display reflects that change—Windows' message magic at work.

When the window procedure receives a WM_WININICHANGE message, it invalidates the window using:

```
InvalidateRect (hwnd, NULL, TRUE) ;
```

When DIGCLOCK receives a WM_TIMER message, it invalidates the window using:

```
InvalidateRect (hwnd, NULL, FALSE) ;
```

A value of TRUE in the last parameter tells Windows to erase the background before drawing the window. A value of FALSE tells Windows simply to draw over the existing background. We use FALSE when processing WM_TIMER messages because this approach reduces flickering of the display. You may be wondering why we need to use the TRUE value at all.

A TRUE value is necessary when processing WM_WININICHANGE messages because the length of the displayed strings can change by several characters if you switch the time format from 12 hours to 24 hours. However, the largest change that occurs as a result of a WM_TIMER message is two characters—for instance, when the date advances from 12/31/95 to 1/1/96—and the formatted string that *WndPaint* uses for the display has a couple of blanks on each end to account for this change in length and the proportional font.

We could also have DIGCLOCK process WM_TIMECHANGE messages, which notify applications of changes to the system date or time. Because DIGCLOCK is updated every second by WM_TIMER messages, this is unnecessary. Processing WM_TIMECHANGE messages would make more sense for a clock that was updated every minute.

Building an Analog Clock

An analog clock program needn't concern itself with internationalization, but the complexity of the graphics more than make up for that simplification. To get it right, you'll need to know how to use mapping modes and even some trigonometry. The ANACLOCK program is shown in Figure 7-7, and its screen display is shown in Figure 7-8 on page 351.

ANACLOCK.MAK

```
#------------------------
# ANACLOCK.MAK make file
#------------------------

anaclock.exe : anaclock.obj
    $(LINKER) $(GUIFLAGS) -OUT:anaclock.exe anaclock.obj $(GUILIBS)

anaclock.obj : anaclock.c
    $(CC) $(CFLAGS) anaclock.c
```

Figure 7-7. *The ANACLOCK program.*   *(continued)*

ANACLOCK.C

```
/*-------------------------------------------
   ANACLOCK.C -- Analog Clock Program
                 (c) Charles Petzold, 1996
   -------------------------------------------*/

#include <windows.h>
#include <string.h>
#include <time.h>
#include <math.h>

#define ID_TIMER    1
#define TWOPI       (2 * 3.14159)

LRESULT CALLBACK WndProc (HWND, UINT, WPARAM, LPARAM) ;

int WINAPI WinMain (HINSTANCE hInstance, HINSTANCE hPrevInstance,
                    PSTR szCmdLine, int iCmdShow)
     {
     static char szAppName[] = "AnaClock" ;
     HWND        hwnd ;
     MSG         msg ;
     WNDCLASSEX  wndclass ;

     wndclass.cbSize        = sizeof (wndclass) ;
     wndclass.style         = CS_HREDRAW | CS_VREDRAW ;
     wndclass.lpfnWndProc   = WndProc ;
     wndclass.cbClsExtra    = 0 ;
     wndclass.cbWndExtra    = 0 ;
     wndclass.hInstance     = hInstance ;
     wndclass.hIcon         = NULL ;
     wndclass.hCursor       = LoadCursor (NULL, IDC_ARROW) ;
     wndclass.hbrBackground = (HBRUSH) GetStockObject (WHITE_BRUSH) ;
     wndclass.lpszMenuName  = NULL ;
     wndclass.lpszClassName = szAppName ;
     wndclass.hIconSm       = NULL ;

     RegisterClassEx (&wndclass) ;

     hwnd = CreateWindow (szAppName, "Analog Clock",
                          WS_OVERLAPPEDWINDOW,
                          CW_USEDEFAULT, CW_USEDEFAULT,
                          CW_USEDEFAULT, CW_USEDEFAULT,
                          NULL, NULL, hInstance, NULL) ;

     if (!SetTimer (hwnd, ID_TIMER, 1000, NULL))
```

(continued)

```
                 {
            MessageBox (hwnd, "Too many clocks or timers!", szAppName,
                      MB_ICONEXCLAMATION | MB_OK) ;
            return FALSE ;
            }

       ShowWindow (hwnd, iCmdShow) ;
       UpdateWindow (hwnd) ;

       while (GetMessage (&msg, NULL, 0, 0))
            {
            TranslateMessage (&msg) ;
            DispatchMessage (&msg) ;
            }
       return msg.wParam ;
       }

void SetIsotropic (HDC hdc, int cxClient, int cyClient)
     {
     SetMapMode (hdc, MM_ISOTROPIC) ;
     SetWindowExtEx (hdc, 1000, 1000, NULL) ;
     SetViewportExtEx (hdc, cxClient / 2, -cyClient / 2, NULL) ;
     SetViewportOrgEx (hdc, cxClient / 2,  cyClient / 2, NULL) ;
     }

void RotatePoint (POINT pt[], int iNum, int iAngle)
     {
     int   i ;
     POINT ptTemp ;

     for (i = 0 ; i < iNum ; i++)
          {
          ptTemp.x = (int) (pt[i].x * cos (TWOPI * iAngle / 360) +
                            pt[i].y * sin (TWOPI * iAngle / 360)) ;

          ptTemp.y = (int) (pt[i].y * cos (TWOPI * iAngle / 360) -
                            pt[i].x * sin (TWOPI * iAngle / 360)) ;

          pt[i] = ptTemp ;
          }
     }

void DrawClock (HDC hdc)
     {
     int   iAngle ;
     POINT pt[3] ;
```

(continued)

```
      for (iAngle = 0 ; iAngle < 360 ; iAngle += 6)
          {
          pt[0].x =   0 ;
          pt[0].y = 900 ;

          RotatePoint (pt, 1, iAngle) ;

          pt[2].x = pt[2].y = iAngle % 5 ? 33 : 100 ;

          pt[0].x -= pt[2].x / 2 ;
          pt[0].y -= pt[2].y / 2 ;

          pt[1].x  = pt[0].x + pt[2].x ;
          pt[1].y  = pt[0].y + pt[2].y ;

          SelectObject (hdc, GetStockObject (BLACK_BRUSH)) ;

          Ellipse (hdc, pt[0].x, pt[0].y, pt[1].x, pt[1].y) ;
          }
      }

void DrawHands (HDC hdc, struct tm *datetime, BOOL bChange)
      {
      static POINT pt[3][5] = { 0, -150, 100, 0, 0, 600, -100, 0, 0, -150,
                                0, -200,  50, 0, 0, 800,  -50, 0, 0, -200,
                                0,    0,   0, 0, 0,   0,    0, 0, 0,  800 } ;
      int          i, iAngle[3] ;
      POINT        ptTemp[3][5] ;

      iAngle[0] = (datetime->tm_hour * 30) % 360 + datetime->tm_min / 2 ;
      iAngle[1] =  datetime->tm_min  *  6 ;
      iAngle[2] =  datetime->tm_sec  *  6 ;

      memcpy (ptTemp, pt, sizeof (pt)) ;

      for (i = bChange ? 0 : 2 ; i < 3 ; i++)
          {
          RotatePoint (ptTemp[i], 5, iAngle[i]) ;

          Polyline (hdc, ptTemp[i], 5) ;
          }
      }

LRESULT CALLBACK WndProc (HWND hwnd, UINT iMsg, WPARAM wParam, LPARAM lParam)
      {
      static int          cxClient, cyClient ;
```

(continued)

```
static struct tm    dtPrevious ;
BOOL                bChange ;
HDC                 hdc ;
PAINTSTRUCT         ps ;
time_t              lTime ;
struct tm           *datetime ;

switch (iMsg)
    {
    case WM_CREATE :
        time (&lTime) ;
        datetime = localtime (&lTime) ;

        dtPrevious = * datetime ;
        return 0 ;

    case WM_SIZE :
        cxClient = LOWORD (lParam) ;
        cyClient = HIWORD (lParam) ;
        return 0 ;

    case WM_TIMER :
        time (&lTime) ;
        datetime = localtime (&lTime) ;

        bChange = datetime->tm_hour != dtPrevious.tm_hour ||
                  datetime->tm_min  != dtPrevious.tm_min ;

        hdc = GetDC (hwnd) ;

        SetIsotropic (hdc, cxClient, cyClient) ;

        SelectObject (hdc, GetStockObject (WHITE_PEN)) ;
        DrawHands (hdc, &dtPrevious, bChange) ;

        SelectObject (hdc, GetStockObject (BLACK_PEN)) ;
        DrawHands (hdc, datetime, TRUE) ;

        ReleaseDC (hwnd, hdc) ;

        dtPrevious = *datetime ;
        return 0 ;

    case WM_PAINT :
        hdc = BeginPaint (hwnd, &ps) ;

        SetIsotropic (hdc, cxClient, cyClient) ;
```

(continued)

```
              DrawClock      (hdc) ;
              DrawHands      (hdc, &dtPrevious, TRUE) ;

              EndPaint (hwnd, &ps) ;
              return 0 ;

       case WM_DESTROY :
              KillTimer (hwnd, ID_TIMER) ;
              PostQuitMessage (0) ;
              return 0 ;
       }
    return DefWindowProc (hwnd, iMsg, wParam, lParam) ;
    }
```

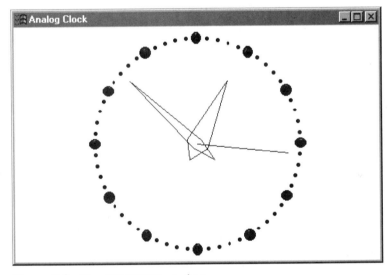

Figure 7-8. *The ANACLOCK window.*

The isotropic mapping mode is ideal for such an application, and setting it is the responsibility of the *SetIsotropic* function in ANACLOCK.C. After calling *SetMapMode*, the function sets the window extents to 1000, and the viewport extents to half the width of the client area and the negative of half the height of the client area. The viewport origin is set to the center of the client area. As I discussed in Chapter 4, this creates a Cartesian coordinate system with the point (0, 0) in the center of the client area, and extending 1000 units in all directions.

The *RotatePoint* function is where the trigonometry comes into play. The three parameters to the function are an array of one or more points, the number of points in that array, and the angle of rotation in degrees. The function rotates the points clockwise (as is appropriate for a clock) around the origin. For example, if the point passed to the function is (0,

100)—that is, the position of 12:00—and the angle is 90 degrees, then the point is converted to (100, 0)—which is 3:00. It does this using the formulas:

```
x' = x * cos (a) + y * sin (a)
y' = y * cos (a) - x * sin (a)
```

The *RotatePoint* function is useful for drawing both the dots of the clock face and the clock hands, as we'll see shortly.

The *DrawClock* function draws the 60 clock face dots starting with the one at the top (12:00 high). Each of them is 900 units from the origin, so the first is located at the point (0, 900) and each subsequent one is 6 additional clockwise degrees from the vertical. Twelve of the dots are 100 units in diameter; the rest are 33 units. The dots are drawn using the *Ellipse* function.

The *DrawHands* function draws the hour, minute, and second hands of the clock. The coordinates defining the outlines of the hands (as they appear when pointing straight up) are stored in an array of POINT structures. Depending on the time, these coordinates are rotated using the *RotatePoint* function and displayed with the Windows *Polyline* function. Notice that the hour and minutes hands are displayed only if the *bChange* parameter to *DrawHands* is TRUE. When the program updates the clock hands, in most cases the hour and minute hands will not need to be redrawn.

Now let's turn our attention to the window procedure. During the WM_CREATE message, the window procedure obtains the current time and also stores it in the variable named *dtPrevious*. This variable will later be used to determine if the hour or minute has changed from the previous updating.

The first time the clock is drawn is during the first WM_PAINT message. That's just a matter of calling the *SetIsotropic*, *DrawClock*, and *DrawHands* functions, the latter with the *bChange* parameter set to TRUE.

During the WM_TIMER message, *WndProc* first obtains the new time and determines if the hour and minute hands need to be redrawn. If so, all the hands are drawn with a white pen using the previous time, effectively erasing them. Otherwise, only the second hand is erased using the white pen. Then, all the hands are drawn with a black pen.

WINDOWS STANDARD TIME

If you've been scouting around the Windows function references, you may be wondering why the Windows *GetCurrentTime* function is not used in DIGCLOCK and ANACLOCK. The answer is that *GetCurrentTime* tells you about "Windows time" rather than real time. This is the time (in milliseconds) since the beginning of the current Windows session. *GetCurrentTime* is used mostly for calculating a difference from the time returned from *GetMessageTime*. You can use these two calls while processing a message to determine how long the message was in the message queue before you retrieved it for processing.

ANIMATION

In Chapter 4, we examined some techniques for using bitmaps and memory device contexts. Because the display of small bitmaps is quite fast, you can use bitmaps (in combination with the Windows timer) for some rudimentary animation.

Yes, it's time for the bouncing-ball program. The BOUNCE program, shown in Figure 7-9, constructs a ball that bounces around in the window's client area. The program uses the timer to pace the ball. The ball itself is a bitmap. The program first creates the ball by creating the bitmap, selecting it into a memory device context, and then making simple GDI function calls. The program draws the bitmapped ball on the display using a bit-block transfer from another memory device context.

BOUNCE.MAK

```
#----------------------
# BOUNCE.MAK make file
#----------------------

bounce.exe : bounce.obj
     $(LINKER) $(GUIFLAGS) -OUT:bounce.exe bounce.obj $(GUILIBS)

bounce.obj : bounce.c
     $(CC) $(CFLAGS) bounce.c
```

BOUNCE.C

```
/*------------------------------------------
   BOUNCE.C -- Bouncing Ball Program
           (c) Charles Petzold, 1996
  ------------------------------------------*/

#include <windows.h>

LRESULT CALLBACK WndProc (HWND, UINT, WPARAM, LPARAM) ;

int WINAPI WinMain (HINSTANCE hInstance, HINSTANCE hPrevInstance,
                    PSTR szCmdLine, int iCmdShow)
     {
     static char szAppName[] = "Bounce" ;
     HWND        hwnd ;
     MSG         msg ;
     WNDCLASSEX  wndclass ;
```

Figure 7-9. *The BOUNCE program.*

(continued)

```
    wndclass.cbSize        = sizeof (wndclass) ;
    wndclass.style         = CS_HREDRAW | CS_VREDRAW ;
    wndclass.lpfnWndProc   = WndProc ;
    wndclass.cbClsExtra    = 0 ;
    wndclass.cbWndExtra    = 0 ;
    wndclass.hInstance     = hInstance ;
    wndclass.hIcon         = LoadIcon (NULL, IDI_APPLICATION) ;
    wndclass.hCursor       = LoadCursor (NULL, IDC_ARROW) ;
    wndclass.hbrBackground = (HBRUSH) GetStockObject (WHITE_BRUSH) ;
    wndclass.lpszMenuName  = NULL ;
    wndclass.lpszClassName = szAppName ;
    wndclass.hIconSm       = LoadIcon (NULL, IDI_APPLICATION) ;

    RegisterClassEx (&wndclass) ;

    hwnd = CreateWindow (szAppName, "Bouncing Ball",
                    WS_OVERLAPPEDWINDOW,
                    CW_USEDEFAULT, CW_USEDEFAULT,
                    CW_USEDEFAULT, CW_USEDEFAULT,
                    NULL, NULL, hInstance, NULL) ;

    if (!SetTimer (hwnd, 1, 50, NULL))
        {
        MessageBox (hwnd, "Too many clocks or timers!",
                szAppName, MB_ICONEXCLAMATION | MB_OK) ;
        return FALSE ;
        }

    ShowWindow (hwnd, iCmdShow) ;
    UpdateWindow (hwnd) ;

    while (GetMessage (&msg, NULL, 0, 0))
        {
        TranslateMessage (&msg) ;
        DispatchMessage (&msg) ;
        }
    return msg.wParam ;
    }

LRESULT CALLBACK WndProc (HWND hwnd, UINT iMsg, WPARAM wParam, LPARAM lParam)
    {
    static HBITMAP hBitmap ;
    static int     cxClient, cyClient, xCenter, yCenter, cxTotal, cyTotal,
                   cxRadius, cyRadius, cxMove, cyMove, xPixel, yPixel ;
    HBRUSH         hBrush ;
```

(continued)

```
HDC          hdc, hdcMem ;
int          iScale ;

switch (iMsg)
     {
     case WM_CREATE :
          hdc = GetDC (hwnd) ;
          xPixel = GetDeviceCaps (hdc, ASPECTX) ;
          yPixel = GetDeviceCaps (hdc, ASPECTY) ;
          ReleaseDC (hwnd, hdc) ;
          return 0 ;

     case WM_SIZE :
          xCenter = (cxClient = LOWORD (lParam)) / 2 ;
          yCenter = (cyClient = HIWORD (lParam)) / 2 ;

          iScale = min (cxClient * xPixel, cyClient * yPixel) / 16 ;

          cxRadius = iScale / xPixel ;
          cyRadius = iScale / yPixel ;

          cxMove = max (1, cxRadius / 2) ;
          cyMove = max (1, cyRadius / 2) ;

          cxTotal = 2 * (cxRadius + cxMove) ;
          cyTotal = 2 * (cyRadius + cyMove) ;

          if (hBitmap)
               DeleteObject (hBitmap) ;

          hdc = GetDC (hwnd) ;
          hdcMem = CreateCompatibleDC (hdc) ;
          hBitmap = CreateCompatibleBitmap (hdc, cxTotal, cyTotal) ;
          ReleaseDC (hwnd, hdc) ;

          SelectObject (hdcMem, hBitmap) ;
          Rectangle (hdcMem, -1, -1, cxTotal + 1, cyTotal + 1) ;

          hBrush = CreateHatchBrush (HS_DIAGCROSS, 0L) ;
          SelectObject (hdcMem, hBrush) ;
          SetBkColor (hdcMem, RGB (255, 0, 255)) ;
          Ellipse (hdcMem, cxMove, cyMove, cxTotal - cxMove,
                                           cyTotal - cyMove) ;
          DeleteDC (hdcMem) ;
          DeleteObject (hBrush) ;
          return 0 ;
```

(continued)

```
        case WM_TIMER :
            if (!hBitmap)
                break ;

            hdc = GetDC (hwnd) ;
            hdcMem = CreateCompatibleDC (hdc) ;
            SelectObject (hdcMem, hBitmap) ;

            BitBlt (hdc, xCenter - cxTotal / 2,
                        yCenter - cyTotal / 2, cxTotal, cyTotal,
                    hdcMem, 0, 0, SRCCOPY) ;

            ReleaseDC (hwnd, hdc) ;
            DeleteDC (hdcMem) ;

            xCenter += cxMove ;
            yCenter += cyMove ;

            if ((xCenter + cxRadius >= cxClient) ||
                (xCenter - cxRadius <= 0))
                    cxMove = -cxMove ;

            if ((yCenter + cyRadius >= cyClient) ||
                (yCenter - cyRadius <= 0))
                    cyMove = -cyMove ;
            return 0 ;

        case WM_DESTROY :
            if (hBitmap)
                DeleteObject (hBitmap) ;

            KillTimer (hwnd, 1) ;
            PostQuitMessage (0) ;
            return 0 ;
        }
    return DefWindowProc (hwnd, iMsg, wParam, lParam) ;
    }
```

BOUNCE reconstructs the ball whenever the program gets a WM_SIZE message. This requires a memory device context compatible with the video display:

```
hdcMem = CreateCompatibleDC (hdc) ;
```

The diameter of the ball is one-sixteenth of either the height or the width of the client area, whichever is shorter. However, the program constructs a bitmap that is larger than the ball: On each of its four sides, the bitmap extends beyond the ball's dimensions by one-half of the ball's radius:

```
        hBitmap = CreateCompatibleBitmap (hdc, cxTotal, cyTotal) ;
```

After the bitmap is selected into a memory device context, the entire bitmap is colored white for the background:

```
        Rectangle (hdcMem, -1, -1, xTotal + 1, yTotal + 1) ;
```

A diagonally hatched brush is selected into the memory device context, and the ball is drawn in the center of the bitmap:

```
        Ellipse (hdcMem, xMove, yMove, xTotal - xMove, yTotal - yMove) ;
```

The margins around the edges of the ball effectively erase the previous image of the ball when the ball is moved. Redrawing the ball at another position requires only a simple *BitBlt* call using the ROP code of SRCCOPY:

```
        BitBlt (hdc, xCenter - xTotal / 2,
                     yCenter - yTotal / 2, xTotal, yTotal,
                     hdcMem, 0, 0, SRCCOPY) ;
```

BOUNCE demonstrates the simplest way to move an image around the display, but this approach isn't satisfactory for general purposes. If you're interested in animation, you'll want to explore some of the other ROP codes (such as SRCINVERT) that perform an exclusive OR operation on the source and destination. Other techniques for animation involve the Windows palette (and the *AnimatePalette* function) and the *CreateDIBSection* function.

Chapter 8

Child Window Controls

Chapter 6 showed programs in the CHECKER series that display a grid of rectangles. When you click the mouse in a rectangle, the program draws an X. When you click again, the X disappears. Although the CHECKER1 and CHECKER2 versions of this program use only one main window, the CHECKER3 version uses a child window for each rectangle. The rectangles are maintained by a separate window procedure called *ChildWndProc*.

If we wanted to, we could add a facility to *ChildWndProc* to send a message to its parent window procedure (*WndProc*) whenever a rectangle is checked or unchecked. Here's how: The child window procedure can determine the window handle of its parent by calling *GetParent*:

```
hwndParent = GetParent (hwnd) ;
```

where *hwnd* is the window handle of the child window. It can then send a message to the parent window procedure:

```
SendMessage (hwndParent, iMsg, wParam, lParam) ;
```

What would *iMsg* be set to? Well, anything you want, really, as long as the numeric value is within the range WM_USER to 0x7FFF. These numbers represent messages that do not conflict with the predefined WM_ messages. Perhaps for this message the child window could set *wParam* to its child window ID. The *lParam* could then be set to a 1 if the child window were being checked and a 0 if it were being unchecked. That's one possibility.

This in effect creates a "child window control." The child window processes mouse and keyboard messages and notifies the parent window when the child window's state has changed. In this way, the child window becomes an input device for the parent window. It encapsulates a specific functionality with regard to its graphical appearance on the screen, its response to user input, and its method of notifying another window when an important input event has occurred.

Although you can create your own child window controls, you can also take advantage of several predefined window classes (and window procedures) that your program can use to create standard child window controls that you've undoubtedly seen in other Windows-based programs. These controls take the form of buttons, check boxes, edit boxes, list boxes, combo boxes, text strings, and scroll bars. For instance, if you want to put a button labeled "Recalculate" in a corner of your spreadsheet program, you can create it with a single *CreateWindow* call. You don't have to worry about the mouse logic or button painting logic or making the button "flash" when it's clicked. That's all done in Windows. All you have to do is trap WM_COMMAND messages—that's how the button informs your window procedure when it has been triggered.

Is it really that simple? Well, almost.

Child window controls are used most often in dialog boxes. As you'll see in Chapter 11, the position and size of the child window controls are defined in a dialog box template contained in the program's resource script. You can also use predefined child window controls on the surface of a normal window's client area. You create each child window with a *CreateWindow* call and adjust the position and size of the child windows with calls to *MoveWindow*. The parent window procedure sends messages to the child window controls, and the child window controls send messages back to the parent window procedure.

As we've been doing since Chapter 2, to create your normal application window, you first define a window class and register it with Windows using *RegisterClassEx*. You then create the window based on that class using *CreateWindow*. When you use one of the predefined controls, however, you do not register a window class for the child window. The class already exists within Windows and has one of these names: "button," "static," "scrollbar," "edit," "listbox," or "combobox." You simply use the name as the window class parameter in *CreateWindow*. The window style parameter to *CreateWindow* defines more precisely the appearance and functionality of the child window control. Windows contains the window procedures that process messages to the child windows based on these classes.

Using child window controls directly on the surface of your window involves tasks of a lower level than are required for using child window controls in dialog boxes, where the dialog box manager adds a layer of insulation between your program and the controls themselves. In particular, you'll discover that the child window controls you create on the surface of your window have no built-in facility to move the input focus from one control to another using the Tab key or cursor movement keys. A child window control can obtain the input focus, but once it does, it won't freely relinquish the input focus back to the parent window. This is a problem we'll struggle with throughout this chapter.

THE BUTTON CLASS

We'll begin our exploration of the button window class with a program called BTNLOOK ("button look"), which is shown in Figure 8-1. BTNLOOK creates 10 child window button controls, one for each of the 10 standard styles of buttons.

BTNLOOK.MAK

```
#----------------------
# BTNLOOK.MAK make file
#----------------------

btnlook.exe : btnlook.obj
     $(LINKER) $(GUIFLAGS) -OUT:btnlook.exe btnlook.obj $(GUILIBS)

btnlook.obj : btnlook.c
     $(CC) $(CFLAGS) btnlook.c
```

BTNLOOK.C

```
/*-------------------------------------------
   BTNLOOK.C -- Button Look Program
                (c) Charles Petzold, 1996
   -------------------------------------------*/

#include <windows.h>

struct
    {
    long style ;
    char *text ;
    }
    button[] =
    {
    BS_PUSHBUTTON,      "PUSHBUTTON",
    BS_DEFPUSHBUTTON,   "DEFPUSHBUTTON",
    BS_CHECKBOX,        "CHECKBOX",
    BS_AUTOCHECKBOX,    "AUTOCHECKBOX",
    BS_RADIOBUTTON,     "RADIOBUTTON",
    BS_3STATE,          "3STATE",
    BS_AUTO3STATE,      "AUTO3STATE",
    BS_GROUPBOX,        "GROUPBOX",
    BS_AUTORADIOBUTTON, "AUTORADIO",
```

Figure 8-1. *The BTNLOOK program.*

(continued)

```
    BS_OWNERDRAW,        "OWNERDRAW"
    } ;

#define NUM (sizeof button / sizeof button[0])

LRESULT CALLBACK WndProc (HWND, UINT, WPARAM, LPARAM) ;

int WINAPI WinMain (HINSTANCE hInstance, HINSTANCE hPrevInstance,
                PSTR szCmdLine, int iCmdShow)
    {
    static char szAppName[] = "BtnLook" ;
    HWND        hwnd ;
    MSG         msg ;
    WNDCLASSEX  wndclass ;

    wndclass.cbSize        = sizeof (wndclass) ;
    wndclass.style         = CS_HREDRAW | CS_VREDRAW ;
    wndclass.lpfnWndProc   = WndProc ;
    wndclass.cbClsExtra    = 0 ;
    wndclass.cbWndExtra    = 0 ;
    wndclass.hInstance     = hInstance ;
    wndclass.hIcon         = LoadIcon (NULL, IDI_APPLICATION) ;
    wndclass.hCursor       = LoadCursor (NULL, IDC_ARROW) ;
    wndclass.hbrBackground = (HBRUSH) GetStockObject (WHITE_BRUSH) ;
    wndclass.lpszMenuName  = NULL ;
    wndclass.lpszClassName = szAppName ;
    wndclass.hIconSm       = LoadIcon (NULL, IDI_APPLICATION) ;

    RegisterClassEx (&wndclass) ;

    hwnd = CreateWindow (szAppName, "Button Look",
                        WS_OVERLAPPEDWINDOW,
                        CW_USEDEFAULT, CW_USEDEFAULT,
                        CW_USEDEFAULT, CW_USEDEFAULT,
                        NULL, NULL, hInstance, NULL) ;

    ShowWindow (hwnd, iCmdShow) ;
    UpdateWindow (hwnd) ;

    while (GetMessage (&msg, NULL, 0, 0))
        {
        TranslateMessage (&msg) ;
        DispatchMessage (&msg) ;
        }
    return msg.wParam ;
    }
```

(continued)

```
LRESULT CALLBACK WndProc (HWND hwnd, UINT iMsg, WPARAM wParam, LPARAM lParam)
    {
    static char   szTop[]    = "iMsg              wParam        lParam",
                  szUnd[]    = "____              _____        _____",
                  szFormat[] = "%-16s%04X-%04X    %04X-%04X",
                  szBuffer[50] ;
    static HWND   hwndButton[NUM] ;
    static RECT   rect ;
    static int    cxChar, cyChar ;
    HDC           hdc ;
    PAINTSTRUCT   ps ;
    int           i ;
    TEXTMETRIC    tm ;

    switch (iMsg)
        {
        case WM_CREATE :
            hdc = GetDC (hwnd) ;
            SelectObject (hdc, GetStockObject (SYSTEM_FIXED_FONT)) ;
            GetTextMetrics (hdc, &tm) ;
            cxChar = tm.tmAveCharWidth ;
            cyChar = tm.tmHeight + tm.tmExternalLeading ;
            ReleaseDC (hwnd, hdc) ;

            for (i = 0 ; i < NUM ; i++)
                hwndButton[i] = CreateWindow ("button", button[i].text,
                    WS_CHILD | WS_VISIBLE | button[i].style,
                    cxChar, cyChar * (1 + 2 * i),
                    20 * cxChar, 7 * cyChar / 4,
                    hwnd, (HMENU) i,
                    ((LPCREATESTRUCT) lParam) -> hInstance, NULL) ;
            return 0 ;

        case WM_SIZE :
            rect.left   = 24 * cxChar ;
            rect.top    =  2 * cyChar ;
            rect.right  = LOWORD (lParam) ;
            rect.bottom = HIWORD (lParam) ;
            return 0 ;

        case WM_PAINT :
            InvalidateRect (hwnd, &rect, TRUE) ;

            hdc = BeginPaint (hwnd, &ps) ;
            SelectObject (hdc, GetStockObject (SYSTEM_FIXED_FONT)) ;
```

(continued)

363

```
                    SetBkMode (hdc, TRANSPARENT) ;

                    TextOut (hdc, 24 * cxChar, cyChar, szTop, sizeof (szTop) - 1) ;
                    TextOut (hdc, 24 * cxChar, cyChar, szUnd, sizeof (szUnd) - 1) ;

                    EndPaint (hwnd, &ps) ;
                    return 0 ;

          case WM_DRAWITEM :
          case WM_COMMAND :
                    ScrollWindow (hwnd, 0, -cyChar, &rect, &rect) ;

                    hdc = GetDC (hwnd) ;
                    SelectObject (hdc, GetStockObject (SYSTEM_FIXED_FONT)) ;

                    TextOut (hdc, 24 * cxChar, cyChar * (rect.bottom /
                              cyChar - 1),
                              szBuffer,
                              wsprintf (szBuffer, szFormat,
                              iMsg == WM_DRAWITEM ? "WM_DRAWITEM" : "WM_COMMAND",
                              HIWORD (wParam), LOWORD (wParam),
                              HIWORD (lParam), LOWORD (lParam))) ;

                    ReleaseDC (hwnd, hdc) ;
                    ValidateRect (hwnd, &rect) ;

                    break ;

          case WM_DESTROY :
                    PostQuitMessage (0) ;
                    return 0 ;
          }
     return DefWindowProc (hwnd, iMsg, wParam, lParam) ;
     }
```

As you click on each button, the button sends a WM_COMMAND message to the parent window procedure, which is the familiar *WndProc*. BTNLOOK's *WndProc* displays the *wParam* and *lParam* parameters of this message on the right half of the client area, as shown in Figure 8-2.

The button with the style BS_OWNERDRAW is displayed on this window only with a background shading because this is a style of button that the program is responsible for drawing. The button indicates it needs drawing by WM_DRAWITEM messages containing an *lParam* message parameter that is a pointer to a structure of type DRAWITEMSTRUCT. These messages are also displayed in BTNLOOK. (I'll discuss owner-draw buttons in more detail later in this chapter.)

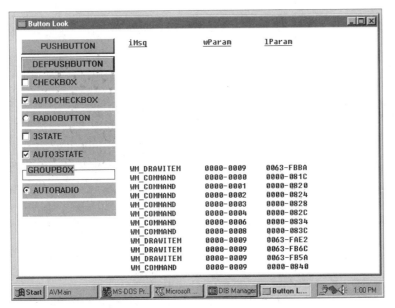

Figure 8-2. *The BTNLOOK display.*

Creating the Child Windows

BTNLOOK defines a structure called *button* that contains button window styles and descriptive text strings for each of the 10 types of buttons. The button window styles all begin with the letters BS, which stand for "button style."

The 10 button child windows are created in a *for* loop during WM_CREATE message processing in *WndProc*. The *CreateWindow* call uses the following parameters:

Class name	"button"
Window text	button[i].text
Window style	WS_CHILD ¦ WS_VISIBLE ¦ button[i].style
x position	cxChar
y position	cyChar * (1 + 2 * i)
Width	20 * cxChar
Height	7 * cyChar / 4
Parent window	hwnd
Child window ID	(HMENU) i
Instance handle	((LPCREATESTRUCT) lParam) -> hInstance
Extra parameters	NULL

The class name parameter is the predefined name. The window style uses WS_CHILD, WS_VISIBLE, and one of the ten button styles (BS_PUSHBUTTON, BS_DEFPUSHBUTTON, and so forth) that are defined in the *button* structure. The window text parameter (which for a normal window is the text that appears in the title bar) is text that will be displayed with each button. I've simply used text that identifies the button style.

The *x* position and *y* position parameters indicate the placement of the upper left corner of the child window relative to the upper left corner of the parent window's client area. The width and height parameters specify the width and height of each child window.

The child window ID parameter should be unique for each child window. This ID helps your window procedure identify the child window when processing WM_COMMAND messages from it. Notice that the child window ID is passed in the *CreateWindow* parameter normally used to specify the program's menu, so it must be cast to an HMENU.

The instance handle parameter of the *CreateWindow* call looks a little strange, but we're taking advantage of the fact that during a WM_CREATE message *lParam* is actually a pointer to a structure of type CREATESTRUCT ("creation structure") that has a member *hInstance*. So we cast *lParam* into a pointer to a CREATESTRUCT structure and get *hInstance* out.

(Some Windows programs use a global variable named *hInst* to give window procedures access to the instance handle available in *WinMain*. In *WinMain*, you need simply set:

```
hInst = hInstance ;
```

before creating the main window. In the CHECKER3 program in Chapter 6 we used *GetWindowLong* to obtain the instance handle:

```
GetWindowLong (hwnd, GWL_HINSTANCE)
```

Any of these methods is fine.)

After the *CreateWindow* call, we needn't do anything more with these child windows. The button window procedure within Windows maintains the buttons for us and handles all repainting jobs. (The exception is the button with the BS_OWNERDRAW style; as I'll discuss later, this button style requires the program to draw the button.) At the program's termination, Windows destroys these child windows when the parent window is destroyed.

The Child Talks to Its Parent

When you run BTNLOOK, you see the different button types displayed on the left side of the client area. As I mentioned earlier, when you click a button with the mouse, the child window control sends a WM_COMMAND message to its parent window. BTNLOOK traps the WM_COMMAND message and displays the values of *wParam* and *lParam*. Here's what they mean:

LOWORD (*wParam*)	Child window ID
HIWORD (*wParam*)	Notification code
lParam	Child window handle

If you're converting programs written for the 16-bit versions of Windows, be aware that these message parameters have been altered to accommodate 32-bit handles.

The child window ID is the value passed to *CreateWindow* when the child window is created. In BTNLOOK these IDs are 0 through 9 for the 10 buttons displayed in the client area. The child window handle is the value that Windows returns from the *CreateWindow* call.

The notification code is a submessage code that the child window uses to tell the parent window in more detail what the message means. The possible values of button notification codes are defined in the Windows header files:

Button Notification Code Identifier	Value
BN_CLICKED	0
BN_PAINT	1
BN_HILITE	2
BN_UNHILITE	3
BN_DISABLE	4
BN_DOUBLECLICKED	5

The notification codes 1 to 5 are for an obsolete button style called BS_USERBUTTON, so you'll only see BN_CLICKED codes.

You'll notice that when you click a button with the mouse, a dashed line surrounds the text of the button. This indicates that the button has the input focus. All keyboard input now goes to the child window button control rather than to the main window. However, when the button control has the input focus, it ignores all keystrokes except the Spacebar, which now has the same effect as a mouse click.

The Parent Talks to Its Child

Although BTNLOOK does not demonstrate this fact, a window procedure can also send messages to the child window control. Five button-specific messages are defined in the Windows header files; each begins with the letters "BM," which stand for "button message." These are:

```
BM_GETCHECK
BM_SETCHECK
BM_GETSTATE
BM_SETSTATE
BM_SETSTYLE
```

The BM_GETCHECK and BM_SETCHECK messages are sent by a parent window to a child window control to get and set the check mark of check boxes and radio buttons. The BM_GETSTATE and BM_SETSTATE messages refer to the normal or "pushed" state of a window when you click it with the mouse or press it with the Spacebar. (We'll see how these messages work when we look at each type of button.) The BM_SETSTYLE message lets you change the button style after the button is created.

Each child window has a window handle and an ID that is unique among its siblings. Knowing one of these items allows you to get the other. If you know the window handle of the child, you can obtain the ID using:

```
id = GetWindowLong (hwndChild, GWL_ID) ;
```

The CHECKERS3 program in Chapter 6 showed that a window can maintain data in a special area reserved when registering the window class. The area that saves the child window ID is reserved by Windows when the child window is created. You can also use:

```
id = GetDlgCtrlID (hwndChild) ;
```

Even though the "Dlg" part of the function name refers to a dialog box, this is really a general purpose function.

Knowing the ID, you can get the child window handle:

```
hwndChild = GetDlgItem (hwndParent, id) ;
```

Push Buttons

The first two buttons shown in BTNLOOK are "push" buttons. A push button is a rectangle enclosing text specified in the window text parameter of the *CreateWindow* call. The rectangle takes up the full height and width of the dimensions given in the *CreateWindow* or *MoveWindow* call. The text is centered within the rectangle.

Push-button controls are used mostly to trigger an immediate action without retaining any type of on/off indication. The two types of push-button controls have window styles called BS_PUSHBUTTON and BS_DEFPUSHBUTTON. The "DEF" in BS_DEFPUSHBUTTON stands for "default." When used to design dialog boxes, BS_PUSHBUTTON controls and BS_DEFPUSHBUTTON controls function differently from one another. When used as child window controls, however, the two types of push buttons function the same way, although BS_DEFPUSHBUTTON has a heavier outline.

A push button looks best when its height is 7/4 times the height of a SYSTEM_FONT character, which is what BTNLOOK uses. The push button's width must accommodate at least the width of the text plus two additional characters.

When the mouse cursor is inside the push button, pressing the mouse button causes the button to repaint itself using 3D-style shading to appear as if it's been depressed. Releasing the mouse button restores the original appearance and sends a WM_COMMAND message to the parent window with notification code BN_CLICKED. As with the other button types, when a push button has the input focus, a dashed line surrounds the text, and pressing and releasing the Spacebar has the same effect as pressing and releasing the mouse button.

You can simulate a push-button flash by sending the window a BM_SETSTATE message. This causes the button to be depressed:

```
SendMessage (hwndButton, BM_SETSTATE, 1, 0) ;
```

This call causes the button to return to normal:

```
SendMessage (hwndButton, BM_SETSTATE, 0, 0) ;
```

The *hwndButton* window handle is the value returned from the *CreateWindow* call.

You can also send a BM_GETSTATE message to a push button. The child window control returns the current state of the button—TRUE if the button is depressed and FALSE (or 0) if normal. Most applications do not require this information, however. And because push buttons do not retain any on/off information, the BM_SETCHECK and BM_GETCHECK messages are not used.

Check Boxes

A check box is a square box with text; the text usually appears to the right of the check box. (If you include the BS_LEFTTEXT style when creating the button, the text appears to the left.) Check boxes are usually incorporated in an application to allow a user to select options. The check box commonly functions as a toggle switch: Clicking the box once causes a check mark to appear; clicking again toggles the check mark off.

The two most common styles for a check box are BS_CHECKBOX and BS_AUTO-CHECKBOX. When you use the BS_CHECKBOX style, you must set the check mark yourself by sending the control a BM_SETCHECK message. The *wParam* parameter is set to 1 to create a check mark and to 0 to remove it. You can obtain the current check state of the box by sending the control a BM_GETCHECK message. You might use code like this to toggle the X mark when processing a WM_COMMAND message from the control:

```
SendMessage ((HWND) lParam, BM_SETCHECK, (WPARAM)
            !SendMessage ((HWND) lParam, BM_GETCHECK, 0, 0), 0) ;
```

Notice the *!* operator in front of the second *SendMessage* call. The *lParam* value is the child window handle passed to your window procedure in the WM_COMMAND message. When you later need to know the state of the button, send it another BM_GETCHECK message. Or you can retain the current check state in a static variable in your window procedure. You can also initialize a BS_CHECKBOX check box with an X by sending it a BM_SETCHECK message:

```
SendMessage (hwndButton, BM_SETCHECK, 1, 0) ;
```

For the BS_AUTOCHECKBOX style, the button control itself toggles the check mark on and off. Your window procedure can ignore WM_COMMAND messages. When you need the current state of the button, send the control a BM_GETCHECK message:

```
iCheck = (int) SendMessage (hwndButton, BM_GETCHECK, 0, 0) ;
```

The value of *iCheck* is TRUE or nonzero if the button is checked, FALSE or 0 if not.

The other two check box styles are BS_3STATE and BS_AUTO3STATE. As their names indicate, these styles can display a third state as well—a gray color within the check box—which occurs when you send the control a WM_SETCHECK message with *wParam* equal to 2. The gray color indicates to the user that the selection is indeterminate or irrelevant. In this case, the check box cannot be checked—that is, it's disabled. However, the check box control continues to send messages to the parent when the box is clicked. Better methods for disabling a check box are described later.

The check box is aligned with the rectangle's left edge and is centered within the top and bottom dimensions of the rectangle that were specified during the *CreateWindow* call. Clicking anywhere within the rectangle causes a WM_COMMAND message to be sent to the parent. The minimum height for a check box is one character height. The minimum width is the number of characters in the text plus two.

Radio Buttons

A radio button looks very much like a check box except that it is shaped like a circle rather than a box. A heavy dot within the circle indicates that the radio button has been checked. The radio button has the window style BS_RADIOBUTTON or BS_AUTORADIOBUTTON, but the latter is used only in dialog boxes. In dialog boxes, groups of radio buttons are conventionally used to indicate mutually exclusive options. Unlike check boxes, radio buttons do not work as toggles—that is, when you click a radio button a second time, its state remains unchanged.

When you receive a WM_COMMAND message from a radio button, you should display its check by sending it a BM_SETCHECK message with *wParam* equal to 1:

```
SendMessage (hwndButton, BM_SETCHECK, 1, 0) ;
```

For all other radio buttons in the same group, you can turn off the checks by sending them BM_SETCHECK messages with *wParam* equal to 0:

```
SendMessage (hwndButton, BM_SETCHECK, 0, 0) ;
```

Group Boxes

The group box, style BS_GROUPBOX, is an oddity in the button class. It neither processes mouse or keyboard input nor sends WM_COMMAND messages to its parent. The group box is a rectangular outline with its window text at the top. Group boxes are often used to enclose other button controls.

Changing the Button Text

You can change the text in a button (or in any other window) by calling *SetWindowText*:

```
SetWindowText (hwnd, pszString) ;
```

where *hwnd* is a handle to the window whose text is being changed and *pszString* is a pointer to a null-terminated string. For a normal window, this text is the text of the title bar. For a button control, it's the text displayed with the button.

You can also obtain the current text of a window:

```
iLength = GetWindowText (hwnd, pszBuffer, iMaxLength) ;
```

The *iMaxLength* parameter specifies the maximum number of characters to copy into the buffer pointed to by *pszBuffer*. The function returns the string length copied. You can prepare your program for a particular text length by first calling:

```
iLength = GetWindowTextLength (hwnd) ;
```

Visible and Enabled Buttons

To receive mouse and keyboard input, a child window must be both visible (displayed) and enabled. When a child window is visible but not enabled, Windows displays the text in gray rather than black.

If you do not include WS_VISIBLE in the window class when creating the child window, the child window will not be displayed until you make a call to *ShowWindow*:

```
ShowWindow (hwndChild, SW_SHOWNORMAL) ;
```

If you include WS_VISIBLE in the window class, you do not need to call *ShowWindow*. However, you can hide the child window by a call to *ShowWindow*:

```
ShowWindow (hwndChild, SW_HIDE) ;
```

You can determine if a child window is visible by a call to:

```
IsWindowVisible (hwndChild) ;
```

You can also enable and disable a child window. By default, a window is enabled. You can disable it by calling:

```
EnableWindow (hwndChild, FALSE) ;
```

For button controls, this has the effect of graying the button text string. The button no longer responds to mouse or keyboard input. This is the best method for indicating that a button option is currently unavailable.

You can reenable a child window by calling:

```
EnableWindow (hwndChild, TRUE) ;
```

You can determine whether a child window is enabled by calling:

```
IsWindowEnabled (hwndChild) ;
```

Buttons and Input Focus

As I noted earlier in this chapter, push buttons, check boxes, radio buttons, and owner-draw buttons receive the input focus when they are clicked with the mouse. The control indicates it has the input focus by a dashed line surrounding the text. When the child window control gets the input focus, the parent window loses it; all keyboard input then goes to the control rather than to the parent window. However, the child window control responds only to the Spacebar, which now functions like the mouse. This situation presents an obvious problem: Your program has lost control of keyboard processing. Let's see what we can do about it.

As I discussed in Chapter 5, when Windows switches the input focus from one window (such as a parent) to another (such as a child window control), it first sends a WM_KILL-FOCUS message to the window losing the input focus. The *wParam* parameter is the handle of the window that is to receive the input focus. Windows then sends a WM_SETFOCUS message to the window receiving the input focus, with *wParam* the handle of the window losing the input focus. (In both cases, *wParam* may be NULL, which indicates that no window has or is receiving the input focus.)

A parent window can prevent a child window control from getting the input focus by processing WM_KILLFOCUS messages. Assume that the array *hwndChild* contains the window handles of all child windows. (These were saved in the array during the *CreateWindow* calls that created the windows.) NUM is the number of child windows:

```
case WM_KILLFOCUS :
    for (i = 0 ; i < NUM ; i++)
        if (hwndChild[i] == (HWND) wParam)
            {
            SetFocus (hwnd) ;
            break ;
            }
    return 0 ;
```

In this code, when the parent window detects that it's losing the input focus to one of its child window controls, it calls *SetFocus* to restore the input focus to itself.

Here's a simpler (but less obvious) way of doing it:

```
case WM_KILLFOCUS :
    if (hwnd == GetParent ((HWND) wParam))
        SetFocus (hwnd) ;
    return 0 ;
```

Both these methods have a shortcoming, however: They prevent the button from responding to the Spacebar, because the button never gets the input focus. A better approach would be to let the button get the input focus but also to include the facility for the user to move from button to button using the Tab key. At first this sounds impossible, but I'll show you how to accomplish it with a technique called "window subclassing" in the COLORS1 program shown later in this chapter.

CONTROLS AND COLORS

As you can see in Figure 8-2, the display of many of the buttons doesn't look quite right. The push buttons are fine, but the others are drawn with a rectangular gray background that simply shouldn't be there. This is because the buttons are designed to be displayed in dialog boxes, and in Windows 95, dialog boxes have a gray surface. Our window has a white surface because that's how we defined it in the WNDCLASS structure:

```
wndclass.hbrBackground = (HBRUSH) GetStockObject (WHITE_BRUSH) ;
```

We've been doing this because we've often been displaying text to the client area, and GDI uses the text color and background color defined in the default device context. These are always black and white. To make the appearance of these buttons look a little better, we must either change the color of the client area to agree with the background color of the buttons, or somehow change the button background color to be white.

The first step is to understand Windows' use of "system colors."

System Colors

Windows maintains 25 system colors for painting various parts of the display. You can obtain and set these colors using *GetSysColor* and *SetSysColors*. Identifiers defined in the Windows header files specify the system color. Setting a system color with *SetSysColors* changes it only for the current Windows session.

You can change some (but not all) system colors using the Display section of the Windows Control Panel or by modifying the *[colors]* section in the WIN.INI file. The *[colors]* section uses keywords for the 25 system colors (different from the *GetSysColor* and *SetSys-Colors* identifiers) followed by red, green, and blue values that can range from 0 to 255. The following table shows how the 25 system colors are identified using the constants used for *GetSysColor* and *SetSysColors* and also the WIN.INI keywords. The table is arranged sequentially by the values of the COLOR_ constants beginning with 0 and ending with 24:

GetSysColor and SetSysColors	*WIN.INI*
COLOR_SCROLLBAR	Scrollbar
COLOR_BACKGROUND	Background
COLOR_ACTIVECAPTION	ActiveTitle
COLOR_INACTIVECAPTION	InactiveTitle
COLOR_MENU	Menu
COLOR_WINDOW	Window
COLOR_WINDOWFRAME	WindowFrame
COLOR_MENUTEXT	MenuText

(continued)

continued

GetSysColor and SetSysColors	WIN.INI
COLOR_WINDOWTEXT	WindowText
COLOR_CAPTIONTEXT	TitleText
COLOR_ACTIVEBORDER	ActiveBorder
COLOR_INACTIVEBORDER	InactiveBorder
COLOR_APPWORKSPACE	AppWorkspace
COLOR_HIGHLIGHT	Hilight
COLOR_HIGHLIGHTTEXT	HilightText
COLOR_BTNFACE	ButtonFace
COLOR_BTNSHADOW	ButtonShadow
COLOR_GRAYTEXT	GrayText
COLOR_BTNTEXT	ButtonText
COLOR_INACTIVECAPTIONTEXT	InactiveTitleText
COLOR_BTNHIGHLIGHT	ButtonHilight
COLOR_3DDKSHADOW	ButtonDkShadow
COLOR_3DLIGHT	ButtonLight
COLOR_INFOTEXT	InfoText
COLOR_INFOBK	InfoWindow

Default values for these 25 colors are provided by the display driver. Windows uses these default values unless they are overriden by the *[colors]* section of WIN.INI, which can be changed through the Control Panel.

Now for the bad news: Although many of these colors seem self-explanatory (for example COLOR_BACKGROUND is the color of the desktop area behind all the windows), the use of system colors in Windows 95 has become quite chaotic. In the old days, Windows was much simpler visually than it is today. Indeed, prior to Windows 3.0, only the first 13 system colors shown above were defined. With the increased use of more visually complex controls using three-dimensional appearances, more system colors were needed.

The Button Colors

This problem is particularly evident for buttons: COLOR_BTNFACE is used for the main surface color of the push buttons and the background color of the others. (This is also the system color used for dialog boxes and message boxes.) COLOR_BTNSHADOW is used for suggesting a shadow at the right and bottom sides of the push buttons and the insides of the check box squares and radio button circles. For push buttons, COLOR_BTNTEXT is used for the text color; for the others it's COLOR_WINDOWTEXT. Several other system colors are also used for various parts of the button designs.

So, if we want to display buttons on the surface of our client area, one way to avoid the color clash is to yield to these system colors. To begin, you use COLOR_BTNFACE for the background of your client area when defining the window class:

```
wndclass.hbrBackground = (HBRUSH) (COLOR_BTNFACE + 1) ;
```

You can try this in the BTNLOOK program. Windows understands that when the value of *hbrBackground* in the WNDCLASSEX structure is this low in value, it actually refers to a system color rather than an actual handle. Windows requires that you add 1 when you use these identifiers when specifying them in the *hbrBackground* field of the WNDCLASSEX structure, but doing so has no purpose other than to prevent the value from being NULL. If the system color happens to be changed while your program is running, the surface of your client area will be invalidated, and Windows will use the new COLOR_BTNFACE value.

But now we've caused another problem. When you display text using *TextOut*, Windows uses values defined in the device context for the text background color (which erases the background behind the text) and the text color. The default values are white (background) and black (text) regardless of both the system colors and the *hbrBackground* field of the window class structure. So you need to use *SetTextColor* and *SetBkColor* to change your text and text background colors to the system colors. You do this after you obtain the handle to a device context:

```
SetBkColor (hdc, GetSysColor (COLOR_BTNFACE)) ;
SetTextColor (hdc, GetSysColor (COLOR_WINDOWTEXT)) ;
```

Now the client-area background, text background, and text color are all consistent with the button colors.

The WM_CTLCOLORBTN Message

We've seen how we can adjust our client area color and text color to the background colors of the buttons. Can we adjust the colors of the buttons to the colors we prefer in our program? Well, in theory, yes, but in practice, no.

What you probably *don't* want to do is use *SetSysColors* to change the appearance of the buttons. This will affect all programs currently running under Windows; it's something users would not appreciate very much.

A better approach (again, in theory) is to process the WM_CTLCOLORBTN message. This is a message that button controls send to the parent window procedure when the child window is about to paint its client area. The parent window can use this opportunity to alter the colors that the child window procedure will use for painting. (In 16-bit versions of Windows, a message called WM_CTLCOLOR was used for all controls. This has been replaced with separate messages for each type of standard control.)

When the parent window procedure receives a WM_CTLCOLORBTN message, the *wParam* message parameter is the handle to the button's device context, *lParam* is the button's window handle. When the parent window procedure gets this message, the button control has already obtained its device context. When processing a WM_CTLCOLORBTN message in your window procedure, you:

■ Optionally set a text color using *SetTextColor*.

■ Optionally set a text background color using *SetBkColor*.

■ Return a brush handle to the child window.

In theory, the child window uses the brush for coloring a background. It is your responsibility to destroy the brush when it is no longer needed.

Here's the problem with WM_CTLCOLORBTN: Only the push buttons and owner-draw buttons send WM_CTLCOLORBTN to their parent windows, and only owner-draw buttons respond to the parent window processing of the message using the brush for coloring the background. This is fairly useless because the parent window is responsible for drawing owner-draw buttons anyway.

Later on in this chapter, we'll examine cases in which messages similar to WM_CTL-COLORBTN but applying to other types of controls are more useful.

Owner-Draw Buttons

If you wish to have total control over the visual appearance of a button but don't want to bother with keyboard and mouse logic, you can create a button with the BS_OWNERDRAW style. This is demonstrated in the OWNERDRW program shown in Figure 8-3.

```
OWNERDRW.MAK

#- - - - - - - - - - - - - - - - - - - - - -
# OWNERDRW.MAK make file
#- - - - - - - - - - - - - - - - - - - - - -

ownerdrw.exe : ownerdrw.obj
     $(LINKER) $(GUIFLAGS) -OUT:ownerdrw.exe ownerdrw.obj $(GUILIBS)

ownerdrw.obj : ownerdrw.c
     $(CC) $(CFLAGS) ownerdrw.c
```

```
OWNERDRW.C

/*- - - - - - - - - - - - - - - - - - - - - - - - - - - - - - - - - - - -
     OWNERDRW.C -- Owner-Draw Button Demo Program
                   (c) Charles Petzold, 1996
     - - - - - - - - - - - - - - - - - - - - - - - - - - - - - - - - - -*/
```

Figure 8-3. *The OWNERDRW program.*   *(continued)*

```
#include <windows.h>

#define IDC_SMALLER      1
#define IDC_LARGER       2

#define BTN_WIDTH        (8 * cxChar)
#define BTN_HEIGHT       (4 * cyChar)

LRESULT CALLBACK WndProc (HWND, UINT, WPARAM, LPARAM) ;

HINSTANCE hInst ;

int WINAPI WinMain (HINSTANCE hInstance, HINSTANCE hPrevInstance,
                    PSTR szCmdLine, int iCmdShow)
     {
     static char szAppName[] = "OwnerDrw" ;
     MSG         msg ;
     HWND        hwnd ;
     WNDCLASSEX  wndclass ;

     hInst = hInstance ;

     wndclass.cbSize        = sizeof (wndclass) ;
     wndclass.style         = CS_HREDRAW | CS_VREDRAW ;
     wndclass.lpfnWndProc   = WndProc ;
     wndclass.cbClsExtra    = 0 ;
     wndclass.cbWndExtra    = 0 ;
     wndclass.hInstance     = hInstance ;
     wndclass.hIcon         = LoadIcon (NULL, IDI_APPLICATION) ;
     wndclass.hCursor       = LoadCursor (NULL, IDC_ARROW) ;
     wndclass.hbrBackground = (HBRUSH) GetStockObject (WHITE_BRUSH) ;
     wndclass.lpszMenuName  = szAppName ;
     wndclass.lpszClassName = szAppName ;
     wndclass.hIconSm       = LoadIcon (NULL, IDI_APPLICATION) ;

     RegisterClassEx (&wndclass) ;

     hwnd = CreateWindow (szAppName, "Owner-Draw Button Demo",
                          WS_OVERLAPPEDWINDOW,
                          CW_USEDEFAULT, CW_USEDEFAULT,
                          CW_USEDEFAULT, CW_USEDEFAULT,
                          NULL, NULL, hInstance, NULL) ;

     ShowWindow (hwnd, iCmdShow) ;
     UpdateWindow (hwnd) ;
```

(continued)

```
      while (GetMessage (&msg, NULL, 0, 0))
           {
           TranslateMessage (&msg) ;
           DispatchMessage (&msg) ;
           }
      return msg.wParam ;
      }

void Triangle (HDC hdc, POINT pt[])
      {
      SelectObject (hdc, GetStockObject (BLACK_BRUSH)) ;
      Polygon (hdc, pt, 3) ;
      SelectObject (hdc, GetStockObject (WHITE_BRUSH)) ;
      }

LRESULT CALLBACK WndProc (HWND hwnd, UINT iMsg, WPARAM wParam, LPARAM lParam)
      {
      static HWND      hwndSmaller, hwndLarger ;
      static int       cxClient, cyClient, cxChar, cyChar ;
      int              cx, cy ;
      LPDRAWITEMSTRUCT pdis ;
      POINT            pt[3] ;
      RECT             rc ;

      switch (iMsg)
           {
           case WM_CREATE :
                cxChar = LOWORD (GetDialogBaseUnits ()) ;
                cyChar = HIWORD (GetDialogBaseUnits ()) ;

                           // Create the owner-draw pushbuttons

                hwndSmaller = CreateWindow ("button", "",
                                WS_CHILD | WS_VISIBLE | BS_OWNERDRAW,
                                0, 0, BTN_WIDTH, BTN_HEIGHT,
                                hwnd, (HMENU) IDC_SMALLER, hInst, NULL) ;

                hwndLarger = CreateWindow ("button", "",
                                WS_CHILD | WS_VISIBLE | BS_OWNERDRAW,
                                0, 0, BTN_WIDTH, BTN_HEIGHT,
                                hwnd, (HMENU) IDC_LARGER, hInst, NULL) ;
                return 0 ;

           case WM_SIZE :
                cxClient = LOWORD (lParam) ;
                cyClient = HIWORD (lParam) ;
```

(continued)

```
                    // Move the buttons to the new center

        MoveWindow (hwndSmaller, cxClient / 2 - 3 * BTN_WIDTH  / 2,
                                 cyClient / 2 -     BTN_HEIGHT / 2,
                                 BTN_WIDTH, BTN_HEIGHT, TRUE) ;

        MoveWindow (hwndLarger,  cxClient / 2 +     BTN_WIDTH  / 2,
                                 cyClient / 2 -     BTN_HEIGHT / 2,
                                 BTN_WIDTH, BTN_HEIGHT, TRUE) ;
        return 0 ;

case WM_COMMAND :
     GetWindowRect (hwnd, &rc) ;

                    // Make the window 10% smaller or larger

     switch (wParam)
          {
          case IDC_SMALLER :
               rc.left   += cxClient / 20 ;
               rc.right  -= cxClient / 20 ;
               rc.top    += cyClient / 20 ;
               rc.bottom -= cyClient / 20 ;

               break ;

          case IDC_LARGER :
               rc.left   -= cxClient / 20 ;
               rc.right  += cxClient / 20 ;
               rc.top    -= cyClient / 20 ;
               rc.bottom += cyClient / 20 ;

               break ;
          }

     MoveWindow (hwnd, rc.left, rc.top, rc.right - rc.left,
                                        rc.bottom - rc.top, TRUE) ;
     return 0 ;

case WM_DRAWITEM :
     pdis = (LPDRAWITEMSTRUCT) lParam ;

                    // Fill area with white and frame it black

     FillRect (pdis->hDC, &pdis->rcItem,
               (HBRUSH) GetStockObject (WHITE_BRUSH)) ;
```

(continued)

```
            FrameRect (pdis->hDC, &pdis->rcItem,
                    (HBRUSH) GetStockObject (BLACK_BRUSH)) ;

                // Draw inward and outward black triangles

    cx = pdis->rcItem.right  - pdis->rcItem.left ;
    cy = pdis->rcItem.bottom - pdis->rcItem.top  ;

    switch (pdis->CtlID)
        {
        case IDC_SMALLER :
                pt[0].x = 3 * cx / 8 ;  pt[0].y = 1 * cy / 8 ;
                pt[1].x = 5 * cx / 8 ;  pt[1].y = 1 * cy / 8 ;
                pt[2].x = 4 * cx / 8 ;  pt[2].y = 3 * cy / 8 ;

                Triangle (pdis->hDC, pt) ;

                pt[0].x = 7 * cx / 8 ;  pt[0].y = 3 * cy / 8 ;
                pt[1].x = 7 * cx / 8 ;  pt[1].y = 5 * cy / 8 ;
                pt[2].x = 5 * cx / 8 ;  pt[2].y = 4 * cy / 8 ;

                Triangle (pdis->hDC, pt) ;

                pt[0].x = 5 * cx / 8 ;  pt[0].y = 7 * cy / 8 ;
                pt[1].x = 3 * cx / 8 ;  pt[1].y = 7 * cy / 8 ;
                pt[2].x = 4 * cx / 8 ;  pt[2].y = 5 * cy / 8 ;

                Triangle (pdis->hDC, pt) ;

                pt[0].x = 1 * cx / 8 ;  pt[0].y = 5 * cy / 8 ;
                pt[1].x = 1 * cx / 8 ;  pt[1].y = 3 * cy / 8 ;
                pt[2].x = 3 * cx / 8 ;  pt[2].y = 4 * cy / 8 ;

                Triangle (pdis->hDC, pt) ;

                break ;

        case IDC_LARGER :

                pt[0].x = 5 * cx / 8 ;  pt[0].y = 3 * cy / 8 ;
                pt[1].x = 3 * cx / 8 ;  pt[1].y = 3 * cy / 8 ;
                pt[2].x = 4 * cx / 8 ;  pt[2].y = 1 * cy / 8 ;

                Triangle (pdis->hDC, pt) ;

                pt[0].x = 5 * cx / 8 ;  pt[0].y = 5 * cy / 8 ;
```

(continued)

```
                            pt[1].x = 5 * cx / 8 ;   pt[1].y = 3 * cy / 8 ;
                            pt[2].x = 7 * cx / 8 ;   pt[2].y = 4 * cy / 8 ;

                            Triangle (pdis->hDC, pt) ;

                            pt[0].x = 3 * cx / 8 ;   pt[0].y = 5 * cy / 8 ;
                            pt[1].x = 5 * cx / 8 ;   pt[1].y = 5 * cy / 8 ;
                            pt[2].x = 4 * cx / 8 ;   pt[2].y = 7 * cy / 8 ;

                            Triangle (pdis->hDC, pt) ;

                            pt[0].x = 3 * cx / 8 ;   pt[0].y = 3 * cy / 8 ;
                            pt[1].x = 3 * cx / 8 ;   pt[1].y = 5 * cy / 8 ;
                            pt[2].x = 1 * cx / 8 ;   pt[2].y = 4 * cy / 8 ;

                            Triangle (pdis->hDC, pt) ;

                            break ;
                       }

                  // Invert the rectangle if the button is selected

            if (pdis->itemState & ODS_SELECTED)
                  InvertRect (pdis->hDC, &pdis->rcItem) ;

                  // Draw a focus rectangle if the button has the focus

            if (pdis->itemState & ODS_FOCUS)
                       {
                       pdis->rcItem.left   += cx / 16 ;
                       pdis->rcItem.top    += cy / 16 ;
                       pdis->rcItem.right  -= cx / 16 ;
                       pdis->rcItem.bottom -= cy / 16 ;

                       DrawFocusRect (pdis->hDC, &pdis->rcItem) ;
                       }

            return 0 ;

       case WM_DESTROY :
            PostQuitMessage (0) ;
            return 0 ;
       }
  return DefWindowProc (hwnd, iMsg, wParam, lParam) ;
  }
```

This program contains two buttons in the center of its client area, as shown in Figure 8-4. The button on the left has four triangles pointing to the center of the button. Clicking the button decreases the size of the window by 10%. The button on the right has four triangles pointing outward, and clicking this button increases the window size by 10%.

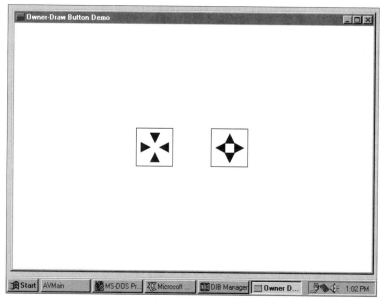

Figure 8-4. *The OWNERDRW display.*

Most programs that use the BS_OWNERDRAW button style to draw their own buttons often use small bitmaps for the button images. The OWNERDRW program, however, simply draws the triangles on the surface of the buttons.

During the WM_CREATE message, OWNERDRW obtains the average width and height of the system font by calling the *GetDialogBaseUnits* function. This is a function often very handy for obtaining this information. OWNERDRW then creates two buttons with the BS_OWNERDRAW style; the buttons are given a width of eight times the system font and four times the system font height. (When using predefined bitmaps to draw buttons, it's useful to know that these dimensions create buttons that are 64 pixels by 64 pixels on a VGA.) The buttons are not yet positioned. During the WM_SIZE message, OWNERDRW positions the buttons in the center of the client area by calling *MoveWindow*.

Clicking on the buttons causes them to generate WM_COMMAND messages. To process the WM_COMMAND message, OWNERDRW calls *GetWindowRect* to store the position and size of the entire window (not only the client area) in a RECT (rectangle) structure. This position is relative to the screen. OWNERDRW then adjusts the fields of this rectangle structure depending on whether the left or right button was clicked. Then the program repositions and resizes the window by calling *MoveWindow*. This generates another WM-_SIZE message, and the buttons are repositioned in the center of the client area.

If this were all the program did, it would be entirely functional but the buttons would not be visible. A button created with the BS_OWNERDRAW style sends its parent window a WM_DRAWITEM message whenever the button needs to be repainted. This occurs when the button is first created, when it is pressed or released, when it gains or loses the input focus, and whenever else it needs repainting.

During the WM_DRAWITEM message, the *lParam* message parameter is a pointer to a structure of type DRAWITEMSTRUCT. The OWNERDRW program stores this pointer in a variable named *pdis*. This structure contains the information necessary for a program to draw the button. (The same structure is also used for owner-draw list boxes and menu items.) The structure fields important for working with buttons are *hDC* (the device context for the button), *rcItem* (a RECT structure providing the size of the button), *CtlID* (the control window ID), and *itemState* (which indicates whether the button is pushed or has the input focus).

OWNERDRW begins WM_DRAWITEM processing by calling *FillRect* to erase the surface of the button with a white brush, and *FrameRect* to draw a black frame around the button. Then, OWNERDRW draws four black-filled triangles on the button by calling *Polygon*. That's the normal case.

If the button is currently being pressed, then a bit of the *itemState* field of the DRAWITEMSTRUCT will be set. You can test this bit using the ODS_SELECTED constant. If the bit is set, OWNERDRW inverts the colors of the button by calling *InvertRect*. If the button has the input focus, then the ODS_FOCUS bit of the *itemState* field will be set. In this case, OWNERDRW draws a dotted rectangle just inside the periphery of the button by calling *DrawFocusRect*.

A word of warning when using owner-draw buttons: Windows obtains a device context for you and includes it as a field of the DRAWITEMSTRUCT structure. Leave the device context in the same state you found it. Any GDI objects selected into the device context must be unselected. Also, be careful not to draw outside the rectangle defining the boundaries of the button.

THE STATIC CLASS

You create a static child window control by using "static" as the window class in the *CreateWindow* function. These are fairly benign child windows. They do not accept mouse or keyboard input, and they do not send WM_COMMAND messages back to the parent window. (When you move or click the mouse over a static child window, the child window traps the WM_NCHITTEST message and returns a value of HTTRANSPARENT to Windows. This causes Windows to send the same WM_NCHITTEST message to the underlying window, which is usually the parent. The parent usually passes the message to *DefWindowProc*, where it is converted to a client-area mouse message.)

The first six static window styles simply draw a rectangle or a frame in the client area of the child window. In the table at the top of the following page, the "RECT" static styles (left column) are filled-in rectangles; the three "FRAME" styles (right column) are rectangular outlines that are not filled in:

SS_BLACKRECT	SS_BLACKFRAME
SS_GRAYRECT	SS_GRAYFRAME
SS_WHITERECT	SS_WHITEFRAME

"BLACK," "GRAY," and "WHITE" do not mean the colors are black, gray, and white. Rather, the colors are based on system colors as shown here:

Static Control	*System Color*
BLACK	COLOR_3DDKSHADOW
GRAY	COLOR_BTNSHADOW
WHITE	COLOR_BTNHIGHLIGHT

The window text field of the *CreateWindow* call is ignored for these styles. The upper left corner of the rectangle begins at the *x* position and *y* position coordinates relative to the parent window. (You can also use styles of SS_ETCHEDHORZ, SS_ETCHEDVERT, or SS_ETCHEDFRAME to create a shadowed-looking frame with the "gray" and "white" colors.)

The static class also includes three text styles: SS_LEFT, SS_RIGHT, and SS_CENTER. These create left-justified, right-justified, and centered text. The text is given in the window text parameter of the *CreateWindow* call, and it can be changed later using *SetWindowText*. When the window procedure for static controls displays this text, it uses the *DrawText* function with DT_WORDBREAK, DT_NOCLIP, and DT_EXPANDTABS parameters. The text is wordwrapped within the rectangle of the child window.

The background of these three text-style child windows is normally COLOR_BTNFACE, and the text itself is COLOR_WINDOWTEXT. You can intercept WM_CTLCOLORSTATIC messages to change the text color by calling *SetTextColor* and the background color by calling *SetBkColor* and by returning the handle to the background brush. This will be demonstrated in the COLORS1 program shown shortly.

Finally, the static class also includes the window styles SS_ICON and SS_USERITEM. However, these have no meaning when used as child window controls. We'll look at them again when discussing dialog boxes.

THE SCROLLBAR CLASS

When the subject of scroll bars first came up in Chapter 3 while I was designing the SYSMETS series of programs, I discussed some of the differences between "window scroll bars" and "scroll bar controls." SYSMETS uses window scroll bars, which appear at the right and bottom of the window. You add window scroll bars to a window by including the identifier

WS_VSCROLL or WS_HSCROLL or both in the window style when creating the window. Now we're ready to make some scroll bar controls, which are child windows that can appear anywhere in the client area of the parent window. You create child window scroll bar controls by using the predefined window class "scrollbar" and one of the two scroll bar styles, SBS_VERT or SBS_HORZ.

Unlike the button controls (and the edit and list box controls to be discussed later), scroll bar controls do not send WM_COMMAND messages to the parent window. Instead, they send WM_VSCROLL and WM_HSCROLL messages, just like window scroll bars. When processing the scroll bar messages, you can differentiate between window scroll bars and scroll bar controls by the *lParam* parameter. It will be 0 for window scroll bars and the scroll bar window handle for scroll bar controls. The high and low words of the *wParam* parameter have the same meaning for window scroll bars and scroll bar controls.

Although window scroll bars have a fixed width, Windows uses the full rectangle dimensions given in the *CreateWindow* call (or later in the *MoveWindow* call) to size the scroll bar controls. You can make long, thin scroll bar controls or short, pudgy scroll bar controls.

If you want to create scroll bar controls that have the same dimensions as window scroll bars, you can use *GetSystemMetrics* to obtain the height of a horizontal scroll bar:

```
GetSystemMetrics (SM_CYHSCROLL) ;
```

or the width of a vertical scroll bar:

```
GetSystemMetrics (SM_CXVSCROLL) ;
```

(The scroll bar window style identifiers SBS_LEFTALIGN, SBS_RIGHTALIGN, SBS_TOP-ALIGN, and SBS_BOTTOMALIGN are documented to give standard dimensions to scroll bars. However, these styles work only for scroll bars in dialog boxes.)

You can set the range and position of a scroll bar control with the same calls used for window scroll bars:

```
SetScrollRange (hwndScroll, SB_CTL, iMin, iMax, bRedraw) ;
SetScrollPos (hwndScroll, SB_CTL, iPos, bRedraw) ;
SetScrollInfo (hwndScroll, SB_CTL, &si, bRedraw) ;
```

The difference is that window scroll bars use a handle to the main window as the first parameter and SB_VERT or SB_HORZ as the second parameter.

Amazingly enough, the system color named COLOR_SCROLLBAR is no longer used for scroll bars. The end buttons and thumb are based on COLOR_BTNFACE, COLOR_BTNHIGHLIGHT, COLOR_BTNSHADOW, COLOR_BTNTEXT (for the little arrows), COLOR_BTNSHADOW, and COLOR_BTNLIGHT. The large area between the two end buttons is based on a combination of COLOR_BTNFACE and COLOR_BTNHIGHLIGHT.

If you trap WM_CTLCOLORSCROLLBAR messages, you can return a brush from the message to override the color used for this area. Let's do it.

The COLORS1 Program

To see some uses of scroll bars and static child windows—and also to explore color in more depth—we'll use the COLORS1 program, shown in Figure 8-5. COLORS1 displays three scroll bars in the left half of the client area labeled "Red," "Green," and "Blue." As you scroll the scroll bars, the right half of the client area changes to the composite color indicated by the mix of the three primary colors. The numeric values of the three primary colors are displayed under the three scroll bars.

COLORS1.MAK

```
#----------------------
# COLORS1.MAK make file
#----------------------

colors1.exe : colors1.obj
     $(LINKER) $(GUIFLAGS) -OUT:colors1.exe colors1.obj $(GUILIBS)

colors1.obj : colors1.c
     $(CC) $(CFLAGS) colors1.c
```

COLORS1.C

```
/*-------------------------------------------
   COLORS1.C -- Colors Using Scroll Bars
               (c) Charles Petzold, 1996
   -------------------------------------------*/

#include <windows.h>
#include <stdlib.h>

LRESULT CALLBACK WndProc    (HWND, UINT, WPARAM, LPARAM) ;
LRESULT CALLBACK ScrollProc (HWND, UINT, WPARAM, LPARAM) ;

WNDPROC fnOldScr[3] ;
HWND    hwndScrol[3], hwndLabel[3], hwndValue[3], hwndRect ;
int     color[3], iFocus ;

int WINAPI WinMain (HINSTANCE hInstance, HINSTANCE hPrevInstance,
                    PSTR szCmdLine, int iCmdShow)
     {
     static char  szAppName[] = "Colors1" ;
```

Figure 8-5. *The COLORS1 program.*   *(continued)*

```
static char *szColorLabel[] = { "Red", "Green", "Blue" } ;
HWND         hwnd ;
int          i ;
MSG          msg ;
WNDCLASSEX   wndclass ;

wndclass.cbSize        = sizeof (wndclass) ;
wndclass.style         = CS_HREDRAW | CS_VREDRAW ;
wndclass.lpfnWndProc   = WndProc ;
wndclass.cbClsExtra    = 0 ;
wndclass.cbWndExtra    = 0 ;
wndclass.hInstance     = hInstance ;
wndclass.hIcon         = LoadIcon (NULL, IDI_APPLICATION) ;
wndclass.hCursor       = LoadCursor (NULL, IDC_ARROW) ;
wndclass.hbrBackground = CreateSolidBrush (0L) ;
wndclass.lpszMenuName  = NULL ;
wndclass.lpszClassName = szAppName ;
wndclass.hIconSm       = LoadIcon (NULL, IDI_APPLICATION) ;

RegisterClassEx (&wndclass) ;

hwnd = CreateWindow (szAppName, "Color Scroll",
                    WS_OVERLAPPEDWINDOW,
                    CW_USEDEFAULT, CW_USEDEFAULT,
                    CW_USEDEFAULT, CW_USEDEFAULT,
                    NULL, NULL, hInstance, NULL) ;

hwndRect = CreateWindow ("static", NULL,
                    WS_CHILD | WS_VISIBLE | SS_WHITERECT,
                    0, 0, 0, 0,
                    hwnd, (HMENU) 9, hInstance, NULL) ;

for (i = 0 ; i < 3 ; i++)
    {
    hwndScroll[i] = CreateWindow ("scrollbar", NULL,
                    WS_CHILD | WS_VISIBLE | WS_TABSTOP | SBS_VERT,
                    0, 0, 0, 0,
                    hwnd, (HMENU) i, hInstance, NULL) ;

    hwndLabel[i] = CreateWindow ("static", szColorLabel[i],
                    WS_CHILD | WS_VISIBLE | SS_CENTER,
                    0, 0, 0, 0,
                    hwnd, (HMENU) (i + 3), hInstance, NULL) ;
```

(continued)

```
                      hwndValue[i] = CreateWindow ("static", "0",
                                     WS_CHILD | WS_VISIBLE | SS_CENTER,
                                     0, 0, 0, 0,
                                     hwnd, (HMENU) (i + 6), hInstance, NULL) ;

                 fnOldScr[i] = (WNDPROC) SetWindowLong (hwndScroll[i], GWL_WNDPROC,
                                                (LONG) ScrollProc) ;

                 SetScrollRange (hwndScroll[i], SB_CTL, 0, 255, FALSE) ;
                 SetScrollPos   (hwndScroll[i], SB_CTL, 0, FALSE) ;
                 }

          ShowWindow (hwnd, iCmdShow) ;
          UpdateWindow (hwnd) ;

          while (GetMessage (&msg, NULL, 0, 0))
               {
               TranslateMessage (&msg) ;
               DispatchMessage  (&msg) ;
               }
          return msg.wParam ;
          }

LRESULT CALLBACK WndProc (HWND hwnd, UINT iMsg, WPARAM wParam, LPARAM lParam)
     {
     static COLORREF crPrim[3] = {   RGB (255, 0, 0), RGB (0, 255, 0),
                                 RGB (0, 0, 255) } ;
     static HBRUSH    hBrush[3], hBrushStatic ;
     static int       cyChar ;
     static RECT      rcColor ;
     char             szbuffer[10] ;
     int              i, cxClient, cyClient ;

     switch (iMsg)
          {
          case WM_CREATE :
               for (i = 0 ; i < 3 ; i++)
                    hBrush[i] = CreateSolidBrush (crPrim[i]) ;

               hBrushStatic = CreateSolidBrush (
                              GetSysColor (COLOR_BTNHIGHLIGHT)) ;

               cyChar = HIWORD (GetDialogBaseUnits ()) ;
               return 0 ;
```

(continued)

388

```
case WM_SIZE :
     cxClient = LOWORD (lParam) ;
     cyClient = HIWORD (lParam) ;

     SetRect (&rcColor, cxClient / 2, 0, cxClient, cyClient) ;

     MoveWindow (hwndRect, 0, 0, cxClient / 2, cyClient, TRUE) ;

     for (i = 0 ; i < 3 ; i++)
          {
          MoveWindow (hwndScroll[i],
               (2 * i + 1) * cxClient / 14, 2 * cyChar,
               cxClient / 14, cyClient - 4 * cyChar, TRUE) ;

          MoveWindow (hwndLabel[i],
               (4 * i + 1) * cxClient / 28, cyChar / 2,
               cxClient / 7, cyChar, TRUE) ;

          MoveWindow (hwndValue[i],
               (4 * i + 1) * cxClient / 28,
               cyClient - 3 * cyChar / 2,
               cxClient / 7, cyChar, TRUE) ;
          }
     SetFocus (hwnd) ;
     return 0 ;

case WM_SETFOCUS :
     SetFocus (hwndScroll[iFocus]) ;
     return 0 ;

case WM_VSCROLL :
     i = GetWindowLong ((HWND) lParam, GWL_ID) ;

     switch (LOWORD (wParam))
          {
          case SB_PAGEDOWN :
               color[i] += 15 ;
                                        // fall through
          case SB_LINEDOWN :
               color[i] = min (255, color[i] + 1) ;
               break ;

          case SB_PAGEUP :
               color[i] -= 15 ;
                                        // fall through
          case SB_LINEUP :
```

(continued)

```
                    color[i] = max (0, color[i] - 1) ;
                    break ;

               case SB_TOP :
                    color[i] = 0 ;
                    break ;

               case SB_BOTTOM :
                    color[i] = 255 ;
                    break ;

               case SB_THUMBPOSITION :
               case SB_THUMBTRACK :
                    color[i] = HIWORD (wParam) ;
                    break ;

               default :
                    break ;
               }
          SetScrollPos  (hwndScroll[i], SB_CTL, color[i], TRUE) ;
          SetWindowText (hwndValue[i], itoa (color[i], szbuffer, 10)) ;

          DeleteObject ((HBRUSH)
               SetClassLong (hwnd, GCL_HBRBACKGROUND,
                    (LONG) CreateSolidBrush (
                              RGB (color[0], color[1], color[2])))) ;

          InvalidateRect (hwnd, &rcColor, TRUE) ;
          return 0 ;

     case WM_CTLCOLORSCROLLBAR :
          i = GetWindowLong ((HWND) lParam, GWL_ID) ;

          return (LRESULT) hBrush[i] ;

     case WM_CTLCOLORSTATIC :
          i = GetWindowLong ((HWND) lParam, GWL_ID) ;

          if (i >= 3 && i <= 8)      // static text controls
               {
               SetTextColor ((HDC) wParam, crPrim[i % 3]) ;
               SetBkColor ((HDC) wParam,
                         GetSysColor (COLOR_BTNHIGHLIGHT));

               return (LRESULT) hBrushStatic ;
               }
```

(continued)

```
                    break ;

          case WM_SYSCOLORCHANGE :
                 DeleteObject (hBrushStatic) ;

                 hBrushStatic = CreateSolidBrush (
                                 GetSysColor (COLOR_BTNHIGHLIGHT)) ;
                 return 0 ;

          case WM_DESTROY :
                 DeleteObject ((HBRUSH)
                    SetClassLong (hwnd, GCL_HBRBACKGROUND,
                       (LONG) GetStockObject (WHITE_BRUSH))) ;

                 for (i = 0 ; i < 3 ; DeleteObject (hBrush[i++])) ;

                 DeleteObject (hBrushStatic) ;

                 PostQuitMessage (0) ;
                 return 0 ;
          }
     return DefWindowProc (hwnd, iMsg, wParam, lParam) ;
     }

LRESULT CALLBACK ScrollProc (HWND hwnd, UINT iMsg, WPARAM wParam, LPARAM lParam)
     {
     int i = GetWindowLong (hwnd, GWL_ID) ;

     switch (iMsg)
          {
          case WM_KEYDOWN :
                 if (wParam == VK_TAB)
                    SetFocus (hwndScrol[(i +
                       (GetKeyState (VK_SHIFT) < 0 ? 2 : 1)) % 3]) ;
                 break ;

          case WM_SETFOCUS :
                 iFocus = i ;
                 break ;
          }
     return CallWindowProc (fnOldScr[i], hwnd, iMsg, wParam, lParam) ;
     }
```

COLORS1 puts its children to work. The program uses 10 child window controls: 3 scroll bars, 6 windows of static text, and 1 static rectangle. COLORS1 traps WM_CTLCOLOR-SCROLLBAR messages to color the interior sections of the three scroll bars red, green, and blue and WM_CTLCOLORSTATIC messages to color the static text.

You can scroll the scroll bars using either the mouse or the keyboard. You can use COLORS1 as a development tool in experimenting with color and choosing attractive (or, if you prefer, ugly) colors for your own Windows programs. The COLORS1 display is shown in Figure 8-6, unfortunately reduced to gray shades for the printed page.

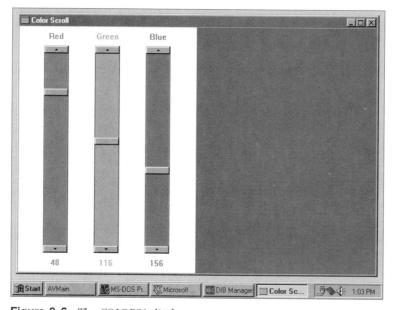

Figure 8-6. *The COLORS1 display.*

COLORS1 doesn't process WM_PAINT messages. Virtually all of the work in COLORS1 is done by the child windows.

The color shown on the right half of the client area is actually the window's background color. A static child window with style SS_WHITERECT blocks out the left half of the client area. The three scroll bars are child window controls with the style SBS_VERT. These scroll bars are positioned on top of the SS_WHITERECT child. Six more static child windows of style SS_CENTER (centered text) provide the labels and the color values. COLORS1 creates its normal overlapped window and the ten child windows within the *WinMain* function using *CreateWindow*. The SS_WHITERECT and SS_CENTER static windows use the window class "static"; the three scroll bars use the window class "scrollbar."

The *x* position, *y* position, width, and height parameters of the *CreateWindow* calls are initially set to 0 because the position and sizing depend on the size of the client area, which is not yet known. COLORS1's window procedure resizes all ten child windows using *MoveWindow* when it receives a WM_SIZE message. So whenever you resize the COLORS1 window, the size of the scroll bars changes proportionally.

When the *WndProc* window procedure receives a WM_VSCROLL message, the high word of the *lParam* parameter is the handle to the child window. We can use *GetWindowLong* to get the child window ID number:

```
i = GetWindowLong (1Param, GWW_ID) ;
```

For the three scroll bars, we have conveniently set the ID numbers to 0, 1, and 2, so *WndProc* can tell which scroll bar is generating the message.

Because the handles to the child windows were saved in arrays when the windows were created, *WndProc* can process the scroll bar message and set the new value of the appropriate scroll bar using the *SetScrollPos* call:

```
SetScrollPos (hwndScrol[i], SB_CTL, color[i], TRUE) ;
```

WndProc also changes the text of the child window at the bottom of the scroll bar:

```
SetWindowText (hwndValue[i], itoa (color[i], szbuffer, 10)) ;
```

The Automatic Keyboard Interface

Scroll bar controls can also process keystrokes, but only if they have the input focus. The following table shows how keyboard cursor keys translate into scroll bar messages:

Cursor Key	*Scroll Bar Message* **wParam** *Value*
Home	SB_TOP
End	SB_BOTTOM
Page Up	SB_PAGEUP
Page Down	SB_PAGEDOWN
Left or Up	SB_LINEUP
Right or Down	SB_LINEDOWN

In fact, the SB_TOP and SB_BOTTOM scroll bar messages can be generated only by using the keyboard. If you want a scroll bar control to obtain the input focus when the scroll bar is clicked with the mouse, you must include the WS_TABSTOP identifier in the window style parameter of the *CreateWindow* call. When a scroll bar has the input focus, a blinking gray block is displayed on the scroll bar thumb.

To provide a full keyboard interface to the scroll bars, however, some more work is necessary. First, the *WndProc* window procedure must specifically give a scroll bar the input focus. It does this by processing the WM_SETFOCUS message, which the parent window receives when it obtains the input focus. *WndProc* simply sets the input focus to one of the scroll bars:

```
SetFocus (hwndScroll[iFocus]) ;
```

But you also need some way to get from one scroll bar to another by using the keyboard, preferably by using the Tab key. This is more difficult, because once a scroll bar has the input focus, it processes all keystrokes. But the scroll bar cares only about the cursor keys; it ignores the Tab key. The way out of this dilemma lies in a technique called "window subclassing." We'll use it to add a facility to COLORS1 to jump from one scroll bar to another using the Tab key.

Window Subclassing

The window procedure for the scroll bar controls is somewhere inside Windows. However, you can obtain the address of this window procedure by a call to *GetWindowLong* using the GWL_WNDPROC identifier as a parameter. Moreover, you can set a new window procedure for the scroll bars by calling *SetWindowLong*. This technique, called "window subclassing," is very powerful. It lets you hook into existing window procedures, process some messages within your own program, and pass all other messages to the old window procedure.

The window procedure that does preliminary scroll bar message processing in COLORS1 is called *ScrollProc*; it is toward the end of the COLORS1.C listing. Because *ScrollProc* is a function within COLORS1 that is called by Windows, it must be defined as a CALLBACK.

For each of the three scroll bars, COLORS1 uses *SetWindowLong* to set the address of the new scroll bar window procedure and also obtain the address of the existing scroll bar window procedure:

```
fnOldScr[i] = (WNDPROC) SetWindowLong (hwndScroll[i], GWL_WNDPROC,
                                          (LONG) ScrollProc)) ;
```

Now the function *ScrollProc* gets all messages that Windows sends to the scroll bar window procedure for the three scroll bars in COLORS1 (but not, of course, for scroll bars in other programs). The *ScrollProc* window procedure simply changes the input focus to the next (or previous) scroll bar when it receives a Tab or Shift-Tab keystroke. It calls the old scroll bar window procedure using *CallWindowProc*.

Coloring the Background

When COLORS1 defines its window class, it gives the background of its client area a solid black brush:

```
wndclass.hbrBackground = CreateSolidBrush (0L) ;
```

When you change the settings of COLORS1's scroll bars, the program must create a new brush and put the new brush handle in the window class structure. Just as we were able to get and set the scroll bar window procedure using *GetWindowLong* and *SetWindowLong*, we can get and set the handle to this brush using *GetClassWord* and *SetClassWord*.

You can create the new brush and insert the handle in the window class structure and then delete the old brush:

```
DeleteObject ((HBRUSH)
    SetClassLong (hwnd, GCL_HBRBACKGROUND, (LONG)
        CreateSolidBrush (RGB (color[0], color[1], color[2])))) ;
```

The next time Windows recolors the background of the window, Windows will use this new brush. To force Windows to erase the background, we invalidate the right half of the client area:

```
InvalidateRect (hwnd, &rcColor, TRUE) ;
```

The TRUE (nonzero) value as the third parameter indicates that we want the background erased before repainting.

InvalidateRect causes Windows to put a WM_PAINT message in the message queue of the window procedure. Because WM_PAINT messages are low priority, this message will not be processed immediately if you are still moving the scroll bar with the mouse or the cursor keys. Alternatively, if you want the window to be updated immediately after the color is changed, you can add the statement:

```
UpdateWindow (hwnd) ;
```

after the *InvalidateRect* call. But this might slow down keyboard and mouse processing.

COLORS1's *WndProc* function doesn't process the WM_PAINT message but passes it to *DefWindowProc*. Window's default processing of WM_PAINT messages simply involves calling *BeginPaint* and *EndPaint* to validate the window. Because we specified in the *InvalidateRect* call that the background should be erased, the *BeginPaint* call causes Windows to generate a WM_ERASEBKGND (erase background) message. *WndProc* ignores this message also. Windows processes it by erasing the background of the client area using the brush specified in the window class.

It's always a good idea to clean up before termination, so during processing of the WM_DESTROY message, *DeleteObject* is called once more:

```
DeleteObject ((HBRUSH)
    SetClassLong (hwnd, GCL_HBRBACKGROUND,
        (LONG) GetStockObject (WHITE_BRUSH))) ;
```

Coloring the Scroll Bars and Static Text

In COLORS1, the interiors of the three scroll bars and the text in the six text fields are colored red, green, and blue. The coloring of the scroll bars is accomplished by processing WM_CTL-COLORSCROLLBAR messages.

In *WndProc* we define a static array of three handles to brushes:

```
static HBRUSH hBrush[3] ;
```

During processing of WM_CREATE, we create the three brushes:

```
for (i = 0 ; i < 3 ; i++)
    hBrush[i] = CreateSolidBrush (crPrim[i]) ;
```

where the *crPrim* array contains the RGB values of the three primary colors. During the WM_CTLCOLORSCROLLBAR processing, the window procedure returns one of these three brushes:

```
case WM_CTLCOLORSCROLLBAR :
    i = GetWindowLong ((HWND) lParam, GWW_ID) ;
    return (LRESULT) hBrush[i] ;
```

These brushes must be destroyed during processing of the WM_DESTROY message:

```
for (i = 0 ; i < 3 ; DeleteObject (hBrush[i++])) ;
```

The text in the static text fields is colored similarly by processing the WM_CTLCOLOR-STATIC message and calling *SetTextColor*. The text background is set using *SetBkColor* with the system color COLOR_BTNHIGHLIGHT. This causes the text background to be the same color as the static rectangle control behind the scroll bars and text displays. For static text controls, this text background color applies only to the rectangle behind each character in the string, and not to the entire width of the control window. To accomplish this, the window procedure must also return a handle to a brush of the COLOR_BTNHIGHLIGHT color. This brush is named *hBrushStatic* and is created during the WM_CREATE message and destroyed during the WM_DESTROY message.

By creating a brush based on the COLOR_BTNHIGHLIGHT color during the WM_-_CREATE message and using it through the duration of the program, we've exposed ourselves to a little problem. If the COLOR_BTNHIGHLIGHT color is changed while the program is running, the color of the static rectangle will change, and the text background color will change, but the whole background of the text window controls will remain the old COLOR-_BTNHIGHLIGHT color.

To fix this problem, COLORS1 also processes the WM_SYSCOLORCHANGE message by simply recreating *hBrushStatic* using the new color.

THE EDIT CLASS

The edit class is in some ways the simplest predefined window class and in other ways the most complex. When you create a child window using the class name "edit," you define a rectangle based on the *x* position, *y* position, width, and height parameters of the *Create-Window* call. This rectangle contains editable text. When the child window control has the input focus, you can type text, move the cursor, select portions of text using either the mouse or the Shift key and a cursor key, delete selected text to the clipboard by pressing Ctrl-X, copy text by pressing Ctrl-C, and insert text from the clipboard by pressing Ctrl-V.

One of the simplest uses of edit controls is for single-line entry fields. But edit controls are not limited to single lines, as I'll demonstrate in the POPPAD1 program shown in Figure 8-7. As we encounter various other topics in this book, the POPPAD program will be enhanced to use menus, dialog boxes (to load and save files), and printers. The final version will be a simple but complete text editor with surprisingly little overhead required in our code.

POPPAD1.MAK

```
#----------------------
# POPPAD1.MAK make file
#----------------------


poppad1.exe : poppad1.obj
     $(LINKER) $(GUIFLAGS) -OUT:poppad1.exe poppad1.obj $(GUILIBS)


poppad1.obj : poppad1.c
     $(CC) $(CFLAGS) poppad1.c
```

POPPAD1.C

```
/*------------------------------------------------------------
   POPPAD1.C -- Popup Editor using child window edit box
                (c) Charles Petzold, 1996
   ------------------------------------------------------------*/

#include <windows.h>

LRESULT CALLBACK WndProc (HWND, UINT, WPARAM, LPARAM);

char szAppName[] = "PopPad1" ;

int WINAPI WinMain (HINSTANCE hInstance, HINSTANCE hPrevInstance,
                    PSTR szCmdLine, int iCmdShow)
     {
     HWND        hwnd ;
     MSG         msg ;
     WNDCLASSEX  wndclass ;

     wndclass.cbSize        = sizeof (wndclass) ;
     wndclass.style         = CS_HREDRAW | CS_VREDRAW ;
```

Figure 8-7. *The POPPAD1 program.* *(continued)*

```
        wndclass.lpfnWndProc    = WndProc ;
        wndclass.cbClsExtra     = 0 ;
        wndclass.cbWndExtra     = 0 ;
        wndclass.hInstance      = hInstance ;
        wndclass.hIcon          = LoadIcon (NULL, IDI_APPLICATION) ;
        wndclass.hCursor        = LoadCursor (NULL, IDC_ARROW) ;
        wndclass.hbrBackground  = (HBRUSH) GetStockObject (WHITE_BRUSH) ;
        wndclass.lpszMenuName   = NULL ;
        wndclass.lpszClassName  = szAppName ;
        wndclass.hIconSm        = LoadIcon (NULL, IDI_APPLICATION) ;

        RegisterClassEx (&wndclass) ;

        hwnd = CreateWindow (szAppName, szAppName,
                        WS_OVERLAPPEDWINDOW,
                        CW_USEDEFAULT, CW_USEDEFAULT,
                        CW_USEDEFAULT, CW_USEDEFAULT,
                        NULL, NULL, hInstance, NULL) ;

        ShowWindow (hwnd, iCmdShow) ;
        UpdateWindow (hwnd) ;

        while (GetMessage (&msg, NULL, 0, 0))
            {
            TranslateMessage (&msg) ;
            DispatchMessage (&msg) ;
            }
        return msg.wParam ;
        }

LRESULT CALLBACK WndProc (HWND hwnd, UINT iMsg, WPARAM wParam, LPARAM lParam)
        {
        static HWND hwndEdit ;

        switch (iMsg)
            {
            case WM_CREATE :
                hwndEdit = CreateWindow ("edit", NULL,
                        WS_CHILD | WS_VISIBLE | WS_HSCROLL | WS_VSCROLL |
                            WS_BORDER | ES_LEFT | ES_MULTILINE |
                            ES_AUTOHSCROLL | ES_AUTOVSCROLL,
                        0, 0, 0, 0,
                        hwnd, (HMENU) 1,
                        ((LPCREATESTRUCT) lParam) -> hInstance, NULL) ;
                return 0 ;
```

(continued)

```
          case WM_SETFOCUS :
               SetFocus (hwndEdit) ;
               return 0 ;

          case WM_SIZE :
               MoveWindow (hwndEdit, 0, 0, LOWORD (lParam),
                                          HIWORD (lParam), TRUE) ;
               return 0 ;

          case WM_COMMAND :
               if (LOWORD (wParam) == 1)
                    if (HIWORD (wParam) == EN_ERRSPACE !!
                        HIWORD (wParam) == EN_MAXTEXT)
                              MessageBox (hwnd,
                                     "Edit control out of space.",
                                     szAppName, MB_OK ! MB_ICONSTOP) ;
               return 0 ;

          case WM_DESTROY :
               PostQuitMessage (0) ;
               return 0 ;
          }
     return DefWindowProc (hwnd, iMsg, wParam, lParam) ;
     }
```

POPPAD1 is a multiline editor (without any file I/O just yet) in less than 100 lines of C. (One drawback, however, is that the predefined multiline edit control is limited to 32 KB of text.) As you can see, POPPAD1 itself doesn't do very much. The predefined edit control is doing quite a lot. In this form, the program lets you explore what edit controls can do without any help from a program.

The Edit Class Styles

As noted earlier, you create an edit control using "edit" as the window class in the *CreateWindow* call. The window style is WS_CHILD plus several options. As in static child window controls, the text in edit controls can be either left-justified, right-justified, or centered. You specify this formatting with the window styles ES_LEFT, ES_RIGHT, and ES_CENTER.

By default, an edit control has a single line. You can create a multiline edit control with the window style ES_MULTILINE. For a single-line edit control, you can normally enter text only to the end of the edit control rectangle. To create an edit control that automatically scrolls horizontally, you use the style ES_AUTOHSCROLL. For a multiline edit control, text wordwraps unless you use the ES_AUTOHSCROLL style, in which case you must press the Enter key to start a new line. You can also include vertical scrolling in a multiline edit control by using the style ES_AUTOVSCROLL.

When you include these scrolling styles in multiline edit controls, you might also want to add scroll bars to the edit control. You do so by using the same window style identifiers as for nonchild windows: WS_HSCROLL and WS_VSCROLL.

By default, an edit control does not have a border. You can add one by using the style WS_BORDER.

When you select text in an edit control, Windows displays it in reverse video. When the edit control loses the input focus, however, the selected text is no longer highlighted. If you want the selection to be highlighted even when the edit control does not have the input focus, you can use the style ES_NOHIDESEL.

When POPPAD1 creates its edit control, the style is given in the *CreateWindow* call as:

```
WS_CHILD ¦ WS_VISIBLE ¦ WS_HSCROLL ¦ WS_VSCROLL ¦
    WS_BORDER ¦ ES_LEFT ¦ ES_MULTILINE ¦
    ES_AUTOHSCROLL ¦ ES_AUTOVSCROLL
```

In POPPAD1 the dimensions of the edit control are later defined by a call to *MoveWindow* when *WndProc* receives a WM_SIZE message. The size of the edit control is simply set to the size of the main window:

```
MoveWindow (hwndEdit, 0, 0, LOWORD (lParam),
                           HIWORD (lParam), TRUE) ;
```

For a single-line edit control, the height of the control must accommodate the height of a character. If the edit control has a border (as most do), use $1\frac{1}{2}$ times the height of a character (including external leading).

Edit Control Notification

Edit controls send WM_COMMAND messages to the parent window procedure. The meanings of the *wParam* and *lParam* variables are the same as for button controls:

Parameter	Description
LOWORD (*wParam*)	Child window ID
HIWORD (*wParam*)	Notification code
lParam	Child window handle

The notification codes are shown below:

EN_SETFOCUS	Edit control has gained the input focus
EN_KILLFOCUS	Edit control has lost the input focus
EN_CHANGE	Edit control's contents will change
EN_UPDATE	Edit control's contents have changed
EN_ERRSPACE	Edit control has run out of space

EN_MAXTEXT	Edit control has run out of space on insertion
EN_HSCROLL	Edit control's horizontal scroll bar has been clicked
EN_VSCROLL	Edit control's vertical scroll bar has been clicked

POPPAD1 traps only EN_ERRSPACE and EN_MAXTEXT notification codes and displays a message box.

The edit control stores text in the memory space of its parent window's program. As I noted above, the contents of an edit control are limited to about 32 KB.

Using the Edit Controls

If you use several single-line edit controls on the surface of your main window, you'll need to use window subclassing to move the input focus from one control to another. You can accomplish this much as COLORS1 does, by intercepting Tab and Shift-Tab keystrokes. (Another example of window subclassing is shown later in this chapter in the HEAD program.) How you handle the Enter key is up to you. You can use it the same way as the Tab key or as a signal to your program that all the edit fields are ready.

If you want to insert text into an edit field, you can do so using *SetWindowText*. Getting text out of an edit control involves *GetWindowTextLength* and *GetWindowText*. We'll see examples of these facilities in our later revisions to the POPPAD program.

Messages to an Edit Control

We won't cover all the messages you can send to an edit control using *SendMessage*, because there are quite a few of them, and several will be used in the later POPPAD revisions. Here's a broad overview.

These messages let you cut, copy, or clear the current selection. A user selects the text to be acted upon by using the mouse or the Shift key and a cursor key, thus highlighting the selected text in the edit control:

```
SendMessage (hwndEdit, WM_CUT, 0, 0) ;
SendMessage (hwndEdit, WM_COPY, 0, 0) ;
SendMessage (hwndEdit, WM_CLEAR, 0, 0) ;
```

WM_CUT removes the current selection from the edit control and sends it to the clipboard. WM_COPY copies the selection to the clipboard but leaves it intact in the edit control. WM_CLEAR deletes the selection from the edit control without passing it to the clipboard.

You can also insert clipboard text into the edit control at the cursor position:

```
SendMessage (hwndEdit, WM_PASTE, 0, 0) ;
```

You can obtain the starting and ending positions of the current selection:

```
SendMessage (hwndEdit, EM_GETSEL, (WPARAM) &iStart,
                                  (LPARAM) &iEnd) ;
```

The ending position is actually the position of the last selected character plus 1. You can select text:

```
SendMessage (hwndEdit, EM_SETSEL, iStart, iEnd) ;
```

You can also replace a current selection with other text:

```
SendMessage (hwndEdit, EM_REPLACESEL, 0, (LPARAM) szString) ;
```

For multiline edit controls, you can obtain the number of lines:

```
iCount = SendMessage (hwndEdit, EM_GETLINECOUNT, 0, 0) ;
```

For any particular line, you can obtain an offset from the beginning of the edit buffer text:

```
iOffset = SendMessage (hwndEdit, EM_LINEINDEX, iLine, 0) ;
```

Lines are numbered starting at 0. An *iLine* value of -1 returns the offset of the line containing the cursor. You obtain the length of the line from:

```
iLength = SendMessage (hwndEdit, EM_LINELENGTH, iLine, 0) ;
```

and copy the line itself into a buffer using:

```
iLength = SendMessage (hwndEdit, EM_GETLINE, iLine,
                       (LPARAM) szBuffer) ;
```

THE LISTBOX CLASS

The final predefined child window control I'll discuss in this chapter is the list box. A list box is a collection of text strings displayed as a scrollable columnar list within a rectangle. A program can add or remove strings in the list by sending messages to the list box window procedure. The list box control sends WM_COMMAND messages to its parent window when an item in the list is selected. The parent window can then determine which item has been selected.

List boxes are most commonly used in dialog boxes, for example, the dialog box called up by selecting Open from the File menu. The list box displays files in the current directory and can also display other subdirectories. A list box can be either single selection or multiple selection. The latter allows the user to select more than one item from the list box. When a list box has the input focus, it displays a dashed line surrounding an item in the list box. This cursor does not indicate the selected item in the list box. The selected item is indicated by highlighting, which displays the item in reverse video.

In a single-selection list box, the user can select the item that the cursor is positioned on by pressing the Spacebar. The arrow keys move both the cursor and the current selection and can scroll the contents of the list box. The Page Up and Page Down keys also scroll the list box by moving the cursor but not the selection. Pressing a letter key moves the cursor and the selection to the first (or next) item that begins with that letter. An item can also be selected by clicking or double-clicking the mouse on the item.

In a multiple-selection list box, the Spacebar toggles the selection state of the item where the cursor is positioned. (If the item is already selected, it is deselected.) The arrow keys deselect all previously selected items and move the cursor and selection just as in single-selection list boxes. However, the Ctrl key and the arrow keys can move the cursor without moving the selection. The Shift key and arrow keys can extend a selection.

Clicking or double-clicking an item in a multiple-selection list box deselects all previously selected items and selects the clicked item. Clicking an item while pressing the Shift key, however, toggles the selection state of the item without changing the selection state of any other item.

List Box Styles

You create a list box child window control with *CreateWindow* using "listbox" as the window class and WS_CHILD as the window style. This default list box style, however, does not send WM_COMMAND messages to its parent, meaning that a program would have to interrogate the list box (via messages to the list box controls) regarding the selection of items within the list box. Therefore, list box controls almost always include the list box style identifier LBS_NOTIFY, which allows the parent window to receive WM_COMMAND messages from the list box. If you want the list box control to sort the items in the list box, you can also use LBS_SORT, another common style.

By default, list boxes are single selection. If you want to create a multiple-selection list box, you use the style LBS_MULTIPLESEL.

Normally, a list box updates itself when a new item is added to the scroll box list. You can prevent this by including the style LBS_NOREDRAW. You will probably not want to use this style, however. Instead, you can temporarily prevent repainting of a list box control by using the WM_SETREDRAW message that I'll describe a little later.

By default, the list box window procedure displays only the list of items without any border around it. You can add a border with the window style identifier WS_BORDER. And to add a vertical scroll bar for scrolling through the list with the mouse, you use the window style identifier WS_VSCROLL.

The Windows header files define a list box style called LBS_STANDARD that includes the most commonly used styles. It is defined as:

```
(LBS_NOTIFY ¦ LBS_SORT ¦ WS_VSCROLL ¦ WS_BORDER)
```

You can also use the WS_SIZEBOX and WS_CAPTION identifiers, but these will allow the user to resize the list box and to move it around its parent's client area.

The width of a list box should accommodate the width of the longest string plus the width of the scroll bar. You can get the width of the vertical scroll bar using:

```
GetSystemMetrics (SM_CXVSCROLL) ;
```

You can calculate the height of the list box by multiplying the height of a character by the number of items you want to appear in view. A list box does not use external leading when spacing lines of text.

Putting Strings in the List Box

After you've created the list box, the next step is to put text strings in it. You do this by sending messages to the list box window procedure using the *SendMessage* call. The text strings are generally referenced by an index number that starts at 0 for the topmost item. In the examples that follow, *hwndList* is the handle to the child window list box control, and *iIndex* is the index value. In cases where you pass a text string in the *SendMessage* call, the *lParam* parameter is a pointer to a null-terminated string.

In most of these examples, the *SendMessage* call can return LB_ERRSPACE (defined as −2) if the window procedure runs out of available memory space to store the contents of the list box. *SendMessage* returns LB_ERR (−1) if an error occurs for other reasons and LB_OKAY (0) if the operation is successful. You can test *SendMessage* for a nonzero value to detect either of the two errors.

If you use the LBS_SORT style (or if you are placing strings in the list box in the order that you want them to appear), the easiest way to fill up a list box is with the LB_ADDSTRING message:

```
SendMessage (hwndList, LB_ADDSTRING, 0, (LPARAM) szString) ;
```

If you do not use LBS_SORT, you can insert strings into your list box by specifying an index value with LB_INSERTSTRING:

```
SendMessage (hwndList, LB_INSERTSTRING, iIndex, (LPARAM) szString) ;
```

For instance, if *iIndex* is equal to 4, *szString* becomes the new string with an index value of 4—the fifth string from the top (because counting starts at 0). Any strings below this point are pushed down. An *iIndex* value of −1 adds the string to the bottom. You can use LB_INSERTSTRING with list boxes that have the LBS_SORT style, but the list box contents will not be re-sorted. (You can also insert strings into a list box using the LB_DIR message, which is discussed in detail toward the end of this chapter.)

You can delete a string from the list box by specifying the index value with the LB_DELETESTRING message:

```
SendMessage (hwndList, LB_DELETESTRING, iIndex, 0) ;
```

You can clear out the list box using LB_RESETCONTENT:

```
SendMessage (hwndList, LB_RESETCONTENT, 0, 0) ;
```

The list box window procedure updates the display when an item is added to or deleted from the list box. If you have a number of strings to add or delete, you may want to temporarily inhibit this action by turning off the control's redraw flag:

```
SendMessage (hwndList, WM_SETREDRAW, FALSE, 0) ;
```

After you've finished, you can turn the redraw flag back on:

```
SendMessage (hwndList, WM_SETREDRAW, TRUE, 0) ;
```

A list box created with the LBS_NOREDRAW style begins with the redraw flag turned off.

Selecting and Extracting Entries

The *SendMessage* calls that carry out the tasks shown below usually return a value. If an error occurs, this value is set to LB_ERR (defined as −1).

After you've put some items into a list box, you can find out how many items are in the list box:

```
iCount = SendMessage (hwndList, LB_GETCOUNT, 0, 0) ;
```

Some of the other calls are different for single-selection and multiple-selection list boxes. Let's first look at single-selection list boxes.

Normally, you'll let a user select from a list box. But if you want to highlight a default selection, you can use:

```
SendMessage (hwndList, LB_SETCURSEL, iIndex, 0) ;
```

Setting *iIndex* to −1 in this call deselects all items.

You can also select an item based on its initial characters:

```
iIndex = SendMessage (hwndList, LB_SELECTSTRING, iIndex,
                      (LPARAM) szSearchString) ;
```

The *iIndex* given as the *lParam* parameter to the *SendMessage* call is the index following which the search begins for an item with initial characters that match *szSearchString*. An *iIndex* value of −1 starts the search from the top. *SendMessage* returns the index of the selected item, or LB_ERR if no initial characters match *szSearchString*.

When you get a WM_COMMAND message from the list box (or at any other time), you can determine the index of the current selection using LB_GETCURSEL:

```
iIndex = SendMessage (hwndList, LB_GETCURSEL, 0, 0) ;
```

The *iIndex* value returned from the call is LB_ERR if no item is selected.

You can determine the length of any string in the list box:

```
iLength = SendMessage (hwndList, LB_GETTEXTLEN, iIndex, 0) ;
```

and copy the item into the text buffer:

```
iLength = SendMessage (hwndList, LB_GETTEXT, iIndex,
                       (LPARAM) szBuffer) ;
```

In both cases, the *iLength* value returned from the call is the length of the string. The *szBuffer* array must be large enough for the length of the string and a terminating NULL. You may want to use LB_GETTEXTLEN to first allocate some memory to hold the string.

For a multiple-selection list box, you cannot use LB_SETCURSEL, LB_GETCURSEL, or LB_SELECTSTRING. Instead, you use LB_SETSEL to set the selection state of a particular item without affecting other items that may also be selected:

```
SendMessage (hwndList, LB_SETSEL, wParam, iIndex) ;
```

The *wParam* parameter is nonzero to select and highlight the item and 0 to deselect it. If the *lParam* parameter is −1, all items are either selected or deselected. You can also determine the selection state of a particular item using:

```
iSelect = SendMessage (hwndList, LB_GETSEL, iIndex, 0) ;
```

where *iSelect* is set to nonzero if the item indexed by *iIndex* is selected and 0 if it is not.

Receiving Messages from List Boxes

When a user clicks on a list box with the mouse, the list box receives the input focus. A parent window can give the input focus to a list box control by using:

```
SetFocus (hwndList) ;
```

When a list box has the input focus, the cursor movement keys, letter keys, and Spacebar can also be used to select items from the list box.

A list box control sends WM_COMMAND messages to its parent. The meanings of the *wParam* and *lParam* variables are the same as for the button and edit controls:

LOWORD (*wParam*)	Child window ID
HIWORD (*wParam*)	Notification code
lParam	Child window handle

The notification codes and their values are as follows:

LBN_ERRSPACE	−2
LBN_SELCHANGE	1
LBN_DBLCLK	2
LBN_SELCANCEL	3
LBN_SETFOCUS	4
LBN_KILLFOCUS	5

The list box control sends the parent window LBN_SELCHANGE and LBN_DBLCLK codes only if the list box window style includes LBS_NOTIFY.

The LBN_ERRSPACE code indicates that the list box control has run out of space. The LBN_SELCHANGE code indicates that the current selection has changed; these messages occur as the user moves the highlight through the list box, toggles the selection state with the Spacebar, or clicks an item with the mouse. The LBN_DBLCLK code indicates that a list box item has been double-clicked with the mouse. (The notification code values for LBN_SELCHANGE and LBN_DBLCLK refer to the number of mouse clicks.)

Depending on your application, you may want to use either LBN_SELCHANGE or LBN_DBLCLK messages or both. Your program will get many LBN_SELCHANGE messages, but LBN_DBLCLK messages occur only when the user double-clicks with the mouse. If your program uses double-clicks, you'll need to provide a keyboard interface that duplicates LBN_DBLCLK.

A Simple List Box Application

Now that you know how to create a list box, fill it with text items, receive messages from the list box, and extract strings, it's time to program an application. The ENVIRON program, shown in Figure 8-8, uses a list box in its client area to display the name of your current MS-DOS environment variables (such as PATH, COMSPEC, and PROMPT). As you select a variable, the name and the environment string are displayed across the top of the client area.

ENVIRON.MAK

```
#----------------------
# ENVIRON.MAK make file
#----------------------

environ.exe : environ.obj
     $(LINKER) $(GUIFLAGS) -OUT:environ.exe environ.obj $(GUILIBS)

environ.obj : environ.c
     $(CC) $(CFLAGS) environ.c
```

ENVIRON.C

```
/*-------------------------------------------
   ENVIRON.C -- Environment List Box
                (c) Charles Petzold, 1996
   -------------------------------------------*/

#include <windows.h>
#include <stdlib.h>
#include <string.h>

#define  MAXENV   4096
```

Figure 8-8. *The ENVIRON program.*

(continued)

```
LRESULT CALLBACK WndProc (HWND, UINT, WPARAM, LPARAM) ;

int WINAPI WinMain (HINSTANCE hInstance, HINSTANCE hPrevInstance,
                    PSTR szCmdLine, int iCmdShow)
     {
     static char szAppName[] = "Environ" ;
     HWND        hwnd ;
     MSG         msg ;
     WNDCLASSEX  wndclass ;

     wndclass.cbSize        = sizeof (wndclass) ;
     wndclass.style         = CS_HREDRAW | CS_VREDRAW ;
     wndclass.lpfnWndProc   = WndProc ;
     wndclass.cbClsExtra    = 0 ;
     wndclass.cbWndExtra    = 0 ;
     wndclass.hInstance     = hInstance ;
     wndclass.hIcon         = LoadIcon (NULL, IDI_APPLICATION) ;
     wndclass.hCursor       = LoadCursor (NULL, IDC_ARROW) ;
     wndclass.hbrBackground = (HBRUSH) (COLOR_WINDOW + 1) ;
     wndclass.lpszMenuName  = NULL ;
     wndclass.lpszClassName = szAppName ;
     wndclass.hIconSm       = LoadIcon (NULL, IDI_APPLICATION) ;

     RegisterClassEx (&wndclass) ;

     hwnd = CreateWindow (szAppName, "Environment List Box",
                          WS_OVERLAPPEDWINDOW,
                          CW_USEDEFAULT, CW_USEDEFAULT,
                          CW_USEDEFAULT, CW_USEDEFAULT,
                          NULL, NULL, hInstance, NULL) ;

     ShowWindow (hwnd, iCmdShow) ;
     UpdateWindow (hwnd) ;

     while (GetMessage (&msg, NULL, 0, 0))
          {
          TranslateMessage (&msg) ;
          DispatchMessage (&msg) ;
          }
     return msg.wParam ;
     }

LRESULT CALLBACK WndProc (HWND hwnd, UINT iMsg, WPARAM wParam, LPARAM lParam)
     {
     static char szBuffer[MAXENV + 1] ;
     static HWND hwndList, hwndText ;
     HDC         hdc ;
```

(continued)

```
int        i ;
TEXTMETRIC  tm ;

switch (iMsg)
     {
     case WM_CREATE :
          hdc = GetDC (hwnd) ;
          GetTextMetrics (hdc, &tm) ;
          ReleaseDC (hwnd, hdc) ;

          hwndList = CreateWindow ("listbox", NULL,
                         WS_CHILD | WS_VISIBLE | LBS_STANDARD,
                         tm.tmAveCharWidth, tm.tmHeight * 3,
                         tm.tmAveCharWidth * 16 +
                              GetSystemMetrics (SM_CXVSCROLL),
                         tm.tmHeight * 5,
                         hwnd, (HMENU) 1,
                         (HINSTANCE) GetWindowLong (hwnd,
                                             GWL_HINSTANCE),
                         NULL) ;

          hwndText = CreateWindow ("static", NULL,
                         WS_CHILD | WS_VISIBLE | SS_LEFT,
                         tm.tmAveCharWidth,          tm.tmHeight,
                         tm.tmAveCharWidth * MAXENV, tm.tmHeight,
                         hwnd, (HMENU) 2,
                         (HINSTANCE) GetWindowLong (hwnd,
                                             GWL_HINSTANCE),
                         NULL) ;

          for (i = 0 ; environ[i] ; i++)
               {
               if (strlen (environ[i]) > MAXENV)
                    continue ;
               *strchr (strcpy (szBuffer, environ [i]), '=') = '\0' ;
               SendMessage (hwndList, LB_ADDSTRING, 0,
                              (LPARAM) szBuffer) ;
               }
          return 0 ;

     case WM_SETFOCUS :
          SetFocus (hwndList) ;
          return 0 ;

     case WM_COMMAND :
          if (LOWORD (wParam) == 1 && HIWORD (wParam) == LBN_SELCHANGE)
```

(continued)

```
                         {
                         i = SendMessage (hwndList, LB_GETCURSEL, 0, 0) ;
                         i = SendMessage (hwndList, LB_GETTEXT, i,
                                                       (LPARAM) szBuffer) ;

                         strcpy (szBuffer + i + 1, getenv (szBuffer)) ;
                         *(szBuffer + i) = '=' ;

                         SetWindowText (hwndText, szBuffer) ;
                         }
                    return 0 ;

               case WM_DESTROY :
                    PostQuitMessage (0) ;
                    return 0 ;
               }
          return DefWindowProc (hwnd, iMsg, wParam, lParam) ;
          }
```

ENVIRON creates two child windows: a list box with the style LBS_STANDARD and a static window with the style SS_LEFT (left-justified text). ENVIRON uses the *environ* variable (declared external in STDLIB.H) to obtain the list of environment strings, and it uses the message LB_ADDSTRING to direct the list box window procedure to place each string in the list box.

When you run ENVIRON, you can select an environment variable using the mouse or the keyboard. Each time you change the selection, the list box sends a WM_COMMAND message to the parent window, which is *WndProc*. When *WndProc* receives a WM-_COMMAND message, it checks to see whether the low word of *wParam* is 1 (the child ID of the list box) and whether the high word of *wParam* (the notification code) is equal to LBN_SELCHANGE. If so, it obtains the index of the selection using the LB_GETCURSEL message and the text itself—the environment variable name—using LB_GETTEXT. The ENVIRON program uses the C function *getenv* to obtain the environment string corresponding to that variable and *SetWindowText* to pass this string to the static child window control, which displays the text.

Note that ENVIRON cannot use the index returned from LB_GETCURSEL to index the *environ* variable and obtain the environment string. Because the list box has an LBS_SORT style (included in LBS_STANDARD), the indices no longer match.

Listing Files

I've been saving the best for last: LB_DIR, the most powerful list box message. This fills the list box with a file directory list, optionally including subdirectories and valid disk drives:

```
SendMessage (hwndList, LB_DIR, iAttr, (LPARAM) szFileSpec) ;
```

Using file attribute codes

The *iAttr* parameter is a file attribute code. The least significant byte is the normal file attribute code when making MS-DOS function calls:

iAttr	Value	Attribute
DDL_READWRITE	0x0000	Normal file
DDL_READONLY	0x0001	Read-only file
DDL_HIDDEN	0x0002	Hidden file
DDL_SYSTEM	0x0004	System file
DDL_DIRECTORY	0x0010	Subdirectory
DDL_ARCHIVE	0x0020	File with archive bit set

The next highest byte provides a little bit of additional control over the items desired:

iAttr	Value	Option
DDL_DRIVES	0x4000	Include drive letters
DDL_EXCLUSIVE	0x8000	Exclusive search only

When the *iAttr* value of the LB_DIR message is DDL_READWRITE, the list box lists normal files, read-only files, and files with the archive bit set. This is consistent with the logic used by MS-DOS function calls to find files. When the value is DDL_DIRECTORY, the list includes child subdirectories in addition to these files with the directory names in square brackets. A value of DDL_DRIVES ¦ DDL_DIRECTORY expands the list to include all valid drives where the drive letters are shown between dashes.

Setting the topmost bit of *iAttr* lists the files with the indicated flag while excluding normal files. For a Windows file backup program, for instance, you might want to list only files that have been modified since the last backup. Such files have their archive bits set, so you would use DDL_EXCLUSIVE ¦ DDL_ARCHIVE.

Ordering file lists

The *lParam* parameter is a pointer to a file specification string such as "*.*". This file specification does not affect the subdirectories that the list box includes.

You'll want to use the LBS_SORT message for list boxes with file lists. The list box will first list files satisfying the file specification and then (optionally) list valid disk drives in the form:

```
[-A-]
```

411

and (also optionally) subdirectory names. The first subdirectory listing will take the form:

```
[..]
```

This "double-dot" subdirectory entry lets the user back up one level toward the root directory. (The entry will not appear if you're listing files in the root directory.) Finally, the specific subdirectory names are listed in the form:

```
[SUBDIR]
```

If you do not use LBS_SORT, the filenames and subdirectory names are intermixed and the drive letters appear at the bottom of the list box.

A *Head* for Windows

A well-known UNIX utility called *head* displays the beginning lines of a file. Let's use a list box to write a similar program for Windows. HEAD, shown in Figure 8-9, lists all files and child subdirectories in the list box. You can choose a file to display by double-clicking on the filename with the mouse or by pressing the Enter key when the filename is selected. You can also change the subdirectory using either of these methods. The program displays up to 8 KB of the beginning of the file in the right side of the client area of HEAD's window.

```
HEAD.MAK

#--------------------
# HEAD.MAK make file
#--------------------

head.exe : head.obj
     $(LINKER) $(GUIFLAGS) -OUT:head.exe head.obj $(GUILIBS)

head.obj : head.c
     $(CC) $(CFLAGS) head.c
```

```
HEAD.C

/*-----------------------------------------------------
   HEAD.C -- Displays beginning (head) of file
             (c) Charles Petzold, 1996
   -----------------------------------------------*/

#include <windows.h>
#include <string.h>
#include <direct.h>
```

Figure 8-9. *The HEAD program.*

(continued)

```
#define  MAXPATH    256
#define  MAXREAD    8192

LRESULT CALLBACK WndProc  (HWND, UINT, WPARAM, LPARAM) ;
LRESULT CALLBACK ListProc (HWND, UINT, WPARAM, LPARAM) ;

WNDPROC fnOldList ;

int WINAPI WinMain (HINSTANCE hInstance, HINSTANCE hPrevInstance,
                    PSTR szCmdLine, int iCmdShow)
     {
     static char szAppName[] = "Head" ;
     HWND        hwnd ;
     MSG         msg ;
     WNDCLASSEX  wndclass ;

     wndclass.cbSize        = sizeof (wndclass) ;
     wndclass.style         = CS_HREDRAW | CS_VREDRAW ;
     wndclass.lpfnWndProc   = WndProc ;
     wndclass.cbClsExtra    = 0 ;
     wndclass.cbWndExtra    = 0 ;
     wndclass.hInstance     = hInstance ;
     wndclass.hIcon         = LoadIcon (NULL, IDI_APPLICATION) ;
     wndclass.hCursor       = LoadCursor (NULL, IDC_ARROW) ;
     wndclass.hbrBackground = (HBRUSH) (COLOR_BTNFACE + 1) ;
     wndclass.lpszMenuName  = NULL ;
     wndclass.lpszClassName = szAppName ;
     wndclass.hIcon         = LoadIcon (NULL, IDI_APPLICATION) ;

     RegisterClassEx (&wndclass) ;

     hwnd = CreateWindow (szAppName, "File Head",
                          WS_OVERLAPPEDWINDOW | WS_CLIPCHILDREN,
                          CW_USEDEFAULT, CW_USEDEFAULT,
                          CW_USEDEFAULT, CW_USEDEFAULT,
                          NULL, NULL, hInstance, NULL) ;

     ShowWindow (hwnd, iCmdShow) ;
     UpdateWindow (hwnd) ;

     while (GetMessage (&msg, NULL, 0, 0))
          {
          TranslateMessage (&msg) ;
          DispatchMessage (&msg) ;
          }
     return msg.wParam ;
     }
```

(continued)

```
LRESULT CALLBACK WndProc (HWND hwnd, UINT iMsg, WPARAM wParam, LPARAM lParam)
     {
     static BOOL      bValidFile ;
     static char      sReadBuffer[MAXREAD], szFile[MAXPATH] ;
     static HWND      hwndList, hwndText ;
     static OFSTRUCT  ofs ;
     static RECT      rect ;
     char             szBuffer[MAXPATH + 1] ;
     HDC              hdc ;
     int              iHandle, i ;
     PAINTSTRUCT      ps ;
     TEXTMETRIC       tm ;

     switch (iMsg)
          {
          case WM_CREATE :
               hdc = GetDC (hwnd) ;
               SelectObject (hdc, GetStockObject (SYSTEM_FIXED_FONT)) ;
               GetTextMetrics (hdc, &tm) ;
               ReleaseDC (hwnd, hdc) ;

               rect.left = 20 * tm.tmAveCharWidth ;
               rect.top  =  3 * tm.tmHeight ;

               hwndList = CreateWindow ("listbox", NULL,
                         WS_CHILDWINDOW | WS_VISIBLE | LBS_STANDARD,
                         tm.tmAveCharWidth, tm.tmHeight * 3,
                         tm.tmAveCharWidth * 13 +
                              GetSystemMetrics (SM_CXVSCROLL),
                         tm.tmHeight * 10,
                         hwnd, (HMENU) 1,
                         (HINSTANCE) GetWindowLong (hwnd,
                                                 GWL_HINSTANCE),
                         NULL) ;

               hwndText = CreateWindow ("static",
                         getcwd (szBuffer, MAXPATH),
                         WS_CHILDWINDOW | WS_VISIBLE | SS_LEFT,
                         tm.tmAveCharWidth,             tm.tmHeight,
                         tm.tmAveCharWidth * MAXPATH, tm.tmHeight,
                         hwnd, (HMENU) 2,
                         (HINSTANCE) GetWindowLong (hwnd,
                                                 GWL_HINSTANCE),
                         NULL) ;
```

(continued)

```
        fnOldList = (WNDPROC) SetWindowLong (hwndList, GWL_WNDPROC,
                                          (LPARAM) ListProc) ;

     SendMessage (hwndList, LB_DIR, 0x37, (LPARAM) "*.*") ;
     return 0 ;

case WM_SIZE :
     rect.right  = LOWORD (lParam) ;
     rect.bottom = HIWORD (lParam) ;
     return 0 ;

case WM_SETFOCUS :
     SetFocus (hwndList) ;
     return 0 ;

case WM_COMMAND :
     if (LOWORD (wParam) == 1 && HIWORD (wParam) == LBN_DBLCLK)
          {
          if (LB_ERR == (i = SendMessage (hwndList,
                                    LB_GETCURSEL, 0, 0L)))
               break ;

          SendMessage (hwndList, LB_GETTEXT, i,
                       (LPARAM) szBuffer) ;

          if (-1 != OpenFile (szBuffer, &ofs, OF_EXIST | OF_READ))
               {
               bValidFile = TRUE ;
               strcpy (szFile, szBuffer) ;
               getcwd (szBuffer, MAXPATH) ;
               if (szBuffer [strlen (szBuffer) - 1] != '\\')
                    strcat (szBuffer, "\\") ;
               SetWindowText (hwndText,
                              strcat (szBuffer, szFile)) ;
               }
          else
               {
               bValidFile = FALSE ;
               szBuffer [strlen (szBuffer) - 1] = '\0' ;
               chdir (szBuffer + 1) ;
               getcwd (szBuffer, MAXPATH) ;
               SetWindowText (hwndText, szBuffer) ;
               SendMessage (hwndList, LB_RESETCONTENT, 0, 0L) ;
               SendMessage (hwndList, LB_DIR, 0x37,
                            (LONG) "*.*") ;
               }
```

(continued)

```
                        InvalidateRect (hwnd, NULL, TRUE) ;
                        }
                   return 0 ;

              case WM_PAINT :
                   hdc = BeginPaint (hwnd, &ps) ;
                   SelectObject (hdc, GetStockObject (SYSTEM_FIXED_FONT)) ;
                   SetTextColor (hdc, GetSysColor (COLOR_BTNTEXT)) ;
                   SetBkColor   (hdc, GetSysColor (COLOR_BTNFACE)) ;

                   if (bValidFile && -1 != (iHandle =
                             OpenFile (szFile, &ofs, OF_REOPEN | OF_READ)))
                        {
                        i = _lread (iHandle, sReadBuffer, MAXREAD) ;
                        _lclose (iHandle) ;
                        DrawText (hdc, sReadBuffer, i, &rect, DT_WORDBREAK |
                             DT_EXPANDTABS | DT_NOCLIP | DT_NOPREFIX) ;
                        }
                   else
                        bValidFile = FALSE ;

                   EndPaint (hwnd, &ps) ;
                   return 0 ;

              case WM_DESTROY :
                   PostQuitMessage (0) ;
                   return 0 ;
              }
         return DefWindowProc (hwnd, iMsg, wParam, lParam) ;
         }

LRESULT CALLBACK ListProc (HWND hwnd, UINT iMsg, WPARAM wParam, LPARAM lParam)
     {
     if (iMsg == WM_KEYDOWN && wParam == VK_RETURN)

          SendMessage (GetParent (hwnd), WM_COMMAND, 1,
                    MAKELONG (hwnd, LBN_DBLCLK)) ;

     return CallWindowProc (fnOldList, hwnd, iMsg, wParam, lParam) ;
     }
```

In ENVIRON, when we selected an environment variable—either with a mouse click or with the keyboard—the program displayed an environment string. However, if we used this select-display approach in HEAD, the program would be too slow because it would continually need to open and close files as you moved the selection through the list box. Instead, HEAD requires that the file or subdirectory be double-clicked. This presents a bit of a problem because list box controls have no automatic keyboard interface that corresponds to a mouse double-click. As we know, we should provide keyboard interfaces when possible.

The solution? Window subclassing, of course. The list box subclass function in HEAD is called *ListProc*. It simply looks for a WM_KEYDOWN message with *wParam* equal to VK_RETURN and sends a WM_COMMAND message with an LBN_DBLCLK notification code back to the parent. The WM_COMMAND processing in *WndProc* uses the Windows function *OpenFile* to check for the selection from the list. If *OpenFile* returns an error, the selection is not a file, so it's probably a subdirectory. HEAD then uses *chdir* to change the subdirectory. It sends an LB_RESETCONTENT message to the list box to clear out the contents and an LB_DIR message to fill the list box with files from the new subdirectory.

The WM_PAINT message processing in *WndProc* opens the file using the Windows *OpenFile* function. This returns an MS-DOS handle to the file that can be passed to the Windows functions *_lread* and *_lclose*. The contents of the file are displayed using *DrawText*.

Section III

Using Resources

Chapter 9

Icons, Cursors, Bitmaps, and Strings

Most Windows-based programs include a customized icon that Windows displays in the upper left corner of the title bar of the application window. Windows also displays a program's icon when the program is listed in the Start menu or shown in the task bar at the bottom of the screen or listed in Windows Explorer. Some programs—most notably graphical drawing tools such as Windows Paint—use customized mouse cursors to represent different operations of the program. Very many Windows programs use menus and dialog boxes. Along with scroll bars, menus and dialog boxes are the bread and butter of the standardized Windows user interface.

Icons, cursors, menus, and dialog boxes are all related. They are all types of Windows "resources." Resources are data and they are stored in a program's .EXE file, but they do not reside in what we normally think of as an executable program's data area. That is, the resources are not immediately accessible using variables defined in the program source code. They must be explicitly loaded into memory from the .EXE file.

When Windows loads a program's code and data into memory for execution, it usually leaves the resources on disk. Only when Windows needs a particular resource does it load the resource into memory. Indeed, you may have noticed this dynamic loading of resources when working with Windows programs. When you invoke a program's dialog box for the first time, Windows usually accesses the disk to copy the dialog box resource from the program's .EXE file into memory.

In this book I'll be discussing these resources:

- Icons

- Cursors

- Bitmaps

- Character strings

- User-defined resources

- Menus

- Keyboard accelerators

- Dialog boxes

The first five resources in the list are discussed in this chapter. Menus and keyboard accelerators are covered in Chapter 10 and dialog boxes in Chapter 11.

COMPILING RESOURCES

During program development, resources are defined in a "resource script," which is an ASCII text file with the extension .RC. The resource script can contain ASCII representations of resources and can also reference other files (either ASCII or binary files) that contain other resources. The resource compiler (RC.EXE) compiles the resource script into a binary form, which is a file with the extension .RES. By specifying the .RES file in the LINK command line, you can cause LINK to include the compiled resources in the .EXE file along with the normal program code and data from the .OBJ and .LIB files.

On a command line, you can compile a .RC resource script into a binary .RES file by executing:

```
RC -r -DWIN32 filename.RC
```

This command creates a binary file named *filename.RES*. Most Windows programmers give the resource script the same name as the program itself.

In the command line shown above, the -r parameter causes the resource compiler to create the .RES file and store it on disk. This is optional, but it's almost always what you want to do. The -DWIN32 parameter defines a constant (WIN32) that indicates that the compiled resources should be stored in the 32-bit file format appropriate for Windows 95 and Windows NT. One implication of defining the WIN32 constant is that text strings appearing in menus and dialog boxes are stored in Unicode format, with 2 bytes per character. If you do a hexadecimal dump of a .RES file, you'll see all the ASCII characters in menu and dialog box text separated by zeros. Don't be alarmed—it's normal.

Prior to Windows 95, the resource compiler was also responsible for adding the compiled resources to the .EXE file created by the linker. The linker provided with the Windows 95 version of Visual C++ performs the entire job. Simply include the .RES filename along with the .OBJ file (or files) in the LINK command line.

The procedure of compiling resources is reflected in a new section of our by-now familiar make file. Along with compiling the .C source code files, you compile the resources like so:

```
progname.res : progname.rc [progname.h] [and other files]
    $(RC) $(RCVARS) progname.rc
```

The RC and RCVARS macros are defined by environment variables to be "rc" and "-r -DWIN32", respectively. I've indicated that a .H header file may also be a dependent file. Within the resource script, you can indeed include a header file. This header file is usually also included in the .C source code file and defines identifiers used by the program to reference the resources. I've also indicated that the dependent file list possibly includes "other files." These are files referenced from within the resource script. Generally, they are binary files that contain icons, cursors, or bitmap images.

The RC.EXE resource compiler uses a preprocessor that can fold added or subtracted constants, recognize /* and */ as comment delimiters, and recognize the C preprocessor directives *#define, #undef, #ifdef, #ifndef, #include, #if, #elif, #else,* and *#endif.* The *#include* directive works a little differently than in normal C programs. (We'll examine this in greater detail in Chapter 11.)

When using resources, another change in the make file is that the .RES file (along with any .OBJ files) becomes a dependent file for the .EXE target.

ICONS AND CURSORS

Let's begin by looking at a sample program that uses two resources—an icon and a cursor. RESOURC1, shown in Figure 9-1, displays a customized icon when the program is minimized and uses a customized cursor when the mouse is in RESOURC1's client area. RESOURC1 also draws its icon in several rows and columns within the client area.

RESOURC1.MAK

```
#-----------------------
# RESOURC1.MAK make file
#-----------------------

resourc1.exe : resourc1.obj resourc1.res
    $(LINKER) $(GUIFLAGS) -OUT:resourc1.exe \
    resourc1.obj resourc1.res $(GUILIBS)
```

Figure 9-1. *The RESOURC1 program, including an icon and a cursor.* (continued)

```
resourc1.obj : resourc1.c
    $(CC) $(CFLAGS) resourc1.c

resourc1.res : resourc1.rc resourc1.ico resourc1.cur
    $(RC) $(RCVARS) resourc1.rc
```

RESOURC1.C

```c
/*---------------------------------------------------------------
    RESOURC1.C -- Icon and Cursor Demonstration Program No. 1
                  (c) Charles Petzold, 1996
   ---------------------------------------------------------------*/

#include <windows.h>

LRESULT CALLBACK WndProc (HWND, UINT, WPARAM, LPARAM) ;

char       szAppName[] = "Resourc1" ;
HINSTANCE hInst ;

int WINAPI WinMain (HINSTANCE hInstance, HINSTANCE hPrevInstance,
                    PSTR szCmdLine, int iCmdShow)
    {
    HWND        hwnd ;
    MSG         msg ;
    WNDCLASSEX wndclass ;

    wndclass.cbSize        = sizeof (wndclass) ;
    wndclass.style         = CS_HREDRAW | CS_VREDRAW ;
    wndclass.lpfnWndProc   = WndProc ;
    wndclass.cbClsExtra    = 0 ;
    wndclass.cbWndExtra    = 0 ;
    wndclass.hInstance     = hInstance ;
    wndclass.hIcon         = LoadIcon (hInstance, szAppName) ;
    wndclass.hCursor       = LoadCursor (hInstance, szAppName) ;
    wndclass.hbrBackground = (HBRUSH) (COLOR_WINDOW + 1) ;
    wndclass.lpszMenuName  = NULL ;
    wndclass.lpszClassName = szAppName ;
    wndclass.hIconSm       = LoadIcon (hInstance, szAppName) ;

    RegisterClassEx (&wndclass) ;

    hInst = hInstance ;
```

(continued)

424

```
        hwnd = CreateWindow (szAppName, "Icon and Cursor Demo",
                        WS_OVERLAPPEDWINDOW,
                        CW_USEDEFAULT, CW_USEDEFAULT,
                        CW_USEDEFAULT, CW_USEDEFAULT,
                        NULL, NULL, hInstance, NULL) ;

     ShowWindow (hwnd, iCmdShow) ;
     UpdateWindow (hwnd) ;

     while (GetMessage (&msg, NULL, 0, 0))
          {
          TranslateMessage (&msg) ;
          DispatchMessage (&msg) ;
          }
     return msg.wParam ;
     }

LRESULT CALLBACK WndProc (HWND hwnd, UINT iMsg, WPARAM wParam, LPARAM lParam)
     {
     static HICON hIcon ;
     static int   cxIcon, cyIcon, cxClient, cyClient ;
     HDC          hdc ;
     PAINTSTRUCT  ps ;
     int          x, y ;

     switch (iMsg)
          {
          case WM_CREATE :
               hIcon = LoadIcon (hInst, szAppName) ;
               cxIcon = GetSystemMetrics (SM_CXICON) ;
               cyIcon = GetSystemMetrics (SM_CYICON) ;
               return 0 ;

          case WM_SIZE :
               cxClient = LOWORD (lParam) ;
               cyClient = HIWORD (lParam) ;
               return 0 ;

          case WM_PAINT :
               hdc = BeginPaint (hwnd, &ps) ;

               for (y = cyIcon ; y < cyClient ; y += 2 * cyIcon)
                    for (x = cxIcon ; x < cxClient ; x += 2 * cxIcon)
                         DrawIcon (hdc, x, y, hIcon) ;
```

(continued)

```
            EndPaint (hwnd, &ps) ;
            return 0 ;

      case WM_DESTROY :
            PostQuitMessage (0) ;
            return 0 ;
      }
   return DefWindowProc (hwnd, iMsg, wParam, lParam) ;
   }
```

RESOURC1.RC

```
/*-------------------------------
   RESOURC1.RC resource script
   ----------------------------*/

resourc1  ICON    resourc1.ico
resourc1  CURSOR  resourc1.cur
```

RESOURC1.ICO

RESOURC1.CUR

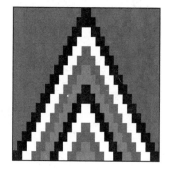

You can create icons and cursors using Microsoft Developer Studio or any other integrated development environment for Windows. They are saved in a binary format. Icons have an .ICO extension and cursors have a .CUR extension. These files are referred to in the RESOURC1.RC resource script.

The Image Editor

The tool you use to create icons, cursors, and bitmaps is often called an "image editor," and it is one of the most important development tools in any Windows integrated development environment. Icons and cursors are both variations of bitmaps, so it will be helpful to examine bitmaps first.

A "bitmap" is an array of bits where one or more bits corresponds to each display pixel. In a monochrome bitmap, each pixel requires one bit. (In the simplest case, a 1 bit represents white and a 0 bit represents black. However, bitmaps are often used in logical operations rather than merely to create simple drawings.) In a color bitmap, multiple bits correspond to each pixel to represent color. Image editors generally support the creation of monochrome bitmaps and 16-color bitmaps. In a 16-color bitmap, 4 bits are required for each pixel.

A bitmap may have any number of rows and columns, but some image editors may limit the size they can manage. Bitmaps are stored in files with a .BMP extension. You can also create icons and cursors in an image editor.

In theory, Windows displays icons and cursors on the screen in a pixel size that depends on the resolution of the video display. This ensures that the icons and cursors are neither too large nor too small. However, due to the overwhelming preponderance of Video Graphics Array (VGA) video adaptors using a screen size of 640 pixels horizontally by 480 pixels vertically, icon and cursor sizes are now not quite as variable as they used to be.

Under Windows 95, there are two sizes of icons—standard and small. On a VGA display, the standard icons are 32 pixels wide by 32 pixels high and the small icons are 16 pixels square. The small icons are used at the left of an application's title bar to invoke the system menu, in the system task bar at the bottom of the screen, and in the program listings in the Start menu. The icons appearing on the desktop are standard size. In Windows Explorer, and in the Start menu, a user can optionally select standard or small icons.

A program can obtain the horizontal (X) and vertical (Y) pixel dimensions of icons and cursors using the *GetSystemMetrics* function with parameters of SM_CXICON and SM_CYICON (for regular icons), SM_CXSMICON and SM_CYSMICON (for small icons), and SM_CXCURSOR and SM_CYCURSOR for mouse cursors. On most video displays, the dimensions of regular icons and cursors are identical.

The image editor included in Developer Studio can create an .ICO file with up to three different icon images:

- Standard: 32 pixels square with 16 colors
- Monochrome: 32 pixels square in black and white
- Small: 16 pixels square with 16 colors

The icons and cursor shown in the programs in this chapter are all monochrome. You don't need to create icon images in all three formats. Internally, Windows can create a small icon from a standard icon by simply eliminating every other row and column. On monochrome displays (now almost entirely obsolete), Windows can approximate the colors using gray shades.

When you create an icon image in one of the three formats, the image editor actually stores it as two bitmaps—a monochrome bitmap "mask" and a monochrome or color bitmap image. Icons are always rectangular, but this mask allows the icon to appear to be nonrectangular. That is, part of the icon allows the background against which the icon is displayed to be visible. The icon can also contain areas that invert the background color. For a monochrome icon, the following table shows how the image editor constructs the two bitmaps that describe the icon:

Color:	Black	White	Screen	Inverse Screen
Mask Bitmap:	0	0	1	1
Image Bitmap:	0	1	0	1

When displaying the icon, Windows first uses a bitwise AND operation of the display and the first bitmap. The display pixels corresponding to 0 bits from the first bitmap all become 0s, which are black. The display pixels corresponding to 1 bits remain the same. This is shown in the following logic table:

	Display Pixel	
Mask Bit	0	1
0	0	0
1	0	1

Next, Windows performs a bitwise exclusive OR operation of the image bitmap and the display. A 0 in the second bitmap leaves the display pixel the same; a 1 in the second bitmap inverts the display pixel. Here's the logic table:

	Display Pixel	
Image Bit	***0***	***1***
0	0	1
1	1	0

Using C notation for the operations, the display is altered by the following formula:

```
Display = (Display & Mask) ^ Image
```

For a 16-color icon, the mask bitmap is still monochrome and constructed as shown above. The image bitmap contains 4 bits per pixel to represent 16 colors. All four bits are set to 1 for areas of the icon that invert the background.

Earlier I said that when talking about bitmaps, 0 does not necessarily mean black, and 1 does not necessarily mean white. As you can see here, it depends on how Windows uses the bitmaps.

In RESOURC1, I've defined the window class to make the background of the client area be COLOR_WINDOW. You may want to change the window color in the Windows Control Panel to see how the icon and cursor invert colors.

Getting a Handle on Icons

A resource script references the icon file with a statement that looks like this:

```
myicon ICON iconfile.ico
```

where ICONFILE.ICO is the name of the icon file. This statement assigns the name "myicon" to the icon. In your C program, you use the *LoadIcon* function to obtain a handle to the icon. *LoadIcon* requires two parameters. The first is the instance handle of your program, generally called *hInstance* in *WinMain*. Windows needs this handle to determine which .EXE file contains the icon resource. The second parameter is the icon name from the resource script, in the form of a pointer to a null-terminated string. *LoadIcon* returns a value of type HICON, which is defined in WINDOWS.H.

Here is the relationship between the icon name in the resource script and the *LoadIcon* statement in your C program:

> Resource script: ***myicon*** *ICON iconfile.ico*
>
> Program source: *hIcon = LoadIcon (hInstance, "**myicon**") ;*

Don't worry about uppercase and lowercase here. The resource compiler converts the name in the resource script file to uppercase and inserts the name in the resource table of the program's .EXE file header. The first time you call *LoadIcon*, Windows converts the string in the second parameter to uppercase and searches the resource table of the .EXE file for a matching name.

You may also use a number (a 16-bit unsigned WORD) instead of a name. This number is called an ID number for the icon. Here's how it's done:

Resource script: ***125*** *ICON iconfile.ico*

Program source: *hIcon = LoadIcon (hInstance, MAKEINTRESOURCE (**125**)) ;*

MAKEINTRESOURCE ("make an integer into a resource string") is a macro defined in the Windows header files that converts a number into a pointer, but with the top 16 bits set to zero. That's how Windows knows that the second parameter to *LoadIcon* is a number rather than a pointer to a character string.

Sample programs presented earlier in this book use predefined icons:

```
LoadIcon (NULL, IDI_APPLICATION) ;
```

Windows knows that this is a predefined icon because the *hInstance* parameter is set to NULL. IDI_APPLICATION happens also to be defined in the Windows header files in terms of MAKEINTRESOURCE:

```
#define IDI_APPLICATION MAKEINTRESOURCE (32512)
```

The predefined icons and cursors are part of the display driver file.

You can also reference the icon name using a third method that combines the string method and the number method:

Resource script: ***125*** *ICON iconfile.ico*

Program source: *hIcon = LoadIcon (hInstance, "**#125**") ;*

Windows recognizes the initial # character as prefacing a number in ASCII form.

How about a fourth method? This one uses a macro definition in a header file that is included (using the *#include* directive) in both the resource script and your program:

Header file: *#define myicon 125*

Resource script: ***myicon*** *ICON iconfile.ico*

Program source: *hIcon = LoadIcon (hInstance, MAKEINTRESOURCE (**myicon**)) ;*

Be careful when you use this method! Although case does not matter when the icon name is a character string, case does make a difference for identifiers that are generated from *#define* statements.

Using ID numbers rather than names for icons reduces the .EXE file size and probably speeds up the *LoadIcon* call just a bit. Moreover, if your program uses many icons, you'll find it easier to store the ID numbers in an array.

Using Icons in Your Program

Although Windows uses icons in several ways to denote a program, many Windows programs specify an icon only when defining the window class:

```
wndclass.hIcon    = LoadIcon (hInstance, "MyIcon") ;
    .
    .
    .
wndclass.hIconSm = LoadIcon (hInstance, "MySmIcon") ;
```

You can reference the same standard-size icon in both statements and Windows will simply adjust the size when displaying the small icon. If you later want to change the program's icon, you can do so using *SetClassLong*. Let's assume you had a second icon in your resource script:

```
anothericon ICON iconfil2.ico
```

You can substitute this icon for "myicon" with the statement:

```
SetClassLong (hwnd, GCL_HICON, LoadIcon (hInstance, "anothericon")) ;
```

You can change the small icon with GCL_HICONSM. If you save the icon handle from a *LoadIcon* call, you can also draw the icon on the client area of your window:

```
DrawIcon (hdc, x, y, hIcon) ;
```

Windows itself uses the *DrawIcon* function when displaying your program's icon in the icon area. Windows obtains the handle to the icon from the window class structure. You can obtain the handle in the same way:

```
DrawIcon (hdc, x, y, GetClassLong (hwnd, GGL_HICON)) ;
```

The RESOURC1 sample program uses the same icon for the window class and for displaying in its client area. In the resource script the icon is given the same name as the program:

```
resourc1  ICON  resourc1.ico
```

Because the character string "Resourc1" is stored in the array *szAppName* and is already used in the program for the window class name, the *LoadIcon* call is simply:

```
LoadIcon (hInstance, szAppName) ;
```

You'll notice that *LoadIcon* is called three times in RESOURC1 for the same icon, twice when defining the window class in *WinMain* and again when obtaining a handle to the icon while processing the WM_CREATE message in *WndProc*. Calling *LoadIcon* three times presents no problem: Both calls return the same handle. Windows actually loads the icon only once from the .EXE file.

Using Alternate Cursors

The statements that you use to specify a cursor in your resource script and to obtain a handle to a cursor in your program are very similar to the icon statements shown above:

Resource script: ***mycursor*** *CURSOR cursfile.cur*

Program source: *hCursor = LoadCursor (hInstance, "**mycursor**") ;*

The other methods shown for icons (using ID numbers and MAKEINTRESOURCE) work with cursors also. The Windows header files include a *typedef* definition for HCURSOR that you can use for storing the cursor handle.

You can use the cursor handle obtained from *LoadCursor* when setting the *hCursor* member of the window class structure:

```
wndclass.hCursor = LoadCursor (hInstance, "mycursor") ;
```

This causes the mouse cursor to be displayed as your customized cursor when the mouse is within the client area of your window.

If you use child windows, you may want the cursor to appear differently, depending on the child window below the cursor. If your program defines the window class for these child windows, you can use different cursors for each class by appropriately setting the *hCursor* field in each window class. And if you use predefined child window controls, you can alter the *hCursor* field of the window class using:

```
SetClassLong (hwndChild, GCL_HCURSOR,
        LoadCursor (hInstance, "childcursor") ;
```

If you separate your client area into smaller logical areas without using child windows, you can use *SetCursor* to change the mouse cursor:

```
SetCursor (hCursor) ;
```

You should call *SetCursor* during processing of the WM_MOUSEMOVE message. Otherwise, Windows uses the cursor specified in the window class to redraw the cursor when it is moved.

RESOURC1 uses the name of the program for the name of the cursor:

```
resourc1  CURSOR  resourc1.cur
```

When RESOURC1.C defines the window class, the following *szAppName* variable is used for *LoadCursor*:

```
wndclass.hCursor = LoadCursor (hInstance, szAppName) ;
```

Bitmaps: Pictures in Pixels

We've already talked about the use of bitmaps in icons and cursors. Windows also includes a resource type called BITMAP.

Bitmaps are used for two major purposes. The first is to draw pictures on the display. For instance, the Windows display driver files contain lots of tiny bitmaps used for drawing the arrows in scroll bars, the check marks in pull-down menus, the pictures on the sizing buttons, check boxes, and radio buttons. You can use bitmaps in menus (as discussed in Chapter 10) and application toolbars (as discussed in Chapter 12). Programs such as Paint use bitmaps to display a graphics menu.

The second major use of bitmaps is to create brushes. Brushes, you'll recall, are patterns of pixels that Windows uses to fill an area of the display.

Using Bitmaps and Brushes

The RESOURC2 program, shown in Figure 9-2, is an enhanced version of RESOURC1 that includes a monochrome bitmap resource used to create a brush for the background of the client area. The bitmap was created in an image editor with dimensions of 8 by 8, which is the minimum size for a brush.

RESOURC2.MAK

```
#-----------------------
# RESOURC2.MAK make file
#-----------------------

resourc2.exe : resourc2.obj resourc2.res
    $(LINKER) $(GUIFLAGS) -OUT:resourc2.exe \
    resourc2.obj resourc2.res $(GUILIBS)

resourc2.obj : resourc2.c
    $(CC) $(CFLAGS) resourc2.c

resourc2.res : resourc2.rc resourc2.ico resourc2.cur resourc2.bmp
    $(RC) $(RCVARS) resourc2.rc
```

RESOURC2.C

```c
/*-------------------------------------------------------------
   RESOURC2.C -- Icon and Cursor Demonstration Program No. 2
                 (c) Charles Petzold, 1996
   -------------------------------------------------------------*/

#include <windows.h>

LRESULT CALLBACK WndProc (HWND, UINT, WPARAM, LPARAM) ;

char       szAppName[] = "Resourc2" ;
HINSTANCE hInst ;

int WINAPI WinMain (HINSTANCE hInstance, HINSTANCE hPrevInstance,
                    PSTR szCmdLine, int iCmdShow)
    {
    HBITMAP    hBitmap ;
    HBRUSH     hBrush ;
    HWND       hwnd ;
    MSG        msg ;
    WNDCLASSEX wndclass ;
```

Figure 9-2. *The RESOURC2 program, including an icon, a cursor, and a bitmap.* *(continued)*

```
       hBitmap = LoadBitmap (hInstance, szAppName) ;
       hBrush = CreatePatternBrush (hBitmap) ;

       wndclass.cbSize        = sizeof (wndclass) ;
       wndclass.style         = CS_HREDRAW | CS_VREDRAW ;
       wndclass.lpfnWndProc   = WndProc ;
       wndclass.cbClsExtra    = 0 ;
       wndclass.cbWndExtra    = 0 ;
       wndclass.hInstance     = hInstance ;
       wndclass.hIcon         = LoadIcon (hInstance, szAppName) ;
       wndclass.hCursor       = LoadCursor (hInstance, szAppName) ;
       wndclass.hbrBackground = hBrush ;
       wndclass.lpszMenuName  = NULL ;
       wndclass.lpszClassName = szAppName ;
       wndclass.hIconSm       = LoadIcon (hInstance, szAppName) ;

       RegisterClassEx (&wndclass) ;

       hInst = hInstance ;

       hwnd = CreateWindow (szAppName, "Icon and Cursor Demo",
                            WS_OVERLAPPEDWINDOW,
                            CW_USEDEFAULT, CW_USEDEFAULT,
                            CW_USEDEFAULT, CW_USEDEFAULT,
                            NULL, NULL, hInstance, NULL) ;

       ShowWindow (hwnd, iCmdShow) ;
       UpdateWindow (hwnd) ;

       while (GetMessage (&msg, NULL, 0, 0))
            {
            TranslateMessage (&msg) ;
            DispatchMessage (&msg) ;
            }

       DeleteObject ((HGDIOBJ) hBrush) ;          // clean-up
       DeleteObject ((HGDIOBJ) hBitmap) ;

       return msg.wParam ;
       }

LRESULT CALLBACK WndProc (HWND hwnd, UINT iMsg, WPARAM wParam, LPARAM lParam)
     {
     static HICON hIcon ;
     static int   cxIcon, cyIcon, cxClient, cyClient ;
```

(continued)

```
     HDC        hdc ;
     PAINTSTRUCT ps ;
     int        x, y ;

     switch (iMsg)
         {
         case WM_CREATE :
             hIcon = LoadIcon (hInst, szAppName) ;
             cxIcon = GetSystemMetrics (SM_CXICON) ;
             cyIcon = GetSystemMetrics (SM_CYICON) ;
             return 0 ;

         case WM_SIZE :
             cxClient = LOWORD (lParam) ;
             cyClient = HIWORD (lParam) ;
             return 0 ;

         case WM_PAINT :
             hdc = BeginPaint (hwnd, &ps) ;

             for (y = cyIcon ; y < cyClient ; y += 2 * cyIcon)
                 for (x = cxIcon ; x < cxClient ; x += 2 * cxIcon)
                     DrawIcon (hdc, x, y, hIcon) ;

             EndPaint (hwnd, &ps) ;
             return 0 ;

         case WM_DESTROY :
             PostQuitMessage (0) ;
             return 0 ;
         }
     return DefWindowProc (hwnd, iMsg, wParam, lParam) ;
     }
```

RESOURC2.RC

```
/*-----------------------------
   RESOURC2.RC resource script
  -----------------------------*/

resourc2  ICON    resourc2.ico
resourc2  CURSOR  resourc2.cur
resourc2  BITMAP  resourc2.bmp
```

(continued)

RESOURC2.ICO

RESOURC2.CUR

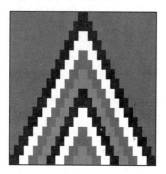

RESOURC2.BMP

The bitmap resource is included in the resource script in the same format as the icon and cursor:

```
resourc2 BITMAP resourc2.bmp
```

The *LoadBitmap* function used in *WinMain* is similar to the *LoadIcon* and *LoadCursor* calls. It returns a handle to a bitmap:

```
hBitmap = LoadBitmap (hInstance, szAppName) ;
```

This handle is then used to create a pattern brush. The brush is based on the bitmap:

```
hBrush = CreatePatternBrush (hBitmap) ;
```

When Windows fills an area of the display with this brush, the bitmap is repeated horizontally and vertically every eight pixels. We want to use this brush to color the background of the client area, which we accomplish when defining the window class:

```
wndclass.hbrBackground = hBrush ;
```

The major difference between bitmaps and other resources is of practical significance and can be simply stated: Bitmaps are GDI objects. Proper program structure dictates that they should be deleted when they are no longer needed or before the program terminates. In RESOURC2 this is done at the end of *WinMain*:

```
DeleteObject ((HGDIOBJ) hBrush) ;
DeleteObject ((HGDIOBJ) hBitmap) ;
```

CHARACTER STRINGS

Having a resource for character strings may seem odd at first. Certainly we haven't had any problem using regular old character strings defined as variables right in our source code.

Character string resources are primarily for easing the translation of your program to other languages. As you'll discover in the next two chapters, menus and dialog boxes are also part of the resource script. If you use character string resources rather than put strings directly into your source code, all text that your program uses will be in one file—the resource script. If the text in this resource script is translated, all you need do to create a foreign-language version of your program is relink the program and add the translated resources to the .EXE file. This method is much safer than messing around with your source code. (Of course, you could also choose to define all your character strings as macros and store them in a header file. This method also avoids altering source code during language translations.)

Using Character String Resources

The character string resources are defined in your resource script using the keyword STRINGTABLE:

```
STRINGTABLE
    {
    id1, "character string 1"
    id2, "character string 2"
    [other string definitions]
    }
```

The resource script can contain only one string table. Each string can be only one line long with a maximum of 255 characters. The strings cannot contain any C-style control characters except for \t (tab). However, the strings *can* contain octal constants:

Tab	\011
Linefeed	\012
Carriage return	\015

These control characters are recognized by the *DrawText* and *MessageBox* functions.

Your program can use the *LoadString* call to copy a string resource into a buffer in the program's data segment:

```
LoadString (hInstance, id, szBuffer, iMaxLength) ;
```

The *id* parameter refers to the ID number that precedes each string in the resource script; *szBuffer* is a pointer to a character array that receives the character string; and *iMaxLength* is the maximum number of characters to transfer into *szBuffer*. The string ID numbers that precede each string are generally macro identifiers defined in a header file. Many Windows programmers use the prefix *IDS_* to denote an ID number for a string. Sometimes a filename or other information must be embedded in the string when the string is displayed. In this case you put C formatting characters in the string and use it as a formatting string in *sprintf* or *wsprintf*.

Using Strings with *MessageBox*

Let's look at an example of a program that uses three character strings to display three error messages in a message box. A header file that we'll call PROGRAM.H defines three identifiers for these messages:

```
#define IDS_FILENOTFOUND 1
#define IDS_FILETOOBIG   2
#define IDS_FILEREADONLY 3
```

The resource script looks like this:

```
#include "program.h"
[other resource script]
STRINGTABLE
    {
    IDS_FILENOTFOUND,   "File %s not found."
    IDS_FILETOOBIG,     "File %s too large to edit."
    IDS_FILEREADONLY,   "File %s is read-only."
    }
```

The C source code file also includes this header file and defines a function to display a message box. (I'm assuming that *szAppName* is a global variable that contains the program name and that *hInst* is a global variable that contains the instance handle of your program.)

```
#include "program.h"
[other program lines]
OkMessage (HWND hwnd, int iErrorNumber, char *szFileName)
    {
    char szFormat[40] ;
    char szBuffer[60] ;

    LoadString (hInst, iErrorNumber, szFormat, 40) ;
```

```
    sprintf (szBuffer, szFormat, szFilename) ;

    return MessageBox (hwnd, szBuffer, szAppName,
                      MB_OK | MB_ICONEXCLAMATION) ;
    }
```

To display a message box containing the "file not found" message, the program calls:

```
OkMessage (hwnd, IDS_FILENOTFOUND, szFileName) ;
```

USER-DEFINED RESOURCES

The "user-defined resource" is convenient for attaching miscellaneous data to your .EXE file and obtaining access to that data within the program. The data can be in any format you want—text or binary. The Windows functions used to access user-defined resources return a pointer to the data when Windows loads the data into memory. You can do whatever you want with that data. You'll probably find that this is a more convenient way to store and access miscellaneous data rather than the alternative, which is storing it in other files and accessing it with file input functions.

For instance, suppose you have a file called PROGHELP.TXT that contains "help" text for your program. This file needn't be a pure ASCII file: It can also contain binary data, such as pointers that would aid your program in referencing various sections of this file. Reference this file with a statement in your resource script that looks like this:

```
helptext TEXT proghelp.txt
```

The names *helptext* (the name of the resource) and TEXT (the type of the resource) in this statement can be any names you want. I've capitalized TEXT simply to make it look like the ICON, CURSOR, and BITMAP statements. What we're doing here is making up our own type of resource, called TEXT.

During program initialization (for example, during processing of the WM_CREATE message), you can obtain a handle to this resource:

```
hResource = LoadResource (hInstance,
        FindResource (hInstance, "TEXT", "helptext")) ;
```

The variable *hResource* is defined with type HGLOBAL. Despite its name, *LoadResource* does not actually load the resource into memory just yet. The *LoadResource* and *FindResource* functions used together like this are essentially equivalent to the *LoadIcon* and *LoadCursor* functions. In fact, *LoadIcon* and *LoadCursor* use the *LoadResource* and *FindResource* functions.

You can use numbers rather than names for the resource name and resource type. The numbers can be converted to far pointers in the *FindResource* call using MAKEINTRESOURCE. The numbers used for the resource type must be greater than 255. (Windows uses numbers between 1 and 9 when calling *FindResource* for existing resource types.)

When you need access to the text, call *LockResource*:

```
pHelpText = LockResource (hResource) ;
```

LockResource loads the resource into memory (if it has not already been loaded), and then it returns a pointer to it. When you've finished with the resource, you can free it from memory:

```
FreeResource (hResource) ;
```

The resource will also be freed when your program terminates, even if you don't call *FreeResource*.

Let's look at a sample program that uses three resources—an icon, a string table, and a user-defined resource. The POEPOEM program, shown in Figure 9-3, displays the text of Edgar Allan Poe's "Annabel Lee" in its client area. The user-defined resource is the file POEPOEM.ASC, which contains the text of the poem. The text file is terminated with a backslash (\).

POEPOEM.MAK

```
#-----------------------
# POEPOEM.MAK make file
#-----------------------

poepoem.exe : poepoem.obj poepoem.res
     $(LINKER) $(GUIFLAGS) -OUT:poepoem.exe poepoem.obj poepoem.res $(GUILIBS)

poepoem.obj : poepoem.c poepoem.h
     $(CC) $(CFLAGS) poepoem.c

poepoem.res : poepoem.rc poepoem.ico poepoem.asc poepoem.h
     $(RC) $(RCVARS) poepoem.rc
```

POEPOEM.C

```
/*-----------------------------------------------------
    POEPOEM.C -- Demonstrates User-Defined Resource
               (c) Charles Petzold, 1996
    -----------------------------------------------*/

#include <windows.h>
#include "poepoem.h"
```

Figure 9-3. *The POEPOEM program, including an icon and a user-defined resource.*   *(continued)*

```
LRESULT CALLBACK WndProc (HWND, UINT, WPARAM, LPARAM) ;

char      szAppName[10] ;
char      szCaption[35] ;
HINSTANCE hInst ;

int WINAPI WinMain (HINSTANCE hInstance, HINSTANCE hPrevInstance,
                    PSTR szCmdLine, int iCmdShow)
     {
     HWND         hwnd ;
     MSG          msg ;
     WNDCLASSEX wndclass ;

     LoadString (hInstance, IDS_APPNAME, szAppName, sizeof (szAppName)) ;
     LoadString (hInstance, IDS_CAPTION, szCaption, sizeof (szCaption)) ;

     wndclass.cbSize        = sizeof (wndclass) ;
     wndclass.style         = CS_HREDRAW | CS_VREDRAW ;
     wndclass.lpfnWndProc   = WndProc ;
     wndclass.cbClsExtra    = 0 ;
     wndclass.cbWndExtra    = 0 ;
     wndclass.hInstance     = hInstance ;
     wndclass.hIcon         = LoadIcon (hInstance, szAppName) ;
     wndclass.hCursor       = LoadCursor (NULL, IDC_ARROW) ;
     wndclass.hbrBackground = (HBRUSH) GetStockObject (WHITE_BRUSH) ;
     wndclass.lpszMenuName  = NULL ;
     wndclass.lpszClassName = szAppName ;
     wndclass.hIconSm       = LoadIcon (hInstance, szAppName) ;

     RegisterClassEx (&wndclass) ;

     hInst = hInstance ;

     hwnd = CreateWindow (szAppName, szCaption,
                     WS_OVERLAPPEDWINDOW | WS_CLIPCHILDREN,
                     CW_USEDEFAULT, CW_USEDEFAULT,
                     CW_USEDEFAULT, CW_USEDEFAULT,
                     NULL, NULL, hInstance, NULL) ;

     ShowWindow (hwnd, iCmdShow) ;
     UpdateWindow (hwnd) ;

     while (GetMessage (&msg, NULL, 0, 0))
```

(continued)

```
            {
        TranslateMessage (&msg) ;
        DispatchMessage (&msg) ;
            }
     return msg.wParam ;
     }

LRESULT CALLBACK WndProc (HWND hwnd, UINT iMsg, WPARAM wParam, LPARAM lParam)
     {
     static char    *pText ;
     static HGLOBAL hResource ;
     static HWND    hScroll ;
     static int     iPosition, cxChar, cyChar, cyClient, iNumLInes, xScroll ;
     char           szPoemRes[15] ;
     HDC            hdc ;
     PAINTSTRUCT    ps ;
     RECT           rect ;
     TEXTMETRIC     tm ;

     switch (iMsg)
          {
          case WM_CREATE :
               hdc = GetDC (hwnd) ;
               GetTextMetrics (hdc, &tm) ;
               cxChar = tm.tmAveCharWidth ;
               cyChar = tm.tmHeight + tm.tmExternalLeading ;
               ReleaseDC (hwnd, hdc) ;

               xScroll = GetSystemMetrics (SM_CXVSCROLL) ;

               hScroll = CreateWindow ("scrollbar", NULL,
                         WS_CHILD | WS_VISIBLE | SBS_VERT,
                         0, 0, 0, 0,
                         hwnd, (HMENU) 1, hInst, NULL) ;

               LoadString (hInst, IDS_POEMRES, szPoemRes,
                                  sizeof (szPoemRes)) ;

               hResource = LoadResource (hInst,
                         FindResource (hInst, szPoemRes, "TEXT")) ;

               pText = (char *) LockResource (hResource) ;

               iNumLInes = 0 ;

               while (*pText != '\\' && *pText != '\0')
```

(continued)

```
               {
          if (*pText == '\n')
               iNumLInes ++ ;
          pText = AnsiNext (pText) ;
          }
     *pText = '\0' ;

     SetScrollRange (hScroll, SB_CTL, 0, iNumLInes, FALSE) ;
     SetScrollPos   (hScroll, SB_CTL, 0, FALSE) ;
     return 0 ;

case WM_SIZE :
     MoveWindow (hScroll, LOWORD (lParam) - xScroll, 0,
          xScroll, cyClient = HIWORD (lParam), TRUE) ;
     SetFocus (hwnd) ;
     return 0 ;

case WM_SETFOCUS :
     SetFocus (hScroll) ;
     return 0 ;

case WM_VSCROLL :
     switch (wParam)
          {
          case SB_TOP :
               iPosition = 0 :
               break ;
          case SB_BOTTOM :
               iPosition = iNumLInes ;
               break ;
          case SB_LINEUP :
               iPosition -= 1 ;
               break ;
          case SB_LINEDOWN :
               iPosition += 1 ;
               break ;
          case SB_PAGEUP :
               iPosition -= cyClient / cyChar ;
               break ;
          case SB_PAGEDOWN :
               iPosition += cyClient / cyChar ;
               break ;
          case SB_THUMBPOSITION :
               iPosition = LOWORD (lParam) ;
               break ;
```

(continued)

```
                              }
                    iPosition = max (0, min (iPosition, iNumLInes)) ;
                    if (iPosition != GetScrollPos (hScroll, SB_CTL))
                         {
                         SetScrollPos (hScroll, SB_CTL, iPosition, TRUE) ;
                         InvalidateRect (hwnd, NULL, TRUE) ;
                         }
                    return 0 ;

          case WM_PAINT :
               hdc = BeginPaint (hwnd, &ps) ;

               pText = (char *) LockResource (hResource) ;

               GetClientRect (hwnd, &rect) ;
               rect.left += cxChar ;
               rect.top  += cyChar * (1 - iPosition) ;
               DrawText (hdc, pText, -1, &rect, DT_EXTERNALLEADING) ;

               EndPaint (hwnd, &ps) ;
               return 0 ;

          case WM_DESTROY :
               FreeResource (hResource) ;
               PostQuitMessage (0) ;
               return 0 ;
          }
     return DefWindowProc (hwnd, iMsg, wParam, lParam) ;
     }
```

POEPOEM.RC

```
/*--------------------------------
   POEPOEM.RC resource script
   ---------------------------*/

#include "poepoem.h"

poepoem     ICON    poepoem.ico
AnnabelLee  TEXT    poepoem.asc

STRINGTABLE
     {
     IDS_APPNAME, "poepoem"
     IDS_CAPTION, """Annabel Lee"" by Edgar Allen Poe"
     IDS_POEMRES, "AnnabelLee"
     }
```

444

(continued)

POEPOEM.ICO

POEPOEM.H

```
/*------------------------
   POEPOEM.H header file
----------------------*/

#define IDS_APPNAME 0
#define IDS_CAPTION 1
#define IDS_POEMRES 2
```

POEPOEM.ASC

```
It was many and many a year ago,
   In a kingdom by the sea,
That a maiden there lived whom you may know
   By the name of Annabel Lee;
And this maiden she lived with no other thought
   Than to love and be loved by me.
I was a child and she was a child
   In this kingdom by the sea,
But we loved with a love that was more than love --
   I and my Annabel Lee --
With a love that the winged seraphs of Heaven
   Coveted her and me.
And this was the reason that, long ago,
   In this kingdom by the sea,
A wind blew out of a cloud, chilling
   My beautiful Annabel Lee;
So that her highborn kinsmen came
   And bore her away from me,
To shut her up in a sepulchre
   In this kingdom by the sea.
```

(continued)

```
The angels, not half so happy in Heaven,
    Went envying her and me --
Yes! that was the reason (as all men know,
    In this kingdom by the sea)
That the wind came out of the cloud by night,
    Chilling and killing my Annabel Lee.
But our love it was stronger by far than the love
    Of those who were older than we --
    Of many far wiser than we --
And neither the angels in Heaven above
    Nor the demons down under the sea
Can ever dissever my soul from the soul
    Of the beautiful Annabel Lee:
For the moon never beams, without bringing me dreams
    Of the beautiful Annabel Lee;
And the stars never rise, but I feel the bright eyes
    Of the beautiful Annabel Lee:
And so, all the night-tide, I lie down by the side
Of my darling -- my darling -- my life and my bride,
    In her sepulchre there by the sea --
    In her tomb by the sounding sea.
                                              [May, 1849]
```

In the POEPOEM.RC resource script, the user-defined resource is given the type TEXT and the name *AnnabelLee*:

```
AnnabelLee  TEXT  poepoem.asc
```

During WM_CREATE processing in *WndProc*, a handle to the resource is obtained using *FindResource* and *LoadResource*. The resource is locked using *LockResource*, and a small routine replaces the backslash (\) at the end of the file with a 0. This is for the benefit of the *DrawText* function used later during the WM_PAINT message

Note the use of a child window scroll bar control rather than a window scroll bar: The child window scroll bar control has an automatic keyboard interface, so no WM_KEY-DOWN processing is required in POEPOEM.

POEPOEM also uses three character strings, the IDs of which are defined in the POEPOEM.H header file. The IDS_APPNAME and IDS_CAPTION strings are loaded into global static variables using *LoadString*:

```
LoadString (hInstance, IDS_APPNAME, szAppName, sizeof (szAppName)) ;
LoadString (hInstance, IDS_CAPTION, szCaption, sizeof (szCaption)) ;
```

Now that we've defined all the character strings used in POEPOEM as resources, we've made it easier for translators to convert the program to a foreign-language version. Of course, they'd also have to translate the text of "Annabel Lee"—which would, I suspect, be a somewhat more difficult task.

Chapter 10

Menus and Accelerators

Do you remember the Monty Python skit about the cheese shop? Here's how it goes: A guy comes into a cheese shop and wants a particular type of cheese. Of course, the shop doesn't have it. So he asks for another type of cheese, and another, and another, and another (eventually totaling about 40 types of cheese), and still the answer is: No, no, no, no, no. Ultimately, there's a shooting involved.

This whole unfortunate incident could have been avoided through the use of menus. A menu is a list of available options. A menu tells a hungry eater what the kitchen can serve up, and—for a Windows program—tells the user what operations an application is capable of performing.

A menu is probably the most important part of the consistent user interface that Windows programs offer, and adding a menu to your program is a relatively easy part of Windows programming. You simply define the structure of the menu in your resource script and assign a unique ID number to each menu item. You specify the name of the menu in the window class structure. When the user chooses a menu item, Windows sends your program a WM_COMMAND message containing that ID. But we won't stop with that simple example. One of the more interesting things you can do with menus is display bitmaps in the menu rather than character strings, so we'll take a detailed look at how that is done.

This chapter also covers "keyboard accelerators." These are key combinations that are used primarily to duplicate menu functions.

MENUS

A window's menu bar is displayed immediately below the title bar. This menu bar is sometimes called a program's "main menu" or the "top-level menu." Items listed in the top-level menu usually invoke a drop-down menu, which is also called a "popup menu" or a "submenu." You may also define multiple nestings of popups: that is, an item on a popup menu can invoke another popup menu. Sometimes items in popup menus invoke a dialog box for more information. (Dialog boxes are covered in the next chapter.) Most parent windows have, to the far left of the title bar, a display of the program's small icon. This icon invokes the system menu, which is really another popup menu.

Menu items in popups can be "checked," which means that Windows draws a small check mark to the left of the menu text. Check marks let the user know which program options have been chosen from the menu. These options can be mutually exclusive, but they don't have to be. Top-level menu items cannot be checked.

Menu items in the top-level menu or in popup menus can be "enabled," "disabled," or "grayed." The words "active" and "inactive" are sometimes used synonymously with "enabled" and "disabled." Menu items flagged as enabled or disabled look the same to the user, but a grayed menu item is displayed in gray text.

From the perspective of the user, enabled, disabled, and grayed menu items can all be "selected" (highlighted). That is, the user can click the mouse on a disabled menu item, or move the reverse-video cursor bar to a disabled menu item, or trigger the menu item using the item's key letter. However, from the perspective of your program, enabled, disabled, and grayed menu items function differently. Windows sends your program a WM_COMMAND message only for enabled menu items. You use disabled and grayed menu items for options that are not currently valid. If you want to let the user know the option is not valid, make it grayed.

Menu Structure

When you create or change menus in a program, it's useful to think of the top-level menu and each popup menu as being separate menus. The top-level menu has a menu handle, each popup menu within a top-level menu has its own menu handle, and the system menu (which is also a popup) has a menu handle.

Each item in a menu is defined by three characteristics. The first characteristic is what appears in the menu. This is either a text string or a bitmap. The second characteristic is either an ID number that Windows sends to your program in a WM_COMMAND message or a popup menu that Windows displays when the user chooses that menu item. The third characteristic describes the attribute of the menu item, including whether the item is disabled, grayed, or checked.

The Menu Template

You can create a menu in three different ways. The most common (and the easiest) is to define the menu in your resource script in the form of a menu template, for example:

```
MyMenu MENU
    {
    [menu list]
    }
```

MyMenu is the name of the menu. You reference this name in the window class structure. Usually, the menu name is the same as the application name.

Within the curly brackets you may use MENUITEM or POPUP statements. The format of the MENUITEM statement is:

```
MENUITEM "&Text", id [, options]
```

and the format of the POPUP statement is:

```
POPUP "&Text" [, options]
    {
    [menu list]
    }
```

Instead of curly brackets, you can use BEGIN and END if you wish. The text displayed for each menu must be enclosed in double quotation marks. An ampersand (&) causes the character that follows it to be underlined when Windows displays the menu. This is also the character Windows searches for when you select a menu item using the Alt key. If you don't include an ampersand in the text, no underline will appear, and Windows will use instead the first letter of the text for Alt-key searches.

The options on the MENUITEM and POPUP statements that appear in the top-level menu list are as follows:

- ■ GRAYED—The menu item is inactive, and it does not generate a WM_COMMAND message. The text is grayed.

- ■ INACTIVE—The menu item is inactive, and it does not generate a WM_COMMAND message. The text is displayed normally.

- ■ MENUBREAK—This item and the following items appear on a new line of the menu.

- ■ HELP—This item and the following items are right-justified.

Options can be combined using the C bitwise OR symbol (¦), but GRAYED and INACTIVE cannot be used together. MENUBREAK is uncommon in a top-level menu, because

Windows automatically separates a top-level menu into multiple lines if the window is too narrow to fit the entire menu.

Following a POPUP statement in the main menu, the left and right brackets (or the BEGIN and END keywords) block off a list of items in the popup. The following statements are allowed in a popup definition:

```
MENUITEM "text", id [, options]
```

and:

```
MENUITEM SEPARATOR
```

and:

```
POPUP "text" [, options]
```

MENUITEM SEPARATOR draws a horizontal line in the popup menu. This line is often used to separate groups of related options.

For items in popup menus, you can use the columnar tab character \t in the character string. Text following the \t is placed in a new column spaced far enough to the right to accommodate the longest text string in the first column of the popup. We'll see how this works when discussing keyboard accelerators toward the end of this chapter. A \a right-justifies the text that follows it. The options for MENUITEM in a popup are as follows:

- CHECKED—A check mark appears to the left of the text.

- GRAYED—The menu item is inactive, and it does not generate a WM_COMMAND message. The text is grayed.

- INACTIVE—The menu item is inactive, and it does not generate a WM_COMMAND message. The text is displayed normally.

- MENUBREAK—This item and the following items appear in a new column of the menu.

- MENUBARBREAK—This item and the following items appear in a new column of the menu. A vertical line separates the columns.

GRAYED and INACTIVE cannot be used together. MENUBREAK and MENUBARBREAK cannot be used together. You should use either MENUBREAK or MENUBARBREAK when the number of items in a popup are "taller" than can be displayed in a single column.

The id values in the MENUITEM statements are the numbers that Windows sends to the window procedure in menu messages. The id values should be unique within a menu. Instead of using numbers, you'll probably want to use identifiers defined in a header file. By convention, these identifiers begin with the letters IDM ("ID for a Menu").

Referencing the Menu in Your Program

Many Windows applications have only one menu in the resource script. The program makes reference to this menu in the definition of the window class:

```
wndclass.lpszMenuName = "MyMenu" ;
```

Programmers often use the name of the program as the name of the menu so that the same character string can also be used for the window class, the name of the program's icon, and the name of the menu. However, you can also use a number (or a macro identifier) for the menu rather than a name. The resource script would look like this:

```
45 MENU
    {
    [menu definition]
    }
```

In this case, the assignment statement for the *lpszMenuName* field of the window class structure can be either:

```
wndclass.lpszMenuName = MAKEINTRESOURCE (45) ;
```

or:

```
wndclass.lpszMenuName = "#45" ;
```

Although specifying the menu in the window class is the most common way to reference a menu resource, you have alternatives. A Windows application can load a menu resource into memory with the *LoadMenu* function, which is similar to the *LoadIcon* and *LoadCursor* functions described in Chapter 9. If you use a name for the menu in the resource script, *LoadMenu* returns a handle to the menu:

```
hMenu = LoadMenu (hInstance, "MyMenu") ;
```

If you use a number, the *LoadMenu* call takes either this form:

```
hMenu = LoadMenu (hInstance, MAKEINTRESOURCE (45)) ;
```

or this form:

```
hMenu = LoadMenu (hInstance, "#45") ;
```

You can then specify this menu handle as the ninth parameter to *CreateWindow*.

```
hwnd = CreateWindow ("MyClass", "Window Caption",
            WS_OVERLAPPEDWINDOW,
            CW_USEDEFAULT,CW_USEDEFAULT,
            CW_USEDEFAULT,CW_USEDEFAULT,
            NULL,
            hMenu,
            hInstance,
            NULL) ;
```

In this case, the menu specified in the *CreateWindow* call overrides any menu specified in the window class. You can think of the menu in the window class as being a default menu for the windows based on the window class if the ninth parameter to *CreateWindow* is NULL. Therefore, you can use different menus for several windows based on the same window class.

You can also have a NULL menu in the window class and a NULL menu in the *CreateWindow* call and assign a menu to a window after the window has been created:

```
SetMenu (hwnd, hMenu) ;
```

This form lets you dynamically change a window's menu. We'll see an example of this in the NOPOPUPS program shown later in this chapter.

Any menu that is attached to a window is destroyed when the window is destroyed. Any menus not attached to a window should be explicitly destroyed by calls to *DestroyMenu* before the program terminates.

Menus and Messages

Windows usually sends a window procedure several different messages when the user selects a menu item. In most cases your program can ignore many of these messages and simply pass them to *DefWindowProc*. One such message is WM_INITMENU with the following parameters:

wParam	*lParam*
Handle to main menu	0

The value of *wParam* is the handle to your main menu even if the user is selecting an item from the system menu. Windows programs generally ignore the WM_INITMENU message. Although the message exists to give you the opportunity to change the menu before an item is chosen, I suspect any changes to the top-level menu at this time would be very disconcerting to the user.

Your program also receives WM_MENUSELECT messages. A program can receive many WM_MENUSELECT messages as the user moves the cursor or mouse among the menu items. As we'll see in Chapter 12, this is helpful for implementing a status bar that contains a full text description of the menu option. The parameters that accompany WM_MENUSELECT are as follows:

LOWORD (wParam)	*HIWORD (wParam)*	*lParam*
Selected item: Menu ID or popup menu handle	Selection flags	Handle to menu containing selected item

WM_MENUSELECT is a menu-tracking message. The low word of *wParam* tells you what item of the menu is currently selected (highlighted). The "selection flags" in the high word of *wParam* can be a combination of the following: MF_GRAYED, MF_DISABLED, MF-_CHECKED, MF_BITMAP, MF_POPUP, MF_HELP, MF_SYSMENU, and MF_MOUSESELECT. You may want to use WM_MENUSELECT if you need to change something in the client area of your window based on the movement of the highlight among the menu items. Most programs pass this message to *DefWindowProc*.

When Windows is ready to display a popup menu, it sends the window procedure a WM_INITMENUPOPUP message with the following parameters:

wParam	*LOWORD (lParam)*	*HIWORD (lParam)*
Popup menu handle	Popup index	1 for system menu, 0 otherwise

This message is important if you need to enable or disable items in a popup menu before it is displayed. For instance, suppose your program can copy text from the clipboard using the Paste command on a popup menu. When you receive a WM_INITMENUPOPUP message for that popup, you should determine if the clipboard has text in it. If it doesn't, you should gray the Paste menu item. We'll see an example of this in the revised POPPAD program shown toward the end of this chapter.

The most important menu message is WM_COMMAND. This message indicates that the user has chosen an enabled menu item from your window's menu. You'll recall from Chapter 8 that WM_COMMAND messages also result from child window controls. If you happen to use the same ID codes for menus and child window controls, you can differentiate between them by value of *lParam*, which will be 0 for a menu item:

	LOWORD (wParam)	*HIWORD (wParam)*	*lParam*
Menu:	Menu ID	0	0
Control:	Control ID	Notification code	Child window handle

The WM_SYSCOMMAND message is similar to the WM_COMMAND message except that WM_SYSCOMMAND signals that the user has chosen an enabled menu item from the system menu:

	LOWORD (wParam)	*HIWORD (wParam)*	*lParam*
System menu:	Menu ID	0	0 (If the WM_SYSCOMMAND message is the result of a mouse click, then LOWORD (lParam) and HIWORD (lParam) refer respectively to the X and Y screen coordinates of the mouse cursor.)

The menu ID indicates which item on the system menu has been chosen. For the predefined system menu items, the bottom four bits should be masked out. The resultant value will be one of the following: SC_SIZE, SC_MOVE, SC_MINIMIZE, SC_MAXIMIZE, SC_NEXTWIN-DOW, SC_PREVWINDOW, SC_CLOSE, SC_VSCROLL, SC_HSCROLL, SC_ARRANGE, SC_RESTORE, and SC_TASKLIST. In addition, the low word of *wParam* can be SC_MOUSE-MENU or SC_KEYMENU.

If you add menu items to the system menu, the low word of *wParam* will be the menu ID that you define. To avoid conflicts with the predefined menu IDs, use values below 0xF000. It is important that you pass normal WM_SYSCOMMAND messages to *DefWindowProc*. If you do not, you'll effectively disable the normal system menu commands.

The final message we'll discuss is WM_MENUCHAR, which isn't really a menu message at all. Windows sends this message to your window procedure in one of two circumstances: if the user presses Alt and a character key that does not correspond to a menu item, or, when a popup is displayed, if the user presses a character key that does not correspond to an item in the popup. The parameters that accompany the WM_MENUCHAR message are as follows:

LOWORD (wParam)	HIWORD (wParam)	lParam
ASCII code	Selection code	Handle to menu

The selection code is:

- 0—No popup is displayed.
- MF_POPUP—Popup is displayed.
- MF_SYSMENU—System menu popup is displayed.

Windows programs usually pass this message to *DefWindowProc*, which normally returns a 0 to Windows, which causes Windows to beep. We'll see a use for the WM_MENUCHAR message in the GRAFMENU program shown later in this chapter.

A Sample Program

Let's look at a simple example. The MENUDEMO program, shown in Figure 10-1, has five items in the main menu—File, Edit, Background, Timer, and Help. Each of these items has a popup. MENUDEMO does the simplest and most common type of menu processing, which involves trapping WM_COMMAND messages and checking the low word of *wParam*.

MENUDEMO.MAK

```
#-----------------------
# MENUDEMO.MAK make file
#-----------------------

menudemo.exe : menudemo.obj menudemo.res
     $(LINKER) $(GUIFLAGS) -OUT:menudemo.exe menudemo.obj \
     menudemo.res $(GUILIBS)

menudemo.obj : menudemo.c menudemo.h
     $(CC) $(CFLAGS) menudemo.c

menudemo.res : menudemo.rc menudemo.h
     $(RC) $(RCVARS) menudemo.rc
```

MENUDEMO.C

```c
/*-------------------------------------------
   MENUDEMO.C -- Menu Demonstration
                 (c) Charles Petzold, 1996
   -------------------------------------------*/

#include <windows.h>
#include "menudemo.h"

LRESULT CALLBACK WndProc (HWND, UINT, WPARAM, LPARAM) ;

char szAppName[] = "MenuDemo" ;

int WINAPI WinMain (HINSTANCE hInstance, HINSTANCE hPrevInstance,
                    PSTR szCmdLine, int iCmdShow)
     {
     HWND         hwnd ;
     MSG          msg ;
     WNDCLASSEX wndclass ;

     wndclass.cbSize        = sizeof (wndclass) ;
     wndclass.style         = CS_HREDRAW | CS_VREDRAW ;
     wndclass.lpfnWndProc   = WndProc ;
     wndclass.cbClsExtra    = 0 ;
     wndclass.cbWndExtra    = 0 ;
     wndclass.hInstance     = hInstance ;
```

Figure 10-1. *The MENUDEMO program.*   *(continued)*

```
     wndclass.hIcon         = LoadIcon (NULL, IDI_APPLICATION) ;
     wndclass.hCursor       = LoadCursor (NULL, IDC_ARROW) ;
     wndclass.hbrBackground = (HBRUSH) GetStockObject (WHITE_BRUSH) ;
     wndclass.lpszMenuName  = szAppName ;
     wndclass.lpszClassName = szAppName ;
     wndclass.hIconSm       = LoadIcon (NULL, IDI_APPLICATION) ;

     RegisterClassEx (&wndclass) ;

     hwnd = CreateWindow (szAppName, "Menu Demonstration",
                     WS_OVERLAPPEDWINDOW,
                     CW_USEDEFAULT, CW_USEDEFAULT,
                     CW_USEDEFAULT, CW_USEDEFAULT,
                     NULL, NULL, hInstance, NULL) ;

     ShowWindow (hwnd, iCmdShow) ;
     UpdateWindow (hwnd) ;

     while (GetMessage (&msg, NULL, 0, 0))
          {
          TranslateMessage (&msg) ;
          DispatchMessage (&msg) ;
          }
     return msg.wParam ;
     }

LRESULT CALLBACK WndProc (HWND hwnd, UINT iMsg, WPARAM wParam, LPARAM lParam)
     {
     static int  iColorID[5] = { WHITE_BRUSH, LTGRAY_BRUSH, GRAY_BRUSH,
                                 DKGRAY_BRUSH, BLACK_BRUSH } ;
     static int  iSelection = IDM_WHITE ;
     HMENU       hMenu ;

     switch (iMsg)
          {
          case WM_COMMAND :
               hMenu = GetMenu (hwnd) ;

               switch (LOWORD (wParam))
                    {
                    case IDM_NEW :
                    case IDM_OPEN :
                    case IDM_SAVE :
                    case IDM_SAVEAS :
```

(continued)

```
                MessageBeep (0) ;
                return 0 ;

        case IDM_EXIT :
                SendMessage (hwnd, WM_CLOSE, 0, 0L) ;
                return 0 ;

        case IDM_UNDO :
        case IDM_CUT :
        case IDM_COPY :
        case IDM_PASTE :
        case IDM_DEL :
                MessageBeep (0) ;
                return 0 ;

        case IDM_WHITE :                // Note: Logic below
        case IDM_LTGRAY :               //    assumes that IDM_WHITE
        case IDM_GRAY :                 //    through IDM_BLACK are
        case IDM_DKGRAY :               //    consecutive numbers in
        case IDM_BLACK :                //    the order shown here.

                CheckMenuItem (hMenu, iSelection, MF_UNCHECKED) ;
                iSelection = LOWORD (wParam) ;
                CheckMenuItem (hMenu, iSelection, MF_CHECKED) ;

                SetClassLong (hwnd, GCL_HBRBACKGROUND,
                        (LONG) GetStockObject
                            (iColorID[LOWORD (wParam) - IDM_WHITE])) ;

                InvalidateRect (hwnd, NULL, TRUE) ;
                return 0 ;

        case IDM_START :
                if (SetTimer (hwnd, 1, 1000, NULL))
                    {
                    EnableMenuItem (hMenu, IDM_START, MF_GRAYED) ;
                    EnableMenuItem (hMenu, IDM_STOP, MF_ENABLED) ;
                    }
                return 0 ;

        case IDM_STOP :
                KillTimer (hwnd, 1) ;
                EnableMenuItem (hMenu, IDM_START, MF_ENABLED) ;
                EnableMenuItem (hMenu, IDM_STOP,  MF_GRAYED) ;
```

(continued)

```
                              return 0 ;

                   case IDM_HELP :
                        MessageBox (hwnd, "Help not yet implemented!",
                                   szAppName, MB_ICONEXCLAMATION | MB_OK) ;
                        return 0 ;

                   case IDM_ABOUT :
                        MessageBox (hwnd, "Menu Demonstration Program.",
                                   szAppName, MB_ICONINFORMATION | MB_OK) ;
                        return 0 ;
                   }
              break ;

         case WM_TIMER :
              MessageBeep (0) ;
              return 0 ;

         case WM_DESTROY :
              PostQuitMessage (0) ;
              return 0 ;
         }
    return DefWindowProc (hwnd, iMsg, wParam, lParam) ;
    }
```

MENUDEMO.RC

```
/*---------------------------
   MENUDEMO.RC resource script
   ---------------------------*/

#include "menudemo.h"

MenuDemo MENU
    {
    POPUP "&File"
        {
        MENUITEM "&New",                    IDM_NEW
        MENUITEM "&Open...",                IDM_OPEN
        MENUITEM "&Save",                   IDM_SAVE
        MENUITEM "Save &As...",             IDM_SAVEAS
        MENUITEM SEPARATOR
        MENUITEM "E&xit",                   IDM_EXIT
        }
```

(continued)

```
    POPUP "&Edit"
        {
        MENUITEM "&Undo",                 IDM_UNDO
        MENUITEM SEPARATOR
        MENUITEM "Cu&t",                  IDM_CUT
        MENUITEM "&Copy",                 IDM_COPY
        MENUITEM "&Paste",                IDM_PASTE
        MENUITEM "De&lete",               IDM_DEL
        }
    POPUP "&Background"
        {
        MENUITEM "&White",                IDM_WHITE, CHECKED
        MENUITEM "&Lt Gray",              IDM_LTGRAY
        MENUITEM "&Gray",                 IDM_GRAY
        MENUITEM "&Dk Gray",              IDM_DKGRAY
        MENUITEM "&Black",                IDM_BLACK
        }
    POPUP "&Timer"
        {
        MENUITEM "&Start"                 IDM_START
        MENUITEM "S&top"                  IDM_STOP,  GRAYED
        }
    POPUP "&Help"
        {
        MENUITEM "&Help...",              IDM_HELP
        MENUITEM "&About MenuDemo...",    IDM_ABOUT
        }
    }
```

MENUDEMO.H

```
/*-------------------------
   MENUDEMO.H header file
   ----------------------*/

#define IDM_NEW      1
#define IDM_OPEN     2
#define IDM_SAVE     3
#define IDM_SAVEAS   4
#define IDM_EXIT     5

#define IDM_UNDO    10
#define IDM_CUT     11
#define IDM_COPY    12
```

(continued)

```
#define IDM_PASTE     13
#define IDM_DEL       14

#define IDM_WHITE     20
#define IDM_LTGRAY    21
#define IDM_GRAY      22
#define IDM_DKGRAY    23
#define IDM_BLACK     24

#define IDM_START     30
#define IDM_STOP      31

#define IDM_HELP      40
#define IDM_ABOUT     41
```

Identifiers for all menu IDs are defined in MENUDEMO.H. This file must be specified (using a *#include* statement) in both the resource script file and the C source code file. The identifiers begin with IDM. The ID numbers defined for the menu items need not be consecutive. However, if you process these IDs in your program using switch and case statements, keep in mind that the C compiler can best optimize this code using jump tables if you use consecutive menu ID numbers.

The MENUDEMO program simply beeps when it receives a WM_COMMAND message for most items in the File and Edit popups. The Background popup lists five stock brushes that MENUDEMO can use to color the background. In the MENUDEMO.RC resource script the White menu item (with a menu ID of IDM_WHITE) is flagged as CHECKED, which places a check mark next to the item. In MENUDEMO.C, the value of *iSelection* is initially set to IDM_WHITE.

The five brushes on the Background popup menu are mutually exclusive. When MENUDEMO.C receives a WM_COMMAND message where the low word of *wParam* is one of these five items on the Background popup, it must remove the check mark from the previously chosen background color and add a check mark to the new background color. To do this, it first gets a handle to its menu:

```
hMenu = GetMenu (hwnd) ;
```

The *CheckMenuItem* function is used to uncheck the currently checked item:

```
CheckMenuItem (hMenu, iSelection, MF_UNCHECKED) ;
```

The *iSelection* value is set to the low word of *wParam*, and the new background color is checked:

```
iSelection = LOWORD (wParam) ;
CheckMenuItem (hMenu, iSelection, MF_CHECKED) ;
```

The background color in the window class is then replaced with the new background color, and the window client area is invalidated. Windows erases the window using the new background color.

The Timer popup lists two options—Start and Stop. Initially, the Stop option is grayed (as indicated in the menu definition for the resource script). When you choose the Start option, MENUDEMO tries to start a timer and, if successful, grays the Start option and makes the Stop option active:

```
EnableMenuItem (hMenu, IDM_START, MF_GRAYED) ;
EnableMenuItem (hMenu, IDM_STOP,  MF_ENABLED) ;
```

On receipt of a WM_COMMAND message with the low word of *wParam* equal to IDM_STOP, the MENUDEMO program kills the timer, activates the Start option, and grays the Stop option:

```
EnableMenuItem (hMenu, IDM_START, MF_ENABLED) ;
EnableMenuItem (hMenu, IDM_STOP,  MF_GRAYED) ;
```

Notice that it's impossible for MENUDEMO to receive a WM_COMMAND message with the low word of *wParam* equal to IDM_START while the timer is going. Similarly, it's impossible to receive a WM_COMMAND with the low word of *wParam* equal to IDM_STOP while the timer is not going.

When MENUDEMO receives a WM_COMMAND message with the low word of the *wParam* parameter equal to IDM_ABOUT or IDM_HELP, it displays a message box. (In the next chapter, we'll change this to a dialog box.)

When MENUDEMO receives a WM_COMMAND message with the low word of *wParam* equal to IDM_EXIT, it sends itself a WM_CLOSE message. This is the same message that *DefWindowProc* sends the window procedure when it receives a WM_SYSCOMMAND message with *wParam* equal to SC_CLOSE. We'll examine this more in the POPPAD2 program shown toward the end of this chapter.

Menu Etiquette

The format of the File and Edit popups in MENUDEMO is quite similar to the formats in other Windows programs. One of the objectives of Windows is to provide a user with a recognizable interface that does not require relearning basic concepts for each program. It certainly helps if the File and Edit menus look the same in every Windows program and use the same letters for selection in combination with the Alt key.

Beyond the File and Edit popups, the menus of most Windows programs will be different. When designing a menu you should look at existing Windows programs and aim for some consistency. Of course, if you think these other programs are wrong and you know the right way to do it, nobody's going to stop you. Also keep in mind that revising a menu usually requires revising only the resource script and not your program code. You can move menu items around at a later time without many problems.

Although your program menu can have MENUITEM statements on the top level, these are not typical because they can be too easily chosen by mistake. If you do this, use an exclamation point after the text string to indicate that the menu item does not invoke a popup.

Defining a Menu the Hard Way

Defining a menu in a program's resource script is usually the easiest way to add a menu in your window, but it's not the only way. You can dispense with the resource script and create a menu entirely within your program using two functions called *CreateMenu* and *AppendMenu*. After you finish defining the menu, you can pass the menu handle to *CreateWindow* or use *SetMenu* to set the window's menu.

Here's how it's done. *CreateMenu* simply returns a handle to a new menu:

```
hMenu = CreateMenu () ;
```

The menu is initially empty. *AppendMenu* inserts items into the menu. You must obtain a different menu handle for the top-level menu item and for each popup. The popups are constructed separately; the popup menu handles are then inserted into the top-level menu. The code shown in Figure 10-2 creates a menu in this fashion; in fact, it is the same menu as in the MENUDEMO program.

```
hMenu = CreateMenu () ;

hMenuPopup = CreateMenu () ;

AppendMenu (hMenuPopup, MF_STRING,    IDM_NEW,    "&New") ;
AppendMenu (hMenuPopup, MF_STRING,    IDM_OPEN,   "&Open...") ;
AppendMenu (hMenuPopup, MF_STRING,    IDM_SAVE,   "&Save") ;
AppendMenu (hMenuPopup, MF_STRING,    IDM_SAVEAS, "Save &As...") ;
AppendMenu (hMenuPopup, MF_SEPARATOR, 0,          NULL) ;
AppendMenu (hMenuPopup, MF_STRING,    IDM_EXIT,   "E&xit") ;

AppendMenu (hMenu, MF_POPUP, (UINT) hMenuPopup, "&File") ;

hMenuPopup = CreateMenu () ;

AppendMenu (hMenuPopup, MF_STRING,    IDM_UNDO,   "&Undo") ;
AppendMenu (hMenuPopup, MF_SEPARATOR, 0,          NULL) ;
AppendMenu (hMenuPopup, MF_STRING,    IDM_CUT,    "Cu&t") ;
AppendMenu (hMenuPopup, MF_STRING,    IDM_COPY,   "&Copy") ;
AppendMenu (hMenuPopup, MF_STRING,    IDM_PASTE,  "&Paste") ;
AppendMenu (hMenuPopup, MF_STRING,    IDM_DEL,    "De&lete") ;
```

Figure 10-2. *C code that creates the same menu as used in the MENUDEMO program but without requiring a resource script file.*   *(continued)*

```
    AppendMenu (hMenu, MF_POPUP, (UINT) hMenuPopup, "&Edit") ;

hMenuPopup = CreateMenu () ;

AppendMenu (hMenuPopup, MF_STRING ¦ MF_CHECKED, IDM_WHITE,  "&White") ;
AppendMenu (hMenuPopup, MF_STRING,              IDM_LTGRAY, "&Lt Gray") ;
AppendMenu (hMenuPopup, MF_STRING,              IDM_GRAY,   "&Gray") ;
AppendMenu (hMenuPopup, MF_STRING,              IDM_DKGRAY, "&Dk Gray") ;
AppendMenu (hMenuPopup, MF_STRING,              IDM_BLACK,  "&Black") ;

AppendMenu (hMenu, MF_POPUP, (UINT) hMenuPopup, "&Background") ;

hMenuPopup = CreateMenu () ;

AppendMenu (hMenuPopup, MF_STRING,             IDM_START, "&Start") ;
AppendMenu (hMenuPopup, MF_STRING ¦ MF_GRAYED, IDM_STOP,  "S&top") ;
AppendMenu (hMenu, MF_POPUP, (UINT) hMenuPopup, "&Timer") ;

hMenuPopup = CreateMenu () ;

AppendMenu (hMenuPopup, MF_STRING, IDM_HELP,  "&Help...") ;
AppendMenu (hMenuPopup, MF_STRING, IDM_ABOUT, "&About MenuDemo...") ;

AppendMenu (hMenu, MF_POPUP, (UINT) hMenuPopup, "&Help") ;
```

I think you'll agree that the resource script menu template is easier and clearer. I'm not recommending that you define a menu in this way, only showing that it can be done. Certainly you could cut down on the code size substantially by using some arrays of structures containing all the menu item character strings, IDs, and flags. But if you do that, you might as well take advantage of the third method Windows provides for defining a menu.

A Third Approach to Defining Menus

The *LoadMenuIndirect* function accepts a pointer to a structure of type MENUITEMTEM-PLATE and returns a handle to a menu. This function is used within Windows to construct a menu after loading the normal menu template from a resource script. If you're brave, you can try using it yourself.

Floating Popup Menus

You can also make use of menus without having a top-level menu bar. You can instead cause a popup menu to appear on top of any part of the screen. One approach is to invoke this popup menu in response to a click of the right mouse button. However, menu items must still be selected with the left mouse button. The POPMENU program in Figure 10-3, beginning on the following page, shows how this is done.

POPMENU.MAK

```
#----------------------
# POPMENU.MAK make file
#----------------------


popmenu.exe : popmenu.obj popmenu.res
    $(LINKER) $(GUIFLAGS) -OUT:popmenu.exe popmenu.obj \
    popmenu.res $(GUILIBS)

popmenu.obj : popmenu.c popmenu.h
    $(CC) $(CFLAGS) popmenu.c

popmenu.res : popmenu.rc popmenu.h
    $(RC) $(RCVARS) popmenu.rc
```

POPMENU.C

```
/*-------------------------------------------
    POPMENU.C -- Popup Menu Demonstration
                 (c) Charles Petzold, 1996
   -------------------------------------------*/

#include <windows.h>
#include "popmenu.h"

LRESULT CALLBACK WndProc (HWND, UINT, WPARAM, LPARAM) ;

char       szAppName[] = "PopMenu" ;
HINSTANCE hInst ;

int WINAPI WinMain (HINSTANCE hInstance, HINSTANCE hPrevInstance,
                    PSTR szCmdLine, int iCmdShow)
    {
    HWND       hwnd ;
    MSG        msg ;
    WNDCLASSEX wndclass ;

    wndclass.cbSize        = sizeof (wndclass) ;
    wndclass.style         = CS_HREDRAW | CS_VREDRAW ;
    wndclass.lpfnWndProc   = WndProc ;
    wndclass.cbClsExtra    = 0 ;
    wndclass.cbWndExtra    = 0 ;
    wndclass.hInstance     = hInstance ;
    wndclass.hIcon         = LoadIcon (NULL, IDI_APPLICATION) ;
```

Figure 10-3. *The POPMENU program.*   *(continued)*

```
    wndclass.hCursor        = LoadCursor (NULL, IDC_ARROW) ;
    wndclass.hbrBackground = (HBRUSH) GetStockObject (WHITE_BRUSH) ;
    wndclass.lpszMenuName  = NULL ;
    wndclass.lpszClassName = szAppName ;
    wndclass.hIconSm        = LoadIcon (NULL, IDI_APPLICATION) ;

    RegisterClassEx (&wndclass) ;

    hInst = hInstance ;

    hwnd = CreateWindow (szAppName, "Popup Menu Demonstration",
                         WS_OVERLAPPEDWINDOW,
                         CW_USEDEFAULT, CW_USEDEFAULT,
                         CW_USEDEFAULT, CW_USEDEFAULT,
                         NULL, NULL, hInstance, NULL) ;

    ShowWindow (hwnd, iCmdShow) ;
    UpdateWindow (hwnd) ;

    while (GetMessage (&msg, NULL, 0, 0))
        {
        TranslateMessage (&msg) ;
        DispatchMessage (&msg) ;
        }
    return msg.wParam ;
    }

LRESULT CALLBACK WndProc (HWND hwnd, UINT iMsg, WPARAM wParam, LPARAM lParam)
    {
    static HMENU hMenu ;
    static int   iColorID[5] = { WHITE_BRUSH,  LTGRAY_BRUSH, GRAY_BRUSH,
                                 DKGRAY_BRUSH, BLACK_BRUSH } ;
    static int   iSelection = IDM_WHITE ;
    POINT        point ;

    switch (iMsg)
        {
        case WM_CREATE :
            hMenu = LoadMenu (hInst, szAppName) ;
            hMenu = GetSubMenu (hMenu, 0) ;
            return 0 ;

        case WM_RBUTTONDOWN :
            point.x = LOWORD (lParam) ;
            point.y = HIWORD (lParam) ;
```

(continued)

```
            ClientToScreen (hwnd, &point) ;

            TrackPopupMenu (hMenu, 0, point.x, point.y, 0, hwnd, NULL) ;
            return 0 ;

    case WM_COMMAND :
        switch (LOWORD (wParam))
            {
            case IDM_NEW :
            case IDM_OPEN :
            case IDM_SAVE :
            case IDM_SAVEAS :
            case IDM_UNDO :
            case IDM_CUT :
            case IDM_COPY :
            case IDM_PASTE :
            case IDM_DEL :
                 MessageBeep (0) ;
                 return 0 ;

            case IDM_WHITE :            // Note: Logic below
            case IDM_LTGRAY :           //    assumes that IDM_WHITE
            case IDM_GRAY :             //    through IDM_BLACK are
            case IDM_DKGRAY :           //    consecutive numbers in
            case IDM_BLACK :            //    the order shown here.

                 CheckMenuItem (hMenu, iSelection, MF_UNCHECKED) ;
                 iSelection = LOWORD (wParam) ;
                 CheckMenuItem (hMenu, iSelection, MF_CHECKED) ;

                 SetClassLong (hwnd, GCL_HBRBACKGROUND,
                     (LONG) GetStockObject
                         (iColorID[LOWORD (wParam) - IDM_WHITE])) ;

                 InvalidateRect (hwnd, NULL, TRUE) ;
                 return 0 ;

            case IDM_ABOUT :
                 MessageBox (hwnd,
                          "Popup Menu Demonstration Program.",
                          szAppName,
                          MB_ICONINFORMATION | MB_OK) ;
                 return 0 ;
```

(continued)

```
                              case IDM_EXIT :
                                   SendMessage (hwnd, WM_CLOSE, 0, 0) ;
                                   return 0 ;

                              case IDM_HELP :
                                   MessageBox (hwnd, "Help not yet implemented!",
                                               szAppName,
                                               MB_ICONEXCLAMATION | MB_OK) ;
                                   return 0 ;
                              }
                         break ;

                    case WM_DESTROY :
                         PostQuitMessage (0) ;
                         return 0 ;
                    }
               return DefWindowProc (hwnd, iMsg, wParam, lParam) ;
               }
```

POPMENU.RC

```
/*---------------------------
   POPMENU.RC resource script
   ---------------------------*/

#include "popmenu.h"

PopMenu MENU
     {
     POPUP ""
          {
          POPUP "&File"
               {
               MENUITEM "&New",                IDM_NEW
               MENUITEM "&Open...",            IDM_OPEN
               MENUITEM "&Save",               IDM_SAVE
               MENUITEM "Save &As...",         IDM_SAVEAS
               MENUITEM SEPARATOR
               MENUITEM "E&xit",               IDM_EXIT
               }
          POPUP "&Edit"
               {
               MENUITEM "&Undo",               IDM_UNDO
```

(continued)

```
                    MENUITEM SEPARATOR
                    MENUITEM "Cu&t",                  IDM_CUT
                    MENUITEM "&Copy",                 IDM_COPY
                    MENUITEM "&Paste",                IDM_PASTE
                    MENUITEM "De&lete",               IDM_DEL
                    }
              POPUP "&Background"
                    {
                    MENUITEM "&White",                IDM_WHITE, CHECKED
                    MENUITEM "&Lt Gray",              IDM_LTGRAY
                    MENUITEM "&Gray",                 IDM_GRAY
                    MENUITEM "&Dk Gray",              IDM_DKGRAY
                    MENUITEM "&Black",                IDM_BLACK
                    }
              POPUP "&Help"
                    {
                    MENUITEM "&Help...",              IDM_HELP
                    MENUITEM "&About PopMenu...",     IDM_ABOUT
                    }
              }
        }
```

POPMENU.H

```
/*-----------------------
   POPMENU.H header file
   ----------------------*/

#define IDM_NEW      1
#define IDM_OPEN     2
#define IDM_SAVE     3
#define IDM_SAVEAS   4
#define IDM_EXIT     5

#define IDM_UNDO     10
#define IDM_CUT      11
#define IDM_COPY     12
#define IDM_PASTE    13
#define IDM_DEL      14

#define IDM_WHITE    20
#define IDM_LTGRAY   21
#define IDM_GRAY     22
```

(continued)

```
#define IDM_DKGRAY   23
#define IDM_BLACK    24

#define IDM_HELP     30
#define IDM_ABOUT    31
```

The POPMENU.RC resource script defines a menu very similar to the one in MENUDEMO.RC. The difference is that the top-level menu contains only one item—a popup that invokes the File, Edit, Background, and Help options.

During the WM_CREATE message in *WndProc*, POPMENU obtains a handle to this popup menu:

```
hMenu = LoadMenu (hInst, szAppName) ;
hMenu = GetSubMenu (hMenu, 0) ;
```

During the WM_RBUTTONDOWN message, POPMENU obtains the position of the mouse pointer, converts the position to screen coordinates, and passes the coordinates to *TrackPopupMenu*:

```
point.x = LOWORD (lParam) ;
point.y = HIWORD (lParam) ;
ClientToScreen (hwnd, &point) ;

TrackPopupMenu (hMenu, 0, point.x, point.y, 0, hwnd, NULL) ;
```

Windows then displays the popup menu with the items File, Edit, Background, and Help. Selecting any of these options causes the nested popup menus to appear to the right. The menu functions the same as a normal menu.

Using the System Menu

Parent windows created with a style that includes WS_SYSMENU have a system menu box at the left of the title bar. If you like, you can modify this menu. For instance, you can add your own menu commands to the system menu. While this is not recommended, modifying the system menu is often a quick-and-dirty way to add a menu to a short program without defining it in the resource script. The only restriction is this: The ID numbers you use to add commands to the system menu must be lower than 0xF000. Otherwise, they will conflict with the IDs that Windows uses for the normal system menu commands. And remember: When you process WM_SYSCOMMAND messages in your window procedure for these new menu items, you must pass the other WM_SYSCOMMAND messages to *DefWindowProc*. If you don't, you'll effectively disable all normal options on the system menu.

The program POORMENU ("Poor Person's Menu"), shown in Figure 10-4, beginning on the following page, adds a separator bar and three commands to the system menu. The last of these commands removes the additions.

POORMENU.MAK

```
#-----------------------
# POORMENU.MAK make file
#-----------------------


poormenu.exe : poormenu.obj
    $(LINKER) $(GUIFLAGS) -OUT:poormenu.exe poormenu.obj $(GUILIBS)

poormenu.obj : poormenu.c
    $(CC) $(CFLAGS) poormenu.c
```

POORMENU.C

```
/*-------------------------------------------
   POORMENU.C -- The Poor Person's Menu
                (c) Charles Petzold, 1996
   -------------------------------------------*/

#include <windows.h>

#define IDM_ABOUT   1
#define IDM_HELP    2
#define IDM_REMOVE  3

LRESULT CALLBACK WndProc (HWND, UINT, WPARAM, LPARAM) ;

static char szAppName[] = "PoorMenu" ;

int WINAPI WinMain (HINSTANCE hInstance, HINSTANCE hPrevInstance,
                    PSTR szCmdLine, int iCmdShow)
     {
     HMENU       hMenu ;
     HWND        hwnd ;
     MSG         msg ;
     WNDCLASSEX wndclass ;

     wndclass.cbSize        = sizeof (wndclass) ;
     wndclass.style         = CS_HREDRAW | CS_VREDRAW ;
     wndclass.lpfnWndProc   = WndProc ;
     wndclass.cbClsExtra    = 0 ;
     wndclass.cbWndExtra    = 0 ;
     wndclass.hInstance     = hInstance ;
     wndclass.hIcon         = LoadIcon (NULL, IDI_APPLICATION) ;
     wndclass.hCursor       = LoadCursor (NULL, IDC_ARROW) ;
```

Figure 10-4. *The POORMENU program.*   *(continued)*

```
          wndclass.hbrBackground = (HBRUSH) GetStockObject (WHITE_BRUSH) ;
          wndclass.lpszMenuName  = NULL ;
          wndclass.lpszClassName = szAppName ;
          wndclass.hIconSm       = LoadIcon (NULL, IDI_APPLICATION) ;

          RegisterClassEx (&wndclass) ;

          hwnd = CreateWindow (szAppName, "The Poor-Person's Menu",
                              WS_OVERLAPPEDWINDOW,
                              CW_USEDEFAULT, CW_USEDEFAULT,
                              CW_USEDEFAULT, CW_USEDEFAULT,
                              NULL, NULL, hInstance, NULL) ;


          hMenu = GetSystemMenu (hwnd, FALSE) ;

          AppendMenu (hMenu, MF_SEPARATOR, 0,           NULL) ;
          AppendMenu (hMenu, MF_STRING,    IDM_ABOUT,  "About...") ;
          AppendMenu (hMenu, MF_STRING,    IDM_HELP,   "Help...") ;
          AppendMenu (hMenu, MF_STRING,    IDM_REMOVE, "Remove Additions") ;

          ShowWindow (hwnd, iCmdShow) ;
          UpdateWindow (hwnd) ;

          while (GetMessage (&msg, NULL, 0, 0))
               {
               TranslateMessage (&msg) ;
               DispatchMessage (&msg) ;
               }
          return msg.wParam ;
          }

LRESULT CALLBACK WndProc (HWND hwnd, UINT iMsg, WPARAM wParam, LPARAM lParam)
     {
     switch (iMsg)
          {
          case WM_SYSCOMMAND :
               switch (LOWORD (wParam))
                    {
                    case IDM_ABOUT :
                         MessageBox (hwnd, "A Poor-Person's Menu Program.",
                                     szAppName, MB_OK | MB_ICONINFORMATION) ;
                         return 0 ;

                    case IDM_HELP :
                         MessageBox (hwnd, "Help not yet implemented!",
```

(continued)

```
                                    szAppName, MB_OK | MB_ICONEXCLAMATION) ;
                    return 0 ;

               case IDM_REMOVE :
                    GetSystemMenu (hwnd, TRUE) ;
                    return 0 ;
               }
          break ;

     case WM_DESTROY :
          PostQuitMessage (0) ;
          return 0 ;
     }
     return DefWindowProc (hwnd, iMsg, wParam, lParam) ;
}
```

The three menu IDs are defined near the top of POORMENU.C:

```
#define IDM_ABOUT    1
#define IDM_HELP     2
#define IDM_REMOVE   3
```

After the program's window has been created, POORMENU obtains a handle to the system menu:

```
hMenu = GetSystemMenu (hwnd, FALSE) ;
```

When you first call *GetSystemMenu*, you should set the second parameter to FALSE in preparation for modifying the menu.

The menu is altered with four *AppendMenu* calls:

```
AppendMenu (hMenu, MF_SEPARATOR, 0,          NULL) ;
AppendMenu (hMenu, MF_STRING,    IDM_ABOUT,  "About...") ;
AppendMenu (hMenu, MF_STRING,    IDM_HELP,   "Help...") ;
AppendMenu (hMenu, MF_STRING,    IDM_REMOVE, "Remove Additions") ;
```

The first *AppendMenu* call adds the separator bar. Choosing the Remove Additions menu item causes POORMENU to remove these additions, which it accomplishes simply by calling *GetSystemMenu* again with the second parameter set to TRUE:

```
GetSystemMenu (hwnd, TRUE) ;
```

The standard system menu has the options Restore, Move, Size, Minimize, Maximize, Close, and Switch To. These generate WM_SYSCOMMAND messages with *wParam* equal to SC_RESTORE, SC_MOVE, SC_SIZE, SC_MINIMIZE, SC_MAXIMIZE, SC_CLOSE, and SC-_TASKLIST. Although Windows programs do not normally do so, you can process these messages yourself rather than pass them on to *DefWindowProc*. You can also disable or remove some of these standard options from the system menu using methods described below. The Windows documentation also includes some standard additions to the system menu. These use the identifiers SC_NEXTWINDOW, SC_PREVWINDOW, SC_VSCROLL, SC_HSCROLL, and SC_ARRANGE. You might find it appropriate to add these commands to the system menu in some applications.

Changing the Menu

We've already seen how the *AppendMenu* function can be used to define a menu entirely within a program and to add menu items to the system menu. Prior to Windows 3.0, you would have been forced to use the *ChangeMenu* function for this job. *ChangeMenu* was so versatile that it was one of the most complex functions in all of Windows. In Windows 95, *ChangeMenu* is still available, but its functionality has been divided among five new functions:

- ■ *AppendMenu*—adds a new item to the end of a menu.

- ■ *DeleteMenu*—deletes an existing item from a menu and destroys the item.

- ■ *InsertMenu*—inserts a new item into a menu.

- ■ *ModifyMenu*—changes an existing menu item.

- ■ *RemoveMenu*—removes an existing item from a menu.

The difference between *DeleteMenu* and *RemoveMenu* is important if the item is a popup menu. *DeleteMenu* destroys the popup menu—but *RemoveMenu* does not.

Other Menu Commands

Here are some more functions useful for working with menus.

When you change a top-level menu item, the change is not shown until Windows redraws the menu bar. You can force this redrawing by calling:

```
DrawMenuBar (hwnd) ;
```

Notice that the parameter to *DrawMenuBar* is a handle to the window rather than a handle to the menu.

You can obtain the handle to a popup menu using:

```
hMenuPopup = GetSubMenu (hMenu, iPosition) ;
```

where *iPosition* is the index (starting at 0) of the popup within the top-level menu indicated by *hMenu*. You can then use the popup menu handle with other functions (such as *AppendMenu*).

You can obtain the current number of items in a top-level or popup menu using:

```
iCount = GetMenuItemCount (hMenu) ;
```

You can obtain the menu ID for an item in a popup menu from:

```
id = GetMenuItemID (hMenuPopup, iPosition) ;
```

where *iPosition* is the position (starting at 0) of the item within the popup.

In MENUDEMO you saw how to check or uncheck an item in a popup menu using:

```
CheckMenuItem (hMenu, id, iCheck) ;
```

In MENUDEMO, *hMenu* was the handle to the top-level menu, *id* was the menu ID, and the value of *iCheck* was either MF_CHECKED or MF_UNCHECKED. If *hMenu* is a handle to a popup menu, then the *id* parameter can be a positional index rather than a menu ID. If an index is more convenient, you include MF_BYPOSITION in the third parameter. For instance:

```
CheckMenuItem (hMenu, iPosition, MF_CHECKED | MF_BYPOSITION) ;
```

The *EnableMenuItem* function works similarly to *CheckMenuItem* except the third parameter is MF_ENABLED, MF_DISABLED, or MF_GRAYED. If you use *EnableMenuItem* on a top-level menu item that has a popup, you must also use the MF_BYPOSITION identifier in the third parameter because the menu item has no menu ID. We'll see an example of *EnableMenuItem* in the POPPAD program shown later in this chapter. *HiliteMenuItem* is similar to *CheckMenuItem* and *EnableMenuItem* but uses MF_HILITE and MF_UNHILITE. This highlighting is the reverse video that Windows uses when you move among menu items. You do not normally need to use *HiliteMenuItem*.

What else do you need to do with your menu? Have you forgotten what character string you used in a menu? You can refresh your memory by calling:

```
iByteCount = GetMenuString (hMenu, id, pString, iMaxCount, iFlag) ;
```

The *iFlag* is either MF_BYCOMMAND (where *id* is a menu ID) or MF_BYPOSITION (where *id* is a positional index). The function copies up to *iMaxCount* bytes of the character string into *pString* and returns the number of bytes copied.

Or perhaps you'd like to know what the current flags of a menu item are:

```
iFlags = GetMenuState (hMenu, id, iFlag) ;
```

Again, *iFlag* is either MF_BYCOMMAND or MF_BYPOSITION. The *iFlags* return value is a combination of all the current flags. You can determine the current flags by testing against the MF_DISABLED, MF_GRAYED, MF_CHECKED, MF_MENUBREAK, MF_MENUBARBREAK, and MF_SEPARATOR identifiers.

Or maybe by this time you're a little fed up with menus. In that case you'll be pleased to know that if you no longer need a menu in your program, you can destroy it:

```
DestroyMenu (hMenu) ;
```

This invalidates the menu handle.

An Unorthodox Approach to Menus

Now let's step a little off the beaten path. Instead of having drop-down menus in your program, how about creating multiple top-level menus without any popups and switching between the top-level menus using the *SetMenu* call? The NOPOPUPS program, shown in Figure 10-5, demonstrates how to do it. This program includes File and Edit items similar to those that MENUDEMO uses but displays them as alternate top-level menus.

NOPOPUPS.MAK

```
#------------------------
# NOPOPUPS.MAK make file
#------------------------

nopopups.exe : nopopups.obj nopopups.res
     $(LINKER) $(GUIFLAGS) -OUT:nopopups.exe nopopups.obj \
     nopopups.res $(GUILIBS)

nopopups.obj : nopopups.c nopopups.h
     $(CC) $(CFLAGS) nopopups.c

nopopups.res : nopopups.rc nopopups.h
     $(RC) $(RCVARS) nopopups.rc
```

NOPOPUPS.C

```
/*----------------------------------------------------
   NOPOPUPS.C -- Demonstrates No-Popup Nested Menu
                 (c) Charles Petzold, 1996
   ----------------------------------------------------*/

#include <windows.h>
#include "nopopups.h"

LRESULT CALLBACK WndProc (HWND, UINT, WPARAM, LPARAM) ;

int WINAPI WinMain (HINSTANCE hInstance, HINSTANCE hPrevInstance,
                    PSTR szCmdLine, int iCmdShow)
     {
     static char szAppName[] = "NoPopUps" ;
     HWND        hwnd ;
     MSG         msg ;
     WNDCLASSEX  wndclass ;
```

Figure 10-5. *The NOPOPUPS program.*

(continued)

```
     wndclass.cbSize        = sizeof (wndclass) ;
     wndclass.style         = CS_HREDRAW | CS_VREDRAW ;
     wndclass.lpfnWndProc   = WndProc ;
     wndclass.cbClsExtra    = 0 ;
     wndclass.cbWndExtra    = 0 ;
     wndclass.hInstance     = hInstance ;
     wndclass.hIcon         = LoadIcon (NULL, IDI_APPLICATION) ;
     wndclass.hCursor       = LoadCursor (NULL, IDC_ARROW) ;
     wndclass.hbrBackground = (HBRUSH) GetStockObject (WHITE_BRUSH) ;
     wndclass.lpszMenuName  = NULL ;
     wndclass.lpszClassName = szAppName ;
     wndclass.hIconSm       = LoadIcon (NULL, IDI_APPLICATION) ;

     RegisterClassEx (&wndclass) ;

     hwnd = CreateWindow (szAppName, "No-Popup Nested Menu Demonstration",
                          WS_OVERLAPPEDWINDOW,
                          CW_USEDEFAULT, CW_USEDEFAULT,
                          CW_USEDEFAULT, CW_USEDEFAULT,
                          NULL, NULL, hInstance, NULL) ;

     ShowWindow (hwnd, iCmdShow) ;
     UpdateWindow (hwnd) ;

     while (GetMessage (&msg, NULL, 0, 0))
          {
          TranslateMessage (&msg) ;
          DispatchMessage (&msg) ;
          }
     return msg.wParam ;
     }

LRESULT CALLBACK WndProc (HWND hwnd, UINT iMsg, WPARAM wParam, LPARAM lParam)
     {
     static HMENU hMenuMain, hMenuEdit, hMenuFile ;
     HINSTANCE     hInstance ;

     switch (iMsg)
          {
          case WM_CREATE :
               hInstance = (HINSTANCE) GetWindowLong (hwnd, GWL_HINSTANCE) ;

               hMenuMain = LoadMenu (hInstance, "MenuMain") ;
               hMenuFile = LoadMenu (hInstance, "MenuFile") ;
```

(continued)

476

```
            hMenuEdit = LoadMenu (hInstance, "MenuEdit") ;

            SetMenu (hwnd, hMenuMain) ;
            return 0 ;

      case WM_COMMAND :
            switch (LOWORD (wParam))
                  {
                  case IDM_MAIN :
                        SetMenu (hwnd, hMenuMain) ;
                        return 0 ;

                  case IDM_FILE :
                        SetMenu (hwnd, hMenuFile) ;
                        return 0 ;

                  case IDM_EDIT :
                        SetMenu (hwnd, hMenuEdit) ;
                        return 0 ;

                  case IDM_NEW :
                  case IDM_OPEN :
                  case IDM_SAVE :
                  case IDM_SAVEAS :
                  case IDM_UNDO :
                  case IDM_CUT :
                  case IDM_COPY :
                  case IDM_PASTE :
                  case IDM_DEL :
                        MessageBeep (0) ;
                        return 0 ;
                  }
            break ;

      case WM_DESTROY :
            SetMenu (hwnd, hMenuMain) ;
            DestroyMenu (hMenuFile) ;
            DestroyMenu (hMenuEdit) ;

            PostQuitMessage (0) ;
            return 0 ;
      }
return DefWindowProc (hwnd, iMsg, wParam, lParam) ;
}
```

(continued)

NOPOPUPS.RC

```
/*-----------------------------
   NOPOPUPS.RC resource script
-----------------------------*/

#include "nopopups.h"

MenuMain MENU
    {
    MENUITEM "MAIN:",        0,      INACTIVE
    MENUITEM "&File...",     IDM_FILE
    MENUITEM "&Edit...",     IDM_EDIT
    }

MenuFile MENU
    {
    MENUITEM "FILE:",        0,      INACTIVE
    MENUITEM "&New",         IDM_NEW
    MENUITEM "&Open...",     IDM_OPEN
    MENUITEM "&Save",        IDM_SAVE
    MENUITEM "Save &As...",  IDM_SAVEAS
    MENUITEM "(&Main)",      IDM_MAIN
    }

MenuEdit MENU
    {
    MENUITEM "EDIT:",        0,      INACTIVE
    MENUITEM "&Undo",        IDM_UNDO
    MENUITEM "Cu&t",         IDM_CUT
    MENUITEM "&Copy",        IDM_COPY
    MENUITEM "&Paste",       IDM_PASTE
    MENUITEM "De&lete",      IDM_DEL
    MENUITEM "(&Main)",      IDM_MAIN
    }
```

NOPOPUPS.H

```
/*-----------------------
   NOPOPUPS.H header file
-----------------------*/

#define IDM_NEW    1
#define IDM_OPEN   2
#define IDM_SAVE   3
```

(continued)

```
#define IDM_SAVEAS    4

#define IDM_UNDO      5
#define IDM_CUT       6
#define IDM_COPY      7
#define IDM_PASTE     8
#define IDM_DEL       9

#define IDM_MAIN     10
#define IDM_EDIT     11
#define IDM_FILE     12
```

The resource script has three menus rather than one. When the window procedure processes the WM_CREATE message, Windows loads each menu resource into memory:

```
hMenuMain = LoadMenu (hInstance, "MenuMain") ;
hMenuFile = LoadMenu (hInstance, "MenuFile") ;
hMenuEdit = LoadMenu (hInstance, "MenuEdit") ;
```

Initially, the program displays the main menu:

```
SetMenu (hwnd, hMenuMain) ;
```

The main menu lists the three options using the character strings "MAIN:", "File...", and "Edit..." However, "MAIN:" is disabled, so it doesn't cause WM_COMMAND messages to be sent to the window procedure. The File and Edit menus begin "FILE:" and "EDIT:" to identify these as submenus. The last item in the File and Edit menus is the character string "(Main)"; this option indicates a return to the main menu. Switching among these three menus is simple:

```
case WM_COMMAND :
     switch (LOWORD (wParam))
          {
          case IDM_MAIN :
               SetMenu (hwnd, hMenuMain) ;
               return 0 ;

          case IDM_FILE :
               SetMenu (hwnd, hMenuFile) ;
               return 0 ;

          case IDM_EDIT :
               SetMenu (hwnd, hMenuEdit) ;
               return 0 ;

          [other program lines]
          }
     break ;
```

During the WM_DESTROY message, NOPOPUPS sets the program's menu to the Main menu and destroys the File and Edit menus with calls to *DestroyMenu*. The Main menu is destroyed automatically when the window is destroyed.

USING BITMAPS IN MENUS

Character strings are not the only way to display a menu item. You can also use a bitmap. If you immediately recoiled at the thought of pictures of file folders, paste jars, and trash cans in a menu, don't think of pictures. Think instead of how useful menu bitmaps might be for a drawing program. Think of using different fonts and font sizes, line widths, hatch patterns, and colors in your menus.

The program we're going to examine is called GRAFMENU ("graphics menu"). The top-level menu is shown in Figure 10-6. The enlarged block letters are obtained from 40-by-16-pixel monochrome bitmap files created in the Developer Studio's image editor and saved as .BMP files; they could be pictures instead. Choosing FONT from the menu invokes a popup containing three options—Courier New, Arial, and Times New Roman. These are the standard Windows TrueType fonts and each is displayed in its respective font (Figure 10-7). These bitmaps were created in the program using a technique involving a memory device context.

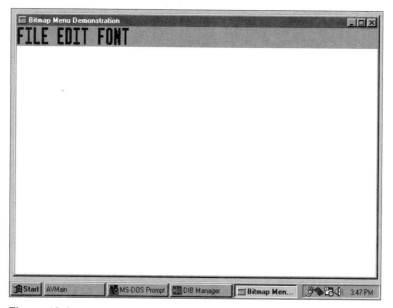

Figure 10-6. *The GRAFMENU program's top-level menu.*

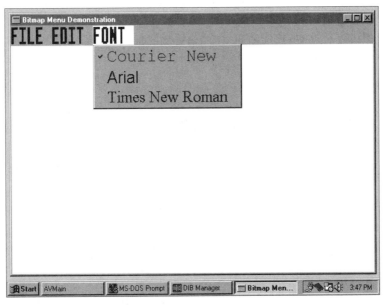

Figure 10-7. *The GRAFMENU program's popup FONT menu.*

Finally, when you pull down the system menu, you see that you have access to some "help" information, with the word "Help" perhaps mirroring the desperation of a new user (Figure 10-8). This 64-by-64-pixel monochrome bitmap was created in the Developer Studio's image editor.

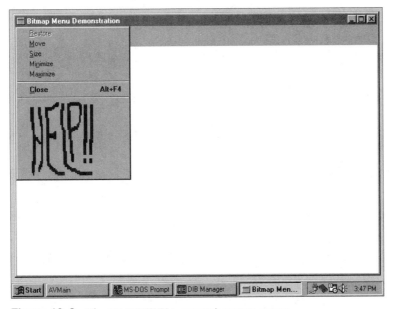

Figure 10-8. *The GRAFMENU program's system menu.*

The GRAFMENU program, including the four bitmaps created in the image editor, is shown in Figure 10-9.

GRAFMENU.MAK

```
#-----------------------
# GRAFMENU.MAK make file
#-----------------------

grafmenu.exe : grafmenu.obj grafmenu.res
     $(LINKER) $(GUIFLAGS) -OUT:grafmenu.exe \
     grafmenu.obj grafmenu.res $(GUILIBS)

grafmenu.obj : grafmenu.c grafmenu.h
     $(CC) $(CFLAGS) grafmenu.c

grafmenu.res : grafmenu.rc grafmenu.h \
     editlabl.bmp filelabl.bmp fontlabl.bmp bighelp.bmp
     $(RC) $(RCVARS) grafmenu.rc
```

GRAFMENU.C

```c
/*-------------------------------------------------
     GRAFMENU.C -- Demonstrates Bitmap Menu Items
                   (c) Charles Petzold, 1996
   -------------------------------------------------*/

#include <windows.h>
#include <string.h>
#include "grafmenu.h"

LRESULT CALLBACK WndProc  (HWND, UINT, WPARAM, LPARAM) ;
HBITMAP StretchBitmap (HBITMAP) ;
HBITMAP GetBitmapFont (int) ;

char szAppName[] = "GrafMenu" ;

int WINAPI WinMain (HINSTANCE hInstance, HINSTANCE hPrevInstance,
                    PSTR szCmdLine, int iCmdShow)
     {
     HBITMAP    hBitmapHelp, hBitmapFile, hBitmapEdit,
                hBitmapFont, hBitmapPopFont[3] ;
     HMENU      hMenu, hMenuPopup ;
```

Figure 10-9. *The GRAFMENU program.*   *(continued)*

```
HWND        hwnd ;
int         i ;
MSG         msg ;
WNDCLASSEX wndclass ;

wndclass.cbSize        = sizeof (wndclass) ;
wndclass.style         = CS_HREDRAW | CS_VREDRAW ;
wndclass.lpfnWndProc   = WndProc ;
wndclass.cbClsExtra    = 0 ;
wndclass.cbWndExtra    = 0 ;
wndclass.hInstance     = hInstance ;
wndclass.hIcon         = LoadIcon (NULL, IDI_APPLICATION) ;
wndclass.hCursor       = LoadCursor (NULL, IDC_ARROW) ;
wndclass.hbrBackground = (HBRUSH) GetStockObject (WHITE_BRUSH) ;
wndclass.lpszMenuName  = NULL ;
wndclass.lpszClassName = szAppName ;
wndclass.hIconSm       = LoadIcon (NULL, IDI_APPLICATION) ;

RegisterClassEx (&wndclass) ;

hMenu = CreateMenu () ;

hMenuPopup = LoadMenu (hInstance, "MenuFile") ;
hBitmapFile = StretchBitmap (LoadBitmap (hInstance, "BitmapFile")) ;
AppendMenu (hMenu, MF_BITMAP | MF_POPUP, (int) hMenuPopup,
            (PSTR) (LONG) hBitmapFile) ;

hMenuPopup = LoadMenu (hInstance, "MenuEdit") ;
hBitmapEdit = StretchBitmap (LoadBitmap (hInstance, "BitmapEdit")) ;
AppendMenu (hMenu, MF_BITMAP | MF_POPUP, (int) hMenuPopup,
            (PSTR) (LONG) hBitmapEdit) ;

hMenuPopup = CreateMenu () ;

for (i = 0 ; i < 3 ; i++)
    {
    hBitmapPopFont[i] = GetBitmapFont (i) ;
    AppendMenu (hMenuPopup, MF_BITMAP, IDM_COUR + i,
                (PSTR) (LONG) hBitmapPopFont[i]) ;
    }

hBitmapFont = StretchBitmap (LoadBitmap (hInstance, "BitmapFont")) ;
AppendMenu (hMenu, MF_BITMAP | MF_POPUP, (int) hMenuPopup,
            (PSTR) (LONG) hBitmapFont) ;
```

(continued)

```
    hwnd = CreateWindow (szAppName, "Bitmap Menu Demonstration",
                    WS_OVERLAPPEDWINDOW,
                    CW_USEDEFAULT, CW_USEDEFAULT,
                    CW_USEDEFAULT, CW_USEDEFAULT,
                    NULL, hMenu, hInstance, NULL) ;

    hMenu = GetSystemMenu (hwnd, FALSE);
    hBitmapHelp = StretchBitmap (LoadBitmap (hInstance, "BitmapHelp")) ;
    AppendMenu (hMenu, MF_SEPARATOR, NULL,      NULL) ;
    AppendMenu (hMenu, MF_BITMAP,    IDM_HELP, (PSTR) (LONG) hBitmapHelp) ;

    ShowWindow (hwnd, iCmdShow) ;
    UpdateWindow (hwnd) ;

    while (GetMessage (&msg, NULL, 0, 0))
         {
         TranslateMessage (&msg) ;
         DispatchMessage (&msg) ;
         }

    DeleteObject (hBitmapHelp) ;
    DeleteObject (hBitmapEdit) ;
    DeleteObject (hBitmapFile) ;
    DeleteObject (hBitmapFont) ;

    for (i = 0 ; i < 3 ; i++)
         DeleteObject (hBitmapPopFont[i]) ;

    return msg.wParam ;
    }

HBITMAP StretchBitmap (HBITMAP hBitmap1)
    {
    BITMAP      bm1, bm2 ;
    HBITMAP     hBitmap2 ;
    HDC         hdc, hdcMem1, hdcMem2 ;
    TEXTMETRIC tm ;

    hdc = CreateIC ("DISPLAY", NULL, NULL, NULL) ;
    GetTextMetrics (hdc, &tm) ;
    hdcMem1 = CreateCompatibleDC (hdc) ;
    hdcMem2 = CreateCompatibleDC (hdc) ;
    DeleteDC (hdc) ;
```

(continued)

```
        GetObject (hBitmap1, sizeof (BITMAP), (PSTR) &bm1) ;


     bm2 = bm1 ;
     bm2.bmWidth      = (tm.tmAveCharWidth * bm2.bmWidth) / 4 ;
     bm2.bmHeight     = (tm.tmHeight       * bm2.bmHeight) / 8 ;
     bm2.bmWidthBytes = ((bm2.bmWidth + 15) / 16) * 2 ;


     hBitmap2 = CreateBitmapIndirect (&bm2) ;


     SelectObject (hdcMem1, hBitmap1) ;
     SelectObject (hdcMem2, hBitmap2) ;


     StretchBlt (hdcMem2, 0, 0, bm2.bmWidth, bm2.bmHeight,
                 hdcMem1, 0, 0, bm1.bmWidth, bm1.bmHeight, SRCCOPY) ;


     DeleteDC (hdcMem1) ;
     DeleteDC (hdcMem2) ;
     DeleteObject (hBitmap1) ;


     return hBitmap2 ;
     }

HBITMAP GetBitmapFont (int i)
     {
     static char   *szFaceName[3] = { "Courier New", "Arial",
                                       "Times New Roman" } ;
     static LOGFONT lf ;
     HBITMAP        hBitmap ;
     HDC            hdc, hdcMem ;
     HFONT          hFont ;
     SIZE           size ;
     TEXTMETRIC     tm ;


     hdc = CreateIC ("DISPLAY", NULL, NULL, NULL) ;
     GetTextMetrics (hdc, &tm) ;


     lf.lfHeight = 2 * tm.tmHeight ;
     strcpy ((char *) lf.lfFaceName, szFaceName[i]) ;


     hdcMem = CreateCompatibleDC (hdc) ;
     hFont = (HFONT) SelectObject (hdcMem, CreateFontIndirect (&lf)) ;
     GetTextExtentPoint (hdcMem, szFaceName[i],
                     strlen (szFaceName[i]), &size) ;
```

(continued)

```
        hBitmap = CreateBitmap (size.cx, size.cy, 1, 1, NULL) ;
        SelectObject (hdcMem, hBitmap) ;

        TextOut (hdcMem, 0, 0, szFaceName[i], strlen (szFaceName[i])) ;

        DeleteObject (SelectObject (hdcMem, hFont)) ;
        DeleteDC (hdcMem) ;
        DeleteDC (hdc) ;

        return hBitmap ;
        }

LRESULT CALLBACK WndProc (HWND hwnd, UINT iMsg, WPARAM wParam, LPARAM lParam)
        {
        HMENU       hMenu ;
        static int  iCurrentFont = IDM_COUR ;

        switch (iMsg)
             {
             case WM_CREATE :
                  CheckMenuItem (GetMenu (hwnd), iCurrentFont, MF_CHECKED) ;
                  return 0 ;

             case WM_SYSCOMMAND :
                  switch (LOWORD (wParam))
                       {
                       case IDM_HELP :
                            MessageBox (hwnd, "Help not yet implemented!",
                                        szAppName, MB_OK | MB_ICONEXCLAMATION) ;
                            return 0 ;
                       }
                  break ;

             case WM_COMMAND :
                  switch (LOWORD (wParam))
                       {
                       case IDM_NEW :
                       case IDM_OPEN :
                       case IDM_SAVE :
                       case IDM_SAVEAS :
                       case IDM_UNDO :
                       case IDM_CUT :
                       case IDM_COPY :
```

(continued)

486

```
                           case IDM_PASTE :
                           case IDM_DEL :
                                MessageBeep (0) ;
                                return 0 ;


                           case IDM_COUR :
                           case IDM_ARIAL :
                           case IDM_TIMES :
                                hMenu = GetMenu (hwnd) ;
                                CheckMenuItem (hMenu, iCurrentFont, MF_UNCHECKED) ;
                                iCurrentFont = LOWORD (wParam) ;
                                CheckMenuItem (hMenu, iCurrentFont, MF_CHECKED) ;
                                return 0 ;

                           }
                      break ;

             case WM_DESTROY :
                  PostQuitMessage (0) ;
                  return 0 ;
             }
        return DefWindowProc (hwnd, iMsg, wParam, lParam) ;
        }
```

GRAFMENU.RC

```
/*-----------------------------
   GRAFMENU.RC resource script
   -----------------------------*/

#include "grafmenu.h"

BitmapEdit BITMAP editlabl.bmp
BitmapFile BITMAP filelabl.bmp
BitmapFont BITMAP fontlabl.bmp
BitmapHelp BITMAP bighelp.bmp

MenuFile MENU
    {
    MENUITEM "&New",        IDM_NEW
    MENUITEM "&Open...",    IDM_OPEN
    MENUITEM "&Save",       IDM_SAVE
    MENUITEM "Save &As...", IDM_SAVEAS
    }
```

(continued)

```
MenuEdit MENU
    {
    MENUITEM "&Undo",        IDM_UNDO
    MENUITEM SEPARATOR
    MENUITEM "Cu&t",         IDM_CUT
    MENUITEM "&Copy",        IDM_COPY
    MENUITEM "&Paste",       IDM_PASTE
    MENUITEM "De&lete",      IDM_DEL
    }
```

GRAFMENU.H

```
/*-----------------------
   GRAFMENU.H header file
   ---------------------*/

#define IDM_NEW      1
#define IDM_OPEN     2
#define IDM_SAVE     3
#define IDM_SAVEAS   4

#define IDM_UNDO     5
#define IDM_CUT      6
#define IDM_COPY     7
#define IDM_PASTE    8
#define IDM_DEL      9

#define IDM_COUR     10
#define IDM_ARIAL    11
#define IDM_TIMES    12

#define IDM_HELP     13
```

EDITLABL.BMP

FILELABL.BMP

(continued)

FONTLABL.BMP

BIGHELP.BMP

Two Methods of Creating Bitmaps for Menus

To insert a bitmap into a menu, you use *AppendMenu* or *InsertMenu*. Where does this bitmap come from? It can come from one of two places. First, you can create a bitmap using the Developer Studio's image editor and include the bitmap file in your resource script. Within the program, you can use *LoadBitmap* to load the bitmap resource into memory and use *AppendMenu* or *InsertMenu* to attach it to the menu. There's a problem with this approach, however. The bitmap will not be suitable for all types of video resolutions and aspect ratios; you have to stretch the loaded bitmap to account for this. Alternatively, you can create the bitmap right in the program and attach it to the menu.

Both of these methods sound a lot more difficult than they actually are. We don't have to mess around with the actual bits themselves. Windows provides functions that let us manipulate bitmaps cleanly using the memory device context.

The Memory Device Context

When you use GDI calls (such as *TextOut*) to write on the client area of your window, you're actually writing to a block of memory (the video display memory) that is organized much like a giant bitmap. The width and height of this bitmap are equal to the resolution of the video display. The manner in which multiple bits define color is also defined by the video adapter. If you think about it, Windows should also be able to pretend that a block of regular memory is video display memory. It should be able to write to this memory the same way it writes on the screen. We should then be able to use this block of memory as a bitmap.

That's exactly what a memory device context is. It helps us draw on and manipulate bitmaps in a Windows program. Here are the steps involved:

1. Create a memory device context using the *CreateCompatibleDC* call. Initially, the display surface of this memory device context contains one monochrome pixel. You can think of this device context as being 1 pixel high and 1 pixel wide, with two colors (black and white).

2. Create an uninitialized bitmap using *CreateBitmap, CreateBitmapIndirect,* or *CreateCompatibleBitmap.* When you create the bitmap, you specify the height and width and the color organization. However, the pixels of the bitmap need not actually represent anything yet. Save the handle to the bitmap.

3. Select the bitmap into the memory device context using *SelectObject.* Now the memory device context has a display surface that is the size of the bitmap with the same number of colors as defined by the bitmap.

4. Use GDI functions to draw on the memory device context the same way you use GDI functions to draw on a normal device context. Anything you draw within the display surface of the memory device context is actually drawn on the bitmap selected into the device context.

5. Delete the memory device context. You are left with a handle to a bitmap that contains a pixel representation of what you drew on the memory device context.

Creating a Bitmap with Text

The *GetBitmapFont* function in GRAFMENU takes a parameter of 0, 1, or 2 and returns a handle to a bitmap. This bitmap contains the string "Courier New," "Arial," or "Times New Roman" in the appropriate font and about twice the size of the normal system font. Let's see how *GetBitmapFont* does it. (The code that follows is not the same as that in the GRAF-MENU.C file. For purposes of clarity, I've replaced references to the *szFaceName* array with the values appropriate for Arial.)

The first step is to determine the size of the system font by using the TEXTMETRIC structure:

```
hdc = CreateIC ("DISPLAY", NULL, NULL, NULL) ;
GetTextMetrics (hdc, &tm) ;
```

Certain fields of this TEXTMETRIC structure must be modified to make it describe a larger Arial font in a logical font structure:

```
lf.lfHeight = 2 * tm.tmHeight ;
strcpy ((char *) lf.lfFaceName, "Arial") ;
```

The next step is to get a device context for the screen and create a memory device context compatible with the screen:

```
hdcMem = CreateCompatibleDC (hdc) ;
```

The handle to the memory device context is *hdcMem*. Next, we create a font based on the modified *lf* structure and select that font into the memory device context:

```
hFont = (HFONT) SelectObject (hdcMem, CreateFontIndirect (&lf)) ;
```

Now when we write some text to the memory device context, Windows will use the TrueType Arial font selected into the device context.

But this memory device context still has a one-pixel monochrome device surface. We have to create a bitmap large enough for the text we want to display on it. You can obtain the dimensions of the text through *GetTextExtentPoint* and create a bitmap based on these dimensions with *CreateBitmap*:

```
GetTextExtentPoint (hdcMem, "Arial", 5, &size) ;
hBitmap = CreateBitmap (size.cx, size.cy, 1, 1, NULL) ;
SelectObject (hdcMem, hBitmap) ;
```

This device context now has a monochrome display surface exactly the size of the text. Now all we have to do is write the text to it. You've seen this function before:

```
TextOut (hdcMem, 0, 0, "Arial", 5) ;
```

We're finished except for cleaning up. To do so, we select the system font (with handle *hFont*) back into the device context using *SelectObject*, and we delete the previous font handle that *SelectObject* returns, which is the handle to the Arial font:

```
DeleteObject (SelectObject (hdcMem, hFont)) ;
```

Now we can also delete the two device contexts:

```
DeleteDC (hdcMem) ;
DeleteDC (hdc) ;
```

We're left with a bitmap that has the text "Arial" in an Arial font.

Scaling Bitmaps

The memory device context also comes to the rescue when we need to scale fonts to a different display resolution or aspect ratio. I created the four bitmaps used in GRAFMENU to be the correct size for a display that has a system font height of 8 pixels and width of 4 pixels. For other system font dimensions, the bitmap has to be stretched. This is done in GRAFMENU's *StretchBitmap* function.

The first step is to get the device context for the screen, obtain the text metrics for the system font, and create two memory device contexts:

```
hdc = CreateIC ("DISPLAY", NULL, NULL, NULL) ;
GetTextMetrics (hdc, &tm) ;
hdcMem1 = CreateCompatibleDC (hdc) ;
hdcMem2 = CreateCompatibleDC (hdc) ;
DeleteDC (hdc) ;
```

The bitmap handle passed to the function is *hBitmap1*. The program can obtain the dimensions of this bitmap using *GetObject*:

```
GetObject (hBitmap1, sizeof (BITMAP), (PSTR) &bm1) ;
```

This copies the dimensions into a structure *bm1* of type BITMAP. The structure *bm2* is set equal to *bm1*, and then certain fields are modified based on the system font dimensions:

```
bm2 = bm1 ;
bm2.bmWidth      = (tm.tmAveCharWidth * bm2.bmWidth)  / 4 ;
bm2.bmHeight     = (tm.tmHeight       * bm2.bmHeight) / 8 ;
bm2.bmWidthBytes = ((bm2.bmWidth + 15) / 16) * 2 ;
```

Then a new bitmap with handle *hBitmap2* can be created that is based on the altered dimensions:

```
hBitmap2 = CreateBitmapIndirect (&bm2) ;
```

You can then select these two bitmaps into the two memory device contexts:

```
SelectObject (hdcMem1, hBitmap1) ;
SelectObject (hdcMem2, hBitmap2) ;
```

We want to copy the first bitmap to the second bitmap and stretch it in the process. This involves the *StretchBlt* call:

```
StretchBlt (hdcMem2, 0, 0, bm2.bmWidth, bm2.bmHeight,
            hdcMem1, 0, 0, bm1.bmWidth, bm1.bmHeight, SRCCOPY) ;
```

Now the second bitmap has the properly scaled bitmap. We'll use that one in the menu. Cleanup is simple:

```
DeleteDC (hdcMem1) ;
DeleteDC (hdcMem2) ;
DeleteObject (hBitmap1) ;
```

Putting the Menu Together

GRAFMENU's *WinMain* function uses the *StretchBitmap* and *GetBitmapFont* functions when constructing the menu. GRAFMENU has two menus already defined in the resource script. These will become popups for the File and Edit options.

GRAFMENU begins by obtaining a handle to an empty menu:

```
hMenu = CreateMenu () ;
```

The popup menu for File (containing the four options New, Open, Save, and Save As) is loaded from the resource script:

```
hMenuPopup = LoadMenu (hInstance, "MenuFile") ;
```

The bitmap containing the word "FILE" is also loaded from the resource script and stretched using *StretchBitmap*:

```
hBitmapFile = StretchBitmap (LoadBitmap (hInstance, "BitmapFile")) ;
```

The bitmap handle and popup menu handle become parameters in the *AppendMenu* call:

```
AppendMenu (hMenu, MF_BITMAP | MF_POPUP, (int) hMenuPopup,
            (PSTR) (LONG) hBitmapFile) ;
```

The same procedure is followed for the Edit menu:

```
hMenuPopup = LoadMenu (hInstance, "MenuEdit") ;
hBitmapEdit = StretchBitmap (LoadBitmap (hInstance, "BitmapEdit")) ;
AppendMenu (hMenu, MF_BITMAP | MF_POPUP, (int) hMenuPopup,
            (PSTR) (LONG) hBitmapEdit) ;
```

The popup menu for the three fonts is constructed from calls to the *GetBitmapFont* function:

```
hMenuPopup = CreateMenu () ;
for (i = 0 ; i < 3 ; i++)
    {
    hBitmapPopFont[i] = GetBitmapFont (i) ;
    AppendMenu (hMenuPopup, MF_BITMAP, IDM_COUR + i,
                (PSTR) (LONG) hMenuPopupFont[i]) ;
    }
```

The popup is then added to the menu:

```
hBitmapFont = StretchBitmap (LoadBitmap (hInstance, "BitmapFont")) ;
AppendMenu (hMenu, MF_BITMAP | MF_POPUP, (int) hMenuPopup,
            (PSTR) (LONG) hBitmapFont) ;
```

The window menu is complete. Now you can include *hMenu* in the *CreateWindow* call:

```
hwnd = CreateWindow (szAppName, "Bitmap Menu Demonstration",
                     WS_OVERLAPPEDWINDOW,
                     CW_USEDEFAULT, CW_USEDEFAULT,
                     CW_USEDEFAULT, CW_USEDEFAULT,
                     NULL, hMenu, hInstance, NULL) ;
```

After *hwnd* is available, GRAFMENU can alter the system menu. GRAFMENU first obtains a handle to it:

```
hMenu = GetSystemMenu (hwnd, FALSE) ;
```

This loads the "Help" bitmap and stretches it to an appropriate size:

```
hBitmapHelp = StretchBitmap (LoadBitmap (hInstance, "BitmapHelp")) ;
```

This adds a separator bar and the stretched bitmap to the system menu:

```
AppendMenu (hMenu, MF_SEPARATOR, NULL, NULL) ;
AppendMenu (hMenu, MF_BITMAP, IDM_HELP, (PSTR) (LONG) hBitmapHelp) ;
```

Remember that bitmaps are GDI objects and must be explicitly deleted before your program terminates. You accomplish this after GRAFMENU exits from its message loop:

```
DeleteObject (hBitmapHelp) ;
DeleteObject (hBitmapEdit) ;
DeleteObject (hBitmapFile) ;
DeleteObject (hBitmapFont) ;

for (i = 0 ; i < 3 ; i++)
     DeleteObject (hBitmapPopFont[i]) ;
```

I'll conclude this section with a couple of miscellaneous notes:

- In a top-level menu, Windows adjusts the menu bar height to accommodate the tallest bitmap. Other bitmaps (or character strings) are aligned at the top of the menu bar. The size of the menu bar obtained from:

    ```
    GetSystemMetrics (SM_CYMENU)
    ```
    is no longer valid after you put bitmaps in a top-level menu.

- As you can see from playing with GRAFMENU, you can use check marks with bitmapped menu items in popups, but the check mark is of normal size. If that bothers you, you can create a customized check mark and use *SetMenuItem-Bitmaps*.

- Another approach to using non-text (or text in a font other than the system font) on a menu is the "owner-draw" menu.

Adding a Keyboard Interface

Now we have another problem. When the menu contains text, Windows automatically adds a keyboard interface. You can select a menu item using the Alt key in combination with a letter of the character string. But once you put a bitmap in a menu, you've eliminated that keyboard interface. Even if the bitmap says something, Windows doesn't know about it.

This is where the WM_MENUCHAR message comes in handy. Windows sends a WM_MENUCHAR message to your window procedure when you press Alt with a character key that does not correspond to a menu item. We need to intercept WM_MENUCHAR messages and check the low word of *wParam* (the ASCII character of the pressed key). If this corresponds to a menu item, we have to return a long integer back to Windows where the high word is set to 2 and the low word is set to the index of the menu item we want associated with that key. Windows does the rest.

KEYBOARD ACCELERATORS

Described as simply as possible, keyboard accelerators are key combinations that generate WM_COMMAND (or in some cases WM_SYSCOMMAND) messages. Most often, programs use keyboard accelerators to duplicate the actions of common menu options. (However, keyboard accelerators can also perform nonmenu functions.) For instance, some Windows programs have an Edit menu that includes a Delete option; these programs conventionally assign the Del key as a keyboard accelerator for this option. The user can choose the Delete option from the menu by pressing an Alt-key combination or can use the keyboard accelerator by simply pressing the Del key. When the window procedure receives a WM-_COMMAND message, it does not have to determine whether the menu or the keyboard accelerator was used.

Why You Should Use Keyboard Accelerators

You may ask: Why should I use keyboard accelerators? Why can't I simply trap WM_KEY-DOWN or WM_CHAR messages and duplicate the menu functions myself? What's the advantage? For a single-window application, you can certainly trap keyboard messages, but you get certain advantages from using keyboard accelerators: You don't need to duplicate the menu and keyboard accelerator logic.

For applications with multiple windows and multiple window procedures, keyboard accelerators become very important. As we've seen, Windows sends keyboard messages to the window procedure for the window that currently has the input focus. For keyboard accelerators, however, Windows sends the WM_COMMAND message to the window procedure whose handle is specified in the Windows function *TranslateAccelerator.* Generally, this will be your main window, the same window that has the menu, which means that the logic for acting upon keyboard accelerators does not have to be duplicated in every window procedure.

This advantage becomes particularly important if you use modeless dialog boxes (discussed in the next chapter) or child windows on your main window's client area. If a particular keyboard accelerator is defined to move among windows, then only one window procedure has to include this logic. The child windows do not receive WM_COMMAND messages from the keyboard accelerators.

Some Rules on Assigning Accelerators

In theory, you can define a keyboard accelerator for almost any virtual key or character key in combination with the Shift key, Ctrl key, or Alt key. However, you should try to achieve some consistency with other applications and avoid interfering with Windows' use of the keyboard. You should avoid using Tab, Enter, Esc, and the Spacebar in keyboard accelerators because these are often used for system functions.

The most common use of keyboard accelerators is for items on the program's Edit menu. The recommended keyboard accelerators for these items changed between Windows 3.0 and Windows 3.1, so it's become common to support both the old and the new accelerators, as shown in the following table:

Function	Old Accelerator	New Accelerator
Undo	Alt+Backspace	Ctrl+Z
Cut	Shift+Del	Ctrl+X
Copy	Ctrl+Ins	Ctrl+C
Paste	Shift+Ins	Ctrl+V
Delete or Clear	Del	Del

Another common accelerator is the F1 function key to invoke help. Avoid use of the F4, F5, and F6 keys because these are often used for special functions in Multiple Document Interface (MDI) programs (which are discussed in Chapter 18).

The Accelerator Table

Keyboard accelerator tables are defined in your .RC resource script. The general form is shown here:

```
MyAccelerators ACCELERATORS
    {
    [accelerator definitions]
    }
```

This accelerator table name is *MyAccelerators*. The ACCELERATORS table does not include load and memory options. You can have multiple ACCELERATORS tables in your resource script.

Each keyboard accelerator you define requires a different line in the table. There are four types of accelerator definitions:

```
"char",  id          [,SHIFT] [,CONTROL] [,ALT]
"^char", id          [,SHIFT] [,CONTROL] [,ALT]
nCode,   id, ASCII    [,SHIFT] [,CONTROL] [,ALT]
nCode,   id, VIRTKEY   [,SHIFT] [,CONTROL] [,ALT]
```

In these examples, *"char"* means a single character enclosed in double quotation marks, and *"^char"* is the character ^ and a single character in double quotation marks. The *id* number performs a function similar to the menu ID in a menu definition. It is the value that Windows sends to your window procedure in the WM_COMMAND message to identify the accelerator. These are usually identifiers defined in a header file. Keyboard accelerators almost always select options in popup menus. When the keyboard accelerator duplicates a menu command, use the same ID for both the menu and the accelerator. When the keyboard accelerator does not duplicate a menu command, use a unique ID.

In the first type of accelerator definition, the keyboard accelerator is a case-sensitive match of the character within double quotes:

```
"char",  id          [,SHIFT] [,CONTROL] [,ALT]
```

If you want to define a keyboard accelerator for that key in combination with one or more of the Shift, Ctrl, and ALT keys, simply add SHIFT, CONTROL, and/or ALT.

In the second type of definition, the keyboard accelerator is the character in combination with the Ctrl key:

```
"^char", id          [,SHIFT] [,CONTROL] [,ALT]
```

This type is the same as the first type when the CONTROL keyword is used with the character alone.

The third and fourth types use a number (*nCode*) rather than a character in quotes:

```
nCode,   id, ASCII      [,SHIFT] [,CONTROL] [,ALT]
nCode,   id, VIRTKEY    [,SHIFT] [,CONTROL] [,ALT]
```

This number is interpreted as either a case-sensitive ASCII code or a virtual key code, depending on the ASCII or VIRTKEY keyword.

The most common keyboard accelerators are the second and fourth types. You use the second type for character keys in combination with Ctrl. For example, this defines an accelerator for Ctrl+A:

```
"^A", id
```

Use the fourth type for virtual key codes such as function keys. This defines an accelerator for the Ctrl-F9 combination:

```
VK_F9, wid, VIRTKEY, CONTROL
```

The identifier VK_F9 is defined in the Windows header files as the virtual key code for the F9 key, so you have to include the statement:

```
#include <windows.h>
```

near the top of the resource script.

The first and third types of definition shown above are rarely used. If you want to use them, watch out for case-sensitivity. Windows does a case-sensitive match on the *"char"* or *nCode* based on the character you press. When you add the SHIFT keyword, Windows checks to see if the Shift key is depressed. This situation sometimes causes results you may not anticipate. For instance, if *"char"* is *"A"*, the keyboard accelerator is invoked when you press the A key with the Shift key down or Caps Lock on, but not both. If you use *"A"* with SHIFT, the A key must be pressed with Shift down, but the accelerator can't be invoked at all when Caps Lock is on. Similarly, *"a"* by itself is a keyboard accelerator for the unshifted A key or for the A key with both Shift down and Caps Lock on. But *"a"* with SHIFT invokes the accelerator only when Shift is down and Caps Lock is on.

When you define keyboard accelerators for a menu item, you should include the key combination in the menu item text. The tab (\t) character separates the text from the accelerator so that the accelerators align in a second column. To notate accelerator keys in a menu, use the text Ctrl, Shift, or Alt followed by a plus sign and the key. For example:

- F6
- Shift+F6
- Ctrl+F6

Loading the Accelerator Table

Within your program, you use the *LoadAccelerators* function to load the accelerator table into memory and obtain a handle to it. The *LoadAccelerators* statement is very similar to the *LoadIcon*, *LoadCursor*, *LoadBitmap*, and *LoadMenu* statements.

First, define a handle to an accelerator table as type HACCEL:

```
HACCEL hAccel ;
```

Then load the accelerator table:

```
hAccel = LoadAccelerators (hInstance, "MyAccelerators") ;
```

As with icons, cursors, bitmaps, and menus, you can use a number for the accelerator table name and then use that number in the *LoadAccelerators* statement with the MAKEINT-RESOURCE macro or preceded by a # character and enclosed in quotation marks.

Translating the Keystrokes

We will now tamper with three lines of code that are common to almost all the Windows programs that we've created so far in this book. The code is the standard message loop:

```
while (GetMessage (&msg, NULL, 0, 0))
     {
     TranslateMessage (&msg) ;
     DispatchMessage (&msg) ;
     }
```

Here's how we change it to use the keyboard accelerator table:

```
while (GetMessage (&msg, NULL, 0, 0))
     {
     if (!TranslateAccelerator (hwnd, hAccel, &msg))
          {
          TranslateMessage (&msg) ;
          DispatchMessage (&msg) ;
          }
     }
```

The *TranslateAccelerator* function determines if the message stored in the *msg* message structure is a keyboard message. If it is, the function searches for a match in the accelerator table whose handle is *hAccel*. If it finds a match, it calls the window procedure for the window whose handle is *hwnd*. If the keyboard accelerator ID corresponds to a menu item in the system menu, then the message is WM_SYSCOMMAND. Otherwise, the message is WM_COMMAND.

When *TranslateAccelerator* returns, the return value is nonzero if the message has been translated (and already sent to the window procedure) and 0 if not. If *Translate-Accelerator* returns a nonzero value, you should not call *TranslateMessage* and *Dispatch-Message* but rather loop back to the *GetMessage* call.

The *hwnd* parameter in *TranslateMessage* looks a little out of place because it's not required in the other three functions in the message loop. Moreover, the message structure itself (the structure variable *msg*) has a member named *hwnd*, which is also a handle to a window. Here's why the function is a little different:

The fields of the *msg* structure are filled in by the *GetMessage* call. When the second parameter of *GetMessage* is NULL, the function retrieves messages for all windows belonging to the application. When *GetMessage* returns, the *hwnd* member of the *msg* structure is the window handle of the window that will get the message. However, when *TranslateAccelerator* translates a keyboard message into a WM_COMMAND or WM_SYSCOMMAND message, it replaces the *msg.hwnd* window handle with the window handle *hwnd* specified as the first parameter to the function. That is how Windows sends all keyboard accelerator messages to the same window procedure even if another window in the application currently has the input focus. *TranslateAccelerator* does not translate keyboard messages when a modal dialog box or message box has the input focus because messages for these windows do not come through the program's message loop.

In some cases in which another window in your program (such as a modeless dialog box) has the input focus, you may not want keyboard accelerators to be translated. You'll see how to handle this situation in the next chapter.

Receiving the Accelerator Messages

When a keyboard accelerator corresponds to a menu item in the system menu, *Translate-Accelerator* sends the window procedure a WM_SYSCOMMAND message. Otherwise, *TranslateAccelerator* sends the window procedure a WM_COMMAND message. The following table shows the types of WM_COMMAND messages you can receive for keyboard accelerators, menu commands, and child window controls:

	LOWORD (wParam)	*HIWORD (wParam)*	*lParam*
Accelerator:	Accelerator ID	1	0
Menu:	Menu ID	0	0
Control:	Control ID	Notification code	Child window handle

If the keyboard accelerator corresponds to a menu item, the window procedure also receives WM_INITMENU, WM_INITMENUPOPUP, and WM_MENUSELECT messages, just as if the menu option had been chosen. Programs usually enable and disable items in a popup menu when processing WM_INITMENUPOPUP, so you still have that facility when using keyboard accelerators. If the keyboard accelerator corresponds to a disabled or grayed menu item, however, *TranslateAccelerator* does not send the window procedure a WM_COMMAND or WM_SYSCOMMAND message.

If the active window is minimized, *TranslateAccelerator* sends the window procedure WM_SYSCOMMAND messages—but not WM_COMMAND messages—for keyboard accelerators that correspond to enabled system menu items. *TranslateAccelerator* also sends that window procedure WM_COMMAND messages for accelerators that do not correspond to any menu items.

POPPAD with a Menu and Accelerators

In Chapter 8, we created a program called POPPAD1 that uses a child window edit control to implement a rudimentary notepad. In this chapter, we'll add File and Edit menus and call it POPPAD2. The Edit items will all be functional; we'll finish the *File* functions in Chapter 11 and the *Print* function in Chapter 15. POPPAD2 is shown in Figure 10-10.

POPPAD2.MAK

```
#-----------------------
# POPPAD2.MAK make file
#-----------------------

poppad2.exe : poppad2.obj poppad2.res
     $(LINKER) $(GUIFLAGS) -OUT:poppad2.exe poppad2.obj poppad2.res $(GUILIBS)

poppad2.obj : poppad2.c poppad2.h
     $(CC) $(CFLAGS) poppad2.c

poppad2.res : poppad2.rc poppad2.h poppad2.ico
     $(RC) $(RCVARS) poppad2.rc
```

POPPAD2.C

```
/*---------------------------------------------------------
   POPPAD2.C -- Popup Editor Version 2 (includes menu)
                (c) Charles Petzold, 1996
   ---------------------------------------------------------*/

#include <windows.h>
#include "poppad2.h"
```

Figure 10-10. *The POPPAD2 program.*

```
LRESULT CALLBACK WndProc (HWND, UINT, WPARAM, LPARAM) ;

char szAppName[] = "PopPad2" ;

int WINAPI WinMain (HINSTANCE hInstance, HINSTANCE hPrevInstance,
                    PSTR szCmdLine, int iCmdShow)
    {
    HACCEL      hAccel ;
    HWND        hwnd ;
    MSG         msg ;
    WNDCLASSEX wndclass ;

    wndclass.cbSize        = sizeof (wndclass) ;
    wndclass.style         = CS_HREDRAW | CS_VREDRAW ;
    wndclass.lpfnWndProc   = WndProc ;
    wndclass.cbClsExtra    = 0 ;
    wndclass.cbWndExtra    = 0 ;
    wndclass.hInstance     = hInstance ;
    wndclass.hIcon         = LoadIcon (hInstance, szAppName) ;
    wndclass.hCursor       = LoadCursor (NULL, IDC_ARROW) ;
    wndclass.hbrBackground = (HBRUSH) GetStockObject (WHITE_BRUSH) ;
    wndclass.lpszMenuName  = szAppName ;
    wndclass.lpszClassName = szAppName ;
    wndclass.hIconSm       = LoadIcon (NULL, IDI_APPLICATION) ;

    RegisterClassEx (&wndclass) ;

    hwnd = CreateWindow (szAppName, szAppName,
                         WS_OVERLAPPEDWINDOW,
                         GetSystemMetrics (SM_CXSCREEN) / 4,
                         GetSystemMetrics (SM_CYSCREEN) / 4,
                         GetSystemMetrics (SM_CXSCREEN) / 2,
                         GetSystemMetrics (SM_CYSCREEN) / 2,
                         NULL, NULL, hInstance, NULL) ;

    ShowWindow (hwnd, iCmdShow) ;
    UpdateWindow (hwnd) ;

    hAccel = LoadAccelerators (hInstance, szAppName) ;

    while (GetMessage (&msg, NULL, 0, 0))
        {
        if (!TranslateAccelerator (hwnd, hAccel, &msg))
            {
            TranslateMessage (&msg) ;
```

(continued)

```
                    DispatchMessage (&msg) ;
                    }
            }
     return msg.wParam ;
     }

AskConfirmation (HWND hwnd)
     {
     return MessageBox (hwnd, "Really want to close PopPad2?",
                    szAppName, MB_YESNO | MB_ICONQUESTION) ;
     }

LRESULT CALLBACK WndProc (HWND hwnd, UINT iMsg, WPARAM wParam, LPARAM lParam)
     {
     static HWND hwndEdit ;
     int        iSelect, iEnable ;

     switch (iMsg)
          {
          case WM_CREATE :
               hwndEdit = CreateWindow ("edit", NULL,
                    WS_CHILD | WS_VISIBLE | WS_HSCROLL | WS_VSCROLL |
                         WS_BORDER | ES_LEFT | ES_MULTILINE |
                         ES_AUTOHSCROLL | ES_AUTOVSCROLL,
                    0, 0, 0, 0,
                    hwnd, (HMENU) 1,
                    ((LPCREATESTRUCT) lParam)->hInstance, NULL) ;
               return 0 ;

          case WM_SETFOCUS :
               SetFocus (hwndEdit) ;
               return 0 ;

          case WM_SIZE :
               MoveWindow (hwndEdit, 0, 0, LOWORD (lParam),
                                          HIWORD (lParam), TRUE) ;
               return 0 ;

          case WM_INITMENUPOPUP :
               if (lParam == 1)
                    {
                    EnableMenuItem ((HMENU) wParam, IDM_UNDO,
                         SendMessage (hwndEdit, EM_CANUNDO, 0, 0) ?
                              MF_ENABLED : MF_GRAYED) ;
```

(continued)

502

```
                    EnableMenuItem ((HMENU) wParam, IDM_PASTE,
                         IsClipboardFormatAvailable (CF_TEXT) ?
                              MF_ENABLED : MF_GRAYED) ;

                    iSelect = SendMessage (hwndEdit, EM_GETSEL, 0, 0) ;

                    if (HIWORD (iSelect) == LOWORD (iSelect))
                         iEnable = MF_GRAYED ;
                    else
                         iEnable = MF_ENABLED ;

                    EnableMenuItem ((HMENU) wParam, IDM_CUT,   iEnable) ;
                    EnableMenuItem ((HMENU) wParam, IDM_COPY,  iEnable) ;
                    EnableMenuItem ((HMENU) wParam, IDM_DEL,   iEnable) ;

                    return 0 ;
                    }
          break ;

     case WM_COMMAND :

          if (lParam)
               {
               if (LOWORD (lParam) == 1 &&
                    (HIWORD (wParam) == EN_ERRSPACE ||
                    HIWORD (wParam) == EN_MAXTEXT))
                         MessageBox (hwnd,
                                   "Edit control out of space.",
                                   szAppName, MB_OK | MB_ICONSTOP) ;
               return 0 ;
               }

          else switch (LOWORD (wParam))
                    {
                    case IDM_NEW :
                    case IDM_OPEN :
                    case IDM_SAVE :
                    case IDM_SAVEAS :
                    case IDM_PRINT :
                         MessageBeep (0) ;
                         return 0 ;

                    case IDM_EXIT :
                         SendMessage (hwnd, WM_CLOSE, 0, 0) ;
                         return 0 ;
```

(continued)

```
                    case IDM_UNDO :
                         SendMessage (hwndEdit, WM_UNDO, 0, 0) ;
                         return 0 ;

                    case IDM_CUT :
                         SendMessage (hwndEdit, WM_CUT, 0, 0) ;
                         return 0 ;

                    case IDM_COPY :
                         SendMessage (hwndEdit, WM_COPY, 0, 0) ;
                         return 0 ;

                    case IDM_PASTE :
                         SendMessage (hwndEdit, WM_PASTE, 0, 0) ;
                         return 0 ;

                    case IDM_DEL :
                         SendMessage (hwndEdit, WM_CLEAR, 0, 0) ;
                         return 0 ;

                    case IDM_SELALL :
                         SendMessage (hwndEdit, EM_SETSEL, 0, -1) ;
                         return 0 ;

                    case IDM_HELP :
                         MessageBox (hwnd, "Help not yet implemented!",
                              szAppName, MB_OK | MB_ICONEXCLAMATION) ;
                         return 0 ;

                    case IDM_ABOUT :
                         MessageBox (hwnd,
                              "POPPAD2 (c) Charles Petzold, 1996",
                              szAppName, MB_OK | MB_ICONINFORMATION) ;
                         return 0 ;
                    }
               break ;

     case WM_CLOSE :
          if (IDYES == AskConfirmation (hwnd))
               DestroyWindow (hwnd) ;
          return 0 ;

     case WM_QUERYENDSESSION :
          if (IDYES == AskConfirmation (hwnd))
               return 1 ;
```

(continued)

504

```
            else
                return 0 ;

        case WM_DESTROY :
            PostQuitMessage (0) ;
            return 0 ;
        }
    return DefWindowProc (hwnd, iMsg, wParam, lParam) ;
    }
```

POPPAD2.RC

```
/*----------------------------
   POPPAD2.RC resource script
   ------------------------*/

#include <windows.h>
#include "poppad2.h"

PopPad2 ICON poppad2.ico

PopPad2 MENU
    {
    POPUP "&File"
        {
        MENUITEM "&New",              IDM_NEW
        MENUITEM "&Open...",          IDM_OPEN
        MENUITEM "&Save",             IDM_SAVE
        MENUITEM "Save &As...",       IDM_SAVEAS
        MENUITEM SEPARATOR
        MENUITEM "&Print",            IDM_PRINT
        MENUITEM SEPARATOR
        MENUITEM "E&xit",             IDM_EXIT
        }
    POPUP "&Edit"
        {
        MENUITEM "&Undo\tCtrl+Z",     IDM_UNDO
        MENUITEM SEPARATOR
        MENUITEM "Cu&t\tCtrl+X",      IDM_CUT
        MENUITEM "&Copy\tCtrl+C",     IDM_COPY
        MENUITEM "&Paste\tCtrl+V",    IDM_PASTE
        MENUITEM "De&lete\tDel",      IDM_DEL
        MENUITEM SEPARATOR
        MENUITEM "&Select All",       IDM_SELALL
        }
```

(continued)

```
        POPUP "&Help"
            {
            MENUITEM "&Help...",           IDM_HELP
            MENUITEM "&About PopPad2...", IDM_ABOUT
            }
        }

PopPad2 ACCELERATORS
    {
    "^Z",        IDM_UNDO
    VK_BACK,     IDM_UNDO,   VIRTKEY, ALT
    "^X",        IDM_CUT
    VK_DELETE, IDM_CUT,      VIRTKEY, SHIFT
    "^C",        IDM_COPY
    VK_INSERT, IDM_COPY,     VIRTKEY, CONTROL
    "^V",        IDM_PASTE
    VK_INSERT, IDM_PASTE,    VIRTKEY, SHIFT
    VK_DELETE, IDM_DEL,      VIRTKEY
    VK_F1,       IDM_HELP,   VIRTKEY
    }
```

POPPAD2.H

```
/*---------------------
   POPPAD2.H header file
   ---------------------*/

#define IDM_NEW      1
#define IDM_OPEN     2
#define IDM_SAVE     3
#define IDM_SAVEAS   4
#define IDM_PRINT    5
#define IDM_EXIT     6

#define IDM_UNDO    10
#define IDM_CUT     11
#define IDM_COPY    12
#define IDM_PASTE   13
#define IDM_DEL     14
#define IDM_SELALL  15

#define IDM_HELP    20
#define IDM_ABOUT   22
```

(continued)

POPPAD2.ICO

The POPPAD2.RC resource script file contains the menu and the accelerator table. You'll notice that the accelerators are all indicated within the character strings of the Edit popup menu following the tab (\t) character.

Enabling Menu Items

The major job in the window procedure now involves enabling and graying the options in the Edit menu, which is done when processing the WM_INITMENUPOPUP. First, the program checks to see if the Edit popup is about to be displayed. Because the position index of Edit in the menu (starting with File at 0) is 1, *lParam* equals 1 if the Edit popup is about to be displayed.

To determine if the Undo option can be enabled, POPPAD2 sends an EM_CANUNDO message to the edit control. The *SendMessage* call returns nonzero if the edit control can perform an Undo action, in which case the option is enabled; otherwise, the option is grayed:

```
EnableMenuItem ((HMENU) wParam, IDM_UNDO,
    SendMessage (hwndEdit, EM_CANUNDO, 0, 0) ?
        MF_ENABLED : MF_GRAYED) ;
```

The Paste option should be enabled only if the clipboard currently contains text. We can determine this through the *IsClipboardFormatAvailable* call with the CF_TEXT identifier:

```
EnableMenuItem ((HMENU) wParam, IDM_PASTE,
    IsClipboardFormatAvailable (CF_TEXT) ?
        MF_ENABLED : MF_GRAYED) ;
```

The Cut, Copy, and Delete options should be enabled only if text in the edit control has been selected. Sending the edit control an EM_GETSEL message returns an integer containing this information:

```
iSelect = SendMessage (hwndEdit, EM_GETSEL, 0, 0) ;
```

The low word of *iSelect* is the position of the first selected character; the high word of *iSelect* is the position of the character following the selection. If these two words are equal, no text has been selected:

```
if (HIWORD (iSelect) == LOWORD (iSelect))
    iEnable = MF_GRAYED ;
else
    iEnable = MF_ENABLED ;
```

The value of *iEnable* is then used for the Cut, Copy, and Delete options:

```
EnableMenuItem ((HMENU) wParam, IDM_CUT,   iEnable) ;
EnableMenuItem ((HMENU) wParam, IDM_COPY,  iEnable) ;
EnableMenuItem ((HMENU) wParam, IDM_DEL,   iEnable) ;
```

Processing the Menu Options

Of course, if we were not using a child window edit control for POPPAD2, we would now be faced with the problems involved with actually implementing the Undo, Cut, Copy, Paste, Delete, and Select All options from the Edit menu. But the edit control makes this process easy because we merely send the edit control a message for each of these options:

```
case IDM_UNDO :
    SendMessage (hwndEdit, WM_UNDO, 0, 0) ;
    return 0 ;

case IDM_CUT :
    SendMessage (hwndEdit, WM_CUT, 0, 0) ;
    return 0 ;

case IDM_COPY :
    SendMessage (hwndEdit, WM_COPY, 0, 0) ;
    return 0 ;

case IDM_PASTE :
    SendMessage (hwndEdit, WM_PASTE, 0, 0) ;
    return 0 ;

case IDM_DEL :
    SendMessage (hwndEdit, WM_CLEAR, 0, 0) ;
    return 0 ;

case IDM_SELALL :
    SendMessage (hwndEdit, EM_SETSEL, 0, -1) ;
    return 0 ;
```

Notice that we could have simplified this even further by making the values of IDM_UNDO, IDM_CUT, and so forth, equal to the values of the corresponding window messages WM_UNDO, WM_CUT, and so forth.

The About option on the File popup invokes a simple message box:

```
case IDM_ABOUT :
    MessageBox (hwnd,
         "POPPAD2 (c) Charles Petzold, 1996",
         szAppName, MB_OK | MB_ICONINFORMATION) ;
    return 0 ;
```

In Chapter 11, we'll make this a dialog box. A message box is also invoked when you select the Help option from this menu or when you press the F1 accelerator key.

The Exit option sends the window procedure a WM_CLOSE message:

```
case IDM_EXIT :
    SendMessage (hwnd, WM_CLOSE, 0, 0) ;
    return 0 ;
```

That is precisely what *DefWindowProc* does when it receives a WM_SYSCOMMAND message with *wParam* equal to SC_CLOSE.

In previous programs, we have not processed the WM_CLOSE messages in our window procedure but have simply passed them to *DefWindowProc*. *DefWindowProc* does something very simple with WM_CLOSE: It calls the *DestroyWindow* function. Rather than send WM_CLOSE messages to *DefWindowProc*, however, POPPAD2 processes them. This fact is not so important now, but it will become very important in Chapter 11 when POPPAD can actually edit files:

```
case WM_CLOSE :
    if (IDYES == AskConfirmation (hwnd))
        DestroyWindow (hwnd) ;
    return 0 ;
```

AskConfirmation is a function in POPPAD2 that displays a message box asking for confirmation to close the program:

```
AskConfirmation (HWND hwnd)
    {
    return MessageBox (hwnd, "Do you really want to close Poppad2?",
                  szAppName, MB_YESNO | MB_ICONQUESTION) ;
    }
```

The message box (as well as the *AskConfirmation* function) returns IDYES if the Yes button is selected. Only then does POPPAD2 call *DestroyWindow*. Otherwise, the program is not terminated.

If you want confirmation before terminating a program, you must also process WM_QUERYENDSESSION messages. Windows begins sending every window procedure a WM_QUERYENDSESSION message when the user ends a Windows session. If any window procedure returns 0 from this message, the Windows session is not terminated. Here's how we handle WM_QUERYENDSESSION:

```
case WM_QUERYENDSESSION :
    if (IDYES == AskConfirmation (hwnd))
        return 1 ;
    else
        return 0 ;
```

The WM_CLOSE and WM_QUERYENDSESSION messages are the only two messages you have to process if you want to ask for user confirmation before ending a program. That's why we made the Exit menu option in POPPAD2 send the window procedure a WM_CLOSE message—by doing so, we avoided having to ask for confirmation at yet a third point.

If you process WM_QUERYENDSESSION messages, you may also be interested in the WM_ENDSESSION message. Windows sends this message to every window procedure that has previously received a WM_QUERYENDSESSION message. The *wParam* parameter is 0 if the session fails to terminate because another program has returned 0 from WM_QUERY-ENDSESSION. The WM_ENDSESSION message essentially answers the question: I told Windows it was OK to terminate me, but did I really get terminated?

Although I've included the normal New, Open, Save, and Save As options in POPPAD2's File menu, they are currently nonfunctional. To process these commands, we need to use dialog boxes. You're now ready to learn about them.

Chapter 11

Dialog Boxes

Dialog boxes are most often used for obtaining additional input from the user beyond what can be easily managed through a menu. The programmer indicates that a menu item invokes a dialog box by adding an ellipsis (...) to the menu item.

A dialog box generally takes the form of a popup window containing various child window controls. The size and placement of these controls are specified in a "dialog box template" in the program's resource script file. Microsoft Windows 95 is responsible for creating the dialog box popup window and the child window controls, and for providing a window procedure to process dialog box messages (including all keyboard and mouse input). The code within Windows that does all this is sometimes referred to as the "dialog box manager."

Many of the messages that are processed by the dialog box window procedure within Windows are also passed to a function within your own program, called a "dialog box procedure" or "dialog procedure." This function is similar to a normal window procedure, but with some important differences. Generally, you will not be doing very much within the dialog procedure except initializing the child window controls when the dialog box is created, processing messages from the child window controls, and ending the dialog box.

The subject of dialog boxes would normally be a big one because it involves the use of child window controls. However, we have already explored child window controls in Chapter 8. When you use child window controls in dialog boxes, the Windows dialog box manager picks up many of the responsibilities that we assumed in Chapter 8. In particular, the problems we encountered with passing the input focus between the scroll bars in the COLORS1 program do not occur with dialog boxes. Windows handles all the logic necessary to shift input focus between controls in a dialog box.

However, adding a dialog box to a program is not a trivial undertaking. It involves changes to several files—the dialog box template goes in the resource script file, the dialog box procedure goes in the source code file, and identifiers used in the dialog box often go in the program's header file. We'll begin with a simple dialog box to give you a feel for the interconnections between these various pieces.

MODAL DIALOG BOXES

Dialog boxes are either "modal" or "modeless." The modal dialog box is the most common. When your program displays a modal dialog box, the user cannot switch between the dialog box and another window in your program. The user must explicitly end the dialog box, usually by clicking a push button marked either OK or Cancel. The user can, however, generally switch to another program while the dialog box is still displayed. Some dialog boxes (called "system modal") do not allow even this. System modal dialog boxes must be ended before the user does anything else in Windows.

Creating an "About" Dialog Box

Even if a Windows program requires no user input, it will often have a dialog box that is invoked by an About option on the menu. This dialog box displays the name and icon of the program, a copyright notice, a push button labeled OK, and perhaps other information. The first program we'll look at does nothing except display an About dialog box. The ABOUT1 program is shown in Figure 11-1.

ABOUT1.MAK

```
#----------------------
# ABOUT1.MAK make file
#----------------------

about1.exe : about1.obj about1.res
    $(LINKER) $(GUIFLAGS) -OUT:about1.exe about1.obj about1.res $(GUILIBS)

about1.obj : about1.c about1.h
    $(CC) $(CFLAGS) about1.c

about1.res : about1.rc about1.h about1.ico
    $(RC) $(RCVARS) about1.rc
```

Figure 11-1. *The ABOUT1 program.*

(continued)

ABOUT1.C

```
/*-------------------------------------------
   ABOUT1.C -- About Box Demo Program No. 1
               (c) Charles Petzold, 1996
   -------------------------------------------*/

#include <windows.h>
#include "about1.h"

LRESULT CALLBACK WndProc      (HWND, UINT, WPARAM, LPARAM) ;
BOOL    CALLBACK AboutDlgProc (HWND, UINT, WPARAM, LPARAM) ;

int WINAPI WinMain (HINSTANCE hInstance, HINSTANCE hPrevInstance,
                    PSTR szCmdLine, int iCmdShow)
     {
     static char  szAppName[] = "About1" ;
     MSG          msg ;
     HWND         hwnd ;
     WNDCLASSEX   wndclass ;

     wndclass.cbSize        = sizeof (wndclass) ;
     wndclass.style         = CS_HREDRAW | CS_VREDRAW ;
     wndclass.lpfnWndProc   = WndProc ;
     wndclass.cbClsExtra    = 0 ;
     wndclass.cbWndExtra    = 0 ;
     wndclass.hInstance     = hInstance ;
     wndclass.hIcon         = LoadIcon (hInstance, szAppName) ;
     wndclass.hCursor       = LoadCursor (NULL, IDC_ARROW) ;
     wndclass.hbrBackground = (HBRUSH) GetStockObject (WHITE_BRUSH) ;
     wndclass.lpszMenuName  = szAppName ;
     wndclass.lpszClassName = szAppName ;
     wndclass.hIconSm       = LoadIcon (hInstance, szAppName) ;

     RegisterClassEx (&wndclass) ;

     hwnd = CreateWindow (szAppName, "About Box Demo Program",
                          WS_OVERLAPPEDWINDOW,
                          CW_USEDEFAULT, CW_USEDEFAULT,
                          CW_USEDEFAULT, CW_USEDEFAULT,
                          NULL, NULL, hInstance, NULL) ;

     ShowWindow (hwnd, iCmdShow) ;
     UpdateWindow (hwnd) ;
```

(continued)

```
        while (GetMessage (&msg, NULL, 0, 0))
             {
             TranslateMessage (&msg) ;
             DispatchMessage (&msg) ;
             }
        return msg.wParam ;
        }

LRESULT CALLBACK WndProc (HWND hwnd, UINT iMsg, WPARAM wParam, LPARAM lParam)
        {
        static WNDPROC    lpfnAboutDlgProc ;
        static HINSTANCE hInstance ;

        switch (iMsg)
             {
             case WM_CREATE :
                  hInstance = ((LPCREATESTRUCT) lParam)->hInstance ;
                  return 0 ;

             case WM_COMMAND :
                  switch (LOWORD (wParam))
                       {
                       case IDM_ABOUT :
                            DialogBox (hInstance, "AboutBox", hwnd, AboutDlgProc) ;
                            return 0 ;
                       }
                  break ;

             case WM_DESTROY :
                  PostQuitMessage (0) ;
                  return 0 ;
             }
        return DefWindowProc (hwnd, iMsg, wParam, lParam) ;
        }

BOOL CALLBACK AboutDlgProc (HWND hDlg, UINT iMsg, WPARAM wParam,
                                                  LPARAM lParam)
        {
        switch (iMsg)
             {
             case WM_INITDIALOG :
                  return TRUE ;

             case WM_COMMAND :
                  switch (LOWORD (wParam))
                       {
                       case IDOK :
```

(continued)

514

```
                        case IDCANCEL :
                                EndDialog (hDlg, 0) ;
                                return TRUE ;
                        }
                break ;
        }
    return FALSE ;
    }
```

ABOUT1.RC

```
/*---------------------------
   ABOUT1.RC resource script
   --------------------------*/

#include <windows.h>
#include "about1.h"

About1 ICON about1.ico

About1 MENU
    {
    POPUP "&Help"
        {
        MENUITEM "&About About1...",        IDM_ABOUT
        }
    }

AboutBox DIALOG  20, 20, 160, 80
    STYLE WS_POPUP | WS_DLGFRAME
    {
    CTEXT "About1"                     -1,   0, 12, 160,  8
    ICON  "About1"                     -1,   8,  8,   0,  0
    CTEXT "About Box Demo Program"     -1,   0, 36, 160,  8
    CTEXT "(c) Charles Petzold, 1996"  -1,   0, 48, 160,  8
    DEFPUSHBUTTON "OK"                 IDOK, 64, 60,  32, 14, WS_GROUP
    }
```

ABOUT1.H

```
/*---------------------
   ABOUT1.H header file
   ---------------------*/

#define IDM_ABOUT       1
```

(continued)

ABOUT1.ICO

The Dialog Box Template

The first job involved in adding a dialog box to a program is designing the dialog box template. This template can go directly into the resource script file, or it can be in a separate file that by convention uses the extension .DLG (for "dialog"). If you put the template in a separate file, you include the line:

```
rcinclude filename.dlg
```

in the resource script file.

You can create the dialog box template manually in a text editor, or you can use any automated tool. The output of these tools is not of publishable quality, so I'll show dialog box templates that look as if they were created manually.

The dialog box template for ABOUT1 looks like this:

```
AboutBox DIALOG  20, 20, 160, 80
        STYLE WS_POPUP ¦ WS_DLGFRAME
        {
        CTEXT "About1"                  -1,   0, 12, 160,  8
        ICON  "About1"                  -1,   8,  8,   0,  0
        CTEXT "About Box Demo Program"  -1,   0, 36, 160,  8
        CTEXT "(c) Charles Petzold, 1996" -1,  0, 48, 160,  8
        DEFPUSHBUTTON "OK"              IDOK, 64, 60,  32, 14, WS_GROUP
        }
```

The first line gives the dialog box a name (in this case, *AboutBox*). As is the case for other resources, you can use a number instead. The name is followed by the keyword DIALOG and four numbers. The first two numbers are the *x*- and *y*-coordinates of the upper left corner of the dialog box, relative to the client area of its parent when the dialog box is invoked by the program. The second two numbers are the width and height of the dialog box.

These coordinates and sizes are not in units of pixels. They are instead based on a special coordinate system used only for dialog box templates. The numbers are based on the size of a system font character: x-coordinates and width are expressed in units of $\frac{1}{4}$ an average character width; y-coordinates and height are expressed in units of $\frac{1}{8}$ the character height. Thus for this particular dialog box, the upper left corner of the dialog box is 5 characters from the left edge of the main window's client area and $2\frac{1}{2}$ characters from the top edge. It is 40 characters wide and 10 characters high.

This coordinate system allows you to use coordinates and sizes that will retain the general dimensions and look of the dialog box regardless of the resolution of the video display. Because system font characters are often approximately twice as high as they are wide, the dimensions of both the x-axis and the y-axis are about the same.

The function *GetDialogBaseUnits* lets you determine the system font sizes that the dialog manager uses. For a standard VGA (perhaps the most common video adapter used in Windows), *GetDialogBaseUnits* returns a character width of 8 and a character height of 16. Because dialog box units are $\frac{1}{4}$ the width of an average character and $\frac{1}{8}$ the height, each dialog box unit corresponds to 2 pixels on a VGA. This is a good rule to remember if the idea of dialog box units seems too abstract at times. But don't rely on it.

The STYLE statement in the template is similar to the style field of a *CreateWindow* call. Using WS_POPUP and WS_DLGFRAME is normal for modal dialog boxes, but we'll explore some alternatives later on.

Within the left and right brackets, you define the child window controls that will appear in the dialog box. This dialog box uses three types of child window controls: CTEXT (centered text), ICON (an icon), and DEFPUSHBUTTON (a default push button). The format of these statements is:

```
control-type "text" id, xPos, yPos, xWidth, yHeight [, iStyle]
```

The *iStyle* value at the end is optional; it specifies additional window styles using identifiers defined in the Windows header files.

These CTEXT, ICON, and DEFPUSHBUTTON identifiers are used only in dialog boxes. They are shorthand for a particular window class and window style. For example, CTEXT indicates that the class of the child window control is "static" and that the style is:

```
WS_CHILD ¦ SS_CENTER ¦ WS_VISIBLE ¦ WS_GROUP
```

Although this is the first time we've encountered the WS_GROUP identifier, we used the WS_CHILD, SS_CENTER, and WS_VISIBLE window styles when creating static child window text controls in the COLORS1 program in Chapter 8.

For the icon, the text field is the name of the program's icon resource, which is also defined in the ABOUT1 resource script. For the push button, the text field is the text that appears inside the push button. This text is equivalent to the text specified as the second parameter in a *CreateWindow* call when you create a child window control in a program.

The *id* field is a value that the child window uses to identify itself when sending messages (usually WM_COMMAND messages) to its parent. The parent window of these child window controls is the dialog box window itself, which sends these messages to a window procedure in Windows. However, this window procedure also sends these messages to the dialog box procedure that you'll include in your program. The *id* values are equivalent to the child window IDs used in the *CreateWindow* function when we created child windows in Chapter 8. Because the text and icon controls do not send messages back to the parent window, these values are set to −1. The *id* value for the push button is IDOK, which is defined in the Windows header files as 1.

The next four numbers set the position of the child window control (relative to the upper left corner of the dialog box's client area) and the size. The position and size are expressed in units of ¼ the average width and ⅛ the height of a system font character. The width and height values are ignored for the ICON statement.

The DEFPUSHBUTTON statement in the dialog box template includes the window style WS_GROUP in addition to the window style implied by the DEFPUSHBUTTON keyword. I'll have more to say about WS_GROUP (and the related WS_TABSTOP style) when discussing the second version of this program, ABOUT2, a bit later.

The Dialog Box Procedure

The dialog box procedure within your program handles messages to the dialog box. Although it looks very much like a window procedure, it is not a true window procedure. The window procedure for the dialog box is within Windows. That window procedure calls your dialog box procedure with many of the messages that it receives. Here's the dialog box procedure for ABOUT1:

```
BOOL CALLBACK AboutDlgProc (HWND hDlg, UINT iMsg, WPARAM wParam, LPARAM lParam)
    {
    switch (iMsg)
        {
        case WM_INITDIALOG :
            return TRUE ;

        case WM_COMMAND :
            switch (LOWORD (wParam))
                {
                case IDOK :
                case IDCANCEL :
                    EndDialog (hDlg, 0) ;
                    return TRUE ;
                }
            break ;
        }
    return FALSE ;
    }
```

The parameters to this function are the same as those for a normal window procedure; as with a window procedure, the dialog box procedure must be defined as a CALLBACK function. Although I've used *hDlg* for the handle to the dialog box window, you can use *hwnd* instead if you like. Let's note first the differences between this function and a window procedure:

- A window procedure returns an LRESULT; a dialog box procedure returns a BOOL (which is defined in the Windows header files as an *int*).

- A window procedure calls *DefWindowProc* if it does not process a particular message; a dialog box procedure returns TRUE (nonzero) if it processes a message and FALSE (0) if it does not.

- A dialog box procedure does not need to process WM_PAINT or WM_DESTROY messages. A dialog box procedure will not receive a WM_CREATE message; instead, the dialog box procedure performs initialization during the special WM_INITDIALOG message.

The WM_INITDIALOG message is the first message the dialog box procedure receives. This message is sent only to dialog box procedures. If the dialog box procedure returns TRUE, then Windows sets the input focus to the first child window control in the dialog box that has a WS_TABSTOP style (which I'll explain in the discussion of ABOUT2). In this dialog box, the first child window control that has a WS_TABSTOP style is the push button. Alternatively, during the processing of WM_INITDIALOG, the dialog box procedure can use *SetFocus* to set the focus to one of the child window controls in the dialog box and then return FALSE.

The only other message this dialog box processes is WM_COMMAND. This is the message the push-button control sends to its parent window either when the button is clicked with the mouse or when the Spacebar is pressed while the button has the input focus. The ID of the control (which we set to IDOK in the dialog box template) is in the low word of *wParam*. For this message, the dialog box procedure calls *EndDialog*, which tells Windows to destroy the dialog box. For all other messages, the dialog box procedure returns FALSE to tell the dialog box window procedure within Windows that our dialog box procedure did not process the message.

The messages for a modal dialog box don't go through your program's message queue, so you needn't worry about the effect of keyboard accelerators within the dialog box.

Invoking the Dialog Box

During the processing of WM_CREATE in *WndProc*, ABOUT1 obtains the program's instance handle and stores it in a static variable:

```
hInstance = ((LPCREATESTRUCT) lParam)->hInstance ;
```

ABOUT1 checks for WM_COMMAND messages where the low word of *wParam* is equal to IDM_ABOUT. When it gets one, the program calls *DialogBox*:

```
DialogBox (hInstance, "AboutBox", hwnd, AboutDlgProc) ;
```

This function requires the instance handle (saved during WM_CREATE), the name of the dialog box (as defined in the resource script), the parent of the dialog box (which is the program's main window), and the address of the dialog procedure. If you use a number rather than a name for the dialog box template, you can convert it to a string using the MAKEINTRESOURCE macro.

Selecting "About About1..." from the menu displays the dialog box, as shown in Figure 11-2. You can end this dialog box by clicking the OK button with the mouse, by pressing the Spacebar, or by pressing Enter. For any dialog box that contains a default push button, Windows sends a WM_COMMAND message to the dialog box, with the low word of *wParam* equal to the ID of the default push button when Enter or the Spacebar is pressed.

The *DialogBox* function you call to display the dialog box will not return control to *WndProc* until the dialog box is ended. The value returned from *DialogBox* is the second parameter to the *EndDialog* function called within the dialog box procedure. (This value is not used in ABOUT1 but is used in ABOUT2.) *WndProc* can then return control to Windows.

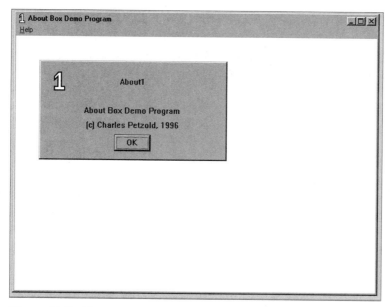

Figure 11-2. *The ABOUT1 program's dialog box.*

Even when the dialog box is displayed, *WndProc* can continue to receive messages. In fact, you can send messages to *WndProc* from within the dialog box procedure. ABOUT1's main window is the parent of the dialog box popup window, so the *SendMessage* call in *AboutDlgProc* would start off like this:

```
SendMessage (GetParent (hDlg), . . . ) ;
```

More on the Dialog Box Style

The window style of the dialog box is specified in the STYLE line of the dialog box template. For ABOUT1, we used a style that is most common for modal dialog boxes:

```
STYLE WS_POPUP ¦ WS_DLGFRAME
```

However, you can also experiment with other styles. For example, you can try:

```
STYLE WS_POPUP ¦ WS_CAPTION
```

This creates a dialog box with a title bar and a normal window border. The title bar allows the user to move the dialog box around the display by using the mouse. When you use WS_CAPTION, the *x*- and *y*-coordinates specified in the DIALOG statement are the coordinates of the dialog box's client area, relative to the upper left corner of the parent window's client area. The title bar will be shown above the *y*-coordinate.

If you have a title bar, you can put text in it using the CAPTION statement in the dialog box template:

```
CAPTION "Dialog Box Caption"
```

following the STYLE statement. Or while processing the WM_INITDIALOG message in the dialog procedure, you can use:

```
SetWindowText (hDlg, "Dialog Box Caption") ;
```

If you use the WS_CAPTION style, you can also add a system menu box with the WS_SYSMENU style:

```
STYLE WS_POPUP ¦ WS_CAPTION ¦ WS_SYSMENU
```

This style allows the user to select Move or Close from the system menu.

Adding WS_THICKFRAME to the style allows the user to resize the dialog box, although resizing is unusual for a dialog box. If you don't mind being a little unusual, you can also try adding WS_MAXIMIZEBOX to the STYLE statement.

The STYLE statement is not required. If you do not include a STYLE or CAPTION statement in the template, the default style is:

```
WS_POPUP ¦ WS_BORDER
```

But this is rather dull looking. WS_DLGFRAME produces much more attractive results. If you include a CAPTION statement with a STYLE statement, the default style is:

```
WS_POPUP | WS_CAPTION | WS_SYSMENU
```

You can also add a menu to a dialog box by specifying:

```
MENU menu-name
```

in the dialog box template. The argument is either the name or number of a menu in the resource script. Menus are highly uncommon for modal dialog boxes. If you use one, be sure that all the ID numbers in the menu and the dialog box controls are unique.

The FONT statement lets you set something other than the system font for use with dialog box text.

Although the dialog box window procedure is normally within Windows, you can use one of your own window procedures to process dialog box messages. To do so, you specify a window class name in the dialog box template:

```
CLASS "class-name"
```

This approach is rare, but we'll use it in the HEXCALC program shown later in this chapter.

When you call *DialogBox* specifying the name of a dialog box template, Windows has almost everything it needs to create a popup window by calling the normal *CreateWindow* function. Windows obtains the coordinates and size of the window, the window style, the caption, and the menu from the dialog box template. Windows gets the instance handle and the parent window handle from the parameters to *DialogBox*. The only other piece of information it needs is a window class (assuming the dialog box template does not specify one). Windows registers a special window class for dialog boxes. The window procedure for this window class has access to the pointer to your dialog box procedure (which you provide in the *DialogBox* call), so it can keep your program informed of messages that this popup window receives. Of course, you can create and maintain your own dialog box by creating the popup window yourself. Using *DialogBox* is simply an easier approach.

More on Defining Controls

In the dialog box template in ABOUT1.RC, we used the shorthand notation CTEXT, ICON, and DEFPUSHBUTTON to define the three types of child window controls we wanted in the dialog box. There are others you can use. Each type implies a particular predefined window class and a window style. The table on the facing page shows the equivalent window class and window style for each of the control types:

Control Type	*Window Class*	*Window Style*
PUSHBUTTON	button	BS_PUSHBUTTON ¦ WS_TABSTOP
DEFPUSHBUTTON	button	BS_DEFPUSHBUTTON ¦ WS_TABSTOP
CHECKBOX	button	BS_CHECKBOX ¦ WS_TABSTOP
RADIOBUTTON	button	BS_RADIOBUTTON ¦ WS_TABSTOP
GROUPBOX	button	BS_GROUPBOX ¦ WS_TABSTOP
LTEXT	static	SS_LEFT ¦ WS_GROUP
CTEXT	static	SS_CENTER ¦ WS_GROUP
RTEXT	static	SS_RIGHT ¦ WS_GROUP
ICON	static	SS_ICON
EDITTEXT	edit	ES_LEFT ¦ WS_BORDER ¦ WS_TABSTOP
SCROLLBAR	scrollbar	SBS_HORZ
LISTBOX	listbox	LBS_NOTIFY ¦ WS_BORDER ¦ WS_VSCROLL
COMBOBOX	combobox	CBS_SIMPLE ¦ WS_TABSTOP

The RC resource compiler is the only program that understands this shorthand notation. In addition to the window styles shown above, each of these controls has the style:

```
WS_CHILD ¦ WS_VISIBLE
```

For all these control types except EDITTEXT, SCROLLBAR, LISTBOX, and COMBOBOX, the format of the control statement is:

```
control-type "text", id, xPos, yPos, xWidth, yHeight [, iStyle]
```

For EDITTEXT, SCROLLBAR, LISTBOX, and COMBOBOX, the format is:

```
control-type id, xPos, yPos, xWidth, yHeight [, iStyle]
```

which excludes the text field. In both statements, the *iStyle* parameter is optional.

In Chapter 8, I discussed rules for determining the width and height of predefined child window controls. You might want to refer back to that chapter for these rules, keeping in mind that sizes specified in dialog box templates are always in terms of $1/4$ the average character width and $1/8$ the character height.

The "style" field of the control statements is optional. It allows you to include other window style identifiers. For instance, if you wanted to create a check box consisting of text to the left of a square box, you could use:

```
CHECKBOX "text", id, xPos, yPos, xWidth, yHeight, BS_LEFTTEXT
```

While the shorthand notation for child window controls is convenient, it is also incomplete. You can't create a child window edit control without a border, for example. For this reason, the RC resource compiler also recognizes a generalized control statement that looks like this:

```
CONTROL "text", id, "class", iStyle, xPos, yPos, xWidth, yHeight
```

This statement allows you to create any type of child window control by specifying the window class and the complete window style. For example, instead of using:

```
PUSHBUTTON "OK", IDOK, 10, 20, 32, 14
```

you can use:

```
CONTROL "OK", IDOK, "button", WS_CHILD ¦ WS_VISIBLE ¦
        BS_PUSHBUTTON ¦ WS_TABSTOP, 10, 20, 32, 14
```

When the resource script is compiled, these two statements are encoded identically in the .RES file and the .EXE file.

When you use CONTROL statements in a dialog box template, you don't need to include the WS_CHILD and WS_VISIBLE styles. Windows includes these in the window style when creating the child windows. The format of the CONTROL statement also clarifies what the Windows dialog manager does when it creates a dialog box. First, as I described earlier, it creates a popup window whose parent is the window handle that was provided in the *DialogBox* function. Then for each control in the dialog template, the dialog box manager creates a child window. The parent of each of these controls is the popup dialog box. The CONTROL statement shown above is translated into a *CreateWindow* call that looks like this:

```
CreateWindow ("button", "OK",
    WS_CHILD ¦ WS_VISIBLE ¦ BS_PUSHBUTTON ¦ WS_TABSTOP,
    10 * cxChar / 4, 20 * cyChar / 8,
    32 * cxChar / 4, 14 * cyChar / 8,
    hDlg, IDOK, hInstance, NULL) ;
```

where *cxChar* and *cyChar* are the width and height of a system font character in pixels. The *hDlg* parameter is returned from the *CreateWindow* call that creates the dialog box window. The *hInstance* parameter is obtained from the original *DialogBox* call.

A More Complex Dialog Box

The simple dialog box in ABOUT1 demonstrates the basics of getting a dialog box up and running; now let's try something a little more complex. The ABOUT2 program, shown in Figure 11-3, demonstrates how to manage controls (in this case, radio buttons) within a dialog box procedure and also how to paint on the client area of the dialog box.

ABOUT2.MAK

```
#---------------------
# ABOUT2.MAK make file
#---------------------

about2.exe : about2.obj about2.res
    $(LINKER) $(GUIFLAGS) -OUT:about2.exe about2.obj about2.res $(GUILIBS)

about2.obj : about2.c about2.h
    $(CC) $(CFLAGS) about2.c

about2.res : about2.rc about2.h about2.ico
    $(RC) $(RCVARS) about2.rc
```

ABOUT2.C

```
/*--------------------------------------------
   ABOUT2.C -- About Box Demo Program No. 2
              (c) Charles Petzold, 1996
   --------------------------------------------*/

#include <windows.h>
#include "about2.h"

LRESULT CALLBACK WndProc        (HWND, UINT, WPARAM, LPARAM) ;
BOOL    CALLBACK AboutDlgProc (HWND, UINT, WPARAM, LPARAM) ;

int iCurrentColor  = IDD_BLACK,
    iCurrentFigure = IDD_RECT ;

int WINAPI WinMain (HINSTANCE hInstance, HINSTANCE hPrevInstance,
                    PSTR szCmdLine, int iCmdShow)
    {
    static char  szAppName[] = "About2" ;
    MSG          msg ;
    HWND         hwnd ;
    WNDCLASSEX   wndclass ;

    wndclass.cbSize       = sizeof (wndclass) ;
    wndclass.style        = CS_HREDRAW | CS_VREDRAW ;
    wndclass.lpfnWndProc  = WndProc ;
    wndclass.cbClsExtra   = 0 ;
    wndclass.cbWndExtra   = 0 ;
    wndclass.hInstance    = hInstance ;
```

Figure 11-3. *The ABOUT2 program.* *(continued)*

525

```
        wndclass.hIcon         = LoadIcon (hInstance, szAppName) ;
        wndclass.hCursor       = LoadCursor (NULL, IDC_ARROW) ;
        wndclass.hbrBackground = (HBRUSH) GetStockObject (WHITE_BRUSH) ;
        wndclass.lpszMenuName  = szAppName ;
        wndclass.lpszClassName = szAppName ;
        wndclass.hIconSm       = LoadIcon (hInstance, szAppName) ;

        RegisterClassEx (&wndclass) ;

        hwnd = CreateWindow (szAppName, "About Box Demo Program",
                        WS_OVERLAPPEDWINDOW,
                        CW_USEDEFAULT, CW_USEDEFAULT,
                        CW_USEDEFAULT, CW_USEDEFAULT,
                        NULL, NULL, hInstance, NULL) ;

        ShowWindow (hwnd, iCmdShow) ;
        UpdateWindow (hwnd) ;

        while (GetMessage (&msg, NULL, 0, 0))
            {
            TranslateMessage (&msg) ;
            DispatchMessage (&msg) ;
            }
        return msg.wParam ;
        }

void PaintWindow (HWND hwnd, int iColor, int iFigure)
        {
        static COLORREF crColor[8] = { RGB (0,    0, 0), RGB ( 0,   0, 255),
                                       RGB (0,   255, 0), RGB ( 0, 255, 255),
                                       RGB (255,   0, 0), RGB (255,   0, 255),
                                       RGB (255, 255, 0), RGB (255, 255, 255) } ;
        HBRUSH          hBrush ;
        HDC             hdc ;
        RECT            rect ;

        hdc = GetDC (hwnd) ;
        GetClientRect (hwnd, &rect) ;
        hBrush = CreateSolidBrush (crColor[iColor - IDD_BLACK]) ;
        hBrush = (HBRUSH) SelectObject (hdc, hBrush) ;

        if (iFigure == IDD_RECT)
            Rectangle (hdc, rect.left, rect.top, rect.right, rect.bottom) ;
        else
            Ellipse  (hdc, rect.left, rect.top, rect.right, rect.bottom) ;
```

(continued)

```
    DeleteObject (SelectObject (hdc, hBrush)) ;
    ReleaseDC (hwnd, hdc) ;
    }

void PaintTheBlock (HWND hCtrl, int iColor, int iFigure)
    {
    InvalidateRect (hCtrl, NULL, TRUE) ;
    UpdateWindow (hCtrl) ;
    PaintWindow (hCtrl, iColor, iFigure) ;
    }

LRESULT CALLBACK WndProc (HWND hwnd, UINT iMsg, WPARAM wParam, LPARAM lParam)
    {
    static HINSTANCE hInstance ;
    PAINTSTRUCT      ps ;

    switch (iMsg)
        {
        case WM_CREATE :
            hInstance = ((LPCREATESTRUCT) lParam)->hInstance ;
            return 0 ;

        case WM_COMMAND :
            switch (LOWORD (wParam))
                {
                case IDM_ABOUT :
                    if (DialogBox (hInstance, "AboutBox", hwnd,
                                   AboutDlgProc))
                        InvalidateRect (hwnd, NULL, TRUE) ;
                    return 0 ;
                }
            break ;

        case WM_PAINT :
            BeginPaint (hwnd, &ps) ;
            EndPaint (hwnd, &ps) ;

            PaintWindow (hwnd, iCurrentColor, iCurrentFigure) ;
            return 0 ;

        case WM_DESTROY :
            PostQuitMessage (0) ;
            return 0 ;
        }
```

(continued)

```
        return DefWindowProc (hwnd, iMsg, wParam, lParam) ;
        }

BOOL CALLBACK AboutDlgProc (HWND hDlg, UINT iMsg, WPARAM wParam,
                                                   LPARAM lParam)
     {
     static HWND hCtrlBlock ;
     static int  iColor, iFigure ;

     switch (iMsg)
          {
          case WM_INITDIALOG :
               iColor  = iCurrentColor ;
               iFigure = iCurrentFigure ;

               CheckRadioButton (hDlg, IDD_BLACK, IDD_WHITE, iColor) ;
               CheckRadioButton (hDlg, IDD_RECT,  IDD_ELL,   iFigure) ;

               hCtrlBlock = GetDlgItem (hDlg, IDD_PAINT) ;

               SetFocus (GetDlgItem (hDlg, iColor)) ;
               return FALSE ;

          case WM_COMMAND :
               switch (LOWORD (wParam))
                    {
                    case IDOK :
                         iCurrentColor  = iColor ;
                         iCurrentFigure = iFigure ;
                         EndDialog (hDlg, TRUE) ;
                         return TRUE ;

                    case IDCANCEL :
                         EndDialog (hDlg, FALSE) ;
                         return TRUE ;

                    case IDD_BLACK :
                    case IDD_RED :
                    case IDD_GREEN :
                    case IDD_YELLOW :
                    case IDD_BLUE :
                    case IDD_MAGENTA :
                    case IDD_CYAN :
                    case IDD_WHITE :
                         iColor = LOWORD (wParam) ;
                         CheckRadioButton (hDlg, IDD_BLACK, IDD_WHITE,
                                           LOWORD (wParam)) ;
```

(continued)

```
                                    PaintTheBlock (hCtrlBlock, iColor, iFigure) ;
                                    return TRUE ;

                          case IDD_RECT :
                          case IDD_ELL :
                               iFigure = wParam ;
                               CheckRadioButton (hDlg, IDD_RECT, IDD_ELL,
                                              LOWORD (wParam)) ;
                               PaintTheBlock (hCtrlBlock, iColor, iFigure) ;
                               return TRUE ;

                          }
                     break ;

               case WM_PAINT :
                    PaintTheBlock (hCtrlBlock, iColor, iFigure) ;
                    break ;
               }
          return FALSE ;
          }
```

ABOUT2.RC

```
/*---------------------------
   ABOUT2.RC resource script
   -----------------------*/

#include <windows.h>
#include "about2.h"

about2 ICON about2.ico

About2 MENU
     {
     POPUP "&Help"
          {
          MENUITEM "&About About2...",          IDM_ABOUT
          }
     }

#define TABGRP (WS_TABSTOP | WS_GROUP)

AboutBox DIALOG 20, 20, 140, 188
     STYLE WS_POPUP | WS_DLGFRAME
     {
```

(continued)

```
CTEXT        "About2"              -1,        0,  12, 140,   8
ICON         "About2"              -1,        8,   8,   0,   0
CTEXT        "About Box Demo Program" -1, 4,  36, 130,   8
CTEXT        ""                    IDD_PAINT, 68,  54,  60,  60
GROUPBOX     "&Color"             -1,        4,  50,  54, 112
RADIOBUTTON "&Black"              IDD_BLACK,  8,  60,  40,  12, TABGRP
RADIOBUTTON "B&lue"               IDD_BLUE,   8,  72,  40,  12
RADIOBUTTON "&Green"              IDD_GREEN,  8,  84,  40,  12
RADIOBUTTON "Cya&n"              IDD_CYAN,   8,  96,  40,  12
RADIOBUTTON "&Red"               IDD_RED,    8, 108,  40,  12
RADIOBUTTON "&Magenta"           IDD_MAGENTA, 8, 120,  40,  12
RADIOBUTTON "&Yellow"            IDD_YELLOW, 8, 132,  40,  12
RADIOBUTTON "&White"             IDD_WHITE,  8, 144,  40,  12
GROUPBOX     "&Figure"           -1,       68, 120,  60,  40, WS_GROUP
RADIOBUTTON "Rec&tangle"         IDD_RECT,  72, 134,  50,  12, TABGRP
RADIOBUTTON "&Ellipse"           IDD_ELL,   72, 146,  50,  12
DEFPUSHBUTTON "OK"               IDOK,      20, 168,  40,  14, WS_GROUP
PUSHBUTTON   "Cancel"            IDCANCEL,  80, 168,  40,  14, WS_GROUP
}
```

ABOUT2.H

```
/*--------------------
   ABOUT2.H header file
---------------------*/

#define IDM_ABOUT        1

#define IDD_BLACK       10
#define IDD_BLUE        11
#define IDD_GREEN       12
#define IDD_CYAN        13
#define IDD_RED         14
#define IDD_MAGENTA     15
#define IDD_YELLOW      16
#define IDD_WHITE       17

#define IDD_RECT        20
#define IDD_ELL         21

#define IDD_PAINT       30
```

(continued)

ABOUT2.ICO

The About box in ABOUT2 has two groups of radio buttons. One group is used to select a color, and the other group is used to select either a rectangle or an ellipse. The rectangle or ellipse is shown in the dialog box with the interior colored with the current color selection. If you press the OK button, the dialog box is ended, and the program's window procedure draws the selected figure in its own client area. If you press Cancel, the client area of the main window remains the same. The dialog box is shown in Figure 11-4. Although the ABOUT2 dialog box uses the predefined identifiers IDOK and IDCANCEL for the two push buttons, each of the radio buttons has its own identifier beginning with the letters IDD ("ID for dialog box control"). These identifiers are defined in ABOUT2.H.

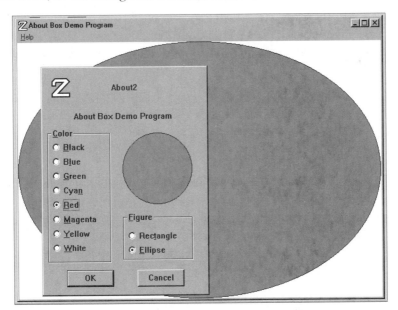

Figure 11-4. *The ABOUT2 program's dialog box.*

Working with Dialog Box Controls

In Chapter 8, you discovered that most child window controls send WM_COMMAND messages to the parent window. (The exception is scroll bar controls.) You also saw that the parent window can alter child window controls (for instance, checking or unchecking radio buttons or check boxes) by sending messages to the controls. You can similarly alter controls in a dialog box procedure. If you have a series of radio buttons, for example, you can check and uncheck the buttons by sending them messages. However, Windows also provides several shortcuts when working with controls in dialog boxes. Let's look at the way in which the dialog box procedure and the child window controls communicate.

The dialog box template for ABOUT2 is shown in the ABOUT2.RC resource script in Figure 11-3. The GROUPBOX control is simply a frame with a title (either Color or Figure) that surrounds each of the two groups of radio buttons. The eight radio buttons in the first group are mutually exclusive, as are the two radio buttons in the second group.

When one of the radio buttons is clicked with the mouse (or when the Spacebar is pressed while the radio button has the input focus), the child window sends its parent a WM_COMMAND message with the low word of *wParam* set to the ID of the control. The high word of *wParam* is a notification code and the *lParam* value is the window handle of the control. For a radio button, this notification code is BN_CLICKED, or 0. The dialog box window procedure in Windows then passes this WM_COMMAND message to the dialog box procedure within ABOUT2.C. When the dialog box procedure receives a WM_COMMAND message for one of the radio buttons, it turns on the check mark for that button and turns off the check marks for all the other buttons in the group.

You might recall from Chapter 8 that checking and unchecking a button requires that you send the child window control a BM_SETCHECK message. To turn on a button check mark, you use:

```
SendMessage (hwndCtrl, BM_SETCHECK, 1, 0) ;
```

To turn off the check mark, you use:

```
SendMessage (hwndCtrl, BM_SETCHECK, 0, 0) ;
```

The *hwndCtrl* parameter is the window handle of the child window button control.

But this method presents a little problem in the dialog box procedure, because you don't know the window handles of all the radio buttons. You know only the one from which you're getting the message. Fortunately, Windows provides you with a function to obtain the window handle of a dialog box control using the dialog box window handle and the control ID:

```
hwndCtrl = GetDlgItem (hDlg, id) ;
```

(You can also obtain the ID value of a control from the window handle by using this function:

```
id = GetWindowLong (hwndCtrl, GWL_ID) ;
```

but this is rarely necessary.)

You'll notice in the ABOUT2.H header file shown in Figure 11-3 that the ID values for the eight colors are sequential from IDD_BLACK to IDD_WHITE. This arrangement helps in processing the WM_COMMAND messages from the radio buttons. For a first attempt at checking and unchecking the radio buttons, you might try something like the following in the dialog box procedure:

```
static int iColor ;
[other program lines]
case WM_COMMAND :
     switch (LOWORD (wParam))
          {
          [other program lines]
          case IDD_BLACK :
          case IDD_RED :
          case IDD_GREEN :
          case IDD_YELLOW :
          case IDD_BLUE :
          case IDD_MAGENTA :
          case IDD_CYAN :
          case IDD_WHITE :
               iColor = LOWORD (wParam) ;

               for (i = IDD_BLACK ; i <= IDD_WHITE ; i++)
                   SendMessage (GetDlgItem (hDlg, i),
                       BM_SETCHECK, i == LOWORD (wParam), 0) ;
               return TRUE ;
          [other program lines]
```

This approach works satisfactorily. You've saved the new color value in *iColor*, and you've also set up a loop that cycles through all the ID values for the eight colors. You obtain the window handle of each of these eight radio button controls and use *SendMessage* to send each handle a BM_SETCHECK message. The *wParam* value of this message is set to 1 only for the button that sent the WM_COMMAND message to the dialog box window procedure.

The first shortcut is the special dialog box procedure *SendDlgItemMessage*:

```
SendDlgItemMessage (hDlg, id, iMsg, wParam, lParam) ;
```

It is equivalent to:

```
SendMessage (GetDlgItem (hDlg, id), id, wParam, lParam) ;
```

Now the loop would look like this:

```
for (i = IDD_BLACK ; i <= IDD_WHITE ; i++)
    SendDlgItemMessage (hDlg, i, BM_SETCHECK, i == LOWORD (wParam), 0) ;
```

That's a little better. But the real breakthrough comes when you discover the *CheckRadioButton* function:

```
CheckRadioButton (hDlg, idFirst, idLast, idCheck) ;
```

This function turns off the check marks for all radio button controls with IDs from *idFirst* to *idLast* except for the radio button with an ID of *idCheck*, which is checked. The IDs must be sequential. So we can get rid of the loop entirely and use:

```
CheckRadioButton (hDlg, IDD_BLACK, IDD_WHITE, LOWORD (wParam)) ;
```

That's how it's done in the dialog box procedure in ABOUT2.

A similar shortcut function is provided for working with check boxes. If you create a CHECKBOX dialog window control, you can turn the check mark on and off using the function:

```
CheckDlgButton (hDlg, idCheckbox, iCheck) ;
```

If *iCheck* is set to 1, the button is checked; if it's set to 0, the button is unchecked. You can obtain the status of a check box in a dialog box using:

```
iCheck = IsDlgButtonChecked (hDlg, idCheckbox) ;
```

You can either retain the current status of the check mark as a static variable within the dialog box procedure, or you can do something like this to toggle the button on a WM_COMMAND message:

```
CheckDlgButton (hDlg, idCheckbox,
    !IsDlgButtonChecked (hDlg, idCheckbox)) ;
```

If you define a BS_AUTOCHECKBOX control, then you don't need to process the WM_COMMAND message at all. You can simply obtain the current status of the button using *IsDlgButtonChecked* before terminating the dialog box.

The OK and Cancel Buttons

ABOUT2 has two push buttons, labeled OK and Cancel. In the dialog box template in ABOUT2.RC, the OK button has an ID of IDOK (defined in the Windows header files as 1) and the Cancel button has an ID of IDCANCEL (defined as 2). The OK button is the default:

```
DEFPUSHBUTTON "OK"      IDOK,    20, 168, 40, 14, WS_GROUP
PUSHBUTTON    "Cancel" IDCANCEL, 80, 168, 40, 14, WS_GROUP
```

This arrangement is normal for OK and Cancel buttons in dialog boxes; having the OK button as the default helps out with the keyboard interface. Here's how: Normally, you would end the dialog box by clicking one of these buttons with the mouse or pressing the Spacebar when the desired button has the input focus. However, the dialog box window procedure also generates a WM_COMMAND message when the user presses Enter, regardless of which control has the input focus. The low word of *wParam* is set to the ID value of the default push button in the dialog box unless another push button has the input focus. In that case, the low word of *wParam* is set to the ID of the push button with the input focus. If no push button in the dialog box is the default push button, then Windows sends the dialog box procedure a WM_COMMAND message with the low word of *wParam* equal to IDOK. If the user presses the Esc key or Ctrl-Break, Windows sends the dialog box procedure a WM_COMMAND message with the low word of *wParam* equal to IDCANCEL. So you don't have to add separate keyboard logic to the dialog box procedure, because the keystrokes that normally terminate a dialog box are translated by Windows into WM_COMMAND messages for these two push buttons.

The *AboutDlgProc* function handles these two WM_COMMAND messages by calling *EndDialog*:

```
switch (LOWORD (wParam))
    {
    case IDOK :
        iCurrentColor  = iColor ;
        iCurrentFigure = iFigure ;
        EndDialog (hDlg, TRUE) ;
        return TRUE ;

    case IDCANCEL :
        EndDialog (hDlg, FALSE) ;
        return TRUE ;
```

ABOUT2's window procedure uses the global variables *iCurrentColor* and *iCurrentFigure* when drawing the rectangle or ellipse in the program's client area. *AboutDlgProc* uses the static local variables *iColor* and *iFigure* when drawing the figure within the dialog box.

Notice the different value in the second parameter of *EndDialog*. This is the value that is passed back as the return value from the original *DialogBox* function in *WndProc*:

```
case IDM_ABOUT :
    if (DialogBox (hInstance, "AboutBox", hwnd, AboutDlgProc))
        InvalidateRect (hwnd, NULL, TRUE) ;
    return 0 ;
```

If *DialogBox* returns TRUE (nonzero), meaning that the OK button was pressed, then the *WndProc* client area needs to be updated with the new figure and color. These were saved in the global variables *iCurrentColor* and *iCurrentFigure* by *AboutDlgProc* when it received a WM_COMMAND message with the low word of *wParam* equal to IDOK. If *DialogBox* returns FALSE, the main window continues to use the original settings of *iCurrentColor* and *iCurrentFigure*.

TRUE and FALSE are commonly used in *EndDialog* calls to signal to the main window procedure whether the user ended the dialog box with OK or Cancel. However, the parameter to *EndDialog* is actually an *int*, and *DialogBox* returns an *int*, so it's possible to return more information in this way than simply TRUE or FALSE.

Tab Stops and Groups

In Chapter 8, we used window subclassing to add a facility to COLORS1 that let us move from one scroll bar to another by pressing the Tab key. In a dialog box, window subclassing is unnecessary: Windows does all the logic for moving the input focus from one control to another. However, you have to help out by using the WS_TABSTOP and WS_GROUP window styles in the dialog box template. For all controls that you want to access using the Tab key, specify WS_TABSTOP in the window style. If you refer back to the table on page 523, you'll notice that many of the controls include WS_TABSTOP as a default, while others do not. Generally the controls that do not include the WS_TABSTOP style (particularly the static controls) should not get the input focus because they can't do anything with it. Unless you set the input focus to a specific control in a dialog box during processing of the WM_INITDIALOG message and return FALSE from the message, Windows sets the input focus to the first control in the dialog box that has the WS_TABSTOP style.

The second keyboard interface that Windows adds to a dialog box involves the cursor movement keys. This interface is of particular importance with radio buttons. After you use the Tab key to move to the currently checked radio button within a group, you need to use the cursor movement keys to change the input focus from that radio button to other radio buttons within the group. You accomplish this by using the WS_GROUP window style. For a particular series of controls in the dialog box template, Windows will use the cursor movement keys to shift the input focus from the first control that has the WS_GROUP style up to (but not including) the next control that has the WS_GROUP style. Windows will cycle from the last control in a dialog box to the first control if necessary to find the end of the group.

By default, the controls LTEXT, CTEXT, RTEXT, and ICON include the WS_GROUP style, which conveniently marks the end of a group. You often have to add WS_GROUP styles to other types of controls.

Let's look at the dialog box template in ABOUT2.RC:

```
AboutBox DIALOG 20, 20, 140, 188
    STYLE WS_POPUP ¦ WS_DLGFRAME
    {
    CTEXT       "About2"              -1,        0, 12, 140,   8
    ICON        "About2"              -1,        8,  8,   0,   0
    CTEXT       "About Box Demo Program" -1, 4,  36, 130,   8
    CTEXT       ""                    IDD_PAINT, 68, 54,  60,  60
    GROUPBOX    "&Color"              -1,        4, 50,  54, 112
    RADIOBUTTON "&Black"              IDD_BLACK, 8, 60,  40,  12, TABGRP
    RADIOBUTTON "B&lue"               IDD_BLUE,  8, 72,  40,  12
```

```
RADIOBUTTON  "&Green"      IDD_GREEN,    8,  84,  40,  12
RADIOBUTTON  "Cya&n"       IDD_CYAN,     8,  96,  40,  12
RADIOBUTTON  "&Red"        IDD_RED,      8, 108,  40,  12
RADIOBUTTON  "&Magenta"    IDD_MAGENTA,  8, 120,  40,  12
RADIOBUTTON  "&Yellow"     IDD_YELLOW,   8, 132,  40,  12
RADIOBUTTON  "&White"      IDD_WHITE,    8, 144,  40,  12
GROUPBOX     "&Figure"     -1,          68, 120,  60,  40, WS_GROUP
RADIOBUTTON  "Rec&tangle"  IDD_RECT,    72, 134,  50,  12, TABGRP
RADIOBUTTON  "&Ellipse"    IDD_ELL,     72, 146,  50,  12
DEFPUSHBUTTON "OK"         IDOK,        20, 168,  40,  14, WS_GROUP
PUSHBUTTON   "Cancel"      IDCANCEL,    80, 168,  40,  14, WS_GROUP
}
```

To simplify the appearance of the template, an identifier is defined in ABOUT2.RC that combines WS_TABSTOP and WS_GROUP:

```
#define TABGRP (WS_TABSTOP | WS_GROUP)
```

The four controls that have the WS_TABSTOP style are the first radio buttons of each group (explicitly included) and the two push buttons (by default). When you first invoke the dialog box, these are the four controls you can move among using the Tab key.

Within each group of radio buttons, you use the cursor movement keys to change the input focus and the check mark. For example, the first radio button control (Black) in the Color group box and the Figure group box control have the WS_GROUP style. This means that you can use the cursor movement keys to move the focus from the Black radio button up to (but not including) the Figure group box. Similarly, the first radio button control (Rectangle) in the Figure group box and the DEFPUSHBUTTON control have the WS_GROUP style, so you can use the cursor movement keys to move between the two radio buttons in this group: Rectangle and Ellipse. Both push buttons get the WS_GROUP style to prevent the cursor movement keys from doing anything when the push buttons have the input focus.

When using ABOUT2, the dialog box manager in Windows performs some magic in the two groups of radio buttons. As expected, the cursor movement keys within a group of radio buttons shift the input focus and send a WM_COMMAND message to the dialog box procedure. But when you change the checked radio button within the group, Windows also assigns the newly checked radio button the WS_TABSTOP style. The next time you tab to that group, Windows will set the input focus to the checked radio button.

An ampersand (&) in the text field causes the letter that follows to be underlined and adds another keyboard interface. You can move the input focus to any of the radio buttons by pressing the underlined letter. By pressing C (for the Color group box) or F (for the Figure group box), you can move the input focus to the currently checked radio button in that group.

Although programmers normally let the dialog box manager take care of all this, Windows includes two functions that let you search for the next or previous tab stop or group item. These functions are:

```
      hwndCtrl = GetNextDlgTabItem (hDlg, hwndCtrl, bPrevious) ;
```

and:

```
      hwndCtrl = GetNextDlgGroupItem (hDlg, hwndCtrl, bPrevious) ;
```

If *bPrevious* is TRUE, the functions return the previous tab stop or group item; if FALSE, they return the next tab stop or group item.

Painting on the Dialog Box

ABOUT2 also does something relatively unusual: It paints on the dialog box. Let's see how this works. Within the dialog box template in ABOUT2.RC, a blank text control is defined with a position and size for the area we want to paint:

```
      CTEXT   ""   IDD_PAINT, 68, 54, 60, 60
```

This area is 15 characters wide and $7\frac{1}{2}$ characters high. Because this control has no text, all that the window procedure for the "static" class does is erase the background when the child window control has to be repainted.

When the current color or figure selection changes or when the dialog box itself gets a WM_PAINT message, the dialog box procedure calls *PaintTheBlock*, which is a function in ABOUT2.C:

```
      PaintTheBlock (hCtrlBlock, iColor, iFigure) ;
```

The window handle *hCtrlBlock* had been set during the processing of the WM_INITDIALOG message:

```
      hCtrlBlock = GetDlgItem (hDlg, IDD_PAINT) ;
```

Here's the *PaintTheBlock* function:

```
      void PaintTheBlock (HWND hCtrl, int iColor, int iFigure)
           {
           InvalidateRect (hCtrl, NULL, TRUE) ;
           UpdateWindow (hCtrl) ;
           PaintWindow (hCtrl, iColor, iFigure) ;
           }
```

This invalidates the child window control, flags it as updated, and then calls another function in ABOUT2 called *PaintWindow*.

The *PaintWindow* function obtains a device context handle for *hCtrl* and draws the selected figure, filling it with a colored brush based on the selected color. The size of the child window control is obtained from *GetClientRect*. Although the dialog box template defines the size of the control in terms of characters, *GetClientRect* obtains the dimensions in pixels. You can also use the function *MapDialogRect* to convert the character coordinates in the dialog box to pixel coordinates in the client area.

We're not really painting the dialog box's client area—we're actually painting the client area of the child window control. Whenever the dialog box gets a WM_PAINT message, the child window control is invalidated and then updated to make it believe that its client area is now valid. We then paint on top of it.

Using Other Functions with Dialog Boxes

Most functions that you can use with child windows you can also use with controls in a dialog box. For instance, if you're feeling devious, you can use *MoveWindow* to move the controls around the dialog box and force the user to chase them around with the mouse.

Sometimes you need to dynamically enable or disable certain controls in a dialog box, depending on the settings of other controls. This call:

```
EnableWindow (hwndCtrl, bEnable) ;
```

enables the control when *bEnable* is TRUE (nonzero) and disables it when *bEnable* is FALSE (0). When a control is disabled, it receives no keyboard or mouse input. Don't disable a control that has the input focus.

Defining Your Own Controls

Although Windows assumes much of the responsibility for maintaining the dialog box and child window controls, various methods let you slip some of your own code into this process. We've already seen a method that allows you to paint on the surface of a dialog box. You can also use window subclassing (discussed in Chapter 8) to alter the operation of child window controls.

You can also define your own child window controls and use them in a dialog box. For example, suppose you don't particularly care for the normal rectangular push buttons and would prefer to create elliptical push buttons. You can do this by registering a window class and using your own window procedure to process messages for your customized child window. You then specify this window class in a CONTROL statement in the dialog box template. The ABOUT3 program, shown in Figure 11-5, does exactly that.

ABOUT3.MAK

```
#---------------------
# ABOUT3.MAK make file
#---------------------

about3.exe : about3.obj about3.res
    $(LINKER) $(GUIFLAGS) -OUT:about3.exe about3.obj about3.res $(GUILIBS)
```

Figure 11-5. *The ABOUT3 program.*

(continued)

```
about3.obj : about3.c about3.h
    $(CC) $(CFLAGS) about3.c

about3.res : about3.rc about3.h about3.ico
    $(RC) $(RCVARS) about3.rc
```

ABOUT3.C

```c
/*----------------------------------------------
   ABOUT3.C -- About Box Demo Program No. 3
               (c) Charles Petzold, 1996
   ----------------------------------------------*/

#include <windows.h>
#include "about3.h"

LRESULT CALLBACK WndProc (HWND, UINT, WPARAM, LPARAM) ;
BOOL    CALLBACK AboutDlgProc (HWND, UINT, WPARAM, LPARAM) ;
LRESULT CALLBACK EllipPushWndProc (HWND, UINT, WPARAM, LPARAM) ;

int WINAPI WinMain (HINSTANCE hInstance, HINSTANCE hPrevInstance,
                    PSTR szCmdLine, int iCmdShow)
     {
     static char  szAppName[] = "About3" ;
     MSG          msg ;
     HWND         hwnd ;
     WNDCLASSEX   wndclass ;

     wndclass.cbSize        = sizeof (wndclass) ;
     wndclass.style         = CS_HREDRAW | CS_VREDRAW ;
     wndclass.lpfnWndProc   = WndProc ;
     wndclass.cbClsExtra    = 0 ;
     wndclass.cbWndExtra    = 0 ;
     wndclass.hInstance     = hInstance ;
     wndclass.hIcon         = LoadIcon (hInstance, szAppName) ;
     wndclass.hCursor       = LoadCursor (NULL, IDC_ARROW) ;
     wndclass.hbrBackground = (HBRUSH) GetStockObject (WHITE_BRUSH) ;
     wndclass.lpszMenuName  = szAppName ;
     wndclass.lpszClassName = szAppName ;
     wndclass.hIconSm       = LoadIcon (hInstance, szAppName) ;

     RegisterClassEx (&wndclass) ;

     wndclass.cbSize        = sizeof (wndclass) ;
     wndclass.style         = CS_HREDRAW | CS_VREDRAW ;
```

(continued)

```
        wndclass.lpfnWndProc    = EllipPushWndProc ;
        wndclass.cbClsExtra     = 0 ;
        wndclass.cbWndExtra     = 0 ;
        wndclass.hInstance      = hInstance ;
        wndclass.hIcon          = NULL ;
        wndclass.hCursor        = LoadCursor (NULL, IDC_ARROW) ;
        wndclass.hbrBackground  = (HBRUSH) (COLOR_BTNFACE + 1) ;
        wndclass.lpszMenuName   = NULL ;
        wndclass.lpszClassName  = "EllipPush" ;
        wndclass.hIconSm        = NULL ;

        RegisterClassEx (&wndclass) ;

        hwnd = CreateWindow (szAppName, "About Box Demo Program",
                             WS_OVERLAPPEDWINDOW,
                             CW_USEDEFAULT, CW_USEDEFAULT,
                             CW_USEDEFAULT, CW_USEDEFAULT,
                             NULL, NULL, hInstance, NULL) ;

        ShowWindow (hwnd, iCmdShow) ;
        UpdateWindow (hwnd) ;

        while (GetMessage (&msg, NULL, 0, 0))
             {
             TranslateMessage (&msg) ;
             DispatchMessage (&msg) ;
             }
        return msg.wParam ;
        }

LRESULT CALLBACK WndProc (HWND hwnd, UINT iMsg, WPARAM wParam, LPARAM lParam)
        {
        static HINSTANCE hInstance ;

        switch (iMsg)
             {
             case WM_CREATE :
                  hInstance = ((LPCREATESTRUCT) lParam)->hInstance ;
                  return 0 ;

             case WM_COMMAND :
                  switch (LOWORD (wParam))
                       {
                       case IDM_ABOUT :
                            DialogBox (hInstance, "AboutBox", hwnd,
```

(continued)

```
                                        AboutDlgProc) ;
                        return 0 ;
                    }
                break ;

            case WM_DESTROY :
                PostQuitMessage (0) ;
                return 0 ;
        }
    return DefWindowProc (hwnd, iMsg, wParam, lParam) ;
    }

BOOL CALLBACK AboutDlgProc (HWND hDlg, UINT iMsg, WPARAM wParam, LPARAM lParam)
    {
    switch (iMsg)
        {
        case WM_INITDIALOG :
            return TRUE ;

        case WM_COMMAND :
            switch (LOWORD (wParam))
                {
                case IDOK :
                    EndDialog (hDlg, 0) ;
                    return TRUE ;
                }
            break ;
        }
    return FALSE ;
    }

LRESULT CALLBACK EllipPushWndProc (HWND hwnd, UINT iMsg, WPARAM wParam,
                                                       LPARAM lParam)
    {
    char        szText[40] ;
    HBRUSH      hBrush ;
    HDC         hdc ;
    PAINTSTRUCT ps ;
    RECT        rect ;

    switch (iMsg)
        {
        case WM_PAINT :
            GetClientRect (hwnd, &rect) ;
```

(continued)

```
                GetWindowText (hwnd, szText, sizeof (szText)) ;

                hdc = BeginPaint (hwnd, &ps) ;

                hBrush = CreateSolidBrush (GetSysColor (COLOR_WINDOW)) ;
                hBrush = (HBRUSH) SelectObject (hdc, hBrush) ;
                SetBkColor (hdc, GetSysColor (COLOR_WINDOW)) ;
                SetTextColor (hdc, GetSysColor (COLOR_WINDOWTEXT)) ;

                Ellipse (hdc, rect.left, rect.top, rect.right, rect.bottom) ;
                DrawText (hdc, szText, -1, &rect,
                            DT_SINGLELINE | DT_CENTER | DT_VCENTER) ;

                DeleteObject (SelectObject (hdc, hBrush)) ;

                EndPaint (hwnd, &ps) ;
                return 0 ;

          case WM_KEYUP :
                if (wParam != VK_SPACE)
                     break ;
                                        // fall through
          case WM_LBUTTONUP :
                SendMessage (GetParent (hwnd), WM_COMMAND,
                     GetWindowLong (hwnd, GWL_ID), (LPARAM) hwnd) ;
                return 0 ;
          }
     return DefWindowProc (hwnd, iMsg, wParam, lParam) ;
     }
```

ABOUT3.RC

```
/*---------------------------
   ABOUT3.RC resource script
 ---------------------------*/

#include <windows.h>
#include "about3.h"

about3 ICON about3.ico

About3 MENU
    {
    POPUP "&Help"
        {
```

(continued)

```
            MENUITEM "&About About3...",         IDM_ABOUT
            }
        }

#define TABGRP (WS_TABSTOP ! WS_GROUP)

AboutBox DIALOG  20, 20, 160, 80
    STYLE WS_POPUP ! WS_DLGFRAME
    {
    CTEXT    "About3"                          -1,  0, 12, 160,  8
    ICON     "About3"                          -1,  8,  8,   0,  0
    CTEXT    "About Box Demo Program"          -1,  0, 36, 160,  8
    CTEXT    "(c) Charles Petzold, 1996"       -1,  0, 48, 160,  8
    CONTROL  "OK" IDOK, "EllipPush",   TABGRP,     64, 60,  32, 14
    }
```

ABOUT3.H

```
/*-----------------------
   ABOUT3.H header file
 -----------------------*/

#define IDM_ABOUT       1
```

ABOUT3.ICO

The window class we'll be registering is called "EllipPush" ("elliptical push button"). Rather than use a DEFPUSHBUTTON statement in the dialog box template, we use a CONTROL statement that specifies this window class:

```
CONTROL "OK" IDOK, "EllipPush", TABGRP, 64, 60, 32, 14
```

The dialog box manager uses this window class in a *CreateWindow* call when creating the child window control in the dialog box.

The ABOUT3.C program registers the "EllipPush" window class in *WinMain*:

```
wndclass.cbSize        = sizeof (wndclass) ;
wndclass.style         = CS_HREDRAW | CS_VREDRAW ;
wndclass.lpfnWndProc   = EllipPushWndProc ;
wndclass.cbClsExtra    = 0 ;
wndclass.cbWndExtra    = 0 ;
wndclass.hInstance     = hInstance ;
wndclass.hIcon         = NULL ;
wndclass.hCursor       = LoadCursor (NULL, IDC_ARROW) ;
wndclass.hbrBackground = (HBRUSH) (COLOR_BTNFACE + 1) ;
wndclass.lpszMenuName  = NULL ;
wndclass.lpszClassName = "EllipPush" ;
wndclass.hIconSm       = NULL ;

RegisterClassEx (&wndclass) ;
```

The window class specifies that the window procedure is *EllipPushWndProc*, which is also in ABOUT3.C.

The *EllipPushWndProc* window procedure processes only three messages: WM_PAINT, WM_KEYUP, and WM_LBUTTONUP. During the WM_PAINT message, it obtains the size of its window from *GetClientRect* and obtains the text that appears in the push button from *GetWindowText*. It uses the Windows functions *Ellipse* and *DrawText* to draw the ellipse and the text.

The processing of the WM_KEYUP and WM_LBUTTONUP messages is very simple:

```
case WM_KEYUP :
     if (wParam != VK_SPACE)
          break ;
                              // fall through
case WM_LBUTTONUP :
     SendMessage (GetParent (hwnd), WM_COMMAND,
          GetWindowLong (hwnd, GWL_ID), (LPARAM) hwnd) ;
     return 0 ;
```

The window procedure obtains the handle of its parent window (the dialog box) using *GetParent* and sends a WM_COMMAND message with *wParam* equal to the control's ID. The ID is obtained using *GetWindowLong*. The dialog box window procedure then passes this message on to the dialog box procedure within ABOUT3. The result is a customized push button, as shown in Figure 11-6 on the following page. You can use this same method to create other customized controls for dialog boxes.

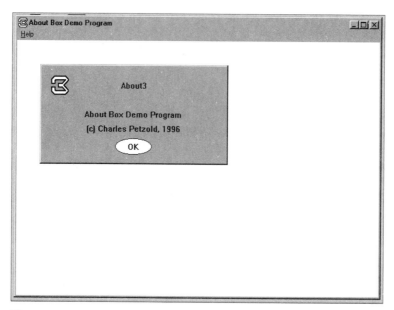

Figure 11-6. *A customized push button created by ABOUT3.*

Is that all there is to it? Well, not really. *EllipPushWndProc* is a bare-bones version of the logic generally involved in maintaining a child window control. For instance, the button doesn't flash like normal push buttons. To invert the colors on the interior of the push button, the window procedure would have to process WM_KEYDOWN (from the Spacebar) and WM_LBUTTONDOWN messages. The window procedure should also capture the mouse on a WM_LBUTTONDOWN message and release the mouse (and return the button's interior color to normal) if the mouse is moved outside the child window's client area while the button is still depressed. Only if the button is released while the mouse is captured should the child window send a WM_COMMAND message back to its parent.

EllipPushWndProc also does not process WM_ENABLE messages. As mentioned above, a dialog box procedure can disable a window using the *EnableWindow* function. The child window would then display gray rather than black text to indicate that it has been disabled and cannot receive messages.

If the window procedure for a child window control needs to store data that are different for each created window, it can do so by using a positive value of *cbWndExtra* in the window class structure. This reserves space in the internal window structure that can be accessed by using *SetWindowWord*, *SetWindowLong*, *GetWindowWord*, and *GetWindowLong*.

MESSAGE BOXES

Let's take a breather here. We've been looking at ways to customize dialog boxes. Now let's look at an alternative to dialog boxes—the message box. We began using message boxes way back in Chapter 7, but we haven't yet examined them in detail.

A message box is an appropriate and easy-to-use alternative to a dialog box when you need a simple response from the user. The general syntax is:

```
iItem = MessageBox (hwndParent, szText, szCaption, iType) ;
```

The message box has a caption (the character string *szCaption*), one or more lines of text (*szText*), one or more buttons, and (optionally) a predefined icon. One of the buttons is a default. The *iItem* value returned from *MessageBox* indicates the button that was clicked.

The *hwndParent* parameter is generally the handle to the window that creates the message box. The input focus will be set to this window when the message box is destroyed. If you don't have a window handle available or you don't want the input focus to go to one of your windows, you can use NULL for the handle. If you use a message box within a dialog box, use the dialog box window handle (which we've been calling *hDlg*) for this parameter.

The *szText* parameter is a long pointer to NULL-terminated text that appears in the body of the message box. Windows breaks this text into several lines if necessary. You can also include tab characters in the text, and you can define your own line breaks using carriage returns or linefeeds or both. The *szCaption* string is generally the name of the application.

The *iType* parameter is a collection of flags joined by the C bitwise OR operator. The first group of flags specifies the push buttons to appear at the bottom of the message box: MB_OK (the default), MB_OKCANCEL, MB_YESNO, MB_YESNOCANCEL, MB_RETRY-CANCEL, MB_ABORTRETRYIGNORE, and MB_HELP. These flags allow for a maximum of four buttons. The second group of flags specifies which of the buttons is the default: MB_DEF-BUTTON1 (the default), MB_DEFBUTTON2, MB_DEFBUTTON3, and MB_DEFBUTTON4.

The third group of flags specifies the icon to appear in the message box: MB_ICONINFORMATION (which is the same as MB_ICONASTERISK), MB_ICONWARNING (the same as MB_ICONEXCLAMATION), MB_ICONERROR (the same as MB_ICONSTOP and MB_ICONHAND), and MB_ICONQUESTION. There is no default. If you omit one of these flags, the message box has no icon. You should use the information icon for a status message, the warning point for a reminder, the question mark for questioning if the user really wants to do something, and the error icon for a signal of serious problems.

The fourth set of flags governs whether the message box is application modal, in which case the user can switch to another application without ending the message box, or system modal, which requires the user to end the message box before doing anything else. The flags are MB_APPLMODAL (the default) and MB_SYSTEMMODAL. Finally, you can use a fifth flag,

MB_NOFOCUS, which displays the message box but does not give it the input focus.

Depending on which button is clicked, the message box returns one of these identifiers: IDOK, IDCANCEL, IDYES, IDNO, IDRETRY, IDIGNORE, IDHELP, or IDABORT.

Popup Information

One handy use of a message box during program development is to provide information to you while the program is executing. It would be ideal if you could use a message box much as you use *printf* in C programs for MS-DOS, with a formatting string and a variable number of arguments. And in fact, you can create a function that lets you do this:

```
void OkMsgBox (char *szCaption, char *szFormat, ...)
    {
    char  szBuffer[256] ;
    char *pArguments ;

    pArguments = (char *) &szFormat + sizeof (szFormat) ;
    vsprintf (szBuffer, szFormat, pArguments) ;
    MessageBox (NULL, szBuffer, szCaption, MB_OK) ;
    }
```

The *vsprintf* function is similar to *sprintf* except that it uses a pointer to a series of arguments (*pArguments*) rather than the arguments themselves. *OkMsgBox* sets *pArguments* to the arguments on the stack when *OkMsgBox* is called. The first parameter to *OkMsgBox* is the message box caption, the second parameter is a format string, and the third and subsequent parameters are the values to be displayed. Let's say you want a message box to appear every time the window procedure gets a WM_SIZE message. Your code might look like this:

```
case WM_SIZE :
     OkMsgBox ("WM_SIZE Message",
               "wParam = %04X-%04X, lParam = %04X-%04X",
               HIWORD (wParam), LOWORD (wParam),
               HIWORD (lParam), LOWORD (lParam)) ;
     [other program lines]
     return 0 ;
```

This displays the values of *wParam* and *lParam* within the message box.

MODELESS DIALOG BOXES

At the beginning of this chapter, I explained that dialog boxes can be either "modal" or "modeless." So far we've been looking at modal dialog boxes, the more common of the two types. Modal dialog boxes (except system modal dialog boxes) allow the user to switch between the dialog box and other programs. However, the user cannot switch to another window in the program until the modal dialog box is destroyed. Modeless dialog boxes allow the user to switch between the dialog box and the window that created it as well as between the dialog box and other programs. The modeless dialog box is thus more akin to the regular popup windows that your program might create.

Modeless dialog boxes are preferred when the user would find it convenient to keep the dialog box displayed for a while. For instance, word processors often use modeless dialog boxes for the text Find and Replace dialogs. If the Find dialog box were modal, the user would have to choose Find from the menu, enter the string to be found, end the dialog box to return to the document, and then repeat the entire process to search for another occurrence of the same string. Allowing the user to switch between the document and the dialog box is much more convenient.

As you've seen, modal dialog boxes are created using *DialogBox*. The function returns a value only after the dialog box is destroyed. It returns the value specified in the second parameter of the *EndDialog* call that was used within the dialog box procedure to terminate the dialog box. Modeless dialog boxes are created using *CreateDialog*. This function takes the same parameters as *DialogBox*:

```
hDlgModeless = CreateDialog (hInstance, szTemplate, hwndParent,
                             DialogProc) ;
```

The difference is that the *CreateDialog* function returns immediately with the window handle of the dialog box. Normally, you store this window handle in a global variable.

Although the use of the names *DialogBox* with modal dialog boxes and *CreateDialog* with modeless dialog boxes may seem arbitrary, you can remember which is which by keeping in mind that modeless dialog boxes are similar to normal windows. *CreateDialog* should remind you of the *CreateWindow* function, which creates normal windows.

Differences Between Modal and Modeless Dialog Boxes

Working with modeless dialog boxes is similar to working with modal dialog boxes, but there are several important differences:

■ Modeless dialog boxes usually include a title bar and a system menu icon. The STYLE statement in the dialog box template for a modeless dialog box will look something like this:

```
STYLE WS_POPUP | WS_CAPTION | WS_SYSMENU | WS_VISIBLE
```

The title bar and system menu allow the user to move the modeless dialog box to another area of the display using either the mouse or the keyboard. You don't normally provide a title bar and system menu with a modal dialog box, because the user can't do anything in the underlying window anyway.

■ Notice that the WS_VISIBLE style is included in our sample STYLE statement. If you omit WS_VISIBLE, you must call *ShowWindow* after the *CreateDialog* call:

```
hDlgModeless = CreateDialog (  . . .  ) ;
ShowWindow (hDlgModeless, SW_SHOW) ;
```

If you neither include WS_VISIBLE nor call *ShowWindow*, the modeless dialog box will not be displayed. In overlooking this fact, programmers who have mastered modal dialog boxes often experience difficulties when they first try to create a modeless dialog box.

■ Unlike messages to modal dialog boxes and message boxes, messages to modeless dialog boxes come through your program's message queue. The message loop must be altered to pass these messages to the dialog box window procedure. Here's how you do it: When you use *CreateDialog* to create a modeless dialog box, you should save the dialog box handle returned from the call in a global variable (for instance, *hDlgModeless*). Change your message loop to look like this:

```
while (GetMessage (&msg, NULL, 0, 0))
     {
     if (hDlgModeless == 0 || !IsDialogMessage (hDlgModeless, &msg))
          {
          TranslateMessage (&msg) ;
          DispatchMessage  (&msg) ;
          }
     }
```

If the message is intended for the modeless dialog box, then *IsDialog-Message* sends it to the dialog box window procedure and returns TRUE (non-zero); otherwise, it returns FALSE (0). The *TranslateMessage* and *DispatchMessage* functions should be called only if *hDlgModeless* is 0 or if the message is not for the dialog box. If you use keyboard accelerators for your program's window, then the message loop looks like this:

```
while (GetMessage (&msg, NULL, 0, 0))
     {
     if (hDlgModeless == 0 || !IsDialogMessage (hDlgModeless, &msg))
        {
        if (!TranslateAccelerator (hwnd, hAccel, &msg))
           {
           TranslateMessage (&msg) ;
           DispatchMessage  (&msg) ;
           }
        }
     }
```

Because global variables are initialized to 0, *hDlgModeless* will be 0 until the dialog box is created, thus ensuring that *IsDialogMessage* is not called with an invalid window handle. You must take the same precaution when you destroy the modeless dialog box, as explained below.

The *hDlgModeless* variable can also be used by other parts of the program as a test of the existence of the modeless dialog box. For example, other windows in the program can send messages to the dialog box while *hDlgModeless* is not equal to 0.

■ Use *DestroyWindow* rather than *EndDialog* to end a modeless dialog box. When you call *DestroyWindow*, set the *hDlgModeless* global variable to 0.

The user customarily terminates a modeless dialog box by choosing Close from the system menu. Although the Close option is enabled, the dialog box window procedure within Windows does not process the WM_CLOSE message. You must do this yourself in the dialog box procedure:

```
case WM_CLOSE :
    DestroyWindow (hDlg) ;
    hDlgModeless = 0 ;
    break ;
```

Note the difference between these two window handles: The *hDlg* parameter to *DestroyWindow* is the parameter passed to the dialog box procedure; *hDlgModeless* is the global variable returned from *CreateDialog* that you test within the message loop.

You can also allow a user to close a modeless dialog box using push buttons. Use the same logic as for the WM_CLOSE message. Any information that the dialog box must "return" to the window that created it can be stored in global variables.

The New COLORS Program

The COLORS1 program described in Chapter 8 created nine child windows to display three scroll bars and six text items. At that time, the program was one of the more complex we had developed. Converting COLORS1 to use a modeless dialog box makes the program—and particularly its *WndProc* function—almost ridiculously simple. The revised COLORS2 program is shown in Figure 11-7.

COLORS2.MAK

```
#---------------------
# COLORS2.MAK make file
#---------------------
```

Figure 11-7. *The COLORS2 program.*

(continued)

```
colors2.exe : colors2.obj colors2.res
    $(LINKER) $(GUIFLAGS) -OUT:colors2.exe colors2.obj colors2.res $(GUILIBS)

colors2.obj : colors2.c
    $(CC) $(CFLAGS) colors2.c

colors2.res : colors2.rc
    $(RC) $(RCVARS) colors2.rc
```

COLORS2.C

```c
/*-------------------------------------------------
   COLORS2.C -- Version using Modeless Dialog Box
                (c) Charles Petzold, 1996
   -------------------------------------------------*/

#include <windows.h>

LRESULT CALLBACK WndProc       (HWND, UINT, WPARAM, LPARAM) ;
BOOL    CALLBACK ColorScrDlg (HWND, UINT, WPARAM, LPARAM) ;

HWND hDlgModeless ;

int WINAPI WinMain (HINSTANCE hInstance, HINSTANCE hPrevInstance,
                    PSTR szCmdLine, int iCmdShow)
    {
    static char  szAppName[] = "Colors2" ;
    HWND         hwnd ;
    MSG          msg ;
    WNDCLASSEX   wndclass ;

    wndclass.cbSize        = sizeof (wndclass) ;
    wndclass.style         = CS_HREDRAW | CS_VREDRAW ;
    wndclass.lpfnWndProc   = WndProc ;
    wndclass.cbClsExtra    = 0 ;
    wndclass.cbWndExtra    = 0 ;
    wndclass.hInstance     = hInstance ;
    wndclass.hIcon         = LoadIcon (NULL, IDI_APPLICATION) ;
    wndclass.hCursor       = LoadCursor (NULL, IDC_ARROW) ;
    wndclass.hbrBackground = CreateSolidBrush (0L) ;
    wndclass.lpszMenuName  = NULL ;
    wndclass.lpszClassName = szAppName ;
```

(continued)

```
        wndclass.hIconSm        = LoadIcon (NULL, IDI_APPLICATION) ;

    RegisterClassEx (&wndclass) ;

    hwnd = CreateWindow (szAppName, "Color Scroll",
                         WS_OVERLAPPEDWINDOW | WS_CLIPCHILDREN,
                         CW_USEDEFAULT, CW_USEDEFAULT,
                         CW_USEDEFAULT, CW_USEDEFAULT,
                         NULL, NULL, hInstance, NULL) ;

    ShowWindow (hwnd, iCmdShow) ;
    UpdateWindow (hwnd) ;

    hDlgModeless = CreateDialog (hInstance, "ColorScrDlg", hwnd, ColorScrDlg) ;

    while (GetMessage (&msg, NULL, 0, 0))
        {
        if (hDlgModeless == 0 || !IsDialogMessage (hDlgModeless, &msg))
            {
            TranslateMessage (&msg) ;
            DispatchMessage  (&msg) ;
            }
        }
    return msg.wParam ;
    }

LRESULT CALLBACK WndProc (HWND hwnd, UINT iMsg, WPARAM wParam, LPARAM lParam)
    {
    switch (iMsg)
        {
        case WM_DESTROY :
            DeleteObject (
                (HGDIOBJ) SetClassLong (hwnd, GCL_HBRBACKGROUND,
                    (LONG) GetStockObject (WHITE_BRUSH))) ;

            PostQuitMessage (0) ;
            return 0 ;
        }
    return DefWindowProc (hwnd, iMsg, wParam, lParam) ;
    }

BOOL CALLBACK ColorScrDlg (HWND hDlg, UINT iMsg, WPARAM wParam, LPARAM lParam)
    {
    static int iColor[3] ;
```

(continued)

```
HWND      hwndParent, hCtrl ;
int       iCtrlID, iIndex ;

switch (iMsg)
    {
    case WM_INITDIALOG :
        for (iCtrlID = 10 ; iCtrlID < 13 ; iCtrlID++)
            {
            hCtrl = GetDlgItem (hDlg, iCtrlID) ;
            SetScrollRange (hCtrl, SB_CTL, 0, 255, FALSE) ;
            SetScrollPos   (hCtrl, SB_CTL, 0, FALSE) ;
            }
        return TRUE ;

    case WM_VSCROLL :
        hCtrl   = (HWND) lParam ;
        iCtrlID = GetWindowLong (hCtrl, GWL_ID) ;
        iIndex  = iCtrlID - 10 ;
        hwndParent = GetParent (hDlg) ;

        switch (LOWORD (wParam))
            {
            case SB_PAGEDOWN :
                iColor[iIndex] += 15 ;          // fall through
            case SB_LINEDOWN :
                iColor[iIndex] = min (255, iColor[iIndex] + 1) ;
                break ;
            case SB_PAGEUP :
                iColor[iIndex] -= 15 ;          // fall through
            case SB_LINEUP :
                iColor[iIndex] = max (0, iColor[iIndex] - 1) ;
                break ;
            case SB_TOP :
                iColor[iIndex] = 0 ;
                break ;
            case SB_BOTTOM :
                iColor[iIndex] = 255 ;
                break ;
            case SB_THUMBPOSITION :
            case SB_THUMBTRACK :
                iColor[iIndex] = HIWORD (wParam) ;
                break ;
            default :
                return FALSE ;
            }
        SetScrollPos  (hCtrl, SB_CTL,      iColor[iIndex], TRUE) ;
```

(continued)

```
                    SetDlgItemInt (hDlg,  iCtrlID + 3, iColor[iIndex], FALSE) ;

                    DeleteObject (
                         (HGDIOBJ) SetClassLong (hwndParent, GCL_HBRBACKGROUND,
                              (LONG) CreateSolidBrush (
                                   RGB (iColor[0], iColor[1], iColor[2])))) ;

                    InvalidateRect (hwndParent, NULL, TRUE) ;
                    return TRUE ;
               }
          return FALSE ;
          }
```

COLORS2.RC

```
/*----------------------------
   COLORS2.RC resource script
   --------------------------*/

#include <windows.h>

#define SBS_VERT_TAB (SBS_VERT | WS_TABSTOP)

ColorScrDlg DIALOG  8, 16, 124, 132
     STYLE WS_POPUP | WS_CAPTION | WS_SYSMENU | WS_VISIBLE
     CAPTION "Color Scroll Scrollbars"
     {
     CONTROL "&Red",   -1, "static",    SS_CENTER,    10,   4, 24,   8
     CONTROL "",       10, "scrollbar", SBS_VERT_TAB, 10,  16, 24, 100
     CONTROL "0",      13, "static",    SS_CENTER,    10, 120, 24,   8
     CONTROL "&Green", -1, "static",    SS_CENTER,    50,   4, 24,   8
     CONTROL "",       11, "scrollbar", SBS_VERT_TAB, 50,  16, 24, 100
     CONTROL "0",      14, "static",    SS_CENTER,    50, 120, 24,   8
     CONTROL "&Blue",  -1, "static",    SS_CENTER,    90,   4, 24,   8
     CONTROL "",       12, "scrollbar", SBS_VERT_TAB, 90,  16, 24, 100
     CONTROL "0",      15, "static",    SS_CENTER,    90, 120, 24,   8
     }
```

Although the original COLORS1 program displayed scroll bars that were based on the size of the window, the new version keeps them at a constant size within the modeless dialog box, as shown in Figure 11-8 on the following page. The dialog box template in COLORS2.RC uses CONTROL statements for all nine child windows in the dialog box. The modeless dialog box is created in COLORS2's *WinMain* function following the *UpdateWindow* call for the program's main window. Note that the window style for the main window includes WS_CLIPCHILDREN, which allows the program to repaint the main window without erasing the dialog box.

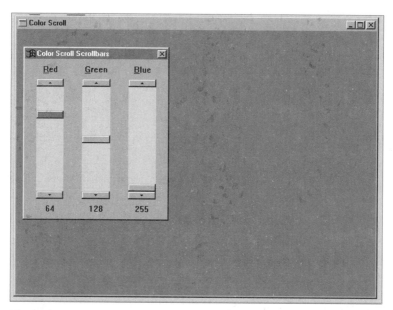

Figure 11-8. *The COLORS2 display.*

The dialog box window handle returned from *CreateDialog* is stored in the global variable *hDlgModeless* and tested during the message loop, as described above. In this program, however, it isn't necessary to store the handle in a global variable or to test the value before calling *IsDialogMessage*. The message loop could have been written like this:

```
while (GetMessage (&msg, NULL, 0, 0))
     {
     if (!IsDialogMessage (hDlgModeless, &msg))
          {
          TranslateMessage (&msg) ;
          DispatchMessage  (&msg) ;
          }
     }
```

Because the dialog box is created before the program enters the message loop and the dialog box is not destroyed until the program terminates, the value of *hDlgModeless* will always be valid. I included the logic in case you want to add some code to the dialog box window procedure to destroy the dialog box:

```
case WM_CLOSE :
     DestroyWindow (hDlg) ;
     hDlgModeless = 0 ;
     break ;
```

In the original COLORS1 program, *SetWindowText* set the values of the three numeric labels after converting the integers to text with *itoa*. The code looked like this:

```
SetWindowText (hwndValue[i], itoa (color[i], szBuffer, 10)) ;
```

The value of *i* was the ID number of the current scroll bar being processed, and *hwndValue* was an array containing the window handles of the three static text child windows for the numeric values of the colors.

The new version uses *SetDlgItemInt* to set each text field of each child window to a number:

```
SetDlgItemInt (hDlg, iCtrlID + 3, iColor[iIndex], FALSE) ;
```

(Although *SetDlgItemInt* and its companion, *GetDlgItemInt*, are most often used with edit controls, they can also be used to set the text field of other controls, such as static text controls.) The *iCtrlID* variable is the ID number of the scroll bar; adding 3 to the number converts it to the ID for the corresponding numeric label. The third parameter is the color value. Normally, the fourth parameter would be set to TRUE to indicate that numbers greater than 32,767 should be displayed as negatives. For this program, however, the values range from 0 to 255, so the fourth parameter has no effect.

In the process of converting COLORS1 to COLORS2, we passed more and more of the work to Windows. The earlier version called *CreateWindow* ten times; the new version calls *CreateWindow* once and *CreateDialog* once. But if you think that we've reduced our *CreateWindow* calls to a minimum, get a load of this next program.

HEXCALC: Window or Dialog Box?

Perhaps the epitome of lazy programming is the HEXCALC program, shown in Figure 11-9. This program doesn't call *CreateWindow* at all, never processes WM_PAINT messages, never obtains a device context, and never processes mouse messages. Yet it manages to incorporate a 10-function hexadecimal calculator with a full keyboard and mouse interface in fewer than 150 lines of source code. The calculator is shown in Figure 11-10 on page 562.

HEXCALC.MAK

```
#----------------------
# HEXCALC.MAK make file
#----------------------

hexcalc.exe : hexcalc.obj hexcalc.res
    $(LINKER) $(GUIFLAGS) -OUT:hexcalc.exe hexcalc.obj hexcalc.res $(GUILIBS)

hexcalc.obj : hexcalc.c
    $(CC) $(CFLAGS) hexcalc.c

hexcalc.res : hexcalc.rc hexcalc.ico
    $(RC) $(RCVARS) hexcalc.rc
```

Figure 11-9. *The HEXCALC program.* *(continued)*

HEXCALC.C

```
/*------------------------------------------
   HEXCALC.C -- Hexadecimal Calculator
              (c) Charles Petzold, 1996
   ------------------------------------------*/

#include <windows.h>
#include <limits.h>
#include <stdlib.h>
#include <string.h>
#include <ctype.h>

LRESULT CALLBACK WndProc (HWND, UINT, WPARAM, LPARAM) ;

int WINAPI WinMain (HINSTANCE hInstance, HINSTANCE hPrevInstance,
                    PSTR szCmdLine, int iCmdShow)
     {
     static char   szAppName[] = "HexCalc" ;
     HWND          hwnd ;
     MSG           msg ;
     WNDCLASSEX    wndclass ;

     wndclass.cbSize        = sizeof (wndclass) ;
     wndclass.style         = CS_HREDRAW | CS_VREDRAW;
     wndclass.lpfnWndProc   = WndProc ;
     wndclass.cbClsExtra    = 0 ;
     wndclass.cbWndExtra    = DLGWINDOWEXTRA ;
     wndclass.hInstance     = hInstance ;
     wndclass.hIcon         = LoadIcon (hInstance, szAppName) ;
     wndclass.hCursor       = LoadCursor (NULL, IDC_ARROW) ;
     wndclass.hbrBackground = (HBRUSH) (COLOR_WINDOW + 1) ;
     wndclass.lpszMenuName  = NULL ;
     wndclass.lpszClassName = szAppName ;
     wndclass.hIconSm       = LoadIcon (hInstance, szAppName) ;

     RegisterClassEx (&wndclass) ;

     hwnd = CreateDialog (hInstance, szAppName, 0, NULL) ;

     ShowWindow (hwnd, iCmdShow) ;

     while (GetMessage (&msg, NULL, 0, 0))
          {
          TranslateMessage (&msg) ;
```

(continued)

```
            DispatchMessage (&msg) ;
            }
      return msg.wParam ;
      }

void ShowNumber (HWND hwnd, UINT iNumber)
      {
      char szBuffer[20] ;

      SetDlgItemText (hwnd, VK_ESCAPE, strupr (ltoa (iNumber, szBuffer, 16))) ;
      }

DWORD CalcIt (UINT iFirstNum, int iOperation, UINT iNum)
      {
      switch (iOperation)
            {
            case '=' : return iNum ;
            case '+' : return iFirstNum +  iNum ;
            case '-' : return iFirstNum -  iNum ;
            case '*' : return iFirstNum *  iNum ;
            case '&' : return iFirstNum &  iNum ;
            case '¦' : return iFirstNum ¦  iNum ;
            case '^' : return iFirstNum ^  iNum ;
            case '<' : return iFirstNum << iNum ;
            case '>' : return iFirstNum >> iNum ;
            case '/' : return iNum ? iFirstNum / iNum : UINT_MAX ;
            case '%' : return iNum ? iFirstNum % iNum : UINT_MAX ;
            default  : return 0 ;
            }
      }

LRESULT CALLBACK WndProc (HWND hwnd, UINT iMsg, WPARAM wParam, LPARAM lParam)
      {
      static BOOL  bNewNumber = TRUE ;
      static int   iOperation = '=' ;
      static UINT  iNumber, iFirstNum ;
      HWND         hButton ;

      switch (iMsg)
            {
            case WM_KEYDOWN :                       // left arrow --> backspace
                 if (wParam != VK_LEFT)
                      break ;
                 wParam = VK_BACK ;
                                                    // fall through
```

(continued)

```
case WM_CHAR :
    if ((wParam = toupper (wParam)) == VK_RETURN)
        wParam = '=' ;

    hButton = GetDlgItem (hwnd, wParam) ;

    if (hButton != NULL)
        {
        SendMessage (hButton, BM_SETSTATE, 1, 0) ;
        SendMessage (hButton, BM_SETSTATE, 0, 0) ;
        }
    else
        {
        MessageBeep (0) ;
        break ;
        }
                                    // fall through
case WM_COMMAND :
    SetFocus (hwnd) ;

    if (LOWORD (wParam) == VK_BACK)         // backspace
        ShowNumber (hwnd, iNumber /= 16) ;

    else if (LOWORD (wParam) == VK_ESCAPE)  // escape
        ShowNumber (hwnd, iNumber = 0) ;

    else if (isxdigit (LOWORD (wParam)))    // hex digit
        {
        if (bNewNumber)
            {
            iFirstNum = iNumber ;
            iNumber = 0 ;
            }
        bNewNumber = FALSE ;

        if (iNumber <= UINT_MAX >> 4)
            ShowNumber (hwnd, iNumber = 16 * iNumber + wParam -
                (isdigit (wParam) ? '0' : 'A' - 10)) ;
        else
            MessageBeep (0) ;
        }
    else                                    // operation
        {
        if (!bNewNumber)
            ShowNumber (hwnd, iNumber =
                CalcIt (iFirstNum, iOperation, iNumber)) ;
```

(continued)

```
                    bNewNumber = TRUE ;
                    iOperation = LOWORD (wParam) ;
                    }
               return 0 ;

          case WM_DESTROY :
               PostQuitMessage (0) ;
               return 0 ;
          }
     return DefWindowProc (hwnd, iMsg, wParam, lParam) ;
     }
```

HEXCALC.RC

```
/*----------------------------
   HEXCALC.RC resource script
----------------------------*/

#include <windows.h>

HexCalc ICON hexcalc.ico

HexCalc DIALOG 32768, 0, 102, 122
     STYLE WS_OVERLAPPED | WS_CAPTION | WS_SYSMENU | WS_MINIMIZEBOX
     CLASS "HexCalc"
     CAPTION "Hex Calculator"
     {
     PUSHBUTTON "D",      68,  8,  24, 14, 14
     PUSHBUTTON "A",      65,  8,  40, 14, 14
     PUSHBUTTON "7",      55,  8,  56, 14, 14
     PUSHBUTTON "4",      52,  8,  72, 14, 14
     PUSHBUTTON "1",      49,  8,  88, 14, 14
     PUSHBUTTON "0",      48,  8, 104, 14, 14
     PUSHBUTTON "0",      27, 26,   4, 50, 14
     PUSHBUTTON "E",      69, 26,  24, 14, 14
     PUSHBUTTON "B",      66, 26,  40, 14, 14
     PUSHBUTTON "8",      56, 26,  56, 14, 14
     PUSHBUTTON "5",      53, 26,  72, 14, 14
     PUSHBUTTON "2",      50, 26,  88, 14, 14
     PUSHBUTTON "Back",    8, 26, 104, 32, 14
     PUSHBUTTON "C",      67, 44,  40, 14, 14
     PUSHBUTTON "F",      70, 44,  24, 14, 14
     PUSHBUTTON "9",      57, 44,  56, 14, 14
     PUSHBUTTON "6",      54, 44,  72, 14, 14
     PUSHBUTTON "3",      51, 44,  88, 14, 14
```

(continued)

```
PUSHBUTTON "+",        43, 62,  24, 14, 14
PUSHBUTTON "-",        45, 62,  40, 14, 14
PUSHBUTTON "*",        42, 62,  56, 14, 14
PUSHBUTTON "/",        47, 62,  72, 14, 14
PUSHBUTTON "%",        37, 62,  88, 14, 14
PUSHBUTTON "Equals",   61, 62, 104, 32, 14
PUSHBUTTON "&&",       38, 80,  24, 14, 14
PUSHBUTTON "¦",       124, 80,  40, 14, 14
PUSHBUTTON "^",        94, 80,  56, 14, 14
PUSHBUTTON "<",        60, 80,  72, 14, 14
PUSHBUTTON ">",        62, 80,  88, 14, 14
}
```

HEXCALC.ICO

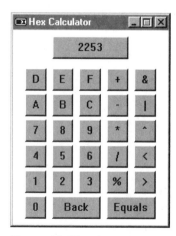

Figure 11-10. *The HEXCALC display.*

HEXCALC is a normal infix notation calculator that uses C notation for the operations. It works with unsigned 32-bit integers and does addition, subtraction, multiplication, division, and remainders; bitwise AND, OR, and exclusive OR operations; and left and right bit shifts. Division by 0 causes the result to be set to FFFFFFFF.

You can use either the mouse or keyboard with HEXCALC. You begin by "clicking in" or typing the first number (up to eight hexadecimal digits), then the operation, and then the second number. You can then show the result by clicking the Equals button or by pressing either the Equals key or the Enter key. To correct your entries, you use the Back button or the Backspace or Left Arrow key. Click the "display" box or press the Esc key to clear the current entry.

What's so strange about HEXCALC is that the window displayed on the screen seems to be a hybrid of a normal overlapped window and a modeless dialog box. On the one hand, all the messages to HEXCALC are processed in a function called *WndProc* that appears to be a normal window procedure. The function returns a long, it processes the WM_DESTROY message, and it calls *DefWindowProc* just like a normal window procedure. On the other hand, the window is created in *WinMain* with a call to *CreateDialog* using a dialog box template from HEXCALC.RC. So is HEXCALC a normal overlapped window or a modeless dialog box?

The simple answer is that a dialog box *is* a window. Normally, Windows uses its own internal window procedure to process messages to a dialog box popup window. Windows then passes these messages to a dialog box procedure within the program that creates the dialog box. In HEXCALC we are forcing Windows to use the dialog box template to create a popup window, but we're processing messages to that window ourselves.

A closer look at HEXCALC.RC will reveal how this is done. The top of the dialog box template looks like this:

```
HexCalc DIALOG 32768, 0, 102, 122
        STYLE WS_OVERLAPPED ! WS_CAPTION ! WS_SYSMENU ! WS_MINIMIZEBOX
        CLASS "HexCalc"
        CAPTION "Hex Calculator"
```

Notice the identifiers, such as WS_OVERLAPPED and WS_MINIMIZEBOX, which we might use to create a normal window using a *CreateWindow* call. The CLASS statement is the crucial difference between this dialog box and the others we've created so far. When we omitted this statement in previous dialog box templates, Windows registered a window class for the dialog box and used its own window procedure to process the dialog box messages. The inclusion of a CLASS statement here tells Windows to send the messages elsewhere—specifically, to the window procedure specified in the "HexCalc" window class.

The "HexCalc" window class is registered in the *WinMain* function of HEXCALC, just like a window class for a normal window. However, note this very important difference: The *cbWndExtra* field of the WNDCLASS structure is set to DLGWINDOWEXTRA. This is essential for dialog procedures that you register yourself.

After registering the window class, *WinMain* calls *CreateDialog*:

```
hwnd = CreateDialog (hInstance, szAppName, 0, NULL) ;
```

The second parameter (the string "HexCalc") is the name of the dialog box template. The third parameter, which is normally the window handle of the parent window, is set to 0 because the window has no parent. The last parameter, which is normally the address of the dialog procedure, isn't required because Windows won't be processing the messages and hence can't send them to a dialog procedure.

This *CreateDialog* call in conjunction with the dialog box template is effectively translated by Windows into a *CreateWindow* call that does the equivalent of this:

```
hwnd = CreateWindow ("HexCalc", "Hex Calculator",
        WS_OVERLAPPED | WS_CAPTION | WS_SYSMENU | WS_MINIMIZEBOX,
        CW_USEDEFAULT, CW_USEDEFAULT,
        102 * 4 / cxChar, 122 * 8 / cyChar,
        NULL, NULL, hInstance, NULL) ;
```

The *cxChar* and *cyChar* variables are the width and height of a system font character.

We reap an enormous benefit from letting Windows make this *CreateWindow* call: Windows will not stop at creating the 1 popup window but will also call *CreateWindow* for all 29 child window push-button controls defined in the dialog box template. All these controls send WM_COMMAND messages to the window procedure of the parent window, which is none other than *WndProc*. This is an excellent technique for creating a window that must contain a collection of child windows.

Creatively Using Control IDs

HEXCALC contains no header file with identifiers for all the ID numbers of the child window controls in the dialog box template. We can dispense with this file because the ID number for each of the push-button controls is set to the ASCII code of the text that appears in the control. This means that *WndProc* can treat WM_COMMAND messages and WM_CHAR messages in much the same way. In each case, *wParam* is the ASCII code of the button.

Of course, a little massaging of the keyboard messages is necessary. *WndProc* traps WM_KEYDOWN messages to translate the Left Arrow key to a Backspace key. During processing of WM_CHAR messages, *WndProc* converts the character code to uppercase and the Enter key to the ASCII code for the Equals key.

The validity of a WM_CHAR message is checked by calling *GetDlgItem*. If the *GetDlgItem* function returns 0, then the keyboard character is not one of the ID numbers defined in the dialog box template. If the character is one of the IDs, however, the appropriate button is flashed by sending it a couple of BM_SETSTATE messages:

```
hButton = (SetDlgItem(hwnd, wParam) ;
if (hButton != NULL)
    {
```

```
          SendMessage (hButton, BM_SETSTATE, 1, 0) ;
          SendMessage (hButton, BM_SETSTATE, 0, 0) ;
          }
```

This adds a nice touch to HEXCALC's keyboard interface, and with a minimum of effort.

When *WndProc* processes WM_COMMAND messages, it always sets the input focus to the parent window:

```
case WM_COMMAND :
     SetFocus (hwnd) ;
```

Otherwise, the input focus would be shifted to one of the buttons whenever it was clicked with the mouse.

THE COMMON DIALOG BOXES

One of the primary goals of Windows was to promote a standardized user interface. For many common menu items, this happened fairly quickly. Almost every software manufacturer adopted the Alt-File-Open selection to open a file. However, the actual file-open dialog boxes were often quite dissimilar.

Beginning with Windows 3.1, a solution to this problem became available, and it continues to be supported under Windows 95. This is an enhancement called the "common dialog box library." This library consists of several functions that invoke standard dialog boxes for opening and saving files, searching and replacing, choosing colors, choosing fonts (all of which I'll demonstrate in this chapter), and printing (which I'll demonstrate in Chapter 15).

To use these functions, you basically initialize the fields of a structure and pass a pointer to the structure to a function in the common dialog box library. The function creates and displays the dialog box. When the user makes the dialog box go away, the function you called returns control to your program, and you obtain information from the structure you passed to it.

The COMMDLG.H header file defines the functions and the structures that are necessary for using these dialog boxes. COMDLG32.LIB is the common dialog box import library, and COMDLG32.DLL is the dynamic link library containing the dialog box templates and procedures.

POPPAD Revisited

When we added a menu to POPPAD in Chapter 10, several standard menu options were left unimplemented. We are now ready to add logic to POPPAD to open files, read them in, and save the edited files on disk. In the process, we'll also add font selection and search and replace logic to POPPAD.

The files that contribute to the POPPAD3 program are shown in Figure 11-11.

POPPAD3.MAK

```
#----------------------
# POPPAD3.MAK make file
#----------------------

poppad3.exe : poppad.obj    popfile.obj   popfind.obj \
              popfont.obj popprnt0.obj poppad.res
    $(LINKER) $(GUIFLAGS) -OUT:poppad3.exe poppad.obj popfile.obj \
              popfind.obj popfont.obj popprnt0.obj poppad.res $(GUILIBS)

poppad.obj : poppad.c poppad.h
    $(CC) $(CFLAGS) poppad.c

popfile.obj : popfile.c
    $(CC) $(CFLAGS) popfile.c

popfind.obj : popfind.c
    $(CC) $(CFLAGS) popfind.c

popfont.obj : popfont.c
    $(CC) $(CFLAGS) popfont.c

popprnt0.obj : popprnt0.c
    $(CC) $(CFLAGS) popprnt0.c

poppad.res : poppad.rc poppad.h poppad.ico
    $(RC) $(RCVARS) poppad.rc
```

POPPAD.C

```
/*----------------------------------------
    POPPAD.C -- Popup Editor
              (c) Charles Petzold, 1996
   ----------------------------------------*/

#include <windows.h>
#include <commdlg.h>
#include <stdlib.h>
#include "poppad.h"

#define EDITID   1
#define UNTITLED "(untitled)"
```

Figure 11-11. *The POPPAD3 program.*   *(continued)*

```
LRESULT CALLBACK WndProc        (HWND, UINT, WPARAM, LPARAM) ;
BOOL    CALLBACK AboutDlgProc (HWND, UINT, WPARAM, LPARAM) ;

            // Functions in POPFILE.C

void PopFileInitialize (HWND) ;
BOOL PopFileOpenDlg      (HWND, PSTR, PSTR) ;
BOOL PopFileSaveDlg      (HWND, PSTR, PSTR) ;
BOOL PopFileRead         (HWND, PSTR) ;
BOOL PopFileWrite        (HWND, PSTR) ;

            // Functions in POPFIND.C

HWND PopFindFindDlg      (HWND) ;
HWND PopFindReplaceDlg   (HWND) ;
BOOL PopFindFindText     (HWND, int *, LPFINDREPLACE) ;
BOOL PopFindReplaceText (HWND, int *, LPFINDREPLACE) ;
BOOL PopFindNextText     (HWND, int *) ;
BOOL PopFindValidFind    (void) ;

            // Functions in POPFONT.C

void PopFontInitialize   (HWND) ;
BOOL PopFontChooseFont   (HWND) ;
void PopFontSetFont      (HWND) ;
void PopFontDeinitialize (void) ;

            // Functions in POPPRNT.C

BOOL PopPrntPrintFile (HINSTANCE, HWND, HWND, PSTR) ;

            // Global variables

static char szAppName[] = "PopPad" ;
static HWND hDlgModeless ;

int WINAPI WinMain (HINSTANCE hInstance, HINSTANCE hPrevInstance,
                    PSTR szCmdLine, int iCmdShow)
    {
    MSG         msg ;
    HWND        hwnd ;
    HACCEL      hAccel ;
    WNDCLASSEX  wndclass ;

    wndclass.cbSize         = sizeof (wndclass) ;
    wndclass.style          = CS_HREDRAW | CS_VREDRAW ;
```

(continued)

```
      wndclass.lpfnWndProc   = WndProc ;
      wndclass.cbClsExtra    = 0 ;
      wndclass.cbWndExtra    = 0 ;
      wndclass.hInstance     = hInstance ;
      wndclass.hIcon         = LoadIcon (hInstance, szAppName) ;
      wndclass.hCursor       = LoadCursor (NULL, IDC_ARROW) ;
      wndclass.hbrBackground = (HBRUSH) GetStockObject (WHITE_BRUSH) ;
      wndclass.lpszMenuName  = szAppName ;
      wndclass.lpszClassName = szAppName ;
      wndclass.hIconSm       = LoadIcon (hInstance, szAppName) ;

      RegisterClassEx (&wndclass) ;

      hwnd = CreateWindow (szAppName, NULL,
                           WS_OVERLAPPEDWINDOW,
                           CW_USEDEFAULT, CW_USEDEFAULT,
                           CW_USEDEFAULT, CW_USEDEFAULT,
                           NULL, NULL, hInstance, szCmdLine) ;

      ShowWindow (hwnd, iCmdShow) ;
      UpdateWindow (hwnd) ;

      hAccel = LoadAccelerators (hInstance, szAppName) ;

      while (GetMessage (&msg, NULL, 0, 0))
          {
          if (hDlgModeless == NULL || !IsDialogMessage (hDlgModeless, &msg))
              {
              if (!TranslateAccelerator (hwnd, hAccel, &msg))
                  {
                  TranslateMessage (&msg) ;
                  DispatchMessage (&msg) ;
                  }
              }
          }
      return msg.wParam ;
      }

void DoCaption (HWND hwnd, char *szTitleName)
      {
      char szCaption[64 + _MAX_FNAME + _MAX_EXT] ;

      wsprintf (szCaption, "%s - %s", szAppName,
                szTitleName[0] ? szTitleName : UNTITLED) ;
```

(continued)

```
    SetWindowText (hwnd, szCaption) ;
    }

void OkMessage (HWND hwnd, char *szMessage, char *szTitleName)
    {
    char szBuffer[64 + _MAX_FNAME + _MAX_EXT] ;

    wsprintf (szBuffer, szMessage, szTitleName[0] ? szTitleName : UNTITLED) ;

    MessageBox (hwnd, szBuffer, szAppName, MB_OK | MB_ICONEXCLAMATION) ;
    }

short AskAboutSave (HWND hwnd, char *szTitleName)
    {
    char szBuffer[64 + _MAX_FNAME + _MAX_EXT] ;
    int  iReturn ;

    wsprintf (szBuffer, "Save current changes in %s?",
              szTitleName[0] ? szTitleName : UNTITLED) ;

    iReturn = MessageBox (hwnd, szBuffer, szAppName,
                          MB_YESNOCANCEL | MB_ICONQUESTION) ;

    if (iReturn == IDYES)
        if (!SendMessage (hwnd, WM_COMMAND, IDM_SAVE, 0L))
            iReturn = IDCANCEL ;

    return iReturn ;
    }

LRESULT CALLBACK WndProc (HWND hwnd, UINT iMsg, WPARAM wParam, LPARAM lParam)
    {
    static BOOL       bNeedSave = FALSE ;
    static char       szFileName[_MAX_PATH] ;
    static char       szTitleName[_MAX_FNAME + _MAX_EXT] ;
    static HINSTANCE  hInst ;
    static HWND       hwndEdit ;
    static int        iOffset ;
    static UINT       iMsgFindReplace ;
    int               iSelBeg, iSelEnd, iEnable ;
    LPFINDREPLACE     pfr ;

    switch (iMsg)
        {
```

(continued)

```
            case WM_CREATE :
                 hInst = ((LPCREATESTRUCT) lParam) -> hInstance ;

                          // Create the edit control child window

                 hwndEdit = CreateWindow ("edit", NULL,
                          WS_CHILD | WS_VISIBLE | WS_HSCROLL | WS_VSCROLL |
                              WS_BORDER | ES_LEFT | ES_MULTILINE |
                              ES_NOHIDESEL | ES_AUTOHSCROLL | ES_AUTOVSCROLL,
                          0, 0, 0, 0,
                          hwnd, (HMENU) EDITID, hInst, NULL) ;

                 SendMessage (hwndEdit, EM_LIMITTEXT, 32000, 0L) ;

                          // Initialize common dialog box stuff

                 PopFileInitialize (hwnd) ;
                 PopFontInitialize (hwndEdit) ;

                 iMsgFindReplace = RegisterWindowMessage (FINDMSGSTRING) ;

                          // Process command line

                 lstrcpy (szFileName, (PSTR)
                          (((LPCREATESTRUCT) lParam)->lpCreateParams)) ;

                 if (strlen (szFileName) > 0)
                     {
                     GetFileTitle (szFileName, szTitleName,
                              sizeof (szTitleName)) ;

                     if (!PopFileRead (hwndEdit, szFileName))
                          OkMessage (hwnd, "File %s cannot be read!",
                                    szTitleName) ;
                     }

                 DoCaption (hwnd, szTitleName) ;
                 return 0 ;

            case WM_SETFOCUS :
                 SetFocus (hwndEdit) ;
                 return 0 ;

            case WM_SIZE :
                 MoveWindow (hwndEdit, 0, 0, LOWORD (lParam),
                                        HIWORD (lParam), TRUE) ;
```

(continued)

```
          return 0 ;

case WM_INITMENUPOPUP :
     switch (lParam)
          {
          case 1 :          // Edit menu

                    // Enable Undo if edit control can do it

               EnableMenuItem ((HMENU) wParam, IDM_UNDO,
                    SendMessage (hwndEdit, EM_CANUNDO, 0, 0L) ?
                         MF_ENABLED : MF_GRAYED) ;

                    // Enable Paste if text is in the clipboard

               EnableMenuItem ((HMENU) wParam, IDM_PASTE,
                    IsClipboardFormatAvailable (CF_TEXT) ?
                         MF_ENABLED : MF_GRAYED) ;

                    // Enable Cut, Copy, and Del if text is selected

               SendMessage (hwndEdit, EM_GETSEL, (WPARAM) &iSelBeg,
                                              (LPARAM) &iSelEnd) ;

               iEnable = iSelBeg != iSelEnd ? MF_ENABLED : MF_GRAYED ;

               EnableMenuItem ((HMENU) wParam, IDM_CUT,   iEnable) ;
               EnableMenuItem ((HMENU) wParam, IDM_COPY,  iEnable) ;
               EnableMenuItem ((HMENU) wParam, IDM_CLEAR, iEnable) ;
               break ;

          case 2 :          // Search menu

                    // Enable Find, Next, and Replace if modeless
                    //    dialogs are not already active

               iEnable = hDlgModeless == NULL ?
                         MF_ENABLED : MF_GRAYED ;

               EnableMenuItem ((HMENU) wParam, IDM_FIND,    iEnable) ;
               EnableMenuItem ((HMENU) wParam, IDM_NEXT,    iEnable) ;
               EnableMenuItem ((HMENU) wParam, IDM_REPLACE, iEnable) ;
               break ;
          }
     return 0 ;
```

(continued)

```
case WM_COMMAND :
                    // Messages from edit control

     if (lParam && LOWORD (wParam) == EDITID)
          {
          switch (HIWORD (wParam))
               {
               case EN_UPDATE :
                    bNeedSave = TRUE ;
                    return 0 ;

               case EN_ERRSPACE :
               case EN_MAXTEXT :
                    MessageBox (hwnd, "Edit control out of space.",
                              szAppName, MB_OK | MB_ICONSTOP) ;
                    return 0 ;
               }
          break ;
          }

     switch (LOWORD (wParam))
          {
                    // Messages from File menu

          case IDM_NEW :
               if (bNeedSave && IDCANCEL ==
                         AskAboutSave (hwnd, szTitleName))
                    return 0 ;

               SetWindowText (hwndEdit, "\0") ;
               szFileName[0]  = '\0' ;
               szTitleName[0] = '\0' ;
               DoCaption (hwnd, szTitleName) ;
               bNeedSave = FALSE ;
               return 0 ;

          case IDM_OPEN :
               if (bNeedSave && IDCANCEL ==
                         AskAboutSave (hwnd, szTitleName))
                    return 0 ;

               if (PopFileOpenDlg (hwnd, szFileName, szTitleName))
                    {
                    if (!PopFileRead (hwndEdit, szFileName))
                         {
                         OkMessage (hwnd, "Could not read file %s!",
                                   szTitleName) ;
```

(continued)

```
                         szFileName[0] = '\0' ;
                         szTitleName[0] = '\0' ;
                         }
               }

          DoCaption (hwnd, szTitleName) ;
          bNeedSave = FALSE ;
          return 0 ;

     case IDM_SAVE :
          if (szFileName[0])
               {
               if (PopFileWrite (hwndEdit, szFileName))
                    {
                    bNeedSave = FALSE ;
                    return 1 ;
                    }
               else
                    OkMessage (hwnd, "Could not write file %s",
                                     szTitleName) ;

               return 0 ;
               }
                                        // fall through
     case IDM_SAVEAS :
          if (PopFileSaveDlg (hwnd, szFileName, szTitleName))
               {
               DoCaption (hwnd, szTitleName) ;

               if (PopFileWrite (hwndEdit, szFileName))
                    {
                    bNeedSave = FALSE ;
                    return 1 ;
                    }
               else
                    OkMessage (hwnd, "Could not write file %s",
                                     szTitleName) ;

               }
          return 0 ;

     case IDM_PRINT :
          if (!PopPrntPrintFile (hInst, hwnd, hwndEdit,
                                 szTitleName))
               OkMessage (hwnd, "Could not print file %s",
                                szTitleName) ;
          return 0 ;
```

(continued)

```
                  case IDM_EXIT :
                       SendMessage (hwnd, WM_CLOSE, 0, 0) ;
                       return 0 ;

                            // Messages from Edit menu

                  case IDM_UNDO :
                       SendMessage (hwndEdit, WM_UNDO, 0, 0) ;
                       return 0 ;

                  case IDM_CUT :
                       SendMessage (hwndEdit, WM_CUT, 0, 0) ;
                       return 0 ;

                  case IDM_COPY :
                       SendMessage (hwndEdit, WM_COPY, 0, 0) ;
                       return 0 ;

                  case IDM_PASTE :
                       SendMessage (hwndEdit, WM_PASTE, 0, 0) ;
                       return 0 ;

                  case IDM_CLEAR :
                       SendMessage (hwndEdit, WM_CLEAR, 0, 0) ;
                       return 0 ;

                  case IDM_SELALL :
                       SendMessage (hwndEdit, EM_SETSEL, 0, -1) ;
                       return 0 ;

                            // Messages from Search menu

                  case IDM_FIND :
                       SendMessage (hwndEdit, EM_GETSEL, NULL,
                                                     (LPARAM) &iOffset) ;

                       hDlgModeless = PopFindFindDlg (hwnd) ;
                       return 0 ;

                  case IDM_NEXT :
                       SendMessage (hwndEdit, EM_GETSEL, NULL,
                                                     (LPARAM) &iOffset) ;

                       if (PopFindValidFind ())
                            PopFindNextText (hwndEdit, &iOffset) ;
                       else
                            hDlgModeless = PopFindFindDlg (hwnd) ;
```

(continued)

```
                              return 0 ;

                  case IDM_REPLACE :
                       SendMessage (hwndEdit, EM_GETSEL, NULL,
                                                   (LPARAM) &iOffset) ;

                       hDlgModeless = PopFindReplaceDlg (hwnd) ;
                       return 0 ;

                  case IDM_FONT :
                       if (PopFontChooseFont (hwnd))
                            PopFontSetFont (hwndEdit) ;

                       return 0 ;

                            // Messages from Help menu

                  case IDM_HELP :
                       OkMessage (hwnd, "Help not yet implemented!", "\0") ;
                       return 0 ;

                  case IDM_ABOUT :
                       DialogBox (hInst, "AboutBox", hwnd, AboutDlgProc) ;
                       return 0 ;
                  }
             break ;

     case WM_CLOSE :
          if (!bNeedSave || IDCANCEL != AskAboutSave (hwnd, szTitleName))
               DestroyWindow (hwnd) ;

          return 0 ;

     case WM_QUERYENDSESSION :
          if (!bNeedSave || IDCANCEL != AskAboutSave (hwnd, szTitleName))
               return 1 ;

          return 0 ;

     case WM_DESTROY :
          PopFontDeinitialize () ;
          PostQuitMessage (0) ;
          return 0 ;

     default :
```

(continued)

```
                        // Process "Find-Replace" iMsgs

          if (iMsg == iMsgFindReplace)
               {
               pfr = (LPFINDREPLACE) lParam ;

               if (pfr->Flags & FR_DIALOGTERM)
                    hDlgModeless = NULL ;

               if (pfr->Flags & FR_FINDNEXT)
                    if (!PopFindFindText (hwndEdit, &iOffset, pfr))
                         OkMessage (hwnd, "Text not found!", "\0") ;

               if (pfr->Flags & FR_REPLACE !!
                    pfr->Flags & FR_REPLACEALL)
                    if (!PopFindReplaceText (hwndEdit, &iOffset, pfr))
                         OkMessage (hwnd, "Text not found!", "\0") ;

               if (pfr->Flags & FR_REPLACEALL)
                    while (PopFindReplaceText (hwndEdit, &iOffset, pfr)) ;

               return 0 ;
               }
          break ;
     }
     return DefWindowProc (hwnd, iMsg, wParam, lParam) ;
     }

BOOL CALLBACK AboutDlgProc (HWND hDlg, UINT iMsg, WPARAM wParam, LPARAM lParam)
     {
     switch (iMsg)
          {
          case WM_INITDIALOG :
               return TRUE ;

          case WM_COMMAND :
               switch (LOWORD (wParam))
                    {
                    case IDOK :
                         EndDialog (hDlg, 0) ;
                         return TRUE ;
                    }
               break ;
          }
     return FALSE ;
     }
```

(continued)

POPFILE.C

```c
/*---------------------------------------------
   POPFILE.C -- Popup Editor File Functions
  ---------------------------------------------*/

#include <windows.h>
#include <commdlg.h>
#include <stdlib.h>
#include <stdio.h>

static OPENFILENAME ofn ;

void PopFileInitialize (HWND hwnd)
     {
     static char szFilter[] = "Text Files (*.TXT)\0*.txt\0"  \
                              "ASCII Files (*.ASC)\0*.asc\0" \
                              "All Files (*.*)\0*.*\0\0";

     ofn.lStructSize       = sizeof (OPENFILENAME) ;
     ofn.hwndOwner         = hwnd ;
     ofn.hInstance         = NULL ;
     ofn.lpstrFilter       = szFilter ;
     ofn.lpstrCustomFilter = NULL ;
     ofn.nMaxCustFilter    = 0 ;
     ofn.nFilterIndex      = 0 ;
     ofn.lpstrFile         = NULL ;         // Set in Open and Close functions
     ofn.nMaxFile          = _MAX_PATH ;
     ofn.lpstrFileTitle    = NULL ;         // Set in Open and Close functions
     ofn.nMaxFileTitle     = _MAX_FNAME + _MAX_EXT ;
     ofn.lpstrInitialDir   = NULL ;
     ofn.lpstrTitle        = NULL ;
     ofn.Flags             = 0 ;            // Set in Open and Close functions
     ofn.nFileOffset       = 0 ;
     ofn.nFileExtension    = 0 ;
     ofn.lpstrDefExt       = "txt" ;
     ofn.lCustData         = 0L ;
     ofn.lpfnHook          = NULL ;
     ofn.lpTemplateName    = NULL ;
     }

BOOL PopFileOpenDlg (HWND hwnd, PSTR pstrFileName, PSTR pstrTitleName)
     {
     ofn.hwndOwner         = hwnd ;
     ofn.lpstrFile         = pstrFileName ;
```

(continued)

```
        ofn.lpstrFileTitle      = pstrTitleName ;
        ofn.Flags               = OFN_HIDEREADONLY | OFN_CREATEPROMPT ;

        return GetOpenFileName (&ofn) ;
        }

BOOL PopFileSaveDlg (HWND hwnd, PSTR pstrFileName, PSTR pstrTitleName)
        {
        ofn.hwndOwner           = hwnd ;
        ofn.lpstrFile           = pstrFileName ;
        ofn.lpstrFileTitle      = pstrTitleName ;
        ofn.Flags               = OFN_OVERWRITEPROMPT ;

        return GetSaveFileName (&ofn) ;
        }

static long PopFileLength (FILE *file)
        {
        int iCurrentPos, iFileLength ;

        iCurrentPos = ftell (file) ;

        fseek (file, 0, SEEK_END) ;

        iFileLength = ftell (file) ;

        fseek (file, iCurrentPos, SEEK_SET) ;

        return iFileLength ;
        }

BOOL PopFileRead (HWND hwndEdit, PSTR pstrFileName)
        {
        FILE *file ;
        int   iLength ;
        PSTR  pstrBuffer ;

        if (NULL == (file = fopen (pstrFileName, "rb")))
            return FALSE ;

        iLength = PopFileLength (file) ;

        if (NULL == (pstrBuffer = (PSTR) malloc (iLength + 1)))
            {
            fclose (file) ;
```

(continued)

```
          return FALSE ;
          }

     fread (pstrBuffer, 1, iLength, file) ;
     fclose (file) ;
     pstrBuffer[iLength] = '\0' ;

     SetWindowText (hwndEdit, pstrBuffer) ;
     free (pstrBuffer) ;

     return TRUE ;
     }

BOOL PopFileWrite (HWND hwndEdit, PSTR pstrFileName)
     {
     FILE *file ;
     int   iLength ;
     PSTR  pstrBuffer ;

     if (NULL == (file = fopen (pstrFileName, "wb")))
          return FALSE ;

     iLength = GetWindowTextLength (hwndEdit) ;

     if (NULL == (pstrBuffer = (PSTR) malloc (iLength + 1)))
          {
          fclose (file) ;
          return FALSE ;
          }

     GetWindowText (hwndEdit, pstrBuffer, iLength +1) ;

     if (iLength != (int) fwrite (pstrBuffer, 1, iLength, file))
          {
          fclose (file) ;
          free (pstrBuffer) ;
          return FALSE ;
          }

     fclose (file) ;
     free (pstrBuffer) ;

     return TRUE ;
     }
```

(continued)

POPFIND.C

```
/*-----------------------------------------------------------
   POPFIND.C -- Popup Editor Search and Replace Functions
-------------------------------------------------------------*/

#include <windows.h>
#include <commdlg.h>
#include <string.h>
#define MAX_STRING_LEN   256

static char szFindText [MAX_STRING_LEN] ;
static char szReplText [MAX_STRING_LEN] ;

HWND PopFindFindDlg (HWND hwnd)
     {
     static FINDREPLACE fr ;          // must be static for modeless dialog!!!

     fr.lStructSize      = sizeof (FINDREPLACE) ;
     fr.hwndOwner        = hwnd ;
     fr.hInstance        = NULL ;
     fr.Flags            = FR_HIDEUPDOWN | FR_HIDEMATCHCASE | FR_HIDEWHOLEWORD ;
     fr.lpstrFindWhat    = szFindText ;
     fr.lpstrReplaceWith = NULL ;
     fr.wFindWhatLen     = sizeof (szFindText) ;
     fr.wReplaceWithLen  = 0 ;
     fr.lCustData        = 0 ;
     fr.lpfnHook         = NULL ;
     fr.lpTemplateName   = NULL ;

     return FindText (&fr) ;
     }

HWND PopFindReplaceDlg (HWND hwnd)
     {
     static FINDREPLACE fr ;          // must be static for modeless dialog!!!

     fr.lStructSize      = sizeof (FINDREPLACE) ;
     fr.hwndOwner        = hwnd ;
     fr.hInstance        = NULL ;
     fr.Flags            = FR_HIDEUPDOWN | FR_HIDEMATCHCASE | FR_HIDEWHOLEWORD ;
     fr.lpstrFindWhat    = szFindText ;
     fr.lpstrReplaceWith = szReplText ;
     fr.wFindWhatLen     = sizeof (szFindText) ;
     fr.wReplaceWithLen  = sizeof (szReplText) ;
     fr.lCustData        = 0 ;
     fr.lpfnHook         = NULL ;
```

(continued)

```
        fr.lpTemplateName   = NULL ;

    return ReplaceText (&fr) ;
    }

BOOL PopFindFindText (HWND hwndEdit, int *piSearchOffset, LPFINDREPLACE pfr)
    {
    int  iLength, iPos ;
    PSTR pstrDoc, pstrPos ;

            // Read in the edit document

    iLength = GetWindowTextLength (hwndEdit) ;

    if (NULL == (pstrDoc = (PSTR) malloc (iLength + 1)))
        return FALSE ;

    GetWindowText (hwndEdit, pstrDoc, iLength + 1) ;

            // Search the document for the find string

    pstrPos = strstr (pstrDoc + *piSearchOffset, pfr->lpstrFindWhat) ;
    free (pstrDoc) ;

            // Return an error code if the string cannot be found

    if (pstrPos == NULL)
        return FALSE ;

            // Find the position in the document and the new start offset

    iPos = pstrPos - pstrDoc ;
    *piSearchOffset = iPos + strlen (pfr->lpstrFindWhat) ;

            // Select the found text

    SendMessage (hwndEdit, EM_SETSEL, iPos, *piSearchOffset) ;
    SendMessage (hwndEdit, EM_SCROLLCARET 0, 0) ;

    return TRUE ;
    }

BOOL PopFindNextText (HWND hwndEdit, int *piSearchOffset)
    {
    FINDREPLACE fr ;
```

(continued)

```
            fr.lpstrFindWhat = szFindText ;

        return PopFindFindText (hwndEdit, piSearchOffset, &fr) ;
        }

BOOL PopFindReplaceText (HWND hwndEdit, int *piSearchOffset, LPFINDREPLACE pfr)
        {
                // Find the text

        if (!PopFindFindText (hwndEdit, piSearchOffset, pfr))
            return FALSE ;

                // Replace it

        SendMessage (hwndEdit, EM_REPLACESEL, 0, (LPARAM) pfr->lpstrReplaceWith) ;

        return TRUE ;
        }

BOOL PopFindValidFiMnd (void)
        {
        return *szFindText != '\0' ;
        }
```

POPFONT.C

```
/*-------------------------------------------
   POPFONT.C -- Popup Editor Font Functions
  -------------------------------------------*/

#include <windows.h>
#include <commdlg.h>

static LOGFONT logfont ;
static HFONT   hFont ;

BOOL PopFontChooseFont (HWND hwnd)
    {
    CHOOSEFONT cf ;

    cf.lStructSize      = sizeof (CHOOSEFONT) ;
    cf.hwndOwner        = hwnd ;
    cf.hDC              = NULL ;
    cf.lpLogFont        = &logfont ;
    cf.iPointSize       = 0 ;
    cf.Flags            = CF_INITTOLOGFONTSTRUCT | CF_SCREENFONTS
                                                 | CF_EFFECTS ;
```

(continued)

```
    cf.rgbColors        = 0L ;
    cf.lCustData        = 0L ;
    cf.lpfnHook         = NULL ;
    cf.lpTemplateName   = NULL ;
    cf.hInstance        = NULL ;
    cf.lpszStyle        = NULL ;
    cf.nFontType        = 0 ;                    // Returned from ChooseFont
    cf.nSizeMin         = 0 ;
    cf.nSizeMax         = 0 ;

    return ChooseFont (&cf) ;
    }

void PopFontInitialize (HWND hwndEdit)
    {
    GetObject (GetStockObject (SYSTEM_FONT), sizeof (LOGFONT),
                                             (PSTR) &logfont) ;
    hFont = CreateFontIndirect (&logfont) ;
    SendMessage (hwndEdit, WM_SETFONT, (WPARAM) hFont, 0) ;
    }

void PopFontSetFont (HWND hwndEdit)
    {
    HFONT hFontNew ;
    /RECT rect ;

    hFontNew = CreateFontIndirect (&logfont) ;
    SendMessage (hwndEdit, WM_SETFONT, (WPARAM) hFontNew, 0) ;
    DeleteObject (hFont) ;
    hFont = hFontNew ;
    GetClientRect (hwndEdit, &rect) ;
    InvalidateRect (hwndEdit, &rect, TRUE);
    }

void PopFontDeinitialize (void)
    {
    DeleteObject (hFont) ;
    }
```

POPPRNT0.C

```
/*----------------------------------------------------------------
   POPPRNT0.C -- Popup Editor Printing Functions (dummy version)
   ----------------------------------------------------------------*/

#include <windows.h>
```

(continued)

```
BOOL PopPrntPrintFile (HINSTANCE hInst, HWND hwnd, HWND hwndEdit,
                                      PSTR pstrTitleName)
     {
     return FALSE ;
     }
```

POPPAD.RC

```
/*---------------------------
   POPPAD.RC resource script
   --------------------------*/

#include <windows.h>
#include "poppad.h"

PopPad ICON "poppad.ico"

PopPad MENU
     {
     POPUP "&File"
          {
          MENUITEM "&New\tCtrl+N",          IDM_NEW
          MENUITEM "&Open...\tCtrl+O",      IDM_OPEN
          MENUITEM "&Save\tCtrl+S",         IDM_SAVE
          MENUITEM "Save &As...",           IDM_SAVEAS
          MENUITEM SEPARATOR
          MENUITEM "&Print...\tCtrl+P",     IDM_PRINT
          MENUITEM SEPARATOR
          MENUITEM "E&xit",                 IDM_EXIT
          }
     POPUP "&Edit"
          {
          MENUITEM "&Undo\tCtrl+Z",         IDM_UNDO
          MENUITEM SEPARATOR
          MENUITEM "Cu&t\tCtrl+X",          IDM_CUT
          MENUITEM "&Copy\tCtrl+C",         IDM_COPY
          MENUITEM "&Paste\tCtrl+V",        IDM_PASTE
          MENUITEM "De&lete\tDel",          IDM_CLEAR
          MENUITEM SEPARATOR
          MENUITEM "&Select All",           IDM_SELALL
          }
     POPUP "&Search"
          {
```

(continued)

```
            MENUITEM "&Find...\tCtrl+F",    IDM_FIND
            MENUITEM "Find &Next\tF3",      IDM_NEXT
            MENUITEM "R&eplace...\tCtrl+R", IDM_REPLACE
            }
      POPUP "F&ormat"
            {
            MENUITEM "&Font...",            IDM_FONT
            }
      POPUP "&Help"
            {
            MENUITEM "&Help",               IDM_HELP
            MENUITEM "&About PopPad...",     IDM_ABOUT
            }
      }

PopPad ACCELERATORS
      {
      "^N",        IDM_NEW
      "^O",        IDM_OPEN
      "^S",        IDM_SAVE
      "^P",        IDM_PRINT
      "^Z",        IDM_UNDO
      VK_BACK,     IDM_UNDO,  VIRTKEY, ALT
      "^X",        IDM_CUT
      VK_DELETE,   IDM_CUT,   VIRTKEY, SHIFT
      "^C",        IDM_COPY
      VK_INSERT,   IDM_COPY,  VIRTKEY, CONTROL
      "^V",        IDM_PASTE
      VK_INSERT,   IDM_PASTE, VIRTKEY, SHIFT
      VK_DELETE,   IDM_CLEAR, VIRTKEY
      "^F",        IDM_FIND
      VK_F3,       IDM_NEXT,  VIRTKEY
      "^R",        IDM_REPLACE
      VK_F1,       IDM_HELP,  VIRTKEY
      }

AboutBox DIALOG  20, 20, 160, 80
      STYLE WS_POPUP | WS_DLGFRAME
      {
      CTEXT "PopPad"                              -1,  0, 12, 160,  8
      ICON  "PopPad"                              -1,  8,  8,   0,  0
      CTEXT "Popup Editor for Microsoft Windows" -1,  0, 36, 160,  8
      CTEXT "Copyright (c) Charles Petzold, 1996" -1,  0, 48, 160,  8
      DEFPUSHBUTTON "OK"                         IDOK, 64, 60,  32, 14, WS_GROUP
      }
```

(continued)

```
PrintDlgBox DIALOG 20, 20, 100, 76
    STYLE WS_POPUP ¦ WS_CAPTION ¦ WS_SYSMENU ¦ WS_VISIBLE
    CAPTION "PopPad"
    {
    CTEXT "Sending",                     -1,  0, 10, 100,  8
    CTEXT "",                  IDD_FNAME,  0, 20, 100,  8
    CTEXT "to print spooler.",           -1,  0, 30, 100,  8
    DEFPUSHBUTTON "Cancel",     IDCANCEL, 34, 50,  32, 14, WS_GROUP
    }
```

POPPAD.H

```
/*----------------------
   POPPAD.H header file
----------------------*/

#define IDM_NEW         10
#define IDM_OPEN        11
#define IDM_SAVE        12
#define IDM_SAVEAS      13
#define IDM_PRINT       14
#define IDM_EXIT        15

#define IDM_UNDO        20
#define IDM_CUT         21
#define IDM_COPY        22
#define IDM_PASTE       23
#define IDM_CLEAR       24
#define IDM_SELALL      25

#define IDM_FIND        30
#define IDM_NEXT        31
#define IDM_REPLACE     32

#define IDM_FONT        40

#define IDM_HELP        50
#define IDM_ABOUT       51

#define IDD_FNAME       10
```

(continued)

POPPAD.ICO

To avoid duplicating source code in Chapter 15, I've added printing to the menu in POPPAD.RC along with some other support.

POPPAD.C contains all the basic source code for the program. POPFILE.C has the code to invoke the File Open and File Save dialog boxes, and it also contains the file I/O routines. POPFIND.C contains the search and replace logic. POPFONT.C has the font selection logic. POPPRNT0.C doesn't do very much: POPPRNT0.C will be replaced with POPPRNT.C in Chapter 15 to create the final POPPAD program.

Let's look at POPPAD.C first. You'll notice in *WinMain* that the *szCmdLine* parameter is used as the last field of the *CreateWindow* call. This string might contain a filename that was entered as a command-line parameter to POPPAD3 when the program was executed. During processing of the WM_CREATE message in *WndProc*, this filename is passed to the *PopFileRead* function located in POPFILE.C.

POPPAD.C maintains two filename strings: The first (stored in *WndProc* using the name *szFileName*) is the fully qualified drive, path, and filename. The second (stored as *szTitleName*) is the filename by itself. This is used in the *DoCaption* function in POPPAD3 to display the filename in the title bar of the window and is used in the *OKMessage* and *AskAboutSave* functions to display message boxes to the user.

POPFILE.C contains several functions to display the File Open and File Save dialog boxes and to perform the actual file I/O. The dialog boxes are displayed using the functions *GetOpenFileName* and *GetSaveFileName*, located in the common dialog box dynamic link library (COMDLG32.DLL). Both of these functions use a structure of type OPENFILENAME, defined in COMMDLG.H. In POPFILE.C, a global variable named *ofn* is used for this structure. Most of the fields of *ofn* are initialized in the *PopFileInitialize* function, which POPPAD.C calls when processing the WM_CREATE message in *WndProc*.

It's convenient to make *ofn* a static global structure because *GetOpenFileName* and *GetSaveFileName* return some information to the structure that should be used in subsequent calls to these functions.

Although common dialog boxes have a lot of options—including setting your own dialog box template and hooking into the dialog box procedure—my use of the File Open and File Save dialog boxes in POPFILE.C is quite basic. The only fields of the OPENFILENAME structure that are set are *lStructSize* (the size of the structure), *hwndOwner* (the dialog box's owner), *lpstrFilter* (which I'll discuss shortly), *lpstrFile* and *nMaxFile* (a pointer to a buffer to receive the fully qualified filename and the size of that buffer), *lpstrFileTitle* and *nMaxFileTitle* (a buffer and its size for the filename by itself), *Flags* (which sets options for the dialog box), and *lpstrDefExt* (which is set to a text string containing the default filename extension if the user does not specify one when typing a filename in the dialog box).

When the user selects Open from the File menu, POPPAD3 calls POPFILE's *PopFileOpenDlg* function, passing to it the window handle, a pointer to the filename buffer, and a pointer to the file title buffer. *PopFileOpenDlg* sets the *hwndOwner*, *lpstrFile*, and *lpstrFileTitle* fields of the OPENFILENAME structure appropriately, sets *Flags* to OFN_HIDE-READONLY ¦ OFN_CREATEPROMPT, and then calls *GetOpenFileName*, which displays the familiar dialog box shown in Figure 11-12. The default File Open dialog box includes a check box that allows the user to designate that a file is to be opened as "read only"; the OFN_HIDEREADONLY flag causes GetOpenFileName to hide this check box.

When the user ends this dialog box, the *GetOpenFileName* function returns. The OFN_CREATEPROMPT flag instructs *GetOpenFileName* to display a message box asking the user whether the file should be created if the selected file does not exist.

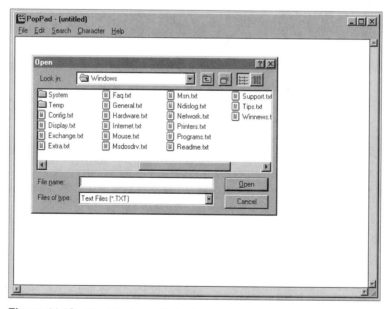

Figure 11-12. *The File Open dialog box.*

The combo box in the lower left corner lists the types of files that will be displayed in the file list. This is known as a "filter." The user can change the filter by selecting another file type from the combo box list. In the *PopFileInitialize* function in POPFILE.C, I define a filter in the variable *szFilter* for three types of files: text files with the extension .TXT, ASCII files with the extension .ASC, and all files. The *lpstrFilter* field of the OPENFILENAME structure is set to this filter.

If the user changes the filter when the dialog box is active, the *nFilterIndex* field of OPENFILENAME reflects the user's choice. Because the structure is stored as a static variable, the next time the dialog box is invoked, the filter will be set to the selected file type.

The *PopFileSaveDlg* function in POPFILE.C is similar. It sets the *Flags* parameter to OFN_OVERWRITEPROMPT and calls *GetSaveFileName* to invoke the File Save dialog box. The OFN_OVERWRITEPROMPT flag causes a message box to be displayed asking the user whether a file should be overwritten if the selected file already exists. The other functions in POPFILE.C perform file I/O using the standard C library functions. (I'll discuss file I/O in Windows 95 in more detail in Chapter 13.)

Changing the Font

In Chapter 4, I promised that I'd show you how your program can easily allow a user to select a font. It's shown in POPFONT.C.

During the WM_CREATE message, POPPAD3 calls *PopFontInitialize* in POPFONT.C. This function obtains a LOGFONT structure based on the system font, creates a font from it, and sends a WM_SETFONT message to the edit control to set a new font. (Although the default edit control font is the system font, the *PopFontInitialize* function creates a new font for the edit control because eventually the font will be deleted, and it wouldn't be wise to delete the stock system font.)

When POPPAD3 receives a WM_COMMAND message for the program's font option, it calls *PopFontChooseFont*. This function initializes a CHOOSEFONT structure and then calls *ChooseFont* to display the font selection dialog box. If the user presses the OK button, *ChooseFont* will return TRUE. POPPAD3 then calls *PopFontSetFont* to set the new font in the edit control. The old font is deleted.

Finally, during the WM_DESTROY message, POPPAD3 calls *PopFontDeinitialize* to delete the last font that *PopFontSetFont* created.

Search and Replace

The common dialog box library also includes two dialog boxes for the text search and replace functions. These two functions (*FindText* and *ReplaceText*) use a structure of type FINDREPLACE. The POPFIND.C file shown in Figure 11-11 has two routines (*PopFindFindDlg* and *PopFindReplaceDlg*) to call these functions, and it also has a couple of functions to search through the text in the edit control and to replace text.

There are a few considerations with using the search and replace functions. First, the dialog boxes they invoke are modeless dialog boxes, which means you should alter your message loop to call *IsDialogMessage* when the dialog boxes are active. Second, the FINDREPLACE structure you pass to *FindText* and *ReplaceText* must be a static variable; because the dialog box is modeless, the functions return after the dialog box is displayed rather than after it's destroyed. Nevertheless, the dialog box procedure must be able to continue to access the structure.

Third, while the *FindText* and *ReplaceText* dialogs are displayed, they communicate with the owner window through a special message. The message number can be obtained by calling the *RegisterWindowMessage* function with the FINDMSGSTRING parameter. This is done while processing the WM_CREATE message in *WndProc*, and the message number is stored in a static variable.

While processing the default message case, *WndProc* compares the message variable with the value returned from *RegisterWindowMessage*. The *lParam* message parameter is a pointer to the FINDREPLACE structure, and the *Flags* field indicates whether the user has used the dialog box to find text or replace text or whether the dialog box is terminating. POPPAD3 calls the *PopFindFindText* and *PopFindReplaceText* functions in POPFIND.C to perform the search and replace functions.

The One Function Call Windows Program

So far I've shown two programs that let you view selected colors: COLORS1 in Chapter 8 and COLORS2 in this chapter. Now it's time for COLORS3, a program that makes only one Windows function call. The COLORS3 source code is shown in Figure 11-13.

The one Windows function that COLORS3 calls is *ChooseColor*, another function in the common dialog box library. It displays the dialog box shown in Figure 11-14. Color selection is similar to that in COLORS1 and COLORS2, but it's somewhat more interactive.

COLORS3.MAK

```
#----------------------
# COLORS3.MAK make file
#----------------------

colors3.exe : colors3.obj
    $(LINKER) $(GUIFLAGS) -OUT:colors3.exe colors3.obj $(GUILIBS)

colors3.obj : colors3.c
    $(CC) $(CFLAGS) colors3.c
```

Figure 11-13. *The COLORS3 program.*

(continued)

COLORS3.C

```
//*----------------------------------------------
   COLORS3.C -- Version using Common Dialog Box
                (c) Charles Petzold, 1996
   ----------------------------------------------*/

#include <windows.h>
#include <commdlg.h>

int WINAPI WinMain (HINSTANCE hInstance, HINSTANCE hPrevInstance,
                    PSTR szCmdLine, int iCmdShow)
     {
     static CHOOSECOLOR cc ;
     static COLORREF    crCustColors[16] ;

     cc.lStructSize    = sizeof (CHOOSECOLOR) ;
     cc.hwndOwner      = NULL ;
     cc.hInstance      = NULL ;
     cc.rgbResult      = RGB (0x80, 0x80, 0x80) ;
     cc.lpCustColors   = crCustColors ;
     cc.Flags          = CC_RGBINIT | CC_FULLOPEN ;
     cc.lCustData      = 0L ;
     cc.lpfnHook       = NULL ;
     cc.lpTemplateName = NULL ;

     return ChooseColor (&cc) ;
     }
```

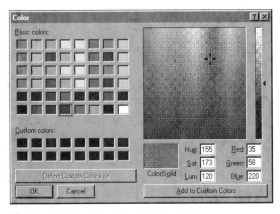

Figure 11-14. *The COLORS3 display.*

The *ChooseColor* function uses a structure of type CHOOSECOLOR and an array of 16 COLORREFs (DWORDs) to store custom colors that the user selects from the dialog box. The *rgbResult* field can be initialized to a color value that will be displayed if the CC_RGBINIT flag is set in the *Flags* field. When using the function normally, the *rgbResult* field will be set to the color that the user selects.

Notice that the *hwndOwner* field of the Color dialog box is set to NULL. When the *ChooseColor* function calls *DialogBox* to display the dialog box, the third parameter to *DialogBox* is also set to NULL. This is perfectly legitimate. It means that the dialog box is not owned by another window. The caption in the dialog box will appear in the task bar, and the dialog box will seem to function much like a normal window.

You can also use this technique with your own dialog boxes in your own programs. It's possible to make a Windows program that only creates a dialog box and does all processing within the dialog box procedure.

Chapter 12

The Modern User Interface

Each major release of Microsoft Windows offered user-interface enhancements, and Windows 95 is no exception, offering a host of features to improve ease-of-use. The various forms of Windows Explorer (which include the Network Neighborhood and the Control Panel) simplify the navigation of hard drives, network resources, and windows that control system settings. A new shell tightly integrates the old MS-DOS file system into a name space that includes network file and print servers. The most visible part of the file system is the desktop (available at the command-line prompt as \WINDOWS\DESKTOP), which provides a user-defined view into available programs and files. Another visible part of the file system is the Start menu (residing at \WINDOWS\Start Menu), which provides a hierarchy of menus as an alternative to the desktop for organizing program and data files.

To simplify the creation of Windows programs that match the elegant user-interface of the system shell, Microsoft created the common control library. Of the seventeen common controls, some—such as toolbars and status bars—have been around for many years in many applications built by developers willing to create a set from scratch (or use the set provided by class libraries such as the Microsoft Foundation Class (MFC) Library or Borland's OWL class library). Other common controls, such as the hierarchical tree view and the configurable list view, were first introduced with Windows 95. Figure 12-1 summarizes the common controls, sorted into four categories: frame controls, compound dialog controls, Windows Explorer controls, and miscellaneous controls.

Category	Control	Description
Frame Window Controls		Controls commonly used within a frame window.
	Toolbar	Holds command shortcut buttons.
	Tooltip	Provides quick help to users by displaying text in a floating window.
	Status bar	Information window normally placed at the bottom of an application's frame window.
Compound Dialog Boxes		Controls for property sheets and wizards.
	Property page	A modeless dialog box used as a single page in a property sheet or a wizard.
	Property sheet	Container for multiple property pages.
Windows Explorer Controls		Controls for building Windows Explorer-like user interfaces.
	Tree view	Displays hierarchically organized list (like the left pane of Windows Explorer).
	List view	Displays lists of items identified by bitmap plus text data (like the right pane of Windows Explorer).
Miscellaneous Controls		
	Animation	Plays animation sequences to show progress of long operations.
	Drag list	A list box that supports simple drag/drop to itself or to other drag list boxes. (*Not* an OLE-aware drag/drop container.)
	Header	Displays a horizontal window for column labels (used by the list view control).
	Hot-Key	Displays feedback for run-time definition of accelerator keys.
	Image list	Non-window control for storing a set of raster (bitmap, cursor, and icon) images.
	Progress bar	Displays progress for long operations as a percent of task completed.
	Rich edit	An edit control supporting multiple fonts and basic OLE container features.

Figure 12-1. *Controls supported by COMCTL32.DLL.* *(continued)*

Category	*Control*	*Description*
	Tab	Displays list of items for selection. Tabs are used by property sheets to select property pages. The Windows 95 task bar is a tab control, which uses buttons instead of tabs.
	Trackbar	A scrollbar substitute for selecting a value in a specific range.
	Up-Down	A scrollbar substitute consisting of two arrows (but no scrollbar body) for incrementing or decrementing a value in an accompanying "buddy" edit control.

This chapter covers the basics for working with all of these controls and then focuses on the first two categories—frame controls and compound dialog controls—which represent a set that every Windows application will use. The other two categories—Windows Explorer controls and miscellaneous controls—are discussed in some detail in Nancy Cluts' book, *Programming the Windows 95 User Interface* (Microsoft Press, 1995).

COMMON CONTROL BASICS

Each common control—with the single exception of the image list—is implemented as a window class. In this way, common controls are similar to the predefined dialog box controls introduced with the first version of Windows. Both types of controls are created by calling *CreateWindow*, fine-tuned with class-specific style flags, manipulated with class-specific messages, and arranged by making regular window-manipulation API calls. Both types of controls also send their parents notification messages to inform them of interesting events.

A difference between common controls and predefined controls is the specific message sent for notifications. Predefined controls send WM_COMMAND notification messages, while common controls (with just a few exceptions) send WM_NOTIFY messages. While the delivery mechanism differs slightly, the idea behind both notification messages is the same: something interesting has happened that the parent window might want to respond to.

The most important point to remember when working with a control from either set is this: a control is a window, and everything you already know about manipulating windows applies to manipulating controls. Also remember that everything you already know about working with the predefined dialog controls applies to working with the common controls. In fact, one common control, the rich edit control, is basically a souped-up edit control, supporting the same basic set of control styles, messages, and notifications as the original (plus a few more to support its new features). What you already know about working with the regular edit control will help you go that much further when working with the rich edit control.

As with the predefined controls, the advantage of using common controls is that you get a lot of features—each is a self-contained "black box"—with a minimum of effort on your part. The key challenge to exploiting common controls is understanding the control and figuring out the exact feature set that's built in versus the added work you'd have to do to get some desired behavior or appearance. Once you know what is possible, only a little arm wrestling is required to get a control working for you.

Library Initialization

With the exception of the rich edit control, the common controls reside in COMCTL32.DLL, which first shipped with Microsoft Windows NT 3.51 and Windows 95. (While the name of this DLL might suggest to you that a 16-bit common control library exists somewhere, as of this writing Microsoft doesn't plan to release a 16-bit version of the common control library. Microsoft did briefly make available some details of a similar control library that shipped with Windows for Workgroups 3.11, but that library was never officially supported and does not exist in current Microsoft operating systems.)

To use any common control, a program first calls the *InitCommonControls* function, which registers common control window classes using the *RegisterClass* function. *InitCommonControls* takes no parameters and has no return value:

```
InitCommonControls () ;
```

The declaration for this function, along with other declarations needed to use the common control library, resides in COMMCTRL.H. This file is not part of the core files referenced from WINDOWS.H, so any source file that refers to common control functions, data types, or symbolic constants must explicitly include it:

```
#include <commctrl.h>
```

To aid the linker in locating common control functions, some reference must be made to the common control static link library, COMCTL32.LIB. Your development environment might already include such a reference. You'll know soon enough if it's missing, however, as the linker will display a message like the following one:

```
error: unresolved external symbol __imp__InitCommonControls@0
```

To fix this problem, add COMCTL32.LIB to the list of linker libraries.

Because of its size and complexity, the rich edit control resides in its own dynamic link library: RICHED32.DLL. (Microsoft doesn't plan to ship a RICHED16.DLL.) The rich edit control registers itself when this library loads, which you request with a call to the *LoadLibrary* function:

```
LoadLibrary ("RICHED32.DLL") ;
```

Rich edit declarations reside in RICHEDIT.H, and OLE-specific declarations for the rich edit control are in RICHOLE.H.

Creating Common Controls

The most obvious way to create a common control window is to call the *CreateWindow* or *CreateWindowEx* function. (The *CreateWindowEx* function is identical to *Create Window*, except that it has an additonal "extended style" parameter. The extended window styles for common controls are discussed in the next section.) For example, this call creates a toolbar:

```
HWND hwndToolBar = CreateWindow (TOOLBARCLASSNAME,
                      NULL,
                      CCS_TOP    ¦
                      WS_CHILD   ¦
                      WS_VISIBLE ¦
                      WS_BORDER  ¦
                      WS_CLIPSIBLINGS,
                      0, 0, 0, 0,
                      hwndParent,
                      (HMENU) 1,
                      hInst,
                      0 ) ;
```

A few of the parameters in this function call deserve further explanation. The class name doesn't appear in quotes because it's a symbolic constant whose definition depends on the character set selected at program build time. For the ANSI character set, TOOLBAR-CLASSNAME is replaced by "ToolbarWindow32"; and when the UNICODE character set is being used, an "L" is placed before this name (L"ToolbarWindow32") to create a UNICODE string. All common control classes are defined this way.

Most of the time, common controls are created as child windows, which explains the WS_CHILD style flag and the assignment of the parent window handle, *hwndParent*. As in this example, child windows are often created with an initial location (*x, y*) and size (*cx, cy*) of zero, and then resized when the parent window changes size (that is, when the parent window gets a WM_SIZE message).

An alternative to calling *CreateWindow* is to call a control-specific creation function, which typically performs some convenient initialization. An example of a control-specific creation function is *CreateToolbarEx*, which creates a toolbar *and* adds buttons to the toolbar. In other cases, such as with property sheets and property pages, no class name is available so a specific creation function is required: *PropertySheet* creates a property sheet, and *CreatePropertySheetPage* creates individual property pages. Image lists are created by calling *ImageList_Create*, a control-specific function that's required because image lists themselves are not windows. Figure 12-2 summarizes common control class names and creation functions.

Category/Control	Control Class	Control Creation Function
Frame window controls:		
Toolbar	TOOLBARCLASSNAME	*CreateToolbarEx*
Tooltip	TOOLTIPS_CLASS	None
Status bar	STATUSCLASSNAME	*CreateStatusWindow*
Animation	ANIMATE_CLASS	None
Progress bar	PROGRESS_CLASS	None
Compound dialog controls:		
Property page	None	*CreatePropertySheetPage*
Property sheet	None	*PropertySheet*
Explorer controls:		
Tree view	WC_TREEVIEW	None
List view	WC_LISTVIEW	None
Image list	None	*ImageList_Create*
Miscellaneous controls:		
Drag list	"listbox" (ANSI) or L"listbox" (UNICODE)	*MakeDragList*
Header	WC_HEADER	None
Hot-Key	HOTKEY_CLASS	None
Rich edit	"RichEdit" (ANSI) or L"RichEdit" (UNICODE)	None
Tab	WC_TABCONTROL	None
Trackbar	TRACKBAR_CLASS	None
Up-Down	UPDOWN_CLASS	*CreateUpDownControl*

Figure 12-2. *Common control class names and creation functions.*

Common Control Styles

Much of the hard work in creating any kind of window—whether your own window, a predefined control, or a common control—involves selecting the correct set of style flags. (As a refresher, style flags are combined with the C bitwise OR operator and passed together as one of two parameters to *CreateWindowEx*: either the first—*dwExStyle*—or the fourth—*dwStyle*—parameter.) It's hard work because the style flags control a wide range of features including window appearance (or failure to appear when WS_VISIBLE is inadvertently omitted), window behavior, and certain kinds of interactions between windows.

When creating common controls, there are four sets of style flags to consider: generic window style (WS_) flags, generic common control style (CCS_) flags, control-specific style flags, and extended style (WS_EX_) flags. The first of these three types is passed to *CreateWindowEx*'s fourth parameter; the last type is passed as *CreateWindowEx*'s first parameter.

Generic window styles

Generic window styles have names that start with WS_ and can affect windows of any class. Of the twenty or so window styles, seven apply to common controls: WS_CHILD, WS_VISIBLE, WS_DISABLED, WS_BORDER, WS_TABSTOP, WS_CLIPCHILDREN, and WS_CLIPSIBLINGS.

Every common control window will use the WS_CHILD style bit, which makes the control a child of some parent window on whose pixels the common control resides. When the control sends notification messages, it sends them to its parent. Child windows are destroyed automatically when their parent window is destroyed.

The WS_VISIBLE style flag allows a window to appear (although the presence of this flag doesn't insure that a window won't be hidden behind other windows). A common programming error involves forgetting to include the WS_VISIBLE style flag, which has sent many a programmer on a frantic search—through books and magazines and to online services—for the cause of the "missing" window. Modify a window's visibility after creation by calling *ShowWindow* or *SetWindowPos*.

The WS_DISABLED flag disables a window, which prevents it from receiving mouse and keyboard input. The most common use of this flag is to disable a control in a dialog box; upon being disabled, most controls change their appearance to let the user know that they are not available. For example, the OK button in a File Open dialog is disabled when the filename edit control is empty. That button only becomes enabled when some text is typed for the filename. Once a window has been created, calls to the *EnableWindow* function enable and disable a window.

The WS_BORDER style bit provides a thin border around a control.

When a control is in a dialog box, the WS_TABSTOP style bit makes the control part of the tab order for keyboard input.

The WS_CLIPCHILDREN and WS_CLIPSIBLINGS style bits protect a child window's drawing surface from outside disruption. "Clipping" refers to the enforcement of drawing boundaries between windows. While clipping is always enabled for overlapped and popup windows, by default clipping is *disabled* for child windows. The WS_CLIPCHILDREN style bit enables clipping when a child window's parent is drawing, thus preventing the parent window from drawing on its child. The WS_CLIPSIBLINGS style bit enables clipping between sibling windows to prevent "sibling rivalry"—fighting between two sibling windows over the pixels occupied by overlapping areas. When working with child windows, these two styles help solve otherwise inexplicable problems in the appearance of the child windows.

Extended window styles

The extended window styles have names starting with WS_EX_, and are passed as the first parameter to *CreateWindowEx*. Of the 27 extended style bits, 3 apply to the child window creation: WS_EX_CLIENTEDGE, WS_EX_STATICEDGE, and WS_EX_NOPARENTNOTIFY.

The WS_EX_CLIENTEDGE and WS_EX_STATICEDGE style flags support a 3D look. Their proper use allows an application to look good next to other Windows 95 applications. Note that these style flags are supported only on Windows 95 and versions of Windows NT that run with the Windows 95 shell. (These flags have no effect on earlier operating system versions.)

The WS_EX_CLIENTEDGE style flag creates a "sunken" client area for an application's main workspace—for example, the text window of a word processing program. Since most controls, such as toolbars and status windows, are created *outside* this area, avoid this style bit for toolbar parents and status window parents. Also, avoid the WS_EX_OVERLAPPED-WINDOW style flag, which includes WS_EX_CLIENTEDGE as part of its definition.

The WS_EX_STATICEDGE style flag creates a sunken look for output-only windows. For example, the notification window on the Windows 95 task bar—the tiny window on the right side of the task bar containing status icons and the clock—uses this style. You'll use this flag with such common controls as progress bars and animation windows. Also, any output-only control embedded in a status window or in a toolbar will probably use this style flag, since its unique look is readily understood by experienced Windows 95 users.

The WS_EX_NOPARENTNOTIFY style bit requests that a child window not send WM_PARENTNOTIFY messages to its parent window. Without this bit, a child window sends notifications to its parent when the child is created, destroyed, or gets a mouse down message. Dialog box controls are always created with this style bit to cut down on message traffic overhead.

Generic common control styles

The common control library provides a set of style values with a CCS_ prefix for use with toolbars, status windows, and header controls. Included in this set are CCS_ADJUSTABLE, CCS_BOTTOM, CCS_NODIVIDER, CCS_NOMOVEY, CCS_NOPARENTALIGN, CCS_NORESIZE, and CCS_TOP. Since the meaning of these styles are specific to individual controls, further discussion will wait for control-specific coverage in the next section.

Control-specific styles

Just as the predefined dialog controls have control-specific styles—such as BS_PUSH-BUTTON, ES_MULTILINE, LBS_SORT—so do the Windows 95 common controls. As with predefined controls, each common control style has a unique prefix, all of which are summarized in Figure 12-3 on the facing page. The simpler common controls have no control-specific style flags defined.

Detailed coverage of individual control-specific styles appears later in this chapter where individual controls are discussed.

Category/Control	Style Flag Prefix	Example
Frame window controls:		
Toolbar	TBSTYLE_	TBSTYLE_ALTDRAG
Tooltip	None	
Status bar	SBARS_	SBARS_SIZEGRIP
Animation	ACS_	ACS_AUTOPLAY
Progress bar	None	
Compound dialog controls:		
Property page	None	
Property sheet	None	
Explorer controls:		
Tree view	TVS_	TVS_HASBUTTONS
List view	LVS_	LVS_ALIGNLEFT
Image list	None	
Miscellaneous controls:		
Drag list	None	
Header	HDS_	HDS_BUTTONS
Hot-Key	None	
Rich edit	ES_	ES_DISABLENOSCROLL
Tab	TCS_	TCS_BUTTONS
Trackbar	TBS_	TBS_AUTOTICKS
Up-Down	UDS_	UDS_ALIGNLEFT

Figure 12-3. *Common control style flag prefixes.*

Sending Messages to Common Controls

Once a common control window has been created, you send messages to manage its operation. As you might expect, this involves calling *SendMessage* with its familiar four parameters: window handle, message ID, *wParam* value, and *lParam* value. Just as there are control-specific styles, there are control-specific messages.

As an alternative to calling *SendMessage*, you can use a set of C-language macros defined in COMMCTRL.H that accept a message-specific set of parameters, combine values as needed (packing, for example, two *shorts* into an *lParam*), and then call *SendMessage*. The return value is also cast, to minimize extraneous noise from the compiler when, for example, the LRESULT value returned by *SendMessage* doesn't match the expected return type.

As an example of how convenient these macros make sending messages to controls, consider the TVM_INSERTITEM message for adding an item to a tree view control. This message adds a single item to a tree view control. Here's what the call to send this message looks like using *SendMessage*:

```
hItem = (HTREEITEM) SendMessage (hwndTV, TVM_INSERTITEM,
                       0, (LPARAM) (LPTV_INSERTSTRUCT) &tvis) ;
```

Here's how to send the same message using the *TreeView_InsertItem* macro:

```
hItem = TreeView_InsertItem (hwndTV, &tvis) ;
```

The macro is easier to read (providing both the target window class name and the message name), it requires only half the keystrokes, and it produces the same result because it expands to a *SendMessage* call with the exact same casting. Given a choice between the two, the macro call is hard to turn down.

(If you're interested in using a set of similar macros for the predefined controls, you'll find that a set has been defined in WINDOWSX.H While the macros are not explicitly documented in any help file, they are fairly self-explanatory and reasonably easy to use. Like the set of macros for the common controls, the macros in WINDOWSX.H will make your code simpler to write and to read.)

As useful as these macros are, the Win32 files unfortunately include definitions for only half of the common controls. COMMCTRL.H contains only macro definitions for the following classes: animation, header, list view, property sheets (in PRSHT.H), tree view, and the tab control.

Since the message macros are so useful, you'll find a set for the other common controls on the companion CD-ROM. Included are macros for the following classes: hot-key control, progress bar, rich edit control, status bar, toolbar, tooltip, trackbar, and up-down control. Look for the file \PETZOLD\CHAP12\COMCTHLP.H.

You'll also find a program on the companion CD-ROM, CTLMACRO, which catalogs all common control message macros. As shown in figure 12-4, CTLMACRO organizes all common control macros into a hierarchy that's accessible through a single tree view control. When you locate the message you need, click on the Copy button to copy the macro to the clipboard. From there, it's a simple matter to paste the macro into your favorite program editor.

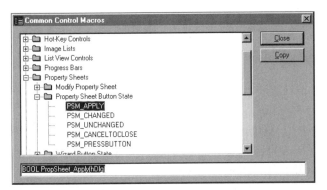

Figure 12-4. *The CTLMACRO program provides quick access to common control message macros.*

Notification Messages from Common Controls

As with predefined controls, common controls talk back to their parent window via notification messages. Notification messages tell the parent window that something of interest has happened to the window: the user has clicked the control, typed text, provided the control with the keyboard focus, or moved the focus away from the control.

Unlike predefined controls, which send notifications as WM_COMMAND messages, common controls send notifications as WM_NOTIFY messages. So if you're adding a common control to existing code, you're not likely to mix up notification handling for a predefined control with that of a common control. WM_NOTIFY messages also avoid confusion with menu notifications, which also arrive in the form of WM_COMMAND messages.

However, not all common control notifications arrive as a WM_NOTIFY message. In particular, toolbars—which use WM_NOTIFY for most notifications—send WM_COMMAND messages when a toolbar button is pushed. Since toolbars are meant to supplement menu selections, a common set of WM_COMMAND handling code—which previously supported menus and accelerators—can now seamlessly accept toolbar button messages. Another exception is up-down controls, which also send a WM_VSCROLL or WM_HSCROLL message when an up-down button is clicked.

While each common control has its own unique set of notification codes, a common set of notifications has also been defined. The set appears in the following table:

Notification Code	Description
NM_CLICK	User has clicked the left mouse button.
NM_DBLCLK	User has double-clicked the left mouse button.
NM_KILLFOCUS	Control has lost the keyboard focus.
NM_OUTOFMEMORY	Out-of-memory error.
NM_RCLICK	User has clicked the right mouse button.
NM_RDBLCLK	User has double-clicked the right mouse button.
NM_RETURN	User has pressed the Enter key.
NM_SETFOCUS	Control has gained the keyboard focus.

Not every common control will necessarily send each of the common notifications when you might think it makes sense for them to. For example, tab controls don't send the focus-related notifications (NM_KILLFOCUS and NM_SETFOCUS). As you work with each common control, you'll have to work out which set of notifications that particular type of control sends.

One solution to the puzzle of what notifications get sent by a specific common control class is to trap every WM_NOTIFY message and output the associated notification code to a debug window. This task is simplified by the fact that the notification codes from each common control are defined in a unique range, so a simple table lookup can be used to properly interpret the meaning of a notification code from any common control. No matter what common control you're working with, then, you can handle the WM_NOTIFY message as follows to send output to (for example) the debugging stream via the *Output-DebugString* function. To see the results of this function in the Win32 API, you must run your program in a debugger:

```
case WM_NOTIFY :
    {
    int idCtrl = (int) wParam ;
    LPNMHDR pnmh = (LPNMHDR) lParam ;

#ifdef _DEBUG
        // Dump notifications to debug stream (debugger)
        LPSTR pText ;
        if (QueryNotifyText (pnmh->code, &pText))
            {
            OutputDebugString (pText) ;
            OutputDebugString ("\r\n") ;
            }
#endif
    [other program lines]
    return 0 ;
    }
```

Each sample program in this chapter handles the WM_NOTIFY message in a manner simi-lar to that shown here. The declarations needed to call *QueryNotifyText* function are as follows:

```
typedef struct tagCONTROLNOTIFICATIONS
    {
    UINT  nCode ;
    LPSTR pName ;
    } CONTROLNOTIFICATIONS ;


BOOL QueryNotifyText (UINT nNotifyCode, LPSTR *pName) ;
```

The function and data definitions for *QueryNotifyText* are as follows:

```
#include <windows.h>
#include <windowsx.h>
#include <commctrl.h>
#include <prsht.h>
#include "notify.h"

CONTROLNOTIFICATIONS cnLookupTable[] =
    {
    NM_OUTOFMEMORY,          "NM_OUTOFMEMORY",
    NM_CLICK,                "NM_CLICK",
    NM_DBLCLK,               "NM_DBLCLK",
    NM_RETURN,               "NM_RETURN",
    NM_RCLICK,               "NM_RCLICK",
    NM_RDBLCLK,              "NM_RDBLCLK",
    NM_SETFOCUS,             "NM_SETFOCUS",
    NM_KILLFOCUS,            "NM_KILLFOCUS",
    LVN_ITEMCHANGING,        "LVN_ITEMCHANGING",
    LVN_ITEMCHANGED,         "LVN_ITEMCHANGED",
    LVN_INSERTITEM,          "LVN_INSERTITEM",
    LVN_DELETEITEM,          "LVN_DELETEITEM",
    LVN_DELETEALLITEMS,      "LVN_DELETEALLITEMS",
    LVN_BEGINLABELEDITA,     "LVN_BEGINLABELEDITA",
    LVN_BEGINLABELEDITW,     "LVN_BEGINLABELEDITW",
    LVN_ENDLABELEDITA,       "LVN_ENDLABELEDITA",
    LVN_ENDLABELEDITW,       "LVN_ENDLABELEDITW",
    LVN_COLUMNCLICK,         "LVN_COLUMNCLICK",
    LVN_BEGINDRAG,           "LVN_BEGINDRAG",
    LVN_BEGINRDRAG,          "LVN_BEGINRDRAG",
    LVN_GETDISPINFOA,        "LVN_GETDISPINFOA",
    LVN_GETDISPINFOW,        "LVN_GETDISPINFOW",
    LVN_SETDISPINFOA,        "LVN_SETDISPINFOA",
    LVN_SETDISPINFOW,        "LVN_SETDISPINFOW",
```

(continued)

```
LVN_KEYDOWN,              "LVN_KEYDOWN",
HDN_ITEMCHANGINGA,        "HDN_ITEMCHANGINGA",
HDN_ITEMCHANGINGW,        "HDN_ITEMCHANGINGW",
HDN_ITEMCHANGEDA,         "HDN_ITEMCHANGEDA",
HDN_ITEMCHANGEDW,         "HDN_ITEMCHANGEDW",
HDN_ITEMCLICKA,           "HDN_ITEMCLICKA",
HDN_ITEMCLICKW,           "HDN_ITEMCLICKW",
HDN_ITEMDBLCLICKA,        "HDN_ITEMDBLCLICKA",
HDN_ITEMDBLCLICKW,        "HDN_ITEMDBLCLICKW",
HDN_DIVIDERDBLCLICKA,     "HDN_DIVIDERDBLCLICKA",
HDN_DIVIDERDBLCLICKW,     "HDN_DIVIDERDBLCLICKW",
HDN_BEGINTRACKA,          "HDN_BEGINTRACKA",
HDN_BEGINTRACKW,          "HDN_BEGINTRACKW",
HDN_ENDTRACKA,            "HDN_ENDTRACKA",
HDN_ENDTRACKW,            "HDN_ENDTRACKW",
HDN_TRACKA,               "HDN_TRACKA",
HDN_TRACKW,               "HDN_TRACKW",
TVN_SELCHANGINGA,         "TVN_SELCHANGINGA",
TVN_SELCHANGINGW,         "TVN_SELCHANGINGW",
TVN_SELCHANGEDA,          "TVN_SELCHANGEDA",
TVN_SELCHANGEDW,          "TVN_SELCHANGEDW",
TVN_GETDISPINFOA,         "TVN_GETDISPINFOA",
TVN_GETDISPINFOW,         "TVN_GETDISPINFOW",
TVN_SETDISPINFOA,         "TVN_SETDISPINFOA",
TVN_SETDISPINFOW,         "TVN_SETDISPINFOW",
TVN_ITEMEXPANDINGA,       "TVN_ITEMEXPANDINGA",
TVN_ITEMEXPANDINGW,       "TVN_ITEMEXPANDINGW",
TVN_ITEMEXPANDEDA,        "TVN_ITEMEXPANDEDA",
TVN_ITEMEXPANDEDW,        "TVN_ITEMEXPANDEDW",
TVN_BEGINDRAGA,           "TVN_BEGINDRAGA",
TVN_BEGINDRAGW,           "TVN_BEGINDRAGW",
TVN_BEGINRDRAGA,          "TVN_BEGINRDRAGA",
TVN_BEGINRDRAGW,          "TVN_BEGINRDRAGW",
TVN_DELETEITEMA,          "TVN_DELETEITEMA",
TVN_DELETEITEMW,          "TVN_DELETEITEMW",
TVN_BEGINLABELEDITA,      "TVN_BEGINLABELEDITA",
TVN_BEGINLABELEDITW,      "TVN_BEGINLABELEDITW",
TVN_ENDLABELEDITA,        "TVN_ENDLABELEDITA",
TVN_ENDLABELEDITW,        "TVN_ENDLABELEDITW",
TVN_KEYDOWN,              "TVN_KEYDOWN",
TTN_NEEDTEXTA,            "TTN_NEEDTEXTA",
TTN_NEEDTEXTW,            "TTN_NEEDTEXTW",
TTN_SHOW,                 "TTN_SHOW",
TTN_POP,                  "TTN_POP",
TCN_KEYDOWN,              "TCN_KEYDOWN",
TCN_SELCHANGE,            "TCN_SELCHANGE",
TCN_SELCHANGING,          "TCN_SELCHANGING",
```

(continued)

```
        TBN_GETBUTTONINFOA,     "TBN_GETBUTTONINFOA",
        TBN_GETBUTTONINFOW,     "TBN_GETBUTTONINFOW",
        TBN_BEGINDRAG,          "TBN_BEGINDRAG",
        TBN_ENDDRAG,            "TBN_ENDDRAG",
        TBN_BEGINADJUST,        "TBN_BEGINADJUST",
        TBN_ENDADJUST,          "TBN_ENDADJUST",
        TBN_RESET,              "TBN_RESET",
        TBN_QUERYINSERT,        "TBN_QUERYINSERT",
        TBN_QUERYDELETE,        "TBN_QUERYDELETE",
        TBN_TOOLBARCHANGE,      "TBN_TOOLBARCHANGE",
        TBN_CUSTHELP,           "TBN_CUSTHELP",
        UDN_DELTAPOS,           "UDN_DELTAPOS",
        PSN_SETACTIVE,          "PSN_SETACTIVE",
        PSN_KILLACTIVE,         "PSN_KILLACTIVE",
        PSN_APPLY,              "PSN_APPLY",
        PSN_RESET,              "PSN_RESET",
        PSN_HELP,               "PSN_HELP",
        PSN_WIZBACK,            "PSN_WIZBACK",
        PSN_WIZNEXT,            "PSN_WIZNEXT",
        PSN_WIZFINISH,          "PSN_WIZFINISH",
        PSN_QUERYCANCEL,        "PSN_QUERYCANCEL"
        } ;

int NOTIFY_COUNT = sizeof (cnLookupTable) /
                   sizeof (CONTROLNOTIFICATIONS) ;


//------------------------------------------------------------
// QueryNotifyText: Convert notification codes into text
//------------------------------------------------------------
BOOL QueryNotifyText (UINT nNotifyCode, LPSTR *pName)
     {
     BOOL bFound = FALSE ;
     int  iNotify ;

     for (iNotify = 0 ; iNotify < NOTIFY_COUNT ; iNotify++)
          {
          if (cnLookupTable[iNotify].nCode == nNotifyCode)
               {
               *pName = cnLookupTable[iNotify].pName ;
               return TRUE ;
               }
          }

     // Unknown notification code
     *pName = "** Unknown **" ;
     return FALSE ;
     }
```

FRAME WINDOW CONTROLS

Three common controls are often used with frame windows: toolbars, tooltips, and status bars. Figure 12-5 shows examples of each of these as implemented in the GADGETS sample program.

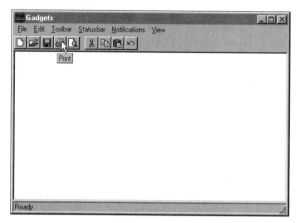

Figure 12-5. *The GADGETS program, showing the toolbar, tooltip, and status bar frame window common controls.*

Toolbars

A toolbar is a child window, typically placed just below a program's menu, that holds buttons for commonly requested menu commands and program options. Toolbar buttons themselves are not windows but rather are graphic objects drawn using a bitmap on the surface of the toolbar window.

The labels on toolbar buttons are either a bitmap or a bitmap supplemented with a text label. (The current implementation does not support buttons with text-only labels.) A toolbar sets the size of all buttons the same, and it sets the size of buttons with text labels to be large enough to accommodate the longest label. For this reason, you'll likely want to choose short character strings for text labels to avoid oversized buttons.

In addition to buttons, a toolbar can also hold other child window controls, such as a combo box. Create the contained control with a call to *CreateWindow*, specifying the toolbar as the contained control's parent window. As Nancy Cluts points out in *Programming the Windows 95 User Interface*, the only real obstacle to putting a control on a toolbar is reserving enough pixel real estate. That is accomplished by adding separators as placeholders for the contained control. Just as separators in menus are defined in the menu definition with a special flag—the SEPARATOR keyword—toolbar button separators are created by creating toolbar buttons with the TBSTYLE_SEP button style flag. A dozen or so separators are required to reserve sufficient space for a combo box in a toolbar.

Creating a Toolbar

Create a toolbar either by calling *CreateWindow* and specifying the TOOLBARCLASSNAME class name or by calling *CreateToolbarEx*, which creates a toolbar and initializes a set of buttons. Here's how the *CreateToolbarEx* function is defined:

```
HWND CreateToolbarEx (HWND hwnd, DWORD ws, UINT wID,
        int nBitmaps, HINSTANCE hBMInst,
        UINT wBMID, LPCTBBUTTON lpButtons,
        int  iNumButtons, int dxButton,
        int dyButton, int dxBitmap,
        int dyBitmap, UINT uStructSize) ;
```

The first three parameters are used in a call that *CreateToolbarEx* makes to *CreateWindow*: *hwnd* is the parent window, *ws* holds window styles flags, and *wID* is the child ID of the toolbar child window.

The next three parameters are used to load the bitmap resource, which holds button face images (multiple images are packed in a single row in the same bitmap): *nBitmaps* is the number of images in the bitmap, and *hBMInst* and *wBMID* identify the bitmap resource to load.

lpButtons is a pointer to an array of TBBUTTON elements, and *iNumButtons* identifies the number of elements in the array. Each TBBUTTON element defines the bitmap, the command ID, the button type, and the initial button state for each toolbar button.

The size of each button is set based on the bitmap image size (*dxBitmap*, *dyBitmap*). The minimum width of a button is *dxBitmap* + 7 pixels, and the minimum height is *dyBitmap* + 7 pixels. Optionally, you can set *dxButton* and *dyButton* to force a button larger than this minimum; otherwise, set *dxButton* and *dyButton* to zero.

The version of the toolbar is based on the size of the TBBUTTON structure, which you indicate with the last parameter—*uStructSize*—which must be set to *sizeof (TBBUTTON)*.

On creation, a toolbar sets its size and location to the "right" values: the height is set to accommodate its buttons, its width is set to the width of its parent window's client area, and its location is set to the top of its parent window. Coercing a toolbar to behave differently requires modification of its window styles, as discussed in the next section.

Toolbar window styles

A toolbar's major features are controlled by setting the toolbar window style flags. A mix of generic (CCS_) style flags and toolbar-specific (TBSTYLE_) style flags are allowed, as shown in the table on the following page:

Category	Style Flag	Description
Appearance	CCS_NODIVIDER	Disables drawing of highlight on top edge of toolbar.
	TBSTYLE_WRAPABLE	Supports multirow toolbar.
Auto-move in y-axis	CCS_TOP	Places toolbar at top of parent window (default), adjusting width to parent window and height to button size.
	CCS_BOTTOM	Places toolbar at bottom of parent window, adjusting width to parent window client area and height to button size.
	CCS_NOMOVEY	Sets initial x-position (at left border of parent) but not initial y-position, adjusting width to parent window client area and height to button size.
Disable auto-move/auto-size	CCS_NOPARENTALIGN	Toolbar sets its own height, but not its location or width. To handle properly, post a message to resize after creation.
	CCS_NORESIZE	Disables all auto-move and auto-size features. This disables the following style flags: CCS_TOP, CCS_BOTTOM, CCS_NOMOVEY, and CCS_NOPARENTALIGN. You must explicitly move and size the toolbar.
Toolbar customizing	CCS_ADJUSTABLE	Supports Click-Shift to move buttons and double-click to display customization dialog box. (For details, see discussion of customizing a toolbar beginning on page 624.)
	TBSTYLE_ALTDRAG	Modifies CCS_ADJUSTABLE toolbar so that Alt-Click (instead of Shift-Click) moves buttons.
Tooltip support	TBSTYLE_TOOLTIPS	Creates a tooltip control.

The only default style flag is CCS_TOP, which sets the toolbar at the top of its parent window's client area when the toolbar is created. After that, the parent window can request the toolbar to resize and relocate itself by sending a TB_AUTOSIZE message, which toolbar parents typically do on receipt of a WM_SIZE message. Aside from sending the resize request message, toolbars with a CCS_TOP or CCS_BOTTOM flag are quite self-sufficient and require no other maintenance. The presence of style flags that disable a toolbar's auto-move and auto-size features requires a little more work to maintain the toolbar as its parent window resizes.

Two style flags modify the appearance of a toolbar. The first, CCS_NODIVIDER, removes a highlighted border that's intended to separate the buttons on a CCS_TOP toolbar from an application's menu. For toolbars drawn at other locations (such as a second toolbar drawn under the first toolbar), you'll probably want to hide the border. The same is true for windows with a toolbar but no menu—the border just doesn't look right. The other appearance-modifying style, TBSTYLE_WRAPABLE, allows a toolbar to wrap buttons and occupy multiple rows. Without this flag, buttons that are too long to fit in a single line are clipped from view and become unavailable to users.

Three style flags control movement along the *y*-axis: CCS_TOP (default), CCS_BOTTOM, and CCS_NOMOVEY. These flags control how a toolbar places itself in its parent window at creation time and also when it receives a TB_AUTOSIZE message. The CCS_NOMOVEY flag causes a toolbar to adjust only its width (to fit within its parent's client area), its height, and its location along the *x*-axis, leaving it up to you to explicitly move the toolbar along the *y*-axis, either with the desired *y*-axis value in the call to *CreateWindow* or with a call to a function like *MoveWindow* after the toolbar has been created. A toolbar with this flag would be useful as a second toolbar residing immediately under a CCS_TOP toolbar.

Two other style flags restrict the auto-move and auto-size features of a toolbar. With the CCS_NOPARENTALIGN style flag, a toolbar sets its own height to accommodate the size of its buttons—but you must set the toolbar's location and width. The CCS_NORESIZE flag completely disables any movement or resizing of a toolbar. This flag would be useful when using a toolbar as a dialog box control, when it must fit within a specific space without resizing itself. This flag would also be useful to set two or more toolbars next to each other in the same row.

The CCS_ADJUSTABLE style flag creates a toolbar that a user can modify on the fly. Buttons can be dragged around the toolbar or dragged off the toolbar with a Shift-Click. A double-click summons the Customize Toolbar dialog box, for adding, deleting, and moving toolbar buttons. (This dialog also appears when a toolbar receives a TB_CUSTOMIZE message.) Customization requires the parent window to respond to a few notification messages—TBN_QUERYINSERT and TBN_QUERYDELETE, among others—sent by the toolbar, which ask permission before inserting or deleting buttons. For a customizable toolbar, the TBSTYLE_ALTDRAG flag changes the button movement user interface from Shift-Click to Alt-Click, in those instances when Shift-Click has other meanings.

The TBSTYLE_TOOLTIPS style flag requests the toolbar to create a tooltip control, which displays a tiny window for text hints about each button. The toolbar's parent window gets a TTN_NEEDTEXT notification (which comes in the form of a WM_NOTIFY message) when the tooltip needs text for specific buttons.

Defining button face images

The toolbar window procedure parses a single bitmap into multiple images needed for button faces subject to this restriction: all images must be the same size. Bitmaps with more than one image must place the image on the same row—that is, the second image appears to the right of the first image, the third is on the right of the second, and so on. While the *CreateToolbarEx* function accepts only one bitmap identifier, you can add bitmaps to a toolbar—with one or more button images per bitmap—by sending the toolbar a TB_ADDBITMAP message.

The common control library has two sets of bitmaps with ready-to-use button images. One set of bitmaps contains button images that correspond to the File and Edit menus; the second set contains button images for different types of views. Each set provides the same set of bitmaps in two sizes: large (24 by 24) and small (16 by 16). To access these bitmaps, you specify a special value, HINST_COMMCTRL, for the bitmap resource instance handle (*hBMInst*) parameter to *CreateToolbarEx* (or in the appropriate structure for the TB_ADDBITMAP message). For the bitmap ID parameter, *wBMID*, select from the following table:

Bitmap Resource ID	Description
IDB_STD_SMALL_COLOR	File and Edit menu images for 16-by-16 button images.
IDB_STD_LARGE_COLOR	File and Edit menu images for 24-by-24 button images.
IDB_VIEW_SMALL_COLOR	View menu images for 16-by-16 button images.
IDB_VIEW_LARGE_COLOR	View menu images for 24-by-24 button images.

The two "standard" (IDB_STD_SMALL_COLOR and IDB_STD_LARGE_COLOR) bitmaps each contain 15 images. Connecting a specific image to a toolbar button involves setting the zero-based image index in the *iBitmap* member of the button's corresponding TBBUTTON structure. When using the standard bitmaps, pick an index from this set of symbolic constants: STD_CUT, STD_COPY, STD_PASTE, STD_UNDO, STD_REDOW, STD_DELETE, STD_FILENEW, STD_FILEOPEN, STD_FILESAVE, STD_PRINTPRE, STD_PROPERTIES, STD_HELP, STD_FIND, STD_REPLACE, and STD_PRINT.

The two "view" (IDB_VIEW_SMALL_COLOR and IDB_VIEW_LARGE_COLOR) bitmaps each contain 12 images. Select button image indexes using these symbolic constants: VIEW_LARGEICONS, VIEW_SMALLICONS, VIEW_LIST, VIEW_DETAILS, VIEW_SORT-NAME, VIEW_SORTSIZE, VIEW_SORTDATE, VIEW_SORTTYPE, VIEW_PARENTFOLDER, VIEW_NETCONNECT, VIEW_NETDISCONNECT, and VIEW_NEWFOLDER.

When using one of these four bitmaps, you don't need to set the button size (*dxButton*, *dyButton*) or bitmap size (*dxBitmap*, *dyBitmap*) because *CreateToolbarEx* recognizes these bitmaps and sets the sizes.

Filling the TBBUTTON array

The creation of a toolbar with its bitmap sets the stage for defining individual toolbar buttons. For that, you need an array of TBBUTTON elements, with each element defining a single toolbar button. After a toolbar has been created, you can define additional buttons by sending a TB_ADDBUTTONS message to a toolbar or by inserting buttons between existing buttons with a TB_INSERTBUTTON message.

TBBUTTON is defined in COMMCTRL.H as:

```
typedef struct _TBBUTTON
    {
    int iBitmap ;
    int idCommand ;
    BYTE fsState ;
    BYTE fsStyle ;
    BYTE bReserved[2] ;
    DWORD dwData ;
    int iString ;
    } TBBUTTON ;
```

Note that this definition differs from the one given in the Win32 help database, which excludes the *bReserved* member. When performing a block initialization of TBBUTTON members, you'll have to include two extra members to properly initialize the array.

The *iBitmap* member of TBBUTTON is the zero-based index of the button image to use. When using bitmaps provided with the common control library, you'll use the STD_ and VIEW_ constants in this member. A given toolbar defines its own image indices based on the order in which bitmaps are added.

TBBUTTON's *idCommand* identifies a button's command identifier. When a button is pushed, it sends a WM_COMMAND message with *idCommand* in the message's *wParam* parameter.

fsState and *fsStyle* indicate initial state and style of a button. "Button styles" are persistent for the life of a button; "button states" can be set when a button is created and modified either by user action or by messages sent to the toolbar. Here are the five toolbar button styles:

Button Styles	Description
TBSTYLE_BUTTON	Button acts like a pushbutton (can click but doesn't stay down—the default).
TBSTYLE_SEP	Separator to create space between other buttons or to reserve space for child window controls (such as a combo box).
TBSTYLE_CHECK	Button behaves like a check box (toggles between up and down for each click).
TBSTYLE_GROUP	Button is member of a group of radio-button-like buttons (supports mutually exclusive selection).
TBSTYLE_CHECKGROUP	Combines TBSTYLE_CHECK and TBSTYLE_GROUP.

The five styles combine to produce roughly the equivalent of the three basic types of dialog box buttons: push buttons, check boxes, and radio buttons.

There are six toolbar button states:

Button States	Description
TBSTATE_CHECKED	A check box–style button is in the down state.
TBSTATE_PRESSED	Any kind of button is in down state.
TBSTATE_ENABLED	Button is enabled (can receive mouse input).
TBSTATE_HIDDEN	Button is hidden (completely disappears and its space is occupied by other buttons).
TBSTATE_INDETERMINATE	Button in "maybe" state; it appears gray but can still be clicked.
TBSTATE_WRAP	In a TBSTYLE_WRAPABLE toolbar, the toolbar wraps after this button.

Each of these states can be accessed using a pair of toolbar-specific messages: one to query the state and one to set the state. For example, you can query the enabled state for a specific button by sending a TB_ISBUTTONENABLED message; send a TB_ENABLEBUTTON message to either enable or disable a button.

The *dwData* member of TBBUTTON is an optional 4-byte field for your use. For example, you can store a pointer in this member to hold button-specific data. Once set, you query the value of *dwData* by sending a TB_GETBUTTON message, but you cannot change a button's *dwData* value once a button has been created.

The *iString* member of TBBUTTON is the zero-based index of a button's text label. You add strings to a toolbar's string list by sending a TB_ADDSTRING message.

An example of toolbar creation

Here's an example of creating a toolbar with small (16-by-16) button face images taken from a standard bitmap provided by the common control library:

```
HWND hwndToolBar = CreateToolbarEx (hwndParent,
                    WS_CHILD | WS_VISIBLE |
                    WS_CLIPSIBLINGS | CCS_TOP |
                    TBSTYLE_TOOLTIPS,
                    1, 0,
                    HINST_COMMCTRL,
                    IDB_STD_SMALL_COLOR,
                    tbb,
                    5, 0, 0, 0, 0,
                    sizeof (TBBUTTON)) ;
```

The thirteen parameters to *CreateToolbarEx* allow it to create a toolbar child window, load a single bitmap resource as a source of button face images, create five toolbar buttons, request tooltip support, and establish the expected version of the toolbar window.

Here is the TBBUTTON array required to define the attributes of individual toolbar buttons:

```
TBBUTTON tbb[] =
    {
    STD_FILENEW,  1, TBSTATE_ENABLED, TBSTYLE_BUTTON, 0, 0, 0, 0,
    STD_FILEOPEN, 2, TBSTATE_ENABLED, TBSTYLE_BUTTON, 0, 0, 0, 0,
    STD_FILESAVE, 3, TBSTATE_ENABLED, TBSTYLE_BUTTON, 0, 0, 0, 0,
    STD_PRINT,    4, TBSTATE_ENABLED, TBSTYLE_BUTTON, 0, 0, 0, 0,
    STD_PRINTPRE, 5, TBSTATE_ENABLED, TBSTYLE_BUTTON, 0, 0, 0, 0,
    } ;
```

An alternative to calling *CreateToolbarEx* would be to call *CreateWindow* to create the toolbar and then send individual messages to initialize various aspects of the toolbar. Here's code that accomplishes the same results as the previous call to *CreateToolbarEx:*

```
HWND hwndToolBar = CreateWindow (TOOLBARCLASSNAME,
                    NULL,
                    WS_CHILD | WS_VISIBLE |
                    WS_CLIPSIBLINGS | CCS_TOP |
                    TBSTYLE_TOOLTIPS,
                    0, 0, 0, 0,
                    hwndParent,
                    (HMENU) 1,
                    hInst,
                    0) ;
```

(continued)

```
// Set version with TBBUTTON size
ToolBar_ButtonStructSize (hwnd) ;

ToolBar_AddBitmap (hwnd, 1, &tbbitmap) ;

// Create buttons
ToolBar_AddButtons (hwnd, 5, tbb) ;
```

The only additional data definition required is a structure of type TBADDBITMAP, which identifies the instance handle and resource identifier of the toolbar bitmap:

```
TBADDBITMAP tbbitmap =
    {
    HINST_COMMCTRL, IDB_STD_SMALL_COLOR,
    } ;
```

Once a toolbar has been created, it sends its parent window a WM_COMMAND message whenever one of its buttons is clicked. Other than responding to such messages, the only other housekeeping chore required for a toolbar control is to request it to change its size whenever its parent changes size.

Moving and sizing toolbars

Toolbars have an auto-size and auto-placement feature that comes into play when you send a toolbar a TB_AUTOSIZE message. You'll normally send this message when the toolbar's parent window changes size—that is, receives a WM_SIZE message:

```
SendMessage (hwndToolBar, TB_AUTOSIZE, 0, 0L) ;
```

Alternatively, you could use the message macros provided in COMCTHLP.H on the companion CD-ROM:

```
ToolBar_AutoSize (hwndToolBar) ;
```

A toolbar's response to this message depends on its style flags. With a CCS_TOP and CCS_BOTTOM, for example, a toolbar sets its own size and location. At the other extreme, a toolbar with a CCS_NORESIZE flag ignores this message and requires you to explicitly set its size and location.

Supporting a tooltip control

A tooltip control is a tiny window containing helpful text. Typically, tooltip controls are activated when the mouse cursor pauses over a specific area such as a toolbar button; however, it's possible to activate a tooltip at any time. The tooltip control keeps track of a list of "hot" areas—which, in the context of a tooltip, is called a "tool"—that can either be a rectangular area in a window, or an entire window. A tooltip can appear for a tool that resides in any type of window, although our main concern is tooltips within toolbars.

Toolbars created with a TBSTYLE_TOOLTIPS style flag have a tooltip control, and each button added to the toolbar is registered as a tooltip tool. To modify a toolbar's tooltip control—for example, to add a combo box control to the tool list—fetch the tooltip window handle by sending a TB_GETTOOLTIPS message to the toolbar. You then modify the tooltip control by sending tooltip control messages (marked with a TTM_ prefix) directly to the tooltip control.

When a tooltip becomes activated over a toolbar, the tooltip sends a request for the text to display by sending the toolbar a WM_NOTIFY message with a notification code of TTN_NEEDTEXT. The toolbar forwards this message to the toolbar's parent window, which replies by filling in a supplied TOOLTIPTEXT structure. Here's an example of how to respond to this request for three toolbar buttons and a combo box that resides on the toolbar window:

```
case WM_NOTIFY :
    {
    LPNMHDR pnmh = (LPNMHDR) lParam ;
    LPSTR    pReply ;

    // Fetch tooltip text
    if (pnmh->code == TTN_NEEDTEXT)
        {
        LPTOOLTIPTEXT lpttt = (LPTOOLTIPTEXT) lParam ;
        switch (lpttt->hdr.idFrom)
            {
            case 0 :
                pReply = "First Button" ;
                break ;

            case 1 :
                pReply = "Second Button" ;
                break ;

            case 2 :
                pReply = "Third Button" ;
                break ;

            default :
                if (lpttt->uFlags & TTF_IDISHWND) &&
                    lpttt->hdr.idFrom == (UINT) hwndCombo)
                    {
                    pReply = "Combo Box" ;
                    }
                else
                    {
                    pReply = "Unknown" ;
                    }
            }
        lstrcpy (lpttt->szText, pReply) ;
        }
    }
```

One odd feature of this code fragment is that WM_NOTIFY's *lParam* parameter gets cast to two different pointer types: a pointer to an NMHDR and a pointer to a TOOLTIPTEXT. This can be explained by the fact that all WM_NOTIFY messages pass an NMHDR structure containing details that apply to every type of common control. When control-specific (or notification-code specific) details must be provided, those details get supplied after the NMHDR data—which is another way of saying that the provided data structure— TOOLTIPTEXT here—has an NMHDR structure as its first data member.

WINUSER.H defines NMHDR as follows:

```
typedef struct tagNMHDR
    {
    HWND  hwndFrom ;
    UINT  idFrom ;
    UINT  code ;
    } NMHDR ;


typedef NMHDR FAR *LPNMHDR ;
```

The third member of this structure, *code*, holds the notification code—that is, the reason the WM_NOTIFY message was sent in the first place—and it can be a generic notification code (like NM_CLICK or NM_SETFOCUS) or a class-specific code (such as TTN_NEEDTEXT in this example). The *hwndFrom* member identifies the window that sent the message, and *idFrom* is either the window ID or the ID of the specific item (such as a toolbar button) on whose behalf the message was sent.

When a tooltip sends a TTN_NEEDTEXT notification, it passes a pointer to a data structure unique to this notification code: TOOLTIPTEXT. This structure is defined in COMMCTRL.H as follows:

```
typedef struct tagTOOLTIPTEXTA
    {
    NMHDR     hdr ;
    LPSTR     lpszText ;
    char      szText[80] ;
    HINSTANCE hinst ;
    UINT      uFlags ;
    } TOOLTIPTEXTA, FAR *LPTOOLTIPTEXTA ;
```

The first member, *hdr*, holds the NMHDR data that must be supplied for every WM_NOTIFY message.

On receipt of a TTN_NEEDTEXT message, the first task is to check which button (or window) has been selected. This is accomplished by checking the NMHDR structure's *idFrom* member, which will be either a button index when the mouse is over a button or a window handle when the mouse is over a child window on the toolbar. The *uFlags* member holds the flag TTF_IDISHWND to indicate that the identifier is a window handle and not a button index.

On receipt of a TTN_NEEDTEXT notification, there are three ways to supply text to the tooltip control: by returning a pointer to the string in the *lpszText* member, by copying the string to the *szText* buffer, or by identifying a string resource. As with other resources, you identify the string resource with an instance handle and a unique identifier. Copy the instance handle to the *hinst* member, and the identifier to the *lpszText* member, using the MAKEINTRESOURCE macro:

```
lptttt->hinst = hInstance ;
lptttt->lpszText = MAKEINTRESOURCE (100) ;
```

Adding a child window to a toolbar

Toolbars support only buttons, so to put something other than a button on a toolbar, you must create a child window. One of the more common types of windows added to toolbars are combo boxes; therefore, combo boxes will be the focus of this discussion (although any type of window can reside on a toolbar). Since the basics of creating child windows is covered in Chapter 8, I'll cover some refinements here: making room in the toolbar for a child window, resizing the toolbar, and providing tooltip support.

Making room for a child window in a toolbar

In *Programming the Windows 95 User Interface*, Nancy Cluts suggests adding separators (buttons with the TBSTYLE_SEP style) as placeholders when creating a child window in a toolbar. You'll have to experiment to figure out the right number of separators, but for the sake of comparison, the GADGETS sample program, which appears later in this chapter, uses 20 separators to allocate space for its combo box.

The presence of separators makes it easy to calculate coordinates for the window, which you'll need for the call to *CreateWindow*. Send the TB_GETITEMRECT message to get the pixel coordinates of any item in a toolbar—buttons or separators—and you get back the four coordinates of the item's rectangle. Here's how GADGETS calculates the space available for its combo box using message macros from COMCTHLP.H (found on the companion CD-ROM):

```
RECT r ;
int x, y, cx, cy ;

// Calculate coordinates for combo box
ToolBar_GetItemRect (hwndTB, 0, &r) ;
x = r.left ;
y = r.top ;
ToolBar_GetItemRect (hwndTB, 18, &r) ;
cx = r.right - x + 1 ;
```

Setting the upper left corner of the control at (*x, y*) lines the control up with the toolbar buttons. Since GADGETS placed 20 separators on its toolbar, querying the location of the 19th (or 18th for zero-based counting) leaves a single separator's width between the right of the combo box and the first button.

The only other value needed to place a child window on a toolbar is the height, which for most controls will probably be the button height ($r.bottom - r.top + 1$) returned by the TB_GETITEMRECT message. But a combo box behaves a little differently from other types of windows, since its edit (or static) control sizes itself to accommodate its font, and the height passed to *CreateWindow* is, instead, the allowable height for its drop-down window. Setting a value large enough to accommodate several lines makes sense, which you can do in a device-independent way by basing your calculations on font metric data returned by the *GetTextMetrics* function. GADGETS punts and hard-codes this value as:

```
cy = 100 ;
```

Toolbar control creation

There are a few caveats when you create a child window on a toolbar. Some are obvious, such as making sure to include the WS_VISIBLE and WS_CHILD style flags. Without WS_VISIBLE, the call might succeed but the control won't appear. The WS_CHILD style flag creates a child window, which must have a parent on whose pixels the child window resides. That raises the issue of which window should be the parent of the child window.

The obvious choice of parent for a toolbar window is the toolbar itself, but this can create strange problems. In particular, predefined controls send notification messages (in the form of WM_COMMAND messages) to their parent, which can have unexpected effects. For example, the GADGETS program crashed consistently on Windows 95 when its toolbar combo box was created with the toolbar as its parent and the combo box window ID set to 101. (Oddly enough, that combination never caused a problem on Windows NT 3.51. Closer inspection revealed an operating-system-specific version of COMCTL32.DLL.) While changing the control ID seemed to solve the problem, it leaves open the possibility (however remote) that a future version of the common control library will use whatever child ID we select and cause the same problem all over again. And yet, the toolbar *must* be the window's parent for it to live on the toolbar.

The solution to this apparent contradiction is to specify another window as the window's parent in the call to *CreateWindow*—preferably one for which you own the window procedure. After the child window has been created, place the child window on the toolbar by calling *SetParent*. Dialog controls are apparently very loyal and send their WM_COMMAND notification messages to their original parent window, which allows you to process the notifications yourself. So notification messages go to one window, and yet the child window physically resides on another window—the toolbar. GADGETS does this two-step as follows:

```
hwndCombo = CreateWindow ("combobox",
               NULL,
               WS_CHILD | WS_VISIBLE |
               CBS_DROPDOWN,
               x, y, cx, cy,
```

```
            hwndParent,
            (HMENU) 100,
            hInst,
            0) ;

// Set toolbar as combobox window parent
SetParent (hwndCombo, hwndTB) ;
```

Resizing a toolbar with a child window

Another complication caused by toolbar-based child windows has to do with making sure the toolbar is tall enough to accommodate the window. Incidentally, this seems more of a problem for the old Windows shell—such as seen on Windows NT 3.51—and not on the newer Windows 95 shell. Since some of your users may be using this version of Windows NT, you will want to be sure to test your code in both environments.

The simplest solution, which works for every type of control *except* combo boxes, is to resize the window itself. A combo box is fussier because it resizes itself to accommodate its current font. So, indirectly at least, you can control the size of a combo box by setting its font. This you accomplish by creating a font of the correct size and providing it to the combo box in the form of a WM_SETFONT "shrinking pill" message. As long as a control is shorter than toolbar buttons, the TB_AUTOSIZE message will handle all the fuss of adjusting the toolbar to changes in the size of its parent window. (See the earlier discussion on moving and sizing toolbars.)

When you cannot coerce a child window to be smaller, you must make the toolbar larger. GADGETS demonstrates this approach and is the basis for this discussion.

To gain full control over a toolbar's size and location, create the toolbar with the CCS_NORESIZE style flag. In spite of what the name might suggest, this flag prevents a toolbar from both resizing itself *and* from moving itself. With this flag set, the TB_AUTOSIZE message does nothing, so moving and resizing the toolbar is entirely up to you. When the parent window receives a WM_SIZE message, you must calculate the required location (x, y) and size (cx, cy) for the window and make the change by calling a routine such as *MoveWindow*.

For an application with a single toolbar at the top of its parent window, the location is easy: (0, 0). The width is also straightforward, since WM_SIZE provides the parent's width in the low word of *wParam*. To resize a toolbar in response to a WM_SIZE message, something like the following is needed:

```
case WM_SIZE :
    {
    int cx = LOWORD (lParam) ;
    MoveWindow (hwndToolBar, 0, 0, cx, cyToolBar, TRUE) ;
    [other program lines]
    return 0 ;
    }
```

The missing piece is the toolbar height (*cyToolBar*). GADGETS' solution involves two queries: one to the combo box size and the other to the toolbar item size plus a fudge factor of 5 (apparently the margin that's been hard-coded into the toolbar). The toolbar height is the larger of the two values:

```
// Calculate toolbar height
GetWindowRect (hwndCombo, &r) ;
cyToolBar = r.bottom - r.top + 1 ;
cyToolBar += y ;
cyToolBar += (2 * GetSystemMetrics (SM_CYBORDER)) ;
ToolBar_GetItemRect (hwndTB, 0, &r) ;
cyToolBar = max (cyToolBar, r.bottom + 5) ;
```

Tooltip support for a child window

Aside from handling the tooltip's TTN_NEEDTEXT notification, making tooltips operational for toolbar buttons is effortless. For a child window in a toolbar, one added step is required: adding the child window to the tool list maintained by the tooltip control.

Adding a new tool to a tooltip's tool list involves sending the tooltip a TTM_ADDTOOL message. But first, a handle to the toolbar's tooltip is needed, which a toolbar provides when it's sent a TB_GETTOOLTIP message:

```
hwndTT = ToolBar_GetToolTips (hwndToolBar) ;
```

The TTM_ADDTOOL message requires a pointer to a TOOLINFO structure, which describes a tool to a tooltip control. TOOLINFO is defined in COMMCTRL.H as follows:

```
typedef struct tagTOOLINFOA
    {
    UINT cbSize ;
    UINT uFlags ;
    HWND hwnd ;
    UINT uId ;
    RECT rect ;
    HINSTANCE hinst ;
    LPSTR lpszText ;
    } TOOLINFOA, NEAR *PTOOLINFOA, FAR *LPTOOLINFOA ;
```

Assign the size of TOOLINFO to the *cbSize* member, which provides control-specific version information to the tooltip control. Neglecting to fill this value causes the tooltip control to ignore the message.

The *uFlags* field does allow some refinements to the tool definition. One flag, TTF_IDISHWND, is required when passing a child window handle as a tool. It indicates that the item identifier field, *uId*, is a window handle. Another flag, TTF_CENTERTIP, causes the tooltip to center itself under a tool rather than according to the default, which is below and to the right of the mouse cursor. A third flag, TTF_SUBCLASS, requests the tooltip control to subclass the tool window to watch mouse **message** traffic. Without this flag, you'd have to construct some other mechanism to transmit mouse message details to the tooltip control.

A third field, *hwnd*, identifies the window that contains the tool, which in this context is (of course) the toolbar.

The *uId* field is an arbitrary identifier that a tool creator (such as the toolbar) assigns to each tool. For example, a toolbar assigns a zero-based index for each of its buttons, and the toolbar passes that index to the tooltip when adding each button to the tooltip's list. When this identifier holds a window handle, as it will when an entire child window makes up a tool, the TTF_IDISHWND flag in the *uFlags* field notifies the tooltip of that fact.

A tool's location in its parent window is identified with *rect*, which allows the tooltip control to do the hit-testing for individual buttons within the toolbar window. When an entire window is a tool—that is, when the TTF_IDISHWND flag is set—this field is ignored.

The actual text to display for a tool gets defined with a combination of the *hinst* and *lpszText* fields, which identify a string resource. As an alternative, you may request a TTN_NEEDTEXT notification by setting *lpszText* to LPSTR_TEXTCALLBACK.

Here is how GADGETS adds tooltip support for the combo box in its toolbar:

```
TOOLINFO ti ;
ZeroMemory (&ti, sizeof (TOOLINFO)) ;
ti.cbSize = sizeof (TOOLINFO) ;
ti.uFlags = TTF_IDISHWND | TTF_CENTERTIP | TTF_SUBCLASS ;
ti.hwnd   = hwndToolBar ;
ti.uId    = (UINT) (HWND) hwndComboBox ;
ti.lpszText = LPSTR_TEXTCALLBACK ;
bSuccess = ToolTip_AddTool (hwndTT, &ti) ;
```

One point worth mentioning about combo boxes is that they are a combination of two or more controls: the combo box container, an edit or static control, and a list box. To provide complete tooltip support, the visible components should be added to the tooltip's list of tools. GADGETS adds tooltip support for the edit control, as follows:

```
// Add tooltip for combo box's edit control
hwndEdit = GetWindow (hwndComboBox, GW_CHILD) ;
ti.cbSize = sizeof (TOOLINFO) ;
ti.uFlags = TTF_IDISHWND | TTF_CENTERTIP | TTF_SUBCLASS ;
ti.hwnd   = hwndToolBar ;
ti.uId    = (UINT) (HWND) hwndEdit ;
ti.lpszText = LPSTR_TEXTCALLBACK ;
bSuccess = ToolTip_AddTool (hwndTT, &ti) ;
```

Once a tooltip control knows about a child window, the tooltip appears when the mouse pauses over the child window for a moment. There's a bit of magic to this detection, made possible by a subclass procedure requested with the TTF_SUBCLASS flag. The subclass procedure watches for mouse messages—and when it detects one, it sends a TTM_RELAYEVENT message to the tooltip.

If for some reason you decide not to use the subclass technique—perhaps because it interferes with subclassing already being performed—there are several alternative approaches to take. You can modify the window procedure of the child control and simply forward a TTM_RELAYEVENT message on receipt of a mouse message. You can also add a WH_GETMESSAGE hook to look for mouse messages for your specific window. Perhaps the easiest alternative is to add a tiny piece of code to your program's message loop. As the primary gateway for mouse (along with keyboard, timer, and paint) messages to enter a program, it's a good choice when the TTF_SUBCLASS flag doesn't meet your needs. Here's what GADGETS' message loop would look like if it didn't use this flag:

```
while (GetMessage (&msg, NULL, 0, 0))
    {
    if (pMsg->hwnd == hwndCombo || pMsg->hwnd == hwndEdit)
        {
        if (pMsg->message >= WM_MOUSEFIRST &&
            pMsg->message <= WM_MOUSELAST)
            {
            ToolTip_RelayEvent (hwndTT, pMsg) ;
            }
        }

    TranslateMessage (&msg) ;
    DispatchMessage (&msg) ;
    }
```

Customizing a toolbar

Toolbars are modifiable at run time by end users. The primary mechanism for doing this is the Customize Toolbar dialog box, shown in figure 12-6. This dialog shows two lists: one of available buttons and one of the buttons currently on the toolbar. Users can click on the Add and Remove buttons to move items between the two lists. In addition, both list boxes are drag list boxes so that a user can pick up and drag objects within a list or from one list to the other. Summon this dialog box by sending a TB_CUSTOMIZE message to a toolbar.

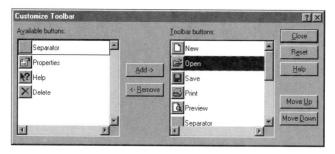

Figure 12-6. *The Customize Toolbar dialog box.*

Two style flags provide access to a toolbar's features via mouse input. A toolbar created with the CCS_ADJUSTABLE flag displays the customization dialog in response to a double-click on the body of the toolbar. (This flag is not required to summon the customization dialog under program control; as noted in the previous paragraph, simply send the TB_CUSTOMIZE message.) In addition, users can move buttons on a toolbar by picking them up with a Shift-Click and dropping them at a different location on the toolbar. Users can delete buttons by clicking them and dragging them off the toolbar. The TBSTYLE_ALTDRAG flag modifies button dragging to begin with the Alt-Click (as is done with Microsoft Word for Windows) instead of Shift-Click.

The key to toolbar customization is proper handling of the associated notification messages. Even before the customization dialog shows itself, it sends three initial types of queries: TBN_QUERYINSERT, TBN_QUERYDELETE, and TBN_GETBUTTONINFO. The associated notification messages are summarized in the following table:

Toolbar Customization Notification	*Description*
TBN_BEGINADJUST and TBN_ENDADJUST	The life of the customize dialog is bracketed between these two notifications.
TBN_QUERYINSERT	Asks whether it's okay to insert a button at a specified position. When the customize dialog first starts, reply TRUE; otherwise, the dialog disappears.
TBN_QUERYDELETE	Asks whether it's okay to delete a button. Reply TRUE for "yes" and FALSE for "no."
TBN_GETBUTTONINFO	A series of these messages asks for information about all buttons that can be displayed in the toolbar. Those currently not on the toolbar are put on a list of available buttons.
TBN_TOOLBARCHANGE	Toolbar buttons have been moved, deleted, or inserted.
TBN_RESET	User has clicked Reset button on customization dialog.
TBN_CUSTHELP	User has clicked Help button on customization dialog.

The TBN_QUERYINSERT notification asks whether any new button can be inserted into the toolbar. If the answer is "no" (a return value of zero or FALSE), the dialog briefly flashes on screen and disappears, which can be disturbing to a user. To ensure that the customization dialog box sticks around, then, you need to respond to this first query with a "yes" (non-zero or TRUE) reply:

```
case WM_NOTIFY :
    {
    LPNMHDR pnmh = (LPNMHDR) lParam ;

    // Allow toolbar to be customized
    if (pnmh->code == TBN_QUERYINSERT)
        {
        return 1 ;
        }
```

A set of TBN_QUERYDELETE notifications—one per toolbar button—are sent, asking whether individual buttons can be deleted or not. The reply causes enabling and disabling of the Remove push button: TRUE allows a toolbar button to be deleted, and FALSE prevents it from being deleted.

A series of TBN_GETBUTTONINFO notifications provide the toolbar's parent a chance to identify all the buttons that could possibly reside in the toolbar. For each request, you provide a TBBUTTON description of possible buttons along with a string that describes the button in the Customize Toolbar dialog box list box. A return of TRUE means that you've filled in the structure and want to receive this notification again. A return of FALSE indicates there are no more buttons. The results of this query fill the "Available buttons" list box, but only buttons currently not in the toolbar will actually appear on this list. Here's the long way to reply to this message for two buttons:

```
LPTBNOTIFY ptbn = (LPTBNOTIFY) lParam ;
switch (ptbn->iItem)
    {
    case 0 :
        lstrcpy (ptbn->pszText, "Help") ;
        ptbn->tbButton.iBitmap = STD_HELP ;
        ptbn->tbButton.idCommand = 11 ;
        ptbn->tbButton.fsState = TBSTATE_ENABLED ;
        ptbn->tbButton.fsStyle = TBSTYLE_BUTTON ;
        ptbn->tbButton.dwData = 0 ;
        ptbn->tbButton.iString = 10 ;
        return 1 ;
    case 1 :
        lstrcpy (ptbn->pszText, "Delete") ;
        ptbn->tbButton.iBitmap = STD_DELETE ;
        ptbn->tbButton.idCommand = 12 ;
        ptbn->tbButton.fsState = TBSTATE_ENABLED ;
        ptbn->tbButton.fsStyle = TBSTYLE_BUTTON ;
        ptbn->tbButton.dwData = 0 ;
        ptbn->tbButton.iString = 11 ;
        return 1 ;
    default :
        return 0 ;
    }
```

Since you've probably already got an array of TBBUTTONs, the quicker way to reply to this message is to use *memcpy* to copy a TBBUTTON for each notification received. Here's how GADGETS handles this:

```
lstrcpy (ptbn->pszText, GetString (ptbn->iItem)) ;
memcpy (&ptbn->tbButton, &tbb[iButton], sizeof (TBBUTTON)) ;
```

Status Bars

Status bars are output-only windows often residing at the bottom of a program's main window. The most common use of a status bar is to provide helpful tips as a user browses menu items—like a waiter providing pithy comments on this or that selection on a restaurant menu. When a menu is not being browsed, programs often display supplementary program information in the status bar. Details like the state of shift keys—Caps Lock, Num Lock, and Scroll Lock—are often displayed, along with program-specific information like the current page, line, or column in a word processing program.

The common control status bar is bimodal, so it is able to handle the two basic uses of a status bar—menu item description and other program status information—with a minimum of conflict. In menu description mode ("simple mode"), the status bar becomes a raised bar to display a single text line. In program status mode, the status bar displays one or more text panes, each of which is called a status bar "part." Individual status bar parts can be created as recessed, pop out, or borderless. In addition, you can add child windows (such as a clock window or a progress bar window) to a status bar. When switching between simple mode and non-simple mode, the status bar stores one set of hidden panes while displaying one set of visible panes.

Creating a status bar

The simplest way to create a status bar is to call *CreateStatusWindow*:

```
hwndStatusBar = CreateStatusWindow (WS_CHILD |
                    WS_VISIBLE |
                    WS_CLIPSIBLINGS |
                    CCS_BOTTOM,
                    "Ready",
                    hwndParent,
                    2) ;
```

This function calls *CreateWindow* to create a child window with *hwndParent* as its parent window, with window text of "Ready" (which the status bar displays in its first pane), a child ID of 2, and window style flags as defined in the first parameter.

The table on the following page summarizes style flags that can be used to fine-tune a status bar. You'll probably always use SBARS_SIZEGRIP, since it creates the diagonal hatch grip that users expect. The rest of the style flags modify the initial size or location of a status bar so that it can reside somewhere other than the default CCS_BOTTOM, which puts a status bar at the bottom of its parent window's client area.

Category	Style Flag	Description
Appearance	SBARS_SIZEGRIP	Display diagonal hatch grip on right side of status bar to suggest "resize by grabbing here" feature.
Initial location	CCS_TOP	Place status bar at top of parent window.
	CCS_BOTTOM	Place status bar at bottom of parent window (the default).
	CCS_NOMOVEY	Disable moving along y-axis.
Disable auto-move/auto-size	CCS_NOPARENTALIGN	Status bar only sets its own height (cy). It doesn't set its own location (x, y) or width (cx). To handle properly, post a message to resize after creation.
	CCS_NORESIZE	Disables all auto-move and auto-size features, and disables CCS_TOP, CCS_BOTTOM, CCS_NOMOVEY, CCS_NOPARENTALIGN. You must explicitly move and size the status bar.

Moving and sizing a status bar

When a status bar's parent window changes size (when the parent gets a WM_SIZE message), the status bar must be moved and resized to stay at the bottom of its parent's client area. While the toolbar common control (discussed earlier in this chapter) resizes itself in response to the TB_AUTOSIZE message, no equivalent exists for status bars. Instead, you must provide some code like the following:

```
case WM_SIZE :
    {
    int cxParent = LOWORD (lParam) ;
    int cyParent = HIWORD (lParam) ;
    int x, y, cx, cy ;
    RECT rWindow ;

    // Keep status window height the same
    GetWindowRect (hwndStatusBar, &rWindow) ;
    cy = rWindow.bottom - rWindow.top ;

    x = 0 ;
    y = cyParent - cy ;
    cx = cxParent ;
    MoveWindow (hwndStatusBar, x, y, cx, cy, TRUE) ;
    }
```

This code keeps the height of the status bar the same and modifies its width and location to appropriately cover the expected area of its parent.

Supporting menu browsing

Users expect Windows programs to display helpful status bar text as menus are browsed to determine which menu item provides some needed service. Even a casual Windows user quickly learns that one-word menu item names hide more than they reveal. And while experienced users readily understand the role of standard menu commands, they'll still get stuck on trying to make sense of program-specific menu items.

A window's menu sends a WM_MENUSELECT message as a user browses the items in a menu and—as was discussed in Chapter 10—a WM_COMMAND message when a specific menu item is actually chosen. To support the display of helpful menu hints, you respond to the first of these, the WM_MENUSELECT message.

To simplify the process of handling this message and displaying text in a status bar, the common control library provides the *MenuHelp* routine. This routine assumes the presence of menu help text in a string table and a data structure to cross-reference menu items to string table IDs. The *MenuHelp* routine is defined as follows:

```
void MenuHelp (UINT      uMsg,        // WM_MENUSELECT
               WPARAM     wParam,      // wParam parameter
               LPARAM     lParam,      // lParam parameter
               HMENU      hMainMenu,   // Main menu handle
               HINSTANCE  hInst,       // Instance handle
               HWND       hwndStatus,  // Status bar handle
               UINT FAR   *lpwIDs) ;   // String table array
```

The first parameter, *uMsg*, must be WM_MENUSELECT, although the presence of this parameter (and notes in the Win32 documentation) suggest that help handling the WM_COMMAND message was contemplated when this routine was designed. Pass the *wParam* and *lParam* window procedure parameters as the second and third parameters. Taken together, these three parameters describe which part of the menu system a user is browsing and whether it's a menu item, popup menu, or system menu.

The sixth parameter, *hwndStatus*, is a handle to the status bar window. The *MenuHelp* function sends a control-specific message, SB_SIMPLE, to set the status bar to one-pane (request simple) mode and to display the appropriate text. Later, when the user quits browsing, *MenuHelp* sends another SB_SIMPLE message to return the status bar to multipane (nonsimple) mode.

MenuHelp uses the other three parameters—*hMainMenu*, *hInst*, and *lpwIDs*—to determine which string to display as different menu items are browsed. The *hInst* parameter identifies the module—which could be a DLL's instance handle or the currently running program's instance handle—that owns the string table containing menu strings (which, as you might expect, get loaded with a call to *LoadString*).

The trick to getting *MenuHelp* to work properly is sending the right value for the fourth and seventh parameters: *hMainMenu* and *lpwIDs*. Setting this up and getting it right is a bit tricky because there are three kinds of items to consider: menu commands, popup menus, and the system menu. Another complication is that the Win32 documentation suggests that *lpwIDs* is an array that *MenuHelp* searches; while it makes sense to use an array to store string resource base values, you'll have to parse the array yourself because the *MenuHelp* function does not do it for you.

Browsing menu items

The *MenuHelp* function calculates the resource string ID for a menu item by adding the command ID value (obtained from the low word of *wParam*) to the value referenced by *lpwIDs*. For example, the following call to *MenuHelp* displays string resource number 125 in the status bar:

```
UINT uiStringBase = 100 ;
WPARAM wParam = 25 ;
MenuHelp (WM_MENUSELECT, wParam, lParam, NULL,
          hInst, hwndStatus, &uiStringBase) ;
```

As this example shows, the menu handle value—*hMainMenu*—can be NULL for the display of menu command items since *MenuHelp* doesn't use this value in its calculations.

The simplest way to match menu command items to resource strings is to assign both the same values. That allows you to set the string base value to zero and ignore it.

Browsing popup menu items

For popup menus, the *MenuHelp* function calculates the status bar resource string by adding the zero-based index of the popup menu to the value referenced by the *lpwIDs* parameter. For this to work properly, *MenuHelp*'s fourth parameter—*hMainMenu*—must be the handle to the popup menu's parent. A structure like the following one provides a convenient way to map menu handles to a resource string base:

```
typedef struct tagPOPUPSTRING
    {
    HMENU hMenu ;
    UINT  uiString ;
    } POPUPSTRING ;
```

In the GADGETS program, in which three menus contain popup menus, this data structure is defined as:

```
POPUPSTRING popstr[5] ;
```

and is initialized at status bar creation time as follows:

```
HMENU hMainMenu = GetMenu (hwndParent) ;
popstr[0].hMenu    = hMainMenu ;
popstr[0].uiString = IDS_MAIN_MENU ;
```

```
popstr[1].hMenu    = GetSubMenu (hMainMenu, 2) ;
popstr[1].uiString = IDS_TOOLBAR_MENU ;
popstr[2].hMenu    = GetSubMenu (hMainMenu, 3) ;
popstr[2].uiString = IDS_STATUSBAR_MENU ;
popstr[3].hMenu    = NULL ;
popstr[3].uiString = 0 ;
```

On receipt of a WM_MENUSELECT message, the *lParam* parameter contains the parent menu handle. Getting *MenuHelp* to fetch the correct string resource involves searching the array yourself and passing the address as *MenuHelp*'s last parameter. Here's how GADGETS performs this:

```
if ((fuFlags & MF_POPUP) &&
    (!(fuFlags & MF_SYSMENU)))
    {
    for (iMenu = 1 ; iMenu < MAX_MENUS ; iMenu++)
        {
        if ((HMENU) lParam == popstr[iMenu].hMenu)
            {
            hMainMenu = (HMENU) lParam ;
            break ;
            }
        }
    }
```

For this to work properly, *hMainMenu* must be set as the handle of the popup menu's parent menu. While we're interested in handling our own popup menus, we expressly exclude handling for the system menu.

Browsing the system menu

The *MenuHelp* function provides helpful status bar text for the system menu and system menu items. All it requires is the *wParam* and *lParam* parameters from the WM_MENUSELECT message, just as they are passed for the other types of menu items. Also, the value of *hMainMenu* must be a value besides the actual system menu handle; NULL works just fine.

Example

Putting all the pieces together for menu items, popup menus, and the system menu, here's how GADGETS handles the WM_MENUSELECT message for proper display of helpful status bar text:

```
LRESULT
Statusbar_MenuSelect (HWND hwnd, WPARAM wParam, LPARAM lParam)
    {
    UINT fuFlags = (UINT) HIWORD (wParam) ;
    HMENU hMainMenu = NULL ;
    int iMenu = 0 ;
```

(continued)

```
// Handle non-system popup menu descriptions
if ((fuFlags & MF_POPUP) &&
    (!(fuFlags & MF_SYSMENU)))
    {
    for (iMenu = 1 ; iMenu < MAX_MENUS ; iMenu++)
        {
        if ((HMENU) lParam == popstr[iMenu].hMenu)
            {
            hMainMenu = (HMENU) lParam ;
            break ;
            }
        }
    }

// Display helpful text in status bar
MenuHelp (WM_MENUSELECT, wParam, lParam, hMainMenu, hInst,
          hwndStatusBar, &((UINT) popstr[iMenu].hMenu)) ;

return 0 ;
}
```

The GADGETS Program

The GADGETS sample program pulls together the three controls discussed: toolbars, tooltips, and status bars. As shown in Figure 12-7, GADGETS has a toolbar with a combo box, and a status bar with a sizing grip. It also has a client window that contains a list box for the display of all notification codes received for each of these three controls. To help make sense of the different styles for toolbars and status bars, GADGETS lets you enable and disable these style flags to show the immediate effect of each style flag. Figure 12-8 shows the GADGETS source files.

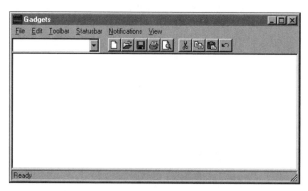

Figure 12-7. *The GADGETS display.*

GADGETS.MAK

```
#----------------------
# GADGETS.MAK make file
#----------------------

gadgets.exe : gadgets.obj notifdef.obj statbar.obj \
              toolbar.obj tooltip.obj gadgets.res
    $(LINKER) $(GUIFLAGS) -OUT:gadgets.exe gadgets.obj \
    notifdef.obj statbar.obj toolbar.obj tooltip.obj \
    gadgets.res $(GUILIBS)

gadgets.obj : gadgets.c comcthlp.h gadgets.h
    $(CC) $(CFLAGS) gadgets.c

notifdef.obj : notifdef.c notifdef.h
    $(CC) $(CFLAGS) notifdef.c

statbar.obj : statbar.c comcthlp.h gadgets.h
    $(CC) $(CFLAGS) statbar.c

toolbar.obj : toolbar.c comcthlp.h gadgets.h notifdef.h
    $(CC) $(CFLAGS) toolbar.c

tooltip.obj : tooltip.c comcthlp.h gadgets.h notifdef.h
    $(CC) $(CFLAGS) tooltip.c

gadgets.res : gadgets.rc gadgets.ico
    $(RC) $(RCVARS) gadgets.rc
```

GADGETS.H

```
// Resource definitions
#define IDM_FILE_NEW            100     // -- Menu commands --
#define IDM_FILE_OPEN           101
#define IDM_FILE_SAVE           102
#define IDM_FILE_SAVEAS         103
#define IDM_FILE_PRINT          104
#define IDM_FILE_PREVIEW        105
#define IDM_FILE_EXIT           106
#define IDM_EDIT_UNDO           200
#define IDM_EDIT_CUT            201
#define IDM_EDIT_COPY           202
#define IDM_EDIT_PASTE          203
```

Figure 12-8. *The GADGETS source files.*   *(continued)*

```
#define IDM_EDIT_PROP                   204
#define IDM_TB_HELP                     250
#define IDM_TB_DELETE                   251
#define IDM_IGNORESIZE                  300
#define IDM_STRINGS                     301
#define IDM_LARGEICONS                  302
#define IDM_SMALLICONS                  303
#define IDM_NODIVIDER                   400
#define IDM_WRAPABLE                    401
#define IDM_TOP                         402
#define IDM_BOTTOM                      403
#define IDM_NOMOVEY                     404
#define IDM_NOPARENTALIGN               405
#define IDM_NORESIZE                    406
#define IDM_ADJUSTABLE                  407
#define IDM_ALTDRAG                     408
#define IDM_TOOLTIPS                    409
#define IDM_TB_CHECK                    500
#define IDM_TB_ENABLE                   501
#define IDM_TB_HIDE                     502
#define IDM_TB_INDETERMINATE            503
#define IDM_TB_PRESS                    504
#define IDM_TB_BUTTONCOUNT              505
#define IDM_TB_GETROWS                  506
#define IDM_TB_CUSTOMIZE                507
#define IDM_STAT_IGNORESIZE             600
#define IDM_STAT_SIZEGRIP               700
#define IDM_STAT_TOP                    701
#define IDM_STAT_BOTTOM                 702
#define IDM_STAT_NOMOVEY                703
#define IDM_STAT_NOPARENTALIGN          704
#define IDM_STAT_NORESIZE               705
#define IDM_ST_GETBORDERS               800
#define IDM_ST_GETPARTS                 801
#define IDM_ST_SETTEXT                  802
#define IDM_ST_SIMPLE                   803
#define IDM_NOTIFICATIONS_CLEAR         900
#define IDM_VIEW_TOOLBAR                1000
#define IDM_VIEW_STATUS                 1001
#define IDM_VIEW_NOTIFICATIONS          1002
#define IDM_COMBOBOX                    4000
#define IDI_APP                         101    // -- Icons --
#define IDS_MAIN_MENU                   71     // -- Strings --
#define IDS_MAIN_MENU1                  72
#define IDS_MAIN_MENU2                  73
#define IDS_MAIN_MENU3                  74
```

(continued)

```
#define IDS_MAIN_MENU4                  75
#define IDS_MAIN_MENU5                  76
#define IDS_TOOLBAR_MENU                80
#define IDS_TOOLBAR_MENU1               81
#define IDS_TOOLBAR_MENU2               82
#define IDS_TOOLBAR_MENU3               83
#define IDS_STATUSBAR_MENU              90
#define IDS_STATUSBAR_MENU1             91
#define IDS_STATUSBAR_MENU2             92
#define IDS_STATUSBAR_MENU3             93


#define IDC_TB_COMBOBOX                 2000  // -- Toolbar combo box


// Toolbar functions
HWND InitToolBar (HWND hwndParent) ;
HWND RebuildToolBar (HWND hwndParent, WORD wFlag) ;
void ToolBarMessage (HWND hwndTB, WORD wMsg) ;
LRESULT ToolBarNotify (HWND hwnd, WPARAM wParam, LPARAM lParam) ;


// Tooltip functions
BOOL InitToolTip (HWND hwndToolBar, HWND hwndComboBox) ;
BOOL RelayToolTipMessage (LPMSG pMsg) ;
void CopyToolTipText (LPTOOLTIPTEXT lpttt) ;


// Status bar functions
HWND InitStatusBar (HWND hwndParent) ;
HWND RebuildStatusBar (HWND hwndParent, WORD wFlag) ;
void StatusBarMessage (HWND hwndSB, WORD wMsg) ;
LRESULT Statusbar_MenuSelect (HWND, WPARAM, LPARAM) ;


// Notification window functions
HWND ViewNotificationsToggle (HWND hwnd) ;
void DisplayNotificationDetails (WPARAM wParam, LPARAM lParam) ;
void ClearNotificationList () ;
```

NOTIFDEF.H

```
typedef struct tagCONTROLNOTIFICATIONS
    {
    UINT  nCode ;
    LPSTR pName ;
    } CONTROLNOTIFICATIONS ;


BOOL QueryNotifyText (UINT nNotifyCode, LPSTR *pName) ;
void DisplayText (LPSTR pText) ;
```

(continued)

GADGETS.C

```
/*-----------------------------------------
    GADGETS.C -- Gadgets for a frame window
                 (c) Paul Yao, 1996
    -----------------------------------------*/
#include <windows.h>
#include <windowsx.h>
#include <commctrl.h>
#include "comcthlp.h"
#include "gadgets.h"

LRESULT CALLBACK WndProc (HWND, UINT, WPARAM, LPARAM) ;
LRESULT CALLBACK ClientWndProc (HWND, UINT, WPARAM, LPARAM) ;

char szAppName[]  = "Gadgets" ;
BOOL bIgnoreSize = FALSE ;
HINSTANCE hInst ;
HWND hwndClient = NULL ;
HWND hwndToolBar = NULL ;
HWND hwndStatusBar = NULL ;
HWND hwndNotify = NULL ;

extern DWORD dwToolBarStyles ;
extern BOOL bStrings ;
extern BOOL bLargeIcons ;
extern BOOL bComboBox ;
extern DWORD dwStatusBarStyles ;
extern int cyToolBar ;

//------------------------------------------------------------------
int WINAPI WinMain (HINSTANCE hInstance, HINSTANCE hPrevInstance,
                    PSTR lpszCmdLine, int cmdShow)
    {
    HWND        hwnd ;
    MSG         msg ;
    WNDCLASSEX  wc ;

    hInst = hInstance ;

    wc.cbSize        = sizeof (wc) ;
    wc.lpszClassName = szAppName ;
    wc.hInstance     = hInstance ;
    wc.lpfnWndProc   = WndProc ;
    wc.hCursor       = LoadCursor (NULL, IDC_ARROW) ;
    wc.hIcon         = LoadIcon (hInst, MAKEINTRESOURCE (IDI_APP)) ;
    wc.lpszMenuName  = "MAIN" ;
```

(continued)

```
       wc.hbrBackground = (HBRUSH) (COLOR_WINDOW + 1) ;
       wc.style         = 0 ;
       wc.cbClsExtra    = 0 ;
       wc.cbWndExtra    = 0 ;
       wc.hIconSm       = LoadIcon (hInst, MAKEINTRESOURCE (IDI_APP)) ;


       RegisterClassEx (&wc) ;

       wc.lpszClassName = "ClientWndProc" ;
       wc.hInstance     = hInstance ;
       wc.lpfnWndProc   = ClientWndProc ;
       wc.hCursor       = LoadCursor (NULL, IDC_ARROW) ;
       wc.hIcon         = LoadIcon (NULL, IDI_APPLICATION) ;
       wc.lpszMenuName  = NULL ;
       wc.hbrBackground = (HBRUSH) (COLOR_WINDOW + 1) ;
       wc.style         = 0 ;
       wc.cbClsExtra    = 0 ;
       wc.cbWndExtra    = 0 ;
       wc.hIconSm       = LoadIcon (NULL, IDI_APPLICATION) ;


       RegisterClassEx (&wc) ;

       hwnd = CreateWindowEx (0L,
                             szAppName, szAppName,
                             WS_OVERLAPPEDWINDOW,
                             CW_USEDEFAULT, CW_USEDEFAULT,
                             CW_USEDEFAULT, CW_USEDEFAULT,
                             NULL, NULL, hInstance, NULL) ;
       ShowWindow (hwnd, cmdShow) ;
       UpdateWindow (hwnd) ;

       InitCommonControls () ;

       while (GetMessage (&msg, NULL, 0, 0))
            {
            TranslateMessage (&msg) ;
            DispatchMessage (&msg) ;
            }
       return msg.wParam ;
       }

//-------------------------------------------------------------------
void MenuCheckMark (HMENU hmenu, int id, BOOL bCheck)
     {
     int iState ;
     iState = (bCheck) ? MF_CHECKED : MF_UNCHECKED ;
```

(continued)

```
        CheckMenuItem (hmenu, id, iState) ;
        }


//-----------------------------------------------------------------
LRESULT CALLBACK
WndProc (HWND hwnd, UINT mMsg, WPARAM wParam, LPARAM lParam)
    {
    switch (mMsg)
        {
        case WM_CREATE :
            {
            // Create toolbar (source resides in toolbar.c)
            hwndToolBar = InitToolBar (hwnd) ;

            // Create status bar (source resides in statbar.c)
            hwndStatusBar = InitStatusBar (hwnd) ;

            // Create client window (contains notify list)
            hwndClient = CreateWindowEx (WS_EX_CLIENTEDGE,
                            "ClientWndProc", NULL,
                            WS_CHILD ¦ WS_VISIBLE, 0, 0, 0, 0,
                            hwnd, (HMENU) 4, hInst, NULL) ;

            return 0 ;
            }

        case WM_COMMAND :
            {
            // Toolbar button commands
            if (LOWORD (wParam) < 300)
                {
                char ach[80] ;
                wsprintf (ach, "Got Command (%d)", wParam) ;
                MessageBox (hwnd, ach, szAppName, MB_OK) ;
                break ;
                }

            // Menu item commands
            switch (LOWORD (wParam))
                {
                // Toolbar settings
                case IDM_STRINGS :
                case IDM_LARGEICONS :
                case IDM_SMALLICONS :
                case IDM_NODIVIDER :
                case IDM_WRAPABLE :
                case IDM_TOP :
                case IDM_BOTTOM :
```

(continued)

```
        case IDM_NOMOVEY :
        case IDM_NOPARENTALIGN :
        case IDM_NORESIZE :
        case IDM_ADJUSTABLE :
        case IDM_ALTDRAG :
        case IDM_TOOLTIPS :
        case IDM_COMBOBOX :
             DestroyWindow (hwndToolBar) ;
             hwndToolBar = RebuildToolBar (hwnd,
                                            LOWORD (wParam)) ;

             break ;

        // Toolbar messages
        case IDM_TB_CHECK :
        case IDM_TB_ENABLE :
        case IDM_TB_HIDE :
        case IDM_TB_INDETERMINATE :
        case IDM_TB_PRESS :
        case IDM_TB_BUTTONCOUNT :
        case IDM_TB_GETROWS :
        case IDM_TB_CUSTOMIZE :
             ToolBarMessage (hwndToolBar, LOWORD (wParam)) ;
             break ;

        // Status bar settings
        case IDM_STAT_SIZEGRIP :
        case IDM_STAT_TOP :
        case IDM_STAT_BOTTOM :
        case IDM_STAT_NOMOVEY :
        case IDM_STAT_NOPARENTALIGN :
        case IDM_STAT_NORESIZE :
             DestroyWindow (hwndStatusBar) ;
             hwndStatusBar =
                  RebuildStatusBar (hwnd, LOWORD (wParam)) ;
             break ;

        // Status bar messages
        case IDM_ST_GETBORDERS :
        case IDM_ST_GETPARTS :
        case IDM_ST_SETTEXT :
        case IDM_ST_SIMPLE :
             StatusBarMessage (hwndStatusBar, LOWORD (wParam)) ;
             break ;

        // Toggle display of toolbar
        case IDM_VIEW_TOOLBAR :
```

(continued)

```
            {
            RECT r ;

            if (hwndToolBar && IsWindowVisible (hwndToolBar))
                {
                ShowWindow (hwndToolBar, SW_HIDE) ;
                }
            else
                {
                ShowWindow (hwndToolBar, SW_SHOW) ;
                }

            // Resize other windows
            GetClientRect (hwnd, &r) ;
            PostMessage (hwnd, WM_SIZE, 0,
                        MAKELPARAM (r.right, r.bottom)) ;

            break ;
            }

      // Toggle display of status bar
      case IDM_VIEW_STATUS :
            {
            RECT r ;

            if (hwndStatusBar &&
                IsWindowVisible (hwndStatusBar))
                {
                ShowWindow (hwndStatusBar, SW_HIDE) ;
                }
            else
                {
                ShowWindow (hwndStatusBar, SW_SHOW) ;
                }

            // Resize other windows
            GetClientRect (hwnd, &r) ;
            PostMessage (hwnd, WM_SIZE, 0,
                        MAKELPARAM (r.right, r.bottom)) ;

            break ;
            }

      // Toggle display of notifications window
      case IDM_VIEW_NOTIFICATIONS :
            hwndNotify = ViewNotificationsToggle (hwndClient) ;
            break ;
```

(continued)

```
                    // Toggle ignore WM_SIZE to show auto-size/auto-move
                    case IDM_IGNORESIZE :
                    case IDM_STAT_IGNORESIZE :
                         {
                         RECT r ;

                         bIgnoreSize = !bIgnoreSize ;
                         if (bIgnoreSize)
                             {
                             ShowWindow (hwndClient, SW_HIDE) ;
                             }
                         else
                             {
                             ShowWindow (hwndClient, SW_SHOW) ;
                             GetClientRect (hwnd, &r) ;
                             PostMessage (hwnd, WM_SIZE, 0,
                                          MAKELPARAM (r.right, r.bottom)) ;
                             }
                         break ;
                         }

                    // Clear contents of notification window
                    case IDM_NOTIFICATIONS_CLEAR :
                         ClearNotificationList () ;
                         break ;
                    }

          return 0 ;
          }

     case WM_INITMENU :
          {
          BOOL bCheck ;
          HMENU hmenu = (HMENU) wParam ;

          MenuCheckMark (hmenu, IDM_IGNORESIZE, bIgnoreSize) ;
          MenuCheckMark (hmenu, IDM_STAT_IGNORESIZE, bIgnoreSize) ;

          // Toolbar menu items
          MenuCheckMark (hmenu, IDM_STRINGS, bStrings) ;
          MenuCheckMark (hmenu, IDM_LARGEICONS, bLargeIcons) ;
          MenuCheckMark (hmenu, IDM_SMALLICONS, !bLargeIcons) ;
          MenuCheckMark (hmenu, IDM_COMBOBOX, bComboBox) ;

          bCheck = (dwToolBarStyles & CCS_NODIVIDER) ;
          MenuCheckMark (hmenu, IDM_NODIVIDER, bCheck) ;
```

(continued)

```
                bCheck = (dwToolBarStyles & TBSTYLE_WRAPABLE) ;
                MenuCheckMark (hmenu, IDM_WRAPABLE, bCheck) ;

                bCheck = ((dwToolBarStyles & 3) == CCS_TOP) ;
                MenuCheckMark (hmenu, IDM_TOP, bCheck) ;

                bCheck = ((dwToolBarStyles & 3) == CCS_BOTTOM) ;
                MenuCheckMark (hmenu, IDM_BOTTOM, bCheck) ;

                bCheck = ((dwToolBarStyles & 3) == CCS_NOMOVEY) ;
                MenuCheckMark (hmenu, IDM_NOMOVEY, bCheck) ;

                bCheck = (dwToolBarStyles & CCS_NOPARENTALIGN) ;
                MenuCheckMark (hmenu, IDM_NOPARENTALIGN, bCheck) ;

                bCheck = (dwToolBarStyles & CCS_NORESIZE) ;
                MenuCheckMark (hmenu, IDM_NORESIZE, bCheck) ;

                bCheck = (dwToolBarStyles & CCS_ADJUSTABLE) ;
                MenuCheckMark (hmenu, IDM_ADJUSTABLE, bCheck) ;

                bCheck = (dwToolBarStyles & TBSTYLE_ALTDRAG) ;
                MenuCheckMark (hmenu, IDM_ALTDRAG, bCheck) ;

                bCheck = (dwToolBarStyles & TBSTYLE_TOOLTIPS) ;
                MenuCheckMark (hmenu, IDM_TOOLTIPS, bCheck) ;

                // Status bar menu items
                bCheck = (dwStatusBarStyles & SBARS_SIZEGRIP) ;
                MenuCheckMark (hmenu, IDM_STAT_SIZEGRIP, bCheck) ;

                bCheck = ((dwStatusBarStyles & 3) == CCS_TOP) ;
                MenuCheckMark (hmenu, IDM_STAT_TOP, bCheck) ;

                bCheck = ((dwStatusBarStyles & 3) == CCS_BOTTOM) ;
                MenuCheckMark (hmenu, IDM_STAT_BOTTOM, bCheck) ;

                bCheck = ((dwStatusBarStyles & 3) == CCS_NOMOVEY) ;
                MenuCheckMark (hmenu, IDM_STAT_NOMOVEY, bCheck) ;

                bCheck = (dwStatusBarStyles & CCS_NOPARENTALIGN) ;
                MenuCheckMark (hmenu, IDM_STAT_NOPARENTALIGN, bCheck) ;

                bCheck = (dwStatusBarStyles & CCS_NORESIZE) ;
                MenuCheckMark (hmenu, IDM_STAT_NORESIZE, bCheck) ;

                // View menu items
```

(continued)

```
        bCheck = IsWindowVisible (hwndToolBar) ;
        MenuCheckMark (hmenu, IDM_VIEW_TOOLBAR, bCheck) ;

        bCheck = IsWindowVisible (hwndStatusBar) ;
        MenuCheckMark (hmenu, IDM_VIEW_STATUS, bCheck) ;

        bCheck = (hwndNotify != NULL) ;
        MenuCheckMark (hmenu, IDM_VIEW_NOTIFICATIONS, bCheck) ;
        return 0 ;
        }

case WM_MENUSELECT :
     return Statusbar_MenuSelect (hwnd, wParam, lParam) ;

case WM_DESTROY :
     PostQuitMessage (0) ;
     return 0 ;

case WM_NOTIFY :
     {
     LPNMHDR pnmh = (LPNMHDR) lParam ;
     int idCtrl = (int) wParam ;

     // Display notification details in notify window
     DisplayNotificationDetails (wParam, lParam) ;

     // Toolbar notifications
     if ((pnmh->code >= TBN_LAST) &&
         (pnmh->code <= TBN_FIRST))
           {
           return ToolBarNotify (hwnd, wParam, lParam) ;
           }

     // Fetch tooltip text
     if (pnmh->code == TTN_NEEDTEXT)
           {
           LPTOOLTIPTEXT lpttt = (LPTOOLTIPTEXT) lParam ;
           CopyToolTipText (lpttt) ;
           }

     return 0 ;
     }

case WM_SIZE :
     {
     int cx = LOWORD (lParam) ;
```

(continued)

```
            int cy = HIWORD (lParam) ;
            int cyStatus ;
            int cyTB ;
            int x, y ;
            DWORD dwStyle ;
            RECT rWindow ;

            // Ignore size message to allow auto-move and auto-size
            //    features to be more clearly seen
            if (bIgnoreSize)
                return 0 ;

            // Adjust toolbar size
            if (IsWindowVisible (hwndToolBar))
                {
                dwStyle = GetWindowLong (hwndToolBar, GWL_STYLE) ;
                if (dwStyle & CCS_NORESIZE)
                    {
                    MoveWindow (hwndToolBar,
                                0, 0, cx, cyToolBar, FALSE) ;
                    }
                else
                    {
                    ToolBar_AutoSize (hwndToolBar) ;
                    }
                InvalidateRect (hwndToolBar, NULL, TRUE) ;
                GetWindowRect (hwndToolBar, &rWindow) ;
                ScreenToClient (hwnd, (LPPOINT) &rWindow.left) ;
                ScreenToClient (hwnd, (LPPOINT) &rWindow.right) ;
                cyTB = rWindow.bottom - rWindow.top ;
                }
            else
                {
                cyTB = 0 ;
                }

            // Adjust status bar size
            if (IsWindowVisible (hwndStatusBar))
                {
                GetWindowRect (hwndStatusBar, &rWindow) ;
                cyStatus = rWindow.bottom - rWindow.top ;
                MoveWindow (hwndStatusBar, 0, cy - cyStatus,
                                    cx, cyStatus, TRUE) ;
                }
            else
                {
                cyStatus = 0 ;
                }
```

(continued)

```
                    // Adjust client window size
                    x = 0 ;
                    y = cyTB ;
                    cy = cy - (cyStatus + cyTB) ;
                    MoveWindow (hwndClient, x, y, cx, cy, TRUE) ;
                    return 0 ;
                    }

          default :
               return (DefWindowProc (hwnd, mMsg, wParam, lParam)) ;
          }
     }

//------------------------------------------------------------------
LRESULT CALLBACK
ClientWndProc (HWND hwnd, UINT mMsg, WPARAM wParam, LPARAM lParam)
     {
     static COLORREF crBack ;
     static HBRUSH hbr ;

     switch (mMsg)
          {
          case WM_CREATE :
               hwndNotify = ViewNotificationsToggle (hwnd) ;
               crBack = GetSysColor (COLOR_APPWORKSPACE) ;
               hbr = CreateSolidBrush (crBack) ;
               return 0 ;

          case WM_DESTROY :
               DeleteObject (hbr) ;
               return 0 ;

          case WM_CTLCOLORLISTBOX :
                    {
                    DefWindowProc (hwnd, mMsg, wParam, lParam) ;
                    SetBkColor ((HDC) wParam, crBack) ;
                    SetBkMode ((HDC) wParam, TRANSPARENT) ;
                    return (LRESULT) (HBRUSH) hbr ;
                    }

          case WM_SIZE :
                    {
                    HWND hwndNotify = GetWindow (hwnd, GW_CHILD) ;
                    int cx = LOWORD (lParam) ;
                    int cy = HIWORD (lParam) ;
```

(continued)

645

```
                    // Ignore if notification window is absent
                    if (hwndNotify != NULL)
                        {
                        MoveWindow (hwndNotify, 0, 0, cx, cy, TRUE) ;
                        }

                    return 0 ;
                    }

          default :
               return (DefWindowProc (hwnd, mMsg, wParam, lParam)) ;
          }
     }
```

TOOLBAR.C

```
/*-----------------------------------------

   TOOLBAR.C -- Toolbar helper functions
                (c) Paul Yao, 1996
   -----------------------------------------*/
#include <windows.h>
#include <commctrl.h>
#include "comcthlp.h"
#include "gadgets.h"
#include "notifdef.h"


HWND hwndCombo ;
HWND hwndEdit ;
HWND hwndToolTip ;
HWND hwndTB ;

int cyToolBar ;

BOOL bComboBox   = FALSE ;
BOOL bStrings    = FALSE ;
BOOL bLargeIcons = FALSE ;

DWORD dwToolBarStyles = WS_CHILD | WS_VISIBLE | WS_CLIPSIBLINGS |
                        CCS_TOP | CCS_NODIVIDER | TBSTYLE_TOOLTIPS ;

extern HINSTANCE hInst ;

char szTbStrings[]  = "New\0Open\0Save\0Print\0Preview\0"
                      "Cut\0Copy\0Paste\0Undo\0Properties\0"
                      "Help\0Delete\0" ;
```

(continued)

```
TBBUTTON tbb[] =
   {
   0, 0, TBSTATE_ENABLED, TBSTYLE_SEP, 0, 0, 0, 0,
   0, 0, TBSTATE_ENABLED, TBSTYLE_SEP, 0, 0, 0, 0,
   0, 0, TBSTATE_ENABLED, TBSTYLE_SEP, 0, 0, 0, 0,
   0, 0, TBSTATE_ENABLED, TBSTYLE_SEP, 0, 0, 0, 0,
   0, 0, TBSTATE_ENABLED, TBSTYLE_SEP, 0, 0, 0, 0,
   0, 0, TBSTATE_ENABLED, TBSTYLE_SEP, 0, 0, 0, 0,
   0, 0, TBSTATE_ENABLED, TBSTYLE_SEP, 0, 0, 0, 0,
   0, 0, TBSTATE_ENABLED, TBSTYLE_SEP, 0, 0, 0, 0,
   0, 0, TBSTATE_ENABLED, TBSTYLE_SEP, 0, 0, 0, 0,
   0, 0, TBSTATE_ENABLED, TBSTYLE_SEP, 0, 0, 0, 0,
   0, 0, TBSTATE_ENABLED, TBSTYLE_SEP, 0, 0, 0, 0,
   0, 0, TBSTATE_ENABLED, TBSTYLE_SEP, 0, 0, 0, 0,
   0, 0, TBSTATE_ENABLED, TBSTYLE_SEP, 0, 0, 0, 0,
   0, 0, TBSTATE_ENABLED, TBSTYLE_SEP, 0, 0, 0, 0,
   0, 0, TBSTATE_ENABLED, TBSTYLE_SEP, 0, 0, 0, 0,
   0, 0, TBSTATE_ENABLED, TBSTYLE_SEP, 0, 0, 0, 0,
   0, 0, TBSTATE_ENABLED, TBSTYLE_SEP, 0, 0, 0, 0,
   0, 0, TBSTATE_ENABLED, TBSTYLE_SEP, 0, 0, 0, 0,
   0, 0, TBSTATE_ENABLED, TBSTYLE_SEP, 0, 0, 0, 0,
   0, 0, TBSTATE_ENABLED, TBSTYLE_SEP, 0, 0, 0, 0,
   STD_FILENEW, IDM_FILE_NEW, TBSTATE_ENABLED, TBSTYLE_BUTTON,
      0, 0, 0, 0,
   STD_FILEOPEN, IDM_FILE_OPEN, TBSTATE_ENABLED, TBSTYLE_BUTTON,
      0, 0, 0, 1,
   STD_FILESAVE, IDM_FILE_SAVE, TBSTATE_ENABLED, TBSTYLE_BUTTON,
      0, 0, 0, 2,
   STD_PRINT, IDM_FILE_PRINT, TBSTATE_ENABLED, TBSTYLE_BUTTON,
      0, 0, 0, 3,
   STD_PRINTPRE, IDM_FILE_PREVIEW, TBSTATE_ENABLED, TBSTYLE_CHECK,
      0, 0, 0, 4,

   0, 0, TBSTATE_ENABLED, TBSTYLE_SEP, 0, 0, 0, 0,

   STD_CUT, IDM_EDIT_CUT, TBSTATE_ENABLED, TBSTYLE_CHECKGROUP,
      0, 0, 0, 5,
   STD_COPY, IDM_EDIT_COPY, TBSTATE_ENABLED, TBSTYLE_CHECKGROUP,
      0, 0, 0, 6,
   STD_PASTE, IDM_EDIT_PASTE, TBSTATE_ENABLED, TBSTYLE_CHECKGROUP,
      0, 0, 0, 7,
   STD_UNDO, IDM_EDIT_UNDO, TBSTATE_ENABLED, TBSTYLE_BUTTON,
      0, 0, 0, 8,
   STD_PROPERTIES, IDM_EDIT_PROP, TBSTATE_ENABLED, TBSTYLE_CHECK,
      0, 0, 0, 9,
```

(continued)

```
            STD_HELP, IDM_TB_HELP, TBSTATE_ENABLED, TBSTYLE_BUTTON,
                0, 0, 0, 10,
            STD_DELETE, IDM_TB_DELETE, TBSTATE_ENABLED, TBSTYLE_BUTTON,
                0, 0, 0, 11,
            } ;

int nCust[] = { 21, 22, 23, 24, 25, 27, 28, 29, 30, 31, 32, 33, -1} ;

TBADDBITMAP tbStdLarge[] =
        {
        HINST_COMMCTRL, IDB_STD_LARGE_COLOR,
        } ;

TBADDBITMAP tbStdSmall[] =
        {
        HINST_COMMCTRL, IDB_STD_SMALL_COLOR,
        } ;

//-------------------------------------------------------------------
LPSTR GetString (int iString)
        {
        int i, cb ;
        LPSTR pString ;

        // Cycle through to requested string
        pString = szTbStrings ;
        for (i = 0 ; i < iString ; i++)
            {
            cb = lstrlen (pString) ;
            pString += (cb + 1) ;
            }

        return pString ;
        }

//-------------------------------------------------------------------
LRESULT ToolBarNotify (HWND hwnd, WPARAM wParam, LPARAM lParam)
        {
        LPNMHDR pnmh = (LPNMHDR) lParam ;
        int idCtrl = (int) wParam ;

        // Allow toolbar to be customized
        if ((pnmh->code == TBN_QUERYDELETE) ||
            (pnmh->code == TBN_QUERYINSERT))
            {
            return 1 ; // We always say "yes"
            }
```

(continued)

```
      // Provide details of allowable toolbar buttons
      if (pnmh->code == TBN_GETBUTTONINFO)
           {
           LPTBNOTIFY ptbn = (LPTBNOTIFY) lParam ;
           int iButton = nCust[ptbn->iItem] ;

           if (iButton != -1)
                {
                lstrcpy (ptbn->pszText, GetString (ptbn->iItem)) ;
                memcpy (&ptbn->tbButton, &tbb[iButton], sizeof (TBBUTTON)) ;
                return 1 ;
                }
           }

      return 0 ;
      }

//-------------------------------------------------------------------
HWND InitToolBar (HWND hwndParent)
      {
      int   iNumButtons ;
      LPTBBUTTON ptbb ;

      if (bComboBox)
           {
           ptbb = &tbb[0] ;
           iNumButtons = 31 ;
           }
      else
           {
           ptbb = &tbb[21] ;
           iNumButtons = 10 ;
           }

      UINT uiBitmap = (bLargeIcons) ? IDB_STD_LARGE_COLOR :
                                      IDB_STD_SMALL_COLOR ;
      hwndTB = CreateToolbarEx (hwndParent,
                   dwToolBarStyles,
                   1, 15,
                   HINST_COMMCTRL,
                   uiBitmap,
                   ptbb,
                   iNumButtons,
                   0, 0, 0, 0,
                   sizeof (TBBUTTON)) ;
```

(continued)

```
    // If requested, add to string list
    if (bStrings)
        ToolBar_AddString (hwndTB, 0, szTbStrings) ;

    // Store handle to tooltip control
    hwndToolTip = ToolBar_GetToolTips (hwndTB) ;

    // Insert combo box into toolbar
    if (bComboBox)
        {
        RECT r ;
        int x, y, cx, cy ;

        // Calculate coordinates for combo box
        ToolBar_GetItemRect (hwndTB, 0, &r) ;
        x = r.left ;
        y = r.top ;
        cy = 100 ;
        ToolBar_GetItemRect (hwndTB, 18, &r) ;
        cx = r.right - x + 1 ;

        hwndCombo = CreateWindow ("combobox",
                        NULL,
                        WS_CHILD | WS_VISIBLE |
                        CBS_DROPDOWN,
                        x, y, cx, cy,
                        hwndParent,
                        (HMENU) IDC_TB_COMBOBOX,
                        hInst,
                        0) ;

        // Set toolbar as combo box window parent
        SetParent (hwndCombo, hwndTB) ;

        SendMessage (hwndCombo, CB_ADDSTRING, 0, (LPARAM) "One") ;
        SendMessage (hwndCombo, CB_ADDSTRING, 0, (LPARAM) "Two") ;
        SendMessage (hwndCombo, CB_ADDSTRING, 0, (LPARAM) "Three") ;

        // Calculate toolbar height
        GetWindowRect (hwndCombo, &r) ;
        cyToolBar = r.bottom - r.top + 1 ;
        cyToolBar += y ;
        cyToolBar += (2 * GetSystemMetrics (SM_CYBORDER)) ;
        ToolBar_GetItemRect (hwndTB, 0, &r) ;
        cyToolBar = max (cyToolBar, r.bottom + 5) ;
```

(continued)

```
                // If toolbar has tooltips, initialize
                if (dwToolBarStyles & TBSTYLE_TOOLTIPS)
                    InitToolTip (hwndTB, hwndCombo) ;
            }

        return hwndTB ;
        }

//-------------------------------------------------------------------
void static FlipStyleFlag (LPDWORD dwStyle, DWORD flag)
        {
        if (*dwStyle & flag)  // Flag on -- turn off
            {
            *dwStyle &= (~flag) ;
            }
        else                  // Flag off -- turn on
            {
            *dwStyle != flag ;
            }
        }

//-------------------------------------------------------------------
HWND RebuildToolBar (HWND hwndParent, WORD wFlag)
        {
        HWND hwndTB ;
        RECT r ;

        switch (wFlag)
            {
            case IDM_STRINGS :
                bStrings = !bStrings ;
                break ;

            case IDM_LARGEICONS :
                bLargeIcons = TRUE ;
                break ;

            case IDM_SMALLICONS :
                bLargeIcons = FALSE ;
                break ;

            case IDM_NODIVIDER :
                FlipStyleFlag (&dwToolBarStyles, CCS_NODIVIDER) ;
                break ;
```

(continued)

```
        case IDM_WRAPABLE :
            FlipStyleFlag (&dwToolBarStyles, TBSTYLE_WRAPABLE) ;
            break ;

        case IDM_TOP :
            dwToolBarStyles &= 0xFFFFFFFC ;
            dwToolBarStyles != CCS_TOP ;
            break ;

        case IDM_BOTTOM :
            dwToolBarStyles &= 0xFFFFFFFC ;
            dwToolBarStyles != CCS_BOTTOM ;
            break ;

        case IDM_NOMOVEY :
            dwToolBarStyles &= 0xFFFFFFFC ;
            dwToolBarStyles != CCS_NOMOVEY ;
            break ;

        case IDM_NOPARENTALIGN :
            FlipStyleFlag (&dwToolBarStyles, CCS_NOPARENTALIGN) ;
            break ;

        case IDM_NORESIZE :
            FlipStyleFlag (&dwToolBarStyles, CCS_NORESIZE) ;
            break ;

        case IDM_ADJUSTABLE :
            FlipStyleFlag (&dwToolBarStyles, CCS_ADJUSTABLE) ;
            break ;

        case IDM_ALTDRAG :
            FlipStyleFlag (&dwToolBarStyles, TBSTYLE_ALTDRAG) ;
            break ;

        case IDM_TOOLTIPS :
            FlipStyleFlag (&dwToolBarStyles, TBSTYLE_TOOLTIPS) ;
            break ;

        case IDM_COMBOBOX :
            bComboBox = (!bComboBox) ;
        }

    hwndTB = InitToolBar (hwndParent) ;
```

(continued)

```
        // Post parent a WM_SIZE message to resize children
        GetClientRect (hwndParent, &r) ;
        PostMessage (hwndParent, WM_SIZE, 0,
                     MAKELPARAM (r.right, r.bottom)) ;


        return hwndTB ;
        }



//-------------------------------------------------------------------
void ToolBarMessage (HWND hwndTB, WORD wMsg)
        {
        switch (wMsg)
             {
             case IDM_TB_CHECK :
                  {
                  int nState = ToolBar_GetState (hwndTB, 1) ;
                  BOOL bCheck = (!(nState & TBSTATE_CHECKED)) ;
                  ToolBar_CheckButton (hwndTB, 1, bCheck) ;
                  break ;
                  }

             case IDM_TB_ENABLE :
                  {
                  int nState = ToolBar_GetState (hwndTB, 2) ;
                  BOOL bEnabled = (!(nState & TBSTATE_ENABLED)) ;
                  ToolBar_EnableButton (hwndTB, 2, bEnabled) ;
                  break ;
                  }

             case IDM_TB_HIDE :
                  {
                  int nState = ToolBar_GetState (hwndTB, 3) ;
                  BOOL bShow = (!(nState & TBSTATE_HIDDEN)) ;
                  ToolBar_HideButton (hwndTB, 3, bShow) ;
                  break ;
                  }

             case IDM_TB_INDETERMINATE :
                  {
                  int nState = ToolBar_GetState (hwndTB, 4) ;
                  BOOL bInd = (!(nState & TBSTATE_INDETERMINATE)) ;
                  ToolBar_Indeterminate (hwndTB, 4, bInd) ;
                  break ;
                  }
```

(continued)

```
        case IDM_TB_PRESS :
            {
            int nState = ToolBar_GetState (hwndTB, 5) ;
            BOOL bPress = (!(nState & TBSTATE_PRESSED)) ;
            ToolBar_PressButton (hwndTB, 5, bPress) ;
            break ;
            }

        case IDM_TB_BUTTONCOUNT :
            {
            int nButtons = ToolBar_ButtonCount (hwndTB) ;
            char ach[80] ;
            wsprintf (ach, "Button Count = %d", nButtons) ;
            MessageBox (GetParent (hwndTB), ach,
                        "TB_BUTTONCOUNT", MB_OK) ;
            break ;
            }

        case IDM_TB_GETROWS :
            {
            int nRows = ToolBar_GetRows (hwndTB) ;
            char ach[80] ;
            wsprintf (ach, "Row Count = %d", nRows) ;
            MessageBox (GetParent (hwndTB), ach,
                        "TB_GETROWS", MB_OK) ;
            break ;
            }

        case IDM_TB_CUSTOMIZE :
            // ToolBar_Customize (hwndTB) ;
            SendMessage (hwndTB, TB_CUSTOMIZE, (LPARAM) &tbb[25], 5) ;
            break ;
        }
    }
```

TOOLTIP.C

```
/*-----------------------------------------
    TOOLTIP.C -- Tooltip helper functions
                 (c) Paul Yao, 1996
   ------------------------------------------*/
#include <windows.h>
#include <commctrl.h>
#include "comcthlp.h"
#include "notifdef.h"
#include "gadgets.h"
```

(continued)

```
extern BOOL bComboBox ;
extern char szTbStrings[] ;
extern HINSTANCE hInst ;
extern HWND hwndEdit ;
extern HWND hwndCombo ;
extern HWND hwndEdit ;
static HWND hwndTT ;

// Map toolbar button command to string index
int CommandToString[] =
    { IDM_FILE_NEW, IDM_FILE_OPEN, IDM_FILE_SAVE, IDM_FILE_PRINT,
      IDM_FILE_PREVIEW, IDM_EDIT_CUT, IDM_EDIT_COPY, IDM_EDIT_PASTE,
      IDM_EDIT_UNDO, IDM_EDIT_PROP, IDM_TB_HELP, IDM_TB_DELETE, -1
    } ;

//-----------------------------------------------------------------
BOOL InitToolTip (HWND hwndToolBar, HWND hwndComboBox)
    {
    BOOL bSuccess ;
    TOOLINFO ti ;

    // Fetch handle to tooltip control
    hwndTT = ToolBar_GetToolTips (hwndToolBar) ;
    if (hwndTT == NULL)
        return FALSE ;

    // Add tooltip for main combo box
    ZeroMemory (&ti, sizeof (TOOLINFO)) ;
    ti.cbSize = sizeof (TOOLINFO) ;
    ti.uFlags = TTF_IDISHWND | TTF_CENTERTIP | TTF_SUBCLASS ;
    ti.hwnd   = hwndToolBar ;
    ti.uId    = (UINT) (HWND) hwndComboBox ;
    ti.lpszText = LPSTR_TEXTCALLBACK ;
    bSuccess = ToolTip_AddTool (hwndTT, &ti) ;
    if (!bSuccess)
        return FALSE ;

    // Add tooltip for combo box's edit control
    hwndEdit = GetWindow (hwndComboBox, GW_CHILD) ;
    ti.uId    = (UINT) (HWND) hwndEdit ;
    bSuccess = ToolTip_AddTool (hwndTT, &ti) ;

    return bSuccess ;
    }
```

(continued)

```
//-------------------------------------------------------------------------
void CopyToolTipText (LPTOOLTIPTEXT lpttt)
    {
    int i ;
    int iButton = lpttt->hdr.idFrom ;
    int cb ;
    int cMax ;
    LPSTR pString ;
    LPSTR pDest = lpttt->lpszText ;

    // Check for combo box window handles
    if (lpttt->uFlags & TTF_IDISHWND)
        {
        if ((iButton == (int) hwndCombo) ||
            (iButton == (int) hwndEdit))
            {
            lstrcpy (pDest, "1-2-3 ComboBox") ;
            return ;
            }
        }

    // Map command ID to string index
    for (i = 0 ; CommandToString[i] != -1 ; i++)
        {
        if (CommandToString[i] == iButton)
            {
            iButton = i ;
            break ;
            }
        }

    // To be safe, count number of strings in text
    pString = szTbStrings ;
    cMax = 0 ;
    while (*pString != '\0')
        {
        cMax++ ;
        cb = lstrlen (pString) ;
        pString += (cb + 1) ;
        }

    // Check for valid parameter
    if (iButton > cMax)
        {
        pString = "Invalid Button Index" ;
        }
```

(continued)

```
    else
        {
        // Cycle through to requested string
        pString = szTbStrings ;
        for (i = 0 ; i < iButton ; i++)
            {
            cb = lstrlen (pString) ;
            pString += (cb + 1) ;
            }
        }

    lstrcpy (pDest, pString) ;
    }
```

STATBAR.C

```
/*-------------------------------------------
   STATBAR.C -- Status bar helper functions
                (c) Paul Yao, 1996
   -------------------------------------------*/
#include <windows.h>
#include <commctrl.h>
#include "comcthlp.h"
#include "gadgets.h"

typedef struct tagPOPUPSTRING
    {
    HMENU hMenu ;
    UINT uiString ;
    } POPUPSTRING ;

#define MAX_MENUS 5

static POPUPSTRING popstr[MAX_MENUS] ;

DWORD dwStatusBarStyles = WS_CHILD | WS_VISIBLE |
                          WS_CLIPSIBLINGS | CCS_BOTTOM |
                          SBARS_SIZEGRIP ;
extern HINSTANCE hInst ;
extern HWND hwndStatusBar ;

//--------------------------------------------------------------------
HWND InitStatusBar (HWND hwndParent)
```

(continued)

```
    {
    HWND hwndSB ;
    // Initialize values for WM_MENUSELECT message handling
    HMENU hMenu = GetMenu (hwndParent) ;
    HMENU hMenuTB = GetSubMenu (hMenu, 2) ;
    HMENU hMenuSB = GetSubMenu (hMenu, 3) ;
    popstr[0].hMenu   = 0 ;
    popstr[0].uiString = 0 ;
    popstr[1].hMenu   = hMenu ;
    popstr[1].uiString = IDS_MAIN_MENU ;
    popstr[2].hMenu   = hMenuTB ;
    popstr[2].uiString = IDS_TOOLBAR_MENU ;
    popstr[3].hMenu   = hMenuSB ;
    popstr[3].uiString = IDS_STATUSBAR_MENU ;
    popstr[4].hMenu   = 0 ;
    popstr[4].uiString = 0 ;

    hwndSB = CreateStatusWindow (dwStatusBarStyles,
                                 "Ready",
                                 hwndParent,
                                 2) ;
    return hwndSB ;
    }

//---------------------------------------------------------------
void static FlipStyleFlag (LPDWORD dwStyle, DWORD flag)
    {
    if (*dwStyle & flag)  // Flag on -- turn off
        {
        *dwStyle &= (~flag) ;
        }
    else                  // Flag off -- turn on
        {
        *dwStyle |= flag ;
        }
    }
//---------------------------------------------------------------
HWND RebuildStatusBar (HWND hwndParent, WORD wFlag)
    {
    HWND hwndSB ;
    RECT r ;

    switch (wFlag)
        {
        case IDM_STAT_SIZEGRIP :
            FlipStyleFlag (&dwStatusBarStyles, SBARS_SIZEGRIP) ;
            break ;
```

(continued)

```
                 case IDM_STAT_TOP :
                     dwStatusBarStyles &= 0xFFFFFFFC ;
                     dwStatusBarStyles |= CCS_TOP ;
                     break ;

                 case IDM_STAT_BOTTOM :
                     dwStatusBarStyles &= 0xFFFFFFFC ;
                     dwStatusBarStyles |= CCS_BOTTOM ;
                     break ;

                 case IDM_STAT_NOMOVEY :
                     dwStatusBarStyles &= 0xFFFFFFFC ;
                     dwStatusBarStyles |= CCS_NOMOVEY ;
                     break ;

                 case IDM_STAT_NOPARENTALIGN :
                     FlipStyleFlag (&dwStatusBarStyles, CCS_NOPARENTALIGN) ;
                     break ;

                 case IDM_STAT_NORESIZE :
                     FlipStyleFlag (&dwStatusBarStyles, CCS_NORESIZE) ;
                     break ;
             }

     hwndSB = InitStatusBar (hwndParent) ;

     // Post parent a WM_SIZE message to resize children
     GetClientRect (hwndParent, &r) ;
     PostMessage (hwndParent, WM_SIZE, 0,
                 MAKELPARAM (r.right, r.bottom)) ;

     return hwndSB ;
     }


//-------------------------------------------------------------------
void StatusBarMessage (HWND hwndSB, WORD wMsg)
     {
     switch (wMsg)
         {
         case IDM_ST_GETBORDERS :
             {
             char ach[180] ;
             int aiBorders[3] ;
```

(continued)

```
                    Status_GetBorders (hwndSB, &aiBorders) ;
                    wsprintf (ach, "Horiz Width = %d\n"
                            "Vert Width = %d\n"
                            "Separator Width = %d",
                            aiBorders[0], aiBorders[1],
                            aiBorders[2]) ;
                    MessageBox (GetParent (hwndSB), ach,
                            "SB_GETBORDERS", MB_OK) ;
                    break ;
                    }

            case IDM_ST_GETPARTS :
                    {
                    char ach[80] ;
                    int nParts = Status_GetParts (hwndSB, 0, 0) ;
                    wsprintf (ach, "Part Count = %d", nParts) ;
                    MessageBox (GetParent (hwndSB), ach,
                            "SB_GETPARTS", MB_OK) ;
                    break ;
                    }

            case IDM_ST_SETTEXT :
                    Status_SetText (hwndSB, 0, 0,
                                "SB_SETTEXT Message Sent") ;
                    break ;

            case IDM_ST_SIMPLE :
                    {
                    static BOOL bSimple = TRUE ;
                    Status_Simple (hwndSB, bSimple) ;
                    bSimple = (!bSimple) ;
                    break ;
                    }
            }
    }


//--------------------------------------------------------------------------
LRESULT
Statusbar_MenuSelect (HWND hwnd, WPARAM wParam, LPARAM lParam)
    {
    UINT fuFlags = (UINT) HIWORD (wParam) ;
    HMENU hMainMenu = NULL ;
    int iMenu = 0 ;

    // Handle non-system popup menu descriptions
    if ((fuFlags & MF_POPUP) &&
```

(continued)

```
        (!(fuFlags & MF_SYSMENU)))
        {
        for (iMenu = 1 ; iMenu < MAX_MENUS ; iMenu++)
            {
            if ((HMENU) lParam == popstr[iMenu].hMenu)
                {
                hMainMenu = (HMENU) lParam ;
                break ;
                }
            }
        }

    // Display helpful text in status bar
    MenuHelp (WM_MENUSELECT, wParam, lParam, hMainMenu, hInst,
            hwndStatusBar, (UINT *) &popstr[iMenu]) ;

    return 0 ;
    }
```

NOTIFDEF.C

```
/*-------------------------------------------------
    NOTIFDEF.C -- Support notification detail window
                 (c) Paul Yao, 1996
    -------------------------------------------------*/
#include <windows.h>
#include <windowsx.h>
#include <commctrl.h>
#include <prsht.h>
#include "notifdef.h"

CONTROLNOTIFICATIONS cnLookupTable[] =
    {
    NM_OUTOFMEMORY,        "NM_OUTOFMEMORY",
    NM_CLICK,              "NM_CLICK",
    NM_DBLCLK,             "NM_DBLCLK",
    NM_RETURN,             "NM_RETURN",
    NM_RCLICK,             "NM_RCLICK",
    NM_RDBLCLK,            "NM_RDBLCLK",
    NM_SETFOCUS,           "NM_SETFOCUS",
    NM_KILLFOCUS,          "NM_KILLFOCUS",
    LVN_ITEMCHANGING,      "LVN_ITEMCHANGING",
    LVN_ITEMCHANGED,       "LVN_ITEMCHANGED",
    LVN_INSERTITEM,        "LVN_INSERTITEM",
    LVN_DELETEITEM,        "LVN_DELETEITEM",
```

(continued)

```
LVN_DELETEALLITEMS,      "LVN_DELETEALLITEMS",
LVN_BEGINLABELEDITA,     "LVN_BEGINLABELEDITA",
LVN_BEGINLABELEDITW,     "LVN_BEGINLABELEDITW",
LVN_ENDLABELEDITA,       "LVN_ENDLABELEDITA",
LVN_ENDLABELEDITW,       "LVN_ENDLABELEDITW",
LVN_COLUMNCLICK,         "LVN_COLUMNCLICK",
LVN_BEGINDRAG,           "LVN_BEGINDRAG",
LVN_BEGINRDRAG,          "LVN_BEGINRDRAG",
LVN_GETDISPINFOA,        "LVN_GETDISPINFOA",
LVN_GETDISPINFOW,        "LVN_GETDISPINFOW",
LVN_SETDISPINFOA,        "LVN_SETDISPINFOA",
LVN_SETDISPINFOW,        "LVN_SETDISPINFOW",
LVN_KEYDOWN,             "LVN_KEYDOWN",
HDN_ITEMCHANGINGA,       "HDN_ITEMCHANGINGA",
HDN_ITEMCHANGINGW,       "HDN_ITEMCHANGINGW",
HDN_ITEMCHANGEDA,        "HDN_ITEMCHANGEDA",
HDN_ITEMCHANGEDW,        "HDN_ITEMCHANGEDW",
HDN_ITEMCLICKA,          "HDN_ITEMCLICKA",
HDN_ITEMCLICKW,          "HDN_ITEMCLICKW",
HDN_ITEMDBLCLICKA,       "HDN_ITEMDBLCLICKA",
HDN_ITEMDBLCLICKW,       "HDN_ITEMDBLCLICKW",
HDN_DIVIDERDBLCLICKA,    "HDN_DIVIDERDBLCLICKA",
HDN_DIVIDERDBLCLICKW,    "HDN_DIVIDERDBLCLICKW",
HDN_BEGINTRACKA,         "HDN_BEGINTRACKA",
HDN_BEGINTRACKW,         "HDN_BEGINTRACKW",
HDN_ENDTRACKA,           "HDN_ENDTRACKA",
HDN_ENDTRACKW,           "HDN_ENDTRACKW",
HDN_TRACKA,              "HDN_TRACKA",
HDN_TRACKW,              "HDN_TRACKW",
TVN_SELCHANGINGA,        "TVN_SELCHANGINGA",
TVN_SELCHANGINGW,        "TVN_SELCHANGINGW",
TVN_SELCHANGEDA,         "TVN_SELCHANGEDA",
TVN_SELCHANGEDW,         "TVN_SELCHANGEDW",
TVN_GETDISPINFOA,        "TVN_GETDISPINFOA",
TVN_GETDISPINFOW,        "TVN_GETDISPINFOW",
TVN_SETDISPINFOA,        "TVN_SETDISPINFOA",
TVN_SETDISPINFOW,        "TVN_SETDISPINFOW",
TVN_ITEMEXPANDINGA,      "TVN_ITEMEXPANDINGA",
TVN_ITEMEXPANDINGW,      "TVN_ITEMEXPANDINGW",
TVN_ITEMEXPANDEDA,       "TVN_ITEMEXPANDEDA",
TVN_ITEMEXPANDEDW,       "TVN_ITEMEXPANDEDW",
TVN_BEGINDRAGA,          "TVN_BEGINDRAGA",
TVN_BEGINDRAGW,          "TVN_BEGINDRAGW",
```

(continued)

```
        TVN_BEGINRDRAGA,      "TVN_BEGINRDRAGA",
        TVN_BEGINRDRAGW,      "TVN_BEGINRDRAGW",
        TVN_DELETEITEMA,      "TVN_DELETEITEMA",
        TVN_DELETEITEMW,      "TVN_DELETEITEMW",
        TVN_BEGINLABELEDITA,  "TVN_BEGINLABELEDITA",
        TVN_BEGINLABELEDITW,  "TVN_BEGINLABELEDITW",
        TVN_ENDLABELEDITA,    "TVN_ENDLABELEDITA",
        TVN_ENDLABELEDITW,    "TVN_ENDLABELEDITW",
        TVN_KEYDOWN,          "TVN_KEYDOWN",
        TTN_NEEDTEXTA,        "TTN_NEEDTEXTA",
        TTN_NEEDTEXTW,        "TTN_NEEDTEXTW",
        TTN_SHOW,             "TTN_SHOW",
        TTN_POP,              "TTN_POP",
        TCN_KEYDOWN,          "TCN_KEYDOWN",
        TCN_SELCHANGE,        "TCN_SELCHANGE",
        TCN_SELCHANGING,      "TCN_SELCHANGING",
        TBN_GETBUTTONINFOA,   "TBN_GETBUTTONINFOA",
        TBN_GETBUTTONINFOW,   "TBN_GETBUTTONINFOW",
        TBN_BEGINDRAG,        "TBN_BEGINDRAG",
        TBN_ENDDRAG,          "TBN_ENDDRAG",
        TBN_BEGINADJUST,      "TBN_BEGINADJUST",
        TBN_ENDADJUST,        "TBN_ENDADJUST",
        TBN_RESET,            "TBN_RESET",
        TBN_QUERYINSERT,      "TBN_QUERYINSERT",
        TBN_QUERYDELETE,      "TBN_QUERYDELETE",
        TBN_TOOLBARCHANGE,    "TBN_TOOLBARCHANGE",
        TBN_CUSTHELP,         "TBN_CUSTHELP",
        UDN_DELTAPOS,         "UDN_DELTAPOS",
        PSN_SETACTIVE,        "PSN_SETACTIVE",
        PSN_KILLACTIVE,       "PSN_KILLACTIVE",
        PSN_APPLY,            "PSN_APPLY",
        PSN_RESET,            "PSN_RESET",
        PSN_HELP,             "PSN_HELP",
        PSN_WIZBACK,          "PSN_WIZBACK",
        PSN_WIZNEXT,          "PSN_WIZNEXT",
        PSN_WIZFINISH,        "PSN_WIZFINISH",
        PSN_QUERYCANCEL,      "PSN_QUERYCANCEL"
        } ;

int NOTIFY_COUNT = sizeof (cnLookupTable) / sizeof (CONTROLNOTIFICATIONS) ;
static HWND hwndNotify = NULL ;

extern HINSTANCE hInst ;
```

(continued)

```
//----------------------------------------------------------------
// QueryNotifyText: Convert notification codes into text
//----------------------------------------------------------------
BOOL QueryNotifyText (UINT nNotifyCode, LPSTR *pName)
    {
    BOOL bFound = FALSE ;
    int  iNotify ;

    for (iNotify = 0 ; iNotify < NOTIFY_COUNT ; iNotify++)
        {
        if (cnLookupTable[iNotify].nCode == nNotifyCode)
            {
            *pName = cnLookupTable[iNotify].pName ;
            return TRUE ;
            }
        }

    // Unknown notification code
    *pName = "** Unknown **" ;
    return FALSE ;
    }


//----------------------------------------------------------------
// ViewNotificationsToggle: Display/hide notification window
//----------------------------------------------------------------
HWND ViewNotificationsToggle (HWND hwnd)
    {
    int x, y, cx, cy ;
    RECT rWindow ;

    if (hwndNotify)
        {
        DestroyWindow (hwndNotify) ;
        hwndNotify = NULL ;
        }
    else
        {
        GetClientRect (hwnd, &rWindow) ;
        x = 0 ;
        y = 0 ;
        cx = rWindow.right  - rWindow.left ;
        cy = rWindow.bottom - rWindow.top ;
        hwndNotify = CreateWindowEx (0L,
                        "LISTBOX", NULL,
                        LBS_NOINTEGRALHEIGHT |
```

(continued)

```
                                    WS_CHILD    |
                                    WS_VISIBLE  |
                                    WS_VSCROLL,
                                    x, y, cx, cy,
                                    hwnd, (HMENU) 1, hInst, NULL) ;
          }

     return hwndNotify ;
     }

//-----------------------------------------------------------------
void DisplayText (LPSTR pText)
     {
     int iIndex ;

     if (hwndNotify == NULL)
          return ;

     iIndex = ListBox_AddString (hwndNotify, pText) ;
     ListBox_SetTopIndex (hwndNotify, iIndex) ;
     }

//-----------------------------------------------------------------
void DisplayNotificationDetails (WPARAM wParam, LPARAM lParam)
     {
     LPNMHDR pnmh ;
     LPSTR   pName ;

     if (hwndNotify == NULL)
          return ;

     pnmh = (LPNMHDR) lParam ;
     QueryNotifyText (pnmh->code, &pName) ;
     DisplayText (pName) ;
     }

//-----------------------------------------------------------------
void ClearNotificationList ()
     {
     if (hwndNotify == NULL)
          return ;

     ListBox_ResetContent (hwndNotify) ;
     }
```

(continued)

GADGETS.RC

```
#include "gadgets.h"
#include <windows.h>

IDI_APP ICON    DISCARDABLE     "gadgets.ico"

MAIN MENU DISCARDABLE
    {
    POPUP "&File"
        {
        MENUITEM "&New",                        IDM_FILE_NEW
        MENUITEM "&Open",                       IDM_FILE_OPEN
        MENUITEM "&Save",                       IDM_FILE_SAVE
        MENUITEM "Save &As...",                 IDM_FILE_SAVEAS
        MENUITEM SEPARATOR
        MENUITEM "&Print...",                   IDM_FILE_PRINT
        MENUITEM "Print Pre&view...",           IDM_FILE_PREVIEW
        MENUITEM SEPARATOR
        MENUITEM "&Exit",                       IDM_FILE_EXIT
        }
    POPUP "&Edit"
        {
        MENUITEM "&Undo\tCtrl+Z",               IDM_EDIT_UNDO
        MENUITEM SEPARATOR
        MENUITEM "&Cut\tCtrl+X",                IDM_EDIT_CUT
        MENUITEM "&Copy\tCtrl+C",               IDM_EDIT_COPY
        MENUITEM "&Paste\tCtrl+V",              IDM_EDIT_PASTE
        MENUITEM SEPARATOR
        MENUITEM "Pr&operties",                 IDM_EDIT_PROP
        }
    POPUP "&Toolbar"
        {
        POPUP "St&yles"
            {
            MENUITEM "CCS_NODIVIDER",                IDM_NODIVIDER
            MENUITEM "TBSTYLE_WRAPABLE",             IDM_WRAPABLE
            MENUITEM SEPARATOR
            MENUITEM "CCS_TOP",                      IDM_TOP
            MENUITEM "CCS_BOTTOM",                   IDM_BOTTOM
            MENUITEM "CCS_NOMOVEY",                  IDM_NOMOVEY
            MENUITEM SEPARATOR
            MENUITEM "CCS_NOPARENTALIGN",            IDM_NOPARENTALIGN
            MENUITEM "CCS_NORESIZE",                 IDM_NORESIZE
            MENUITEM SEPARATOR
```

(continued)

```
                    MENUITEM "CCS_ADJUSTABLE",                    IDM_ADJUSTABLE
                    MENUITEM "TBSTYLE_ALTDRAG",                   IDM_ALTDRAG
                    MENUITEM SEPARATOR
                    MENUITEM "TBSTYLE_TOOLTIPS",                  IDM_TOOLTIPS
                    }
                MENUITEM "&Ignore WM_SIZE",            IDM_IGNORESIZE
                MENUITEM SEPARATOR
                POPUP "&Messages"
                    {
                    MENUITEM "TB_CHECKBUTTON",                 IDM_TB_CHECK
                    MENUITEM "TB_ENABLEBUTTON",                IDM_TB_ENABLE
                    MENUITEM "TB_HIDEBUTTON",                  IDM_TB_HIDE
                    MENUITEM "TB_INDETERMINATE",               IDM_TB_INDETERMINATE
                    MENUITEM "TB_PRESSBUTTON",                 IDM_TB_PRESS
                    MENUITEM SEPARATOR
                    MENUITEM "TB_BUTTONCOUNT",                 IDM_TB_BUTTONCOUNT
                    MENUITEM "TB_GETROWS",                     IDM_TB_GETROWS
                    MENUITEM SEPARATOR
                    MENUITEM "TB_CUSTOMIZE",                   IDM_TB_CUSTOMIZE
                    }
                MENUITEM SEPARATOR
                MENUITEM "&Large Icons",              IDM_LARGEICONS
                MENUITEM "&Small Icons",              IDM_SMALLICONS
                MENUITEM SEPARATOR
                MENUITEM "S&trings",                  IDM_STRINGS
                MENUITEM "&Combo Box",                IDM_COMBOBOX
                }
        POPUP "&Statusbar"
            {
            POPUP "&Styles"
                {
                MENUITEM "SBARS_SIZEGRIP",                 IDM_STAT_SIZEGRIP
                MENUITEM SEPARATOR
                MENUITEM "CCS_TOP",                        IDM_STAT_TOP
                MENUITEM "CCS_BOTTOM",                     IDM_STAT_BOTTOM
                MENUITEM "CCS_NOMOVEY",                    IDM_STAT_NOMOVEY
                MENUITEM SEPARATOR
                MENUITEM "CCS_NOPARENTALIGN",              IDM_STAT_NOPARENTALIGN
                MENUITEM "CCS_NORESIZE",                   IDM_STAT_NORESIZE
                }
            MENUITEM "&Ignore WM_SIZE",            IDM_STAT_IGNORESIZE
            MENUITEM SEPARATOR
            POPUP "&Messages"
                {
                MENUITEM "SB_GETBORDERS",                  IDM_ST_GETBORDERS
                MENUITEM "SB_GETPARTS",                    IDM_ST_GETPARTS
```

(continued)

```
                    MENUITEM "SB_SETTEXT",                    IDM_ST_SETTEXT
                    MENUITEM SEPARATOR
                    MENUITEM "SB_SIMPLE",                     IDM_ST_SIMPLE
                    }
              }
        POPUP "&Notifications"
              {
              MENUITEM "&Clear",                             IDM_NOTIFICATIONS_CLEAR
              }
        POPUP "&View"
              {
              MENUITEM "&Toolbar",                           IDM_VIEW_TOOLBAR
              MENUITEM "&Status Bar",                        IDM_VIEW_STATUS
              MENUITEM "&Notifications",                     IDM_VIEW_NOTIFICATIONS
              }
        }

STRINGTABLE DISCARDABLE
     {
     IDS_MAIN_MENU
          "Create, open, save, print documents or quit program"
     IDS_MAIN_MENU1          "Undo, cut, copy, paste, and properties"
     IDS_MAIN_MENU2          "Toolbar styles, messages, and creation options"
     IDS_MAIN_MENU3          "Status bar styles and messages"
     IDS_MAIN_MENU4          "Clear notifications window"
     IDS_MAIN_MENU5
          "Show or hide toolbar, status bar, and notifications window"
     IDS_TOOLBAR_MENU        "Set toolbar styles and re-create toolbar"
     IDS_TOOLBAR_MENU1       "placeholder"
     IDS_TOOLBAR_MENU2       "placeholder"
     IDS_TOOLBAR_MENU3       "Send messages to toolbar"
     IDS_STATUSBAR_MENU      "Set status bar styles and re-create status bar"
     IDS_STATUSBAR_MENU1     "placeholder"
     IDS_STATUSBAR_MENU2     "placeholder"
     IDS_STATUSBAR_MENU3     "Send messages to status bar"
     IDM_FILE_NEW            "Creates a new document"
     IDM_FILE_OPEN           "Open an existing document"
     IDM_FILE_SAVE           "Save the active document"
     IDM_FILE_SAVEAS         "Save the active document with a new name"
     IDM_FILE_PRINT          "Prints the active document"
     IDM_FILE_PREVIEW        "Displays full pages as they will be printed"
     IDM_FILE_EXIT           "Quits program"
     IDM_EDIT_UNDO           "Reverse the last action"
     IDM_EDIT_CUT
          "Cuts the selection and puts it on the Clipboard"
```

(continued)

```
        IDM_EDIT_COPY
            "Copies the selection and puts it on the Clipboard"
        IDM_EDIT_PASTE
            "Inserts the Clipboard contents at the insertion point"
        IDM_EDIT_PROP
            "Opens property sheet for currently selected item"
        IDM_IGNORESIZE
            "Toggle WM_SIZE handling to show autosize/auto move"
        IDM_STRINGS              "Creates toolbar with strings"
        IDM_LARGEICONS           "Creates toolbar with large icons"
        IDM_SMALLICONS           "Creates toolbar with small icons"
        IDM_COMBOBOX             "Creates toolbar with combobox"
        IDM_NODIVIDER            "Toggle divider above toolbar"
        IDM_WRAPABLE             "Toggle toolbar resizing for narrow window"
        IDM_TOP                  "Toggle placing toolbar at top of parent"
        IDM_BOTTOM               "Toggle placing toolbar at bottom of parent"
        IDM_NOMOVEY              "Toggle inhibit moving window on Y-axis"
        IDM_NOPARENTALIGN        "Toggle inhibit aligning to parent"
        IDM_NORESIZE             "Toggle inhibit any sizing or moving"
        IDM_ADJUSTABLE           "Toggle ability for user to customize toolbar"
        IDM_ALTDRAG              "Toggle Alt-click to drag buttons"
        IDM_TOOLTIPS             "Toggle tooltip support"
        IDM_TB_CHECK             "Toggle button 0 checked state"
        IDM_TB_ENABLE            "Toggle button 1 enabled state"
        IDM_TB_HIDE              "Toggle button 2 hidden state"
        IDM_TB_INDETERMINATE     "Toggle button 3 indeterminate state"
        IDM_TB_PRESS             "Toggle button 4 pressed state"
        IDM_TB_BUTTONCOUNT       "Query button count"
        IDM_TB_GETROWS           "Query row count"
        IDM_TB_CUSTOMIZE         "Request customize dialog box"
        IDM_STAT_IGNORESIZE
            "Toggle WM_SIZE handling to show autosize/auto move"
        IDM_STAT_SIZEGRIP        "Status bar to have sizing grip"
        IDM_STAT_TOP             "Toggle placing status bar at top of parent"
        IDM_STAT_BOTTOM          "Toggle placing status bar at bottom of parent"
        IDM_STAT_NOMOVEY         "Toggle inhibit moving window on Y-axis"
        IDM_STAT_NOPARENTALIGN   "Toggle inhibit aligning to parent"
        IDM_STAT_NORESIZE        "Toggle inhibit any sizing or moving"
        IDM_ST_GETBORDERS        "Query size of status bar borders"
        IDM_ST_GETPARTS          "Query number of status bar parts"
        IDM_ST_SETTEXT           "Set text in status bar"
        IDM_ST_SIMPLE            "Toggle status bar simple state"
        IDM_NOTIFICATIONS_CLEAR  "Clear contents of notification window"
        IDM_VIEW_TOOLBAR         "Show/hide toolbar"
        IDM_VIEW_STATUS          "Show/hide status bar"
        IDM_VIEW_NOTIFICATIONS   "Show/hide notification window"
        }
```

(continued)

GADGETS.ICO

GADGETS creates a toolbar, a status bar, and a client window when its main window gets a WM_CREATE message. The location at creation time of each window doesn't matter, since a WM_SIZE message always follows a WM_CREATE and that's when GADGETS repositions its child windows.

GADGETS' client window holds a list box for displaying details of notification (WM_NOTIFY) messages received by the main window. These messages are sent from each of the three common controls—the toolbar, status bar, and tooltip control—when each encounters a noteworthy event. The toolbar sends notifications of mouse clicks and toolbar customization queries; the status bar sends notification queries as well; the tooltip control asks for text for the tooltip window when the mouse cursor pauses over a toolbar tool.

The first two popup menus—the File and Edit menus—are dummy menus to mimic the actions of toolbar buttons. The other four menus—Toolbar, Statusbar, Notifications, and View—control features that GADGETS is supposed to demonstrate. Some experimentation will show each major feature of toolbars, status bars, and tooltips.

Controlling GADGETS' toolbar

GADGETS lets you see the relationships between the three factors that affect toolbars (and other controls): window styles, control-specific messages, and notification messages. Set window styles by selecting the Styles submenu from the Toolbar menu, send control-specific messages by selecting the Messages submenu from the Toolbar menu, and view notifications displayed in the client-area-sized list box. You control the presence of various toolbar features—icon size, presence of strings, and presence of a combo box—via other options on the Toolbar menu.

At startup, GADGETS' toolbar has small icons, tooltip support, no strings, and no combo box. It resides at the top of its parent window, but the auto-size and auto-move features can be fine-tuned by setting various toolbar styles. When you experiment with toolbar location, you may wish to disable GADGETS' positioning of the toolbar by selecting the appropriate menu option.

GADGETS sends a sample set of toolbar messages to its toolbar. Most of the messages are for tweaking individual buttons, such as TB_CHECKBUTTON to check and uncheck a button, and TB_ENABLEBUTTON to enable and disable buttons. Two query messages let you ask for the number of buttons and the number of rows.

The TB_CUSTOMIZE message summons the Customize Toolbar dialog box, which lets a user add or remove toolbar items. The key to proper operation of the customization dialog is to provide proper replies to toolbar notifications: TBN_QUERYINSERT, TBN_QUERYDELETE, and TBN_GETBUTTONINFO. When you customize GADGETS' toolbar, watch the flow of notification messages to get a feel for the sequence and flow of these requests.

Controlling GADGETS' status bar

GADGETS has a menu for controlling status bar styles and sending it messages. This menu has a much smaller set of commands than does the toolbar menu, since status bars are somewhat simpler than toolbars.

The most interesting aspect of GADGETS' status bar has to do with how GADGETS handles the WM_MENUSELECT message to display helpful text in the status window. All status bar strings reside in GADGETS' string table. To simplify the mapping of menu item command IDs to string resource IDs, the two are the same. For example, the command ID for the File Open menu command is defined by IDM_FILE_OPEN, which is also the string resource ID for the string "Open an existing document".

To provide helpful text when a popup menu is selected, GADGETS maps menu handles to string IDs. GADGETS has ten popup menus, which are all owned by three parent menus: the main menu bar, the toolbar popup menu, and the status bar menu. The string resource status bar descriptions for the popup menus in these parent menus start with strings IDS_MAIN_MENU, IDS_TOOLBAR_MENU, and IDS_STATUSBAR_MENU. GADGETS maps parent menu handles to these three values, passing them to the *MenuHelp* function to display the right string of text.

PROPERTY SHEETS

"Property sheets"—sometimes called "tabbed dialogs"—provide the ability to combine several dialog boxes in a single, compound dialog box. In a property sheet, an individual dialog is called a "property page." Figure 12-9 shows the Display Properties property sheet that's available on the Windows 95 desktop. (To access this property sheet, summon the shell context menu with a right mouse click and select the "Properties" menu item.) The various pages in this property sheet allow a user to fine-tune desktop options such as the wallpaper, screen saver, colors, and fonts, and also modify display driver settings to change available colors, device resolution, and even the current display driver.

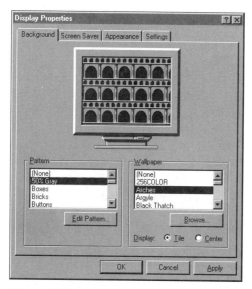

Figure 12-9. *The Display Properties property sheet.*

A property sheet provides the ability to modify all the settings for a complex object—such as the display screen in this example—from a group of property pages that are all conveniently connected together. Every page has its own tab, on which a user clicks to call up a specific page. An optional Apply button lets a user preview changes without dismissing the property sheet. If the results aren't satisfactory, another change can be made—perhaps back to the original setting—while the property sheet is still available.

Another type of compound dialog box related to property sheets is the *wizard*. A wizard is a set of dialogs that accept user input in a specific sequence to accomplish some specific task. Figure 12-10 shows the first of six pages in the Windows 95 Add Printer Wizard, which through a sequence of dialogs allows a user to enter all the details needed to install a new system printer. The programming interface for wizards is the same as for property sheets, although the user interface is a bit different: the OK and Cancel buttons are replaced with Back and Next buttons. These buttons provide the only way to navigate between wizard pages (instead of the tabs used on property sheets). On the last page, wizards display a Finish button which, when clicked, dismisses the wizard to allow the execution of the task for which the wizard was requested to begin.

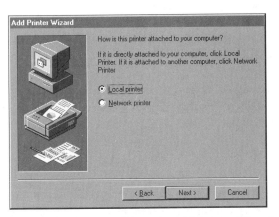

Figure 12-10. *A page from the Add Printer Wizard.*

Creating Property Sheets

To create a property sheet, you collect the elements you'd otherwise need to create a set of individual dialog boxes—dialog templates and dialog procedures—and then fill in some data structures and call *PropertySheet*. Each property page requires its own dialog box template to describe the layout of individual controls. Each property page also needs its own dialog box procedure, which handles the dialog initialization (WM_INITDIALOG) message and also handles the notification (WM_COMMAND) messages sent from controls. Property page dialog procedures handle a third message, WM_NOTIFY, which serves as a notification about changes in the state of the property sheet itself.

These elements are organized using two data structures, one for each property page and a header structure that describes overall property sheet attributes. You define the attributes of each property page with the PROPSHEETPAGE data structure and a set of property pages using an array of PROPSHEETPAGE structures. A pointer to the property page structures gets included in a PROPSHEETHEADER data structure, which holds property sheet attributes.

Property page dialog templates

The dialog box templates used for property pages are almost identical to the ones you'd use to create normal dialog boxes. A property page dialog template contains regular predefined window controls such as edits, list boxes, and push buttons; it could also contain common controls, such as animation, drag list, trackbars, and up-down controls. As with regular dialog box templates, each control in a property page template has a unique control ID that you trade at run time—via *GetDlgItem*—for a window handle.

One difference between normal dialog templates and property page templates is that property page templates typically don't contain push buttons such as OK and Cancel. The property sheet creates and maintains a set of push buttons that are shared by all property pages. The default buttons for a regular property sheet are OK, Cancel, and Apply, although you can set a flag to inhibit the Apply button if it doesn't suit your needs. You can also set a flag to request that the property sheet display a Help button, which will be enabled for property pages that support help. Wizards use a slightly different set of buttons: Back and Next to traverse the wizard's pages, and a Finish button on the last page.

Another dialog template issue involves the size and shape of individual property page dialogs. Within a given property sheet, you'll want a similar size and shape for all pages since the property sheet adjusts its own size to accommodate the widest and the tallest property page. Fine-tuning the layout of dialog box templates is always a time-consuming and tedious task; in the context of property sheets, you have even more work to do in coordinating the layout of different dialog templates.

The PROPSHEETPAGE structure

Once you've created the dialog box template for each property page and have at least a skeleton of a dialog box procedure, the next step in creating a property sheet is to fill out a PROPSHEETPAGE structure for each property page. PROPSHEETPAGE is defined in PRSHT.H as follows:

```
typedef struct _PROPSHEETPAGE
    {
    DWORD            dwSize ;             // = sizeof (PROPSHEETPAGE)
    DWORD            dwFlags ;
    HINSTANCE        hInstance ;
    union
        {
        LPCSTR           pszTemplate ;  // Default
        LPCDLGTEMPLATE pResource ;      // PSP_DLGINDIRECT
        } DUMMYUNIONNAME ;
    union
        {
        HICON        hIcon ;            // PSP_USEHICON
        LPCSTR       pszIcon ;          // PSP_USEICONID
        } DUMMYUNIONNAME2 ;
    LPCSTR           pszTitle ;         // PSP_USETITLE
    DLGPROC          pfnDlgProc ;
    LPARAM           lParam ;
    LPFNPSPCALLBACKA pfnCallback ;      // PSP_USECALLBACK
    UINT FAR *pcRefParent ;             // PSP_USEREFPARENT
    } PROPSHEETPAGE, FAR *LPPROPSHEETPAGE ;
```

The comments in this listing provide notes on each member. The presence of a PSP_ flag indicates the flag that must be included in the *dwFlags* field to activate a given data structure member. Here are details about the meaning of individual members of PROPSHEETPAGE:

- *dwSize*—tags the current version of the property page; should be set to *sizeof (PROPSHEETPAGE)*.

- *dwFlags*—holds one or more PSP_ flags combined with the C bitwise OR operator. Most flags control whether a member of the PROPSHEETPAGE structure should be used or ignored. Two additional flags not used for this purpose are PSP_HASHELP and PSP_RTLREADING. The PSP_HASHELP flag enables the Help button when a given page is active (the PSH_HASHELP flag must be present in PROPSHEETHEADER for the Help button to appear). PSP_RTLREADING makes the property page use right-to-left reading (for Hebrew or Arabic).

- *hInstance*—identifies the executable file from which resources, including dialog box templates (*pszTemplate*) and icons (*pszIcon*), are loaded.

- The dialog box template is identified by *pszTemplate* (the default) for templates loaded from a resource, or by *pResource* (requires PSP_DLGINDIRECT in *dwFlags*) for templates loaded from memory.

- An icon can optionally be displayed in the tab of the property page. The icon can either be identified by an icon handle, *hIcon* (requires PSP_USEHICON in *dwFlags*), or by icon resource ID, *pszIcon* (requires PSP_USEICONID in *dwFlags*).

- The default title from a property page tab is the title specified in the dialog template, unless PSP_USETITLE is set in *dwFlags* which causes *pszTitle* to be used instead.

- *pfnDlgProc*—specifies the dialog procedure for the property page.

- *lParam*—specifies an initialization value passed to the property page's callback function, identified by the *pfnCallback* parameter.

- *pfnCallback* is a callback function (requires PSP_USECALLBACK in *dwFlags*) called before a property page is created and after it is destroyed.

- *pcRefParent* identifies a reference count for the property sheet. It's a pointer to a UINT that is incremented when property pages are created and decremented when property pages are destroyed. At any moment in time, the value referenced by this pointer lets you know exactly how many property pages are present.

This chapter's property sheet sample, PROPERTY, fills its array of PROPSHEETPAGE structures as follows:

```
PROPSHEETPAGE   pspage[2] ;
// Zero out property page data structure
ZeroMemory (&pspage, 2 * sizeof (PROPSHEETPAGE)) ;
```

(continued)

```
// Init window style page data
pspage[0].dwSize      = sizeof (PROPSHEETPAGE) ;
pspage[0].dwFlags     = PSP_USECALLBACK | PSP_USEICONID ;
pspage[0].hInstance   = hInst ;
pspage[0].pszTemplate = MAKEINTRESOURCE (IDD_STYLES) ;
pspage[0].pszIcon     = MAKEINTRESOURCE (IDI_PAGE1) ;
pspage[0].pfnDlgProc  = StyleDlgProc ;
pspage[0].lParam      = (LPARAM) &dwChildStyle ;
pspage[0].pfnCallback = StylePageProc ;

// Init extended window style page data
pspage[1].dwSize      = sizeof (PROPSHEETPAGE) ;
pspage[1].dwFlags     = PSP_USECALLBACK | PSP_USEICONID |
                        PSP_HASHELP ;
pspage[1].hInstance   = hInst ;
pspage[1].pszTemplate = MAKEINTRESOURCE (IDD_EXSTYLES) ;
pspage[1].pszIcon     = MAKEINTRESOURCE (IDI_PAGE2) ;
pspage[1].pfnDlgProc  = ExStyleDlgProc ;
pspage[1].lParam      = (LPARAM) &dwChildExStyle ;
pspage[1].pfnCallback = ExStylePageProc ;
```

The *pfnDlgProc* member of PROPSHEETPAGE holds a pointer to a dialog box procedure. In addition to the two messages, WM_INITDIALOG and WM_COMMAND, that most dialog box procedures handle, property page dialog procedures must handle a third message, WM_NOTIFY. Here's a skeleton dialog box procedure for a property page:

```
BOOL CALLBACK
EmptyPageDlgProc (HWND hwndDlg, UINT msg,
               WPARAM wParam, LPARAM lParam)
    {
    switch (msg)
        {
        case WM_INITDIALOG :
            [dialog initialization]
            break ;

        case WM_COMMAND :
            [notifications from regular dialog controls]
            break ;

        case WM_NOTIFY :
            {
            LPNMHDR pnmh = (LPNMHDR) lParam ;
            [property sheet notifications]
            }
        }
    }
```

The *pfnCallback* member of PROPSHEETPAGE refers to a callback function that gets called before an individual property page is created and right after it is destroyed. One reason to use this function is to be able to fetch the *lParam* member of PROPSHEETPAGE, which holds an initialization value sent from the creator of the property page to the property page (such as a pointer to the data to be modified). Here's a skeleton of the property page callback function:

```
static LPARAM InputData ;

UINT CALLBACK
EmptyPageProc (HWND hwnd, UINT uMsg, LPPROPSHEETPAGE ppsp)
     {
     switch (uMsg)
          {
          case PSPCB_CREATE :
               InputData = ppsp->lParam ;
               return TRUE ;

          case PSPCB_RELEASE :
               return 0 ;
          }
     }
```

In the current implementation, the window handle parameter, *hwnd*, is always NULL; *uMsg* is PSPCB_CREATE for the call before the property page is created and PSPCB_RELEASE for the call after the property page has been destroyed. Although the creation notification is sent only if a property page is actually created, the release notification always gets sent to every property page (whether or not a particular property page was created).

After filling in an array of PROPSHEETPAGE structures, the next step in creating a property sheet is to reference that array in the *ppsp* member of the property sheet header structure, PROPSHEETHEADER.

The PROPSHEETHEADER structure

The PROPSHEETHEADER structure is defined in PRSHT.H as follows:

```
typedef struct _PROPSHEETHEADER
     {
     DWORD          dwSize ;          // = sizeof (PROPSHEETHEADER)
     DWORD          dwFlags ;
     HWND           hwndParent ;
     HINSTANCE      hInstance ;
     union
          {
          HICON     hIcon ;           // PSH_USEHICON
          LPCSTR    pszIcon ;         // PSH_USEICONID
```

(continued)

```
        }DUMMYUNIONNAME ;
LPCSTR        pszCaption ;
UINT          nPages ;
union
    {
    UINT        nStartPage ;     // (Default)
    LPCSTR      pStartPage ;     // PSH_USEPSTARTPAGE
    }DUMMYUNIONNAME2 ;
union
    {
    LPCPROPSHEETPAGE ppsp ;      // PSH_PROPSHEETPAGE
    HPROPSHEETPAGE FAR *phpage ;
    }DUMMYUNIONNAME3 ;
PFNPROPSHEETCALLBACK pfnCallback ; // PSH_USECALLBACK
} PROPSHEETHEADER, FAR *LPPROPSHEETHEADER ;
```

The comments in this listing provide notes on each member. The presence of a PSH_ flag in a comment indicates a flag that must be included in the *dwFlags* field to activate a given data structure member. Here are details about the meaning of individual members of PROPSHEETHEADER.

- *dwSize* identifies the size of PROPSHEETHEADER for version control. It should be set to *sizeof (PROPSHEETHEADER)*.

- *dwFlags* holds one or more PSH_ flags combined with the C bitwise OR operator. Some flags control whether a particular member of PROPSHEETHEADER is used as indicated in the previous listing. Details of other flags appear below.

- *hwndParent* identifies the property sheet's parent window. For modal property sheets, the parent window is disabled.

- For property sheets that use resources (such as icons), the *hInstance* parameter identifies the module from which resources are to be loaded.

- A property sheet can optionally have an icon, identified either by the icon handle, *hIcon* (requires PSH_USEHICON in *dwFlags*), or an icon resource, *pszIcon* (requires PSH_USEICONID in *dwFlags*).

- The property sheet caption is defined by the string *pszCaption*.

- The number of pages in a property sheet (and the size of the property page array) is *nPages*.

- The first property sheet page to display is either *nStartPage*, a zero-based index, or *pStartPage* (requires PSH_USEPSTARTPAGE in *dwFlags*), the caption of the first page to be displayed.

- The pages of a property sheet are defined using one of two types of arrays. The first alternative is an array of handles to property sheet pages as returned by

CreatePropertySheetPage (the default) and identified by *phpage*. The second choice is an array of PROPSHEETPAGE structures (requiring the PSH_PROP-SHEETPAGE flag in *dwFlags*) identified by *ppsp*.

■ In addition to the dialog box procedures for each property page, the property sheet itself can have a callback function that is called before any pages on the property sheet are created. This function is identified by *pfnCallback*.

The *dwFlags* member allows fine-tuning of a property sheet. Several of the flags indicate whether a particular member of PROPSHEETHEADER should be used or ignored. In the previous listing of that structure, individual members are marked with the names of flags. The other flags are summarized in the following table:

Flag	Meaning
PSH_HASHELP	Displays the Help button in the property sheet, which is enabled when a page with the PSP_HASHELP flag is active. When clicked, it sends a WM_NOTIFY message with a PSN_HELP notification code.
PSH_MODELESS	Creates a modeless property sheet.
PSH_NOAPPLYNOW	Hides the Apply button.
PSH_PROPTITLE	Appends the word "Properties" in the title bar after the title defined by the *pszCaption* member of PROPSHEETHEADER.
PSH_WIZARD	Creates a wizard instead of a property sheet.

The *PropertySheet* function

The function that actually creates a property sheet is *PropertySheet*, which takes a single parameter: a pointer to a PROPSHEETHEADER structure. Property sheets are modal by default, so the *PropertySheet* function returns TRUE when the user clicks OK and FALSE when the user clicks Cancel. A call to *PropertySheet* looks like a typical call to *DialogBox*:

```
if (PropertySheet (&pshead))
    {
    [user clicked OK -- accept changes]
    }
else
    {
    [user clicked Cancel -- abandon changes]
    }
```

To create a modeless property sheet, create the property sheet by calling *PropertySheet* with the PSH_MODELESS flag in the property sheet header structure. Instead of returning a Boolean value, *PropertySheet* returns a handle to the property sheet window:

```
// Create modeless property sheet -- returns HWND
HWND hwndPropSheet = (HWND) PropertySheet (&pshead) ;
```

Property Page Dialog Box Procedures

Each property page has its own dialog box procedure. On creation of a property page, the dialog procedure receives a WM_INITDIALOG message, in response to which a dialog procedure initializes the controls in the page. The property sheet takes a lazy approach to creating individual property pages, however, and doesn't create them until they are needed. For this reason, a particular property page won't get a WM_INITDIALOG message when the property sheet is first created and if a particular property page never becomes active, its dialog procedure won't get a WM_INITDIALOG message.

As with the dialog procedures in regular dialog boxes, property page dialog procedures receive WM_COMMAND notifications for their controls. But without the OK and Cancel buttons of regular dialogs, you shouldn't call *EndDialog* from a property page dialog procedure to dismiss either the property page or the property sheet. Instead, rely on the property sheet to destroy each page when the user dismisses the property sheet.

The WM_NOTIFY message

The property sheet sends a WM_NOTIFY message to notify dialog procedures of significant changes in the state of a property sheet. This message identifies when a page is activated and when it is deactivated. For property pages that require validation of individual controls, the deactivation notification provides the opportunity to check values and optionally to prevent the property page from being deactivated when invalid values are present. A WM_NOTIFY message also gets sent when the user clicks the OK or Apply button—requesting that the changes be applied—or the Cancel button to request that changes be ignored. When a property sheet is created as a wizard, a third set of WM_NOTIFY messages inform the dialog procedure of clicks on wizard buttons: Back, Next, or Finish.

The *lParam* of the WM_NOTIFY message holds a pointer to an NMHDR; the *code* member of this data structure identifies the reason for the notification. This code skeleton handles all available property sheet notifications:

```
case WM_NOTIFY :
     {
     LPNMHDR pnmh = (LPNMHDR) lParam ;
     switch (pnmh->code)
```

(continued)

```
        {
        case PSN_SETACTIVATE :
            [property page activated]
            break ;

        case PSN_KILLACTIVE :
            [property page deactivated]
            break ;

        case PSN_APPLY :
            [user clicked OK or Apply]
            break ;

        case PSN_RESET :
            [user clicked Cancel]
            break ;

        case PSN_QUERYCANCEL :
            [user clicked Cancel -- Ok?]
            break ;

        case PSN_HELP :
            [user clicked Help]
            break ;

        case PSN_WIZBACK :
            [user clicked Back on wizard]
            break ;

        case PSN_WIZNEXT :
            [user clicked Next on wizard]
            break ;

        case PSN_WIZFINISH :
            [user clicked Finish on wizard]
            break ;
        }
    }
```

The meanings of individual property page notifications are summarized in the table on the following page:

Notification Code	User Action	Description
PSN_APPLY	User clicked OK button (dismisses property page) or Apply button (doesn't dismiss property page). Active and inactive pages get this, but only if the page has been created.	Acceptance of requested changes.
PSN_HELP	Help button	
PSN_KILLACTIVE	User has either dismissed property page, moved to another property page, or clicked Apply button.	Notification to validate contents of page; can prevent page from being dismissed when invalid values detected.
PSN_QUERYCANCEL	Cancel button	Asks whether user can cancel property sheet.
PSN_RESET	Cancel button	Notification to ignore all actions since Apply button was last clicked.
PSN_SETACTIVE	User has either started property page and current page is first active, picked a new active page, or clicked Apply button (which deactivates and reactivates page).	Notification that a page is active.
PSN_WIZBACK	User has clicked the Back button on a wizard.	
PSN_WIZFINISH	User has clicked the Finish button on a wizard.	
PSN_WIZNEXT	User has clicked the Next button on a wizard.	

The most important of these notifications is PSN_APPLY, which means that the user has clicked the OK or Apply button. Requested changes should be accepted. This notification replaces the WM_COMMAND message with the IDOK control ID in a normal dialog. Unlike a normal dialog, however, you don't call *EndDialog* from within a property page dialog (because doing so causes the property page to disappear). You leave it up to the property sheet itself to manage the creation and destruction of individual property pages.

PSN_APPLY is sent when either of two buttons are clicked—OK or Apply—and in most cases you apply the changes and don't try to distinguish one from the other. However, there is a situation in which the cases are handled differently: for a modeless property sheet, you must destroy the property sheet when the OK button is clicked. Here's how to do that:

```
// Check for modeless property sheet
if (IsWindowEnabled (hwndMain))
    {
    LPPSHNOTIFY psh = (LPPSHNOTIFY) lParam ;
    HWND hwndPropSheet ;

    // Click Apply button means no destroy
    if (pnmh->code == PSN_APPLY && psh->lParam == 0)
        return TRUE ;

    // Clicking OK or Cancel, destroy property sheet
    hwndPropSheet = GetParent (hwndDlg) ;
    DestroyWindow (hwndPropSheet) ;
    hwndModeless = NULL ;
    }
```

The PSN_APPLY and PSN_RESET notifications are broadcast to the dialog procedure for every active and inactive property page in a property sheet—subject to one restriction: The property page must have been created. Since the property sheet takes a lazy approach to creating individual property pages, only creating them when the user tries to activate a page for the first time, it's possible (and quite common) to have a property sheet in which a particular property page dialog procedure doesn't receive a WM_NOTIFY message. In practice, what this means is that a property page dialog will always receive a WM_INIT-DIALOG message—so it can initialize all its controls—before it receives a WM_NOTIFY message.

Controlling property sheets

Controlling a property sheet involves sending it messages, for which you need a handle to the property sheet itself. Property page dialog procedures receive a handle to individual property pages, which are child windows of the property sheet. Receiving a handle to a property sheet requires a call to *GetParent*:

```
// Fetch handle to property sheet
HWND hwndPropSheet = GetParent (hwndDlg) ;
```

With this handle, you call *SendMessage*—something easily accomplished with the property sheet macros provided in PRSHT.H.

The following table summarizes available property sheet messages:

Category	Message	Description
Activate page	PSM_SETCURSEL	Notification to activate the page identified by zero-based index or property page handle.
	PSM_SETCURSELID	Notification to activate the page identified by page resource ID.
Button state	PSM_APPLY	Simulates user clicking the Apply button, which causes all existing pages to receive a WM_NOTIFY message with a PSN_APPLY notification code.
	PSM_CANCELTOCLOSE	Disables Cancel button and changes text of OK button to Close.
	PSM_CHANGED	Sets "dirty flag" for current page. If dirty flag is set for any page, Apply button is enabled; otherwise, it is disabled.
	PSM_UNCHANGED	Clears "dirty flag" for current page; see PSM_CHANGED, above.
	PSM_PRESSBUTTON	Simulates user pressing property sheet button.
	PSM_SETFINISHTEXT	Enables Finish button on wizard and sets its text.
	PSM_SETWIZBUTTONS	Enables wizard buttons.
Edit page list	PSM_ADDPAGE	Adds page to property sheet.
	PSM_REMOVEPAGE	Deletes page from property sheet.
Query	PSM_GETTABCONTROL	Fetches handle to tab control.
	PSM_GETCURRENTPAGEHWND	Fetches window handle to current property page window.

(continued)

Category	Message	Description
	PSM_QUERYSIBLINGS	On receipt of this message, the property sheet sends a PSM_QUERYSIBLINGS message to the dialog procedure for all existing property pages. (The term "existing" means that the user has visited the page, causing the dialog procedure to receive a WM_INITDIALOG message.)
Change requires reboot	PSM_REBOOTSYSTEM	Set flag to cause *Property-Sheet* function to return ID_PSREBOOTSYSTEM.
	PSM_RESTARTWINDOWS	Set flag to cause *Property-Sheet* function to return ID_PSRESTARTWINDOWS.
Miscellaneous	PSM_ISDIALOGMESSAGE	Enables keyboard interface to modeless property sheet (see discussion beginning on page 686).
	PSM_SETTITLE	Sets title on property sheet.

Enabling and disabling the Apply button

The Apply button is disabled when a property sheet is created and must be explicitly enabled from the dialog box procedures for individual property pages when a user changes some data. Notify the property sheet that data has changed by sending a PSM_CHANGED message. Revoke changes (and disable the Apply button) by sending a PSM_UNCHANGED message to the property sheet. Using the PRSHT.H message macros, here's how to send this message to a property sheet:

```
hwndSheet = GetParent (hwndDlg) ;
PropSheet_Changed (hwndSheet, hwndDlg) ;
```

The property sheet keeps a "changed" bit for each property page, so that the Apply button gets enabled whenever *any* property page declares that its contents have changed, regardless of which page happens to be visible at a given moment.

Applying changes

When the user clicks either the OK or Apply button, it's time to engage whatever changes have been requested. The two events should be handled in the same way, even though a click on the OK button dismisses the property sheet, while a click on the Apply button doesn't. One way to combine the handling of the two changes into one operation is to send a message to the parent window requesting that changes be applied. This is different from the way a modal dialog would be handled in a typical Windows program, which would just wait for a return from the *DialogBox* function before initiating any changes in the main program. In fact, it's more akin to the way that changes from a modeless dialog would be handled.

The notification from an OK button click and an Apply button click are the same. The dialog procedures for existing property pages—pages that the user has visited and whose dialog procedures have received a WM_INITDIALOG message—will get a WM_NOTIFY message with a PSN_APPLY notification code. The reasonable response is to write whatever changes have taken place and send a message to the parent window.

To make a property sheet behave more like a modal dialog box, hide the Apply button by creating the property sheet with the PSH_NOAPPLYNOW style flag. (Formerly, "Apply Now" was the button title.) Applying the changes then involves watching the return value from *PropertySheet*: clicking OK returns a value of TRUE, clicking Cancel returns a value of FALSE.

Property sheet help

There are two mechanisms for requesting help on a property sheet: the Help button and the F1 key. The Help button only appears on property sheets created with a PSH_HASHELP creation flag, and it remains disabled until a property page with a PSP_HASHELP flag is active. Clicks on the Help button cause a WM_NOTIFY message with a PSN_HELP notification code to be sent to the property page dialog procedure. You'll presumably respond to this message by displaying a help window with tips for using a particular property page.

Every Win32 window supports the F1 help key. The default window procedure responds to unhandled F1 key hits by sending a WM_HELP message to a window's parent window. For this reason, nothing special is required to enable F1-key help support aside from handling the WM_HELP message.

Handling a modeless property sheet

Just as most dialog boxes are modal dialogs, most property sheets are modal. Should you desire a modeless property sheet, a few extra changes are required. To obtain a modeless dialog in the first place, specify the PSH_MODELESS flag in the PROPSHEETHEADER structure. Other than that, the other changes are the same you need to make for a modeless dialog box.

To enable the keyboard interface for a modeless dialog box, you call *IsDialogMessage*. This function filters the message loop for keyboard messages. On receipt of a keyboard message, the control holding the keyboard focus receives a WM_GETDLGCODE message essentially asking it, "What kinds of keyboard input do you want?" Based on the reply, the control might get the keyboard or—in response to the Tab key, Alt plus a mnemonic, or arrow keys—the focus gets moved to the next non-static control in the dialog's tab order.

For a modeless property sheet, send a PSM_ISDIALOGMESSAGE message to the property sheet parent instead of calling *IsDialogMessage*. A program with a modeless property sheet, then, will have a message loop like the following:

```
while (GetMessage (&msg, NULL, 0, 0))
    {
    if ((hwndModeless) &&
        (!(PropSheet_IsDialogMessage (hwndModeless, &msg))))
        continue ;

    TranslateMessage (&msg) ;
    DispatchMessage (&msg) ;
    }
```

This code assumes that *hwndModeless* either has a handle to the modeless property sheet when it's present or a NULL when the property sheet isn't present.

Setting wizard buttons

When creating a wizard instead of a property sheet, the dialog procedure for each property page must control the wizard buttons. While a property sheet has an OK and a Cancel button, wizards have Back and Next buttons. Both buttons remain enabled unless you explicitly disable them. And on the last page of a wizard, users expect to see a Finish button in place of a Next button.

To control the setting of wizard buttons, send a PSM_SETWIZBUTTONS message with the *lParam* set to some combination of three values: PSWIZB_NEXT, PSWIZB_BACK, and PSWIZB_FINISH. The right time to send this message is when a wizard page becomes active, which a property page dialog knows about because the dialog procedure receives a PSN_SETACTIVE notification in the form of a WM_NOTIFY message. In response to a PSN_SETACTIVE notification, a wizard can prevent a page from becoming active by returning −1. Alternatively, by returning the resource ID of a specific wizard page, that wizard page is the next one to become active. Otherwise, a return value of 0 allows a particular wizard page to be activated.

When the first page of a wizard becomes active, disable the Back button by sending a PSM_SETWIZBUTTONS message with the PSWIZB_NEXT flag in the *lParam*. The *PropSheet_SetWizButtons* macro provides one way to send this message:

```
// Enable Next button on wizard page
if (bWizard && pnmh->code == PSN_SETACTIVE)
    {
    HWND hwndSheet = GetParent (hwndDlg) ;
    PropSheet_SetWizButtons (hwndSheet, PSWIZB_NEXT) ;
    }
```

On the last page of a wizard, enable the Back button and change the text of the Next button to "Finish" by sending a PSM_SETWIZBUTTONS message with *lParam* set to PSWIZB_BACK combined with PSWIZB_FINISH using the C bitwise OR operator.

```
// Enable Back and Finish buttons on wizard page
if (bWizard && pnmh->code == PSN_SETACTIVE)
    {
    HWND hwndSheet = GetParent (hwndDlg) ;
    PropSheet_SetWizButtons (hwndSheet, PSWIZB_BACK !
                                        PSWIZB_FINISH) ;
    }
```

The PROPERTY Program

Figure 12-11 and Figure 12-12 show the two property pages on the property sheet created by PROPERTY, a property sheet sample. Taken together, the property pages define all the generic style flags (WS_ and WS_EX_) that can be passed to the *CreateWindowEx* function. PROPERTY's main window shows two windows: One ("First Window") is created with the style flags that are edited in the property sheet. Another window ("Second Window") exists to show the effects of certain window clipping style flags (WS_CLIPSIBLINGS) in preventing "sibling rivalry" when two child windows share the same pixels. In addition to showing the basics of building property sheets, PROPERTY shows the workings of most of the window creation style flags. The listings for PROPERTY appear in Figure 12-13.

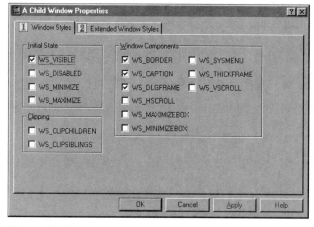

Figure 12-11. *The Window Styles property page.*

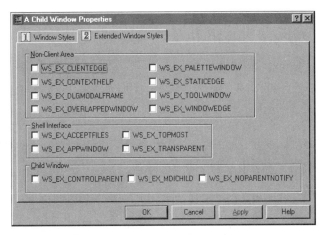

Figure 12-12. *The Extended Window Styles property page.*

PROPERTY.MAK

```
#-----------------------
# PROPERTY.MAK make file
#-----------------------


property.exe : property.obj helper.obj notify.obj \
            page1.obj page2.obj sheet.obj property.res
    $(LINKER) $(GUIFLAGS) -OUT:property.exe property.obj \
    helper.obj notify.obj page1.obj page2.obj sheet.obj \
    property.res $(GUILIBS)


property.obj : property.c comcthlp.h property.h
    $(CC) $(CFLAGS) property.c


helper.obj : helper.c property.h
    $(CC) $(CFLAGS) helper.c


notify.obj : notify.c notify.h
    $(CC) $(CFLAGS) notify.c


page1.obj : page1.c helper.h notify.h property.h
    $(CC) $(CFLAGS) page1.c


page2.obj : page2.c helper.h notify.h property.h
    $(CC) $(CFLAGS) page2.c


sheet.obj : sheet.c comcthlp.h property.h
    $(CC) $(CFLAGS) sheet.c
```

Figure 12-13. *The PROPERTY program.*

(continued)

```
property.res : property.rc property.ico
    $(RC) $(RCVARS) property.rc
```

PROPERTY.H

```
// Menu item identifiers
#define IDM_OVERLAPPED    100
#define IDM_POPUP         101
#define IDM_CHILD         102
#define IDM_WIZARD        200
#define IDM_HASHELP       201
#define IDM_MODELESS      202
#define IDM_MULTILINETABS 203
#define IDM_NOAPPLYNOW    204
#define IDM_PROPTITLE     205
#define IDM_RTLREADING    206

// Dialog template IDs
#define IDD_STYLES                       101
#define IDD_EXSTYLES                     102

// Icon IDs
#define IDI_PAGE1                        103
#define IDI_PAGE2                        104

// Dialog Control IDs
#define IDC_BORDER                       1000
#define IDC_CAPTION                      1001
#define IDC_VISIBLE                      1005
#define IDC_DISABLED                     1006
#define IDC_DLGFRAME                     1007
#define IDC_MINIMIZE                     1008
#define IDC_MAXIMIZE                     1009
#define IDC_HSCROLL                      1010
#define IDC_MAXIMIZEBOX                  1011
#define IDC_MINIMIZEBOX                  1012
#define IDC_SYSMENU                      1013
#define IDC_THICKFRAME                   1014
#define IDC_VSCROLL                      1015
#define IDC_CLIPCHILDREN                 1016
#define IDC_CLIPSIBLINGS                 1017
#define IDC_CLIENTEDGE                   1018
#define IDC_CONTEXTHELP                  1019
#define IDC_DLGMODALFRAME                1020
#define IDC_EXOVERLAPPED                 1021
#define IDC_PALETTE                      1022
```

(continued)

690

```
#define IDC_STATICEDGE          1023
#define IDC_TOOLWINDOW          1024
#define IDC_WINDOWEDGE          1025
#define IDC_ACCEPTFILES         1026
#define IDC_APPWINDOW           1027
#define IDC_TOPMOST             1028
#define IDC_TRANSPARENT         1029
#define IDC_CONTROLPARENT       1030
#define IDC_MDICHILD            1031
#define IDC_NOPARENTNOTIFY      1032
#define IDM_WINDOW_PROPERTIES   40001
#define IDC_STATIC              -1
#define IDI_APP                 1000


// Private message
#define PM_CREATEWINDOW    WM_APP


// Property Sheet Functions (in SHEET.C)
BOOL CreatePropertySheet (HWND hwndParent) ;


// Property Page Functions (in PAGE1.C and PAGE2.C)
UINT CALLBACK StylePageProc (HWND, UINT, LPPROPSHEETPAGE) ;
BOOL CALLBACK StyleDlgProc (HWND, UINT, WPARAM, LPARAM) ;
UINT CALLBACK ExStylePageProc (HWND, UINT, LPPROPSHEETPAGE) ;
BOOL CALLBACK ExStyleDlgProc (HWND, UINT, WPARAM, LPARAM) ;
```

HELPER.H

```
void SetButtonCheck (HWND hwndDlg, int CtrlID, BOOL bCheck) ;
BOOL QueryButtonCheck (HWND hwndDlg, int CtrlID) ;
```

PROPERTY.C

```
/*-----------------------------------------
   PROPERTY.C -- Property sheet example
                 (c) Paul Yao, 1996
   -----------------------------------------*/
#include <windows.h>
#include <windowsx.h>
#include <commctrl.h>
#include "comcthlp.h"
#include "property.h"


LRESULT CALLBACK WndProc (HWND, UINT, WPARAM, LPARAM) ;
```

(continued)

```
char szAppName[]  = "Property Sheet" ;
HINSTANCE hInst ;
HWND hwndMain = NULL ;
HWND hwndChild = NULL ;
HWND hwndModeless = NULL ;

HICON hiconApp ;  // Application icon
BOOL bWizard ;    // Flag whether PSH_WIZARD is set

// Values modified by property sheet
DWORD dwChildStyle = WS_CHILD | WS_VISIBLE | WS_BORDER | WS_CAPTION ;
DWORD dwChildExStyle = 0L ;

// Value modified by menu item selection
DWORD dwSheetStyles = PSH_PROPTITLE ;

//-----------------------------------------------------------------------
int WINAPI WinMain (HINSTANCE hInstance, HINSTANCE hPrevInstance,
                    PSTR lpszCmdLine, int cmdShow)
     {
     HWND        hwnd ;
     MSG         msg ;
     WNDCLASSEX wc ;

     hInst = hInstance ;
     hiconApp = LoadIcon (hInst, MAKEINTRESOURCE (IDI_APP)) ;

     ZeroMemory (&wc, sizeof (WNDCLASSEX)) ;
     wc.cbSize        = sizeof (wc) ;
     wc.lpszClassName = "MAIN" ;
     wc.hInstance     = hInstance ;
     wc.lpfnWndProc   = WndProc ;
     wc.hCursor       = LoadCursor (NULL, IDC_ARROW) ;
     wc.hIcon         = hiconApp ;
     wc.lpszMenuName  = "MAIN" ;
     wc.hbrBackground = (HBRUSH) (COLOR_APPWORKSPACE + 1) ;
     wc.hIconSm       = hiconApp ;

     RegisterClassEx (&wc) ;

     wc.lpszClassName = "CHILD" ;
     wc.lpfnWndProc   = DefWindowProc ;
     wc.hCursor       = LoadCursor (NULL, IDC_IBEAM) ;
     wc.hIcon         = NULL ;
     wc.lpszMenuName  = NULL ;
     wc.hbrBackground = (HBRUSH) (COLOR_WINDOW + 1) ;
     wc.hIconSm       = NULL ;
```

(continued)

```
        RegisterClassEx (&wc) ;

        hwndMain =
        hwnd = CreateWindowEx (WS_EX_OVERLAPPEDWINDOW, "MAIN",
                               szAppName, WS_OVERLAPPEDWINDOW,
                               CW_USEDEFAULT, CW_USEDEFAULT,
                               CW_USEDEFAULT, CW_USEDEFAULT,
                               NULL, NULL, hInstance, NULL) ;

        ShowWindow (hwnd, cmdShow) ;
        UpdateWindow (hwnd) ;

        InitCommonControls () ;

        while (GetMessage (&msg, NULL, 0, 0))
             {
             if ((hwndModeless) &&
                 ((PropSheet_IsDialogMessage (hwndModeless, &msg))))
                 continue ;

             TranslateMessage (&msg) ;
             DispatchMessage (&msg) ;
             }
        return msg.wParam ;
        }

//-------------------------------------------------------------------
void MenuCheckMark (HMENU hmenu, int id, BOOL bCheck)
        {
        int iState ;
        iState = (bCheck) ? MF_CHECKED : MF_UNCHECKED ;
        CheckMenuItem (hmenu, id, iState) ;
        }

//-------------------------------------------------------------------
void static FlipFlag (LPDWORD dwStyle, DWORD flag)
        {
        if (*dwStyle & flag)  // Flag on -- turn off
            {
            *dwStyle &= (~flag) ;
            }
        else                  // Flag off -- turn on
            {
            *dwStyle |= flag ;
            }
        }
```

(continued)

693

```
//------------------------------------------------------------------
LRESULT CALLBACK
WndProc (HWND hwnd, UINT mMsg, WPARAM wParam, LPARAM lParam)
    {
    switch (mMsg)
        {
        case WM_CREATE :
            hwndChild = CreateWindowEx (dwChildExStyle, "CHILD",
                                        "First Window", dwChildStyle,
                                        0, 0, 0, 0, hwnd, (HMENU) 1,
                                                    hInst, NULL) ;


            CreateWindowEx (dwChildExStyle, "CHILD", "Second Window",
                            WS_CLIPSIBLINGS | dwChildStyle,
                            10, 10, 200, 50, hwnd,
                            (HMENU) 2, hInst, NULL) ;
            return 0 ;

        case WM_COMMAND :
            {
            switch (LOWORD (wParam))
                {
                case IDM_WINDOW_PROPERTIES :
                    {
                    BOOL bRet ;

                    // If modeless, activate existing property sheet
                    if (hwndModeless)
                        {
                        SetActiveWindow (hwndModeless) ;
                        break ;
                        }

                    // Are we creating a wizard?
                    bWizard = (dwSheetStyles & PSH_WIZARD) ;

                    // Create actual property sheet
                    bRet = CreatePropertySheet (hwnd) ;

                    // Store handle if modeless
                    if (dwSheetStyles & PSH_MODELESS)
                        {
                        hwndModeless = (HWND) bRet ;
                        break ;
                        }
```

(continued)

```
                          break ;
                          }

              case IDM_WIZARD :
                   FlipFlag (&dwSheetStyles, PSH_WIZARD) ;
                   break ;

              case IDM_HASHELP :
                   FlipFlag (&dwSheetStyles, PSH_HASHELP) ;
                   break ;

              case IDM_MODELESS :
                   FlipFlag (&dwSheetStyles, PSH_MODELESS) ;
                   break ;

              case IDM_NOAPPLYNOW :
                   FlipFlag (&dwSheetStyles, PSH_NOAPPLYNOW) ;
                   break ;

              case IDM_PROPTITLE :
                   FlipFlag (&dwSheetStyles, PSH_PROPTITLE) ;
                   break ;

              case IDM_RTLREADING :
                   FlipFlag (&dwSheetStyles, PSH_RTLREADING) ;
                   break ;
                   }
              return 0 ;
         }

    case WM_DESTROY :
         PostQuitMessage (0) ;
         return 0 ;

    case WM_INITMENU :
         {
         BOOL bCheck ;
         HMENU hmenu = (HMENU) wParam ;

         bCheck = (dwSheetStyles & PSH_WIZARD) ;
         MenuCheckMark (hmenu, IDM_WIZARD, bCheck) ;

         bCheck = (dwSheetStyles & PSH_HASHELP) ;
         MenuCheckMark (hmenu, IDM_HASHELP, bCheck) ;
```

(continued)

```
                    bCheck = (dwSheetStyles & PSH_MODELESS) ;
                    MenuCheckMark (hmenu, IDM_MODELESS, bCheck) ;

                    bCheck = (dwSheetStyles & PSH_NOAPPLYNOW) ;
                    MenuCheckMark (hmenu, IDM_NOAPPLYNOW, bCheck) ;

                    bCheck = (dwSheetStyles & PSH_PROPTITLE) ;
                    MenuCheckMark (hmenu, IDM_PROPTITLE, bCheck) ;

                    bCheck = (dwSheetStyles & PSH_RTLREADING) ;
                    MenuCheckMark (hmenu, IDM_RTLREADING, bCheck) ;

                    return 0 ;
                    }

          case WM_SETFOCUS :
                    SetFocus (hwndChild) ;
                    return 0 ;

          case WM_SIZE :
                    {
                    int cxWidth  = LOWORD (lParam) ;
                    int cyHeight = HIWORD (lParam) ;
                    int x, y, cx, cy ;

                    x  = cxWidth  / 4 ;
                    cx = cxWidth  / 2 ;
                    y  = cyHeight / 4 ;
                    cy = cyHeight / 2 ;

                    MoveWindow (hwndChild, x, y, cx, cy, TRUE) ;
                    return 0 ;
                    }

          case PM_CREATEWINDOW :
                    {
                    RECT rClient ;
                    LPARAM l ;

                    DestroyWindow (hwndChild) ;
                    hwndChild = CreateWindowEx (dwChildExStyle, "CHILD",
                                        "First Window", dwChildStyle,
                                        0, 0, 0, 0, hwnd, (HMENU) 1,
                                                    hInst, NULL) ;
```

(continued)

696

```
                // Send ourselves a WM_SIZE to resize child window
                GetClientRect (hwnd, &rClient) ;
                l = MAKELPARAM (rClient.right, rClient.bottom) ;
                SendMessage (hwnd, WM_SIZE, 0, l) ;
                return 0 ;
                }

        default :
            return (DefWindowProc (hwnd, mMsg, wParam, lParam)) ;
        }
    }
```

SHEET.C

```
/*---------------------------------------------
   SHEET.C -- Property sheet page functions
            (c) Paul Yao, 1996
   ---------------------------------------------*/
#include <windows.h>
#include <windowsx.h>
#include <commctrl.h>
#include "comcthlp.h"
#include "property.h"


extern DWORD dwChildStyle ;
extern DWORD dwChildExStyle ;
extern DWORD dwSheetStyles ;
extern char szAppName[] ;
extern HINSTANCE hInst ;
extern HICON hiconApp ;


//------------------------------------------------------------------
int CALLBACK PropSheetProc (HWND hwndDlg, UINT uMsg, LPARAM lParam)
    {
    switch (uMsg)
        {
        case PSCB_INITIALIZED :
            // Process PSCB_INITIALIZED
            break ;

        case PSCB_PRECREATE :
            // Process PSCB_PRECREATE
            break ;
```

(continued)

```
            default :
                // Unknown message
                break ;
            }

        return 0 ;
        }


//----------------------------------------------------------------------
BOOL CreatePropertySheet (HWND hwndParent)
    {
    PROPSHEETHEADER pshead ;
    PROPSHEETPAGE   pspage[2] ;

    // Initialize property sheet HEADER data
    ZeroMemory (&pshead, sizeof (PROPSHEETHEADER)) ;
    pshead.dwSize  = sizeof (PROPSHEETHEADER) ;
    pshead.dwFlags = dwSheetStyles      |
                     PSH_PROPSHEETPAGE  |
                     PSH_USECALLBACK    |
                     PSH_USEHICON ;
    pshead.hwndParent  = hwndParent ;
    pshead.hInstance   = hInst ;
    pshead.hIcon       = hiconApp ;
    pshead.pszCaption  = "A Child Window" ;
    pshead.nPages      = 2 ;
    pshead.nStartPage  = 0 ;
    pshead.ppsp        = pspage ;
    pshead.pfnCallback = PropSheetProc ;

    // Zero out property PAGE data
    ZeroMemory (&pspage, 2 * sizeof (PROPSHEETPAGE)) ;

    // PAGE 1 -- window style page
    pspage[0].dwSize      = sizeof (PROPSHEETPAGE) ;
    pspage[0].dwFlags     = PSP_USECALLBACK | PSP_USEICONID ;
    pspage[0].hInstance   = hInst ;
    pspage[0].pszTemplate = MAKEINTRESOURCE (IDD_STYLES) ;
    pspage[0].pszIcon     = MAKEINTRESOURCE (IDI_PAGE1) ;
    pspage[0].pfnDlgProc  = StyleDlgProc ;
    pspage[0].lParam      = (LPARAM) &dwChildStyle ;
    pspage[0].pfnCallback = StylePageProc ;

    // PAGE 2 -- extended window style page
    pspage[1].dwSize      = sizeof (PROPSHEETPAGE) ;
```

(continued)

698

```
        pspage[1].dwFlags      = PSP_USECALLBACK | PSP_USEICONID |
                                 PSP_HASHELP ;
        pspage[1].hInstance    = hInst ;
        pspage[1].pszTemplate  = MAKEINTRESOURCE (IDD_EXSTYLES) ;
        pspage[1].pszIcon      = MAKEINTRESOURCE (IDI_PAGE2) ;
        pspage[1].pfnDlgProc   = ExStyleDlgProc ;
        pspage[1].lParam       = (LPARAM) &dwChildExStyle ;
        pspage[1].pfnCallback  = ExStylePageProc ;

        // --------- Create & display property sheet ---------

        return PropertySheet (&pshead) ;
        }
```

PAGE1.C

```
/*-----------------------------------
   PAGE1.C -- Property sheet page 1
             (c) Paul Yao, 1996
   -----------------------------------*/
#include <windows.h>
#include <prsht.h>
#include "property.h"
#include "notify.h"
#include "helper.h"

static LPDWORD pTheStyles ;
extern BOOL bWizard ;
extern HWND hwndMain ;
extern HWND hwndModeless ;

DWORD FetchStyles (HWND hwndDlg) ;

//-------------------------------------------------------------------
UINT CALLBACK
StylePageProc (HWND  hwnd, UINT uMsg, LPPROPSHEETPAGE ppsp)
    {
    switch (uMsg)
        {
        case PSPCB_CREATE :
            // Store pointer to style data
            pTheStyles = (LPDWORD) ppsp->lParam ;
            return TRUE ;
```

(continued)

```
                case PSPCB_RELEASE :
                    return 0 ;
                }

        return 0 ;
        }


//-------------------------------------------------------------------------
BOOL CALLBACK
StyleDlgProc (HWND hwndDlg, UINT msg, WPARAM wParam, LPARAM lParam)
        {
    switch (msg)
            {
        case WM_INITDIALOG :
                {
                BOOL bCheck ;
                DWORD dwOrigStyle = *pTheStyles ;

                bCheck = (dwOrigStyle & WS_VISIBLE) ;
                SetButtonCheck (hwndDlg, IDC_VISIBLE, bCheck) ;

                bCheck = (dwOrigStyle & WS_DISABLED) ;
                SetButtonCheck (hwndDlg, IDC_DISABLED, bCheck) ;

                bCheck = (dwOrigStyle & WS_MINIMIZE) ;
                SetButtonCheck (hwndDlg, IDC_MINIMIZE, bCheck) ;

                bCheck = (dwOrigStyle & WS_MAXIMIZE) ;
                SetButtonCheck (hwndDlg, IDC_MAXIMIZE, bCheck) ;

                bCheck = (dwOrigStyle & WS_CLIPCHILDREN) ;
                SetButtonCheck (hwndDlg, IDC_CLIPCHILDREN, bCheck) ;

                bCheck = (dwOrigStyle & WS_CLIPSIBLINGS) ;
                SetButtonCheck (hwndDlg, IDC_CLIPSIBLINGS, bCheck) ;

                bCheck = (dwOrigStyle & WS_BORDER) ;
                SetButtonCheck (hwndDlg, IDC_BORDER, bCheck) ;

                bCheck = (dwOrigStyle & WS_CAPTION) ;
                SetButtonCheck (hwndDlg, IDC_CAPTION, bCheck) ;

                bCheck = (dwOrigStyle & WS_DLGFRAME) ;
                SetButtonCheck (hwndDlg, IDC_DLGFRAME, bCheck) ;
```

(continued)

```
        bCheck = (dwOrigStyle & WS_HSCROLL) ;
        SetButtonCheck (hwndDlg, IDC_HSCROLL, bCheck) ;

        bCheck = (dwOrigStyle & WS_MAXIMIZEBOX) ;
        SetButtonCheck (hwndDlg, IDC_MAXIMIZEBOX, bCheck) ;

        bCheck = (dwOrigStyle & WS_MINIMIZEBOX) ;
        SetButtonCheck (hwndDlg, IDC_MINIMIZEBOX, bCheck) ;

        bCheck = (dwOrigStyle & WS_SYSMENU) ;
        SetButtonCheck (hwndDlg, IDC_SYSMENU, bCheck) ;

        bCheck = (dwOrigStyle & WS_THICKFRAME) ;
        SetButtonCheck (hwndDlg, IDC_THICKFRAME, bCheck) ;

        bCheck = (dwOrigStyle & WS_VSCROLL) ;
        SetButtonCheck (hwndDlg, IDC_VSCROLL, bCheck) ;

        return TRUE ;
}

case WM_COMMAND :
    {
    WORD wNotifyCode = HIWORD (wParam) ;
    WORD wID = LOWORD (wParam) ;
    HWND hwndSheet ;

    switch (wID)
        {
        case IDC_VISIBLE :
        case IDC_DISABLED :
        case IDC_MINIMIZE :
        case IDC_MAXIMIZE :
        case IDC_CLIPCHILDREN :
        case IDC_CLIPSIBLINGS :
        case IDC_BORDER :
        case IDC_CAPTION :
        case IDC_DLGFRAME :
        case IDC_HSCROLL :
        case IDC_MAXIMIZEBOX :
        case IDC_MINIMIZEBOX :
        case IDC_SYSMENU :
        case IDC_THICKFRAME :
```

(continued)

```
                        case IDC_VSCROLL :
                            hwndSheet = GetParent (hwndDlg) ;
                            PropSheet_Changed (hwndSheet, hwndDlg) ;
                            break ;
                        }
                    return TRUE ;
                    }

            case WM_HELP :
                // Catch F1 key strike
                MessageBox (hwndDlg, "WM_HELP Message Received",
                            "StyleDlgProc", MB_OK) ;
                return TRUE ;

            case WM_NOTIFY :
                {
                LPNMHDR pnmh = (LPNMHDR) lParam ;

                // Handle OK and Apply buttons
                if (pnmh->code == PSN_APPLY)
                    {
                    HWND hwndPS ;
                    HWND hwndActive ;

                    // Overwrite current style value
                    *pTheStyles = FetchStyles (hwndDlg) ;

                    // Tell main window to re-create child window
                    hwndPS = GetParent (hwndDlg) ;
                    hwndActive = PropSheet_GetCurrentPageHwnd (hwndPS) ;

                    // Only re-create if we're the active page
                    if (hwndDlg == hwndActive)
                        PostMessage (hwndMain, PM_CREATEWINDOW, 0, 0L) ;
                    }

                // Destroy modeless dialog on OK or Cancel
                if ((IsWindowEnabled (hwndMain)) &&
                    (pnmh->code == PSN_APPLY || pnmh->code == PSN_RESET))
                    {
                    LPPSHNOTIFY psh = (LPPSHNOTIFY) lParam ;
                    HWND hwndPropSheet ;

                    // Ignore Apply button
                    if (pnmh->code == PSN_APPLY && psh->lParam == 0)
                        return TRUE ;
```

(continued)

```
                        // Clicking OK or Cancel, destroy property sheet
                        hwndPropSheet = GetParent (hwndDlg) ;
                        DestroyWindow (hwndPropSheet) ;
                        hwndModeless = NULL ;
                        }

                  // Enable Next button on wizard page
                  if (bWizard && pnmh->code == PSN_SETACTIVE)
                        {
                        HWND hwndSheet = GetParent (hwndDlg) ;
                        PropSheet_SetWizButtons (hwndSheet, PSWIZB_NEXT) ;
                        }
                  return TRUE ;
                  }

            default :
                  return FALSE ;
            }
      }

//------------------------------------------------------------------
DWORD FetchStyles (HWND hwndDlg)
      {
      DWORD dwStyle = WS_CHILD ;

      if (QueryButtonCheck (hwndDlg, IDC_VISIBLE))
            {
            dwStyle |= WS_VISIBLE ;
            }

      if (QueryButtonCheck (hwndDlg, IDC_DISABLED))
            {
            dwStyle |= WS_DISABLED ;
            }

      if (QueryButtonCheck (hwndDlg, IDC_MINIMIZE))
            {
            dwStyle |= WS_MINIMIZE ;
            }

      if (QueryButtonCheck (hwndDlg, IDC_MAXIMIZE))
            {
            dwStyle |= WS_MAXIMIZE ;
            }
```

(continued)

```
if (QueryButtonCheck (hwndDlg, IDC_CLIPCHILDREN))
    {
    dwStyle |= WS_CLIPCHILDREN ;
    }

if (QueryButtonCheck (hwndDlg, IDC_CLIPSIBLINGS))
    {
    dwStyle |= WS_CLIPSIBLINGS ;
    }

if (QueryButtonCheck (hwndDlg, IDC_BORDER))
    {
    dwStyle |= WS_BORDER ;
    }

if (QueryButtonCheck (hwndDlg, IDC_CAPTION))
    {
    dwStyle |= WS_CAPTION ;
    }

if (QueryButtonCheck (hwndDlg, IDC_DLGFRAME))
    {
    dwStyle |= WS_DLGFRAME ;
    }

if (QueryButtonCheck (hwndDlg, IDC_HSCROLL))
    {
    dwStyle |= WS_HSCROLL ;
    }

if (QueryButtonCheck (hwndDlg, IDC_MAXIMIZEBOX))
    {
    dwStyle |= WS_MAXIMIZEBOX ;
    }

if (QueryButtonCheck (hwndDlg, IDC_MINIMIZEBOX))
    {
    dwStyle |= WS_MINIMIZEBOX ;
    }

if (QueryButtonCheck (hwndDlg, IDC_SYSMENU))
    {
    dwStyle |= WS_SYSMENU ;
    }
```

(continued)

```
    if (QueryButtonCheck (hwndDlg, IDC_THICKFRAME))
        {
        dwStyle |= WS_THICKFRAME ;
        }

    if (QueryButtonCheck (hwndDlg, IDC_VSCROLL))
        {
        dwStyle |= WS_VSCROLL ;
        }

    return dwStyle ;
    }
```

PAGE2.C

```
/*-----------------------------------
   PAGE2.C -- Property sheet page 2
            (c) Paul Yao, 1996
   -----------------------------------*/
#include <windows.h>
#include <commctrl.h>
#include "property.h"
#include "notify.h"
#include "helper.h"

static LPDWORD pTheExStyles ;
extern BOOL bWizard ;
extern HWND hwndMain ;
extern HWND hwndModeless ;

DWORD FetchExStyles (HWND hwndDlg) ;

//-------------------------------------------------------------------
UINT CALLBACK
ExStylePageProc (HWND  hwnd, UINT uMsg, LPPROPSHEETPAGE ppsp)
    {
    switch (uMsg)
        {
        case PSPCB_CREATE :
            // Store pointer to extended style data
            pTheExStyles = (LPDWORD) ppsp->lParam ;
            return TRUE ;
```

(continued)

```
                    case PSPCB_RELEASE :
                        break ;
                    }

             return 0 ;
             }

//---------------------------------------------------------------------
BOOL CALLBACK
ExStyleDlgProc (HWND hwndDlg, UINT msg, WPARAM wParam, LPARAM lParam)
         {
         switch (msg)
                {
                case WM_INITDIALOG :
                    {
                    BOOL bCheck ;
                    DWORD dwOrigStyle = *pTheExStyles ;

                    bCheck = (dwOrigStyle & WS_EX_CLIENTEDGE) ;
                    SetButtonCheck (hwndDlg, IDC_CLIENTEDGE, bCheck) ;

                    bCheck = (dwOrigStyle & WS_EX_CONTEXTHELP) ;
                    SetButtonCheck (hwndDlg, IDC_CONTEXTHELP, bCheck) ;

                    bCheck = (dwOrigStyle & WS_EX_DLGMODALFRAME) ;
                    SetButtonCheck (hwndDlg, IDC_DLGMODALFRAME, bCheck) ;

                    bCheck = (dwOrigStyle & WS_EX_OVERLAPPEDWINDOW) ;
                    SetButtonCheck (hwndDlg, IDC_EXOVERLAPPED, bCheck) ;

                    bCheck = (dwOrigStyle & WS_EX_PALETTEWINDOW) ;
                    SetButtonCheck (hwndDlg, IDC_PALETTE, bCheck) ;

                    bCheck = (dwOrigStyle & WS_EX_STATICEDGE) ;
                    SetButtonCheck (hwndDlg, IDC_STATICEDGE, bCheck) ;

                    bCheck = (dwOrigStyle & WS_EX_TOOLWINDOW) ;
                    SetButtonCheck (hwndDlg, IDC_TOOLWINDOW, bCheck) ;

                    bCheck = (dwOrigStyle & WS_EX_WINDOWEDGE) ;
                    SetButtonCheck (hwndDlg, IDC_WINDOWEDGE, bCheck) ;

                    bCheck = (dwOrigStyle & WS_EX_ACCEPTFILES) ;
                    SetButtonCheck (hwndDlg, IDC_ACCEPTFILES, bCheck) ;

                    bCheck = (dwOrigStyle & WS_EX_APPWINDOW) ;
                    SetButtonCheck (hwndDlg, IDC_APPWINDOW, bCheck) ;
```

(continued)

```
                   bCheck = (dwOrigStyle & WS_EX_TOPMOST) ;
                   SetButtonCheck (hwndDlg, IDC_TOPMOST, bCheck) ;

                   bCheck = (dwOrigStyle & WS_EX_TRANSPARENT) ;
                   SetButtonCheck (hwndDlg, IDC_TRANSPARENT, bCheck) ;

                   bCheck = (dwOrigStyle & WS_EX_CONTROLPARENT) ;
                   SetButtonCheck (hwndDlg, IDC_CONTROLPARENT, bCheck) ;

                   bCheck = (dwOrigStyle & WS_EX_MDICHILD) ;
                   SetButtonCheck (hwndDlg, IDC_MDICHILD, bCheck) ;

                   bCheck = (dwOrigStyle & WS_EX_NOPARENTNOTIFY) ;
                   SetButtonCheck (hwndDlg, IDC_NOPARENTNOTIFY, bCheck) ;

                   return TRUE ;
                   }

          case WM_COMMAND :
               {
               WORD wNotifyCode = HIWORD (wParam) ;
               WORD wID = LOWORD (wParam) ;
               HWND hwndSheet ;

               switch (wID)
                   {
                   case IDC_CLIENTEDGE :
                   case IDC_CONTEXTHELP :
                   case IDC_DLGMODALFRAME :
                   case IDC_EXOVERLAPPED :
                   case IDC_PALETTE :
                   case IDC_STATICEDGE :
                   case IDC_TOOLWINDOW :
                   case IDC_WINDOWEDGE :
                   case IDC_ACCEPTFILES :
                   case IDC_APPWINDOW :
                   case IDC_TOPMOST :
                   case IDC_TRANSPARENT :
                   case IDC_CONTROLPARENT :
                   case IDC_MDICHILD :
                   case IDC_NOPARENTNOTIFY :
                        hwndSheet = GetParent (hwndDlg) ;
                        PropSheet_Changed (hwndSheet, hwndDlg) ;
                        break ;
                   }
               return TRUE ;
               }
```

(continued)

```
case WM_HELP :
    // Catch F1 key strike
    MessageBox (hwndDlg, "WM_HELP Message Received",
                "ExStyleDlgProc", MB_OK) ;
    return TRUE ;

case WM_NOTIFY :
    {
    LPNMHDR pnmh = (LPNMHDR) lParam ;

    // Handle Finish button on wizard page
    if (pnmh->code == PSN_WIZFINISH)
        {
        HWND hwndPS ;

        hwndPS = GetParent (hwndDlg) ;
        PropSheet_Apply (hwndPS) ;
        return TRUE ;
        }

    // Handle OK and Apply buttons
    if (pnmh->code == PSN_APPLY || pnmh->code == PSN_RESET)
        {
        HWND hwndPS ;
        HWND hwndActive ;

        // Overwrite current style value
        *pTheExStyles = FetchExStyles (hwndDlg) ;

        // Tell main window to re-create child window
        hwndPS = GetParent (hwndDlg) ;
        hwndActive = PropSheet_GetCurrentPageHwnd (hwndPS) ;

        // Only re-create if we're the active page
        if (hwndDlg == hwndActive)
            PostMessage (hwndMain, PM_CREATEWINDOW, 0, 0L) ;
        }

    // Destroy modeless dialog on OK or Cancel
    if ((IsWindowEnabled (hwndMain)) &&
        (pnmh->code == PSN_APPLY || pnmh->code == PSN_RESET))
        {
        LPPSHNOTIFY psh = (LPPSHNOTIFY) lParam ;
        HWND hwndPropSheet ;

        // Ignore Apply button
        if (pnmh->code == PSN_APPLY && psh->lParam == 0)
```

(continued)

```
                    return TRUE ;

                // Clicking OK or Cancel, destroy property sheet
                hwndPropSheet = GetParent (hwndDlg) ;
                DestroyWindow (hwndPropSheet) ;
                hwndModeless = NULL ;
            }

            // Enable Back and Finish buttons on wizard page
            if (bWizard && pnmh->code == PSN_SETACTIVE)

                {
                HWND hwndSheet = GetParent (hwndDlg) ;
                PropSheet_SetWizButtons (hwndSheet, PSWIZB_BACK |
                                                    PSWIZB_FINISH) ;

                }

            // Support for Help button
            if (pnmh->code == PSN_HELP)
                {
                MessageBox (hwndDlg, "PSN_HELP Notification Received",
                            "ExStyleDlgProc", MB_OK) ;
                }

            return TRUE ;
            }

        default :
            return FALSE ;
        }
    }

//--------------------------------------------------------------------
DWORD FetchExStyles (HWND hwndDlg)
    {
    DWORD dwStyle = 0L ;

    if (QueryButtonCheck (hwndDlg, IDC_CLIENTEDGE))
        {
        dwStyle |= WS_EX_CLIENTEDGE ;
        }

    if (QueryButtonCheck (hwndDlg, IDC_CONTEXTHELP))
        {
        dwStyle |= WS_EX_CONTEXTHELP ;
        }
```

(continued)

```
if (QueryButtonCheck (hwndDlg, IDC_DLGMODALFRAME))
    {
    dwStyle != WS_EX_DLGMODALFRAME ;
    }

if (QueryButtonCheck (hwndDlg, IDC_EXOVERLAPPED))
    {
    dwStyle != WS_EX_OVERLAPPEDWINDOW ;
    }

if (QueryButtonCheck (hwndDlg, IDC_PALETTE))
    {
    dwStyle != WS_EX_PALETTEWINDOW ;
    }

if (QueryButtonCheck (hwndDlg, IDC_STATICEDGE))
    {
    dwStyle != WS_EX_STATICEDGE ;
    }

if (QueryButtonCheck (hwndDlg, IDC_TOOLWINDOW))
    {
    dwStyle != WS_EX_TOOLWINDOW ;
    }

if (QueryButtonCheck (hwndDlg, IDC_WINDOWEDGE))
    {
    dwStyle != WS_EX_WINDOWEDGE ;
    }

if (QueryButtonCheck (hwndDlg, IDC_ACCEPTFILES))
    {
    dwStyle != WS_EX_ACCEPTFILES ;
    }

if (QueryButtonCheck (hwndDlg, IDC_APPWINDOW))
    {
    dwStyle != WS_EX_APPWINDOW ;
    }

if (QueryButtonCheck (hwndDlg, IDC_TOPMOST))
    {
    dwStyle != WS_EX_TOPMOST ;
    }

if (QueryButtonCheck (hwndDlg, IDC_TRANSPARENT))
    {
    dwStyle != WS_EX_TRANSPARENT ;
    }
```

(continued)

```
    if (QueryButtonCheck (hwndDlg, IDC_CONTROLPARENT))
        {
        dwStyle |= WS_EX_CONTROLPARENT ;
        }

    if (QueryButtonCheck (hwndDlg, IDC_MDICHILD))
        {
        dwStyle |= WS_EX_MDICHILD ;
        }

    if (QueryButtonCheck (hwndDlg, IDC_NOPARENTNOTIFY))
        {
        dwStyle |= WS_EX_NOPARENTNOTIFY ;
        }

    return dwStyle ;
    }
```

HELPER.C

```
/*---------------------------------
   HELPER.C -- Helper routines
               (c) Paul Yao, 1996
   ---------------------------------*/
#include <windows.h>
#include <windowsx.h>
#include <commctrl.h>
#include "property.h"

//-------------------------------------------------------------
void SetButtonCheck (HWND hwndDlg, int CtrlID, BOOL bCheck)
    {
    HWND hwndCtrl = GetDlgItem (hwndDlg, CtrlID) ;
    if (bCheck)
        {
        Button_SetCheck (hwndCtrl, BST_CHECKED) ;
        }
    }

//-------------------------------------------------------------
BOOL QueryButtonCheck (HWND hwndDlg, int CtrlID)
    {
    HWND hwndCtrl = GetDlgItem (hwndDlg, CtrlID) ;
    int  nCheck = Button_GetCheck (hwndCtrl) ;
    return (nCheck == BST_CHECKED) ;
    }
```

PROPERTY.RC

```
#include "property.h"
#include <windows.h>


IDI_APP                    ICON    DISCARDABLE    "PROPERTY.ICO"
IDI_PAGE1                  ICON    DISCARDABLE    "page1.ico"
IDI_PAGE2                  ICON    DISCARDABLE    "page2.ico"


MAIN MENU DISCARDABLE
    {
    POPUP "&Property-Sheet-Styles"
        {
        MENUITEM "PSH_WIZARD",                  IDM_WIZARD
        MENUITEM SEPARATOR
        MENUITEM "PSH_HASHELP",                 IDM_HASHELP
        MENUITEM "PSH_MODELESS",                IDM_MODELESS
        MENUITEM "PSH_NOAPPLYNOW",              IDM_NOAPPLYNOW
        MENUITEM "PSH_PROPTITLE",               IDM_PROPTITLE
        MENUITEM "PSH_RTLREADING",              IDM_RTLREADING
        }
    POPUP "&Window"
        {
        MENUITEM "Properties",                  IDM_WINDOW_PROPERTIES
        }
    }


IDD_STYLES DIALOG DISCARDABLE  0, 0, 292, 127
STYLE DS_MODALFRAME | WS_POPUP | WS_CAPTION | WS_SYSMENU
CAPTION "Window Styles"
FONT 8, "MS Sans Serif"
    {
    GROUPBOX    "&Initial State",IDC_STATIC,7,7,94,69
    CONTROL     "WS_VISIBLE",IDC_VISIBLE,"Button",BS_AUTOCHECKBOX |
                WS_TABSTOP,14,21,55,10
    CONTROL     "WS_DISABLED",IDC_DISABLED,"Button",BS_AUTOCHECKBOX |
                WS_TABSTOP,14,35,64,10
    CONTROL     "WS_MINIMIZE",IDC_MINIMIZE,"Button",BS_AUTOCHECKBOX |
                WS_TABSTOP,14,49,60,10
    CONTROL     "WS_MAXIMIZE",IDC_MAXIMIZE,"Button",BS_AUTOCHECKBOX |
                WS_TABSTOP,14,63,62,10
    GROUPBOX    "&Clipping",IDC_STATIC,7,80,94,42
    CONTROL     "WS_CLIPCHILDREN",IDC_CLIPCHILDREN,"Button",
                BS_AUTOCHECKBOX | WS_TABSTOP,14,94,79,10
```

(continued)

```
        CONTROL      "WS_CLIPSIBLINGS",IDC_CLIPSIBLINGS,"Button",
                     BS_AUTOCHECKBOX ¦ WS_TABSTOP,14,108,75,10
        GROUPBOX     "&Window Components",IDC_STATIC,115,7,170,98
        CONTROL      "WS_BORDER",IDC_BORDER,"Button",BS_AUTOCHECKBOX ¦
                     WS_TABSTOP,123,21,60,10
        CONTROL      "WS_CAPTION",IDC_CAPTION,"Button",BS_AUTOCHECKBOX ¦
                     WS_TABSTOP,123,35,60,10
        CONTROL      "WS_DLGFRAME",IDC_DLGFRAME,"Button",BS_AUTOCHECKBOX ¦
                     WS_TABSTOP,123,49,68,10
        CONTROL      "WS_HSCROLL",IDC_HSCROLL,"Button",BS_AUTOCHECKBOX ¦
                     WS_TABSTOP,123,63,71,10
        CONTROL      "WS_MAXIMIZEBOX",IDC_MAXIMIZEBOX,"Button",
                     BS_AUTOCHECKBOX ¦ WS_TABSTOP,123,77,93,10
        CONTROL      "WS_MINIMIZEBOX",IDC_MINIMIZEBOX,"Button",
                     BS_AUTOCHECKBOX ¦ WS_TABSTOP,123,91,90,10
        CONTROL      "WS_SYSMENU",IDC_SYSMENU,"Button",BS_AUTOCHECKBOX ¦
                     WS_TABSTOP,200,21,72,10
        CONTROL      "WS_THICKFRAME",IDC_THICKFRAME,"Button",BS_AUTOCHECKBOX ¦
                     WS_TABSTOP,200,35,77,10
        CONTROL      "WS_VSCROLL",IDC_VSCROLL,"Button",BS_AUTOCHECKBOX ¦
                     WS_TABSTOP,200,49,74,10
    }

IDD_EXSTYLES DIALOG DISCARDABLE  0, 0, 330, 161
STYLE DS_MODALFRAME ¦ WS_POPUP ¦ WS_CAPTION ¦ WS_SYSMENU
CAPTION "Extended Window Styles"
FONT 8, "MS Sans Serif"
    {
    GROUPBOX     "&Non-Client Area",IDC_STATIC,7,7,263,71
    CONTROL      "WS_EX_CLIENTEDGE",IDC_CLIENTEDGE,"Button",
                 BS_AUTOCHECKBOX ¦ WS_TABSTOP,14,21,113,10
    CONTROL      "WS_EX_CONTEXTHELP",IDC_CONTEXTHELP,"Button",
                 BS_AUTOCHECKBOX ¦ WS_TABSTOP,14,35,116,10
    CONTROL      "WS_EX_DLGMODALFRAME",IDC_DLGMODALFRAME,"Button",
                 BS_AUTOCHECKBOX ¦ WS_TABSTOP,14,49,121,10
    CONTROL      "WS_EX_OVERLAPPEDWINDOW",IDC_EXOVERLAPPED,"Button",
                 BS_AUTOCHECKBOX ¦ WS_TABSTOP,14,63,127,10
    CONTROL      "WS_EX_PALETTEWINDOW",IDC_PALETTE,"Button",
                 BS_AUTOCHECKBOX ¦ WS_TABSTOP,149,21,113,10
    CONTROL      "WS_EX_STATICEDGE",IDC_STATICEDGE,"Button",
                 BS_AUTOCHECKBOX ¦ WS_TABSTOP,149,35,102,10
    CONTROL      "WS_EX_TOOLWINDOW",IDC_TOOLWINDOW,"Button",
                 BS_AUTOCHECKBOX ¦ WS_TABSTOP,149,49,101,10
    CONTROL      "WS_EX_WINDOWEDGE",IDC_WINDOWEDGE,"Button",
                 BS_AUTOCHECKBOX ¦ WS_TABSTOP,149,63,102,10
```

(continued)

```
GROUPBOX      "&Shell Interface",IDC_STATIC,8,80,214,39
CONTROL       "WS_EX_ACCEPTFILES",IDC_ACCEPTFILES,"Button",
              BS_AUTOCHECKBOX | WS_TABSTOP,14,90,97,10
CONTROL       "WS_EX_APPWINDOW",IDC_APPWINDOW,"Button",
              BS_AUTOCHECKBOX | WS_TABSTOP,14,104,96,10
CONTROL       "WS_EX_TOPMOST",IDC_TOPMOST,"Button",BS_AUTOCHECKBOX |
              WS_TABSTOP,118,90,88,10
CONTROL       "WS_EX_TRANSPARENT",IDC_TRANSPARENT,"Button",
              BS_AUTOCHECKBOX | WS_TABSTOP,118,104,102,10
GROUPBOX      "&Child Window",IDC_STATIC,7,121,316,33
CONTROL       "WS_EX_CONTROLPARENT",IDC_CONTROLPARENT,"Button",
              BS_AUTOCHECKBOX | WS_TABSTOP,14,135,105,10
CONTROL       "WS_EX_MDICHILD",IDC_MDICHILD,"Button",BS_AUTOCHECKBOX |
              WS_TABSTOP,124,135,77,10
CONTROL       "WS_EX_NOPARENTNOTIFY",IDC_NOPARENTNOTIFY,"Button",
              BS_AUTOCHECKBOX | WS_TABSTOP,206,135,111,10
}
```

PAGE1.ICO

PAGE2.ICO

(continued)

PROPERTY.ICO

In response to the WM_CREATE message, PROPERTY's main window creates two child windows. The window with the "First Window" caption is the window of primary interest. This window is resized when its parent is resized to ensure it occupies one-ninth of its parent's client area. When style flags are changed, the parent window receives a private message, PM_CREATEWINDOW, in response to which the parent window destroys the existing child window, creates a new child window with the requested styles, and then sends itself a WM_SIZE message to force a resizing of the child window.

The style flags for creating the child window are stored in two global variables defined in PROPERTY.C:

```
DWORD dwChildStyle = WS_CHILD | WS_VISIBLE |
                     WS_BORDER | WS_CAPTION ;
DWORD dwChildExStyle = 0L ;
```

Pointers to each of these variables are passed to each property page in the *lParam* field of the PROPSHEETPAGE structure. For example, here's how *dwChildStyle* is passed to the first property page (in SHEET.C):

```
pspage[0].lParam = (LPARAM) &dwChildStyle ;
```

The first property page retrieves this value in its page procedure (*StylePageProc*). Located in PAGE1.C, this function is called right before the property page itself is created with a PSPCB_CREATE message code. This pointer gets stored in a global variable that's been declared as *static*, and which therefore has a scope limited to the current source file:

```
// Store pointer to style data
pTheStyles = (LPDWORD) ppsp->lParam ;
```

where *ppsp* is a pointer to the property page structure, PROPSHEETPAGE, passed to the property page function.

Each property page has a pointer to the data that it is responsible for editing, so when it's time to apply changes, each property page dialog procedure writes the changes back to the source. It would have been just as easy to use global variables—a common practice when creating regular dialog boxes. But we use the *lParam* parameter to show how a "remote" property page—such as one that resides in a dynamic link library—could be initialized using nothing more than the contents of the PROPSHEETPAGE structure.

Within the property page dialog procedures, most of the interesting things occur in response to a WM_NOTIFY message. When the OK or Apply button gets clicked, a notification code of PSN_APPLY gets sent to the dialog procedures. As was mentioned earlier, property pages are created in a fairly conservative fashion—that is, they are created as users activate individual pages. Only pages that have been created actually receive notifications, which means that when the window styles property sheet is dismissed, the two dialog procedures might only receive one PSN_APPLY notification between them. Or, they might get two if both pages have been created.

This creates the possibility that two PSN_APPLY notifications might be received. To ensure that changes are applied only once, each dialog procedure checks whether it's the active property page before sending a PM_CREATEWINDOW request to the program's main window. This is done by sending a PSM_GETCURRENTPAGEHWND message to the property sheet, which returns a handle to the active property page. The request to re-create the child window is sent out—via *PostMessage*, to avoid timing problems—only from the dialog procedure for the currently active property page:

```
HWND hwndPS = GetParent (hwndDlg) ;
HWND hwndActive = PropSheet_GetCurrentPageHwnd (hwndPS) ;

// Only re-create if we're the active page
if (hwndDlg == hwndActive)
    PostMessage (hwndMain, PM_CREATEWINDOW, 0, 0L) ;
```

What PROPERTY shows is that most of what you already know about handling dialogs also applies to property sheets. A few refinements have been added to deal with different scenarios—creating wizards, modeless property sheets, and using a different set of buttons—that are sometimes useful to application developers.

The Kernel and the Printer

Chapter 13

Memory Management and File I/O

If you are learning Windows programming for the first time with Windows 95, you are a very fortunate person. You simply do not know how lucky you are. In fact, the lessons you will learn from this chapter can be summarized in one sentence: When working with memory and files, you will rarely (if ever) need to use anything other than the standard C run-time library.

The reason I advise the use of the C library functions (such as *malloc, free, fopen, fclose,* and so forth) is that they are clean and simple, you probably already know how to use them, and you are probably very comfortable with them. But most importantly, there are no problems when you use these functions in your Windows 95 programs. As we'll see shortly, this was not always the case.

Memory management and file input/output (I/O) are two of the most rudimentary services that a simple non-graphical operating system (such as MS-DOS) provides to application programs. A third is tasking, which can be as simple as loading a program from a disk file into memory and starting it running. After these three services, perhaps the fourth most important is keeping track of the date and time.

The system services provided by the Windows 95 kernel are much more extensive, including dynamic linking (covered in this book in Chapter 19); multitasking, multithreading, and thread synchronization (Chapter 14); interprocess communication or IPC (Chapters 16, 17, and 20); as well as some other features that did not make the cut for this book.

Although using C library functions is convenient, it is also possible to write a Windows 95 program without using any C library functions at all. Any library function that requires a call to the operating system (such as the memory management and file I/O functions) has a corresponding (and usually more versatile) operating system function. Which route you choose—operating system functions or C library functions—is up to you, and it is possible to mix and match.

MEMORY: GOOD, BAD, AND UGLY

To see how far Windows has progressed in the past ten years, it is both interesting and amusing to read the minimum system requirements for the November 1985 release of Windows 1.0: "320K memory, DOS 2.0 or higher, two double-sided disk drives, graphics adapter card." These requirements simply reflected the type of machine that most users were running at the time. In retrospect, Microsoft's success at getting Windows to run at all under this limited environment was quite miraculous. Memory management in Windows 1.0 was very bizarre, and often downright ugly, but it *did* work…at least most of the time.

Segmented Memory

Windows 1.0 was designed for the Intel 8086 and 8088 microprocessors. Internally, these were 16-bit microprocessors that were capable of addressing 1 megabyte of memory. In IBM compatibles, the video display and the system ROM-based BIOS (Basic Input/Output System) reserved the top 384 KB of this address space, leaving the maximum RAM space for programs and data at the infamous 640-KB level.

Addressing a megabyte of memory requires a 20-bit address (2^{20} is 1,048,576). In the 8086 and 8088, this 20-bit physical address was formed from two 16-bit values, a segment address and an offset address. The microprocessor stored four segment addresses: for code, data, the stack, and an extra. A 20-bit physical address was formed by shifting a segment address left by four bits and adding an offset address:

	Segment:	ssssssssssssssss0000
+	Offset:	0000oooooooooooooooo
=	Address:	aaaaaaaaaaaaaaaaaaaa

This creates a 20-bit address that can access up to 1 MB of memory (2 to the 20th power).

If the segment registers are kept constant, a program uses only 16-bit offset addresses for accessing the code and data. (Due to the architecture of C, the stack segment was set the same as the data segment used to store static variables.) Each of these two segments addresses 64 KB of memory. For a single-tasking operating system where programs require only 64 KB of code and 64 KB of data, this worked reasonably well.

As application programs became more sophisticated (and hence larger), multiple segments were required for code and/or data. This forced the manufacturers of C compilers to define near (or short) pointers, which were 16 bits wide and used a default code or data segment, and far (or long) pointers, which were 32 bits wide and included both an offset address and an explicit segment address. However, this 32-bit address could not directly address memory. Nor could the address be incremented without logic that observed when the offset address rolled over and mandated an adjustment to the segment address. Also, the manufacturers of C compilers had to define different programming models: small (one code segment and one data segment), medium (multiple code segments), compact (multiple data segments), large (multiple code and data segments), and huge (same as large but with built-in address increment logic).

MS-DOS itself didn't have much support for memory management. Many early DOS programs simply figured out how much memory was available and used it all. Macho programmers prided themselves on the extent to which they could use the PC hardware directly without bothering with the nuisance of an operating system.

Because Windows 1.0 was a multitasking environment, it was necessary to do something more with memory management than had been provided under MS-DOS. Think about it: As multiple programs are loaded into memory and later exited, memory becomes fragmented. The operating system must move blocks of memory around to consolidate free space. In other words, as I said in the earlier editions of this book: "Multitasking without memory management is like having a party in a closet: You may be able to accommodate some of the earlier arrivals, but once everybody starts mingling, some toes are going to get smashed."

How can this be done? You can't just move a block of code or data in memory with no regard to the application program. It will have the wrong address. Here's where segmented memory came in handy. If programs use only offset addresses, the segment addresses can be changed by the operating system, and that's what the early versions of Windows did.

One implication of this was that Windows programs were basically limited to small or medium models with just one 64-KB segment for data. Programs used near pointers to reference their data segment; the data segment address for a particular process was set as the operating system passed control to the program. This allowed Windows to move the program's data segment and reset the segment address. All far function calls made by a program (including those to operating system functions) were adjusted when code segments used by the program were moved in memory.

A program running under a 16-bit version of Windows could either allocate memory from its own data segment (called "local" memory addressed with just a 16-bit offset pointer) or outside its data segment (called "global" memory addressed with a 32-bit address). In both cases, the memory allocation functions returned a handle to the memory block. Programs had to "lock" the block to anchor the block in memory. The lock function returned a far pointer. After using the memory, the memory block would have to be unlocked. This allowed Windows to move the block when necessary. The locking and unlocking process was often performed during the processing of a single message, and often led to many bugs, as well as undesirable effects on programmers, including premature hair loss, gastro-intestinal disturbances, and insanity.

As is usual with handles, the memory handles were really just pointers to a table in the Windows kernel. The early versions of Windows maintained a memory segment called BURGERMASTER that contained a master handle-to-memory table. This segment was named after a favorite take-out and drive-in restaurant of the early Windows developers, located across a busy highway from the first Microsoft offices in Washington. (I ate at BurgerMaster a few years ago and concluded that the Windows developers must have been pretty fast runners to cross the highway without incident.)

But enough nostalgia. Aside from the historical background, one reason for discussing this awful stuff is that Windows 95 still retains some remnants of this Windows 1.0 addressing scheme. The architecture of Windows 95 has pretty much abandoned it, of course, but it sometimes shows up in the structure and syntax of the function calls.

The problems with short and far addresses in 16-bit versions of Windows also carried over into file I/O. In many cases, a program received a filename from a dialog box. This was a far address. But in the small and medium memory models, the C library functions for file I/O expected near addresses. Similarly, a program that stored data in global memory blocks had to address it with far pointers, and thus file I/O to and from these blocks was awkward. This required that Windows duplicate with function calls all of the MS-DOS assembly language file I/O functions.

Interim Solutions

I know this discussion has already brought back painful memories for veterans of MS-DOS and Windows programming. Another unwelcome blast-from-the-past is probably the Lotus-Intel-Microsoft Expanded Memory Specification (LIM EMS). This specification was usually implemented in a board full of memory that could be addressed in 16-KB blocks through a 64-KB window located in the high space of memory not occupied by the video adapter board or the ROM BIOS. Different blocks of 16-KB memory could be bank-switched in and out of the window. Windows 2.0 supported LIM EMS with several function calls.

By the time Windows 3.0 rolled around, Microsoft was able to support the Intel 286-style "protected mode" (as opposed to "real mode" of the 8086 and 8088 processors discussed above) without causing too many problems to existing programs. In protected mode, the segment address is called a "selector." It is still 16 bits wide, but internal to the 286 it references a 24-bit "base" address that is added to the 16-bit offset address to form a 24-bit physical address capable of addressing 16 megabytes (MB) of memory:

To ease the transition from the earlier versions of Windows, the handle returned from the global memory allocation function was simply the selector. This use of protected mode eased memory management somewhat, but the real goal had to wait.

Finally, 32 Bits and Hassle-Free

Windows 95 requires the presence of an Intel 386, 486, or Pentium microprocessor. These processors use 32-bit memory addressing and are thus capable of accessing 2^{32}, or 4,294,967,296, bytes (4 gigabytes or GB) of physical memory. Of course, most users of Windows 95 don't come close to this limit. According to the Windows 95 carton, the operating system requires only 4 megabytes of memory, but 8 MB is recommended. These days, 16 megabytes is considered to provide ample elbow room for most purposes.

Although the Intel 386, 486, and Pentium microprocessors are still capable of using segmented memory addressing, Windows 95 keeps the segment registers fixed and instead opts for a 32-bit flat addressing scheme. This means that addresses in Windows 95 applications are stored as simple 32-bit values, again allowing the access of 4 GB of memory.

The 32-bit addresses used by Windows 95 application programs to access code and data are *not* the 32-bit physical addresses that the microprocessor uses to address physical memory. The address that the application uses is called a "virtual" address. It is translated to a physical address through a "page table." Application programs can usually ignore this process. (That's one of the reasons operating systems were invented.) Your program seems to sit in a 32-bit address space, and there is nothing strange or awkward you must do to access this memory. However, some of the Windows technical documentation refers to virtual addresses and page tables, so it's helpful to have a good grasp of what's going on.

The physical memory is divided into "pages" that are 4096 (4 KB) bytes in length. Thus, each page begins at an address with the lowest 12 bits equaling zero. A machine equipped with 8 megabytes of memory has 2048 pages. The Windows 95 operating system maintains a collection of page tables (which are themselves 4-KB pages) to translate virtual addresses to physical addresses.

Every process under Windows 95 has its own "directory page," which is a collection of up to 1024 32-bit entries stored contiguously. The physical address of the current directory page is stored in a microprocessor register called CR3, which is changed when Windows 95 switches control between processes. The top 10 bits of a virtual address specifies one of the 1024 possible entries in this directory page. The top 20 bits of the entry in the directory page indicate a physical address of a page table. (The bottom 12 bits of the physical address are set to zero.) This references another page, which also has up to 1024 32-bit entries. The middle 10 bits of the virtual address references one of these entries. Again, the entry has a 20-bit physical address to indicate the starting position of a page frame, which is a physical address. The bottom 12 bits of a virtual address point to a physical position within this page frame.

I know it's confusing at first. Shown symbolically, you can represent a 32-bit virtual address (which is what an application works with) as a 10-bit directory page entry (d), a 10-bit page table entry (p), and a 12-bit offset (o):

dddd-dddd-ddpp-pppp-pppp-oooo-oooo-oooo

For each process, the microprocessor stores a 20-bit value in the CR3 register (r for register):

rrrr-rrrr-rrrr-rrrr-rrrr

The starting physical address of the process's current directory page is:

rrrr-rrrr-rrrr-rrrr-rrrr-0000-0000-0000

Keep in mind that all pages are stored on 4-KB boundaries, so each page begins at an address with the bottom 12 bits equal to zero. The microprocessor first accesses the physical address:

rrrr-rrrr-rrrr-rrrr-rrrr-dddd-dddd-dd00

This location contains another 20-bit value (t for table):

tttt-tttt-tttt-tttt-tttt

which indicates the starting physical address of a page table:

tttt-tttt-tttt-tttt-tttt-0000-0000-0000

The microprocessor then accesses a physical address of:

tttt-tttt-tttt-tttt-tttt-pppp-pppp-pp00

Stored in this area is a 20-bit value of a page frame (f for frame):

ffff-ffff-ffff-ffff-ffff

The final 32-bit physical address is a combination of this page frame with the bottom 12 offset bits of the virtual address:

ffff-ffff-ffff-ffff-ffff-oooo-oooo-oooo

That's the physical address. We're all done.

It may seem as if this is an extensively time-consuming process for translating a virtual address to a physical address, but it's really not. The Intel 386, 486, and Pentium microprocessors have an internal memory cache that can save these page tables right within the processor. The translation actually occurs very quickly without any significant performance hit. The double-paging gives each application a theoretical limit of over one million 4-KB pages.

The advantages to paging are enormous: First, applications are insulated from each other. No process can inadvertently (or maliciously) write over the code or data space of another process, because it cannot even address the other process's memory without the proper CR3 value, and setting this value is only within the domain of the Windows 95 kernel.

Second, this paging mechanism solves one of the most basic problems in a multitasking environment, which is the consolidation of free memory. In a simpler addressing scheme, as multiple programs are executed and exited, memory can become fragmented. If memory is too fragmented, programs cannot run because they don't have enough contiguous memory, even if the amount of total free memory is entirely adequate. With paging, it is not necessary to consolidate free physical memory because pages need not be contiguous. Everything is handled through the manipulation of the page tables. The only waste really comes from the overhead of the page tables themselves and the 4-KB granularity of the pages.

Third, there are extra bits in the 32-bit page-table entries aside from the 20-bit addresses. One bit indicates that the particular page has been accessed (this is called the "accessed" bit); another if the page has been written to (the "dirty" bit). Windows 95 can use these bits to determine if a page of memory can be swapped to a disk file to obtain more free physical memory. Another bit ("present") indicates if the page has been swapped out to disk and must be reloaded into memory.

Another bit ("read/write") indicates if the page can be written to. This bit protects code from errant pointers. For example, if you include the following statement in a Windows program:

```
* (int *) WinMain = 0 ;
```

you will get a message box saying "This program has performed an illegal operation and will be shut down." This bit does not prevent a program from compiling program source code and storing assembly language instructions in memory to be executed, as we'll see.

I have a few further notes about Windows 95 memory management:

Virtual addresses are 32 bits wide. Your program code and data (static, stack, or allocated) will have addresses between 0x00000000 and 0x7FFFFFFF. Windows 95 itself uses addresses from 0x80000000 to 0xFFFFFFFF, and this is where you'll find the entry points to the Windows 95 dynamic link libraries.

The total amount of free memory is determined by the amount of free physical memory and the free area of the hard disk available for page swapping. As is usual with virtual memory management, Windows 95 employs a least-recently-used (LRU) algorithm to determine what pages to swap out to disk. The "accessed" and "dirty" bits help out here. Code pages do not have to be saved to disk; because code pages are non-writable, they can simply be reloaded from the .EXE file or the dynamic link library.

Sometimes you'll see that a disk is being accessed when you move the mouse from the client area of one program to the client area of another. Why is this? Windows has to send mouse movement messages to the second application. If the program's code to process this message is not currently in memory, Windows must reload it from the disk file. If you have several large Windows programs loaded simultaneously and not much memory, you will probably witness some "thrashing" (an inordinate amount of disk activity) as you move from program to program because Windows is reloading previously discarded pages. Sometimes individual programs will suddenly slow down (or stop entirely) while Windows performs swapping.

Code pages can be shared among applications. This is particularly useful for dynamic link libraries. Several programs running at the same time can use the same Windows 95 functions without requiring that the same code be loaded into memory multiple times. Only one copy of the code is necessary.

When you dynamically allocate memory, each block that you allocate does *not* get its own page. Successive allocations of small amounts of memory will be on the same physical page to the nearest 4-bit starting address. (That is, an allocation of one byte uses 16 bytes.) If a particular block is reallocated to a larger size, it may have to be physically moved in memory if something follows it on the page.

Aside from the 4-KB granularity of pages, physical memory cannot become hopelessly fragmented because defragmentation involves only manipulation of the page tables. However, an application's virtual memory *can* become fragmented if an application allocates, reallocates, and frees a great many memory blocks. The 2-GB limit on application code and data is usually sufficient to avoid problems. It is much more likely that a program will run out of physical memory before encountering a limit on virtual memory. But it can happen, and if you have a program where this problem is conceivable, you may want to give serious thought to "movable" memory, which I'll discuss later in this chapter.

Finally, after all of these preliminaries, my advice remains the same: Use the C library functions whenever possible. You have a 32-bit address space. Use it and (if your application is cool enough) abuse the hell out of it.

MEMORY ALLOCATION

Have I sufficiently advised the use of the C library functions to allocate memory? To reinforce this behavior, I'll begin with a brief review:

The C Library Functions

In your programs you can define a pointer (for example, to an array of integers) like so:

```
int *p ;
```

The pointer p is a 32-bit value that is uninitialized. You can get a block of memory for p to point at using the statement:

```
    p = (int *) malloc (1024) ;
```

This allocates a memory block of 1024 bytes, which can store 256 32-bit integers. A NULL pointer indicates that the memory allocation was not successful. You can also allocate this block is by using:

```
    p = (int *) calloc (256, sizeof (int)) ;
```

The two parameters to *calloc* are multiplied by each other to get 1024 bytes. The *calloc* function also has the effect of zeroing out the memory block.

If you need to increase the size of this memory block (perhaps doubling it), you can call:

```
    p = (int *) realloc (p, 2048) ;
```

The pointer is passed to the function, and a pointer (perhaps different in value, particularly if the block is being enlarged) is returned from the function. This syntax indicates that the operating system (in this case Windows 95) may have to move the block in virtual memory. For example, if you allocated a 1024-byte memory block, you may have obtained a virtual address of 0x00750100. You may also have allocated a second memory block and obtained a virtual address of 0x00750504. It is not possible to increase the first memory block to 2048 bytes and continue to use the same virtual address. In this case, Windows 95 will also have to move the block in physical memory to a new page.

Finally, when you're finished with the memory you call:

```
    free (p) ;
```

These are the only four functions defined by the ANSI C specification. C compiler manufacturers often support quite a few more, the most useful probably being *_msize*, which returns the size of an allocated memory block.

Fundamental Windows 95 Memory Allocation

As I mentioned earlier, everything you can do with C library functions you can do with your own code or by making use of Windows 95 kernel functions. Here's the Windows 95 function to allocate a block of memory for pointers to integers:

```
    p = (int *) GlobalAlloc (uiFlags, dwSize) ;
```

The function takes two parameters: a possible series of flags and a byte size of the allocated block. It returns a virtual address that your program can use to address the allocated memory. A NULL value indicates that not enough memory was available for the allocation.

With one exception, for every function that begins with the word *Global*, there is another that begins with the word *Local*. These two sets of functions are identical under Windows 95; the two different prefixes are for compatibility with previous versions of Windows where the *Global* functions returned far pointers and *Local* functions returned near pointers.

Although defined a bit differently, the two parameters to *GlobalAlloc* are both 32-bit unsigned integers. If you set the first parameter to zero, you effectively use this flag:

GMEM_FIXED (equal to zero)

This makes the *GlobalAlloc* function functionally equivalent to the *malloc* function. In earlier versions of Windows, the GMEM_FIXED flag was discouraged because Windows could not move the block in physical memory. In Windows 95, the GMEM_FIXED flag is normal because it returns a virtual address, and the operating system can move the block in physical memory by altering the page table.

You can also use the flag:

GMEM_ZEROINIT

if you'd like every byte in the memory block to be initially set to zero. The succinct GPTR flag combines the GMEM_FIXED and GMEM_ZEROINIT flags as defined in the Windows header files:

```
#define GPTR (GMEM_FIXED | GMEM_ZEROINIT)
```

There is also a reallocation function:

```
p = (int *) GlobalReAlloc (p, dwSize, uiFlags) ;
```

You can use the GMEM_ZEROINIT flag to zero out the new bytes if the memory block is being enlarged.

Here's the function to return the size of the memory block:

```
dwSize = GlobalSize (p) ;
```

and the function to free it:

```
GlobalFree (p) ;
```

Movable Memory

As I mentioned earlier, in previous versions of Windows the GMEM_FIXED parameter was discouraged because it required that Windows keep the memory block fixed in physical memory. In Windows 95, a memory block can be moved in physical memory and retain the same virtual address. Even so, the *GlobalAlloc* function still supports the flag:

GMEM_MOVEABLE

and the shorthand identifier to additionally zero out the memory (as defined in the Windows header files):

```
#define GHND (GMEM_MOVEABLE | GMEM_ZEROINIT)
```

(Note that most dictionaries prefer the spelling "movable" over "moveable," which is what my editors wanted to change the identifier to in the first edition of this book. Unfortunately, the developers of Windows had already etched their spelling preferences in stone—or at least in the Windows header files.)

The GMEM_MOVEABLE flag allows a memory block to be moved in *virtual* memory. This doesn't necessarily mean that the memory block will be moved in physical memory, but the address that the application uses to read and write to the block can change. Does this sound odd? It should, but we'll see how it works shortly.

You may ask: Why do I want to use movable memory if I don't have to? (And you may voice that question with more vehemence after you see what's involved.) One answer is to maintain compatibility with existing Windows source code. A better answer is that you may be nervous about fragmentation of virtual memory. If your program allocates, reallocates, and frees memory like a madman, virtual memory can indeed become fragmented. Will your program ever run out of the 2 GB of virtual memory space before running out of the 4 or 8 or 16 MB of physical memory space? It *could* happen. The problem is exacerbated by the increased tendency for people to run their machines continually. (As we know, screen savers are primarily for the entertainment of the after-hours office janitorial staff.) Programs that keep running for days on end may encounter more memory fragmentation than those designed to run for an hour or two.

If this is a potential problem, then you'll want to use movable memory, and here's how to do it. First, define a pointer and a variable of type GLOBALHANDLE:

```
int *p ;
GLOBALHANDLE hGlobal ;
```

Then allocate the memory, for example:

```
hGlobal = GlobalAlloc (GHND, 1024) ;
```

Notice that no casting is required for the return value from the *GlobalAlloc* function. The function is defined as returning a GLOBALHANDLE variable, because this is the way that *GlobalAlloc* worked in the general case of the pre-95 versions of Windows.

As with any Windows handle, don't worry too much about what the number really means. Just store it. When you need to access that memory block, call:

```
p = (int *) GlobalLock (hGlobal) ;
```

This translates the handle into a pointer. During the time that the block is locked, Windows will fix the address in virtual memory. It will not move. When you are finished accessing the block call:

```
GlobalUnlock (hGlobal) ;
```

This gives Windows 95 the freedom to move the block in virtual memory. To be really compulsively correct about this process (and to experience the torments of early Windows programmers), you should lock and unlock the memory block in the course of a single message.

When you want to free the memory, call *GlobalFree* with the handle rather than the pointer. If you don't currently have access to the handle, use the function:

hGlobal = GlobalHandle (p) ;

You can lock a memory block multiple times before unlocking it. Windows maintains a lock count, and each lock requires a corresponding unlock before the block is free to be moved. Moving a block in virtual memory is not really a copy of bytes from one location to another—it basically involves manipulation of the page tables. The only real reason for allocating a movable block is to prevent fragmentation of virtual memory.

Discardable Memory

If you're brave enough to use the GMEM_MOVEABLE option, you may also be brave enough to use:

GMEM_DISCARDABLE

This option can only be used with GMEM_MOVEABLE. A memory block allocated with this flag can be discarded from physical memory by the Windows kernel when some free space is needed.

This may sound perverse, but think about it for a moment. Memory blocks that contain code are discardable, for example. These blocks are non-writable. Hence, it is faster to load code from the original .EXE file than to swap the code to disk and reload it. If you allocate memory for an unchangeable block of data that can be easily regenerated (usually by loading from a disk file), then you can make it discardable. You'll know it has been discarded when you call *GlobalLock* and get back a NULL pointer. Then you'll regenerate the data.

A memory block cannot be discarded unless the lock count is zero. To deliberately discard a memory block, call:

GlobalDiscard (hGlobal) ;

Miscellaneous Functions and Flags

Another flag available in the *GlobalAlloc* function is GMEM_SHARE or GMEM_DDESHARE (these are the same). As the name indicates, this flag is intended for dynamic data exchange, which I'll discuss in Chapter 17.

GlobalAlloc and *GlobalReAlloc* can also include the GMEM_NODISCARD or GMEM_NOCOMPACT flags. These flags instruct Windows to not discard any memory or not do any movement of memory to satisfy the memory request. Only excessively altruistic programmers use these flags.

The *GlobalReAlloc* function can also change flags (for example to convert a fixed block to movable or vice versa) if the new size is indicated as zero and GMEM_MODIFY is included in the flags parameter.

The *GlobalFlags* function returns a combination of the GMEM_DISCARDABLE, GMEM_DISCARDED, and GMEM_SHARE flags.

Finally, you can call *GlobalMemoryStatus* (the only *Global* function without a similar *Local* function) with a pointer to a structure of type MEMORYSTATUS to determine the amount of physical memory and virtual memory available to your application.

This completes the survey of functions beginning with the prefix *Global*. Windows 95 also supports some functions that you implement yourself or duplicate with C library functions. These are called *FillMemory* (fill with a particular byte), *ZeroMemory* (fill with zeros), and *CopyMemory* and *MoveMemory*, both of which copy memory from one location to another. If the locations overlap, *CopyMemory* may not work correctly. Use *MoveMemory* instead.

Is It Good?

Before you access some memory, you may want to test whether it's valid or not. If the pointer is invalid, your program will experience a protection exception. Testing the pointer first guarantees that this doesn't happen. The *IsBadCodePtr*, *IsBadReadPtr*, *IsBadWritePtr*, and *IsBadStringPtr* functions do this for you. The first of these functions simply accepts a pointer and returns TRUE (non-zero) if the pointer is invalid. The other three accept a pointer as the first parameter and a length in the second parameter. The fourth function also searches for a zero terminator and stops testing the validity of the memory if one is encountered.

Virtual Memory Functions

Windows 95 also supports a collection of functions beginning with the word *Virtual*. These functions allow you much more control over memory. However, only rather esoteric applications will require these functions.

For example, suppose you were writing an integrated development environment that included an in-memory compiler and executor. Among other things, your program would read source code and compile it into a block of memory. You may then want to make that memory block "execute-only," meaning that it couldn't be inadvertently read from or (worse) written to by the program that's just been compiled and is now ready to run. This is something your development environment will want to do to better trap pointer bugs in the user's program. You could also flag certain blocks of memory as "read-only." Both of these jobs are possible with the virtual memory functions, but, like I said, it's a fairly esoteric requirement.

Perhaps a more common need is to reserve a large block of virtual memory for data that may expand greatly as your program is running. Simply doing the normal thing—which is frequently using the C *realloc* function or the Windows *GlobalReAlloc* function to dynamically change the size of an allocated block—may entail a performance hit. The virtual memory management functions may help in avoiding this. Here's how.

In Windows 95 any section of your application's virtual memory can be in one of three different states—"committed" (that is, mapped to an area of physical memory), "free" (available for future allocation), and "reserved," which is somewhere in between. A block of reserved virtual memory is not mapped to any physical memory, but the addresses within the reserved block will not be used unless you want them to be used. This is how you can get a large block of contiguous virtual memory that may or may not be mapped to physical memory as the program is running.

To use the virtual memory functions, your program should know the memory page size. Unlike Windows NT, Windows 95 runs only on Intel microprocessors, and the page size is always 4096 bytes. If your programs will be designed to run under Windows NT also, use the *GetSystemInfo* function to obtain this information. This function takes one parameter, which is a pointer to a structure of type SYSTEM_INFO. The *dwPageSize* field indicates the page size; also of use are the *lpMinimumApplicationAddress* and *lpMaximumApplication-Address* fields, which indicate the minimum and maximum addresses available to an application. For Windows 95, these values are 0x00400000 and 0x7FFFFFFF, respectively.

The *VirtualAlloc* function looks like this:

```
p = VirtualAlloc (pAddr, dwSize, iAllocType, iProtect) ;
```

The first parameter indicates a desired starting base address of virtual memory, and you should set it to NULL the first time you call this function. The second parameter indicates the size. The third parameter can be MEM_RESERVE or MEM_COMMIT to reserve or commit the space. The fourth parameter can be constants beginning with the prefix PAGE_ (such as PAGE_READONLY or PAGE_EXECUTE) to indicate protection of the memory block. Subsequent calls to *VirtualAlloc* can commit or reserve a section of this block. The *VirtualFree* function frees up the virtual memory.

Heap Functions

The final set of memory allocation functions begins with the word *Heap*. These functions create and maintain a contiguous block of virtual memory from which you can allocate smaller sections. You begin by calling the *HeapCreate* function. You then use *HeapAllocate*, *HeapReAllocate*, and *HeapFree* to allocate and free blocks of memory within the heap. The heap can be compacted to consolidate free space.

There is little reason for using the heap functions.

FILE INPUT/OUTPUT

I'm going to say it again: For file input and output use the C library functions whenever possible. I already did this in the POPPAD3 program in Chapter 11 by using *fopen*, *fseek*, *fread*, *fwrite*, and *fclose*.

The Old Way

Working with files under Windows has gradually improved over the years. Back in the days of Windows 1.0 and 2.0, the only documented file I/O function was *OpenFile*, and the officially recommended approach to reading and writing files was to write small assembly language files that directly accessed MS-DOS function calls. Although the use of standard C run-time library functions was possible, in a small or medium model program these functions worked only with near pointers. This was a nuisance for programs that maintained file data in global memory blocks. Even filenames (often obtained from dialog boxes) were accessed by far pointers.

Fortunately, many programmers soon discovered some undocumented functions for working with files using far pointers. These took the names *_lopen*, *_lread*, *_lwrite*, and so forth, and they hooked almost directly into MS-DOS function calls. Beginning with Windows 3.0, these functions were documented, and they were the standard file I/O functions for Windows programming. They are no longer recommended for Windows 95.

The Windows 95 Difference

Several improvements over many earlier versions of Windows to file I/O are provided by Windows 95:

First, like Windows 3.1, Windows 95 provides the common dialog box library that includes File Open and File Save dialog boxes. These were demonstrated in Chapter 11. It is highly recommended that you use these dialogs. They eliminate the need for filename parsing that may be system dependent.

Second, Windows 95 is a 32-bit environment. With relevance here, this means that you can read from a file or write to a file in one big gulp with single *fread* or *fwrite* functions (or their Windows equivalents). Changes to existing code involves eliminating *for* loops.

Third, Windows 95 supports long filenames. The easiest way for your programs to deal with long filenames is to do nothing with them. (How's *that* for simplicity?) The Windows documentation indicates that you should use data returned from *GetVolumeInformation* to dynamically allocate buffers to store filenames. But that's usually a nuisance. I tend to use two constants defined in STDLIB.H: _MAX_PATH (set equal to 260) and _MAX_FNAME (256) to statically allocate the space.

The Windows 95 File I/O Functions

If you do not use the C library functions for file I/O, you can use functions provided by Windows 95. The *CreateFile* function is quite extensive:

```
hFile = CreateFile (szName, dwAccess, dwShare, NULL, dwCreate, dwFlags, 0) ;
```

Despite the name, the function is also used for opening existing files. Moreover, you use the same function for opening pipes (used for IPC) and communications devices.

For files, the first parameter is the filename. The second is either GENERIC_READ or GENERIC_WRITE or both. Using 0 allows you to obtain information about the file but not access it. The *dwShare* parameter can open the file with sharing attributes, allowing other processes to read from (FILE_SHARE_READ) or write to (FILE_SHARE_WRITE) or both.

The *dwCreate* flag is one of several constants, indicating how the file should be opened. These are comprehensive and fairly self explanatory. The CREATE_NEW flag causes the function to fail if the file already exists, while CREATE_ALWAYS deletes the contents of any existing file. Similarly, OPEN_EXISTING fails if the file does not exist, and OPEN_ALWAYS creates the file if it does not exist. TRUNCATE_EXISTING fails if the file does not exist but deletes all the data in an existing file.

The *dwFlags* parameter can be a combination of constants beginning with FILE_ATTRIBUTE and FILE_FLAG for setting file attributes and other behavior.

CreateFile returns a variable of type HANDLE. Eventually you close the file by calling CloseHandle with the file handle. The *ReadFile* and *WriteFile* functions are quite similar:

```
ReadFile (hFile, pBuffer, dwToRead, &dwHaveRead, NULL) ;
WriteFile (hFile, pBuffer, dwToWrite, &dwHaveWritten, NULL) ;
```

The second parameter is a pointer to a buffer containing the data; the third parameter indicates the number of bytes to read from or write to the file; and the fourth parameter is a pointer to a variable that on return from the function indicates the number of bytes actually read or written. (The last parameter is only used with a file opened with FILE_FLAG_OVER-LAPPED flag, a subject beyond the scope of this book.)

Memory-Mapped I/O

Under Windows 95 (and this is one distinct enhancement over the 16-bit versions of Windows), it is possible to read from and write to a file as if it were a block of memory. This may sound a bit odd at first, but it comes in handy at times. Also, this is the recommended technique for sharing memory among two or more processes, as we'll see in Chapter 19, "Dynamic Link Libraries (DLLs)."

This is the simplest approach to file-mapped I/O: You first create the file normally using the *CreateFile* function. Then call:

```
hMap = CreateFileMapping (hFile, NULL, dwProtect, 0, 0, szName) ;
```

The *dwProtect* parameter can be one of the following and should be compatible with the sharing mode of the file: PAGE_READONLY, PAGE_WRITECOPY, PAGE_READWRITE. The last parameter is an optional name, generally used for sharing the data with another process. In that case, *OpenFileMapping* opens the same file with that specified name. Both functions return a HANDLE data type.

When you need to access part of this file, call *MapViewOfFile*:

```
p = MapViewOfFile (hMap, dwAccess, dwHigh, dwLow, dwNumber) ;
```

All or part of the file will be mapped to memory, beginning at a 64-bit offset in the file indicated by *dwHigh* or *dwLow*. (Obviously *dwHigh* will be zero unless you have a file greater than 4 GB in length.) The *dwNumber* parameter indicates the number of bytes you wish to map to memory. The *dwAccess* parameter can be FILE_MAP_WRITE (which also allows reading) or FILE_MAP_READ and should be compatible with the *dwProtect* parameter of the *CreateFileMapping* call.

At this point you can use the pointer returned from the function for accessing or modifying the data in file. The *FlushViewOfFile* function writes any dirty pages of the memory-mapped file back out to disk. The *UnmapViewOfFile* function invalidates the pointer returned from *MapViewOfFile*. You must still close the file using *CloseHandle*.

We'll see an example of this process in the chapter on dynamic link libraries.

Chapter 14

Multitasking
and Multithreading

Multitasking is the ability of an operating system to run multiple programs concurrently. Basically, the operating system uses a hardware clock to allocate "time slices" for each currently running process. If the time slices are small enough—and the machine is not overloaded with many programs trying to do something—it appears to a user as if all the programs are running simultaneously.

Multitasking is nothing new. On large mainframe computers, multitasking is a given. These mainframes often have scores or hundreds of terminals attached to them, and each terminal user should get the impression that he or she has exclusive access to the whole machine. In addition, mainframe operating systems often allow users to "submit jobs to the background," where they are carried out by the machine while the user can work on something else.

Multitasking on personal computers has taken much longer to become a reality. But we now seem to be approaching an era when PC multitasking will also be taken for granted. As I'll discuss shortly, to some extent the 16-bit versions of Windows supported multitasking, and we now have Windows NT and Windows 95, 32-bit versions of Windows that support both true multitasking and—as an extra bonus—multithreading.

Multithreading is the ability of a program to multitask within itself. The program can split itself into separate "threads" of execution that also seem to run concurrently. This concept may at first seem barely useful, but it turns out that programs can use multithreading to perform lengthy jobs in the background without requiring users to take an extended break away from their machines. (Well, sometimes this may *not* be desired. An excuse to take a journey to the watercooler or refrigerator is often welcome!)

737

MODES OF MULTITASKING

In the early days of the PC, some people advocated multitasking for the future, but many others scratched their heads in puzzlement: Of what use is multitasking on a single-user personal computer? Well, it turned out that multitasking was something users wanted without really knowing it.

Multitasking Under DOS?

The Intel 8088 microprocessor used in the original PC was not exactly built for multitasking. Part of the problem (as I discussed in the last chapter) was inadequate memory management. As multiple programs are started up and ended, a multitasking operating system is often called upon to move memory blocks around to consolidate free space. This was not possible on the 8088 in a manner transparent to applications.

DOS itself didn't help much. Designed to be small and to stay out of the way of applications, DOS supported very little beyond loading programs and providing them with access to the file system.

Still, creative programmers in the early days of DOS found a way to overcome those obstacles, mostly with terminate-and-stay-resident (TSR) programs. Some TSRs, like print spoolers, hooked into the hardware timer interrupt to perform true background processing. Others, like popup utilities such as SideKick, could perform a type of task switching—suspending an application while the popup was running. DOS was also progressively enhanced to provide support for TSRs.

Some software vendors attempted to mold task-switching or multitasking shells on top of DOS (such as Quarterdeck's DesqView), but only one of these environments has achieved a large market penetration. That, of course, is Windows.

Non-Preemptive Multitasking

When Microsoft introduced Windows 1.0 in 1985, it was the most sophisticated solution yet devised to go beyond the limitations of DOS. Back then, Windows ran in real mode, but even so, it was able to move memory blocks around in physical memory—a prerequisite for multitasking—in a way that was not quite transparent to applications but almost tolerable.

In a graphical windowing environment, multitasking makes a lot more sense than in a command-line single-user operating system. For example, in classical command-line UNIX, it is possible to execute programs off the command line so that they run in the background. However, any display output from the program must be redirected to a file, or the output will get mixed up with whatever else the user is doing.

A windowing environment allows multiple programs to run together on the same screen. Switching back and forth becomes trivial, and it is also possible to quickly move data from one program to another, for example, to imbed a picture created in a drawing program into a text file maintained by a word processing program. Data transfer has been supported in various ways under Windows, first with the clipboard, then later through Dynamic Data Exchange (DDE), and now through Object Linking and Embedding (OLE).

Yet, the multitasking implemented in the early versions of Windows was not the traditional preemptive time-slicing found in multiuser operating systems. Those operating systems use a system clock to periodically interrupt one task and restart another. The 16-bit versions of Windows supported something called "non-preemptive multitasking." This type of multitasking is made possible because of the message-based architecture of Windows. In the general case, a Windows program would sit dormant in memory until it received a message. These messages were often the direct or indirect result of user input through the keyboard or mouse. After processing the message, the program returned control back to Windows.

The 16-bit versions of Windows did not arbitrarily switch control from one Windows program to another based on a timer tick. Instead, any task-switching took place when a program had finished processing a message and had returned control to Windows. This non-preemptive multitasking is also called "cooperative multitasking" because it requires some cooperation on the part of applications. One Windows program could tie up the whole system if it took a long time processing a message.

Although non-preemptive multitasking has been the general rule in 16-bit Windows, some forms of preemptive multitasking were also present. Windows used preemptive multitasking for running DOS programs and also allowed dynamic link libraries to receive hardware timer interrupts for multimedia purposes.

The 16-bit Windows included several features to help programmers solve—or at least cope with—the limitations of non-preemptive multitasking. The most notorious is, of course, the hourglass mouse cursor. This is not a solution, of course, but just a way of letting the user know that a program is busy working on a lengthy job and that the system will be otherwise unusable for a little while. Another partial solution is the Windows timer, which allows a program to receive a message and do some work at periodic intervals. The timer is often used for clock applications and animation.

Another solution to the limitations of preemptive multitasking is the *PeekMessage* function call, as we saw in Chapter 4 in the RANDRECT program. Normally a program uses the *GetMessage* call to retrieve the next message from its message queue. However, if there are no messages in the message queue, then *GetMessage* will not return until a message is present. *PeekMessage*, on the other hand, returns control to the program even if no messages are pending. Thus, a program can perform a long job and intermix *PeekMessage* calls in the code. The long job will continue running as long as there are no pending messages for the program or any other program.

PM and the Serialized Message Queue

The first attempt by Microsoft (in collaboration with IBM) to implement multitasking in a quasi-DOS/Windows environment was OS/2 and the Presentation Manager (PM). Although OS/2 certainly supported preemptive multitasking, it often didn't seem as if this preemption was carried over into the Presentation Manager. The problem is that PM serialized user input messages from the keyboard and mouse. What this means is that PM would not deliver a keyboard or mouse message to a program until the previous user input message had been fully processed.

Although keyboard and mouse messages are just a few of the many messages a PM (or Windows) program can receive, most of the other messages are the result of a keyboard or mouse event. For example, a menu command message is the result of the user making a menu selection using the keyboard or mouse. The keyboard or mouse message is not fully processed until the menu command message is processed.

The primary reason for the serialized message queue is to allow predictable "type-ahead" and "mouse-ahead" actions by the user. If one of the keyboard or mouse messages causes a shift in input focus from one window to another, then subsequent keyboard messages should go to the window with the new input focus. So, the system doesn't know where to send a subsequent user input message until the previous ones have been processed.

The consensus these days is that it should *not* be possible for one application to tie up the entire system, and that requires a deserialized message queue, which is supported by Windows NT and Windows 95. If one program is busy doing a lengthy job, you can switch the input focus to another program.

The Multithreading Solution

I've been discussing the OS/2 Presentation Manager only because it was the first environment that provided some veteran Windows programmers (such as myself) with their introduction to multithreading. Interestingly enough, the *limitations* of PM's implementation of multithreading provided programmers with essential clues to how multithreaded programs should be architected. Even though these limitations have now largely been lifted from Windows 95, the lessons learned from more limited environments are still quite valid. So let's proceed.

In a multithreaded environment, programs can split themselves into separate pieces (called threads of execution) that run concurrently. The support of threads turned out to be the best solution to the problem of the serialized message queue in the Presentation Manager, and continues to make a whole lot of sense under Windows 95.

In terms of code, a thread is simply represented by a function which might also call other functions in the program. A program begins execution with its main (or primary) thread, which in a traditional C program is the function called *main,* and which in Windows is *WinMain.* Once running, the program can create new threads of execution by making a system call specifying the name of the initial thread function. The operating system pre-emptively switches control among the threads in much the same way it switches control among processes.

In the OS/2 Presentation Manager, each thread could either create a message queue or not. A PM thread must create a message queue if it wishes to create windows from that thread. Otherwise, a thread needn't create a message queue if it is just doing a lot of data crunching or graphics output. Because the non-message-queue threads do not process messages, they cannot hang the system. The only restriction is that a non-message-queue thread cannot send a message to a window in a message-queue thread, or make any function call that causes a message to be sent. (They can, however, *post* messages to message-queue threads.)

Thus, PM programmers learned how to divide their programs into one message-queue thread that created all the windows and processed messages to them, and one or more non-message-queue threads that performed lengthy background tasks. PM programmers also learned about the "$\frac{1}{10}$ second rule." Basically, they were advised that a message-queue thread spend no more than $\frac{1}{10}$ of a second processing any message. Anything that takes longer should be done in a different thread. If all programmers followed this rule, no PM program could hang the system for more than $\frac{1}{10}$ second.

Multithreaded Architecture

I said that the limitations of PM provided programmers with essential clues to understanding how to use multiple threads of execution in a program running under a graphical environment. So here's what I recommend for the architecture of your programs: Your primary thread creates all the windows that your program needs, includes all the window procedures for these windows, and processes all the messages for these windows. Any other threads are simply background crunchers. They do not interact with the user except through communication with the primary thread.

One way to think of this is that the primary thread handles user input (and other messages), perhaps creating secondary threads in the process. These additional threads do the non-user related tasks.

In other words, your program's primary thread is a Governor, and your secondary threads are the Governor's staff. The Governor delegates all the big jobs to his or her staff while maintaining contact with the outside world. Because they are staff members, the secondary threads do not hold their own press conferences. They discreetly do their work, report back to the Governor, and await their next assignment.

Threads within a particular program are all parts of the same process, so they share the process's resources, such as memory and open files. Because threads share the program's memory, they also share static variables. However, each thread has its own stack, so automatic variables are unique to each thread. Each thread also has its own processor state (and math coprocessor state) that is saved and restored during thread switches.

Thread Hassles

Properly designing, coding, and debugging a complex multithreaded application is conceivably one of the most difficult jobs a Windows programmer can encounter. Because a preemptive multitasking system can interrupt a thread at any point to switch control to another thread, any undesirable interaction between two threads may show up only occasionally, seemingly on a random basis.

One common bug in a multithreaded program is called a "race condition." This happens when a programmer assumes that one thread will finish doing something—for example, preparing some data—before another thread needs that data. To help coordinate thread activity, operating systems require various forms of synchronization. One is the semaphore, which allows the programmer to block the execution of a thread at a certain point in the code until another thread signals that it can resume. Similar to semaphores are "critical sections," which are sections of code that cannot be interrupted.

But semaphores can also introduce another common thread-related bug, which is called a "deadlock." This occurs when two threads have blocked each other's execution and they can only unblock that execution by proceeding.

Fortunately, 32-bit programs are more immune to certain problems involving threads than 16-bit programs. For example, suppose one thread executes the simple statement:

```
lCount++ ;
```

where *lCount* is a long 32-bit global variable that is used by other threads. In a 16-bit program, that single statement in C is compiled into two machine code instructions, the first one incrementing the low 16 bits of the variable, and the second adding any carry into the high 16 bits. Suppose the operating system interrupted the thread between those two machine code instructions. If *lCount* was 0x0000FFFF before the first machine code instruction, then *lCount* would be zero at the time the thread was interrupted, and that's the value another thread would see. Only when the thread resumed would *lCount* be incremented to its proper value of 0x00010000.

This is one of those bugs that might cause an operational problem so infrequently that it would never be detected. In a 16-bit program, the proper way to solve it would be to enclose the statement in a critical section, during which the thread cannot be interrupted. In a 32-bit program, however, the statement is fine because it is compiled to a single machine code instruction.

The Windows Advantage

Windows NT and Windows 95 have a deserialized message queue. The implementation of this seems very good: If a program is taking a long time processing a message, then the mouse cursor appears as an hourglass when the mouse is over that program's window, but it changes to a normal arrow when positioned over another program's window. A simple click can bring that other window to the foreground.

The user, however, is still prevented from working with the program doing the big job because the big job is preventing the program from receiving other messages. This is undesirable. A program should be always open to messages, and that requires the use of secondary threads.

In Windows NT and Windows 95 there is no distinction between message-queue threads and non-message-queue threads. Each thread gets its own message queue when the thread is created. This reduces some of the awkward rules for threads in a PM program. (Still, however, in most cases you'll want to process input through message procedures in one thread and pass off long jobs to other threads that do not maintain windows. This structure almost always makes the best sense, as we'll see.)

Still more good news: Windows NT and Windows 95 have a function that allows one thread to kill another thread in the same process. As you'll discover when you begin writing multithreaded code, this is sometimes very convenient. The early versions of OS/2 did not include a "kill thread" function.

The final good news (at least for this topic) is that Windows NT and Windows 95 have implemented something called "thread local storage" (TLS). To understand this, recall that I mentioned earlier that static variables (both global and local to a function) are shared among threads because they sit in the process's data memory space. Automatic variables (which are always local to a function) are unique to each thread because they occupy space on the stack, and each thread has its own stack.

It is sometimes convenient for two or more threads to use the same function, and for these threads to use static variables that are unique to the thread. That's thread local storage. There are a few Windows function calls involved, but Microsoft has also added an extension to the C compiler that makes the use of thread local storage more transparent to the programmer.

New! Improved! Now with Threads!

Now that I've made the case for threads, let's put the subject in proper perspective. Sometimes there's a tendency to use every feature that an operating system has to offer. The worst case is when your boss comes to your desk and says, "I've heard that this new Whatsit thing is really hot. Let's incorporate some Whatsit in our program." And then you spend a week trying to figure out how Whatsit can possibly benefit the application.

The point is—it just doesn't make sense to add multithreading to an application that doesn't need it. Some do not. If your program displays the hourglass cursor for an annoying period of time, or if it uses the *PeekMessage* call to avoid the hourglass cursor, then restructuring the program for multithreading is probably a good idea. Otherwise, you're just making things hard for yourself and possibly introducing new bugs into the code.

There are even some cases where the hourglass cursor might be entirely appropriate. I mentioned earlier the "1/10 second rule." Well, loading a large file into memory may take longer than 1/10 second. Does this mean that file-loading routines should be implemented in separate threads? Not necessarily. When a user commands a program to open a file, he or she usually wants that operation carried out immediately. Putting the file-loading routines in a separate thread simply adds overhead. It's just not worth it, even if you want to boast to your friends that you write multithreaded programs!

WINDOWS 95 MULTITHREADING

Let's jump right into this by examining some simple programs that use multiple threads of execution.

Random Rectangles Revisited

The RNDRCTMT program shown in Figure 14-1 is a multithreaded version of the RANDRECT program shown in Chapter 4. As you'll recall, RANDRECT used the *PeekMessage* loop to display a series of random rectangles.

```
RNDRCTMT.MAK

#------------------------
# RNDRCTMT.MAK make file
#------------------------

rndrctmt.exe : rndrctmt.obj
    $(LINKER) $(GUIFLAGS) -OUT:rndrctmt.exe rndrctmt.obj $(GUILIBS)

rndrctmt.obj : rndrctmt.c
    $(CC) $(CFLAGSMT) rndrctmt.c
```

```
RNDRCTMT.C

/*-----------------------------------------------
   RNDRCTMT.C -- Displays Random Rectangles
                 (c) Charles Petzold, 1996
  -----------------------------------------------*/

#include <windows.h>
#include <process.h>
#include <stdlib.h>

LRESULT CALLBACK WndProc (HWND, UINT, WPARAM, LPARAM) ;

HWND hwnd ;
int  cxClient, cyClient ;
```

Figure 14-1. *The RNDRCTMT program.*   *(continued)*

```
int WINAPI WinMain (HINSTANCE hInstance, HINSTANCE hPrevInstance,
                    PSTR szCmdLine, int iCmdShow)
    {
    static char szAppName[] = "RndRctMT" ;
    MSG         msg ;
    WNDCLASSEX  wndclass ;

    wndclass.cbSize        = sizeof (wndclass) ;
    wndclass.style         = CS_HREDRAW | CS_VREDRAW ;
    wndclass.lpfnWndProc   = WndProc ;
    wndclass.cbClsExtra    = 0 ;
    wndclass.cbWndExtra    = 0 ;
    wndclass.hInstance     = hInstance ;
    wndclass.hIcon         = LoadIcon (NULL, IDI_APPLICATION) ;
    wndclass.hCursor       = LoadCursor (NULL, IDC_ARROW) ;
    wndclass.hbrBackground = (HBRUSH) GetStockObject (WHITE_BRUSH) ;
    wndclass.lpszMenuName  = NULL ;
    wndclass.lpszClassName = szAppName ;
    wndclass.hIconSm       = LoadIcon (NULL, IDI_APPLICATION) ;

    RegisterClassEx (&wndclass) ;

    hwnd = CreateWindow (szAppName, "Random Rectangles",
                         WS_OVERLAPPEDWINDOW,
                         CW_USEDEFAULT, CW_USEDEFAULT,
                         CW_USEDEFAULT, CW_USEDEFAULT,
                         NULL, NULL, hInstance, NULL) ;

    ShowWindow (hwnd, iCmdShow) ;
    UpdateWindow (hwnd) ;

    while (GetMessage (&msg, NULL, 0, 0))
        {
        TranslateMessage (&msg) ;
        DispatchMessage (&msg) ;
        }

    return msg.wParam ;
    }

VOID Thread (PVOID pvoid)
    {
    HBRUSH hBrush ;
    HDC    hdc ;
    int    xLeft, xRight, yTop, yBottom, iRed, iGreen, iBlue ;
```

(continued)

745

```
        while (TRUE)
            {
            if (cxClient != 0 !! cyClient != 0)
                {
                xLeft   = rand () % cxClient ;
                xRight  = rand () % cxClient ;
                yTop    = rand () % cyClient ;
                yBottom = rand () % cyClient ;
                iRed    = rand () & 255 ;
                iGreen  = rand () & 255 ;
                iBlue   = rand () & 255 ;

                hdc = GetDC (hwnd) ;
                hBrush = CreateSolidBrush (RGB (iRed, iGreen, iBlue)) ;
                SelectObject (hdc, hBrush) ;

                Rectangle (hdc, min (xLeft, xRight), min (yTop, yBottom),
                                max (xLeft, xRight), max (yTop, yBottom)) ;

                ReleaseDC (hwnd, hdc) ;
                DeleteObject (hBrush) ;
                }
            }
        }

LRESULT CALLBACK WndProc (HWND hwnd, UINT iMsg,  WPARAM wParam, LPARAM lParam)
    {
    switch (iMsg)
        {
        case WM_CREATE :
            _beginthread (Thread, 0, NULL) ;
            return 0 ;

        case WM_SIZE :
            cxClient = LOWORD (lParam) ;
            cyClient = HIWORD (lParam) ;
            return 0 ;

        case WM_DESTROY :
            PostQuitMessage (0) ;
            return 0 ;
        }
    return DefWindowProc (hwnd, iMsg, wParam, lParam) ;
    }
```

Notice first that there's a small change in the make file. In the compilation step, the CFLAGS variable has been changed to CFLAGSMT. This is the same as CFLAGS except including the flag -MT, which the compiler needs to compile a multithreaded application. In particular, the compiler inserts the LIBCMT.LIB filename in the .OBJ file rather than LIBC.LIB. This information is used by the linker.

The LIBC.LIB and LIBCMT.LIB files contain the C library functions. Some C library functions maintain static data. The *strtok* function, for example, is designed to be called more than once in succession and stores a pointer in static memory. In a multithreaded program, each thread must have its own static pointer in the *strtok* function. Thus, the multithreaded version of this function is a little different from the singlethreaded *strtok* function.

Also notice that I've included the header file PROCESS.H in RNDRCTMT.C. This file defines a function named *_beginthread* that starts up a new thread (as we'll see shortly). The file is not defined unless an _MT identifier is defined, and that's another result of the -MT flag.

In the *WinMain* function, the *hwnd* value returned from *CreateWindow* is stored in a global variable. So also are the *cxClient* and *cyClient* values obtained from the WM_SIZE message in the window procedure.

The window procedure calls *_beginthread* in the easiest way, with simply the address of the thread function (called *Thread*) as the first parameter and zeros for the other parameters. The thread function returns VOID and has a parameter which is a pointer to a VOID. The *Thread* function in RNDRCTMT does not use this parameter.

After the *_beginthread* function is called, the code in that thread function (as well as any other function the thread function may call) runs concurrently with the rest of the code in the program. Two or more threads can use the same function in a process. In this case, the automatic local variables (stored on the stack) are unique to each thread; all static variables are common to all threads in the process. This is how the window procedure can set the global *cxClient* and *cyClient* variables and the *Thread* function can use them.

There are times that you need persistent data unique to more than one thread. Normally, persistent data involves static variables, but in Windows 95 you can use "thread local storage," which I'll discuss later in this chapter.

The Programming Contest Problem

On October 3, 1986, Microsoft held a day-long press briefing for technical editors and writers of computer magazines to discuss their current array of language products, including their first interactive development environment, QuickBASIC 2.0. At that time, Windows 1.0 was less than a year old, and no one knew when we'd get something similar for that environment. (It took quite a few years.) What made this event unique was a little something that Microsoft's public relations folks had cooked up—a programming contest called "Storm the Gates." Bill Gates would be using QuickBASIC 2.0, and the technical computer press people could use whatever language product they might decide to bring.

The particular programming problem used for the contest was picked out of a hat from among several others (designed to require about a half hour to program) submitted by the press contestants. It went something like this:

Create a multitasking simulation consisting of four windows. The first window must show a series of increasing numbers, the second must show a series of increasing prime numbers, and the third must show the Fibonacci series. (The Fibonacci series begins with the numbers 0 and 1, and every successive number is the sum of the two before it—that is, 0, 1, 1, 2, 3, 5, 8, and so forth). These three windows should either scroll or clear themselves when the numbers reach the bottom of the window. The fourth window must display circles of random radii, and the program must terminate with a press of the Escape key.

Of course, in October 1986, such a program running under DOS couldn't be much more than a multitasking *simulation*, and none of the contestants were brave enough—and most not yet knowledgeable enough—to code it for Windows. Moreover, to do so from scratch would almost certainly have taken longer than a half hour!

Most of the people who participated in this contest wrote a program that divided the screen into four areas. The program contained a loop that sequentially updated each window, and then checked if the Escape key had been pressed. As is customary under DOS, the program used 100 percent of CPU processing.

Had it been programmed for Windows 1.0, the result would have looked something like the MULTI1 program shown in Figure 14-2. I say "something like" because I've converted the programming to 32-bit processing. But the structure and very much of the code—aside from variable and function parameter definitions—would have been the same.

MULTI1.MAK

```
#----------------------
# MULTI1.MAK make file
#----------------------

multi1.exe : multi1.obj
     $(LINKER) $(GUIFLAGS) -OUT:multi1.exe multi1.obj $(GUILIBS)

multi1.obj : multi1.c
     $(CC) $(CFLAGS) multi1.c
```

MULTI1.C

```
/*---------------------------------------------
   MULTI1.C -- Multitasking Demo
              (c) Charles Petzold, 1996
   ---------------------------------------*/
```

Figure 14-2. *The MULTI1 program.*

(continued)

```
#include <windows.h>
#include <stdlib.h>
#include <string.h>
#include <math.h>

LRESULT CALLBACK WndProc (HWND, UINT, WPARAM, LPARAM) ;

int cyChar ;

int WINAPI WinMain (HINSTANCE hInstance, HINSTANCE hPrevInstance,
                    PSTR szCmdLine, int iCmdShow)
     {
     static char  szAppName[] = "Multi1" ;
     HWND         hwnd ;
     MSG          msg ;
     WNDCLASSEX   wndclass ;

     wndclass.cbSize        = sizeof (wndclass) ;
     wndclass.style         = CS_HREDRAW | CS_VREDRAW ;
     wndclass.lpfnWndProc   = WndProc ;
     wndclass.cbClsExtra    = 0 ;
     wndclass.cbWndExtra    = 0 ;
     wndclass.hInstance     = hInstance ;
     wndclass.hIcon         = LoadIcon (NULL, IDI_APPLICATION) ;
     wndclass.hCursor       = LoadCursor (NULL, IDC_ARROW) ;
     wndclass.hbrBackground = (HBRUSH) GetStockObject (WHITE_BRUSH) ;
     wndclass.lpszMenuName  = NULL ;
     wndclass.lpszClassName = szAppName ;
     wndclass.hIconSm       = LoadIcon (NULL, IDI_APPLICATION) ;

     RegisterClassEx (&wndclass) ;

     hwnd = CreateWindow (szAppName, "Multitasking Demo",
                          WS_OVERLAPPEDWINDOW,
                          CW_USEDEFAULT, CW_USEDEFAULT,
                          CW_USEDEFAULT, CW_USEDEFAULT,
                          NULL, NULL, hInstance, NULL) ;

     ShowWindow (hwnd, iCmdShow) ;
     UpdateWindow (hwnd) ;
     while (GetMessage (&msg, NULL, 0, 0))
          {
          TranslateMessage (&msg) ;
          DispatchMessage (&msg) ;
          }
```

(continued)

```
      return msg.wParam ;
      }

int CheckBottom (HWND hwnd, int cyClient, int iLine)
     {
     if (iLine * cyChar + cyChar > cyClient)
          {
          InvalidateRect (hwnd, NULL, TRUE) ;
          UpdateWindow (hwnd) ;
          iLine = 0 ;
          }
     return iLine ;
     }

// Window 1: Display increasing sequence of numbers
// -----------------------------------------------

LRESULT APIENTRY WndProc1 (HWND hwnd, UINT iMsg,  WPARAM wParam, LPARAM lParam)
     {
     static int    iNum, iLine ;
     static short  cyClient ;
     char          szBuffer[16] ;
     HDC           hdc ;

     switch (iMsg)
          {
          case WM_SIZE :
               cyClient = HIWORD (lParam) ;
               return 0 ;

          case WM_TIMER :
               if (iNum < 0)
                    iNum = 0 ;

               iLine = CheckBottom (hwnd, cyClient, iLine) ;

               wsprintf (szBuffer, "%d", iNum++) ;

               hdc = GetDC (hwnd) ;
               TextOut (hdc, 0, iLine * cyChar, szBuffer, strlen (szBuffer)) ;
               ReleaseDC (hwnd, hdc) ;

               iLine++ ;

               return 0 ;
          }
```

(continued)

```
        return DefWindowProc (hwnd, iMsg, wParam, lParam) ;
     }

// Window 2: Display increasing sequence of prime numbers
// ----------------------------------------------------------

LRESULT APIENTRY WndProc2 (HWND hwnd, UINT iMsg,  WPARAM wParam, LPARAM lParam)
     {
     static int   iNum = 1, iLine ;
     static short cyClient ;
     char         szBuffer[16] ;
     int          i, iSqrt ;
     HDC          hdc ;

     switch (iMsg)
          {
          case WM_SIZE :
               cyClient = HIWORD (lParam) ;
               return 0 ;

          case WM_TIMER :
               do   {
                    if (++iNum < 0)
                         iNum = 0 ;

                    iSqrt = (int) sqrt (iNum) ;

                    for (i = 2 ; i <= iSqrt ; i++)
                         if (iNum % i == 0)
                              break ;
                    }
               while (i <= iSqrt) ;

               iLine = CheckBottom (hwnd, cyClient, iLine) ;

               wsprintf (szBuffer, "%d", iNum) ;

               hdc = GetDC (hwnd) ;
               TextOut (hdc, 0, iLine * cyChar, szBuffer, strlen (szBuffer)) ;
               ReleaseDC (hwnd, hdc) ;

               iLine++ ;

               return 0 ;
          }
     return DefWindowProc (hwnd, iMsg, wParam, lParam) ;
```

(continued)

```
        }

// Window 3: Display increasing sequence of Fibonacci numbers
// ------------------------------------------------------------

LRESULT APIENTRY WndProc3 (HWND hwnd, UINT iMsg, WPARAM wParam, LPARAM lParam)
      {
      static int    iNum = 0, iNext = 1, iLine ;
      static short  cyClient ;
      char          szBuffer[16] ;
      int           iTemp ;
      HDC           hdc ;

      switch (iMsg)
           {
           case WM_SIZE :
                cyClient = HIWORD (lParam) ;
                return 0 ;

           case WM_TIMER :
                if (iNum < 0)
                     {
                     iNum  = 0 ;
                     iNext = 1 ;
                     }

                iLine = CheckBottom (hwnd, cyClient, iLine) ;

                wsprintf (szBuffer, "%d", iNum) ;

                hdc = GetDC (hwnd) ;
                TextOut (hdc, 0, iLine * cyChar, szBuffer, strlen (szBuffer)) ;
                ReleaseDC (hwnd, hdc) ;

                iTemp = iNum ;
                iNum  = iNext ;
                iNext += iTemp ;

                iLine++ ;

                return 0 ;
           }
      return DefWindowProc (hwnd, iMsg, wParam, lParam) ;
      }
```

(continued)

```
// Window 4: Display circles of random radii
// ----------------------------------------

LRESULT APIENTRY WndProc4 (HWND hwnd, UINT iMsg, WPARAM wParam, LPARAM lParam)
     {
     static short cxClient, cyClient ;
     HDC          hdc ;
     int          iDiameter ;

     switch (iMsg)
         {
         case WM_SIZE :
              cxClient = LOWORD (lParam) ;
              cyClient = HIWORD (lParam) ;
              return 0 ;

         case WM_TIMER :
              InvalidateRect (hwnd, NULL, TRUE) ;
              UpdateWindow (hwnd) ;

              iDiameter = rand() % (max (1, min (cxClient, cyClient))) ;

              hdc = GetDC (hwnd) ;

              Ellipse (hdc, (cxClient - iDiameter) / 2,
                            (cyClient - iDiameter) / 2,
                            (cxClient + iDiameter) / 2,
                            (cyClient + iDiameter) / 2) ;

              ReleaseDC (hwnd, hdc) ;
              return 0 ;
         }
     return DefWindowProc (hwnd, iMsg, wParam, lParam) ;
     }

// Main window to create child windows
// -----------------------------------

LRESULT APIENTRY WndProc (HWND hwnd, UINT iMsg, WPARAM wParam, LPARAM lParam)
     {
     static char    *szChildClass[] = { "Child1", "Child2",
                                         "Child3", "Child4" } ;
     static HWND     hwndChild[4] ;
     static WNDPROC  ChildProc[] = { WndProc1, WndProc2,
                                     WndProc3, WndProc4 } ;
     HINSTANCE       hInstance ;
```

(continued)

```
int          i, cxClient, cyClient ;
WNDCLASSEX   wndclass ;

switch (iMsg)
    {
    case WM_CREATE :
        hInstance = (HINSTANCE) GetWindowLong (hwnd, GWL_HINSTANCE) ;

        wndclass.cbSize        = sizeof (wndclass) ;
        wndclass.style         = CS_HREDRAW | CS_VREDRAW ;
        wndclass.cbClsExtra    = 0 ;
        wndclass.cbWndExtra    = 0 ;
        wndclass.hInstance     = hInstance ;
        wndclass.hIcon         = NULL ;
        wndclass.hCursor       = LoadCursor (NULL, IDC_ARROW) ;
        wndclass.hbrBackground = (HBRUSH) GetStockObject (WHITE_BRUSH) ;
        wndclass.lpszMenuName  = NULL ;
        wndclass.hIconSm       = NULL ;

        for (i = 0 ; i < 4 ; i++)
            {
            wndclass.lpfnWndProc   = ChildProc[i] ;
            wndclass.lpszClassName = szChildClass[i] ;

            RegisterClassEx (&wndclass) ;

            hwndChild[i] = CreateWindow (szChildClass[i], NULL,
                WS_CHILDWINDOW | WS_BORDER | WS_VISIBLE,
                0, 0, 0, 0, hwnd, (HMENU) i, hInstance, NULL) ;
            }

        cyChar = HIWORD (GetDialogBaseUnits ()) ;
        SetTimer (hwnd, 1, 10, NULL) ;
        return 0 ;

    case WM_SIZE :
        cxClient = LOWORD (lParam) ;
        cyClient = HIWORD (lParam) ;

        for (i = 0 ; i < 4 ; i++)
            MoveWindow (hwndChild[i], (i % 2) * cxClient / 2,
                                      (i > 1) * cyClient / 2,
                        cxClient / 2, cyClient / 2, TRUE) ;
        return 0 ;
```

(continued)

```
          case WM_TIMER :
               for (i = 0 ; i < 4 ; i++)
                    SendMessage (hwndChild[i], WM_TIMER, wParam, lParam) ;

               return 0 ;

          case WM_CHAR :
               if (wParam == '\x1B')
                    DestroyWindow (hwnd) ;

               return 0 ;

          case WM_DESTROY :
               KillTimer (hwnd, 1) ;
               PostQuitMessage (0) ;
               return 0 ;
          }
     return DefWindowProc (hwnd, iMsg, wParam, lParam) ;
     }
```

The actual program presents nothing we haven't really seen before. The main window creates four child windows, each of which occupies one quarter of the client area. The main window also sets a Windows timer and sends WM_TIMER messages to each of the four child windows.

Normally a Windows program should maintain enough information to re-create the contents of its window during the WM_PAINT message. MULTI1 doesn't do this, but the windows are drawn and erased so rapidly that I didn't think it necessary.

The prime number generator in *WndProc2* isn't terribly efficient, but it works. A number is prime, of course, if it has no divisors except 1 and itself. To check if a particular number is prime, however, doesn't require dividing by all numbers, and checking for remainders, up to the number being checked, but only up to the square root of that number. That square root calculation is the reason for the unusual introduction of floating point math in an otherwise all integer-based program.

There is nothing really wrong with the MULTI1 program. Using the Windows timer is a fine way to simulate multitasking in earlier versions of Windows and Windows 95. However, the use of the timer sometimes restricts the speed of a program. If the program can update all its windows within a single WM_TIMER message with time to spare, then it's not taking full advantage of the machine.

One possible solution is to perform two or more updates during a single WM_TIMER message. But how many? That would have to depend on the speed of the machine, and that is a major variable. One would not want to write a program tuned only to a 25-Mhz 386 or a 50-Mhz 486 or a 500-Mhz 786.

The Multithreaded Solution

Let's take a look at a multithreaded solution to this programming problem. The MULTI2 program is shown in Figure 14-3.

```
MULTI2.MAK

#---------------------
# MULTI2.MAK make file
#---------------------

multi2.exe : multi2.obj
     $(LINKER) $(GUIFLAGS) -OUT:multi2.exe multi2.obj $(GUILIBS)

multi2.obj : multi2.c
     $(CC) $(CFLAGSMT) multi2.c
```

```
MULTI2.C

/*-----------------------------------------
   MULTI2.C -- Multitasking Demo
              (c) Charles Petzold, 1996
   -----------------------------------------*/

#include <windows.h>
#include <stdlib.h>
#include <string.h>
#include <math.h>
#include <process.h>

typedef struct
     {
     HWND hwnd ;
     int  cxClient ;
     int  cyClient ;
     int  cyChar ;
     BOOL bKill ;
     }
     PARAMS, *PPARAMS ;

LRESULT APIENTRY WndProc (HWND, UINT, WPARAM, LPARAM) ;

int WINAPI WinMain (HINSTANCE hInstance, HINSTANCE hPrevInstance,
                    PSTR szCmdLine, int iCmdShow)
     {
```

Figure 14-3. *The MULTI2 program.*   *(continued)*

```
        static char szAppName[] = "Multi2" ;
        HWND        hwnd ;
        MSG         msg ;
        WNDCLASSEX  wndclass ;

        wndclass.cbSize        = sizeof (wndclass) ;
        wndclass.style         = CS_HREDRAW | CS_VREDRAW ;
        wndclass.lpfnWndProc   = WndProc ;
        wndclass.cbClsExtra    = 0 ;
        wndclass.cbWndExtra    = 0 ;
        wndclass.hInstance     = hInstance ;
        wndclass.hIcon         = LoadIcon (NULL, IDI_APPLICATION) ;
        wndclass.hCursor       = LoadCursor (NULL, IDC_ARROW) ;
        wndclass.hbrBackground = (HBRUSH) GetStockObject (WHITE_BRUSH) ;
        wndclass.lpszMenuName  = NULL ;
        wndclass.lpszClassName = szAppName ;
        wndclass.hIconSm       = LoadIcon (NULL, IDI_APPLICATION) ;

        RegisterClassEx (&wndclass) ;

        hwnd = CreateWindow (szAppName, "Multitasking Demo",
                             WS_OVERLAPPEDWINDOW,
                             CW_USEDEFAULT, CW_USEDEFAULT,
                             CW_USEDEFAULT, CW_USEDEFAULT,
                             NULL, NULL, hInstance, NULL) ;

        ShowWindow (hwnd, iCmdShow) ;
        UpdateWindow (hwnd) ;

        while (GetMessage (&msg, NULL, 0, 0))
             {
             TranslateMessage (&msg) ;
             DispatchMessage (&msg) ;
             }
        return msg.wParam ;
        }

int CheckBottom (HWND hwnd, int cyClient, int cyChar, int iLine)
     {
     if (iLine * cyChar + cyChar > cyClient)
          {
          InvalidateRect (hwnd, NULL, TRUE) ;
          UpdateWindow (hwnd) ;
          iLine = 0 ;
          }
```

(continued)

```
        return iLine ;
        }

// Window 1: Display increasing sequence of numbers
// -----------------------------------------------

void Thread1 (PVOID pvoid)
     {
     int     iNum = 0, iLine = 0 ;
     char    szBuffer[16] ;
     HDC     hdc ;
     PPARAMS pparams ;

     pparams = (PPARAMS) pvoid ;

     while (!pparams->bKill)
          {
          if (iNum < 0)
              iNum = 0 ;

          iLine = CheckBottom (pparams->hwnd,   pparams->cyClient,
                               pparams->cyChar, iLine) ;

          wsprintf (szBuffer, "%d", iNum++) ;

          hdc = GetDC (pparams->hwnd) ;

          TextOut (hdc, 0, iLine * pparams->cyChar,
                   szBuffer, strlen (szBuffer)) ;

          ReleaseDC (pparams->hwnd, hdc) ;

          iLine++ ;
          }
     _endthread () ;
     }

LRESULT APIENTRY WndProc1 (HWND hwnd, UINT iMsg, WPARAM wParam, LPARAM lParam)
     {
     static PARAMS params ;

     switch (iMsg)
          {
          case WM_CREATE :
               params.hwnd = hwnd ;
               params.cyChar = HIWORD (GetDialogBaseUnits ()) ;
```

(continued)

```
              _beginthread (Thread1, 0, &params) ;
              return 0 ;

       case WM_SIZE :
              params.cyClient = HIWORD (lParam) ;
              return 0 ;

       case WM_DESTROY :
              params.bKill = TRUE ;
              return 0 ;
       }
    return DefWindowProc (hwnd, iMsg, wParam, lParam) ;
    }

// Window 2: Display increasing sequence of prime numbers
// -------------------------------------------------------

void Thread2 (PVOID pvoid)
    {
    char    szBuffer[16] ;
    int     iNum = 1, iLine = 0, i, iSqrt ;
    HDC     hdc ;
    PPARAMS pparams ;

    pparams = (PPARAMS) pvoid ;

    while (!pparams->bKill)
        {
        do
            {
            if (++iNum < 0)
                iNum = 0 ;

            iSqrt = (int) sqrt (iNum) ;

            for (i = 2 ; i <= iSqrt ; i++)
                if (iNum % i == 0)
                    break ;
            }
        while (i <= iSqrt) ;

        iLine = CheckBottom (pparams->hwnd,   pparams->cyClient,
                             pparams->cyChar, iLine) ;

        wsprintf (szBuffer, "%d", iNum) ;
```

(continued)

```
                    hdc = GetDC (pparams->hwnd) ;

                    TextOut (hdc, 0, iLine * pparams->cyChar,
                             szBuffer, strlen (szBuffer)) ;

                    ReleaseDC (pparams->hwnd, hdc) ;

                    iLine++ ;
                    }
          _endthread () ;
          }

LRESULT APIENTRY WndProc2 (HWND hwnd, UINT iMsg, WPARAM wParam, LPARAM lParam)
     {
     static PARAMS params ;

     switch (iMsg)
          {
          case WM_CREATE :
               params.hwnd = hwnd ;
               params.cyChar = HIWORD (GetDialogBaseUnits ()) ;
               _beginthread (Thread2, 0, &params) ;
               return 0 ;

          case WM_SIZE :
               params.cyClient = HIWORD (lParam) ;
               return 0 ;

          case WM_DESTROY :
               params.bKill = TRUE ;
               return 0 ;
          }
     return DefWindowProc (hwnd, iMsg, wParam, lParam) ;
     }

// Window 3: Display increasing sequence of Fibonacci numbers
// ----------------------------------------------------------

void Thread3 (PVOID pvoid)
     {
     char      szBuffer[16] ;
     int       iNum = 0, iNext = 1, iLine = 0, iTemp ;
     HDC       hdc ;
     PPARAMS   pparams ;

     pparams = (PPARAMS) pvoid ;
```

(continued)

```
        while (!pparams->bKill)
            {
            if (iNum < 0)
                {
                iNum  = 0 ;
                iNext = 1 ;
                }

            iLine = CheckBottom (pparams->hwnd,   pparams->cyClient,
                                 pparams->cyChar, iLine) ;

            wsprintf (szBuffer, "%d", iNum) ;

            hdc = GetDC (pparams->hwnd) ;

            TextOut (hdc, 0, iLine * pparams->cyChar,
                     szBuffer, strlen (szBuffer)) ;

            ReleaseDC (pparams->hwnd, hdc) ;

            iTemp  = iNum ;
            iNum   = iNext ;
            iNext += iTemp ;

            iLine++ ;
            }
    _endthread () ;
    }

LRESULT APIENTRY WndProc3 (HWND hwnd, UINT iMsg, WPARAM wParam, LPARAM lParam)
    {
    static PARAMS params ;

    switch (iMsg)
        {
        case WM_CREATE :
            params.hwnd = hwnd ;
            params.cyChar = HIWORD (GetDialogBaseUnits ()) ;
            _beginthread (Thread3, 0, &params) ;
            return 0 ;

        case WM_SIZE :
            params.cyClient = HIWORD (lParam) ;
            return 0 ;

        case WM_DESTROY :
```

(continued)

```
                        params.bKill = TRUE ;
                        return 0 ;
                    }
            return DefWindowProc (hwnd, iMsg, wParam, lParam) ;
            }

// Window 4: Display circles of random radii
// -------------------------------------------

void Thread4 (PVOID pvoid)
     {
     HDC      hdc ;
     int      iDiameter ;
     PPARAMS pparams ;

     pparams = (PPARAMS) pvoid ;

     while (!pparams->bKill)
          {
          InvalidateRect (pparams->hwnd, NULL, TRUE) ;
          UpdateWindow (pparams->hwnd) ;

          iDiameter = rand() % (max (1,
                            min (pparams->cxClient, pparams->cyClient))) ;

          hdc = GetDC (pparams->hwnd) ;

          Ellipse (hdc, (pparams->cxClient - iDiameter) / 2,
                        (pparams->cyClient - iDiameter) / 2,
                        (pparams->cxClient + iDiameter) / 2,
                        (pparams->cyClient + iDiameter) / 2) ;

          ReleaseDC (pparams->hwnd, hdc) ;
          }
     _endthread () ;
     }

LRESULT APIENTRY WndProc4 (HWND hwnd, UINT iMsg, WPARAM wParam, LPARAM lParam)
     {
     static PARAMS params ;

     switch (iMsg)
          {
          case WM_CREATE :
               params.hwnd = hwnd ;
               params.cyChar = HIWORD (GetDialogBaseUnits ()) ;
```

(continued)

```
                        _beginthread (Thread4, 0, &params) ;
                        return 0 ;

                   case WM_SIZE :
                        params.cxClient = LOWORD (lParam) ;
                        params.cyClient = HIWORD (lParam) ;
                        return 0 ;

                   case WM_DESTROY :
                        params.bKill = TRUE ;
                        return 0 ;
                   }
              return DefWindowProc (hwnd, iMsg, wParam, lParam) ;
              }


// Main window to create child windows
// -----------------------------------

LRESULT APIENTRY WndProc (HWND hwnd, UINT iMsg, WPARAM wParam, LPARAM lParam)
     {
     static char    *szChildClass[] = { "Child1", "Child2",
                                          "Child3", "Child4" } ;

     static HWND     hwndChild[4] ;
     static WNDPROC  ChildProc[] = { WndProc1, WndProc2,
                                      WndProc3, WndProc4 } ;

     HINSTANCE       hInstance ;
     int             i, cxClient, cyClient ;
     WNDCLASSEX      wndclass ;

     switch (iMsg)
         {
         case WM_CREATE :
              hInstance = (HINSTANCE) GetWindowLong (hwnd, GWL_HINSTANCE) ;

              wndclass.cbSize        = sizeof (wndclass) ;
              wndclass.style         = CS_HREDRAW | CS_VREDRAW ;
              wndclass.cbClsExtra    = 0 ;
              wndclass.cbWndExtra    = 0 ;
              wndclass.hInstance     = hInstance ;
              wndclass.hIcon         = NULL ;
              wndclass.hCursor       = LoadCursor (NULL, IDC_ARROW) ;
              wndclass.hbrBackground = (HBRUSH) GetStockObject (WHITE_BRUSH) ;
              wndclass.lpszMenuName  = NULL ;
              wndclass.hIconSm       = NULL ;

              for (i = 0 ; i < 4 ; i++)
```

(continued)

```
                          {
                          wndclass.lpfnWndProc   = ChildProc[i] ;
                          wndclass.lpszClassName = szChildClass[i] ;

                          RegisterClassEx (&wndclass) ;

                          hwndChild[i] = CreateWindow (szChildClass[i], NULL,
                               WS_CHILDWINDOW | WS_BORDER | WS_VISIBLE,
                               0, 0, 0, 0, hwnd, (HMENU) i, hInstance, NULL) ;
                          }

                     return 0 ;

          case WM_SIZE :
               cxClient = LOWORD (lParam) ;
               cyClient = HIWORD (lParam) ;

               for (i = 0 ; i < 4 ; i++)
                    MoveWindow (hwndChild[i], (i % 2) * cxClient / 2,
                                              (i > 1) * cyClient / 2,
                               cxClient / 2, cyClient / 2, TRUE) ;
               return 0 ;

          case WM_CHAR :
               if (wParam == '\x1B')
                    DestroyWindow (hwnd) ;

               return 0 ;

          case WM_DESTROY :
               PostQuitMessage (0) ;
               return 0 ;
          }
     return DefWindowProc (hwnd, iMsg, wParam, lParam) ;
     }
```

The *WinMain* and *WndProc* functions of MULTI2.C are very similar to those in MULTI1.C. *WndProc* registers four window classes for the four windows, creates those windows, and resizes them during the WM_SIZE message. The only difference in *WndProc* is that it no longer sets the Windows timer or processes WM_TIMER messages.

The big difference in MULTI2 is that each of the child window procedures creates another thread of execution by calling the *_beginthread* function during the WM_CREATE message. In total, the MULTI2 program has five threads of execution that run concurrently. The main thread contains the main window procedure and the four child window procedures. The other four threads use the functions named *Thread1*, *Thread2*, and so forth. These other four threads are responsible for drawing the four windows.

The multithreaded code I showed in the RNDRCTMT program did not use the third-parameter to *_beginthread*. This parameter allows a thread that creates another thread to pass information to the other thread in 32-bit variables. Customarily, this variable is a pointer, and also customarily, it is a pointer to a structure. This allows the creating thread and the new thread to share information without the use of global variables. As you can see, there are no global variables in MULTI2.

For the MULTI2 program, I defined a structure named PARAMS near the top of the program, and a pointer to that structure named PPARAMS. This structure has five fields—a window handle, the width and height of the window, the height of a character, and a Boolean variable named *bKill*. This final structure field allows the creating thread to inform the created thread when it's time to terminate itself.

Let's take a look at *WndProc1*, the child window procedure that displays the sequence of increasing numbers. The window procedure has become very simple. The only local variable is a PARAMS structure. During the WM_CREATE message, it sets the *hwnd* and *cyChar* fields of this structure and calls *_beginthread* to create a new thread using the *Thread1* function, passing to it a pointer to this structure. During the WM_SIZE message, *WndProc1* sets the *cyClient* field of the structure, and during the WM_DESTROY message, it sets the *bKill* field to TRUE. The *Thread1* function concludes by calling *_endthread*. This is not strictly necessary because the thread is destroyed after exiting the thread function. However, *_endthread* is useful to exit a thread deep within some complex levels of processing.

The *Thread1* function does the actual drawing on the window, and it runs concurrently with the other four threads of the program. The function receives a pointer to the PARAMS structure and runs in a *while* loop, checking each time if the *bKill* field is TRUE or FALSE. If FALSE, the function essentially performs the same processing as during the WM_TIMER message in MULTI1.C—formatting the number, obtaining a device context handle, and displaying the number using *TextOut*.

As you'll see when you run MULTI2 under Windows 95, the windows are updated much faster than in MULTI1, indicating the program is using the power of the processor more efficiently. There's another difference between MULTI1 and MULTI2: Usually when you move or size a window, the default window procedure enters a modal loop and all output to the window stops. In MULTI2, the output continues.

Any Problems?

It may seem as if the MULTI2 program is not as bullet-proofed as it could be. To see what I'm getting at, let's look at some multithreaded "flaws" in MULTI2.C, using *WndProc1* and *Thread1* as examples.

WndProc1 runs in the main thread of MULTI2, and *Thread1* runs concurrently with it. The times at which Windows 95 switches between these two threads is variable and unpredictable. Suppose *Thread1* is running and has just executed the code that checks if the *bKill* field of the PARAMS structure is TRUE. It's not, but then Windows 95 switches control to the main thread, at which time the user terminates the program. *WndProc1* receives a WM_DESTROY message and sets the *bKill* parameter to TRUE. Oops! Too late! Suddenly the operating system switches to *Thread1*, and that function attempts to obtain a device context handle to a non-existent window.

It turns out this is not a problem. Windows 95 is sufficiently bullet-proofed so that the graphics functions simply fail without causing any problems.

Proper multithreaded programming techniques involve the use of thread synchronization (and in particular, critical sections), which I'll discuss in more detail shortly. Basically, critical sections are delimited by calls to *EnterCriticalSection* and *LeaveCriticalSection*. If one thread enters a critical section, another thread cannot enter a critical section. The latter thread is blocked on the *EnterCriticalSection* call until the first thread calls *LeaveCriticalSection*.

Another possible problem in MULTI2 is that the main thread could receive a WM_ERASEBKGND or WM_PAINT message during the time that a secondary thread is drawing its output. Again, using a critical section would help prevent any problems that could result from two threads attempting to draw on the same window. But, experimentation seems to show that Windows 95 properly serializes access to the graphics drawing functions. That is, one thread can't draw on a window while another thread is in the middle of doing so.

The Windows 95 documentation warns about one area where graphics functions are *not* serialized, and that involves use of GDI objects, such as pens, brushes, fonts, bitmaps, regions, and palettes. It is possible for one thread to destroy an object that another thread is using. The solution to this problem requires use of a critical section, or better yet, not sharing GDI objects between threads.

The Benefits of Sleep

I've discussed what I consider to be the best architecture of a multithreaded program, which is that the primary thread creates all the program's windows, contains all the window procedures for these windows, and processes all messages to the windows. Secondary threads carry out background jobs or lengthy jobs.

However, suppose you want to do animation in a secondary thread. Normally, animation in Windows is done with WM_TIMER messages. But if a secondary thread does not create a window it cannot receive these messages. Without any timing, the animation would probably run much too fast.

The solution is the *Sleep* function. In effect, a thread calls the *Sleep* function to suspend itself voluntarily. The single parameter is a time in milliseconds. The *Sleep* function call does not return until the specified time has elapsed. During that time, the thread is suspended and is allocated no time slices (although obviously the thread still requires a small amount of processing time during timer ticks when the system must determine if the thread should be resumed). A parameter of 0 to the *Sleep* function causes the thread to forfeit the remainder of its time slice.

When a thread calls *Sleep*, only that thread is suspended for the specified amount of time. The system still runs other threads, either in the same process or another process. I used the *Sleep* function in the SCRAMBLE program in Chapter 4 to slow down the scrambling operation.

Normally, you should not use the *Sleep* function in your primary thread because it slows down message processing, but because SCRAMBLE did not create any windows, there is no problem in using it there.

THREAD SYNCHRONIZATION

About once a year, the traffic lights at the busy intersection outside my apartment window stop working. The result is chaos, and while the cars usually avoid actually hitting each other, they often come close.

We might term the intersection of two roads as a "critical section." A southbound car and a westbound car cannot pass through an intersection at the same time without hitting each other. Depending on the traffic volume, different approaches are taken to solve the problem. For very light traffic at an intersection with high visibility, drivers can be trusted to properly yield. More traffic might require a stop sign, and still heavier traffic would require traffic lights. The traffic lights help coordinate the activity of the intersection (as long as they work, of course).

The Critical Section

In a single-tasking operating system, traditional computer programs don't need traffic lights to help them coordinate their activities. They run as if they owned the road, which they do. There is nothing to interfere with what they do.

Even in a multitasking operating system, most programs seemingly run independently of each other. But some problems could arise. For example, two programs could need to read from and write to the same file at the same time. In such cases, the operating system provides a mechanism of shared files and record locking to help out.

However, in an operating system that supports multithreading the situation gets messy and potentially dangerous. It is not uncommon for two or more threads to share some data. For example, one thread could update one or more variables and another thread could use those variables. Sometimes this poses a problem, and sometimes it doesn't. (Keep in mind that the operating system can only switch control from one thread to another between machine code instructions. If only a single integer is being shared among the threads, then changes to this variable usually occur in a single instruction, and potential problems are minimized.)

However, suppose the threads share several variables or a data structure. Often, these multiple variables or the fields of the structure must be consistent among themselves. The operating system could interrupt a thread in the middle of updating these variables. The thread that uses these variables would then be dealing with inconsistent data.

The result is a collision, and it's not difficult to imagine how an error like this could crash the program. What we need are the programming equivalent of traffic lights to help coordinate and synchronize the thread traffic. That's the critical section. Basically, a critical section is a block of code that should not be interrupted.

There are four functions for using critical sections. To use these functions, you must define a critical section object, which is a global variable of type CRITICAL_SECTION, for example:

```
CRITICAL_SECTION cs ;
```

This CRITICAL_SECTION data type is a structure, but the fields are used only internally to Windows. This critical section object must first be initialized by one of the threads in the program by calling:

```
InitializeCriticalSection (&cs) ;
```

This creates a critical section object named *cs*. The online documentation for this function includes the following warnings: "A critical section object cannot be moved or copied. The process must also not modify the object, but must treat it as logically opaque." This can be translated as "Don't mess around with it, and don't even look at it."

After the critical section object has been initialized, a thread enters a critical section by calling:

```
EnterCriticalSection (&cs) ;
```

At this point, the thread is said to "own" the critical section object. No two threads can own the critical section object at the same time. Thus, if a thread has entered a critical section, the next thread calling *EnterCriticalSection* with the same critical section object will be suspended in the function call. The function will return only when the first thread leaves the critical section by calling:

```
LeaveCriticalSection (&cs) ;
```

At that time, the second thread—suspended in its call to *EnterCriticalSection*—will own the critical section and the function call will return.

When the critical section object is no longer needed by the program, it can be deleted by calling:

```
DeleteCriticalSection (&cs) ;
```

This frees up any system resources that may have been allocated to maintain the critical section object.

This critical section mechanism involves "mutual exclusion" (a term that will come up again as we continue to explore thread synchronization). Only one thread can own a critical section at any time. Thus, one thread can enter a critical section, set the fields of a structure, and exit the critical section. Another thread using the structure would also enter a critical section before accessing the fields of the structure, and then exit the critical section.

Note that you can define multiple critical section objects, say, as *cs1* and *cs2*. For example, if a program has four threads, and the first two threads share some data, they can use one critical section object, and if the other two threads share some other data, they can use a second critical section object.

Note that you should be careful when using a critical section in your main thread. If the secondary thread spends a long time in its own critical section, it could hang the main thread for an inordinate amount of time.

The Mutex Object

One limitation with critical sections is that they may only be used for coordinating threads within a single process. But there are cases where you need to coordinate two different processes that share a resource (such as shared memory). You can't use critical sections for that, and instead you use something oddly called a "mutex object."

The fabricated word "mutex" stands for "mutual exclusion," and that's precisely our goal here. We want to prevent threads of a program from being interrupted while updating or using shared data. Or, to use my earlier analogy, we want southbound traffic and westbound traffic mutually excluded from the intersection.

EVENT SIGNALING

We can define a "big job" as anything a program has to do that might violate the $1/10$ second rule. Obvious big jobs include a spelling check in a word processing program, a file sort or indexing in a database program, a spreadsheet recalculation, printing, and even complex drawing. Of course, as we know by now, the best solution to following the $1/10$ second rule is to farm out big jobs to secondary threads of execution. These secondary threads do not create windows, and hence they are not bound by the $1/10$ second rule.

It is often desirable for the secondary threads to inform the primary thread when they have completed, or for the primary thread to abort the job the secondary thread is doing. That's what we'll examine here.

The BIGJOB1 Program

As a hypothetical big job, I'll use a series of floating-point calculations sometimes known as the "savage" benchmark. This calculation increments an integer in a roundabout manner: It squares a number and takes the square root (canceling out the square), applies *log* and *exp* functions (again canceling each other out), then applies the *atan* and *tan* functions (another canceling out), and finally adds 1 to the result.

The BIGJOB1 program is shown in Figure 14-4.

BIGJOB1.MAK

```
#----------------------
# BIGJOB1.MAK make file
#----------------------


bigjob1.exe : bigjob1.obj
     $(LINKER) $(GUIFLAGS) -OUT:bigjob1.exe bigjob1.obj $(GUILIBS)

bigjob1.obj : bigjob1.c
     $(CC) $(CFLAGSMT) bigjob1.c
```

BIGJOB1.C

```
/*-------------------------------------------
   BIGJOB1.C -- Multithreading Demo
              (c) Charles Petzold, 1996
   -------------------------------------------*/

#include <windows.h>
#include <math.h>
#include <process.h>

#define REP              100000

#define STATUS_READY     0
#define STATUS_WORKING   1
#define STATUS_DONE      2

#define WM_CALC_DONE     (WM_USER + 0)
#define WM_CALC_ABORTED  (WM_USER + 1)

typedef struct
    {
```

Figure 14-4. *The BIGJOB1 program.*

(continued)

```
        HWND hwnd ;
        BOOL bContinue ;
        }
        PARAMS, *PPARAMS ;

LRESULT APIENTRY WndProc (HWND, UINT, WPARAM, LPARAM) ;

int WINAPI WinMain (HINSTANCE hInstance, HINSTANCE hPrevInstance,
                    PSTR szCmdLine, int iCmdShow)
    {
    static char szAppName[] = "BigJob1" ;
    HWND        hwnd ;
    MSG         msg ;
    WNDCLASSEX  wndclass ;

    wndclass.cbSize        = sizeof (wndclass) ;
    wndclass.style         = CS_HREDRAW | CS_VREDRAW ;
    wndclass.lpfnWndProc   = WndProc ;
    wndclass.cbClsExtra    = 0 ;
    wndclass.cbWndExtra    = 0 ;
    wndclass.hInstance     = hInstance ;
    wndclass.hIcon         = LoadIcon (NULL, IDI_APPLICATION) ;
    wndclass.hCursor       = LoadCursor (NULL, IDC_ARROW) ;
    wndclass.hbrBackground = (HBRUSH) GetStockObject (WHITE_BRUSH) ;
    wndclass.lpszMenuName  = NULL ;
    wndclass.lpszClassName = szAppName ;
    wndclass.hIconSm       = LoadIcon (NULL, IDI_APPLICATION) ;

    RegisterClassEx (&wndclass) ;

    hwnd = CreateWindow (szAppName, "Multithreading Demo",
                         WS_OVERLAPPEDWINDOW,
                         CW_USEDEFAULT, CW_USEDEFAULT,
                         CW_USEDEFAULT, CW_USEDEFAULT,
                         NULL, NULL, hInstance, NULL) ;

    ShowWindow (hwnd, iCmdShow) ;
    UpdateWindow (hwnd) ;

    while (GetMessage (&msg, NULL, 0, 0))
        {
        TranslateMessage (&msg) ;
        DispatchMessage (&msg) ;
        }
    return msg.wParam ;
    }
```

(continued)

```
void Thread (PVOID pvoid)
    {
    double  A = 1.0 ;
    INT     i ;
    LONG    lTime ;
    PPARAMS pparams ;

    pparams = (PPARAMS) pvoid ;

    lTime = GetCurrentTime () ;

    for (i = 0 ; i < REP && pparams->bContinue ; i++)
        A = tan (atan (exp (log (sqrt (A * A))))) + 1.0 ;

    if (i == REP)
        {
        lTime = GetCurrentTime () - lTime ;
        SendMessage (pparams->hwnd, WM_CALC_DONE, 0, lTime) ;
        }
    else
        SendMessage (pparams->hwnd, WM_CALC_ABORTED, 0, 0) ;

    _endthread () ;
    }

LRESULT CALLBACK WndProc (HWND hwnd, UINT iMsg, WPARAM wParam, LPARAM lParam)
    {
    static char   *szMessage[] = { "Ready (left mouse button begins)",
                                   "Working (right mouse button aborts)",
                                   "%d repetitions in %ld msec" } ;
    static INT     iStatus ;
    static LONG    lTime ;
    static PARAMS  params ;
    char           szBuffer[64] ;
    HDC            hdc ;
    PAINTSTRUCT    ps ;
    RECT           rect ;

    switch (iMsg)
        {
        case WM_LBUTTONDOWN :
            if (iStatus == STATUS_WORKING)
                {
                MessageBeep (0) ;
                return 0 ;
                }
```

(continued)

```
                  iStatus = STATUS_WORKING ;

                  params.hwnd = hwnd ;
                  params.bContinue = TRUE ;

                  _beginthread (Thread, 0, &params) ;

                  InvalidateRect (hwnd, NULL, TRUE) ;
                  return 0 ;

          case WM_RBUTTONDOWN :
                  params.bContinue = FALSE ;
                  return 0 ;

          case WM_CALC_DONE :
                  lTime = lParam ;
                  iStatus = STATUS_DONE ;
                  InvalidateRect (hwnd, NULL, TRUE) ;
                  return 0 ;

          case WM_CALC_ABORTED :
                  iStatus = STATUS_READY ;
                  InvalidateRect (hwnd, NULL, TRUE) ;
                  return 0 ;

          case WM_PAINT :
                  hdc = BeginPaint (hwnd, &ps) ;

                  GetClientRect (hwnd, &rect) ;

                  wsprintf (szBuffer, szMessage[iStatus], REP, lTime) ;

                  DrawText (hdc, szBuffer, -1, &rect,
                            DT_SINGLELINE | DT_CENTER | DT_VCENTER) ;

                  EndPaint (hwnd, &ps) ;
                  return 0 ;

          case WM_DESTROY :
                  PostQuitMessage (0) ;
                  return 0 ;
          }
     return DefWindowProc (hwnd, iMsg, wParam, lParam) ;
     }
```

This is a fairly simple program, but I think you'll see how it illustrates a generalized approach to doing big jobs in a multithreaded program. To use the BIGJOB1 program, click with the left mouse button on the client area of the window. This begins 100,000 repetitions of the savage calculation, which takes about 8 seconds on a 33-Mhz 386 machine. When the calculation has completed, the elapsed time is displayed in the window. While the calculation is in progress, you can click on the client area with the right mouse button to abort it.

So, let's take a look at how this is done:

The window procedure maintains a static variable called *iStatus* (which can be set to one of three constants defined near the top of the program, beginning with the prefix STA-TUS) indicating whether the program is ready to do a calculation, working on a calculation, or done with a calculation. The program uses the *iStatus* variable during the WM_PAINT message to display an appropriate character string in the center of the client area.

The window procedure also maintains a static structure (of type PARAMS, also defined near the top of the program) to share data between the window procedure and the secondary thread. The structure has only two fields—*hwnd* (the handle of the program's window) and *bContinue*, which is a Boolean variable used to indicate to the thread whether to continue the calculation or not.

When you click on the client area with the left mouse button, the window procedure sets the *iStatus* variable to STATUS_WORKING, and the two fields of the PARAMS structure. The *hwnd* field of the structure is set to the window handle, of course, and *bContinue* is set to TRUE.

The window procedure then creates a secondary thread with a call to _beginthread. The secondary thread function, called *Thread*, begins by calling *GetCurrentTime* to get the elapsed time in milliseconds that Windows has been running. It then enters a *for* loop to do 100,000 repetitions of the savage calculation. Notice also that the thread will drop out of the loop if *bContinue* is ever set to FALSE.

After the *for* loop, the thread function checks whether it's actually completed 100,000 calculations. If it has, it calls *GetCurrentTime* again to get the elapsed time, and then uses *SendMessage* to send the window procedure a program-defined WM_CALC_DONE message with the elapsed time as *lParam*. If the calculation was aborted prematurely (that is, if the *bContinue* field of the PARAMS structure became FALSE during the loop), then the thread sends the window procedure a WM_CALC_ABORTED message. The thread then gracefully ends by calling _endthread.

Within the window procedure, the *bContinue* field of the PARAMS structure is set to FALSE when you click on the client area with the right mouse button. This is how the calculation is aborted before completion.

The window procedure processes the WM_CALC_DONE message by first saving the elapsed time. The processing of both the WM_CALC_DONE and WM_CALC_ABORTED messages continues with a call to *InvalidateRect* to generate a WM_PAINT message and display a new text string in the client area.

It's usually a good idea to include a provision (such as the *bContinue* field in the structure) to allow the thread to terminate gracefully. The *KillThread* function should be used only when graceful termination is awkward. The reason why is that threads can allocate resources, such as memory. If this memory is not freed when the thread terminates, then it will still be allocated. Threads are not processes: Allocated resources are shared among all threads in a process, so they are not automatically freed when the thread terminates. Good programming structure dictates that a thread should free any resources it allocates.

Note also that a third thread may be created while the second thread is still in progress. This could happen if Windows 95 switches control from the second thread to the first thread between the *SendMessage* call and the *_endthread* call, and the window procedure then creates a new thread in response to a mouse click. This is not a problem here, but if it is a problem in one of your own applications, you'll want to use a critical section to avoid thread collisions.

The Event Object

BIGJOB1 creates a thread every time it needs to perform the savage calculation; the thread terminates after doing the calculation.

An alternative is to keep the thread around for the entire duration of the program, and only kick it into action when necessary. This is an ideal application for an event object.

An event object is either "signaled" (also known as "set") or "unsignaled" (also known as "reset"). You create the event object by calling:

```
hEvent = CreateEvent (&sa, fManual, fInitial, pszName) ;
```

The first parameter (a pointer to a SECURITY_ATTRIBUTES structure) and the last parameter (an event object name) are meaningful only when event objects are shared among processes. In a single process, these parameters are generally set to NULL. Set the *fInitial* parameter to TRUE if you want the event object to be initially signaled, and FALSE for initially unsignaled. I'll describe the *fManual* parameter shortly.

To signal an existing event object, call:

```
SetEvent (hEvent) ;
```

To unsignal an event object, call:

```
ResetEvent (hEvent) ;
```

A program generally calls:

```
WaitForSingleObject (hEvent, dwTimeOut) ;
```

with the second parameter set to INFINITE. The function returns immediately if the event object is currently signaled (or set). Otherwise, the function will suspend the thread until the event object becomes signaled. You can set the second parameter to a time-out value in milliseconds so the function returns before the event object becomes signaled.

If the *fManual* parameter of the original *CreateEvent* call is set to FALSE, then the event object becomes automatically unsignaled when the *WaitForSingleObject* function returns. This feature usually makes it unnecessary to use the *ResetEvent* function.

So, now we're equipped to look at BIGJOB2.C, shown in Figure 14-5.

BIGJOB2.MAK

```
#----------------------
# BIGJOB2.MAK make file
#----------------------

bigjob2.exe : bigjob2.obj
     $(LINKER) $(GUIFLAGS) -OUT:bigjob2.exe bigjob2.obj $(GUILIBS)

bigjob2.obj : bigjob2.c
     $(CC) $(CFLAGSMT) bigjob2.c
```

BIGJOB2.C

```
/*--------------------------------------------
   BIGJOB2.C -- Multithreading Demo
               (c) Charles Petzold, 1996
   --------------------------------------------*/

#include <windows.h>
#include <math.h>
#include <process.h>

#define REP              100000

#define STATUS_READY     0
#define STATUS_WORKING   1
#define STATUS_DONE      2

#define WM_CALC_DONE     (WM_USER + 0)
#define WM_CALC_ABORTED  (WM_USER + 1)
```

Figure 14-5. *The BIGJOB2 program.* *(continued)*

```
typedef struct
    {
    HWND    hwnd ;
    HANDLE  hEvent ;
    BOOL    bContinue ;
    }
    PARAMS, *PPARAMS ;

LRESULT CALLBACK WndProc (HWND, UINT, WPARAM, LPARAM) ;

int WINAPI WinMain (HINSTANCE hInstance, HINSTANCE hPrevInstance,
                    PSTR szCmdLine, int iCmdShow)
    {
    static char szAppName[] = "BigJob2" ;
    HWND        hwnd ;
    MSG         msg ;
    WNDCLASSEX  wndclass ;

    wndclass.cbSize        = sizeof (wndclass) ;
    wndclass.style         = CS_HREDRAW | CS_VREDRAW ;
    wndclass.lpfnWndProc   = WndProc ;
    wndclass.cbClsExtra    = 0 ;
    wndclass.cbWndExtra    = 0 ;
    wndclass.hInstance     = hInstance ;
    wndclass.hIcon         = LoadIcon (NULL, IDI_APPLICATION) ;
    wndclass.hCursor       = LoadCursor (NULL, IDC_ARROW) ;
    wndclass.hbrBackground = (HBRUSH) GetStockObject (WHITE_BRUSH) ;
    wndclass.lpszMenuName  = NULL ;
    wndclass.lpszClassName = szAppName ;
    wndclass.hIconSm       = LoadIcon (NULL, IDI_APPLICATION) ;

    RegisterClassEx (&wndclass) ;

    hwnd = CreateWindow (szAppName, "Multithreading Demo",
                         WS_OVERLAPPEDWINDOW,
                         CW_USEDEFAULT, CW_USEDEFAULT,
                         CW_USEDEFAULT, CW_USEDEFAULT,
                         NULL, NULL, hInstance, NULL) ;

    ShowWindow (hwnd, iCmdShow) ;
    UpdateWindow (hwnd) ;

    while (GetMessage (&msg, NULL, 0, 0))
        {
        TranslateMessage (&msg) ;
        DispatchMessage (&msg) ;
        }
```

(continued)

```
        return msg.wParam ;
        }

void Thread (PVOID pvoid)
     {
     double  A = 1.0 ;
     INT     i ;
     LONG    lTime ;
     PPARAMS pparams ;

     pparams = (PPARAMS) pvoid ;

     while (TRUE)
          {
          WaitForSingleObject (pparams->hEvent, INFINITE) ;

          lTime = GetCurrentTime () ;

          for (i = 0 ; i < REP && pparams->bContinue ; i++)
               A = tan (atan (exp (log (sqrt (A * A))))) + 1.0 ;

          if (i == REP)
               {
               lTime = GetCurrentTime () - lTime ;
               SendMessage (pparams->hwnd, WM_CALC_DONE, 0, lTime) ;
               }
          else
               SendMessage (pparams->hwnd, WM_CALC_ABORTED, 0, 0) ;
          }
     }

LRESULT CALLBACK WndProc (HWND hwnd, UINT iMsg, WPARAM wParam, LPARAM lParam)
     {
     static char   *szMessage[] = { "Ready (left mouse button begins)",
                                    "Working (right mouse button aborts)",
                                    "%d repetitions in %ld msec" } ;
     static HANDLE hEvent ;
     static INT    iStatus ;
     static LONG   lTime ;
     static PARAMS params ;
     char          szBuffer[64] ;
     HDC           hdc ;
     PAINTSTRUCT   ps ;
     RECT          rect ;
```

(continued)

```
switch (iMsg)
    {
    case WM_CREATE :
         hEvent = CreateEvent (NULL, FALSE, FALSE, NULL) ;

         params.hwnd = hwnd ;
         params.hEvent = hEvent ;
         params.bContinue = FALSE ;

         _beginthread (Thread, 0, &params) ;

         return 0 ;

    case WM_LBUTTONDOWN :
         if (iStatus == STATUS_WORKING)
             {
             MessageBeep (0) ;
             return 0 ;
             }

         iStatus = STATUS_WORKING ;

         params.bContinue = TRUE ;

         SetEvent (hEvent) ;

         InvalidateRect (hwnd, NULL, TRUE) ;
         return 0 ;

    case WM_RBUTTONDOWN :
         params.bContinue = FALSE ;
         return 0 ;

    case WM_CALC_DONE :
         lTime = lParam ;
         iStatus = STATUS_DONE ;
         InvalidateRect (hwnd, NULL, TRUE) ;
         return 0 ;

    case WM_CALC_ABORTED :
         iStatus = STATUS_READY ;
         InvalidateRect (hwnd, NULL, TRUE) ;
         return 0 ;

    case WM_PAINT :
```

(continued)

```
            hdc = BeginPaint (hwnd, &ps) ;

            GetClientRect (hwnd, &rect) ;

            wsprintf (szBuffer, szMessage[iStatus], REP, lTime) ;

            DrawText (hdc, szBuffer, -1, &rect,
                      DT_SINGLELINE | DT_CENTER | DT_VCENTER) ;

            EndPaint (hwnd, &ps) ;
            return 0 ;

       case WM_DESTROY :
            _endthread () ;
            PostQuitMessage (0) ;
            return 0 ;
       }
   return DefWindowProc (hwnd, iMsg, wParam, lParam) ;
   }
```

The window procedure processes the WM_CREATE message by first creating a non-manual event object that is initialized in the unsignaled (or reset) state. It then creates the thread.

The *Thread* function enters an infinite *while* loop but calls *WaitForSingleObject* at the beginning of the loop. (Notice that the PARAMS structure includes a third field containing the handle to the event object.) Because the event is initially unsignaled, the thread is suspended in the function call. A left mouse button click causes the window procedure to call *SetEvent*. This releases the second thread from the *WaitForSingleObject* call, and it begins the savage calculation. After finishing, the thread calls *WaitForSingleObject* again, but the event object has become unsignaled from the first call. Thus, the thread is suspended until the next mouse click.

Otherwise, the program is almost identical to BIGJOB1.

THREAD LOCAL STORAGE (TLS)

Global variables in a multithreaded program (as well as any allocated memory) are shared among all the threads in the program. Local static variables in a function are also shared among all threads using that function. Local automatic variables in a function are unique to each thread, because they are stored on the stack and each thread has its own stack.

It may be necessary to have persistent storage that is unique to each thread. For example, the C *strtok* function I mentioned earlier in this chapter requires this type of storage. Unfortunately, the C language does not support such storage. But Windows 95 includes four functions that implement a mechanism to do it. This is called thread local storage.

Here's how it works. First, define a structure that contains all the data that needs to be unique among the threads, for example:

```
typedef struct
    {
    int a ;
    int b ;
    }
    DATA, *PDATA ;
```

The primary thread calls *TlsAlloc* to obtain an index value:

```
dwTlsIndex = TlsAlloc () ;
```

This can be stored in a global variable or passed to the thread function in the parameter structure.

The thread function begins by allocating memory for the data structure and calling *TlsSetValue* using the index obtained above:

```
TlsSetValue (dwTlsIndex, GlobalAlloc (GPTR, sizeof (DATA))) ;
```

This associates a pointer with a particular thread and a particular thread index. Now, any function that needs to use this pointer (including the original thread function itself) can include code like so:

```
PDATA pdata ;
[other program lines]
pdata = (PDATA) TlsGetValue (dwTlsIndex) ;
```

Now it can set or use *pdata->a* and *pdata->b*. Before the thread function terminates, it frees the allocated memory:

```
GlobalFree (TlsGetValue (dwTlsIndex)) ;
```

When all the threads using this data have terminated, the primary thread frees the index:

```
TlsFree (dwTlsIndex) ;
```

This process may be confusing at first, so perhaps it might be helpful to see how thread local storage might be implemented. (I have no knowledge of how Windows 95 actually does it, but this is plausible.) First, *TlsAlloc* might simply allocate a block of memory (0 bytes in length) and return an index value that is a pointer to this block. Every time *TlsSetValue* is called with that index, the block of memory is increased by 8 bytes using *GlobalReAlloc*. Stored in these 8 bytes is the ID of the thread calling the function (obtained by calling *GetCurrentThreadId*) and the pointer passed to the *TlsSetValue* function. *TlsGetValue* simply uses the thread ID to search the table and then return the pointer. *TlsFree* frees up the block of memory.

So you see, this is something you could probably easily implement yourself, but it's nice to have the facility already done for us.

Chapter 15

Using the Printer

The concept of device independence may have seemed all well and good in Chapters 3 and 4, when we were using the video display for text and graphics, but how well does the concept hold up for printers and plotters? In general, the news is good. Under Microsoft Windows 95, printers and plotters have a device-independent graphics interface. You can forget about printer control sequences and communications protocols when programming for the printer. Retail Windows programs conspicuously lack the disks of specialized printer drivers that characterize word-processing software and graphics programs for MS-DOS. When a retail Windows program includes printer drivers, they are usually enhanced versions of existing printer drivers.

From a Windows program, you can print text and graphics on paper using the same GDI functions that we've been using for the video display. Many of the issues of device independence that we've explored in Chapters 3 and 4—mostly related to the size and resolution of the display surface and its color capabilities—can be approached and resolved in the same way. Yet a printer or plotter is not simply a display that uses paper rather than a cathode-ray tube. There are some very significant differences. For example, we have never had to consider the problem of a video display not being connected to the display adapter or the problem of the display "running out of screen," but it is common for a printer to be off line or to run out of paper.

Nor have we worried about the video display adapter being incapable of performing certain graphics operations. Either the display adapter can handle graphics or it can't. And if it can't, then it can't be used with Windows at all. But some printers can't print graphics (although they can still be used with Windows), and plotters can do vector graphics but have a real problem with bit-block transfers.

Here are some other issues to consider:

- Printers are slower than video displays. Although we have on occasion tried to tune our programs for best performance, we haven't worried about the time required for the video display to be refreshed. But nobody wants to wait for a printer to finish printing before getting back to work.

- Programs reuse the surface of the video display as they overwrite previous display output with new output. This can't be done on a printer. Instead, a printer must eject a completed page and go on to the next page.

- On the video display, different applications are windowed. On a printer, output from different applications must be separated into distinct documents or print jobs.

To add printer support to the rest of GDI, Windows 95 provides several functions which, for lack of a better name, I'll refer to as print functions. A program calls normal text and graphics functions to "display" on a page in the same way as it displays on the screen. Print functions, such as *StartDoc*, *EndDoc*, *StartPage*, and *EndPage* are responsible for organizing the output and sending it to the printer.

PRINTING, SPOOLING, AND THE PRINT FUNCTIONS

When you use a printer in Windows 95, you're actually initiating a complex interaction involving the GDI32 library module, the printer device driver library module (which has a .DRV extension), and the Windows print spooler, as well as some other modules that get into the act. Before we start programming for the printer, let's examine how this process works.

When an application program wants to begin using a printer, it first obtains a handle to the printer device context using *CreateDC* or *PrintDlg*. This causes the printer device driver library module to be loaded into memory (if it's not present already) and to initialize itself. The program then calls the *StartDoc* function, which signals the beginning of a new document. The *StartDoc* function is handled by the GDI module. The GDI module calls the *Control* function in the printer device driver, telling the device driver to initialize data and prepare for printing.

The call to *StartDoc* begins the process of printing a document; the process ends when the program calls *EndDoc*. These two calls act as bookends for the normal GDI commands that write text or draw graphics to the document pages. Each page is itself a sort of subdocument. A program calls *StartPage* to begin a page and *EndPage* to end the page.

For example, if a program wants to draw an ellipse on a page, it first calls *StartDoc* to begin the print job, then *StartPage* to signal a new page. It then calls *Ellipse*, just as it does when drawing an ellipse on the screen. The GDI module generally stores the GDI calls in a disk-based file, usually in enhanced metafile format, located in the subdirectory indicated by the TEMP environment variable. (If no TEMP variable exists, Windows uses the root directory of the first fixed disk on the system.) The file begins with the characters ~EMF (for "enhanced metafile") and has a .TMP extension. However, as I'll discuss shortly, it's possible for the printer driver to skip this step.

When the application program is finished with the GDI calls that define the first page, the program calls *EndPage*. Now the real work begins. The printer driver must translate the various drawing commands stored in the metafile into output for the printer. The printer output required to define a page of graphics can be very large, particularly if the printer has no high-level page-composition language. For example, a 600-dots-per-inch laser printer using 8½-by-11-inch paper might require more than four megabytes of data to define one page of graphics.

For this reason, printer drivers often implement a technique called "banding," which divides the page into rectangles called bands. (We'll examine banding later in this chapter.) The GDI module obtains the dimensions of each band from the printer driver. It then sets a clipping region equal to this band and calls the printer device driver *Output* function for each of the drawing functions contained in the enhanced metafile. This process is called "playing the metafile into the device driver." The GDI module must play the entire enhanced metafile into the device driver for each band that the device driver defines on the page. After the process is completed, Windows deletes the enhanced metafile.

For each band, the device driver translates these drawing functions into the output necessary to realize them on the printer. The format of this output will be specific to the printer. For dot-matrix printers, it will be a collection of control sequences, including graphics sequences. (For some assistance with constructing this output, the printer driver can call various "helper" routines also located in the GDI module.) For laser printers with a high-level page-composition language (such as PostScript), the printer output will be in that language.

The printer driver passes the printer output for each band to the GDI module, which then stores this printer output in a temporary file also located in the TEMP subdirectory. This file begins with the characters ~SPL and has a .TMP extension. When the entire page is finished, the GDI module makes an interprocess call to the print spooler indicating that a new printed page is ready. The application program then goes on to the next page. When the application is finished with all the pages it must print, it calls *EndDoc* to signal that the print job is completed. Figure 15-1 on the following page shows the interaction of the program, the GDI module, the printer driver, and the print spooler.

The Windows 95 print spooler is actually a collection of several components:

Spooler Component	*Description*
Print Request Router	Routes a data stream to the print provider
Local print provider	Creates spool files destined for a local printer
Network print provider	Creates spool files destined for a network printer

Spooler Component	Description
Print processor	Performs despooling, which is the conversion of spooled device-independent data into a form specific to the target printer
Port monitor	Controls the port to which the printer is connected
Language monitor	Controls printers capable of two-way communication to set device configuration and to monitor printer status

The spooler relieves application programs of much of the work involved with printing. Windows loads the print spooler at startup, so it is already active when a program begins printing. When the program prints a document, the GDI module creates the files that contain printer output. The print spooler's job is to send these files out to the printer. It is notified of a new print job by the GDI module. It then begins reading the file and transferring

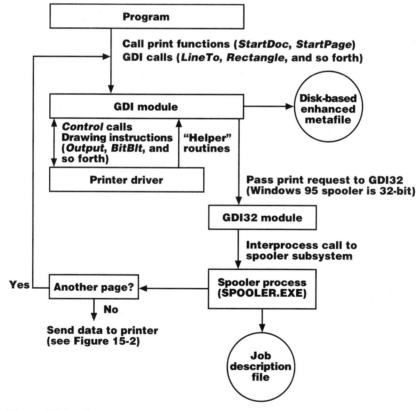

Figure 15-1. *The interaction of the application program, the GDI module, the printer driver, and the spooler.*

it directly to the printer. To transfer the files, the spooler uses various communications functions for the parallel or serial port to which the printer is connected. When the spooler is done sending a file to a printer, it deletes the temporary file holding the output. This process is shown in Figure 15-2.

Most of this process is transparent to the application program. From the perspective of the program, "printing" occurs only during the time required for the GDI module to save all the printer output in disk files. After that—or even before, if printing is handled in a separate thread—the program is freed up to do other things. The actual printing of the document becomes the print spooler's responsibility rather than the program's. From the Printers folder a user can pause print jobs, change their priority, or cancel print jobs. This arrangement allows programs to "print" faster than would be possible if they were printing in real time and had to wait for the printer to finish one page before proceeding to the next.

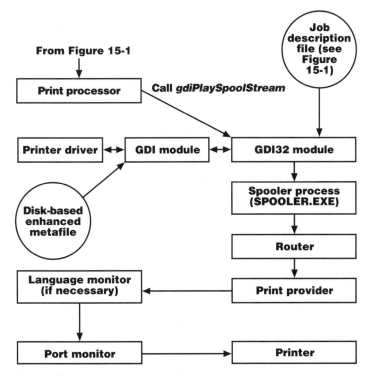

Figure 15-2. *The operation of the print spooler.*

Although I've described how printing works in general, there are some variations on this theme. One is that the print spooler doesn't have to be active in order for Windows programs to use the printer. The user can turn off spooling for a printer from the Details tab of the printer's property sheet.

Why would a user want to bypass the Windows spooler? Well, perhaps the user has a hardware or software print spooler that works faster than the Windows spooler. Or perhaps the printer is on a network that has its own spooler. The general rule is that one spooler is faster than two. Removing the Windows spooler would speed up printing because the printer output doesn't have to be stored on disk. It can go right out to the printer and be intercepted by the external hardware or software print spooler.

If the Windows spooler isn't active, the GDI module doesn't store the printer output from the device driver in a file. Instead, GDI itself sends the output directly to the parallel or serial printer port.

Here's another variation on the general theme. Normally, the GDI module stores all the functions necessary to define a page in an enhanced metafile and then plays this metafile into the printer driver once for each band defined by the driver. If the printer driver doesn't require banding, however, the enhanced metafile isn't created; GDI simply passes the drawing functions directly to the driver. In a further variation, it is also possible for an application to assume responsibility for dividing printer output into bands. This makes the printing code in the application program more complex, but it relieves the GDI module of creating the metafile. Once again, GDI simply passes the functions for each band to the printer driver.

Now perhaps you're starting to see how printing from a Windows program might involve a bit more overhead than that required for using the video display. Several problems can occur—particularly if the GDI module runs out of disk space while creating the metafile or the printer output files. You can either get very involved in reporting these problems to the user and attempting to do something about them, or you can remain relatively aloof.

We'll examine several different approaches to printing in the pages that follow. But first things first—let's begin by obtaining a printer device context.

THE PRINTER DEVICE CONTEXT

Just as you must obtain a handle to a device context before you paint on the video display, you must obtain a printer device context handle before printing. Once you have this handle (and have called *StartDoc* to announce your intention of creating a new document), you can use this printer device context handle the same way you use the video display device context handle—as the first parameter to the various GDI calls we covered in Chapters 3 and 4.

Obtaining a printer device context handle is ordinarily very easy. Most programs simply call the *PrintDlg* function. Besides providing a handle to a device context for the selected printer, this function also gives the user the opportunity to change printers or specify other job characteristics before printing. *PrintDlg*, as we'll discuss later, can save you a lot of work. For now, you may simply want to start printing on the default printer without a dialog, the way NOTEPAD does. For that you must create a printer device context the hard way, with the *CreateDC* function.

In Chapter 4, you learned that you can get a handle to a device context for the entire video display by calling:

```
hdc = CreateDC ("DISPLAY", NULL, NULL, NULL) ;
```

You can obtain a printer device context handle using this same function. However, for a printer device context, the first and third parameters are ignored in Win32. Thus, the general syntax of *CreateDC* for printers is:

```
hdc = CreateDC (NULL, lpszDeviceName, NULL, lpInitializationData) ;
```

The *lpInitializationData* parameter is also generally set to NULL. The *lpszDeviceName* parameter points to a character string that tells Windows the name of the printer device. Before you can set the device name, you must find out what printers are available.

Getting the *CreateDC* Parameters

A system can have more than one printer attached to it. It may even have other programs, such as facsimile software, masquerading as printers. Regardless of the number of attached printers, only one can be considered the "current printer" or the "default printer." This is the most recent printer that the user has chosen from the dialog box invoked by the Print option or otherwise designated using the Printers folder. Many small Windows programs use only this printer for printing.

Windows 95 offers several methods for determining what printers (or pseudoprinters) are attached to the system. We'll look at two methods: Calling the *EnumPrinters* function and searching the WIN.INI file.

The *EnumPrinters* function

Calling *EnumPrinters* is the easiest way to identify printers. The function fills an array of structures that contain information about each attached printer. You even have your choice of three structures, depending on the level of detail you want. The PRINTER_INFO_1 structure provides little more than the name of the printer. PRINTER_INFO_2 offers more information, such as the name of the printer driver, the name of the printer device, and the output port. PRINTER_INFO_5 gives the device name, the port name, and timeout periods. Using this structure has the additional advantage of causing *EnumPrinters* to query the registry rather than open any devices, resulting in faster operation. To create a printer device context, you need only the printer name, so PRINTER_INFO_5 suffices.

Here's an example. The following function calls *EnumPrinters* and returns a device context handle for the default printer:

```
HDC GetPrinterDC (void)
    {
    PRINTER_INFO_5 pinfo5[3] ;
    DWORD          dwNeeded, dwReturned ;
```

```
    if (EnumPrinters (PRINTER_ENUM_DEFAULT, NULL, 5, (LPBYTE) pinfo5,
                  sizeof (pinfo5), &dwNeeded, &dwReturned))
       return CreateDC (NULL, pinfo5[0].pPrinterName, NULL, NULL) ;

    return 0 ;          // EnumPrinters failed, so return null hdc
    }
```

The first parameter in *EnumPrinters* specifies the type of printer objects we're inter-ested in—in this case, we use the flag PRINTER_ENUM_DEFAULT to request information only for the default printer. The third parameter indicates the type of structure we want to fill—1 for PRINTER_INFO_1, 2 for PRINTER_INFO_2, and 5 for PRINTER_INFO_5. The parameter *pinfo5* points to an array of structures, the first of which *EnumPrinters* fills with the device name of the default printer.

There can be only one default printer, so you might be wondering why the above code allocates an array of three PRINTER_INFO_5 structures. Unfortunately, *EnumPrinters* either has a bug or is poorly written, depending on how charitable one feels. Although it correctly fills the first PRINTER_INFO_5 structure of the array, the function requires a buffer larger than a single structure. (Don't believe the documentation.) Increasing the buffer size by a factor of three seems to keep *EnumPrinters* happy.

The *CreateDC* function returns 0 if the printer device context could not be created. This can occur if the printer name is malformed, if Windows can't find the printer driver, or if the output port name is "none" (which means the printer is not connected to an output port). You can, however, obtain an information context for a printer connected to "none" by using *CreateIC* rather than *CreateDC*.

Let's say you need a list of all attached printers, not just the default. *EnumPrinters* can handle that, too, though it requires a bit more work. Just specify a first parameter of PRINTER_ENUM_LOCAL. In Windows 95, this flag causes the function to enumerate all attached printers, both local to the system and available through a network.

To enumerate an unknown number of printers, you should first query *EnumPrinters* to find out how large a buffer it requires. It returns the required size in *dwNeeded*, which you then use to allocate a sufficient buffer:

```
LPPRINTER_INFO_5 ppinfo5 ;
DWORD            dwNeeded, dwReturned ;
BOOL             bErr ;

// First, find out how large an array is needed
EnumPrinters (PRINTER_ENUM_LOCAL, NULL, 5, "", 0, &dwNeeded, &dwReturned) ;

// Next, allocate sufficient heap for the PRINTER_INFO_5 array
ppinfo5 = (LPPRINTER_INFO_5) HeapAlloc (GetProcessHeap (),
                                   HEAP_ZERO_MEMORY, dwNeeded) ;
```

```
// Last, call EnumPrinters again to fill the allocated PRINTER_INFO_5 array
if (ppinfo5)
     bErr = EnumPrinters (PRINTER_ENUM_LOCAL, NULL, 5, (LPBYTE) ppinfo5,
                          dwNeeded, &dwNeeded, &dwReturned)) ;
```

This example fills an allocated array of PRINTER_INFO_5 structures with data for all local and remote printers attached to the system. The first call to *EnumPrinters* intentionally fails, returning the required buffer size in *dwNeeded*. The code then allocates the buffer from the heap and again calls *EnumPrinters*, this time with sufficient buffer space. The actual number of PRINTER_INFO_5 structures that *EnumPrinters* fills—one structure for each attached printer—is returned in *dwReturned*. If *EnumPrinters* returns a value of TRUE, you can present the printer names to the user. (We'll do this shortly in the DEVCAPS2 program.)

Searching the WIN.INI file

Another method for finding attached printers requires you to do a little fishing in the WIN.INI file. The *[windows]* section of WIN.INI lists the default printer with the keyword device. The string that follows contains the device name (required in the *CreateDC* call), driver name, and output port:

```
[windows]
[other lines]
device=IBM Graphics,IBMGRX,LPT1:
```

In this case, the device name is IBM Graphics, the driver name is IBMGRX, and the output port is LPT1.

Here is another way to write our *GetPrinterDC* function to return a printer device context handle. This example uses *GetProfileString* to obtain the device string from WIN.INI, parses it into its three components, and calls *CreateDC* to create a device context for the default printer. Although in Win32 *CreateDC* ignores the driver and port names, the example below illustrates how to extract all names from the string that *GetProfileString* returns:

```
HDC GetPrinterDC ()
    {
    char szPrinter[80] ;
    char *szDevice, *szDriver, *szOutput ;

    GetProfileString ("windows", "device", ",,,", szPrinter, 80) ;

    if (NULL != (szDevice = strtok (szPrinter, "," )) &&
        NULL != (szDriver = strtok (NULL,      ", ")) &&
        NULL != (szOutput = strtok (NULL,      ", ")))
          return CreateDC (szDriver, szDevice, szOutput, NULL) ;

    return 0 ;
    }
```

GetProfileString looks in the *[windows]* section for the keyword *device* and copies up to 80 characters following the equal sign into *szPrinter*. (The third parameter to *GetProfileString* is a default string if Windows can't find the *[windows]* section or the device keyword in WIN.INI.) The string is parsed using the normal C *strtok* function, which breaks a string into tokens. Note that I use only a comma to find the end of the *szDevice* string, because the device name can include embedded blanks. Both a comma and space are used to separate the driver name and output port so that leading or trailing blanks are stripped from these strings. (Using *strtok* is not an entirely satisfactory method of parsing this string, because *strtok* doesn't take into account the multibyte character codes that can be used in versions of Windows for countries in the Far East. If this is of concern, you can use *EnumPrinters* as described above or you can write your own version of *strtok* that uses *CharNext* to advance through the string.)

The *[windows]* section of WIN.INI lists only the default printer, but multiple printers can be listed in the *[devices]* section of WIN.INI. The *[devices]* section looks something like this:

```
[devices]
IBM Graphics=IBMGRX,LPT1:
Generic / Text Only=TTY,output.prn
HP Plotter=HPPLOT,COM1:
Postscript Printer=PSCRIPT,COM2:
```

To the left of each equal sign is the device name; to the right is first the driver name and then the output port. Getting a device context handle using the printer specified in the *[windows]* section of WIN.INI is essentially the same as getting a device context handle using one of the printers from the *[devices]* section, except that the latter is more difficult because you have more than one choice.

For a list of all the attached printers from the *[devices]* section of WIN.INI, including the default listed in the *[windows]* section, call *GetProfileString* with a NULL second parameter:

```
static char szAllDevices[4096] ;
[other program lines]
GetProfileString ("devices", NULL, "", szAllDevices,
                            sizeof (szAllDevices)) ;
```

On return, *szAllDevices* contains a list of the keywords (the device names) in the *[devices]* section. Each keyword is terminated by a NULL except for the final keyword, which is terminated by two NULLs. For the example list shown above, *szAllDevices* would contain (using C notation):

```
IBM Graphics\0Generic / Text Only\0HP Plotter\0Postscript Printer\0\0
```

Let's assume that a user selects one of these devices and that you've set the pointer *szDevice* to the beginning of that device name in *szAllDevices*. You can then use *szDevice* to call *CreateDC* or *CreateIC*. If you also need the driver name and output port, you must obtain the rest of the string by calling *GetProfileString* again:

```
GetProfileString ("devices", szDevice, "", szPrinter, 64) ;
```

Then parse the *szPrinter* string to extract the driver name and the output port name:

```
szDriver = strtok (szPrinter, ", ") ;
szOutput = strtok (NULL     , ", ") ;
```

The valid output ports on a particular system are listed in the *[ports]* section of WIN.INI. You don't need to access this section of WIN.INI to use the printer. You can assume that the user has already identified a particular port for the printer, and you can further assume that the user has properly defined the communications parameters for serial (COM) ports.

The *[ports]* section often looks something like this:

```
[ports]
LPT1:=
LPT2:=
LPT3:=
COM1:=9600,n,8,1
COM2:=1200,n,8,1
output.prn=
```

The OUTPUT.PRN file (or any file with a .PRN extension) can be listed here to direct printer output to a file. This filename can appear as the output port for a printer in the *[windows]* section or *[devices]* section of WIN.INI.

The Revised DEVCAPS Program

The original DEVCAPS1 program in Chapter 4 displays only some of the information available from the *GetDeviceCaps* function for the video display. The new version, shown in Figure 15-3, shows even more information for both the video display and all printers attached to the system. It also displays a dialog that lets you choose one of the printers.

DEVCAPS2.MAK

```
#------------------------
# DEVCAPS2.MAK make file
#------------------------

devcaps2.exe : devcaps2.obj devcaps2.res
    $(LINKER) $(GUIFLAGS) -OUT:devcaps2.exe devcaps2.obj \
        devcaps2.res $(GUILIBS) winspool.lib
```

Figure 15-3. *The DEVCAPS2 program.*   *(continued)*

```
devcaps2.obj : devcaps2.c devcaps2.h
    $(CC) $(CFLAGS) devcaps2.c

devcaps2.res : devcaps2.rc devcaps2.h
    $(RC) $(RCVARS) devcaps2.rc
```

DEVCAPS2.C

```c
/*---------------------------------------------------------------------
   DEVCAPS2.C -- Displays Device Capability Information (Version 2)
                 (c) Charles Petzold, 1996
  ---------------------------------------------------------------------*/

#include <windows.h>
#include <string.h>
#include <stdio.h>
#include "devcaps2.h"

LRESULT CALLBACK WndProc (HWND, UINT, WPARAM, LPARAM) ;
void DoBasicInfo     (HDC, HDC, int, int) ;
void DoOtherInfo     (HDC, HDC, int, int) ;
void DoBitCodedCaps (HDC, HDC, int, int, int) ;

int WINAPI WinMain (HINSTANCE hInstance, HINSTANCE hPrevInstance,
                    PSTR szCmdLine, int iCmdShow)
    {
    static char  szAppName[] = "DevCaps2" ;
    HWND         hwnd ;
    MSG          msg ;
    WNDCLASSEX   wndclass ;

    wndclass.cbSize        = sizeof (wndclass) ;
    wndclass.style         = CS_HREDRAW | CS_VREDRAW ;
    wndclass.lpfnWndProc   = WndProc ;
    wndclass.cbClsExtra    = 0 ;
    wndclass.cbWndExtra    = 0 ;
    wndclass.hInstance     = hInstance ;
    wndclass.hIcon         = LoadIcon (NULL, IDI_APPLICATION) ;
    wndclass.hCursor       = LoadCursor (NULL, IDC_ARROW) ;
    wndclass.hbrBackground = (HBRUSH) GetStockObject (WHITE_BRUSH) ;
    wndclass.lpszMenuName  = szAppName ;
    wndclass.lpszClassName = szAppName ;
    wndclass.hIconSm       = LoadIcon (NULL, IDI_APPLICATION) ;

    RegisterClassEx (&wndclass) ;
```

(continued)

794

```
      hwnd = CreateWindow (szAppName, NULL,
                          WS_OVERLAPPEDWINDOW,
                          CW_USEDEFAULT, CW_USEDEFAULT,
                          CW_USEDEFAULT, CW_USEDEFAULT,
                          NULL, NULL, hInstance, NULL) ;

     ShowWindow (hwnd, iCmdShow) ;
     UpdateWindow (hwnd) ;

     while (GetMessage (&msg, NULL, 0, 0))
          {
          TranslateMessage (&msg) ;
          DispatchMessage (&msg) ;
          }
     return msg.wParam ;
     }

LRESULT CALLBACK WndProc (HWND hwnd, UINT msg, WPARAM wParam, LPARAM lParam)
     {
     static char    szDevice[32], szWindowText[64] ;
     static int     n, cxChar, cyChar,
                    nCurrentDevice = IDM_SCREEN,
                    nCurrentInfo   = IDM_BASIC ;
     static DWORD   dwNeeded, dwReturned ;
     static LPPRINTER_INFO_5 pinfo5 ;

     DWORD          i ;
     HDC            hdc, hdcInfo ;
     HMENU          hMenu ;
     PAINTSTRUCT    ps ;
     TEXTMETRIC     tm ;
     HANDLE         hPrint ;

     switch (msg)
          {
          case WM_CREATE :
               hdc = GetDC (hwnd) ;
               SelectObject (hdc, GetStockObject (SYSTEM_FIXED_FONT)) ;
               GetTextMetrics (hdc, &tm) ;
               cxChar = tm.tmAveCharWidth ;
               cyChar = tm.tmHeight + tm.tmExternalLeading ;
               ReleaseDC (hwnd, hdc) ;

               lParam = 0 ;
                                                  // fall through
```

(continued)

```
case WM_WININICHANGE :
    if (lParam != 0 && lstrcmp ((PSTR) lParam, "devices") != 0)
        return 0 ;

    hMenu = GetSubMenu (GetMenu (hwnd), 0) ;

    while (GetMenuItemCount (hMenu) > 1)
        DeleteMenu (hMenu, 1, MF_BYPOSITION) ;

    // Get a list of all local and remote printers
    //
    // First, find out how large an array is needed; this
    //    call will fail, leaving the required size in dwNeeded
    EnumPrinters (PRINTER_ENUM_LOCAL,
                  NULL, 5, (LPBYTE) "", 0, &dwNeeded,
                  &dwReturned) ;

    // Next, allocate space for PRINTER_INFO_5 array
    if (pinfo5)
        HeapFree (GetProcessHeap (), 0, pinfo5) ;
    pinfo5 = (LPPRINTER_INFO_5) HeapAlloc (GetProcessHeap (),
                                HEAP_NO_SERIALIZE, dwNeeded) ;

    // Last, fill allocated PRINTER_INFO_5 array
    if (!pinfo5 || !EnumPrinters (PRINTER_ENUM_LOCAL,
                       NULL, 5, (LPBYTE) pinfo5, dwNeeded,
                       &dwNeeded, &dwReturned))
        {
        MessageBox (hwnd, "Could not enumerate printers!",
                                    NULL, MB_ICONSTOP) ;
        DestroyWindow (hwnd) ;
        return 0 ;
        }

    for (i = 0, n = IDM_SCREEN + 1 ; i < dwReturned ; i++, n++)
        {
        AppendMenu (hMenu, n % 16 ? 0 : MF_MENUBARBREAK, n,
                                    pinfo5->pPrinterName) ;
        pinfo5++ ;
        }

    AppendMenu (hMenu, MF_SEPARATOR, 0, NULL) ;
    AppendMenu (hMenu, 0, IDM_DEVMODE, "Properties") ;

    wParam = IDM_SCREEN ;

                                        // fall through
```

(continued)

```
case WM_COMMAND :
    hMenu = GetMenu (hwnd) ;

    if (wParam < IDM_DEVMODE)              // IDM_SCREEN & Printers
        {
        CheckMenuItem (hMenu, nCurrentDevice, MF_UNCHECKED) ;
        nCurrentDevice = wParam ;
        CheckMenuItem (hMenu, nCurrentDevice, MF_CHECKED) ;
        }
    else if (wParam == IDM_DEVMODE)     // "Properties" selection
        {
        GetMenuString (hMenu, nCurrentDevice, szDevice,
                       sizeof (szDevice), MF_BYCOMMAND) ;

        if (OpenPrinter (szDevice, &hPrint, NULL))
            {
            PrinterProperties (hwnd, hPrint) ;
            ClosePrinter (hPrint) ;
            }
        }
    else                                  // info menu items
        {
        CheckMenuItem (hMenu, nCurrentInfo, MF_UNCHECKED) ;
        nCurrentInfo = wParam ;
        CheckMenuItem (hMenu, nCurrentInfo, MF_CHECKED) ;
        }
    InvalidateRect (hwnd, NULL, TRUE) ;
    return 0 ;

case WM_INITMENUPOPUP :
    if (lParam == 0)
        EnableMenuItem (GetMenu (hwnd), IDM_DEVMODE,
            nCurrentDevice == IDM_SCREEN ?
                MF_GRAYED : MF_ENABLED) ;
    return 0 ;

case WM_PAINT :
    strcpy (szWindowText, "Device Capabilities: ") ;

    if (nCurrentDevice == IDM_SCREEN)
        {
        strcpy (szDevice, "DISPLAY") ;
        hdcInfo = CreateIC (szDevice, NULL, NULL, NULL) ;
        }
    else
```

(continued)

```
                    {
            hMenu = GetMenu (hwnd) ;
            GetMenuString (hMenu, nCurrentDevice, szDevice,
                           sizeof (szDevice), MF_BYCOMMAND) ;
            hdcInfo = CreateIC (NULL, szDevice, NULL, NULL) ;
                    }

        strcat (szWindowText, szDevice) ;
        SetWindowText (hwnd, szWindowText) ;

        hdc = BeginPaint (hwnd, &ps) ;
        SelectObject (hdc, GetStockObject (SYSTEM_FIXED_FONT)) ;

        if (hdcInfo)
                {
            switch (nCurrentInfo)
                    {
                case IDM_BASIC :
                        DoBasicInfo (hdc, hdcInfo, cxChar, cyChar) ;
                        break ;

                case IDM_OTHER :
                        DoOtherInfo (hdc, hdcInfo, cxChar, cyChar) ;
                        break ;

                case IDM_CURVE :
                case IDM_LINE :
                case IDM_POLY :
                case IDM_TEXT :
                        DoBitCodedCaps (hdc, hdcInfo, cxChar, cyChar,
                            nCurrentInfo - IDM_CURVE) ;
                        break ;
                    }
            DeleteDC (hdcInfo) ;
                }

        EndPaint (hwnd, &ps) ;
        return 0 ;

    case WM_DESTROY :
        if (pinfo5)
            HeapFree (GetProcessHeap (), 0, pinfo5) ;

        PostQuitMessage (0) ;
```

(continued)

```
                    return 0 ;
            }
     return DefWindowProc (hwnd, msg, wParam, lParam) ;
     }

void DoBasicInfo (HDC hdc, HDC hdcInfo, int cxChar, int cyChar)
     {
     static struct
            {
            int    nIndex ;
            char *szDesc ;
            }
            info[] =
            {
            HORZSIZE,       "HORZSIZE       Width in millimeters:",
            VERTSIZE,       "VERTSIZE       Height in millimeters:",
            HORZRES,        "HORZRES        Width in pixels:",
            VERTRES,        "VERTRES        Height in raster lines:",
            BITSPIXEL,      "BITSPIXEL      Color bits per pixel:",
            PLANES,         "PLANES         Number of color planes:",
            NUMBRUSHES,     "NUMBRUSHES     Number of device brushes:",
            NUMPENS,        "NUMPENS        Number of device pens:",
            NUMMARKERS,     "NUMMARKERS     Number of device markers:",
            NUMFONTS,       "NUMFONTS       Number of device fonts:",
            NUMCOLORS,      "NUMCOLORS      Number of device colors:",
            PDEVICESIZE,    "PDEVICESIZE    Size of device structure:",
            ASPECTX,        "ASPECTX        Relative width of pixel:",
            ASPECTY,        "ASPECTY        Relative height of pixel:",
            ASPECTXY,       "ASPECTXY       Relative diagonal of pixel:",
            LOGPIXELSX,     "LOGPIXELSX     Horizontal dots per inch:",
            LOGPIXELSY,     "LOGPIXELSY     Vertical dots per inch:",
            SIZEPALETTE,    "SIZEPALETTE    Number of palette entries:",
            NUMRESERVED,    "NUMRESERVED    Reserved palette entries:",
            COLORRES,       "COLORRES       Actual color resolution:"
            } ;
     char   szBuffer[80] ;
     int    i ;

     for (i = 0 ; i < sizeof (info) / sizeof (info[0]) ; i++)
            TextOut (hdc, cxChar, (i + 1) * cyChar, szBuffer,
                 sprintf (szBuffer, "%-40s%8d", info[i].szDesc,
                      GetDeviceCaps (hdcInfo, info[i].nIndex))) ;
     }

void DoOtherInfo (HDC hdc, HDC hdcInfo, int cxChar, int cyChar)
```

(continued)

```
{
static BITS clip[] =
    {
    CP_RECTANGLE,  "CP_RECTANGLE",      "Can Clip To Rectangle:"
    } ;

static BITS raster[] =
    {
    RC_BITBLT,        "RC_BITBLT",        "Capable of simple BitBlt:",
    RC_BANDING,       "RC_BANDING",       "Requires banding support:",
    RC_SCALING,       "RC_SCALING",       "Requires scaling support:",
    RC_BITMAP64,      "RC_BITMAP64",      "Supports bitmaps >64K:",
    RC_GDI20_OUTPUT,  "RC_GDI20_OUTPUT",  "Has 2.0 output calls:",
    RC_DI_BITMAP,     "RC_DI_BITMAP",     "Supports DIB to memory:",
    RC_PALETTE,       "RC_PALETTE",       "Supports a palette:",
    RC_DIBTODEV,      "RC_DIBTODEV",      "Supports bitmap conversion:",
    RC_BIGFONT,       "RC_BIGFONT",       "Supports fonts >64K:",
    RC_STRETCHBLT,    "RC_STRETCHBLT",    "Supports StretchBlt:",
    RC_FLOODFILL,     "RC_FLOODFILL",     "Supports FloodFill:",
    RC_STRETCHDIB,    "RC_STRETCHDIB",    "Supports StretchDIBits:"
    } ;

static char *szTech[] = { "DT_PLOTTER (Vector plotter)",
                          "DT_RASDISPLAY (Raster display)",
                          "DT_RASPRINTER (Raster printer)",
                          "DT_RASCAMERA (Raster camera)",
                          "DT_CHARSTREAM (Character-stream, PLP)",
                          "DT_METAFILE (Metafile, VDM)",
                          "DT_DISPFILE (Display-file)" } ;
char        szBuffer[80] ;
int         i ;

TextOut (hdc, cxChar, cyChar, szBuffer,
    sprintf (szBuffer, "%-24s%04XH",
        "DRIVERVERSION:", GetDeviceCaps (hdcInfo, DRIVERVERSION))) ;

TextOut (hdc, cxChar, 2 * cyChar, szBuffer,
    sprintf (szBuffer, "%-24s%-40s",
        "TECHNOLOGY:",szTech[GetDeviceCaps (hdcInfo, TECHNOLOGY)])) ;

TextOut (hdc, cxChar, 4 * cyChar, szBuffer,
    sprintf (szBuffer, "CLIPCAPS (Clipping capabilities)")) ;

for (i = 0 ; i < sizeof (clip) / sizeof (clip[0]) ; i++)
    TextOut (hdc, 9 * cxChar, (i + 6) * cyChar, szBuffer,
```

(continued)

```
                    sprintf (szBuffer, "%-16s%-28s %3s",
                         clip[i].szMask, clip[i].szDesc,
                         GetDeviceCaps (hdcInfo, CLIPCAPS) & clip[i].nMask ?
                              "Yes" : "No")) ;


     TextOut (hdc, cxChar, 8 * cyChar, szBuffer,
          sprintf (szBuffer, "RASTERCAPS (Raster capabilities)")) ;

     for (i = 0 ; i < sizeof (raster) / sizeof (raster[0]) ; i++)
          TextOut (hdc, 9 * cxChar, (i + 10) * cyChar, szBuffer,
               sprintf (szBuffer, "%-16s%-28s %3s",
                    raster[i].szMask, raster[i].szDesc,
                    GetDeviceCaps (hdcInfo, RASTERCAPS) & raster[i].nMask ?
                         "Yes" : "No")) ;
     }

void DoBitCodedCaps (HDC hdc, HDC hdcInfo, int cxChar,
                                      int cyChar, int nType)
     {
     static BITS curves[] =
          {
          CC_CIRCLES,     "CC_CIRCLES",     "circles:",
          CC_PIE,         "CC_PIE",         "pie wedges:",
          CC_CHORD,       "CC_CHORD",       "chord arcs:",
          CC_ELLIPSES,    "CC_ELLIPSES",    "ellipses:",
          CC_WIDE,        "CC_WIDE",        "wide borders:",
          CC_STYLED,      "CC_STYLED",      "styled borders:",
          CC_WIDESTYLED,  "CC_WIDESTYLED",  "wide and styled borders:",
          CC_INTERIORS,   "CC_INTERIORS",   "interiors:"
          } ;

     static BITS lines[] =
          {
          LC_POLYLINE,    "LC_POLYLINE",    "polyline:",
          LC_MARKER,      "LC_MARKER",      "markers:",
          LC_POLYMARKER,  "LC_POLYMARKER",  "polymarkers",
          LC_WIDE,        "LC_WIDE",        "wide lines:",
          LC_STYLED,      "LC_STYLED",      "styled lines:",
          LC_WIDESTYLED,  "LC_WIDESTYLED",  "wide and styled lines:",
          LC_INTERIORS,   "LC_INTERIORS",   "interiors:"
          } ;

     static BITS poly[] =
          {
          PC_POLYGON,     "PC_POLYGON",     "alternate fill polygon:",
          PC_RECTANGLE,   "PC_RECTANGLE",   "rectangle:",
```

(continued)

```
              PC_WINDPOLYGON,"PC_WINDPOLYGON","winding number fill polygon:",
              PC_SCANLINE,   "PC_SCANLINE",   "scanlines:",
              PC_WIDE,       "PC_WIDE",       "wide borders:",
              PC_STYLED,     "PC_STYLED",     "styled borders:",
              PC_WIDESTYLED, "PC_WIDESTYLED", "wide and styled borders:",
              PC_INTERIORS,  "PC_INTERIORS",  "interiors:"
              } ;

     static BITS text[] =
              {
              TC_OP_CHARACTER, "TC_OP_CHARACTER", "character output precision:",
              TC_OP_STROKE,    "TC_OP_STROKE",    "stroke output precision:",
              TC_CP_STROKE,    "TC_CP_STROKE",    "stroke clip precision:",
              TC_CR_90,        "TC_CP_90",
                                    "90 degree character rotation:",
              TC_CR_ANY,       "TC_CR_ANY",       "any character rotation:",
              TC_SF_X_YINDEP,  "TC_SF_X_YINDEP",
                                    "scaling independent of X and Y:",
              TC_SA_DOUBLE,    "TC_SA_DOUBLE",
                                    "doubled character for scaling:",
              TC_SA_INTEGER,   "TC_SA_INTEGER",
                                    "integer multiples for scaling:",
              TC_SA_CONTIN,    "TC_SA_CONTIN",
                                    "any multiples for exact scaling:",
              TC_EA_DOUBLE,    "TC_EA_DOUBLE", "double weight characters:",
              TC_IA_ABLE,      "TC_IA_ABLE",   "italicizing:",
              TC_UA_ABLE,      "TC_UA_ABLE",   "underlining:",
              TC_SO_ABLE,      "TC_SO_ABLE",   "strikeouts:",
              TC_RA_ABLE,      "TC_RA_ABLE",   "raster fonts:",
              TC_VA_ABLE,      "TC_VA_ABLE",   "vector fonts:"
              } ;

     static struct
              {
              int   nIndex ;
              char  *szTitle ;
              BITS  (*pbits)[] ;
              short nSize ;
              }
              bitinfo[] =
              {
              CURVECAPS, "CURVCAPS (Curve Capabilities)",
                        (BITS (*)[]) curves, sizeof (curves) /
                                        sizeof (curves[0]),
              LINECAPS,  "LINECAPS (Line Capabilities)",
                        (BITS (*)[]) lines, sizeof (lines) /
                                        sizeof (lines[0]),
```

(continued)

```
            POLYGONALCAPS, "POLYGONALCAPS (Polygonal Capabilities)",
                    (BITS (*)[]) poly, sizeof (poly) / sizeof (poly[0]),
        TEXTCAPS,    "TEXTCAPS (Text Capabilities)",
                    (BITS (*)[]) text, sizeof (text) / sizeof (text[0])
        } ;

    static char szBuffer[80] ;
    BITS (*pbits)[] = bitinfo[nType].pbits ;
    int nDevCaps = GetDeviceCaps (hdcInfo, bitinfo[nType].nIndex) ;
    int  i ;

    TextOut (hdc, cxChar, cyChar, bitinfo[nType].szTitle,
            strlen (bitinfo[nType].szTitle)) ;

    for (i = 0 ; i < bitinfo[nType].nSize ; i++)
        TextOut (hdc, cxChar, (i + 3) * cyChar, szBuffer,
            sprintf (szBuffer, "%-16s %s %-32s %3s",
                (*pbits)[i].szMask, "Can do", (*pbits)[i].szDesc,
                nDevCaps & (*pbits)[i].nMask ? "Yes" : "No")) ;
    }
```

DEVCAPS2.H

```
/*------------------------
   DEVCAPS2.H header file
   ------------------------*/

#define IDM_SCREEN  1

#define IDM_DEVMODE 0x100

#define IDM_BASIC    0x101
#define IDM_OTHER    0x102
#define IDM_CURVE    0x103
#define IDM_LINE     0x104
#define IDM_POLY     0x105
#define IDM_TEXT     0x106

typedef struct
    {
    short  nMask ;
    char  *szMask ;
    char  *szDesc ;
    }
    BITS ;
```

(continued)

DEVCAPS2.RC

```
/*---------------------------------
   DEVCAPS2.RC resource script
   ---------------------------*/

#include "devcaps2.h"

DevCaps2 MENU
    {
    POPUP "&Device"
        {
        MENUITEM "&Screen",                    IDM_SCREEN, CHECKED
        }
    POPUP "&Capabilities"
        {
        MENUITEM "&Basic Information",         IDM_BASIC, CHECKED
        MENUITEM "&Other Information",         IDM_OTHER
        MENUITEM "&Curve Capabilities",        IDM_CURVE
        MENUITEM "&Line Capabilities",         IDM_LINE
        MENUITEM "&Polygonal Capabilities",    IDM_POLY
        MENUITEM "&Text Capabilities",         IDM_TEXT
        }
    }
```

Because DEVCAPS2 obtains only an information context for the printer, you can select printers from DEVCAPS's menu, although each printer may have an output port of "none." If you want to compare the capabilities of different printers, you can first use the Printers folder to add various printer drivers.

The *PrinterProperties* Call

The Device menu of the DEVCAPS2 program includes an option called Properties. To use it, first select a printer from the Device menu, and then select Properties: Up pops a dialog box. Where did the dialog box come from? It is invoked by the printer driver, and—at the very least—it requests that you make a choice of paper size. Most printer drivers also give you a choice of "portrait" or "landscape" mode. In portrait mode (often the default), the short side of the paper is the top; in landscape mode, the long side is the top. If you change this mode, the change is reflected in the information the DEVCAPS2 program obtains from the *GetDeviceCaps* function: The horizontal size and resolution are switched with the vertical size and resolution. Properties dialog boxes for color plotters can be quite extensive, requesting the colors of the pens installed in the plotter and the type of paper (or transparencies) being used.

All printer drivers in Windows 95 contain an exported function called *ExtDeviceMode* that invokes this dialog box and saves the information that the user enters. Some printer drivers store this information in the registry or in their own section of the WIN.INI file, and some don't. Those that store the information have access to it during the next Windows session.

Windows programs that allow the user a choice of printers generally just call *PrintDlg*. This useful function takes care of all the work of communicating with the user and handles any changes the user requests in preparation for printing. *PrintDlg* also invokes the property sheet dialog when the user clicks the Properties button. Try it in WORDPAD. You'll see it's the same dialog as the one that DEVCAPS2 displays.

A program can also display a printer's properties dialog by directly calling the printer driver's *ExtDeviceMode* or *ExtDeviceModePropSheet* functions. However, I don't recommend this. It's far better to invoke the dialog indirectly by calling *PrinterProperties*. This GDI function can access 16-bit printer drivers, whereas your 32-bit program can't (unless you want to write your own thunking layer).

PrinterProperties requires a handle to a printer object, which you get by calling the *OpenPrinter* function. When the user cancels the property sheet dialog, *PrinterProperties* returns. You then retire the printer handle by calling *ClosePrinter*. Here's how DEVCAPS2 does it.

The program first obtains the name of the printer currently selected in the Device menu and saves it in a character array named *szDevice*:

```
GetMenuString (hMenu, nCurrentDevice, szDevice,
               sizeof (szDevice), MF_BYCOMMAND) ;
```

Then it obtains the handle of this device using *OpenPrinter*. If the call is successful, the program next calls *PrinterProperties* to invoke the dialog box, then *ClosePrinter* to retire the device handle:

```
if (OpenPrinter (szDevice, &hPrint, NULL))
    {
    PrinterProperties (hwnd, hPrint) ;
    ClosePrinter (hPrint) ;
    }
```

Checking for *BitBlt* Capability

You can use the *GetDeviceCaps* or *DeviceCapabilities* functions to obtain the size and resolution of the printable area of the page. (In most cases, this area won't be the same as the full size of the paper.) You can also obtain the relative pixel width and height, if you want to do your own scaling.

You can obtain another important printer characteristic from the RC_BITBLT bit of the value returned from *GetDeviceCaps* with a parameter of RASTERCAPS ("raster capabilities"). This bit indicates whether the device is capable of bit-block transfers. Most dot-matrix and laser printers are capable of bit-block transfers, but most plotters are not. Devices that cannot handle bit-block transfers do not support the following GDI functions: *Create-CompatibleDC*, *CreateCompatibleBitmap*, *PatBlt*, *BitBlt*, *StretchBlt*, *GrayString*, *DrawIcon*, *SetPixel*, *GetPixel*, *FloodFill*, *ExtFloodFill*, *FillRgn*, *FrameRgn*, *InvertRgn*, *PaintRgn*, *FillRect*, *FrameRect*, and *InvertRect*. This is the single most important distinction between using GDI calls on a video display and using them on a printer.

THE FORMFEED PROGRAM

We're now ready to print, and we're going to start as simply as possible. In fact, our first printing program does nothing but cause a printer form feed to eject the page. The FORMFEED program, shown in Figure 15-4, demonstrates the absolute minimum requirements for printing.

FORMFEED.MAK

```
#-----------------------
# FORMFEED.MAK make file
#-----------------------

formfeed.exe: formfeed.obj
     $(LINKER) $(GUIFLAGS) -OUT:formfeed.exe formfeed.obj \
     $(GUILIBS) winspool.lib

formfeed.obj: formfeed.c
     $(CC) $(CFLAGS) formfeed.c
```

FORMFEED.C

```
/*-----------------------------------------------
   FORMFEED.C -- Advances printer to next page
                 (c) Charles Petzold, 1996
   -----------------------------------------------*/

#include <windows.h>

HDC  GetPrinterDC (void) ;

int WINAPI WinMain (HINSTANCE hInstance, HINSTANCE hPrevInstance,
                    LPSTR lpszCmdLine, int iCmdShow)
     {
     static DOCINFO di      = { sizeof (DOCINFO), "FormFeed", NULL } ;
     HDC            hdcPrint = GetPrinterDC () ;
```

Figure 15-4. *The FORMFEED program.*

(continued)

```
     if (hdcPrint != NULL)
          {
          if (StartDoc (hdcPrint, &di) > 0)
               if (StartPage (hdcPrint) > 0 && EndPage (hdcPrint) > 0)
                    EndDoc (hdcPrint) ;

          DeleteDC (hdcPrint) ;
          }
     return FALSE ;
     }

HDC GetPrinterDC (void)
     {
     PRINTER_INFO_5 pinfo5[3] ;
     DWORD          dwNeeded, dwReturned ;

     if (EnumPrinters (PRINTER_ENUM_DEFAULT, NULL, 5, (LPBYTE) pinfo5,
                    sizeof (pinfo5), &dwNeeded, &dwReturned))
          return CreateDC (NULL, pinfo5[0].pPrinterName, NULL, NULL) ;

     return 0 ;                    // EnumPrinters failed, so return null hdc
     }
```

FORMFEED includes the *GetPrinterDC* function shown earlier. Other than obtaining the printer device context (and later deleting it), the program calls only the four print functions we discussed earlier in this chapter. FORMFEED first calls *StartDoc* to start a new document. It tests the return value from *StartDoc* and proceeds only if the value is positive:

```
     if (StartDoc (hdcPrint, &di) > 0)
```

The second field of the DOCINFO structure *di* points to a string that identifies the document being printed. As the document prints or while it is waiting to print, this string appears in the Document Name column of the printer's job queue. (To see a list of queued print documents, click the Start button, choose Settings, then Printers, and double-click the printer's icon.) Generally, the identification string includes the name of the application doing the printing and the file being printed. In this case, it's simply the name "FormFeed."

If *StartDoc* is successful (indicated by a positive return value), then FORMFEED calls *StartPage*, followed immediately by a call to *EndPage*. This sequence advances the printer to a new page. Once again, the return values are tested:

```
     if (StartPage (hdcPrint) > 0 && EndPage (hdcPrint) > 0)
```

Finally, if everything has proceeded without error to this point, the document is ended:

```
     EndDoc (hdcPrint) ;
```

Note that the *EndDoc* function is called only if no printing errors have been reported. If one of the other print functions returns an error code, then GDI has already aborted the document. If the printer is not currently printing, such an error code often results in the printer being reset.

Simply testing the return values from the print functions is the easiest way to check for errors. If you want to report a particular error to the user, you must call *GetLastError* to determine the error. (Later in this chapter, we'll look at reporting printer errors with *GetLastError.*) For example, an error occurs if GDI can't find sufficient disk space to store the printer output necessary to trigger the printer to do a form feed. For most printers, this occurrence is extremely unlikely. For your own amusement, however, you might try specifying the PostScript printer driver as your current printer, with the output port OUTPUT.PRN. Run FORMFEED and check the size of the file. (It will be over 8 KB!)

If you've ever written a simple form feed program for MS-DOS, you know that ASCII number 12 activates a form feed for most printers. Why not simply open the printer port using the GDI function *OpenPrinter* and then output an ASCII number 12 using *write?* Well, nothing prevents you from doing this. You have to determine the parallel port or the serial port the printer is attached to—that's available by calling *GetPrinter* with the printer identifier that *OpenPrinter* returns and reading the port identifier from a PRINTER_INFO_5 structure. You then have to determine if another program is currently using the printer. (You don't want the form feed to be output in the middle of a document.) Finally, you have to determine if ASCII number 12 is a form feed character for the connected printer. It isn't universal. In fact, the form feed command in PostScript isn't a 12; it's the word *showpage.*

In short, don't even think about going around Windows; stick with the Windows functions for printing.

PRINTING GRAPHICS AND TEXT

Printing from a Windows program usually involves more overhead than shown in the FORMFEED program, as well as some GDI calls to actually print something. Let's write a program that prints one page of text and graphics. We'll start with the method shown in the FORMFEED program and then add some enhancements. We'll be looking at four versions of this program called PRINT1, PRINT2, PRINT3, and PRINT4. To avoid a lot of duplicated source code, each of these programs will use functions contained in the PRINT.C file, which is shown in Figure 15-5.

```
PRINT.C

/*-------------------------------------------------------------------
    PRINT.C -- Common routines for Print1, Print2, Print3, and Print4
  -------------------------------------------------------------------*/
```

Figure 15-5. *The PRINT.C file of the PRINT1, PRINT2, PRINT3, and PRINT4 programs.*

(continued)

```
#include <windows.h>

LRESULT CALLBACK WndProc (HWND, UINT, WPARAM, LPARAM) ;
BOOL PrintMyPage (HWND) ;

extern HINSTANCE hInst ;
extern char      szAppName[] ;
extern char      szCaption[] ;

int WINAPI WinMain (HINSTANCE hInstance, HINSTANCE hPrevInstance,
                    PSTR szCmdLine, int iCmdShow)
     {
     HWND          hwnd ;
     MSG           msg ;
     WNDCLASSEX    wndclass ;

     wndclass.cbSize        = sizeof (wndclass) ;
     wndclass.style         = CS_HREDRAW | CS_VREDRAW ;
     wndclass.lpfnWndProc   = WndProc ;
     wndclass.cbClsExtra    = 0 ;
     wndclass.cbWndExtra    = 0 ;
     wndclass.hInstance     = hInstance ;
     wndclass.hIcon         = LoadIcon (NULL, IDI_APPLICATION) ;
     wndclass.hCursor       = LoadCursor (NULL, IDC_ARROW) ;
     wndclass.hbrBackground = (HBRUSH) GetStockObject (WHITE_BRUSH) ;
     wndclass.lpszMenuName  = NULL ;
     wndclass.lpszClassName = szAppName ;
     wndclass.hIconSm       = LoadIcon (NULL, IDI_APPLICATION) ;

     RegisterClassEx (&wndclass) ;

     hInst = hInstance ;

     hwnd = CreateWindow (szAppName, szCaption,
                     WS_OVERLAPPEDWINDOW,
                     CW_USEDEFAULT, CW_USEDEFAULT,
                     CW_USEDEFAULT, CW_USEDEFAULT,
                     NULL, NULL, hInstance, NULL) ;

     ShowWindow (hwnd, iCmdShow) ;
     UpdateWindow (hwnd) ;

     while (GetMessage (&msg, NULL, 0, 0))
          {
          TranslateMessage (&msg) ;
          DispatchMessage (&msg) ;
          }
```

(continued)

```
        return msg.wParam ;
        }


HDC GetPrinterDC (void)
     {
     PRINTER_INFO_5 pinfo5[3] ;
     DWORD          dwNeeded, dwReturned ;

     if (EnumPrinters (PRINTER_ENUM_DEFAULT, NULL, 5, (LPBYTE) pinfo5,
                    sizeof (pinfo5), &dwNeeded, &dwReturned))
        return CreateDC (NULL, pinfo5[0].pPrinterName, NULL, NULL) ;

     return 0 ;              // EnumPrinters failed, so return null hdc
     }

void PageGDICalls (HDC hdcPrn, int cxPage, int cyPage)
     {
     static char szTextStr[] = "Hello, Printer!" ;

     Rectangle (hdcPrn, 0, 0, cxPage, cyPage) ;

     MoveToEx (hdcPrn, 0, 0, NULL) ;
     LineTo   (hdcPrn, cxPage, cyPage) ;
     MoveToEx (hdcPrn, cxPage, 0, NULL) ;
     LineTo   (hdcPrn, 0, cyPage) ;

     SaveDC (hdcPrn) ;

     SetMapMode        (hdcPrn, MM_ISOTROPIC) ;
     SetWindowExtEx    (hdcPrn, 1000, 1000, NULL) ;
     SetViewportExtEx (hdcPrn, cxPage / 2, -cyPage / 2, NULL) ;
     SetViewportOrgEx (hdcPrn, cxPage / 2,  cyPage / 2, NULL) ;

     Ellipse (hdcPrn, -500, 500, 500, -500) ;

     SetTextAlign (hdcPrn, TA_BASELINE | TA_CENTER) ;

     TextOut (hdcPrn, 0, 0, szTextStr, sizeof (szTextStr) - 1) ;

     RestoreDC (hdcPrn, -1) ;
     }

LRESULT CALLBACK WndProc (HWND hwnd, UINT msg, WPARAM wParam, LPARAM lParam)
     {
     static int   cxClient, cyClient ;
     HDC          hdc ;
     HMENU        hMenu ;
```

(continued)

810

```
    PAINTSTRUCT  ps ;

switch (msg)
     {
     case WM_CREATE :
          hMenu = GetSystemMenu (hwnd, FALSE) ;
          AppendMenu (hMenu, MF_SEPARATOR, 0, NULL) ;
          AppendMenu (hMenu, 0, 1, "&Print") ;
          return 0 ;

     case WM_SIZE :
          cxClient = LOWORD (lParam) ;
          cyClient = HIWORD (lParam) ;
          return 0 ;

     case WM_SYSCOMMAND :
          if (wParam == 1)
               {
               if (PrintMyPage (hwnd))
                    MessageBox (hwnd, "Could not print page!",
                         szAppName, MB_OK | MB_ICONEXCLAMATION) ;
               return 0 ;
               }
          break ;

     case WM_PAINT :
          hdc = BeginPaint (hwnd, &ps) ;

          PageGDICalls (hdc, cxClient, cyClient) ;

          EndPaint (hwnd, &ps) ;
          return 0 ;

     case WM_DESTROY :
          PostQuitMessage (0) ;
          return 0 ;
     }
  return DefWindowProc (hwnd, msg, wParam, lParam) ;
  }
```

PRINT.C contains the functions *WinMain*, *WndProc*, *GetPrinterDC*, and *PageGDICalls*. The latter function expects to receive a handle to the printer device context and two variables containing the width and height of the printer page. *PageGDICalls* draws a rectangle that encompasses the entire page, two lines between opposite corners of the page, an ellipse in the middle of the page (its diameter half the lesser of the printer height and width), and the text "Hello, Printer!" in the center of this ellipse.

During processing of the WM_CREATE message, *WndProc* adds a Print option to the system menu. Selecting this option causes a call to *PrintMyPage*, a function that we'll enhance over the course of the four versions of the program. *PrintMyPage* returns TRUE (nonzero) if it encounters an error during printing and returns FALSE otherwise. If *PrintMyPage* returns TRUE, *WndProc* displays a message box to inform you of the error.

Bare-Bones Printing

PRINT1, the first version of the printing program, is shown in Figure 15-6. After compiling PRINT1, you can execute it and then select Print from the system menu. If the TEMP variable in your MS-DOS environment indicates a fixed disk (or if you have no TEMP variable), then you should see some disk activity as the GDI module saves the printer output to a temporary file. After PRINT1 has finished, the spooler should begin sending the disk file out to the printer.

Let's look at the code in PRINT1.C. If *PrintMyPage* can't obtain a device context handle for the printer, it returns TRUE, and *WndProc* displays the message box indicating an error. If the function succeeds in obtaining the device context handle, it then determines the horizontal and vertical size of the page in pixels by calling *GetDeviceCaps*:

```
xPage = GetDeviceCaps (hdcPrn, HORZRES) ;
yPage = GetDeviceCaps (hdcPrn, VERTRES) ;
```

This is not the full size of the paper but rather its printable area. After that call, the code in PRINT1's *PrintMyPage* function is structurally the same as the code in FORMFEED, except that PRINT1 calls *PageGDICalls* between the calls to *StartPage* and *EndPage*. Only if the calls to *StartDoc*, *StartPage*, and *EndPage* are successful does PRINT1 call the *EndDoc* print function.

```
PRINT1.MAK

#----------------------
# PRINT1.MAK make file
#----------------------

print1.exe : print.obj print1.obj
    $(LINKER) $(GUIFLAGS) -OUT:print1.exe print.obj print1.obj \
    $(GUILIBS) winspool.lib

print.obj : print.c
    $(CC) $(CFLAGS) print.c

print1.obj : print1.c
    $(CC) $(CFLAGS) print1.c
```

Figure 15-6. *The PRINT1 program.*   *(continued)*

PRINT1.C

```
/*-----------------------------------------
   PRINT1.C -- Bare-Bones Printing
              (c) Charles Petzold, 1996
   ---------------------------------------*/

#include <windows.h>

HDC  GetPrinterDC (void) ;                    // in PRINT.C
void PageGDICalls (HDC, int, int) ;

HINSTANCE hInst ;
char      szAppName[] = "Print1" ;
char      szCaption[] = "Print Program 1" ;

BOOL PrintMyPage (HWND hwnd)
     {
     static DOCINFO di = { sizeof (DOCINFO), "Print1: Printing", NULL } ;
     BOOL          bError = FALSE ;
     HDC           hdcPrn ;
     int           xPage, yPage ;

     if (NULL == (hdcPrn = GetPrinterDC ()))
         return TRUE ;

     xPage = GetDeviceCaps (hdcPrn, HORZRES) ;
     yPage = GetDeviceCaps (hdcPrn, VERTRES) ;

     if (StartDoc (hdcPrn, &di) > 0)
         {
         if (StartPage (hdcPrn) > 0)
             {
             PageGDICalls (hdcPrn, xPage, yPage) ;

             if (EndPage (hdcPrn) > 0)
                 EndDoc (hdcPrn) ;
             else
                 bError = TRUE ;
             }
         }
     else
         bError = TRUE ;

     DeleteDC (hdcPrn) ;
     return bError ;
     }
```

If you try to run PRINT1 when the drive containing the TEMP subdirectory lacks sufficient space to store the full page of graphics output, you'll see an error message from Windows that says: *Windows could not write to the printer spool file. Make sure your disk has enough free space and try again.*

This isn't a calamitous problem—you need only click the OK button to dismiss the message. You can then delete some unused files to make room on the disk as the message suggests. However, if the error occurs when you submit several print jobs in rapid succession, simply waiting a moment before trying to print again may cure the problem. This is because the error can result from the presence in the TEMP subdirectory of other temporary print files created by GDI for printing. Giving the spooler enough time to send these files to the printer and then clean up after itself allows the program currently printing to continue.

Canceling Printing with an Abort Procedure

What if we had inadvertently introduced a bug into PRINT1, causing it to print out a ream of paper instead of a single page? What could we do when the printer began to relentlessly spew out paper? Well, we could always pull the plug. We could also cancel printing from the Printers folder by selecting Settings from the Start menu, choosing Printers, double-clicking on the icon for our demonic printer, and choosing Purge Print Jobs from the Printer menu to abort the printing. (By this time we're ankle-deep in paper.)

While printing, a program should provide the user with a convenient avenue of escape. When spooling is enabled, the opportunity to cancel printing from the printing program doesn't last very long—only until the spooler has received the data and has created a spool file. After that, the program no longer has control over the print process. (The user can still cancel the print job from the Printers folder, however.) If spooling is disabled, the program can abort printing any time up until the printer's buffer receives the last of the print data.

Canceling a print job from within a program requires something called an "abort procedure." The abort procedure is a small exported function in your program. You give Windows the address of this function using the *SetAbortProc* function; GDI then calls the procedure repeatedly during printing, in essence asking, "Shall I continue printing?"

Let's look first at what's required to add an abort procedure to the printing logic and then examine some of the ramifications. The abort procedure is commonly called *AbortProc*, and it takes the following form:

```
BOOL CALLBACK AbortProc (HDC hdcPrn, int iCode)
    {
    [other program lines]
    }
```

Before printing, you must register the abort procedure by calling *SetAbortProc*:

```
SetAbortProc (hdcPrn, AbortProc) ;
```

You make this call before the call to *StartDoc*. You don't need to "unset" the abort procedure after you finish printing.

While processing the *EndPage* call (that is, while playing the enhanced metafile into the device driver and creating the temporary printer output files), GDI frequently calls the abort procedure. The *hdcPrn* parameter is the printer device context handle. The *iCode* parameter is 0 if all is going well or is SP_OUTOFDISK if the GDI module has run out of disk space because of the temporary printer output files.

AbortProc must return TRUE (nonzero) if the print job is to be continued and returns FALSE (0) if the print job is to be aborted. The abort procedure can be as simple as this:

```
BOOL CALLBACK AbortProc (HDC hdcPrn, int iCode)
    {
    MSG    msg ;

    while (PeekMessage (&msg, NULL, 0, 0, PM_REMOVE))
        {
        TranslateMessage (&msg) ;
        DispatchMessage (&msg) ;
        }
    return TRUE ;
    }
```

This function may seem a little peculiar. In fact, it looks suspiciously like a message loop. What's a message loop doing here of all places? Well, it *is* a message loop. You'll note, however, that this message loop calls *PeekMessage* rather than *GetMessage*. I discussed *PeekMessage* in connection with the RANDRECT program in Chapter 4. You'll recall that *PeekMessage* returns control to a program with a message from the program's message queue (just like *GetMessage*) but also returns control if there are no messages waiting in any program's message queue.

The message loop in the *AbortProc* function repeatedly calls *PeekMessage* while *PeekMessage* returns TRUE. This TRUE value means that *PeekMessage* has retrieved a message that can be sent to one of the program's window procedures using *TranslateMessage* and *DispatchMessage*. When there are no more messages in the program's message queue, the return value of *PeekMessage* is then FALSE, so *AbortProc* returns control to Windows.

How Windows Uses *AbortProc*

When a program is printing, the bulk of the work takes place during the call to *EndPage*. Before that call, the GDI module simply adds another record to the disk-based enhanced metafile every time the program calls a GDI drawing function. When GDI gets the *EndPage* call, it plays this metafile into the device driver once for each band the device driver defines on a page. GDI then stores in a file the printer output created by the printer driver. If the spooler isn't active, the GDI module itself must write this printer output to the printer.

During the call to *EndPage*, the GDI module calls the abort procedure you've set. Normally, the *iCode* parameter is 0, but if GDI has run out of disk space because of the presence of other temporary files that haven't been printed yet, then the *iCode* parameter is SP_OUTOFDISK. (You wouldn't normally check this value, but you can if you want.) The abort procedure then goes into its *PeekMessage* loop to retrieve messages from the program's message queue.

If there are no messages in the program's message queue, *PeekMessage* returns FALSE. The abort procedure then drops out of its message loop and returns a TRUE value to the GDI module to indicate that printing should continue. The GDI module then continues to process the *EndPage* call.

The GDI stops the print process if an error occurs, so the main purpose of the abort procedure is to allow the user to cancel printing. For that we also need a dialog box that displays a Cancel button. Let's take these two steps, one at a time. First, we'll add an abort procedure to create the PRINT2 program, and then we'll add a dialog with a Cancel button in PRINT3 to make the abort procedure useful.

Implementing an Abort Procedure

Let's quickly review the mechanics of the abort procedure. You define an abort procedure that looks like this:

```
BOOL CALLBACK AbortProc (HDC hdcPrn, int iCode)
    {
    MSG  msg ;

    while (PeekMessage (&msg, NULL, 0, 0, PM_REMOVE))
        {
        TranslateMessage (&msg) ;
        DispatchMessage (&msg) ;
        }
    return TRUE ;
    }
```

When you want to print something, you give Windows this pointer with the call:

```
SetAbortProc (hdcPrn, AbortProc) ;
```

You make this call before the call to *StartDoc*. And that's it.

Well, not quite. We've overlooked a problem with that *PeekMessage* loop in *AbortProc*—a big problem. *AbortProc* is called only while your program is in the midst of printing. Some very ugly things can happen if you retrieve a message in *AbortProc* and dispatch it to your own window procedure. A user could select Print from the menu again. But the program is already in the middle of the printing routine. A user could load a new file into the program while the program is trying to print the previous file. A user could even quit your program! If that happens, all your program's windows will be destroyed.

You'll eventually return from the printing routine, but you'll have nowhere to go except to a window procedure that's no longer valid.

This stuff boggles the mind. Your program isn't prepared for it. For this reason, when you set an abort procedure, you should first disable your program's window so that it can't receive keyboard and mouse input. You do this with:

```
EnableWindow (hwnd, FALSE) ;
```

This prevents keyboard and mouse input from getting into the message queue. The user therefore can't do anything with your program during the time it's printing. When printing is finished, you reenable the window for input:

```
EnableWindow (hwnd, TRUE) ;
```

So why do we even bother with the *TranslateMessage* and *DispatchMessage* calls in *AbortProc* when no keyboard or mouse messages will get into the message queue in the first place? It's true that the *TranslateMessage* call isn't strictly needed (although it's almost always included). But we must use *DispatchMessage* in case a WM_PAINT message gets in the message queue. If WM_PAINT isn't processed properly with a *BeginPaint* and *EndPaint* pair in the window procedure, the message will remain in the queue and clog up the works, because *PeekMessage* will never return a FALSE.

When you disable your window during the time you're printing, your program remains inert on the display. But a user can switch to another program and do some work there, and the spooler can continue sending output files to the printer.

The PRINT2 program, shown in Figure 15-7, adds an abort procedure (and the necessary support) to the logic in PRINT1. More specifically, PRINT2 adds the abort procedure, a call to the *SetAbortProc* function, and two calls to *EnableWindow*, the first to disable the window and the second to reenable it.

PRINT2.MAK

```
#---------------------
# PRINT2.MAK make file
#---------------------

print2.exe : print.obj print2.obj
    $(LINKER) $(GUIFLAGS) -OUT:print2.exe print.obj print2.obj \
    $(GUILIBS) winspool.lib

print.obj : print.c
    $(CC) $(CFLAGS) print.c

print2.obj : print2.c
    $(CC) $(CFLAGS) print2.c
```

Figure 15-7. *The PRINT2 program.*

(continued)

PRINT2.C

```
/*-------------------------------------------
   PRINT2.C -- Printing with Abort Function
             (c) Charles Petzold, 1996
   -------------------------------------------*/

#include <windows.h>

HDC  GetPrinterDC (void) ;                    // in PRINT.C
void PageGDICalls (HDC, int, int) ;

HINSTANCE hInst ;
char      szAppName[] = "Print2" ;
char      szCaption[] = "Print Program 2 (Abort Function)" ;

BOOL CALLBACK AbortProc (HDC hdcPrn, int iCode)
     {
     MSG msg ;

     while (PeekMessage (&msg, NULL, 0, 0, PM_REMOVE))
          {
          TranslateMessage (&msg) ;
          DispatchMessage (&msg) ;
          }
     return TRUE ;
     }

BOOL PrintMyPage (HWND hwnd)
     {
     static DOCINFO di = { sizeof (DOCINFO), "Print2: Printing", NULL } ;
     BOOL          bError = FALSE ;
     HDC           hdcPrn ;
     short         xPage, yPage ;

     if (NULL == (hdcPrn = GetPrinterDC ()))
          return TRUE ;

     xPage = GetDeviceCaps (hdcPrn, HORZRES) ;
     yPage = GetDeviceCaps (hdcPrn, VERTRES) ;

     EnableWindow (hwnd, FALSE) ;

     SetAbortProc (hdcPrn, AbortProc) ;

     if (StartDoc (hdcPrn, &di) > 0)
```

(continued)

```
        {
        if (StartPage (hdcPrn) > 0)
            {
            PageGDICalls (hdcPrn, xPage, yPage) ;

            if (EndPage (hdcPrn) > 0)
                bError = TRUE ;
            }
        }
    else
        bError = TRUE ;

    if (!bError)
        EndDoc (hdcPrn) ;

    EnableWindow (hwnd, TRUE) ;
    DeleteDC (hdcPrn) ;
    return bError ;
    }
```

Adding a Printing Dialog Box

PRINT2 is not entirely satisfactory. The program doesn't directly indicate when it is print-ing and when it is finished with printing. Only when you poke at the program with the mouse and find that it doesn't respond can you determine that it must still be processing the *PrintMyPage* routine. Nor does PRINT2 give the user the opportunity to cancel the print job while it is spooling.

You're probably aware that most Windows programs give users a chance to cancel a printing operation currently in progress. A small dialog box comes up on the screen; it contains some text and a push button labeled Cancel. The program displays this dialog box during the entire time that GDI is saving the printer output in a disk file or, if the spooler is disabled, while the printer is printing. This is a modeless dialog box, and you must supply the dialog procedure.

This dialog box is often called the "abort dialog box," and the dialog procedure is often called the "abort dialog procedure." To distinguish it more clearly from the "abort procedure," I'll call this dialog procedure the "printing dialog procedure." The abort pro-cedure (with the name *AbortProc*) and the printing dialog procedure (which I'll name *PrintDlgProc*) are two separate exported functions. If you want to print in a professional Windows-like manner, you must have both of these.

These two functions interact as follows: The *PeekMessage* loop in *AbortProc* must be modified to send messages for the modeless dialog box to the dialog box window proce-dure. *PrintDlgProc* must process WM_COMMAND messages to check the status of the Cancel button. If the Cancel button is pressed, it sets a variable called *bUserAbort* to TRUE. The value returned from *AbortProc* is the inverse of *bUserAbort*. You will recall that *AbortProc* returns TRUE to continue printing and FALSE to abort printing. In PRINT2 we always returned TRUE. Now we'll return FALSE if the user clicks the Cancel button in the printing dialog box. This logic is implemented in the PRINT3 program, shown in Figure 15-8.

If you experiment with PRINT3, you may want to temporarily disable print spooling. Otherwise, the Cancel button, which is visible only while the spooler collects data from PRINT3, may disappear too quickly to actually click on it. To disable spooling, select Settings from the Start menu, choose Printers, right-click on the icon for the default printer, and click Properties. You'll find spool settings in the Details tab.

Don't be surprised if things don't come to an immediate halt when you click the Cancel button, especially on a slow printer. The printer has an internal buffer that must drain before the printer stops. Clicking Cancel merely tells GDI not to send any more data to the printer's buffer.

PRINT3.MAK

```
#----------------------
# PRINT3.MAK make file
#----------------------

print3.exe : print.obj print3.obj print.res
    $(LINKER) $(GUIFLAGS) -OUT:print3.exe print.obj print3.obj \
    print.res $(GUILIBS) winspool.lib

print.obj : print.c
    $(CC) $(CFLAGS) print.c

print3.obj : print3.c
    $(CC) $(CFLAGS) print3.c

print.res : print.rc
    $(RC) $(RCVARS) print.rc
```

PRINT3.C

```
/*------------------------------------------
   PRINT3.C -- Printing with Dialog Box
            (c) Charles Petzold, 1996
   ------------------------------------------*/

#include <windows.h>
```

Figure 15-8. *The PRINT3 program.*

(continued)

```
HDC  GetPrinterDC (void) ;                    // in PRINT.C
void PageGDICalls (HDC, int, int) ;


HINSTANCE hInst ;
char      szAppName[] = "Print3" ;
char      szCaption[] = "Print Program 3 (Dialog Box)" ;


BOOL   bUserAbort ;
HWND   hDlgPrint ;

BOOL CALLBACK PrintDlgProc (HWND hDlg, UINT msg, WPARAM wParam, LPARAM lParam)
     {
     switch (msg)
          {
          case WM_INITDIALOG :
               SetWindowText (hDlg, szAppName) ;
               EnableMenuItem (GetSystemMenu (hDlg, FALSE), SC_CLOSE,
                                                            MF_GRAYED) ;

               return TRUE ;


          case WM_COMMAND :
               bUserAbort = TRUE ;
               EnableWindow (GetParent (hDlg), TRUE) ;
               DestroyWindow (hDlg) ;
               hDlgPrint = 0 ;
               return TRUE ;
          }
     return FALSE ;
     }


BOOL CALLBACK AbortProc (HDC hdcPrn, int iCode)
     {
     MSG   msg ;

     while (!bUserAbort && PeekMessage (&msg, NULL, 0, 0, PM_REMOVE))
          {
          if (!hDlgPrint || !IsDialogMessage (hDlgPrint, &msg))
               {
               TranslateMessage (&msg) ;
               DispatchMessage (&msg) ;
               }
          }
     return !bUserAbort ;
     }
```

(continued)

```
BOOL PrintMyPage (HWND hwnd)
    {
    static DOCINFO di = { sizeof (DOCINFO), "Print3: Printing", NULL } ;
    BOOL          bError = FALSE ;
    HDC           hdcPrn ;
    int           xPage, yPage ;

    if (NULL == (hdcPrn = GetPrinterDC ()))
        return TRUE ;

    xPage = GetDeviceCaps (hdcPrn, HORZRES) ;
    yPage = GetDeviceCaps (hdcPrn, VERTRES) ;

    EnableWindow (hwnd, FALSE) ;

    bUserAbort = FALSE ;
    hDlgPrint = CreateDialog (hInst, "PrintDlgBox", hwnd, PrintDlgProc) ;

    SetAbortProc (hdcPrn, AbortProc) ;

    if (StartDoc (hdcPrn, &di) > 0)
        {
        if (StartPage (hdcPrn) > 0)
            {
            PageGDICalls (hdcPrn, xPage, yPage) ;

            if (EndPage (hdcPrn) > 0)
                EndDoc (hdcPrn) ;
            else
                bError = TRUE ;
            }
        }
    else
        bError = TRUE ;

    if (!bUserAbort)
        {
        EnableWindow (hwnd, TRUE) ;
        DestroyWindow (hDlgPrint) ;
        }

    DeleteDC (hdcPrn) ;

    return bError || bUserAbort ;
    }
```

(continued)

PRINT.RC

```
/*---------------------------
    PRINT.RC resource script
  ---------------------------*/

#include <windows.h>

PrintDlgBox DIALOG 40, 40, 120, 40
    STYLE WS_POPUP | WS_CAPTION | WS_SYSMENU | WS_VISIBLE
    {
    CTEXT           "Cancel Printing", -1,  4,  6, 120, 12
    DEFPUSHBUTTON   "Cancel",    IDCANCEL, 44, 22,  32, 14, WS_GROUP
    }
```

Two global variables are added to PRINT3: a BOOL called *bUserAbort* and a handle to the dialog box window called *hDlgPrint*. The *PrintMyPage* function initializes *bUserAbort* to FALSE, and as in PRINT2, the program's main window is disabled. The pointer to *AbortProc* is used in the *SetAbortProc* call, and the pointer to *PrintDlgProc* is used in a *CreateDialog* call. The window handle returned from *CreateDialog* is saved in *hDlgPrint*.

The message loop in *AbortProc* now looks like this:

```
while (!bUserAbort && PeekMessage (&msg, NULL, 0, 0, PM_REMOVE))
    {
    if (!hDlgPrint || !IsDialogMessage (hDlgPrint, &msg))
        {
        TranslateMessage (&msg) ;
        DispatchMessage (&msg) ;
        }
    }
return !bUserAbort ;
```

It calls *PeekMessage* only if *bUserAbort* is FALSE, that is, if the user hasn't yet aborted the printing operation. The *IsDialogMessage* function is required to send the message to the modeless dialog box. As is normal with modeless dialog boxes, the handle to the dialog box window is checked before this call is made. *AbortProc* returns the inverse of *bUserAbort*. Initially, *bUserAbort* is FALSE, so *AbortProc* returns TRUE, indicating that printing is to continue. But *bUserAbort* could be set to TRUE in the printing dialog procedure.

The *PrintDlgProc* function is fairly simple. While processing WM_INITDIALOG, the function sets the window caption to the name of the program and disables the Close option on the system menu. If the user clicks the Cancel button, *PrintDlgProc* receives a WM_COMMAND message:

```
case WM_COMMAND :
     bUserAbort = TRUE ;
     EnableWindow (GetParent (hDlg), TRUE) ;
     DestroyWindow (hDlg) ;
     hDlgPrint = 0 ;
     return TRUE ;
```

Setting *bUserAbort* to TRUE indicates that the user has decided to cancel the printing operation. The main window is enabled, and the dialog box is destroyed. (It is important that you perform these two actions in this order. Otherwise, some other program running under Windows will become the active program, and your program might disappear into the background.) As is normal, *hDlgPrint* is set to 0 to prevent *IsDialogMessage* from being called in the message loop.

The only time this dialog box receives messages is when *AbortProc* retrieves messages with *PeekMessage* and sends them to the dialog box window procedure with *IsDialogMessage*. The only time *AbortProc* is called is when the GDI module is processing the *EndPage* function. If GDI sees that the return value from *AbortProc* is FALSE, it returns control from the *EndPage* call back to *PrintMyPage*. It doesn't return an error code. At that point, *PrintMyPage* thinks that the page is complete and calls the *EndDoc* function. Nothing is printed, however, because the GDI module didn't finish processing the *EndPage* call.

Some cleanup remains. If the user didn't cancel the print job from the dialog box, then the dialog box is still displayed. *PrintMyPage* reenables its main window and destroys the dialog box:

```
if (!bUserAbort)
     {
     EnableWindow (hwnd, TRUE) ;
     DestroyWindow (hDlgPrint) ;
     }
```

Two variables tell you what happened: *bUserAbort* tells you if the user aborted the print job, and *bError* tells you if an error occurred. You can do what you want with these variables. *PrintMyPage* simply performs a logical OR operation to return to *WndProc*:

```
return bError || bUserAbort ;
```

Adding Printing to POPPAD

Now we're ready to add a printing facility to the POPPAD series of programs and declare POPPAD finished. You'll need the various POPPAD files from Chapter 11, plus the two new files in Figure 15-9.

POPPAD.MAK

```
#---------------------
# poppad.MAK make file
#---------------------

poppad.exe : poppad.obj popfile.obj popfind.obj \
             popfont.obj popprnt.obj poppad.res
     $(LINKER) $(GUIFLAGS) -OUT:poppad.exe poppad.obj popfile.obj \
     popfind.obj popfont.obj popprnt.obj poppad.res $(GUILIBS)

poppad.obj : poppad.c poppad.h
     $(CC) $(CFLAGS) poppad.c

popfile.obj : popfile.c
     $(CC) $(CFLAGS) popfile.c

popfind.obj : popfind.c
     $(CC) $(CFLAGS) popfind.c

popfont.obj : popfont.c
     $(CC) $(CFLAGS) popfont.c

popprnt.obj : popprnt.c
     $(CC) $(CFLAGS) popprnt.c

poppad.res : poppad.rc poppad.h poppad.ico
     $(RC) $(RCVARS) poppad.rc
```

POPPRNT.C

```
/*-------------------------------------------------
   POPPRNT.C -- Popup Editor Printing Functions
   -------------------------------------------------*/

#include <windows.h>
#include <commdlg.h>
#include <string.h>
#include "poppad.h"

BOOL bUserAbort ;
HWND hDlgPrint ;

BOOL CALLBACK PrintDlgProc (HWND hDlg, UINT msg, WPARAM wParam, LPARAM lParam)
```

Figure 15-9. *New POPPAD files to add printing capability.*   *(continued)*

```
     {
     switch (msg)
          {
          case WM_INITDIALOG :
               EnableMenuItem (GetSystemMenu (hDlg, FALSE), SC_CLOSE,
                                                        MF_GRAYED) ;
               return TRUE ;

          case WM_COMMAND :
               bUserAbort = TRUE ;
               EnableWindow (GetParent (hDlg), TRUE) ;
               DestroyWindow (hDlg) ;
               hDlgPrint = 0 ;
               return TRUE ;
          }
     return FALSE ;
     }


BOOL CALLBACK AbortProc (HDC hPrinterDC, int iCode)
     {
     MSG msg ;

     while (!bUserAbort && PeekMessage (&msg, NULL, 0, 0, PM_REMOVE))
          {
          if (!hDlgPrint || !IsDialogMessage (hDlgPrint, &msg))
               {
               TranslateMessage (&msg) ;
               DispatchMessage (&msg) ;
               }
          }
     return !bUserAbort ;
     }


BOOL PopPrntPrintFile (HINSTANCE hInst, HWND hwnd, HWND hwndEdit,
                                                  LPSTR szTitleName)
     {
     static DOCINFO  di = { sizeof (DOCINFO), "", NULL } ;
     static PRINTDLG pd ;
     BOOL            bSuccess ;
     LPCTSTR         pstrBuffer ;
     int             yChar, iCharsPerLine, iLinesPerPage, iTotalLines,
                     iTotalPages, iPage, iLine, iLineNum ;
     TEXTMETRIC      tm ;
     WORD            iColCopy, iNonColCopy ;

     pd.lStructSize          = sizeof (PRINTDLG) ;
     pd.hwndOwner            = hwnd ;
```

(continued)

```
    pd.hDevMode             = NULL ;
    pd.hDevNames            = NULL ;
    pd.hDC                  = NULL ;
    pd.Flags                = PD_ALLPAGES ¦ PD_COLLATE ¦ PD_RETURNDC ;
    pd.nFromPage            = 1 ;
    pd.nToPage              = 0xFFFF ;
    pd.nMinPage             = 1 ;
    pd.nMaxPage             = 0xFFFF ;
    pd.nCopies              = 1 ;
    pd.hInstance            = NULL ;
    pd.lCustData            = 0L ;
    pd.lpfnPrintHook        = NULL ;
    pd.lpfnSetupHook        = NULL ;
    pd.lpPrintTemplateName  = NULL ;
    pd.lpSetupTemplateName  = NULL ;
    pd.hPrintTemplate       = NULL ;
    pd.hSetupTemplate       = NULL ;

    if (!PrintDlg (&pd))
        return TRUE ;

    iTotalLines = (short) SendMessage (hwndEdit, EM_GETLINECOUNT, 0, 0L) ;

    if (iTotalLines == 0)
        return TRUE ;

    GetTextMetrics (pd.hDC, &tm) ;
    yChar = tm.tmHeight + tm.tmExternalLeading ;

    iCharsPerLine = GetDeviceCaps (pd.hDC, HORZRES) / tm.tmAveCharWidth ;
    iLinesPerPage = GetDeviceCaps (pd.hDC, VERTRES) / yChar ;
    iTotalPages   = (iTotalLines + iLinesPerPage - 1) / iLinesPerPage ;

    pstrBuffer = (LPCTSTR) HeapAlloc (GetProcessHeap (),
                                HEAP_NO_SERIALIZE, iCharsPerLine + 1) ;

    EnableWindow (hwnd, FALSE) ;

    bSuccess   = TRUE ;
    bUserAbort = FALSE ;

    hDlgPrint = CreateDialog (hInst, (LPCTSTR) "PrintDlgBox", hwnd,
                                                PrintDlgProc) ;
    SetDlgItemText (hDlgPrint, IDD_FNAME, szTitleName) ;
```

(continued)

```
      SetAbortProc (pd.hDC, AbortProc) ;

GetWindowText (hwnd, (PTSTR) di.lpszDocName, sizeof (PTSTR)) ;

if (StartDoc (pd.hDC, &di) > 0)
     {
     for (iColCopy = 0 ;
          iColCopy < ((WORD) pd.Flags & PD_COLLATE ? pd.nCopies : 1) ;
          iColCopy++)
          {
          for (iPage = 0 ; iPage < iTotalPages ; iPage++)
               {
               for (iNonColCopy = 0 ;
                    iNonColCopy < (pd.Flags & PD_COLLATE ?
                                                    1 : pd.nCopies) ;
                    iNonColCopy++)
                    {

                    if (StartPage (pd.hDC) < 0)
                         {
                         bSuccess = FALSE ;
                         break ;
                         }

                    for (iLine = 0 ; iLine < iLinesPerPage ; iLine++)
                         {
                         iLineNum = iLinesPerPage * iPage + iLine ;

                         if (iLineNum > iTotalLines)
                              break ;

                         *(int *) pstrBuffer = iCharsPerLine ;

                         TextOut (pd.hDC, 0, yChar * iLine, pstrBuffer,
                              (int) SendMessage (hwndEdit, EM_GETLINE,
                              (WPARAM) iLineNum, (LPARAM) pstrBuffer)) ;
                         }

                    if (EndPage (pd.hDC) < 0)
                         {
                         bSuccess = FALSE ;
                         break ;
                         }

                    if (bUserAbort)
                         break ;
                    }
```

(continued)

```
                        if (!bSuccess !! bUserAbort)
                              break ;
                        }

                  if (!bSuccess !! bUserAbort)
                        break ;
                  }
            }
      else
            bSuccess = FALSE ;

      if (bSuccess)
            EndDoc (pd.hDC) ;

      if (!bUserAbort)
            {
            EnableWindow (hwnd, TRUE) ;
            DestroyWindow (hDlgPrint) ;
            }

      HeapFree (GetProcessHeap (), 0, (LPVOID) pstrBuffer) ;
      DeleteDC (pd.hDC) ;

      return bSuccess && !bUserAbort ;
      }
```

In keeping with the philosophy of making POPPAD as simple as possible by taking advantage of high-level Windows features, the POPPRNT.C file demonstrates how to use the *PrintDlg* function. This function is included in the common dialog box library and uses a structure of type PRINTDLG.

Normally, a Print option is included on a program's File menu. When the user selects the Print option, a program can initialize the fields of the PRINTDLG structure and call *PrintDlg*.

PrintDlg displays a dialog box that allows the user to select a page range to print. Thus, this dialog box is particularly suitable for programs such as POPPAD that can print multipage documents. The dialog box also provides an edit field to specify the number of copies, and a check box labeled "Collate." Collation affects the page-ordering of multiple copies. For example, if the document is three pages long and the user requests that three copies be printed, the program can print them in one of two orders. Collated copies are in the page order 1, 2, 3, 1, 2, 3, 1, 2, 3. Noncollated copies are in the order 1, 1, 1, 2, 2, 2, 3, 3, 3. It's up to your program to print the copies in the correct order.

The dialog box also allows the user to select a nondefault printer, and it includes a button labeled Properties that invokes a device mode dialog box. At the very least, this allows the user to select portrait or landscape mode.

On return from the *PrintDlg* function, fields of the PRINTDLG structure indicate the range of pages to print and whether multiple copies should be collated. The structure also provides the printer device context handle, ready to be used.

In POPPRNT.C, the *PopPrntPrintFile* function (which is called from POPPAD when the user selects the Print option from the File menu) calls *PrintDlg* and then proceeds to print the file. *PopPrntPrintFile* then performs some calculations to determine the number of characters it can fit on a line and the number of lines it can fit on a page. This process involves calls to *GetDeviceCaps* to determine the resolution of the page and to *GetTextMetrics* for the dimensions of a character.

The program obtains the total number of lines in the document (the variable *iTotalLines*) by sending an EM_GETLINECOUNT message to the edit control. A buffer for holding the contents of each line is allocated from local memory. For each line, the first word of this buffer is set to the number of characters in the line. Sending the edit control an EM_GETLINE message copies a line into the buffer; the line is then sent to the printer device context using *TextOut*.

Notice that the logic to print the document includes two *for* loops for the number of copies. The first uses a variable named *iColCopy* and takes effect when the user has specified collated copies; the second uses the *iNonColCopy* variable and takes effect for noncollated copies.

The program breaks from the *for* loop incrementing the page number if either *StartPage* or *EndPage* returns an error or if *bUserAbort* is TRUE. If the return value of the abort procedure is FALSE, *EndPage* doesn't return an error. For this reason, *bUserAbort* is tested explicitly before the next page is started. If no error is reported, the call to *EndDoc* is made:

```
if (!bError)
     EndDoc (hdcPrn) ;
```

You might want to experiment with POPPAD by printing a multipage file. You can monitor progress from the print job window, which you display by selecting Open from the File menu of the Printers folder. The file being printed first shows up in the print job window after GDI has finished processing the first call to *EndPage*. At that time, the spooler starts sending the file to the printer. If you then cancel the print job from POPPAD, the spooler aborts the printing also—that's a result of returning FALSE from the abort procedure. Once the file appears in the print job window, you can also cancel the printing by selecting Cancel Printing from the Document menu. In that case, the *EndPage* call in progress in POPPAD returns an SP_ERROR error (equal to −1).

Programmers new to Windows often become inordinately obsessed with the *AbortDoc* function. This function is rarely used in printing. As you can see in POPPAD, a user can cancel a print job at almost any time, either through POPPAD's printing dialog box or through the print job window. Neither requires that the program use the *AbortDoc* function. The only time that a call to *AbortDoc* would be allowed in POPPAD is between the call to *StartDoc* and the first call to *EndPage*, but that code goes so quickly that *AbortDoc* isn't necessary.

Figure 15-10 shows the correct sequence of print function calls for printing a multipage document. The best place to check for a *bUserAbort* value of TRUE is after each call to *EndPage*. The *EndDoc* function is used only when the previous print functions have proceeded without error. In fact, once you get an error from any call to a print function, the show is over, and you can go home.

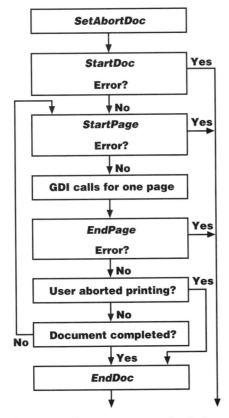

Figure 15-10. *The sequence of calls for printing a document.*

Handling Error Codes

We have been handling the return values from the print functions in a relatively simple manner: If a print function (such as *StartDoc*) returns a negative value, then an error has occurred, and the printing operation is aborted. The negative error code is SP_ERROR (–1), and it is the only value that the Win32 print functions return to indicate failure. By itself, SP_ERROR doesn't tell us much.

You can report errors to the user more precisely by calling *GetLastError* immediately after the error occurs. When called after a print function fails, *GetLastError* returns one of five identifiers defined in WINGDI.H. WINGDI.H also includes an identifier called SP_NOTREPORTED, which is equal to 0x4000. If a bitwise AND of the return value from *GetLastError* with SP_NOTREPORTED is 0, then the error has already been reported to the user. A bitwise OR of the return value of *GetLastError* with SP_NOTREPORTED can be compared with the five error-code identifiers to determine whether the error has been reported or not.

The following fragment shows one method of obtaining a text string identifying the error. It assumes that if a print function such as *StartDoc* returns a negative value, the flag *bError* is set to TRUE. The code tests the flag and calls the function *_GetErrorText* if an error has occurred. It then displays the returned error message to the user. *_GetErrorText* returns NULL if the error has already been reported to the user:

```
if (bError == TRUE)
    {
    pszErrMsg = _GetErrorText () ;
    if (pszErrMsg)
        MessageBox (hwnd, pszErrMsg, NULL, MB_OK) ;
    }
 .

 .

LPCTSTR _GetErrorText (void)
    {
    static LPCTSTR pszErrorText[] = {  "General error",
                                       "Canceled from program",
                                       "Canceled by user",
                                       "Out of disk space",
                                       "Out of memory" } ;
    DWORD dwError = GetLastError () ;

    if ((dwError & SP_NOTREPORTED) == 0)
        return NULL ;

    return pszErrorText[~dwError] ;
    }
```

The five error codes (with some likely causes) are as follows:

- SP_ERROR (0xFFFF, or −1)—Defined as indicating a "general error," this is the only error code that the Win32 print functions return. It indicates that the GDI module or the printer device driver can't begin a document.

- SP_APPABORT (0xFFFE, or −2)—This code is documented as indicating that the program's abort procedure has returned a FALSE value. However, this is the case only if the spooler isn't active. If the spooler is active and if the abort procedure is passed an *iCode* parameter of 0 and then returns a FALSE, *EndPage* will return a positive value.

- SP_USERABORT (0xFFFD, or −3)—This code indicates that the user canceled the printing job from the Printers folder.

- SP_OUTOFDISK (0xFFFC, or −4)—This code indicates that no more disk space is available. You'll encounter this error code if the disk drive containing the TEMP subdirectory can't accommodate any temporary spooler files. If the TEMP subdirectory has some existing temporary spooler files, then the abort procedure is called during an *EndPage* call with an *iCode* parameter of SP_OUTOFDISK. If the abort procedure then returns FALSE, *EndPage* returns SP_ERROR. A subsequent call to *GetLastError* returns SP_OUTOFDISK.

- SP_OUTOFMEMORY (0xFFFB, or −5)—This code indicates that insufficient memory is available for printing.

THE TECHNIQUE OF BANDING

Banding is the technique of defining a page of graphics as a series of separately constructed rectangles called bands. This approach relieves a printer driver of the necessity of constructing an entire bitmapped page image in memory. Banding is most important for raster printers that have no high-level page-composition control, such as dot-matrix printers and some laser printers.

Banding is one of the most misunderstood aspects of programming for the printer in Windows. Part of the problem lies in the documentation for the *GetDeviceCaps* function. The RC_BANDING bit of the value returned from *GetDeviceCaps* with the RASTERCAPS index is documented as "requires banding support." Programmers looking at this documentation assume that their applications must use banding with such printers. But this isn't so. Most of the information available from *GetDeviceCaps* is intended solely for the GDI module. This information allows GDI to determine what the device can do by itself and what it needs help with. The banding requirement falls into this category.

In general, an application program doesn't need to include its own banding logic. As you've seen, when you make GDI calls that define a page of graphics, the GDI module usually stores these calls in an enhanced metafile and then uses banding to set a clipping region before playing this metafile into the printer device driver. This is transparent to the application program. Under certain conditions, however, an application might want to take over the responsibility for doing banding. When an application uses banding, the GDI module doesn't create the intermediary enhanced metafile. Instead, the drawing commands for each band are passed to the printer device driver. There are two advantages to this approach:

- It can slightly increase printing speed. The application needs to call only those GDI functions that draw something in each particular band, which is faster than having the GDI module play the entire enhanced metafile into the device driver for each band.

- It can reduce the disk space normally required for printing. If the application is printing bitmaps but is not doing its own banding, then these bitmaps must be stored in the metafile that GDI creates. This situation can result in a metafile as large as the printer output file that the GDI module eventually creates.

Banding is particularly important for printing bitmaps, because they occupy a large amount of space in the metafile. (Printing a bitmap requires selecting the bitmap into a memory device context and using *BitBlt* or *StretchBlt* to write it to the printer device context.) But banding also further complicates the printing process, as you'll see when we create PRINT4, the final version of our printing program.

Strike Up the Bands

To have your program do its own banding, you must use a GDI function we haven't talked about yet, called *ExtEscape*. The name of this function implies that it is ignored by the GDI module and that it goes straight to the printer driver. In some cases, this is true, but often GDI also does some work during *ExtEscape* calls.

The general syntax of *ExtEscape* is:

```
iResult = ExtEscape (hdcPrinter, iEscapeCode, cbCountIn,
                          psDataIn, cbCountOut, psDataOut) ;
```

The *iEscapeCode* parameter is a subfunction code that is specified using an identifier defined in WINGDI.H. The other four parameters depend on the subfunction. Although the two parameters *psDataIn* and *psDataOut* are declared as pointers to character strings, they sometimes point to structures. To cast the pointers into string pointers, use (LPSTR).

Not all *ExtEscape* subfunctions are implemented in all device drivers. In fact, *ExtEscape* has been designed to be open-ended so that manufacturers of display devices can define their own *ExtEscape* subfunctions to access certain unique facilities of the devices. *ExtEscape* always returns 0 if the subfunction is not implemented and a negative value if an error occurs. A positive value indicates success.

The only *ExtEscape* subfunction that concerns us here is NEXTBAND. This subfunction is used to print a page of print data in a series of rectangular bands. To use NEXTBAND in a call to *ExtEscape*, first define a variable of type RECT:

```
RECT rect ;
```

You'll recall that the RECT structure has four fields named *left, top, right,* and *bottom.* For each page, you start by making an *ExtEscape* call for the subfunction NEXTBAND, passing to it a pointer to *rect.* On return, *rect* contains the coordinates of the first band. The coordinates are always device coordinates (pixels), regardless of the current mapping mode of the printer device context. You make GDI calls to print in that band. You then call the NEXTBAND *ExtEscape* function again to obtain the coordinates of the next band, and you print in that band. When the RECT structure passed to *ExtEscape* is returned empty (all fields set to 0), the page is done.

Here's what the code to print a single page looks like. For simplicity's sake, this code doesn't take into account errors that can be returned from the print functions or checks of the *bUserAbort* value:

```
StartPage (hdcPrn) ;           // Begin one page of print
ExtEscape (hdcPrn, NEXTBAND, 0, NULL, sizeof (rect), (LPSTR) &rect) ;

while (!IsRectEmpty (&rect))
    {
    [call GDI functions to print in band]
    ExtEscape (hdcPrn, NEXTBAND, 0, NULL, sizeof (rect), (LPSTR) &rect) ;
    }

EndPage (hdcPrn) ;             // End the page
```

Each NEXTBAND *ExtEscape* call (except the first) performs a function similar to the *EndPage* call: It signals to the GDI module and to the printer device driver that the entire band has been defined and that it can now be saved in a disk file (or written to the printer if the spooler is not active). The code begins with a call to *StartPage*; it ends with a call to *EndPage* after the loop has run its course.

It's easiest to visualize banding for a dot-matrix printer. Before illustrating the process, we need to make a distinction between the "top of the paper" (which is always the section of the paper printed first) and the "top of the page" (which depends on whether the printer driver is in portrait or landscape mode).

In portrait mode, the top of the page is the same as the top of the paper. The bands go down the page. The *rect.left* value in the RECT structure set by the NEXTBAND *ExtEscape* call is always 0, and *rect.right* is always equal to the width of the printing area in pixels (the value obtained from *GetDeviceCaps* with a HORZRES parameter). For the first band, *rect.top* equals 0. For each successive band, *rect.top* equals the *rect.bottom* value of the previous band. For the last band, *rect.bottom* equals the height of the printing area in pixels. (See Figure 15-11.)

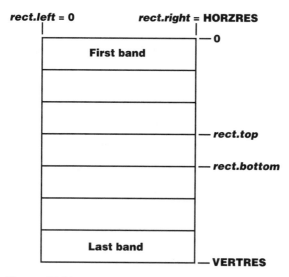

Figure 15-11. *Banding for a dot-matrix printer in portrait mode.*

Thus in each band, you can print from the *rect.left* and *rect.top* coordinates up to (but not including) the *rect.right* and *rect.bottom* coordinates. If you call the function:

```
Rectangle (hdcPrn, rect.left, rect.top, rect.right, rect.bottom) ;
```

the rectangle will be printed on the outermost edges of the band. (Recall that the right and bottom sides of the rectangle drawn by *Rectangle* are actually one pixel short of the points indicated by the last two parameters.)

In landscape mode, the dot-matrix printer must print the document sideways, starting from the left side of the page. The bands are in exactly the same area on the paper, but the rectangle coordinates are different because the left side of the page is now the top of the paper. In landscape mode, *rect.top* is always 0, and *rect.bottom* is a constant equal to the height of the printing area in pixels (the value obtained from *GetDeviceCaps* using the VERTRES parameter). For the first band, *rect.left* equals 0. For the last band, *rect.right* is the width of the printing area in pixels. (See Figure 15-12.)

A laser printer or a plotter might handle banding differently from a dot-matrix printer, because the printer output might not need to be sent to the printer sequentially from the top of the page to the bottom. Although Figures 15-11 and 15-12 represent the normal case, your program shouldn't assume that the banding rectangles will follow these patterns.

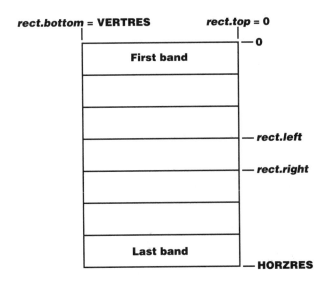

Figure 15-12. *Banding for a dot-matrix printer in landscape mode.*

Separating your printer output into bands might seem like a major headache. But even if you use banding, you don't need to include a lot of banding logic. The band is a clipping region. You can make GDI calls that print outside the band, and Windows will ignore everything except what falls inside the band. This means that for each band, you can make all the GDI calls for the entire page.

You can determine whether a particular driver requires banding support by checking the RC_BANDING bit of the value returned from *GetDeviceCaps* using the RASTERCAPS parameter. As I mentioned before, this information is of concern only to GDI. Whether a driver requires banding support or not, the GDI module always supports the NEXTBAND *ExtEscape* call. If the driver doesn't require banding support, the first NEXTBAND *ExtEscape* call for a page returns a rectangle equal to the size of the printing area. The second NEXTBAND call for a page returns an empty rectangle.

Implementing Banding

The PRINT4 program, shown in Figure 15-13, adds banding to the printing logic in PRINT3. PRINT4 also requires the PRINT.RC file in Figure 15-8 and—like all our PRINT programs—the PRINT.C file in Figure 15-5.

```
#---------------------
# PRINT4.MAK make file
#---------------------
```

Figure 15-13. *The PRINT4 program.*

(continued)

```
print4.exe : print.obj print4.obj print.res
    $(LINKER) $(GUIFLAGS) -OUT:print4.exe print.obj print4.obj \
    print.res $(GUILIBS) winspool.lib

print.obj : print.c
    $(CC) $(CFLAGS) print.c

print4.obj : print4.c
    $(CC) $(CFLAGS) print4.c

print.res : print.rc
    $(RC) $(RCVARS) print.rc
```

PRINT4.C

```c
/*-----------------------------------------
   PRINT4.C -- Printing with Banding
               (c) Charles Petzold, 1996
   -----------------------------------------*/

#include <windows.h>

HDC  GetPrinterDC (void) ;                    // in PRINT.C
void PageGDICalls (HDC, int, int) ;

HINSTANCE hInst ;
char     szAppName[] = "Print4" ;
char     szCaption[] = "Print Program 4 (Banding)" ;

BOOL   bUserAbort ;
HWND   hDlgPrint ;

BOOL CALLBACK PrintDlgProc (HWND hDlg, UINT msg, WPARAM wParam, LPARAM lParam)
     {
     switch (msg)
          {
          case WM_INITDIALOG :
               SetWindowText (hDlg, szAppName) ;
               EnableMenuItem (GetSystemMenu (hDlg, FALSE), SC_CLOSE,
                                                            MF_GRAYED) ;
               return TRUE ;

          case WM_COMMAND :
               bUserAbort = TRUE ;
               EnableWindow (GetParent (hDlg), TRUE) ;
```

(continued)

```
                    DestroyWindow (hDlg) ;
                    hDlgPrint = 0 ;
                    return TRUE ;
            }
      return FALSE ;
      }

BOOL CALLBACK AbortProc (HDC hdcPrn, int iCode)
      {
      MSG   msg ;

      while (!bUserAbort && PeekMessage (&msg, NULL, 0, 0, PM_REMOVE))
            {
            if (!hDlgPrint || !IsDialogMessage (hDlgPrint, &msg))
                  {
                  TranslateMessage (&msg) ;
                  DispatchMessage (&msg) ;
                  }
            }
      return !bUserAbort ;
      }

BOOL PrintMyPage (HWND hwnd)
      {
      static DOCINFO di = { sizeof (DOCINFO), "Print4: Printing", NULL } ;
      BOOL          bError = FALSE ;
      HDC           hdcPrn ;
      RECT          rect ;
      int           xPage, yPage ;

      if (NULL == (hdcPrn = GetPrinterDC ()))
            return TRUE ;

      xPage = GetDeviceCaps (hdcPrn, HORZRES) ;
      yPage = GetDeviceCaps (hdcPrn, VERTRES) ;

      EnableWindow (hwnd, FALSE) ;

      bUserAbort = FALSE ;
      hDlgPrint = CreateDialog (hInst, "PrintDlgBox", hwnd, PrintDlgProc) ;

      SetAbortProc (hdcPrn, AbortProc) ;

      if (StartDoc (hdcPrn, &di) > 0 && StartPage (hdcPrn) > 0 &&
            ExtEscape (hdcPrn, NEXTBAND, 0, NULL, sizeof (rect), (LPSTR) &rect)
            > 0)
```

(continued)

```
          {
     while (!IsRectEmpty (&rect) && !bUserAbort)
          {
          Rectangle (hdcPrn, rect.left, rect.top, rect.right,
                                              rect.bottom) ;
          PageGDICalls (hdcPrn, xPage, yPage) ;

          if (ExtEscape (hdcPrn, NEXTBAND, 0, NULL, sizeof (rect),
               (LPSTR) &rect) < 0)
               {
               bError = TRUE ;              // If error, set flag and
               break ;                      //    break out of loop
               }
          }
     }
else
     bError = TRUE ;

if (!bError)
     {
     if (bUserAbort)
          AbortDoc (hdcPrn) ;
     else
          if (EndPage (hdcPrn))
               EndDoc (hdcPrn) ;
     }

if (!bUserAbort)
     {
     EnableWindow (hwnd, TRUE) ;
     DestroyWindow (hDlgPrint) ;
     }

DeleteDC (hdcPrn) ;

return bError !! bUserAbort ;
}
```

PRINT4 differs from PRINT3 in only a few particulars. You'll notice that the *Rectangle* function prints the rectangle for each band rather than a rectangle on the border of the entire page. This allows you to see where the bands are for a particular printer. The structure of the printing operation looks like this:

```
        if (StartDoc (hdcPrn, &di) > 0 && StartPage (hdcPrn) > 0 &&
            ExtEscape (hdcPrn, NEXTBAND, 0, NULL, sizeof (rect), (LPSTR) &rect) > 0)
             {
            while (!IsRectEmpty (&rect) && !bUserAbort)
                 {
                 [make GDI calls]
                 if (ExtEscape (hdcPrn, NEXTBAND, 0, NULL, sizeof (rect),
                     (LPSTR) &rect) < 0)
                      {
                      bError = TRUE ;           // If error, set flag and
                      break ;                   //   break out of loop
                      }
                 }
             }
        else
             bError = TRUE ;
```

The *while* loop for the band proceeds only if the rectangle isn't empty and if the user hasn't canceled the print job from the dialog box. PRINT4 has to check the return value from each NEXTBAND *ExtEscape* call and set *bError* if *ExtEscape* returns a negative value. If no *ExtEscape* call returns an error, then the print job must either be ended by calling *EndDoc* or be aborted by calling *AbortDoc*. If the user cancels printing during the NEXTBAND loop, then the print job must be aborted using the *AbortDoc* call. Here is the code to do this:

```
     if (!bError)
          {
          if (bUserAbort)
               AbortDoc (hdcPrn) ;
          else
               if (EndPage (hdcPrn))
                    EndDoc (hdcPrn) ;
          }
```

THE PRINTER AND FONTS

Chapter 4 includes a program called JUSTIFY that uses GDI-based fonts to display formatted text. Programs that work with formatted text on the screen usually also need to print this text. In fact, word-processing and desktop publishing programs generally use the display solely to provide a preview of the printed output.

TrueType provides the easiest route to accurately rendering text on the screen as it will appear when printed. One approach you can use is to restrict your program to using only

TrueType fonts. If you enumerate fonts using the *EnumFontFamilies* function, you can check the TRUETYPE_FONTTYPE bit of the *iFontType* parameter to the call-back function. You then use a listbox to display only those fonts with the TRUETYPE_FONTTYPE bit set.

If you let the user choose a font by displaying the dialog box provided by the *ChooseFont* function in the common dialog box library (as demonstrated in the JUSTIFY program in Chapter 4), you can include the CF_TTONLY flag in the *Flags* field of the CHOOSEFONT structure to restrict the list to TrueType fonts.

However, restricting font selection to TrueType may disturb those users who have invested money in downloadable fonts or font cartridges for their laser printers. These printer fonts will not be listed for selection by the user. To display printer fonts in the dialog box created by *ChooseFont*, you should include the CF_PRINTERFONTS constant in the *Flags* field of the CHOOSEFONT structure.

You must also set the *hDC* field of the CHOOSEFONT structure to the device context handle for the printer. The fonts displayed in the list box will then be limited to the internal printer fonts, TrueType fonts, and stroke fonts. (To eliminate the stroke fonts from the listbox, also use the flag CF_NOVECTORFONTS.)

If you let the user choose printer fonts, what you show on the display can only approximate what the printer will print. If the printer offers a 15-point Zapf Chancery font, for example, it can be approximated with a 15-point TrueType font, but the character widths of the TrueType font will not be the same as the Zapf Chancery font. Even for TrueType fonts, there may be rounding errors in character widths that cause differences between the screen display and the printer.

In short, if you're writing a program that must display formatted text destined for a printer, you can count on some work ahead. Here are some guidelines to get you started.

When you display formatted text on the screen, you want to space the text based on how it will eventually be printed. You can use *GetDeviceCaps* and *DeviceCapabilities* to determine the size of the paper and the size of the printable area. For instance, if the paper is 8½ inches wide and the user selects left and right margins of 1 inch, then you want to display text on the screen using a width of 6½ inches. The "logical twips" mapping mode discussed in Chapter 4 is appropriate for this display. There's a catch, however. If the user selects a 15-point font that the printer supports, you might have to approximate that font on the display with, say, a 14-point font—but you can't use this 14-point display font to determine the amount of 15-point text that can fit in one printed line. You must determine this instead based on the printer font. Likewise, you must use the printer font to determine how many lines fit on a page.

To format the display text, you'll need both a handle to the screen device context (to display the text on the screen) and a handle to a printer information context. You don't need a printer device context handle until you actually want to print. Follow these steps:

1. Put together a logical font structure with the typeface name, the type size, and the attributes selected by the user, and select that logical font into the printer information context.

2. Call *GetTextMetrics* for the printer information context to determine the real size and characteristics of the selected printer font. Call *GetTextFace* to obtain the typeface name.

3. Use the information obtained in Step 2 to create another logical font structure based on the size and characteristics of the printer font, and select this logical font into the screen device context. The font now selected into the screen device context closely approximates the font selected into the printer information context.

4. When you write the text to the display, follow the general procedure used in the *Justify* function of the JUSTIFY program. However, go through the *GetTextExtent* and *SetTextJustification* logic using the printer information context, but stop short of *TextOut*. This approach allows you to determine the amount of text that fits in each line and the number of lines that fit on a page.

5. When you have established each line of text as appropriate for the printer, you can call *GetTextExtent* and (possibly) *SetTextJustification* using the screen display context. You then call *TextOut* to display the line.

To print the text, you'll probably use code structured like that in the POPPRNT.C file combined with the logic in the *Justify* function of JUSTIFY.C. You obtain a printer device context and go through the *GetTextExtent* and *SetTextJustification* logic again, this time using *TextOut* to print each line.

Data Exchange and Links

Chapter 16

The Clipboard

The Windows clipboard allows data to be transferred from one program to another. It is a relatively simple mechanism that doesn't require much overhead in either the program that places data in the clipboard or the program that later gets access to it. Windows 95 comes with a clipboard viewer program that shows the current contents of the clipboard. Many programs that deal with documents or other data include an Edit menu with the options Cut, Copy, and Paste. When a user selects Cut or Copy, the program transfers data to the clipboard. This data is in a particular format, such as text, a bitmap, or a metafile. When a user selects Paste from the menu, the program determines if the clipboard contains data in a format that the program can use and, if so, transfers that data from the clipboard to the program.

Programs should not transfer data into or out of the clipboard without an explicit instruction from the user. For example, a user who performs a Cut or a Copy operation in one program should be able to assume that the data will remain in the clipboard until the next Cut or Copy operation.

SIMPLE USE OF THE CLIPBOARD

We'll begin by looking at the code involved for transferring data to the clipboard (Cut and Copy) and getting access to clipboard data (Paste).

The Standard Clipboard Data Formats

Windows supports various standard clipboard formats that have identifiers in the Windows header files. The most common of these are:

- CF_TEXT—a NULL-terminated ANSI character-set character string containing a carriage return and a linefeed character at the end of each line. This is the simplest form of clipboard data. The data to be transferred to the clipboard is stored in a memory block and is transferred using the handle to the block. The memory block becomes the property of the clipboard, and the program that creates the block should not continue to use it.

- CF_BITMAP—a device-dependent bitmap. The bitmap is transferred to the clipboard using the bitmap handle. Again, a program should not continue to use this bitmap after giving it to the clipboard.

- CF_METAFILEPICT—a "metafile picture." This isn't exactly the same as a metafile (described in Chapter 4). Rather, it's a metafile with some additional information in the form of a small structure of type METAFILEPICT. A program transfers a metafile picture to the clipboard using the handle to a memory block containing this structure. The four fields of the METAFILEPICT structure are: *mm* (LONG), the mapping mode for the metafile; *xExt* (LONG) and *yExt* (LONG), in simple terms, the width and height of the metafile image; and *hMF* (HMETAFILE), the handle to the metafile. (I'll discuss the *xExt* and *yExt* fields in detail later in this chapter.) After a program transfers a metafile picture to the clipboard, it should not continue to use either the memory block containing the METAFILEPICT structure or the metafile handle, because both will be under the control of Windows 95.

- CF_ENHMETAFILE—a handle to an enhanced metafile (described in Chapter 4). This format does not use the METAFILEPICT structure.

- CF_SYLK—a memory block containing data in the Microsoft "Symbolic Link" (SYLK) format. This format is used for exchanging data between Microsoft Corporation's Multiplan, Chart, and Excel programs. It is an ASCII format with each line terminated with a carriage return and a linefeed.

- CF_DIF—a memory block containing data in the Data Interchange Format (DIF). This is a format devised by Software Arts for use in transferring data to the VisiCalc spreadsheet program. The format is now under the control of Lotus Corporation. This is also an ASCII format with lines terminated by carriage returns and linefeeds.

The CF_SYLK and CF_DIF formats are conceptually similar to the CF_TEXT format. Character strings containing SYLK or DIF data are not necessarily NULL-terminated, however, because the formats define the end of the data.

- CF_TIFF—a memory block containing data in the Tag Image File Format (TIFF). This is a format devised by Microsoft Corporation, Aldus Corporation, and Hewlett-Packard Company in conjunction with some hardware manufacturers. The format (which describes bitmapped data) is available from Hewlett-Packard.

- CF_OEMTEXT—a memory block containing text data (similar to CF_TEXT) but using the OEM character set.

- CF_DIB—a memory block defining a device-independent bitmap (described in Chapter 4). The memory block begins with a BITMAPINFO structure followed by the bitmap bits.

- CF_PALETTE—a handle to a color palette. This is generally used in conjunction with CF_DIB for defining the color palette used by the bitmap.

Transferring Text to the Clipboard

Let's assume that you want to transfer a character string to the clipboard and that you have a pointer (called *pString*) to this string. You want to transfer *iLength* bytes of this string.

First, allocate a moveable memory block of *iLength* size by using *GlobalAlloc*. Include room for a terminating NULL:

```
hGlobalMemory = GlobalAlloc (GHND | GMEM_DDESHARE, iLength + 1) ;
```

The value of *hGlobalMemory* will be NULL if the block could not be allocated. If the allocation is successful, lock the block to get a pointer to it:

```
pGlobalMemory = GlobalLock (hGlobalMemory) ;
```

Copy the character string into the memory block:

```
for (i = 0 ; i < iLength ; i++)
    *pGlobalMemory++ = *pString++ ;
```

You don't need to add the terminating NULL because the GHND flag for *GlobalAlloc* zeroes out the entire memory block during allocation. Unlock the block:

```
GlobalUnlock (hGlobalMemory) ;
```

Now you have a memory handle that references a memory block containing the NULL-terminated text. To get this into the clipboard, open the clipboard and empty it:

```
OpenClipboard (hwnd) ;
EmptyClipboard () ;
```

Give the clipboard the memory handle using the CF_TEXT identifier, and close the clipboard:

```
SetClipboardData (CF_TEXT, hGlobalMemory) ;
CloseClipboard () ;
```

You're done.

Here are some rules concerning this process:

- Call *OpenClipboard* and *CloseClipboard* while processing a single message. Don't leave the clipboard open any longer than necessary.

- Don't give the clipboard a locked memory handle.

- After you call *SetClipboardData*, don't continue to use the memory block. It no longer belongs to your program, and you should treat the handle as invalid. If you need to continue to access the data, make another copy of it or read it from the clipboard (as described in the next section). You can also continue to reference the block between the *SetClipboardData* call and the *CloseClipboard* call, but you must use the handle that is returned from *SetClipboardData*. Unlock this handle before you call *CloseClipboard*.

Getting Text from the Clipboard

Getting text from the clipboard is only a little more complex than transferring text to the clipboard. You must first determine whether the clipboard does in fact contain data in the CF_TEXT format. One of the easiest methods is to use the call:

```
bAvailable = IsClipboardFormatAvailable (CF_TEXT) ;
```

This function returns TRUE (nonzero) if the clipboard contains CF_TEXT data. We used this function in the POPPAD2 program in Chapter 10 to determine whether the Paste item on the Edit menu should be enabled or grayed. *IsClipboardFormatAvailable* is one of the few clipboard functions that you can use without first opening the clipboard. However, if you later open the clipboard to get this text, you should also check again (using the same function or one of the other methods) to determine if the CF_TEXT data is still in the clipboard.

To transfer the text out, first open the clipboard:

```
OpenClipboard (hwnd) ;
```

Obtain the handle to the memory block referencing the text:

```
hClipMemory = GetClipboardData (CF_TEXT) ;
```

This handle will be NULL if the clipboard doesn't contain data in the CF_TEXT format. This is another way to determine if the clipboard contains text. If *GetClipboardData* returns NULL, close the clipboard without doing anything else.

The handle you receive from *GetClipboardData* doesn't belong to your program—it belongs to the clipboard. The handle is valid only between the *GetClipboardData* and *CloseClipboard* calls. You can't free that handle or alter the data it references. If you need to have continued access to the data, you should make a copy of the memory block.

Here's one method for copying the data into your program. Just allocate a pointer to a memory block of the same size as the clipboard data block:

```
pMyCopy = (char *) malloc (GlobalSize (hClipMemory)) ;
```

Now lock the handle to get a pointer to the clipboard block:

```
pClipMemory = GlobalLock (hClipMemory) ;
```

Now just copy the data:

```
strcpy (pMyCopy, pClipMemory) ;
```

Or you can use some simple C code:

```
while (*pMyCopy++ = *pClipMemory++) ;
```

Unlock the block before closing the clipboard:

```
GlobalUnlock (hClipMemory) ;
CloseClipboard () ;
```

Now you have a pointer called *pMyCopy* that you can later lock to access this data.

Opening and Closing the Clipboard

Only one program can have the clipboard open at any time. The purpose of the *OpenClipboard* call is to prevent the clipboard contents from changing while a program is using the clipboard. *OpenClipboard* returns a BOOL value indicating whether the clipboard was successfully opened. It will not be opened if another application failed to close it. If every program politely opens and then closes the clipboard as quickly as possible when responding to a user command, you'll never run into the problem of being unable to open the clipboard.

However, in the world of impolite programs and pre-emptive multitasking, some problems could arise. Even if your program hasn't lost input focus between the time it's put something into the clipboard and the time the user invokes a Paste option, don't assume that what you've put in there is still there. A background process *could* have accessed the clipboard during that time.

Also, watch out for a more subtle problem involving message boxes: If you can't allocate enough memory to copy something to the clipboard, then you might want to display a message box. If this message box isn't system modal, however, the user can switch to another application while the message box is displayed. You should either make the message box system modal or close the clipboard before you display the message box.

You can also run into problems if you leave the clipboard open while you display a dialog box. Edit fields in a dialog box use the clipboard for cutting and pasting text.

Using the Clipboard with Bitmaps

In using the CF_BITMAP format, you give the clipboard a handle to a device-dependent bitmap when calling *SetClipboardData*. The *GetClipboardData* function returns a handle to a device-dependent bitmap.

If you have a bitmap handle, you can copy the bitmap to the clipboard with the following simple code:

```
OpenClipboard (hwnd) ;
EmptyClipboard () ;
SetClipboardData (CF_BITMAP, hBitmap) ;
CloseClipboard () ;
```

Getting access to the bitmap is also easy:

```
OpenClipboard (hwnd) ;
hBitmap = GetClipboardData (CF_BITMAP) ;
```

If the clipboard does not contain a bitmap, *hBitmap* will be NULL. To make a copy of the bitmap, call *GetObject* to determine the bitmap pixel size and color organization:

```
GetObject (hBitmap, sizeof (BITMAP), (PSTR) &bm) ;
```

Now you can create your own bitmap with the same size and color organization using *CreateBitmapIndirect*:

```
hMyBitmap = CreateBitmapIndirect (&bm) ;
```

Select both bitmaps into memory device contexts created using *CreateCompatibleDC*:

```
hdcMemSrc = CreateCompatibleDC (hdc) ;
SelectObject (hdcMemSrc, hBitmap) ;
hdcMemDst = CreateCompatibleDC (hdc) ;
SelectObject (hdcMemDst, hMyBitmap) ;
```

and call *BitBlt* to copy from the clipboard bitmap to your own:

```
BitBlt (hdcMemDst, 0, 0, bm.bmWidth, bm.bmHeight, hdcMemSrc, 0, 0, SRCCOPY) ;
```

The only cleanup involved is deleting the memory device contexts and closing the clipboard:

```
DeleteDC (hdcMemSrc) ;
DeleteDC (hdcMemDst) ;
CloseClipboard () ;
```

Don't delete the original bitmap because it now belongs to the clipboard.

Programs that work with device-independent bitmaps (DIBs) can also transfer these bitmaps to and obtain them from the clipboard. If your program has a global memory handle referencing a memory block that contains a bitmap definition in DIB format, it can simply pass the handle to *SetClipboardData* with the CF_DIB identifier. After closing the clipboard, the DIB memory block no longer belongs to your program. If your program needs to keep a copy of the DIB, it can make a copy for the clipboard by allocating a memory block of the same size and copying the DIB data. Obtaining a DIB from the clipboard is similar to obtaining text from the clipboard, except that the data is not 0-terminated.

If your program needs to keep its own copy of a bitmap (in either device-independent or device-dependent format) after passing a copy to the clipboard, you might be using lots of memory space to store the two copies. In this case, you'll probably want to use a technique called "delayed rendering" to avoid hogging memory resources. Delayed rendering is discussed later in this chapter.

The Metafile and the Metafile Picture

Using the clipboard for transferring enhanced metafiles is quite simple. The *GetClipboardData* function returns a handle to the enhanced metafile; the *SetClipboardData* function also uses the metafile handle. Need a copy of the metafile? Use the *CopyEnhMetaFile* function. As I said in Chapter 4 and demonstrated again in Chapter 15, the primary improvements of the enhanced metafile format over the old format are that you can easily determine the size of the image and display it appropriately in your window.

The old unenhanced metafiles present a messy problem. If you have a handle to an old-style metafile, how can you determine how large the image will be when you play it? Unless you start digging into the internals of the metafile itself, you can't.

Moreover, when a program obtains an old-style metafile from the clipboard, it has the most flexibility in working with it if the metafile has been designed to be played in an MM_ISOTROPIC or MM_ANISOTROPIC mapping mode. The program that receives the metafile can then scale the image by simply setting viewport extents before playing the metafile. But if the mapping mode is set to MM_ISOTROPIC or MM_ANISOTROPIC within the metafile, then the program that receives the metafile is stuck. The program can make GDI calls only before or after the metafile is played. It can't make a GDI call in the middle of a metafile.

To solve these problems, old-style metafile handles are not directly put into the clipboard and retrieved by other programs. Instead, the metafile handle is part of a "metafile picture," which is a structure of type METAFILEPICT. This structure allows the program that obtains the metafile picture from the clipboard to set the mapping mode and viewport extents itself before playing the metafile.

The METAFILEPICT structure is 16 bytes long and has four fields: *mm*, the mapping mode; *xExt* and *yExt*, the width and height of the metafile image; and *hMF*, the handle to the metafile. For all the mapping modes except MM_ISOTROPIC and MM_ANISOTROPIC, the *xExt* and *yExt* values are the size of the image in units of the mapping mode given by *mm*. With this information, the program that copies the metafile picture structure from the clipboard can determine how much display space the metafile will encompass when it is played. The program that creates the metafile can set these values to the largest *x*-coordinates and *y*-coordinates it uses in the GDI drawing functions that enter the metafile.

For the MM_ISOTROPIC and MM_ANISOTROPIC mapping modes, the *xExt* and *yExt* fields function differently. You will recall from Chapter 4 that a program uses the MM_ISOTROPIC or MM_ANISOTROPIC mapping mode when it wants to use arbitrary logical units in GDI functions independent of the measurable size of the image. A program uses MM_ISOTROPIC when it wants to maintain an aspect ratio regardless of the size of the viewing surface and MM_ANISOTROPIC when it doesn't care about the aspect ratio. You will also recall from Chapter 4 that after a program sets the mapping mode to MM_ISOTROPIC or MM_ANISOTROPIC, it generally makes calls to *SetWindowExtEx* and *SetViewportExtEx*. The *SetWindowExtEx* call uses logical units to specify the units the program wants to use when drawing. The *SetViewportExtEx* call uses device units based on the size of the viewing surface (for instance, the size of the window's client area).

If a program creates an MM_ISOTROPIC or MM_ANISOTROPIC metafile for the clipboard, then the metafile should not itself contain a call to *SetViewportExtEx* because the device units in that call would be based on the display surface of the program creating the metafile and not on the display surface of the program that reads the metafile from the clipboard and plays it. Instead, the *xExt* and *yExt* values should assist the program that obtains the metafile from the clipboard in setting appropriate viewport extents for playing the metafile. But the metafile itself contains a call to set the window extent when the mapping mode is MM_ISOTROPIC or MM_ANISOTROPIC. The coordinates of the GDI drawing functions within the metafile are based on these window extents.

The program that creates the metafile and metafile picture follows these rules:

- The *mm* field of the METAFILEPICT structure is set to specify the mapping mode.

- For mapping modes other than MM_ISOTROPIC and MM_ANISOTROPIC, the *xExt* and *yExt* fields are set to the width and height of the image in units corresponding to the *mm* field. For metafiles to be played in an MM_ISOTROPIC or MM_ANISOTROPIC environment, matters get a little more complex. For MM_ANISOTROPIC, 0 values of *xExt* and *yExt* are used when the program is suggesting neither a size nor an aspect ratio for the image. For MM_ISOTROPIC or MM_ANISOTROPIC, positive values of *xExt* and *yExt* indicate a suggested width and height of the image in units of 0.01 mm (MM_HIMETRIC units). For MM_ISOTROPIC, negative values of *xExt* and *yExt* indicate a suggested aspect ratio of the image but not a suggested size.

- For the MM_ISOTROPIC and MM_ANISOTROPIC mapping modes, the metafile itself contains calls to *SetWindowExtEx* and (possibly) *SetWindowOrgEx*. That is, the program that creates the metafile calls these functions in the metafile device context. Generally, the metafile will not contain calls to *SetMapMode*, *SetViewportExtEx*, or *SetViewportOrgEx*.

- The metafile should be a memory-based metafile, not a disk-based metafile.

Here's some sample code for a program creating a metafile and copying it to the clipboard. If the metafile uses the MM_ISOTROPIC or MM_ANISOTROPIC mapping mode, the first calls in the metafile should be to set the window extents. (The window extents are fixed in the other mapping modes.) Regardless of the mapping mode, the window origin can also be set:

```
hdcMeta = CreateMetaFile (NULL) ;
SetWindowExtEx (hdcMeta, ...) ;
SetWindowOrgEx (hdcMeta, ...) ;
```

The coordinates in the drawing functions of the metafile are based on these window extents and the window origin. After the program uses GDI calls to draw on the metafile device context, the metafile is closed to get a handle to the metafile:

```
hmf = CloseMetaFile (hdcMeta) ;
```

The program also needs to define a pointer to a structure of type METAFILEPICT and allocate a block of memory for this structure:

```
HGLOBAL        hGMem ;
LPMETAFILEPICT pMFP ;
[other program lines]
hGMem = GlobalAlloc (GHND, sizeof (METAFILEPICT)) ;

pMFP = (LPMETAFILEPICT) GlobalLock (hGMem) ;
```

Next, the program sets the four fields of this structure:

```
pMFP->mm   = MM_... ;
pMFP->xExt = ... ;
pMFP->yExt = ... ;
pMFP->hMF  = hmf ;

GlobalUnlock (hGMem) ;
```

The program then transfers the memory block containing the metafile picture structure to the clipboard:

```
OpenClipboard (hwnd) ;
EmptyClipboard () ;
SetClipboardData (CF_METAFILEPICT, hGMem) ;
CloseClipboard () ;
```

Following these calls, the *hGMem* handle (the memory block containing the metafile picture structure) and the *hmf* handle (the metafile itself) become invalid for the program that created them.

Now for the hard part. When a program obtains a metafile from the clipboard and plays this metafile, the following steps must take place:

1.   The program uses the *mm* field of the metafile picture structure to set the mapping mode.

2.   For mapping modes other than MM_ISOTROPIC or MM_ANISOTROPIC, the program uses the *xExt* and *yExt* values to set a clipping rectangle or simply to determine the size of the image. For the MM_ISOTROPIC and MM_AN-ISOTROPIC mapping modes, the program uses *xExt* and *yExt* to set the viewport extents.

3.   The program then plays the metafile.

Here's the code. You first open the clipboard, get the handle to the metafile picture structure, and lock it:

```
OpenClipboard (hwnd) ;
hGMem = GetClipboardData (CF_METAFILEPICT) ;
pMFP = (LPMETAFILEPICT) GlobalLock (hGMem) ;
```

You can then save the attributes of your current device context and set the mapping mode to the *mm* value of the structure:

```
SaveDC (hdc) ;
SetMappingMode (pMFP->mm) ;
```

If the mapping mode isn't MM_ISOTROPIC or MM_ANISOTROPIC, you can set a clipping rectangle to the values of *xExt* and *yExt*. Because these values are in logical units, you have to use *LPtoDP* to convert the coordinates to device units for the clipping rectangle. Or you can simply save the values so that you know how large the image is.

For the MM_ISOTROPIC or MM_ANISOTROPIC mapping mode, you use *xExt* and *yExt* to set the viewport extent. One possible function to perform this task is shown below. This function assumes that *cxClient* and *cyClient* represent the pixel height and width of the area in which you want the metafile to appear if no suggested size is implied by *xExt* and *yExt*.

```
void PrepareMetaFile (HDC hdc, LPMETAFILEPICT pmfp,
                      int cxClient, int cyClient)
    {
    int xScale, yScale, iScale ;

    SetMapMode (hdc, pmfp->mm) ;

    if (pmfp->mm == MM_ISOTROPIC || pmfp->mm == MM_ANISOTROPIC)
        {
        if (pmfp->xExt == 0)
            SetViewportExtEx (hdc, cxClient, cyClient, NULL) ;
        else if (pmfp->xExt > 0)
            SetViewportExtEx (hdc,
```

```
                        pmfp->xExt * GetDeviceCaps (hdc, HORZRES) /
                                GetDeviceCaps (hdc, HORZSIZE) / 100,
                        pmfp->yExt * GetDeviceCaps (hdc, VERTRES) /
                                GetDeviceCaps (hdc, VERTSIZE) / 100,
                        NULL) ;

        else if (pmfp->xExt < 0)
            {
            xScale = 100 * cxClient * GetDeviceCaps (hdc, HORZSIZE) /
                        GetDeviceCaps (hdc, HORZRES) / -pmfp->xExt ;
            yScale = 100 * cyClient * GetDeviceCaps (hdc, VERTSIZE) /
                        GetDeviceCaps (hdc, VERTRES) / -pmfp->yExt ;
            iScale = min (xScale, yScale) ;

            SetViewportExtEx (hdc,
                    -pmfp->xExt * iScale * GetDeviceCaps (hdc, HORZRES) /
                            GetDeviceCaps (hdc, HORZSIZE) / 100,
                    -pmfp->yExt * iScale * GetDeviceCaps (hdc, VERTRES) /
                            GetDeviceCaps (hdc, VERTSIZE) / 100,
                    NULL) ;
            }
        }
    }
```

This code assumes that both *xExt* and *yExt* are 0, greater than 0, or less than 0 (which should be the case). If the extents are 0, no size or aspect ratio is suggested. The viewport extents are set to the area in which you want to display the metafile. Positive values of *xExt* and *yExt* are a suggested image size in units of 0.01 mm. The *GetDeviceCaps* function assists in determining the number of pixels per 0.01 mm, and this value is multiplied by the extent values in the metafile picture structure. Negative values of *xExt* and *yExt* indicate a suggested aspect ratio but not a suggested size. The value *iScale* is first calculated based on the aspect ratio of the size in millimeters corresponding to *cxClient* and *cyClient*. This scaling factor is then used to set a viewport extent in pixels.

With this job out of the way, you can set a viewport origin if you want, play the metafile, and return the device context to normal:

```
PlayMetaFile (pMFP->hMF) ;
RestoreDC (hdc, -1) ;
```

Then you unlock the memory block and close the clipboard:

```
GlobalUnlock (hGMem) ;
CloseClipboard () ;
```

BEYOND SIMPLE CLIPBOARD USE

In using text and bitmaps, you've seen that transferring data to the clipboard requires four calls after the data has been prepared:

```
OpenClipboard (hwnd) ;
EmptyClipboard () ;
SetClipboardData (iFormat, hHandle) ;
CloseClipboard () ;
```

Getting access to this data requires three calls:

```
OpenClipboard (hwnd) ;
hHandle = GetClipboardData (iFormat) ;
[other program lines]
CloseClipboard () ;
```

You can make a copy of the clipboard data or use it in some other manner between the *GetClipboardData* and *CloseClipboard* calls. That approach may be all you'll need for most purposes, but you can also use the clipboard in more sophisticated ways.

Using Multiple Data Items

When you open the clipboard to put data into it, you must call *EmptyClipboard* to signal Windows to free or delete the contents of the clipboard. You can't add something to the existing contents of the clipboard. So in this sense, the clipboard holds only one item at a time.

However, between the *EmptyClipboard* and the *CloseClipboard* calls, you can call *SetClipboardData* several times, each time using a different clipboard format. For instance, if you want to store a short string of text in the clipboard, you can create a metafile device context and write that text to the metafile. You can also create a bitmap large enough to hold the character string, select the bitmap into a memory device context, and write the string to the bitmap. In this way, you make that character string available not only to programs that can read text from the clipboard but also to programs that read bitmaps and metafiles from the clipboard. Moreover, if you select a different font into the metafile device context or memory device context before writing the text, programs that read bitmaps or metafiles will use the string with this different font. (Of course, these programs won't be able to recognize the metafile or bitmap as actually containing a character string.)

If you want to write several handles to the clipboard, you call *SetClipboardData* for each of them:

```
OpenClipboard (hwnd) ;
EmptyClipboard () ;
SetClipboardData (CF_TEXT, hGMemText) ;
SetClipboardData (CF_BITMAP, hBitmap) ;
SetClipboardData (CF_METAFILEPICT, hGMemMFP) ;
CloseClipboard () ;
```

While these three formats of data are in the clipboard, an *IsClipboardFormatAvailable* call with the CF_TEXT, CF_BITMAP, or CF_METAFILEPICT argument will return TRUE. A program can get access to these handles by calling:

```
hGMemText = GetClipboardData (CF_TEXT) ;
```

or:

```
hBitmap = GetClipboardData (CF_BITMAP) ;
```

or:

```
hGMemMFP = GetClipboardData (CF_METAFILEPICT) ;
```

The next time a program calls *EmptyClipboard,* Windows will free or delete all three of the handles retained by the clipboard as well as the metafile that is part of the METAFILEPICT structure.

A program can determine all the formats stored by the clipboard by first opening the clipboard and then calling *EnumClipboardFormats.* Start off by setting a variable *iFormat* to 0:

```
iFormat = 0 ;
OpenClipboard (hwnd) ;
```

Now make successive *EnumClipboardFormats* calls starting with the 0 value. The function will return a positive *iFormat* value for each format currently in the clipboard. When the function returns 0, you're done:

```
while (iFormat = EnumClipboardFormats (iFormat))
     {
     [logic for each iFormat value]
     }
CloseClipboard () ;
```

You can obtain the number of different formats currently in the clipboard by calling:

```
iCount = CountClipboardFormats () ;
```

Delayed Rendering

When you put data into the clipboard, you generally make a copy of the data and give the clipboard a handle to a memory block that contains the copy. For very large data items, this approach can waste memory. If the user never pastes that data into another program, it will continue to occupy memory space until it is replaced by something else.

You can avoid this problem by using a technique called "delayed rendering," in which your program doesn't actually supply the data until another program needs it. Rather than give Windows a handle to the data, you simply use a NULL in the *SetClipboardData* call:

```
OpenClipboard (hwnd) ;
EmptyClipboard () ;
SetClipboardData (iFormat, NULL) ;
CloseClipboard () ;
```

You can have multiple *SetClipboardData* calls using different values of *iFormat*. You can use NULL parameters with some of them and real handles with others.

That's simple enough, but now the process gets a little more complex. When another program calls *GetClipboardData*, Windows will check to see if the handle for that format is NULL. If it is, Windows will send a message to the "clipboard owner" (your program) asking for a real handle to the data. Your program must then supply this handle.

More specifically, the "clipboard owner" is the last window that put data into the clipboard. When a program calls *OpenClipboard*, Windows stores the window handle required by this function. This handle identifies the window that has the clipboard open. On receipt of an *EmptyClipboard* call, Windows establishes this window as the new clipboard owner.

A program that uses delayed rendering has to process three messages in its window procedure: WM_RENDERFORMAT, WM_RENDERALLFORMATS, and WM_DESTROYCLIP-BOARD. Windows sends your window procedure a WM_RENDERFORMAT message when another program calls *GetClipboardData*. The value of *wParam* is the format requested. When you process the WM_RENDERFORMAT message, don't open and empty the clipboard. Simply create a memory block for the format given by *wParam*, transfer the data to it, and call *SetClipboardData* with the correct format and the handle. Obviously, you'll need to retain information in your program in order to construct this data properly when processing WM_RENDERFORMAT. When another program calls *EmptyClipboard*, Windows sends your program a WM_DESTROYCLIPBOARD message. This tells you that the information to construct the clipboard data is no longer needed. You are no longer the clipboard owner.

If your program terminates while it is still the clipboard owner, and the clipboard still contains NULL data handles that your program set with *SetClipboardData*, you'll receive a WM_RENDERALLFORMATS message. You should open the clipboard, empty it, put the data in memory blocks, and call *SetClipboardData* for each format. Then close the clipboard. The WM_RENDERALLFORMATS message is one of the last messages your window procedure receives. It is followed by a WM_DESTROYCLIPBOARD message (because you've rendered all the data) and then the normal WM_DESTROY.

If your program can transfer only one format of data to the clipboard (text, for instance), you can combine the WM_RENDERALLFORMATS and WM_RENDERFORMAT processing. The code will look something like this:

```
case WM_RENDERALLFORMATS :
     OpenClipboard (hwnd) ;
     EmptyClipboard () ;
                                   // fall through
case WM_RENDERFORMAT :
```

```
[put text into global memory block]
SetClipboardData (CF_TEXT, hMem) ;

if (iMsg == WM_RENDERALLFORMATS)
    CloseClipboard () ;
return 0 ;
```

If your program uses several clipboard formats, then you will want to process the WM_RENDERFORMAT message only for the format requested by *wParam*. You don't need to process the WM_DESTROYCLIPBOARD message unless it is burdensome for your program to retain the information necessary to construct the data.

Private Data Formats

So far we've dealt with only the standard clipboard formats defined by Windows. However, you may want to use the clipboard to store a "private data format." Many word processors use this technique to store text that contains font and formatting information.

At first, this concept may seem nonsensical. If the purpose of the clipboard is to transfer data between applications, why should the clipboard contain data that only one application understands? The answer is simple: The clipboard also exists to allow the transfer of data to and from the same program (or perhaps between different instances of the same program), and any program obviously understands its own private formats.

There are several ways to use private data formats. The easiest involves data that is ostensibly in one of the standard clipboard formats (text, bitmap, or metafile) but that has meaning only to your program. In this case, you use one of the following *iFormat* values in your *SetClipboardData* and *GetClipboardData* calls: CF_DSPTEXT, CF_DSPBITMAP, CF_DSP-METAFILEPICT, or CF_DSPENHMETAFILE. The letters DSP stand for "display"—these formats allow Windows' clipboard viewer to display the data as text, a bitmap, or a metafile. However, another program that calls *GetClipboardData* using the normal CF_TEXT, CF_BITMAP, CF_METAFILEPICT, or CF_ENHMETAFILE format won't obtain this data.

If you use one of these formats to put data in the clipboard, you must also use the same format to get the data out. But how do you know if the data is from another instance of your program or from another program using one of these formats? Here's one way: You can first obtain the clipboard owner by calling:

```
hwndClipOwner = GetClipboardOwner () ;
```

You can then get the name of the window class of this window handle:

```
char szClassName[16] ;
[other program lines]
GetClassName (hwndClipOwner, &szClassName, 16) ;
```

If the class name is the same as your program's, then the data was put in the clipboard by another instance of your program.

The second way to use private formats involves the CF_OWNERDISPLAY flag. The memory handle to *SetClipboardData* is NULL:

```
SetClipboardData (CF_OWNERDISPLAY, NULL) ;
```

This is the method that some word processors use to show formatted text in the client area of the clipboard viewer included with Windows 95. Obviously, the clipboard viewer does not know how to display this formatted text. When a word processor specifies the CF_OWNERDISPLAY format, it is also taking responsibility for painting the clipboard viewer's client area.

Because the memory handle is NULL, a program that calls *SetClipboardData* with the CF_OWNERDISPLAY format (the clipboard owner) must process the delayed rendering messages sent to the clipboard owner by Windows as well as five additional messages. These five messages are sent by the clipboard viewer to the clipboard owner:

■ WM_ASKCBFORMATNAME—The clipboard viewer sends this message to the clipboard owner to get a name for the format of the data. The *lParam* parameter is a pointer to a buffer, and *wParam* is the maximum number of characters for this buffer. The clipboard owner must copy the name of the clipboard format into this buffer.

■ WM_SIZECLIPBOARD—This message tells the clipboard owner that the size of the clipboard viewer's client area has changed. The *wParam* parameter is a handle to the clipboard viewer, and *lParam* is a pointer to a RECT structure containing the new size. If the RECT structure contains all zeros, the clipboard viewer is being destroyed or made an icon. Although Windows' clipboard viewer allows only one instance of itself to be running, other clipboard viewers can also send this message to the clipboard owner. Handling these multiple clipboard viewers isn't impossible for the clipboard owner (given that *wParam* identifies the particular viewer), but it isn't easy, either.

■ WM_PAINTCLIPBOARD—This message tells the clipboard owner to update the clipboard viewer's client area. Again, *wParam* is a handle to the clipboard viewer's window. The *lParam* parameter is a handle to a PAINTSTRUCT structure. The clipboard owner can obtain a handle to the clipboard viewer's device context from the *hdc* field of this structure.

■ WM_HSCROLLCLIPBOARD and WM_VSCROLLCLIPBOARD—These messages inform the clipboard owner that a user has scrolled the clipboard viewer's scroll bars. The *wParam* parameter is a handle to the clipboard viewer's window, the low word of *lParam* is the scrolling request and the high word of *lParam* is the thumb position if the low word is SB_THUMBPOSITION.

Handling these messages may look like more trouble than it's worth. However, the process does provide a benefit to the user: When copying text from a word processor to the clipboard, the user will find it comforting to see the text still formatted in the clipboard viewer's client area.

The third way to use private clipboard data formats is to register your own clipboard format name. You supply a name for this format to Windows, and Windows gives your program a number to use as the format parameter in *SetClipboardData* and *GetClipboardData*. Programs that use this method generally also copy data to the clipboard in one of the standard formats. This approach allows the clipboard viewer to display data in its client area (without the hassles involved with CF_OWNERDISPLAY) and permits other programs to copy data from the clipboard.

As an example, let's assume we've written a vector drawing program that copies data to the clipboard in a bitmap format, a metafile format, and its own registered clipboard format. The clipboard viewer will display the metafile. Other programs that can read bitmaps or metafiles from the clipboard will obtain those formats. However, when the vector drawing program itself needs to read data from the clipboard, it will copy the data in its own registered format because that format probably contains more information than the bitmap or metafile.

A program registers a new clipboard format by calling:

```
iFormat = RegisterClipboardFormat (pszFormatName) ;
```

The *iFormat* value is between 0xC000 and 0xFFFF. A clipboard viewer (or a program that obtains all the current clipboard formats by calling *EnumClipboardFormats*) can obtain the ASCII name of this format by calling:

```
GetClipboardFormatName (iFormat, psBuffer, iMaxCount) ;
```

Windows copies up to *iMaxCount* characters into *psBuffer*.

Programmers who use this method for copying data to the clipboard might want to publicize the format name and the actual format of the data. If the program becomes popular, other programs can then copy data in this format from the clipboard.

BECOMING A CLIPBOARD VIEWER

A program that is notified of changes in the clipboard contents is called a "clipboard viewer." You get a clipboard viewer with Windows 95, but you can also write your own clipboard viewer program. Clipboard viewers are notified of changes to the clipboard through messages to the viewer's window procedure.

The Clipboard Viewer Chain

Any number of clipboard viewer applications can be running in Windows at the same time, and they can all be notified of changes to the clipboard. From Windows' perspective, however, there is only one clipboard viewer, which I'll call the "current clipboard viewer." Windows maintains only one window handle to identify the current clipboard viewer, and it sends messages only to that window when the contents of the clipboard change.

Clipboard viewer applications have the responsibility of participating in the "clipboard viewer chain" so that all running clipboard viewer programs receive the messages that Windows sends to the current clipboard viewer. When a program registers itself as a clipboard viewer, that program becomes the current clipboard viewer. Windows gives that program the window handle of the previous current clipboard viewer, and the program saves this handle. When the program receives a clipboard viewer message, it sends that message to the window procedure of the next program in the clipboard chain.

Clipboard Viewer Functions and Messages

A program can become part of the clipboard viewer chain by calling the *SetClipboardViewer* function. If the primary purpose of the program is to serve as a clipboard viewer, the program can call this function during processing of the WM_CREATE message. The function returns the window handle of the previous current clipboard viewer. The program should save that handle in a static variable:

```
static HWND hwndNextViewer ;
[other program lines]

case WM_CREATE :
    [other program lines]

    hwndNextViewer = SetClipboardViewer (hwnd) ;
```

If your program is the first program to become a clipboard viewer during the Windows session, then *hwndNextViewer* will be NULL.

Windows sends a WM_DRAWCLIPBOARD message to the current clipboard viewer (the most recent window to register itself as a clipboard viewer) whenever the contents of the clipboard change. Each program in the clipboard viewer chain should use *SendMessage* to pass this message to the next clipboard viewer. The last program in the clipboard viewer chain (the first window to register itself as a clipboard viewer) will have stored a NULL *hwndNextViewer* value. If *hwndNextViewer* is NULL, the program simply returns without sending the message to another program. (Don't confuse the WM_DRAWCLIPBOARD and WM_PAINTCLIPBOARD messages. The WM_PAINTCLIPBOARD message is sent by a clipboard viewer to programs that use the CF_OWNERDISPLAY clipboard format. The WM_DRAWCLIPBOARD message is sent by Windows to the current clipboard viewer.)

The easiest way to process the WM_DRAWCLIPBOARD message is to send the message to the next clipboard viewer (unless *hwndNextViewer* is NULL) and invalidate the client area of your window:

```
case WM_DRAWCLIPBOARD :
     if (hwndNextViewer)
          SendMessage (hwndNextViewer, iMsg, wParam, lParam) ;

     InvalidateRect (hwnd, NULL, TRUE) ;
     return 0 ;
```

During processing of the WM_PAINT message, you can read the contents of the clipboard by using the normal *OpenClipboard*, *GetClipboardData*, and *CloseClipboard* calls.

When a program wants to remove itself from the clipboard viewer chain, it must call *ChangeClipboardChain*. This function requires the window handle of the program leaving the viewer chain and the window handle of the next clipboard viewer:

```
ChangeClipboardChain (hwnd, hwndNextViewer) ;
```

When a program calls *ChangeClipboardChain*, Windows sends a WM_CHANGECBCHAIN message to the current clipboard viewer. The *wParam* parameter is the handle of the window removing itself from the chain (the first parameter to *ChangeClipboardChain*), and *lParam* is the window handle of the next clipboard viewer after the one removing itself from the chain (the second parameter to *ChangeClipboardChain*).

When your program receives a WM_CHANGECBCHAIN message, you must therefore check to see if *wParam* is equal to the value of *hwndNextViewer* that you've saved. If it is, your program must set *hwndNextViewer* to *lParam*. This action ensures that any future WM_DRAWCLIPBOARD messages you get won't be sent to the window removing itself from the clipboard viewer chain. If *wParam* isn't equal to *hwndNextViewer*, and *hwndNextViewer* isn't NULL, send the message to the next clipboard viewer:

```
case WM_CHANGECBCHAIN :
     if ((HWND) wParam == hwndNextViewer)
          hwndNextViewer = (HWND) lParam ;

     else if (hwndNextViewer)
          SendMessage (hwndNextViewer, iMsg, wParam, lParam) ;
     return 0 ;
```

You shouldn't need to include the *else if* statement, which checks *hwndNextViewer* for a non-NULL value. A NULL *hwndNextViewer* value would indicate that the program executing this code is the last viewer on the chain, in which case the message should never have gotten this far.

If your program is still in the clipboard viewer chain when it is about to terminate, you must remove it from the chain. You can do this during processing of the WM_DESTROY message by calling *ChangeClipboardChain*:

```
case WM_DESTROY :
     ChangeClipboardChain (hwnd, hwndNextViewer) ;
     PostQuitMessage (0) ;
     return 0 ;
```

Windows also has a function that allows a program to obtain the window handle of the first clipboard viewer:

```
hwndViewer = GetClipboardViewer () ;
```

This function isn't normally needed. The return value can be NULL if there is no current clipboard viewer.

Here's an example to illustrate how the clipboard viewer chain works. When Windows first starts up, the current clipboard viewer is NULL:

Current clipboard viewer:	NULL

A program with a window handle of *hwnd1* calls *SetClipboardViewer*. The function returns NULL, which becomes the *hwndNextViewer* value in this program:

Current clipboard viewer:	*hwnd1*
hwnd1's next viewer:	NULL

A second program, with a window handle of *hwnd2*, now calls *SetClipboardViewer* and gets back *hwnd1*:

Current clipboard viewer:	*hwnd2*
hwnd2's next viewer:	*hwnd1*
hwnd1's next viewer:	NULL

A third program (*hwnd3*) and then a fourth (*hwnd4*) also call *SetClipboardViewer* and get back *hwnd2* and *hwnd3*:

Current clipboard viewer:	*hwnd4*
hwnd4's next viewer:	*hwnd3*
hwnd3's next viewer:	*hwnd2*
hwnd2's next viewer:	*hwnd1*
hwnd1's next viewer:	NULL

When the contents of the clipboard change, Windows sends a WM_DRAWCLIPBOARD message to *hwnd4*, *hwnd4* sends the message to *hwnd3*, *hwnd3* sends it to *hwnd2*, *hwnd2* sends it to *hwnd1*, and *hwnd1* returns.

Now *hwnd2* decides to remove itself from the chain by calling:

```
ChangeClipboardChain (hwnd2, hwnd1) ;
```

Windows sends *hwnd4* a WM_CHANGECBCHAIN message with *wParam* equal to *hwnd2* and *lParam* equal to *hwnd1*. Because *hwnd4*'s next viewer is *hwnd3*, *hwnd4* sends this message to *hwnd3*. Now *hwnd3* notes that *wParam* is equal to its next viewer (*hwnd2*), so it sets its next viewer equal to *lParam* (*hwnd1*) and returns. The mission is accomplished. The clipboard viewer chain now looks like this:

Current clipboard viewer:	*hwnd4*
hwnd4's next viewer:	*hwnd3*
hwnd3's next viewer:	*hwnd1*
hwnd1's next viewer:	NULL

A Simple Clipboard Viewer

Clipboard viewers don't have to be as sophisticated as the one provided with Windows 95. A clipboard viewer can, for instance, display a single clipboard format. The CLIPVIEW program, shown in Figure 16-1, is a clipboard viewer that displays only the CF_TEXT format.

CLIPVIEW.MAK

```
#------------------------
# CLIPVIEW.MAK make file
#------------------------

clipview.exe : clipview.obj
     $(LINKER) $(GUIFLAGS) -OUT:clipview.exe clipview.obj $(GUILIBS)

clipview.obj : clipview.c
     $(CC) $(CFLAGS) clipview.c
```

CLIPVIEW.C

```
/*------------------------------------------------
   CLIPVIEW.C -- Simple Clipboard Viewer
                (c) Charles Petzold, 1996
  ------------------------------------------------*/
#include <windows.h>

LRESULT CALLBACK WndProc (HWND, UINT, WPARAM, LPARAM) ;
```

Figure 16-1. *The CLIPVIEW program.* (continued)

```
int WINAPI WinMain (HINSTANCE hInstance, HINSTANCE hPrevInstance,
                    PSTR szCmdLine, int iCmdShow)
    {
    static char   szAppName[] = "ClipView" ;
    HWND          hwnd ;
    MSG           msg ;
    WNDCLASSEX    wndclass

    wndclass.cbSize        = sizeof (wndclass) ;
    wndclass.style         = CS_HREDRAW | CS_VREDRAW ;
    wndclass.lpfnWndProc   = WndProc ;
    wndclass.cbClsExtra    = 0 ;
    wndclass.cbWndExtra    = 0 ;
    wndclass.hInstance     = hInstance ;
    wndclass.hIcon         = NULL ;
    wndclass.hCursor       = LoadCursor (NULL, IDC_ARROW) ;
    wndclass.hbrBackground = (HBRUSH) GetStockObject (WHITE_BRUSH) ;
    wndclass.lpszMenuName  = NULL ;
    wndclass.lpszClassName = szAppName ;
    wndclass.hIconSm       = LoadIcon (NULL, IDI_APPLICATION) ;

    RegisterClassEx (&wndclass) ;

    hwnd = CreateWindow (szAppName, "Simple Clipboard Viewer (Text Only)",
                         WS_OVERLAPPEDWINDOW,
                         CW_USEDEFAULT, CW_USEDEFAULT,
                         CW_USEDEFAULT, CW_USEDEFAULT,
                         NULL, NULL, hInstance, NULL) ;

    ShowWindow (hwnd, iCmdShow) ;
    UpdateWindow (hwnd) ;

    while (GetMessage (&msg, NULL, 0, 0))
        {
        TranslateMessage (&msg) ;
        DispatchMessage (&msg) ;
        }
    return msg.wParam ;
    }

LRESULT CALLBACK WndProc (HWND hwnd, UINT iMsg, WPARAM wParam, LPARAM lParam)
    {
    static HWND hwndNextViewer ;
    HGLOBAL     hGMem ;
    HDC         hdc ;
```

(continued)

```
          PSTR        pGMem ;
          PAINTSTRUCT ps ;
          RECT        rect ;

          switch (iMsg)
               {
               case WM_CREATE :
                    hwndNextViewer = SetClipboardViewer (hwnd) ;
                    return 0 ;

               case WM_CHANGECBCHAIN :
                    if ((HWND) wParam == hwndNextViewer)
                         hwndNextViewer = (HWND) lParam ;

                    else if (hwndNextViewer)
                         SendMessage (hwndNextViewer, iMsg, wParam, lParam) ;

                    return 0 ;

               case WM_DRAWCLIPBOARD :
                    if (hwndNextViewer)
                         SendMessage (hwndNextViewer, iMsg, wParam, lParam) ;

                    InvalidateRect (hwnd, NULL, TRUE) ;
                    return 0 ;

               case WM_PAINT :
                    hdc = BeginPaint (hwnd, &ps) ;
                    GetClientRect (hwnd, &rect) ;
                    OpenClipboard (hwnd) ;

                    hGMem = GetClipboardData (CF_TEXT) ;

                    if (hGMem != NULL)
                         {
                         pGMem = (PSTR) GlobalLock (hGMem) ;
                         DrawText (hdc, pGMem, -1, &rect, DT_EXPANDTABS) ;
                         GlobalUnlock (hGMem) ;
                         }

                    CloseClipboard () ;
                    EndPaint (hwnd, &ps) ;
                    return 0 ;
```

(continued)

```
       case WM_DESTROY :
            ChangeClipboardChain (hwnd, hwndNextViewer) ;
            PostQuitMessage (0) ;
            return 0 ;
       }
     return DefWindowProc (hwnd, iMsg, wParam, lParam) ;
     }
```

The CLIPVIEW program processes WM_CREATE, WM_CHANGECBCHAIN, WM-_DRAWCLIPBOARD, and WM_DESTROY messages as discussed above. The WM_PAINT message simply opens the clipboard and uses *GetClipboardData* with a format of CF_TEXT. If the function returns a memory handle, CLIPVIEW locks it and uses *DrawText* to display the text in its client area.

A clipboard viewer that handles data formats beyond the five standard formats (as the one supplied with Windows 95 does) has additional work to do, such as displaying the names of all the formats currently in the clipboard. You can do this by calling *EnumClipboardFormats* and obtaining the names of the nonstandard formats from *GetClipboardFormatName*. A clipboard viewer that uses the CF_OWNERDISPLAY format must send these four messages to the clipboard to display the data:

WM_PAINTCLIPBOARD   WM_VSCROLLCLIPBOARD

WM_SIZECLIPBOARD   WM_HSCROLLCLIPBOARD

If you want to write such a clipboard viewer, you have to obtain the window handle of the clipboard owner using *GetClipboardOwner* and send that window these messages when you need to update the clipboard viewer's client area.

## Chapter 17

Dynamic Data Exchange (DDE)

Dynamic Data Exchange (DDE) is one of several mechanisms of interprocess communication (IPC) supported under Windows 95. Three other means discussed in this book are the Windows clipboard (which I discuss in Chapter 16), shared memory in dynamic link libraries (Chapter 19), and OLE (Chapter 20). DDE is less ambitious (and less capable) than OLE, but generally easier to implement.

DDE is based on the messaging system built into Windows. Two Windows programs carry on a DDE "conversation" by posting messages to each other. These two programs are known as the "server" and the "client." A DDE server is the program that has access to data that may be useful to other Windows programs. A DDE client is the program that obtains this data from the server.

In Windows 95, programs can optionally use the DDE Management Library (DDEML), which simplifies DDE in several ways. DDEML insulates the program from DDE messaging by providing a high-level function call layer. Programs using DDEML respond to DDE messages using a call-back function. The two methods of using DDE are compatible because DDEML is built on top of the DDE messaging system.

In this chapter, I'll first discuss the traditional approach to DDE and then show how the interprocess-communication problem is solved using DDEML.

A DDE conversation is initiated by the client program. The client broadcasts a message (called WM_DDE_INITIATE) to all currently running Windows programs. This message indicates a general category of data the client needs. A DDE server that has this data can respond to this broadcasted message. At that point, the conversation begins.

A single Windows program can be both a client to one program and a server to another, but this requires two different DDE conversations. A server can deliver data to multiple clients, and a client can obtain data from multiple servers, but again, this requires multiple DDE conversations. To keep these conversations unique and separate, each conversation (on both the client and server sides) uses a different window. Generally, a program that supports DDE will create a hidden child window for each conversation it maintains.

The programs involved in a DDE conversation need not be specifically coded to work with each other. As I'll discuss in the next section of this chapter, generally the writer of a DDE server will publicly document how the data is identified. A user of a program that can act as a DDE client (such as Microsoft Excel) can use this information to establish a DDE conversation between the two programs.

If you write a family of two or more Windows programs that must communicate with each other but not with other Windows programs, you may consider defining your own messaging protocol. However, if two or more of your programs must write as well as read shared data, you must place the data in a memory-mapped file. As we'll see later in this chapter, DDE clients never write data, only read it. A DDE server can therefore safely allocate memory with the *GlobalAlloc* or *HeapAlloc* function.

Because DDE uses the messaging system built into Windows, it fits very naturally in the environment. But this is not to say that DDE is easy to implement. The protocol has many options, and programs must be ready to deal with some rather tricky problems.

BASIC CONCEPTS

When a client asks a server for data, it must be able to identify the type of data it wants. This is done with three character strings, called the "application," the data "topic," and the data "item."

Application, Topic, and Item

The idea of the application, topic, and item is best approached with an example. In the first half of this chapter, I'll show you how to write a Windows DDE server program called DDEPOP1. This program contains population data of the United States from the 1970, 1980, and 1990 censuses. Based on a quadratic extrapolation, the program can calculate the instantaneous ("at this moment") population of any state or of the United States as a whole.

Anybody who writes a DDE server program should document how this data is identified using three character strings:

■ The server application name—In this example, this is simply "DDEPOP1". Each server has only one application name, the name of the program.

■   The topic name—All DDE servers support at least one topic. In the case of DDEPOP1, only one topic is supported, which is identified by the string "US_Population". Conceivably, the DDEPOP1 program could be expanded to include data concerning the square-mile areas of the states, in which case the program would support a second topic named "US_Area".

■   The item name—Within each topic, a DDE server supports one or more data items. In DDEPOP1, the item identifies the state using the standard two-character post office abbreviation, such as "NY" for New York, "CA" for California, and "US" for the total. DDEPOP1 supports 52 items—the 50 states, the District of Columbia ("DC"), and the total.

This documentation is sufficient to use the DDEPOP1 server with another Windows program that can act as a client, for example, Microsoft Excel. To use DDEPOP1 with Microsoft Excel, you can type the following into a spreadsheet cell:

```
=DDEPOP1!US_Population!US
```

These three strings indicate the application, topic, and item (in this case, the total United States population). If DDEPOP1.EXE is not already running, Microsoft Excel will attempt to execute it. (DDEPOP1 must be in the current directory or in a directory listed in the PATH environment variable.) If successful, Excel will initiate a DDE conversation with DDEPOP1, obtain the population data, and display the population as a number in the cell. These population figures can be formatted, graphed, or used in calculations.

What's most interesting is that the population figures will be periodically updated in the spreadsheet. This is known as a "hot link" or (in a slight variation) "warm link." Every 5 seconds, DDEPOP1 recalculates the population data and notifies a client when an item has changed. In the case of the total U.S. population, you'll see the figure increase by 1 about every 15 seconds.

The Types of Conversations

There are three basic types of DDE conversations—cold link, hot link, and warm link. These conversations use DDE messages defined in the DDE.H header file. The simplest of the three conversations is the cold link.

1.   **The Cold Link**

A cold link conversation begins when a client broadcasts a WM_DDE-_INITIATE message identifying the application and topic it requires. (The application and topic may be set to NULL to begin a conversation with any server application or any data topic.) A server application that supports the specified topic responds to the client with a WM_DDE_ACK ("acknowledge") message:

The client then requests a particular data item by posting a WM_DDE-_REQUEST message. If the server can supply this data item, it responds by posting a WM_DDE_DATA message to the client:

I've also indicated here that the client can acknowledge to the server that it has received the WM_DDE_DATA message. This is optional (which I've indicated by putting the WM_DDE_ACK message within parentheses). The server indicates whether it wants this acknowledgment in a flag passed with the WM-_DDE_DATA message. A flag passed with the WM_DDE_ACK message indicates a "positive" acknowledgment.

If the client posts a WM_DDE_REQUEST message to the server, and the server cannot supply the requested data item, then the server posts a "negative" WM_DDE_ACK message to the client:

The DDE conversation continues with the client posting WM _DDE_REQUEST messages to the server—for the same data item or different data items—and the server responding with WM_DDE_DATA or WM_DDE_ACK messages. The conversation is terminated when the client and server post each other WM-_DDE_TERMINATE messages:

Although I've indicated that the client posts the first WM_DDE_TERMINATE message, this is not always the case. The server can post the first WM_DDE-_TERMINATE message, and the client must respond to that.

2. The Hot Link

One problem with the cold link is that the data the server has access to may change with the passing of time. (This is the case with DDEPOP1, which calculates an instantaneous population that can change.) In the cold link, the client does not know when the data changes. The hot link solves this problem.

Again, the DDE conversation begins with a WM_DDE_INITIATE message and a WM_DDE_ACK message:

The client indicates the data item it requires by posting a WM_DDE_ADVISE message to the server. The server responds by posting a WM_DDE_ACK message indicating if it has access to this item:

A positive acknowledgment indicates that the server can supply the data; a negative acknowledgment indicates that it cannot.

At this point, the server is obligated to notify the client whenever the value of the data item changes. This notification uses a WM_DDE_DATA message, to which the client (based on a flag set in the WM_DDE_DATA message) may or may not respond with a WM_DDE_ACK message:

When the client no longer wishes to be advised of updates to the data item, it posts a WM_DDE_UNADVISE message to the server, and the server acknowledges:

The conversation is terminated with the posting of WM_DDE_TERMINATE messages:

The cold link and the hot link are not mutually exclusive. During a single DDE conversation, a client may ask for some data items by using WM_DDE-_REQUEST (for a cold link) and ask for others by using WM_DDE_ADVISE (for a hot link).

3. The Warm Link

The warm link combines elements of the cold link and hot link. The conversation begins as normal:

As with the hot link, the client posts a WM_DDE_ADVISE message to the server, and the server acknowledges either positively or negatively:

However, a flag passed with the WM_DDE_ADVISE message indicates that the client wishes only to be informed of changes in data without immediately receiving the new data item. So the server posts WM_DDE_DATA messages with NULL data whenever the data item changes:

Now the client knows that a particular data item has changed. To obtain this item, the client uses a WM_DDE_REQUEST message, just as in the cold link:

As in the hot link, a client can stop being advised of changes in data items by posting a WM_DDE_UNADVISE message to the server:

The conversation is terminated with the WM_DDE_TERMINATE messages:

These three types of conversations use all the DDE messages except two: WM_DDE-_POKE (in which a client gives a server unsolicited data) and WM_DDE_EXECUTE (in which a client sends a command string to a server). I won't be covering these messages in this chapter.

The DDE.H header file also defines four structures:

- DDEACK (used in the WM_DDE_ACK message)

- DDEADVISE (used in the WM_DDE_ADVISE message)

- DDEDATA (used in the WM_DDE_DATA message)

- DDEPOKE (used in the WM_DDE_POKE message)

I'll deal with the first three structures as I discuss the sample programs in this chapter.

Character Strings and Atoms

I've discussed how a DDE client and server identify data using three character strings—the application, topic, and item. But in the actual messages between the client and server, these character strings do not appear: "Atoms" are used instead.

Atoms are WORD values that refer to character strings in a case-insensitive manner. You can use atoms within your own program for working with character strings, in which case the atom table (the table that references the atom values with the strings) is stored in your program's data space.

You define an atom as follows:

```
ATOM aAtom ;
```

You can add a string to the atom table using the function:

```
aAtom = AddAtom (pString) ;
```

If the character string does not already exist in the atom table, this function adds it and returns a unique value identifying the string. Each atom has a "reference count," which is the number of times *AddAtom* has been called for the same string. The reference count is initially set to 1. If the character string already exists in the atom table (that is, if this is the second or subsequent time that *AddAtom* has been called for the same string), the function returns the number identifying the character string and increments the reference count.

The function:

```
DeleteAtom (aAtom) ;
```

decrements the reference count. When the count is 0, the atom and character string are removed from the atom table.

The function:

```
aAtom = FindAtom (pString) ;
```

will return the atom associated with the character string (or 0 if the string is not in the atom table). This function does not affect the reference count of the atom.

The function:

```
iBytes = GetAtomName (aAtom, pBuffer, iBufferSize) ;
```

returns the character string for an atom. The last parameter indicates the size of the buffer pointed to by the second parameter. The function returns the number of bytes copied to the buffer and does not affect the reference count.

These four functions (there are several others of lesser importance) allow you to work with atoms within your own program. However, because the atom table is stored in your program's data space, the atoms are unique to your program. To use atoms with DDE, you must use another set of four functions, similar to the functions described above:

```
aAtom = GlobalAddAtom (pString) ;
GlobalDeleteAtom (aAtom) ;
aAtom = GlobalFindAtom (pString) ;
iBytes = GlobalGetAtomName (aAtom, pBuffer, iBufferSize) ;
```

The atom table for these atoms is stored in a shared memory space in a dynamic link library within Windows and hence is common to all Windows programs. One program can use *GlobalAddAtom* to add a string to the atom table and pass the atom to another program. This other program can use *GlobalGetAtomName* to obtain the character string associated with the atom. This is how Windows programs identify the DDE application, topic, and item.

The rules regarding the use of atoms with DDE are extremely important: It is not good if an atom that is still required by one program is deleted from the atom table by another program. Neither is it good if atoms that are no longer required are not deleted from the atom table. For this reason, you must be careful about how your program handles atoms.

Atoms are used for the DDE application, topic, and item strings. The data structures that are transferred from one Windows program to another can be allocated either from the heap using *GlobalAlloc* or *HeapAlloc*, or as memory-mapped files. Either method allows the data to be shared among multiple Windows programs. However, I don't recommend using memory-mapped files for DDE conversations because they provide a client the opportunity to overwrite or corrupt the data. By allocating a memory block from the heap, the server ensures the data is "read only" to all clients. The DDE rules that govern which program is responsible for allocating and freeing these memory blocks are also quite strict.

In Win32, *GlobalAlloc* is just a wrapper for *HeapAlloc*, and the memory it reserves is private to the caller. Other processes can't touch it. Even the GMEM_DDESHARE (and GMEM_SHARE) flags make no difference, because *GlobalAlloc* ignores them. So how does a DDE client see the data stored in the server's private memory? It doesn't. When the server posts a WM_DDE_DATA message to a client, Windows makes a copy of the referenced DDEDATA structure that holds the data. The client sees a copy of the allocated memory block, not the block itself.

A DDE SERVER PROGRAM

We are now ready to begin looking at DDEPOP1, the DDE server program that can supply instantaneous state population data to a DDE client. This program is shown in Figure 17-1. Note that although *GlobalAlloc* does not require the GMEM_DDESHARE flag, the source listing below includes the flag for the sake of clarity.

DDEPOP1.MAK

```
#----------------------
# DDEPOP1.MAK make file
#----------------------

ddepop1.exe : ddepop1.obj ddepop1.res
     $(LINKER) $(GUIFLAGS) -OUT:ddepop1.exe ddepop1.obj ddepop1.res $(GUILIBS)

ddepop1.obj : ddepop1.c ddepop.h
     $(CC) $(CFLAGS) ddepop1.c

ddepop1.res : ddepop1.rc ddepop.ico
     $(RC) $(RCVARS) ddepop1.rc
```

DDEPOP.C

```c
/*--------------------------------------------------
   DDEPOP1.C -- DDE Server for Population Data
                (c) Charles Petzold, 1996
   --------------------------------------------------*/

#include <windows.h>
#include <dde.h>
#include <string.h>
#include "ddepop.h"

typedef struct
     {
     unsigned int fAdvise:1 ;
     unsigned int fDeferUpd:1 ;
     unsigned int fAckReq:1 ;
     unsigned int dummy:13 ;
     long         lPopPrev ;
     }
```

Figure 17-1. *The DDEPOP1 program.*   *(continued)*

```
    POPADVISE ;

#define ID_TIMER    1
#define DDE_TIMEOUT 3000

LRESULT CALLBACK WndProc       (HWND, UINT, WPARAM, LPARAM) ;
LRESULT CALLBACK ServerProc    (HWND, UINT, WPARAM, LPARAM) ;
BOOL    CALLBACK TimerEnumProc (HWND, LONG) ;
BOOL    CALLBACK CloseEnumProc (HWND, LONG) ;
BOOL             PostDataMessage (HWND, HWND, int, BOOL, BOOL, BOOL) ;

char      szAppName[]     = "DdePop1" ;
char      szServerClass[] = "DdePop1.Server" ;
HINSTANCE hInst ;

int WINAPI WinMain (HINSTANCE hInstance, HINSTANCE hPrevInstance,
                    PSTR szCmdLine, int iCmdShow)
    {
    HWND        hwnd ;
    MSG         msg ;
    WNDCLASSEX  wndclass ;

    hInst = hInstance ;

            // Register window class

    wndclass.cbSize        = sizeof (wndclass) ;
    wndclass.style         = 0 ;
    wndclass.lpfnWndProc   = WndProc ;
    wndclass.cbClsExtra    = 0 ;
    wndclass.cbWndExtra    = 0 ;
    wndclass.hInstance     = hInstance ;
    wndclass.hIcon         = LoadIcon (hInstance, szAppName) ;
    wndclass.hCursor       = LoadCursor (NULL, IDC_ARROW) ;
    wndclass.hbrBackground = (HBRUSH) GetStockObject (WHITE_BRUSH) ;
    wndclass.lpszMenuName  = NULL ;
    wndclass.lpszClassName = szAppName ;
    wndclass.hIconSm       = LoadIcon (hInstance, szAppName) ;

    RegisterClassEx (&wndclass) ;

            // Register window class for DDE Server

    wndclass.cbSize        = sizeof (wndclass) ;
    wndclass.style         = 0 ;
```

(continued)

```
      wndclass.lpfnWndProc   = ServerProc ;
      wndclass.cbClsExtra    = 0 ;
      wndclass.cbWndExtra    = 2 * sizeof (DWORD) ;
      wndclass.hInstance     = hInstance ;
      wndclass.hIcon         = NULL ;
      wndclass.hCursor       = NULL ;
      wndclass.hbrBackground = NULL ;
      wndclass.lpszMenuName  = NULL ;
      wndclass.lpszClassName = szServerClass ;
      wndclass.hIconSm       = NULL ;

      RegisterClassEx (&wndclass) ;

      hwnd = CreateWindow (szAppName, "DDE Population Server",
                      WS_OVERLAPPEDWINDOW,
                      CW_USEDEFAULT, CW_USEDEFAULT,
                      CW_USEDEFAULT, CW_USEDEFAULT,
                      NULL, NULL, hInstance, NULL) ;

      InitPops () ;                       // initialize 'pop' structure

      SetTimer (hwnd, ID_TIMER, 5000, NULL) ;

      ShowWindow (hwnd, SW_SHOWMINNOACTIVE) ;
      UpdateWindow (hwnd) ;

      while (GetMessage (&msg, NULL, 0, 0))
           {
           TranslateMessage (&msg) ;
           DispatchMessage (&msg) ;
           }

      KillTimer (hwnd, ID_TIMER) ;

      return msg.wParam ;
      }

LRESULT CALLBACK WndProc (HWND hwnd, UINT iMsg, WPARAM wParam, LPARAM lParam)
      {
      static char szTopic[] = "US_Population" ;
      ATOM        aApp, aTop ;
      HWND        hwndClient, hwndServer ;

      switch (iMsg)
```

(continued)

```
          {
          case WM_DDE_INITIATE :

                    // wParam          -- sending window handle
                    // LOWORD (lParam) -- application atom
                    // HIWORD (lParam) -- topic atom

               hwndClient = (HWND) wParam ;

               aApp = GlobalAddAtom (szAppName) ;
               aTop = GlobalAddAtom (szTopic) ;

                    // Check for matching atoms, create window, and
                    //   acknowledge

               if ((LOWORD (lParam) == NULL || LOWORD (lParam) == aApp) &&
                    (HIWORD (lParam) == NULL || HIWORD (lParam) == aTop))
                    {
                    hwndServer = CreateWindow (szServerClass, NULL,
                                           WS_CHILD, 0, 0, 0, 0,
                                           hwnd, NULL, hInst, NULL) ;

                    SetWindowLong (hwndServer, 0, (LONG) hwndClient) ;
                    SendMessage ((HWND) wParam, WM_DDE_ACK,
                              (WPARAM) hwndServer,
                              MAKELPARAM (aApp, aTop)) ;
                    }

                    // Otherwise, delete the atoms just created

               else
                    {
                    GlobalDeleteAtom (aApp) ;
                    GlobalDeleteAtom (aTop) ;
                    }

               return 0 ;

          case WM_TIMER :
          case WM_TIMECHANGE :

                    // Calculate new current populations

               CalcPops () ;
```

(continued)

```
                    // Notify all child windows

            EnumChildWindows (hwnd, &TimerEnumProc, 0L) ;
            return 0 ;

      case WM_QUERYOPEN :
            return 0 ;

      case WM_CLOSE :

                    // Notify all child windows

            EnumChildWindows (hwnd, &CloseEnumProc, 0L) ;

            break ;                        // for default processing

      case WM_DESTROY :
            PostQuitMessage (0) ;
            return 0 ;
      }
    return DefWindowProc (hwnd, iMsg, wParam, lParam) ;
    }

LRESULT CALLBACK ServerProc (HWND hwnd, UINT iMsg, WPARAM wParam, LPARAM lParam)
    {
    ATOM          aItem ;
    char          szItem[10] ;
    DDEACK        DdeAck ;
    DDEADVISE     *pDdeAdvise ;
    DWORD         dwTime ;
    GLOBALHANDLE  hPopAdvise, hDdeAdvise, hCommands, hDdePoke ;
    int           i ;
    UINT          uiLow, uiHi ;
    HWND          hwndClient ;
    MSG           msg ;
    POPADVISE     *pPopAdvise ;
    WORD          cfFormat, wStatus ;

    switch (iMsg)
        {
        case WM_CREATE :

                    // Allocate memory for POPADVISE structures
```

(continued)

```
                    hPopAdvise = GlobalAlloc (GHND, NUM_STATES * sizeof (POPADVISE)) ;

               if (hPopAdvise == NULL)
                    DestroyWindow (hwnd) ;
               else
                    SetWindowLong (hwnd, 4, (LONG) hPopAdvise) ;

               return 0 ;

     case WM_DDE_REQUEST :

                    // wParam          -- sending window handle
                    // LOWORD (lParam) -- data format
                    // HIWORD (lParam) -- item atom

               hwndClient = (HWND) wParam ;
               cfFormat   = LOWORD (lParam) ;
               aItem      = HIWORD (lParam) ;

                    // Check for matching format and data item

               if (cfFormat == CF_TEXT)
                    {
                    GlobalGetAtomName (aItem, szItem, sizeof (szItem)) ;

                    for (i = 0 ; i < NUM_STATES ; i++)
                         if (strcmp (szItem, pop[i].szState) == 0)
                              break ;

                    if (i < NUM_STATES)
                         {
                         GlobalDeleteAtom (aItem) ;
                         PostDataMessage (hwnd, hwndClient, i,
                                        FALSE, FALSE, TRUE) ;
                         return 0 ;
                         }
                    }

                    // Negative acknowledge if no match

               DdeAck.bAppReturnCode = 0 ;
               DdeAck.reserved       = 0 ;
               DdeAck.fBusy          = FALSE ;
               DdeAck.fAck           = FALSE ;
```

(continued)

```
            wStatus = *((WORD *) &DdeAck) ;

            if (!PostMessage (hwndClient, WM_DDE_ACK, (WPARAM) hwnd,
                         PackDDElParam (WM_DDE_ACK, wStatus, aItem)))
                 {
                 GlobalDeleteAtom (aItem) ;
                 }

        return 0 ;

   case WM_DDE_ADVISE :

            // wParam -- sending window handle
            // lParam -- DDEADVISE memory handle & item atom

        UnpackDDElParam (WM_DDE_ADVISE, lParam, &uiLow, &uiHi) ;
        FreeDDElParam (WM_DDE_ADVISE, lParam) ;

        hwndClient = (HWND) wParam ;
        hDdeAdvise = (GLOBALHANDLE) uiLow ;
        aItem      = (ATOM) uiHi ;

        pDdeAdvise = (DDEADVISE *) GlobalLock (hDdeAdvise) ;

            // Check for matching format and data item

        if (pDdeAdvise->cfFormat == CF_TEXT)
             {
             GlobalGetAtomName (aItem, szItem, sizeof (szItem)) ;

             for (i = 0 ; i < NUM_STATES ; i++)
                 if (strcmp (szItem, pop[i].szState) == 0)
                     break ;

                 // Fill in the POPADVISE structure and
                 //     acknowledge
             if (i < NUM_STATES)
                  {
                  hPopAdvise = (GLOBALHANDLE) GetWindowLong (hwnd, 4) ;
                  pPopAdvise = (POPADVISE *)
                                     GlobalLock (hPopAdvise) ;

                  pPopAdvise[i].fAdvise   = TRUE ;
                  pPopAdvise[i].fDeferUpd = pDdeAdvise->fDeferUpd ;
                  pPopAdvise[i].fAckReq   = pDdeAdvise->fAckReq ;
```

(continued)

886

```
                         pPopAdvise[i].lPopPrev  = pop[i].lPop ;

                    GlobalUnlock (hDdeAdvise) ;
                    GlobalFree (hDdeAdvise) ;

                    DdeAck.bAppReturnCode = 0 ;
                    DdeAck.reserved       = 0 ;
                    DdeAck.fBusy          = FALSE ;
                    DdeAck.fAck           = TRUE ;

                    wStatus = *((WORD *) &DdeAck) ;

                    if (!PostMessage (hwndClient, WM_DDE_ACK,
                                      (WPARAM) hwnd,
                                      PackDDElParam (WM_DDE_ACK,
                                                     wStatus, aItem)))
                         {
                         GlobalDeleteAtom (aItem) ;
                         }
                    else
                         {
                         PostDataMessage (hwnd, hwndClient, i,
                                          pPopAdvise[i].fDeferUpd,
                                          pPopAdvise[i].fAckReq,
                                          FALSE) ;
                         }

                    GlobalUnlock (hPopAdvise) ;
                    return 0 ;
                    }
               }


               // Otherwise, post a negative WM_DDE_ACK

     GlobalUnlock (hDdeAdvise) ;

     DdeAck.bAppReturnCode = 0 ;
     DdeAck.reserved       = 0 ;
     DdeAck.fBusy          = FALSE ;
     DdeAck.fAck           = FALSE ;

     wStatus = *((WORD *) &DdeAck) ;

     if (!PostMessage (hwndClient, WM_DDE_ACK, (WPARAM) hwnd,
                    PackDDElParam (WM_DDE_ACK, wStatus, aItem)))
```

(continued)

```
                    {
                    GlobalFree (hDdeAdvise) ;
                    GlobalDeleteAtom (aItem) ;
                    }

          return 0 ;

     case WM_DDE_UNADVISE :

               // wParam          -- sending window handle
               // LOWORD (lParam) -- data format
               // HIWORD (lParam) -- item atom

          hwndClient = (HWND) wParam ;
          cfFormat   = LOWORD (lParam) ;
          aItem      = HIWORD (lParam) ;

          DdeAck.bAppReturnCode = 0 ;
          DdeAck.reserved       = 0 ;
          DdeAck.fBusy          = FALSE ;
          DdeAck.fAck           = TRUE ;

          hPopAdvise  = (GLOBALHANDLE) GetWindowLong (hwnd, 4) ;
          pPopAdvise = (POPADVISE *) GlobalLock (hPopAdvise) ;

               // Check for matching format and data item

          if (cfFormat == CF_TEXT || cfFormat == NULL)
               {
               if (aItem == (ATOM) NULL)
                    for (i = 0 ; i < NUM_STATES ; i++)
                         pPopAdvise[i].fAdvise = FALSE ;
               else
                    {
                    GlobalGetAtomName (aItem, szItem, sizeof (szItem)) ;

                    for (i = 0 ; i < NUM_STATES ; i++)
                         if (strcmp (szItem, pop[i].szState) == 0)
                              break ;

                    if (i < NUM_STATES)
                         pPopAdvise[i].fAdvise = FALSE ;
                    else
                         DdeAck.fAck = FALSE ;
                    }
               }
```

(continued)

```
        else
            DdeAck.fAck = FALSE ;

            // Acknowledge either positively or negatively

        wStatus = *((WORD *) &DdeAck) ;

        if (!PostMessage (hwndClient, WM_DDE_ACK, (WPARAM) hwnd,
                     PackDDElParam (WM_DDE_ACK, wStatus, aItem)))
            {
            if (aItem != (ATOM) NULL)
                GlobalDeleteAtom (aItem) ;
            }

        GlobalUnlock (hPopAdvise) ;
        return 0 ;

case WM_DDE_EXECUTE :

        // Post negative acknowledge

        hwndClient = (HWND) wParam ;
        hCommands  = (GLOBALHANDLE) lParam ;

        DdeAck.bAppReturnCode = 0 ;
        DdeAck.reserved       = 0 ;
        DdeAck.fBusy          = FALSE ;
        DdeAck.fAck           = FALSE ;

        wStatus = *((WORD *) &DdeAck) ;

        if (!PostMessage (hwndClient, WM_DDE_ACK, (WPARAM) hwnd,
                     PackDDElParam (WM_DDE_ACK,
                                    wStatus, (UINT) hCommands)))
            {
            GlobalFree (hCommands) ;
            }
        return 0 ;

case WM_DDE_POKE :

        // Post negative acknowledge

        UnpackDDElParam (WM_DDE_POKE, lParam, &uiLow, &uiHi) ;
        FreeDDElParam (WM_DDE_POKE, lParam) ;
        hwndClient = (HWND) wParam ;
```

(continued)

```
                    hDdePoke  = (GLOBALHANDLE) uiLow ;
                    aItem     = (ATOM) uiHi ;


                    DdeAck.bAppReturnCode = 0 ;
                    DdeAck.reserved       = 0 ;
                    DdeAck.fBusy          = FALSE ;
                    DdeAck.fAck           = FALSE ;

                    wStatus = *((WORD *) &DdeAck) ;

                    if (!PostMessage (hwndClient, WM_DDE_ACK, (WPARAM) hwnd,
                                   PackDDElParam (WM_DDE_ACK, wStatus, aItem)))
                         {
                         GlobalFree (hDdePoke) ;
                         GlobalDeleteAtom (aItem) ;
                         }


                    return 0 ;

          case WM_DDE_TERMINATE :

                    // Respond with another WM_DDE_TERMINATE iMsg

                    hwndClient = (HWND) wParam ;
                    PostMessage (hwndClient, WM_DDE_TERMINATE, (WPARAM) hwnd, 0L) ;
                    DestroyWindow (hwnd) ;
                    return 0 ;

          case WM_TIMER :

                    // Post WM_DDE_DATA iMsgs for changed populations

                    hwndClient = (HWND) GetWindowLong (hwnd, 0) ;
                    hPopAdvise = (GLOBALHANDLE) GetWindowLong (hwnd, 4) ;
                    pPopAdvise = (POPADVISE *) GlobalLock (hPopAdvise) ;

                    for (i = 0 ; i < NUM_STATES ; i++)
                         if (pPopAdvise[i].fAdvise)
                              if (pPopAdvise[i].lPopPrev != pop[i].lPop)
                                   {
                                   if (!PostDataMessage (hwnd, hwndClient, i,
                                                   pPopAdvise[i].fDeferUpd,
                                                   pPopAdvise[i].fAckReq,
                                                   FALSE))
```

(continued)

890

```
                                  break ;

                          pPopAdvise[i].lPopPrev = pop[i].lPop ;
                          }

          GlobalUnlock (hPopAdvise) ;
          return 0 ;

     case WM_CLOSE :

               // Post a WM_DDE_TERMINATE iMsg to the client

          hwndClient = (HWND) GetWindowLong (hwnd, 0) ;
          PostMessage (hwndClient, WM_DDE_TERMINATE, (WPARAM) hwnd, 0L) ;

          dwTime = GetCurrentTime () ;

          while (GetCurrentTime () - dwTime < DDE_TIMEOUT)
               if (PeekMessage (&msg, hwnd, WM_DDE_TERMINATE,
                                WM_DDE_TERMINATE, PM_REMOVE))
                    break ;

          DestroyWindow (hwnd) ;
          return 0 ;

     case WM_DESTROY :
          hPopAdvise = (GLOBALHANDLE) GetWindowLong (hwnd, 4) ;
          GlobalFree (hPopAdvise) ;
          return 0 ;
     }
     return DefWindowProc (hwnd, iMsg, wParam, lParam) ;
     }

BOOL CALLBACK TimerEnumProc (HWND hwnd, LPARAM lParam)
     {
     SendMessage (hwnd, WM_TIMER, 0, 0L) ;

     return TRUE ;
     }

BOOL CALLBACK CloseEnumProc (HWND hwnd, LPARAM lParam)
     {
     SendMessage (hwnd, WM_CLOSE, 0, 0L) ;
```

(continued)

```
       return TRUE ;
       }

BOOL PostDataMessage (HWND hwndServer, HWND hwndClient, int iState,
                      BOOL fDeferUpd, BOOL fAckReq, BOOL fResponse)
       {
       ATOM         aItem ;
       char         szPopulation[16] ;
       DDEACK       DdeAck ;
       DDEDATA      *pDdeData ;
       DWORD        dwTime ;
       GLOBALHANDLE hDdeData ;
       MSG          msg ;
       WORD         wStatus ;

       aItem = GlobalAddAtom (pop[iState].szState) ;

            // Allocate a DDEDATA structure if not deferred update

       if (fDeferUpd)
            {
            hDdeData = NULL ;
            }
       else
            {
            wsprintf (szPopulation, "%ld\r\n", pop[iState].lPop) ;

            hDdeData = GlobalAlloc (GHND | GMEM_DDESHARE,
                                   sizeof (DDEDATA) + strlen (szPopulation)) ;

            pDdeData = (DDEDATA *) GlobalLock (hDdeData) ;

            pDdeData->fResponse = fResponse ;
            pDdeData->fRelease  = TRUE ;
            pDdeData->fAckReq   = fAckReq ;
            pDdeData->cfFormat  = CF_TEXT ;

            lstrcpy ((PSTR) pDdeData->Value, szPopulation) ;

            GlobalUnlock (hDdeData) ;
            }

            // Post the WM_DDE_DATA iMsg
```

(continued)

```
      if (!PostMessage (hwndClient, WM_DDE_DATA, (WPARAM) hwndServer,
                   PackDDElParam (WM_DDE_DATA, (UINT) hDdeData, aItem)))
           {
           if (hDdeData != NULL)
               GlobalFree (hDdeData) ;

           GlobalDeleteAtom (aItem) ;
           return FALSE ;
           }

           // Wait for the acknowledge iMsg if it's requested

      if (fAckReq)
           {
           DdeAck.fAck = FALSE ;

           dwTime = GetCurrentTime () ;

           while (GetCurrentTime () - dwTime < DDE_TIMEOUT)
                {
                if (PeekMessage (&msg, hwndServer, WM_DDE_ACK, WM_DDE_ACK,
                             PM_REMOVE))
                     {
                     wStatus = LOWORD (msg.lParam) ;
                     DdeAck = *((DDEACK *) &wStatus) ;
                     aItem  = HIWORD (msg.lParam) ;
                     GlobalDeleteAtom (aItem) ;
                     break ;
                     }
                }

           if (DdeAck.fAck == FALSE)
                {
                if (hDdeData != NULL)
                     GlobalFree (hDdeData) ;

                return FALSE ;
                }
           }

      return TRUE ;
      }
```

DDEPOP.H

```
/*-------------------------------------------------------------------

   DDEPOP.H header file

   Data from "The World Almanac and Book of Facts 1992," page 75
   ----------------------------------------------------------------*/

#include <time.h>

struct
     {
     char       *szState ;
     long        lPop70 ;
     long        lPop80 ;
     long        lPop90 ;
     long        lPop ;
     long        lPopLast ;
     long double a ;
     long double b ;
     long double c ;
     }
     pop[] = {
          "AL",   3444354,   3894025,   4040587, 0, 0, 0.0, 0.0, 0.0,
          "AK",    302583,    401851,    550043, 0, 0, 0.0, 0.0, 0.0,
          "AZ",   1775399,   2716546,   3665228, 0, 0, 0.0, 0.0, 0.0,
          "AR",   1923322,   2286357,   2350725, 0, 0, 0.0, 0.0, 0.0,
          "CA",  19971069,  23667764,  29760021, 0, 0, 0.0, 0.0, 0.0,
          "CO",   2209596,   2889735,   3294394, 0, 0, 0.0, 0.0, 0.0,
          "CT",   3032217,   3107564,   3287116, 0, 0, 0.0, 0.0, 0.0,
          "DE",    548104,    594338,    666168, 0, 0, 0.0, 0.0, 0.0,
          "DC",    756668,    638432,    606900, 0, 0, 0.0, 0.0, 0.0,
          "FL",   6791418,   9746961,  12937926, 0, 0, 0.0, 0.0, 0.0,
          "GA",   4587930,   5462982,   6478216, 0, 0, 0.0, 0.0, 0.0,
          "HI",    769913,    964691,   1108229, 0, 0, 0.0, 0.0, 0.0,
          "ID",    713015,    944127,   1006749, 0, 0, 0.0, 0.0, 0.0,
          "IL",  11110285,  11427409,  11430602, 0, 0, 0.0, 0.0, 0.0,
          "IN",   5195392,   5490214,   5544159, 0, 0, 0.0, 0.0, 0.0,
          "IA",   2825368,   2913808,   2776755, 0, 0, 0.0, 0.0, 0.0,
          "KS",   2249071,   2364236,   2477574, 0, 0, 0.0, 0.0, 0.0,
          "KY",   3220711,   3660324,   3685296, 0, 0, 0.0, 0.0, 0.0,
          "LA",   3644637,   4206116,   4219973, 0, 0, 0.0, 0.0, 0.0,
          "ME",    993722,   1125043,   1227928, 0, 0, 0.0, 0.0, 0.0,
          "MD",   3923897,   4216933,   4781468, 0, 0, 0.0, 0.0, 0.0,
          "MA",   5689170,   5737093,   6016425, 0, 0, 0.0, 0.0, 0.0,
          "MI",   8881826,   9262044,   9295297, 0, 0, 0.0, 0.0, 0.0,
```

(continued)

```
             "MN",   3806103,   4075970,   4375099, 0, 0, 0.0, 0.0, 0.0,
             "MS",   2216994,   2520770,   2573216, 0, 0, 0.0, 0.0, 0.0,
             "MO",   4677623,   4916766,   5117073, 0, 0, 0.0, 0.0, 0.0,
             "MT",    694409,    786690,    799065, 0, 0, 0.0, 0.0, 0.0,
             "NE",   1485333,   1569825,   1578385, 0, 0, 0.0, 0.0, 0.0,
             "NV",    488738,    800508,   1201833, 0, 0, 0.0, 0.0, 0.0,
             "NH",    737681,    920610,   1109252, 0, 0, 0.0, 0.0, 0.0,
             "NJ",   7171112,   7365011,   7730188, 0, 0, 0.0, 0.0, 0.0,
             "NM",   1017055,   1303302,   1515069, 0, 0, 0.0, 0.0, 0.0,
             "NY",  18241391,  17558165,  17990455, 0, 0, 0.0, 0.0, 0.0,
             "NC",   5084411,   5880095,   6628637, 0, 0, 0.0, 0.0, 0.0,
             "ND",    617792,    652717,    638800, 0, 0, 0.0, 0.0, 0.0,
             "OH",  10657423,  10797603,  10847115, 0, 0, 0.0, 0.0, 0.0,
             "OK",   2559463,   3025487,   3145585, 0, 0, 0.0, 0.0, 0.0,
             "OR",   2091533,   2633156,   2842321, 0, 0, 0.0, 0.0, 0.0,
             "PA",  11800766,  11864720,  11881643, 0, 0, 0.0, 0.0, 0.0,
             "RI",    949723,    947154,   1003464, 0, 0, 0.0, 0.0, 0.0,
             "SC",   2590713,   3120729,   3486703, 0, 0, 0.0, 0.0, 0.0,
             "SD",    666257,    690768,    696004, 0, 0, 0.0, 0.0, 0.0,
             "TN",   3926018,   4591023,   4877185, 0, 0, 0.0, 0.0, 0.0,
             "TX",  11198655,  14225513,  16986510, 0, 0, 0.0, 0.0, 0.0,
             "UT",   1059273,   1461037,   1722850, 0, 0, 0.0, 0.0, 0.0,
             "VT",    444732,    511456,    562758, 0, 0, 0.0, 0.0, 0.0,
             "VA",   4651448,   5346797,   6187358, 0, 0, 0.0, 0.0, 0.0,
             "WA",   3413244,   4132353,   4866692, 0, 0, 0.0, 0.0, 0.0,
             "WV",   1744237,   1950186,   1793477, 0, 0, 0.0, 0.0, 0.0,
             "WI",   4417821,   4705642,   4891769, 0, 0, 0.0, 0.0, 0.0,
             "WY",    332416,    469557,    453588, 0, 0, 0.0, 0.0, 0.0,
             "US", 203302031, 226542203, 248709873, 0, 0, 0.0, 0.0, 0.0
             } ;

#define NUM_STATES (sizeof (pop) / sizeof (pop[0]))

void CalcPops (void)
     {
     int    i ;
     time_t lTime ;

     time (&lTime) ;                    // time in seconds since 1/1/70
     lTime -= 92L * 24 * 60 * 60 ;      // time in seconds since 4/1/70

     for (i = 0 ; i < NUM_STATES ; i++)
          pop[i].lPop = (long) (pop[i].a * lTime * lTime +
                              pop[i].b * lTime +
                              pop[i].c) ;
     }
```

(continued)

```
void InitPops (void)
    {
    int        i ;
    long double ldSec80, ldSec90 ;

    ldSec80 = 3653.0 * 24 * 60 * 60 ;  // seconds from 4/1/70 to 4/1/80
    ldSec90 = 7305.0 * 24 * 60 * 60 ;  // seconds from 4/1/70 to 4/1/90

    for (i = 0 ; i < NUM_STATES ; i++)
        {
        pop[i].a = (ldSec90 * (pop[i].lPop80 - pop[i].lPop70) +
                      ldSec80 * (pop[i].lPop70 - pop[i].lPop90)) /
                     (ldSec90 * ldSec80 * (ldSec80 - ldSec90)) ;

        pop[i].b = (ldSec90 * ldSec90 * (pop[i].lPop70 - pop[i].lPop80) +
                      ldSec80 * ldSec80 * (pop[i].lPop90 - pop[i].lPop70)) /
                     (ldSec90 * ldSec80 * (ldSec80 - ldSec90)) ;

        pop[i].c = pop[i].lPop70 ;
        }

    CalcPops () ;
    }
```

DDEPOP1.RC

```
/*-----------------------------
   DDEPOP1.RC resource script
   -------------------------*/

DdePop1 ICON ddepop.ico
```

DDEPOP.ICO

I described earlier how you can use this server with Microsoft Excel. Later in this chapter I'll show you a DDE client program (called SHOWPOP1) that also uses DDEPOP1 as a server.

The DDEPOP1 Program

You'll notice that the top of the DDEPOP1.C listing contains the line:

```
#include <dde.h>
```

This is the header file that includes the DDE messages and data structures.

The program then defines a structure (called POPADVISE) using a *typedef* statement. I'll discuss later how this structure is used.

In *WinMain*, the program registers two window classes. The first has the class name "DdePop1" and is used for the program's main window. The second has the class name "Dde-Pop1.Server." This second class is used for the child windows that are created to maintain multiple DDE conversations. Each conversation requires its own child window based on this window class.

In this second window class, the *cbWndExtra* field of the WNDCLASSEX structure is set to hold two double words per window. As you'll see, the first will be used to store the window handle of the client with which the server window is communicating. The second will be a handle to a memory block that contains NUM_STATE structures of type POPADVISE.

After DDEPOP1 creates its main window, it calls *InitPops*. This function is located in DDEPOP.H, along with the actual population data and a function called *CalcPops* to calculate the instantaneous populations. DDEPOP1 also calls *SetTimer* to set a 5-second timer to periodically update the *lPop* field of the *pop* structure in DDEPOP.H.

You'll notice that *ShowWindow* is called with the SW_SHOWMINNOACTIVE parameter and that *WndProc* returns 0 from the WM_QUERYOPEN message. This keeps DDEPOP displayed as a button on the taskbar.

The WM_DDE_INITIATE Message

A DDE conversation is initiated by a client by broadcasting a WM_DDE_INITIATE message to all top-level windows. (As you'll see when I discuss the DDE client program later in this chapter, this is accomplished by calling *SendMessage* with an HWND_BROADCAST message as the first parameter.)

The WM_DDE_INITIATE message is handled by a DDE server in its main window procedure. As in every DDE message, the *wParam* parameter is the handle to the window sending the message. This is the window handle of the client. *WndProc* stores this in the variable *hwndClient*.

For the WM_DDE_INITIATE message, the low word of *lParam* is the atom identifying the desired application. This could be NULL if the client wants a response from any server. The high word of *lParam* is the atom identifying the desired topic. Again, this could be NULL if the client wants a response from a server that can supply any topic.

WndProc processes the WM_DDE_INITIATE message by calling *GlobalAddAtom* to add atoms for its application name ("DdePop1") and topic name ("US_Population"). It then checks if the atoms supplied in the low word and high word of *lParam* are NULL or match these atoms.

If the atoms match, then *WndProc* creates a hidden child window based on the "Dde-Pop1.Server" window class. This window (whose window procedure is *ServerProc*) will handle all subsequent DDE messages in the DDE conversation. The first of the two double words reserved for the window is set to the handle of the client using *SetWindowLong*. *WndProc* then acknowledges the WM_DDE_INITIATE message by sending a WM_DDE_ACK message back to the client. The *wParam* parameter is the handle of the just-created server window, and *lParam* contains the atoms identifying the server application name and the topic name. (If the client requested all topics and the server supports multiple topics, then the server would send multiple WM_DDE_ACK messages back to the client, one for each topic it supports.)

A program that receives a WM_DDE_ACK message is responsible for deleting all atoms that accompany the message. *WndProc* calls *GlobalDeleteAtom* for the two atoms it created only if it does not send a WM_DDE_ACK message to the client.

The WM_DDE_INITIATE message and the WM_DDE_ACK message (in response to WM_DDE_INITIATE) are the only two DDE messages that are sent using *SendMessage* rather than posted using *PostMessage*. As we'll see later in this chapter, this means that a client sending a WM_DDE_INITIATE message receives the WM_DDE_ACK response before the original *SendMessage* call has returned.

The *ServerProc* Window Procedure

With the sending of the WM_DDE_ACK message in response to the WM_DDE_INITIATE message, the DDE conversation has begun. As I mentioned, when *WndProc* sends the WM_DDE_ACK message back to the client, it sets the *wParam* parameter to the handle of the child window it creates for the conversation. This means that all subsequent DDE messages occur between the client and this child window, whose window procedure is *ServerProc*.

ServerProc processes its WM_CREATE message by allocating the memory required to hold NUM_STATES structures of type POPADVISE. (I'll discuss how these are used shortly.) The handle to this memory block is stored as the second reserved double word using *SetWindowLong*. This memory block is freed when *ServerProc* receives a WM_DESTROY message.

The WM_DDE_REQUEST Message

A client posts a WM_DDE_REQUEST message to a server when it wants data that is associated with a particular item. This is the type of transaction known as the cold link. The server responds by posting a WM_DDE_DATA message to the client with the data or a

WM_DDE_ACK message if it cannot satisfy the request. Let's look at how *ServerProc* handles the WM_DDE_REQUEST message.

As is usual with DDE messages, the *wParam* parameter accompanying WM_DDE-_REQUEST is the handle to the window posting the message, in this case the client. The low word of the *lParam* parameter is a requested data format. The high word of *lParam* is an atom identifying the requested data item.

The formats of DDE data are the same as clipboard formats, so this low word of *lParam* will most commonly be one of the identifiers beginning with the CF prefix. A client may send multiple WM_DDE_REQUEST messages to a server for the same item but with different formats. The server should respond with a WM_DDE_DATA message for only the formats it supports. Far and away the most common format for DDE data is CF_TEXT, and this is the only format that DDEPOP1 supports.

So, when processing the WM_DDE_REQUEST message, *ServerProc* first checks if the requested format is CF_TEXT. *ServerProc* then calls the *GlobalGetAtomName* function to get the character string associated with the atom passed in the high word of *lParam*. If the client knows what it's doing, this will be a two-character string identifying the state. A *for* loop goes through the states and attempts to match this with the *szState* field of the *pop* structure. If there's a match, *ServerProc* deletes the atom by calling *GlobalDeleteAtom* and then calls *PostDataMessage* (a function towards the end of DDEPOP1 that posts the WM-_DDE_DATA message, which I'll describe shortly). *ServerProc* then returns.

If the requested format is not CF_TEXT, or if there was no match between the item atom and one of the state names, then *ServerProc* posts a negative WM_DDE_ACK message indicating that the data was not available. It does this by setting the *fAck* field of a DDEACK structure (defined in DDE.H) to FALSE. The DDEACK structure is converted to a word, which forms the low word of *lParam*. The high word of *lParam* is the atom for the requested item. *PostMessage* posts the WM_DDE_ACK message to the client.

Notice how the atom is handled here. The documentation for WM_DDE_REQUEST states: "When responding with either a WM_DDE_DATA or WM_DDE_ACK message, the server application can either reuse the *aItem* atom or it can delete the atom and create a new one." What this means is that the state of the global atom table should not be altered by the server—that is, the reference count for the *aItem* atom should not be incremented or decremented.

There are three cases here:

- If the requested format is CF_TEXT and the atom matches one of the state names, then *ServerProc* calls *GlobalDeleteAtom* before calling the function in DDEPOP1.C named *PostDataMessage*. This *PostDataMessage* function (as we'll see shortly) re-creates the atom when posting a WM_DDE_DATA message to the client.

- If the requested format is not CF_TEXT or if the atom does not match one of the state names, then *ServerProc* calls *PostMessage* to deliver a negative WM_DDE_ACK message to the client. The atom is simply reused in this message.

■   However, if this *PostMessage* call fails (perhaps indicating that the client has been unexpectedly terminated), then *ServerProc* deletes the atom because the client cannot.

We are not yet finished with the WM_DDE_REQUEST message because we have not yet examined how DDEPOP1's *PostDataMessage* responds with the WM_DDE_DATA message. That's next.

DDEPOP1's *PostDataMessage* Function

The *PostDataMessage* function towards the end of DDEPOP1.C is responsible for posting a WM_DDE_DATA message to a client. This function is set up to also handle WM_DDE_ADVISE messages (which I'll discuss shortly), so it's a little more complex than if it had to handle only WM_DDE_REQUEST messages.

PostDataMessage has six parameters:

■   *hwndServer*—the window handle of the server

■   *hwndClient*—the window handle of the client

■   *iState*—the index of the *pop* array identifying the state for which population data is requested

■   *fDeferUpd*—which *ServerProc* sets to FALSE when responding to WM_DDE_REQUEST messages

■   *fAckReq*—which *ServerProc* also sets to FALSE in this case

■   *fResponse*—which *ServerProc* sets to TRUE to indicate a response from a WM_DDE_REQUEST message

(I'll discuss the *fDeferUpd* and *fAckReq* parameters shortly when we get to the WM_DDE_ADVISE message. For now, just ignore all parts of *PostDataMessage* when either of these two parameters is set to TRUE.)

The *PostDataMessage* function begins by calling *GlobalAddItem* to create an atom for the two-character state name. (You'll recall that *ServerProc* deleted the atom before calling *PostDataMessage*.) It then calls *wsprintf* to convert the population of the state (updated by *WndProc* within the past 5 seconds) to a character string terminated with a carriage return and linefeed.

PostDataMessage then uses *GlobalAlloc* with the GMEM_DDESHARE option to allocate a block of memory large enough for a DDEDATA structure (defined in DDE.H) with the actual data (the character string *szPopulation*) appended. In the case of *PostDataMessage* being used in response to a WM_DDE_REQUEST message, the fields of the DDEDATA structure are set as follows:

■ The *fResponse* field of the DDEDATA structure is set to TRUE, indicating that the data is in response to a WM_DDE_DATA message.

■ The *fRelease* field is also set to TRUE, indicating that the client should free the memory block just allocated.

■ The *fAckReq* field is set to FALSE, indicating that a WM_DDE_ACK message from the client is not required.

■ The *cfFormat* field is set to CF_TEXT, indicating that the data is in a text format.

■ The *szPopulation* array is copied into the area of the memory block beginning at the *Value* field of the structure.

PostDataMessage then uses *PostMessage* to post a WM_DDE_DATA message to the client. As usual, *wParam* is the handle of the window (the server) sending the message. The *lParam* parameter is a bit more complicated. It identifies a memory object that holds two values: the handle of the memory block containing the DDEDATA structure and the atom identifying the data item (the two-character state name). The identifier in *lParam* is created by calling *PackDDElParam*. The procedure that receives the WM_DDE_DATA message must extract the two data items from the *lParam* memory object by calling *Unpack-DDElParam* and then release the object by calling *FreeDDElParam*.

If *PostMessage* is successful, then we're done. The client is responsible for freeing the memory block and deleting the atom. If *PostMessage* fails (perhaps because the client is no longer with us), *PostDataMessage* frees the memory block it allocated and deletes the atom.

The WM_DDE_ADVISE Message

You are, I trust, beginning to recognize some of the complexities involved in DDE. It gets a little more complex with WM_DDE_ADVISE and the hot link.

The WM_DDE_REQUEST message I've just discussed allows the client to obtain data from the server. But if this data changes (as the instantaneous population will), the client has no way to know that. Allowing the client to know when data has been updated is the purpose of the WM_DDE_ADVISE message. On receipt of this message, a server is responsible for notifying the client when the data has changed. (This notification is accomplished by the server posting WM_DDE_DATA messages to the client.) This can be tricky because the server must "remember" which items the client has asked to be advised on. Moreover, the client will ask that this data be posted in particular ways.

In a WM_DDE_ADVISE message, *lParam* identifies an object that holds both a handle to a global memory block containing a DDEADVISE structure as defined in DDE.H, and the atom identifying the data item. When processing WM_DDE_ADVISE, *ServerProc* calls *UnpackDDElParam* to extract the handle and the atom, and then calls *FreeDDElParam* to free the *lParam* object. It then checks that the *cfFormat* field of the DDEADVISE structure is CF_TEXT. If it is, it obtains the text string referenced by the atom and checks it against the *szState* field of the *pop* structure.

If there's a match, then *ServerProc* gets a pointer to the array of POPADVISE structures that it allocated during the WM_CREATE message. This array has a POPADVISE structure for each state, and there is a different array for each window carrying on a DDE conversation. This array is used to store all information *ServerProc* will need to update items to the client.

The fields of the POPADVISE structure for the selected state are set as follows:

- The *fAdvise* field is set to TRUE. This is simply a flag that indicates that the client wants updated information on this state.

- The *fDeferUpd* ("deferred update") field is set to the value of the same field in the DDEADVISE structure. A TRUE value indicates that the client wants to establish a warm link rather than a hot link. The client will be advised of a change in data without getting the data immediately. (In this case, the server posts a WM_DDE_DATA message with a NULL value rather than a handle to the global memory block containing a DDEDATA structure. The client will later post a normal WM_DDE_REQUEST message to obtain the actual data.) A FALSE value indicates that the client wants the data in the WM_DDE_DATA message.

- The *fAckReq* ("acknowledgment requested") field is set to the value of the same field in the DDEADVISE structure. This is a very tricky value. A TRUE value instructs the server to post the WM_DDE_DATA with the *fAckReq* field of the DDEDATA structure set to TRUE so that the client is required to acknowledge the WM_DDE_DATA message with a WM_DDE_ACK message. A TRUE value does *not* mean that the client is requesting a WM_DDE_ACK message from the server; it's requiring that the server require a WM_DDE_ACK message from the client when later posting the WM_DDE_DATA message.

- The *lPopPrev* field is set to the current population of the state. *ServerProc* uses this field to determine if the client needs notification that the population has changed.

ServerProc is now finished with the DDEADVISE structure and frees the memory block as the documentation for WM_DDE_ADVISE instructs. *ServerProc* must now acknowledge the WM_DDE_ADVISE message by posting a positive WM_DDE_ACK message. The *fAck* field of the DDEACK structure is set to TRUE. If *PostMessage* fails, then *ServerProc* deletes the atom.

If the data format was not CF_TEXT, or if there was no match for the state, then *ServerProc* posts a negative WM_DDE_ACK message. In this case, if the *PostMessage* call fails, *ServerProc* both deletes the atom and frees the DDEADVISE memory block.

In theory, handling of the WM_DDE_ADVISE message is now complete. However, the client has asked that it be notified whenever a data item changes. Given that the client doesn't know any value of the data item, it is necessary for *ServerProc* to post a WM_DDE_DATA message to the client.

It does this using the *PostDataMessage* function, but with the third parameter set to the *fDeferUpd* field of the POPADVISE structure, the fourth parameter set to the *fAckReq* field of the POPADVISE structure, and the last parameter set to FALSE (indicating a WM_DDE_DATA message posted in response to WM_DDE_ADVISE rather than WM_DDE_REQUEST).

It's time for another look at *PostDataMessage*. Toward the beginning of the function, note that if the *fDeferUpd* parameter is TRUE, then the function simply sets *hDdeData* to NULL rather than allocating memory for it.

If the *fAckReq* parameter is TRUE, then *PostDataMessage* waits for a WM_DDE_ACK message from the client after posting the WM_DDE_DATA message. It does this by calling *PeekMessage*. *PostDataMessage* deletes the atom in the WM_DDE_ACK message. If the WM_DDE_ACK message does not arrive within three seconds—or if the message is a negative acknowledgment—then *PostDataMessage* frees the data block containing the DDEDATA structure.

If you think that you can skip over part of this work by assuming that a client will never post a WM_DDE_ADVISE message with the deferred update or acknowledgment requested fields set to TRUE, guess again. Microsoft Excel does precisely that, establishing a warm link with acknowledgments to the WM_DDE_DATA messages.

Updating the Items

After processing a WM_DDE_ADVISE message, a server is required to notify the client when an item has changed. How this works depends on the server. In the case of DDEPOP1, a timer is used to recalculate the populations every 5 seconds. This occurs while processing the WM_TIMER message in *WndProc*.

WndProc then calls *EnumChildWindows* with the *TimerEnumProc* function (located after *ServerProc* in DDEPOP1.C). *TimerEnumProc* sends WM_TIMER messages to all the child windows, all of which will be using the *ServerProc* window procedure.

ServerProc processes the WM_TIMER message by looping through all the states and checking if the POPADVISE structure field *fAdvise* is set to TRUE and the population has changed. If so, it calls *PostDataMessage* to post a WM_DDE_DATA message to the client.

The WM_DDE_UNADVISE Message

The WM_DDE_UNADVISE message instructs a server to stop posting WM_DDE_DATA messages when a data item has changed. The low word of *lParam* is either the data format or NULL, indicating all data formats. The high word of *lParam* is either the item ATOM or NULL to indicate all items.

DDEPOP1 handles the WM_DDE_UNADVISE message by setting the appropriate *fAdvise* fields of the POPADVISE structure to FALSE, and then acknowledging with a positive or negative WM_DDE_ACK message.

The WM_DDE_TERMINATE Message

When a client wishes to terminate the conversation, it posts a WM_DDE_TERMINATE message to the server. The server simply responds with its own WM_DDE_TERMINATE message back to the client. *ServerProc* also destroys the child window on receipt of WM_DDE_TERMINATE because it is no longer needed, and the conversation that the window has maintained is terminated.

ServerProc also processes WM_DDE_POKE and WM_DDE_EXECUTE messages, but in both cases simply responds with a negative acknowledgment.

If DDEPOP1 is closed from its system menu, then it must terminate all DDE conversations with its clients. So, when *WndProc* receives a WM_CLOSE message, it calls *EnumChildWindows* with the *CloseEnumProc* function. *CloseEnumProc* sends WM_CLOSE messages to all the child windows.

ServerProc responds to WM_CLOSE by posting a WM_DDE_TERMINATE message to the client and then waiting for another WM_DDE_TERMINATE message back from the client.

A DDE CLIENT PROGRAM

Now that we've examined a DDE server program that you can use with Microsoft Excel, let's examine a DDE client program that uses DDEPOP1 as a server. This program is called SHOWPOP1 and is shown in Figure 17-2.

```
SHOWPOP1.MAK

#-------------------------
# SHOWPOP1.MAK make file
#-------------------------

showpop1.exe : showpop1.obj
     $(LINKER) $(GUIFLAGS) -OUT:showpop1.exe showpop1.obj $(GUILIBS)

showpop1.obj : showpop1.c showpop.h
     $(CC) $(CFLAGS) showpop1.c
```

Figure 17-2. *The SHOWPOP1 program.* *(continued)*

SHOWPOP1.C

```
/*-------------------------------------------
   SHOWPOP1.C -- DDE Client using DDEPOP1
                (c) Charles Petzold, 1996
   -------------------------------------------*/

#include <windows.h>
#include <dde.h>
#include <stdlib.h>
#include <string.h>
#include "showpop.h"

#define WM_USER_INITIATE (WM_USER + 1)
#define DDE_TIMEOUT      3000

LRESULT CALLBACK WndProc (HWND, UINT, WPARAM, LPARAM) ;

char szAppName[] = "ShowPop1" ;

int WINAPI WinMain (HINSTANCE hInstance, HINSTANCE hPrevInstance,
                    PSTR szCmdLine, int iCmdShow)
     {
     HWND          hwnd ;
     MSG           msg ;
     WNDCLASSEX    wndclass ;

     wndclass.cbSize        = sizeof (wndclass) ;
     wndclass.style         = CS_HREDRAW | CS_VREDRAW ;
     wndclass.lpfnWndProc   = WndProc ;
     wndclass.cbClsExtra    = 0 ;
     wndclass.cbWndExtra    = 0 ;
     wndclass.hInstance     = hInstance ;
     wndclass.hIcon         = LoadIcon (hInstance, szAppName) ;
     wndclass.hCursor       = LoadCursor (NULL, IDC_ARROW) ;
     wndclass.hbrBackground = (HBRUSH) GetStockObject (WHITE_BRUSH) ;
     wndclass.lpszMenuName  = NULL ;
     wndclass.lpszClassName = szAppName ;
     wndclass.hIconSm       = LoadIcon (hInstance, szAppName) ;

     RegisterClassEx (&wndclass) ;

     hwnd = CreateWindow (szAppName, "DDE Client - US Population",
```

(continued)

```
                              WS_OVERLAPPEDWINDOW,
                              CW_USEDEFAULT, CW_USEDEFAULT,
                              CW_USEDEFAULT, CW_USEDEFAULT,
                              NULL, NULL, hInstance, NULL) ;

     ShowWindow (hwnd, iCmdShow) ;
     UpdateWindow (hwnd) ;

     SendMessage (hwnd, WM_USER_INITIATE, 0, 0L) ;

     while (GetMessage (&msg, NULL, 0, 0))
          {
          TranslateMessage (&msg) ;
          DispatchMessage (&msg) ;
          }
     return msg.wParam ;
     }

LRESULT CALLBACK WndProc (HWND hwnd, UINT iMsg, WPARAM wParam, LPARAM lParam)
     {
     static BOOL    fDoingInitiate = TRUE ;
     static char    szServerApp[]  = "DdePop1",
                    szTopic[]      = "US_Population" ;
     static HWND    hwndServer = NULL ;
     static long    cxChar, cyChar ;
     ATOM           aApp, aTop, aItem ;
     char           szBuffer[24], szPopulation[16], szItem[16] ;
     DDEACK         DdeAck ;
     DDEDATA        *pDdeData ;
     DDEADVISE      *pDdeAdvise ;
     DWORD          dwTime ;
     GLOBALHANDLE   hDdeAdvise, hDdeData ;
     HDC            hdc ;
     MSG            msg ;
     PAINTSTRUCT    ps ;
     short          i ;
     long           x, y ;
     TEXTMETRIC     tm ;
     WORD           wStatus ;
     UINT           uiLow, uiHi ;

     switch (iMsg)
          {
          case WM_CREATE :
               hdc = GetDC (hwnd) ;
```

(continued)

906

```
            GetTextMetrics (hdc, &tm) ;
            cxChar = tm.tmAveCharWidth ;
            cyChar = tm.tmHeight + tm.tmExternalLeading ;
            ReleaseDC (hwnd, hdc) ;
            return 0 ;

case WM_USER_INITIATE :

                // Broadcast WM_DDE_INITIATE iMsg

            aApp = GlobalAddAtom (szServerApp) ;
            aTop = GlobalAddAtom (szTopic) ;

            SendMessage (HWND_BROADCAST, WM_DDE_INITIATE, (WPARAM) hwnd,
                        MAKELONG (aApp, aTop)) ;

                // If no response, try loading DDEPOP first

            if (hwndServer == NULL)
                {
                WinExec (szServerApp, SW_SHOWMINNOACTIVE) ;

                SendMessage (HWND_BROADCAST, WM_DDE_INITIATE, (WPARAM) hwnd,
                            MAKELONG (aApp, aTop)) ;
                }

                // Delete the atoms

            GlobalDeleteAtom (aApp) ;
            GlobalDeleteAtom (aTop) ;
            fDoingInitiate = FALSE ;

                // If still no response, display message box

            if (hwndServer == NULL)
                {
                MessageBox (hwnd, "Cannot connect with DDEPOP1.EXE!",
                            szAppName, MB_ICONEXCLAMATION | MB_OK) ;

                return 0 ;
                }

                // Post WM_DDE_ADVISE iMsgs

            for (i = 0 ; i < NUM_STATES ; i++)
```

(continued)

907

```
     {
     hDdeAdvise = GlobalAlloc (GHND | GMEM_DDESHARE,
                              sizeof (DDEADVISE)) ;

     pDdeAdvise = (DDEADVISE *) GlobalLock (hDdeAdvise) ;

     pDdeAdvise->fAckReq   = TRUE ;
     pDdeAdvise->fDeferUpd = FALSE ;
     pDdeAdvise->cfFormat  = CF_TEXT ;

     GlobalUnlock (hDdeAdvise) ;

     aItem = GlobalAddAtom (pop[i].szAbb) ;

     if (!PostMessage (hwndServer, WM_DDE_ADVISE, (WPARAM) hwnd,
                   PackDDElParam (WM_DDE_ADVISE,
                                   (UINT) hDdeAdvise, aItem)))
          {
          GlobalFree (hDdeAdvise) ;
          GlobalDeleteAtom (aItem) ;
          break ;
          }

     DdeAck.fAck = FALSE ;

     dwTime = GetCurrentTime () ;

     while (GetCurrentTime () - dwTime < DDE_TIMEOUT)
          {
          if (PeekMessage (&msg, hwnd, WM_DDE_ACK,
                       WM_DDE_ACK, PM_REMOVE))
               {
               GlobalDeleteAtom (HIWORD (msg.lParam)) ;

               wStatus = LOWORD (msg.lParam) ;
               DdeAck = *((DDEACK *) &wStatus) ;

               if (DdeAck.fAck == FALSE)
                    GlobalFree (hDdeAdvise) ;

               break ;
               }
          }
```

(continued)

```
                    if (DdeAck.fAck == FALSE)
                         break ;

                    while (PeekMessage (&msg, hwnd, WM_DDE_FIRST,
                                            WM_DDE_LAST, PM_REMOVE))
                         {
                         DispatchMessage (&msg) ;
                         }
                    }

          if (i < NUM_STATES)
               {
               MessageBox (hwnd, "Failure on WM_DDE_ADVISE!",
                          szAppName, MB_ICONEXCLAMATION ¦ MB_OK) ;
               }
          return 0 ;

     case WM_DDE_ACK :

               // In response to WM_DDE_INITIATE, save server window

          if (fDoingInitiate)
               {
               UnpackDDElParam (WM_DDE_ACK, lParam, &uiLow, &uiHi) ;
               FreeDDElParam (WM_DDE_ACK, lParam) ;
               hwndServer = (HWND) wParam ;
               GlobalDeleteAtom ((ATOM) uiLow) ;
               GlobalDeleteAtom ((ATOM) uiHi) ;
               }
          return 0 ;

     case WM_DDE_DATA :

               // wParam -- sending window handle
               // lParam -- DDEDATA memory handle & item atom

          UnpackDDElParam (WM_DDE_DATA, lParam, &uiLow, &uiHi) ;
          FreeDDElParam (WM_DDE_DATA, lParam) ;

          hDdeData  = (GLOBALHANDLE) uiLow ;
          pDdeData = (DDEDATA *) GlobalLock (hDdeData) ;
          aItem     = (ATOM) uiHi ;

               // Initialize DdeAck structure
```

(continued)

```
            DdeAck.bAppReturnCode = 0 ;
            DdeAck.reserved       = 0 ;
            DdeAck.fBusy          = FALSE ;
            DdeAck.fAck           = FALSE ;

                // Check for matching format and data item

        if (pDdeData->cfFormat == CF_TEXT)
            {
            GlobalGetAtomName (aItem, szItem, sizeof (szItem)) ;

            for (i = 0 ; i < NUM_STATES ; i++)
                if (strcmp (szItem, pop[i].szAbb) == 0)
                    break ;

            if (i < NUM_STATES)
                {
                strcpy (szPopulation, (char *) pDdeData->Value) ;
                pop[i].lPop = atol (szPopulation) ;
                InvalidateRect (hwnd, NULL, FALSE) ;

                DdeAck.fAck = TRUE ;
                }
            }

            // Acknowledge if necessary

        if (pDdeData->fAckReq == TRUE)
            {
            wStatus = *((WORD *) &DdeAck) ;

            if (!PostMessage ((HWND) wParam, WM_DDE_ACK, (WPARAM) hwnd,
                            PackDDElParam (WM_DDE_ACK,
                                                wStatus, aItem)))
                {
                GlobalDeleteAtom (aItem) ;
                GlobalUnlock (hDdeData) ;
                GlobalFree (hDdeData) ;
                return 0 ;
                }
            }
        else
            {
            GlobalDeleteAtom (aItem) ;
            }
```

(continued)

```
            // Clean up

        if (pDdeData->fRelease == TRUE || DdeAck.fAck == FALSE)
            {
            GlobalUnlock (hDdeData) ;
            GlobalFree (hDdeData) ;
            }
        else
            {
            GlobalUnlock (hDdeData) ;
            }

        return 0 ;

case WM_PAINT :
    hdc = BeginPaint (hwnd, &ps) ;

    for (i = 0 ; i < NUM_STATES ; i++)
        {
        if (i < (NUM_STATES + 1) / 2)
            {
            x = cxChar ;
            y = i * cyChar ;
            }
        else
            {
            x = 44 * cxChar ;
            y = (i - (NUM_STATES + 1) / 2) * cyChar ;
            }

        TextOut (hdc, x, y, szBuffer,
                wsprintf (szBuffer, "%-20s",
                        (PSTR) pop[i].szState)) ;

        x += 36 * cxChar ;

        SetTextAlign (hdc, TA_RIGHT | TA_TOP) ;

        TextOut (hdc, x, y, szBuffer,
                wsprintf (szBuffer, "%10ld", pop[i].lPop)) ;

        SetTextAlign (hdc, TA_LEFT | TA_TOP) ;
        }
```

(continued)

```
        EndPaint (hwnd, &ps) ;
        return 0 ;

case WM_DDE_TERMINATE :

        // Respond with another WM_DDE_TERMINATE iMsg

    PostMessage (hwndServer, WM_DDE_TERMINATE, (WPARAM) hwnd, 0L) ;
    hwndServer = NULL ;
    return 0 ;

case WM_CLOSE :
    if (hwndServer == NULL)
        break ;

        // Post WM_DDE_UNADVISE iMsg

    PostMessage (hwndServer, WM_DDE_UNADVISE, (WPARAM) hwnd,
                MAKELONG (CF_TEXT, NULL)) ;

    dwTime = GetCurrentTime () ;

    while (GetCurrentTime () - dwTime < DDE_TIMEOUT)
        {
        if (PeekMessage (&msg, hwnd, WM_DDE_ACK,
                    WM_DDE_ACK, PM_REMOVE))
            break ;
        }

        // Post WM_DDE_TERMINATE iMsg

    PostMessage (hwndServer, WM_DDE_TERMINATE, (WPARAM) hwnd, 0L) ;

    dwTime = GetCurrentTime () ;

    while (GetCurrentTime () - dwTime < DDE_TIMEOUT)
        {
        if (PeekMessage (&msg, hwnd, WM_DDE_TERMINATE,
                    WM_DDE_TERMINATE, PM_REMOVE))
            break ;
        }

    break ;              // for default processing

case WM_DESTROY :
    PostQuitMessage (0) ;
```

(continued)

```
                    return 0 ;
          }
    return DefWindowProc (hwnd, iMsg, wParam, lParam) ;
    }
```

SHOWPOP.H

```
/*-----------------------
   SHOWPOP.H header file
   -----------------------*/

struct
    {
    char *szAbb ;
    char *szState ;
    long  lPop ;
    }
    pop[] = {
            "AL", "Alabama",            0, "AK", "Alaska",              0,
            "AZ", "Arizona",            0, "AR", "Arkansas",            0,
            "CA", "California",         0, "CO", "Colorado",            0,
            "CT", "Connecticut",        0, "DE", "Delaware",            0,
            "DC", "Dist. of Columbia",  0, "FL", "Florida",             0,
            "GA", "Georgia",            0, "HI", "Hawaii",              0,
            "ID", "Idaho",              0, "IL", "Illinois",            0,
            "IN", "Indiana",            0, "IA", "Iowa",                0,
            "KS", "Kansas",             0, "KY", "Kentucky",            0,
            "LA", "Louisiana",          0, "ME", "Maine",               0,
            "MD", "Maryland",           0, "MA", "Massachusetts",       0,
            "MI", "Michigan",           0, "MN", "Minnesota",           0,
            "MS", "Mississippi",        0, "MO", "Missouri",            0,
            "MT", "Montana",            0, "NE", "Nebraska",            0,
            "NV", "Nevada",             0, "NH", "New Hampshire",       0,
            "NJ", "New Jersey",         0, "NM", "New Mexico",          0,
            "NY", "New York",           0, "NC", "North Carolina",      0,
            "ND", "North Dakota",       0, "OH", "Ohio",                0,
            "OK", "Oklahoma",           0, "OR", "Oregon",              0,
            "PA", "Pennsylvania",       0, "RI", "Rhode Island",        0,
            "SC", "South Carolina",     0, "SD", "South Dakota",        0,
            "TN", "Tennessee",          0, "TX", "Texas",               0,
            "UT", "Utah",               0, "VT", "Vermont",             0,
            "VA", "Virginia",           0, "WA", "Washington",          0,
            "WV", "West Virginia",      0, "WI", "Wisconsin",           0,
            "WY", "Wyoming",            0, "US", "United States Total", 0
            } ;
#define NUM_STATES (sizeof (pop) / sizeof (pop[0]))
```

This program displays the names of the states in its window with the updated populations obtained from DDEPOP1 using the WM_DDE_ADVISE facility. You'll note that SHOWPOP1 contains a structure called *pop* just like DDEPOP1, but this version contains the two-letter state abbreviations, the state names, and a field called *lPop* (initialized with zeros) that will contain the updated populations obtained from DDEPOP1.

SHOWPOP1 carries on only one DDE conversation, so it needs only one window for this conversation, and it uses *WndProc* for this purpose.

Initiating the DDE Conversation

I've chosen to initiate the DDE conversation by sending *WndProc* a user-defined message (which I've called WM_USER_INITIATE) after the *UpdateWindow* call in *WinMain*. Normally a client would initiate the conversation in response to a menu command.

In response to this user-defined message, *WndProc* calls *GlobalAddAtom* to create atoms for the application name of the server ("DdePop1") and the topic name ("US_Population"). *WndProc* broadcasts the WM_DDE_INITIATE message by calling *SendMessage* with an HWND_BROADCAST window handle.

As we've seen, a server that scores a match with the application and topic atoms is required to send a WM_DDE_ACK message back to the client. Because this message is sent using *SendMessage* rather than posted, the client will receive the WM_DDE_ACK message before the original *SendMessage* call with the WM_DDE_INITIATE message has returned. *WndProc* handles the WM_DDE_ACK message by storing the window handle of the server in the variable *hwndServer* and deleting the atoms that accompany the message.

If a client broadcasts a WM_DDE_INITIATE message with NULL application or topic names, it must be prepared to receive multiple WM_DDE_ACK messages from each of the servers that can satisfy the request. In this case, the client must decide which server to use. The others must be posted WM_DDE_TERMINATE messages to terminate the conversation.

It is possible that *hwndServer* will still be NULL after the WM_DDE_INITIATE *SendMessage* call. This means that DDEPOP1 is not running under Windows. In this case, *WndProc* attempts to execute DDEPOP1 by calling *WinExec*. The *WinExec* call searches the current directory and the PATH environment variable to load DDEPOP1. *WndProc* then again broadcasts the WM_DDE_INITIATE message. If *hwndServer* is still NULL, then *WndProc* displays a message box notifying the user of the problem.

Next, for each of the states listed in the *pop* structure, *WndProc* allocates a DDEADVISE structure by calling *GlobalAlloc*. The *fAckReq* ("acknowledgment requested") flag is set to TRUE (indicating that the server should post WM_DDE_DATA messages with the *fAckReq* field in the DDEDATA field set to NULL). The *fDeferUpd* flag is set to FALSE (indicating a hot link rather than a warm link), and the *cfFormat* field is set to CF_TEXT. *GlobalAddAtom* adds an atom for the two-letter state abbreviation.

This structure and the atom are passed to the server when SHOWPOP1 posts the WM__DDE_ADVISE message. If the *PostMessage* call fails (which might happen if DDEPOP1 is suddenly terminated), then SHOWPOP1 frees the memory block, deletes the atom, and exits the loop. Otherwise, SHOWPOP1 waits for a WM_DDE_ACK message by calling *Peek-Message*. As the DDE documentation indicates, the client deletes the atom accompanying the message and also frees the global memory block if the server responds with a negative acknowledgment.

It's quite likely that this WM_DDE_ACK message from the server will be followed by a WM_DDE_DATA message for the item. For this reason, SHOWPOP1 calls *PeekMessage* and *DispatchMessage* to extract any DDE messages from the message queue and dispatch them to *WndProc*.

The WM_DDE_DATA Message

Following the WM_DDE_ADVISE messages, *WndProc* will receive WM_DDE_DATA messages from the server containing updated population data. As I discussed earlier, *lParam* is a memory object containing both a handle to a memory block containing a WM_DDE_DATA structure and the atom identifying the data item. This information is extracted with a call to *UnpackDDElParam*.

SHOWPOP1 checks if the *cfFormat* field of the DDEDATA structure is CF_TEXT. (Of course, we know that DDEPOP1 uses CF_TEXT exclusively, but this is just for the sake of completeness.) It then obtains the text string associated with the item atom by calling *Global-GetAtomName*. This text string is the two-letter state abbreviation.

Using a *for* loop, SHOWPOP1 scans through the states looking for a match. If it finds one, it copies the population data from the DDEDATA structure into the *szPopulation* array, converts it to a long integer using the C function *atol* ("ASCII to long"), stores it in the *pop* structure, and invalidates the window.

All that remains now is cleaning up. If the client requested an acknowledgment of the WM_DDE_DATA message, *WndProc* posts one. If no acknowledgment was requested (or if the *PostMessage* call fails), the *aItem* atom is deleted. If the *PostMessage* call fails, or if there was no match on the state (indicating a negative acknowledgment), or if the *fRelease* flag in the DDEDATA structure is set to TRUE, then SHOWPOP1 frees the memory block.

I originally wrote SHOWPOP1 so that it posted WM_DDE_ADVISE messages with the *fAckReq* field of the DDEADVISE structure set to FALSE. This indicates to the server that the WM_DDE_DATA messages should be posted with the *fAckReq* field of the DDEDATA structure set to FALSE, which in turn indicates to the client that it should not post WM_DDE_ACK messages to the server acknowledging the WM_DDE_DATA messages. This worked fine for normal updates. However, if I changed the system time in Windows while SHOWPOP1 was running, then DDEPOP1 posted 52 WM_DDE_DATA messages to SHOWPOP1 without waiting for acknowledgment. This caused SHOWPOP1's message queue to overflow, and it lost many of the updated populations.

The lesson is clear: If a client wishes to be advised of many data items that can change all at once, it must set the *fAckReq* field of the DDEADVISE structure to TRUE. This is the only safe approach.

The WM_DDE_TERMINATE Message

Handling a WM_DDE_TERMINATE message posted by the server is simple: SHOWPOP1 simply posts another WM_DDE_TERMINATE message back to the client and sets the *hwndServer* variable to NULL (indicating the conversation is over).

If SHOWPOP1 is closed (indicated by a WM_CLOSE message), then the program first posts a WM_DDE_UNADVISE message to the server to prevent any future updates. This uses a NULL item atom to indicate all data items. SHOWPOP1 then posts a WM_DDE-_TERMINATE message to the server and waits for a WM_DDE_TERMINATE message to return back from the server.

THE DDE MANAGEMENT LIBRARY

Because of the complexity that many programmers encountered when using DDE, Microsoft decided to give it a new look and feel beginning with Windows 3.1. The DDE Management Library (DDEML) hides many of the complexities of DDE by encapsulation of messages, atom management, and memory management in a function call interface.

DDEML may appear daunting at first. The DDEML.H and DDE.H header files define 30 function calls beginning with the prefix *Dde*. A program using DDEML also requires a call-back function that can process 16 transaction types. These are constants defined in DDEML.H beginning with the prefix XTYP.

The good news is that DDEML does indeed simplify DDE programming. This will be obvious in the code lengths of the DDEPOP2.C and SHOWPOP2.C source code files, which are functionally equivalent to DDEPOP1 and SHOWPOP1.

Conceptual Differences

There are some terminology and conceptual differences between using classic DDE and using DDEML. First, although DDE transactions are still based on application, topic, and item names, in DDEML the application name is called the "service" name.

Any program that uses DDEML must first register itself with the DDE Management Library by calling *DdeInitialize*. This function obtains an application instance identifier that is passed to all other DDEML functions. When the program terminates, it calls *DdeUn-initialize*.

The most significant difference between classic DDE and DDEML is that a program processes DDE transactions in a call-back function rather than a window procedure. This call-back function is registered with the system in the *DdeInitialize* call.

When passing data from one application to another, a program does not directly allocate shared memory. Instead, the program creates a data handle from a buffer containing the data, through a call to *DdeCreateDataHandle*. The program receiving the data obtains the data from the handle using *DdeAccessData* or *DdeGetData*. The data handle is freed by calling *DdeFreeDataHandle*.

Rather than using atoms, a DDEML program uses string handles, which are stored in variables of type HSZ. The *DdeCreateStringHandle* function creates a string handle from a character string, *DdeQueryString* obtains a string from the handle, *DdeCmpStringHandles* compares the strings represented by two string handles, and *DdeFreeStringHandle* frees a string handle. In some cases, string handles are freed automatically. A program can keep a string handle valid by calling *DdeKeepStringHandle*.

DDE the DDEML Way

Let's jump right into the sample code to see how DDEML works in a real-life application. Figure 17-3 shows the source code for a DDEML server called DDEPOP2, and Figure 17-4 (beginning on page 923) shows the source code for a DDEML client named SHOWPOP2. The DDEPOP2 program also requires the DDEPOP.H and DDEPOP.ICO files from Figure 17-1, and the SHOWPOP2 program requires the SHOWPOP.H file from Figure 17-2.

DDEPOP2.MAK

```
#----------------------
# DDEPOP2.MAK make file
#----------------------

ddepop2.exe : ddepop2.obj ddepop2.res
     $(LINKER) $(GUIFLAGS) -OUT:ddepop2.exe ddepop2.obj ddepop2.res $(GUILIBS)

ddepop2.obj : ddepop2.c ddepop.h
     $(CC) $(CFLAGS) ddepop2.c

ddepop2.res : ddepop2.rc ddepop.ico
     $(RC) $(RCVARS) ddepop2.rc
```

DDEPOP2.C

```
/*---------------------------------------------------
   DDEPOP2.C -- DDEML Server for Population Data
              (c) Charles Petzold, 1996
   ---------------------------------------------------*/
```

Figure 17-3. *The DDEPOP2 program.*   *(continued)*

```
#include <windows.h>
#include <ddeml.h>
#include <string.h>
#include "ddepop.h"

#define WM_USER_INITIATE (WM_USER + 1)
#define ID_TIMER         1

LRESULT  CALLBACK WndProc     (HWND, UINT, WPARAM, LPARAM) ;
HDDEDATA CALLBACK DdeCallback (UINT, UINT, HCONV, HSZ, HSZ,
                                      HDDEDATA, DWORD, DWORD) ;

char      szAppName[] = "DdePop2" ;
char      szTopic[]   = "US_Population" ;
DWORD     idInst ;
HINSTANCE hInst ;
HWND      hwnd ;

int WINAPI WinMain (HINSTANCE hInstance, HINSTANCE hPrevInstance,
                   PSTR szCmdLine, int iCmdShow)
    {
    MSG         msg ;
    WNDCLASSEX  wndclass ;

    wndclass.cbSize        = sizeof (wndclass) ;
    wndclass.style         = 0 ;
    wndclass.lpfnWndProc   = WndProc ;
    wndclass.cbClsExtra    = 0 ;
    wndclass.cbWndExtra    = 0 ;
    wndclass.hInstance     = hInstance ;
    wndclass.hIcon         = LoadIcon (hInstance, szAppName) ;
    wndclass.hCursor       = LoadCursor (NULL, IDC_ARROW) ;
    wndclass.hbrBackground = (HBRUSH) GetStockObject (WHITE_BRUSH) ;
    wndclass.lpszMenuName  = NULL ;
    wndclass.lpszClassName = szAppName ;
    wndclass.hIconSm       = LoadIcon (hInstance, szAppName) ;

    RegisterClassEx (&wndclass) ;

    hwnd = CreateWindow (szAppName, "DDEML Population Server",
                        WS_OVERLAPPEDWINDOW,
                        CW_USEDEFAULT, CW_USEDEFAULT,
                        CW_USEDEFAULT, CW_USEDEFAULT,
                        NULL, NULL, hInstance, NULL) ;

    ShowWindow (hwnd, SW_SHOWMINNOACTIVE) ;
```

(continued)

```
        UpdateWindow (hwnd) ;

                // Initialize for using DDEML

        if (DdeInitialize (&idInst, (PFNCALLBACK) &DdeCallback,
                        CBF_FAIL_EXECUTES | CBF_FAIL_POKES |
                        CBF_SKIP_REGISTRATIONS | CBF_SKIP_UNREGISTRATIONS, 0))
            {
            MessageBox (hwnd, "Could not initialize server!",
                        szAppName, MB_ICONEXCLAMATION | MB_OK) ;

            DestroyWindow (hwnd) ;
            return FALSE ;
            }

                // Set the timer

        SetTimer (hwnd, ID_TIMER, 5000, NULL) ;

                // Start things going

        SendMessage (hwnd, WM_USER_INITIATE, 0, 0L) ;

        while (GetMessage (&msg, NULL, 0, 0))
            {
            TranslateMessage (&msg) ;
            DispatchMessage (&msg) ;
            }

                // Clean up

        DdeUninitialize (idInst) ;
        KillTimer (hwnd, ID_TIMER) ;

        return msg.wParam ;
        }

int GetStateNumber (UINT iFmt, HSZ hszItem)
    {
    char szItem[32] ;
    int  i ;

    if (iFmt != CF_TEXT)
        return -1 ;
```

(continued)

```
        DdeQueryString (idInst, hszItem, szItem, sizeof (szItem), 0) ;

        for (i = 0 ; i < NUM_STATES ; i++)
             if (strcmp (szItem, pop[i].szState) == 0)
                  break ;

        if (i >= NUM_STATES)
             return -1 ;

        return i ;
        }

HDDEDATA CALLBACK DdeCallback (UINT iType, UINT iFmt, HCONV hConv,
                               HSZ hsz1, HSZ hsz2, HDDEDATA hData,
                               DWORD dwData1, DWORD dwData2)
        {
        char szBuffer[32] ;
        int  i ;

        switch (iType)
             {
             case XTYP_CONNECT :            // hsz1 = topic
                                            // hsz2 = service

                  DdeQueryString (idInst, hsz2, szBuffer, sizeof (szBuffer), 0) ;

                  if (0 != strcmp (szBuffer, szAppName))
                       return FALSE ;

                  DdeQueryString (idInst, hsz1, szBuffer, sizeof (szBuffer), 0) ;

                  if (0 != strcmp (szBuffer, szTopic))
                       return FALSE ;

                  return (HDDEDATA) TRUE ;

             case XTYP_ADVSTART :           // hsz1 = topic
                                            // hsz2 = item

                       // Check for matching format and data item

                  if (-1 == (i = GetStateNumber (iFmt, hsz2)))
                       return FALSE ;

                  pop[i].lPopLast = 0 ;
                  PostMessage (hwnd, WM_TIMER, 0, 0L) ;
```

(continued)

920

```
                    return (HDDEDATA) TRUE ;

          case XTYP_REQUEST :
          case XTYP_ADVREQ :                  // hsz1 = topic
                                              // hsz2 = item

                    // Check for matching format and data item

               if (-1 == (i = GetStateNumber (iFmt, hsz2)))
                    return NULL ;

               wsprintf (szBuffer, "%ld\r\n", pop[i].lPop) ;

               return DdeCreateDataHandle (idInst, (unsigned char *) szBuffer,
                                   strlen (szBuffer) + 1,
                                   0, hsz2, CF_TEXT, 0) ;

          case XTYP_ADVSTOP :                 // hsz1 = topic
                                              // hsz2 = item

                    // Check for matching format and data item

               if (-1 == (i = GetStateNumber (iFmt, hsz2)))
                    return FALSE ;

               return (HDDEDATA) TRUE ;
          }

     return NULL ;
     }

LRESULT CALLBACK WndProc (HWND hwnd, UINT iMsg, WPARAM wParam, LPARAM lParam)
     {
     static HSZ hszService, hszTopic ;
     HSZ       hszItem ;
     int       i ;

     switch (iMsg)
          {
          case WM_USER_INITIATE :
               InitPops () ;

               hszService = DdeCreateStringHandle (idInst, szAppName, 0) ;
               hszTopic   = DdeCreateStringHandle (idInst, szTopic,   0) ;

               DdeNameService (idInst, hszService, NULL, DNS_REGISTER) ;
```

(continued)

```
                    return 0 ;

        case WM_TIMER :
        case WM_TIMECHANGE :

                // Calculate new current populations

            CalcPops () ;

            for (i = 0 ; i < NUM_STATES ; i++)
                if (pop[i].lPop != pop[i].lPopLast)
                    {
                    hszItem = DdeCreateStringHandle (idInst,
                                                    pop[i].szState, 0) ;

                    DdePostAdvise (idInst, hszTopic, hszItem) ;

                    DdeFreeStringHandle (idInst, hszItem) ;

                    pop[i].lPopLast = pop[i].lPop ;
                    }

            return 0 ;

        case WM_QUERYOPEN :
            return 0 ;

        case WM_DESTROY :
            DdeNameService (idInst, hszService, NULL, DNS_UNREGISTER) ;
            DdeFreeStringHandle (idInst, hszService) ;
            DdeFreeStringHandle (idInst, hszTopic) ;

            PostQuitMessage (0) ;
            return 0 ;
        }
    return DefWindowProc (hwnd, iMsg, wParam, lParam) ;
    }
```

DDEPOP2.RC

```
/*-------------------------
DDEPOP2.RC resource script
------------------------*/

DdePop2 ICON ddepop.ico
```

SHOWPOP2.MAK

```
#-----------------------
# SHOWPOP2.MAK make file
#-----------------------

showpop2.exe : showpop2.obj
    $(LINKER) $(GUIFLAGS) -OUT:showpop2.exe showpop2.obj $(GUILIBS)

showpop2.obj : showpop2.c showpop.h
    $(CC) $(CFLAGS) showpop2.c
```

SHOWPOP2.C

```
/*---------------------------------------------
   SHOWPOP2.C -- DDEML Client using DDEPOP2
                 (c) Charles Petzold, 1996
   ---------------------------------------------*/

#include <windows.h>
#include <ddeml.h>
#include <stdlib.h>
#include <string.h>
#include "showpop.h"

#define WM_USER_INITIATE (WM_USER + 1)
#define DDE_TIMEOUT       3000

LRESULT  CALLBACK WndProc      (HWND, UINT, WPARAM, LPARAM) ;
HDDEDATA CALLBACK DdeCallback (UINT, UINT, HCONV, HSZ, HSZ,
                               HDDEDATA, DWORD, DWORD) ;

char  szAppName[] = "ShowPop2" ;
DWORD idInst ;
HCONV hConv ;
HWND  hwnd ;

int WINAPI WinMain (HINSTANCE hInstance, HINSTANCE hPrevInstance,
                    PSTR szCmdLine, int iCmdShow)
    {
    MSG          msg ;
    WNDCLASSEX  wndclass ;

    wndclass.cbSize          = sizeof (wndclass) ;
    wndclass.style           = CS_HREDRAW | CS_VREDRAW ;
```

Figure 17-4. *The SHOWPOP2 program.*   *(continued)*

```
wndclass.lpfnWndProc   = WndProc ;
wndclass.cbClsExtra    = 0 ;
wndclass.cbWndExtra    = 0 ;
wndclass.hInstance     = hInstance ;
wndclass.hIcon         = LoadIcon (hInstance, szAppName) ;
wndclass.hCursor       = LoadCursor (NULL, IDC_ARROW) ;
wndclass.hbrBackground = (HBRUSH) GetStockObject (WHITE_BRUSH) ;
wndclass.lpszMenuName  = NULL ;
wndclass.lpszClassName = szAppName ;
wndclass.hIconSm       = LoadIcon (hInstance, szAppName) ;

RegisterClassEx (&wndclass) ;

hwnd = CreateWindow (szAppName, "DDEML Client - US Population",
                WS_OVERLAPPEDWINDOW,
                CW_USEDEFAULT, CW_USEDEFAULT,
                CW_USEDEFAULT, CW_USEDEFAULT,
                NULL, NULL, hInstance, NULL) ;

ShowWindow (hwnd, iCmdShow) ;
UpdateWindow (hwnd) ;

        // Initialize for using DDEML


if (DdeInitialize (&idInst, (PFNCALLBACK) &DdeCallback,
                APPCLASS_STANDARD | APPCMD_CLIENTONLY, 0L))
     {
     MessageBox (hwnd, "Could not initialize client!",
                szAppName, MB_ICONEXCLAMATION | MB_OK) ;

     DestroyWindow (hwnd) ;
     return FALSE ;
     }

        // Start things going

SendMessage (hwnd, WM_USER_INITIATE, 0, 0L) ;

while (GetMessage (&msg, NULL, 0, 0))
     {
     TranslateMessage (&msg) ;
     DispatchMessage (&msg) ;
     }
```

(continued)

```
                    // Uninitialize DDEML

      DdeUninitialize (idInst) ;

      return msg.wParam ;
      }

HDDEDATA CALLBACK DdeCallback (UINT iType, UINT iFmt, HCONV hConv,
                         HSZ hsz1, HSZ hsz2, HDDEDATA hData,
                         DWORD dwData1, DWORD dwData2)
      {
      char szItem[10], szPopulation[16] ;
      int  i ;

      switch (iType)
           {
           case XTYP_ADVDATA :        // hsz1  = topic
                                      // hsz2  = item
                                      // hData = data

                // Check for matching format and data item

                if (iFmt != CF_TEXT)
                    return DDE_FNOTPROCESSED ;

                DdeQueryString (idInst, hsz2, szItem, sizeof (szItem), 0) ;

                for (i = 0 ; i < NUM_STATES ; i++)
                    if (strcmp (szItem, pop[i].szAbb) == 0)
                         break ;

                if (i >= NUM_STATES)
                    return DDE_FNOTPROCESSED ;

                    // Store the data and invalidate the window

                DdeGetData (hData, (unsigned char *) szPopulation,
                          sizeof (szPopulation), 0) ;

                pop[i].lPop = atol (szPopulation) ;

                InvalidateRect (hwnd, NULL, FALSE) ;

                return (HDDEDATA) DDE_FACK ;
```

(continued)

```
            case XTYP_DISCONNECT :
                hConv = NULL ;

                MessageBox (hwnd, "The server has disconnected.",
                            szAppName, MB_ICONASTERISK | MB_OK) ;

                return NULL ;
            }

     return NULL ;
     }

LRESULT CALLBACK WndProc (HWND hwnd, UINT iMsg, WPARAM wParam,  LPARAM lParam)
     {
     static char   szService[] = "DdePop2",
                   szTopic[]   = "US_Population" ;
     static long   cxChar, cyChar ;
     char          szBuffer[24] ;
     HDC           hdc ;
     HSZ           hszService, hszTopic, hszItem ;
     PAINTSTRUCT   ps ;
     int           i ;
     long          x, y ;
     TEXTMETRIC    tm ;

     switch (iMsg)
          {
          case WM_CREATE :
               hdc = GetDC (hwnd) ;
               GetTextMetrics (hdc, &tm) ;
               cxChar = tm.tmAveCharWidth ;
               cyChar = tm.tmHeight + tm.tmExternalLeading ;
               ReleaseDC (hwnd, hdc) ;

               return 0 ;

          case WM_USER_INITIATE :

                       // Try connecting

               hszService = DdeCreateStringHandle (idInst, szService, 0) ;
               hszTopic   = DdeCreateStringHandle (idInst, szTopic,   0) ;

               hConv = DdeConnect (idInst, hszService, hszTopic, NULL) ;
```

(continued)

```
                    // If that doesn't work, load server

if (hConv == NULL)
     {
     WinExec (szService, SW_SHOWMINNOACTIVE) ;

     hConv = DdeConnect (idInst, hszService, hszTopic, NULL) ;
     }

          // Free the string handles

DdeFreeStringHandle (idInst, hszService) ;
DdeFreeStringHandle (idInst, hszTopic) ;

          // If still not connected, display message box

if (hConv == NULL)
     {
     MessageBox (hwnd, "Cannot connect with DDEPOP2.EXE!",
                 szAppName, MB_ICONEXCLAMATION | MB_OK) ;

     return 0 ;
     }

          // Request notification

for (i = 0 ; i < NUM_STATES ; i++)
     {
     hszItem = DdeCreateStringHandle (idInst, pop[i].szAbb, 0) ;

     DdeClientTransaction (NULL, 0, hConv, hszItem, CF_TEXT,
                           XTYP_ADVSTART | XTYPF_ACKREQ,
                           DDE_TIMEOUT, NULL) ;

     DdeFreeStringHandle (idInst, hszItem) ;
     }

if (i < NUM_STATES)
     {
     MessageBox (hwnd, "Failure on WM_DDE_ADVISE!",
                 szAppName, MB_ICONEXCLAMATION | MB_OK) ;
     }

return 0 ;
```

```
case WM_PAINT :
    hdc = BeginPaint (hwnd, &ps) ;

    for (i = 0 ; i < NUM_STATES ; i++)
        {
        if (i < (NUM_STATES + 1) / 2)
            {
            x = cxChar ;
            y = i * cyChar ;
            }
        else
            {
            x = 44 * cxChar ;
            y = (i - (NUM_STATES + 1) / 2) * cyChar ;
            }

        TextOut (hdc, x, y, szBuffer,
                wsprintf (szBuffer, "%-20s",
                        (PSTR) pop[i].szState)) ;

        x += 36 * cxChar ;

        SetTextAlign (hdc, TA_RIGHT | TA_TOP) ;

        TextOut (hdc, x, y, szBuffer,
                wsprintf (szBuffer, "%10ld", pop[i].lPop)) ;

        SetTextAlign (hdc, TA_LEFT | TA_TOP) ;
        }

    EndPaint (hwnd, &ps) ;
    return 0 ;

case WM_CLOSE :
    if (hConv == NULL)
        break ;

            // Stop the advises

    for (i = 0 ; i < NUM_STATES ; i++)
        {
        hszItem = DdeCreateStringHandle (idInst, pop[i].szAbb, 0) ;

        DdeClientTransaction (NULL, 0, hConv, hszItem, CF_TEXT,
                        XTYP_ADVSTOP, DDE_TIMEOUT, NULL) ;
```

(continued)

```
                    DdeFreeStringHandle (idInst, hszItem) ;
               }

               // Disconnect the conversation

          DdeDisconnect (hConv) ;

          break ;              // for default processing

     case WM_DESTROY :
          PostQuitMessage (0) ;
          return 0 ;
     }
     return DefWindowProc (hwnd, iMsg, wParam, lParam) ;
}
```

In *WinMain*, SHOWPOP2 passes the address of its call-back function (called *DdeCallback*) to *DdeInitialize*. The DDEML instance handle is stored in the global variable *idInst*, which must be passed as the first parameter to all other DDEML function calls.

SHOWPOP2 then sends itself a WM_USER_INITIATE message; other initialization occurs in the *WndProc* window procedure. The program calls *DdeCreateStringHandle* twice to create string handles for the server's service name ("DdePop2") and the topic name ("US_Population"). SHOWPOP2 passes these string handles to *DdeConnect* to attempt to initiate a conversation with the DDEPOP2 server. As in SHOWPOP1, if the conversation cannot be initiated, the program calls *WinExec* to load DDEPOP2 and then tries again. Following this, the string handles can be freed with calls to *DdeFreeStringHandle*.

When the DDEPOP2 server starts up, it calls *DdeInitialize* in its *WinMain* function and also calls *SetTimer* to set a 5-second timer for updating the population data. DDEPOP2 then sends its window procedure a WM_USER_INITIATE message. While processing this message, DDEPOP2 initializes the population data and creates two string handles for its service and topic names. *WndProc* then calls *DdeNameService* to register its service name. This prevents the call-back function from receiving any connection requests that do not explicitly name it as a service.

When SHOWPOP2 calls *DdeConnect*, the DDE Management Library calls the call-back function in DDEPOP2 with a transaction type of XTYP_CONNECT. The *hsz1* and *hsz2* parameters to the call-back function are string handles that indicate the topic and service names passed to the *DdeConnect* function. The *DdeCallback* function in DDEPOP2 uses the *DdeQueryString* function to check if the topic and service names match the strings "US_Population" and "DdePop2". If the strings match, *DdeCallback* returns TRUE; otherwise, the function returns FALSE. String handles passed to a call-back function do not need to be freed by the call-back.

When the server's *DdeCallback* function returns TRUE after processing the XTYP-_CONNECT transaction, the DDE conversation has begun. The *DdeConnect* function called

929

by the client (SHOWPOP2) returns a conversation handle, which has a data type of HCONV. This handle is also passed to the server's call-back function in an XTYP_CONNECT-_CONFIRM transaction. The server could save this conversation handle if it wishes, but DDE-POP2 does not.

When we last left SHOWPOP2, it had established a connection with DDEPOP2 by calling *DdeConnect* and freed the string handles for the service and topic names required for that function. SHOWPOP2 then attempts to begin hot links for the populations of each of the 50 states, the District of Columbia, and the entire United States. To do this, SHOWPOP2 enters a loop and calls *DdeCreateStringHandle* for each of the two-character state codes. These are passed, along with the conversation handle, the clipboard format type, and the flag XTYP_ADVSTART to *DdeClientTransaction*. This is the basic function a client uses to obtain data from a server. Each string handle is then freed with a call to *DdeFreeStringHandle*.

When a client engaged in a conversation calls *DdeClientTransaction* with an XTYP-_ADVSTART parameter, the server's call-back function is called by the DDE Management Library with a transaction type of XTYP_ADVSTART. DDEPOP2 simply checks if the clipboard format is CF_TEXT and the item name is a valid two-character state code. (This is done in DDEPOP2's *GetStateNumber* function.) If the item name is valid, DDEPOP2 then sets the population of that state to 0 and posts a WM_TIMER message to its window procedure.

Here's where some of the real magic of DDEML takes place. The DDEPOP2 server has agreed to have a conversation, but it has not saved the conversation handle. The DDEPOP2 call-back has also received XTYP_ADVSTART transactions for particular states, but it has not saved any information about which client in which conversation has requested information about which states.

DDEPOP2 has not saved this information, but the DDE Management Library has. Now let's see what happens when DDEPOP2 updates its population information during WM_TIMER (and WM_TIMECHANGE) processing in *WndProc*. It calls *CalcPops* to calculate new populations, and then checks which population changed. If a population has changed, DDEPOP2 creates a string handle for the two-character state code and then calls *DdePostAdvise* with the topic and item names.

For each conversation where a client has requested a hot link with the topic and item names passed to *DdePostAdvise*, *DdePostAdvise* calls DDEPOP2's own call-back function with an XTYP_ADVREQ transaction type. The *hsz1* and *hsz2* parameters to the call-back function indicate the topic and item names. All the call-back function needs do is return a data handle referencing the new data. To do this, *DdeCallback* formats the population in a string and passes the string buffer to *DdeCreateDataHandle*. This function returns a data handle of type HDDEDATA, which the call-back function simply returns. Data handles returned from a call-back function do not need to be explicitly freed.

When DDEPOP2 returns a data handle from its call-back function in response to an XTYP_ADVREQ transaction, the DDE Management Library calls SHOWPOP2's call-back function with a transaction type of XTYP_ADVDATA. SHOWPOP2 uses the *DdeGetData* function to obtain the population data and stores it. SHOWPOP2 then invalidates its window to update the display.

And that's basically it. When the time comes for SHOWPOP2 to terminate, it calls *Dde-ClientTransaction* for all the states using a transaction type of XTYP_ADVSTOP. DDEPOP2 receives this transaction in its call-back function. SHOWPOP2 then calls *DdeDisconnect* and, after dropping out of its message loop, *DdeUninitialize*. Any cleaning up that the DDE programs failed to do before this function is done automatically by *DdeUninitialize*.

## Chapter 18

The Multiple Document Interface (MDI)

The Multiple Document Interface (MDI) is a specification for applications that handle documents in Microsoft Windows. The specification describes a window structure and user interface that allow the user to work with multiple documents within a single application (such as text documents in a word-processing program or spreadsheets in a spreadsheet program). Simply put, just as Windows maintains multiple application windows within a single screen, an MDI application maintains multiple document windows within a single client area. The first MDI application for Windows was the first Windows version of Microsoft Excel. Both Microsoft Word for Windows and Microsoft Access are MDI applications.

Although the MDI specification has been around since Windows 2, at that time MDI applications were difficult to write and required some very intricate programming work. Since Windows 3, however, much of that work has already been done for you. Windows 95 adds only one new function and one new message to the collection of functions, data structures, and messages that exist for the specific purpose of simplifying MDI applications.

THE ELEMENTS OF MDI

The main application window of an MDI program is conventional: It has a title bar, a menu, a sizing border, a system menu icon, and minimize/maximize icons. The client area, however, is often called a "workspace" and is not directly used to display program output. This workspace may contain multiple child windows, each of which displays a document.

These child windows look much like normal application windows. They have a title bar, a sizing border, a system menu icon, minimize/maximize icons, and possibly scroll bars. None of the document windows has a menu, however. The menu on the main application window applies to the document windows.

Only one document window at a time is active (indicated by a highlighted title bar) and appears in front of all the other document windows. All the document child windows are clipped to the workspace area and never appear outside the application window.

At first, MDI seems a fairly straightforward job for the Windows programmer. All you need to do is create a WS_CHILD window for each document, making the program's main application window the parent of the document window. But with a little exploration of an MDI application such as Microsoft Excel, you'll find some complications that require difficult code. For instance:

■   An MDI document window can be minimized. Its icon appears at the bottom of the workspace. (Generally an MDI application will use different icons for the main application window and each type of document window.)

■   An MDI document window can be maximized. In this case, the title bar of the document window (normally used to show the filename of the document in the window) disappears, and the filename appears appended to the application name in the application window's title bar. The system menu icon of the document window becomes the first item in the top-level menu of the application window. The icon to restore the size of the document window becomes the last item in the top-level menu and appears to the far right.

■   The system keyboard accelerator to close a document window is the same as that to close the main window, except that the Ctrl key is used rather than Alt. That is, Alt-F4 closes the application window while Ctrl-F4 closes the document window. In addition, Ctrl-F6 switches among the child document windows within the active MDI application. Alt-Spacebar invokes the system menu of the main window, as usual. Alt- – (minus) invokes the system menu of the active child document window.

■   When using the cursor keys to move among items on the menu, control normally passes from the system menu to the first item on the menu bar. In an MDI application, control passes from the application system menu to the active document system menu to the first item on the menu bar.

■ If the application is capable of supporting several types of child windows (for example, the worksheet and chart documents in Microsoft Excel), then the menu should reflect the operations associated with that type of document. This requires that the program change the menu when a different document window becomes active. In addition, when no document window exists, the menu should be stripped down to only those operations involved in opening a new document.

■ The top-level menu bar has an item called Window. By convention, this is the last item on the top-level menu bar except for Help. The Window submenu generally has options to arrange the document windows within the workspace. Document windows can be "cascaded" from the upper left or "tiled" so that each document window is fully visible. This submenu also has a list of all the document windows. Selecting one moves that document window to the foreground.

All of these aspects of MDI are supported in Windows 95. Some overhead is required, of course (as will be shown in a sample program), but it isn't anywhere close to the amount of code you'd have to write to support all these features directly.

WINDOWS 95 AND MDI

Some new terminology is necessary when approaching the Windows 95 MDI support. The main application window is called the "frame window." Just as in a conventional Windows program, this is a window of the WS_OVERLAPPEDWINDOW style.

An MDI application also creates a "client window" based on the predefined window class "MDICLIENT." The client window is created by a call to *CreateWindow* using this window class and the WS_CHILD style. The last parameter to *CreateWindow* is a pointer to a small structure of type CLIENTCREATESTRUCT. This client window covers the client area of the frame window and is responsible for much of the MDI support. The color of this client window is the system color COLOR_APPWORKSPACE.

The document windows are called "child windows." You create these windows by initializing a structure of type MDICREATESTRUCT and sending the client window a WM_MDICREATE message with a pointer to this structure.

The document windows are children of the client window, which in turn is a child of the frame window. The parent–child hierarchy is shown in the diagram in Figure 18-1 on the following page.

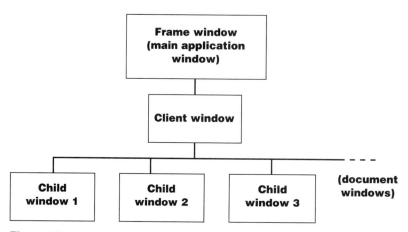

Figure 18-1. *The parent-child hierarchy of a Windows MDI application.*

You need a window class (and window procedure) for the frame window and for each type of child window supported by the application. You don't need a window procedure for the client window because the window class is preregistered.

MDI support of Windows 95 includes one window class, five functions, two data structures, and twelve messages. I've already mentioned the MDI window class, which is MDICLIENT, and the data structures, CLIENTCREATESTRUCT and MDICREATESTRUCT. Two of the five functions replace *DefWindowProc* in MDI applications: Rather than call *DefWindowProc* for all unprocessed messages, a frame window procedure calls *DefFrameProc* and a child window procedure calls *DefMDIChildProc*. Another function specific to MDI, *TranslateMDISysAccel*, is used in the same way as *TranslateAccelerator*, which I discussed in Chapter 10. Windows 3 added the function *ArrangeIconicWindows*, but one of the special MDI messages makes this function unnecessary for MDI programs.

If the MDI child windows in your program conduct any lengthy operations, consider running them in separate threads. This allows the user to switch away from a busy child window and continue working in another while the first window churns away at its task in the background. Windows 95 provides the new *CreateMDIWindow* function specifically for this purpose. A thread calls *CreateMDIWindow* to create an MDI child window; thereafter, the window operates entirely within the context of the thread. A single-threaded program does not require *CreateMDIWindow* to create a child window, since the WM_MDICREATE message accomplishes the same thing.

In the single-threaded sample program coming up, I'll demonstrate nine of the twelve MDI messages. (The other three are not normally required.) These messages begin with the prefix WM_MDI. A frame window sends one of these messages to the client window to perform an operation on a child window or to obtain information about a child window. (For example, a frame window sends a WM_MDICREATE message to a client window to create a child window.) The WM_MDIACTIVATE message is an exception: While a frame window can send this message to the client window to activate one of the child windows, the client window also sends the message to the child windows being activated and deactivated to inform them of this change.

THE SAMPLE PROGRAM

The MDIDEMO program, shown in Figure 18-2, demonstrates the basics of writing an MDI application.

MDIDEMO.MAK

```
#-----------------------
# MDIDEMO.MAK make file
#-----------------------

mdidemo.exe : mdidemo.obj mdidemo.res
    $(LINKER) $(GUIFLAGS) -OUT:mdidemo.exe mdidemo.obj mdidemo.res $(GUILIBS)

mdidemo.obj : mdidemo.c mdidemo.h
    $(CC) $(CFLAGS) mdidemo.c

mdidemo.res : mdidemo.rc mdidemo.h
    $(RC) $(RCVARS) mdidemo.rc
```

MDIDEMO.C

```
/*---------------------------------------------------------
   MDIDEMO.C -- Multiple Document Interface Demonstration
                (c) Charles Petzold, 1996
   ---------------------------------------------------------*/

#include <windows.h>
#include <stdlib.h>
#include "mdidemo.h"

LRESULT CALLBACK FrameWndProc (HWND, UINT, WPARAM, LPARAM) ;
BOOL    CALLBACK CloseEnumProc (HWND, LPARAM) ;
LRESULT CALLBACK HelloWndProc (HWND, UINT, WPARAM, LPARAM) ;
```

Figure 18-2. *The MDIDEMO program.* *(continued)*

```
LRESULT CALLBACK RectWndProc    (HWND, UINT, WPARAM, LPARAM) ;

        // structure for storing data unique to each Hello child window

typedef struct tagHELLODATA
    {
    UINT     iColor ;
    COLORREF clrText ;
    }
    HELLODATA, *LPHELLODATA ;

        // structure for storing data unique to each Rect child window

typedef struct tagRECTDATA
    {
    short cxClient ;
    short cyClient ;
    }
    RECTDATA, *LPRECTDATA ;

        // global variables

char       szFrameClass[] = "MdiFrame" ;
char       szHelloClass[] = "MdiHelloChild" ;
char       szRectClass[]  = "MdiRectChild" ;
HINSTANCE  hInst ;
HMENU      hMenuInit, hMenuHello, hMenuRect ;
HMENU      hMenuInitWindow, hMenuHelloWindow, hMenuRectWindow ;

int WINAPI WinMain (HINSTANCE hInstance, HINSTANCE hPrevInstance,
                    PSTR szCmdLine, int iCmdShow)
    {
    HACCEL      hAccel ;
    HWND        hwndFrame, hwndClient ;
    MSG         msg ;
    WNDCLASSEX  wndclass ;

    hInst = hInstance ;

    if (!hPrevInstance)
        {
                // Register the frame window class
```

(continued)

938

```
wndclass.cbSize         = sizeof (wndclass) ;
wndclass.style          = CS_HREDRAW | CS_VREDRAW ;
wndclass.lpfnWndProc    = FrameWndProc ;
wndclass.cbClsExtra     = 0 ;
wndclass.cbWndExtra     = 0 ;
wndclass.hInstance      = hInstance ;
wndclass.hIcon          = LoadIcon (NULL, IDI_APPLICATION) ;
wndclass.hCursor        = LoadCursor (NULL, IDC_ARROW) ;
wndclass.hbrBackground  = (HBRUSH) (COLOR_APPWORKSPACE + 1) ;
wndclass.lpszMenuName   = NULL ;
wndclass.lpszClassName  = szFrameClass ;
wndclass.hIconSm        = LoadIcon (NULL, IDI_APPLICATION) ;

RegisterClassEx (&wndclass) ;

        // Register the Hello child window class

wndclass.cbSize         = sizeof (wndclass) ;
wndclass.style          = CS_HREDRAW | CS_VREDRAW ;
wndclass.lpfnWndProc    = HelloWndProc ;
wndclass.cbClsExtra     = 0 ;
wndclass.cbWndExtra     = sizeof (HANDLE) ;
wndclass.hInstance      = hInstance ;
wndclass.hIcon          = LoadIcon (NULL, IDI_APPLICATION) ;
wndclass.hCursor        = LoadCursor (NULL, IDC_ARROW) ;
wndclass.hbrBackground  = (HBRUSH) GetStockObject (WHITE_BRUSH) ;
wndclass.lpszMenuName   = NULL ;
wndclass.lpszClassName  = szHelloClass ;
wndclass.hIconSm        = LoadIcon (NULL, IDI_APPLICATION) ;

RegisterClassEx (&wndclass) ;

        // Register the Rect child window class

wndclass.cbSize         = sizeof (wndclass) ;
wndclass.style          = CS_HREDRAW | CS_VREDRAW ;
wndclass.lpfnWndProc    = RectWndProc ;
wndclass.cbClsExtra     = 0 ;
wndclass.cbWndExtra     = sizeof (HANDLE) ;
wndclass.hInstance      = hInstance ;
wndclass.hIcon          = LoadIcon (NULL, IDI_APPLICATION) ;
wndclass.hCursor        = LoadCursor (NULL, IDC_ARROW) ;
wndclass.hbrBackground  = (HBRUSH) GetStockObject (WHITE_BRUSH) ;
```

(continued)

```
          wndclass.lpszMenuName  = NULL ;
          wndclass.lpszClassName = szRectClass ;
          wndclass.hIconSm       = LoadIcon (NULL, IDI_APPLICATION) ;

          RegisterClassEx (&wndclass) ;
          }
               // Obtain handles to three possible menus & submenus

     hMenuInit  = LoadMenu (hInst, "MdiMenuInit") ;
     hMenuHello = LoadMenu (hInst, "MdiMenuHello") ;
     hMenuRect  = LoadMenu (hInst, "MdiMenuRect") ;

     hMenuInitWindow  = GetSubMenu (hMenuInit,  INIT_MENU_POS) ;
     hMenuHelloWindow = GetSubMenu (hMenuHello, HELLO_MENU_POS) ;
     hMenuRectWindow  = GetSubMenu (hMenuRect,  RECT_MENU_POS) ;

               // Load accelerator table

     hAccel = LoadAccelerators (hInst, "MdiAccel") ;

               // Create the frame window

     hwndFrame = CreateWindow (szFrameClass, "MDI Demonstration",
                          WS_OVERLAPPEDWINDOW | WS_CLIPCHILDREN,
                          CW_USEDEFAULT, CW_USEDEFAULT,
                          CW_USEDEFAULT, CW_USEDEFAULT,
                          NULL, hMenuInit, hInstance, NULL) ;

     hwndClient = GetWindow (hwndFrame, GW_CHILD) ;

     ShowWindow (hwndFrame, iCmdShow) ;
     UpdateWindow (hwndFrame) ;

               // Enter the modified message loop

     while (GetMessage (&msg, NULL, 0, 0))
          {
          if (!TranslateMDISysAccel (hwndClient, &msg) &&
              !TranslateAccelerator (hwndFrame, hAccel, &msg))
               {
               TranslateMessage (&msg) ;
               DispatchMessage (&msg) ;
               }
          }
```

(continued)

```
                // Clean up by deleting unattached menus

     DestroyMenu (hMenuHello) ;
     DestroyMenu (hMenuRect) ;

     return msg.wParam ;
     }

LRESULT CALLBACK FrameWndProc (HWND hwnd, UINT iMsg, WPARAM wParam,
                                                    LPARAM lParam)
     {
     static HWND          hwndClient ;
     CLIENTCREATESTRUCT   clientcreate ;
     HWND                 hwndChild ;
     MDICREATESTRUCT      mdicreate ;

     switch (iMsg)
          {
          case WM_CREATE :          // Create the client window

                    clientcreate.hWindowMenu  = hMenuInitWindow ;
                    clientcreate.idFirstChild = IDM_FIRSTCHILD ;

                    hwndClient = CreateWindow ("MDICLIENT", NULL,
                              WS_CHILD | WS_CLIPCHILDREN | WS_VISIBLE,
                              0, 0, 0, 0, hwnd, (HMENU) 1, hInst,
                              (LPSTR) &clientcreate) ;
                    return 0 ;

          case WM_COMMAND :
                    switch (wParam)
                         {
                         case IDM_NEWHELLO :     // Create a Hello child window

                              mdicreate.szClass = szHelloClass ;
                              mdicreate.szTitle = "Hello" ;
                              mdicreate.hOwner  = hInst ;
                              mdicreate.x       = CW_USEDEFAULT ;
                              mdicreate.y       = CW_USEDEFAULT ;
                              mdicreate.cx      = CW_USEDEFAULT ;
                              mdicreate.cy      = CW_USEDEFAULT ;
                              mdicreate.style   = 0 ;
                              mdicreate.lParam  = 0 ;
```

(continued)

```
                hwndChild = (HWND) SendMessage (hwndClient,
                              WM_MDICREATE, 0,
                              (LPARAM) (LPMDICREATESTRUCT) &mdicreate) ;
           return 0 ;

      case IDM_NEWRECT :          // Create a Rect child window

           mdicreate.szClass = szRectClass ;
           mdicreate.szTitle = "Rectangles" ;
           mdicreate.hOwner  = hInst ;
           mdicreate.x       = CW_USEDEFAULT ;
           mdicreate.y       = CW_USEDEFAULT ;
           mdicreate.cx      = CW_USEDEFAULT ;
           mdicreate.cy      = CW_USEDEFAULT ;
           mdicreate.style   = 0 ;
           mdicreate.lParam  = 0 ;

           hwndChild = (HWND) SendMessage (hwndClient,
                              WM_MDICREATE, 0,
                              (LPARAM) (LPMDICREATESTRUCT) &mdicreate) ;
           return 0 ;

      case IDM_CLOSE :            // Close the active window

           hwndChild = (HWND) SendMessage (hwndClient,
                                 WM_MDIGETACTIVE, 0, 0) ;

           if (SendMessage (hwndChild, WM_QUERYENDSESSION, 0, 0))
                SendMessage (hwndClient, WM_MDIDESTROY,
                          (WPARAM) hwndChild, 0) ;
           return 0 ;

      case IDM_EXIT :             // Exit the program

           SendMessage (hwnd, WM_CLOSE, 0, 0) ;
           return 0 ;

                      // messages for arranging windows
      case IDM_TILE :
           SendMessage (hwndClient, WM_MDITILE, 0, 0) ;
           return 0 ;

      case IDM_CASCADE :
           SendMessage (hwndClient, WM_MDICASCADE, 0, 0) ;
           return 0 ;
```

(continued)

```
                    case IDM_ARRANGE :
                         SendMessage (hwndClient, WM_MDIICONARRANGE, 0, 0) ;
                         return 0 ;

                    case IDM_CLOSEALL :          // Attempt to close all children

                         EnumChildWindows (hwndClient, &CloseEnumProc, 0) ;
                         return 0 ;

                    default:                // Pass to active child...

                         hwndChild = (HWND) SendMessage (hwndClient,
                                              WM_MDIGETACTIVE, 0, 0) ;

                         if (IsWindow (hwndChild))
                              SendMessage (hwndChild, WM_COMMAND,
                                        wParam, lParam) ;

                         break ;          // ...and then to DefFrameProc
                    }
               break ;

          case WM_QUERYENDSESSION :
          case WM_CLOSE :                          // Attempt to close all children

               SendMessage (hwnd, WM_COMMAND, IDM_CLOSEALL, 0) ;

               if (NULL != GetWindow (hwndClient, GW_CHILD))
                    return 0 ;

               break ;   // I.e., call DefFrameProc

          case WM_DESTROY :
               PostQuitMessage (0) ;
               return 0 ;
          }
               // Pass unprocessed messages to DefFrameProc (not DefWindowProc)

     return DefFrameProc (hwnd, hwndClient, iMsg, wParam, lParam) ;
     }

BOOL CALLBACK CloseEnumProc (HWND hwnd, LPARAM lParam)
     {
     if (GetWindow (hwnd, GW_OWNER))                // Check for icon title
          return 1 ;
```

(continued)

```
        SendMessage (GetParent (hwnd), WM_MDIRESTORE, (WPARAM) hwnd, 0) ;

        if (!SendMessage (hwnd, WM_QUERYENDSESSION, 0, 0))
            return 1 ;

        SendMessage (GetParent (hwnd), WM_MDIDESTROY, (WPARAM) hwnd, 0) ;
            return 1 ;
        }

LRESULT CALLBACK HelloWndProc (HWND hwnd, UINT iMsg, WPARAM wParam,
                                                    LPARAM lParam)
    {
    static COLORREF clrTextArray[] = { RGB (0,   0, 0), RGB (255, 0,   0),
                                    RGB (0, 255, 0), RGB ( 0, 0, 255),
                                    RGB (255, 255, 255) } ;
    static HWND    hwndClient, hwndFrame ;
    HDC            hdc ;
    HMENU          hMenu ;
    LPHELLODATA    lpHelloData ;
    PAINTSTRUCT    ps ;
    RECT           rect ;

    switch (iMsg)
        {
        case WM_CREATE :
                    // Allocate memory for window private data

            lpHelloData = (LPHELLODATA) HeapAlloc (GetProcessHeap (),
                                                HEAP_ZERO_MEMORY,
                                                sizeof (HELLODATA)) ;

            lpHelloData->iColor  = IDM_BLACK ;
            lpHelloData->clrText = RGB (0, 0, 0) ;
            SetWindowLong (hwnd, 0, (long) lpHelloData) ;

                    // Save some window handles

            hwndClient = GetParent (hwnd) ;
            hwndFrame  = GetParent (hwndClient) ;
            return 0 ;

        case WM_COMMAND :
            switch (wParam)
                {
                case IDM_BLACK :
```

(continued)

```
                    case IDM_RED :
                    case IDM_GREEN :
                    case IDM_BLUE :
                    case IDM_WHITE :
                                    // Change the text color

                         lpHelloData = (LPHELLODATA) GetWindowLong (hwnd, 0) ;

                         hMenu = GetMenu (hwndFrame) ;

                         CheckMenuItem (hMenu, lpHelloData->iColor,
                                            MF_UNCHECKED) ;
                         lpHelloData->iColor = wParam ;
                         CheckMenuItem (hMenu, lpHelloData->iColor,
                                            MF_CHECKED) ;

                         lpHelloData->clrText =
                             clrTextArray[wParam - IDM_BLACK] ;

                         InvalidateRect (hwnd, NULL, FALSE) ;
                    }
               return 0 ;

     case WM_PAINT :
                    // Paint the window

          hdc = BeginPaint (hwnd, &ps) ;

          lpHelloData = (LPHELLODATA) GetWindowLong (hwnd, 0) ;
          SetTextColor (hdc, lpHelloData->clrText) ;

          GetClientRect (hwnd, &rect) ;

          DrawText (hdc, "Hello, World!", -1, &rect,
                    DT_SINGLELINE | DT_CENTER | DT_VCENTER) ;

          EndPaint (hwnd, &ps) ;
          return 0 ;

     case WM_MDIACTIVATE :

                    // Set the Hello menu if gaining focus

          if (lParam == (LPARAM) hwnd)
```

(continued)

```
                    SendMessage (hwndClient, WM_MDISETMENU,
                            (WPARAM) hMenuHello, (LPARAM) hMenuHelloWindow) ;

                    // Check or uncheck menu item

               lpHelloData = (LPHELLODATA) GetWindowLong (hwnd, 0) ;
               CheckMenuItem (hMenuHello, lpHelloData->iColor,
                       (lParam == (LPARAM) hwnd) ? MF_CHECKED : MF_UNCHECKED) ;

                    // Set the Init menu if losing focus

               if (lParam != (LPARAM) hwnd)
                    SendMessage (hwndClient, WM_MDISETMENU, (WPARAM) hMenuInit,
                            (LPARAM) hMenuInitWindow) ;

               DrawMenuBar (hwndFrame) ;
               return 0 ;

          case WM_QUERYENDSESSION :
          case WM_CLOSE :
               if (IDOK != MessageBox (hwnd, "OK to close window?", "Hello",
                                  MB_ICONQUESTION | MB_OKCANCEL))
                    return 0 ;

               break ;    // I.e., call DefMDIChildProc

          case WM_DESTROY :
               lpHelloData = (LPHELLODATA) GetWindowLong (hwnd, 0) ;
               HeapFree (GetProcessHeap (), 0, lpHelloData) ;
               return 0 ;
          }
               // Pass unprocessed message to DefMDIChildProc

     return DefMDIChildProc (hwnd, iMsg, wParam, lParam) ;
     }

LRESULT CALLBACK RectWndProc (HWND hwnd, UINT iMsg, WPARAM wParam,
                                              LPARAM lParam)
     {
     static HWND   hwndClient, hwndFrame ;
     HBRUSH        hBrush ;
     HDC           hdc ;
     LPRECTDATA    lpRectData ;
```

(continued)

```
PAINTSTRUCT  ps ;
int         xLeft, xRight, yTop, yBottom ;
short       nRed, nGreen, nBlue ;

switch (iMsg)
    {
    case WM_CREATE :
                   // Allocate memory for window private data

        lpRectData = (LPRECTDATA) HeapAlloc (GetProcessHeap (),
                                        HEAP_ZERO_MEMORY,
                                        sizeof (RECTDATA)) ;

        SetWindowLong (hwnd, 0, (long) lpRectData) ;

                   // Start the timer going

        SetTimer (hwnd, 1, 250, NULL) ;

                   // Save some window handles

        hwndClient = GetParent (hwnd) ;
        hwndFrame  = GetParent (hwndClient) ;
        return 0 ;

    case WM_SIZE :              // If not minimized, save the window size

        if (wParam != SIZE_MINIMIZED)
            {
            lpRectData = (LPRECTDATA) GetWindowLong (hwnd, 0) ;

            lpRectData->cxClient = LOWORD (lParam) ;
            lpRectData->cyClient = HIWORD (lParam) ;
            }

        break ;         // WM_SIZE must be processed by DefMDIChildProc

    case WM_TIMER :             // Display a random rectangle

        lpRectData = (LPRECTDATA) GetWindowLong (hwnd, 0) ;

        xLeft  = rand () % lpRectData->cxClient ;
        xRight = rand () % lpRectData->cxClient ;
```

(continued)

```
                    yTop    = rand () % lpRectData->cyClient ;
                    yBottom = rand () % lpRectData->cyClient ;
                    nRed    = rand () & 255 ;
                    nGreen  = rand () & 255 ;
                    nBlue   = rand () & 255 ;

                    hdc = GetDC (hwnd) ;
                    hBrush = CreateSolidBrush (RGB (nRed, nGreen, nBlue)) ;
                    SelectObject (hdc, hBrush) ;

                    Rectangle (hdc, min (xLeft, xRight), min (yTop, yBottom),
                                    max (xLeft, xRight), max (yTop, yBottom)) ;

                    ReleaseDC (hwnd, hdc) ;
                    DeleteObject (hBrush) ;
                    return 0 ;

          case WM_PAINT :             // Clear the window

                    InvalidateRect (hwnd, NULL, TRUE) ;
                    hdc = BeginPaint (hwnd, &ps) ;
                    EndPaint (hwnd, &ps) ;
                    return 0 ;

          case WM_MDIACTIVATE :      // Set the appropriate menu
                    if (lParam == (LPARAM) hwnd)
                         SendMessage (hwndClient, WM_MDISETMENU, (WPARAM) hMenuRect,
                                      (LPARAM) hMenuRectWindow) ;
                    else
                         SendMessage (hwndClient, WM_MDISETMENU, (WPARAM) hMenuInit,
                                      (LPARAM) hMenuInitWindow) ;

                    DrawMenuBar (hwndFrame) ;
                    return 0 ;

          case WM_DESTROY :
                    lpRectData = (LPRECTDATA) GetWindowLong (hwnd, 0) ;
                    HeapFree (GetProcessHeap (), 0, lpRectData) ;
                    KillTimer (hwnd, 1) ;
                    return 0 ;
          }
          // Pass unprocessed message to DefMDIChildProc

     return DefMDIChildProc (hwnd, iMsg, wParam, lParam) ;
     }
```

MDIDEMO.RC

```
/*---------------------------
   MDIDEMO.RC resource script
   ---------------------------*/

#include <windows.h>
#include "mdidemo.h"

MdiMenuInit MENU
    {
    POPUP "&File"
        {
        MENUITEM "New &Hello",          IDM_NEWHELLO
        MENUITEM "New &Rectangles",     IDM_NEWRECT
        MENUITEM SEPARATOR
        MENUITEM "E&xit",               IDM_EXIT
        }
    }

MdiMenuHello MENU
    {
    POPUP "&File"
        {
        MENUITEM "New &Hello",          IDM_NEWHELLO
        MENUITEM "New &Rectangles",     IDM_NEWRECT
        MENUITEM "&Close",              IDM_CLOSE
        MENUITEM SEPARATOR
        MENUITEM "E&xit",               IDM_EXIT
        }
    POPUP "&Color"
        {
        MENUITEM "&Black",              IDM_BLACK
        MENUITEM "&Red",                IDM_RED
        MENUITEM "&Green",              IDM_GREEN
        MENUITEM "B&lue",               IDM_BLUE
        MENUITEM "&White",              IDM_WHITE
        }
    POPUP "&Window"
        {
        MENUITEM "&Cascade\tShift+F5",  IDM_CASCADE
        MENUITEM "&Tile\tShift+F4",     IDM_TILE
        MENUITEM "Arrange &Icons",      IDM_ARRANGE
        MENUITEM "Close &All",          IDM_CLOSEALL
        }
    }
```

(continued)

```
MdiMenuRect MENU
    {
    POPUP "&File"
        {
        MENUITEM "New &Hello",          IDM_NEWHELLO
        MENUITEM "New &Rectangles",     IDM_NEWRECT
        MENUITEM "&Close",              IDM_CLOSE
        MENUITEM SEPARATOR
        MENUITEM "E&xit",               IDM_EXIT
        }
    POPUP "&Window"
        {
        MENUITEM "&Cascade\tShift+F5",  IDM_CASCADE
        MENUITEM "&Tile\tShift+F4",     IDM_TILE
        MENUITEM "Arrange &Icons",      IDM_ARRANGE
        MENUITEM "Close &All",          IDM_CLOSEALL
        }
    }

MdiAccel ACCELERATORS
    {
    VK_F5, IDM_CASCADE, VIRTKEY, SHIFT
    VK_F4, IDM_TILE,    VIRTKEY, SHIFT
    }
```

MDIDEMO.H

```
/*-----------------------
   MDIDEMO.H header file
  ----------------------*/

#define EXPORT              __declspec (dllexport)

#define INIT_MENU_POS       0
#define HELLO_MENU_POS      2
#define RECT_MENU_POS       1

#define IDM_NEWHELLO        10
#define IDM_NEWRECT         11
#define IDM_CLOSE           12
#define IDM_EXIT            13

#define IDM_BLACK           20
#define IDM_RED             21
```

(continued)

```
#define IDM_GREEN      22
#define IDM_BLUE       23
#define IDM_WHITE      24

#define IDM_TILE       30
#define IDM_CASCADE    31
#define IDM_ARRANGE    32
#define IDM_CLOSEALL   33

#define IDM_FIRSTCHILD 100
```

MDIDEMO supports two types of extremely simple document windows: One displays "Hello, World!" in the center of its client area, and the other displays a series of random rectangles. (In the source code listings and identifier names, these are referred to as the Hello document and the Rect document.) Different menus are associated with these two types of document windows. The document window that displays "Hello, World!" has a menu that allows you to change the color of the text.

Three Menus

Let's turn first to the MDIDEMO.RC resource script. The resource script defines three menu templates used by the program.

The program displays the MdiMenuInit menu when no document windows are present. This menu simply allows creating a new document or exiting the program.

The MdiMenuHello menu is associated with the document window that displays "Hello, World!" The File submenu allows opening a new document of either type, closing the active document, and exiting the program. The Color submenu lets you set the text color. The Window submenu has options for arranging the document windows in a cascaded or tiled fashion, arranging the document icons, and closing all the windows. This submenu will also list all the document windows as they are created.

The MdiMenuRect menu is associated with the random rectangle document. This is the same as the MdiMenuHello menu except that it does not include the Color submenu.

The MDIDEMO.H header file defines all the menu identifiers as well as three constants:

```
#define INIT_MENU_POS  0
#define HELLO_MENU_POS 2
#define RECT_MENU_POS  1
```

These identifiers indicate the position of the Window submenu in each of the three menu templates. This information is needed by the program to inform the client window where the document list is to appear. Of course, the MdiMenuInit menu doesn't have a Window submenu, so I've indicated that the list should be appended to the first submenu (position 0). The list will never actually be viewed there, however. (You'll see why this is needed when I discuss the program later.)

The IDM_FIRSTCHILD identifier doesn't correspond to a menu item. This is the identifier that will be associated with the first document window in the list that will appear in the Window submenu. This identifier should be greater than all the other menu IDs.

Program Initialization

In MDIDEMO.C, *WinMain* begins by registering window classes for the frame window and the two child windows. The window procedures are called *FrameWndProc, HelloWndProc,* and *RectWndProc.* Normally, different icons should be associated with these window classes. For the purpose of simplicity, I've used the standard IDI_APPLICATION icon for the frame and child.

Note that I've defined the *hbrBackground* field of the WNDCLASSEX structure for the frame window class to be the COLOR_APPWORKSPACE system color. This is not entirely necessary because the client area of the frame window is covered up by the client window, and the client window has this color anyway. However, using this color looks a little better when the frame window is first displayed.

The *lpszMenuName* field is set to NULL for each of these three window classes. For the Hello and Rect child window classes, this is normal. For the frame window class, I've chosen to indicate the menu handle in the *CreateWindow* function when creating the frame window.

The window classes for the Hello and Rect child windows allocate extra space for each window using a nonzero value as the *cbWndExtra* field of the WNDCLASSEX structure. This space will be used to store a pointer to a block of memory (the size of the HELLODATA or RECTDATA structures defined near the top of MDIDEMO.C) used to store information unique to each document window.

Next, *WinMain* uses *LoadMenu* to load the three menus and save their handles in global variables. Three calls to the *GetSubMenu* function obtain handles to the Window submenu to which the document list will be appended. These are also saved in global variables. The *LoadAccelerators* function loads the accelerator table.

A call to *CreateWindow* in *WinMain* creates the frame window. During the WM-_CREATE processing in *FrameWndProc,* the frame window creates the client window. This involves another call to *CreateWindow.* The window class is set to MDICLIENT, which is the preregistered class for MDI client windows. The last parameter to *CreateWindow* must be set to a pointer to a structure of type CLIENTCREATESTRUCT. This structure has two fields:

- *hWindowMenu* is the handle of the submenu to which the document list will be appended. In MDIDEMO, this is *hMenuInitWindow,* which was obtained during *WinMain.* You'll see later how the menu is changed.

- *idFirstChild* is the menu ID to be associated with the first document window in the document list. This is simply IDM_FIRSTCHILD.

Back in *WinMain*, MDIDEMO displays the newly created frame window and enters the message loop. The message loop differs a little from a normal loop: After obtaining the message from the message queue with a call to *GetMessage*, an MDI program passes the message to *TranslateMDISysAccel* (and *TranslateAccelerator* if, like the MDIDEMO program, the program also has menu accelerators).

The *TranslateMDISysAccel* function translates any keystrokes that may correspond to the special MDI accelerators (Ctrl-F6, for example) into a WM_SYSCOMMAND message. If neither *TranslateMDISysAccel* nor *TranslateAccelerator* returns TRUE (indicating that a message was translated by one of these functions), do not call *TranslateMessage* and *DispatchMessage*.

Notice the two window handles passed to *TranslateMDISysAccel* and *Translate-Accelerator*: *hwndClient* and *hwndFrame*, respectively. The *WinMain* function obtains the *hwndClient* window handle by calling *GetWindow* with the GW_CHILD parameter.

CREATING THE CHILDREN

The bulk of *FrameWndProc* is devoted to processing WM_COMMAND messages that signal menu selections. As usual, the *wParam* parameter to *FrameWndProc* contains the menu ID number.

For *wParam* values of IDM_NEWHELLO and IDM_NEWRECT, *FrameWndProc* must create a new document window. This involves initializing the fields of an MDICREATE-STRUCT structure (most of which correspond to *CreateWindow* parameters) and sending the client window a WM_MDICREATE message with *lParam* set to a pointer to this structure. The client window then creates the child document window. *FrameWndProc* could have created the child window directly with a call to *CreateMDIWindow*. For a single-threaded program like MDIDEMO, you can choose whichever method you prefer.

Normally the *szTitle* field of the MDICREATESTRUCT structure would be the filename corresponding to the document. The *style* field can be set to the window styles WS_HSCROLL or WS_VSCROLL or both to include scroll bars in the document window. (It is not necessary to call *ShowScrollBar* to display the scroll bars.) The *style* field can also include WS_MINIMIZE or WS_MAXIMIZE to initially display the document window in a minimized or maximized state.

The *lParam* field of the MDICREATESTRUCT structure provides a way for the frame window and the child window to share some variables. This field could be set to a memory handle that references a block of memory containing a structure. During the WM_CREATE message in the child document window, *lParam* is a pointer to a CREATESTRUCT structure, and the *lpCreateParams* field of this structure is a pointer to the MDICREATESTRUCT structure used to create the window.

On receipt of the WM_MDICREATE message, the client window creates the child document window and adds the title of the window to the bottom of the submenu specified in the MDICLIENTSTRUCT structure used to create the client window. When the

MDIDEMO program creates its first document window, this is the File submenu of the Mdi-MenuInit menu. We'll see later how this document list gets moved to the Window submenu of the MdiMenuHello and MdiMenuRect menus.

Up to nine documents can be listed on the menu, each preceded by an underlined number from 1 to 9. If more than nine document windows are created, this list is followed by a "More windows" item on the menu. This item invokes a dialog box with a list box that lists all the document windows. The maintenance of this document list is one of the nicest features of the Windows 95 MDI support.

MORE FRAME WINDOW MESSAGE PROCESSING

Let's continue with *FrameWndProc* message processing before turning our attention to the child document windows.

When you select Close from the File menu, MDIDEMO closes the active child window. It obtains the handle to the active child window by sending the client window a WM_MDIGETACTIVE message. If the child window responds affirmatively to a WM_QUERY-ENDSESSION message, then MDIDEMO sends the client window a WM_MDIDESTROY message to close the child window.

Processing the Exit option from the File menu requires only that the frame window procedure send itself a WM_CLOSE message.

Processing the Tile, Cascade, and Arrange Icons options from the Window submenu is a snap, requiring only that the WM_MDITILE, WM_MDICASCADE, and WM_MDIICON-ARRANGE messages be sent to the client window.

The Close All option is a little more complex. *FrameWndProc* calls *EnumChild-Windows*, passing a pointer referencing the *CloseEnumProc* function. This function sends a WM_MDIRESTORE message to each child window, followed by a WM_QUERYEND-SESSION and (possibly) a WM_MDIDESTROY message. This is not done for the icon title window, indicated by a non-NULL return of *GetWindow* with the GW_OWNER parameter.

You'll notice that *FrameWndProc* does not process any of the WM_COMMAND messages that signal one of the colors being selected from the Color menu. These messages are really the responsibility of the document window. For this reason, *FrameWndProc* sends all unprocessed WM_COMMAND messages to the active child window so that the child window can process those messages that pertain to its window.

All messages that the frame window procedure chooses not to process must be passed to *DefFrameProc*. This function replaces *DefWindowProc* in the frame window procedure. Even if a frame window procedure traps the WM_MENUCHAR, WM_SETFOCUS, or WM_SIZE messages, these also must be passed to *DefFrameProc*.

Unprocessed WM_COMMAND messages must also be passed to *DefFrameProc*. In particular, *FrameWndProc* does not process any of the WM_COMMAND messages resulting from the user selecting one of the documents from the list in the Window submenu. (The *wParam* values for these options begin with IDM_FIRSTCHILD.) These messages are passed to *DefFrameProc* and processed there.

Notice that the frame window does not need to maintain a list of window handles of all document windows it creates. If ever these handles are needed (such as when processing the Close All option from the menu), they can be obtained using *EnumChildWindows*.

THE CHILD DOCUMENT WINDOWS

Now let's look at *HelloWndProc*, which is the window procedure used for the child document windows that display "Hello, World!"

As with any window class used for more than one window, static variables defined in the window procedure (or any function called from the window procedure) are shared by all windows created based on that window class.

Data that is unique to each window must be stored using a method other than static variables. One such technique involves window properties. Another approach (the one I used) uses memory space reserved by defining a nonzero value in the *cbWndExtra* field of the WNDCLASSEX structure used to register the window class.

In MDIDEMO, I use this space to store a pointer to a block of memory the size of the HELLODATA structure. *HelloWndProc* allocates this memory during the WM_CREATE message, initializes the two fields (which indicate the currently checked menu item and the text color), and stores the memory pointer using *SetWindowLong*.

When processing a WM_COMMAND message for changing the text colors (recall that these messages originate in the frame window procedure), *HelloWndProc* uses *GetWindowLong* to obtain the pointer to the memory block containing the HELLODATA structure. Using this structure, *HelloWndProc* unchecks the checked menu item, checks the selected menu item, and saves the new color.

A document window procedure receives the WM_MDIACTIVATE message whenever the window becomes active or inactive (indicated by whether or not the value in *lParam* holds the window's handle). You'll recall that the MDIDEMO program has three different menus: MdiMenuInit for when no documents are present, MdiMenuHello for when a Hello document window is active, and MdiMenuRect for when a Rect document window is active.

The WM_MDIACTIVATE message provides an opportunity for the document window to change the menu. If *lParam* contains the window's handle (meaning the window is becoming active), *HelloWndProc* changes the menu to MdiMenuHello. If *lParam* holds the handle of another window, *HelloWndProc* changes the menu to MdiMenuInit.

HelloWndProc changes the menu by sending a WM_MDISETMENU message to the client window. The client window processes this message by removing the document list from the current menu and appending it to the new menu. This is how the document list is transferred from the MdiMenuInit menu (which is in effect when the first document is created) to the MdiMenuHello menu. Do not use the *SetMenu* function to change a menu in an MDI application.

Another little chore involves the check marks on the Color submenu. Program options such as this should be unique to each document. For example, you should be able to set black text in one window and red text in another. The menu check marks should reflect the option chosen in the active window. For this reason, *HelloWndProc* unchecks the selected menu item when the window is becoming inactive and checks the appropriate item when the window is becoming active.

The *wParam* and *lParam* values of WM_MDIACTIVATE are the handles of the windows being deactivated and activated, respectively. The window procedure gets the first WM_MDIACTIVATE message with *lParam* set to the handle of the current window when the window is first created and gets the last message with *lParam* set to another value when the window is destroyed. When the user switches from one document to another, the first document window receives a WM_MDIACTIVATE message with *wParam* set to the handle of the first window (at which time the window procedure sets the menu to MdiMenuInit). The second document window receives a WM_MDIACTIVATE message with *lParam* set to the handle of the second window (at which time the window procedure sets the menu to MdiMenuHello or MdiMenuRect as appropriate). If all the windows are closed, the menu is left as MdiMenuInit.

You'll recall that *FrameWndProc* sends the child window a WM_QUERYENDSESSION message when the user selects Close or Close All from the menu. *HelloWndProc* processes the WM_QUERYENDSESSION and WM_CLOSE messages by displaying a message box and asking the user whether the window can be closed. (In a real program, this message box would ask whether a file needed to be saved.) If the user indicates that the window should not be closed, the window procedure returns 0.

During the WM_DESTROY message, *HelloWndProc* frees the memory block allocated during the WM_CREATE message.

All unprocessed messages must be passed on to *DefMDIChildProc* (not *DefWindowProc*) for default processing. Several messages must be passed to *DefMDIChildProc* whether the child window procedure does something with them or not. These are: WM_CHILDACTIVATE, WM_GETMINMAXINFO, WM_MENUCHAR, WM_MOVE, WM_SETFOCUS, WM_SIZE, and WM_SYSCOMMAND.

RectWndProc is fairly similar to *HelloWndProc* in much of the overhead involved, but it's a little simpler (no menu options are involved and the window does not verify with the user whether it can be closed), so I needn't discuss it. But note that *RectWndProc* breaks after processing WM_SIZE so it is passed to *DefMDIChildProc*.

CLEANING UP

In *WinMain*, MDIDEMO uses *LoadMenu* to load the three menus defined in the resource script. Normally Windows will destroy a menu at the time the window to which the menu is attached is destroyed. That takes care of the MdiMenuInit menu. However, menus that are not attached to a window (in MDIDEMO, the Hello and Rect menus) will continue to occupy valuable space in memory, even after the program terminates. For this reason, MDIDEMO calls *DestroyMenu* twice at the end of *WinMain* to get rid of the Hello and Rect menus.

THE POWER OF WINDOW PROCEDURE

Much of the support in Windows 95 for the Multiple Document Interface is encapsulated in the MDICLIENT window class. I think this clearly illustrates the power of the object-oriented architecture of Windows. The client window procedure serves as an intermediary layer between the frame window and the various document windows.

Now let's look at another powerful feature of Windows—dynamic link libraries (DLLs).

Chapter 19

Dynamic Link Libraries

Dynamic link libraries (also called DLLs, dynamic libraries, "dynalink" libraries, or library modules) are one of the most important structural elements of Windows. Most of the disk files associated with Windows are either program modules or dynamic link library modules. So far we've been writing Windows programs; now it's time to take a stab at writing dynamic link libraries. Many of the principles you've learned in writing programs are also applicable to writing these libraries, but there are some important differences.

LIBRARY BASICS

As you've seen, a Windows program is an executable file that generally creates one or more windows and uses a message loop to receive user input. Dynamic link libraries are generally not directly executable, and they usually do not receive messages. They are separate files containing functions that can be called by programs and other DLLs to perform certain jobs. A dynamic link library is brought into action only when another module calls one of the functions in the library.

The term *dynamic linking* refers to the process that Windows uses to link a function call in one module to the actual function in the library module. *Static linking* occurs during program development when you link various object (.OBJ) modules, run-time library (.LIB) files, and usually a compiled resource (.RES) file to create a Windows .EXE file. Dynamic linking instead occurs at run time.

KERNEL32.DLL, USER32.DLL, and GDI32.DLL, the various driver files such as KEY-BOARD.DRV, SYSTEM.DRV, and MOUSE.DRV, and the video and printer drivers are all dynamic link libraries. These are libraries that all Windows programs can use.

Some dynamic link libraries (such as font files) are termed "resource-only." They contain only data (usually in the form of resources) and no code. Thus, one purpose of dynamic link libraries is to provide functions and resources that can be used by many different programs. In a conventional operating system, only the operating system itself contains routines that other programs can call on to do a job. In Windows, the process of one module calling a function in another module is generalized. In effect, by writing a dynamic link library, you are writing an extension to Windows. Or you can think of dynamic link libraries (including those that make up Windows) as extensions to your program.

Although a dynamic link library module may have any extension (such as .EXE or .FON), the standard extension in Microsoft Windows 95 is .DLL. Only dynamic link libraries with the extension .DLL will be loaded automatically by Windows. If the file has another extension, the program must explicitly load the module using the *LoadLibrary* or *LoadLibraryEx* function.

You'll generally find that dynamic link libraries make most sense in the context of a large application. For instance, suppose you write a large accounting package for Windows that consists of several different programs. You'll probably find that these programs use many common routines. You could put these common routines in a normal object library (with the extension .LIB) and add them to each of the program modules during static linking with LINK. But this approach is wasteful, because each of the programs in this package contains identical code for the common routines. Moreover, if you change one of the routines in this library, you'll have to relink all the programs that use the changed routine. If, however, you put these common routines in a dynamic link library called (for instance) ACCOUNT.DLL, you've solved both problems. Only the library module need contain the routines required by all the programs (thus requiring less disk space for the files and less memory space when running two or more of the applications simultaneously), and you can make changes to the library module without relinking any of the individual programs.

Dynamic link libraries can themselves be viable products. For instance, suppose you write a collection of three-dimensional drawing routines and put them in a dynamic link library called GDI3.DLL. If you then interest other software developers in using your library, you can license it to be included with their graphics programs. A user who has several of these programs would need only one GDI3.DLL file.

Library: One Word, Many Meanings

Part of the confusion surrounding dynamic link libraries results from the appearance of the word library in several different contexts. Besides dynamic link libraries, we'll also be talking about "object libraries" and "import libraries."

An object library is a file with the extension .LIB containing code that is added to your program's .EXE file when you run the linker during static linking. For example, in Microsoft Visual C++, the normal C runtime object library that you link with your program is called LIBC.LIB.

An import library is a special form of an object library file. Like object libraries, import libraries have the extension .LIB and are used by the linker to resolve function calls in your source code. However, import libraries contain no code. Instead, they provide the linker with information necessary to set up relocation tables within the .EXE file for dynamic linking. The KERNEL32.LIB, USER32.LIB, and GDI32.LIB files included with the Microsoft compiler are import libraries for Windows functions. If you call *Rectangle* in a program, GDI32.LIB tells LINK that this function is in the GDI32.DLL dynamic link library. This information goes into the .EXE file so that Windows can perform dynamic linking with the GDI32.DLL dynamic link library when your program is executed.

Object libraries and import libraries are used only during program development. Dynamic link libraries are used during run time. A dynamic link library must be present on the disk when a program is run that uses the library. When Windows 95 needs to load a dynamic link library module before running a program that requires it, the library file must be stored in the directory containing the .EXE program, the current directory, the Windows system directory, the Windows directory, or a directory accessible through the PATH string in the MS-DOS environment. (The directories are searched in that order.)

A SIMPLE DLL

As usual, we'll begin very simply. Figure 19-1 shows the necessary source code for a dynamic link library called EDRLIB that contains only one function. The "EDR" of this filename stands for "easy drawing routine," and you can easily add other functions to it that simplify the drawing functions in your applications. The single function in EDRLIB is called *EdrCenterText*, and it simply centers a NULL-terminated text string in a rectangle, much like *DrawText* but without as many parameters.

EDRLIB.MAK

```
#----------------------
# EDRLIB.MAK make file
#----------------------

edrlib.dll : edrlib.obj
     $(LINKER) $(DLLFLAGS) -OUT:edrlib.dll edrlib.obj $(GUILIBS)

edrlib.obj : edrlib.c edrlib.h
     $(CC) $(CFLAGS) edrlib.c
```

Figure 19-1. *The EDRLIB library.* (*continued*)

EDRLIB.H

```
/*---------------------------
     EDRLIB.H header file
---------------------------*/

#define EXPORT extern "C" __declspec (dllexport)

EXPORT BOOL CALLBACK EdrCenterText (HDC, PRECT, PSTR) ;
```

EDRLIB.C

```
/*--------------------------------------------------------
     EDRLIB.C -- Easy Drawing Routine Library module
                 (c) Charles Petzold, 1996
--------------------------------------------------------*/

#include <windows.h>
#include <string.h>
#include "edrlib.h"

int WINAPI DllMain (HINSTANCE hInstance, DWORD fdwReason, PVOID pvReserved)
     {
     return TRUE ;
     }

EXPORT BOOL CALLBACK EdrCenterText (HDC hdc, PRECT prc, PSTR pString)
     {
     int   iLength ;
     SIZE size ;

     iLength = strlen (pString) ;

     GetTextExtentPoint32 (hdc, pString, iLength, &size) ;

     return TextOut (hdc, (prc->right - prc->left - size.cx) / 2,
                          (prc->bottom - prc->top - size.cy) / 2,
                     pString, iLength) ;
     }
```

As you can see, the make file has two differences from the make files we've been using for our applications. First, in the link command line, I've substituted the environment variable DLLFLAGS for GUIFLAGS. This was included in the MSC.BAT file I introduced in Chapter 1 and simply includes the link command-line parameter -DLL. This parameter tells the linker that the resultant file will be a dynamic link library. Also, you'll notice that instead of creating a .EXE file, the make file creates a file named EDRLIB.DLL.

The EDRLIB.H file first defines a macro constant named EXPORT:

```
#define EXPORT extern "C" __declspec (dllexport)
```

Using the EXPORT keyword when defining functions in your dynamic link library will tell the linker that the functions are available for use by other programs. The *EdrCenterText* function is defined in the header file using this EXPORT definition. The function is also defined using the CALLBACK constant, just like a window procedure.

EDRLIB.C also looks a little different from normal Windows C files. It includes a function named *DllMain* rather than *WinMain*. This function is used to perform initialization and de-initialization, as I'll discuss later in this chapter. For our purposes, all we need do right now is return TRUE. And finally, EDRLIB.C contains the *EdrCenterText* function.

When you run

```
NMAKE EDRLIB.MAK
```

on a command line, you'll create EDRLIB.DLL, the dynamic link library. You'll also find two other new files. EDRLIB.LIB is an import library that we'll use shortly. EDRLIB.EXP is an export library that is created as a residue of the linking process. You may delete it.

Does EDRLIB.DLL work? Well, let's try it out. EDRTEST, shown in Figure 19-2, uses EDRLIB.DLL to center a text string in its client area.

```
EDRTEST.MAK

#----------------------
# EDRTEST.MAK make file
#----------------------

edrtest.exe : edrtest.obj edrlib.lib
    $(LINKER) $(GUIFLAGS) -OUT:edrtest.exe edrtest.obj edrlib.lib $(GUILIBS)

edrtest.obj : edrtest.c edrlib.h
    $(CC) $(CFLAGS) edrtest.c
```

```
EDRTEST.C

/*-------------------------------------------------------------
    EDRTEST.C -- Program using EDRLIB dynamic link library
                 (c) Charles Petzold, 1996
   -------------------------------------------------------------*/
```

Figure 19-2. *The EDRTEST program.*

(continued)

```
#include <windows.h>
#include "edrlib.h"

LRESULT CALLBACK WndProc (HWND, UINT, WPARAM, LPARAM) ;

int WINAPI WinMain (HINSTANCE hInstance, HINSTANCE hPrevInstance,
                    PSTR szCmdLine, int iCmdShow)
    {
    static char  szAppName[] = "StrProg" ;
    HWND         hwnd ;
    MSG          msg ;
    WNDCLASSEX   wndclass ;

    wndclass.cbSize        = sizeof (wndclass) ;
    wndclass.style         = CS_HREDRAW | CS_VREDRAW ;
    wndclass.lpfnWndProc   = WndProc ;
    wndclass.cbClsExtra    = 0 ;
    wndclass.cbWndExtra    = 0 ;
    wndclass.hInstance     = hInstance ;
    wndclass.hIcon         = LoadIcon (NULL, IDI_APPLICATION) ;
    wndclass.hCursor       = LoadCursor (NULL, IDC_ARROW) ;
    wndclass.hbrBackground = (HBRUSH) GetStockObject (WHITE_BRUSH) ;
    wndclass.lpszMenuName  = NULL ;
    wndclass.lpszClassName = szAppName ;
    wndclass.hIconSm       = LoadIcon (NULL, IDI_APPLICATION) ;

    RegisterClassEx (&wndclass) ;

    hwnd = CreateWindow (szAppName, "DLL Demonstration Program",
                         WS_OVERLAPPEDWINDOW,
                         CW_USEDEFAULT, CW_USEDEFAULT,
                         CW_USEDEFAULT, CW_USEDEFAULT,
                         NULL, NULL, hInstance, NULL) ;

    ShowWindow (hwnd, iCmdShow) ;
    UpdateWindow (hwnd) ;

    while (GetMessage (&msg, NULL, 0, 0))
        {
        TranslateMessage (&msg) ;
        DispatchMessage (&msg) ;
        }
    return msg.wParam ;
    }

LRESULT CALLBACK WndProc (HWND hwnd, UINT iMsg, WPARAM wParam, LPARAM lParam)
```

(continued)

```
     {
     HDC         hdc ;
     PAINTSTRUCT ps ;
     RECT        rect ;

     switch (iMsg)
          {
          case WM_PAINT :
               hdc = BeginPaint (hwnd, &ps) ;

               GetClientRect (hwnd, &rect) ;

               EdrCenterText (hdc, &rect,
                              "This string was displayed by a DLL") ;

               EndPaint (hwnd, &ps) ;
               return 0 ;

          case WM_DESTROY :
               PostQuitMessage (0) ;
               return 0 ;
          }
     return DefWindowProc (hwnd, iMsg, wParam, lParam) ;
     }
```

This looks like a normal Windows program and it certainly is. Note, however, that EDRTEST.C includes EDRLIB.H to define the *EdrCenterText* function that the program calls during the WM_PAINT message. Also notice that EDRTEST.MAK includes the EDRLIB.LIB file in the link statement. That import library provides the information LINK needs to set up a reference in the EDRTEST.EXE file to the EDRLIB.DLL file.

It is vital to understand that the *EdrCenterText* code is not included in the EDRTEST.EXE file. Instead, there is simply a reference to the EDRLIB.DLL file and the *EdrCenterText* function. EDRTEST.EXE requires EDRLIB.DLL to run.

Including EDRLIB.H in the EDRTEST.C source code file is equivalent to including WINDOWS.H. Including EDRLIB.LIB in the link command line is equivalent to including all the Windows import libraries (such as USER32.LIB), which are listed in the GUILIBS environment variable referenced by the make file. When your program runs, it links with EDLIB.DLL in the same way it links with USER32.DLL. Congratulations! You've just created an extension to Windows 95!

A few words on the subject of dynamic link libraries before we continue... Although I've just categorized a DLL as an extension to Windows 95, it is also an extension to your application program. Everything the DLL does is done on behalf of the application. For example, all memory it allocates is owned by the application. Any windows it creates are owned by the application. Any files it opens are owned by the application. Multiple applications can use the same DLL simultaneously, but under Windows 95 these applications are shielded from interfering with each other. However, if you write a DLL with functions that can be called from multiple threads of a program, you should compile the DLL with the CFLAGSMT environment variable rather than CFLAGS.

Because code is nonwritable, different processes can share the same code in a dynamic link library. The data maintained by a DLL, however, is different for each process. Each process has its own address space for any data the DLL uses. Sharing memory among processes requires extra work (as we'll see).

SHARED MEMORY IN DLLS

It's very nice that Windows 95 isolates applications that are using the same dynamic link libraries at the same time. However, sometimes it's not preferable. You may want to write a DLL that contains some memory that can be shared among various applications, or perhaps multiple instances of the same application. This involves using shared memory (actually a memory-mapped file), which I mentioned in Chapter 13 but promised I'd demonstrate later.

Let's examine how this works with a program called STRPROG ("string program") and the dynamic link library called STRLIB ("string library"). STRLIB has three exported functions that STRPROG calls. Just to make this interesting, one of the functions in STRLIB uses a call-back function defined in STRPROG.

STRLIB is a dynamic link library module that stores and sorts up to 256 character strings. The strings are capitalized and maintained by shared memory in STRLIB. STRPROG can use STRLIB's three functions to add strings, delete strings, and obtain all the current strings from STRLIB. The program has two menu items (Enter and Delete) that invoke dialog boxes to add and delete these strings. STRPROG lists all the current strings stored by STRLIB in STRPROG's client area.

This function defined in STRLIB adds a string to STRLIB's shared memory:

```
EXPORT BOOL CALLBACK AddString (PSTR pStringIn)
```

The parameter *pStringIn* is a pointer to the string. The string is capitalized within the *AddString* function. If an identical string already exists in STRLIB's list of strings, this function adds another copy of the string. *AddString* returns TRUE (nonzero) if it is successful and FALSE (0) otherwise. A FALSE return value can result if the string has a length of 0, if memory could not be allocated to store the string, or if 256 strings are already stored.

This STRLIB function deletes a string from STRLIB's shared memory:

```
EXPORT BOOL CALLBACK DeleteString (PSTR pStringIn)
```

Again, the parameter *pStringIn* is a pointer to the string. If more than one string matches, only the first is removed. *DeleteString* returns TRUE (nonzero) if it is successful and FALSE (0) otherwise. A FALSE return value indicates that the length of the string is 0 or that a matching string could not be found.

This STRLIB function uses a call-back function located in the calling program to enumerate the strings currently stored in STRLIB's shared memory:

```
EXPORT int CALLBACK GetStrings (PSTRCB pfnGetStrCallBack, PVOID pParam)
```

The call-back function must be defined as follows:

```
EXPORT BOOL CALLBACK GetStrCallBack (PSTR pString, PVOID pParam)
```

The *pfnGetStrCallBack* parameter to *GetStrings* points to the call-back function. *GetStrings* calls *GetStrCallBack* once for each string or until the call-back function returns FALSE (0). *GetStrings* returns the number of strings passed to the call-back function. The *pParam* parameter is a pointer to programmer-defined data.

The STRLIB Library

Figure 19-3 shows the three files necessary to create the STRLIB.DLL dynamic link library module.

```
STRLIB.MAK

#---------------------
# STRLIB.MAK make file
#---------------------

strlib.dll : strlib.obj
    $(LINKER) $(DLLFLAGS) -SECTION:shared,rws -OUT:strlib.dll \
            strlib.obj $(GUILIBS)

strlib.obj : strlib.c strlib.h
    $(CC) $(CFLAGS) strlib.c
```

```
STRLIB.H

/*---------------------
   STRLIB.H header file
   ---------------------*/

typedef BOOL (CALLBACK *PSTRCB) (PSTR, PVOID) ;
#define MAX_STRINGS 256

#define EXPORT  extern "C" __declspec (dllexport)

EXPORT BOOL CALLBACK AddString    (PSTR) ;
EXPORT BOOL CALLBACK DeleteString (PSTR) ;
EXPORT int  CALLBACK GetStrings   (PSTRCB, PVOID) ;
```

Figure 19-3. *The STRLIB library.*

(continued)

STRLIB.C

```c
/*-------------------------------------------------
   STRLIB.C -- Library module for STRPROG program
               (c) Charles Petzold, 1996
   -------------------------------------------------*/

#include <windows.h>
#include "strlib.h"

#pragma data_seg ("shared")

PSTR pszStrings[MAX_STRINGS] = { NULL } ;
int  iTotal = 0 ;

#pragma data_seg ()

int WINAPI DllMain (HINSTANCE hInstance, DWORD fdwReason, PVOID pvReserved)
    {
    int i ;

    switch (fdwReason)
        {
        // Nothing to do when process (or thread) begins

        case DLL_PROCESS_ATTACH :
        case DLL_THREAD_ATTACH :
        case DLL_THREAD_DETACH :
            break ;

        // When process terminates, free any remaining blocks

        case DLL_PROCESS_DETACH :
            for (i = 0 ; i < iTotal ; i++)
                UnmapViewOfFile (pszStrings[i]) ;
            break ;
        }

    return TRUE ;
    }

EXPORT BOOL CALLBACK AddString (PSTR pStringIn)
    {
    HANDLE hString ;
    PSTR    pString ;
```

(continued)

```
    int    i, iLength, iCompare ;

    if (iTotal == MAX_STRINGS - 1)
        return FALSE ;

    iLength = strlen (pStringIn) ;
    if (iLength == 0)
        return FALSE ;

    hString = CreateFileMapping ((HANDLE) -1, NULL, PAGE_READWRITE,
                                 0, 1 + iLength, NULL) ;
    if (hString == NULL)
        return FALSE ;

    pString = (PSTR) MapViewOfFile (hString, FILE_MAP_WRITE, 0, 0, 0) ;
    strcpy (pString, pStringIn) ;
    AnsiUpper (pString) ;

    for (i = iTotal ; i > 0 ; i--)
        {
        iCompare = strcmpi (pStringIn, pszStrings[i - 1]) ;

        if (iCompare >= 0)
            break ;

        pszStrings[i] = pszStrings[i - 1] ;
        }

    pszStrings[i] = pString ;

    iTotal++ ;
    return TRUE ;
    }

EXPORT BOOL CALLBACK DeleteString (PSTR pStringIn)
    {
    int i, j, iCompare ;

    if (0 == strlen (pStringIn))
        return FALSE ;

    for (i = 0 ; i < iTotal ; i++)
        {
        iCompare = lstrcmpi (pszStrings[i], pStringIn) ;
```

(continued)

```
                if (iCompare == 0)
                    break ;
            }

        // If given string not in list, return without taking action

        if (i == iTotal)
            return FALSE ;

        // Else free memory occupied by the string and adjust list downward

        UnmapViewOfFile (pszStrings[i]) ;

        for (j = i ; j < iTotal ; j++)
            pszStrings[j] = pszStrings[j + 1] ;

        pszStrings[iTotal--] = NULL ;     // Destroy unused pointer
        return TRUE ;
        }

EXPORT int CALLBACK GetStrings (PSTRCB pfnGetStrCallBack, PVOID pParam)
        {
        BOOL bReturn ;
        int  i ;

        for (i = 0 ; i < iTotal ; i++)
            {
            bReturn = pfnGetStrCallBack (pszStrings[i], pParam) ;

            if (bReturn == FALSE)
                return i + 1 ;
            }
        return iTotal ;
        }
```

The Library Entry/Exit Point

As you can see in STRLIB.C, we've now made some use of *DllMain*. This function is called when the library first begins and when it terminates. Although I also included a *DllMain* function in EDRLIB.C, it's not really necessary; a function that performs identically would have been included by the linker by default.

The first parameter to *DllMain* is the instance handle of the library. If your library uses resources that require an instance handle (such as *DialogBox*), you should save *hInstance* as a global variable. The last parameter to *DllMain* is reserved by the system.

The *fdwReason* parameter can be one of four values that indicate why Windows 95 is calling the *DllMain* function. In the following discussion, keep in mind that a single program can be loaded multiple times and run together under Windows. Each time a program is loaded, it is considered a separate process.

An *fdwReason* value of DLL_PROCESS_ATTACH indicates that the dynamic link library has been mapped into the address space of a process. This is a cue for the library to do any initialization tasks it requires to service subsequent requests from the process. Such initialization may include memory allocation, for example. During the time that a process is running, *DllMain* is called with a DLL_PROCESS_ATTACH parameter only once during the lifetime of that process. Any other process using the same dynamic link library causes another call to *DllMain* with a DLL_PROCESS_ATTACH parameter, but that's on behalf of the new process.

If the initialization is successful, *DllMain* should return a nonzero value. Returning zero will cause Windows to not run the program.

When *fdwReason* has a value of DLL_PROCESS_DETACH, it means that the dynamic link library is no longer needed by the process. This provides an opportunity for the library to clean up after itself. Under Windows 95 this is not strictly necessary, but it's a good programming practice.

Similarly, when *DllMain* is called with an *fdwReason* parameter of DLL_THREAD-_ATTACH, it means that an attached process has created a new thread. When the thread terminates, Windows calls *DllMain* with an *fdwReason* parameter of DLL_THREAD_DETACH. Be aware that it's possible to get a DLL_THREAD_DETACH call without an earlier DLL-_THREAD_ATTACH call if the dynamic link library is attached to a process after the thread has been created.

The thread still exists when *DllMain* is called with a parameter of DLL_THREAD-_DETACH. The dynamic link library can even send the thread messages during this process. But it shouldn't use *PostMessage*, because the thread will probably be gone before the message is retrieved.

Aside from the *DllMain* function, STRLIB contains only the three functions that it will export to be used by other programs. All these functions are defined as EXPORT. This causes LINK to list them in the STRLIB.LIB import library.

The STRPROG Program

The STRPROG program, shown in Figure 19-4, is fairly straightforward. The two menu options (Enter and Delete) invoke dialog boxes that allow you to enter a string. STRPROG then calls *AddString* or *DeleteString*. When the program needs to update its client area, it calls *GetStrings* and uses the function *GetStrCallBack* to list the enumerated strings.

STRPROG.MAK

```
#-----------------------
# STRPROG.MAK make file
#-----------------------

strprog.exe : strprog.obj strprog.res strlib.lib
    $(LINKER) $(GUIFLAGS) -OUT:strprog.exe strprog.obj strprog.res \
            strlib.lib $(GUILIBS)

strprog.obj : strprog.c strprog.h strlib.h
    $(CC) $(CFLAGS) strprog.c

strprog.res : strprog.rc strprog.h
    $(RC) $(RCVARS) strprog.rc
```

STRPROG.C

```
/*-----------------------------------------------------------
    STRPROG.C -- Program using STRLIB dynamic link library
                    (c) Charles Petzold, 1996
    -----------------------------------------------------------*/

#include <windows.h>
#include <string.h>
#include "strprog.h"
#include "strlib.h"

#define MAXLEN 32
#define WM_DATACHANGE WM_USER

typedef struct
    {
    HDC  hdc ;
    int  xText ;
    int  yText ;
    int  xStart ;
    int  yStart ;
    int  xIncr ;
    int  yIncr ;
    int  xMax ;
    int  yMax ;
    }
    CBPARAM ;
```

Figure 19-4. *The STRPROG program.*

(continued)

```
LRESULT CALLBACK WndProc (HWND, UINT, WPARAM, LPARAM) ;

char szAppName[] = "StrProg" ;
char szString[MAXLEN] ;

int WINAPI WinMain (HINSTANCE hInstance, HINSTANCE hPrevInstance,
                    PSTR szCmdLine, int iCmdShow)
     {
     HWND         hwnd ;
     MSG          msg ;
     WNDCLASSEX   wndclass ;

     wndclass.cbSize        = sizeof (wndclass) ;
     wndclass.style         = CS_HREDRAW | CS_VREDRAW ;
     wndclass.lpfnWndProc   = WndProc ;
     wndclass.cbClsExtra    = 0 ;
     wndclass.cbWndExtra    = 0 ;
     wndclass.hInstance     = hInstance ;
     wndclass.hIcon         = LoadIcon (NULL, IDI_APPLICATION) ;
     wndclass.hCursor       = LoadCursor (NULL, IDC_ARROW) ;
     wndclass.hbrBackground = (HBRUSH) GetStockObject (WHITE_BRUSH) ;
     wndclass.lpszMenuName  = szAppName ;
     wndclass.lpszClassName = szAppName ;
     wndclass.hIconSm       = LoadIcon (NULL, IDI_APPLICATION) ;

     RegisterClassEx (&wndclass) ;

     hwnd = CreateWindow (szAppName, "DLL Demonstration Program",
                          WS_OVERLAPPEDWINDOW,
                          CW_USEDEFAULT, CW_USEDEFAULT,
                          CW_USEDEFAULT, CW_USEDEFAULT,
                          NULL, NULL, hInstance, NULL) ;

     ShowWindow (hwnd, iCmdShow) ;
     UpdateWindow (hwnd) ;

     while (GetMessage (&msg, NULL, 0, 0))
          {
          TranslateMessage (&msg) ;
          DispatchMessage (&msg) ;
          }
     return msg.wParam ;
     }

BOOL CALLBACK DlgProc (HWND hDlg, UINT iMsg, WPARAM wParam, LPARAM lParam)
```

(continued)

```
    {
switch (iMsg)
     {
     case WM_INITDIALOG :
          SendDlgItemMessage (hDlg, IDD_STRING, EM_LIMITTEXT,
                              MAXLEN - 1, 0) ;
          return TRUE ;

     case WM_COMMAND :
          switch (wParam)
               {
               case IDOK :
                    GetDlgItemText (hDlg, IDD_STRING, szString, MAXLEN) ;
                    EndDialog (hDlg, TRUE) ;
                    return TRUE ;

               case IDCANCEL :
                    EndDialog (hDlg, FALSE) ;
                    return TRUE ;
               }
     }
return FALSE ;
}

BOOL CALLBACK EnumCallBack (HWND hwnd, LPARAM lParam)
{
char szClassName[16] ;

GetClassName (hwnd, szClassName, sizeof (szClassName)) ;

if (0 == strcmp (szClassName, szAppName))
    SendMessage (hwnd, WM_DATACHANGE, 0, 0) ;

return TRUE ;
}

BOOL CALLBACK GetStrCallBack (PSTR pString, CBPARAM *pcbp)
{
TextOut (pcbp->hdc, pcbp->xText, pcbp->yText,
         pString, strlen (pString)) ;

if ((pcbp->yText += pcbp->yIncr) > pcbp->yMax)
    {
    pcbp->yText = pcbp->yStart ;
    if ((pcbp->xText += pcbp->xIncr) > pcbp->xMax)
```

(continued)

```
                    return FALSE ;
            }
    return TRUE ;
    }

LRESULT CALLBACK WndProc (HWND hwnd, UINT iMsg, WPARAM wParam, LPARAM lParam)
    {
    static HINSTANCE  hInst ;
    static int        cxChar, cyChar, cxClient, cyClient ;
    CBPARAM           cbparam ;
    HDC               hdc ;
    PAINTSTRUCT       ps ;
    TEXTMETRIC        tm ;

    switch (iMsg)
        {
        case WM_CREATE :
            hInst = ((LPCREATESTRUCT) lParam)->hInstance ;
            hdc   = GetDC (hwnd) ;
            GetTextMetrics (hdc, &tm) ;
            cxChar = (int) tm.tmAveCharWidth ;
            cyChar = (int) (tm.tmHeight + tm.tmExternalLeading) ;
            ReleaseDC (hwnd, hdc) ;

            return 0 ;

        case WM_COMMAND :
            switch (wParam)
                {
                case IDM_ENTER :
                    if (DialogBox (hInst, "EnterDlg", hwnd, &DlgProc))
                        {
                        if (AddString (szString))
                            EnumWindows (&EnumCallBack, 0) ;
                        else
                            MessageBeep (0) ;
                        }
                    break ;

                case IDM_DELETE :
                    if (DialogBox (hInst, "DeleteDlg", hwnd, &DlgProc))
                        {
                        if (DeleteString (szString))
                            EnumWindows (&EnumCallBack, 0) ;
```

(continued)

975

```
                         else
                                MessageBeep (0) ;
                          }
                    break ;
               }
          return 0 ;

     case WM_SIZE :
          cxClient = (int) LOWORD (lParam) ;
          cyClient = (int) HIWORD (lParam) ;
          return 0 ;

     case WM_DATACHANGE :
          InvalidateRect (hwnd, NULL, TRUE) ;
          return 0 ;

     case WM_PAINT :
          hdc = BeginPaint (hwnd, &ps) ;

          cbparam.hdc   = hdc ;
          cbparam.xText = cbparam.xStart = cxChar ;
          cbparam.yText = cbparam.yStart = cyChar ;
          cbparam.xIncr = cxChar * MAXLEN ;
          cbparam.yIncr = cyChar ;
          cbparam.xMax  = cbparam.xIncr * (1 + cxClient / cbparam.xIncr) ;
          cbparam.yMax  = cyChar * (cyClient / cyChar - 1) ;

          GetStrings ((PSTRCB) GetStrCallBack, (PVOID) &cbparam) ;

          EndPaint (hwnd, &ps) ;
          return 0 ;

     case WM_DESTROY :
          PostQuitMessage (0) ;
          return 0 ;
     }
return DefWindowProc (hwnd, iMsg, wParam, lParam) ;
}
```

STRPROG.RC

```
/*---------------------------
   STRPROG.RC resource script
   ---------------------------*/
```

(continued)

```
#include <windows.h>
#include "strprog.h"

StrProg MENU
    {
    MENUITEM   "&Enter!",  IDM_ENTER
    MENUITEM   "&Delete!", IDM_DELETE
    }

EnterDlg DIALOG 24, 24, 190, 44
    STYLE WS_POPUP | WS_DLGFRAME
    {
    LTEXT          "&Enter:", 0,            4,  8,  24,  8
    EDITTEXT                  IDD_STRING,  32,  6, 154, 12
    DEFPUSHBUTTON  "Ok",      IDOK,        44, 24,  32, 14
    PUSHBUTTON     "Cancel",  IDCANCEL,   114, 24,  32, 14
    }

DeleteDlg DIALOG 24, 24, 190, 44
    STYLE WS_POPUP | WS_DLGFRAME
    {
    LTEXT          "&Delete:", 0,            4,  8,  28,  8
    EDITTEXT                   IDD_STRING,  36,  6, 150, 12
    DEFPUSHBUTTON  "Ok",       IDOK,        44, 24,  32, 14
    PUSHBUTTON     "Cancel",   IDCANCEL,   114, 24,  32, 14
    }
```

STRPROG.H

```
/*-----------------------
   STRPROG.H header file
   -----------------------*/

#define IDM_ENTER     1
#define IDM_DELETE    2
#define IDD_STRING    0x10
```

STRPROG.C includes the STRPROG.H header file, which simply defines the constants used in the STRPROG.RC resource script. It also includes the STRLIB.H header file; this defines the three functions in STRLIB that STRPROG will use.

Running STRPROG

Once you've created STRLIB.DLL and STRPROG.EXE, you're ready to run STRPROG. Before you do so, be sure that STRLIB.DLL is in the current directory or a directory that is accessible by Windows (as discussed earlier). Windows must be able to load STRLIB.DLL when you execute STRPROG. If Windows can't find STRLIB.DLL, it will display a message box telling you about the problem.

When you execute STRPROG.EXE, Windows performs fix-ups to functions in external library modules. Many of these functions are in the normal Windows dynamic link libraries. But Windows also sees that the program calls three functions from STRLIB, so Windows loads the STRLIB.DLL file into memory and calls STRLIB's initialization routine. The calls within STRPROG to these three functions are dynamically linked to the functions in STRLIB. You can then use STRPROG to add and delete strings from STRLIB's internal table. STRPROG's client area shows the strings currently in the table.

The calls from STRPROG to the *AddString*, *DeleteString*, and *GetStrings* functions in STRLIB are very efficient and have no more overhead than calls to any other external module. In fact, the link between STRPROG and STRLIB is as efficient as if the three functions in STRLIB were simply in STRPROG itself. So what? you say. Why do I have to make this a dynamic link library? Can't I include these three routines in STRPROG.EXE?

Well, you could. In one sense, STRLIB is nothing more than an extension of STRPROG. However, you may be interested to see what happens when you execute a second instance of STRPROG. STRLIB stores the character strings and their pointers in shared memory, which lets all instances of STRPROG share this data. Let's look at how it's done.

Sharing Data Among STRPROG Instances

Windows erects a wall around the address space of a Win32 process. Normally, data in an address space is private, invisible to other processes. But running multiple instances of STRPROG shows that STRLIB has no trouble sharing its data with all instances of the program. When you add or delete a string in a STRPROG window, the change is immediately reflected in the other windows.

STRLIB shares two types of data: the strings and the pointers to the strings. For the sake of illustration, it uses a different sharing method for each type. We've already encountered one method in Chapter 13. STRLIB stores each string in a memory-mapped file, making the string visible to all processes.

As for the string pointers, STRLIB keeps them in a special section of memory that it designates as shared:

```
#pragma data_seg ("shared")
PSTR pszStrings[MAX_STRINGS] = { NULL } ;
int  iTotal = 0 ;
#pragma data_seg ()
```

The first *#pragma* statement creates the data section, here named *shared*. You can name the section whatever you wish, though the linker sees only the first eight characters. All initialized variables after the *#pragma* go into the *shared* section. The second *#pragma* statement marks the end of the section. It's important to specifically initialize the variables; otherwise the compiler puts them in the normal uninitialized section rather than in *shared*.

The linker has to be told about *shared*. On the linker command line, specify the -SECTION parameter like this:

```
-SECTION:shared,rws
```

The "rws" letters indicate the section has read, write, and shared attributes.

Now all instances of STRPROG see one instance of the strings and pointers. The *EnumCallBack* function in STRPROG serves to notify all STRPROG's instances that the contents of STRLIB's data segments have changed. *EnumWindows* causes Windows to call *EnumCallBack* with handles to all parent windows. *EnumCallBack* then checks to see if the class name of each window equals "StrProg"; if it does, the function sends the window a privately defined WM_DATACHANGE message. And you can easily imagine an enhanced version of STRLIB managing a database that is shared by several instances of the same program or by single instances of different programs.

SOME LIBRARY RESTRICTIONS

I mentioned earlier that a dynamic link library module doesn't receive messages. However, a library module can call *GetMessage* and *PeekMessage*. The messages the library pulls from the queue with these functions are actually messages for the program that called the library function. In general, the library works on behalf of the program calling it, a rule that holds for most Windows functions that a library calls.

A dynamic link library can load resources (such as icons, strings, and bitmaps) either from the library file or from the file of the program that calls the library. The functions that load resources require an instance handle. If the library uses its own instance handle (which is passed to the library during initialization), then the library can obtain resources from its own file. To load resources from the calling program's .EXE file, the library function requires the instance handle of the program calling the function.

Registering window classes and creating windows in a library can be a little tricky. Both the window class structure and the *CreateWindow* call require an instance handle. Although you can use the library module's instance handle in creating the window class and the window, the window messages still go through the message queue of the program calling the library when the library creates the window. If you must create window classes and windows within a library, it's probably best to use the calling program's instance handle.

Because messages for modal dialog boxes are retrieved outside a program's message loop, you can create a modal dialog box in a library by calling *DialogBox*. The instance handle can be that of the library, and the *hwndParent* parameter to *DialogBox* can be set to NULL.

DYNAMIC LINKING WITHOUT IMPORTS

Rather than have Windows perform dynamic linking when your program is first loaded into memory, you can link a program with a library module while the program is running. For instance, you would normally call the *Rectangle* function like this:

```
Rectangle (hdc, xLeft, yTop, xRight, yBottom) ;
```

This works because the program has been linked with the GDI32.LIB import library, which supplied the address of *Rectangle*.

You can also call *Rectangle* in a very roundabout manner. You first use *typedef* to define a function type for *Rectangle*:

```
typedef BOOL (WINAPI *PFNRECT) (HDC, int, int, int, int) ;
```

You then define two variables:

```
HANDLE  hLibrary ;
PFNRECT pfnRectangle ;
```

Now you set *hLibrary* to the handle of the library and *pfnRectangle* to the address of the *Rectangle* function:

```
hLibrary = LoadLibrary ("GDI32.DLL") ;
pfnRectangle = (PFNRECT) GetProcAddress (hLibrary, "Rectangle") ;
```

The *LoadLibrary* function returns NULL if the library file can't be found or some other error occurs. Now you can call the function and then free the library:

```
pfnRectangle (hdc, xLeft, yTop, xRight, yBottom) ;
FreeLibrary (hLibrary) ;
```

Although this technique of run-time dynamic linking doesn't make much sense for the *Rectangle* function, it will definitely come in handy when you don't know the name of the library module until run time.

The code above uses the *LoadLibrary* and *FreeLibrary* functions. Windows maintains "reference counts" for all library modules. *LoadLibrary* causes the reference count to be incremented. The reference count is also incremented when Windows loads any program that uses the library. *FreeLibrary* causes the reference count to be decremented, as does the termination of an instance of a program that uses this library. When the reference count is 0, Windows can discard the library from memory, because the library is no longer needed.

RESOURCE-ONLY LIBRARIES

Any function in a dynamic link library that Windows programs or other libraries can use must be exported. However, a dynamic link library need not contain any exported functions. What would such a DLL contain? The answer is resources.

Let's say you're working on a Windows application that requires a number of bitmaps. Normally you would list these in the resource script of the program and load them into memory with the *LoadBitmap* function. But perhaps you want to create several sets of bitmaps, each set customized for one of the major display adapters used with Windows. It would make most sense to store these different sets of bitmaps in different files, because a user would need only one set of bitmaps on the fixed disk. These files are resource-only libraries.

Figure 19-5 shows how to create a resource-only library file called BITLIB.DLL that contains nine bitmaps. The BITLIB.RC file lists all the separate bitmap files and assigns each one a number. To create BITLIB.DLL, you need nine bitmaps named BITMAP1.BMP, BITMAP2.BMP, and so forth. You can use the bitmaps provided on the companion CD-ROM or create them yourself in the Windows PAINT program.

BITLIB.MAK

```
#---------------------
# BITLIB.MAK make file
#---------------------

bitlib.dll : bitlib.obj bitlib.res
    $(LINKER) $(DLLFLAGS) -OUT:bitlib.dll bitlib.obj bitlib.res $(GUILIBS)

bitlib.obj : bitlib.c
    $(CC) $(CFLAGS) bitlib.c

bitlib.res : bitlib.rc
    $(RC) $(RCVARS) bitlib.rc
```

BITLIB.C

```
/*------------------------------------------------------------
   BITLIB.C -- Code entry point for BITLIB dynamic link library
               (c) Charles Petzold, 1996
   ------------------------------------------------------------*/

#include <windows.h>
```

Figure 19-5. *The BITLIB library.*

(continued)

```
int WINAPI DllMain (HINSTANCE hInstance, DWORD fdwReason, PVOID pvReserved)
    {
    return TRUE ;
    }
```

BITLIB.RC

```
/*---------------------------
   BITLIB.RC resource script
--------------------------*/

1 BITMAP bitmap1.bmp
2 BITMAP bitmap2.bmp
3 BITMAP bitmap3.bmp
4 BITMAP bitmap4.bmp
5 BITMAP bitmap5.bmp
6 BITMAP bitmap6.bmp
7 BITMAP bitmap7.bmp
8 BITMAP bitmap8.bmp
9 BITMAP bitmap9.bmp
```

The SHOWBIT program, shown in Figure 19-6, reads the bitmap resources from BITLIB and draws them in the upper-left corner of the client area. You can cycle through the bitmaps by pressing a key on the keyboard.

SHOWBIT.MAK

```
#----------------------
# SHOWBIT.MAK make file
#----------------------

showbit.exe : showbit.obj
    $(LINKER) $(GUIFLAGS) -OUT:showbit.exe showbit.obj $(GUILIBS)

showbit.obj : showbit.c
    $(CC) $(CFLAGS) showbit.c
```

SHOWBIT.C

```
/*------------------------------------------------------------
   SHOWBIT.C -- Shows bitmaps in BITLIB dynamic link library
                (c) Charles Petzold, 1996
--------------------------------------------------------------*/
```

Figure 19-6. *The SHOWBIT program.*   *(continued)*

```
#include <windows.h>

LRESULT CALLBACK WndProc (HWND, UINT, WPARAM, LPARAM) ;

int WINAPI WinMain (HINSTANCE hInstance, HINSTANCE hPrevInstance,
                    PSTR szCmdLine, int iCmdShow)
     {
     static char  szAppName[] = "ShowBit" ;
     HWND         hwnd ;
     MSG          msg ;
     WNDCLASSEX   wndclass ;

     wndclass.cbSize        = sizeof (wndclass) ;
     wndclass.style         = CS_HREDRAW | CS_VREDRAW ;
     wndclass.lpfnWndProc   = WndProc ;
     wndclass.cbClsExtra    = 0 ;
     wndclass.cbWndExtra    = 0 ;
     wndclass.hInstance     = hInstance ;
     wndclass.hIcon         = LoadIcon (NULL, IDI_APPLICATION) ;
     wndclass.hCursor       = LoadCursor (NULL, IDC_ARROW) ;
     wndclass.hbrBackground = (HBRUSH) GetStockObject (WHITE_BRUSH) ;
     wndclass.lpszMenuName  = NULL ;
     wndclass.lpszClassName = szAppName ;
     wndclass.hIconSm       = LoadIcon (NULL, IDI_APPLICATION) ;

     RegisterClassEx (&wndclass) ;

     hwnd = CreateWindow (szAppName, "Show Bitmaps from BITLIB (Press Key)",
                          WS_OVERLAPPEDWINDOW,
                          CW_USEDEFAULT, CW_USEDEFAULT,
                          CW_USEDEFAULT, CW_USEDEFAULT,
                          NULL, NULL, hInstance, NULL) ;

     ShowWindow (hwnd, iCmdShow) ;
     UpdateWindow (hwnd) ;

     while (GetMessage (&msg, NULL, 0, 0))
          {
          TranslateMessage (&msg) ;
          DispatchMessage (&msg) ;
          }
     return msg.wParam ;
     }

void DrawBitmap (HDC hdc, int xStart, int yStart, HBITMAP hBitmap)
     {
     BITMAP bm ;
```

(continued)

```
        HDC     hMemDC ;
        POINT  pt ;

        hMemDC = CreateCompatibleDC (hdc) ;
        SelectObject (hMemDC, hBitmap) ;
        GetObject (hBitmap, sizeof (BITMAP), (PSTR) &bm) ;
        pt.x = bm.bmWidth ;
        pt.y = bm.bmHeight ;

        BitBlt (hdc, xStart, yStart, pt.x, pt.y, hMemDC, 0, 0, SRCCOPY) ;

        DeleteDC (hMemDC) ;
        }

LRESULT CALLBACK WndProc (HWND hwnd, UINT iMsg, WPARAM wParam, LPARAM lParam)
        {
        static HINSTANCE   hLibrary ;
        static int         iCurrent = 1 ;
        HBITMAP            hBitmap ;
        HDC                hdc ;
        PAINTSTRUCT        ps ;

        switch (iMsg)
            {
            case WM_CREATE :
                if ((hLibrary = LoadLibrary ("BITLIB.DLL")) == NULL)
                    DestroyWindow (hwnd) ;

                return 0 ;

            case WM_CHAR :
                if (hLibrary)
                    {
                    iCurrent ++ ;
                    InvalidateRect (hwnd, NULL, TRUE) ;
                    }
                return 0 ;

            case WM_PAINT :
                hdc = BeginPaint (hwnd, &ps) ;

                if (hLibrary)
                    {
                    if (NULL == (hBitmap = LoadBitmap (hLibrary,
                                        MAKEINTRESOURCE (iCurrent))))
                        {
                        iCurrent = 1 ;
```

(continued)

```
                                hBitmap = LoadBitmap (hLibrary,
                                               MAKEINTRESOURCE (iCurrent)) ;
                                }

                    if (hBitmap)
                            {
                            DrawBitmap (hdc, 0, 0, hBitmap) ;
                            DeleteObject (hBitmap) ;
                            }
                    }

            EndPaint (hwnd, &ps) ;
            return 0 ;

    case WM_DESTROY :
            if (hLibrary)
                    FreeLibrary (hLibrary) ;

            PostQuitMessage (0) ;
            return 0 ;
        }
    return DefWindowProc (hwnd, iMsg, wParam, lParam) ;
    }
```

During processing of the WM_CREATE message, the SHOWBIT program gets a handle to BITLIB.DLL:

```
if ((hLibrary = LoadLibrary ("BITLIB.DLL")) == NULL)
    DestroyWindow (hwnd) ;
```

If BITLIB.DLL isn't in the current directory, Windows will search for it as discussed earlier in this chapter. If it can't find the library at that point, Windows displays a message box noting the problem. When the user presses OK, *LoadLibrary* returns a NULL value, in which case SHOWBIT terminates.

SHOWBIT can obtain a handle to a bitmap by calling *LoadBitmap* with the library handle and the number of the bitmap:

```
hBitmap = LoadBitmap (hLibrary, MAKEINTRESOURCE (iCurrent)) ;
```

This returns an error if the bitmap corresponding to the number *iCurrent* isn't valid or if not enough memory exists to load the bitmap.

While processing the WM_DESTROY message, SHOWBIT frees the library:

```
FreeLibrary (hLibrary) ;
```

When the last instance of SHOWBIT terminates, the reference count of BITLIB.DLL drops to 0 and the memory it occupies is freed.

Chapter 20

What's This Thing Called OLE?

OLE is a set of standards for building connectable component software. One OLE standard is the Component Object Model (COM) specification, a blueprint for the binary connections between components. Another defining element of OLE is a set of dynamic link libraries that are part of Windows 95 and Windows NT. Microsoft has arranged for third parties—including Digital, Software AG, and Bristol Technologies—to port some of the technologies from these libraries to other operating system platforms. But the set of services provided by OLE is not static. Just as Microsoft has continually enhanced and extended the Windows operating system, so too will Microsoft continue to evolve OLE to accommodate a broader range of application integration needs. As of this writing, for example, Network OLE is slated to appear as part of Windows NT version 4.0; it will enable component connections across network boundaries.

OLE allows a degree of integration between software modules that previously had required proprietary knowledge and therefore represents the first step in creating a world of interchangeable software components. In such a world, a user would be able to combine a word processing edit window from one vendor with a spelling checker from a second vendor to a print preview component from yet a third software provider.

At present, just a few categories of standard OLE connections have been established. And yet, the architecture of OLE not only allows for more categories, but makes new families of connections inevitable. Prior to Windows 95, the four most common categories of OLE connections were compound document support, OLE Automation, OLE Controls, and the Extended Messaging Applications Programming Interface (Extended MAPI). Windows

95 introduced a new family of OLE components, *shell extensions*, for creating tight integration between application software and the Windows 95 desktop. Another OLE-aware component introduced with Windows 95 is the rich edit control, a dialog box control that provides a simple compound document container.

A compound document container creates compound documents, which can hold data from many different, unrelated applications. Containers communicate with "object server" applications to negotiate the two-way movement of data between a server and a compound document. An example of a compound document is when a portion of an Excel spreadsheet is embedded in a Microsoft Word for Windows document. In this example, the Excel spreadsheet data is an *embedded object*, and Word for Windows provides a *compound document container*. This example doesn't show OLE at its best, however, since it's easy to suspect collusion when two products from the same company cooperate closely. That OLE's compound document support is truly universal is demonstrated when programs from many vendors—Adobe PageMaker or Micrografx Designer, for example—provide the same compound document support as Microsoft Word. Each of the container applications can hold Excel spreadsheet objects, Corel Draw drawing objects, Visio diagrams, or data objects from any OLE-compliant object server.

Automation provides a mechanism for defining a set of macro primitives. Macro primitives consist of methods (another term for function calls) and properties (that is, data elements that can be read from or written to or that can be read-only or write-only). The term "automation object" refers to an OLE component that provides a macro primitive. An "automation controller" manipulates the methods and properties of an automation object. Through the OLE-defined standards for automation, programming environments such as Microsoft's Visual Basic, Borland's Delphi, or PowerSoft's Power Builder let you create automation controllers to provide centralized control of work distributed among specialized applications.

OLE Controls are a third type of standard OLE component; they are like dialog box controls in that they are essentially special purpose child windows. Instead of residing in dialog boxes, however, OLE controls reside within *OLE control containers*. OLE controls are automation objects and export their own macro primitives. OLE controls are like compound document objects in that they can save state information in a file created and managed by their container application. OLE controls recognize *ambient properties*, attributes like background color and current font, which allow them to visually blend into their container. OLE controls have the ability to send event notifications to the control container, in that way, they are like Visual Basic controls, which send events to trigger responses. In fact, Microsoft has publicly announced that Visual Basic controls (VBXs) will not be supported in the 32-bit world and is encouraging all VBX developers to upgrade their Win16 VBXs to Win32 OLE controls.

The common element among all standard OLE connections is that they are glued together with the OLE Component Object Model (COM). COM is an object-oriented specification for defining *interfaces*, the contact points between components. COM provides the foundation on which all OLE features are built.

Before I go further, be forewarned that the set of services considered part of OLE is very large—and still growing! Since there isn't room in this chapter to cover all aspects of OLE, the focus will be on the fundamentals of the Component Object Model. Along the way, you'll see two OLE servers (one a private component and one a public component) and two OLE client programs. For more detailed coverage on a wide range of OLE programming topics, see *Inside OLE* by Kraig Brockschmidt (Microsoft Press, 1995).

OLE BASICS

Tapping into OLE component support requires following basic rules of the road.

Connecting to the OLE Libraries

Before any OLE operations can be performed, a Win32 process must connect to the OLE libraries. Any module within a process—whether a program or a DLL—can make the connection. Since multiple attempts to connect are benign, and since the developer of one module can't be sure if other modules have made a connection, every module that relies on the OLE libraries should attempt to establish a connection on behalf of each process in which it runs.

The most common way to connect to the OLE libraries is by calling *OleInitialize*:

```
HRESULT hr = OleInitialize (NULL) ;
if (FAILED (hr))
    {
    // Error handling
    }
```

The single parameter to *OleInitialize* must be NULL (other values were valid in 16-bit OLE, but NULL is the only valid value in 32-bit OLE). This function sets up the OLE services for the current process, then calls an additional setup function, *CoInitialize*, to initialize the Component Object Model library. This library provides low-level services for component creation and cleanup.

In a few cases, you may wish to bypass *OleInitialize* and call *CoInitialize* directly. For example, you'd connect to OLE by calling *CoInitialize* when building a custom OLE component that requires only the most basic COM services. A key benefit is a smaller memory footprint since only a subset of the OLE DLLs actually gets loaded into memory. The call to *CoInitialize* is identical to the call to *OleInitialize*:

```
HRESULT hr = CoInitialize (NULL) ;
if (FAILED (hr))
    {
    // Error handling
    }
```

Each OLE component that attempts to create a connection to the OLE libraries should disconnect itself before terminating if no failure code was returned in the connection attempt. *OleUninitialize* is the disconnect function for *OleInitialize*, and *CoUninitialize* is the disconnect function for *CoInitialize*. As you might expect, *OleUninitialize* calls *CoUninitialize*, so a component only calls the disconnect function matching the connect function it called.

The return value for both initialization functions, of type HRESULT, notifies the caller of success or failure. The preceding code fragments show the use of the FAILED macro to catch a failure. An opposite macro, SUCCEEDED, returns TRUE on success. Almost every OLE function returns a value of type HRESULT. A few guidelines will help to properly interpret its meaning.

Deciphering Result Codes

A common theme throughout OLE is the use of a standard return type, HRESULT, for almost every OLE library call and almost every OLE interface call. The OLE include files define this type as:

```
typedef LONG HRESULT ;
```

Although referred to as a "result handle," it's not a typical handle that references an object. Instead, it's a 32-bit value made up of bit fields, as shown in Figure 20-1.

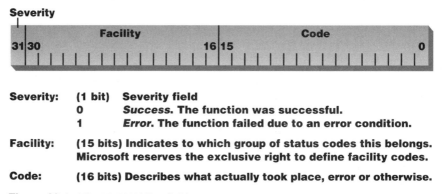

Severity: (1 bit) **Severity field**
0   *Success*. The function was successful.
1   *Error*. The function failed due to an error condition.

Facility: (15 bits) Indicates to which group of status codes this belongs. Microsoft reserves the exclusive right to define facility codes.

Code: (16 bits) Describes what actually took place, error or otherwise.

Figure 20-1. *The HRESULT bit fields.*

The most important field in an HRESULT is the Severity field, which indicates success or failure. The SUCCEEDED and FAILED macros determine success or failure based solely on this field.

The Facility field identifies the component which flagged the error. (Please note that to avoid conflicting with facility codes from Microsoft, do not create your own facility codes.) At present, as indicated in the table at the top of the facing page, only a few facilities are defined:

Facility Name	Facility Value	Description
FACILITY_NULL	0	Used for broadly applicable common status codes that have no specific grouping. (E.g., S_OK belongs to this facility.)
FACILITY_RPC	1	Result from underlying remote procedure call implementation.
FACILITY_DISPATCH	2	Result related to *IDispatch* interface.
FACILITY_STORAGE	3	Result related to persistent storage. Result codes less than 256 have same meaning as MS-DOS error codes.
FACILITY_ITF	4	Most commonly specified facility; meaning is interface-specific.
FACILITY_WIN32	7	Result originates from Win32 *GetLastError* function.
FACILITY_WINDOWS	8	Result from Microsoft-defined interface.
FACILITY_CONTROL	10	Result related to OLE controls.

Details are provided in the Code field, bits 0 through 15. For a failure, this field holds the error code. And even for success, as we'll see shortly, there are sometimes shades of success worth discerning.

The layout of bits in HRESULT codes may be implementation-dependent. To determine success or failure, rely only on the FAILED and SUCCEEDED macros. To fetch the facility for an error code, use the HRESULT_FACILITY macro. And for the error code, use the HRESULT_CODE macro. This will ensure that your OLE code will be more easily portable, for example, from Windows 95 to the Apple Macintosh, to UNIX, to VMS, and to every other platform onto which OLE gets ported.

As an example of HRESULT values, this table summarizes *CoInitialize* and *OleInitialize* return values:

Return Value	Binary Value	Description
S_OK	0x00000000L	Indicates the library was initialized successfully.
S_FALSE	0x00000001L	Indicates that the library is already initialized.
E_OUTOFMEMORY	0x8007000E	Failure due to out-of-memory condition.
E_INVALIDARG	0x80070057	Failure due to invalid argument.
E_UNEXPECTED	0x8000FFFF	Failure due to unexpected error.

When a module attempts to initialize the OLE libraries, the return of S_OK and S_FALSE indicates a successful result. The first successful initialization call in a process returns S_OK. Subsequent calls don't affect the already initialized libraries, reflected in the S_FALSE return value. The "S_" prefix stands for "Success," an accurate designation for both result codes since both mean that OLE is ready to use. Of course, a module can always check for specific values for cases when, for example, a debugging tool needs to be the first module to initialize the OLE libraries.

The OLE documentation lists several result codes for most functions, but a function can (and often does) fail with result codes other than those listed in the documentation for specific functions. The hard way to figure out the meaning of the resulting HRESULT code involves searching the OLE include files. An easier way is to call *FormatMessage*, which is a Win32 routine for converting message codes (or in this case, an OLE result handle) into a human-readable string. Here's a wrapper function for *FormatMessage* that accepts an OLE or Win32 error code and provides a text description of the code:

```
// DisplayErrorString: Fetch explanation for
//   Win32 and OLE error codes
void DisplayErrorString (DWORD dwError, BOOL bDebugger)
    {
    CHAR achBuffer[120] ;
    FormatMessage (FORMAT_MESSAGE_FROM_SYSTEM, NULL,
                    dwError,
                    LANG_SYSTEM_DEFAULT,
                    achBuffer, 120,
                    NULL) ;

    if (bDebugger)
        {
        OutputDebugString (achBuffer) ;
        }
    else
        {
        MessageBox (NULL, achBuffer, "DescribeError", MB_OK) ;
        }
    }
```

This function takes two parameters: *dwError* is the HRESULT value returned by an OLE function, and *bDebugger* is a Boolean value indicating where to send output. If *bDebugger* is TRUE, output goes to the debugger's output window (if no debugger is running, such output disappears) or to a message box.

Incidentally, the OLE HRESULT values have been integrated into the Win32 error codes, as you can tell by perusing the Win32 include file, WINERROR.H. One difference between the way that OLE and Win32 handle error codes is that most OLE functions return an HRESULT value directly, whereas Win32 functions don't directly return an error code. For Win32 functions, such error codes are available by calling *GetLastError.* This function returns the current error code for the last function that failed on the current thread. Some Win32 routines clear the error code—to set it to a known state before calling other Win32 routines that might fail—so an immediate check on this code is necessary before calling other Win32 functions.

So far, we've touched on two basic OLE programming points: First, to use OLE as a component you must first connect to the OLE libraries. Second, proper interpretation of the HRESULT return code is necessary to distinguish successful connections from unsuccessful ones. Once connected to the OLE libraries, a module has two available choices: connect to an OLE interface (that is, become a client to an OLE interface), or make an OLE interface available for others to use (that is, become a server for an OLE interface). Most OLE-aware programs do both. To help you decide which you should consider first, the next section introduces the fundamentals of OLE interfaces. OLE interfaces are created by following the *Component Object Model (COM)* specification and therefore are also sometimes called *COM Interfaces.*

Component Object Model (COM) Interfaces

The Component Object Model (COM) is a specification for building an OLE-aware component. COM provides a definition for the fundamental bindings required between interface provider and interface user. All OLE interfaces—whether for compound documents, OLE Automation, OLE Controls, Windows 95 shell extensions, or Extended MAPI—are built according to the COM specification.

COM interfaces provide a single solution to a problem that previously had been addressed by many solutions—namely, connecting software components running in different processes or on different computers. The challenge, simply stated, is to efficiently connect components separated by an address space boundary, a network boundary, or no boundary at all. (As of this writing, Network OLE has not been released but is expected shortly after this book goes to press.) OLE interfaces provide for both inter-process and inter-machine cases while also efficiently handling connections between components running in the *same* address space. A single solution to all three connectivity cases means that developers can ignore differences based solely on component location and instead can focus on the task at hand. This is analogous to the way telephones are used: people communicate using a single mechanism—the telephone handset—whether in different rooms of the same building, on different sides of the same continent, or on different hemispheres of the same planet.

As with all good designs, interfaces combine several things together. Interfaces are at the same time a contract for services, the binary connection between the provider for a service and the user of that service, and a mechanism for supporting out-of-process connections (that is, both inter-process and inter-machine connections). What ties these aspects together is a set of core functions that all interfaces share. Each of these points deserves closer consideration.

An interface is a contract for services

An interface is a contract for services provided by one component (the "server") and used by another (the "client"). As such, the only code associated with an interface definition consists of a set of functions prototypes—function return values, function names, and function parameters. The contract specifies *what* services are provided, but not *how* they are to be provided. The details of the implementation are hidden from view—that is, *encapsulated*—within the service provider.

For example, here are the function prototypes for *IMalloc*, OLE's memory allocation interface:

Function Prototype	Description
void *Alloc (ULONG cb) ;	Allocate *cb* bytes.
void *Realloc (void *pv, ULONG cb) ;	Resize *pv* memory to *cb* bytes.
void Free (void *pv) ;	Free memory referenced by *pv*.
ULONG GetSize (void *pv) ;	Query memory size.
int DidAlloc (void *pv) ;	Allocated by this allocator?
void HeapMinimize (void) ;	Defragment memory.

The services provided by such an allocator—the "what"—are obvious to any programmer experienced with dynamic memory allocation. But the *implementation*—that is, *how* the requests get satisfied—is not specified. An *IMalloc* implementor on Windows 95 could use any available Win32 mechanism including the page allocator (*VirtualAlloc*) for large objects, the heap allocator (*HeapAlloc*) for small objects, or a Win16 API-compatible allocator (*GlobalAlloc* or *LocalAlloc*) for an allocator compatible with both the Win16 and Win32 APIs. An implementor could even call C run-time allocation functions to create a portable *IMalloc* independent of the Win32 API.

One point worth mentioning about *IMalloc* concerns the naming standard for interfaces. Following the Hungarian notation naming style, interface names have an "I" prefix: for example, *IStorage*, *IOleObject*, and *IDataObject*. This is similar to the use of the "C" prefix with Microsoft MFC library class names (*CWinApp*, *CFrameWnd*) or the "T" prefix with Borland OWL class names (*TApplication*, *TWindow*).

While the details of how an interface gets implemented are hidden from view, the binary contact point between a client and a server is quite visible and clearly defined.

An interface defines a binary contact point

At its core, the binary implementation of an interface is a function pointer array. A server for an interface like *IMalloc* implements individual functions and builds an array of function pointers. A client expects to access server functions via such an array.

The specific connection that servers provide to clients is a *pointer to an array of function pointers*. In C, array syntax provides one way to create a function pointer array. An *IMalloc* server could allocate an array of function pointers as follows:

```
// Define generic function pointer type
typedef (* PFNINTERFACE) () ;

// Allocate an array of function pointers
PFNINTERFACE allocator[6] = { Alloc, Realloc, Free,
                              GetSize, DidAlloc,
                              HeapMinimize } ;
```

and then return the critical connection—the pointer to the array of function pointers—to any client that calls:

```
PFNINTERFACE *FetchAllocator ()
    {
    return &allocator ;
    }
```

The problem with array syntax is that calls to *IMalloc* functions are clumsy and error prone. The return type must be cast, no parameter checking can take place, and an array index replaces a function name. A call to *Alloc* requesting 20 bytes, for example, looks like this:

```
PFNINTERFACE *pAlloc = FetchAllocator () ;
void *pData = (void *) pAlloc[0] (20) ;
```

With parameter type checking disabled, calls like the following don't generate any warning or error messages:

```
// Error: Wrong parameter type!!
pData = (void *) pMalloc[0] ("20 bytes") ;

// Error: Wrong number of parameters!!
pData = (void *) pMalloc[0] (20, 30, 40, 50, 60) ;
```

A better approach involves using a structure containing function pointers. Taking this approach involves declarations like the following:

```
// Specifically-typed function pointer types
typedef void * (* PFNALLOC) (ULONG) ;
typedef void * (* PFNREALLOC) (void *, ULONG) ;
typedef void   (* PFNFREE) (void *) ;
```

```
typedef ULONG   (* PFNGETSIZE) (void *) ;
typedef int     (* PFNDIDALLOC) (void *) ;
typedef void    (* PFNHEAPMINIMIZE) (void) ;

// Define structure containing function pointers
typedef struct tagALLOCATOR
    {
    PFNALLOC          Alloc ;
    PFNREALLOC        Realloc ;
    PFNFREE           Free ;
    PFNGETSIZE        GetSize ;
    PFNDIDALLOC       DidAlloc ;
    PFNHEAPMINIMIZE   HeapMinimize ;
    } ALLOCATOR ;

ALLOCATOR imalloc = { Alloc, Realloc, Free,
                      GetSize, DidAlloc,
                      HeapMinimize } ;

ALLOCATOR *FetchAllocator ()
    {
    return &imalloc ;
    }
```

While not using explicit array syntax, the actual layout of the binary image mimics the function array in the earlier example.

More to the point, the use of a structure—while perhaps somewhat complicated to define—makes calls easy and natural. In particular, casting of return types is not required, function names can be used to make function calls, and parameter type checking for the compiler is fully operational. Here is a call to allocate 20 bytes:

```
ALLOCATOR *pAlloc = FetchAllocator () ;
void *pData = pAlloc->Alloc (20) ;
```

The best approach to take—and the one adopted for OLE interfaces—is to use the array of function pointers created automatically when a C++ class is declared. A function pointer array is created for all "virtual" functions—those functions prefixed with a *virtual* keyword. The presence of function prototypes in a C++ class declaration provides parameter checking without an endless stream of function pointer *typedef*s:

```
class IMalloc
    {
    virtual void  *Alloc (ULONG cb) ;
    virtual void  *Realloc (void *pv, ULONG cb) ;
    virtual void   Free (void *pv) ;
    virtual ULONG  GetSize (void *pv) ;
    virtual int    DidAlloc (void *pv) ;
    virtual void   HeapMinimize (void) ;
    } ;
```

One slight complication arises from the use of C++ classes. In particular, when calling such functions from C, the C++ object requires an additional level of indirection to reference the function table. What effectively gets created is an *IMalloc *** instead of a simple *IMalloc ** pointer. Another complication is that a pointer to the component object must be passed as a first parameter, to simulate the implicit passing of a *this* pointer that all C++ object functions expect. Here's how to call an *IMalloc* interface function in C:

```
IMalloc *pMalloc = FetchMalloc () ;
void *pData = pMalloc->lpVtbl->Alloc (pMalloc, 20) ;
```

Setting aside these additional complications, the core of the binary definition of an interface—the function table array—is the same.

An important aspect of OLE interfaces is inter-process and inter-machine support, covered together in this introduction to OLE as simply "remotable connections."

An interface is a remotable connection

To the client, the binary interface—the function array—stays the same whether a client/server connection runs *in-process* or crosses a process or network boundary. When a server is running with its client in the same process, a single function array unites calls from the client to functions in the server. When calling a server *out-of-process*, the client stills sees a function array. There are two types of out-of-process servers: *local servers* run in a different address space on the same machine, and *remote servers* run on a different machine altogether. To a caller, the difference between local and remote services are transparent. A server provides the necessary support mechanism so that its interfaces can provide a seamless connection—across a process boundary or across a network boundary—without the client knowing or caring where the "real" work is done.

The OLE libraries provide much of the support required for running remote. In the address space of the client process, a function array is constructed and connected to a set of surrogate *proxy functions*. Proxy functions, which are the logical equivalent of call forwarding in a telephone system, wrap parameters into a package to be shipped to the "real" interface in the server address space. In the server address space, a set of *stub functions* unwraps the package and call actual server functions using the passed parameters.

The packing, transport, and unpacking work performed by proxy and stub functions is called *marshaling*. OLE provides default marshaling support for all OLE-defined interfaces using a built-in remote procedure call (RPC) mechanism for cross-process and cross-network calls. If you define a custom interface—that is, a new interface not part of the OLE standard—your interface isn't inherently remotable.

To make a custom interface remotable, OLE allows you two choices. The first is to write an Interface Definition Language (IDL) script that describes your interface and pass it through the Microsoft IDL compiler. This compiler generates the proxy and stub function code which you compile into a DLL. The second choice is to control all aspects of the marshaling yourself, which allows you to use any transport mechanism—such as shared memory, Windows messages, named pipes, RPC, Morse code, and so on. This option is called "custom marshaling," which means that OLE itself is not at all involved in cross-process or cross-network calls."

An OLE interface function table contains two sets of functions: interface-generic functions and interface-specific functions. The preceding *IMalloc* interface example showed only functions specific to the task of memory allocation. What is missing are three generic functions, discussed in the next section, that occupy the first three positions of every OLE interface function array.

Every OLE interface has these three functions

Every OLE interface has a common set of interface functions, which support basic housekeeping on behalf of the underlying OLE component: *QueryInterface*, *AddRef*, and *Release*. Together, these three functions make up their own interface, called *IUnknown*:

```
class IUnknown
    {
    virtual HRESULT QueryInterface (REFIID iid, void **ppv) ;
    virtual ULONG   AddRef () ;
    virtual ULONG   Release () ;
    } ;
```

The rationale for an interface named "Unknown" reflects the fact that interfaces are accessed by pointers, and it's helpful to be able to create a generic pointer. Akin to the C/C++ *void* *, a "generic pointer" provides a minimum set of known things that can be accomplished with any interface. In particular, you'll encounter OLE functions that can return different kinds of interface pointers. Such functions are often prototyped to return an *IUnknown* *.

For the sake of simplicity, the *IMalloc* interface introduced earlier did not include the three interface functions. A more accurate *IMalloc* declaration references *IUnknown* as a base class from which all its members are inherited:

```
class IMalloc : public IUnknown
    {
    virtual void  *Alloc (ULONG cb) ;
    virtual void  *Realloc (void *pv, ULONG cb) ;
    virtual void   Free (void *pv) ;
    virtual ULONG GetSize (void *pv) ;
    virtual int    DidAlloc (void *pv) ;
    virtual void   HeapMinimize (void) ;
    } ;
```

NOTE to C Programmers

Through the mechanism of C++ class inheritance, the addition of "*: public IUnknown*" to the definition of *IMalloc* prefixes all *IUnknown* elements to the *IMalloc* class. Nine member functions make up *IMalloc*'s virtual function table, and these nine define the binary connection to this interface.

In addition to the six memory management functions, the *IMalloc* interface also provides three functions not related to memory management. As you'll see, these three functions provide important glue for OLE components. Like any other interface, *IUnknown* represents a contract for services. But because this interface is always present in every other interface—in C++ terms, *IUnknown* is a base interface for every other OLE interface—*IUnknown* defines services that every OLE interface must provide. Understanding the meaning of this contract is important whether you are implementing a client or server program.

IUnknown Services

While exposed by individual interfaces, the three *IUnknown* functions really represent OLE component services rather than interface-specific services. The two basic services are: management of component lifetime, and access to multiple interfaces in a single component. (Note: The term "OLE component" is equivalent to the term "OLE object" used in the OLE specifications.)

Manage "component lifetime"

Component lifetime refers to the need for components to shut down when not needed. Without this crucial step, even the most RAM-rich system will eventually run out of memory. The basic mechanics are straightforward: every OLE component (aka OLE object) maintains a reference count that starts at 1 when the component is created. Calls to *QueryInterface* and *AddRef* increment the reference count, and calls to *Release* decrement the reference count. When the count goes to zero, a component terminates, releasing all its owned system resources.

In the simplest case, a call to *Release* is all that's needed to disconnect a client from an interface. Every interface supports this function, which means you don't have to figure out interface-specific or component-specific termination functions; one function fits all interfaces. The following code demonstrates connecting to, using, and disconnecting from one implementation of *IMalloc*, the OLE task allocator. OLE components use this allocator for memory allocated by one component and freed by another:

```
char    *pData ;
HRESULT hr ;
IMalloc *pMalloc ;
```

```
// Connect to task allocator
hr = CoGetMalloc (1, &pMalloc) ;
if (SUCCEEDED (hr))
    {
    // Allocate memory
    pData = pMalloc->Alloc (cbBytes) ;
    if (pData)
        {
        lstrcpy (pData, pSource) ;
        }
    // Disconnect from task allocator
    pMalloc->Release () ;
    }
```

Calling *IMalloc::Release* doesn't free allocated memory, but decrements a reference count on the allocator component. To free memory, call *IMalloc*'s *Free* member function:

```
hr = CoGetMalloc (1, &pMalloc) ;
if (SUCCEEDED (hr))
    {
    pMalloc->Free (pData) ;
    pMalloc->Release () ;
    }
```

To simplify access to the task allocator, two simpler wrapper functions have been added to the OLE libraries: *CoTaskMemAlloc* and *CoTaskMemFree*. Allocate memory with:

```
pData = CoTaskMemAlloc (cbBytes) ;
```

Free this memory with:

```
CoTaskMemFree (pData) ;
```

More complex management of component lifetime occurs when many different parts of a client rely on interface services. Part of the complexity arises from the simple fact that programmers typically are not used to managing object lifetime by reference count, although there are two similar chores that programmers are experienced with: in the programming world, managing GDI objects; in the human world, communicating via a telephone conference call.

A GDI drawing object—a pen, a brush, a font, and so forth—must be explicitly created and explicitly deleted. (Even though Windows 95 and Windows NT clean up such objects when a process terminates, it's still a good programming practice to clean up after yourself.) That is, every call to GDI to create a green pen:

```
hpenGreen = CreatePen (PS_SOLID, 1, RGB (0, 255, 0)) ;
```

requires a matching call to delete that pen:

```
DeleteObject (hpenGreen) ;
```

From the perspective of reference counting, GDI objects never have a reference count with a value higher than 1.

The disadvantage of this approach is that two programs—say PageMaker and Visio—might each create identical green pens. Or different subsystems in each program—the user-interface, the printing engine, bitmap support, and metafile support—might each create their own green pens. Ten such pens might be created, resulting in a waste of system resources.

If, however, GDI used a reference count-based mechanism to track systemwide pen creation, the second and subsequent requests to create green pens would result in the reference count being incremented on the first green pen. The benefit is reduced system overhead since, after all, one green pen can do the work of ten green pens. If GDI pens were implemented as OLE components, the creation of every pen after the first would boil down to this call to the green pen component:

```
pPenGreen->AddRef () ;
```

Each call would increment the pen reference count. Each call to *DeleteObject* would decrement the reference count by causing a call to:

```
pPenGreen->Release () ;
```

until the reference count was zero so that the green pen would be destroyed. Reference count–based control of component lifetime allows each client of a component to have a defined beginning and end to its connection to that component. (As a side note, it's worth pointing out that GDI under Windows 95 uses a reference count mechanism to minimize redundant objects, though not one based on OLE interfaces.)

The reference count represents an independent connection to a component. It's not unlike how you might handle a conference call from your company to the president of your company's best customer. Perhaps you (as your company's technology spokesperson) are contacted to answer a question. At that point, there's just a reference count of one.

If the conversation turned to testing methodology, you might ask the test manager—your coworker in the next office—to join the call. When he picks up the phone and says "Hello," it's like a call to *AddRef*—the conference call reference count is 2. When the subject turns to documentation issues, you might ask the documentation manager to pick up a phone to be added to the conference call. When she says "Hello," the reference count gets bumped to 3. Your customer knows that three employees of his software supplier are on the line. Only under the most awkward situations would the president think of hanging up the phone unexpectedly, which would be analogous to an OLE server crashing. At some point, your customer is satisfied with what your team has told him, and he wants to speak to your sales manager to place the order. When the sales manager gets on the line, his "Hello" bumps the conference call reference count up to 4.

When you, the testing manager, and the documentation manager can get a word in, you each say "Good-bye" and hang up. Each farewell is analogous to a call to *Release*. The conference call continues, however, analogous to a component staying around in memory. Finally, when the sales manager gets the go-ahead for the big order, he says "Good-bye" to the customer and hangs up. The reference count for the conference call is now zero, and your customer can now hang up.

While conceptually simple, the mechanics of getting reference counting correct take time and effort. Shutting down at the right time requires interface clients to properly account for all connections, whether they be explicit or implicit. When an interface client fails to properly manage component lifetime, strange results can occur: failure to disconnect from a connection leaves components in memory; disconnecting too early leaves one party in an unexpected state.

Managing component lifetime is merely one of the tasks performed by the *IUnknown* member functions. Another important task, support for multiple interfaces in a single component, is the next subject for discussion.

Support for multiple interfaces

OLE's Component Object Model architecture allows individual components to provide more than one interface—at the binary level, more than one array of function pointers. The primary advantage of multiple interfaces is the ability to expose a wider range of services than can be exposed in a single interface. Interfaces, after all, are contracts for services, so the ability to have multiple interfaces is simply the ability to provide more than one type of service. The primary mechanism for obtaining pointers to a component's interfaces is the *QueryInterface* function.

Since *QueryInterface* is itself an interface function, it cannot be called to fetch the first interface pointer from a component. It can, however, be used to obtain the second and subsequent interface pointers from a component. The first interface pointer from a component almost always is returned from a call to one of several C-callable (non-interface) functions. In an earlier example, *CoGetMalloc* fetched an *IMalloc* pointer for the OLE library's task allocator component:

```
HRESULT hr ;
IMalloc *pMalloc ;

// Connect to task allocator
hr = CoGetMalloc (1, &pMalloc) ;
```

After the first interface pointer has been acquired, subsequent interface pointers are accessed by calling the *QueryInterface* member of any existing interface. *QueryInterface* is declared:

```
HRESULT QueryInterface (REFIID iid, void **ppv) ;
```

■ *iid* is a pointer to an interface identifier (IID).

■ *ppv* points to the memory location for the function's return value. The return value for a supported interface is an interface pointer of the requested type. A request for an unsupported interface produces a NULL return value.

If you search through the Win32 include files, you'll see that an IID is defined as a GUID (globally unique identifier), which itself is defined in WTYPES.H, a Win32 include file, as:

```
typedef struct  _GUID
    {
    DWORD Data1 ;
    WORD  Data2 ;
    WORD  Data3 ;
    BYTE  Data4[8] ;
    }  GUID ;
```

This is basically a 16-byte value for uniquely identifying interfaces.

If an OLE component were a building, the IID would be the telephone extension of the party to whom you wish to speak. In such a world, the call to *QueryInterface* is a request to be transferred to a new party within the same organization (component) as the party to whom you are already speaking. The names of the interfaces are like the names of departments—accounting, human resources, legal, development, testing, and so on. Here is a tiny portion of a telephone directory that lists the standard extensions for departments encountered in OLE components:

Interface Name	*IID*
IUnknown	{00000000-0000-0000-C000-000000000046}
IClassFactory	{00000001-0000-0000-C000-000000000046}
IMalloc	{00000002-0000-0000-C000-000000000046}
IMarshal	{00000003-0000-0000-C000-000000000046}

It's important to keep in mind that the human-readable name ("IUnknown") is for your convenience, but your OLE clients and servers use the binary digits to distinguish one interface from another. Fortunately, you rarely have to deal with these long sequences of numbers, since all interface IDs have symbolic constants. The symbolic names add an "IID_" prefix to the interface name, so that IID_IUnknown refers to the binary interface for the *IUnknown* interface. For example, a client that had an *IMalloc* pointer to a component would make a call like the following to fetch a pointer to the *IMarshal* interface:

```
LPMARSHAL pMarshal ;
HRESULT hr = pMalloc->QueryInterface (IID_IMarshal, &pMarshal) ;
```

Keep in mind that this call is first a query: "Do you support the *IMarshal* interface?" The answer is either "Yes" (HRESULT of S_OK) or "No" (HRESULT of E_NOINTERFACE). The reason is that there are hundreds of interfaces, and no component supports them all.

If the requested interface is supported, the returned HRESULT is S_OK. In a successful query, two things happen: A pointer is returned to the location referenced by the second parameter (*pMarshal* in this example), and the reference count to the component is incremented. The reference count increase is due to the fact that a new connection to the component has been created. Closing the connection requires a subsequent call to *Release*:

```
pMarshal->Release () ;
```

If, on the other hand, the requested interface is *not* supported, *QueryInterface* returns E_NOINTERFACE. In this case, a pointer is not returned and the reference count isn't incremented. What will happen, however, is that the *QueryInterface* function overwrites the return value pointer—*pMarshal* in this case—with a NULL value to make sure that it has a known value.

One important benefit of this query capability is that clients of an OLE component can perform a run-time query of a component's capabilities. The presence of an interface means the associated features are present, and its absence means the features are not present.

Related to this benefit is a relatively simple upgrade path for an OLE component. New features, however, are never added by expanding the functions in an interface; once an interface has been defined, the number of features it contains can never change! Instead, new features are added by adding new interfaces. Existing interfaces are left intact to continue supporting clients that expect their presence.

Is OLE a Client/Server Specification?

One question that programmers starting to work with OLE ask concerns whether OLE is a client/server specification. As you may recall from Chapter 17, DDE is a client/server specification. In fact, OLE version 1.0 used DDE as its transport mechanism. In that version, DDE messages carried requests from OLE client to OLE server, and OLE servers replied with more DDE messages that referenced DDE-defined global (*GlobalAlloc*) memory.

While "client" and "server" were often used in the context of OLE 1.0, the evolution of OLE has caused these terms to be used only in a general sense. When two components interact, both are often simultaneously clients (consumers of an interface) as well as servers (providers of an interface). In particular, in the context of compound documents, the term "client" has been replaced with "container application." In the context of OLE Automation, the term "automation controller" is used instead of "automation client." And while "server" is still used, a qualifying prefix—"object server" or "automation server"—specifies the context of the service provided.

The terms client and server are useful when trying to understand a specific OLE interface. In particular, these terms provide a useful framework for answering a common question that often comes up when writing OLE-aware programs: Which interfaces must one implement? and which ones are implemented by someone else?

A PRIVATE COMPONENT SERVER

It's time to take a look at IMALLOC, a dynamic link library (DLL) that demonstrates how to implement an interface. To keep the focus on interface essentials, this example has been kept simple on several counts. First, OLE's memory management interface, *IMalloc*, was chosen because most programmers already understand memory allocation services. Second, IMALLOC does very little real memory work since it delegates memory tasks to the Win32 private heap functions (*HeapCreate, HeapAlloc*, and so forth). And finally, we start with a *private component*—one accessible only through a proprietary mechanism—because, as you'll see later in PUBMEM, making a public component adds additional complexity that can be deferred for now.

Although IMALLOC is a simple component example, it is by no means trivial. In particular, it shows elements you'll need when defining any OLE interface. This includes a representative implementation of the three *IUnknown* interface functions: *QueryInterface*, *AddRef*, and *Release*. It shows the use of special macros that create portable interface declarations for support with C and C++ on a variety of operating system platforms, including Microsoft Windows 95, Microsoft Windows NT, Apple Macintosh, and other systems that will host OLE.

Private components are OLE components that are only visible through private means. IMALLOC, for example, provides access to its interface through a private, exported entry point. This example is a DLL, but another use for private components would be an entire application made up of a sea of private COM components. The key benefit is the encapsulation provided by a clear boundary between component client and component server. What defines an OLE component, after all, is the creation of interfaces that follow the OLE standards—not the public availability of interfaces.

After perusing the source files to IMALLOC, you might be tempted to declare that it isn't an OLE component after all. For one thing, it doesn't make any calls to the OLE libraries. Without a single call to *OleInitialize* (or *CoInitialize*), you might wonder by what right is IMALLOC an OLE component? Simple. IMALLOC's interface was built according to the Component Object Model specification, an OLE standard. Since it doesn't require OLE library services, IMALLOC gets by without initializing—and without incurring the overhead of loading—the OLE libraries. But IMALLOC provides a standard OLE interface, which will become clear when we incorporate that interface into our public component sample, PUBMEM, later in this chapter. IMALLOC's interface code requires almost no changes to operate flawlessly in a public OLE component.

IMALLOC is implemented in C++, which makes sense for interface implementations because the binary layout of an OLE interface exactly matches the layout of a C++ object. While it's possible to implement an interface in plain C, it requires some tedious steps that the C++ compiler does automatically. To get a sense of what programming for OLE is like in C, take a look at CALLER, which appears later in this chapter. It's the client program that loads and calls IMALLOC.DLL. The program files for IMALLOC are shown in Figure 20-2.

IMALLOC.MAK

```
#-----------------------
# IMALLOC.MAK make file
#-----------------------

imalloc.dll : imalloc.obj
    $(LINKER) $(DLLFLAGS) -OUT:imalloc.dll imalloc.obj $(GUILIBS) uuid.lib

imalloc.obj : imalloc.cpp
    $(CC) $(CFLAGS) imalloc.cpp
```

IMALLOC.CPP

```
/*-----------------------------------------------
    IMALLOC.CPP -- Define an imalloc interface
                   (c) Paul Yao, 1996
    -----------------------------------------------*/
#include <windows.h>
#include "imalloc.h"

//-----------------------------------------------------------
// CreateAllocator -- Exported function to create allocator
//-----------------------------------------------------------
EXPORT LPMALLOC CreateAllocator ()
    {
    DAlloc *pAllocator = new DAlloc () ;
    if (pAllocator != NULL && pAllocator->Initialize ())
        {
        pAllocator->AddRef () ;
        }
    else
        {
        delete pAllocator ;
        }
```

Figure 20-2. *The IMALLOC library.*   *(continued)*

```
        return (LPMALLOC) pAllocator ;
        }

//------------------------------------------------------------------
DAlloc::DAlloc ()
        {
    RefCount = 0 ;
    hHeap = NULL ;
        }

//------------------------------------------------------------------
DAlloc::~DAlloc ()
        {
    if (hHeap)
            HeapDestroy (hHeap) ;
        }

//------------------------------------------------------------------
BOOL DAlloc::Initialize ()
        {
    hHeap = HeapCreate (0, 4096, 65535) ;

    return (BOOL) hHeap ;
        }

//------------------------------------------------------------------
STDMETHODIMP
DAlloc::QueryInterface (REFIID riid, LPVOID FAR *ppvObject)
        {
    // Always initialize "out" parameters to NULL
    *ppvObject = NULL ;

    // Everyone supports IUnknown
    if (riid == IID_IUnknown)
        *ppvObject = (LPUNKNOWN) this ;

    // We support IMalloc
    if (riid == IID_IMalloc)
        *ppvObject = (LPMALLOC) this ;

    if (*ppvObject == NULL)
            {
        // Interface not supported
        return E_NOINTERFACE ;
            }
```

(continued)

```
        else
            {
            // Interface supported, so increment reference count
            ((LPUNKNOWN) *ppvObject)->AddRef () ;
            return S_OK ;
            }
        }

//------------------------------------------------------------------
STDMETHODIMP_ (ULONG)
DAlloc::AddRef (void)
    {
    return ++RefCount ;
    }

//------------------------------------------------------------------
STDMETHODIMP_ (ULONG)
DAlloc::Release (void)
    {
    if (0L != --RefCount)
        return RefCount ;

     delete this ;
     return 0L ;
     }

//------------------------------------------------------------------
STDMETHODIMP_ (void *)
DAlloc::Alloc (ULONG cb)
    {
    return HeapAlloc (hHeap, HEAP_ZERO_MEMORY, cb) ;
    }

//------------------------------------------------------------------
STDMETHODIMP_ (void *)
DAlloc::Realloc (void *pv, ULONG cb)
    {
    return HeapReAlloc (hHeap, HEAP_ZERO_MEMORY, pv, cb) ;
    }

//------------------------------------------------------------------
STDMETHODIMP_ (void)
DAlloc::Free (void *pv)
    {
    HeapFree (hHeap, 0, pv) ;
    }
```

(continued)

```
//--------------------------------------------------------------------
STDMETHODIMP_ (ULONG)
DAlloc::GetSize (void *pv)
    {
    return HeapSize (hHeap, 0, pv) ;
    }


//--------------------------------------------------------------------
STDMETHODIMP_ (int)
DAlloc::DidAlloc (void *pv)
    {
    PROCESS_HEAP_ENTRY phe ;

    ZeroMemory (&phe, sizeof (PROCESS_HEAP_ENTRY)) ;

    while (HeapWalk (hHeap, &phe))
        {
        if (phe.lpData == pv)
            return 1 ;
        }

    return 0 ;
    }


//--------------------------------------------------------------------
STDMETHODIMP_ (void)
DAlloc::HeapMinimize (void)
    {
    HeapCompact (hHeap, 0) ;
    }
```

IMALLOC.H

```
//--------------------------------------------------------------------
// C Interface to private allocator
//--------------------------------------------------------------------
#define EXPORT extern "C" __declspec (dllexport)


EXPORT LPMALLOC CreateAllocator () ;


//--------------------------------------------------------------------
// Implementation of allocator interface
//--------------------------------------------------------------------
#undef  INTERFACE
#define INTERFACE DAlloc
```

(continued)

```
DECLARE_INTERFACE_ (DAlloc, IMalloc)
    {
    // *** IUnknown methods ***
    STDMETHOD  (QueryInterface) (THIS_ REFIID riid, LPVOID FAR *ppv) ;
    STDMETHOD_ (ULONG, AddRef)  (THIS) ;
    STDMETHOD_ (ULONG, Release) (THIS) ;

    // *** IMalloc methods ***
    STDMETHOD_ (void *, Alloc)        (THIS_ ULONG cb) ;
    STDMETHOD_ (void *, Realloc)      (THIS_ void *pv, ULONG cb) ;
    STDMETHOD_ (void,   Free)         (THIS_ void *pv) ;
    STDMETHOD_ (ULONG,  GetSize)      (THIS_ void *pv) ;
    STDMETHOD_ (int,    DidAlloc)     (THIS_ void *pv) ;
    STDMETHOD_ (void,   HeapMinimize) (THIS) ;

#ifndef CINTERFACE
public :
    DAlloc () ;
    ~DAlloc () ;
    BOOL Initialize () ;

private :
    ULONG  RefCount ;
    HANDLE hHeap ;
#endif
    } ;
```

To see the allocator in action, run CALLER.EXE, which loads and runs IMALLOC.DLL.

IMALLOC.DLL

As a private OLE component, IMALLOC exposes its *IMalloc* interface by an interface pointer returned from a private exported function, *CreateAllocator*. The interface functions themselves don't need to be exported because the returned interface pointer provides complete access to all interface functions. *CreateAllocator* allocates an instance of *DAlloc*, a C++ object that wraps around a private Win32 heap, and whose virtual function table corresponds to the binary standard defined for the *IMalloc* interface. A pointer to a *DAlloc* object is an *IMalloc* interface pointer, which makes this cast in *CreateAllocator* legitimate:

```
return (LPMALLOC) pAllocator ;
```

Since it's defined within a C++ source file, *CreateAllocator* requires special handling to disable C++ name mangling and provide C-callable bindings, which is what these lines from IMALLOC.H accomplish:

```
#define EXPORT extern "C"  __declspec (dllexport)

EXPORT LPMALLOC CreateAllocator () ;
```

The EXPORT keyword is the same as the one we defined in Chapter 19.

NOTE TO C PROGRAMMERS

IMALLOC was written in C++, so a few terms and conventions might not be familiar to you. Within the *CreateAllocator* function, the *new* operator allocates space for a *DAlloc* object (by calling *malloc*) and then calls its *constructor* function, *DAlloc::DAlloc*, which performs initialization of the object's data members. The *delete* operator, called from *CreateAllocator* if initialization fails, de-allocates the object's memory in case of error. It is comparable to a call to *free*, followed by a call to the object's *destructor* (or cleanup) function, *DAlloc::~DAlloc*.

The *scope operator* (::) assigns a function to a C++ class. In IMALLOC, this notation makes the *GetSize* function a member of the *DAlloc* class:

```
DAlloc::GetSize (...)
```

While all function names prefixed with *DAlloc::* are members of *DAlloc*, not all member functions have entries in *DAlloc*'s function table; only those functions declared with the *virtual* keyword do. In IMALLOC.H, the STDMETHOD and STDMETHOD_ macros (which are described in detail later) include the *virtual* keyword.

A word on the difference between *IMalloc* and *DAlloc* is in order. As a contract for services, an interface cannot have an implementation directly associated with it. In C++ terms, this requirement is satisfied by making all interfaces pure abstract classes—that is, pure interface, with no implementation. So *DAlloc* (the "D" prefix stands for "derived class") uses *IMalloc* for a base class, from which it inherits its virtual function members.

But with three extra member functions—*DAlloc*, *~DAlloc*, and *Initialize*—and two extra data members—*RefCount* and *hHeap*—is *DAlloc* a legitimate implementation of *IMalloc*? The answer is, "yes." The three extra functions are not *virtual functions* (that is, they are not declared with the *virtual* keyword), so they don't affect the layout of the virtual function table which—in OLE terms—is what makes up the interface function table. Since *DAlloc* has an interface function table that matches the table required to fulfill that defined for *IMalloc*, the three extra functions are incidental. As for the data members, these are ignored since OLE interfaces are defined as stateless (data-free) C++ classes. *DAlloc* can use its data members for its own purposes, since they don't get in the way of fulfilling the contract required for an OLE interface in general or the *IMalloc* interface in particular.

Those Funky Macros

One aspect of defining an interface that can at first be perplexing is the use of a set of macros like DECLARE_INTERFACE, STDMETHOD, and THIS. The reason these macros are used is to make OLE code—both client and server code—portable. These macros help enhance OLE interface portability in two ways: First, the macros have both a C and a C++ definition to allow an interface to be accessible from both languages. Second, the macros help support OLE portability to different operating system platforms.

When OLE was being developed, the first C++ compilers had just started to become available. At the time, C was a more widely used language than C++, so the creators of OLE wanted to ensure that either language could be used. An example will help provide an idea of how these macros hide C to C++ differences. Using the macros, the *IUnknown* interface is declared as follows:

```
#undef  INTERFACE
#define INTERFACE IUnknown
DECLARE_INTERFACE (IUnknown)
     {
     STDMETHOD  (QueryInterface) (THIS_
                                  REFIID riid,
                                  LPVOID FAR *ppvObj) PURE ;
     STDMETHOD_ (ULONG, AddRef)  (THIS) PURE ;
     STDMETHOD_ (ULONG, Release) (THIS) PURE ;
     } ;
```

Many interface definition macros have two versions: the regular version and the enhanced version whose name has an underscore (_) suffix. The declaration of *IUnknown* shows a pair of examples: STDMETHOD and STDMETHOD_. Both declare interface functions as *virtual* and that use a specific calling convention (*__stdcall* in Win32). But STDMETHOD indicates a return type of HRESULT. Other return types must be specified as a parameter to the STDMETHOD_ macro.

The following table summarizes the role of the interface declaration and definition macros:

Macro Name	*Description*
DECLARE_INTERFACE	Declares an interface with no base class (for example, see accompanying *IUnknown* declaration).
DECLARE_INTERFACE_	Declares an interface with a base class (for example, see *DAlloc* in IMALLOC.CPP).
PURE	In C++, adds an "=0" at end of virtual function declaration for pure (no-implementation) virtual function. In C, which has no equivalent, is a no-op.
STDMETHOD	Declares the calling convention (*__stdcall* in Win32) and HRESULT return type in an interface declaration. When compiled for C++, such functions are also virtual functions, which means they are assigned a spot in the C++ class virtual function table/ OLE interface function table.

(continued)

Macro Name	Description
STDMETHOD_	The same as STDMETHOD, above, except that return types other than HRESULT are provided for.
STDMETHODIMP	Defines a member function that returns HRESULT.
STDMETHODIMP_	Defines a member function that returns a type other than HRESULT.
THIS	A placeholder for interface functions that take no parameters. In C++, THIS is replaced by *void*. In C, THIS is replaced by a pointer to the referenced object, which provides that the correct bindings call a member function of a C++ class from C.
THIS_	A placeholder for interface functions that take one or more parameters. In C++, THIS_ is empty. In C, it is replaced by the pointer discussed in the previous entry for THIS, followed by a comma.

When the preceding *IUnknown* interface declaration is run through the preprocessor as a C++ declaration, the following emerges:

```
struct IUnknown
    {
    virtual HRESULT __stdcall QueryInterface (const IID *riid,
                                              void **ppv)=0 ;
    virtual ULONG __stdcall AddRef (void)=0 ;
    virtual ULONG __stdcall Release (void)=0 ;
    } ;
```

While you might expect *class* and not *struct* at the start of this declaration, the difference is that a struct is simply a class where members are public by default. The *__stdcall* keyword defines the setup and cleanup of the stack frame. The *virtual* keyword defines a virtual function, necessary for functions to be included in the C++ virtual function table/ OLE interface function table. Finally, the "=0" replaces the PURE keyword, which makes this a pure virtual class—that is, an interface-only class that cannot itself be instantiated.

The resulting C declaration for *IUnknown* is a little more involved, since two structures are created. In spite of this difference from the C++ code, at the binary level the output when both are compiled is the same. This is so because OLE's component object model defines a binary standard for interface bindings. Here is the corresponding *IUnknown* code in C:

```
typedef struct IUnknown
    {
    const struct IUnknownVtbl *lpVtbl ;
    } IUnknown ;
```

```
typedef const struct IUnknownVtbl IUnknownVtbl ;
const struct IUnknownVtbl
    {
    HRESULT (__stdcall * QueryInterface) (IUnknown *This,
                                          const IID *riid,
                                          void **ppd)
    ULONG (__stdcall * AddRef) (IUnknown *This) ;
    ULONG (__stdcall * Release) (IUnknown *This) ;
    } ;
```

The C implementation adds an *IUnknown *This* parameter to the start of the parameter list for each function. This matches the implicit *this* pointer always passed to C++ class member functions. While it may seem odd, it is in fact necessary for C code to match the C++ implementation. The source files to CALLER.EXE, our next sample and the program that calls IMALLOC.DLL, show how this extra parameter must be specified when a C caller references a C++ class function.

Portability between platforms means making provision for subtle, platform-specific keywords. For example, the Win16 OLE interfaces require the *__far* and *__pascal* keywords to create proper bindings. In Win32, these two keywords are replaced with *__stdcall* as the calling convention for all interface functions. The macros provide a placeholder for keywords that you might not anticipate as you create OLE components that might eventually run on an Apple Macintosh system, on UNIX implementations of OLE, or on OS/400, VMS, or MSV. A platform-specific set of include files will match environment-specific keywords where they are needed.

Services Provided by *IUnknown*

While IMALLOC.DLL demonstrates an implementation of the *IMalloc* interface, its most interesting feature is its implementation of the three *IUnknown* member functions and the two services those functions provide: managing of component lifetime and supporting a multi-interface component.

Managing component lifetime

The life of an OLE component is determined by one private data member and two interface functions. The data member is the reference count—a ULONG value named *RefCount* in *DAlloc*—and the two interface functions are *AddRef* and *Release*.

IMALLOC creates an allocator component when *CreateAllocator*, a private component creation function, is called. The related lines of code within *CreateAllocator* are as follows:

```
DAlloc *pAllocator = new DAlloc () ;
if (pAllocator != NULL && pAllocator->Initialize ())
    {
    pAllocator->AddRef () ;
```

```
        }
else
        {
        delete pAllocator ;
        }
```

When the object is created, its reference count is initialized to zero within *DAlloc*'s constructor function. At the same time, the handle to the Win32 heap is set to NULL:

```
DAlloc::DAlloc ()
        {
        RefCount = 0 ;
        hHeap = NULL ;
        }
```

C++ coding is simplified by limiting the work done in class constructors to initializing data members, as just shown. The reason is that constructors have no easy way to notify the object creator of failure conditions, so only work that cannot fail is performed. Tasks that can fail are often delegated to specialized initialization functions, like *DAlloc*'s *Initialize* function, which creates the Win32 heap required to satisfy *IMalloc* allocation requests.

Once *CreateAllocator* has successfully created and initialized a *DAlloc* object, it increments the reference count by calling *AddRef*. This function is defined as:

```
STDMETHODIMP_ (ULONG)
DAlloc::AddRef (void)
        {
        return ++RefCount ;
        }
```

Now you see why this function returns a value other than HRESULT: it lets the caller know the current value of the reference count (but this can be used only for debugging purposes).

The only other call to *AddRef* in IMALLOC occurs in *QueryInterface*. When a pointer to a component interface is returned by *QueryInterface*, it calls *AddRef* so that the count of connections from the component to the outside world is correctly maintained.

While there are two places in IMALLOC that call *AddRef*, there aren't any calls to *Release*. Only the component client calls this function, which makes sense given that it can end the life of a component. Here are the core lines from that function:

```
STDMETHODIMP_ (ULONG)
DAlloc::Release ()
        {
        if (0L != --RefCount)
            return RefCount ;

        delete this ;
        return 0L ;
        }
```

When the reference count goes to zero, the call to the *delete* operator causes the component to free itself and to call its destructor function, *DAlloc::~DAlloc*. Within that function, the Win32 heap gets destroyed:

```
if (hHeap)
    HeapDestroy (hHeap) ;
```

That should make it clear that decrementing the reference count to zero—that is, freeing the object—can have irreversible effects.

While the *IUnknown* members of an OLE component provide the means to manage component lifetime, it's up to the component's client to correctly call these member functions at the right time. Too few calls to *Release* results in a component that occupies memory needlessly. Too many calls result in an object disappearing before it should. It's clear that getting the reference count just right is an important task for client software to perform.

From this look at an implementation of the *IUnknown* member functions, some general guidelines should suggest themselves. First, every call to *AddRef* must be matched with a call to *Release*. Since *QueryInterface* calls *AddRef*, every call to *QueryInterface* must also be matched with a call to *Release*.

Supporting a multi-interface component

From the perspective of an OLE interface server, the *QueryInterface* function is the component's central switchboard for routing requests for interface connections. Here is the *QueryInterface* function from IMALLOC.CPP:

```
STDMETHODIMP
DAlloc::QueryInterface (REFIID riid, LPVOID FAR *ppvObject)
    {
    // Always initialize "out" parameters to NULL
    *ppvObject = NULL ;

    // Everyone supports IUnknown
    if (riid == IID_IUnknown)
        *ppvObject = (LPUNKNOWN) this ;

    // We support IMalloc
    if (riid == IID_IMalloc)
        *ppvObject = (LPMALLOC) this ;

    if (*ppvObject == NULL)
        {
        // Interface not supported
        return E_NOINTERFACE ;
        }
    else
        {
        // Interface supported, so increment reference count
```

```
            ((LPUNKNOWN) *ppvObject)->AddRef () ;
            return S_OK ;
            }
      }
```

Like most OLE interface functions, the return value from *QueryInterface* is HRESULT. Two return values are defined, both of which indicate that no unexpected errors were encountered: S_OK means that the component supports the interface, and a pointer to that interface is returned. E_NOINTERFACE means that the interface isn't supported, and a NULL interface pointer returned.

Because of its out-of-process support, OLE function parameters and interface parameters are categorized as *in, out,* or *in/out.* Relative to the function being called, an "in" parameter has one-way incoming data, an "out" parameter has one-way outgoing data, and an "in/out" parameter provides both incoming data and return data. This simple categorization helps cut down the volume of data that needs to be transported across a process or network boundary. One-way parameters—"in" and "out"—only need transport half of the time, while the two-way parameters, in/out, must be copied both before and after a function call.

QueryInterface has one "in" parameter (*riid*) and one "out" parameter (*ppvObject*). To maintain consistency, the COM specification says that any out parameter that is a pointer must always be set to a known value. That's the reason that the first line of *QueryInterface* sets *ppvObject* to NULL:

```
// Always initialize "out" parameters to NULL
*ppvObject = NULL ;
```

If the requested interface is not supported, then NULL is the correct pointer value. If, on the other hand, an interface is supported, the NULL value is overwritten with a pointer to the requested interface.

When an interface is supported, a pointer to that interface is returned. Then, to ensure that the reference count for the interface is correctly maintained, a call is made to the interface's *AddRef* member:

```
((LPUNKNOWN) *ppvObject)->AddRef () ;
```

This is particularly important for clients of an OLE component to realize, since a successful call to *QueryInterface* always requires a matching call to *Release* to allow the component to know when it's safe to terminate itself.

Even though IMALLOC.DLL supports only one interface, in fact *QueryInterface* responds as if two interfaces are supported: *IUnknown* and *IMalloc.* From the perspective of the client, though, two interfaces are in fact supported: one that controls the underlying component and one that provides memory allocation services. The fact that both use the same virtual function table is a design choice that is integral to COM architecture.

It's not too hard to imagine how *QueryInterface* could provide connections to additional interfaces. The pure mechanics of what *QueryInterface* would do are straightforward. The addition of an *if* statement to check for specific interface ID values allow any number of new interfaces to be supported, such as one for IID_IMarshal in this example:

```
// We support IMarshal
if (riid == IID_IMarshal)
      *ppvObject = (LPMARSHAL) pMarshal ;
```

What's not obvious is the relationship of the interface referenced by *pMarshal* to a specific *DAlloc::QueryInterface* function. There are several answers to this, which unfortunately are beyond the scope of this discussion. Briefly, though, the C++ object that supports the *IMarshal* interface—call it *DMarshal*—might be *contained* in *DAlloc*. Or, through multiple inheritance, multiple supported interfaces would share a common set of *IUnknown* functions. Whatever specific implementation is chosen, to the component client the view is the same: *QueryInterface* provides the central switchboard services to create connections to a component's supported interfaces.

To get a perspective on how a client could make use of IMALLOC's private component, we next take a look at CALLER. It also shows how straight C code can be used to access OLE services.

A PRIVATE COMPONENT CLIENT

The CALLER.EXE program shows how the client of a private component creates an interface connection, calls interface functions, and disconnects from the interface. While IMALLOC showed the details of interface creation—the server point of view—CALLER shows the details of interface consumer—the client perspective. Of the two, the client perspective is the easiest to grasp. Aside from issues associated with proper management of server lifetime—provided by *IUnknown* interface functions—the client perspective is familiar to any programmer who has used a function library: identify the required function, select the proper parameters, and check the return value for success or failure.

In one respect, the view of a COM interface is different from that of other programming interfaces such as Windows' Win32 API or the C run-time library: While other APIs provide a sea of functions related perhaps by function name (*strcpy*, *strlen*, *strcat*, and so on) or by a common first parameter (*MoveWindow*, *FindWindow*, *ShowWindow*, and so on),

COM interface functions define distinct boundaries from other sets of functions. In an object server, this aspect revealed itself in the way that all interface functions are virtual functions of the same interface. In the client of an interface, this relatedness makes itself known by the fact that all interface functions are accessed through a common pointer to the interface functions.

CALLER.EXE also shows how to access a COM interface from C. It takes a tiny bit more effort—meaning a bit more typing. For example, here's the C++ code to access the *Alloc* member of an *IMalloc* interface:

```
LPSTR pData = (LPSTR) pMalloc->Alloc (cbdata) ;
```

A comparable call from C looks like this:

```
LPSTR pData = (LPSTR) pMalloc->lpVtbl->Alloc (pMalloc, cbdata) ;
```

That's not an overwhelming amount of extra typing, but it does represent extra effort and therefore greater risk of making an error.

An obvious solution would be to wrap such calls into a set of interface-specific macros. This might be useful to a development group that planned to retrofit a large legacy C application with calls to OLE interfaces. For example, for the preceding call to *IMalloc::Alloc*, a wrapper macro like this could be defined:

```
#ifdef __cplusplus
#define ALLOC (pInt, cbSize) (pInt##->Alloc (cbSize##))
#else
#define ALLOC (pInt, cbSize) \
            (pInt##->lpVtbl->Alloc (pInt##, cbSize##))
#endif
```

A common syntax could then be used to call *IMalloc::Alloc* from either C or C++:

```
LPSTR pData = (LPSTR) ALLOC (pMalloc, cbdata) ;
```

Such a call saves no effort for the C++ programmer (and is arguably more confusing since it reflects a nonstandard way to access a C++ class). For the C programmer, however, a set of such macros would eliminate redundant typing.

CALLER demonstrates calls to IMALLOC interfaces by allocating memory and storing the values in one of ten slots. As shown in Figure 20-3, CALLER displays the contents of each slot in its main window. Just to keep things interesting, CALLER uses two allocators: one accessed through the *IMalloc* interface provided by IMALLOC.DLL and the other the regular C run-time library functions. Figure 20-4 shows the CALLER source files.

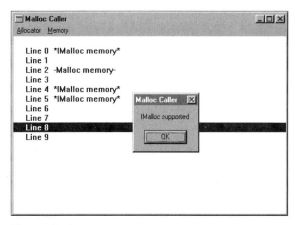

Figure 20-3. *The CALLER display.*

CALLER.MAK

```
#----------------------
# CALLER.MAK make file
#----------------------

caller.exe : caller.obj caller.res imalloc.lib
    $(LINKER) $(GUIFLAGS) -OUT:caller.exe caller.obj caller.res \
            imalloc.lib $(GUILIBS) uuid.lib

caller.obj : caller.c caller.h imalloc.h
    $(CC) -DCINTERFACE $(CFLAGS) caller.c

caller.res : caller.rc caller.h
    $(RC) $(RCVARS) caller.rc
```

CALLER.C

```
/*-----------------------------------------------
    CALLER.C -- Call into private OLE component
                (c) Paul Yao, 1996
    -----------------------------------------------*/
#include <windows.h>
#include "caller.h"
#include "imalloc.h"

LRESULT CALLBACK WndProc (HWND, UINT, WPARAM, LPARAM) ;
```

Figure 20-4. *The CALLER program.*   *(continued)*

```
char szWndClass[] = "CallerWindow" ;
char szAppName[]  = "Malloc Caller" ;

//---------------------------------------------------------------------
int WINAPI WinMain (HINSTANCE hInstance, HINSTANCE hPrevInstance,
                    PSTR lpszCmdLine, int cmdShow)
     {
     HWND        hwnd ;
     MSG         msg ;
     WNDCLASSEX  wc ;

     wc.cbSize        = sizeof (wc) ;
     wc.lpszClassName = szWndClass ;
     wc.hInstance     = hInstance ;
     wc.lpfnWndProc   = WndProc ;
     wc.hCursor       = LoadCursor (NULL, IDC_ARROW) ;
     wc.hIcon         = LoadIcon (NULL, IDI_APPLICATION) ;
     wc.lpszMenuName  = "MAIN" ;
     wc.hbrBackground = (HBRUSH) (COLOR_WINDOW + 1) ;
     wc.style         = 0 ;
     wc.cbClsExtra    = 0 ;
     wc.cbWndExtra    = 0 ;
     wc.hIconSm       = LoadIcon (NULL, IDI_APPLICATION) ;

     RegisterClassEx (&wc) ;

     hwnd = CreateWindowEx (0L, szWndClass, szAppName,
                           WS_OVERLAPPEDWINDOW,
                           CW_USEDEFAULT, CW_USEDEFAULT,
                           CW_USEDEFAULT, CW_USEDEFAULT,
                           NULL, NULL, hInstance, NULL) ;

     ShowWindow (hwnd, cmdShow) ;
     UpdateWindow (hwnd) ;

     while (GetMessage (&msg, NULL, 0, 0))
          {
          TranslateMessage (&msg) ;
          DispatchMessage (&msg) ;
          }
     return msg.wParam ;
     }

//---------------------------------------------------------------------
LRESULT CALLBACK
WndProc (HWND hwnd, UINT iMsg, WPARAM wParam, LPARAM lParam)
```

(continued)

```
     {
static int       iCurLine = 0 ;
static LPMALLOC  pMalloc = NULL ;
static LPSTR     szLine[10] ;
static RECT      rHit[10] ;

switch (iMsg)
     {
     case WM_CREATE :
          // Initialize data pointer array
          ZeroMemory (szLine, sizeof (szLine)) ;
          return 0 ;

     case WM_COMMAND :
          switch (LOWORD (wParam))
               {
               case IDM_CREATE :
                    pMalloc = CreateAllocator () ;
                    if (pMalloc == NULL)
                         {
                         MessageBox (hwnd, "Error: No allocator",
                                     szAppName, MB_OK) ;
                         return 0 ;
                         }

                    InvalidateRect (hwnd, NULL, TRUE) ;
                    return 0 ;

               case IDM_DESTROY :
                    {
                    int i ;

                    // Mark allocated blocks as invalid
                    for (i = 0 ; i < 10 ; i++)
                         {
                         if ((szLine[i] != NULL) &&
                            (pMalloc->lpVtbl->DidAlloc (pMalloc,
                                                    szLine[i])))
                              {
                              szLine[i] = NULL ;
                              }
                         }

                    // Disconnect from & free allocator
                    pMalloc->lpVtbl->Release (pMalloc) ;
```

(continued)

```
            pMalloc = NULL ;

            InvalidateRect (hwnd, NULL, TRUE) ;
            return 0 ;
            }

       case IDM_IUNKNOWN :
            {
            LPUNKNOWN pUnk ;
            HRESULT hr =
                 pMalloc->lpVtbl->QueryInterface (pMalloc,
                                                  IID_IUnknown,
                                                  (void **)&pUnk) ;
            if (SUCCEEDED (hr))
                 {
                 pUnk->lpVtbl->Release (pUnk) ;
                 MessageBox (hwnd, "IUnknown supported",
                             szAppName, MB_OK) ;
                 }
            else
                 {
                 MessageBox (hwnd, "IUnknown not supported",
                             szAppName, MB_OK) ;
                 }
            return 0 ;
            }

       case IDM_IMALLOC :
            {
            LPUNKNOWN pUnk ;
            HRESULT hr =
                 pMalloc->lpVtbl->QueryInterface (pMalloc,
                                                  IID_IMalloc,
                                                  (void **)&pUnk) ;
            if (SUCCEEDED (hr))
                 {
                 pUnk->lpVtbl->Release (pUnk) ;
                 MessageBox (hwnd, "IMalloc supported",
                             szAppName, MB_OK) ;
                 }
            else
                 {
                 MessageBox (hwnd, "IMalloc not supported",
                             szAppName, MB_OK) ;
                 }
```

(continued)

```
                              return 0 ;
                              }

                    case IDM_IMARSHAL :
                         {
                         LPUNKNOWN pUnk ;
                         HRESULT hr =
                              pMalloc->lpVtbl->QueryInterface (pMalloc,
                                                               IID_IMarshal,
                                                               (void **)&pUnk) ;
                         if (SUCCEEDED (hr))
                              {
                              pUnk->lpVtbl->Release (pUnk) ;
                              MessageBox (hwnd, "IMarshal supported",
                                        szAppName, MB_OK) ;
                              }
                         else
                              {
                              MessageBox (hwnd, "IMarshal not supported",
                                        szAppName, MB_OK) ;
                              }
                         return 0 ;
                         }

                    case IDM_ALLOCATE_CUSTOM :
                         if (szLine[iCurLine] != NULL)
                              {
                              MessageBox (hwnd, "Error: Free First",
                                        szAppName, MB_OK) ;
                              return 0 ;
                              }

                         // Allocate from IAllocate interface
                         szLine[iCurLine] =
                              (char *) pMalloc->lpVtbl->Alloc (pMalloc, 100) ;
                         lstrcpy (szLine[iCurLine], "*IMalloc memory*") ;

                         InvalidateRect (hwnd, NULL, TRUE) ;
                         return 0 ;

                    case IDM_ALLOCATE_DEFAULT :
                         if (szLine[iCurLine] != NULL)
                              {
                              MessageBox (hwnd, "Error: Free First",
                                        szAppName, MB_OK) ;
```

(continued)

```
                         return 0 ;
                         }

                    // Allocate from default heap
                    szLine[iCurLine] = (char *) malloc (100) ;
                    lstrcpy (szLine[iCurLine], "-Malloc memory-") ;

                    InvalidateRect (hwnd, NULL, TRUE) ;
                    return 0 ;

               case IDM_FREE :
                    if (szLine[iCurLine] == NULL)
                         {
                         MessageBox (hwnd, "Error: Nothing to free",
                                        szAppName, MB_OK) ;
                         return 0 ;
                         }

                    if (pMalloc == NULL)
                         {
                         goto FreeMalloc ;
                         }

                    // Free allocated object
                    if (pMalloc->lpVtbl->DidAlloc (pMalloc,
                                             szLine[iCurLine]))
                         {
                         pMalloc->lpVtbl->Free (pMalloc,
                                             szLine[iCurLine]) ;
                         }
                    else
                         {
          FreeMalloc:
                         free (szLine[iCurLine]) ;
                         }

                    szLine[iCurLine] = NULL ;

                    InvalidateRect (hwnd, NULL, TRUE) ;
                    return 0 ;
                    }

     case WM_DESTROY :
          // Disconnect from & free allocator
          if (pMalloc)
```

(continued)

```
            {
            pMalloc->lpVtbl->Release (pMalloc) ;
            pMalloc = NULL ;
            }

      PostQuitMessage (0) ;  // Handle application shutdown
      return 0 ;

case WM_INITMENU :
      {
      HMENU hMenu = (HMENU) wParam ;
      if (pMalloc)
            {
            EnableMenuItem (hMenu, IDM_CREATE,          MF_GRAYED) ;
            EnableMenuItem (hMenu, IDM_DESTROY,         MF_ENABLED) ;
            EnableMenuItem (hMenu, IDM_ALLOCATE_CUSTOM, MF_ENABLED) ;
            EnableMenuItem (hMenu, IDM_IUNKNOWN,        MF_ENABLED) ;
            EnableMenuItem (hMenu, IDM_IMALLOC,         MF_ENABLED) ;
            EnableMenuItem (hMenu, IDM_IMARSHAL,        MF_ENABLED) ;
            }
      else
            {
            EnableMenuItem (hMenu, IDM_CREATE,          MF_ENABLED) ;
            EnableMenuItem (hMenu, IDM_DESTROY,         MF_GRAYED) ;
            EnableMenuItem (hMenu, IDM_ALLOCATE_CUSTOM, MF_GRAYED) ;
            EnableMenuItem (hMenu, IDM_IUNKNOWN,        MF_GRAYED) ;
            EnableMenuItem (hMenu, IDM_IMALLOC,         MF_GRAYED) ;
            EnableMenuItem (hMenu, IDM_IMARSHAL,        MF_GRAYED) ;
            }
      return 0 ;
      }

case WM_LBUTTONDOWN :
      {
      int i ;
      int x = LOWORD (lParam) ;
      int y = HIWORD (lParam) ;
      POINT pt = { x, y } ;

      for (i = 0 ; i < 10 ; i++)
            {
            if (PtInRect (&rHit[i], pt))
                  {
                  if (iCurLine != i)  // Minimize screen blink
```

(continued)

```
                          {
                          InvalidateRect (hwnd, &rHit[iCurLine], TRUE) ;
                          InvalidateRect (hwnd, &rHit[i], TRUE) ;
                          iCurLine = i ;
                          }
                  break ;
                  }
              }
          }
          return 0 ;
      }

case WM_PAINT :
      {
      char          szBuff[10] ;
      COLORREF      crText, crBack ;
      HDC           hdc ;
      int           cc ;
      int           i ;
      int           XCount, XText, Y ;
      int           cyLineHeight ;
      PAINTSTRUCT   ps ;
      RECT          rOpaque ;
      TEXTMETRIC    tm ;

      hdc = BeginPaint (hwnd, &ps) ;

      // Fetch line height
      GetTextMetrics (ps.hdc, &tm) ;
      cyLineHeight = tm.tmHeight + tm.tmExternalLeading ;

      // Fetch current text colors
      crText = GetTextColor (ps.hdc) ;
      crBack = GetBkColor (ps.hdc) ;

      XCount = tm.tmAveCharWidth * 3 ;
      XText  = XCount + tm.tmAveCharWidth * 7 ;
      Y      = tm.tmHeight ;

      for (i = 0 ; i < 10 ; i++, Y += cyLineHeight)
          {
          // Set colors to highlight current line
          if (i == iCurLine)
              {
              SetTextColor (ps.hdc, crBack) ;
```

(continued)

```
                        SetBkColor (ps.hdc, crText) ;

                        SetRect (&rOpaque, 0, Y, 9999, Y + cyLineHeight) ;
                        ExtTextOut (ps.hdc, 0, 0, ETO_OPAQUE, &rOpaque,
                                    NULL, 0, NULL ) ;
                        }
                  else
                        {
                        SetTextColor (ps.hdc, crText) ;
                        SetBkColor (ps.hdc, crBack) ;
                        }

                  // Display line count
                  cc = wsprintf (szBuff, "Line %d", i) ;
                  TextOut (ps.hdc, XCount, Y, szBuff, cc) ;

                  // Display text if a string has been defined
                  if (szLine[i] != NULL)
                        {
                        cc = lstrlen (szLine[i]) ;
                        TextOut (ps.hdc, XText, Y, szLine[i], cc) ;
                        }

                  // Calculate hit test rectangle
                  SetRect (&rHit[i], 0, Y, 9999, Y + cyLineHeight) ;
                  }

            EndPaint (hwnd, &ps) ;
            return 0 ;
            }
      default :
            return DefWindowProc (hwnd, iMsg, wParam, lParam) ;
      }
}
```

CALLER.H

```
#define IDM_CREATE            1
#define IDM_DESTROY           2
#define IDM_IUNKNOWN          3
#define IDM_IMALLOC           4
#define IDM_IMARSHAL          5
#define IDM_ALLOCATE_CUSTOM   6
#define IDM_ALLOCATE_DEFAULT  7
#define IDM_FREE              8
#define IDM_CHECK             9
```

(continued)

CALLER.RC

```
#include "callpub.h"

MAIN MENU
    {
    POPUP "&Allocator"
        {
        MENUITEM "&Create",                        IDM_CREATE
        MENUITEM "&Destroy",                       IDM_DESTROY
        MENUITEM SEPARATOR
        MENUITEM "QueryInterface IID_IUnknown", IDM_IUNKNOWN
        MENUITEM "QueryInterface IID_IMalloc",  IDM_IMALLOC
        MENUITEM "QueryInterface IID_IMarshal", IDM_IMARSHAL
        }

    POPUP "&Memory"
        {
        MENUITEM "&Allocate (IMalloc)", IDM_ALLOCATE_CUSTOM
        MENUITEM "&Allocate (malloc)",  IDM_ALLOCATE_DEFAULT
        MENUITEM "&Free",               IDM_FREE
        }
    }
```

CALLER makes no direct use of the OLE libraries and so, like IMALLOC.DLL before it, CALLER doesn't initialize the OLE libraries. (That changes when CALLER gets upgraded to CALLPUB later in this chapter; just as IMALLOC's descendant, PUBMEM, also must rely on the OLE libraries and so issues the appropriate initialization and termination functions.)

All of CALLER's access to *IMalloc* interface services are through menu selections, which put you in complete control of what is called and when it is called. The first thing to do when running CALLER is to create an allocation component by selecting Create from the Allocator menu. This calls IMALLOC's *CreateAllocator* function, which returns the interface pointer required to access IMALLOC's allocator interface.

In response to the Destroy command on the Allocator menu, the allocation component is destroyed by decrementing its reference count with a call to *Release*:

```
pMalloc->lpVtbl->Release (pMalloc) ;
pMalloc = NULL ;
```

It's a good idea to set the value of an interface pointer that's just been released to NULL. This ensures that you won't be able to use it again without generating an exception (which is a bug you'll hopefully catch before shipping your software.)

CALLER exercises the *QueryInterface* member of the allocator to check for supported interfaces. From the client's perspective, it's important to always call *Release* when a call to

QueryInterface provides an interface pointer. Otherwise, you risk leaving a component in memory with its reference count greater than zero when its client thinks it has shut down.

We next turn our attention to what's involved in building a public component server.

A PUBLIC COMPONENT SERVER

PUBMEM.DLL demonstrates the creation of a public OLE component server. The difference between a public and a private component is not in the interface itself; in fact, the public *IMalloc* interface provided by PUBMEM is identical (with one small change) to the private interface provided earlier in the IMALLOC sample. A public OLE component is a component created from a public OLE component class.

A public OLE component class requires the coordination of several elements. A component class has a unique class identifier (CLSID) and a registry entry that ties the class ID to the installed EXEs and DLLs. The component itself must provide a standard mechanism for creating a component on demand called a *class factory*. A class factory is itself a private OLE component, created by a call to a DLL server's *DllGetClassObject* exported entry point, which provides services for the *IClassFactory* interface. The OLE libraries periodically call a second entry point, *DllCanUnloadNow*, to check whether it's safe for the DLL housing the component to terminate. While more complex than that of a private component, a class factory provides a generic mechanism for exposing multiple types of component classes with each able to provide multiple different interfaces. The source files of PUBMEM appear in Figure 20-5.

PUBMEM.MAK

```
#----------------------
# PUBMEM.MAK make file
#----------------------

pubmem.dll : pubmem.obj classfac.obj compobj.obj
    $(LINKER) /EXPORT:DllGetClassObject /EXPORT:DllCanUnloadNow \
    $(DLLFLAGS) -OUT:pubmem.dll pubmem.obj \
    classfac.obj compobj.obj $(GUILIBS) uuid.lib ole32.lib

pubmem.obj : pubmem.cpp pubmem.h
    $(CC) $(CFLAGS) pubmem.cpp

classfac.obj : classfac.cpp pubmem.h
    $(CC) $(CFLAGS) classfac.cpp

compobj.obj : compobj.cpp pubmem.h
    $(CC) $(CFLAGS) compobj.cpp
```

Figure 20-5. *The PUBMEM library.* (continued)

PUBMEM.CPP

```
/*-------------------------------------------------
    PUBMEM.CPP -- Define a public imalloc component
                 (c) Paul Yao, 1996
    -------------------------------------------------*/
#include <windows.h>
#include "pubmem.h"

extern int cObject ;

//-----------------------------------------------------------------
// CreateAllocator -- Exported function to create allocator
//-----------------------------------------------------------------
EXPORT LPMALLOC CreateAllocator ()
    {
    DAlloc *pAllocator = NULL ;

    pAllocator = new DAlloc () ;
    if (pAllocator != NULL && pAllocator->Initialize ())
        {
        pAllocator->AddRef () ;
        }
    else
        {
        delete pAllocator ;
        }

    return (LPMALLOC) pAllocator ;
    }

//-----------------------------------------------------------------
DAlloc::DAlloc ()
    {
    RefCount = 0 ;
    hHeap = NULL ;
    }

//-----------------------------------------------------------------
DAlloc::~DAlloc ()
    {
    if (hHeap)
        HeapDestroy (hHeap) ;
    }
```

(continued)

```
//-------------------------------------------------------------
BOOL DAlloc::Initialize ()
    {
    hHeap = HeapCreate (0, 4096, 65535) ;
    return (BOOL) hHeap ;
    }


//-------------------------------------------------------------
STDMETHODIMP
DAlloc::QueryInterface (REFIID riid, LPVOID FAR *ppvObject)
    {
    // Always initialize "out" parameters to NULL
    *ppvObject = NULL ;

    // Everyone supports IUnknown
    if (riid == IID_IUnknown)
        *ppvObject = (LPUNKNOWN) this ;

    // We support IMalloc
    if (riid == IID_IMalloc)
        *ppvObject = (LPMALLOC) this ;

    if (*ppvObject == NULL)
        {
        // Interface not supported
        return E_NOINTERFACE ;
        }
    else
        {
        // Interface supported, so increment reference count
        ((LPUNKNOWN) *ppvObject )->AddRef () ;
        return S_OK ;
        }
    }


//-------------------------------------------------------------
STDMETHODIMP_ (ULONG)
DAlloc::AddRef (void)
    {
    return ++RefCount ;
    }


//-------------------------------------------------------------
STDMETHODIMP_ (ULONG)
DAlloc::Release (void)
```

(continued)

```
        {
    if (0L != RefCount)
        return RefCount ;

    --cObject ;
    delete this ;
    return 0L ;
    }

//-------------------------------------------------------------------
STDMETHODIMP_ (void *)
DAlloc::Alloc (ULONG cb)
    {
    return HeapAlloc (hHeap, HEAP_ZERO_MEMORY, cb) ;
    }

//-------------------------------------------------------------------
STDMETHODIMP_ (void *)
DAlloc::Realloc (void *pv, ULONG cb)
    {
    return HeapReAlloc (hHeap, HEAP_ZERO_MEMORY, pv, cb) ;
    }

//-------------------------------------------------------------------
STDMETHODIMP_ (void)
DAlloc::Free (void *pv)
    {
    HeapFree (hHeap, 0, pv) ;
    }

//-------------------------------------------------------------------
STDMETHODIMP_ (ULONG)
DAlloc::GetSize (void *pv)
    {
    return HeapSize (hHeap, 0, pv) ;
    }

//-------------------------------------------------------------------
STDMETHODIMP_ (int)
DAlloc::DidAlloc (void *pv)
    {
    PROCESS_HEAP_ENTRY phe ;
    ZeroMemory (&phe, sizeof (PROCESS_HEAP_ENTRY)) ;

    while (HeapWalk (hHeap, &phe))
```

(continued)

```
            {
            if (p he.lpData == pv)
                return 1 ;
            }

        return 0 ;
        }

//-------------------------------------------------------------------
STDMETHODIMP_ (void)
DAlloc::HeapMinimize (void)
        {
        HeapCompact (hHeap, 0) ;
        }
```

CLASSFAC.CPP

```
/*----------------------------------------------
    CLASSFAC.CPP -- OLE Class Factory component
                    (c) Paul Yao, 1996
    ----------------------------------------------*/
#include <windows.h>
#include <initguid.h>
#include "pubmem.h"

extern int cObject ;
extern int cLockCount ;

//-------------------------------------------------------------------
DClassFactory::DClassFactory ()
        {
        RefCount = 0 ;
        }

//-------------------------------------------------------------------
DClassFactory::~DClassFactory ()
        {
        }

//-------------------------------------------------------------------
STDMETHODIMP
DClassFactory::QueryInterface (REFIID riid, LPVOID FAR *ppvObj)
        {
        // Init recipient's pointer
        *ppvObj = NULL ;
```

(continued)

```
    // If asking for IUnknown, we can provide
    if (riid == IID_IUnknown)
        *ppvObj = (LPUNKNOWN) this ;

    // If asking for IClassFactory, we can provide
    if (riid == IID_IClassFactory)
        *ppvObj = (LPCLASSFACTORY) this ;

    // Make sure reference count reflects access
    if (*ppvObj == NULL)
        {
        // Interface not supported
        return E_NOINTERFACE ;
        }
    else
        {
        // Interface supported to increment reference count
        ((LPUNKNOWN) *ppvObj)->AddRef () ;
        return S_OK ;
        }
    }

//-----------------------------------------------------------------
STDMETHODIMP_ (ULONG)
DClassFactory::AddRef ()
    {
    return ++RefCount ;
    }

//-----------------------------------------------------------------
STDMETHODIMP_ (ULONG)
DClassFactory::Release ()
    {
    if (0L != --RefCount)
        return RefCount ;

    delete this ;
    return 0L ;
    }

//-----------------------------------------------------------------
STDMETHODIMP
DClassFactory::CreateInstance (LPUNKNOWN pUnkOuter, REFIID riid,
                        LPVOID FAR *ppvObject)
    {
```

(continued)

```
        // Initialize return pointer
        *ppvObject = NULL ;

        // If trying to aggregate, fail
        if (pUnkOuter != NULL)
            return CLASS_E_NOAGGREGATION ;

        // Create memory allocation object
        LPMALLOC pMalloc = CreateAllocator () ;

        if (pMalloc == NULL)
            {
            return E_OUTOFMEMORY ;
            }
        else
            {
            // Fetch interface requested by caller
            HRESULT hr = pMalloc->QueryInterface (riid, ppvObject) ;

            // Decrement reference count produced by CreateAllocator
            pMalloc->Release () ;

            // Increment count of objects
            if (SUCCEEDED (hr))
                ++cObject ;

            return hr ;
            }
        }

//---------------------------------------------------------------------
STDMETHODIMP
DClassFactory::LockServer (BOOL fLock)
    {
    if (fLock)
        {
        ++cLockCount ;
        }
    else
        {
        --cLockCount ;
        }
    return NOERROR ;
    }
```

(continued)

COMPOBJ.CPP

```
/*-------------------------------------------------
    COMPOBJ.CPP -- Component Object registration
                     (c) Paul Yao, 1996
    ---------------------------------------------*/
#include <windows.h>
#include "pubmem.h"

int cObject    = 0 ;
int cLockCount = 0 ;

//-----------------------------------------------------------------
HRESULT APIENTRY
DllGetClassObject (REFCLSID rclsid, REFIID riid, LPVOID *ppvObj)
    {
    // Initialize "out" pointer to known value
    *ppvObj = NULL ;

    if (rclsid != CLSID_ALLOCATOR)
        {
        return CLASS_E_CLASSNOTAVAILABLE ;
        }

    DClassFactory *pClassFactory = new DClassFactory () ;
    if (pClassFactory == NULL)
        {
        return E_OUTOFMEMORY ;
        }
    else
        {
        return pClassFactory->QueryInterface (riid, ppvObj) ;
        }
    }

//-----------------------------------------------------------------
HRESULT APIENTRY
DllCanUnloadNow (void)
    {
    if (cObject > 0 || cLockCount > 0)
        {
        return S_FALSE ;
        }
```

(continued)

```
    else
        {
        return S_OK ;
        }
    }
```

PUBMEM.H

```
//------------------------------------------------------------------
// C Interface to private allocator
//------------------------------------------------------------------
#define EXPORT extern "C" __declspec (dllexport)

EXPORT LPMALLOC CreateAllocator () ;

// {308D0430-1090-11cf-B92A-00AA006238F8}
DEFINE_GUID (CLSID_ALLOCATOR,
    0x308d0430, 0x1090, 0x11cf, 0xb9,
    0x2a, 0x0, 0xaa, 0x0, 0x62, 0x38, 0xf8) ;


//------------------------------------------------------------------
// Implementation of allocator interface
//------------------------------------------------------------------
#undef  INTERFACE
#define INTERFACE DAlloc

DECLARE_INTERFACE_ (DAlloc, IMalloc)
    {
    // *** IUnknown methods ***
    STDMETHOD  (QueryInterface) (THIS_ REFIID riid, LPVOID FAR *ppv) ;
    STDMETHOD_ (ULONG, AddRef)  (THIS) ;
    STDMETHOD_ (ULONG, Release) (THIS) ;

    // *** IMalloc methods ***
    STDMETHOD_ (void *, Alloc)        (THIS_ ULONG cb) ;
    STDMETHOD_ (void *, Realloc)      (THIS_ void *pv, ULONG cb) ;
    STDMETHOD_ (void,   Free)         (THIS_ void *pv) ;
    STDMETHOD_ (ULONG,  GetSize)      (THIS_ void *pv) ;
    STDMETHOD_ (int,    DidAlloc)     (THIS_ void *pv) ;
    STDMETHOD_ (void,   HeapMinimize) (THIS) ;

#ifndef CINTERFACE
```

(continued)

```
public :
    DAlloc () ;
    ~DAlloc () ;
    BOOL Initialize () ;
private :
    ULONG RefCount ;
    HANDLE hHeap ;
#endif
    } ;


// Class Factory
#undef  INTERFACE
#define INTERFACE DClassFactory

DECLARE_INTERFACE_ (DClassFactory, IClassFactory)
    {
    // *** IUnknown methods ***
    STDMETHOD  (QueryInterface) (THIS_ REFIID riid, LPVOID FAR *ppv) ;
    STDMETHOD_ (ULONG, AddRef)  (THIS) ;
    STDMETHOD_ (ULONG, Release) (THIS) ;

    // *** IClassFactory methods ***
    STDMETHOD (CreateInstance) (THIS_ LPUNKNOWN pUnkOuter,
                                REFIID riid, LPVOID FAR *ppvObject) ;
    STDMETHOD (LockServer)     (THIS_ BOOL fLock) ;

#ifndef CINTERFACE
public :
    DClassFactory () ;
    ~DClassFactory () ;
private :
    ULONG RefCount ;
#endif
    } ;
```

PUBMEM has two exported entry points: *DllGetClassObject* and *DllCanUnloadNow*. Because the OLE libraries expect a DLL server to expose these exact function names, we can't define these functions using the EXPORT keyword. Instead, we expose these functions by using the /EXPORT linker option in the PUBMEM.MAK make file. *DllGetClassObject* provides the mechanism for exposing the class factory. *DllCanUnloadNow* is called when the OLE libraries want to query whether a specific server has any existing connections or whether it's safe to shut down a server and remove it from memory. Both will be discussed shortly; but first, let's take a look at the registry—a key element in making an OLE component public.

Role of the Registry

The registry is a central depository for systemwide persistent state in Windows 95 and Windows NT. The registry was first introduced in Windows 3.1 to publish OLE class details, default extensions for the system shell, and a few odd DDE commands. In Windows 95 and Windows NT, the registry is the replacement for state that used to reside in .INI files, such as currently installed hardware, control panel options, and settings of user preferences for application software. While significant differences exist between how each operating system uses the registry, OLE-related registry entries are the same in both systems.

The registry is structured as a hierarchy of keys, subkeys, and values. On Windows 95, the defined root keys include HKEY_CLASSES_ROOT, HKEY_CURRENT_USER, HKEY_LOCAL_MACHINE, HKEY_USERS, HKEY_CURRENT_CONFIG, and HKEY_DYN_DATA. (Windows NT provides only the first four.) Data about OLE components reside in HKEY_CLASSES_ROOT. (As a side note, the true location of this hierarchy is HKEY_LOCAL_MACHINE\SOFTWARE\Classes, but for compatibility with Windows 3.1 OLE applications, OLE classes were given their own surrogate root node.)

The root keys of HKEY_CLASSES_ROOT consist of three types of entries: file extensions, class names, and system entries. File extension entries start with a period (.) to associate a file with a compound document server (for example, ".vsd" to Visio Corporation's Visio). Class names provide human-readable identifiers for OLE component classes, for which two uses currently exist. The first use for class names is to support OLE 1.0 compound document servers; this use is identified with class names like "Visio.Drawing.4". The second use for class names is OLE automation. Automation macro primitives create OLE automation objects by name—in this context a class name is called a "Program ID" or just "ProgID." For example, using the "Visio.Application" ProgID, a Visual Basic program can create and manipulate Visio objects via automation methods and properties.

There are three kinds of system registry entries, each of which are the roots of their own hierarchies: *TypeLib*, *Interface*, and CLSID. The *TypeLib* hierarchy identifies the location of currently installed type libraries, which are databases that describe the contents of OLE components. Used extensively for automation support, a type library describes the function prototypes for all supported interfaces and also includes references to help files so that development tools can bring up the appropriate help page to help macro programmers make proper use of automation servers.

The *Interface* hierarchy contains a list—sorted by interface ID—of all interfaces installed on a system. It provides the human-readable name for the interface (*IUnknown*, *IMalloc*, and so forth) and details about each interface (the number of functions and the base class for each interface).

The final hierarchy, the CLSID hierarchy, provides details of all currently installed (public) OLE components. A CLSID is a class identifier. Like interface IDs (IID and REFIID data types), class IDs (CLSID and REFCLSID data types) are 128-bit (16 hex digit) numbers that provide a machine-readable way to uniquely identify a component class. Like the IID type, the CLSID is a GUID type:

```
typedef struct _GUID
    {
    DWORD Data1 ;
    WORD Data2 ;
    WORD Data3 ;
    BYTE Data4[8] ;
    }   GUID ;
```

A CLSID is like a telephone number of a specific OLE component. Our earlier discussion of interface IDs (IIDs) compared IIDs with an extension used for interdepartmental calls within the same business. From that perspective, the CLSID provides a way to call from one business to another—in OLE terms, from one component to another component. Just as locating a specific person working for a specific company often requires you to first dial the company's main number and then request an extension, connecting to a specific interface in a specific component requires you to first identify the CLSID to access the component and then the IID to get to the desired interface.

Continuing with the telephone analogy, the registry is like a worldwide telephone book of OLE components. A component can be referenced by file extension, class name, or class ID. Of these three types of entries, the class ID entry is the most important since details of the component's module (.DLL or .EXE) are stored in the CLSID hierarchy. While you (or your setup software) will need to create entries in the hierarchy, you don't need to access the hierarchy programmatically. Instead, you make calls to the OLE libraries that accept a class ID, search the registry, and load the desired component on your behalf.

The following registry entry makes PUBMEM's component publicly available:

```
\HKEY_CLASSES_ROOT\
    CLSID\
        {308D0430-1090-11cf-B92A-00AA006238F8}\
            InprocServer32 = C:\PETZOLD\CHAP20\PUBMEM.DLL
```

InprocServer32 means that the file being referred to is a 32-bit DLL. Other keywords include *LocalServer32* for a 32-bit EXE, *InprocServer* for a 16-bit DLL, and *LocalServer* for a 16-bit EXE. To publish the presence of these other types of servers, additional registry entries are required.

There are two ways to add registry entries: call the registry API or use a tool which in turn calls the registry API. To add an entry to the registry without writing any code, run the registry editor. There's a version for each Microsoft operating system: on Windows NT 3.51, run REGEDT32.EXE; and on Windows 95, run REGEDIT.EXE. As mentioned elsewhere in this chapter, OLE-related entries appear under the HKEY_CLASSES_ROOT hierarchy.

Programmatically, you modify the registry by calling the various registry-editing functions, the functions with a "Reg" prefix. Each new level in the registry hierarchy is represented by HKEY, a handle to a registry key. Registering the public memory allocator, PUBMEM.DLL, involves opening an existing registry key (*RegOpenKeyEx*), creating two new keys (*RegCreateKeyEx*), setting one value (*RegSetValueEx*), and then closing the three opened keys (*RegCloseKey*). Assuming that the component server resides at C:\PETZOLD\CHAP20-\PUBMEM.DLL, the code for registering PUBMEM.DLL appears in Figure 20-6.

```
{
DWORD    dwDisp ;
HKEY     hkMain ;
HKEY     hkClass ;
HKEY     hkPath ;
LPCTSTR  lpClsid = "{308D0430-1090-11cf-B92A-00AA006238F8}" ;
LPCTSTR  lpPath  = "InprocServer32" ;
LPTSTR   lpValue = "C:\\PETZOLD\\CHAP20\\PUBMEM.DLL" ;

// Open "HKEY_CLASSES_ROOT\CLSID"
RegOpenKeyEx (HKEY_CLASSES_ROOT,
             "CLSID",
             0,
             KEY_ALL_ACCESS,
             &hkMain) ;

// Add \HKEY_CLASSES_ROOT\CLSID\{308...8F8}
RegCreateKeyEx (hkMain,
             lpClsid,
             0,
             "",
             REG_OPTION_NON_VOLATILE,
             KEY_ALL_ACCESS,
             NULL,
             &hkClass,
             &dwDisp) ;

if (dwDisp == REG_CREATED_NEW_KEY)
    {
    // Add \...\{308...8F8}\InprocServer32
    RegCreateKeyEx (hkClass,
                 lpPath,
                 0,
                 "",
                 REG_OPTION_NON_VOLATILE,
                 KEY_ALL_ACCESS,
                 NULL,
```

Figure 20-6. *Registering PUBMEM.DLL*   *(continued)*

```
                            &hkPath,
                            &dwDisp) ;

        RegSetValueEx (hkPath,
                            "",
                            0,
                            REG_SZ,
                            (CONST BYTE *) lpValue,
                            lstrlen (lpValue) + 1) ;


        }

    RegCloseKey (hkPath) ;
    RegCloseKey (hkClass) ;
    RegCloseKey (hkMain) ;
    }
```

The registry allows clients to access a public component server by knowing only the component's CLSID. Let's take a closer look at the generation of unique values and coding techniques for this data type.

Mechanics of CLSID Generation and Use

A unique class ID for an OLE component is as important to the overall operation of OLE components as unique telephone numbers are to the overall operation of a telephone system. Without special arrangements, two businesses can't share a telephone number, and the same is true of OLE components: each requires a unique class ID to avoid complications. The problem increases with Network OLE, since the probability of collisions between redundant class IDs increases when more computers—each with their own OLE components—get added to the equation.

The solution used for OLE components comes, in fact, from the world of networked computing. The Open Software Foundation (OSF) created "Universally Unique Identifiers" (UUIDs) for their Distributed Computing Environment (DCE) standard. In OLE programming, UUIDs are called GUIDs and are used both for component class identifiers (CLSIDs) and interface identifiers (IIDs).

You generate a unique GUID—for identifying either component classes, or your own custom interfaces—by running the GUIDGEN or UUIDGEN utility. As described by Kraig Brockschmidt in *Inside OLE*, this program generates unique values using various combinations of a network card's unique IEEE identifier, the current date, the current time, and a counter (for high-frequency allocation requests). The result is a number with a very low probability of duplication by different developers.

The GUIDGEN utility generates a unique GUID and places the value on the clipboard in CF_TEXT format in one of several forms, including an MFC-specific format, a native OLE (non-MFC) format, and as a registry-formatted GUID string. Here's the GUIDGEN-output used by PUBMEM to identify the *IMalloc* allocator component class:

```
// {308D0430-1090-11cf-B92A-00AA006238F8}
DEFINE_GUID (CLSID_ALLOCATOR, \
    0x308d0430, 0x1090, 0x11cf, 0xb9, \
    0x2a, 0x0, 0xaa, 0x0, 0x62, 0x38, 0xf8) ;
```

The commented line shows the format expected by the registry, which includes dashes at specific locations plus the starting and ending curly braces. The symbolic identifier, CLSID_ALLOCATOR, was added to the results created by GUIDGEN as a name appropriate to PUBMEM's component.

To make proper use of the DEFINE_GUID macro requires a tiny bit of care because it has two different definitions. The standard one refers to the GUID name as an *extern* value. In one—and only one—of your source files, you must refer to the other definition, which is most easily done by including INITGUID.H prior to the appearance of the DEFINE_GUID macro:

```
// Redefine DEFINE_GUID to allocate GUID memory
#include <initguid.h>

// Allocate and initialize CLSID_ALLOCATOR
DEFINE_GUID (CLSID_ALLOCATOR, \
    0x308d0430, 0x1090, 0x11cf, 0xb9, \
    0x2a, 0x0, 0xaa, 0x0, 0x62, 0x38, 0xf8) ;
```

When creating an OLE client/server connection, a CLSID value gets passed from the client to the OLE libraries, which passes the value on to the server. The client uses the class ID to request access to a specific component. The OLE libraries use the class ID to search the system registry for the location of the program or DLL associated with that class ID. When the component is finally found, an element within a DLL component server—the class factory—validates that the server supports the requested CLSID. Once that validation has been performed, it is the class factory itself that creates the requested components and provides the first interface pointer to the client.

The Class Factory Component

A class factory is a private OLE component that supports two interfaces: *IUnknown* and *IClassFactory*. It is a private component because it has no class ID and its presence is not advertised in the system registry. As with the allocator in IMALLOC, clients access a class factory through a private entry point: *DllGetClassObject*. Unlike IMALLOC's allocator, however, it is normally the OLE libraries themselves that access this entry point and create the class factory.

The *DllGetClassObject* function has the following prototype:

```
HRESULT
DllGetClassObject (REFCLSID rclsid,
                   REFIID riid,
                   LPVOID *ppv) ;
```

- *rclsid* identifies the desired class (CLSID) value.

- *riid* identifies the desired interface (IID) value, normally IID_ClassFactory.

- *ppv* points to the location where the return value is to be written.

From this single exported entry point, a DLL server can support many different classes. The first parameter to *DllGetClassObject*, *rclsid*, lets the server know which specific class should be created. Like the *QueryInterface* function, when *DllGetClassObject* can provide the requested interface, it copies an interface pointer—normally, an *IClassFactory* interface pointer—to the location specified by the last parameter. If a request cannot be filled, that parameter receives a *NULL* value.

The primary purpose of *DllGetClassObject* is to check for support for a specific class (*rclsid*) and a specific interface (*riid*). If the requested class is supported, PUBMEM's *DllGetClassObject* creates a class factory. Then the class factory's *QueryInterface* function is called—as much to increment its reference count as to check that the requested interface is, in fact, supported. PUBMEM's version of this function is as follows:

```
HRESULT APIENTRY
DllGetClassObject (REFCLSID rclsid, REFIID riid, LPVOID *ppvObj)
    {
    // Initialize "out" pointer to known value
    *ppvObj = NULL ;

    if (rclsid != CLSID_ALLOCATOR)
        {
        return CLASS_E_CLASSNOTAVAILABLE ;
        }

    DClassFactory *pClassFactory = new DClassFactory () ;
    if (pClassFactory == NULL)
        {
        return E_OUTOFMEMORY ;
        }
    else
        {
        return pClassFactory->QueryInterface (riid, ppv) ;
        }
    }
```

Just like *QueryInterface*, *DllGetClassObject* sets the returned interface pointer to NULL if the requested class or the requested class factory interface isn't supported.

The *IClassFactory* interface itself is defined as follows:

```
#undef  INTERFACE
#define INTERFACE IClassFactory

DECLARE_INTERFACE_ (IClassFactory, IUnknown)
    {
    // *** IUnknown methods ***
    STDMETHOD (QueryInterface)  (THIS_
                                 REFIID riid,
                                 LPVOID FAR *ppvObj) PURE ;
    STDMETHOD_ (ULONG, AddRef)  (THIS) PURE ;
    STDMETHOD_ (ULONG, Release) (THIS) PURE ;

    // *** IClassFactory methods ***
    STDMETHOD (CreateInstance)  (THIS_
                                 LPUNKNOWN pUnkOuter,
                                 REFIID riid,
                                 LPVOID FAR *ppvObject) PURE ;
    STDMETHOD (LockServer)      (THIS_ BOOL fLock) PURE ;
    } ;
```

Like all OLE interfaces, *IClassFactory* has the common set of *IUnknown* member functions. This as much as anything else is what makes *IClassFactory* its own separate and distinct component. To maintain this distinction between server objects and class factory objects, a *QueryInterface* to a class factory should not produce a pointer to a server object. And vice versa—*QueryInterface* to a server object should not produce a class factory interface pointer. Instead, the class factory stands apart as a unique component that can be created and used as needed.

There are two *IClassFactory*-specific services: component creation and server lock count control.

When a client wishes to create an instance of a component, the *CreateInstance* member is called. However, most clients won't call this function directly. Instead, clients call the OLE library helper function, *CoCreateInstance*, to request the creation of an OLE component. This function is defined:

```
STDAPI
CoCreateInstance (REFCLSID rclsid,    // Class identifier
                  LPUNKNOWN pUnkOuter, // Outer unknown
                  DWORD dwClsContext,  // Server context
                  REFIID riid,         // Interface identifier
                  LPVOID *ppv);        // Return value
```

■ *rclsid* identifies the class ID of the component to create.

■ *pUnkOuter* identifies the outer *IUknown* to create aggregate objects.

■ *dwClsContext* identifies the context of the server component. Choices include a combination of CLSCTX_INPROC_SERVER for a DLL-server, CLSCTX_INPROC-_HANDLER for a DLL-handler (proxy for an out-of-process server), and CLSCTX_LOCAL_SERVER for a local server (different process on the same machine). As of this writing, no flag has been assigned for a network server.

■ *riid* identifies the requested interface to return.

■ *ppv* points to the location for the returned interface value, in case of success in component creation, or NULL if component could not be created with the requested interface.

The *IClassFactory* function *LockServer* both increments and decrements a server lock count. It combines in a single server function the tasks performed by *IUnknown*'s *AddRef* and *Release* members for interfaces. Except for this very important fact: a server never shuts itself down like a component object will. This raises an important issue in server implementation: the controlling of the server lifetime.

Controlling Server Lifetime

Server lifetime is just as important an issue to a server implementor as component lifetime is to a component implementor. It is as much an issue in a single-component server like PUBMEM as it is for a multi-component server. The mechanism for controlling both is identical. Our focus is on DLL-based server lifetime. While the server lifetime motivating factors for EXE-based servers are the same, the implementation details are quite different. (For details, see Brockschmidt's "*Inside OLE*".)

A server DLL is loaded into memory like any other Windows DLL—with a call to *LoadLibrary*. The fact that the OLE libraries provide their own version of this function, *CoLoadLibrary*, doesn't change the fact that an entity outside the DLL loads the DLL. (*CoLoadLibrary* was created to help simplify porting OLE to non-Windows platforms.) A subsequent call to *CoFreeLibrary* will unload the DLL from memory.

DLL server lifetime is an issue because the client doesn't directly load the server library into memory—the OLE libraries do. So it's up to the OLE libraries to unload the servers at the correct time. But most interactions between client and server ignore the OLE libraries, which therefore cannot know when the proper time has arrived to remove a DLL server from memory—except by asking.

The OLE libraries periodically call the server's *DllCanUnloadNow* entry point to ascertain whether the time has come to unload the server. This function replies with "Yes" (S_OK) or "No" (S_FALSE):

```
HRESULT APIENTRY DllCanUnloadNow (void)
    {
    if (cObject > 0 !! cLockCount > 0)
        {
        return S_FALSE ;
        }
    else
        {
        return S_OK ;
        }
    }
```

The answer is based on one of two factors: whether any components exist and whether the client has locked the server in memory. This latter device is meant to override the situation in which no component exists but—to avoid the overhead of reloading a DLL into memory—a client wishes a server to avoid shutting down.

Lock count on a server is controlled through the *LockServer* member of *IClassFactory*. This function does little more than increment and decrement a lock count, which is little more than a global variable maintained by the server. Here is PUBMEM's implementation of *IClassFactory::LockServer*:

```
STDMETHODIMP
DClassFactory::LockServer (BOOL fLock)
    {
    if (fLock)
        {
        ++cLockCount ;
        }
    else
        {
        --cLockCount ;
        }
    return NOERROR ;
    }
```

The other factor that controls server lifetime is the count of components. In PUBMEM, this count is incremented within *DClassFactory::CreateInstance* upon successful creation of the requested OLE component:

```
// Create memory allocation object
LPMALLOC pMalloc = CreateAllocator () ;

if (pMalloc == NULL)
    {
    return E_OUTOFMEMORY ;
    }
```

```
else
    {
    // Fetch interface requested by caller
    HRESULT hr = pMalloc->QueryInterface (riid, ppvObject) ;

    // Decrement reference count produced by CreateAllocator
    pMalloc->Release () ;

    // Increment count of objects
    If (SUCCEEDED (hr))
        ++cObject ;

    return hr ;
    }
```

This count gets decremented when a component destroys itself, which occurs in *IMalloc*'s *Release* member when its reference count goes to zero:

```
STDMETHODIMP_ (ULONG)
DAlloc::Release (void)
    {
    if (0L != RefCount) ;
        return RefCount ;

    --cObject ;
    delete this ;
    return 0L ;
    }
```

Incidentally, this is the only required change when converting the private component to a public component.

It's time to look at what's involved in creating a client to a public component, which is what the next sample program demonstrates.

A PUBLIC COMPONENT CLIENT

This public component client, CALLPUB.EXE, was created from the private component client, CALLER.EXE. Both call an OLE server component that provides an *IMalloc* interface to allocate and free blocks of memory to hold character strings.

While there were quite a few modifications required to convert a private server into a public server—special entry points and a class factory—only one minor change was required to convert a client of a private component into a client of a public component. Instead of calling the private component creation function, CALLPUB calls an OLE library function—*CoCreateInstance*—whose sole purpose is to create components.

The source files that make up CALLPUB appear in Figure 20-7, beginning on the following page.

CALLPUB.MAK

```
#----------------------
# CALLPUB.MAK make file
#----------------------

callpub.exe : callpub.obj callpub.res pubmem.lib
    $(LINKER) $(GUIFLAGS) -OUT:callpub.exe callpub.obj callpub.res \
    pubmem.lib $(GUILIBS) uuid.lib ole32.lib

callpub.obj : callpub.c callpub.h pubmem.h
    $(CC) -DCINTERFACE $(CFLAGS) callpub.c

callpub.res : callpub.rc callpub.h
    $(RC) $(RCVARS) callpub.rc
```

CALLPUB.C

```c
/*-----------------------------------------------
   CALLPUB.C -- Call into public OLE component
                (c) Paul Yao, 1996
   -----------------------------------------------*/
#include <windows.h>
#include <initguid.h>
#include "pubmem.h"
#include "callpub.h"

LRESULT CALLBACK WndProc (HWND, UINT, WPARAM, LPARAM) ;

char szWndClass[] = "CallerWindow" ;
char szAppName[]  = "Calls Public Malloc" ;

//-------------------------------------------------------------------
int WINAPI WinMain (HINSTANCE hInstance, HINSTANCE hPrevInstance,
                PSTR lpszCmdLine, int cmdShow)
    {
    HWND        hwnd ;
    MSG         msg ;
    WNDCLASSEX  wc ;

    wc.cbSize        = sizeof (wc) ;
    wc.lpszClassName = szWndClass ;
    wc.hInstance     = hInstance ;
    wc.lpfnWndProc   = WndProc ;
    wc.hCursor       = LoadCursor (NULL, IDC_ARROW) ;
```

Figure 20-7. *The CALLPUB program.*   *(continued)*

```
    wc.hIcon         = LoadIcon (NULL, IDI_APPLICATION) ;
    wc.lpszMenuName  = "MAIN" ;
    wc.hbrBackground = (HBRUSH) (COLOR_WINDOW + 1) ;
    wc.style         = 0 ;
    wc.cbClsExtra    = 0 ;
    wc.cbWndExtra    = 0 ;
    wc.hIconSm       = LoadIcon (NULL, IDI_APPLICATION) ;

    RegisterClassEx (&wc) ;

    hwnd = CreateWindowEx (0L, szWndClass, szAppName,
                        WS_OVERLAPPEDWINDOW,
                        CW_USEDEFAULT, CW_USEDEFAULT,
                        CW_USEDEFAULT, CW_USEDEFAULT,
                        NULL, NULL, hInstance, NULL) ;
    ShowWindow (hwnd, cmdShow) ;
    UpdateWindow (hwnd) ;

    // Connect to OLE libraries
    HRESULT hr = CoInitialize (NULL) ;
    if (FAILED (hr))
        {
        // Fail app initialization
        return FALSE ;
        }

    while (GetMessage (&msg, NULL, 0, 0))
        {
        TranslateMessage (&msg) ;
        DispatchMessage (&msg) ;
        }

    // Disconnect from OLE libraries
    CoUninitialize () ;

    return msg.wParam ;
    }

//-----------------------------------------------------------------
LRESULT CALLBACK
WndProc (HWND hwnd, UINT iMsg, WPARAM wParam, LPARAM lParam)
    {
    static int       iCurLine = 0 ;
    static LPMALLOC  pMalloc = NULL ;
    static LPSTR     szLine[10] ;
    static RECT      rHit[10] ;
```

(continued)

```
switch (iMsg)
    {
    case WM_CREATE :
        // Initialize data pointer array
        ZeroMemory (szLine, sizeof (szLine)) ;
        return 0 ;

    case WM_COMMAND :
        switch (LOWORD (wParam))
            {
            case IDM_CREATE :
                {
                HRESULT hr =
                    CoCreateInstance (CLSID_ALLOCATOR,
                                      NULL,
                                      CLSCTX_INPROC_SERVER,
                                      IID_IMalloc,
                                      (void **) &pMalloc) ;

                if (FAILED (hr))
                    {
                    MessageBox (hwnd, "Error: No allocator",
                                szAppName, MB_OK) ;
                    return 0 ;
                    }

                InvalidateRect (hwnd, NULL, TRUE) ;
                return 0 ;
                }

            case IDM_DESTROY :
                {
                int i ;

                // Mark allocated blocks as invalid
                for (i = 0 ; i < 10 ; i++)
                    {
                    if ((szLine[i] != NULL) &&
                        (pMalloc->lpVtbl->DidAlloc (pMalloc,
                                                    szLine[i])))
                        {
                        szLine[i] = NULL ;
                        }
                    }
                // Disconnect from & free allocator
                pMalloc->lpVtbl->Release (pMalloc) ;
```

(continued)

```
                pMalloc = NULL ;

                InvalidateRect (hwnd, NULL, TRUE) ;
                return 0 ;
                }

case IDM_IUNKNOWN :
        {
        LPUNKNOWN pUnk ;
        HRESULT hr =
                pMalloc->lpVtbl->QueryInterface (pMalloc,
                        IID_IUnknown,
                        (void **) &pUnk) ;
        if (SUCCEEDED (hr))
                {
                pUnk->lpVtbl->Release (pUnk) ;
                MessageBox (hwnd, "IUnknown supported",
                            szAppName, MB_OK) ;
                }
        else
                {
                MessageBox (hwnd, "IUnknown not supported",
                            szAppName, MB_OK) ;
                }
        return 0 ;
        }

case IDM_IMALLOC :
        {
        LPUNKNOWN pUnk ;
        HRESULT hr =
                pMalloc->lpVtbl->QueryInterface (pMalloc,
                        IID_IMalloc,
                        (void **) &pUnk) ;

        if (SUCCEEDED (hr))
                {
                pUnk->lpVtbl->Release (pUnk) ;
                MessageBox (hwnd, "IMalloc supported",
                            szAppName, MB_OK) ;
                }
        else
                {
                MessageBox (hwnd, "IMalloc not supported",
                            szAppName, MB_OK) ;
```

(continued)

```
                }
            return 0 ;
            }

        case IDM_IMARSHAL :
            {
            LPUNKNOWN pUnk ;
            HRESULT hr =
                 pMalloc->lpVtbl->QueryInterface (pMalloc,
                        IID_IMarshal,
                        (void **) &pUnk) ;
            if (SUCCEEDED (hr))
                 {
                 pUnk->lpVtbl->Release (pUnk) ;
                 MessageBox (hwnd, "IMarshal supported",
                            szAppName, MB_OK) ;
                 }
            else
                 {
                 MessageBox (hwnd, "IMarshal not supported",
                            szAppName, MB_OK) ;
                 }
            return 0 ;
            }

        case IDM_ALLOCATE_CUSTOM :
            if (szLine[iCurLine] != NULL)
                 {
                 MessageBox (hwnd, "Error: Free First",
                            szAppName, MB_OK) ;
                 return 0 ;
                 }

            // Allocate from IMalloc interface
            szLine[iCurLine] =
                 (char *) pMalloc->lpVtbl->Alloc (pMalloc, 100) ;
            lstrcpy (szLine[iCurLine], "*IMalloc memory*") ;

            InvalidateRect (hwnd, NULL, TRUE) ;
            return 0 ;

        case IDM_ALLOCATE_DEFAULT :
            if (szLine[iCurLine] != NULL)
                 {
                 MessageBox (hwnd, "Error: Free First",
                            szAppName, MB_OK) ;
```

(continued)

```
                                        return 0 ;
                                        }

                            // Allocate from default heap
                            szLine[iCurLine] = (char *) malloc (100) ;
                            lstrcpy (szLine[iCurLine], "-Malloc memory-") ;

                            InvalidateRect (hwnd, NULL, TRUE) ;
                            return 0 ;

                    case IDM_FREE :
                            if (szLine[iCurLine] == NULL)
                                    {
                                    MessageBox (hwnd, "Error: Nothing to free",
                                                szAppName, MB_OK) ;
                                    return 0 ;
                                    }

                            if (pMalloc == NULL)
                                    {
                                    goto FreeMalloc ;
                                    }

                            // Free allocated object
                            if (pMalloc->lpVtbl->DidAlloc (pMalloc,
                                                        szLine[iCurLine]))
                                    {
                                    pMalloc->lpVtbl->Free (pMalloc,
                                                        szLine[iCurLine]) ;
                                    }
                            else
                                    {
            FreeMalloc:
                                    free (szLine[iCurLine]) ;
                                    }

                            szLine[iCurLine] = NULL ;

                            InvalidateRect (hwnd, NULL, TRUE) ;
                            return 0 ;
                        }

        case WM_DESTROY :
            // Disconnect from & free allocator
            if (pMalloc)
```

(continued)

```
                    {
                    pMalloc->lpVtbl->Release (pMalloc) ;
                    pMalloc = NULL ;
                    }

          PostQuitMessage (0) ;  // Handle application shutdown
          return 0 ;

     case WM_INITMENU :
          {
          HMENU hMenu = (HMENU) wParam ;
          if (pMalloc)
               {
               EnableMenuItem (hMenu, IDM_CREATE,         MF_GRAYED) ;
               EnableMenuItem (hMenu, IDM_DESTROY,        MF_ENABLED) ;
               EnableMenuItem (hMenu, IDM_ALLOCATE_CUSTOM, MF_ENABLED) ;
               EnableMenuItem (hMenu, IDM_IUNKNOWN,       MF_ENABLED) ;
               EnableMenuItem (hMenu, IDM_IMALLOC,        MF_ENABLED) ;
               EnableMenuItem (hMenu, IDM_IMARSHAL,       MF_ENABLED) ;
               }
          else
               {
               EnableMenuItem(hMenu, IDM_CREATE,          MF_ENABLED) ;
               EnableMenuItem(hMenu, IDM_DESTROY,         MF_GRAYED) ;
               EnableMenuItem(hMenu, IDM_ALLOCATE_CUSTOM, MF_GRAYED) ;
               EnableMenuItem(hMenu, IDM_IUNKNOWN,        MF_GRAYED) ;
               EnableMenuItem(hMenu, IDM_IMALLOC,         MF_GRAYED) ;
               EnableMenuItem(hMenu, IDM_IMARSHAL,        MF_GRAYED) ;
               }
          return 0 ;
          }

     case WM_LBUTTONDOWN :
          {
          int i ;
          int x = LOWORD (lParam) ;
          int y = HIWORD (lParam) ;
          POINT pt = { x, y } ;

          for (i = 0 ; i < 10 ; i++)
               {
               if (PtInRect (&rHit[i], pt))
                    {
                    if (iCurLine != i)  // Minimize screen blink
                         {
                         InvalidateRect (hwnd, &rHit[iCurLine], TRUE) ;
```

(continued)

```
                              InvalidateRect (hwnd, &rHit[i], TRUE) ;
                              iCurLine = i ;
                              }
                     break ;
                     }
               }
          }
     return 0 ;
     }

case WM_PAINT :
     {
     char           szBuff[10] ;
     COLORREF       crText, crBack ;
     HDC            hdc ;
     int            cc ;
     int            i ;
     int            XCount, XText, Y ;
     int            cyLineHeight ;
     PAINTSTRUCT    ps ;
     RECT           rOpaque ;
     TEXTMETRIC     tm ;

     hdc = BeginPaint (hwnd, &ps) ;

     // Fetch line height
     GetTextMetrics (ps.hdc, &tm) ;
     cyLineHeight = tm.tmHeight + tm.tmExternalLeading ;

     // Fetch current text colors
     crText = GetTextColor (ps.hdc) ;
     crBack = GetBkColor (ps.hdc) ;

     XCount = tm.tmAveCharWidth * 3 ;
     XText  = XCount + tm.tmAveCharWidth * 7 ;
     Y      = tm.tmHeight ;

     for (i = 0 ; i < 10 ; i++, Y += cyLineHeight)
          {
          // Set colors to highlight current line
          if (i == iCurLine)
               {
               SetTextColor (ps.hdc, crBack) ;
               SetBkColor (ps.hdc, crText) ;

               SetRect (&rOpaque, 0, Y, 9999, Y + cyLineHeight) ;
```

(continued)

SECTION V DATA EXCHANGE AND LINKS

```
                        ExtTextOut(ps.hdc, 0, 0, ETO_OPAQUE, &rOpaque,
                                NULL, 0, NULL ) ;
                    }
                else
                    {
                    SetTextColor (ps.hdc, crText) ;
                    SetBkColor (ps.hdc, crBack) ;
                    }

                // Display line count
                cc = wsprintf (szBuff, "Line %d", i) ;
                TextOut (ps.hdc, XCount, Y, szBuff, cc) ;

                // Display text if a string has been defined
                if (szLine[i] != NULL)
                    {
                    cc = lstrlen (szLine[i]) ;
                    TextOut (ps.hdc, XText, Y, szLine[i], cc) ;
                    }

                // Calculate hit test rectangle
                SetRect (&rHit[i], 0, Y, 9999, Y + cyLineHeight) ;
                }

        EndPaint (hwnd, &ps) ;
        return 0 ;
        }

    default :
        return DefWindowProc (hwnd, iMsg, wParam, lParam) ;
    }
}
```

CALLPUB.H

```
#define IDM_CREATE           1
#define IDM_DESTROY          2
#define IDM_IUNKNOWN         3
#define IDM_IMALLOC          4
#define IDM_IMARSHAL         5
#define IDM_ALLOCATE_CUSTOM  6
#define IDM_ALLOCATE_DEFAULT 7
#define IDM_FREE             8
#define IDM_CHECK            9
```

(continued)

CALLPUB.RC

```
#include "callpub.h"

MAIN MENU
    {
    POPUP "&Allocator"
        {
        MENUITEM "&Create",                         IDM_CREATE
        MENUITEM "&Destroy",                        IDM_DESTROY
        MENUITEM SEPARATOR
        MENUITEM "QueryInterface IID_IUnknown", IDM_IUNKNOWN
        MENUITEM "QueryInterface IID_IMalloc",  IDM_IMALLOC
        MENUITEM "QueryInterface IID_IMarshal", IDM_IMARSHAL
        }

    POPUP "&Memory"
        {
        MENUITEM "&Allocate (IMalloc)", IDM_ALLOCATE_CUSTOM
        MENUITEM "&Allocate (malloc)",  IDM_ALLOCATE_DEFAULT
        MENUITEM "&Free",               IDM_FREE
        }
    }
```

Since it makes a call to an OLE library function, CALLPUB initializes the OLE libraries from *WinMain* at startup:

```
// Connect to OLE libraries
HRESULT hr = CoInitialize (NULL) ;
if (FAILED (hr))
    {
    // Fail app initialization
    return FALSE ;
    }
```

and disconnects from OLE before terminating:

```
// Disconnect from OLE libraries
CoUninitialize () ;
```

Both calls are necessary because CALLPUB gets its *IMalloc* interface pointer from the PUBMEM component server by calling *CoCreateInstance*:

```
HRESULT hr =
    CoCreateInstance (CLSID_ALLOCATOR,
                      NULL,
                      CLSCTX_INPROC_SERVER,
                      IID_IMalloc,
                      (void **) &pMalloc) ;
```

```
if (FAILED (hr))
    {
    MessageBox (hwnd, "Error: No allocator",
                szAppName, MB_OK) ;
    return 0 ;
    }
```

This OLE library function searches the registry for the component which can provide the CLSID_ALLOCATOR class, a symbol defined in PUBMEM.H. To force this symbol to allocate memory instead of simply referencing an extern value, the list of include files referenced by PUBMEM includes:

```
#include <initguid.h>
#include "pubmem.h"
```

When this book was being written, three contexts were defined (the *dwClsContext* parameter in *CoCreateInstance*) for the type of server to run. CLSCTX_INPROC_SERVER, which is what PUBMEM requests, is a stand-alone DLL server. Another type of DLL server, CLSCTX_INPROC_HANDLER, is a local handler for an out-of-process server. It serves as an in-process (faster, lower overhead) surrogate until the out-of-process server is actually needed. The third type of context, CLSCTX_LOCAL_SERVER, runs as a separate process on the same machine.

Unlike the private *CreateAllocator* function, which always returns a pointer to an *IMalloc* interface, *CoCreateInstance* lets the caller specify the type of interface to be returned. PUBMEM requests IID_IMalloc, the interface IID for *IMalloc*. But it equally could have requested IID_IUnknown and then performed a *QueryInterface* for the *IMalloc* pointer and achieved the same result. Of course, if two interface pointers were held by a client, two calls to *Release* would eventually be required to properly decrement the reference count.

FINAL WORDS

This introduction to the basics of OLE's Component Object Model (COM) should provide you sufficient background to begin working with the OLE technologies wherever you find them. Whether creating compound document containers or servers, automation objects or controllers, OLE control containers, or OLE controls, all rely on the COM-style interfaces described in this chapter. The Windows 95 shell services are only available via COM interfaces. Even if you rely on a class library, such as Microsoft's MFC or Borland's OWL, if you drill down just a bit you'll find COM peeking up at you.

From the time that Windows 95 was just a glimmer in the eyes of its developers, Microsoft has been sending software developers a consistent message: the future is Win32 and OLE. With the arrival of Windows 95 and the promise of OLE Technologies to come, it's clear that the future has already come upon us.

You now have what you need to build the great Windows applications of tomorrow.

Index

L

N

O

X–Z

CHARLES PETZOLD

Not too long ago, a top-secret squad from Microsoft Press set out on a mission. Their sole objective was simple: They were to find that person who was most dissatisfied with Microsoft's technical documentation about programming for Windows and who had attempted to rectify the problem by writing more clearly and succinctly and accurately about Windows-based programming than any other human on this planet.

Although the target of their search lived some 3,000 miles away from Microsoft's headquarters in Redmond, Washington, he was easy to find. The culprit was a freelance writer, and all of the proof was in print. He had written the very first magazine article about programming for Windows in the December, 1986, issue of *Microsoft Systems Journal*. He had subsequently written numerous articles about Windows programming for *MSJ* and in his long-running "Environments" column for *PC Magazine*. He had also written a best-selling computer book for none other than Microsoft Press, a book entitled *Programming Windows*, first published in 1988 and later revised twice over, and translated into nine languages. In May, 1994, he was one of seven people (and the only author) to be given a Windows Pioneer Award from *Windows Magazine* and Microsoft Corporation for his contribution to the success of Microsoft Windows. The final conclusive piece of evidence came when the Microsoft squad interrogated Windows application programmers around the world on how they had first learned their trade. These programmers uniformly replied: "The Petzold Book."

Charles Petzold was definitely the guy they were after. So, when the Microsoft Press goon squad invaded Petzold's tiny studio apartment in New York City, he was helpless to resist. The Microsofties also warned him that if he did not become compliant with Windows 95, more severe repercussions might come his way.

Petzold had no choice but to agree to revise his book for Windows 95, even though he was hot at work on the Great American Novel. The real bummer for Petzold is that he's also under contract to write books for Microsoft Press on graphics programming and multimedia programming under Windows, but he hopes to finish these two books before the next millennium. The Great American Novel may take a few years longer.

PAUL YAO

A programmer since 1975, Paul Yao has spent the last ten years bringing high-quality technical data on Windows software development to the light of day in his workshops, numerous articles, books, and lectures.

As president of The Paul Yao Company, his leadership in the Microsoft Windows arena dates from 1986, when he coauthored the first book published on Windows programming. His firm's educational emphasis was inspired by Paul's work on a team that created the first publicly available training course on Windows-based programming. That early focus has allowed Paul to continue creating educational opportunities. In 1990, Paul created The Power Programming Workshops. Since then, Paul has traveled the globe presenting on-site workshops on Native OLE, Printer Device Drivers, Win32, Win16, and MFC to groups of C and C++ programmers.

Paul is a contributing editor at *Microsoft Systems Journal,* where he has published numerous articles, among them the first public article on Windows NT–based programming. Paul's most recent book is *Foundations of Visual C++ Programming for Windows 95*, coauthored with his brother, Joseph Yao.

The manuscript for this book was prepared and submitted to Microsoft Press in electronic form. Text files were prepared using Microsoft Word 6.0 for Windows. Pages were composed by Microsoft Press using Adobe PageMaker 5.0 for Windows, with text in Garamond and display type in Helvetica Black. Composed pages were delivered to the printer as electronic prepress files.

Cover Graphic Designer

Gregory Erickson

Cover Illustrator

Glenn Mitsui

Interior Graphic Designer

Kim Eggleston

Interior Graphic Artist

Travis Beaven

Principal Compositor

Barb Runyan

Indexer

Lynn Armstrong
of Shane–Armstrong Information Services

The Paul Yao Company

Looking for a Window Beyond This Book?

Every day, while you're busy trying to stay on top of your workload, the breeze continues to blow through the technology world. New techniques and versions come along. You can come up for air and discover things have changed.

That's why The Paul Yao Company offers expert workshops on the Microsoft® Windows® operating system revealing the secrets of system internals. We'll help you breathe fresh air into your coding and open up new programming opportunities. It's the training you need to stay on top of your profession. So don't let another day pass you by.

**Contact
The Paul Yao Company
for more information:
1.800.942.3535.**

1075 Bellevue Way NE, Suite 300
Bellevue, WA 98004-4276 USA

Voice 1.800.942.3535 • Fax 206.828.6312
e-mail: CIS: 76111.232@compuserve.com
International customers, please call 206.747.1355

The Paul Yao Company
Shedding Light on Windows Programming

1.800.942.3535

T h e   P a u l   Y a o   C o m p a n y

Your Window of Opportunity...

If you would like information on any

of our workshops, call us toll-free at

1.800.942.3535,

or simply fill out this form,

and fax it to: 206.828.6312.

Shed some light on these workshop subjects:

The Power Programming Workshops™ on Microsoft® Windows®. Send in this form for more information on any of these workshop topics.

- ☐ C++ and MFC
- ☐ Win32® for Windows® 95 and Windows NT™
- ☐ Native OLE
- ☐ Printer Device Drivers for Windows 95
- ☐ Win16

I am also interested in the following technical topics:

The Paul Yao Company, based in Seattle, has been training Windows programmers since 1986, when its founder and president, Paul Yao, coauthored the first book ever published on programming for Windows. This focus on Microsoft Windows training has allowed The Paul Yao Company to take a leading role in the growth and development of technical training opportunities and material.

Name

Company

Address

City

State   ZIP

E-Mail Address

Phone

Fax

Building DLLs for C/C++ Programmers
A multimedia technical brief on CD-ROM.

- ☐ A practical introduction to building DLLs, including tips and techniques for avoiding common pitfalls, errors, and traps. Covers building DLLs for Win16, Windows 95, and Windows NT. Includes sample source code to speed your own DLL development.

The Paul Yao Company
Shedding Light on Windows Programming

CALL 1.800.942.3535
FAX 206.828.6312

Microsoft, Windows, and Win32 are registered trademarks and Windows NT is a trademark of Microsoft Corporation.

IMPORTANT—READ CAREFULLY BEFORE OPENING SOFTWARE PACKET(S). By opening the sealed packet(s) containing the software, you indicate your acceptance of the following Microsoft License Agreement.

MICROSOFT LICENSE AGREEMENT

(Book Companion Disks)

This is a legal agreement between you (either an individual or an entity) and Microsoft Corporation. By opening the sealed software packet(s) you are agreeing to be bound by the terms of this agreement. If you do not agree to the terms of this agreement, promptly return the unopened software packet(s) and any accompanying written materials to the place you obtained them for a full refund.

MICROSOFT SOFTWARE LICENSE

1. GRANT OF LICENSE. Microsoft grants to you the right to use one copy of the Microsoft software program included with this book (the "SOFTWARE") on a single terminal connected to a single computer. The SOFTWARE is in "use" on a computer when it is loaded into the temporary memory (i.e., RAM) or installed into the permanent memory (e.g., hard disk, CD-ROM, or other storage device) of that computer. You may not network the SOFTWARE or otherwise use it on more than one computer or computer terminal at the same time.

2. COPYRIGHT. The SOFTWARE is owned by Microsoft or its suppliers and is protected by United States copyright laws and international treaty provisions. Therefore, you must treat the SOFTWARE like any other copyrighted material (e.g., a book or musical recording) except that you may either (a) make one copy of the SOFTWARE solely for backup or archival purposes, or (b) transfer the SOFTWARE to a single hard disk provided you keep the original solely for backup or archival purposes. You may not copy the written materials accompanying the SOFTWARE.

3. OTHER RESTRICTIONS. You may not rent or lease the SOFTWARE, but you may transfer the SOFTWARE and accompanying written materials on a permanent basis provided you retain no copies and the recipient agrees to the terms of this Agreement. You may not reverse engineer, decompile, or disassemble the SOFTWARE. If the SOFTWARE is an update or has been updated, any transfer must include the most recent update and all prior versions.

4. DUAL MEDIA SOFTWARE. If the SOFTWARE package contains both 3.5" and 5.25" disks, then you may use only the disks appropriate for your single-user computer. You may not use the other disks on another computer or loan, rent, lease, or transfer them to another user except as part of the permanent transfer (as provided above) of all SOFTWARE and written materials.

5. SAMPLE CODE. If the SOFTWARE includes Sample Code, then Microsoft grants you a royalty-free right to reproduce and distribute the sample code of the SOFTWARE provided that you: (a) distribute the sample code only in conjunction with and as a part of your software product; (b) do not use Microsoft's or its authors' names, logos, or trademarks to market your software product; (c) include the copyright notice that appears on the SOFTWARE on your product label and as a part of the sign-on message for your software product; and (d) agree to indemnify, hold harmless, and defend Microsoft and its authors from and against any claims or lawsuits, including attorneys' fees, that arise or result from the use or distribution of your software product.

DISCLAIMER OF WARRANTY

The SOFTWARE (including instructions for its use) is provided "AS IS" WITHOUT WARRANTY OF ANY KIND. MICROSOFT FURTHER DISCLAIMS ALL IMPLIED WARRANTIES INCLUDING WITHOUT LIMITATION ANY IMPLIED WARRANTIES OF MERCHANTABILITY OR OF FITNESS FOR A PARTICULAR PURPOSE. THE ENTIRE RISK ARISING OUT OF THE USE OR PERFORMANCE OF THE SOFTWARE AND DOCUMENTATION REMAINS WITH YOU.

IN NO EVENT SHALL MICROSOFT, ITS AUTHORS, OR ANYONE ELSE INVOLVED IN THE CREATION, PRODUCTION, OR DELIVERY OF THE SOFTWARE BE LIABLE FOR ANY DAMAGES WHATSOEVER (INCLUDING, WITHOUT LIMITATION, DAMAGES FOR LOSS OF BUSINESS PROFITS, BUSINESS INTERRUPTION, LOSS OF BUSINESS INFORMATION, OR OTHER PECUNIARY LOSS) ARISING OUT OF THE USE OF OR INABILITY TO USE THE SOFTWARE OR DOCUMENTATION, EVEN IF MICROSOFT HAS BEEN ADVISED OF THE POSSIBILITY OF SUCH DAMAGES. BECAUSE SOME STATES/COUNTRIES DO NOT ALLOW THE EXCLUSION OR LIMITATION OF LIABILITY FOR CONSEQUENTIAL OR INCIDENTAL DAMAGES, THE ABOVE LIMITATION MAY NOT APPLY TO YOU.

U.S. GOVERNMENT RESTRICTED RIGHTS

The SOFTWARE and documentation are provided with RESTRICTED RIGHTS. Use, duplication, or disclosure by the Government is subject to restrictions as set forth in subparagraph (c)(1)(ii) of The Rights in Technical Data and Computer Software clause at DFARS 252.227-7013 or subparagraphs (c)(1) and (2) of the Commercial Computer Software — Restricted Rights 48 CFR 52.227-19, as applicable. Manufacturer is Microsoft Corporation, One Microsoft Way, Redmond, WA 98052-6399.

If you acquired this product in the United States, this Agreement is governed by the laws of the State of Washington.

Should you have any questions concerning this Agreement, or if you desire to contact Microsoft Press for any reason, please write: Microsoft Press, One Microsoft Way, Redmond, WA 98052-6399.